THE
SCIENCE OF SOCIETY

THE

SCIENCE OF SOCIETY

PUBLISHED UNDER THE AUSPICES OF THE SUMNER CLUB
ON THE FOUNDATION ESTABLISHED
IN MEMORY OF
PHILIP HAMILTON McMILLAN OF THE CLASS OF 1894
YALE COLLEGE

THE
SCIENCE OF SOCIETY

BY

WILLIAM GRAHAM SUMNER
*Late Professor of Political and Social Science
in Yale University*

AND

ALBERT GALLOWAY KELLER
*Professor of the Science of Society
in Yale University*

VOLUME III

NEW HAVEN
YALE UNIVERSITY PRESS
LONDON: HUMPHREY MILFORD: OXFORD UNIVERSITY PRESS
1929

First published, September, 1927
Second printing, March, 1929

CONTENTS

VOLUME III

PART V

SELF-PERPETUATION

* An asterisk after a section-number indicates that there is in the *Case-Book* a section corresponding to that number.

Part VI

Self-Gratification

CONTENTS

EXPLANATORY NOTE

Inasmuch as the authors aim always at a display of the inter-connection of society's institutions—to that end employing a re-iteration of cross-reference—it seems proper to equip each volume not alone with its own table of contents but also with those of pre-ceding and succeeding volumes. For this reason the following Tables of Contents of Volumes I, II, and IV are here inserted.

CONTENTS

VOLUME I

Preface.

PART I

INTRODUCTORY

* An asterisk after a section-number indicates that there is in the *Case-Book* a section corresponding to that number.

Part III

Self-Maintenance: Regulative Organization

Chapter XIV. Antagonisms and War.

PART V

SOCIETAL SELF-PERPETUATION

CHAPTER XLI

WHAT MADE MARRIAGE

§331. **The Condition of Bi-sexuality.** To its material environment of things and of men, society has made adjustment through folkways and mores which have tended to form about nuclei or cores of interests and to be shaped into consistent structures; thus arose the industrial, the military, and the regulative organizations. In exactly the same manner, in this case in response to an environment of spirits, was evolved the religious organization. In its development each of these organizations presents a series comparable to those of the animal-world described by organic evolutionists. Some account of these series in the field of the several organizations just mentioned is now before the reader, and there should have been revealed to him something of their essential nature and lines of development. There yet remains one outstanding life-condition of the race, not so much environmental as internal or intrinsic, which is present in consequence of the fact that *Homo* is bi-sexual. To bi-sexuality as well as to nature, fellow-man, or spirit-world, must adjustment be made. It is perhaps a waste of labor to try to state the consequences of that which never happened or will ever happen; but there is some enlightenment to be gained by reflecting on how society's evolution and life would have been altered if *Homo* had been uni-sexual like certain other organisms or if there had been three sexes, as is virtually the case with some insects. The fact of bi-sexuality has constituted a condition of life calling for the development of folkways, mores, and institutions in adjustment to it. The sexes must live in proximity. Children must be reared. How can these necessary results be attained in consonance with societal welfare? In a word, mankind in society faces the imperative impulse toward self-perpetuation, along with that toward self-maintenance; and in the one case as in the other there has been worked out automatically a system whereby, when all has been said in criticism of it, society has perpetuated itself unto this day.

By way of setting foot at once upon the firm ground of reality, we begin with biological facts. Human reproduction is primarily a natural, physical function. Solely as such it belongs to biology and is to be studied without reference to mental, societal, or ethical considerations. It is a natural fact which has no moral quality any more than has eating, breathing, or sleeping, an animal-function which must be treated as other such functions are, entirely within the horizon of organic life; any question of morals in connection with it concerns only the manner in which men use it. "Nature" (to personify, for convenience sake, "natural law") seems to care only, though fanatically, that life shall be passed on and on. Behind reproduction she has placed the stress of a dominating passion[1] and in thousands of ways she has sought to render propagation—in fact, exuberant propagation—inevitable. She cares nothing for the individual interest and even less for canons of human propriety; it is the race-interest, calling for numbers, that is the absorbing consideration.

Though human reproduction is basically physical, it is a function whose range extends beyond the biological; it has intimate connection with mental states and operations, so that it reacts upon the experiences of the human individual; it is directly influenced by mental states and operations and it also produces them. Attended by a great nature-urge, it excites the attendant passions of covetousness, ambition, love of domination, vanity, jealousy, destructiveness of human life; favored by the health and welfare of the organism, it powerfully affects that health and welfare, and is often most intimately interwoven with all the life-interests of the individual.

Nor do the consequences of this function stop with the individual. Inasmuch as two persons of opposite sex must coöperate, it cannot be exercised without the existence of relations between individuals which affect the life, welfare, and happiness of each; and when a child is born there are usually three persons who are now related in life and interest. From being a biological process, reproduction has thus opened out through its consequences into the societal field; for a family presently exists, and the family is the unit-cluster of societal organization. Societal organization is therefore a natural fact, in that it grows inevitably and originally

[1] Lippert, *Kgchte.*, I, 16.

out of sex-functions and, when once begun, its extension and complication up to the highest degree are only a question of time. The family is a miniature society and its relations to sex-union are readily apprehended; but not even the larger aggregate, the tribe or state, can remain unaffected by the facts and acts of reproduction. It must take cognizance of them as a condition of its life and well-being.

If, however, for the sake of special study, we set aside the biological function of sex-union and concentrate upon the mental reactions inseparable in actual living from reproduction and parenthood, together with the societal contacts and relations inevitable between father, mother, and child or between consanguine societal groups or between the society and any of its parts, we must remain aware that we are merely making distinctions for convenience of analysis and exposition. The biological, mental, and societal elements in the self-perpetuation of society are inseparable in life; no one of them can be neglected in a proper study of the subject.

§332. **Conflict of Interests.** The reproductive function so powerfully affects welfare—it is so prolific in pleasure and in pain and its discharge is enforced by so dominant a need—that, becoming for the earliest of men the interest-center of a great group of mores, it enforced upon the most primitive of societies the development of a sex-code and sex-policy. The simpler aspects of the sex-mores have been indicated in a previous connection;[2] and though the more massive institutional developments out of them are yet to come, we must take, at this point, a sort of anticipatory view of the range upon which we are about to enter, even though our covering generalities may seem somewhat vague prior to the examination of the series of institutional forms the sense of which they sum up. The passions which were in play in and around reproduction produced conflicts of will and interest resulting in strife and harm to the society; so that, both unconsciously and consciously, rights came to be defined in the mores and sanctions developed, in avoidance of attendant pain and misery; then through the tie of generations the sex-codes, like the other codes of conduct, were connected with the ghosts of ancestors and so

[2] §60, above; Sumner, *Folkways*, ch. IX.

received their more than human authority. In the first sex-codes of which we know, the man already has right of dominion over a woman or women—rights sanctioned by the consensus of group-members, including both the living and the dead. These rights are in form property-rights, guaranteed by the taboo. Out of these rights and sanctions in the mores has developed the institution of marriage as a component, historical, necessary part of the societal organization. The institution has been made up of traditions, rules, conventions, customs, and ordinances; it has had standards of propriety, truth, right, and justice; it has retained sanctions in group-force and in religion. At any time and place there has been a form of entering into wedlock, with notions of what is right and decent and authority to enforce these convictions by punishments.

"The mores determine what marriage shall be, who may enter into it, in what way they may enter into it, divorce, and all details of proper conduct in the family relation. In regard to all these matters it is evident that custom governs and prescribes. When positive institutions and laws are made they always take up, ordain, and regulate what the mores have long previously made facts in the social order. In the administration of law also, especially by juries, domestic relations are controlled by the mores. The decisions rendered by judges utter in dogmatic or sententious form the current notions of truth and right about these relations. Our terms 'endogamy,' 'mother-family,' 'polyandry,' etc., are only descriptive terms for a summary of the folkways which have been established in different groups and which are capable of classification. . . . The definition of marriage consists in stating what, at any time and place, the mores have imposed as regulations on the relations of a man and woman who are coöperatively carrying on the struggle for existence and the reproduction of the species.

"No laws can do more than specify ways of entering into wedlock, and the rights and duties of the parties in wedlock to each other, which the society will enforce. These, however, are but indifferent externals. All the intimate daily play of interests, emotions, character, taste, etc., are beyond the reach of the bystanders, and that play is what makes wedlock what it is for every pair. Nevertheless the relations of the parties are always deeply controlled by the current opinions in the society, the prevalent ethical standards, the approval or condemnation passed by the bystanders on cases between husbands and wives, and by the precepts and traditions of the old. Thus the mores hold control over individual taste and caprice, and individual experience reacts against the control. All the problems of marriage are in the intimate relations. When they affect large numbers they are brought under the solution of the mores. Therefore the history of marriage is to be interpreted by the mores, and its philosophy must be sought in the fact that it is an ever-moving product of the mores."[3]

   [3] Sumner, *Folkways*, §§357, 363, 364; chs. VII, IX, X, XII, XIII.

It is significant that, despite all regulation, marriage is now, in popular language, attributed to fate. It is a "lottery." It is more likely to be controlled by enthusiasm than by judgment and the parties to it yield their will to what seems inevitable yet doubtful as to consequences. In considering the evolution of marriage it is necessary to recognize the fact that the problem of it is yet unsolved; the adjustments hitherto attained in any generality have been far from perfect. In particular, one should recur to the truth that while the laws and mores can control certain rights and interests in regard to it, they cannot determine the relations of two married persons to one another. Yet it is on these that all the validity and sense of the institution ultimately rest. It is necessary always to bear in mind that marriage remains a relation of exclusive, "pitiless intimacy" between man and woman. All that the law can deal with is external and the mores cannot exercise any immediate control over that which may remain indefinitely secret within the walls of the home. Many a husband or wife has been racked for a life-time within the secure shelter of domestic privacy. The things bystanders can know and discuss are trivial. The essence of the relation is an affair of character, temperament, breeding, sense, and discipline.

Although the shaping of all the notions and ordinances has been at the call of expediency, still the interests of the parties to the marriage—including parents and ancestors of the contractants, remoter relatives, the group, children, and remoter posterity—have never been all accordant. In fact, the interests of the others as against the immediate parties have been maintained by parents, chiefs, priests, and legislators. The institution of marriage has always been such that individuals have rebelled against it as against a yoke under which they were brought before they knew what it was and in subjection to interests other than their own. It has often been found that marriage, being, as an elaborate product of societal evolution, highly conventional, was in disaccord with nature,[4] with human nature, and with ideals of happiness, so that it has distorted life for the individual and frustrated his most cherished purposes. The institution has often been constructed, at any rate in certain of its details, upon doctrines and maxims

[4] Keller, *Soc. Evol.*, 28 ff.

which were not and could not be verified by experience; and so it has seemed to be based upon falsehood and to constitute no less than a trap for the inexperienced. All this has produced inconsistencies and conflicts of interest.

The interests of the individual and of the race were felt to be in conflict long before they were seen to be so. Self-maintenance and self-perpetuation combine as a burden on man. Here are two cumulative tasks, antagonistic to one another. Self-maintenance is individual, but carried on socially; self-perpetuation is social but secured by individual impulse. Nature does not care much for the older generation or for individual self-realization. She wants the germ-plasm to be passed on. Rather than sacrifice any chances of race-perpetuation, she imposes checks upon most forms of individual self-realization in favor of reproduction; the driving force of sex-passion, for instance, is calculated to render the individual obtuse to the call of career and to practical considerations in general. Driven by instinct, he lightly assumes serious material handicaps and "hostages to fortune" in the race which he, as an individual, is to run and in the battle which he must fight. The married man may come to envy the ease, possessions, and opportunities of unattached friends. On the other hand, preoccupation with the individual interest may easily defeat its own end by causing one to renounce or to postpone, with excess of ambition, caution, or selfishness, those durable satisfactions in life which go with home and family. At one end of the scale is unreflecting surrender to nature's call and at the other an over-sophistication, resistive to that call and capable of betraying the very individual interest which it sets out to serve—capable of producing a situation which may become, as the years winnow out the essentials of life, an unending source of disappointment and self-recrimination.

The broadest set of conflicting interests involved in marriage is that existing between individual and race; and closely connected with it is the diversity of interest between parents and offspring.[5] It is impossible to serve the race-interest and the individual interest fully at the same time, though capital overcomes the antagonism to a considerable degree, for it is the rich who can sustain the

---

[5] Spencer, *Prin. Soc.,* I, §336.

burden of the race-interest, the cost of children, with the least strain. It is clear also that the parents and relatives, not being subject to the natural impulsions of the immediate parties to a marriage but more coolly reckoning in such considerations as those of property, family-pride, and many other similarly practical matters, may represent a set of interests quite in conflict with those of the immediate parties.[6] The disposition of the ghostly ancestors, keen for their own eidolistic interests, introduces another element into the complication, an element which, with the development of religion and in the hands of the priests, assumes an almost controlling rôle. And finally—not to prolong the list or unduly to anticipate future topics[7]—the group at large has likewise its interest in the marriage of any and every group-member. It is not a matter of indifference to the tribe that the man A marries the woman B; for with their entrance into that status are involved questions of legitimacy of children, inheritance of property, and jural relations of many sorts of which the regulative organization must take cognizance if it is to maintain order. Here is where the interest of chiefs and legislators enters into marriage.

Two persons must be singularly free from social relations if they can even be wedded, to say nothing of living in matrimony, without reference to anything save their own personal choice. Objections and recommendations, from relatives and others, may be interposed on all sides. Religion, property, rank, age, health, various duties, and numerous other relations of life in society produce reasons why one marriage seems advantageous and another objectionable for a given person. In the case of princes and princesses, especially in the eighteenth century, marriages were difficult and very rarely happy because so narrowly restricted and so arbitrarily dictated by the code of the royal group. There were only two or three women in the world whom a given prince might marry. It was a shock to the orthodox when Bismarck set the code aside. Novels are prone to deal with the moral conflicts which arise from conditions lying in the mores when these interfere with personal romantic choice.

[6] Chs. XLVI, XLVII, below.   [7] §§341, 365, below.

§333. **Inconsistency in the Sex-Mores.** These collisions of interest are due to the complexity of societal relations that attends upon the reproductive function—a function upon whose discharge nature compellingly insists and which, none the less, as respects its consequences, has been largely removed from nature. Nature calls for marriage in the early twenties, let us say, as she calls for animal-mating at the period of fresh and vigorous maturity; but the conventions and mores, of which the animals are relieved, counsel delay. Natural and societal expediency confront one another. Here is an inconsistency of a serious order, though its solution is an inveterate one: for not through liberty of impulse but through restraint do men adjust and forward themselves in human society. This leads us to say that it is under the institution evolving from the mores that all the ethics fall; and the inevitable war of ethics with nature is only one more striking example of the general disaccord of things resulting from the entrance of a new grade of evolution in which the basis of selection is societal rather than natural.[8]

The inconsistencies do not lie solely within the range where the natural and the societal meet. Within the mores, entirely outside of nature, there has existed with regard to this basic matter of bi-sexuality and its derivatives the most striking of disharmonies, one resulting in veritable obscurantism. Bi-sexuality, one of the most fundamental of life-conditions, must be adjusted to by society through the mores; and yet the mores have demanded silence, or even ignorance, concerning the facts about sex. The actual life-conditions are, as it were, jacketed in the mores, so that they do not appear and are not considered, while the convention which envelops them is taken into account as if it were the real ultimate. This is a further case of conventionalization.[9] It needs but little reflection for anyone of sound mind to come to the realization that sex is for the individual a life-condition of the utmost significance and pregnant of the highest satisfaction or the deepest pain. It is a stock human interest. Literature plays about the love-motive so consistently that the novel or drama which lacks that motive and is still popular is singled out as an almost unique performance. What is everybody's interest must be

[8] Keller, *Soc. Evol.*, 187 ff.   [9] §324, above.

deeply significant to the group; and every society, as a condition of its well-being, must have some sort of expediency in its sex-mores and sex-policy. There is no society that does not need the best possible charting of the reefs and shifting shoals represented by both the constant and the newly appearing maladjustments attendant upon the inevitable proximity and association of the two sexes. Knowledge of conditions is at a premium in this diffi-cult matter.

And yet it would appear that modern western society has over a long period exacted ignorance of sex-matters in those who ad-here to its standard code of mores. Restrictions of decency and propriety in respect to sex and reproduction doubtless rose from experience of expediency; it is true, nevertheless, that ignorance, including misinformation, has prevailed in this field and has been maintained by strong sanctions in the name of morals and with the complacency of virtue. Words and subjects connected with reproduction have been strongly tabooed, not only for those who lay claim to culture and manners but also in the daily press that caters to and sets the mode for the less reflecting, in public schools, and in public gatherings of all kinds. Obscenity is still scented in lectures or books not technically medical that offer reliable information concerning sex and reproduction, although not much fault is found with highly suggestive novels and plays that travesty the truth. It would appear that within the range of sex-phenomena, which is admittedly a range of peril to individual and to society, the theory has been that ignorance and unbal-lasted fancy are the best policy. It may be that certain appalling exhibitions of unreserve in the life of today represent an uncon-scious reaction against an equally appalling prudery.

Then, to complete the picture of inconsistency, the code has made it a conventional virtue to exalt love and marriage while interdicting objective examination of either. It is a trait of human nature that "all which is unknown is assumed to be magnificent," and it would seem as if, in the case of marriage, special advantage had been taken of this weakness, so that matters of the highest moment to society must not be much talked about except in a species of romantic hyperbole. Even if this phase is now passing, its irrationality will long persist.

§334*. **The Making of Marriage.** It is the first and most important anthropological fact about the human race that it consists of two distinct and complementary sexes. This sex-difference, which usually passes in our current thinking as a mere incidental dissimilarity impairing in no respect the unity of the race, is in fact a distinction which produces a cleavage through the whole societal structure. The life-experience, angle of vision, interest, and attitude toward life are so different in the sexes that male and female might well be regarded, purely on the basis of these divergences, as two varieties of the same species living in constant mutual presence. This is what strikes one most impressively when he comes at the matter as a student of social relations. Yet sex-differentiation, as the reader well knows,[10] is deeper and wider and rests upon divergences that are more fundamental than the social ones. It is doubtful whether any man ever understood any woman since the world began. Perhaps the experienced physician comes nearest to comprehending. At any rate he knows that she will act in such and such a manner, just as gunpowder will explode under certain conditions. He also knows by observation and through tact how to deal with her. But it is doubtful if he enters at all into what lies back of the concrete expressions upon which he builds his diagnosis and treatment. He simply knows, as most laymen do not, how the mechanism will act under given conditions.

The point where primary physical differences merge into settled secondary distinctions and then again into societal differentiation cannot be defined; one set of facts conditions the other and the normal evolutionary zone of transition is conspicuous. Speaking very generally and inclusively, in view of evidence past and to come, it can be said that in physical functions, mental characteristics, practical aptitudes and disabilities, ethical traits, and capacity for the discharge of societal duties the two sexes are diverse, complementary to one another, and mutual in their coöperative activities.[11]

Between the sexes, thus differently endowed, nature has placed an attraction that has secured the perpetuation of the race. This passion of sex is strong enough, on its occasion, to neutralize the

10 §§57 ff., above.

11 Ellis, *Man and Woman*, 20, 300, 354, 369; Geddes and Thompson, *Evol. of Sex*, 37, 270; Campbell, *Nervous Org., passim.*

impulse of self-preservation and to make against the pursuit of the very struggle for existence. From it results the sex-act. Since the process of reproduction belongs, as a physiological process, to natural science, neither it nor the sex-act concerns the social sciences. What forces brought male and female together in that act is a question that the biologist may set for himself; but that which the student of society wants to resolve is this: What forces brought man and woman together into a coöperative societal relation and, even more particularly, held them in and to that relation?

It would appear at first sight that the sexes were drawn together by nature and that their union might be accepted as a primordial fact. This is one of those things that "must have been," but were not; that "stand to reason," but do not square with the evidence. It is manifest to brief reflection that there are disadvantages to the individual in this relation and that he would not enter it, much less stay in it even for a short time, unless under it interests were satisfied over and above the dissatisfactions attendant. This is but a corollary of the general case of socialization; in short, marriage is a typical case of antagonistic coöperation.[12]

There is some danger in talking of "motives" when primitive folk are under discussion. Most of their actions are in the mores and are performed with a minimum of the reflection and judgment which the term "motive" may imply. As well consider that some motive of the bee takes form in accuracy of comb-construction as to believe that human motive led to sex-taboos or family-institutions. After the course of development has been traversed it is possible to survey it and rationalize upon it, assigning reason and motive for that which, though taking place without premeditation, must nevertheless have had antecedents or premises of some sort, mistaken or not. If one uses the colorless word "interest" and says as little as possible about motive, he will come nearer to the representation of actualities. What interests, then, existed to bring about the more or less enduring association of the sexes in marriage? In short, what made marriage?

First of all, marriage is not in nature and is therefore not an

12 §§7, 8, 16, above.

inevitable natural sequel of sex-passion or a necessary accompaniment of reproduction. This is a case of the obvious that needs stressing. Marriage and mating are two different things.[13] Passion does not explain the endurance of the marital relation nowadays and it has never done so in the past. Mere mating never made a family. Reproduction occurred prior to marriage; a wedding-ceremony is not necessary to secure it. Though marriage is, in one of its aspects, society's way of keeping sex-passion within bounds, that is only one of the reasons for its existence. Probably the coöperation of man and woman would have been developed in some form if it had been totally disassociated from reproduction. "Sex union rests upon the incitement of the very most primary instinct and stands nearest the group of reflex-phenomena; marriage, as the foundation of the family organization of whatsoever kind, is always the creation of societal self-maintenance. The two stand, in origin and aim, far apart."[14] If animal-passion is differentiated from love and considered alone, it is seen to have been probably less effective to bring about marriage on the primitive stage than it has later become. Sex-feeling is not so dominant and bestial among savages as certain detractors of "lower" races would have us believe; indeed, savages are not seldom reported to be sexually cold. They do not live in a state of preoccupation with sex any more than do the animals. Sex is to them too much a matter of course; only when it is shrouded in mystery does it challenge the fancy and invite a sort of absorption.

"The indifference of [African] natives to human physical beauty, which practically amounts to its total elimination as a factor in the relations between the sexes, has often been commented upon. A native whose attention you draw to the handsome features of another native—either woman or man—always responds vaguely, indifferently, never emphatically, rather giving the impression that he does not quite understand what you mean. It is significant that there exists, in the Swahili language, no word which expresses handsome, or beautiful, exclusively."[15] "A pure-blooded Indian," says Morgan,[16] "has very little animal passion"; it is in the half-breed that "it is sensibly augmented and when the second generation is reached with a cross giving three-quarters white blood, it becomes excessive and tends to indiscriminate licentiousness." Among Australians the over-amorous are held in much contempt.[17] Javanese men are

13 Lippert, *Kgchte.*, I, 70; Vinogradoff, *Hist. Jurispr.*, I, 203.
14 Lippert, *Kgchte.*, I, 70.
15 Coudenhove, in *Atl. Mo.*, CXXXII, 197.
16 In *Smithson. Contrib. to Knowledge*, XVII, 206.
17 Spencer and Gillen, *Nat. Tr. Cent. Aust.*, 471.

characterized by "coldness and apathy" toward the women.[18] Many other cases could be cited.[19] It is civilized people who become preoccupied with sex to the extent of bandying charges of sexual immorality, not only against savages but against heretics and hostile sects.[20]

Whatever the sex-susceptibilities of the most backward peoples, passion scarcely figures among their incentives to marriage; indeed, as Starcke[21] notes, "if marriage were decided by the sexual relations, it would be difficult to understand for what reasons marriages were contracted in those communities in which an altogether licentious sexual life is permitted to the unmarried." In all communities, he adds, there is a distinction between sexual relations and marriage; man does not care, apparently, to isolate all the women with whom he holds sexual intercourse in the same way that he isolates his wives. "Sexual considerations were not the basis of marriage"; intercourse between man and wife "is only one of its attributes." The widespread tolerance of unchastity in the young serves to place the sex-relation out of alignment with marriage.[22] Letourneau[23] speaks of "free and transient unions broken as soon as made, experimental marriages, three-quarter marriages, and marriages for a term, all of which show the very slight importance attached to sexual union by man in a low stage of development." Jealousy was excited only "when the man was afraid he should lose his wife."[24]

There is, in fact, nothing in the physical sex-relation which could render union enduring. It is transient, episodical, not calculated to support "the heavy burden of the social order"; it is of the moment and may be succeeded by repulsion. Compared with the action of hunger, vanity, and ghost-fear, that of sex-passion is gusty and spasmodic. It is nothing upon which to build a permanent institution. If it were the only ground of marriage, then when it had passed there would be no marriage. At lovers' vows the gods laugh. It cannot rank with the other socializing forces in the steadiness of its pressure. It is not that which made marriage.

If the sex-act is followed into its biological consequences, there yet remains but little upon which to base an enduring relation between man and woman. It is true that reproduction entails the mother-child connection and that this, being in nature, is guaranteed by the strong instinct of mother-love. But the relation between mother and child is not enough to make marriage or a fam-

[18] Crawford, *Hist. Ind. Archip.*, I, 41-42.

[19] Abel, *New Guinea*, 42; Ellis, *Tshi*, 285; Riedel, in *Bijd.*, XXXV, 79; Stevens, in *Ztsft. f. Eth.*, XXVIII, 180 ff.; Kubary, *Pelauer*, 64; Finsch, "Ponapé," in *Ztsft. f. Eth.*, XII, 318. Some cases in Westermarck, *Marriage*, II, 24-25; Müller, *Sex. Leben*, 55.

[20] Lea, *Inquis.*, I, 85-86, 101; II, 150, 258, 322, 335, 357, 373, 376, 408, 429, 474; III, 97, 127; Lea, *Sac. Celib.*, 414-415; Lecky, *Europ. Morals*, I, 414.

[21] *Prim. Fam.*, 256, 231, 241.   [22] §§344, 365, 366, below.

[23] *Marriage*, 69.   [24] Starcke, *Prim. Fam.*, 255.

ily; to do that the man has to be drawn in and retained; and there seems to be nothing of an instinctive or emotional order competent to secure his adherence. For him the sex-relation has no consequences on the order of the maternal instinct; he does not need the relief of suckling; it is only through mores and institutions of societal creation that responsibility for children is brought home to the father. Marriage and the family, in all their varieties and ramifications, are societal and institutional, not natural.

This becomes the more evident when it is realized that there was for the primitive man no obvious or necessary association between the sex-relation and the birth of children, for that connection is not a fact of observation but of intelligence and knowledge. How could the savage, especially with his stock of daimonistic prepossessions, ever arrive at a comprehension of the relation between the two? If not, then offspring could not belong to the man by any such association as was furnished by the familiar fact of parturition. It has generally been assumed[25] that a man and woman came together through sex-attraction, that parenthood was understood, and that, in particular, fatherhood was a self-evident fact. These assumptions, as appears upon a moment's candid reflection, are unwarranted. This being understood, it is the more evident that the association of man and woman in marriage could not have come about as a sequel of the sex-act and so in the course of nature.

A number of cases have appeared under totemism[26] illustrative of primitive theories concerning procreation. The most thorough treatment of this topic is that of Malinowski;[27] though he has special reference to the Trobriand Islands, his interpretations are more than local. The real cause of pregnancy is always a *baloma* or ghost, who enters a woman's body; all babies are made in Tuma, the spirit-land. Then there is a set of beliefs about reincarnation which imply "a pronounced association between the sea and the spirit children"; the spirits of the dead go into the sea, and mature unmarried girls have to observe various precautions when bathing. The spirits are in the sea-scum or in certain stones. Also in the inland villages the most usual way of becoming pregnant is to receive a spirit while in the water. "Often whilst bathing a woman will feel that something has touched her, or even hurt her. She will say, 'A fish has bitten me.' In fact, it was the *waiwaia* entering or being inserted into her." It is generally a female *baloma* that inserts the spirit or *waiwaia*, and she must always be of maternal kin to the woman. "It might seem quite safe to say that the belief in reincarnation, and the views about a

---

25 Mucke, *Horde,* 21, 155, 177, 187, is an exception; Lippert, *Kgchte.,* I, 78.
26 §260, above.		27 In JAI, XLVI, 403-418.

spirit child being inserted into, or entering, the womb of the mother, exclude any knowledge of the physiological process of impregnation. But any drawing of conclusions, or arguing by the law of logical contradiction, is absolutely futile in the realm of belief, whether savage or civilized. Two beliefs, quite contradictory to each other on logical grounds, may coexist, while a perfectly obvious inference from a very firm tenet may be simply ignored. Thus the only safe way for an ethnological inquirer is to investigate every detail of native belief, and to mistrust any conclusion obtained by inference only."

The author investigates these details, concluding that "the broad assertion that the natives are entirely ignorant of the existence of physiological impregnation may be laid down quite safely and correctly. . . . One distinction must be made at the outset: the distinction between impregnation, that is the idea of the father having a share in building up the body of the child on the one hand, and the purely physical action of sexual intercourse on the other. Concerning the latter, the view held by the natives may be formulated thus: it is necessary for the woman to have gone through sexual life before she can bear a child. . . . It is clear that only the knowledge of the first fact . . . would have any influence in shaping native ideas about kinship. As long as the father does nothing to form the body of the child (in the ideas of a people), there can be no question of consanguinity in the agnatic line. A mere mechanical share in opening up the child's way into the womb, and out of it, is of no fundamental importance. The state of knowledge in Kiriwina is just at the point where there is a vague idea as to some *nexus* between sexual connection and pregnancy, whereas there is no idea whatever concerning the man's contribution towards the new life which is being formed in the mother's body. . . . When I asked who was the father of an illegitimate child, there was only one answer, that there was no father, as the girl was not married. If, then, I asked, in quite plain terms, who is the physiological father, the question was not understood, and when the subject was discussed still further, and the question put in this form: 'There are plenty of unmarried girls, why did this one get with child, and the others not?' the answer would be: 'It is a *baloma* who gave her this child.' And here again I was often puzzled by some remarks, pointing to the view that an unmarried girl is especially exposed to the danger of being approached by a *baloma,* if she is very unchaste. Yet the girls deem it much better precaution to avoid directly any exposure to the *baloma* by not bathing at high tide, etc., than indirectly to escape the danger by being too scrupulously chaste."

The author did not leave the subject at this. "When, instead of merely asking about the . . . pregnancy, I directly advanced the embryological view of the matter, I found the natives absolutely ignorant of the process suggested. To the simile of a seed being planted in the soil and the plant growing out of the seed, they remained quite irresponsive. They were curious, indeed, and asked whether this was 'the white man's manner of doing it,' but they were quite certain that this was not the 'custom' of Kiriwina." They had no conception of the properties of the spermatic discharge. A tale is told of a native who had been away from his wife for two years and returned to find a child which had been born a couple of months before. "He cheerfully accepted it as his own, and did not understand any taunts or allusions made by some white men, who asked him whether he had not better repudiate, or, at least, thoroughly thrash his wife. He found it not in the slightest degree suspicious or suggestive that his wife became pregnant about a year after his departure." The fact is that the sex-relation is regarded as a means of pleasure merely. "I found that, undoubtedly, a girl of very loose conduct would be more likely to have a child, and that if a girl could be found who had never had intercourse, she certainly could have no child. The knowledge seemed to be as complete here as the ignorance was previously, and the very same men seemed to take, in turn, two contradictory points of view. I discussed the matter as thoroughly as I could, and it seemed to me as if the natives would say *yes* or *no,* according to whether the subject was approached from the side of knowledge or of ignorance." The final solution was that a virgin is "closed" or "shut up"; whatever method produces dilatation prepares her for the entrance of the *waiwaia.* "Thus I was taught to make the essential distinction between the idea of the mechanical action of intercourse, which covers all the natives know about the natural conditions of pregnancy, and the knowledge of impregnation, of the man's share in creating the new life . . . a fact of which the natives have not even the slightest glimpse." They do not fret over the case of the animals, "because the native never troubles about consistently carrying over his beliefs into domains where they do not naturally belong. He does not trouble about questions referring to animal after-life, and he has no views about their coming into the world. Those problems are settled with reference to man, but that is their proper domain, and beyond that they ought not to be extended."

Malinowski recalls that this ignorance of physical fatherhood was first discovered by Spencer and Gillen in Australia, and that the subject has been exhaustively covered by Hartland.[28] "The existence of complete ignorance, of the type discovered by Spencer and Gillen, among the most advanced Papuo-Melanesians, and its probable existence among all the Papuo-Melanesians, seems to indicate a much wider range of distribution and a much greater permanence through the higher stages of development than could be assumed hitherto." Nor is this a case of religious ideas obscuring facts. "The garden magic does not by any means 'obscure' the natives' causal knowledge of the nexus between proper clearing of the scrub, manuring the ground with ashes, watering, etc. The two sets of facts run parallel in his mind, and the one in no way 'obscures' the other." There is no reason for incredulity as to this ignorance of natural processes if one realizes how long it has taken to arrive at a knowledge of embryology; and yet "we have authors who, after this state of mind has been found positively among natives, receive the news with scepticism, and try to account for the native state of mind in the most devious manner. The way from the absolute ignorance to the exact knowledge is far, and must be passed gradually." Furthermore, among savage races sexual life begins very early and is carried on intensely; there is no singularity about it, so that it is an outstanding, rare matter. Sexual life is a normal state and no one looks for its consequences. It is to the native like eating and drinking. "How is he to realize that the very act which a woman performs almost as often as eating and drinking will, once, twice or three times in her life, cause her to become pregnant?" The natives are keen enough. "Some of my native informants very clearly pointed out to me the lack of consistency in my argument when I bluntly stated that it is not the *baloma* that produce pregnancy, but that it is caused by something like a seed being thrown on soil. I remember that I was almost directly challenged to account for the discrepancy why the cause which was repeated daily, or almost so, produced effects so rarely. . . . Some knowledge of the mental mechanism of the native, and of the cir-

28 *Primitive Paternity.*

cumstances under which he has to carry out his observations on this subject, ought to persuade anyone that no other state of things could exist, and that no far-fetched explanation or theories are necessary to account for it."

A few actual cases may be added in confirmation of Malinowski's remarkable presentation. Among certain Australians it is believed that a child may come without intercourse—an act merely preparing the woman to receive the child which has a mystic ancestral-spirit origin; they "have no idea of procreation as being directly associated with sexual intercourse, and firmly believe that children can be born without this taking place."[29] The Queensland natives could not understand the methods of preventing fertilization in animals.[30] They do not recognize human paternity, but say that "a woman begets children because (a) she has been sitting over a fire, on which she has roasted a particular species of black bream, which must have been given her by the prospective father; (b) she has purposely gone a hunting and caught a certain kind of bull-frog; (c) some man may have told her to be in an interesting condition; (d) she may dream of having a child put beside her."[31] "The parents of a child are the man and woman (or women) with whom the child lives, who care for him and provide him with food. A child may have two or more mothers, either simultaneously or in succession. He can have only one father at a time, but may have two or more successively." This is a case of monandrous union.[32] "A child enters a family in one of three ways: (1) as the child of the wife at the time of the marriage; (2) by birth, being born of the wife and accepted of the husband (who generally has the right to say if the new-born infant shall live or not); (3) by adoption. . . . It is sometimes necessary to distinguish the blood-mother . . . from other mothers. And it is similarly necessary sometimes to distinguish a child's own father, who is defined as the husband of the mother at the time of the birth. It is necessary to give this definition, as some Australian tribes appear to hold that there is no physiological relationship between father and child."[33]

"The people of the Murray Islands carry the custom of adoption to what seems to us an absurd extreme, and children are transferred from family to family in a way for which the people can give no adequate reason, nor can any adequate reason be found in the other features of the social or religious institutions of the people. I do not wish to go so far as to suggest that this custom of adoption may be a survival of a state of society in which children were largely common to the women of the group so far as nurture was concerned; but this is possible, and in any case this wholesale adoption may help the civilized person to understand that people of low culture may have different ideas in connexion with parentage from those prevalent among ourselves."[34] In Melanesia, if a girl becomes pregnant, she may escape punishment by asserting that some man has "thrown his hate" upon her, has put himself in relation to the ghosts, and these have caused the pregnancy.[35] "Intercourse is recognized as the cause of children, although single girls who become preg-

[29] Spencer and Gillen, *Nat. Tr. Cent. Aust.,* 265; Spencer and Gillen, *North. Tr. Cent. Aust.,* 145, 330, 331.

[30] Roth, *Queensland Aborig.,* 178-179.

[31] Read, in JAI, XLVIII, 153 (quoting Roth, *N. Queensland Eth.,* Bull. 5, §81).

[32] §345, below.

[33] Brown, in JAI, XLVIII, 223.

[34] Rivers, *Soc. Org.,* 186.

[35] Von Pfeil, *Südsee,* 143.

nant have a curious habit of blaming some or other portion of their diet."[36] Elsewhere, "there is no ignorance as to the cause of conception, no strange fancies of virgin births"; nevertheless, the ghosts "resemble human beings both in their outward appearance and in their nature, so that no one hesitates to believe that they can give rise to human children, or at least that they have done so in the past."[37]

On the northwest coast of North America the idea is common that women become pregnant by eating.[38] An Arab girl is represented as telling her father that she became pregnant by drinking what he had forbidden her, namely, water containing powdered bone from a skull.[39] Legends of the introduction of marriage recount how children had had only mothers and that their descent was made bilateral.[40] It may be noted that, with such beliefs, extra-marital pregnancy could not be treated as very remarkable or wrong. The breath is sometimes supposed to be procreative.[41] The idea of impregnation by the sun is not uncommon in legends.[42] Fables that represent infants as brought by birds or beasts may be survivals of the notion that a bird or beast brought the soul to the new-born infant—from the creative original water in which were all germs of life, as one version has it. Legends about virgin-birth, however rarefied and symbolical, have their connection with the topic of uncertainty about procreation; these symbolic fabrics are not woven by fancy out of nothing.[43] Any such uncertainty, especially about fatherhood, tends to remove sex-considerations as a basic factor in marriage.

It is not to be inferred from what precedes that among savages a man and a woman never preferred and selected each other; such selection has unquestionably played a constant part in mating. It does that upon any stage of culture, only upon the primitive stage preference is generally exercised outside or beside the marriage relation as such; love-wife and labor-wife, concubine and slave, might always be beside the status-wife; and the love-wife was often, perhaps regularly, only incidentally the status-wife. It cannot be established that personal attraction had much to do with making marriage. Marriage is a serious matter—too serious to be settled on the basis of mere inclination. An African uncle pleaded before a judge that his nephew could not inherit from his father because his parents married for love; "there is no encouragement to foolishness of this kind in Cameroon, where legal marriage consists in purchase."[44] It is possible to collect cases of sex-

---

36 Seligmann, *Melanesians,* 704.

37 Jenness and Ballentyne, *D'Entrecasteaux,* 104-105.

38 Niblack, in USNM, 1888, 379.

39 Meissner, *Neuarabische Geschichten,* 87.

40 Wilken, in VG, I, 129 ff.; the cases cited by Bachofen are rehearsed.

41 Preuss, in *Globus,* LXXXVI, 362-363.

42 Frazer, *Golden Bough,* II, 237.

43 §456, below.   44 Kingsley, *Travels W. Afr.,* 486.

preference in primitive marriage,[45] and we shall cite what we have; but it is necessary to realize both that romantic love is a comparatively modern phenomenon and also that there is a natural tendency to ascribe to all forms of savage behavior a depth and content of feeling which are really a projection from the mind of the observer.

Of the Australians it is said that a "very common error is that there exists no settled love or lasting affection between the sexes."[46] "Love-marriages are not seldom among the Papuans of British New Guinea."[47] The Bushmen, in the absence of much property, give effect to personal inclination in marriage.[48] The Yakuts have love-songs which manifest a well-defined ideal of physical beauty; "sometimes they also speak in honour of mental and moral qualities, such as a pure heart, cleverness, accessibility, industry on the part of men, and on the part of women, tenderness, self-sacrifice, and modesty." Yet in practice they rather dissociate love from marriage; "evidently in marriage they consider it superfluous."[49] A form of love-marriage, based upon the Hindu *gandharva* form, is found in the Indian Archipelago.[50] In Borneo marriage may be a "union of two persons out of love and confidence."[51] In Formosa, "marriages are real love marriages, but marriage obligations are treated lightly."[52] Among the Indians of the Mexican border, "a degree of mutual pleasing may be considered essential."[53] Mason,[54] who likes to see savage life in its "best light," finds several cases of romance among backward tribes. In Albania, on the other hand, "husband and wife had rarely or never seen one another previous to marriage. I never heard of a case in which a youth refused the bride provided for him. When I remarked on this, the people said: 'Why should he? A woman is a woman; God has made them all alike.' Of the girls they said cheerfully, 'Oh! they get used to it after a week or two.' Such a thing as romantic affection appears to exist but rarely."[55]

When they have got used to each other, the savage spouses may come to cherish considerable mutual affection, as a pair of examples will show. Conjugal affection is not, however, relevant to the subject before us. It is the result of long use, wont, and dependence upon mutual coöperation, and does not go back to sex-difference so much as to the fact of having lived together. The following examples must not be taken as typical of primitive life.

[45] Westermarck, *Marr.*, II, 24-25.

[46] Smyth, *Vict.*, I, 29.　　　　[47] Krieger, *Neu-Guinea*, 297.

[48] Fritsch, *Eingeb. S.-Afr.*, 444, 228.

[49] Sieroshevski-Sumner, in JAI, XXXI, 97.

[50] Wilken, in VG, I, 465 ff.　　　　[51] Schwaner, *Borneo*, I, 194.

[52] Wirth, in AA, X, 365.

[53] Hrdlička, in BAE, Bull. XXXIV, 47; Brinton, "Concep. of Love in some Amer. languages," in *Americanist*, 410-432.

[54] *Woman's Share*, 211, 258.　　　　[55] Durham, in JAI, XL, 460.

"Real affection between husband and wife is by no means uncommon, and we cannot too often be mindful of the fact that instances of the reverse, however numerous they may be, must by no means be accepted as the rule. There are infinitely more numerous cases in which conjugal ties are faithfully observed, and these must be regarded as the rule."[56] This somewhat indefinite statement is rather out of character for this author. Fletcher and LaFlesche[57] recount a touching incident, to which we have not encountered a parallel. "One can sometimes judge of the light by the depth of the shadow cast. An old Omaha man stood beside a husband whose wife lay dead. The mourner sat wailing, holding the woman's cold hand and calling her by the endearing terms that are not uttered to the living. 'Where shall I go, now you are gone?' he cried. 'My grandson,' said the old man, 'it is hard to lose one's mother, to see one's children die, but the sorest trial that can come to a man is to see his wife lie dead. My grandson, before she came to you no one was more willing to bring water for you; now that she has gone you will miss her care. If you have ever spoken harshly to her the words will come back to you and bring you tears. The old men who are gone have taught us that no one is so near, no one can ever be so dear, as a wife; when she dies her husband's joy dies with her. I am old; I have felt these things; I know the truth of what I say.'"

Much has been made of the Hector and Andromache picture as an ideal of wedded bliss; it stands out in the setting of its age as a remarkable and exceptional instance. Occasionally there is, in the tragedians, an Alcestis. There is, however, danger of reading into isolated passages that which is not there. It is said that to marry for love is not praiseworthy; if one thus marries beneath him, he leaves his children degraded.[58] Pericles did not, knowing the charm of woman's society, seek Aspasia to get it; he found out from her what it might be—grace, delicacy, refinement, gaiety. Only in the modern age could it be written of love that it is "a Force illimitable, unconquerable and inexplicable. . . . Upon our own atom of a universe it is given the generic name of Love and its existence is that which the boldest need not defy, the most profound need not attempt to explain with clarity, the most brilliantly sophistical to argue away. Its forms of beauty, triviality, magnificence, imbecility, loveliness, stupidity, holiness, purity and bestiality neither detract from nor add to its unalterable power. . . . Men who were as gods have been uplifted or broken by it, fools have trifled with it, brutes have sullied it, saints have worshipped, poets sung and wits derided it."[59]

These instances, sometimes however with significant reservation, indicate the existence of sex-preference in actual marriage; and the evidence as to woman's power of choice[60] supports the case. Nevertheless the disconnection between love and marriage is much more common and regular. The general tenor of all that is to follow about marriage and the family forbids the assumption that love is a more than contributory factor in the early evolution

[56] Dundas, C., in JAI, XLV, 275.   [57] In BAE, XXVII, 327.
[58] Seymour, Hom. Age, 151; Keller, Hom. Soc., 219; Euripides, Alcestis, 152 ff., 620 ff., and Heracleidæ, 297 ff.; Weinhold, Altnord. Leben, 254.
[59] Burnett, The Head of the House of Coombe, ch. XXXII.
[60] §§359, 386, below.

of marriage. It would appear that other ties, especially those of blood, occupied the place of an attraction between the sexes capable of leading, under marriage, to conjugal affection.[61] Here is a pronounced difference in the mores, as well as of emotional nature, from standards to which we are used. It is another way of meeting life-conditions. The affections of the savage are different in direction and scope from those of the civilized European. "That the Africans are affectionate," writes Miss Kingsley,[62] "I am fully convinced. This affection does not lie precisely on the same lines as that of Europeans, I allow. It is not with them so deeply linked with sex; but the love between mother and child, man and man, brother and sister, woman and woman, is deep, true, and pure." Grief at loss of a spouse is formal and ritual;[63] a Polynesian widow has been known to prostitute herself while her funeral-wounds were still fresh upon neck, breast, and arms.[64]

§335. Marriage and Maintenance. When we turn to cases of unions in whose formation considerations of sex-passion or affection are ignored, we find them both regular and concurrent in their emphasis upon the maintenance-interest. Woman becomes indispensable to man "not on account of an impulse which is suddenly aroused and as quickly disappears, but on account of a necessity which endures as long as life itself, namely the need of food."[65] Marriage is primarily a form of coöperation in self-maintenance and its bond is tighter or looser according to the advantages of the partnership under the existing circumstances. It will be noted that the whole matter is generally envisaged from the standpoint of the man, whom no usage ever so consistently bound, or of parents and relatives; this is likely to rule out other than practical considerations. Woman's influence upon her own destiny, except for certain powers which she acquired under the so-called matriarchate, is usually exercised indirectly.[66] She cannot make herself over as an animal nor can she seize forthwith what she wants; but she has always been able to bring pressure to bear upon man to which he, generally unwittingly, has yielded.

61 §427, below.
62 *W. Afr. Studies*, 168; Junker, *Reise*, II, 505; Eyre, *Cent. Aust.*, II, 214.
63 §224, above.
64 Letourneau, *Marriage*, 254.
65 Starcke, *Prim. Fam.*, 257.
66 Ch. L, and §415, below.

Even the fact that she is regarded as a chattel and is roughly treated has not prevented that consummation.

The Australian needs a wife for a comfortable life, as a beast of burden, a food-producer, and an unresisting victim of the violent outbursts of passion which he dare not vent upon his male comrades.[67] When asked why they want women, the men mention the work they expect them to do.[68] In Melanesia the wife's usefulness in field-labors and the like weighs much more heavily in the scale than her personal attractiveness.[69] On Tikopia Island it was the domestic establishment that was the central feature of marriage. "At marriage it is customary for both man and woman to take the name of the house in which they live, husband and wife being distinguished by different prefixes, and if they go to live in a new house they will both acquire new names. In connection with this custom of taking the name of a house, one does not say, 'I am going to the house of so and so,' but simply to the house, mentioning its name. A man will not say that he is going to see Paerongore but that he is going to Rongore."[70] The Kaffir thinks the Christian wife, married for love, is a shameful thing; she is like a cat, the only thing that is not bought, but got as a gift.[71] Among the Ama-Xosa a young man must have a wife in order to get wealth and position. He regards her only for her worth in this respect, and as a laborer and beast of burden. When he buys her, he regards it as an investment of capital which he is to exploit. This is the usual view with savages. A youth takes a fancy to a certain girl and has overtures made to get her as wife; but in such case he has to pay several oxen more than under ordinary circumstances, "and since cattle are on the average nearer to their hearts than women, such a proceeding is not common."[72] In Matabeleland, "the native, in many instances, enters into marriage as a business speculation, just as the white man engages in and carries on commerce through the medium of money."[73]

"Amongst the Tshi-speaking tribes, as amongst most uncivilized peoples, love, as understood by the people of Europe, has no existence. There is here no romantic sentiment, and the relation between the sexes is ordinarily quite passionless."[74] The passion is reserved for property. In the Kenya Colony, "marriage with the tribe is an avowed economic partnership, and were it not for the ceremonies which the parties undergo might well be said not to exist. . . . Other than economic and ceremonial bonds of marriage there are no marriage bonds. . . . Apart from the ceremonies, and it is suggested that they imply fertility only, marriage with the tribe seems to be a commercial transaction and an economic partnership."[75] Among the Hovas of Madagascar, "the idea of love between husband and wife was hardly thought of; . . . the marriage state was regarded chiefly as a matter of mutual convenience, each party carefully retaining separately his or her property."[76] In northeast Africa, there are few unmarried people, for that status would render it impossible to

[67] Oldfield, in *Trans. Ethnol. Soc. London* (1865), III, 25a.
[68] Eyre, *Cent. Aust.*, II, 321.
[69] Von Pfeil, *Südsee*, 155; Danks, in JAI, XVIII, 293.
[70] Rivers, *Melan. Soc.*, I, 344.
[71] Middlebrook, in *Globus*, LXXV, 271.
[72] Fritsch, *Eingeb. S.-Afr.*, 112, 113, 136, 141.
[73] Prestage, in *Folklore*, XII, 328.   [74] Ellis, *Tshi*, 285.
[75] Barton, in JAI, LIII, 69, 73.   [76] Sibree, *Great Afr. Isl.*, 250.

become well off or rich—the goal of all operations for the northeast African. And, "since the wife represents a considerable money-value, such a treasure never remains unlifted."[77]

The Samoyed "never cares for beauty, but chooses one equal to himself in rank and property." "In the North Chin Hills the only question asked by the parents of the young man regarding the girl is as to how quickly and thoroughly she can clear a hillside of weeds or how long it takes her to plant a patch of millet. In the south, however, marriage has much wider interests, and is usually arranged with the diplomatic view of strengthening the position of chiefs and consolidating the power of clans."[78] Among the Tamils, neither bride nor groom has any freedom of choice: "the betrothal is a simple piece of business, which the parents close with each other, and thus nothing is so incomprehensible to the Tamil as our modern love-lyric would be, if he had the opportunity to know about it."[79] The Laws of Manu brand marriage by voluntary union as bad.[80] "Like the Hindu, the Singhalese marries early; and, like the former, with him too it is not an affair of the heart between the two chief participators but a sober, business agreement between their parents. Marrying is above all an affair of interest, not of feeling."[81]

Among the Usbeks, the common man wants a good worker; hence he does not marry a young woman.[82] Yakut marriages "are brought about without the participation or consent of the young people. Only an extreme repugnance to each other on the part of the two, as a consequence of which a passionate and stubborn protest is manifested, may sometimes win attention. If such a protest is made by the man, it more frequently is respected, but they compel daughters, even grown women and widows, by force, and without discussion, to enter into marriage against their will. For this purpose they beat them, or threaten to drive them out destitute from the house. The author mentions a case in which a man compelled the widow of his brother to take as her husband a man whom she did not like, by the threat to take away her children and property from her."[83] With the Kirghiz, marriage is a method of acquiring wealth and connections.[84] Of the Pelew Islands, Kubary[85] says: "Love is to be seen, although seldom openly exhibited through a marriage-union. The latter is regarded as a piece of sober business, the former being left to the youth. Viewed as an institution, marriage secures support to the husband; and to the wife, or rather to her parents, a steady control of advantages. . . . If the wife can do better in the business of marriage elsewhere, she leaves her husband without hesitation."

In choosing a wife the Greenlander pays no heed to love or to beauty in the bride or even to what little property she may bring; "far more decisive in the suitor's choice is skill in house-keeping."[86] Morgan,[87] who denies to the native

[77] Paulitschke, *Nordost-Afr.*, I, 195.
[78] Czaplicka, *Aborig. Siberia,* 123; Carey and Tuck, *Chin Hills,* I, 189, 190.
[79] Gehring, *Süd-Indien,* 74.
[80] Bühler, *Laws of Manu,* III, 39-41.
[81] Schmidt, *Ceylon,* 253.
[82] *Russian Ethnog.* (Russ.), II, 641.
[83] Sieroshevski-Sumner, in JAI, XXXI, 97.
[84] *Russian Ethnog.* (Russ.), II, 188.
[85] *Pelauer,* 53-54, 59.   [86] Fries, *Grönland,* 111.
[87] In *Smithson. Contrib. to Knowledge,* XVII, 207.

Indian the passion of love, continues: "This fact is sufficiently proved by the universal prevalence of the custom of disposing of the females in marriage without their knowledge or participation in the arrangement." Among the Seri "the man is a suitor not so much from personal inclination as from tribal incentive, and while mating is in minor measure an expression of mutual attachment, it is so regulated as to inure to the benefit of the tribe. . . . These characteristics stand for the primitive form of marriage, so far as known in America; yet it is worthy of special note that the essential and fundamental characteristic is the collective motive under which marriage is prescribed for the welfare of the group, rather than inspired by individual appetite and selfish inclination." Among the North American Indians, "marital unions depend everywhere on economic considerations."[88]

An antithesis to romance occurs among the Guiana Indians: "When their young men arrive at a marriageable age they hand over to them the oldest widows in the place for wives, and when they are left widowers they give them a young girl. . . . To marry a boy and a girl is to join a pair of fools who don't know how to conduct themselves, whereas by marrying the young man to an old woman she teaches him as to how the house has to be managed and how he must work to live. When he becomes a widower and marries a young girl, she benefits by his instructions." Examples of this custom of taking an older and then a younger wife, so that a man often has the two contemporaneously, are found throughout the Guianas; the younger may be only six or seven years old and "subserves the former in all domestic employments until the time of puberty."[89]

Among the ancient Greeks, "a union from personal liking . . . was unheard of save in the most exceptional cases." In old Iceland, analogous political considerations determined the choice of a wife.[90] The Bulgars saw in marriage that through which "a material force was brought to the house for the accomplishment of labor. And so the chief consideration was whether the girl was industrious in labor and capable of it. . . . Nearly the whole burden of the domestic economy rests on the shoulders of the wife."[91] "The Bulgar proverb: 'Take a wife that she may carry you in her hands,' characterizes the aim of the south Slav marriage." Boys of thirteen to eighteen are married to older girls in order to provide the house as early as possible with female agricultural laborers. The paterfamilias has sex-relations with these daughters-in-law.[92]

The union of the sexes is primarily industrial. It has largely so remained through history and is of that character now. In so far as it has become conjugal, parental, poetical, emotional, or ethical, that is due to advance of civilization and belongs to the higher grades of the cultured.

That their marriages are not exclusively or even typically for love between the sexes, does not distinguish the savages sharply

88 McGee, in AA, IX, 378, 379; Lowie and Farrand, in HAI, I, 808.
89 Roth, in BAE, XXXVIII, 679.
90 Blümner, *Gr. Privatalterth.*, 260 ff.; Kålund, in *Aarbøger*, 1870, 295.
91 Strauss, *Bulgaren*, 299; *Russian Ethnog.* (Russ.), II, 482.
92 Simkhovitsch, *Feldgemeinschaft in Russland*, 358.

from the civilized. Though affection for children appears on all
stages and though marriage is often contracted with offspring in
view, children generally subserve some interest, economic or religious,[93] and that is what they are wanted for. The full evidence
for rejecting affection as the controlling motive to marriage will
come out only as the whole subject of societal self-perpetuation
is developed; but enough facts have now been set down to render
an inference as to love making marriage a precarious one. And if
contemporary primitives exhibit a substantial unanimity in ignoring the love-interest or at best in subordinating it decisively to
other considerations, it could not have held a more important
place in that remote, inferential past, when the institutions of self-
perpetuation were forming. Motives of a material order must perforce precede sentiment. All the sanctions of religion and the state
are unable to insure stability to an institution which embraces two
wills and controls two lives, uniting them in a pitiless intimacy
and sparing from its influence no interest or sentiment of which
men and women are capable. But capital and property come
nearer to stabilizing the relation than anything else. Capital, says
Lippert,[94] as a store of supplies relieving men from anxiety about
maintenance, sets free the imagination to find attractions in the
human form and so awakens sex-emotions of a more refined order.
It would be a case of reading modern ideas into minds that could
not harbor them and into experiences that did not contain them
to talk of the primitive woman being, through mutual trust and
esteem, a "comrade" to man in marriage. The mores of that time
separated the sexes by barriers that rendered companionship in
the spiritual sense impossible. Man and woman have never fully
understood each other. It was necessity rather than free inclination, and not seldom necessity diametrically opposed to inclination, which produced sex-association in marriage.

§336. The Subjection of Woman. It is coercion rather than
attraction for which we must look in the evolution of institutions;[95] the first point to consider is how woman was forced into
enduring union with man. Upon her, as upon female animals in

[93] §409, below. [94] *Kgchte.*, I, 437.
[95] §§7, 11, 16, 64, 71, 81, 101, 112, 197, above.

general, a certain aloofness was imposed by her sex, though just what Crawley[96] means when he says that "there are grounds for ascribing to woman an almost instinctive physical dread of the male sex," is not crystal-clear. A more definite reason for aloofness, rooting in the mores rather than in instinct, lay in the sense of shame on account of special sex-functions which were regarded as unwelcome peculiarities and therefore as a cause for abashment. It is only at the top of civilization that men have ceased to regard women at the same time with contempt and with dread on account of what is feminine. Women have not yet ceased to feel a certain shame which was originally a product, in the mores, of the way men regarded them. A person who is deformed or disfigured generally withdraws from a sense of difference and inferiority; and the usages of primitive society inculcated this feeling in women from birth. They accepted it as a fact to which their whole lives must conform.[97] Herein lie certain of the sex-barriers to which allusion has just been made. Others are to be noted in the sex-differences already recounted and in those yet to come.[98] Envisaged as a whole, they furnish the strongest of evidence as to the antagonistic nature of sex-coöperation in marriage. Only necessity could have swept them aside.

If woman's aloofness was a matter of sex, so was her need of man's coöperation or better, perhaps, her inability to resist man's coercion to coöperation. This was not due so much as is sometimes assumed to the original quality of her secondary sex-characteristics of size and bodily strength, whereby she must be weaker than man. There are a number of cases where primitive woman is reported as holding her own with man when it has come to direct physical collision.

It appears that among the savages the secondary sex-characters are less marked, so that it is often difficult to distinguish the sexes upon the criterion of general appearance.[99] In Australian fights between bodies of men and bodies of women, "it was not at all certain which would be victorious, for at

[96] In JAI, XXIV, 221.   [97] Sumner, in *Coll. Ess.*, I, ch. III.
[98] §§57 ff., above, and 378 ff., below.
[99] Ranke, *Mensch*, II, 92, 115; Peschel, *Races*, 83; Brinton, *Races*, 37; Ellis, *Man and Woman*, 2, 4; Hagen, *Papua's*, 157; Fritsch, *Eingeb. S.-Afr.*, 39, 299, 398, 415; Pechuël-Lösche, *Loango*, 8; Henning, in *Globus*, LXXII, 102; Nachtigal, *Sahara*, II, 590; Rockhill, in USNM, 1893, 674; Mackenzie, *Voyages*, 208; Lumholtz, in *Scribner's Mag.*, XVI, 296.

times the women gave the men a severe drubbing with their yam-sticks."[100] In Togo, men are often hen-pecked and disciplined at their wives' hands by force.[101] An East Greenlander, it is reported, who tried to flog his wife, ended by being flogged by her.[102] The Shastika men "are conspicuously smaller and weaker than the women"; they degenerate by reason of contact with the whites, and are bogus dandies and sports.[103] The Núkuóro women are so robust that a man who undertakes to beat his wife may get the worst of it.[104] In his desire to acquire a strong worker for wife, the man sets in motion a sort of selection of the sturdy type of woman. An Indian woman, thrown on her own resources, has supported herself with ease during the winter.[105]

The great necessity of woman lay less in herself as an individual than in herself as a mother. The primary association of human beings is that of mother and child; it is in nature and is due to the prolongation of sex-feeling into maternal love. The struggle for existence was just as hard for a woman as for a man and the woman had the burden of the child besides. Whatever her robustness as an individual, maternity put the female under a decisive handicap. She could escape neither the child-bearing nor the ensuing burden bound upon her by mother-love. This is why her necessity was greater than man's. It was rather the consequences of sex than the fact of sex which enforced association upon her on terms commensurate with the degree to which her need outweighed man's. In fact, woman's rights have for ages depended upon the swaying to and fro of advantage in this matter of association.

Mother-love is an emotion which goes with sex and constitutes a burden and handicap for the female, upon whom the species-interest thus rests with disproportionate weight. Some writers hold that the tie between man and woman is a sort of instinctive affection developed by natural selection and they make much of the behavior of certain birds and mammals where the relation of pairs is supposed to be more or less durable because of their joint relation to offspring.[106] But inferences as to primitive traits based upon animal-behavior are extremely shaky;[107] and there is, in any case, no need of them here, for the strength of the societal interests leading to marriage will be seen to offer something en-

[100] Howitt, in JAI, XVIII, 58.
[101] Pater N., in Globus, LXXIX, 352.
[102] Holm, Ethnol. Skizze, 55.
[103] Powers, in Contrib. Amer. Ethnol., III, 243.
[104] Kubary, Núkuóro, 35.   [105] Hearne, Journey, 262.
[106] Westermarck, Marr., I, 29 ff.   [107] §456, below.

tirely positive as against the vague and unverifiable inferences concerning the father's parental instinct. What we find is that nature has assigned to the female the bearing, suckling, and early maintenance of the child. As for male instincts of protection to offspring, they have left no clear traces in ethnography.

The Tasmanian women "are only too happy if . . . the little beings, who owe to them their birth, are not snatched from their arms; for, in times of dearth, to which, through a too dry or too wet year, these savages, who are completely destitute of foresight, are exposed, it frequently happens that the children are abandoned in the middle of the woods, because the father dreads hunger, or prefers to keep the dog which aids him in hunting down the game."[108] To the father-child relation we shall return,[109] but not to find much evidence of philoprogenitiveness on the part of the man.

There is nothing inferential about mother-love. It was put there by nature in the interest of offspring. The human mother shares it with other animals; with her it is and always has been as evident, instinctive, and unreasoning as with them. It has not rested upon knowledge of procreation or of blood-kinship but on the facts of physical connection. It is, as the writers reiterate, an extension of organic sex-life.[110] This veritable passion is of greater duration where infancy is prolonged, and so human mother-love— and human paternal affection too, after the father has been drawn into the range of family life—normally extends over a typically longer period after birth than is the case with other animal-species.[111]

Mother-love, being an instinct, does not originate in the mores; though they generally support it, they may modify its quality or even suppress it, as is the case of Melanesian mothers who often kill their infants to get rid of the trouble they bring,[112] or some modern wives who resent the intrusion of children upon a career or a life of pleasure. The maternal instinct, colliding with the interests of self-maintenance, self-gratification, or religion, may be nullified or thwarted; witness the religious celibacy of priestesses or nuns. It may be strong enough to deny itself, as where, for instance, the Indian women in Spanish America killed their children

---

[108] Roth, *Tasmania*, 167.   [109] §§409, 410, 419, below.
[110] Geddes and Thompson, *Evol. of Sex*, 291.
[111] For the evolutionary aspect of prolongation of infancy see Fiske, *Destiny of Man*.
[112] Von Pfeil, *Südsee*, 18.

or renounced motherhood rather than subject their offspring to the misery awaiting them. In any case this sentiment renders woman less free and independent in the battle of life. There are few cases where mother-love is absent or where it is not far stronger than paternal affection. Not conceiving it necessary to cite evidence of its prevalence and power, we shall list the few cases encountered where it seems to be weak, absent, or nullified.

In South Australia women of a certain district "would preferably rear a male child, but lack almost all maternal feeling."[113] In fear of a power superior to their own, a certain people of New Guinea fled to the mountain-tops before the English, and the women "discarded their babies because they hampered their progress."[114] Among certain Papuans, "there is no word for 'Love.' I know of no animal, except the duck, which is more careless in attending to its young, than the average Papuan mother. How many of them survive infancy and early childhood is a marvel. . . . I do not mean you to understand that there is no kindness shown by mothers to their children. I mean that their interest never rises to what we know as love." And again: "I cannot speak to you in detail of the terrible cruelty which is practised sometimes by mothers, toward their young daughters. . . . Under certain circumstances, the Papuan mother regards the most revolting brutality as necessary, because it is the custom to practise it. Custom here is stronger than natural affection."[115] In West Africa, captive women would leave their newly-born infants in the lurch and run away; one woman threw her suckling infant into the water, before our eyes, and then tried to escape." "The black mother is an excellent mother whilst the child is very young, like most animals. Directly the child begins to grow up, she has no further use for it, and it has to look after itself, like the offspring of any other animal."[116]

Doubtless the emotion of the mother has been much idealized; in particular there is a tendency to read into primitive affections, especially this one, a depth, quality, and intensity that are the product of evolved mores. Yet even among savages its strength may be judged by the resistance it sometimes offers to the mores of the group. The mother-instinct could not be crushed even by the privilege and prestige of the Polynesian Arreoi society, for, although its female members enjoyed a care-free position and high honor, they often withdrew from it merely to have the satisfaction of caring for their children. And even when, in accord with the prescriptions of the society, they had put their own children to death, they would adopt those of others and nurse them in the

[113] Stationmaster, in JAI, XXIV, 177.
[114] Chinnery, in JAI, XLIX, 40.   [115] Abel, *New Guinea*, 42.
[116] Lessner, in *Globus*, LXXXVI, 393; Stigand, *Elephant*, 208, 209.

tenderest manner.[117] Heathen myths and legends go back for the lowest terms of society to a mother with a child; if a beginning is made with man, as in the Hebrew story, woman has to be derived from him by some grotesque invention. The mother-child motif is a basic one in the thought and fancy of mankind.

§337. Sex-Coöperation. By reason then of her special necessity, a necessity resting upon the fact that she is physically and emotionally attached to offspring as man is not, woman needs a degree of coöperation that man does not. It is easily conceivable that this want tended to push her toward marriage and to hold her in it, and perhaps just as conceivable that it tended occasionally to produce uni-sexual coöperation, as in the long-house system under the mother-family.[118] The historical fact is that under any form of marriage woman is held to that form with greater insistence than is man; there has always existed in this respect a dual standard of obligation and of morality. Woman is thus enchained, of course, by the impersonal stress of the mores; then behind these lies the sanction of man's superior strength—of physique, weapons, training, discipline, *esprit de corps*, organization. Even if woman entered marriage deliberately and willingly because of her special need, she could not get out of it freely if relieved of that exigency. Experience of sex-coöperation had impressed the man with a sense of its value and the organized males could coerce any woman to stay in it. Man can force woman to contribute to his advantage; woman cannot thus force man. The fact is that she lacks, in part, the direction of her own life-career, for it is often controlled by her nearest male relatives according to their interest, not hers. The question is as to the status of woman, not that of man. This is a fact of commanding importance.[119] Those who hold to a creed of primitive equality and justice should try to fit their dogma to this case. If we speak of equality, do we mean in domestic life, in social activity, in trade and industry, in civil and political affairs, in religious rites, or in

[117] Lippert, *Kgchte.*, I, 213; this author cites several original sources, to which should be added Cook, *First Voy.*, in Pinkerton, *Coll.*, XL, 520, and especially Moerenhout, *Voyage aux îles du Grand Océan*, I, 484 ff., cited in Letourneau, *Soc.*, 55; Letourneau, *Morale*, 141.

[118] §416, below.   [119] §§64, 65, above.

all of these? As for justice and fairness, they are modern ideas belonging to civilized life which have no sense here. Inequality of sex and of age is the most obvious fact of the societal situation.

All this gets into the mores and under the sanction of the group, including both living and dead. The force employed by way of sanction to the arrangement makes it a societal institution. Here is faced the crude but undeniable fact that those human relations of marriage and the family, which are now viewed with reverence and are experienced with the highest of earthly satisfactions, began with material interest, selfishness, and coercion of the weaker.

The case of man forms a sort of obverse to that of woman, as has appeared by implication in preceding paragraphs. Factors impelling toward marriage and holding the individual in it occur to the mind much more readily in connection with woman than with man. Woman is the special case where man is the general one. Man is the freer agent; apparently the union of man and woman endured as long as the man did not break it. In fact, the salient aspect of the question: What made marriage? is: What brought man into it? and especially: What held him in and to it? It was not sex-passion, as has been seen; nor sex-affection, however idyllic certain of the cases, sometimes rather sentimentally reported, may seem to be; not paternal affection, least of all where paternity is uncertain, where the father is not regarded as blood-related to the children, or where he will sell wife or children to realize self-interest.[120] Not for nothing, however, does the emotional and impatient savage in marrying give up freedom and take on duties; the mores that stress him to do that, however little he deliberates over his action, have large expediency and compelling reason behind them. For man the interest subserved by marriage is personal and direct where for woman it is more complex and also indirect, by way of the child. If man's interest were not served under marriage, he would and could keep out of it; there is nothing else to hold him; he is under no such special sex-coercion as is woman. It is in the conditions of the struggle for existence and maintenance that we must look to discover his compulsion.

If the sex-interest is not that which made marriage, there is left

120 §409, below.

only the maintenance-interest; if it is not love that made marriage, it must be hunger. For the other socializing forces, vanity and ghost-fear, while they have certainly borne their part in forming the institution,[121] are not nearly enough primordial to stand beside the two that have been considered. Since marriage becomes now a sort of organization evolved basically for societal self-maintenance, we are thrown back, for further analysis, upon ground already covered in considering sex-differentiation and sex-coöperation.[122] From that discussion it appears that the sexes are capable of specialization of function and so of coöperation to mutual advantage. This advantage is a most apt criterion for societal selection to work upon. Since the chances of preservation were greater for both sexes in coöperation than apart, variations opening the way to the expedient adjustment tended to persist and to accumulate. The antagonistic coöperation of the sexes was inevitable and constituted the beginning of industrial and societal organization. This general consideration is enough to explain broadly the association of the sexes in marriage, as well as association of human beings in general.[123] Add to it the especial necessity of the woman, and the outlines of the marriage-institution are already there.

These outworkings of society's evolution were all in the mores, so that when men became aware of their significance, their origins were long past.[124] No detailed account can be given of the variations just alluded to and no one can get back to view the details of human behavior in the formative period of sex-association. One can infer, and that is all; but he can form productive inferences if he cleaves to the facts. We infer that the primitive form of sex-association consisted of a man and a woman (or women), the latter remaining by the trysting-place or fire, caring for the young, and gathering what food she could from a restricted area, while the man wandered farther afield for a more enticing quarry.

"The unrestrainedness and irresponsibility of the man, on the one side, and on the other the fetters of mother-love caused the capacities of the two sexes for getting a living to develop in different directions." The products were mutually desirable, although the methods of production were not in accord. So long as the animal-food consisted of worms, shellfish, and the like, both

121 §341, below.   122 Ch. V, above.
123 §§8, 10, 16, above.   124 Sumner, *Folkways*, §7.

sexes were on a more nearly equal footing; but when the man got better weapons and could hunt on a bigger scale, a differentiation took place. She wanted his game, while he, in time of need, wanted her vegetable products; hence there arose in marriage a sort of double economy.[125]

Any reconstruction of these long-past conditions[126] is obviously schematic, being a composite drawn from the most primitive societies known. In its simplicity and well-roundedness it describes no case which could be found; only varieties and modifications of it are presented in fact, for the good reason that it is no more than a composite type drawn from a variety of cases. It furnishes, nevertheless, a starting-point and a primary definition of marriage.

With the main strand of the marriage-institution, which is economic, we shall try to twist in the accessory ones which, in their variety and come-and-go, relieve the pattern of all monotony. If marriage were merely a form of self-maintenance, there could be no reason for setting it apart from the industrial and other maintenance-organizations, for separate and special treatment. Around the maintenance-interest in marriage, however, there plays the sex-interest, which is a specific characteristic of marriage and the family. It forms a second main thread running through the organization for self-perpetuation and differentiating it from any purely economic structure. There is here no single central factor such as the aleatory element, and the economic and sexual interests now alternate and again unite in forming the nucleus of various succeeding topics. What we have in self-perpetuation is a very special type of self-maintenance characterized by the bi-sexuality of the coöperators. There appears in it a series of relationships in which now the economic and again the purely sexual seem to set the tone. There is a destiny worked out for woman;[127] it is in the mores and she knows no other. Very likely it is also in nature, so that when the mores relax and allow of careers like those of men, many women are no more than generally and superficially, not genuinely and personally, interested. Then there are the interests connected with children, family-relationships, descent, ostentation, property, rights, and religion, which all help to form the aspect of marriage in any place and time. If the main interest in

[125] Lippert, *Kgchte.*, II, 27.   [126] §63, above.
[127] §§61, 62, above.

the making of marriage is here analyzed out, that is done for the
sake of eventually seeing the whole in some order and perspective.
The artificially isolated factors must then be allowed to run together and intertwine again before there is present the living,
recognizable institution which we seek to understand.

CHAPTER XLII

THE MARRIAGE-INSTITUTION

§338. Scope of the Institution. "Marriage" is commonly and loosely used as synonymous with "matrimony," "wedding," "nuptials." The so-called marriage service in the Anglican prayer-book is entitled: "Form of Solemnization of Matrimony"; but matrimony is the equivalent of wedlock and describes a state or status of life within an institution; and its solemnization or consecration can consist in nothing else than in living in it faithfully according to the theory and standards of the group at the time. Wedding is the public act of pledge or promise, with attendant ritual, by which two persons enter upon the status of wedlock, so far as their friends and neighbors, the society, state, and church are concerned; the wedding is a fact and an act upon which rights, property, status of children, and societal sanctions depend. Nuptials include the wedding and the actual beginnings of fulfilment of the intentions declared at the wedding.

If there is to be any clarity in terminology, "marriage" should be used for the institution which includes all these facts and acts as parts, and also courtship, betrothal, divorce, and other details of inception, fulfilment, and dissolution, as well. That is, the marriage-institution is the organization for societal self-perpetuation and is parallel to the industrial organization for societal self-maintenance. Marriage is a societal organization by virtue of the regulations in the mores to which it is subject; so soon as there is any regulation not "in nature," the institution has begun to be. Starcke,[1] after asserting that sexual considerations were not the basis of marriage, says that when the woman's sexual freedom is limited, then the field of sex-relation becomes marriage. Since there never was a time when mankind existed and when natural reproduction did not exist, and since there evidently was a period when regulation within the societal order had not yet come into existence, it follows that the race once reproduced without mar-

---

[1] *Prim. Fam.,* 268; Sumner, *Folkways,* ch. X.

riage. With human association came the folkways and mores and out of the latter developed the institution in its several forms.

Though "marriage" is the only available term to cover the whole institution for societal self-perpetuation, it properly denotes also the union of the sexes. Marriage has meant in all ages the association of a man and woman for the struggle for livelihood and the procreation of children, within the limits and conditions and in the mode set by the mores of the group at the time. It is understood that any such definition must be, as in the case of religion, a statement of lowest terms—one including nothing more than what is common both to the crudest and the most evolved forms. Thus the refined idea and ideal of "wife," as held by the high-minded of our day, differs greatly from the conception implied in the above definition of marriage. The idea is a late one: woman was to her husband slave, servant, property, partner, plaything, child-bearer, long before she was friend or better self or soul-mate or affinity.

Though it is not worth while to assemble and criticize numbers of definitions of marriage, several comments from ethnographers and systematists may be cited for the light they throw upon the conditions which we have sought to cover in our definition. One competent observer writes that "marriage, with the savage, is not a contract between two individuals; it is a natural state into which he is born, and therewith he has to be content."[2] "Even the smallest black child who can talk seems full of knowledge as to all his relations, animate and inanimate, the marriage taboos, and the rest of their complicated system."[3] Marriage is a social state, depending on birth.[4] To remain unmarried after a certain age is a disgrace; and fathers sometimes understate the age of their daughters to spare them and themselves from criticism.[5] Mating, even among very backward tribes, "is so regulated as to inure to the benefit of the tribe" as that is provided for in the mores.[6] This piece of observation reveals marriage in its setting in the mores, its form unconsciously developed in the evolution of the local society and accepted as a matter of course, than which no other is considered or conceived; by being who he is, the Australian marries whom he does.[7] "Marriage must be regarded as a legal institution; sexual intercourse between husband and wife is only one of its attributes."[8] Emphasis upon the complementary nature of the sexes appears in viewing primitive marriage as "an association of two persons of opposite sex, looking to the supplementing of their sexual onesidedness."[9] Definitions trail off into a fringe of the eccentric, whimsical, transcendental, metaphysical, and lunatic.

[2] Fison, in AAAS, 1892, 693.   [3] Parker, Euahlayi, 11.
[4] Fison and Howitt, Kamilaroi, 50; Letourneau, Marriage, 271 ff.
[5] Wilken, in VG, I, 448; Tamura, Warum Heiraten Wir? 9.
[6] McGee, in AA, IX, 378, 379.   [7] §261, above.
[8] Starcke, Prim. Fam., 241.   [9] Mucke, Horde, 73-74.

Where "God's purpose" in marriage is invoked,[10] we meet a sort of topic not proper to scientific investigation.

One set of definitions lays stress upon the agency of offspring in making marriage. It is "a more or less durable connection between male and female lasting beyond the mere act of propagation till after the birth of the off-spring."[11] "The criterion of marriage is, aside from sexual intercourse which it has in common with prostitution, and aside from procreation of children which it shares with free love, the rearing, in true and mutual aid, by their true parents, of children procreated by these parents."[12] Some writers seem to feel that having and rearing children is in nature, that the presence of children lends durability to a marriage, and thus that marriage is, to some degree, in nature. They seem to feel that somehow nature has taken a kindly hand in making marriage. From the standpoint of nature it is of no consequence whether or not male and female have taken public vows and entered into a life-status. All nature seems to care about is that there shall be a maximum of impregnation, gestation, birth, and preservation of the young to maturity; and then a repetition of the cycle. The contention will stand reiteration that marriage is in the mores and so is a product of societal evolution and not of the organic process; one of the first efforts of a student of human society should be to realize and then never lose sight of the distinction between these two types of evolution.

A very painstaking collector of instances[13] concludes that "every possible experiment, compatible with the duration of savage or barbarous societies, has been tried, or is still practiced, amongst various races, without the least thought of the moral ideas generally prevailing in Europe, and which our metaphysicians proclaim as innate and necessary." The conditions and active forces under which mankind reproduces are very numerous and complicated, calling for various forms of adjustment. Hence single rules of action which are put forward as necessary and sufficient to assure society of strong members can never be correct or adequate. On the contrary, men live in such a network of co-operating, counteracting, and compensating forces that they can generalize as to policy only on the basis of broad principles of hygiene and life-conduct. Whatever fundamentals there are can be derived only from inspection of the whole evolutionary series of adaptations. The race has for ages helplessly and blunderingly tried out all sorts of variations in the effort to get some expedient or endurable adjustment to the life-condition of bi-sexuality. No generalization is worth much that does not take notice of them

[10] Rodgers, *Domestic Rel.*, 2.   [11] Westermarck, *Marriage*, I, 71.
[12] Schroeder, *Geschlechtl. Ordnung*, 100.
[13] Letourneau, *Marriage*, 344.

all. To cover such a series of variations in the mores the definition
of marriage has to be stripped to fundamentals that it may remain inclusive.

No definition built on the principle of a greatest common factor
can include all the features of marriage as developed under high
culture. Marriage has always provided, and never more than today, one of the few grand ranges for idealization.[14] The institution has been developed by it. On all the higher grades of society
there floats in the realm of phantasy a conception of the marriage-relation which is ideal, romantic, poetic, never realized, but
yet the most enthusiastic dream which mortals have ever imagined. To bring it to actuality would require youth, health, wealth,
beauty, talent, and power without limit or end. In fairy tales and
romance these conditions have been represented to be true because
otherwise the selected ideal of love and union could not be set
forth. In the world of reality, inevitabilities have come in to destroy the illusion: age, sickness, childlessness, poverty, and the
rest of the ills of life. Men say: "We have missed it, but it is real";
or: "We could and should have realized it if only this or that had
been different in our lot." Few, if any, ever do or can realize the
ideal of marriage that runs through our literature and is professed as a matter of faith in our intercourse with one another.

Marriage cannot be defined on the basis of such idealization.
The loftiest conception of it which has yet attained some realization in the practical life of families is that of the fusion of two
lives and interests for the fuller satisfaction of the interests and
desires of each, and with especial reference to the procreation and
nurture of children. In dealing with the evolution of marriage, it
cannot be defined on the basis of such an evolved and refined conception. If, repeating our definition in a somewhat more explicit
form, we say that marriage is the institutional relation of man
and woman, when more or less durable, as created by the mores,
defined by the taboo, and enforced by society, we have what might
be called the highest common factor of all forms in the evolutionary series that deserve the name of marriage. If idealization were
to be provided for, the definition would be indefinitely narrowed
in scope. Nevertheless it is the idealization or, from another angle,

14 §430, below.

the discontent, that leads to change and new adjustment. Those who because of wealth or other form of power can do so, try out variations. Then the mores may reach forth to embrace them and the taboo may give them sanction if they prevail over the old ways and the latter die out.

There exists also, in regard to marriage, a large element of "pathos," in the original Greek sense of the word. Pathos is not sentimentalism nor yet holiness; it is something of both. The subject of marriage is one of large interest to society and at the same time of intense personal interest. It is thought expedient, in the interest of society, to maintain in regard to it a certain set of opinions and feelings; and if anyone criticizes these on the score that their truth is debatable, he is frowned upon. The subject becomes conventional. It is protected by the current agreement not to handle it freely. Certain sentiments in regard to it are nursed in literature, sermons, lectures, and periodicals. Certain ways of talking about it are made customary and are practised by those who desire to do and say what they or others suppose is favorable to the welfare of society. Novels and plays, seeking popularity, reiterate the view which is conventional and current and thus support and further inculcate it.[15] All this makes marriage a subject by itself and, since it is in its nature mysterious and as it has in it an inevitable element of chance, thus luck and personal happiness, hope and trust, and an optimism which cannot help being blind are its usual concomitants. Herein lies the element of pathos. It complicates the inconsistencies present in the field.[16] It is not all bad and it is by no means all false but for the present purpose the important fact is that it is not all true. Pathos has a practical expediency in that it protects marriage from tampering and tinkering and lends it stability. Its effect is identical, whatever the institution to which it attaches. The scientist must recognize its presence in the field and guard himself against becoming subject to its criticism-stifling influence; he must not be led to treat marriage or any other institution otherwise than on its merits.

§339. The Regulation of the Sex-Impulse. Sex-passion takes hold of the highest and lowest parts of human nature, both physi-

[15] Sumner, *Folkways*, §180.   [16] §333, above.

cal and mental. In its strength it is the culmination of vitality, vigor, power, hope, command of life; growth and development are at full tide. The fashion in the modern age is to exalt it in a somewhat idealized form, so that sex-attraction is taking the position in marriage once held by considerations of property and service. This brings impulse rather than calculation to the fore. There is no question but that sex-passion is environed by perils to both individual and society; excess, abuse, and vice are visited by frightful consequences. There is in sex-relations an immense range which forms, as it were, a closed circle, sweeping from the most unbridled self-indulgence (never reaching satisfaction but forever opening new vistas of extravagance on the mental side while progressively destroying powers of gratification on the physical) to ascetic self-denial, glorification of virginity, and negation of all indulgence as sinful. The last has often issued in prurient abuse. This passion, when thoroughly aroused, represents the acme of impulse; it must needs have surpassed all other impulses, in its period, or the race would long since have perished. Just because the sex-function in so many ways contravenes the immediate life-interests of the individual,[17] must it have been powerfully developed under nature. It is so preoccupying among animals that if it were not periodic it is difficult to see how they could have pursued the struggle for existence with success. The fact that it is not periodic for mankind,[18] renders control all the more needful; and in human society it meets another sort of check characteristic of societal, not of organic evolution.[19]

It is utterly false to maintain that to neglect the function of any member or to deny satisfaction to any natural appetite is a crime against one's self; that every human being has a claim or right not only to be allowed to satisfy any natural desire but to be able to do so; that it is his duty to do so.[20] This view is highly anti-social. The life of man is set within limits and under controls which are as essential as liberty; at the boundaries of his circum-

[17] §332, above.

[18] See, however, Westermarck, *Marriage,* I, 78-79, 81-86, 96-97, 100; Mucke, *Horde,* 68-69; Hill, in JAI, XVIII, 93.

[19] Keller, *Soc. Evol.,* 25 ff.

[20] Bebel, *Die Frau u. der Socialismus,* 76-77. This is, "by virtue of the power of its suggestion, one of the most pernicious books that a noble-hearted enthusiast ever wrote." Gruber, cited in "Moral und Hygiene," in *Umschau,* IV, 846.

scription he beats against disease and death. Discipline or law is the inevitable correlative of liberty, for the only liberty that has worth—in fact, the only genuine liberty that exists—is liberty under law.[21] The welfare of man in society is in the satisfaction of needs and appetites within lines laid down. Property may be got, not by murdering the possessor and stealing but by acquisition within the code; so sex-impulse may be gratified, not by license and tyranny but in the institution and within the mores.

Sex-passion in its unbridled satisfaction is destructive to the individual and therefore to the society because it enervates in mind and body the active and responsible component members of the latter. From the standpoint of society sex-passion is only a means of self-perpetuation and children are the sole object of it. That is all that is expected of it, and in order that it shall properly discharge its function its aberrations must be controlled, as they are, automatically in the mores. Sex-passion is a field of severe moral discipline; it is mighty and yet must be controlled. Man did not make it what it is, nor is the discipline to which it is subjected in society the fault of any person or any class; it is an automatic development, to the interest of society, in the mores. The man or class that rebels against its presence in societal life is as reasonable as he who revolts against the force of gravitation.

Restraint of the sex-impulse in the interest of society is always in evidence, whatever the population-situation—whether it calls for numbers or the reverse. The ultimate consequences of pain, disease, and death prove restraint necessary and enforce it. In the interest of society even the tongue must be bridled and held to truth; anger must be kept in check and impulsive behavior subjected to convention. Everyone by reason of living in society must submit to a limitation of independence and freedom by something outside of his personality. It is these limitations on conduct that create institutions by way of the mores. The reaction of man on his own earthly career has reached its greatest triumph in the subjection of the sex-impulse to the written and unwritten laws of propriety, decency, and restraint. The selfish passion of adults has been disciplined by a thousand injunctions and prohibitions and the ensuing institutions of marriage and the family have been

[21] Sumner, *Coll. Ess.*, II, 156 ff.

raised to be springs of personal satisfaction, reacting, not through the senses alone but through the most refined aptitudes for enjoyment of which civilization has rendered man capable.

The evolution of civilization reveals a long series of successes in the discipline of sex-passion. Sometimes a restraint, having been pushed beyond measure, has been relaxed; sometimes it has weakened and been tightened up. It is far from being true that that is more wholesome which is more stringent, or that more happy which is more free. Conscious or unconscious in its development, discipline is always there. The most obvious of regulation is by law; but the laws are only selected and codified mores[22] and they exercise no more than a rough and incomplete control of externals.

§340. Function of Marriage. There is no question but that marriage has had as one of its chief functions the regulation of the sex-impulse and of sex-relations. All institutions are regulative through the applications of the taboo which builds them, and they are identifiable and distinguishable upon the basis of the range within which they operate. There would be no occasion for setting marriage off from the industrial organization and property if it were not for the fact of human bi-sexuality. The function of marriage is to take care of human relationships which exist as a consequence of the division of the race into two sexes. It cannot perform that function, however, without becoming involved in the meshwork of institutional structure as a whole. We hasten to envisage this situation in more concrete guise.

Rivers[23] is of the opinion that the dominant function of marriage is its regulation of descent, inheritance, and succession: "The institution of marriage has two great functions: it is the means of regulating sexual relations, and it is the means of regulating descent, inheritance, and succession. In civilised communities the former function is so predominant in the minds of most, and especially in the minds of the non-legal, that it is perhaps rarely recognised that at lower levels of culture the latter function is at least equally, and probably more, important. When the history of marriage has been fully traced out, it will almost certainly be found that its function as a regulator of descent, inheritance and succession has played the chief part, and that its function in the regulation of sexual relations remained indefinite long after the institution had reached a high degree of definiteness as a regulator of other

22 §181, above.
23 *Melan. Soc.*, II, 145; and *Soc. Org.*, 37-38.

social relations. In other words, the primary and fundamental function of marriage is the determination of the place which each newly born individual is to take in the social structure of the community into which he or she is born." In another place the author puts his case from a slightly different angle: "Each child, by virtue of being born as a child of a marriage, takes its place in the social structure. Certain members of the group are its relatives; others are not necessarily relatives, but they belong to the same clan or moiety; certain members of the opposite sex are possible mates, while others are for-bidden: all these and other such relationships are determined by an act of birth into a family group. Looked at from this point of view, marriage may be an institution of the most definite and highly organized kind, although in its rôle as a regulator of sexual relations it may be of a very lax and imperfect order."

Marriage offers a sort of framework upon which personal and group-relations having to do with industry, property, war, gov-ernment, and religion, when these have an element of the sexual in them, are plotted and apportioned. The interrelations between marriage and these other institutions will be indicated in the next topic. Society has automatically utilized the trunk-line and branchings of the blood-kinship that follows upon propagation in order to transfer along them, without disorder, both property and social position—inheritance and succession. Rights have formed as a sort of accretion along the same lines. Marriage, we repeat, but provides a convenient, preëxistent schematization of personal and group-relationships consequent upon bi-sexuality, of which regulation in the broad interests of society can make apt use.[24] Adult man and woman, with their complementary capaci-ties, move into a maintenance-organization wherein their work, rights, and duties are apportioned; and within this one-sided or mutual monopoly sexual relations take place, just as eating and sleeping take place. Children are born, and are allocated with the pair (or with the mother alone) and with each other, as blood-kin. The process goes on until there is a network of personal and group-relations. What shall be done with a person's property, when he dies, or with the office he has won? The nearest recourse is to let what he has had remain with those whom he has had. Hence inheritance and succession attend upon descent, which fol-lows blood, the conception of unity of blood being consequent upon a certain sexual union.

This framework or plan of things is not to be shattered be-

[24] See §261, above, for a similar utilization of preëxisting categories.

cause it does not suit everyone. In marriage, as in other institutions, interests are reduced to harmony or something approaching it by limitation in the form of the taboo. The mores define a relation between man and wife and then between the two of them, severally or conjointly, and their children and others in the group;[25] the taboo, being a prohibition of any action by anybody which would violate these relations, is a guard and guarantee of them. Rights are the results. Jealousy, in its primitive form, is a sentiment of personal vanity by which individuals are driven to defend these rights. Adultery is a violation of the taboo on the wife; since among many primitive peoples the wife is property, this crime is found to be assimilated with theft. Incest is sex-union in contravention to the taboo as to who may not marry. Prostitution is total disregard of the general and institutional taboo on the sex-relation. Force imposed these limitations just as in the case of property; force, causing as it did a certain set of relations to exist through generations, was what made the institution; and all the facts and relations, together with the emotions and reflections produced by them, have passed into the history and evolution of the institution as it has come down to the present.

The marriage-institution, with the swarm of mores and taboos by which it is buttressed, is a most astonishing result of the reaction of man on his life-experience and of the institutional effects which can be produced by the inconscient struggle of mankind to adjust life-arrangements to life-conditions under the test of societal expediency. No wonder that society insists upon suppressing departures from the norms of its code. It has done that in both direct and abrupt and also in indirect and subtle ways, but toleration of variations in the matter of sex-relations has been a vanishing quantity.

If anyone could have bidden defiance to the mores of his time it was the revered and almost deified Goethe. When he took a mistress and lived openly with her, he was doing what a number of eminent men of his day were doing. Yet after some years he married her and legitimized their children. Not even his supreme genius and his extraordinary personality and popularity could exempt him from the penalties exacted by society. We have his own word for it.

"A younger friend . . . had confided to the master that he was soon to be

25 §425, below.

married, although he . . . was much inclined to follow the example which Goethe had set, had he not felt that, just because he was an underling, he was in duty bound to tread the ordinary paths. To this Goethe replied: 'First, however, I will give my blessing to a speedy marriage, as soon as your cabin has some sort of a foundation and roof. All that you say about that I subscribe to word for word, for I can well assert that everything bad, or worst, which meets us within the law, whether natural or civil, corporeal or economic, never equals even the thousandth part of the misfortunes that we have to fight through if we go ahead outside or beside the law, or perhaps even in contravention of law and custom, and yet at the same time feel the necessity of remaining in equilibrium with ourselves, with others, and with the moral world-order.' "26

Rising disharmony causes unrest, agitation, and change until a new adjustment is reached. Agitation disturbs the poise of the institution and injures its effectiveness in securing comfort to those living under it. Particularly is this true when the agitation takes rise in whimsical or imaginary interests; the canon law and much of the law derived from it represents the propaganda of clerics who, though they renounced marriage and had no experience of it, yet, by reason of their dogmas, did not hesitate to visit it with contempt. However rational the aims of some of the advocates of sacerdotal celibacy, doctrinaires came to have in their heads artificial and absurd notions of the intrinsic merit of celibacy and asceticism, all of which set about them an horizon of fictions and incongruities. Through books of casuistry, preaching, and the confessional they forced their ideas into the stock Christian mores. This brought war with realities and the inevitable curse of unhappiness.

Whatever the regulations were by which, at any stage, the marriage-institution was constituted and however little they provided for the love-interest, the latter has always been somewhat in evidence as a sort of factor of variation. The case is one of nature crossing convention. Personal inclination may be said to have acted as a solvent to keep the institution mobile and changeful until in modern times love has come to be, ideally, the cardinal principle of the whole. It would appear that this is thought to inaugurate a final and solid basis for the institution; but the contrary is the case. In view of the frivolities of divorce, the relative sterility of the cultured, the dissatisfaction of women with their traditional destiny, socialistic discontent with the family-organi-

26 Geiger, *Goethe und die Seinen,* 110.

zation, and other like indications, it would seem that the institution never was more in question as to its sense, purpose, and nature than in the modern age; that the experience in it was never more unsatisfactory than now; and that all this is perhaps most strikingly true where marriage is most left to the predetermination of the chief parties, who are assumed to act from irresistible personal inclination.

In view of the automatic play of interests in the marriage-institution, it is grotesque to assert that reproduction is altruistic and society-regarding, as contrasted with nutrition, which is egoistic and self-regarding. "Nutrition is everywhere egotistic; but reproduction is invariably altruistic in its character."[27] It would be unprofitable to spend any time upon this class of assertion if we could not thereby become clearer as to the real nature of societal functions—on the principle that finding what and where a thing is not is one way of discovering what and where it is. There is a jumble of terms invented by those who meditate and introspect instead of pursuing real study: individualistic, egoistic, social, altruistic, self-regarding, others-regarding, race-regarding— which is most favorable to muddled thinking and to dabbling in "sociological" discussion on the part of half-educated people. Today there is no easier way to play at being cultivated than to acquire a facility in juggling with such terms, every one of which, although it may be full of meaning, is of an abstract character which allows it readily to become hollow and false. Let us look briefly into the typical case of nutrition versus reproduction.

Reproduction (self-perpetuation), we are told, is altruistic. But it covers two things: the sex-relation and, incidental to it, the production of offspring. The former is the result of an appetite quite as self-centered as the hunger that impels to nutrition and, in its natural manifestations, far more selfish and more absorbing to the subject of it and more tyrannical toward its object. Need we go into detail concerning the action of a passion that sweeps the individual into an acme of self-absorption? If we disregard the conventionalities, pretenses, and assumptions by which we fence off this entire subject and then look squarely at what we know to be the facts in any society that exists now or ever has existed, we know that the non-egoistic, in the sense of the societal, aspect of the sex-relation has never won more than a very slight sway over a very few people for a small part of life.

As for "nutrition" (self-maintenance) being egoistic, it is true, first of all, that nutrition leads on to reproduction—whether we think of the savage who

27 Browne, in PSM, XLIV, 674.

has won food enough, or of the civilized man who, having wealth and satiety on the side of property, turns his care, effort, and ambition to marriage and family. In any case, if reproduction has taken place, nutrition must then be provided by somebody for the children; the effort merges necessarily and insensibly into societal, coöperative processes and becomes a societal, "altruistic" function. If nutrition includes the process of winning supplies (effort) and that of consuming them (satisfaction), then the case is one of imperfect analysis, which is the cause and ground of the whole controversy. Here are simply pulsations of concentration and diffusion of effort and satisfaction in the process of which it is only individual and societal aspects that are presented.

There are stages of society, and cases in all stages, where a population-policy calls for fecundity; but this societal interest, as affording a motive-force for procreation, is insignificant as compared with the pressure toward self-satisfaction. When offspring are a burden—one which increases with advancing civilization[28]—that gives an entirely different aspect to sex-passion. In its consequences the self-regarding act proves to be a cause and compulsion to sacrifice, the greatest in nature, that of parents for offspring. And the sacrifice rolls up on itself; for the more one sacrifices for an object the more he loves it, and the more he loves the more will he sacrifice. That this appears as an unpremeditated consequence, as a burden entailed by a satisfaction (whereas in nutrition the effort comes first and leads up to the satisfaction), is true in all but a small minority of cases in all stages of civilization. Reproduction is societal only in the sense that by it the continued existence of society is assured; but this fact is of subordinate interest or of no interest to the individual. He is not taking on a burden of sacrifice for the society; he could live his own life without children, though without them society could not live on in its life.

Man never has the race in view; it is himself and his that he considers. At a time sex-passion drives him out of himself to another. Children widen still further the range of his interest outside of himself. This non-self-interest is capable of immense range, from an incidental occasion to a life-long absorption in wife and children which contributes the motive of effort and the crown of existence. Thus from his gratification of a self-centered appetite, incidentally and beyond his will (for men and women rarely anticipate the absorption arising out of parenthood), have come into existence persons and relations to persons which react upon him. His energy and emotions, however, though they have gone out beyond himself, are yet limited; the more intense his family-affections and interests the more sharply are they drawn against everybody else. The family is the node, core, or ganglion in which the individual and the societal meet. The societal forces are brought into action incidentally, unintentionally, and therefore unintelligently in the satisfaction of the individual, and the society is produced unawares. Man loves his wife, then his children, not the race. In gratifying himself, then them, he is inevitably drawn into societal activities and becomes "others-regarding." He gives, but only to take for himself and them. Thus the family may be regarded, if one cares to look at it in that way, as the interlacing-point of egoism and altruism.

Nutrition and reproduction cannot then be set in antithesis to one another, as one being individual and the other societal; and

[28] §§25, 42, 43, above, and 402, 403, below.

all inferences from the assumption that this antithesis exists must be regarded as unsound.

§341. **Marriage and the Other Institutions.** Marriage, together with all other institutions of society, shows close relations with co-existing societal forms; for all of these, arising out of the mores, are subject to a strain of consistency with one another.[29] Every wide fluctuation or convulsion in the mores has important consequences in the effects upon the relation of the sexes, the status of woman, the stability of marriage, and the integrity of the family. A realization of the mutual relations of institutions is something that comes from a study of their details rather than from a general inspection of their nature; nevertheless, to get a true sense of their endless interplay, one must be looking for the interrelations as he reviews the details. We call attention, thus in advance, to certain of these interrelations.

It has been seen that marriage and self-maintenance are so vitally allied that the former looks like a special case of the latter;[30] and that alliance is epitomized in some sort in the almost inextricable interweaving of marriage and property. Marriage has had a far more dramatic history, for the interest in it has been enthusiastic and vivid where that in property has been more matter-of-fact and solid. In the latter there has been much less chance for ideal and theory, inasmuch as variations in this range of the societal field are more definitely and sharply tested up.[31] But the two have reacted upon each other at every stage, as the cases accumulated through coming pages will demonstrate. Rights in property and in marriage develop and are suspended together,[32] as witness the Russian Soviet's decrees: it has been proposed to recognize common-law marriage, though the period of living together "must be a reasonably long one" if the couple desires that the union be legalized by the courts.

The *Atlantic Monthly* publishes an article by "A Woman Resident in Russia," which demonstrates the principle that when men tamper with private property they strike also at the family. The latter was regarded as a "bourgeois" institution and the revolutionists set out, in 1917, to abolish it. There was a law proposed in 1925 to do away with certain of these "bourgeois" limitations on

[29] Sumner, *Folkways*, §5.
[31] Keller, *Soc. Evol.*, 129 ff.

[30] §335, above.
[32] §362, below, and *Case-Book*, §344.

freedom. Opposition centered about four points: "(1) that it would abolish marriage; (2) that it would destroy the family; (3) that it would legalize polygamy and polyandry; (4) that it would ruin the peasants. . . . Krilenko, the Soviet public prosecutor, who had a very large share in the framing of the bill and is one of its most passionate advocates, argued that there is neither necessity, importance, or even utility in the registration of a marriage. 'Why should the State know who marries whom?' he exclaimed. 'Of course, if living together and not registration is taken as the test of a married state, polygamy and polyandry may exist; but the State can't put up any barriers against this. Free love is the ultimate aim of a socialistic State; in that State marriage will be free from any kind of obligation, including economic, and will turn into an absolutely free union of two beings. Meanwhile, though our aim is the free union, we must recognize that marriage involves certain economic responsibilities, and that's why the law takes upon itself the defense of the weaker partner, from the economic standpoint.' "[33] To be aligned with the ambitious program of abolishing private property and marriage is the accompanying assault on religion. That these institutions will all have to go, if the effort to annihilate any one of them is to succeed, is a truth that has probably been revealed to offhand statesmen like Krilenko.

It will be seen that in many cases the wife or child seems almost to be property pure and simple, as a slave or an animal is property. Marriage and property will be found linked together in the bride-price, in the dowry, in marriage-stipulations in general, in the transitional and the lasting forms of the family, in inheritance, in the alignment of adultery and theft, and in the rights accorded the woman and child.[34] Not only is one tempted at times to list marriage under self-maintenance; he meets with the reflection also that marriage is sometimes no more than a species of property.[35]

Marriage and property are thus continually influencing each other and running parallel. Not precisely and concordantly, however; for it is not to be forgotten that historical institutions have never developed logically and harmoniously. In a theoretical view it is clear that all parts of an institution should develop harmoniously and contemporaneously and that all relations between institutions should move into line duly, in proper sequence, and at the

[33] Assoc. Press despatch, June 12, 1925; "The Russian Effort to Abolish Marriage," in *Atl. Mo.*, CXXXVIII, 108 ff.

[34] Instances of the interrelation of marriage and property are scattered throughout Letourneau's collections, especially in his *Evolution of Marriage* (ch. IV, and 51-52, 54, 60, 70, 107-108, 118, 119-121, 131, 147, 199, 204-206, 311, 323, 326, 347, 352-354) and *Evolution of Property* (33, 34, 104-105, 153, 323, 336, 365).

[35] Vinogradoff, *Hist. Jurispr.*, I, 197.

right juncture, if all is to go prosperously and with the best results. No such state or operation has been realized in history. On the contrary, the evolution is disjointed and jerky, and states occur in which different institutions or different parts of them are out of gear with each other on account of the presence of survivals or maladjustments.

In general, property acts as a stabilizer to marriage. It is like the lead keel of the yacht, which hangs, heavy and solid, under the surface, keeping the superstructure right side up and steady amidst the squalls. Gusts of passion have often enough threatened the stability of the marriage-relation but it has been maintained in the face of emotional unheaval by the very real and tangible property-interest involved. The stable, practical, clearly-seen interest steadies the wavering, flighty, sentimental, idealized one. Property is a sort of gyroscope to marriage.

A single illustration will carry the point for the moment. The Dyak groom must deposit a value of twenty to three hundred and twenty dollars in the hands of the girl's parents. This is to keep the groom on the right track in future, for if he is untrue to his wife, she gets the deposit. Let there be a small slip with a shamaness or harlot and the wife appropriates it. Such slips are easily made, for these women of loose life come to the feasts where everyone is drunk, and they are beautiful and seductive. The path of the man is thorny, the more so as the custom is not reciprocal, the woman depositing no such forfeit.[36]

Self-perpetuation and self-gratification are closely interwoven. In many cases the unmarried have no standing in the community; the unattached Korean, for instance, is called a half-man and is deficient in social status.

"The Korean is nobody until he is married. He is a being of no account, a 'hobbledehoy.' The wedding-day is the entrance on respectability and manhood, and marks a leap upwards on the social ladder. . . . His name takes the equivalent of 'Mr.' after it; honorifics must be used in addressing him—in short, from being 'nobody' he becomes a 'somebody.' "[37]

It is essential to the distinction of the individual that he shall enter the marriage-institution. Since a man cannot secure a wife until he has won glory in some way, by taking a head or a scalp or performing some other deed of valor, the possession of a wife or wives is a badge of distinction. Puberty-ceremonies antecedent

[36] Perelaer, *Dyaks*, 49.   [37] Bishop, *Korea*, 114-115.

to marriageability test the man and often the woman;[38] and the
parties who fail to exhibit the qualities called for by the mores
remain in a sort of contemptible minority. They are not of age
and lack the dignity of majority. Ornamental deformations, fashions of many kinds, and various other societal phenomena classifiable under self-gratification[39] are intertwined with considerations
of sex and marriage. Stories, narrative and dramatic, iterate and
reiterate the love-motive, playing with undying interest about this
unparalleled crisis in human life; the other great crises of birth
and death, though not neglected, inspire a different sort of interest.

The connection between marriage and religion seems to the
modern observer very close; in fact, it is thought by many that
the latter really makes the former. An occasional enthusiast is
persuaded that "marriages are made in Heaven," and more than
a few contractants would not consider themselves married if there
had been no religious ceremony. This idea, however, is a late one,
for it is only in modern times that the church has introduced into
the mores the idea that marriage is a religious matter.[40] At a very
early period, it is true, religion entered into this field, as into all
other societal departments, in its functions as sanction of the
mores. The aleatory element is conspicuous in marriage; luck and
happiness are at stake in all stages. Concerning the other two of
the great life-crises, just alluded to, the individual has nothing to
say, while upon the outcome of his marriage, which is more or less
in his own hands, really depends the character of his career. This
has been realized in a dim sort of way by men of all periods and
of a consequence the most elaborate of precautions, from a daimonological point of view, have been taken to avoid bad luck and
secure good fortune. Fate in marriage is largely on the knees of
the gods: "Easily recognizable is the offspring of the man to
whom the son of Kronos has allotted happiness in his birth and
marriage."[41]

Marriage remains in the mores and is sanctioned as are other
forms of association, such as friendship, partnership, and brotherhood, by invocation of the supernatural. In West Bengal, girls

---

[38] §§163, 282, above, and 365, below.   [39] §§444 ff., below.
[40] §§372 ff., and ch. LIX, below.   [41] Homer, *Odyssey*, IV, 207-209.

cement their friendship by a religious ceremony.[42] Thus was marriage solemnized by a rite. Inherently inessential to it, this rite
and ritual came to be regarded, because of the exceeding importance to society of that which they sanctioned, as actually creative of the institution. This is but one more striking case of the
infiltration of the religious idea and ceremonial through the body
of the mores; so thorough was that permeation that religion has
been thought to be the creator of mores, morals, and institutions
in general. The reader will encounter, as he goes on, the various
ways in which recourse was taken to religion in connection with
marriage: how horoscopes were cast to determine the fitness of
the parties and the suitability of the wedding-day; how the wedding-ceremony was loaded with precautions and survivals; how
sterility was avoided and fecundity assured; and how family-life,
the blood-bond, inheritance, and even divorce were sanctioned in
general and in their various detail by daimonological practice.
And it is true that marriage and religion relax together.[43]

"At the time of betrothal the prospective bridegroom goes to the house of the
parents of the girl and eats and drinks there. He is accompanied by a person
called *anisu*"—an old man or woman—"who drinks and eats before the prospective bridegroom does so and blesses the match. This is no doubt to assure,
if possible, that any evil influences attending the proposed marriage shall fall
on the *anisu*, who is old and therefore unimportant or less susceptible, rather
than on the bridegroom, just as the reaping and sowing of crops are initiated
by old persons who have in any case little to expect of life, are of little value
to the community as fighting, working, or breeding units, or perhaps who are
so tough as to be able the better to withstand evil influences, for it is clear
that young infants are the most vulnerable."[44]

As respects the relation of marriage to the regulative organization it may be noted, first, that "marriage is no product of law.
It is an institution which began with man and its origin lies far
beyond any human ordinances."[45] This is an approach to saying
that it is in the mores. The necessary conditions of marriage are
in its own nature; those prescribed by law cannot annul it. The
basic fact in this connection is that marriage has jural consequences for the enforcement of which all must look to government
and law. It is held to be a shame that two people should be living
together without having duly engaged that their relation shall

42 Hopkins, *Relig. India*, 535, note.　　43 §163, above.
44 Hutton, *Sema Nagas*, 238-239.　　45 Freisen, *Kanon. Eherechts*, 91.

last out their lives, that is, without having put it out of their power into that of the state to terminate their relationship. Rights have to be defined in the relation: between man and wife, parents and children, and other parties whose interests are involved. Particularly in question are rights to property and so the whole matter of legitimacy. Marriage is a case of presumptions and assumptions. Who questions them? Another heir might.

Laws, contemplating as they do classes of cases, not of persons, must show some uniformity; they enforce consistency in the mores. They take care of types, where the mores cover the variations or fringes. Then laws must fail to cover all cases. Many people, regarding marriage as an affair of religion, construe it according to their sect-codes which are numerous and various. How can law allow for such variations and yet keep the uniformity that belongs to it, and secure the integrity of the state? This situation, coupled with the broad interest of any society in the marriage relation and its consequences,[46] is enough to insure the constant preoccupation of government and law with marriage. The two tighten and relax together.[47]

In Australia, to take a wife without the formal sanction of the local organization is punishable by death.[48] Among the ancients marriage was "only a political institution destined to furnish citizens for the fatherland"—"only the sacrifice of a personal pleasure to public duty."[49] "The powers involved in this matter are not confined to the mere ceremony of the marriage, and do not end with the decree of divorce. They embrace the whole range of domestic life, involving the family relations. They extend to the powers exercised by a court of chancery with regard to guardianship of minors, and the custody, maintenance, and education of children. They extend to the distribution and division of the property, real and personal, belonging to the husband or wife, or to which the children may be entitled, under the provisions of a will, or by right of descent or inheritance, in case there is no will. They involve questions of legitimacy. When the student takes up his law-book and refers to the separate heads under which these matters are familiarly classed by text-writers on the subject of jurisprudence, he will comprehend the vast extent of power which they cover."[50]

Sir Charles Dundas[51] found this relation between laws and marriage so well-balanced that changes in the former threw the latter into utter confusion. "Of

46 §332, above.   47 *Case-Book,* §344.
48 Howitt and Fison, in JAI, XIV, 156.
49 Schmidt, *Soc. Civ.,* 28, 38-39; Jolly, *Sec. Mariages,* 38.
50 Snyder, *Geog. of Marriage,* 178-179.
51 In JAI, XLV, 284.

all questions in native law the most difficult to investigate is that of marriage, partly because inflexible rules regarding the relations between two persons are difficult to maintain, and partly because it is in this direction that native law seems first to fall into disuse. I have taken pains to arrive at the original customs and views on this subject, not only because the present corruption of these cannot be regarded as permanent or legal, but also because after several years of daily experience of questions arising out of native marriages, I have been forced to the conclusion that the original customs are the only ones capable of maintaining marriage as it is understood by the natives."

In any case the modern fact is that the consent of the state remains the one essential sanction of marriage or of its dissolution. Propriety and decency may be in the mores but legitimacy is in law. The most ardent believer in the religious sanction of marriage must get a license and there must be publicity of some kind. The free-love and casual unions called for by certain types of religion are not legitimate; nor is polygamy tolerated because it has been approved or suggested by revelation. The civil ceremony, legally signalizing the entrance into a relation from which so many societal consequences flow and which must therefore be a matter of civil record and control, is entirely sufficient to secure legitimacy, even though it does not, in the eyes of many, meet the demands of propriety. Physicians must, under penalty, promptly record births; both physician and clergyman are really civil officers. Society, through the regulative system, conserves its interest in the mating of the sexes with a rigor and jealousy befitting the significance of that interest.

§342*. Normality of Marriage. For most members of a primitive community, marriage is as normal an event in life as is the mating of animals. When celibacy occurs, it is an exception for which there is some sufficient reason. The only right and proper thing to do at a certain stage in life is to enter wedlock; it is something into which people grow as they grow into youth, or maturity, or old age. In fact, there is a tendency to hurry the young into the status—some say, as a precaution against premarital unchastity or elopement—and delay incites to ridicule, contempt, or suspicion. The general rule is that the young marry as soon as they are physically fit to do so; indeed, if the interests at stake seem to demand it, sexual maturity is set aside as a precondition.

In New Britain girls are married at eleven and twelve; and "the result of such an early union for the girl has been dreadful."[52] In the New Hebrides the age is six or eight, and there is child-betrothal where the little girl works and cooks for the betrothed.[53] On the Congo the girl is eligible for marriage at ten.[54] The Wapagoro boy marries at seven or eight and pays the bride-price when his wife becomes sexually mature.[55] In Fezzan "not seldom are ten or twelve year old mothers seen suckling their little children."[56]

In India children are sometimes espoused even before birth.[57] Into such arrangements, and into child-marriage in general, consideration of property and family-connections enter.[58] "An unmarried woman cannot attain the blessedness of Nirvana and it is reckoned against the parents as a mortal sin to retain an unmarried daughter in the house." Marriage comes at the age of from six to eight, and rich people contract even "suckling-marriages" where the bride may even be less than a year old. There occur marriages of such children to older men and the results are disastrous. The child-brides are anxious and terrified but receive no sympathy.[59] Marriage is indispensable to the female, while to the male it represents the status of householder, "the second and most respectable of the four by which with them the different periods of human life are distinguished. It completes for the man the regenerating ceremonies, expiatory, as is believed, of the sinful taint that every child is supposed to contract in the parent's womb. . . . Thus religion and law coöperate with the climate in its favor."[60] It is impossible to be too early in arranging a satisfactory marriage for one's children; this led to child-marriage, even in ancient times.[61]

Wilken[62] thinks child-marriages in the Malay Archipelago are a sort of prophylaxis against abduction. The custom is widespread in this region. The Dyak or Batak girl is often betrothed at birth and married at six, though she continues with her parents until fullgrown. Child-marriages occur particularly between persons who are designated by the *adat* (mores) as spouses; an older girl may thus be married to a boy who is a mere infant, but who must marry her as the daughter of his mother's brother. The girl comes to live with his parents until he is grown, and is called "daughter-in-law at the rice-block," indicative of the nature of her labors. Child-marriage occurs along with practices of abduction and also when they have become obsolete. Child-betrothal in some cases serves also to withdraw from a girl the right to sex-license. "Blood-friendship, wealth, esteem, noble descent, etc., together with the parents' fear of seeing their plans later, perhaps, frustrated, when the children attain to discretion and independence, are also motives for the contracting of marriages in such tender years."[63]

[52] Danks, in JAI, XVIII, 288.
[53] Ella, in AAAS, 1892, 623; Leggatt, in AAAS, 1892, 704.
[54] Ward, in JAI, XXIV, 289.   [55] Fabry, in *Globus,* XCI, 221.
[56] Rohlfs, in *Mitth. J. Perthes' Geog. Anst.,* Ergänzheft., V, 9.
[57] Thurston, *S. India,* 97; Scott, "Kaikadis," in JASB, IV, 361.
[58] Risley, *Ethnog. Ind.,* I, 178; Modi, in JASB, VII, 78-79.
[59] Gehring, *Süd-Indien,* 78, 79, 80; Kipling, *Naulahka,* chs. XIII, XIV, XV.
[60] Anon., "Child Marriage," in JASB, II, 232, 233, 234.
[61] Jolly, in *Grundr. d. Indo-Ar. Philol.,* II, Heft 8, pp. 54, 58; Monier-Williams, *Brāhmanism,* 354.
[62] *Vkde.,* 277; Wilken, in VG, I, 469-470, 473, 153.
[63] Schwaner, *Borneo,* I, 194.

The conclusion has been ventured that the marriage-age of women depends upon the degree of civilization. It must not be forgotten that maturity comes earlier in some climates than in others and that the custom may not be so deleterious as we should, at first sight, conclude; Juliet is represented as not yet fourteen.[64] Observers, however, instance many ill effects of child-marriage and it could not fail to be selected out under competition, persisting regularly only among declining peoples and in isolation. Particularly to be noted, however, is the prevalence in the field of economic and other social motives rather than mere sex-passion. This is the more strikingly exemplified in marriages of the dead. Here the theory seems to be that everyone should enter the status; if he has failed to do so through death, he should still have his marriage.

Of certain Africans it is reported: "So truly to them is marriage the union of the male and female principle in nature, the sole right and perfect human relationship that they even unite with one another in the spirit-world by special arrangements and rites, young lads and girls who died unmarried."[65] "At a funeral of an unmarried Toda girl, which I witnessed, the corpse was made to go through a form of a marriage ceremony." This is described.[66] Other of the preconditions to marriage are carried out with the dead.[67] Marco Polo[68] noted the Tatar custom of marrying the dead. "If any man have a daughter who dies before marriage, and another man have had a son also die before marriage, the parents of the two arrange a grand wedding between the dead lad and lass. And marry them they do, making a regular contract! And when the contract papers are made out they put them in the fire, in order that the parties in the other world may know the fact, and so look on each other as man and wife. And the parents thenceforward consider themselves sib [kin] to each other just as if their children had lived and married. Whatever may be agreed on between the parties as dowry, those who have had to pay it cause to be painted on pieces of paper, and then put these in the fire, saying that in that way the dead person will get all the real articles in the other world." Survivals of marriage of the dead are seen in the so-called "Totenhochzeit," where the funeral is in part the replica of a marriage-ceremony and the dead boy is provided with a wife or the girl is dressed as a bride.[69]

These cases of marriage of the dead not only bring into strong relief the idea of marriage as a status natural to all, to which all

[64] Shakespeare, *Romeo and Juliet*, Act I, sc. III.
[65] Gutmann, in *Globus*, XCII, 49.   [66] Thurston, *S. India*, 105-106.
[67] Reclus, *Prim. Folk*, 159.
[68] *Book of Ser Marco Polo* (Yule's ed.), I, 234-235.
[69] Kaindl, in *Globus*, LXXXVIII, 305-306, and in LXXXVII, 324.

have a sort of right, but afford striking evidence as to projectivism and beliefs about the nature of the soul and of sacrifice.[70]

That marriage is regarded by primitive people as a normal status for everyone can be demonstrated in no better way than by reviewing the prevalent sentiment about marriage and the reasons for such cases of celibacy as are to be found.

The Fijians believe that those who die unmarried are shut out of the spirit-world. "Of all Fijian spirits, that of a bachelor is most hardly used. Nanggnangga, the bitter hater of bachelors, undertakes to see after their souls; and so untiring is his watch that, it is said, no unwedded spirit has ever yet reached the Elysium of Fiji." The unlucky soul is seized by the aforesaid spirit "and, for the unpardonable offence of bachelorhood, is dashed in pieces on a large black stone, just as one shatters rotten fire-wood." "Laughable or tragic as the folk-belief conceives of the lot of the old maid, always there is revealed most unmistakably in it that . . . to be married and have children is the object for which man, more especially woman, is here on earth, and no happiness is allotted to her who has failed of that goal."[71] Jenness and Ballentyne[72] record, for the D'Entrecasteaux Islands, the following astonishing exception: "The percentage of the unmarried in the district examined was 43 per cent, and as the conditions in this respect seem to be much the same everywhere, this figure can be taken as approximately correct for all places."

"I do not recollect having seen or heard of an African spinster, and bachelors of mature age are rare in the extreme. The African can hardly imagine adult life as anything but a state of matrimony. Even impotent men are found to have wives whom they permit to consort with other men. Indeed the African is to such an extent dependent on women that he is hopeless and helpless without them, a fact which gives the women an influence and power which if not obvious is none the less actual and to be reckoned with."[73] "The African thinks that a man cannot live without a woman. And I have heard them, both on the Lower Congo and the Upper, solemnly discuss whether we were properly made as we always refused to accept their offers of women."[74] Such facts, as one of these authors remarks, bear strongly upon the status of women.[75]

The Kaffirs have a term of reproach which is applied to all marriageable women without husbands. It is never used in connection with a married woman, however loose her character, nor to a girl. It signifies that there is something wrong with the woman: that she has never had a husband, or is separated from the one she has had, or is a widow who has left her late husband's place.[76] A Fulbe who clings to his dignity must be married or have female slaves; otherwise he is an object of contempt. European travellers have suffered in this way by not being mated. And "not only in the Fulbe kingdom but everywhere in the Sudan—yes, among most savage and half-civilized tribes, the same view prevails; and so it would be quite debatable whether one had not better use the social status of the bachelor than that of woman as a criterion between

[70] §§206, 209, 228, 229, 234, above.
[71] Wilken, in VG, III, 223-224, note (he quotes Williams, *Fiji*, I, 244-245).
[72] *D'Entrecasteaux*, 48.
[73] Dundas, C., in JAI, LI, 249.   [74] Weeks, in JAI, XXXIX, 449.
[75] Ch. LI, below.   [76] Kropf, *Kaffir-Engl. Dict.*, 75.

savage and civilized."[77] Junker[78] tells of a daughter who caused her father much distress by refusing to marry; she attempted suicide during Junker's visit. "Marriage and life together with wife and children . . . is a necessity for the northeast African from which no one withdraws or can withdraw." There are no bachelors or old maids. Remaining single removes all chance of self-preservation, especially in old age; one cannot become rich or even well-to-do. Where there is a superfluity of women some go miserably unmarried.[79]

In India only eldest sons can marry equal-caste women. The larger proportion of Brahman women are mercilessly doomed, "notwithstanding the high estimation in which the Hindus hold marriage, to perpetual celibacy, with all its risks and privations. Many of these females live and die unmarried: yet, strange to say, the corpse undergoes all the ceremonies of marriage. To prevent their falling into unchastity they are closely shut up and guarded. Occasionally they do fall, and then are irrevocably expelled from family, friends, and society. In such case they must join the lower castes, to whom they were formerly sold as slaves and concubines, or go over to the Roman Catholic or Syrian Christians, uniting with someone in marriage."[80] Into these caste-matters the religious element evidently enters with power. In ancient Persia the girl normally married at fifteen. To have children was a duty and a blessing and it was a heavy sin to evade or prevent marriage; "a young woman who faded and aged unmarried was only a tiresome burden in the parental home; it even seems that she experienced much ridicule and indignity, in any case general disregard."[81]

On the island of Nias a good many remain unmarried owing, however, to inability to raise the bride-price on the part of the young men and avarice on the part of the fathers of the young women; highly placed young women have especial difficulty. The same is true elsewhere in the Archipelago. Yet the rule is to marry as soon as puberty is reached, and the unmarried, especially women, are held in low esteem. "What are they good for?" the natives ask, thus indicating that the unmarried are beings who have not attained their destiny.[82]

Among the American Indians unmarried men and women of eighteen and even twenty are found;[83] "occasionally a man possessed such a character that no woman would marry him, and more rarely a woman would remain unmarried"—in one case a woman was regarded for that reason as possessing supernatural powers.[84]

Religious and especially sacerdotal celibacy[85] is a practice that generally goes with a more developed civilization. Chinese law enjoins priestly celibacy, Buddhist and Taoist alike, under severe penalties.[86] It is a tragedy to approach spinsterhood in Japan. Three young women, aged 25, 24, and 23, respectively, recently leaped to death in the crater of the Asana volcano in despondency over their prospects.[87] A woman who enters a certain religious

[77] Goldstein, in *Globus*, XCIV, 62.   [78] *Reisen*, III, 291.
[79] Paulitschke, *Nordost-Afr.*, I, 195.
[80] Mateer, in JAI, XII, 300.   [81] Geiger, *Ostiran. Kult.*, 240.
[82] Wilken, in VG, I, 449, 450.
[83] Hrdlička, in BAE, Bull. XXXIV, 48.
[84] Russell, in BAE, XXVI, 184.   [85] §281, above.
[86] Medhurst, in *Trans. China Br. Roy. Asiat. Soc.*, pt. IV, 18.
[87] Assoc. Press despatch, July 25, 1925.

order of the Zuñis is not allowed to marry.[88] The Aztec priesthood was reckoned in the millions, and its celibacy was sanctioned by the death-penalty. Similarly with the brides of the Sun in Peru, and certain women in some Brazilian tribes, who deserted woman's duties and copied the ways of men.[89] Sacerdotal celibacy existed in classical antiquity as a rare but holy thing; the Vestal Virgins afford an example. But attempts were made to combat it.[90] Later on came the well-known Catholic system, developed largely upon the dogma that chastity is better than marriage, though the latter is to be preferred to fornication.[91] In Albania virginity could be chosen in order to avoid an undesired marriage.[92] However, most peoples have retained the old contempt for the bachelor and the barren woman, and especially the notion of the old maid's or bachelor's destiny after death—a selection of weird, fantastic, and repulsive occupations. A tax on the bachelor has been one of the least of his present or prospective troubles.[93]

On the basis of his copious collections, Westermarck[94] concludes that abstinence, or at least, voluntary abstinence, is almost unheard of in a state of nature and that marriage is almost universal among nature-peoples. The condition of the unmarried is deplorable in both this life and the next, for both themselves and their families. Hence the marriage, in due time, of Chinese males who die in infancy or boyhood to the spirits of females who departed before the marriageable age. Marriage is a religious duty and celibacy is an impiety. Westermarck lays the increase of celibacy in recent decades to the absence of polygamy; the difficulty in supporting a family, as children come to be a liability instead of an asset; the delay occasioned by intellectual preparation for life; the higher development of feeling; the presence of other interests; the development of mental faculties, which, he thinks, weakens desire. Because of the inevitable disparity in the representation of the sexes, a hundred men in Europe may choose amongst one hundred and three or four women, so that three or four per cent of females are doomed to a single life. It may be added that in consequence of the World War some countries have experienced a much greater disparity.

[88] Stevenson, in BAE, V, 540. [89] Müller, *Sex. Leben,* 70-71, 73.
[90] Müller, *Sex. Leben,* 67-68; Schmidt, *Soc. Civ.,* 452; Letourneau, *Marriage,* ch. XII.
[91] Roguin, *Mariage,* 17, 18; I Cor., VII, 9; Schroeder, *Geschlechtl. Ordnung,* 64; Gide, *Femme,* 214.
[92] Lane, *Shala,* 172.
[93] Klugmann, *Frau im Talmud,* 32, note; Schroeder, *Geschlechtl. Ordnung,* 60, note.
[94] *Marriage,* I, ch. X, 337, 361, 374.

Through the earlier stretches of societal evolution, as it appears to us, the compound unit of man-plus-woman, since it includes constituents complementary one to the other, formed a combination with high survival-value.[95] For those who might remain outside of it there was small chance in the whole field of self-maintenance except in a parasitic capacity. The reputation and destiny of the unmarried who did not occupy a position exempting them from economic activities have been noted; it was virtually the religious functionaries alone who could be celibate and yet holy, revered, and subsidized—and not even they until a certain advance in societal self-maintenance had been made which would allow of contribution to their support.

Nature's stress urges the human animal to mate. Society has set its approval upon certain ways of mating which, with their accessories of ritual, come to form the institution of marriage. Within this institution, in its local form, all are expected to live as they must live within the local industrial, governmental, or religious organization. All grow up into their relations with the enclosing institution as a matter of course; all are, in fact, born into this phase of society's life as they are born into other phases. Anyone who refuses to bear his part in society's self-perpetuation exhibits a sort of monstrous irrationality of variation from the normal, and runs counter to the massive interests of society, not to say of nature. To the bulk of the society, impelled without resistance or reflection by the natural and societal forces, such variation cannot seem otherwise than a senseless and criminal procedure and a menace to general welfare—unnatural, antisocial, sacrilegious. Though savages may not use these terms, they feel strongly, though vaguely, that departure from time-hallowed and ancestor-sanctioned tradition is very bad.

The right thing to do is to marry and have progeny and neither men nor gods have any patience with the person who does not do the right thing, unless, indeed, there supervenes some consideration of supernatural potency to justify the abnormal course and make it holy. It takes something of unearthly power to do this; the strength of the institution is proved by the nature of the sanction required for challenging it with impunity. It may be said,

[95] §§63, 69, above.

then, that for ages marriage was the normal destiny of all mankind. In order to be in society at all, people had to be in all the phases of its life, endlessly interconnected as these have been seen to be.

CHAPTER XLIII

THE FORMATIVE STAGE

§343*. **Rudimentary Regulation.** The existence of the marriage-institution means restriction upon the sex-relation. If there ever was a time of no restriction, that was a time when marriage was absent. Since available evidence leads to the conclusion that there was less of regulation upon the earlier stages of institutional evolution than later, it is a logical inference that the slight restriction encountered under the most primitive of conditions was preceded by no regulation at all—none, that is to say, in the mores. It is unprofitable to cite the instincts of animals in this connection, for we are not talking about instincts but conventions; and, besides, the animal-series fails to present any consistent trend in the matter of mating that leads up to the human form.[1] In all events we are but slightly interested in inferential stages; our concern is to show that there occur actual cases of relative unregulation, together with what look like survivals of the same, and that, starting with these as a sort of base-line, the evolution of the marriage-institution has been the evolution of restriction. Though the following cases establish the fact that several degrees of lack of regulation occur, yet it must be realized, in scanning such evidence, that the eye of the original observer is likely to have been caught by the staring looseness of the sex-relation rather than by the scanty and at times obscure outlines of societal control. Regulation is regulation even though unplanned and though the regulated are not aware of the fact.

Of certain African pygmies it is reported: "One cannot speak even of a family-institution, for they follow their animal-instincts wholly, without restraint."[2] Among the African Bushmen there is no regulation of the family-tie and infidelity is no crime. Any man may dismiss the woman with whom he has associated or take one from a weaker man.[3] Communalism in wives among various African tribes is reported by classical authors. Herodotus[4] says of one

[1] §456, below.
[2] Von Schkopp, in *Globus,* LXXXIII, 285.
[3] Lichtenstein, *S. Afr.,* II, 48.
[4] *History,* bk. IV, §§180, 172; Strabo, *Geog.,* XVI, 775. A number of such instances are to be found in Mucke, *Horde,* 71; Post, *Geschlechtsgenoss.,* 18,

of them: "They make use of their women in common and associate with them after the manner of cattle, without living in domestic fashion with them."

Among the Yakuts unions inside the kin-group were exceedingly free and non-permanent.[5] In Tibet, free and unceremonious unions were quite common amongst the lower class.[6] The Keriahs of Central India have no word for marriage.[7] There is no "closed marriage" among certain low and rude tribes of the Nilgherry hills.[8] A passage from Wilken[9] reads: "We find it reported of the Poggi Islanders that the contracting of a marriage is unknown to them; in this respect they live with each other entirely according to inclination. The women as a whole are, as it were, the property of the men as a whole and the men, conversely, are the property of the women." Wilken's ethnographic cases are mostly examples of what we call monandry. Another people entirely unacquainted with marriage are the Lubus, who turn to love with entire freedom and unite indiscriminately according to the inspiration of the moment. Communal marriage exists likewise among the Orang Sakai of Malacca. A girl remains for a time and in turn with each man of the tribe until she has made the round of all the men and comes back to the first; then the process begins all over again. Among the Alfurs and Borneans there are a few tribes that contract no marriages; of one tribe in Borneo it is said that "the men and women all live here in marriageless association."[10]

Lippert,[11] gathering together notices in ancient literature, shows how in the complete circuit of the Mediterranean either direct evidence or survivals show the existence of communalism in women. Legendary materials must be handled with reservations but their consensus is significant. "Moreover, it is not alone in the works of the ancients that examples of a total lack of individual marriage is to be found. We are informed that in Russia in the oldest times the men utilized the women without distinction, so that no woman had her appointed husband."[12]

Evidence of this order is conclusive for a very slight degree of regulation, if not of utter promiscuity; however, cases of no regulation at all, that is, of the utter absence of marriage, are about as rare in ethnography as those of no religion. The context of rather sweeping assertions generally reveals some limitation upon so-called "promiscuity," expressed, implied, or possible; and the totality of evidence of relative unregulation is insignificant compared with the bulk of well-attested cases of rigid restriction with

20; Lippert, *Kgchte.,* II, 12; Saint-Martin, *Nord de l'Afrique,* 52-53; Letourneau, *Marriage,* index, *sub* "promiscuity."

[5] Sieroshevski-Sumner, in JAI, XXXI, 568.

[6] Kawaguchi, in *Century Mag.,* XLV, 391.

[7] Dalton, in *Trans. Ethnol. Soc.,* VI, 25.

[8] Wilutzky, *Mann u. Weib,* 19.

[9] *Vkde.,* 263; in VG, I, 131-135, where several examples are cited; Roth, *Sarawak,* II, cxcix.

[10] Schwaner, *Borneo,* II, 168; Wilken, in VG, I, 310, 375, note.

[11] *Kgchte.,* II, 15 ff.

[12] Post, *Geschlechtsgenoss.,* 18 (quoted without reference from Bastian).

which the primitive mores surround the association of the sexes. This does not mean that a state of promiscuity cannot be inferred; it means that it cannot be demonstrated on the basis of available ethnographic data. The present purpose does not call for entrance upon perilous speculative reconstructions of the inferential or upon conjecture that can only multiply controversies impossible of settlement;[13] we are interested solely in establishing a base-line of original looseness of sex-relation from which to start in tracing the development of the institution through restriction. We should leave it at that except for the existence of certain marriage-customs which need explanation and can get it, in our opinion, only on the theory that they are survivals of a state of minimal regulation. They have been called "survivals of promiscuity." That term does not repel us in any way; the reason why we do not subscribe to it is because we do not think it accurate. What men did before the formation of society is a matter of considerable indifference to us; there may have been a state of promiscuity then; but we cannot see that any human society could have established itself or could have long endured without subjecting the sex-relation to control. We prefer, therefore, to speak of minimal regulation or relative unregulation rather than of promiscuity.

The instances of asserted survivals of and reversions to communalism in women[14] are to be treated ultimately with some fullness because they shed much light, in various connections, upon the general subject of marriage. All available cases are not, however, concentrated at this point; they are dis-

[13] Frazer (*Golden Bough*, pt. I, vol. II, 98 ff.) interprets cases of loose relation as instances of sympathetic magic; Westermarck (*Marr.*, I, chs. III-IX) gives considerable space to "a criticism of the hypothesis of promiscuity" and thinks he has disproved it; Letourneau (*Marr.*, ch. III, 292) regards promiscuity as very rare and believes that alleged cases of it are often the results of faulty observation or are anomalies. Achelis (in *Ztsft. f. Erdkunde*, XXV, 303) says there never was any "lawful promiscuity" and that no one has ever believed in it. Kohler (*Urgchte. d. Ehe*, 14) thinks communalistic marriage customs afforded socializing ties at a time when there were no others.

[14] Some idea of the promiscuity-controversy may be gained from the following: Bachofen, *Das Mutterrecht;* MacLennan, *Primitive Marriage;* Lubbock, *Origin of Civilisation;* Morgan, *Systems of Consanguinity;* Post, *Geschlechtsgenossenschaften;* Mucke, *Horde und Familie;* Kohler, *Urgeschichte der Ehe;* Lippert, *Kulturgeschichte;* Peschel, *Races;* Ratzel, *Völkerkunde;* Brinton, *Races and Peoples;* Starcke, *Primitive Family;* Spencer, *Principles of Sociology.*

tributed where they will serve to better advantage. They will be encountered here and there, wherever they will help to an understanding of the nature, conditions, and evolution of the marriage-institution rather than contribute to controversy concerning origins. Those which are cited here should inform the reader sufficiently concerning the bearing upon such controversies of instances which, as he meets them in other connections, will serve to complete the picture of minimal regulation.

In "expiation for marriage,"[15] the existing regulations as to sex-relations are violated at the time when a woman is taken to wife; on that occasion a broader right to her seems to be asserted on the part of the males of her group, before she shall pass under the monopoly of a husband. All that the latter gains the rest lose and certain customs are accepted as expiation for this invasion of a once common right.

A striking feature of the Australian marriage customs is that "particular men representative of the woman's own moiety, and of the half of the tribe to which she does not belong, have access to her, and always in a particular order, according to which those who, in the present state of the tribe, have lawfully the right to her come last." This practice occurs just at the "particular time when a woman is being, so to speak, handed over to one particular man. . . . The individuals who are thus privileged vary from tribe to tribe, but in all cases the striking feature is that, for the time being, the existence of what can only be described as partial promiscuity can clearly be seen."[16] Elsewhere in Australia the girl is dragged away, resisting, by the groom and a friend whose qualification is that he "would have been eligible as her husband had she been promised to him." One or more men join these two; then the groom returns to camp and the other men consummate the marriage. "When the girl is brought back, there is a continuation of the *jus primæ noctis,* in which all males in the camp participate, even to the nearest relatives." But if, after she is taken possession of by her husband, the bride attempts to run away, she is beaten or cut with a knife; as a wife no one else has any longer any right of access to her.[17] In one tribe of New Guinea, the bride and groom after the wedding take a walk; the first man who meets them has relations with the bride and gives the groom a present.[18] Herodotus[19] reports of a tribe in the western Sahara region that they have wives in common and that when a marriage (exclusive union) occurs, the bride must entertain all the guests in turn, each of whom is bound to give her a present.

Among certain Indians, marriage is often made difficult for a young man because he must buy off with valuable gifts all those who have a right to the girl in question.[20] Of the gilds or societies of North America it is recorded that a man who bought his way into a higher circle must yield his wife to the

15 So called by Lubbock, in *Origin Civil.,* ch. III; Wilken, in VG, I, 205 ff., has a number of examples.

16 Spencer and Gillen, *Nat. Tr. Cent. Aust.,* 111, 96.

17 Howitt, in JAI, XX, 60; Spencer and Gillen, *Nat. Tr. Cent. Aust.,* 92, 93.

18 Haddon, in JAI, L, 260.   19 *Hist.,* IV, 172.

20 Fletcher, in *Globus,* LXXIII, 256.

THE FORMATIVE STAGE 1551

sellers of the degree; among the Mandans this produced community of wives.[21] A similar group-right to wives of members appeared in Cuba.[22] A curious custom is the *casa das tintas* (house of the dyes) or *kumbeh* of West Africa. It is a show-house for the prospective bride, where she is displayed and instructed. Exhibition or advertisement of marriageable girls is not uncommon;[23] in this case not only may the girl not be disposed of to a husband until she has been exhibited but she may refuse no man. The presents she gets from her visitors often constitute a rich dower. Only that maiden to whom a prince has laid claim from her childhood is exempt from this public ceremony.[24] The case has aspects that recall sacral or sacrificial harlotry and the dower by prostitution.[25]

A reversal of the sex-rôle is occasionally found which tends to throw doubt upon the expiation-theory. The Bechuana groom is reported as spending the first night, not with the bride but with the maidens of the kraal.[26] Among the peasants in mediæval south Germany the groom was buffeted and cudgelled at the wedding by men and boys; and "in some places the common women also come to the wedding; and the bride has to ransom her husband from them."[27]

It is thought by some that customs of defloration and of the *jus primæ noctis* represent survivals of expiation for marriage. If so, priest or chief must be taken as representing a collective group-right; this may be true but if it is, the survival has fallen into such decay and uncertainty that it has lost convincing power. There are other and more plausible explanations for both practices.[28]

On certain occasions, notably in connection with religious festivals, all forms of sex-regulation are set aside or much relaxed. It appears that a reversion to ancient custom is supposed to exert a coercive or propitiatory influence upon the ghosts and gods.[29]

This belief is particularly prevalent in Australia where, though even in the earliest time a woman belonged to a man (monandry) and there was no communal marriage, yet at the initiation-festivals or other similar occasions the rules were suspended, promiscuous relations were the order of the time, and parents and husbands even made gain of daughters and wives. License was granted to youths at initiation; they were not allowed to marry but were free of the women, even those normally under taboo to them.[30] When a girl of the Dieri is married out of the tribe a great corroborree is held. "The festivities last several days, during which there is free intercourse between the sexes without regard to existing marriage relations. Strangling is the penalty for jealousy shown at such times," though it may crop out afterward and give rise to many bloody affrays. The rules are similarly relaxed upon the entertainment

---

[21] Ratzel, *Vkde.*, II, 624.   [22] Fewkes, in AA, VI, 588.
[23] §361, below.
[24] Bastian, *Deut. Exped.*, I, 44-45, 152, 175-177; Lippert, *Kgchte.*, II, 13 ff.
[25] §§296, above, and 364, below.   [26] Ratzel, *Vkde.*, I, 188.
[27] Hagelstange, *Süddeut. Bauernleben,* 66, 67.
[28] §§365, 366, below; Kohler, *Urgchte. d. Ehe,* 140.
[29] §277, above; Kohler, *Urgchte. d. Ehe,* 139.
[30] Cunow, *Australneger,* 126; Howitt, in JAI, XII, 497; Howitt and Fison, in JAI, XII, 36.

of a mission from another tribe, the women being generally the mediators in tribal quarrels. Upon reconciliation there is general license "even between those of the same totem, provided they are not within prohibited degrees of kinship." The incest-taboo[31] is too old and strong to be relaxed. The ceremony of oaths and ordeals in connection with alliances forms another occasion for "low animal intercourse without fear or favour."[32] In some cases "liberty is accorded only to those parties who would be permitted to marry each other in conformity with the tribal laws."[33]

Access to women-messengers, in event of tribal agreements, appears in Australia; a party intent on reprisal is offered the use of the women in conciliation; and punishment of a woman for infringement of a taboo is sometimes accomplished by making her, for a time, common property to all the men.[34]

Reversions under terror also occur. The *aurora australis* frightens the Kurnai exceedingly; they all "swing the 'dead hand' towards the alarming portent, shouting such words as these: 'Send it away! send it away! do not let it burn us up!' . . . It is very suggestive that on this occasion there was a temporary reversion to intersexual communism; *i.e.*, by exchange of wives. This exchange is connected with a supposed impending supernatural calamity which the deceased 'ancestors' were able to prevent, and it is probably that they were supposed to have caused it. Taking this view the temporary reversion to intersexual communism appears like a propitiatory or expiatory ceremony."[35] Ceremonies constituting reversions to obsolete customs, with which the ancestors were familiar and would presumably be pleased, are common enough in religion.[36] In New Guinea "in ordinary circumstances an initiation is a time of somewhat general license, promiscuous intercourse being permitted between any initiated man and woman."[37]

Among the Mexican Tarahumari the women are chaste; "only at their feasts, when they regularly become intoxicated, they, as well as the men, seem to lose all shame."[38]

Until the year 408 A.D. licentious dances occurred at the feasts of Flora and at the Saturnalia.[39] Cases of license occur in Russian history, particularly on the eve of certain great Christian festivals.[40] Wilken[41] cites the May festival of license. Later, May was thought to be a bad month to marry in, trivial reasons being cited. The author thinks the honor accorded to courtesans is significant of former looseness of sex-relations. Again, it is the ceremonial nature of such practices that lend them survivalistic significance. Other instances of relaxation of restriction are cited by Frazer.[42]

[31] §349, below.
[32] Howitt, in JAI, XX, 59, 70, 72; Gason, in JAI, XXIV, 173. Other cases in Fison and Howitt, *Kamilaroi*, 201-202; Eyre, *Cent. Aust.*, 320-321; Spencer and Gillen, *Nat. Tr. Cent. Aust.*, 96, 97; Starcke, *Prim. Fam.*, 122.
[33] Mathews, in JAI, XXVI, 272.
[34] Spencer and Gillen, *Nat. Tr. Cent. Aust.*, 97, 98, 196.
[35] Howitt, in JAI, XIII, 189.   [36] §324, above.
[37] Chinnery, in JAI, XLV, 77.
[38] Lumholtz, in *Intern. Cong. Anthrop.*, 1893, 106.
[39] McCabe, *St. Augustine*, 340, 341.
[40] Petri, *Anthrop.* (Russ.), 435.   [41] In VG, I, 218.
[42] *Golden Bough*, II ("The Magic Art"), ch. XI.

Two thoughtful writers on Australian customs[43] give it as their opinion that the practices above illustrated are "only capable of any satisfactory explanation on the hypothesis that they indicate the temporary recognition of certain general rights which existed in the time prior to that of the form of group marriage of which we have such clear traces yet lingering amongst the tribes. We do not mean that they afford direct evidence of the former existence of actual promiscuity, but they do afford evidence leading in that direction, and certainly point back to a time when there existed wider marital relations than obtain at the present time—wider than those which are shown in the form of group marriage from which the present system is derived." This passage seems to us about to cover the gist of the whole matter; the group-marriage referred to will be considered presently.

§344*. License. The license accorded to the unmarried also bears upon the subject of this chapter—the formative stage. Where license is allowed, marriage appears clearly as a limitation set upon it at the time of entrance into a new life-status, and the marriage-institution as a structure forming under the action of the taboo. Evidence along this line also confirms the position sustained above that something besides sex-satisfaction lay at the basis of marriage.

The cases are numerous and concordant.[44] Australians and Melanesians exhibit many, together with sporadic exceptions;[45] in the Torres Straits islands it was merely "fashion along we folk."[46] In New Georgia and the Murray Islands the offspring of premarital connections are generally killed by the mother;[47] they have no status. Unchastity is apparently universal among the unmarried of both sexes in the Andaman Islands.[48]

Among the Masai, life is dissolute until "at about the age of twenty-five to thirty the Masai warrior selects a girl as his wife, marries, and entirely changes his mode of life."[49] Some of the tribes of Uganda have the same custom as the Masai: until they reach womanhood, the immature girls live with the young fighting men. If one of them has a child, she strangles it as soon

[43] Spencer and Gillen, *Nat. Tr. Cent. Aust.*, 111.
[44] See also collections in Sumner, *Folkways*, chs. IX and XI.
[45] Fison and Howitt, *Kamilaroi*, 201-202; Eyre, *Cent. Aust.*, II, 320; Krieger, *Neu-Guinea*, 174, 395; Finsch, *Ethnol. Erfahr.*, II, 298.
[46] Haddon, in JAI, XIX, 316, 357.
[47] Somerville, in JAI, XXVI, 394, 407; Hunt, in JAI, XXVIII, I, 10, 11.
[48] Man, in JAI, XII, 135.　　　　　　　　[49] Johnston, in JAI, XV, 15.

as it is born, and the father must present the girl and her father each a goat.[50] Among the Alur, if a girl has a child, the man must marry or pay, or her relations may kill him. The bearing of a child lowers her marriage-value but does not hurt her reputation.[51] Again, no girl can marry until she has had a child which she gives to her brother to be his slave; she must buy herself off, as it were, by what we should regard as unchastity.[52] Similar conditions of premarital behavior occur among the Kaffirs, Niger tribes, in the Lake Regions (though some tribes guard their young women closely), in Uganda (where a resulting pregnancy leads to an induced miscarriage), in Kamerun, and Fezzan;[53] among the Tuareg, on the contrary, irregularities of a sister or daughter are punished by death.[54] The Soyots, reindeer nomads of Siberia, have no morals in our sense; from the ages of twelve or thirteen the sexes associate in the freest manner. Parents are glad if an unmarried daughter has a child; it is no shame and they ask the same price for her, perhaps more. All who wish live in freedom; only "in relation to the daily work in the home does a man have as a rule a regularly bought and paid-for wife." Illegitimate children are gladly taken care of by the mother, for children are greatly loved and wanted. These natives thought it quite wrong in the Europeans to repulse their girls; they were nice girls and did not deserve the humiliation.[55]

On the island of Ponapé marital and premarital conditions stand in strong contrast; "in general, the married woman is much respected, the husband always exhibiting jealousy as respects his rights. This procedure contrasts with the libertinage in which the woman lives during the time she remains unmarried. . . . It is an extraordinary phenomenon for a young woman to be able to offer the treasure of virginity to the husband who chooses her."[56] Finsch[57] says that a girl often acts for the benefit of her parents and that, once married, she must be true. This insistence upon fidelity within the marriage-status is common among peoples allowing premarital license and is very significant of the real nature and restrictive function of the marriage-institution.[58]

Among the East Greenlanders it is the childless wife who is disapproved, not the husbandless mother,[59] and the Bering Strait Eskimo allow unmarried females to constitute a law unto themselves.[60] Kohler[61] cites, with references, cases of premarital license, generally followed by virtue in marriage, among the Eskimo and many Indian tribes; he says that a Greenland girl who has had a child wears a special head-ornament indicating, not shame but heightened reputation. The Huron woman passed "a youth of license; an age of drudgery,"[62] and the Sia were easily tolerant of the license of the married as well as the unmarried.[63] Of the California Indians generally it is reported that premarital license prevails, despite the fulminations of the tribal authori-

[50] Johnston, *Uganda*, II, 878.   [51] Stuhlmann, *Mit Emin*, 525.
[52] Wilson and Felkin, *Uganda*, II, 309.
[53] Fritsch, *Eingeb. S.-Afr.*, 95-96; Granville, in JAI, XXVIII, I, 107; Macdonald, in JAI, XXII, 110; Johnston, *Uganda*, II, 610; Conradt, in *Globus*, LXXXI, 336; Rohlfs, in J. Perthes' *Geog. Anstalt*, Ergänzband., V, 9, 10.
[54] Bruun, *Huleboerne*, 246.   [55] Olsen, *Primitivt Folk*, 147, 148.
[56] Pereiro, *Ponapé*, 119, 120.   [57] *Ethnol. Erfahr.*, III, 242.
[58] Post, *Geschlechtsgenoss.*, 29.   [59] Holm, *Ethnol. Skizze*, 54.
[60] Nelson, in BAE, XVIII, pt. I, 292, 360.
[61] *Urgchte. d. Ehe*, 141, 142.
[62] Parkman, *Jesuits*, Introd., xxxiv.   [63] Stevenson, in BAE, XI, 20.

ties; yet after marriage wives are "guarded with a Turkish jealousy."[64] Among some tribes the assumption of the labret means that the initiate is "admitted to the privileges of a member of the community, including as a chief feature communal rights" over the unmarried women.[65] There are reports of premarital license in New Mexico, Yucatan, and British Guiana.[66]

In general, as we leave the most primitive peoples we leave premarital license also. Herodotus[67] reports it of the Thracians. Among the Arabs a woman's price was proportioned to the number of days in the week that the marriage-tie was to be strictly observed. The women were wholly free during the other days, and their husbands were proud of the attention they received.[68] Curious indifference to the premarital experiences of wife or husband appears in Croatia.[69] Toleration is sometimes exhibited for frailty where the professed code is against it.[70] More modern is the fact that certain employments seem to demand a certain premarital unrestraint.[71]

These last cases are verging upon conditions of prostitution. On the whole, premarital chastity of women and, much later and less commonly, of men has gone along with advance in civilization;[72] and prostitution is quite another thing than license preceding marriage. This seems to be the place in which to set down a word about the former practice.

It is exceedingly hard to find among primitive peoples examples of prostitution which deserve the name. Unless it is defined to suit the case, it is by no means "the oldest profession in the world." While there are plenty of instances of premarital license, lending of wives and daughters, and other loose sexual relationships in primitive life, professional harlots are conspicuous only by their absence until there is contact with a "higher" civilization. Wherever women appear as selling their favors for hire there is some special object in view and they incur no contumely by so doing. They are gathering a dowry in perfectly legitimate manner, according to local mores; they are commendably supporting aged parents or filially obeying their behests; they are serving their deities in orthodox fashion. They are breaking no taboos, but are,

[64] Powers, in *Contrib. Amer. Ethnol.*, III, 157.
[65] Dall, in BAE, III, 79 ff.
[66] Winship, in BAE, XIV, pt. I, 521, note; Bancroft, *Nat. Races*, II, 676; Schomburgk, *Brit.-Guiana*, II, 313.
[67] *Hist.*, IV, 176.
[68] Spencer, *Descr. Soc.*, pt. III-A, fol. 8 and fol. 30.
[69] Rhamm, in *Globus*, LXXXII, 104.
[70] Gomme, *Ethnol. in Folklore*, 182.
[71] Mantegazza, *Amori*, 272 (in the coal mines).
[72] §366, below.

on the contrary, acting regularly and in order. There is all the difference in the world between this and prostitution; it is only the censorious white man, with his ethnocentric exaltation of his own code, who has any contempt to express. The reason he finds fault is because it is his destiny to adhere to a set of mores developed along with that civilization which also fathered prostitution as a profession. It is very doubtful whether a primitive mind could make anything out of a play such as "Mrs. Warren's Profession" or understand why, in response to sensational write-ups, thousands could be turned away from the box office; nor why the Lord Chamberlain should first prohibit the play and then, nearly twenty years later, remove the ban.[73]

It is thought significant that sex-disease, which is so regular a concomitant of harlotry, had failed to put in an appearance among most, if not all, primitive folk prior to contact with civilization. Genuine prostitution is, in any case, rare enough among undeveloped peoples to deserve no more notice than we have here accorded it. In this case, as in that of the attribution to savages of gross sensuality, phallicism, and other qualities and practices deemed discreditable, there has been transferred to them uncritically that which has been observed among alien peoples of half-culture or above, who may even exhibit what is often called racial degeneracy.

A pair of citations may illustrate certain of the above contentions. In East Africa, "wives constantly run away from their husbands to the townships and settlements, where they, together with the Nandi, form by far the largest proportion of the common prostitutes for gain. The tribe do not consider their tribal women as prostitutes; a woman becomes a prostitute when she cohabits with other tribes for mercenary purposes, and when she is a common prostitute there is no question of payment by men of her own tribe also living out of the tribal area; her gains she ultimately brings or sends back to her male relatives. The causes of the increasing prostitution of women for gain are first that [where] a man, generally much older than herself, obtains a lien on her when a child as his future wife by a payment of a goat or two, to be followed on marriage by a full payment, by the time of marriage she generally has other affections; second, that a widow cannot re-marry; third, that the woman, who has had an amount of attention in her girlhood, becomes more of a beast of burden on marriage with this tribe than is usual in East Africa, and the men of the tribe are extremely bad husbands. Children born to prostitutes and to women who have become nominal Mohammedans invariably seem to be absorbed in the tribe."[74] In Siberia, "there also exists the custom called by

[73] *Jr. Soc. Hygiene*, X, 499.   [74] Barton, in JAI, LIII, 69.

some anthropologists 'hospitality prostitution,' by which the bed of an un-married girl is offered to a traveller. An old Yukaghir woman explained . . . that this was due to the poor conditions of life among the people, and to the fact that the bed of a married couple was taboo, and hospitality demanded that a good bed be offered to the visitor."[75]

In general, it is unintelligible nonsense to cite savage customs as examples of "immorality." The morality of the backward peoples can be measured only against the standards of their own mores. It can be said that their standards are widely different from our own. An individual man or woman might be called immoral only if he or she violated the code prevalent in the local society. This rarely happens. That savages do not live up to the standards we profess is as irrelevant as that we do not live up to theirs.

There are, in addition to those of general premarital license, also cases connected with special occasions; these are on the order of the instances recently cited of general promiscuity at festivals and celebrations. As such they are equally reversionary.

Youths of one Australian tribe were not permitted to take a wife during the time of initiation or subsequent probation but during the latter they were permitted complete license as regarded the unmarried of the other sex who were such as they might lawfully marry and even those of their own clan and totem. At the Australian fire-totem ceremony similar conditions prevailed,[76] as also in South African puberty-celebrations.[77]

The *morong* of Assam is regarded as possibly a survival of pre-marriage communalism. It is the common barracks for the unmarried and, under one or another local name, has been observed widely over the earth.[78] In Assam, where the *morong* occurs, "from childhood to marriage there is the most complete and recognized sexual liberty. Morals begin with marriage; infidelity afterwards being, I believe, exceedingly rare." When opportunity and inclination offer, they pair off and settle down, going through some public marriage-ceremony. Thus the individuals epitomize race history; the marriage comes as a restriction on complete sexual liberty. These *morongs*, of which there may be in a village eight or ten for young men and four or five for young women, are tabooed to married women; the institution seems jealous of and hostile to marriage as to an innovation. "A noteworthy fact is that children are seldom born until after marriage. If two or three per cent of the grown girls become *enceinte*, their marriage is arranged for, and all parties are as a rule satis-

[75] Czaplicka, *Aborig. Siberia,* 90-91.

[76] Fison and Howitt, in JAI, XII, 37, note (quoted); Fison and Howitt, *Kamilaroi,* 201-202; Eyre, *Cent. Aust.,* II, 320; Spencer and Gillen, *North. Tr. Cent. Aust.,* 378, 381, 391, 392; Starcke, *Prim. Fam.,* 22, note.

[77] Fritsch, *Eingeb. S.-Afr.,* 111 ff.

[78] Webster, *Prim. Secret Societies,* ch. I; §§161, 162, above.

THE SCIENCE OF SOCIETY

fied."[79] Analogous cases are reported from India and the Masai of Africa, and for the Caroline and Pelew Islands.[80] The Bororo men of Brazil seize and retain girls in the men's houses; such girls are not married afterwards to one man but every man of the community holds the place of father to their children.[81]

Inspection of the cases reveals that the girls kept in these clubhouses are generally abducted or are foreigners and that their parents generally receive considerable wealth in the form of gifts while their daughters are in the "armengol" status, as it is called in the Pelew Islands. There are therefore additional aspects to this custom which receive notice elsewhere;[82] and the communalistic aspects cannot be pressed too far. In fact, the men's clubhouses around the world are generally tabooed to women altogether.[83] There is little disapproval of the premarital license involved, which is the main consideration before us. In fact, residence in the Pelew *Bai* is about the only chance a girl has of being thought well brought up and educated. It is regarded as a sacred social duty "and no girl may hold back; if she does so, her parents scold her severely and she cannot find a husband so easily either, for now she is known everywhere in the community as an incapable and stupid girl who is not fit to be a wife. But the others, when they come home, marry speedily."[84] We have here one of the few and novel primitive educational opportunities for women.

These cases of the relations of the unmarried have their survivalistic significance. Whether they support in some degree the inference as to primordial unregulation—and we think that they do—they at any rate contribute most significantly to an understanding of the primitive viewpoint about sex and marriage. They show us what our own system has evolved from. Vinogradoff,[85] speaking of Aryan marriage, says that contract was not a necessary feature of it, "but that it was gradually evolved from loose unions. Indeed, we have the curious spectacle of an institution which begins by being entirely fluid, but settles down more and more on a basis of contract with reciprocal rights and duties." There is nothing more enlightening as to the nature of marriage than to gain some comprehension of the formative period in its evolution.

Peal, in JAI, XXII, 248, 254, 255; Godden, in JAI, XXVII, 49, thinks "probably too much has been made of the custom in relation to sexual intercourse."

[80] Risley, *Ethnog. Ind.*, I, 212; Thomson, in *Proceed. Roy. Geog. Soc.*, VI, 701; Kubary, *Karolinen-arch.*, 244, 245; Kubary, *Pelauer*, 52-53; Semper, *Palau-Ins.*, 324; Christian, *Caroline Isl.*, 290-291; Senfft, in *Globus*, XCI, 149; Senfft, in *Deutsch-Kolonialbl.* 1900, 416 ff.

[81] Von den Steinen, *Zent. Bras.*, 477, 502.

[82] §§162, 163, above, and 365, below.　　[83] Webster, *Prim. Secret Soc.*, ch. I.

[84] Semper, *Palau-Ins.*, 324.　　[85] *Hist. Jurispr.*, I, 239.

§345. **Monandry.** Setting aside what is purely inferential concerning the matter of sex-relations and taking our stand upon the observed facts of ethnography, we can be sure, first of all, that the women of a tribe belong to the men of that tribe and are tabooed to outsiders. Within the tribe, further, a woman generally, if not always, appertained to one man at a time and there was some small duration in sex-association. This accords with the preceding analysis of the expedient sex-combination consequent upon complementary sex-qualities.[86] The simplest ethnographic form of the sex-relation, which is also capable of inclusion under our definition of marriage, is one which may suitably be called monandry. It should be sharply distinguished from monogamy; failure to do that is responsible for a deal of foolishness about "original monogamy."

Man and wife, together with their children, are found living together upon low stages of civilization. Great emphasis has been laid on this fact as proving that the original form of marriage, family, and society was the monogamic father-family. In actuality it is a case of almost complete absence of organization in which the first exceptional and contingent coming-together of individuals by mutual selection, side by side with others who have made no selection, bears only an external resemblance to later institutions. To this resemblance no significance can attach.[87] Monandry is a more or less durable informal monopoly of a woman by one husband (at a time), occurring in a setting of unregulation.[88] It is like the temporary private occupancy of a piece of land where, typically, land is held by all group-members in common. No individual has any special conjugal authority over a woman—that is, all the men have an equal right over her—until she is assigned to some man to whom she is predestined by custom. Such custom rises out of incidental pairings. All the women are tabooed, as a hunting-ground is, to all men outside the group and, even when they are assigned to individual husbands within the group, the right of the latter is subject to the tribal right of his comrades, either in general for a time just when the woman is passing into the status

---

[86] §§63, 69, above.

[87] Brinton, in *Smithson. Rep.*, 1893, 597; Semon, *Aust. Bush,* 231.

[88] Wilken, in VG, II, 342. His cases of unregulation (VG, I, 131-135) are mostly monandry.

of wife or upon special occasions, such as tribal festivals.[89]
Women are under little or no restriction until allotted. Assignment to some particular husband may not exclude licentiousness
in the wife after marriage, the husband often being indifferent if
the trespasser upon his property pays.[90]

There is much more of interest and profit in pursuing the development of marriage forward from monandry as a starting-
point than in trying to penetrate farther back into the range of
the highly inferential. Monandry is the extreme of observable unregulation. It is true that inference leads safely to the conviction
that there was once still less of restriction, that is, a previous
state without combinations of even so loose an order; but what
the arrangements in that far-off time may have been cannot be
said. It must be kept in mind that monandry means "one man at
a time" for each woman; it is not monogyny or monogamy, and
least of all is it pair-marriage. Such a rudimentary form of union,
having some superficial resemblances to monogamy under the
father-family, has been construed by the type of person who hates
to think of the crudity of human and institutional beginnings to
be the genuine pair-marriage which he admires along with the
rest of us;[91] it is now evident that so to construe it is to confuse
two things which exhibit radical differences.

This union under "temporary monogamy"—an actual combination of one man and one woman, not yet institutional, entirely
unstable, lasting, in some cases, only long enough for the man to
be able to claim the children born to the woman[92]—has its similarities to the "syndyasmian," or "coupling-together," form. Morgan's[93] description of the latter recalls and foreshadows several
of the preceding and following contentions about the nature of
marriage and the family.

"The syndyasmian family was special and peculiar. Several of them were
usually found in one house, forming a communal household, in which the principle of communism in living was practiced. The fact of the conjunction of
several such families in a common household is of itself an admission that the
family was too feeble an organization to face alone the hardships of life. . . .
The marriage institution was as peculiar as the family. Men did not seek wives

[89] Herodotus, *Hist.*, I, §126; Strabo, *Geog.*, XI, 513.
[90] Johnston, in JAI, XV, 8.   [91] Grosse, *Familie*, 42, 48.
[92] Howitt and Fison, in JAI, XII, 38.
[93] *Anc. Soc.*, 453-456; Wake, in JAI, XVII, 278.

as they are sought in civilized society, from affection; for the passion of love, which required a higher development than they had attained, was unknown among them. Marriage, therefore, was not founded upon sentiment but upon convenience and necessity. . . . The relation . . . continued during the pleasure of the parties, and no longer. It is for this reason that it is properly distinguished as the pairing family. The husband could put away his wife at pleasure and take another without offence, and the woman enjoyed the equal right of leaving her husband and accepting another, in which the usages of her tribe and gens were not infringed." In separation the wife "left the home of her husband, taking with her their children, who were regarded as exclusively her own, and her personal effects, upon which her husband had no claim; or where the wife's kindred predominated in the communal household, which was usually the case, the husband left the home of his wife. Thus the continuance of the marriage relation remained at the option of the parties. . . . The principal feature which distinguished the syndyasmian from the monogamian family, although liable to numerous exceptions, was the absence of an exclusive cohabitation."

It is impossible to define very sharply that which has not yet taken on definite outlines; and the conception of monandry must remain as vague and full of exceptions as is the status itself. For instance, what Morgan says is colored by the fact that the position of woman, under the system of the mother-family or an approach to it,[94] was in some respects particularly favorable among the Indians of eastern North America. In the monandrous marriage of the more general type the dominance of the men, by reason of their greater physical power and better organization, is more assured. This prevailing inequality occurs in Morgan's field of observation, as well as elsewhere. Monandry is generally a "temporary monogamy" whose duration is in the hands of the man. It is so far from pair-marriage that, as the term monandry implies, a single man may contract temporary unions with several women at the same time, though each woman is held to one man at a time.

"Among the Iroquois, who were barbarians of high mental grade, and among the equally advanced Indian tribes generally, chastity had come to be required of the wife under severe penalties which the husband might inflict; but he did not admit the reciprocal obligation."[95] So in Australia: single pairs cohabited, the woman being bound to fidelity; the man not. In fact, the man might have two or more wives and they might be sisters.[96] "A man and woman are husband and wife when they live together (occupying the same hut or shelter in the camp and sharing one camp-fire), their union being recognized by other members of the tribe."[97] Certain California Indians "may be said to set up and

[94] §416, below.
[96] Smyth, *Vict.*, 325.
[95] Morgan, *Anc. Soc.*, 455.
[97] Brown, in JAI, XLVIII, 223.

dissolve the conjugal estate almost as easily as do the brute beasts. . . . A Wintun generally pays nothing for his wife, but simply 'takes up with her.' Thus the marital relation is extremely loose and easily surrendered."[98] A Botocudo man may have as many wives as he can support, usually three or four but sometimes twelve; these associations are prefaced by no ceremony and are the results of mere agreements.[99] Elsewhere in Brazil "we find, even if not, as with civilized peoples, a marriage, yet a regular union of the sexes. We find rights and duties of the spouses, paternal power, and various grades of relationship. . . . The spiritual or sentimental need is completely subordinated to the corporeal, and the choice goes out always and onesidedly from the man. . . . Horde and tribe listen to no complaint from the spouses, give to neither of the two any guarantee of the durability of their union, and assure no rights. . . . Thus, since this union, analogous to marriage, is, as such, completely withdrawn from the judicial authority and verdict of the chief and the community, it appears as an unconditioned, intrinsic autocracy."[100] Homer[101] regards the atomistic condition of the Cyclopes as characteristic of the most savage type of society and correlative with cannibalism: "Each rules his wives and children, and they pay no heed to one another."

In typical monandry the man has unlimited power over wife and child:[102] it is only with the limitation upon that power, if there is force enough in the mores to carry it, that the woman's rights appear. Woman could only fight, or run away, or resort to cheating and cunning; and, as she could gain little or nothing by the first two expedients, she adopted the last.

An indication of recent monandry in Australia lies in the determination of the portions of a slain kangaroo which the hunter must give his father, sister, and brother. There is no provision for the wife. "She will not get much from her blackfellow unless there is a surplus."[103]

In monandry the female remains with one male for a time; but however brief the period may be, it is considerably longer than that required for the sex-act. Here is a coöperative relation of man and woman that satisfies, though in the lowest of terms, the definition of marriage.[104] The next development is the extension of the duration of the union; for there was that in the mores which made for prolongation. In the syndyasmian form, "when alienation arose between a married pair, and their separation became imminent, the gentile kindred of each attempted a reconciliation of the parties, in which they were often successful; but if they were unable to remove the difficulty, their separation was approved."[105] Marriage evolves, in general, by a progressive lengthening of the period of association.

[98] Powers, in *Contrib. N. Amer. Ethnol.*, III, 317, 238.
[99] Wied, *Brasilien*, II, 38.   [100] Von Martius, *Beiträge*, 102, 103.
[101] *Odyssey*, IX, 114-115; Keller, *Hom. Soc.*, 3-4.
[102] Curr, *Aust. Race*, I, 109; Eyre, *Cent. Aust.*, II, 319.
[103] Palmer, in JAI, XIII, 285.   [104] §338, above.
[105] Morgan, *Anc. Soc.*, 454.

Another long and fruitless controversy, involving the conception of the horde,[106] falls to the ground when it is seen that the monandrous family is the only germ from which a society can develop. The horde is merely an aggregation of such families of the poorest kind, for special purposes, and on special occasions of short duration. Whether to live herd-wise or pair-wise is a question of the mode of the food-quest. The horde and the family are before us both at once; we see their relation to each other, but it is the family, not the horde, which is the primordial societal unit.

§346*. Group-Marriage. If one starts from monandry as the loosest form of sex-association, he comes almost at once upon a primitive system, called "group-marriage," which has been taken by some to be no more than a specially limited communalism or promiscuity. As such it belongs with the rest of the phenomena of unregulation; and it has its likenesses to polyandry.[107] It is a characteristically Australian form and its essence, as bearing upon still more primitive sex-relations, has been summed up as follows:[108]

"We have a number of men belonging [by birth] to one class married collectively to a number of women of the other class [by birth]. This is, in fact, a form of group marriage." The aspect of these Australian marriage arrangements[109] which concerns us here is that the same man has a marital relation to all the women of a particular prescribed group or class (the tribe being divided into such fractions), and one woman has a similar relation to all the men of a similar group or class. The elders, at an initiation-ceremony, allot individual members of these groups to one another as *piraurus*, a re-allotment taking place at each circumcision-ceremony; the parallel to land-allotment under communal holding should be noted. Again, in a case where several men are of the same totem (that is, are tribal brothers, some of them being also real brothers), and one of them has a wife (who must come from the group with which the men's group intermarries), they all call her wife and she calls them all husband, and they all exercise marital rights over her. "Her children call all the men father and all the men are bound to protect the children." Howitt continues: "One is led to the conclusion that the earlier status of marriage in Australian tribes was the cohabitation in common of a number of men of one of the divisions with a number of women of the other division, and that

[106] §147, above.   [107] §397, below.
[108] Howitt, in JAI, XVIII, 34; Howitt, in JAI, XX, 99, 62, 103 (this being the order of quotations); Howitt and Fison, in JAI, XII, 35; Fison, in JAI, XXIV, 368; Fison, in AAAS, 1892, 719; Wake, in JAI, XIII, 154.
[109] §§261, above, and 352, 353, below.

there has been a gradual and probably slow development of individual marriage." It is impossible, in our judgment, to resist this conclusion, unless systematizers are prepared to dispute the testimony and impressions of their own best witnesses, namely, the competent ethnographers in the field.

The prevalence of this primitive form varies in Australia with the terms in which the struggle for existence is set, tending to disappear as they become easier; the man-land ratio is plainly in evidence. "The most backward-standing types of social organization, having descent through the mother and an archaic communal marriage, exist in the dry and desert country; the more developed Kamilaroi type, having descent through the mother, but a general absence of the Pirauru marriage practice, is found in the better watered tracts which are the sources of all the great rivers of East Australia; while the most developed types, having individual marriage, and in which, in almost all cases, descent is counted through the father, are found along the coasts where there is the most permanent supply of water and most food."[110]

A sort of reversion to group-marriage appears in Siberia where a race of higher civilization is bent upon exploiting the native by any device that occurs to it. "Many Russianized families of the Lower Kolyma form actual combinations of group-marriages with Chukchee families; or, properly speaking, the Chukchee consider it as a group-marriage, and the Russians rather as a kind of prostitution. The Chukchee set great value on these relations, because they consider the Russians, notwithstanding all their hunger and need, as belonging to a higher civilization; and the Russians strive to get out of these relatives some reindeer-meat free of cost, also some cheap reindeer-skins and costly peltries of the tundra."[111]

Rivers[112] does not like the term "group-marriage"; he uses "sexual communism," meaning "a social condition in which it is recognised as legitimate that sexual relations shall take place between a group of men and a group of women. Sexual communism may be of two kinds; in one, sexual relations may take place between any man and any woman of the tribe; in the other, they are limited by social groupings within the tribe." Communism in property shows the same categories. Group-marriage "ought to denote a form of marriage in which every male, or, at least, every male member of a generation of one group, is the husband of every female, or, at least, every woman of the corresponding generation of another group; in which, further, the children are regarded as the children of the group, and not of any individual parent; but we have no conclusive evidence that such a form of marriage exists, or has ever existed." There is some evidence for organized sexual communism, however; "in many forms of the classificatory system, a man classes with his own wife in nomenclature all those women whom his wife would call 'sister' in the classificatory sense, and in some cases there is definite evidence that this is not an empty system of terms of address, but implies relations with these women corresponding with those of the wife in the limited sense." There is also organized communism of a sexual order similar to that of group-marriage in connection with age-classes. "Thus, in one part of New Guinea, all the men born within a given period of time form a group, the members of which have various social relationships, duties, privileges, etc., to one another, and among these relations is one that, though each individual member may have an indi-

110 Howitt, in JAI, XVIII, 33.   111 Czaplicka, *Aborig. Siberia,* 75.
112 *Melan. Soc.,* II, 127, 130; *Soc. Org.,* 45, 78-80; 183.

vidual wife, she is shared with all the other members of the age-grade." The age-grade system is rare, but it shows "that sexual group-relations form a potentiality of human nature." The author emphasizes again "the fact that we have clear evidence that existing varieties of mankind practise sexual communism."

A modification of group-marriage occurs where a set of brothers marry a set of sisters, an arrangement which Cæsar[113] reports of the Britons; to this form the Polynesian term *punalua* has been attached.[114] The *punalua* relation "arose from the fact that two or more brothers with their wives, or two or more sisters with their husbands, were inclined to possess each other in common," though the modern use of the term connotes "dear friend" or "intimate companion." Further modifications, such as the common American Indian custom whereby a man has a number of sisters as his wives, will appear under other connections. Cæsar, it should be added, reports that parents and children had spouses in common. In general, such variants seem to be well accounted for by circumstances of the industrial organization, an industrial combination being superposed upon a marital one.[115] Where wedlock was pair-wise, though the housekeeping was conjoint, this system is all but modified away.

Group-marriage is not the same as communal marriage; it is a narrowed and evolved arrangement which points back to the latter. It is the cross-union of a number of persons in two connubial groups. In communal marriage, while all the women of the group are restricted to its male members, each of them is the possible wife of any man in the group. As communal property is really non-property, so is communal marriage really non-marriage; it is the germ of marriage rather than the thing itself. In practice it has very rarely if ever appeared in ethnography otherwise than as monandry. Group-marriage arises after groups and sub-groups with totems have come into being and have become related to each other so that they are either concubitant or taboo, that is, fore-ordained to mate or not to mate with one another. Then group-marriage appears as a relation, pair-wise, between groups. It too is formative of marriage rather than genuine marriage itself.

Reflection over the facts and relations cited in this chapter leads to the conclusion that the formative period for marriage was likewise the formative period for industrial coöperation between the sexes. Barring the survivalistic evidence of unregulation, the rest has been afforded by societies of a low culture and in particular of an undeveloped self-maintenance organization. Monan-

[113] *Bell. Gall.*, V, 14; Schrader, *Aryan*, 394; Müller, *Sex. Leben*, 31; Starcke, *Prim. Fam.*, 138.

[114] Morgan, in *Smithson. Contrib. Knowledge*, XVII, 453, 238, 477.

[115] §§398 ff., below; Lippert, *Kgchte.*, II, 31.

dry, though it could not but have conferred some of the advantages of sex-specialization and coöperation, allowed of no such protraction of relations between man and woman as might have elicited a more perfect mutual adjustment. The economic basis of union was there, but there was not much chance to develop it. It seems that a pair could cleave together for a longer time if they found it desirable, and doubtless the cases in which that was done represented a tendency toward a more permanent partnership. Monandry was, in a sense, a sort of unconscious experimentation. It is a fact, however, illustrated over and over in the history of marriage, that a pair who know that they may not part at will are disposed to get along together by exercising a forbearance for which there is no occasion under conditions of entire freedom. If sex-specialization is any advantage at all in the advancing struggle for existence, then unregulation of the association of the sexes speedily becomes a maladjustment. It seems that it showed itself to be such from the earliest stages of which there is record, for ethnographic evidence of unregulation is slight and that from survivals must carry back to a remote period. Protraction of coöperation between specific individuals being favorable to success in the struggle for existence, stress was automatically exerted in that direction. The attainment of adjustment in societal self-maintenance called for protraction in time of the association of man and woman. Economic conditions thus demanded the regulation of relations between the sexes and the consequent development of a marriage-institution out of original unregulation.

CHAPTER XLIV

EVOLUTION BY RESTRICTION

§347. Action of the Taboo. In the making of marriage the taboo is found discharging its characteristic function of institution-builder. The general sex-taboo may be conceived of as a measure for keeping male and female apart; it has covered more or less the whole intercourse and relation of the sexes: the food-quest, forms of industry, of ornamentation, of religious function. In respect to the union of the sexes, it has defined a wife and matrimony by ordaining the limits upon absolute freedom; then marriage has come, from one angle, to be the specification of the conditions under which, the mode by which, and the persons by whom the sex-taboo might be broken through, and not otherwise; for other violations of the taboo were vice, crime, and sin. Between two extremes, one of which defines the limits on entire freedom of the woman (for it is the woman rather than the man, who constitutes the focussing-point of the taboo) and the other the breaches in her complete restraint, history shows an immense number of intervening stages. The presence of the sex-taboo indicates that men found, as the requirement of expediency, not that the sexes should be brought together by social customs nor that they should be left to do as individuals saw fit (which would mean that societal expediency was not involved at all), but that they should be kept apart. Such restriction evidently runs counter from the outset to the provisions of Nature; the conventions, here again, are typically restrictive of natural impulse. Endogamy and exogamy are resultant doctrines and policies. In a broad way, the status of woman is a composite of the rights and duties, abilities and disabilities of every kind, which women have suffered or enjoyed under the several forms of the sex-taboo.

Taboo of the women to outsiders, communal rights of insiders over them, and monandrous unions in a setting of unregulation constitute the simplest form or germ of the marriage-institution which can be set down as more than inferential. A condition of total unregulation somewhere beyond the reach of available evidence is a reasonable inference. The parallel cited to the hunting-ground, communally held, and to the temporary monopoly of particular pieces of land is significant of the unity of the selective process and also of the essential interrelation of marriage and property.[1] Though monandry may satisfy the definition of marriage[2] in a minimal sort of way; though we use the term group-"marriage"; and while the foregoing forms come under any treatment of the marriage-institution; yet there is in them so little of restriction that they belong, so to speak, only in the vestibule of the evolving structure.

The development of marriage, like that of other institutions, lies, then, in the action of the taboo;[3] for by it the shapeless mass of folkways surrounding the sex-interest is chiselled into distinctive lines. The history of marriage shows that the definition of the institution consists in specifying who may not marry or, more explicitly, whose wife a certain woman may not be. The taboo is always in evidence: it would appear sometimes as if both the primitive and the more developed human society had expended most of their energy in dealing with the sex-relation, so numerous are the varieties of restriction which are to be found in their mores or deliberate policy. One has, however, the same sort of feeling when he is immersed in the study of property or religion. The fact is that in societal evolution variations are rife and, selection being relatively slow, are not weeded out promptly; in ranges where results cannot be so speedily or convincingly verified there must be persisting variations of widely differing expediency and rationality.[4] Having reviewed the most primitive and unregulated of sex-relations, we now come to a survey of the restrictions whose evolution meant the emergence of a real institution.

The broadest set of restrictions as to who shall or shall not marry whom concerns itself with prohibiting marriage without or within a given group, and thus prescribing endogamy (in-marriage) or exogamy (out-marriage). Of these two forms, endogamy is undoubtedly the more primitive; members of isolated or atomistic societies must have mated within their groups or not at all. More specifically, it was the tabooing of the group's women

1 §341, above.   2 §338, above.
3 §§46, 269, above.   4 Keller, Soc. Evol., 48, 129 ff.

against all outsiders that constituted endogamy. Men were under no such taboo; almost never were they forbidden to get women outside and live with them in a manner that meets our covering definition of marriage. Thus usage and law did not exist to render tribal endogamy a complete and rounded institution and no group was ever characterized by it unless it was a weak or isolated one whose members could not capture women from outside. Amid the chaotic conditions surrounding early marriage, the presence of inveterate woman-stealing must always be reckoned. It had much influence upon the form taken by evolving marriage and in far later stages is represented, in survivalistic form, among the wedding-ceremonies.[5]

From the outset, then, exogamy is always working around and about an endogamous system and gradually extending the range of freedom of intermarriage. It brings outsiders in and tends to break down the distinctions between the in-group or we-group and the out-group or others-group. At the same time that it is dissolving the endogamous system, it is also extending its own taboo within that system, as a result of conquest and incorporation or otherwise, so that it comes to set off non-marrying sections within the tribe. At present tribal endogamy, as once known, is to be found only where it is protected by some form of isolation—either geographical, in the mores, or other—from the influences which might procure a more expedient adjustment.

Thus far endogamy and exogamy have been envisaged mainly as characteristic of the tribe. Both terms, however, are relative, their precise meaning at a place and time depending upon the sort of group under consideration. If a group is denominated exogamous, that obviously means that its male members get their wives from outside. Outside of what? May the men not marry women of their own people at all? May an Iroquois brave not have an Iroquois squaw? What we find in practice is that a man regularly marries a woman of his own nation, though he must belong to a different totem or division from hers. This is a case of exogamy with respect to the totem within a general setting of endogamy with respect to the nation. The Hebrews were exogamous as respects blood-kin out to a certain point fixed in the mores (in-

5 §371, below.

cluding the seventh degree of kinship—the descendants of a common great-grandparent) and at the same time endogamous as respects the "Chosen People." They proscribed cousin-marriage on the one side and union with the Gentile on the other. We ourselves are exogamous as respects the family out to and including, according to the convictions of many, first cousins; and we are endogamous as respects race, in that we do not approve of unions that cross the color-line.

Groups are both endogamous and exogamous at the same time: there are two limits set, one within which and one outside which marriage is tabooed. Unions approved by public opinion, that is, matings in accordance with the mores, occur within a sort of belt between an outer and an inner forbidden area.

In the figure, circle A includes the family, let us say, ending with first cousins, and circle B the white race; the belt C is the range of generally approved unions. It should be noted that whereas unions within C meet general

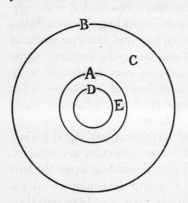

approval, those within the inner circle D (family, including parents and children) inspire repugnance and horror as incestuous, while those within the intervening space E encounter a qualified verdict. And if, beyond B, alien races are graded outward toward a limit of utter savagery, a growing aversion to exogamy is the accompaniment. The marriage of an American to a cultured Mongolian might meet with some slight approval; but marriage with an African Pygmy would be inexplicable and "unnatural." Consider the case of the "squaw-man" of the frontier; in the opinion of the Anglo-Saxon he has lowered himself, though in the codes of other nations, for instance of the Portuguese in Brazil, the crossing of races has evoked little or no censure.

For people who do not believe in international matches, the range of C would be much narrowed; also for those who object to second-cousin unions or marriage between persons of different faith, wealth, or social position. It can readily be seen that the belt C, of approved unions, would shrink to a thin line and then, perhaps, even shorten to a point, in the case of a prince who must marry his equal and at the same time attend to all the punctilios of his class code.

It is evident that hard and fast definition cannot be secured in this evolutionary matter, except in particular and local cases; in such the taboo is wont to be peremptory. Despite the fact that under endogamy there is sometimes a positive injunction, that a person must marry such and such a relation—cousin, or even sister—yet it is the taboo, that is, a negative rather than a positive precept, which is the normal agency of regulation.

Having set forth this preliminary survey of the two policies of in-marriage and out-marriage, we now turn to a detailed consideration of first the one and then the other. In so doing, the numerous facts and immediate inferences from them will seem, perhaps, to be strung on the sexual strand rather than on the economic. The latter may seem to disappear altogether. It is really only overlain and temporarily out of sight. The reader should check up the various glimpses which he will get of it pending the summary at the end of the next chapter.

§348*. Consanguine Marriage. It will open up the subject best to begin with the extreme case of endogamy, thence moving through intermediate forms toward its decline in favor of exogamy. The unit group or society is the kin-group; and so the most elementary form of endogamy is sex-union within that group. Such marriages are called consanguine. There is a vast number of rules about marriage which are unintelligible to us unless we enter into the circle of notions held by those who adhere to the rules. Then we see that most of the taboos are deterrent of consanguine marriage as understood according to the local conception of consanguinity. Of course consanguinity is not all of one degree. If the bonds of relationship or "blood" beyond the most immediate are not known, recognized, or given attention, the kin-group is a family in the narrower sense; and marriage within it is known as incest. Sex-intercourse within it, however unattended by external formalities, is viewed much as marriage would be, that is, it is generally highly reprobated. Incest, as here understood, means close in-breeding. As such, it is found in a number of primitive societies, sometimes prescribed to the exclusion of exogamy or out-breeding and again, far oftener, viewed with the utmost horror and forbidden under the direst penalties.[6] The lat-

---

[6] For a careful review of the topic of consanguineous unions, see Wilken, "Huwelijken tusschen bloedverwanten," in VG, II, 309-352.

ter position is held by the stronger and more advanced societies
which have been long in competition;[7] so that in a study of the
evolution of society and its institutions, the preliminary issue is
found to formulate itself thus: Whence did the taboo on close consanguineous unions arise? It is a debated point; and the available
evidence as to the existence of such unions must be faithfully reviewed. It will be noted, in the course of such a review, that a
number of peoples regard certain unions between persons remotely
consanguineous or not known to be so at all, according to biological standards, with the same horror with which they look upon
the closest consanguine unions. Own cousins have been allowed or
even coerced to marry when remoter kin, or persons not kin at all,
have been forbidden to do so.[8] This is what is meant when people
are said to regard as "incestuous" such a union as that between
persons of spiritual affinity. Incest, in a sense wide enough to
cover cases of this order, could mean only union between persons
who are, according to some arbitrary criterion, "too near" one
another. Although instances will be introduced to illustrate this
point, our use of the word "incest" is confined to cover only relations between parents and children or real brothers and sisters.[9]

In one region of New Guinea "persons of the same name may marry, and
a father may take his step-daughter and his own daughter to wife; but brother
and sister, and cousins do not marry."[10] In the Solomon Islands the union of
two persons having the same tribal mark is regarded as a crime. But the children take the mother's mark. It is therefore theoretically possible and has
been observed in practice that a father may marry and have children by his
own daughter.[11] These first instances are typical of many primitive marriage-
taboos: at the same time they forbid one form of union and allow another,
both being equally consanguine. In some East African tribes men marry their
mothers and sisters, since, being upon the lowest stage of beggary, they are
unable to buy wives from outside their families.[12] Though marriage with a
sister is forbidden, yet "in spite of this it appears to have occurred, even in
the recent past, in times of distress." Poverty presented a choice between
incest and celibacy. Marriage with a half-sister is possible; but the ruling
family, because of such an alliance in the past has to endure such remarks

[7] Keller, Soc. Evol., 81.   [8] §§261, above, and 349, 354, below.
[9] Cases in Tylor, Early Hist., 283; Wilken, in VG, I, 146 ff., 310-311;
Peschel, Vkde., 232 ff.; Sumner, Folkways, ch. XII.
[10] Chalmers, in JAI, XXXIII, 124.
[11] Parkinson, in Dresden K. Zoöl. u. Anth.-Ethnog. Mus., Abhandl. VII,
pt. VI, 6.
[12] French-Sheldon, in JAI, XXI, 361.

as: "They have no shame, and take their own sisters to wife."[13] Again, of another East African tribe: "Brothers marry their sisters and even fathers their daughters, but not a son his own mother," even though he inherits his father's other wives.[14] In Togo sex-relations with half-sisters were regarded as perfectly proper.[15] About this class of cases Starcke[16] notes that if in the primitive family children belonged to the mother's kindred, their legal position with respect to each other being independent, the prohibition of marriage between brothers and sisters (same mother) did not extend to those of half-blood (same father, different mothers). Here would be, then, a formal taboo that takes little account of in-breeding.

Several African cases show a relaxation of the taboo on incest in the case of the royal family. In Gaboon the king was wont to marry his grown daughter, the queen her eldest son—an extreme divagation in the effort to keep the royal blood pure.[17] A prince among the Niam-Niam takes his own daughter to wife, but only with her consent.[18] In Madagascar, there were royal and other marriages between brothers and sisters, but they were "preceded by a ceremony of sprinkling the women with consecrated water, and reciting prayers for happiness and fecundity, as if there was a fear that such unnatural unions would call down upon the parties the anger of the Supreme Being. It should, however, be observed that such marriages were usually made because of the difficulty sometimes occurring of finding a wife of equal rank with the chief or king. There was also often a jealousy of any claimant to the supreme power, on account of the brother of the chief being, of course, older than the chief's own children."[19] The Yukaghir of Siberia "say that in former times marriage was forbidden only between first cousins, and that they do not consider second cousins as consanguineous relatives. The myths often refer to consanguineous marriages, especially between brother and sister" and a modern instance of such union is known.[20]

An astonishing case is where the Balinese married twins of opposite sex together, when they reached puberty. It is not done now but they are still called by a term meaning "betrothed twins." The same custom is reported from old Japan.[21]

In America, the Aleut brother and sister, and sometimes father and daughter, may marry.[22] Brother-sister marriage is said to have been possible in the chieftain's family, among the New England Indians.[23] Of the Sierra Madre tribes it is said that incest between father and daughter is "of daily occurrence." There is no degeneracy; if the parents are strong, the children are also.[24] Even if such cases are not marriages, they are exhibitions of in-breeding. Fraternal incest occurs in Brazil, especially among the smaller and isolated tribes; the more numerous the group, the less is seen of incest. However, it takes place frequently in all grades among the many hordes and tribes on

---

[13] Gutmann, in *Globus*, XCII, 30.
[14] Wilson and Felkin, *Uganda*, II, 49.
[15] Klose, *Togo*, 275.   [16] *Prim. Fam.*, 231.
[17] Bastian, *Afr. Reisen*, 261.   [18] Junker, *Afrika*, III, 291.
[19] §227, above; Sibree, *Great Afr. Isl.*, 252.
[20] Czaplicka, *Aborig. Siberia*, 92.
[21] Wilken, in VG, II, 334; Pfoundes, in JAI, XII, 224.
[22] Reclus, *Prim. Folk*, 65.   [23] Waitz, *Anthrop.*, III, 106.
[24] Dr. M., in *Umschau*, VIII, 496.

the Amazon and Rio Negro and the Caribs "see without a shudder the marriage of parents with their children."[25] Traces of the brother-sister marriage, and especially of endogamous sex-relations, are much more common in Asia and Europe then among the Indians.[26]

A number of cases in which incest is not repugnant to the mores are to be found in antiquity: among Medes, Persians, Egyptians, Hebrews, Greeks, Phrygians, and others.[27] The Hindu divinities Yama and Yami, brother and sister, are represented as conversing on the propriety of a brother-sister union.[28] For certain ecclesiastical offices precisely those persons were in demand who had sprung from such unions;[29] the Zendavesta praises consanguine marriage highly as an ancient custom and a divine ordering. "Among the present-day Persians consanguine marriage is likewise no great exception; here it is plainly a survival out of antiquity."[30] "The object of the institution of consanguine marriage was originally the keeping pure of the blood, the holding-off of alien elements."[31] The Egyptians thought the marriage of brother and sister the most proper, citing the example of Osiris and Isis; in their love-songs the words brother and sister take the sense of lover and mistress.[32] The gods of the Babylonians, Egyptians, and Greeks exhibited incestuous unions of all degrees. Wilken[33] thinks the expression "My sister, oh bride!" in the Song of Solomon is significant and believes that a non-uterine sister was sometimes married.

In the Norse sagas, Niord the Rich, while among the Vans, "had taken his own sister in marriage, for that he was allowed by their law; and their children were Frey and Freyja. But among the Asas it was forbidden to come together in so near relationship."[34] Pagan kings of the Nibelungen period behead wooers of their daughters and sometimes intend to marry the latter after the death of their queens.[35] The incestuous union of Siegmund and Sieglinde is a salient incident in the tale upon which Wagner's Nibelungen Ring is based. The heathen Germans allowed all unions except those between parents and children; if reproof occurs, it is from the standpoint of another time and a different people.[36]

In several parts of Russia a tradition is preserved that in the old days a brother could marry a sister. "Not long ago there lived in the village of Dubensk a very pretty and hard-working girl. Her parents were reluctant to part with her and give her in marriage to a stranger. So they sent her to pay a long visit to her relatives at a distance, and on her return they received her as a complete stranger. From that day forth they obliged her to consider her

[25] Von Martius, *Beiträge*, 115-116, 334, note; Starcke, *Prim. Fam.*, 44.

[26] Bernhöft, *Verwandtsftsnamen*, 15-16, 47.

[27] Maspero, *Hist. Anc.*, I, 50; Justi, *Persien*, 225-226; Müller, *Sacred Books*, IV, pt. I, xlv; Wilken, in VG, I, 148, note.

[28] Hopkins, *Relig. Ind.*, 131.   [29] Tietz, *Blutsverwandsft.*, 8.

[30] Geiger, *Ostiran. Kultur*, 245-247; Schrader, *Aryan*, 392.

[31] Justi, *Persien*, 225-226.

[32] Maspero, *Hist. Anc.*, I, 51; Diodorus, *Hist.*, I, 27.

[33] In VG, II, 341-342. He cites Gen., XX, 12; Levit., XVIII, 16, XX, 21; II Sam., XIII, 13; Ezek., XXII, 11.

[34] "Ynglinga Saga," in Laing, *Sagas*, I, 273; Zenker, *Gesellschaft*, I, 50.

[35] Lichtenberger, *Nibelungen*, 334.

[36] Weinhold, *Deut. Frauen*, I, 359-360; Wilutzky, *Mann u. Weib*, 57-58.

brother as her husband."[37] The Russian military men of the early modern period were reproached because, not marrying, they lived in vice with their sisters, mothers, and daughters.[38] Lea[39] records the case of a canon who contracted incest with a daughter and granddaughter, apparently with entire impunity.

It is worth noting that legends about the beginning of the race, if they go back to one pair, must either go on to incestuous unions in the ensuing generation or nullify their own version of man's origination, as in the Bible.[40]

Among the foregoing cases several have exhibited incest as occurring in ruling families, the intimation being that purity of blood was the object in view. Some writers see in the royal brother-sister marriage an attempt to secure unquestioned legitimacy at a time of transition from mother-descent to father-descent, under the former of which occurs the nephew-right, whereby a sister's son is heir to his uncle, under the latter of which the son succeeds the father. If now son and sister's son are the same person, there can be no flaw in the title.[41] If ruling families, even in Europe, are forced to be endogamous or go outside of their class, it is obvious that the closed circle of Olympus, of half or wholly deified royalty, must resort to consanguine alliances. There remain several instances, some of them classic, which serve to enforce the special case of incest in ruling families.

In Melanesia, consanguineous marriage was regarded as the special privilege of the chiefs; with the common people it was in disfavor.[42] In Tonga and Hawaii the cousin or half-sister marriage existed for reasons of state, probably lest the divine right to rule, resting as it did on the fiction of descent from the gods, be impaired.[43] In the Hawaiian Islands, "the highest kind of chief was one who was the child of brother and sister, who were themselves again the offspring of this kind of marriage. . . . This custom existed side by side with a repugnance among the commoners, not only to marriage with a sister, but with any person with whom blood relationship could be traced."[44] The queen must be a half-sister among some Nigerian tribes, the Nairs of the Malabar coast, the Rajas of Tipura, in some parts of Burma and Siam, among

---

[37] Abercromby, *Finns*, I, 182, 183.

[38] Kostomarov, *Gt. Russians* (Russ.), 154.

[39] *Inquisition*, III, 639.   [40] Gen., IV, 16 ff.

[41] §417, below; Lippert, *Kgchte.*, II, 46 ff.

[42] Rivers, *Melan. Soc.*, I, 382.

[43] Thomson, in JAI, XXIV, 379; other Polynesian cases are cited, with authorities, in Mucke, *Horde*, 89.

[44] Rivers, *Soc. Org.*, 39.

certain Malays of Sumatra, and among the Indians of Hispaniola.[45] "If the king of Teneriffe could not find his equal, he was obliged to marry his sister to prevent the admixture of plebeian blood. Others might marry whom they pleased, except mother or sister."[46]

The two classic cases of royal fraternal incest are those of the Ptolemies and the Incas.[47] In the former dynasty, "they were matched in and in like prize cattle. . . . There are no less than nine cases of close intermarriages distributed among the thirteen Ptolemys."[48] "Cleopatra was the daughter of a brother and sister, great-granddaughter of another brother and sister, and a great-great-granddaughter of Berenice, who was both cousin and half-sister to her husband. She, in accordance with the custom prevailing in the time of the Ptolemies, wedded her younger brother."[49] Concerning the Incas, the old law was that the heir to the throne should marry his eldest sister, legitimate on both sides. According to the chronicles, this was carried out through four-teen generations without the last Incas exhibiting any mental or bodily weakness.[50] Neither they nor Cleopatra were deaf-mute, deformed, or imbecile.

We have been intent upon citing all evidence available to us upon the topic of the closest in-breeding. When it comes to cousin-marriage, or that between uncle and niece, aunt and nephew, the cases are much more numerous and our interest centers chiefly in their bearing upon the broad question as to why endogamy has declined in favor of exogamy. Was in-breeding seen to be a bad thing? The reader should view the following cases with that query in mind.

In Australia the institution of classes had the effect of "actually compelling in-and-in marriage, beyond the degrees of brothers and sisters."[51] On the Gulf of Papua, "persons of the same name may marry and here even cousins may marry, but not brother and sister."[52] In Fiji every man was under an obliga-tion to marry his first cousin, the daughter of his mother's brother.[53] In the New Hebrides, Samoa, and often elsewhere, the proper and suitable marriage is that between children of a brother and sister, while that between the chil-dren of two brothers or two sisters is absolutely forbidden.[54] Evidently the fear of in-breeding has not dictated this common distinction between types of cousin-marriage; in Fiji, "children of sisters are looked upon as brothers and sisters to one another, and not as first cousins; also in the case of the children of brothers"[55]—so that really the prohibition here is against fraternal incest

---

[45] Yule, *Court of Ava,* 86 (where full references are given).

[46] Cook, in AA, II, 478.

[47] Westermarck, *Marriage,* II, 91-93; Letourneau, *Marr.,* ch. IV, 328-329.

[48] Galton, *Hered. Genius,* 151-152; Rawlinson, *Five Mon.,* I, 318; Wester-marck, *Marriage,* II, 225.

[49] Snyder, *Geog. of Marriage,* 41-42.

[50] De la Vega, *Yncas,* I, 308; Tietz, *Blutsverwandsft.,* 8; Westermarck, *Marriage,* II, 95; Mucke, *Horde,* 89; Prescott, *Conq. Peru,* I, 117.

[51] Smyth, *Vict.,* I, 92.

[52] Chalmers, in JAI, XXVII, 332.   [53] Thomson, in JAI, XXIV, 342.

[54] Lawrie, in AAAS, 1892, 709.   [55] Fison, in JAI, XXIV, 361.

which is conceived to attend certain cousin-unions and not others. Evidently there is in evidence here, and in similar cases, a formal interdiction based upon local ideas of relationship.[56]

In Madagascar, the ideas are somewhat different. There "marriage between brothers' children is exceedingly common, and is looked upon as the most proper kind of connection, as keeping property together in the same family. . . . Marriage between brothers' or sisters' children is also allowable on the performance of a slight prescribed ceremony, supposed to remove any impediment from consanguinity; but that of sisters' children, when the sisters have the same mother, is regarded with horror as incest, being emphatically fady or tabooed, and not allowable down to the fifth generation, that is, to the great-great-great-grandchildren of two such sisters."[57] Consanguinity seems to stick to the female line, being relaxed somewhat apologetically in the mixed case. The rule is about the same in another African instance,[58] where, in addition, an uncle may not marry his niece if her mother is his sister by the same mother; otherwise the union is allowed. Among the Koryak of Siberia, "marriage was forbidden only between a father and his daughter and a mother and her son. A son-in-law could marry his mother-in-law, and a father-in-law could marry his daughter-in-law. Marriage was also allowed between first cousins."[59]

A Batak by preference and expectation weds the daughter of his mother's brother, though it is a transgression of the *adat*, or mores, to marry the daughter of a father's sister; a sister's son may marry a brother's daughter but a brother's son may not marry a sister's daughter. Wilken,[60] who reports this state of affairs, together with numerous cases, corroborative and otherwise, thinks it explicable only on the assumption of an original matriarchal system. Tradition holds that formerly a man took the daughter of his father's sister to wife, but that calamities supervened when this was done. It is added that the children of two brothers may not marry.[61] In Sumatra, though the consent of the king is necessary to marry the daughter of a brother or sister, it is never refused.[62]

The Eskimo frequently marry first cousins or remoter blood-relatives with the idea that in such case the wife is nearer to her husband.[63] Among the Caribs of the Antilles "the daughters of a father's or mother's sister are regarded as the wives whom destiny assigns a man."[64] In a Brazilian tribe, "after the death of a man his brother must marry the widow, and the widow's brother must marry her marriageable daughters, if no other bridegroom is found. Certain grades of relationship, for instance between paternal uncle and niece, admit of no marriage."[65] Elsewhere in this region marriages take place even in the near grades of relationship.[66] In British Guiana, a paternal uncle may not marry his niece, though it is allowable to marry a sister's daughter.[67]

[56] §§411, 412, 425, below.
[57] Sibree, *Great Afr. Isl.*, 248-249, 182.
[58] Gutmann, in *Globus*, XCII, 30.   [59] Czaplicka, *Aborig. Siberia*, 89.
[60] In VG, I, 141, 455, 456; II, 227; Tietz, *Blutsverwandsft.*, 14; §417, below.
[61] Meerwaldt, in *Bijd.*, XLI, 203; Marsden, *Sumatra*, 228.
[62] Jacobs, *Groot-Atjeh*, I, 238, note.
[63] Nelson, in BAE, XVIII, pt. I, 291.
[64] Bernhöft, *Verwandsftsnamen*, 62.
[65] Spix u. Martius, *Brasilien*, 1339, note.
[66] Von Martius, *Beiträge*, I, 602.
[67] Schomburgk, *Brit.-Guiana*, II, 318.

In the Old Testament, Nahor marries his brother's daughter, Jacob his two cousins, Amram his paternal aunt.[68] The Book of Jubilees asserts that pious men marry their first cousins on father's or mother's side.[69] The angel tells Tobias that he will ask Raguel (who calls Tobias cousin) to give his daughter to Tobias to wife, "for the right of inheritance doth rather appertain to thee than to any other." Raguel would be liable unto death if he gave her to another.[70] The Semitic attempt to keep the blood pure led to greater toleration of consanguineous unions.[71] "The daughter of the paternal uncle was and is given by preference in marriage to her cousin, among many Bedouin tribes"; hence the custom of calling a first wife, even if entirely unrelated, by that name.[72] Again, a Beduin has the exclusive right to marry his cousin; though he is not obliged to do so, she may not marry another without his consent.[73] In an Arabian story,[74] when a father asks his daughter whether she wishes to marry a suitor, she replies: "He is not one of my cousins nor one of our neighbors who would put restraints upon himself for your sake if I did not please him." From this it appears that in marrying a relative the woman got protection. Modern Jewish practice may be illustrated from the Rothschild family: of fifty-eight recorded marriages of descendants of Mayer Rothschild, just half were those of first cousins. These, as a rule, have been fertile.[75]

In general, in modern times and in civilized countries where there is no religious taboo, cousin-marriage is not prohibited; nevertheless no one can deny that it is the object of some criticism. It is not regarded at all as the normal and natural union, least of all as the inevitable one. Then the idea has become fixed that it is unnatural; that it could not occur in a "state of nature"; that it is an acquired social depravity. How divergent such views are from the truth we have been at some pains to demonstrate by the citation of considerable evidence.

§349*. Taboos of Narrower and Wider Scope. When a series of representative cases has been passed in review, it becomes evident that the closest endogamy has existed in primitive life, without reprobation—in fact, that consanguine marriages and even what we call incestuous unions have been approved and even prescribed. Hence it is possible to set aside forthwith the notion that there exists in man a certain "instinctive" or "natural" abhorrence of such relations. This falls into line with the results at-

[68] Gen., XI, 29; Gen., XXIX, 13, 23, 30; Exod., VI, 20.
[69] Charles, *Bk. of Jubilees*, ch. IV, 15 with note, 16, 20, 27, 28, 33.
[70] *Tobit*, VI, 10, 12.
[71] Hewitt, in *Westminster Rev.*, CXLIII, 258.
[72] Snouck-Hurgronje, in *Bijd.*, XXXV, 449; Tietz, *Blutsverwandsft.*, 13.
[73] Burckhardt, *Bedouins*, 64.   [74] In Von Kremer, *Kgchte.*, II, 97.
[75] "Rothschild," in *Jew. Encycl.*, X, 497.

tained by actual study into the facts about other alleged "instincts," for instance against cannibalism,[76] and other products of speculation unchecked by reference to available facts. Although some idea of the nature of the taboo upon consanguine unions will have been gathered from the cases cited, still we wish to devote some attention to specific cases of that taboo. These are instances of exogamy.

"The social prohibition which forbids the intermarriage of parents and children, or brothers and sisters, is universal through Australia."[77] "Forbidden to have intercourse with blood relations, mothers, sisters, first and second cousins, this religious law is strictly carried out and adhered to under penalty of death." The greatest curse possible, launched only in frenzy or passion, is to call an opponent during a quarrel by a term indicating that he has broken this taboo. "Woe unto the man or woman who should infringe the . . . sacred law."[78] The Fijian shuns his sister "because the woman is *specially* forbidden to him, and her touch would be pollution."[79] In the New Hebrides brothers and sisters and cousins german, may not marry.[80]

One African cosmogony contains the following: "And in the beginning the people married their own sisters. Thereafter they observed that they beat their wives a good deal, and therefore decided: we will no longer marry our sisters, but let one marry the sister of another, in order that each may say, 'If I beat my wife I shall be called to account by her brother and he will mulct me of my property.' If they had gone on further as at the beginning they would have killed their wives, because they said to themselves: 'Even if she dies, what harm? Who will ask me about it!' "[81] Here are some "ills" of incest that even the savage could apprehend. In Uganda, one of the tribes, extending the disapproval of human in-marriage, "held in great abhorrence anything like incest among domestic animals—that is to say, they greatly disapproved of intercourse between a bull-calf and its mother-cow, or between a bull and a cow that were known to be brother and sister. If this occurred, the bull and cow were sent by night to a fetish tree and tied there. The next morning the chief of the tribe appropriated the animals and turned them to his own use."[82] Apparently their transformation into revenue removed the taint. Incest among the Kabyles is considered a crime at once religious and social; wherever it is voluntary, stoning is the punishment. Incestuous relations, in their code, are those between ascendants and descendants in the direct line, and first of all between brother and sister.[83] Since the taboo extends to foster-brother and foster-sister, there cannot be, behind these proscriptions, any perception of biological ills from in-breeding.

"The Nairs respect their elder sisters, who stand in the place of mother to them. They never remain in the same room with their younger sisters; they do not touch or even talk with them, since it might, as they say, give rise to some sinful act, as the girls are young and inconsiderate, while respect for their

---

[76] §§290, 291, above.
[77] Howitt, in JAI, XII, 502.
[78] Gason, in JAI, XXIV, 169.
[79] Wake, in JAI, XIII, 155.
[80] Leggatt, in AAAS, 1892, 705.
[81] Gutmann, in *Globus,* XCII, 30.
[82] Johnston, *Uganda,* II, 719.
[83] Hanoteau et Letourneux, *Kabylie,* II, 170; III, 206.

elder sisters puts an end to any such thought."[84] This is striking evidence of the power of the mores. The Veddahs have a tradition that a painful death is the direct consequence of an incestuous union with elder sisters and aunts.[85] Though the Dyaks practise sex-vice of all description, they yet insist upon drowning those marrying incestuously within the following degrees: parent and child, brother and sister, uncle and niece, aunt and nephew. Cousins are regarded, in Sarawak, as brothers and sisters.[86] In Nukahiva, while the marriage of near kinsfolk was tabooed, sometimes father and daughter or brother and sister lived together. Connection of mother and son was regarded as abominable.[87]

Among the Hudson Bay Eskimo, where much laxity prevails, it is reported that when a man took his mother to wife, public opinion forced him to discard her.[88] "Marriage-taboos between those too nearly related are capable of demonstration even among the very rudest tribes of America."[89] "No one, man or woman, enters the marriage-association out of which he himself springs, even where relations are very loose and approach communalism."[90] Among the Tinneh and Chippeways, while men sometimes marry their mothers, sisters, or daughters, this is not approved by public opinion.[91]

The Laws of Hammurabi punish incest with a daughter by banishment and incest with a mother by burning both parties.[92] The Old Testament Hebrews handled the case with similar ruthlessness.[93] Mohammedan law is very wide in its prohibition, beginning with mother, sister, and daughter.[94] While the Romans interdicted close in-marriage, the classic case in tradition and literature is Greek; incest, says Hermione, is a barbarian custom.[95] What is by many judges regarded as the greatest play ever written, the *Œdipus the King*[96] of Sophocles, is a tragedy of incest with a mother, aggravated by parricide. As both supreme sins were performed unwittingly, the basic tragedy of all is the helpless subjection of man to the aleatory element in life. Œdipus declares that he is blameless; that the fatal situation is due to some ancient curse; that even his father would not have blamed him. The Greek has it that "many a man has associated with his mother in his dreams,"[97] but that was when he was not himself. When he was in a condition of moral responsibility, he would not harbor such a thought. The horror exhibited by Œdipus, his wife-mother, and the Theban people, as the situation is gradually and with matchless skill revealed, is paralleled by the self-punishment of the chief actors and the exaction by the gods of their children's misery and death, as evidence of society's condemnation of such an alliance.

[84] Starcke, *Prim. Fam.*, 229.
[85] Bailey, in *Trans. Ethnol. Soc. London*, II, 295, note.
[86] Perelaer, *Dajaks*, 59.
[87] Ross, in *Smithson. Rep.*, 1866, 310.
[88] Turner, in BAE, XI, 180.   [89] Friederici, in *Globus*, XC, 305.
[90] Bernhöft, *Verwandsftsnamen*, 15-16.
[91] Ross, in *Smithson. Rep.*, 1866, 310.
[92] Müller, *Hammurabi*, 129; Winckler, *Gesetze Ham.*, 28.
[93] Levit., XX, 11.
[94] Schroeder, *Geschlechtl. Ordnung*, 80; Pischon, *Islam*, 9.
[95] Rossbach, *Röm. Ehe*, 421-424; Euripides, *Androm.*, 173 ff.
[96] The story appears also in *The Phœnician Maidens* of Euripides.
[97] Sophocles, *Œd. Kol.*, 266-267, 964 ff.; *Œd. Tyr.*, 981, 982.

In our own mores we can test degrees of revulsion by trying our own feeling about unions in some such order as follows: mother-son, father-daughter (as in Shelley's *Cenci*), brother-sister, step-brother and step-sister, uncle-niece, first cousins, second cousins, and so on. In general, the less the degree of consanguinity, the less the revulsion. What happens is that the powerful stress of sex-passion is actually neutralized by the mores, for the very existence of even sex-attraction between those very closely consanguine is deemed shameful. This case of the suppression of what is perhaps the strongest of human passions by convention forms one of the best illustrations of the disciplinary control exercised by the mores.[98]

Unions between individuals less closely related than parents and children or brothers and sisters are not, as preceding evidence has shown, so consistently under the ban. Nevertheless they are very commonly regarded as incestuous and, as such, are prohibited. Our instances here are illustrative of actual prohibitions; however, there are in addition certain avoidance-customs which have been interpreted as preventatives against consanguineous unions. Brother and younger sister must have nothing to do with one another after the latter reaches sexual maturity; other relations, both by consanguinity and affinity, must not meet, or converse, or have any familiar dealings with one another. That certain males and females are not permitted to eat out of the same dish may be connected with the fact that such an action is often significant of betrothal or marriage.[99] Not all cases of such avoidance can be referred to any one cause, but a number of them seem to be aimed in the direction of out-breeding.

In gathering instances of consanguineous union, one must take pains to notice whether the terms of relationship reported connote real blood-connection as now understood or are merely "classificatory."[100] Where, within some social grouping, all the members of a given age-grade call each other by terms translated as "brother" and "sister," there may exist various degrees of actual blood-kinship between them; and this is true also of terms like "cousin." The classificatory relationships have no special interest in the present connection.

[98] Keller, *Soc. Evol.*, 25 ff.   [99] §§368, 370, 425, below.
[100] §§423, 424, below.

In Australia, "a man cannot marry his blood-cousin, or his daughter's daughter, and a woman cannot marry her blood-cousin or her son's son, notwithstanding the fact that these particular relationships are necessarily located in these very same . . . groups which otherwise would be allowed to join in permanent sex partnership."[101] In some New Guinea tribes, near relatives through the mother and in others through the father may not marry.[102] In Melanesia "the objection to marriage with a sister extended to all those who received the same designation as a sister. . . . There thus seems to have existed among the ordinary people just the same kind of restriction on marriage as is found among most peoples of rude culture who possess wide restrictions on marriage dependent on kinship."[103] The Hottentots punish incest, under which they understand marriage between "children of brothers and sisters of the first or second degrees."[104] In Uganda the laws of consanguinity are very strict; a man is absolutely forbidden to marry any woman of his mother's clan, nor might he marry into his father's except in a case of two very large clans.[105] A man may not marry his cousin; cousins may not, in fact, enter the same house or eat out of the same dish. A man may not take his mother's sister to wife but he will endeavor to support her; "this aunt will, if possible, live with the young man's mother, and be treated by him as analogous to his mother."[106] In West Africa, "a cousin's consanguinity is considered almost the same as that of brother or sister. They cannot marry. Indeed, all lines of consanguinity are carried farther, in prohibition of marriage, than in civilized countries."[107] The Fan has trouble in finding a woman whom he can marry. A man is not to be justified in marrying first cousin or aunt; "and as relationship among the Fans is recognized with both his father and his mother . . . there are an awful quantity of aunts and cousins about from whom he is debarred."[108] The Somals never marry cousins;[109] and the Hovas forbid intermarriage within the fifth degree.[110] The Kabyles extend the taboo widely over relationship by marriage.[111]

The Yakuts, Samoyeds, and Cheremis avoid marriage in the paternal clan; the Ostyaks and Ossetes between those of the same surname.[112] The Chamar of India have a number of rules many of which go back to the taboo of consanguineous unions; marriage is said to be prohibited by some tribes within seven degrees in the descending line. Others say they do not intermarry as long as any previous relationship between the parties is ascertainable.[113] The Khonds think marriage within the same tribe is incest and so they kill all female infants—one reason for infanticide.[114] The law of Manu[115] forbade a

[101] Roth, *N.W. Cent. Queensland*, 182; Ratzel, *Vkde.*, II, 64; Grosse, *Familie*, 60.

[102] Krieger, *Neu-Guinea*, 300.   [103] Rivers, *Melan. Soc.*, I, 382.
[104] Fritsch, *Eingeb. S.-Afr.*, 322.   [105] Roscoe, in JAI, XXXII, 35.
[106] Johnston, *Uganda*, II, 695, 749.   [107] Nassau, *Fetichism*, 4.
[108] Kingsley, *Travels W. Afr.*, 321.
[109] Paulitschke, *Nordost-Afr.*, I, 195.
[110] Müller, *Sex. Leben*, 41.
[111] Hanoteau et Letourneux, *Kabylie*, II, 170; III, 206.
[112] Westermarck, *Marriage*, II, 113-114.
[113] Risley, *Ethnog. India*, I, 169; Jolly, *Recht u. Sitte*, II, 62-63.
[114] §404, below; Hopkins, *Relig. India*, 531.
[115] Bühler, *Manu*, XI, 172.

man to marry the daughter of his father's sister, or of his mother's sister, or of his full brother; "he who marries one of them sinks low." The formal distinction between types of cousin has appeared above and will be accounted for later on.[116] "The Sea Dyaks are very particular as to their prohibited degrees of marriage, and are opposed in principle to the intermarriage of relatives."[117] In the customary laws of the Mohammedan Malays in Sumatra, what they regard as incest is visited with the death-penalty or commutation thereof.[118] The Alfurs taboo intermarriage to the fourth grade.[119]

The Greenlanders' interdiction extends to the third degree; even foster-children brought up in the same household may not marry; and an alien reared within the family-group is counted as a person closely related.[120] The Seneca cannot marry the daughter of his father's sister or of his mother's brother, while the Iroquois excluded collateral marriage in the remotest grades.[121] Among the Pima, uncles and nieces are not permitted to marry, and cousins do not, "out of respect of the parents for each other"; but careful search failed to discover any trace of intratribal groups between which marriage was prohibited.[122] Among the Fuegians, "generally speaking marriages with near kin are held in high abhorrence."[123]

Mohammedan law forbids marriage with aunts, cousins, foster-sisters, relatives-in-law, step-relations, and even nurses.[124] To Roman eyes marriages within the sixth degree of relationship ranked as *nefariæ et incestuosæ nuptiæ*, and this was carried over into the canon law.[125] In Rome the presence of a man at the purification-feast for women constituted incest.[126] "Finally comes the Roman law of the Christian epoch which, under the influence of the Church, interdicted successively the marriage between uncle and niece, aunt and nephew, then between cousins german. But in the Eastern Empire this latter union was authorized."[127] During the Middle Ages restrictions were now tightened now relaxed, and there was great activity in discriminating and proscribing on the part of the canonists and church-authorities. When their proscriptions came into conflict with local usage—of the Germans, for instance—they were relaxed or dispensations were granted.[128]

The so-called "cross-cousin" union has significant bearings upon the explanation of the taboo against consanguineous marriages, for it reveals the fact that that taboo rests upon a mistaken view of biological kinship. It allows the union of cousins

---

[116] §§348, above, and 425, below.   [117] Roth, in JAI, XXI, 133.
[118] Van den Berg, in *Bijd.*, XLIII, 284.
[119] Müller, *Sex. Leben*, 41.
[120] Nansen, *Esk. Life*, 175; Fries, *Grönland*, 111.
[121] Cunow, *Australneger*, 19, 79.   [122] Russell, in BAE, XXVI, 184.
[123] Bridges, in *Voice from S. A.*, XIII, 201.
[124] Schroeder, *Geschlechtl. Ordnung*, 80; Pischon, *Islam*, 9.
[125] Müller, *Sex. Leben*, 41; Rossbach, *Röm. Ehe*, 421-424.
[126] Rossbach, *Röm. Ehe*, 266.
[127] §§353, 425, below; Rivers, *Melan. Soc.*, I, 13; Wilken, in VG, II, 342-343, 348-351.
[128] Schroeder, *Geschlechtl. Ordnung*, 85. For the rules covering wedlock and consanguinity in Scandinavia, see Finsen, in *Annaler*, 1849, 214-221.

who are believed not to be of the same blood whereas it forbids that of other cousins. But if there are ills from cousin-marriage they should appear in both sets of cases alike and lead to a general taboo on all cousin-union. The fact that they do not, reveals the taboo as an arbitrary social measure wholly disconnected with biological ills. The state of the case is briefly this: "The children of two brothers or of two sisters fall into one category and the children of a brother and sister into the other"; the taboo rests upon the former and not upon the latter. The explanation lies in the form of descent recognized; whether in the father-line or the mother-line, children of brothers or of sisters are closely related, while children of brothers are not related to children of sisters. "With exogamy the children of two brothers or of two sisters will or may belong to the same social group, while the children of brother and sister must necessarily belong to different social groups." This situation is plotted out in a subsequent connection;[129] in its pure form as well as in its complications it affords evidence that is not debatable against the view that consanguineous unions were forbidden because of observed ill effects upon offspring. It is not desirable to follow either endogamy or exogamous taboos into the modern period, as the chief point at issue here is concerning the why and how of the evolution shown.

§350*. Cause of the Taboo. In attempting to sum up the evidence about consanguine marriage, what we see is a considerable tolerance among primitive tribes of what we call close consanguine unions, together with a set of taboos upon it which, though sufficient to prevent the closest in-breeding, are inconsistent and ineffective as respects the union of remoter consanguines. In fact, the taboos upon marriages other than those of parents and children or of brothers and sisters, seem to represent adjustments between the societal organization—family-systems, class-systems, totem-groups, or other divisions—and marriage, rather than to reflect concern with in-breeding as a biological matter. The regulations allow what we know to be unions of the same germ-plasm, as in certain cousin-marriages, and forbid others, between relatives-in-law, for instance, where there is no blood-relationship in

129 §§353, 425, below; Roguin, *Mariage,* 83.

evidence. With current ideas of the ills of consanguine marriage in mind, one is likely to refer primitive taboos forbidding it forthwith to a knowledge of adverse physical consequences; yet in the cases reviewed it nowhere appears that prevention of biological degeneration has formed the leading motive, or any motive at all, in restriction.

It is generally impossible, or in the highest degree difficult, to elicit from savages a rational motive for the mores they practise; when they are asserted to have assigned such a motive, there is always the legitimate suspicion that the person reporting on them has read into vague and random answers some persuasion lying, deep of root, in his own mind. To the question, Why? the primitive almost invariably answers by reference to ancestral custom[130] or, perhaps, he relates a myth, which is much the same thing only that the myth can sometimes, though precariously, be interpreted. He does not know why he does thus and so any more than the man on the street knows why he keeps to the right rather than to the left in passing other people. It is "custom 'long we-folks." However, there is a certain amount of evidence as to what primitive people have alleged concerning the ills of consanguine unions and it should be weighed; for in any case there is this elemental rule of exogamy, of taboo against in-marriage, to explain. It must have evolved somewhere along the course of societal evolution and it forms a sharply defined and crucial challenge to the science of society. First of all, what has the savage to say about it?

Several writers on the Australian Dieri report a tradition of theirs about the origin of clans: that at first all relatives married indiscriminately, "until the evil consequences of such unions showed themselves distinctly."[131] The nature of the consequences does not appear; perhaps there was a shortage of kangaroos. Again, it is stated that the Australian cherishes a profound feeling against "mixing the same blood." "No one will be prepared to contend that it is an innate one. It has been arrived at by their ancestors through a course of reasoning which has satisfied them."[132] All we get from these remarks is that the natives have derived, from some source unspecified, a sentiment which they undoubtedly harbor.

According to Hutton,[133] "that the Sema recognises the evils of consanguine-

[130] Sumner, *Folkways,* §1.

[131] Gason, *Dieyerie* (Adelaide, 1874), 13. This is the original; it is cited by Cunow, *Australneger*, 109; Semon, *Aust. Bush*, 227; Fison and Howitt, *Kamilaroi*, 25; Howitt, *S.E. Aust.*, 480 ff.

[132] Howitt, in JAI, XVIII, 10.   [133] *Sema Nagas*, 134.

ous marriage is clear enough, and he describes it as sterile or as resulting in the idiocy or deformity of its offspring, and it is also clear that he considers exogamy a sufficiently effective bar." Wilken[134] challenges any such view; he says that ethnography has arrived at complete certainty on one point, "namely that the taboos of primitive time did not have the object of averting from offspring the actually existing or imagined evil effects of marriage between blood-kin, and that in this therefore the origin of the taboos is not to be sought." Here and there in the Archipelago, as elsewhere, there is a belief that consanguineous unions are harmful, but the asserted cases of ill effects either do not exist at all or, at any rate, not to such a degree as to have caught the attention of nature-peoples. It is the author's opinion that the taboo came first and then, under its influence, the belief in the ill effects. This is precisely the position which we should wish to take; such a process is paralleled all along the line, as, for instance, in the cases of slavery and cannibalism. These instances of close in-breeding in the Archipelago show no ill effects, so far as the author can see, and he cites Arab usage, which has amounted to an age-long series of consanguineous unions without bad results. The Dyaks do not attribute to consanguineous marriage certain ills which travellers lightly refer to that cause, but think misfortunes are due to the breaking of taboo in general. The author cites instances; for instance, an albino child is referable to traffic between a woman and an evil spirit. There is no natural abhorrence of incest in the East Indies; it is a trespass against good mores by which the land becomes unclean and the death of the guilty party is called for in order to appease the higher powers. Such taboos attend on the natural world-order rather than upon the moral; a poor harvest, for example, shows that incest has been committed. The penalty for incest is drowning or burial alive; sometimes there is a sacrifice, the blood being sprinkled toward the sun to allay his wrath, and the flesh constituting a reconciliation-meal for the whole community including the guilty party. There is also a punishment by degradation; a pig-trough is filled and then knocked upon as if to call for the hogs, and the guilty person is made to eat out of it. All the incest-rules point up in exogamy. The view of Morgan and Maine, that exogamy was a reformatory measure, after people saw the results of in-breeding, is worthless.

Of the Maori it is said: "Anyone outside of brother and sister could marry, although marriage of first cousins was greatly disliked. They seem aware of the weakening effect of 'in-breeding.' "[135] Then they were aware of what, as we shall see, is very difficult to prove. A Batak tradition reports that formerly a man married the daughter of his brother's sister, but calamities followed.[136] They are not specified. By the Veddahs "no evil results are anticipated from the union of first cousins."[137]

In old Japan intermarriage between near relatives is deemed inexpedient because the children would be sickly, mentally and physically, and their offspring even more so. This is a better case for the acumen of the partially civil-

---

[134] In VG, I, 140, note, 141 and note, 146 ff., 457, 458, note; II, 352. Wilken's article, "Huwelijken tusschen Bloedverwanten," is a critical review of a publication of the same title by Van der Stok, and was translated into German in *Globus*, LIX; it is in VG, II, 312 ff. Wilken proclaims himself an "anti-consanguinist."

[135] Tregear, in JAI, XIX, 102.   [136] Meerwaldt, in *Bijd.*, XLI, 203.
[137] Bailey, in *Trans. Ethnol. Soc. London,* II, 295, note.

ized in noting the imperceptible; but the marriage of twins, alluded to above, scarcely goes with it.[138] According to a report of the ninth century, A.D., "the Chinese hold that crossing of races produces a sounder offspring, with stronger body, longer life, more robust health, and other advantages."[139] Plutarch[140] asks why marriage of relations is forbidden and suggests several conjectures,

...rly Arabs seem to have opposed in-breed-...ions being: "Marry among strangers, that ...nts."[141] Westermarck[142] cites other cases, ...on of physical degeneracy from close in-

...cuts might see in their animals the advan-...ys, chase out of the herd the young mares ...outside. Their owners, he imagines, would ...haps, in their admiration of their animals, ...Against this guess may be set the follow-...standing the affinity in all their wedlock ...of these robust hill-Beduins. When they ...convenience of marriage within the first ...his we see among cattle, and nevertheless

...ntroduced only with some violence ...ve himself—is extremely slight and ...ly weight can rest upon it and the ...no value. No reasonable grounds ...e peoples to be rationally aware of ...breeding. Rational selection of this order would be a striking anomaly among backward races.[145] Further there is a covering absurdity in the assumption that primitive people have been rationally clear upon a matter concerning which modern scientists, with all their accumulated observations and analyses, are not sure.

Among ethnographers and others who have actually observed human in-marriage there exists no unanimity of opinion that in-breeding is attended by evil results; this being so, it is inconceivable that the savage should have detected with wide generality that which has escaped the trained eye of the educated observer—

[138] Pfoundes, in JAI, XII, 224.
[139] Maçoudi, *Prairies D'Or*, I, 301, 302.
[140] *Moralia*, §108.
[141] Wilken, in VG, II, 45; Wellhausen, "Ehe," in *Gött. Gesell. d. Wissenschaft*, 1893, 441; Von Kremer, *Kgchte.*, II, 105.
[142] *Marriage*, II, 170-181.
[143] Sieroshevski-Sumner, in JAI, XXXI, 559.
[144] Doughty, *Arabia Deserta*, I, 472.
[145] Keller, *Soc. Evol.*, 93 ff.

who, moreover, as a member of a civilized race traditionally suspicious of in-breeding and as an investigator, has his attention directly focussed upon the issue in question.

"The fact of a race of men habitually marrying their first cousins," says Thomson[146] of the Fijians, "promised to exhibit such remarkable features in vital statistics" that a census was taken. The population of twelve villages was not replacing itself by surviving offspring, for though there were 2.94 children to each marriage, only 51.5 per cent of them survived. But of the 133 concubitous families were born 438 children, of whom 232 survived. "In every respect the concubitants [who commonly marry cousins[147]] appear to be the most satisfactory married class. They amount to 29.7 per cent of the population, but they bear 33.3 per cent of the children born, and they rear 34.2 per cent of the children who survive." A Portuguese slave-dealer died in 1849 in Dahomey, leaving four hundred widows and one hundred children. They were interned by the king. In 1863 there were children of the third generation from all degrees of incestuous union. "There was not a single case of deaf-mutism, blindness, cretinism, nor any congenital malformation."[148] There does not seem to result from cousin-marriage in Madagascar "any of those consequences in idiocy and mental disorder of the offspring which we frequently see in European nations as arising from the marriages of first cousins. It is poss ble, however, that to this marrying in and in amongst tribes and families is due, in part at least, the sterility so frequent in Malagasy women, although this is no doubt also largely caused by the too early marriage of young people, and the licentiousness allowed until very lately among the young, and even among mere children."[149]

In India, for nearly three hundred years the members of a certain small community have never, it is said, married out of their caste. "They form a healthy community and are fairer and better looking than most of the Portuguese converts. First cousins may marry, but marriage between second cousins is the rule."[150] Though the Veddahs marry their younger sisters, no traces of malady—insanity, idiocy, epilepsy—are found. "But in other respects the injurious effects of the custom would seem to be plainly discernible. The race is rapidly becoming extinct; large families are all but unknown, and longevity is very rare." This author[151] quotes as follows:[152] "In the Arabian desert, the national type has been preserved by systematic intermarriage. . . . No evil results are anticipated from the union of first cousins; and the experience of ages and of a nation may be trusted." Tietz[153] cites the cases of the Bataks, Arabs, and Beduin, and that of the Ptolemies, previously mentioned, as illustrations of the apparent harmlessness of in-marriage. In the Middle Ages the limitation of marriage to tenants of the same land led to the closest blood-relationship between all in the village;[154] however, this produced no ill effects sufficiently marked to be noted in the records. In a closely endogamous group of six to seven hundred in Schokland, in the Zuider Zee, all the members looked

---

146 In JAI, XXIV, 382, 385.   147 §353, below.
148 Huth, *Marriage of Near Kin,* 145.
149 Sibree, *Great Afr. Isl.,* 248.   150 Dymock, in JASB, II, 17.
151 Bailey, in *Trans. Ethnol. Soc. London,* II, 295-296.
152 Burton, *Pilgrimage,* III, 40-41.
153 *Blutsverwandsft.,* 12-13, 9.   154 Lamprecht, *Beiträge,* 92.

alike and were strong and sound persons with no marked tendency to consti-
tutional disease.[155] A similar case is reported from a peninsula at the mouth
of the Loire, where cousin-marriage was uncommonly frequent.[156] It is noteworthy that official modern censuses offer no evidence as to the ills of in-
breeding.

On the other hand there are cases showing asserted ill effects.[157] The Loyalty
Papuans are said to exhibit "many physical evils" referable to close intermarriage.[158] Von Martius[159] reports the Brazilians as more numerous and less
liable to bodily and mental degeneration where they marry outside the family.
Close intermarriage is reported to have been decidedly injurious to a Galician
Jewish sect, in the matter of disease and backwardness and feeble-mindedness
in children.[160] Ill effects were in some cases conspicuous, in others unobserv-
able, in Danish parishes.[161] "Howe investigated in England seventeen cases of
marriage between very close relations; from these unions 95 children had
sprung, of whom 44 were idiots, 12 scrofulous, 1 deaf, 1 dwarfed, and only
37 sound of body."[162] For economic reasons the noble Venetian families took
to consanguineous unions, and this "was not the most remote cause of the
physical and moral decadence of the patriciate."[163] Reports of similarly caused
degeneration appear from time to time in the press.[164] In a paper read before
the British Medical Association, on consanguineous unions in the Isle of Man,
it is stated that close inbreeding occurs all over the island; that the general
death-rate from tuberculosis is 25.7 per 10,000, or double that of England and
Wales; and that whereas, in an isolated section, where there are only three or
four surnames, the rate is 41.77, in another section, where more strangers come,
it is only 15.19.[165] In another report from a practising physician,[166] we are
told that a closely intermarrying group of mulattoes in Ohio showed fecundity
in the first generation, less in the second, and an increasing sterility in the
third and fourth, together with much disease. In the fourth generation scarcely
one of them was in good health.

Thus the evidence from outside observers is contradictory and
generally vague. Accounts of ill effects seldom inspire confidence,
for they do not convincingly disengage the exact cause or causes
of degeneration. The low estate described may be due to in-breeding; but then it may just as plausibly be referred to other contributing causes. Suspicion of in-breeding lies deep in our tradi-

[155] Tietz, *Blutsverwandsft.*, 15.
[156] Von Fircks, *Bevölkerungslehre*, 233; another in Huth, *Marriage of Near
Kin*, 260.
[157] Westermarck, *Marriage*, II, 230 ff.
[158] Ella, in AAAS, 1892, 628.   [159] *Beiträge*, I, 334.
[160] Ruppin, in *Pol.-Anth. Rev.*, II, 704-706.
[161] Westermarck, *Marriage*, II, 234.
[162] Tietz, *Blutsverwandsft.*, 67.   [163] Molmenti, *Venezia*, I, 393-394.
[164] "Eastman Family," in *Hartford Courant*, Feb. 3, 1905; "Another Idiot
Factory" (Malaga Isl., Maine coast), Assoc. Press despatch, in Feb., 1912.
[165] Report in N. Y. *Times*, Sept. 2, 1900.
[166] Dixon, in *Med. News*, Phila., LXI, 180.

tions. The theory of the harmfulness of close unions comes out clearly in the *Capitularia Regum Francorum*, where it is stated as a matter of fact that from marriages among relatives come blind, crippled, and deformed offspring, and those affected with blear eyes.[167] Deaf-mutism, in particular, is the penalty exacted upon the children. The persuasion that close in-breeding must be bad is so general that one imbued with the traditional view is inclined to single it out forthwith as the factor responsible for degeneracy if it is found to exist along with that condition. Weird views abound within this range of agitated speculation, such as that the ill effects of near-kin marriage come from the anxiety of expectant mothers.[168] On the other hand, where in-marriage exists along with health and strength, the tendency is to regard the instance as exceptional. In general, evidence against the ill effects is likely to be less biased.

The above cases establish, first, that primitive people are not rationally aware of the asserted perils of in-breeding and, second, that observers of consanguine marriage are far from unanimous in the conviction that it results in physical or mental defectiveness. As yet, then, there is no answer to the question as to why the taboo rests so heavily against close endogamy. It is inevitable that this issue must be settled, if at all, on grounds broader and more general than those hitherto covered.

§351. In-breeding in General. For animals, and so for man as an animal, there seems to be no doubt that consistent in-breeding is ultimately dangerous. Darwin[169] says that almost all who have bred animals and have written about it have expressed the strongest belief in the evil effects of constantly breeding in-and-in; and, again, that most plants suffer from self-fertilization. Breeders of higher animals think close mating beyond a certain point dangerous to the welfare of the stock, since the offspring tend to be abnormal or unhealthy.[170] It would appear, in general, that the

167 Tietz, *Blutsverwandsft.*, 26-27.

168 Wilken, in VG, II, 324; Tietz, *Blutsverwandsft.*, 66.

169 *Animals and Plants*, II, 116; *Cross and Self Fertil.*, 439, 458.

170 Geddes and Thompson, *Evol. of Sex*, 74; Tietz, *Blutsverwandsft.*, 31, 32, 34, 40, 43.

stock needs, sooner or later, to be freshened up by the admixture of new blood.[171]

One must not infer too much about human breeding from the processes and results of artificial selection. It is necessary to breed in if the object is to retain or improve a special quality or set of qualities; crossing leads to the loss of the breed. Nor must it be forgotten that, as Darwin[172] told us long ago, the breeder operates from the standpoint of his own wishes or caprices and not with the plant's or animal's good at heart. Often he selects monstrosities as the "fittest" (to his purpose) and produces "saleable defects"; several of our domestic animals have been bred up into a form which would insure their extinction if they were returned to nature. On the other hand, the care with which the breeder proceeds with his selection tends to neutralize any visible ill-effects of his in-breeding; the faulty plants and animals are removed by him and his positive results only are preserved, observed, and admired. Such considerations must be borne in mind in aligning the breeder's in-breeding with human in-breeding. Taking them all into account, it seems safe to say that mating in-and-in comes to have its ills if persisted in too closely and too long.

Nature has provided for a good deal of crossing of strains; isolation means, in general, lack of advance in the scale of being. If variation results from the combination of ancestral elements in the germ-plasm,[173] then the greatest possibilities for new variations, and so for new and improved adaptation, lie in the union of sex-elements whose hereditary constituents are diverse rather than alike. That close endogamy, involving the repeated combination of like elements, is not the law of nature is shown by the endless shadings of characteristics which are the despair of the classifier.

If such considerations be applied to man as an animal, it is clear that he has not been built up to what he is through close in-breeding. Endogamy was consistent only in profound isolation, for woman-capture was unintermittent. There is no such thing as a pure race of men; the shadings here are many and elusive, as elsewhere in nature. No human race of the highest physical quality exists in isolation; on the whole, the most inferior human animals

171 Excellent survey of the whole case in Holmes, *Trend of Race,* ch. XI.
172 *Orig. of Species,* ch. IV.
173 Weismann, *Evol. Theory,* II, chs. XXVIII, XXIX.

are those which have lived under the highest degree of detachment. Hence we cannot fail to conclude that close and continued in-breeding has not permanently favored success in the struggle for existence.

The careful investigations of G. H. Darwin[174] show that the evils ascribed to cousin-marriage are exaggerated, although certain maladies seem to take easy hold upon their offspring. These exhibit an only slightly lowered vitality and higher death-rate, not the specific idiocy, deaf-mutism, infertility, or insanity of popular ascription. Darwin justifies to some extent the belief that "offspring of first cousins are deficient physically whilst at the same time they negative the views of alarmist writers on the subject." Topinard[175] concludes that while the marriage of relations does not produce scrofula, insanity, and other defects, it multiplies and accumulates the same family tendencies, whatever they may be. Galton's researches on hereditary genius might be taken as affording support to the contention that in-breeding has its points. Some difference of opinion exists as to whether in-breeding is or is not worse for savages than for civilized man. Darwin, finding the marriages of first cousins to be four and one-half per cent of the marriages of the aristocracy, three and one-half per cent of those of the middle class, and one and one-half per cent of those of all classes in London, thought that the fact that Englishmen live well limits evil effects.[176] On the other hand savages are more exposed to natural selection, which would weed out defective individuals and so leave less evidence of degeneracy.

There is no doubt that qualities can be accumulated through in-breeding; whether they are to be regarded as favorable or unfavorable depends upon the standpoint from which judgment is passed.

Wilken[177] quotes an eloquent outburst by a French writer: "Here are consanguine parents, full of force and health, exempt from any appreciable infirmity, incapable of giving to their children what they have and giving them on the contrary what they have not, what they have never had—and it is in the presence of such facts that one dares pronounce the word heredity!" The implication is that if parents can pass on what they have not there can be no such thing as heredity. Naturally the case is not so simple as this somewhat irritated writer would have it. Presumably there are no such parents as he figures; probably there are weaknesses in every strain. The passage has the value of a picturesque exaggeration; it throws into relief one of the extremes.

The fact is that, with all the labor that has been put into the study of heredity we still know comparatively little about it. We do know that an understanding of it is of paramount importance to the race of men. It is clear, however, that no one quality can be

[174] "Marriage First Cousins," in *Jr. Statist. Soc.*, XXXVIII.
[175] *Anthropologie*, 397-398.
[176] Westermarck, *Marriage*, II, 235.   [177] In VG, II, 312.

cultivated by itself. There is a sort of compensation here; you cannot breed a horse for strength and speed at the same time, nor cattle for meat and for hide, nor fowls to lay and to set. If in-breeding is attaining success by accumulating certain desirable characteristics, it is likely, at the same time, to be accumulating others of the opposite nature. The accumulation is both positive and negative at the same time and cannot be one or the other exclusively. If all the qualities of uniting individuals were good, in-breeding could but enhance excellence. This, in experience, is never so; hereditary defects are piled up alongside hereditary superiorities; flaws balance off and eventually destroy the favorable qualities, putting an end to their transmission. In fact, it seems as if there were some malign law which decrees that deficiencies shall accumulate faster and fatally outstrip excellences; bodily weaknesses do not have to augment so fast as, for example, mental superiorities in order to offset the latter.

In view of such facts and considerations as have been cited, the informed mind is left somewhat suspicious of close consanguine union, though it does not anticipate the specific defects popularly associated with them. No one could assert that close in-breeding promises more for the race than at least occasional crossing of strains. This is quite another thing, however, from holding that primitive tribes saw the ills of in-breeding clearly enough to rule against them. If we, at this age, find the identification of those ills uncertain and difficult, it is absurd to credit the savage with such knowledge. "The effect of marriages among near kin is a matter about which qualified students of genetics have come to different opinions, and it is hardly probable that primitive peoples have been able to arrive at a valid conclusion on a subject that requires for its solution a refinement of inductive method which is quite alien to the thinking of untrained men."[178]

Assuming that in-breeding is biologically only a little worse than out-breeding, closely endogamous groups are handicapped in the struggle for existence over the exogamous. In that conflict a handicap does not have to be heavy in order to insure defeat. In-breeders will tend, therefore, to disappear, and their mores with them, where competition is keen. They can persist only in isola-

[178] Holmes, *Trend of Race,* 238.

tion. This squares with the facts of ethnography, as representative cases have shown. Through the societal selection resulting from competition the mores of survivors have come to include a strong taboo of close endogamy. The whole process is automatic, however. If the biological consequences of in-breeding are conceded to be bad, these would not be seen and rationally appraised by primitive peoples; it is through the automatic processes of societal evolution, if at all, that the presence of these consequences would evoke restriction.

The presumption is against in-breeding, on biological grounds; but it is not strong and decisive. Any system of endogamy, we repeat, is at least intermittently traversed by the introduction of the stolen woman or by the irregular union. If it were necessary to conclude the case at this point, no satisfactory accounting would have been made for the existence of the taboo against consanguine matings or for the victorious sweep of exogamy.

CHAPTER XLV

ENDOGAMY AND EXOGAMY

§352*. Divisional and Tribal Endogamy. So far, then, as the biological effects of close in-marriage go, it is not conclusively demonstrable that in-breeding is an evil thing, though the presumption is against it. But the case is not yet closed. The biological consequences of close endogamy are not the only ones. Even assuming that there are no necessary ill effects upon physique or mentality traceable to it, there are yet societal results of a far-reaching and significant order. These are consequent upon endogamy as a policy of isolation. It is necessary to work up to them through a review of marriage-usages as exhibited by groups larger than the family or close kindred, to which hitherto the argument has been mainly confined. Such groups are the constituent divisions of tribes and also the tribes themselves. It may be said in general that the farther one gets away from the circle of close consanguinity the commoner does endogamy become.[1] The tribe, among primitive peoples, is quite likely to be endogamous, though woman-stealing is almost always going on and though out of that practice there often develops a *connubium* under which the violent abduction of women is reduced to a regular and peaceful exchange or to purchase and sale.

The tribal divisions alluded to are the divisions, classes, totems, clans,[2] and some others of less consequence. Primitive peoples show a degree of attention to position, adjustment in place, or orientation which is now entirely unrepresented. When villages of independent houses were formed they fell for convenience into two or more parts, opposite to one another, and out of this distribution arose differentiation and adjustment. By an extension of this a sort of encampment-order developed, attended by usages of various sorts. Then there were the constituent kin-groups. These tribal divisions impress one on the face of them as having been constituted primarily to form exogamous bodies within an enclosing endogamous tribe. They look like a deliberate device to

1 §347, fig. 2, above.　　　　2 §§148, 149, 261, above.

secure out-marriage for consanguine groups, for their very definition is largely attained by the taboo prevailing within them against endogamy. Of course they are nothing of the sort but are automatic developments about which we know far more, however little that may be, than the people who practise them. It is mainly within and among these divisions of a tribe that the usages of endogamy and exogamy collide and have to be fought out and compromised. The case, however, is not at all simple, for totems may extend widely beyond tribal lines, rendering sex-relations permissible or tabooed between members of different and even distant peoples. For one intent upon their origins these usages are exceedingly difficult to understand; their development among very backward races, as well as the ability of those who practise them to make distinctions between the marriageable and the unmarriageable on such criteria, taxes credulity; but their existence is unquestionable, and for one who is concerned with their presence and results rather than with their origins they readily yield considerable enlightenment.

The regulation of marriage now under consideration is based chiefly, in fact practically always, upon relationship, and not only proscribes certain unions but enjoins others. Kinship is in play even when membership in clan or other division is taken into account. Nevertheless, whether or not the clan and moiety are ultimately matters of kinship, they discharge a function in regulation, for their members must marry outside of them. Rivers[3] finds that genuine tribal exogamy, if it exists at all, is exceptional; "as we now use the term, exogamy is a custom in which a person may not marry into his or her own moiety or clan (sib) or other constituent group of the tribe. The rule has nothing whatever, so far as is known, to do with the tribe itself, of which the moiety and clan are constituent groups." The whole system of the moiety or clan would be disorganized and the definite and orderly grouping would suffer if exogamy were relaxed. We do not care to take the term exogamy in so restricted a sense, wishing rather to set into contrast the two tendencies of in-marriage and out-marriage as opposite adjustments.

Present interest attaches to the presence of endogamy and the

[3] *Soc. Org.*, 38, 39-42.

entrance of exogamy in aggregations larger than the close kin-group and smaller than the well-developed tribe. Despite the fact that these divisions, in that they so commonly form a sort of framework for exogamy, seem as if devised to subserve that policy, there yet occur cases of divisional endogamy. These impress one as exceptional or survivalistic and as such doubly deserve recording; where the tribe is small and not much differentiated, tribal endogamy naturally goes with them. It makes a great difference whether endogamy is the usage of a small or a large group; if the former, then the group is helped on toward extermination by it.[4] Endogamy in a small society almost inevitably means in-breeding. If an endogamous group were to split up, and if the fragments then perpetuated endogamy as a usage, it would mean disintegration. Exogamy as to such subdivisions, with endogamy as to the original total, would bind them together.

"Endogamy may apparently be a rule in the tribe, if, owing to geographical or social isolation, its members are unable to find mates elsewhere; but usually there is no sentiment against marriages with members of other tribes, and marriages of this kind take place whenever opportunity arises. In such a case there is no point in speaking of the practice as endogamy, for it is not a more or less fixed rule forbidding members of the tribe to seek their mates elsewhere. As an institution endogamy therefore is much less widespread than exogamy."[5] If exogamy is a definite prescription, the same cannot be said, in most cases, of endogamy. "In general endogamy is characterized merely by marrying within the tribe by *choice*, while exogamy is an *obligation* to marry outside."[6] "Endogamy is to be accounted for by the wish of a group to keep together as against outsiders, and, more especially, by the tendency to prevent the dispersion of family property."[7] Such incitements may rise at any time, of course, and, on the small scale, may change exogamy back to endogamy. It is evident that endogamy may be practised either by choice or by necessity, the latter arising out of the circumstances of life and environment and not specifically out of a taboo. If mankind was, in the primor-

---

[4] Von Martius, *Beiträge*, I, 115.   [5] Rivers, *Soc. Org.*, 41.
[6] Wilken, in VG, I, 371-372, 458, note; II, 226; this author believes that exogamy was, in general, prior to endogamy.
[7] Vinogradoff, *Hist. Jurispr.*, I, 211.

dial state, scattered in small groups over a considerable area, this necessity must have been compelling. It is mainly for this reason that we believe endogamy to have preceded exogamy; furthermore, such scattered groups are likely to have been in general ethnocentric and upon terms of suspicion and hostility with other groups.

We come now to cases of endogamy within tribal divisions or small, slightly differentiated tribes; for the present purpose there is small profit in seeking to distinguish sharply between the two.

It may be said concerning Central Australian conditions, that "evidence seems to point back to a time when a man married a woman of his own totem. The references to men and women of one totem always living together in groups would appear to be too frequent and explicit to admit of any other satisfactory explanation." But with the breaking of isolation came exogamy. "It is only, during these early times, when we come into contact with a group of men marching across strange country that we meet, as we might expect to do, with evidence of men having intercourse with women other than those of their own totem."[8] Among the Dieri there is hot opposition to a marriage which removes a girl out of the tribe; and when such a thing takes place a great, apparently expiatory ceremony with extended sex-license occurs.[9] Among one people of Torres Straits, "there was complete intermarriage both within and without the clan. Members of different clans lived together in the same house." But a man of one clan might not wear the totem-badge of another clan.[10] Some of the small British New Guinea tribes are endogamous.[11]

The Galla, a strong and warlike African tribe, have a great horror of exogamy, so they do not marry their slave-women but make them concubines.[12] In Madagascar, "tribes and even families generally marry amongst themselves (with certain exceptions as regards the descendants of sisters, who cannot intermarry down to the seventh generation), so as to keep landed and other property together."[13]

The Yakuts have a tradition of close endogamy,[14] and among certain Ostiaks it is a scandal and a crime to marry out of their name-relation.[15] The Yukaghir have an inclination toward consanguineous marriages, but there are also avoidance-customs that point toward exogamy. These latter, however, could not well lead to a strict exogamy owing to the environment. "As a hunting tribe they frequently have to scatter in various families, or groups of related families, in search of food. In such cases, being isolated and far away from other tribes or clans, they have had to satisfy their sexual desires within the group or even within the family." The authoress[16] suggests that the decline of ex-

8 Spencer and Gillen, *Nat. Tr. Cent. Aust.*, 419, 420.
9 Howitt, in JAI, XX, 59; Howitt, *S.E. Aust.*, 185; §344, above.
10 Haddon, in JAI, XIX, 392.   11 Krieger, *Neu-Guinea*, 297.
12 Paulitschke, *Nordost-Afr.*, I, 257.
13 Sibree, *Great Afr. Isl.*, 185.
14 Sieroshevski-Sumner, in JAI, XXXI, 560, 562.
15 Müller, *Ugrische Volksstamm*, I, 308.
16 Czaplicka, *Aborig. Siberia*, 92, 112.

ogamic custom among the Yakuts may be the result of environment, "which, causing the people to disperse, forces men to take wives from among their own gens."

Hindu castes certainly show endogamy: in one of them, those of common stock show common ancestry within six generations back either of the man or woman.[17] These are occupational groups but may once have been tribal. Of course propinquity and the preservation of craft-secrets may lead to endogamy; there is, however, more to the case than that. "In Africa, the association of endogamy with craft-groups occurs especially in connexion with the occupation of smiths or workers in metal. Among the Masai, Gallas, and other Hamitic, or partially Hamitic, peoples, the smiths form a distinct group, whose marriages are confined strictly within their own body. In many cases . . . the smiths have physical and linguistic characters which suggest that they were once, or are even still, a distinct people. . . . It is probable that these endogamous craft-groups are indigenous peoples who, when a warrior class settled in their country, were given a definite status owing to the usefulness of their occupation, but were not admitted to such intimacy as would be associated with intermarriage."[18] This, of course, applies to the Hindu case. Another caste in India has eleven subdivisions whose members intermarry but do not marry among themselves. The usual rule as to the marriage of cousins appears except that children of two sisters may unite if the sisters were married into separate subdivisions.[19] Among certain hill tribes "the old tribal sense of exogamy seems to be falling into disuse, and many groups which were once exogamous are now endogamous."[20] "A Baloch [Punjab] marries, so far as possible, within the kindred group to which he belongs, the idea being still strongly prevalent among them that numbers are strength, and that the loss of a woman from among a group involves the loss of possible offspring." It is reported that in a certain subdivision of a subdivision of a caste, "their objection to marrying outside their own circle is so strong that, though they are fast dying out because there are so few girls among them, they decline to go to the other sub-divisions for brides."[21] The Veddahs "never marry out of their race, and, with the very smallest cause, the men are exceeding jealous of their most unattractive wives."[22] "The Veddahs afford an example of a people which through the isolation of the family and endogamy has pretty much forfeited its social instincts and has therefore become incapable of rising to a more developed form of civilization."[23]

The Kubus of Sumatra are convinced that they will lose by external association; "they believe firmly that every relation with others than their tribal mates would bring them illnesses."[24] In Malacca, "the woman whom I, according to their idea of the thing, had married (though I had never consummated the marriage) had lost the position which she had formerly occupied, although she was the chief's sister; and she was not permitted to live again upon an equal footing with her relatives because she was degraded through having mar-

---

[17] Scott, in JASB, IV, 369.
[18] Rivers, *Soc. Org.*, 151-152; §72, above.
[19] Modi, in JASB, III, 473 ff.   [20] Crooke, in JAI, XXVIII, 235.
[21] Risley, *Ethnog. India*, I, 64, 129.
[22] Bailey, in *Trans. Eth. Soc. London*, II, 292.
[23] Kohler, *Urgchte. d. Ehe*, 13.
[24] Anon., "Kubus," in *Globus*, XXVI, 46.

ried outside the tribe."[25] The Dyaks and the Alfurs of Celebes are the genuine endogamists of the Archipelago; they and several tribes of Sumatra are reported as having abandoned exogamic rules; they "are going over again rapidly to endogamy."[26] The Alfur of Minahasa seldom marries outside his own district, each district representing a tribe.[27] In Polynesia, "the nobles of different clans belong to one class, and while the clan is usually exogamous, the class always tends to become endogamous."[28]

"Moreover, for the sake of a higher and more important consideration, namely, for the sake of the solidarity of the tribe, endogamy recommends itself even to the suitor and his relations." And a conflict of motives may show that the value of the two systems is relative. "Naturally the parents of the female would rather keep their daughter and her children with them than give her away 'among the enemy'; because they could then more easily put pressure on the son-in-law. For the man, however, this point of view would, on the contrary, be a motive whereby he would prefer not to get his wife from his own camp."[29]

For the isolated Eskimo groups, endogamy is the only possible policy. It is said in general of the American Indians that they "practiced tribal or national endogamy—that is, marriage within the tribe or nation";[30] and Westermarck[31] cites American examples to prove his contention that among many peoples marriage seldom or never occurs outside their own territory. The Bella Coola Indians have relapsed into endogamy of the strictest kind; Boas[32] thinks this is owing to the effort to keep possession of special traditions, which are very jealously guarded but transmissible by marriage. The Mohaves marry very infrequently with other tribes.[33] Among the Sia, "marrying into the clan of either parent is in opposition to the old law; but at present there is nothing for the Sia to do but to break these laws, if they would preserve the remnant of their people, and while such marriages are looked upon with disfavor, it is 'the inevitable.' The young men are watched with jealous eye by their elders that they do not seek brides among other tribes."[34] Among the Seri, perhaps the most primitive people of North America, "tribal endogamy is probably more complete than in any other American tribe now extant—in Seri ethics the deepest vice is conjugal relation with alien peoples, as the noblest virtue is the shedding of alien blood. . . . Inter-clan marriage is continued in order that tribal union may be maintained. Mating or even sporadic connection with aliens is absolutely prohibited, in order that the integrity of the tribe may be preserved." The Seri stock, formerly considerable, is now reduced to a single tribe because of deep-seated animosity to alien peoples and constant warfare.[35] Among certain Brazilian savages, "a fundamental law of the tribe forbids the women association with all who are not of the same tribe." Everywhere in this region "marriage between different tribes is forbidden. The tattoo-marks

[25] Stevens, "Frauenleben, etc.," in *Ztsft. f. Ethnol.*, XXVIII, 178, note.
[26] Wilken, *Vkde.*, 266; Wilken, in VG, I, 371; II, 226.
[27] Wilken, *Vkde.*, 263, 264.   [28] Starcke, *Prim. Fam.*, 89.
[29] Wellhausen, "Ehe," in *Gött. Gesellsft. d. Wissenschaft*, 1893, 438, 437.
[30] Mason, *Woman's Share*, 198.   [31] *Marriage*, II, 47.
[32] In *Folk-Lore*, XI, 303; and in *Amer. Mus. Nat. Hist.*, II, 121.
[33] Kroeber, in AA, IV, 279.   [34] Stevenson, in BAE, XI, 19.
[35] McGee, in AA, IX, 375, 378.

define the limits of permitted marriages, and totemism defines those of prohibited marriages.[36]

Endogamy among the ancient Jews was common, and motived largely in religion;[37] but Solomon had many heathen wives and Samson married, unhappily, a Philistine.[38] Property-considerations entered into certain consanguine unions.[39] "In Arabia one section of a tribe is often nomadic while another is agricultural, but in spite of their kinship the two sections feel themselves very far apart in life and ways of thought, and a nomad girl often refuses to stay with a village husband."[40] Endogamy within the faith or sect is a familiar historical prescription.[41] Certain backward peoples of Russia have remained endogamous.[42] "Probably the Norwegians were formerly exogamic; now the dominant feeling is that natives of the same place should be chosen in marriage and if possible near relatives, even first cousins."[43]

These cases show that it is in general the backward and isolated peoples who cling by tradition to endogamy—which is both a cause and a result of their qualities; and that, where it is practised by other peoples, or classes, or in special cases, there is usually some economic, religious, or other societal reason in evidence. Though under stress there may appear a reversion to it, in the natural course of events it tends to disappear in favor of wider interrelations.

§353*. Divisional and Tribal Exogamy. These tribal subdivisions, as noted, seem as if specially created to realize their typical policy of exogamy. Very frequently a society may be endogamous with respect to the tribe or compounded group (confederacy) while remaining exogamous as regards the intra-tribal divisions.[44] Naturally enough the question is raised as to the nature of the divisions. This has been touched upon before,[45] the conclusion, so far as one could be drawn, being that, in the case of the totems at least, groupings already existed before the rise

[36] Von Martius, Beiträge, I, 404; Starcke, Prim. Fam., 44.

[37] Gen., XXIV, 38; XXVIII, 1, 2; Num., XXXVI, 1-9; Deut., VII, 3; Josh., XXIII, 13; Judges, XIV, 3; Ezra, IX, 12-14; Neh., XIII, 25; I Kings, XI, 2.

[38] Cases of Jews marrying heathen in Exod., II, 21; Judges, III, 5; Ruth, I, 4; Ezra, IX, 1; X, 18, 44; Neh., XIII, 23.

[39] Num., chs. XXVII, XXXVI.   [40] Smith, Relig. Sem., 113.

[41] Schroeder, Geschlechtl. Ordnung, 73, 74; Schmidt, Soc. Civ., etc., 212; Roguin, Mariage, 72, 73.

[42] Russian Ethnog. (Russ.), II, 123.   [43] Nansen, Esk. Life, 175.

[44] Lippert, Kgchte., II, 89 ff.; Rivers, Soc. Org., 40.

[45] §§148, 149, 261, above.

of exogamy which were then available in applying restriction. However this may be—and our argument does not stand or fall thereby—the tribal divisions have their main significance from the fact that there is an elaborate and complicated set of rules to determine the relations of marriage which may or may not be contracted between their members. To these we are about to come.

There are two types of exogamy to be distinguished: where the women of a group go away with alien husbands; and where the latter come into a group and live with wives who belong and stay there. The presence of the one type or the other will be seen to make considerable difference in subsequent arrangements.[46] The whole matter is further complicated with the distinction between the father-family and the mother-family, the former being characterized by the reckoning of blood or descent through males and the latter tracing lineage through females.[47]

With these preliminaries we may turn to the topic of divisional exogamy. The first division to be considered is that of the "class." This term is used to cover intra-group divisions on the basis of age, life-status, totem, and other criteria which are exhibited throughout ethnography. Take the age-classes or "generation-grades"[48] to begin with. In Australia there is a division of the enclosing group into these age-divisions (which are really life-status groups, for the natives do not know their ages), whereby the youth up to marriageability constitute one section, the married adults a second, and the parents of married adults a third.[49] Sexual relations are tabooed outside one's age-group; and that is not all, for within it too restriction prevails, inasmuch as "lateral" selection is limited by the kin-taboo. It is a case of limitation on endogamy carried a step farther than the interdiction of consanguine unions.

"In some parts of the world there are social groups, the composition of which depends either upon the period during which the members are born, or upon the time at which they undergo certain rites, especially that of circumcision. These groups are usually known as age-grades, though this term should perhaps be limited strictly to the grouping of the first kind. A good instance of this variety occurs on the east coast of New Guinea. . . . There is no ceremony of admission to a *kimta*, membership being determined altogether by the time of birth. . . . A *kimta* extends over a wide area, but members of a *kimta* who live in the same settlement are still more closely linked together as *eriam*. To a great extent *eriam* have their property in common, and each member of an *eriam* group has rights of access to the wives of any of his fellows, com-

46 §415, below.   47 §§404, 416, 419, below.
48 Lippert, *Kgchte.*, I, 82 ff.   49 Brown, in JAI, XLIII, 151.

munism in property being thus accompanied by sexual communism of a definite kind. Moreover, the *eriam* relation involves the use of classificatory terms of relationship, a child classing with his father all the *eriam* of his father. There is thus a striking similarity with the relationship which exists, or has existed, in Melanesia, between the members of the moiety or clan. . . . Other examples of age-grades are found in Africa, where they exist among the Masai and other Hamitic or half-Hamitic peoples. Here, however, the event which determines membership is not birth but the time of occurrence of circumcision. . . . In Africa, as in New Guinea, the members of the same age should help one another, and, in the case of the Nandi, this duty seems to be especially incumbent upon members of the same fire. There is also evidence that members of the same fire have right of access to one another's wives. . . . Social groups graded according to age also occur in North America, as among the Hidatsa." The author[50] quoted finds some correlations between these age-grades and the fraternities; and he thinks that the former "may well be survivals of some such condition of social organization as that I suppose to have been the origin of the classificatory system."

When the members of a group are classified by age, there develops a terminology of relationship that seems very strange to us, even though among us it is not unheard of for an older person to address an unrelated younger as "son," "daughter" or a younger an older as "father," "mother." It would seem that the age-grade system implies a defectiveness in the recognition of parenthood; the absence of definite terms might argue lack of understanding; but the eye is on group-relations rather than upon those of individuals.

Within a group, taking myself (ego) as a center, all men of the preceding age-grade are my fathers and all women of that grade are my mothers; those of the same grade are my brothers and sisters; those of the younger stratum my sons and daughters. Relative age supersedes other criteria: thus, male cousins would be father and son if one was a married adult and the other a youth not yet marriageable; and the son of the older of two sisters might be brother of the younger. But, evidently, a real father and daughter or mother and son could never be in the same life-status group; and the taboo on marriage between age-grades alone would prevent this form of incest.

This age-classification takes place within each tribal subdivision. Then comes the provision that the subdivision is exogamous; if it has a totem, its members must marry into another totem, for the totem must be crossed in marriage. And in addition the terms of relationship will vary according as descent is reckoned in the

[50] Rivers, *Soc. Org.*, 136-139, 189-190; he refers to the full account of the age-grades in Schurtz, *Altersklassen und Männerbünde*. On the common fire, see §91, above.

male or female line, conformably to the system as built on the father-family or on the mother-family.

For example, if the father-family is the prevailing form, a man stays in his real father's group. Then all the members of his own life-status stratum are his brothers and sisters; all the men of the older stratum are his fathers and the women his aunts (father's sisters); all on the younger grade are his sons and daughters. As for the subdivision from which his real mother came, all the women of her age-grade are his mothers (any one of them might have been his mother) and all the men his uncles (mother's brothers). The men and women of his own grade are his cousins (uncle's children). His wife belongs to the latter category, since the two subdivisions are under the *connubium*, and he may call all the women in her stratum of her group wives (any one of them may be or might have been his wife). The men of his mother's group will marry his own "sisters," and so they are his brothers-in-law, actually or to be. The younger stratum in the other group are his nephews and nieces (sister's children), who marry his sons or daughters, and their children are his grandchildren.

If descent is in the female line (mother-family) there is a corresponding complexity of relations. It is unnecessary to go into these in this place, where the conditions of exogamy rather than the familial or tribal organization form the topic of discussion. It is to be noted that the arrangement allows of consanguine marriage, though not in the closer degrees.

Tylor[51] has worked out the situation as shown in the accompanying table. Assume first descent in the female line. In class A, let A and a, and in class B,

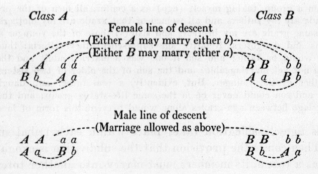

B and b, be a man and a woman. (Capital letters indicate males, small letters, females.) The woman's child follows her class, the man's child is of another. Then sisters a and a have as children A a, who, being of the same class, may not marry; brothers A and A have children B and b, who may not marry; but

[51] In JAI, XVIII, 263.

a brother A and a sister a have children B and a, or b and A, who may marry. Assume now descent in the male line, the man's child being of his class, the woman's not of hers. Then sisters a and a have children B and b, who may not marry; brothers A and A have children A and a, who may not marry; but a brother A and a sister a have children A and b, or B and a, who may marry.

In either case the children of a brother and those of a sister have different totems and are marriageable. It is evident that the distinction between such cousins and other cousins, whose marriage is tabooed, must rest upon considerations other than biological. The totem-relationship has no necessary biological significance.[52] But it is interesting to find a sort of inner regulation, as in the case of some Australians who say that while a brother's and a sister's children belong to marriageable groups, they are "too near" and may not marry.[53]

In Fiji there are two obverse relationships created by group-affiliation and intermarriage, which the reporting ethnographer[54] calls concubitancy and taboo. Concubitants were persons born into marriageability with one another; while others were born sexually tabooed to one another.

Children of sisters or of brothers were looked upon as brothers and sisters to one another and not as first cousins; they were tabooed because fraternal incest was tabooed. They married their concubitants (predestined mates), respectively; that is, the man generally married the daughter of a maternal uncle—though the concubitous relation might include third or even fifth cousins. The offspring of such marriages were then concubitous, and "thenceforward the concubitous and tabu relationships occur in alternate generations."

$$\begin{array}{ccc} A & & B \text{ (brothers)} \\ | & & | \\ X \text{ ($\male$) marries } c \text{ ($\female$)} \longleftarrow \text{(taboo)} \longrightarrow & D \text{ ($\male$) marries } y \text{ ($\female$)} \\ | & & | \\ g \text{ ($\female$)} & \text{marries} & H \text{ ($\male$) (concubitous)} \end{array}$$

A and B are brothers (or one might start with sisters). D and c, being offspring of brothers, are taboo, and marry respectively their concubitants, y and X. Their offspring g and H are concubitous. It is to be noted that, in the first generation, A (or B) has married his concubitant, just as H has married g.

Men and women are born into the relation of concubitancy, that is, of marriageability, as they are born into the atmosphere they breathe; and they can get out of it only with a wrench to the mores, for the grip of the system on the society is close and strong. The case looks like clan-exogamy with tribe-endogamy, but is so much less integrated that it results almost in group-

52 §§348, 349, 260, 261, above.   53 Fison, in JAI, XXIV, 361.
54 Thomson, in JAI, XXIV, 373 ff.

marriage. The following account should be read closely, not only for its main subject matter but for the light it casts upon the conservatism and inertia of the mores; the entrance, in spite of all, of variation in the guise of individual interest; the interpretation of that unwelcome variation in terms of the prevailing code; the enduring interest of the society at large in children and inheritance; and many another matter of significance to which attention has been given in preceding connections.

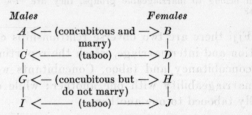

Males   Females
A <— (concubitous and —> B
| marry) |
C <——— (taboo) ———> D
| |
G <— (concubitous but —> H
| do not marry) |
I <——— (taboo) ———> J

"G and H are concubitants, born husband and wife, as were their grandparents A and B, but they grow up and take a dislike to one another and each marries some one else. Yet the system takes no account of such petty interruptions as likes and dislikes. They were born married, and married they must be so far as their children are concerned. They have each married outside the tribe, yet their children I and J are tabu just as much as if G and H had married and they were the offspring of the marriage. G and H have in fact dislocated the system for all posterity, but the system goes on, refusing to admit the injury done to it. The most striking feature of the system is this oppressive intolerance. It is so indifferent to human affections that if a man dares to choose a woman other than the wife provided for him, his disobedience avails him nothing. His concubitant is still his wife, and her children are his children. It will, it is true, give way so far as to recognize as his wife the woman he has chosen, but only on the condition that she becomes his fictitious concubitant, and that all her relatives fall into their places as if she had actually been born his concubitant.

"Since a man who is the concubitant of a woman is necessarily also the concubitant of all her sisters, by a natural evolution, if he marries a woman unrelated to him by blood, and *ipso facto* makes her his concubitant, all her sisters become his concubitants also. In the past they would have been his actual wives, for a man could not take one of several sisters—he was in honor bound to take them all. In the same way a woman and her sisters became the concubitants of all her husband's brothers, and upon his death, she passed naturally to her eldest brother-in-law if he cared to take her. This does not imply polyandry or community among brothers, but rather what is known to anthropologists as Levirate,[55] a woman's marriage to her brother-in-law being contingent on her husband's death."

It must not be understood from the use of the word "obligatory" that con-

[55] §406, below.

cubitancy meant marriage or sex-relations. "The relationship seems to carry with it propriety rather than obligation. Concubitants are born husband and wife, and the system assumes that no individual preference could hereafter destroy that relation; but the obligation does no more than limit the choice of a mate to one or other of the females who are concubitants with the man who desires to marry. It is thus true that in theory the field of choice is very large, for the concubitous relation might include third or even fifth cousins, but in practice the tendency is to marry the concubitant who is next in degree —generally a first cousin—the daughter of a maternal uncle."

The relentless logic of the savage leads to such procedure as the following. Now that free communication exists between the islands, and the men have a far larger field of election, "they are said to choose rather not to marry their concubitants. . . . The result is curious. They do not marry as they did formerly, but they commit adultery either before or after marriage. No sooner is a girl married than her concubitant comes and claims her, and so strong is custom that she seldom repulses him." Such rights have been classified among the "survivals of promiscuity."[56]

As regards the complicated systems of prescriptions and taboos current in Australia,[57] of course the natives cannot explain them. Nevertheless they can live by them: "A native who travelled far and wide through Australia stated that he was furnished with temporary wives by the various tribes with whom he sojourned in his travels; that his right to these women was recognized of course, and that he could always ascertain whether they belonged to the division into which he could legally marry, though the places were one thousand miles apart and the languages quite different."[58] Here is one of those cases where a people reputed by some to be the "lowest" of all mankind come through with an institutional structure which is virtually inexplicable but which they operate with ease. There is at least as much reason to refer it to the supernatural as any of the no more incredible results of organic evolution.

Even a brief review of these Fijian and Australian systems makes it clear that prescriptions and taboos of marriage which seem to us whimsical or grotesque, resting as they do upon a set of ideas which are represented but slightly in our minds, may yet be entirely regular and, as they are better understood, subject to logical analysis just as are all other products of organic and societal evolution. It is also plain that the notion of preventing

[56] §344, above.
[57] Cunow, *Australneger*; Curr, *Aust. Race*, I, 113.
[58] Frazer, *Totem. and Exog.*, I, 63.

consanguineous unions was not the responsible factor behind these systems. What they did was to "place" individuals in society where they could be found and identified when it came to an issue of apportioning or enforcing rights and duties. In particular were they located in their positions in the maintenance-organization. There was little or no reflection over the body of rules evolved; people grew up into a traditional life-status and then acted in it according to the mores, entirely unconscious of the mode of origin or the sense of those mores. The same impression persists as one goes on with the study of endogamy and exogamy on broader lines.

It will have been seen that the sentiment against divisional endogamy is strong and consistent. The conviction that the totem, or whatever the designation of the division may be, must be crossed is held tenaciously and widely. It is not difficult for the prepossessed to construe this as a deep-rooted aversion to biological in-breeding; only when one studies the actual cases does he see the inadequacy of that construction. When it comes to tribal exogamy, which generally means cross-marriage between tribes allied in some way within a wider whole, such as a *connubium* or a confederacy within which endogamy prevails, the case is not markedly dissimilar. The tribes have become, in a real sense, divisions of a comprehensive body. Aside from mere woman-stealing, exogamy always implies a certain peace-bond between the intermarrying groups; the degree to which exogamic relations attain between tribes varies directly with the degree of mutual friendliness and confidence. The existence of *connubium*, as of *commercium*, is both an evidence of acculturation and a powerful factor in building it up.

The following examples are illustrative of divisional and tribal exogamy and are presented as a sort of miscellany supplementary to the detailed cases cited above.

Among the Australians it is a great shame and cause of uproar if marriage occurs within the taboo. A case of adultery, however, is not the society's affair but that of the husband and the adulterer alone. The taboo may extend to both father's and mother's totem.[59] In Victoria, the aboriginal laws forbade a man to marry into his mother's or grandmother's tribe or into an adjoining tribe or into one speaking his own dialect.[60] On Florida Island a chief "imposed a

[59] Cunow, *Australneger*, 43, 84.   [60] Dawson, *Aust. Aborig.*, 27.

heavy fine on the man who had proposed to marry within the prohibited degrees and the offender had to hire an advocate to state his case discreetly, apologize, and beg off a part of the fine."[61] In one part of Melanesia a marriage within the group is regarded as worse than one between brother and sister; under some circumstances the punishment, for the woman, is death.[62] British New Guinea shows some tribes marrying among themselves, some having a *connubium* with their neighbors, and others getting wives solely from without.[63] Chiefs went outside for wives where the common herd might not;[64] thus the eminent, here as elsewhere, fathered variation.

Among the Matabele the rule is so strict against endogamy that those of the same surname may not marry: "A Kumalo cannot marry a Kumalo."[65] Westermarck[66] has collected a number of instances showing that with most Kaffir tribes a marriage within the kin-group is regarded, if not as a punishable crime, at least as a blameworthy offense. In Cameroon a man "does not choose his wife from out his own village because there almost every one is related, but out of another village or out of another tribe altogether."[67] Tradition among the Fantis states that very early some wise seer divided their nation for government into seven tribes. The names of these tribes and the purposes for which they were used indicate a system of totemism, combined with the practice of exogamy, which is considered by the natives to be of the greatest benefit for the improvement of the species.[68] Trilles[69] regards the law of exogamy as a taboo derived from totemic laws; he says that "there can be exogamy without totemism, but when there is totemism, there is exogamy." The Fans are strict exogamists; "thus a man may never marry a woman, not alone of his clan, but not even of his tribe. No more may he espouse a woman of a tribe or clan allied to his own." Wilken[70] also emphasizes this connection, as something that enlists ghost-fear to strengthen the out-marrying policy and make it stable. He sees the individual as originally submerged in the group, a mere atom of it; then the unorganized group breaks up and he goes with this or that kin-group fraction of it. The marriage-taboo shrinks to the size of the constituents that break away and finally applies only to those nearest in blood. Elsewhere wives "are chosen from the women of the neighboring districts, since the usage does not prevail of marrying women of one's own land, not even slaves."[71]

The Yakuts now practice exogamy in the great majority of cases;[72] and the Chukchi marry stranger women gladly and pay high prices for them.[73] In Assam, the chiefs of certain tribes who are great sticklers for custom marry their true wives from other tribes; they may not marry in their own, and women of their own tribes with whom they live are mere concubines whose sons may not become chiefs. The common folk, however, are so "densely packed in the hills, that exogamy has become impossible, and they now all marry within

[61] Codrington, *Melanesians*, 53.
[62] Von Pfeil, *Südsee*, 27.
[63] Krieger, *Neu-Guinea*, 297-298.
[64] Fison, in JAI, XXIV, 370.
[65] Decle, in JAI, XXIII, 84.
[66] *Marriage*, II, 138 ff.; Grosse, *Familie*, 129.
[67] Conradt, in *Globus*, LXXXI, 336.
[68] Connolly, in JAI, XXVI, 132.
[69] *Fân*, 593, 594.
[70] In VG, II, 346, 347-348.
[71] Vannutelli e Citerni, *L'Omo*, 192.
[72] Sieroshevski-Sumner, in JAI, XXI, 573.
[73] Bogoras, in AA, III, 105.

the tribe."[74] Members of certain castes must marry within them, but outside the exogamous subdivision. "Beginning from the bride or bridegroom, six or four degrees exclusive of the couple, i.e., six for the male ancestors and four in case of a female, must be counted without encountering a common progenitor, if marriage between the parties is to be permitted."[75] Under the forbidden degree come also the girl with the same name as the man's mother and the daughter of a religious teacher or pupil. In Bombay the likeness of family-name or fetish-device constitutes a hindrance, since it indicates likeness of stock.[76]

In the case of most peoples, says Starcke,[77] the joint family-group reaches to the seventh degree of kinship—including the descendants of a common great-grandfather; the Karens by preference marry the outermost in that group, namely second cousins. The Chinese inflicted sixty blows for marrying anyone with the same surname, there being about five hundred and thirty surnames distributed amongst the whole Chinese population of the Empire. This means in general that husband and wife must come from different villages. The Chinese code further "debars a man from marrying a kinswoman or connection of any generation senior or junior to that of which he is a member.[78] In Kafiristan a woman may not marry a man of her mother's clan, nor may a man marry into his father's or his father's mother's clan.[79]

Among the Bataks, some Alfurs, and the peoples of Nias, no one may marry inside his tribe.[80] In Malacca, families came to be identified with localities and "even if they lived scattered everywhere in their boats, yet they would say in speaking of themselves that they belonged to that place. Marriage did not change this and it prevailed as an unsubvertible rule that a man and woman from the same place might not marry but must get their spouses from another locality. This rule, like many others, has fallen into oblivion since the area of the Orang-Lâut range has been narrowed to its present boundaries. But even yet the husband is chosen, as far as that is possible, from another place that is as far off as possible."[81] A species of exogamy is shown in a Pelew Islands custom whereby the young women of a community go in a body to the village of another community for a time.[82]

The Iroquois formerly had two marriage-classes; in one, composed of the Wolf, Bear, Beaver, and Turtle totems, these could not, as brothers, intermarry. Similarly with the other class; marriage was from one class to the other. Then this prohibition was relaxed until it applied only within a totem.[83] Among the Siouans, "in every tribe, so far as known, gentile exogamy prevailed—i.e., marriage in the gens was forbidden, under pain of ostracism or still heavier penalty, while the gentes intermarried among one another; in some cases intermarriage between certain tribes was regarded with special

[74] Peal, in JAI, XXII, 254.
[75] Risley, Ethnog. India, I, 86; Collector of Sholapur, in JASB, V, 376.
[76] Jolly, in Grundriss d. Indo-Ar. Phil., II, Heft 8, pp. 62-63.
[77] Prim. Fam., 236.
[78] Medhurst, in Trans. Roy. Asiat. Soc. (China Branch), pt. IV, 21, 22; Westermarck, Marriage, II, 115; DeGroot, Kongsiwezen, 105-106.
[79] Robertson, in JAI, XXVII, 76.   [80] Wilken, Vkde., 263-264.
[81] Stevens, in Ztsft. f. Ethnol., XXVIII, 174-175.
[82] Kubary, Pelauer, 53.   [83] Morgan, League of Iroq., 83.

favor."[84] Among the Cheyennes, in old times the rule against marriage inside the tribe was absolute. In marrying, a pair first investigated their relationship, for kinship, no matter how distant, was a bar. Great was their embarrassment if related persons found themselves in courtship.[85] The Tlinkit phratries are exogamous.[86]

Specific cases of the *connubium* or intermarriage-treaty are to be found in the Old Testament.[87] There were prohibitions of exogamy and infringements of them, as was seen under the preceding topic; "when Levites and priests married foreign women we recognize how little attention was paid to these commands."[88] And *connubium* with aliens was sometimes advocated: "Thou shalt not abhor an Edomite; for he is thy brother: thou shalt not abhor an Egyptian; because thou wast a stranger in his land. The children of the third generation that are born unto them shall enter into the assembly of the Lord."[89] Among the Greeks and Romans no one could marry within the gens;[90] "among the Romans the prohibition of marriage between kin received the greatest extension among the ancients—indeed the greatest next to that of the canon law."[91]

§354. Miscellaneous Restrictions.

There are marriage-prescriptions and restrictions which, though they do not come as types under endogamy or exogamy, should be illustrated here before entering upon the generalizations to be derived from the whole topic of restrictions on marriage. They throw into sharper relief the irrelevancy of the ascription of marriage-taboos to the fear of close in breeding.

It is a sin in some localities for a younger brother to marry before an older does, or a younger sister before an older. This is the reason why the older brother celebrates a sham marriage with a tree-shoot that the younger may marry without committing sin. In Assam the younger brother may not marry before the elder without the latter's written consent. After giving this the elder is himself forbidden to marry, since he has forfeited his right.[92] In Sumatra, if a younger sister is married first, the husband pays a customary due for passing over the elder.[93] There is a certain solidarity about a set of brothers or sisters, concentrated in the eldest: under polyandry[94] the younger brothers share the elder's wife; and marriage to an older sister often means marriage to the younger as well. Under polygyny a man may marry two sisters, as Jacob did; again, while two brothers may marry two sisters, the latter may not be the wives of one man either at the same time or successively.[95]

[84] McGee, in BAE, XV, 178; Dorsey, in BAE, III, 255 ff.

[85] Grinnell, *Cheyenne*, I, 91, 93.   [86] Niblack, in USNM, 1888, 246.

[87] Gen., XXXIV, 16.   [88] Maurer, *Vkde.*, I, 150, 152.

[89] Deut., XXIII, 7-8.   [90] Wilken, in VG, I, 404.

[91] Schroeder, *Geschlechtl. Ordnung*, 80, 81.

[92] Jolly, in *Grundriss d. Indo-Ar. Phil.*, II, Heft 8, p. 59; Starcke, *Prim. Fam.*, 136.

[93] Marsden, *Sumatra*, 229.   [94] §397, below.

[95] Scott, in JASB, IV, 359.

There are all sorts of interdictions upon the marriage of relatives-in-law, which cannot possibly rest upon observation of the ills of in-breeding. The most strikingly irrational case is the prohibition of marriage to a deceased wife's sister.

An occasional tribe forbids such a marriage, for example, the Igorrotes of Luzon.[96] "It seems that in Brazil, as in England, marriage with a sister-in-law is . . . interdicted without possible recourse."[97] It is allowed in Australia, though a deceased wife's daughter by a former husband is tabooed;[98] while in Uganda "a man has the prescriptive right to be offered the refusal one after the other of the younger sisters of his wife or wives as they come to marriageable age; and these girls cannot be handed over to other applicants until their brother-in-law has declined them." This custom, the author[99] remarks, would be very distasteful to those in England who oppose marriage with a deceased wife's sister. Plainly such a marriage is, other things being equal, the most rational marriage possible and even some of the savages see its advantage: the Sea Dyaks accord it parental approval in order to bring up the children as one family.[100] Among the Pima Indians the widower customarily married his wife's sister. "Supposing that she does not like the man and does not wish to marry him?" the writer inquired. Thereupon the answer was given with an air of superior wisdom: "She always wants to."[101] Plainly the modern taboo comes from the Old Testament; among the ancient Hebrews, however, a man might not take his dead brother's wife, though he was under obligation to beget a son by her for that brother.[102] It is not perfectly certain that the Scripture proscribes marriage with the deceased wife's sister[103] but the taboo got into the Theodosian Code;[104] and thus a twist in the mores was perpetuated for ages under conservative influences, chiefly sacerdotal.[105] For years the British House of Commons would vote to repeal this senseless vagary and the Lords would sustain it. In 1907, marriage with a deceased wife's sister was legalized, but union with a deceased husband's brother remained under the ban.[106] It is astonishing to review the precepts that have been laid down for modern men and women by reference to the Pentateuch. They have often amounted to a gratuitous thwarting of interests and happiness. If the stepmother is traditionally "no more gentle than a viper" to the children of a deceased wife; if she becomes a synonym for malevolence,[107] so that a dangerous

[96] Blumentritt, *Igorroten*, 96.

[97] Roguin, *Mariage*, 91.

[98] Dawson, *Aust. Aborig.*, 27.

[99] Johnston, *Uganda*, II, 747.

[100] Wilken, in VG, I, 312.

[101] Russell, in BAE, XXVI, 184.

[102] Levit., XX, 21; §402, below.

[103] Deut., XXVII, 23; this passage has been interpreted to taboo the "deceased wife's sister"; its real meaning seems to be much in question.

[104] *Codicis Theodosiani*, bk. III, ch. XII, §2.

[105] Rathenau, in *Ztsft. f. Vergl. Rechtswiss.*, XV, 309. A typical recent fulmination is Puller, *Marriage with a Deceased Wife's Sister, Forbidden by the Laws of God and of the Church.* See Johnston, *Veneerings*, chs. XV ff.

[106] 7 Edw. VII, c. 47, quoted in "Prohibited Degrees," in *New Internat. Encyclopædia.*

[107] Huxley, *T. H. Huxley*, II, 231-233; Euripides, *Alcestis*, 309-310; Æschylus, *Prometheus*, 727.

promontory is called "hostile to sailors and a step-mother of ships," it would seem that even a rudimentary intelligence would perceive the advantage of a second mother who was already well-disposed to her dead sister's offspring.

The Ostiak will marry a brother's widow, a step-mother, or step-daughter, and they take sisters from another family; only the fathers of bride and groom must not be of the same tribe.[108] In Java and Madura, marriages between foster-parent and foster-child and even between relations by adoption within forbidden degrees are contrary to the mores.[109] In Rome of Caracalla's time, though marriage with a step-mother was improper, the Emperor bade the mores defiance.[110] In western Europe a groomsman might not marry any one of the bride's family whom the groom's brother might not marry.[111] Interdiction of the marriage of god-parents is another irrational variation in the code.

A common form of taboo on marriage is that which proscribes unions between members of different social classes. "As a general rule it can be said that with the people of the Indian Archipelago the difference in station is taken into strict consideration in marrying, to the extent that not alone unions between free and unfree, but also those between the aristocracy or nobility and the common people are disapproved, here and there even forbidden."[112] Again, occupation plays its rôle in marriage-alliances, and this runs out into whimsical absurdities: "In one part of India marriage is prohibited between those fishing tribes which, in making their nets, lay their meshes from right to left, and those which lay them from left to right. A class of milkmen have turned out of their caste those of their trade who make butter without having first boiled the milk, and give their daughters to wife only to those who make butter in the same way as they themselves do. In Cuttack, the most southern part of Bengal, the potters who turn their wheel sitting down, and who make small pots, may not intermarry with those who turn the wheel standing, and who make large pots."[113]

A number of taboos on marriage are based upon considerations of religion and property—considerations which have appeared incidentally above. In West Africa families whose fetishes bear the same name may not intermarry.[114] "Whoever has been circumcised according to the Mohammedan law, cannot hope to make a good match in Bongoland."[115] Conditional curses of the dying act as a bar, transmitted from generation to generation.[116] The Greenlanders hold that there is a spiritual affinity between a deceased person and one named after him, and so perhaps between two of the same generation having the same name. Nansen[117] thinks that this may explain the bar to marriage between two persons of the same name which is generally supposed to rest on an assumed blood-kinship. It is probably unnecessary further to illustrate property-considerations as a bar to marriage;[118] life and literature are witness to their power.

[108] Müller, *Ugrische Volksstamm*, I, 308.
[109] Van den Berg, in *Bijd.*, XLI, 491.
[110] Gubernatis, *Usi Nuz.*, 97, note.
[111] Maine, *Early Law*, 257, 258.   [112] Wilken, in VG, I, 461.
[113] Ihering, *Evol. of Aryan*, 64; Nathubhai, in JASB, III, 422.
[114] Bastian, *Deut. Exped.*, I, 173-174.
[115] Schweinfurth, *Heart of Afr.*, I, 302.
[116] Gutmann, in *Globus*, XCII, 30.   [117] *Esk. Life*, 175, 230.
[118] §§341, above, and 361-364, 381, 395, below.

Selection by rank and property is a caricature of that selection by equality of education, culture, and breeding which assures conformity of ideas and standards. Rank and property may keep a good pair apart, but their greatest evil is when they push two ill-mated people together, as often in royal alliances. Yet economic restraints on marriage may amount to a selection whereby only the more competent marry.

§355*. The Ascendancy of Exogamy. The cases cited sufficiently illustrate the regulations set upon the association of the sexes as respects in-marriage and out-marriage. It is now possible to generalize somewhat as to endogamy and exogamy, recalling at the same time some of our preliminary statements. The terms are evidently not precise; like other words they cover, "not a point, but a territory."[119] They bear a number of connotations according to how one answers the query: "Endogamous (or exogamous) with respect to what?"

Says Powell:[120] "What has been called by some ethnologists endogamy and exogamy are co-relative parts of one regulation"; the Wyandots, for example, "like all other tribes, are born both endogamous and exogamous." The clan, where clans exist, is generally exogamous; but the inclusive tribe is endogamous; "we can no longer regard exogamy and endogamy as a twofold conception, defining social ordinances which are directly opposed to each other."[121] "Every savage man is exogamous with relation to the class or clan to which he may belong, and he is to a certain extent endogamous in relation to the tribe to which he belongs, that is, he marries within that tribe."[122] Again: "Exogamy marks one sphere as too restricted for the limits of marriage; endogamy prescribes the bounds beyond which it shall not go." From another angle, "exogamy prohibits marriage between persons who are so nearly related that they have no legal independence of each other; endogamy prohibits the marriage of persons whose legal status is too remote from each other."[123]

Thus endogamy and exogamy take on various aspects; but if one does not try to contrast them except as opposite tendencies in any given case, they may be viewed in evolutionary perspective and their expediency appraised.

In practice it is exogamy that needs explanation. Endogamy, like poverty, is primordial; exogamy, like wealth, developed out of the primordial.[124] With small, segregated, and hostile groups

119 Whitney, *Life and Growth of Lang.*, 110.
120 In BAE, I, 63.   121 Starcke, *Prim. Fam.*, 222.
122 Powell, in BAE, III, lxi.   123 Starcke, *Prim. Fam.*, 233, 241.
124 §49, above.

of men, endogamy was inevitable, as it still is where isolation persists; exogamy characterizes developing peoples. The origin of exogamy is at best highly inferential and speculative. "My own conviction," says an able observer and writer,[125] "is that we shall never be able to arrive at certainty as to the origin of exogamy, and that our best plan is to accept the fact, confessing our inability to account for it." This is rather a counsel of despair. Exogamy is so ancient that it is probably not possible to fix upon any definite transitions from endogamy to the more expedient system; still there are considerations enough, among those adduced by writers who have undertaken to explain the origin of exogamy, to indicate lines of variation toward it. Endogamy, plainly enough, was a sort of monopoly-policy, whereby not only the women, but also the property and, in the case of royal endogamy, the political power, were confined from straying outside certain limits. There are advantages, however, in breaking any monopoly, and the more stringent it is the more attractive are the gains to be attained from thwarting it. To have a woman from outside was to possess a wife without rights guaranteed by her relations. Property obtained by raiding could be handled with small regard for intra-group regulations. There was no title to it that was so little encumbered by obligation as that which arose from seizure by force; for there were no counter-claimants recognized. There is no question but that the introduction of stolen women had characteristic effects upon any local form of marriage. Enterprising groups, which were succeeding better than others, naturally turned their surplus energy to appropriation from neighbors.

While, therefore, no specific origin of exogamy seems identifiable, the sense of the whole situation made for its development. If this is understood, we may go on to consider the intrinsic values of the system, without concerning ourselves so much as to how it was set in operation. However that may have been, there is a sufficient stretch of evolution open for study, during which exogamy has been in vogue, to allow of a pretty accurate assessment of its superiorities as an adjustment, in comparison with the system which it superseded.

[125] Fison, in JAI, XXIV, 370.

Generalizing upon the actual cases, we find primitive people sometimes prescribing but with far greater unanimity proscribing the union of near kin. The taboo is sharper and more consistent in proportion as the degree of consanguinity is higher. Even in the case of consanguineous marriages, however, the taboos enforcing out-marriage are found not to have been aimed at all consciously or directly at in-breeding. Of two cousin-marriages, equally consanguineous, and therefore equally deleterious if in-breeding is evil, one is forbidden and the other prescribed; and latterly cases have been reviewed where the taboo is strict against marriages exhibiting no degree of consanguinity at all. If the evidence is scanned without preoccupation due to a prior adherence to some theory or traditional doctrine, it is seen that the taboo rests, not upon demonstrable consanguinity and fear of its biological consequences but in every case upon some apparently arbitrary societal regulation of whose origin and sense the peoples in question are entirely ignorant. Anything that is put inferentially behind such regulation, that is, behind the mores, must go clear beyond the ethnographical facts. In view of the lack of specific information as to the origins of the mores, a scientist can no more than infer from their observed expediency or inexpediency toward the reason for their development and persistence or their decline. Such procedure, though it does not reveal the germs of institutions, yet shows them, irrespective of their origins, as living and evolving adjustments of society to its life-conditions.

The broadest perspective of the facts exhibits exogamy with respect to family, clan, or other limited group as correlative with advancing culture. It has prevailed over the closer forms of endogamy as did the mammal over the marsupial, except where the latter have been protected from competition and selection by being isolated.[126] Some of the ethnographers cited have stated specifically or by implication that exogamy has advanced with better communications or that endogamy has reasserted itself where some form of isolation has developed.

"It is only among the smiths, despised and turned back upon themselves, among the hunting-families that live in isolation, and among . . . those who

126 Keller, Soc. Evol., 62-64.

have for a long time operated as pure tillers, that close in-breeding is a behest of the impulse toward self-preservation."[127]

If close endogamy is a losing and exogamy a winning policy, then what does the latter do for those who practise it whereby it has attained, through their survival and success, so dominant a position? For our purposes, exogamy may be assumed to have begun. The variation is there. Now why is it favored by societal selection over the preceding endogamy? It must have shown in practice expediencies detectible under analysis which assured to its exponents superiorities over those who adhered to the older mores.

§356. The Expediency of Exogamy.

The superiorities of exogamy are societal rather than biological. While the latter may and do remain in dispute, the former are unassailable. Concerning the prevalence of endogamy as against that of exogamy, "it will be seen that there is a period in the growth of society when it is a political question of the first importance. While the vast forest or prairie still affords abundant food for a scanty population, small hordes may wander, or groups of households may be set up, each little tribe or settlement cut off from the rest, and marrying within its own border. But when tribes begin to adjoin and press on one another [when the man-land ratio changes[128]] and quarrel, then the difference between marrying-in and marrying-out becomes patent. Endogamy is a policy of isolation, cutting off a horde or village, even from the parent stock whence it separated, if only a generation or two back. Among tribes of low culture there is but one means known of keeping up permanent alliance, and that means is intermarriage. Exogamy, enabling a growing tribe to keep itself compact by constant unions between its spreading clans, enables it to overmatch any number of small intra-marrying groups, isolated and helpless. Again and again in the world's history, savage tribes must have had plainly before their minds the simple practical alternative between marrying-out and being killed out. Even far on in culture, the political value of intermarriage remains." A missionary among the Maori, says the

[127] Kaiser, in *Archiv. f. Rassen- u. Gesellsfts-Biol.*, III, 221.
[128] §2, above.

author[129] we are quoting, in order to end their wars, taught them exogamy between tribes. Exogamy is "an institution which resists the tendency of uncultured populations to disintegrate, cementing them into nations capable of living together in peace and holding together in war, till they reach the period of higher military and political organisation." Exogamy thus fosters a variation in societal organization till it can become permanent. Endogamy tends to hold for society what it has—the one talent—while exogamy means a reaching-out toward the new. Endogamy is conservative while exogamy is progressive.

Still more fundamental than the political services of exogamy to society is its promotion of civilization in general. Out-marriage was a prime factor in acculturation at a time when other acculturative agencies were feeble or non-existent. "Trade and the practice of exogamy were the main factors in breaking down the barriers that separated one community from another."[130] It is not by chance that the Latin terms *commercium* and *connubium* came to be linked together in a formula; interchange of goods and of wives went along side by side. The reader will recall that civilization is a function not alone of numbers, but of the contact of numbers as well.[131] Endogamy provided for no contacts, while exogamy secured them in regular, frequent, and peaceable form; then followed the contagion of ideas or what has been called the "cross-fertilization of culture."

"Modern civilisation tends more or less to lower or pull down the barriers which separate races, nations, the adherents of different religions, and the various classes of society. It has therefore made the endogamous rules less stringent and less restricted, it has widened the limit within which a man or woman may marry and generally marries. This process has been one of vast importance in man's history. Largely originating in race- or class-pride or in religious intolerance, the endogamous rules have in their turn helped to keep up and strengthen these feelings, whereas frequent intermarriages must have the very opposite effect."[132]

Sometimes the effect of contact resulting from exogamy is complicated by the racial factor. "The effect of intermarriage between Malays and aboriginal women is one which at first would hardly be expected, viz., that it is the higher race—the Malay—that is chiefly affected by it. . . . The first Malay adventurers were probably more numerous in males than females. In many places the Chinese tend to absorb the Malays in their turn. The more civilised and

---

[129] Tylor, in JAI, XVIII, 267, 268; Tylor, in *Nineteenth Century*, XL, 93.
[130] Jenness and Ballentyne, *D'Entrecasteaux*, 39.
[131] §26, above.   [132] Westermarck, *Marriage*, II, 68.

wealthy races thin those below them of their women, and necessity drives the latter to make up the loss wherever it is possible to do so, in some measure at the expense of those still lower. This is one of those fundamental facts of ethnography which should be borne in mind in speculating on the gradual extinction of aboriginal races, when comparatively civilised colonies come into contact with them."[133]

Setting aside other acculturative agencies for the sake of isolating effects, let there be assumed three groups, A, B, and C, which are endogamous and therefore bereft of contacts with the outside world. Each group has its code or sum of mores which has been automatically developed in response to life-conditions. Let these sums, for the three groups, be represented by x, y, and z, respectively. There will be some variation, perhaps a good deal of it, between x, y, and z, as A, B, and C pursue their intra-group evolution in isolation from the rest. Plainly no one of the three will go far.

Let it now be supposed that group A begins to get women, by stealing, trading, or *connubium*, from B. These women bring with them the mores of the group in which they have been reared, including its language, arts of life, traditions, and the rest. If it were true, as some contend, that primitive woman was the repository of all the industrial arts, the case would be the stronger; but that contention has not been conceded.[134] Women are, however, agencies of direct transmission of the mores and of acculturation. Part of what they bring from B appeals to the members of A and is adopted forthwith; this part will doubtless include chiefly the maintenance-mores.[135] Further, the incoming women from B have over the next generation in A an influence which is at least equal to that of the men of A and the children grow up naturally into the possession of a good part of the mores of both A and B. If intermarriage is kept up, group A, by taking women from B, comes to possess the sum of the civilization of both groups, or x + y; and group B acquires a similar combination.

It is true enough that the differences in the mores of neighboring groups on the primitive stage may be small as compared with those shown by more developed peoples, but the fact of diversity is more important than its degree. The thin edge of the wedge precedes and opens the cleft for an increasing effect.

[133] Skeat and Blagden, *Malay Penin.*, II, 57-58.
[134] §§68, 69, above. [135] Keller, *Soc. Evol.*, 129 ff.

If now exogamy spreads to cover A, B, and C, each of these groups will get culture represented by x + y + z. The greater the extension of exogamy, the more effective is the cross-fertilization of culture, so that at length groups A, B, C, and the rest of the intermarrying groups up to N will possess most if not all of the civilization x + y + z . . . n. In fact, this series ought to include somewhere, beyond the mere addition, also the element of multiplication, for culture under such circumstances seems to take on a geometrical ratio of increase. It rolls up on itself. Along with it go peaceful relations and toleration; then contacts multiply, the process is speeded up, and the general level of culture rises ever more rapidly.

Even in the case where a man went always to his mother's tribe for a wife, "and was indeed under an obligation to marry his first cousin, the daughter of his mother's brother," the chief families of the two tribes "became closely interwoven, and in time came to have the same gods."[136] Before they pooled their divinities, they had doubtless traded many other elements of culture.

It is evident that endogamous groups, whether or not they are biologically handicapped, are at a great disadvantage, as compared with exogamous groups, in their capacity for societal or cultural adjustments. Whatever the condition of their germ-plasm stream, they are on a lower plane as respects the variation, selection, and transmission of the mores; and the result cannot be uncertain. Annihilation or subjugation lie at hand for the endogamous societies if they come into competition; stagnation if they are isolated; and presently the mores, except those of non-competing groups, are characterized by exogamy. It becomes the prosperity-policy.

It is necessary now to cast a retrospective glance along the line upon which we have come. The biological assessment of exogamy was somewhat inconclusive; not so, however, that which has taken into account societal expediency. For when exogamy has become the unrivalled welfare-policy, it is then in order to view endogamy with disfavor and at length, when the sanction of religion shall have come to be imposed, with horror. The more inveterate the taboo, the more nearly does it seem to approach

136 Thomson, in JAI, XXIV, 342.

"nature" or "second nature," and the more likely is it to be termed "instinctive" because that is what men are wont to call any tendency whose origin is too remote to be readily determined. It is a human trait to employ wise-sounding substitutes and wild guesses instead of the plain: I do not know.

If endogamy is bad, the extremest endogamy is worse. The argument returns in the end to that with which it started. Disapproval of remoter consanguineous unions heightens to horror when it comes to incest. The whole matter is, nevertheless, on the societal plane and in the mores, not on the biological plane and in instinct. Exogamy, as a member of the Bengal Civil Service infers, "was more probably the result of the survival of the fittest than due to a recognition by primitive savages of the evils of interbreeding."[137] To war must be accredited a considerable service in the promotion of exogamy, discharged through its selective action upon endogamous societies. We cannot explain our horror of incest any more than we can tell why we are sickened by the thought of having eaten certain substances, for instance, the flesh of a dog or of a man, which some tribes of the earth regard as of extreme delicacy. All these cases have been in the code of our society for untold ages; there is nothing "instinctive" about them. An instinct does not have to be instructed. We recur to the extreme and classic case for final illustration. That a man may commit incest unwittingly, live on in unhallowed relations happily, usefully, and honorably, and feel revulsion and suffer obloquy only when the historical facts are found out, is the essence of the profoundest human tragedy. If an Œdipus could have had an "instinct," or if the mores had been those of Egyptian rather than of Hellenic Thebes, there would have been no revulsion or tragedy at all.

[137] Crooke, reported in JAI, XXII, 141.

CHAPTER XLVI

MARRIAGE-PRELIMINARIES

§357. The Manner of Marriage. The treatment of marriage amounts to a survey of restrictions laid, in the mores, upon unregulated relations of the sexes. The marriage-institution develops out of a set of taboos imposed by the necessities of societal life and is restrictive of freedom. The limitations which have been examined are those which determine who may or may not marry; and now comes another set that covers the manner of entering the status of matrimony. The mores of endogamy and exogamy concern the *who;* those which come next concern the *how;* and in due course others will be encountered which determine the *how many.* The *how* of marriage covers all the proceedings which initiate the status and culminate in the wedding and attendant ceremonies; beyond these lie the mores of the family.

Perhaps it may be permitted to enforce again at this point an aspect of marriage in its earlier stages which is strange enough to be readily left out of account by a good many moderns, namely, that the individual so merges into the primitive society that it is not he or she who marries, but the community. The French understand this as respects the family-group:

"Family and position count for everything here in France. It is not one little individual choosing another little individual; we are more serious than you in that. It is one family choosing another. It is two *foyers* coming together to found a third."[1]

This is the situation among primitive peoples, except that it is the clan or larger kin-group rather than the family in any limited sense that does the marrying. In many tribes the young grow up into marriage as they do into adulthood or old age; by reason of the passage of time a boy or girl arrives at puberty, passes through certain ceremonies, and pairs off with some mate predestined to him or her by the automatic allotment of an inveterate societal order.

[1] Sedgwick, *The Little French Girl*, 244.

"When a boy is growing up he learns which girl is to be his wife. To the father of this girl he owes certain duties, the chief being that he must make him presents from time to time. This man is his father-in-law, and . . . is in some cases his mother's brother. At the same time the man has a secondary right to a number of other girls. If the girl betrothed to him should die, he will have a try to obtain one of these, and therefore he must devote some attention to their fathers, making them presents from time to time, and going to visit them. It is this fact that seems to determine the social relations of a man with his various *kaga*. They are all prospective fathers-in-law. A man owes the same sort of duties to all the men whom he calls *kaga*, but the recognition of these duties is more intense in some cases than in others."[2]

This suppression of the individual, as it might be called, is but another aspect of the group-solidarity that appears in communalism of various types, in the penalization of the whole for the misdemeanors of the one, and in many another range or detail of the mores. The primitive society could not persist unless it made a united stand against the perils that menaced it; what each individual did was of a significance to societal life apparent to everyone. Hence all must conform to a central direction, as in an army, and all did so as a matter of course, much as does a veteran soldier who has been in the ranks so long that it would be unnatural for him to depart from disciplinary usage.

§358*. "Capture-Marriage." At some far time there must have been an absence of customary preliminaries to the sex-relation. There was mere appropriation of women by men, as of any other variety of loot or property, and sometimes captured women were divided or communalized among the raiders just as quarry among hunters.[3] It was even necessary, in exceptional cases, for a man to ward off the claims of his near relatives to a wife got from abroad.[4] The so-called "marriage by capture" is really no marriage at all; it is pure dominion, and the captured woman is exactly on a par with the captured animal in that she is wholly, without any customary rights, the possession of her captor. He can do as he likes and assumes no obligations. It is typical of capture, especially from alien possessors, that it gives a title going back to first principles, anterior to all institutional usages and needing no explanation or defense. That a captured woman

2 Brown, in JAI, XLIII, 156 (West Australia).
3 Crauford, in JAI, XXIV, 181.
4 Sieroshevski, *Yakuts* (Russ.), 552 ff.

becomes a consort is entirely incidental; it is one of her uses to bear children. We must not allow modern mores to make us see more in the mere sex-relation of primitive peoples than they themselves have seen.

Violent seizure of the possessions of out-groupers has been in the order of events from the earliest stages. To take away what others had was one of the elemental methods of the struggle for existence, easily paralleled among animals; and by reason of woman's relatively weaker and more helpless condition and because also as a working-force and a child-producer she represented a high value, she became one of the chief forms of booty sought in predatory raids. Hence it is to be expected, just as war preceded trade, that the capture of the out-groupers' women, like that of their property, should antedate peaceful arrangements and last on long after relations within a group had become subject to regulation and surrounded with form and ceremonial— ceremonial, however, in which survivals of capture have long persisted.

Though capture is not wholly an inter-group phenomenon, as one might suppose, yet intra-group capture is much more likely to be preserved in survivalistic form within a more or less defined ceremonial than to occur in stark actuality; but under exceptional circumstances it does appear.

Among certain Indians of Brazil wife-stealing goes on inside the tribe, not between tribe and tribe.[5] "The method of capture so frequently described as characteristic of Australian tribes, is the very rarest way in which a Central Australian secures a wife. While it does not often happen that a man forcibly takes a woman from some one else within his own group, yet it does sometimes happen, especially when the man from whom the woman is taken has been remiss in certain religious observances."[6] Among the Slavs capture is exhibited as the dominant feature of sex-union. In the eighteenth century it was the usual thing and is still in many localities. In one district, women are seized out of parties of dancers at the time of festivals, in the forests as they gather fungi, at the river when they are washing. This is an intra-tribal phenomenon, as there is no trace of exogamy.[7]

The rarity of intra-group capture is readily understood, for no society can without peril to its existence surrender its character as a peace-group. The cases which will appear later on show that

[5] Von den Steinen, *Zent. Bras.*, 500.
[6] Spencer and Gillen, *Nat. Tr. Cent. Aust.*, 555.
[7] Rhamm, in *Globus*, LXXXII, 272.

where capture or abduction is practised inside the group it is done to evade exactions, especially of property, connected with the regular ceremonial or is survivalistic, probably of inter-group capture between groups long compounded into one society. The existence of any peace-association is in peril if property-stealing of any and all kinds is not suppressed.

Although woman-capture from other groups is rather common, the practice is limited, even more than is property-raiding, by fear of reprisal. Forays even upon a weaker tribe might be made only in cases of direst necessity, as lives were generally lost.[8] It is true that there was always a strong motive for wife-stealing in the fact that the stolen wife had no troublesome rights as did the status-wife; she was property or slave.[9]

In central Australia, "at times a woman may be captured from another group, though this . . . is of rare occurrence, and is usually associated with an avenging party, the women captured by which, who are almost sure to be the wives of men killed, are allotted to certain members of the avenging party."[10] In one part of south Australia, all the men exercise rights over a captured woman;[11] she belongs to them all. "On rare occasions a wife is captured from another tribe. . . . At present, as the stealing of a female from a neighboring tribe would involve the whole tribe of the thief in war for his sole benefit, and as the possession of the female would lead to constant attacks, tribes set themselves very generally against the practice."[12] Where exchange of women is in vogue, the unhappy non-possessor of exchangcable female relations is miserable and constantly under suspicion. It is feared "that he may violently seize a girl of a neighbouring tribe, and thus provoke a war." If he does, there follows much wrangling and he is subjected to a species of ordeal-duel.[13]

Among the North American Indians, "the women fell to the victors, and so it might even come about that sometimes the men and women of a tribe spoke different tongues. Among the Caribs, who stole women, husbands and wives had different languages."[14] In South America, "wife-capture not seldom occurs. The chief of the Miranhas, with whom I dwelt, had stolen his wife from a neighboring tribe." Certain tribes abduct maidens and wives from others and thus lay the foundation for deadly hatred. Among the Arecunas, "the possession of the most beautiful of the captured girls was accorded to the bravest warrior."[15]

Capture occurred among the Hebrews: the captive became wife after a

8 Reid, in *Cosmopolitan Mag.*, XXVIII, 451.
9 Gumplowicz, *Soc.*, 108.
10 Spencer and Gillen, *Nat. Tr. Cent. Aust.*, 555.
11 Crauford, in JAI, XXIV, 181.
12 Curr, *Aust. Race*, I, 108.   13 Smyth, *Vict.*, I, 79.
14 Bernhöft, *Verwandsftsnamen*, 61; Waitz, *Anthrop.*, III, 55.
15 Von Martius, *Beiträge*, I, 107, 620.

month of mourning for her father and mother; she then shaved her head, cut her nails, and put off the raiment of captivity.[16] Marriage by purchase, after capture, led to a *connubium,* though it was speedily broken.[17] The relation between marriage and war is seen where David, at Saul's command, bought the latter's daughter with two hundred exuvial trophies of the Philistines.[18] Again the Benjaminites lay in wait for and seized the women of Shiloh, taking them as wives.[19] Even the Talmudists aver that "there is no marriage without strife."[20]

As the Tatars appropriated a captive woman by putting a kerchief around her neck and shooting an arrow over her head, so the ancient Greeks thrust a javelin through the hair of a woman taken "at the spear's point."[21] The word for female slave in Homer means "taken with the spear," and while such a slave became generally no more than a concubine, she could be formally married by her captor.[22] The legendary material of the Greeks and Romans is full of wife-capture: consider the case of the captured Andromache or the rape of the Sabines. Capture occurred in militaristic Sparta.[23]

The severity of the old Norse and German penalties on woman-stealing attests its persistence.[24] The Frisian law provides that "if the abductor fled with the stolen woman out of the house into another, from this to a third, and thence to the church, the judge should burn down the three houses, break into the church, and take out the robber."[25] "In the early Middle Ages the forcible abduction of a woman . . . was regarded as one of the weightiest crimes." Most of the tribal codes visited woman-stealing with a money fine corresponding to the purchase-price of a free girl. "Herein is very clearly revealed the after-working of the oldest form of marriage-making, capture-marriage."[26]

In the foregoing cases the stealing was for the sake of getting consorts; it is by exception that a situation occurs where, as on the island of Yap, "woman-stealing for the purpose of marriage is not known but only for that of prostitution."[27] Analogous to this is a case occurring among the Kaffirs: the noble families go and stay with the chief as his guests, he attending to all their wants. One of these is women, and they are furnished by a troop of young men who go out and seize unmarried girls. These are let go after several days and their places filled by new seizures. The frequent and more or less serious quarrels ensuing have led to the abandonment of the custom.[28]

Though genuine capture is not so common in ethnography, all the indications point to its prevalence on the earliest stages. Mock-capture and other survivals cannot be accounted for without inferring that there was a period during which the stamp of violence had been firmly impressed upon the mores.[29] If violence

---

[16] Deut., XXI, 10-13.
[17] Gen., XXXIV, 12; Hosea, III, 2.
[18] II Sam., III, 14.
[19] Judges, XXI.
[20] Bergel, *Eheverhältn.,* 15.
[21] Reclus, *Prim. Folk,* 130.
[22] Keller, *Hom. Soc.,* 220-221, 279-281 (full references to text are given).
[23] Plutarch, *Lycurgus,* 15; Beloch, *Griech. Gchte.,* I, 41.
[24] Wilutsky, *Mann u. Weib,* 139.
[25] Stammler, *Stellung d. Frauen,* 11.
[26] Rudeck, *Gchte. d. Oeffentl. Sittl.,* 174, 175.
[27] Senfft, in *Globus,* XCI, 141.
[28] Fritsch, *Eingeb. S.-Afr.,* 95.
[29] Mucke, *Horde,* 125, where a number of cases are cited.

had not existed in the code of a preceding age, it is difficult indeed to account for its presence, real or feigned, in such generality and profusion in later ceremony; had capture been sporadic and in contravention of all custom, it could not have made for itself such a place in the forms surrounding marriage. On the other hand, if it was once well-nigh universal, either in the very primitive code or in reaction against some irksome system, its well-attested presence as a survival-symbol is naturally and fully explicable. Of course transitional cases occur where there are real deeds of violence in woman-stealing intermingled with the modified and survivalistic forms. Though mock-capture might logically come under the topic of wedding-ceremonies,[30] it may conveniently be detached for present treatment, forming as it does a transition from violence to composition through property-compensation.

Rivers[31] has, as usual, certain views that narrow the subject down to more specific considerations. "The capture of women from other tribes undoubtedly exists, but there is no evidence that it has taken any prominent part either in determining forms of social organization or features of the ritual of marriage. It is from features of this ritual, such as mock fights, that most of the evidence for the supposed wide prevalence of marriage by capture has been derived, but most of these customs are capable of a different explanation, and in some cases this different explanation is conspicuous. Thus, the prominent part taken by the cross-cousin of the bride in such ritual conflicts in Southern India leaves little doubt that the explanation is to be found in the former existence of cross-cousin marriage. . . . When a person other than her cross-cousin marries a girl he often had to satisfy her cross-cousin by some kind of payment, and the mock conflict is almost certainly only another form of recognition of his rights. I have advanced a similar explanation for the ritual capture of Melanesia, where this form of marriage was followed in order to evade the exclusive monopoly of the old men." All such side-lights as this passage affords should be turned upon the subject; similarly the views of Wilken[32] deserve special mention. He believes that abduction was naturally an insult to the group, but more especially to the parents and kin of the girl, which ought to be wiped out in blood. In primitive times, composition of such a wrong was common, and it appeared, here also, in the form of property-compensation, which he regards as the original of the bride-price, the latter not being a real purchase-price in the beginning. Only under exogamy and the patriarchate did it become such. Further, he concludes that child-marriage is closely connected with abduction, being a device of a girl's disposers to force her into the sort of a union which they chose. Where forcible abduction was common, this resource was utilized most. Schwaner[33] expresses it as the result of "the fear of parents lest their plans might perchance later on be frustrated when

[30] §371, below.   [31] Soc. Org., 46-47.
[32] In VG, I, 433, 469, 470, 479.
[33] Borneo, I, 194-195; Perelaer, Dajaks, 47.

their children come to discretion and independence." Wilken sees abduction as a natural phenomenon accompanying endogamy, provided the maternal family exists—a situation in which a man normally goes to live with the woman's family and the children follow her. If the man can forcibly bring the woman to his village, then he is absolved from some of his disabilities, but has to pay compensation. Cases are cited from the East Indies.

It is not so easy to distinguish between mock-capture and elopement. Theoretically the latter implies that the woman goes voluntarily. Cases where willingness is explicitly in evidence will be held over for the next topic; but it should be noted that the mock-resistance or passivity of a consenting woman does not go with elopement.

There are many pretended fights in Australia over a woman who has been bought, bartered for, or presented as a gift in advance.[34] A young man to whom a girl is promised, gets the parental permission and then abducts her, she resisting as much as possible. The marriage is consummated by friends of the groom who stand in a certain relationship to the bride. "The women used to boast of the resistance which they made" before being ceremonially stolen. They have a special term for such ceremonial.[35] In northeastern New Guinea, "the young husband must buy his wife from her father; but before this he . . . abducts her into the forest, there to conceal her in a hut. He must then hide himself well, for . . . the girl's father has the right to kill him at sight. The acquaintances of the young husband therefore negotiate for him and come to an agreement as to the price for which the father will give up the daughter. The father appears thereafter as reconciled and lets the young people return from the bush."[36] In some tribes "the young men waylay the girls they admire, and endeavour, by force or persuasion, or the offering of presents, to obtain their consent. This method often leads to amusing incidents, as the girls have the privilege of scratching and fighting their would-be lovers to any extent, and the lover may not retaliate, as he would bring down upon his woolly head the anger of the girl's parents."[37] Although this is really a phenomenon of courtship, the violence-element is apparent. The Fiji young man and his comrades seize the girl betrothed to him.[38] Melanesians in general sometimes steal wives, the union being made legal by payments to her relatives.[39]

In Uganda, "if the father shows any reluctance to hand over the betrothed girl, the suitor sends a band of young men who capture her and bring her to his village. If this act is attempted during the daytime, the young men of the girl's village and her brothers turn out to fight the suitor's party with sticks. The girl screams a great deal and makes many loud protests, but usually allows herself to be captured. This act of violence is only resorted to if the girl's father is avaricious."[40] Among Bechuana wedding-ceremonies, "there is

[34] Ratzel, *Vkde.*, II, 70.   [35] Howitt, *S.E. Aust.*, 193.
[36] Von Pfeil, *Südsee*, 316-317.
[37] Hardy and Elkington, *S. Seas*, 40.
[38] Fison, in JAI, XIV, 30.   [39] Ratzel, *Vkde.*, II, 275.
[40] Johnston, *Uganda*, II, 747-748.

one of casting an arrow into the hut of the bridegroom, which is worthy of notice as symbolic,"[41] that is, survivalistic.

Abduction among the Malays seems always to be compounded for by subsequent payment. In its mildest form the suitor sends a dagger to the girl's parents, together with an offer to pay double the usual expenses. There are mimic combats and barring of the groom's passage by a rope.[42] Abduction is a resort in order to force better terms for the groom, sometimes with collusion, the bride-price being stated out of vanity to have been exorbitant.[43] "Abduction," says Wilken,[44] "actual or pretended, is spread universally over the Archipelago"; he cites many examples. In Java, for instance, it is customary for the groom "to seize his bride before the house-door about the hips with both arms and thus carry her into the house." The analogy with Greek and Roman procedure is alluded to and Rossbach[45] is quoted: "The young woman enters marriage under coercion; she must be torn away from the bosom of her mother and led away by force. At the door of the house she resists once more and the conductors of the bride, who hold her by the arm, must drag her in by force." When the woman follows the man in marriage, the commonest form in the Archipelago as elsewhere, there are three proceedings to distinguish, corresponding to the Roman *traditio, deductio in domum,* and *confarreatio.* In the first the bride is given to the groom by her father, in the second is brought in procession to his home, in the third is taken into the family-bond of the man. In the East Indies, the pretended abduction takes the place of the ceremonies of the *traditio* and *deductio.*[46] Wilken thinks that the deferring of consummation[47] may be due to the bride's duty of formal resistance. Again, as in a former case, the suitor rushes in and binds himself to the girl he wishes; and in this posture and with bared *kris* he awaits the appearance of the parents, who have to choose between consent and their daughter's death. They know he is in earnest and hasten to give consent.[48] A case like this may strike one, at first sight, as simply sporadic; but it is what was regularly done when consent was not forthcoming, and at an earlier time of raid and rape all consent must have been withheld. A return to the shadow of former conditions evokes an approximation of former practice.

Among the Eskimo, the girl must pretend to resist being married; they were shocked to hear that a European girl said yes when asked.[49] The American Indians almost always bought their wives; sometimes, however, the youth, having settled with the parents of the girl, forced her to go with him into the forest for several days. The Kootenay suitor, "in the olden times," entered the girl's lodge and when found there was threatened; but the matter was easily composed.[50] Among the Cheyennes, the bride is lifted over the threshold on

---

[41] Conder, in JAI, XVI, 83.

[42] Skeat, in *Folk Lore,* XI, 306-307.   [43] Ratzel, *Vkde.,* II, 431.

[44] *Vkde.,* 277; in VG, I, 176-177; 487, 488, 498 including note 50, 500, 532, 533.

[45] *Röm. Ehe,* 359-360.

[46] Vinogradoff, *Hist. Jurispr.,* I, 242 ff.

[47] §374, below.

[48] Van Eck, in *Ind. Gids.,* 1881, II, 840.

[49] Nansen, *Esk. Life,* 139.

[50] Anon., "Northwest Ind.," in PSM, XLIII, 824.

entering the groom's dwelling.[51] If the Abipone bride resisted, she was brought to her husband in a sack; generally parents did not force the girl.[52] In other districts there was, at least in semblance, an abduction, or the girl might run away and escape the marriage unless caught.[53]

Capture-ceremonies have been not uncommon in Europe. The Roman form has been alluded to; it has been "explained" by the guesses of old-style classical writers; for instance, the bride must not touch the threshold, as that would be a profanation of a spot sacred to Vesta, the goddess of virginity.[54] Among the old Slavs, "capture-marriage occurred after conference and therefore with the assent of the girl and also of her parents; hence the whole is shown to be a sort of ceremony which probably had the object only of evading the trouble and costs to the suitor in the case of wife-purchase." It was not an out-and-out deed of violence.[55] In Russia, "one of the many acts in the long drama, as it were, which is performed at every peasant wedding, consists in a representation of the attack and defence of the bride."[56] If a suitor richer than the accepted one appears, Votyak parents help him steal their daughter. Woman-stealing in an emergency is practised by the Mordvins. Again, at a marriage the members of the groom's and the bride's parties go by different names, remaining hostile to one another during the festivities and seeking by songs and jests to insult one another.[57] In Albania the bride must struggle and "carries with her from her home one invariable gift—a pair of fire-tongs."[58] The Bulgarians sometimes evade the giving of many presents to neighbors and relatives at a wedding by abduction; elopement serves the same purpose.[59] Similarly in southern Rumania, abduction of a sort is enforced by the groom's impatience or by thrift.[60] On one of the Balearic Islands, the bride is kidnapped with the consent of her parents. Sometimes this is not followed by marriage; but there is no reproach on return and no reputations are impaired.[61] Several graphic cases are cited by Tylor.[62]

§359*. Elopement. Abduction shades into elopement in many particulars. It is hardly exact to say that capture is against the will of the bride, while elopement is not; the captured girl may be willing, even though she resists and deplores her fate, for that is called for by the mores and constitutes propriety. Again, the willing girl may not with propriety appear to consent, though she may not be required by usage to struggle and lament; she may remain, at least to appearance, merely passive. Where elopement

[51] Grinnell, *Cheyenne,* I, 144.   [52] Ratzel, *Vkde.,* II, 618.

[53] Von Martius, *Beiträge,* I, 599-600; Ehrenreich, in *Berl. Mus. Vkde.,* 1891, 65.

[54] Dezobry, *Rome,* III, 11.

[55] Rhamm, in *Globus,* LXXXII, 272.

[56] Ralston, *Songs of Russ.,* 285.

[57] *Russian Ethnog.* (Russ.), I, 193, 269, 300; II, 223.

[58] Lane, *Shala,* 40.   [59] Strauss, *Bulgaren,* 310.

[60] Lazär, in *Globus,* XCIV, 318.   [61] Vuillier, *Forgotten Isles,* 137.

[62] *Anth.,* 403-404.

is customary—and among some tribes it attends every marriage as part of the ceremony[63]—it cannot be invariable that the woman is willing; she may merely acquiesce in going through the form prescribed by the mores. In general, however, elopement implies volition on her part, even though capture does not imply that she is unwilling.

This is an aspect of the matter which, though secondary, we wish here to emphasize. There would be no object in citing numbers of cases of elopement, which is often very like abduction also in the formal combats that attend upon it and in other respects, if there could not be brought to light at the same time a further salient aspect of the marriage-relation. It has been so prevalently assumed that woman has no voice in determining her destiny, especially in marriage, that the real truth of the matter needs reiterated demonstration. Special attention is to be accorded to the position of woman, her powers and disabilities, in a later connection;[64] and we shall then wish to recall such exhibitions of her control over her own destiny as will appear in the case of elopement. Elopement belongs here as constituting one of the preliminaries of marriage; but an important strand of interpretation will connect what is immediately to come with general considerations regarding the status of woman that are not yet developed. The reader is urged to survey the following cases with the query in mind as to how far woman is mistress of her own destiny. It is likewise important to note to what extent children of both sexes are really able to evade parental domination.[65] Wilken[66] thinks that child-marriage was a parental expedient to secure plans for marrying children from interference through abduction or elopement.

In Australia, elopement is a method intermediate between that of "charming" and that of capture, for in the case of charming the initiative may be assumed by the woman.[67] It is thought that the claim of the old men to regulate the relations of the young ones to their tribal wives formed a special stimulus to elopement.[68] "There are strong reasons for believing, that when the continent was only partially occupied, elopements from within the tribe

---

[63] Milne, *Eastern Clan*, 128 ff., 400 ff.; Rivers, *Soc. Org.*, 46.

[64] Chs. L-LII, below.   [65] §§379, 384, below.

[66] In VG, I, 152, 153, 175, 176.

[67] Spencer and Gillen, *Nat. Tr. Cent. Aust.*, 556.

[68] Howitt and Fison, in JAI, XII, 39.

were frequent, and that those who eloped proceeded into the unpeopled wilds, and there established themselves."[69] Among the southeastern tribes, elopement was practised by "those who might lawfully marry, if the necessary consent had been obtained on both sides." A combat ensued, which was not always ceremonial but rather in expiation for injury done to the woman's brothers in depriving them of a valuable asset. Elopement was also in many cases a matter of wife-trading. In certain tribes, the man with few exceptions "could acquire a wife in one way only, namely, by running off with her secretly and with her own consent. Marriage, therefore, was by elopement, and this was brought about in different ways." Two young men, each with an unmarried sister, could, with the sisters' consent (for in this tribe the choice of a husband rested altogether with the woman), arrange a double elopement.[70]

In Victoria the elopement is accompanied by scenes that baffle description. Women tear their cheeks with their nails; the nearer relatives hack at their own heads with hatchets. Pursuit of the couple, who have taken to the bush, is organized; and they know in what direction to go, for the young man has confided to someone, as a great secret, the proposed route. On their return to camp the girl is cruelly handled by the women, every one of whom must lay a hand on her, and the young man must fight all comers. He is generally worsted, often standing quietly while men and women strike him until he falls to the ground stunned. When the girl is able to walk—for she is sometimes speared through the feet—the elopement is repeated. At length, with some variation of tactics, the pair have their way.[71] The cases vary; sometimes the elopement is successful if the runaways once reach the man's camp or if the woman escapes to him twice.[72] In Queensland two lovers whose union is not sanctioned by the camp-council may elope; then after a month or two they return, are gashed and beaten, though never fatally hurt, for upon that blood-revenge would necessarily follow.[73]

In southeast Australia there was a sort of medicine-man who aided elopements by his spells. When he had made a spell strong enough the youth might run off with the girl, "but there must first be a formality showing that the final choice was with her. Stealing to the back of her parents' camp, where she was sitting, he touched her with a long stick, and she, being ready to run away, pulled the end as a signal. The youth then left, and the girl, having her outfit ready, flitted after him. . . . The old people winked at the elopement but punished the young folks when they came back." In this case the local restrictions were so thoroughgoing that almost the only chance of getting married at all was by foregoing parental consent, and the office of the special elopement-functionary "arose in time to lend a sanction to the proceedings."[74]

In New Guinea, "abductions take place, but only with the consent of the woman. The pair then flee into the forest or even into a neighboring village. If the relatives of the seducer can pay well, they let the affair take care of itself and leave the pair together. In other cases it is not so easily smoothed out." If all is well, the parents and other parties involved cut their foreheads till the blood runs as a sign that they belong to each other.[75] Elsewhere it very

[69] Curr, *Aust. Race*, I, 108.
[71] Smyth, *Vict.*, I, 83-84.
[73] Roth, *N.W. Cent. Queensland*, 181.
[74] Howitt, *S.E. Aust.*, 149-150; Howitt, in JAI, XVI, 36, 38, note.
[75] Krieger, *Neu-Guinea*, 173, 392.

[70] Howitt, *S.E. Aust.*, 245, 273.
[72] Cunow, *Australneger*, 34, 98.

rarely happens that early betrothals come to anything. The girl usually finds that she likes some other boy better than the one her parents have chosen. She has her remedy. The day before the marriage-ceremony she disappears into the bush with the man of her choice and when they return the next morning they are legally man and wife.[76] On the Murray Islands, elopement is followed by a mock fight and a conference on purchase-price.[77] In New Georgia, "if a man and a girl fall in love with one another, and the man is poor, and cannot afford to pay, they go away and hide together in the bush, until the parents cease to be offended, when they return to society, a married couple."[78] So too there are "marriages by flight," where parents refuse consent.[79]

There is evidently an aspect to elopement in which it is presented as a method of evading or lowering the purchase-price of a wife. It might be asked why the man should pay at all if he can be married for nothing; upon reflection, however, it is evident that something desirable is sacrificed by the recourse to elopement. It is the right thing to go through the regular ceremony and it is often almost solely in the impossibility of so doing that a makeshift is adopted. Many people nowadays feel that a civil or unceremonious marriage is no marriage at all. When the wedding-ceremonies are studied, plenty of examples are encountered where the parties are willing enough to pay for the display, privileges, and even discomforts attending the ceremony prescribed by the mores as regular and proper. When it is a case of irregularity or nothing, the variation appears.

It is "a mistake to imagine that a [Kaffir] girl is sold by her father in the same manner and with the same authority with which he would dispose of a cow."[80] Among the Veddahs, the young man, after having an understanding with the girl, carries her off from the parental cave or hut; this is the practice of the youthful and weaker groom as against the stronger house-father.[81]

Among the Palaungs of Farther India, elopement is an integral part of the wedding-ceremonies.[82] In the Indian Archipelago the native women have a good deal to say about their disposal in marriage. Sometimes the relations of a girl want to marry her, against her inclination, to an older or wealthier man, because of the higher price he is willing to pay for her. "But for the girl there is often, in such a case, a saving provision sanctioned by the *adat* [mores]. She may, provided she is in possession of a love-guerdon, run away to the giver of it, who is obliged to accept her; and his relatives have then only to see to it that they come to an understanding with the owners of the girl about the purchase-price. . . . Indeed, if her parents wish to force their daughter to a marriage, she can of herself escape the fate of a union she does not desire by

[76] Guise, in JAI, XXVIII, 208.
[78] Somerville, in JAI, XXVI, 406.
[80] Westermarck, *Marriage,* II, 303.
[82] Milne, *Eastern Clan,* 128 ff., 400 ff.

[77] Hunt, in JAI, XXVIII, 9-10.
[79] Czaplicka, *Aborig. Siberia,* 74.
[81] Sarasin, *Weddas,* 461.

letting herself be abducted by her lover. Then we can say that among the various peoples with whom abduction exists as a lawful form of marriage, the girls have more control over their hands than one would, at first sight, taking the grade of evolution into consideration, suppose."[83] The Sumatrans allow a similar power of self-disposal which, "from a spirit of indulgence and humanity which few codes can boast, has the sanction of the laws. The father has left only the power of dictating the mode of marriage; he cannot take his daughter away if the lover is willing to comply with the custom in such cases. The girl must be lodged, unviolated, in the home of some respectable family till the relations are advised of the *enlèvement*, and settle the terms. If, however, upon immediate pursuit, they are overtaken upon the road, she may be forced back, but not after she has taken sanctuary."[84]

Among the Sioux Indians, "marriages by elopement are considered undignified, and different terms are applied to a marriage by elopement and one by parental consent."[85] Sometimes among the Omahas a man elopes with a woman; but her kindred have no cause for anger if he takes her as a wife.[86] In Paraguay, "very often when their marriage is not acquiesced in and the lovers do not wish to be separated, they flee out of the village and build their home afar from their relatives."[87] In such cases elopement is not so much a variation within the system as a complete abrogation of it.

In the Caucasus those who cannot pay for a wife steal one, which is considered very honorable. But the stealing must be with the woman's consent and done with great boldness. If caught, the abductor may have to pay for it with his life and certainly with his back. Among the Tatars of eastern Russia, the groom must steal his bride even though there is no necessity for it. The girl quits her father's house forever and goes to a trysting-place, where her lover meets her and takes her home. The parents on both sides have known about it all the time and could have stopped it; they have, in fact, made ready for it. The next day, when the parents of the bride set out in pursuit, they go straight to the house of the groom; there they are met as honored guests, a bargain is made about the bride-money, and there is a feast.[88] In Bosnia and Herzogovina, especially among the poorer people, capture or elopement is a means of evading the bride-price or the larger costs of a public wedding. Often the abduction is arranged between the families.[89]

Elopement appears as a short-cut through unsupportable ceremonial and as a sort of defiance of the traditional code. It is essentially unconventional, though it may work into the very body of convention. It is a good illustration of the genesis of variation in the mores and of the survival of a variation under conditions where it secures a better realization of interests. With the less rigorous demands of modern systems, its utility has virtually disappeared.

[83] Wilken, in VG, I, 466-468; Wilken, *Vkde.*, 279.
[84] Marsden, *Sumatra*, 260.   [85] Dorsey, in BAE, XV, 242.
[86] Dorsey, in BAE, III, 260.   [87] Koch, in *Globus*, LXXXI, 106.
[88] *Russian Ethnog.* (Russ.), II, 355, 133.
[89] Rhamm, in *Globus*, LXXXII, 272.

§360. Exchange of Women. Wife-capture led to vengeance, then to intertribal compromise, compact, and purchase; in fact, marriage by capture, exchange, and purchase was about the only form of primitive intertribal relation. Exchange, here, as in the development of trade out of antecedent robbery, was a new adjustment, more expedient than those attended by violence.[90] It might be said that endogamy must have existed where the relations of tribes were so hostile that intermarriage was impossible, and yet their comparative strength such that stealing from each other was too dangerous. We lay no stress upon the sentimental considerations introduced by some writers to explain the resistance of relatives or even that of the bride: for instance, that her grief at marriage may be because home-bonds are relaxed or broken and that a fitting symbol is found in the resistance of her kinsfolk.[91]

Groups which customarily intermarry are said to be under the *connubium*, as those who trade goods of another sort with one another are under the *commercium;* the two practices, as has been repeatedly noted, tend to go together.[92] Exchange of women may take place, of course, within a group. This transitional form is not widely in evidence, though it is quite common in Australia and is represented here and there in other parts of the world. It is important to note that when it is the custom to marry a relative, as in the cross-cousin marriage, no property passes, except in those cases in which the orthodox marriage does not take place, but some other woman is taken to wife. In marriage by exchange the most usual form is that in which brother and sister marry sister and brother. This practice may co-exist with marriage by purchase, and there is reason to believe that, in some cases, it is only a means of avoiding the expense attendant on the marriage-payments.[93]

"A common custom in . . . most Australian tribes is the exchange of sisters." The exchange of women has a special name; by it a man secures a wife for his son by making an arrangement with another man with regard to the latter's daughter.[94] "For the most part those who have no female relatives

90 Lippert, *Kgchte.*, II, 86; §§76, 77, above.
91 Starcke, *Prim. Fam.*, 218; Westermarck, *Marriage*, II, 252.
92 §356, above.   93 Rivers, *Soc. Org.*, 46.
94 Brown, in JAI, XLIII, 156 (a number of cases are cited); Spencer and Gillen, *Nat. Tr. Cent. Aust.*, 554.

to give in exchange have to go without wives"; and the exchangeable relative is usually a sister.[95] "Any two young men of different tribes and classes, having each a sister or cousin, may agree, with the consent of their chiefs, to exchange the young women and marry them. This is done without any previous courtship, or consent on the part of the women, even although they may be perfect strangers to the men, and they must submit."[96] In another locality, the principal old man in the camp tells the bridegroom that he can have the girl he wants and at the same time gives him a piece of string with a knot tied in it. If the bridegroom has a sister whom the bride's brother wishes to marry, two knots are tied in the string by the old man, one at each end. The bridegroom keeps this until he is able to hand it to his brother-in-law along with his sister or another woman as wife; for he considers it his duty to provide his brother-in-law with a wife if possible.[97] Much ceremony may surround the exchange. When the matter is at last arranged, the young man's father says to his son, "Here is your sister; take her, and go and get your wife." Sometimes the girl rebelled and eloped with some other man whom she liked. As often in cases of elopement, "if they could escape and remain away until a child was born, nothing would be done to them, especially if the man could find a sister to exchange for her."[98]

In Sumatra, in lieu of paying the bride-price, a barter-transaction takes place in which one virgin "is given in exchange for another; and it is not unusual to borrow a girl for this purpose, from a friend or relation, the borrower binding himself to replace her, or pay her *jujur* [bride-price], when required. A man who has a son and daughter gives the latter in exchange for a wife to the former. The person who receives her disposes of her as his own child, or marries her himself. A brother will give his sister in exchange for a wife, or, in default of such, procure a cousin for the purpose."[99]

Wife-exchange between groups cannot develop upon the basis of any such meticulous *quid pro quo*. As neighboring groups steal from each other, there exists a sort of mutuality which furnishes the basis for an agreement creating a jural relation, superseding violence and retaliation and establishing peace and order. Such a *connubium*, even though broken at once,[100] tends presently to supersede what went before and may lead on to intertribal amalgamation, as in the Roman-Sabine tradition. Illustrative examples have appeared under the topic of exogamy, in the preceding chapter.

It will be noted that all these forms of wife-getting are correlative with the general societal status and are altered as it is altered. These changes all go on together and also in various combinations because they support each other and work out into a general con-

[95] Curr, *Aust. Race*, I, 107; Cunow, *Australneger*, 98.
[96] Dawson, *Aust. Aborig.*, 34; Smyth, *Vict.*, I, 77.
[97] Bonney, in JAI, XIII, 129.   [98] Howitt, *S.E. Aust.*, 263.
[99] Marsden, *Sumatra*, 259.   [100] Gen., XXXIV, 16.

sistency in the mores. In particular is it evident that maintenance-considerations are present throughout capture, elopement, and exchange. They are various ways of acquiring a prime possession indispensable in the pursuit of well-being. The element of sexual preference is not seldom pronounced in elopement; yet the latter is a stock way of dodging the bride-price and might well have been attached to the topic of purchase. Among peoples who have not yet built up high barriers against the chances of life, marriage is a serious matter and a focus of material considerations. What we have called the economic strand underlies all the rest in the fabric of marriage and appears clearly, upon slight reflection, in the foregoing preliminaries to wedlock. It is even more prominently to the fore in purchase and dowry.

CHAPTER XLVII

PURCHASE AND DOWRY

§361*. Wife-Purchase. It is clear that capture, abduction, and exchange are different phases of the same thing, while elopement is a sort of general expedient for evading the burdens and discomforts of orthodox procedure. The line of evolution leads next to wife-purchase, where the bride-price is a commutation of preceding violence, much as the blood-price is a substitute for retaliation in kind. It is stated that with the replacement of capture by purchase, real marriage-ceremonies, with their reminiscences of capture, mock fights, and the like, begin.[1] It is to be recalled yet again that capture by violence outside the in-group has existed independently of all forms of the marriage-institution from the earliest times. It is primordial in the sense that one can think of no beginning for it. By the side of institutional marriage it always offered higher gratification to the greed and vanity of man. Since the out-group from which a woman had been stolen could advance no recognized adverse claim, whereas under *connubium* or endogamy a certain reciprocity of obligation existed, capture was the best title to a woman, as plunder of an outsider was the best title to property. Captive women have been in evidence irregularly in all early societies by the side of wives of status. Thus there is no sharp distinction of "stages" here any more than in other parts of the field; "capture-marriage" did not cease at some point of time, to be succeeded by some other form, any more than did the stone-age or the hunting-stage.

Marriage by purchase is the prevalent primitive form, constituting a mean between capture at one end of the scale and dowry at the other. It is based upon the general alignment of woman with property, though this idea is expressed now in crude and brutal guise and again in attenuated and refined form. Nor is every case where property passes, where, for instance, the bridegroom makes presents to the bride's relatives, an example of marriage by purchase. Gifts are made to win favor and consent, as in the case of

[1] Schroeder, *Geschlechtl. Ordnung*, 335.

requests in general, or to atone for capture or elopement, or to repay parents for the expenses of the girl's rearing, or to reimburse the loss of her services, or to buy the right to beget children by her and include them in one's own tribe.[2] Under endogamy and the mother-family, especially if the man goes to the woman's group, the only sense of gifts to her parents, kinsmen, or herself is to win favor and acceptance. They are marks of respect and recognition and are the antithesis of abduction and elopement. It is in exogamy and under the father-family, especially if a man takes his wife from her tribe to his own, that payments are most genuinely purchase; for in that case the woman is lost to her own people just as a thing bought becomes as nothing to its former owner. The relation of purchase to capture is often traceable: "*coemptio*," says Wilken,[3] "was developed from *raptus*"; the former is often attended with ceremonies of resentment as if it were the latter.

A wife was a need imposed on a man at maturity not so much by nature as by the mores. The bride-price was an obstacle in the overcoming of which many were led into debt and even debt-slavery, producing social effects of a durable order. The fact of wife-purchase is so common as to call for little illustration; but there is a variety about it that deserves notice. Though the bride-price is generally paid in cattle or some other form of money, it may be rendered in service, in high social connections, or in any other form of value for value. Payment may be made all at one time or in instalments over a short or long period. It is this variety rather than the fact itself of purchase that calls for illustration.

Among certain Australians, a man continues during his lifetime to pay a sort of tribute to his wife's group; this contrasts with the ordinary practice in Australia of paying a lump sum.[4] In general wife-sale is not prevalent among the Melanesians; in cases where it occurs and the wife is divorced, her father must repay the bride-price as soon as he has obtained a similar sum from another son-in-law.[5] In fact, there is actual sale which is not so denominated: most of the tribes of British New Guinea "do not like to hear the word purchase-price used with reference to marriage. They say that what the bridegroom gives the father for the girl is purely a voluntary present, to the making of which nobody is forced."[6] The gift is sometimes of great value. A wife

[2] Smith, *Kinship*, 108.   [3] In VG, I, 478.
[4] Spencer and Gillen, *Nat. Tr. Cent. Aust.*, 470.
[5] Ratzel, *Vkde.*, II, 275.   [6] Krieger, *Neu-Guinea*, 297-298.

can be bought in Papua for a shell nose-ornament. "The possessor of one of these ornaments could easily buy a wife for it, and sometimes it is paid as tribute money by one who may have to pay blood-money, or is unable to give the statutory pig as atonement for a murder."[7] The natives of Torres Straits allow a divorced wife to "marry again, but the new husband would have to pay the old one, who must share the purchase goods with the woman's parents."[8]

In Africa, marriage has the prevailing character of purchase.[9] It has been noted before that a Kaffir despises a wife taken for love, that is, without payment, and compares her with a cat, which is the only animal got for nothing.[10] Zulu women are proud of the price they bring.[11] A woman retains certain rights and the cattle given for her are quite as much a guarantee of the husband's good behavior as the price he pays for his wife. She keeps the cattle if he illtreats or deserts her; he keeps them under like circumstances on her part. Thus is property the stabilizer of marriage.[12] The property-idea enters also when the father is assumed to be compensated through the bride-price for the loss of a daughter's services.[13] Among the Matabele, "the husband does not pay for his wife before marriage, but when she bears a child, it belongs to her father unless the husband pays to his father-in-law according to his means. Sometimes a man will go and ask for a girl and give cattle to her father; but this does not dispense with the necessity of giving them when a child is born."[14] This instance raises the query as to what is bought. Again, among many peoples, "the first-born child was surrendered to the father-in-law as purchase money for the wife."[15] We shall see in other connections[16] the importance attached to the birth of children as constituting one of the real fruitions and justifications of marriage. That wife-purchase in Africa is not yet obsolete is indicated by a recent news item which announces that "five pounds sterling, and no more, is to be the price of a wife, according to a recently ratified convention between the Governments of Great Britain and Liberia."[17] There is even a sort of purchase by trophies, recalling the case of Samson in the Old Testament.[18] This is a variation upon the test of the man for fitness to enter the marital state.[19]

Sir Charles Dundas[20] has applied his acute intelligence to this subject, with the result of clarifying several of its general aspects, as well as of setting the East African situation in the proper light. It must be understood that he uses the word "dowry" in the sense of bride-price. "The only legalisation of marriage is through payment of dowry." The amount may be determined by what was

[7] Pratt, in *Nat. Geog. Mag.*, XVIII, 569.
[8] Haddon, in JAI, XIX, 397.   [9] Ratzel, *Vkde.*, I, 153.
[10] Middlebrook, in *Globus*, LXXV, 271.
[11] Ratzel, *Vkde.*, I, 254.   [12] §341, above.
[13] MacDonald, in JAI, XIX, 270; Kropf, *Kaffir-Eng. Dict.*, 208.
[14] Decle, in JAI, XXIII, 84.   [15] Starcke, *Prim. Fam.*, 146.
[16] §§390, 392, 409, below.   [17] N. Y. *Times*, June 7, 1921.
[18] Waitz, *Anthrop.*, II, 515; II Sam., III, 14.
[19] §§163, above, and 365, below.
[20] In JAI, XLV, 285-286, 288-291; and in JAI, LI, 254-257, 262, 265.

paid for the bride's mother. "I am strongly inclined to think that dowry and bloodmoney for a woman are intended to be identical, and that formerly in all these tribes there was a fixed amount of dowry, but as the latter is a matter of daily transaction, it has through the fluctuation of wealth become less definite, while blood-money has remained at the original figure. Were it not so, it would be inconsistent that a man should pay thirty goats for the life of a woman for whom her husband paid, perhaps, seventy goats. If I am right in this it gives an instance of the manner in which inconsistencies arise in native custom, because it is sub-jected to a change in one direction and not in another. Dowry is seldom paid in full at once; it may be paid in installments before and after marriage; the husband may not be in a position to pay his wife's bride-price until his own daughter is married. Still, absolute rights over a woman and her children are accorded only when the whole price has been paid; if he retains them under other conditions it is because his father-in-law has received what will stand as proof of the agreement and the woman elects to stay with him. . . . A wife usually resents being married without dowry, this being a slight upon her, and if, therefore, nothing has been paid and the woman declines to live with him, the husband's claim is generally reckoned to be invalid. . . . When once full dowry has been paid, the husband's sole claim to the woman is unquestioned. . . . Divorce and return of dowry may be taken as one and the same thing. . . . The marriage is annulled so soon as the dowry is returned. . . . It should be noted that while a father is almost bound to pay for a wife for his son, in the event of a divorce, dowry is claimed by, and belongs to, the son and not the father. . . . When dowry is returned it is always understood that the husband has the right to demand back the identical cattle or sheep or goats given by him. . . . In many cases, however, the father has already disposed of the animals, and then follows com-plicated litigation. The original owner will expect those who have since received them to return the animals, and it is altogether according to their ideas inequitable that a man's cattle should be with anyone with whom he has no connection. In many cases I have known the elders to order cattle to be restored after they have passed through five or six hands; in others they have required the first recipient to redeem them from the subsequent owners. . . . The fact is that formerly cattle received in dowry were never parted with. It was considered most shameful to sell such animals, as this alone could sever all connection between the daughter and her parental village. . . . Under such circumstances, of course, no complication could arise, and the present-day confusion is an example of how a breach of custom creates an impossible position when allowed to become a rule."

The author thinks "it is to be regretted that Europeans have not given sufficient consideration to this subject—in fact, we are apt to regard native marriage merely as a commercial transaction. So long as we speak of 'purchasing wives' we shall probably continue to think of matrimony among natives as a matter of sale and barter. I must refer here to the old custom under which cattle received in dowry were not parted with, and this seems to suggest that dowry was considered far more in the light of a pawn or security than as a purchase price. If women were bought and sold as any animal might be, then they could also be traded and transferred, but this is certainly not so. On the contrary, there are very definite rules to make marriage even more permanent than with us. Careful consideration will . . . show that a woman is in no way regarded as a chattel, or, if we insist that dowry is only a purchase price, we must admit that once a woman is sold she ceases to be a chattel and becomes a wife in every sense of the word." Breaches of old custom are referable in no slight degree to European misunderstanding; "our attitude towards native matrimony has been identical with our manner of treating any other commercial transaction, and when we think of the hundreds of cases thus dealt with, we cannot be surprised if we ourselves have given marriage the stamp of trade, until this has well-nigh superseded every other consideration. . . . It may be that some fathers will seek to exact the utmost value, and to that end they may be prone to close with the highest bidder, but he will as often as not be frustrated by his daughter's choice, and it is always regarded as shameful. The remark, 'Are you trading with your child?' will generally bring the father to reason. Another consideration which opposes commercialism in the matter of matrimony is the fact that immediate payment of the whole dowry is rarely demanded. . . . In various ways the poverty of a man need not be an impediment to his marriage; even if the cupidity of the father is not to be overcome, the tribal authorities will always sanction it if the young people elope." But one case of wife-sale is available: in one tribe, "if a man has liquidated a debt for his parents-in-law, and subsequently gets into debt himself, he may sell his wife"; but this is simply an alternative to becoming a slave for debt. "I rather incline to think that when the term 'to buy a wife' is used in Africa this is an expression introduced by Europeans."

Dundas agrees with Wilken (below) that while "the frequent recurrence of practices reminiscent of wife robbery suggest a time not so remote when this was actually customary, . . . it seems possible that at some time the robberies, or rather the fights ensuing thereon, were compounded by a payment, which is now called dowry. Another view taken is that dowry represents compensation for the loss of a worker in the family"—the "loss of services." Furthermore, since in default of payment for the wife her parents have a claim to her children, "a right which is more definitely admitted than is the right to take back the woman herself," the dowry appears to be a payment for children. In any case, "it is the payment of dowry which gives legitimacy to the children." Where children belong to the mother's master, if she is a slave, and also if dowry has not been paid for the wife, there is "a revival of the idea that offspring always belong to the female unless the father has acquired a right of marriage and payment of dowry."

Barton[21] speaks of the first bride-payments being made when a girl is not yet weaned, the natives stating that thus "the girl will appreciate her future from an early age and avoid the 'fast' life of her sisters in the rest of the tribal area; the presumption is not proved in practice and is mainly responsible for the constant matrimonial discords." By this payment a man acquires a lien on the girl for the rest of her life; she may marry and have grown-up children while he delays over his right, but if he can establish the fact of that first payment, she and her children go without demur to him provided he pays a bride-price equal to that paid by the usurper. "A man will never forego a lien of this nature, whether he has a number of wives, much property, or is impoverished." Again, in the Congo region, "as there were so many debts among them a person would sometimes (and it was not uncommon) marry and pay this marriage 'money' without a single slave actually passing between

21 In JAI, LIII, 70.

them. . . . I have known more than one case in which the father of the girl has had the debt worked gradually back to himself, and in giving his daughter in marriage he has received nothing, but has paid some of his creditors."[22]

Among the reindeer-nomads of the Yenesei the woman is plainly bought and her position is low; for a good girl a value of one horse, worth fifty to sixty rubles, is given. Most of the natives have but one wife, though there is no restriction except ability to buy.[23] Among the Gilyaks on the east coast of Saghalien only forty per cent are female. Girls are bought when very small, even as infants, and reared for the purchaser.[24] Among the Yakuts the bride-price is strongly entrenched in the mores: it "is shared by the parents, older brothers, uncles, and guardians of the bride, and, in the case of orphan working girls, by the master. Each gets something, be it ever so little, as a recognition of surrender by him of a claim on the woman. Not a single well-bred Yakut girl would consent to go to her husband without a bride-price. She would be degraded in her own eyes and according to the views of her people. It would mean that she was not worth any price, was friendless, or an outcast. It can be understood, therefore, that the Yakut women look down upon the Russian women, who, as they say, pay somebody to take them."[25] The Chukchi suitor may serve some years, tending reindeer, instead of paying; but even after being received into the family, he is sometimes dismissed by a displeased father.[26] Among the Kirghiz the bride-price, very significantly, is calculated upon the payment for the murder of a woman;[27] when married, she is as if dead, so far as value to her father goes, and the loss is recompensed on that basis.[28]

The views of Wilken,[29] with special reference to conditions in the Indian Archipelago, are quite as significant as those of Dundas. Marriage is, in Buru, a transaction between two groups, whereby the *fenna* (clan) of the groom recompenses that of the bride for the loss of a member. The bride is therefore bought not by the groom but by his group, nor have her parents a right to the full payment, though they get the major part. If a man dies before he has discharged whatever obligations are his, the *fenna* to which he belongs must do so. Wilken's reiterated contention is that the bride-price is in essence no purchase-price, but a compensation or a sort of reconciliation-offering succeeding the injury done to the bride's group, especially when force has been used. The feast, as well as the exchange of betel, is a sign of such

[22] Weeks, in JAI, XXXIX, 440-441.
[23] Olsen, *Primitivt Folk,* 146; the ruble is about fifty cents.
[24] Miroliubov, *Eight Years in Sakhalin* (Russ.), 86.
[25] Sieroshevski-Sumner, in JAI, XXXI, 85.
[26] Ratzel, *Vkde.,* II, 767; Bogoras, in AA, III, 104, 105.
[27] *Russian Ethnog.* (Russ.), II, 188.   [28] Hiekisch, *Tungusen,* 87.
[29] In VG, I, 44-46, 174 ff., 334, 340-344, 378, 379, 478, 737 ff.; II, 206, 232, 233, 234, 244-245, 344, 228, 230-231; I, 180-183.

reconciliation. "As far as our Indian Archipelago is concerned, there is in that region scarcely a tribe with which marriage does not rest upon the giving of a bride-price" in this sense. The Batak gives his wife names indicating that she is more appreciated than a mere bought chattel, calling her "means of food-getting," "disher-up of food." The fact is that the bride-price is analogous to wergeld and is, even when a genuine purchase-price, a survival of the reconciliation-gift; in some cases there is a choice between revenge and compensation, here as in the case of murder, and recourse is taken to the former if compensation is not promptly forthcoming or if, what is much the same thing, the priest is not on hand to bless the union. Later, when the reconciliation-element is forgotten, the payment is interpreted as a purchase. There is naturally no bride-price under the matrilineal system, where the woman remains at home, the man goes to her, and there is no abduction to avenge; this mother-line marriage is like debt-slavery for the man, the word for it signifying to live with a creditor and be under obligation to help him. When a group pays for a bride for one of its members, his widow stays in his tribe and any one of his fellows has the right to marry her without further payment. Brothers have the preference, but in default of them, other relations have the next right; this situation, under the patriarchate, naturally admits of no divorce. Where a man cannot pay the bride-price, and so goes to his wife, he may transform this matrilineal marriage into a patrilineal by payment. That the bride-price is no purchase-price is evidenced by the ensuing position of the woman; she often has an approximately equal position in the family and a large influence in public life; and it certainly is not such when it is paid to the woman herself, as happens in several tribes. It is out of the *raptus* that the *coemptio* developed. When it comes to a marriage with a slave, it appears that in a union between a free woman and a slave man, where there is no bride-price, the children belong to the mother and follow her status; in one between a free man and a slave woman, without bride-price, the children follow the status of the mother and are slaves of her master; in a marriage between a free man and a slave woman, with bride-price (meaning the sum that frees her from her owner), the children follow the status of the father.

Where the regular patriarchal bride-price is in force, the children belong to the master of the wife—that is, to her husband in the first instance, then to his group which at least contributed toward the bride-price; the mother's group has no claim to them, even when the bride-price has not been paid in full and the man may be a debt-slave for it to the wife's father. These children are responsible for their mother's bride-price, as well as for any other paternal debts, if the father dies; they are thus closely identified with him. Where the system is not so firmly patriarchal, only those children belong to the father who are born after the whole of the price has been paid. Neglect to pay the bride-price sometimes amounts to the same as delinquency in settling fines in compensation, say for murder or incendiarism, in the above-mentioned result of enslavement.

The author quoted cites many instances in support of the above contentions, among them one which illustrates picturesquely the entrance of vanity into the bride-price situation. In southern Sumatra, the highest bride-price is demanded for the daughter of a district head-man and amounts to about $800. Considerably less, about $320, is asked for the daughter of the chief of a village, and only $80 for an ordinary woman. People are, from motives of vanity, wont to overvalue the bride-price. "Not seldom it is even observed that the names only of the costly objects of which the bride-price must be composed, are announced, and that on delivery these objects are replaced by others of little value, for example, where a carabao or a kris with a gold sheath is in question, a piece of cotton or a belt respectively. It appears to be chiefly in the case of marriages which are the sequel of abduction that such practices take place." This fact points again to the abduction as a device to escape heavy expenses. Finally, the author cites a May-Day auction of the girls of many German villages, wherein the most beautiful are carried off by the richest young men, unless great personal affection leads the less well-to-do to greater money-sacrifices. The one who succeeds in his bid for some girl has the exclusive right to dance with her all spring and summer. This custom represents the imitation in play of the serious happenings of life; "the way in which these symbolic marriages . . . are formed allow us to see, as in a mirror, how in earlier times marriages came about in earnest."

The Tlinkits of Alaska "adopted the dowry [bride-price] system that prevailed in the time of Jacob. This is just as sacred in their eyes as the Christian system is to us. Under it native men and women have lived together thirty, forty and fifty years in good faith, and reared large families. They could not have done better had they been married by a dozen priests. And yet we meet white people who regard the native system as a system of fornication."[30] Among the Guiana Indians, "marriage by purchase, either in the shape of presents, work done, etc., was of common usage. . . . In one thing there is more or less agreement among all the (Orinoco) nations, and that is their

[30] Jones, *Thlingets,* 214.

daughters are salable, that the bridegroom must pay the parents for the trouble taken in rearing them, and also for the solicitude and care with which they will henceforth work for their husbands. . . . By whatever means the Warrau may have secured his first wife, his second, third, and fourth ones are obtained by presents (i.e., purchase). If the wife is old, an event which usually already takes place at 20 years of age, the man looks out for another from the little girls of 7 and 8 years of age. He hands the child over to the eldest wife for instruction, who teaches her the household duties until such time as she enters upon all the rights and cares of a married woman." A story is told of "an old Carib father coming to claim compensation from his son-in-law for the loss of his daughter's services and of his subsequent claim for the child. The unwritten law of Carib usage was decidedly in the old man's favor and he received compensation for that child. For each succeeding birth he could, if he chose, reappear like an unquiet spirit, make a similar demand, and be supported therein by the custom of his nation."[31]

Service is always a commutation of the bride-price, as in the case of Jacob,[32] who is represented as serving fourteen years for two sisters; in Assam very generally, "a youth having taken a fancy to a girl of his own or a neighboring village, has to serve in her parents' home for a certain length of time, varying from one to two or more years, before he can marry her."[33] Elsewhere he may serve three years or, if wealthy, pay two or three hundred rupees down.[34] A survival occurs where, though he buys his wife, the groom must live a few days after marriage in the home of the bride's parents.[35] Purchase after capture is a manner of composing enmities and checking violence.[36] Other considerations appear as equivalents for an actual bride-price. An Arab father, in one case, would give his daughter in marriage if he might name all her sons and give all her daughters in marriage.[37] In Homer,[38] Agamemnon offers his daughter to Achilles without price, and indeed will go much farther and give a dower (or bribe), if Achilles will return to the field and discharge those services to the expedition which mean the difference between its failure and success and so between its leader's humiliation or glory. Here, too, good connections, as well as services of various kinds, may be reckoned as purchase-value; or the bride's father may retain a child.

The bride-price may be so high that, as in one recorded case, the father spent an eighth of his wealth—ten buffaloes—at the marriage of his son; again, it may be only "a small present."[39] The bride-price may be paid to the bride's father and the "milk money" to her mother.[40] A curious case is where the bridegroom-elect gives his prospective father-in-law a written document promising him money and two daughters in consideration of the bride he is about to receive. "Should no daughters be born, his sons have to fulfill their father's pledge and give up two of their daughters to their grandparents, or to their descendants. The object of this custom is to get two girls back for one

[31] Roth, in BAE, XXXVIII, 670.   [32] Gen., XIX, 20, 30.
[33] Woodthorpe, in JAI, XI, 205.
[34] Lewin, S.E. India, 234; a rupee is about thirty-two cents.
[35] Godden, in JAI, XXVI, 175.   [36] Gen., XXXIV, 9, 12.
[37] Wellhausen, in Gött. Gesell. Wiss., 1893, 479.
[38] Iliad, IX, 283 ff.; Keller, Hom. Soc., 213.
[39] Modi, in JASB, VII, 79; Risley, Ethnog. Ind., I, 213.
[40] Thurston, S. India, 82.

given." Should no children be born, extra money must be paid, and if the man cannot do that, his relatives club together and discharge the debt.[41] The details of this case evince a family-solidarity strange to us.

It is hardly necessary to say, in view of the tenor of preceding cases, that the poor and obscure man often gets short shrift when it comes to marriage. Wealth and rank receive their recognition, even among the African Bushmen, for their prominent old men take the young and attractive women.[42]

In one African tribe, "poor men cannot marry at all, not even the poorest girl. Therefore among this nature-people are not seldom to be found bachelors who can never marry. It is easily understood that they are the butts of the people, and particularly of the women." Venality and sycophancy to wealth are in the order of things, and "the man with only one wife is the object of cynical ridicule. . . . The chief's son gets the gladdest consent; the poor man is most emphatically turned away. The girls speak straight out: 'Let me rather die than marry a poor man.' Poverty is regarded by them as the greatest shame because it forces them to hard work; and stupidity is in their eyes worse than wickedness. And so they exhort a woman: 'Rather than give life to a dunce, bring forth a ruffian!'"[43] Stupidity is evidently inferred from its fruits—ill success and poverty.

The girl's family, in order to enhance her attractiveness and so to raise her purchase-price, sometimes practises a sort of advertising device, the bride-show.

Among certain Somals, the bride is decorated in pompous style for the sake of appearance and display. She is led about on foot or horseback, covered with oils and perfumes, in order to play upon the groom's feelings so that he may voluntarily increase his marriage-gifts to the bride or that a higher price may be wrung from him. Poor people present their daughters thus, in the midst of friends, all reeking with perfumes to make the atmosphere bewitching.[44]

The bride-show is practised also for the sake of increasing dowry. This is like an auction. Among the people of Cathay the poorest, we are told, are not able to give dower to their daughters. The latter are brought into the market-place with the noise of war-trumpets, are exposed to view, and married to such as like them best.[45] This bride-show for dower-collection is regarded by Lippert[46] as a survival of primitive communism in women; he quotes a Slavic case.[47] The girl who wants to marry is presented in a well-lighted room amongst her friends, and is visited by wooers who pay each a piece of money—the kreuzer being called a ducat and presented as such, thus raising the nominal value of the gift. Such a girl often gets together a considerable sum, since

---

[41] Gunthorpe, in JASB, I, 413.   [42] Hahn, in *Globus*, XVIII, 122.

[43] Gutmann, in *Globus*, XCII, 2.

[44] Paulitschke, *Nordost-Afr.*, I, 199.

[45] Eden, *Three First Books on Amer.*, 24.

[46] *Kgchte.*, II, 20, 21.

[47] Rajacsich, *Leben d. Südslaven*, 166, 167, 180 ff.

she is sometimes visited by several swains on the same day. These presents remain to the girl in case the wooing comes to nothing. In this region dowry is not customary, except that the wedding-guests contribute. In some German districts the custom still remains of having a bride-show on the evening of the wedding-day, when every respectable guest may claim a dance with the bride, giving a piece of money, which, however, goes to pay the musicians. In Lappland a bride remains for eight days before the wedding in the house of the groom, veiled; anyone who wishes may see her by giving a few kopecks.[48]

Whether or not this ceremony is survivalistic of "expiation for marriage,"[49] it represents a way of manipulating the bride-price, or providing a dowry. Evidently sentiment does not engross the primitive minds to the exclusion of property-interests.

§362. Transitional Forms. Although purchase in some more or less crass form has existed in civilized states until very recently and despite the fact that cases of it can still be found, nevertheless relatively backward peoples have learned to adjust property-interests in marriage by arrangements other than the bride-price. Those interests cannot ever be ignored, since they are vitally and obviously involved; still the prescription of a certain method for meeting them, such as the bride-price, may become less insistent. It is a fact that purchase may bear so unequally upon a society as to produce classes, because only the wealthy can buy the daughters of the wealthy, yet the bride-price, when institutional, may become fixed independently of the riches or poverty of the parties;[50] it was so in the Middle Ages, when a few coins, often owned and kept by the church, were used survivalistically. But whatever is done in mitigation and readjustment, the property-interests repose solidly at the basis of things.

The prevailing notion until within two or three centuries has been that a mere promise can never be a firm basis for marriage; that love is a transitory emotion; and that what is requisite to make a real marriage, that is, an institutional union founded upon permanent, positive, and tangible interests, is a property-guarantee. One of the Danish kings, it is recounted, introduced marriage by purchase in order to give firmness to the marriage-tie.[51] Thus the struggle for existence, along with its projection, the mainte-

---

48 Frijs, in *Globus*, XXII, 54.   49 §§343, 344, above.
50 Veth, *Borneo's Wester-Afdeeling*, II, 268.
51 Saxo Grammaticus, *Danish Hist.*, V, 88.

nance-mores, is again seen to constitute the underpinning of societal life. It is not possible to divorce marriage and property; to pretend to do so is affectation and falsehood. Novels and poems have presented marriage as if it were a question only as to whether a man and woman are attractive to each other. Everyone knows, on a moment's reflection, that the societal issue at stake in marriage, for the contractants as well as for society, is whether the pair can pay their way. There are those who act without regard to this consideration. The consequences prove their folly.

Transitional forms in the marriage-institution are the better understood if this abiding correlation of the mores of maintenance and of perpetuation is never lost to sight. When, in the course of evolution, the terms of the struggle for existence came to be less harsh, it began to be felt that the making of gain from a daughter was base. Then the mores were bound to swing away from wife-purchase, and distinctions were developed between the price paid for an object bought and a pledge given in valuable things, that is, the bride-price was re-envisaged. It became a forfeit which the man could not demand back if he divorced the woman for no fault of hers. Property-control over him was the only available check; it alone furnished a counterpart of his domination of wife and children. The ceremony of purchase was what produced a transfer of status, a tie of relationship that was not of blood, and a jural fact accordant with the jural concepts current in society. When a basic expedient of this order begins to seem crude, it is "interpreted," much as religious dogmas have been. Again and again one encounters the interpreted version of a crude and primitive actuality; and he regularly finds a general indisposition to recognize the genetic relationship between the now accepted version and that of which it is a rendition. It offends taste to refer a refined and high-minded practice to its primitive antecedents; one is solemnly told that the evolved form has been specially created or revealed and that its manifest family-likeness with the older practice is "symbolic."[52]

In capture the man assumes no obligation at all; it is a case of pure dominion, prerogative, authority, power; in purchase the case may be the same but rarely is. Capture is individual; in pur-

[52] §456, below.

chase, although the father takes the bride-price, he may yet make stipulations. There is no one to stand by or avenge the captured woman; when, however, a groom buys a "wife," he gets a person whose rights, however slight they may be, are defined in the mores and by the taboo, just as now a man takes a "wife" as a wife is defined, as respects rights and duties, in contemporary mores and law. The bride-price brings in the rest of society, as it were, beginning with the wife's kin, to say how the relationship between man and wife, now no longer an affair of the captor alone, shall be arranged. Thus in the course of development from capture to purchase, limitations inhering in the mores are accumulated against the man; the taboo, proceeding by its usual process of proscription and exclusion, works out into the formation of a real institution where before there was none. This is in line with the regular course of institutional development, under action of the taboo, leading from monandry toward a more strictly ordered relation of the sexes. The transition from capture to purchase also shows, especially in the mock-resistance stage, what Tylor[53] calls a practical meaning: "It does justice between weaker and stronger groups; for as soon as the rule is admitted that resistance is to be merely formal the weaker gains the power of equitable retaliation."

As the mores about marriage pass on from phase to phase the ethics and standards of vanity conform to them. In our code it is shocking that a girl should be bought like a slave or abducted by force; under a régime of capture, however, the woman's honor and pride, whatever her real feeling for the man or about the union, required that she should be forced against resistance to go with the man. Then she was not responsible. Propriety demanded also that her relatives should put up a real or feigned resistance. Where marriage by purchase exists, a girl is justly proud of the price she brings; she would be despised if she cost nothing. This is only human nature. If a dozen civilized men of the eighteenth century had been seized by Barbary pirates and sold off at auction, there would be some small self-complacency at being bid up higher than the rest and some shamefacedness at bringing up the rear of the appraisal.

[53] In *Nineteenth Cent.*, XL, 95.

General transitions of this sort are always highly significant in the evolutionary process. There is a special one to which we now come, namely, the transition from purchase to dowry. These two methods appear at first sight to be directly opposed one to the other, for in the one the wife is bought and in the other, even in its modern manifestations, it might be said that the husband is bought. The sentiment of the Yakut women, who despised the Russian brides because they had to pay someone to take them,[54] shows how the latter method looks to those who practise the former. And yet the two systems are only different ways of attending to that constant and abiding thing, the property-interest in marriage, and they may actually appear together in the same transaction. As the cases show,[55] the groom gives the bride-price and then the receiver thereof hands something back, either to the groom or to the bride or to both together.

This seems irrational, but it is only the inconsistency of the variation that has come into being alongside established usage. It is a transitional stage where the old custom persists because it is the time-honored mode of institutional marriage, just as the primitive apron is worn beneath the skirt or trousers. The older usage is "real" in the mores and in rights, while the new one is a reflection of a developed paternal interest going with an increased paternal wealth and power, first, probably, under the father-family. When the bride passes into the hands of a husband who gets with her a dower returnable in case she is divorced or maltreated, her father has a hold upon him that makes for a stability and peace in the marriage-relation which it could not otherwise have. The bride-price encroaches upon the material resources of the husband just when he is about to need them most. If the father takes it, his rights are satisfied, his authority recognized, and concession is made to the code. If thereafter he gives the bride or the pair an outfit, he helps to found a new household entirely apart from existing ones.

When the groom gives cattle, the bride's father may give cattle too—only the groom must actually bring all he gives, not that number minus what are to be returned. The bride-price and the

54 Sieroshevski-Sumner, in JAI, XXXI, 85; §361, above.
55 §364, below.

dowry are actual, concrete things. Sometimes the dowry is composed of other constituents than those of the bride-price or even of other units of the same thing—other cows, for example. The idea of the dowry, in such a case, is of something else, apart from the bride-price; the two must be kept separate and identifiable. The dowry lies, for some time, as a variation, in the range of individual will and power, while the bride-price is set, and at a conventional figure, in the established code. The groom brings twenty cows, let us say; the father gives ten other cows or ten of those which have been brought. There is no composite transaction whereby the groom is allowed to subtract ten and bring only ten. That would improperly mix things that should stand visibly separate before all men. When the code says twenty it does not mean ten. Everyone knows A's cows, and also B's, and their presence elsewhere than in A's or B's possession serves as a sort of memorandum of contract. They have been paid for some special customary consideration. Their transfer stabilizes the relation which they signalize. There is no cancellation or settlement by differences. There is no parallel to the Christmas gift-giving of two unimaginative and thought-thrifty parties who agree that each shall assume that he has received five dollars from the other and get himself something with it.

§363*. The "Ambil-Anak." A typical transitional form lying somewhere between purchase and dowry, and of which an exceptionally full description is available, is the *ambil-anak* union of Sumatra. Over against it is set the *jujur* form, or marriage with bride-price, which is the regular type. It is to Wilken[56] chiefly that we owe the portrayal and analysis of the *ambil-anak* and its relation to the *jujur*, and we shall follow his treatment somewhat closely.

The peoples of south Sumatra are under the patriarchal system:[57] the regular practice is for the bride to leave her own family and go over to that of her husband for good and all, her children belonging to her husband's family. *Mulier est finis familiæ.* But this is not always the case. The patriarchal régime is not based upon the blood-relationship of father and child; it is the control over the woman that forms its foundation. Marriage is a purchase and the

[56] "Huwelijks- en Erfrecht" (Zuid-Sumatra), in VG, II, 223 ff.
[57] §419, below.

child belongs to the man, not because he has begotten it but because he is the owner of the wife. "Out of this there follows of itself that when the woman has not come in this manner under the control of the man—*in manum mariti*—but has remained *in patria potestate,* the children are not the father's, do not belong to his family, but make a part of the family, the tribe, of the mother. Among a number of peoples . . . with whom marriages with the bride-price, *cum manu,* are the rule, there appear marriages *sine manu,* or without payment of bride-price. Not alone, therefore, through the sons but also through the daughters, who in their marriage have remained *in patria potestate,* is the race in this case carried forward."

It is necessary first to understand clearly the nature of the common form of marriage, the *jujur.* This is generally paid in goods, which are overvalued in order to bring the nominal figure up to the demands of the *adat,* or code; other such thrifty devices are employed, generally in cases of marriages following abduction. Economic conditions thus break over the mores, just as where, in sacrifices, only the poorer parts of the animal are offered up; in fact, the economic conditions are about the only ones which regularly modify the code.[58]

Although the *jujur* must be settled before going forward to the wedding, credit can be given on security, this leading often to debt-slavery. The man must remain with his parents-in-law till the bride-price is paid in full, sometimes over a set period of seven years during which he works for them. If he never succeeds in paying up, his children, in some localities, remain in service until his daughters make good, through the bride-price paid for them, what is still owed for their mother. After the *jujur* is paid, however, the father may not interfere, even when the daughter is badly used. To meet this situation germs of a dowry are developed: a small part of the price "is usually, from motives of delicacy or friendship, left unpaid, and so long as that is the case relationship is understood to subsist between the two families. The parents of the woman have a right to interfere on occasion of her ill-treatment; the husband is liable to be fined for wounding her; and there are other limitations on his absolute rights." If the sum is finally paid, which seldom happens except in cases of violent quarrel, the tie of relationship is said to be broken and the woman becomes to all intents the slave of her lord. As long as the daughter is not "wholly sold," there is a reservation of rights of interference.

The widow for whom a bride-price has been paid is at the disposal of her husband's relatives; they can keep her or marry her off with or without *jujur.* One man had seven young widows of his brothers at disposal. If the widow can repay the *jujur* money, she may go back to her family but must leave her children behind; if they are too young to be separated from the mother, she keeps them till they grow older and is then paid something for rearing them. Divorce is next to impossible under the *jujur* unless the wife remains childless; among the Bataks, in such case, the *jujur* must be restored or the bride replaced. Where divorce is allowed more freely, the bride-price must be repaid double. The general rule in all cases is that the children stay with the father; they are shown to be his by their obligation to discharge his debts in their persons, to say nothing of his right to sell them into slavery.

This outline of the *jujur* may serve as a type of the marriage with bride-price, or *cum manu;* it resumes to some degree the instances of marriage by

[58] §§266, 288, above; Keller, *Soc. Evol.,* 143 ff.

purchase cited above. Now over against this form, and in the same region, there exists marriage without a bride-price, or *sine manu*. "In this marriage the woman remains in the house of her parents, which the man enters, and the children belong to the mother's family. Under the mother-family,[59] of course, only marriages of this order could take place; then with the transition to the patriarchate they at first persisted, so that a situation was created where marriages *sine manu* appeared at the same time with those *cum manu*." Under this system there existed the idea that the race could be carried forward just as well in the male as in the female line. Gradually that view altered, the marriages *cum manu* and the patriarchal system became commoner; then the notion gained strength that the race must be preserved first of all through sons and that only in default of them could daughters come into consideration. Here a daughter might be regarded as a son, with a son's rights and duties; or as nil, the rights and duties passing over to her sons. Hence the marriage *sine manu* declined and finally became wholly exceptional, constituting no more than a recourse or last resort under conditions where a daughter had to be called upon to maintain the stock.

Such a form of marriage has several local names, but is generally known as *ambil-anak* or *ambel-anak* (child-receiving, or child-adoption; the word *lengit*, conveying the idea that the man thus marrying is lost to his own people, being often appended). This form is a good deal more than a survival out of the mother-family system, where the husband goes to the wife's home; even if it is an old form, it is used to effect a new adjustment. The *jujur*, as a purchase-price for the removal of the wife from her family, had no reason for existence if she were not removed. Hence the *ambil-anak* marriage is a modification ·of the prevalent *jujur*, for local and particular reasons, rather than the persistence of a matriarchal form.

The adoption-idea is indicated by the term itself. In one district there is even a fiction connected with this form of marriage that the young man comes into the house as an own child, while the own daughter is regarded as a daughter-in-law. "When a man marries after the custom, called *ambil-anak*, he pays no money to the father of the bride, but becomes one of his family, and is entirely upon the footing of a son; the father of his wife being thenceforward answerable for his debts, etc., in the same manner as his own children. The married man becomes entirely separated from his original family, and gives up the right of inheritance. It is, however, in the powers of the father of the wife to divorce from her his adopted son whenever he thinks proper, in which case the husband is not entitled to any of his children, nor to any effects other than simply the clothes on his back: but if the wife is willing to still live with him, and he is able to redeem her and the children by paying the father one hundred dollars, it is not at the option of the father to refuse accepting this sum; and in that case the marriage becomes a *kulo* or *jujur*, and is subject to the same rules."[60]

The cases cited by Wilken show the *ambil-anak* marriage referable in nearly all instances to a lack of male descendants which causes the female to be called in to carry on the line. The groom virtually pays the bride-price in his renunciation of inheritance and other rights in his own family and the bride's father collects it in the services performed by the daughter's husband and in the

59 §416, below.
60 Marsden, *Sumatra*, 235, 236, 262-263.

children born to hold up his family. He does not want it in any other form and would not receive it if offered, for the receipt of it would make the marriage like the *jujur* form which he is engaged in evading. He wants to "hold up the house, and may even announce his plans and publicly call for candidates, hammering on a basin the while. This is sometimes done when an own son is young or sickly." These types of marriage *sine manu* are sometimes entered into when the man is too poor to pay the bride-price and does not revolt at evasion; in that case the *ambil-anak* is a somewhat demeaning form.[61] It is only in cases of this order, when the *ambil-anak* is not a resort to uphold the family-line, that the man can take his wife away on payment of the bride-price. Even so, he may not take the children; he has not had the *manus* over his wife, who has been *in patria potestate,* and the children are not his. Yet there are possibilities of composition. "If he has not daughters by the marriage, he may redeem himself and wife, by paying her *jujur;* but if there are daughters before they become emancipated, the difficulty is enhanced, because the family are likewise entitled to their value. It is common, however, when they are upon good terms, to release him, on the payment of one *jujur,* or at most with an addition of an *adat* of fifty dollars. With this addition, he may insist upon a release, whilst his daughters are not marriageable."[62]

Under certain conditions the rule that the children of an *ambil-anak* union belong exclusively to the mother is modified. They may be evenly divided between the parents on each side; the death of man or wife results in such division. The first and third children commonly go to the mother, the second and fourth to the father. If the number of children is uneven, the youngest is left with the mother as long as it needs her care and then can choose for itself between the parents. An only daughter remains with the mother. If an only child of an *ambil-anak* marriage marries and has children, they are divided among the two grandparents. Marriage with division of the children does not reduce the man as does the regular form; under it also the woman may follow the man if he goes back to his family. If he pays the *jujur,* she must go; even if he does not, she may go if her parents agree. Again, a man has a right to assign one child, a son if there are several, to his own family: "commonly this is done when the man expects a heritage from his side and does not want to let it be entirely lost to his descendants."

It is to be noted by way of completing the case that, along with the Sumatran *jujur* and *ambil-anak* forms, exists also the transition to a "parental" system, where, among other things, children belong equally to both parents, inheriting from both alike. No bride-price is paid, and though the man goes to live with his wife, he is not obliged to stay there. In case of separation the children are divided. There is here also a small beginning of dowry, a little marriage-gift, running from ten to two hundred gulden (four to eighty dollars); it is thought that a greater sum makes the marriage more stable. This dowry, found chiefly in larger settlements and along the coast, would seem to go with advancing civilization. The man does not have to pay for the whole wedding-feast, or any of it; in some cases the bride pays two-thirds, while in others she would be ashamed to accept any aid from the man. "This marriage is a regular treaty between the parties, on the footing of equality."[63] Only

[61] Müller, *Sex. Leben,* 17.
[62] Marsden, *Sumatra,* 263; Mucke, *Horde,* 209, 213, 226, note.
[63] Marsden, *Sumatra,* 263, 225 ff.

when a poor young man marries a rich girl, does he become the plaything of his parents-in-law. If the woman is convinced that she is the head of the establishment, she calls the man "my wife" and institutes divorce-proceedings if she wishes. The Dutch government put the *jujur* under penalty in 1862, the result being that while the word was no longer used, the custom was re-christened and remained. But the legal prohibitions coincided in some cases with the natural change to the "parental" form and hastened it somewhat.[64]

In general it may be said that the whole complexion of a marriage depends on whether the woman goes to the man or the man to the woman. "The main fact," says Vinogradoff,[65] "is residence." The inferior goes to the superior, as a rule, and the character of the resulting association reflects this preliminary procedure. Under the mother-family the man goes to the woman and there is no bride-price, unless his services during his presence on sufferance and good behavior be accounted as such. With the coming of the father-family, the wife, either purchased or with a dowry, generally goes to the husband; and intermediate forms, such as have now been presented, represent adjustments to local conditions as respects movement and status of both parties in the realization of interests.

§364*. Dowry. This word, employed by some writers as the equivalent of bride-price, is here used to cover what is given to the receivers of the bride; what goes along with her; her *dot*. By a series of transitional practices wife-purchase passes into what looks very like husband-purchase. It then becomes the duty of a right-minded man, instead of collecting a price for daughter or sister, to exert himself to the utmost in providing her with the dowry which alone will make her marriage proper and honorable; this done, a brother may, in deep satisfaction by reason of duty accomplished, virtuously look about for a family willing to give him, along with a daughter, enough capital to start a new establishment. The dowry-system is familiar; the illustrations to be given are selected in order to exhibit its initial stages and ethnic varieties rather than the mature institution. To be noted are the gifts of the father to the daughter, which remain her property, the return-gifts at receipt of the bride-price, and other approaches toward the true dowry which have been referred to, but

64 Wilken, in VG, II, 261-263, 266-267.
65 *Hist. Jurispr.*, I, 195; §415, below.

without much illustration, under the preceding topic of transitional forms.[66]

Among the Matabele if the girl's father is rich enough, he gives her an ox or cow, and the husband takes note of the gift in a certain ceremonial form.[67] In Uganda a father receives flour, beer, and sheep, and later gives his daughter anklets and a hoe. Again, the groom's father gives ten head of cattle to the bride's father and the latter, on taking his daughter to her husband's house, restores three of the ten.[68] "It is customary in Theraka for a rich man to return twenty out of the thirty goats paid for his daughter, nominally a gift to the bride, but in actual fact they are given to the husband. Among the Tetu Akikuyu three goats, and in Ndia four goats, are returned when the woman has borne a child, but in all cases this is merely a gift and cannot be claimed. The father is entitled to expect liberal hospitality in his daughter's village, and this is claimed almost as a right."[69] "A Yao once asked me if Europeans make presents to the father of their fiancée. When I told him that it is the other way, and that the father gives the daughter money for her married establishment, and that her friends give her presents, he inquired: 'Is this because the parents of the girl are afraid that, perhaps, if they give her nothing, later, when the two have been married for some years, and a quarrel arises, the husband might say to his wife: "What! You dare quarrel with me, and yet when I married you, you had nothing, and I gave you everything!"?' "[70] In West Africa, dowry makes all the difference between marriage and harlotry.[71] In Borku, "the bridegroom gives his father-in-law at the betrothal a certain number, varying according to the family's wealth and rank, of female camels, of which the bride gets back about half under the form of dower. The groom has to provide the marriage feast, while the girl's father fits out the new household with a supply of grain and butter."[72] In northeast Africa, where there is bride-purchase, "a father-in-law who is growing wealthier commonly turns over half of this sum to the new pair and thereby announces his consent to the marriage." Among the Somal, the bride's father gets a fair price, "in return for which he has the duty of building a hut for the future pair and giving them some furniture. The complete purchase-price reaches generally two or three horses and about two hundred sheep. It often occurs that a father blessed with daughters turns this price over to the girl and gives her a new outfit over and above."[73] "A noble Tibboo gives a horse along with his daughter when she is married."[74] In modern Egypt the bride gets property which she can take away if divorced; thus she "cannot with truth be said to be purchased."[75]

Among the Chukchi, "when a son-in-law takes his wife home without quarreling with her father he is usually given some reindeer, the number of which depends upon the quality of work done by the young man during his period

[66] §362, above.   [67] Decle, in JAI, XXIII, 84.
[68] Johnston, *Uganda*, II, 609-610, 632.
[69] Dundas, C., in JAI, XLV, 286.
[70] Coudenhove, in *Atl. Mo.*, CXXXII, 189.
[71] Nassau, *Fetichism*, 6.   [72] Nachtigal, *Sahara*, II, 177.
[73] Paulitschke, *Nordost-Afr.*, I, 197, 198; II, 286.
[74] Rohlfs, in *Mitth. J. Perthes' Geog. Anstalt*, Ergänzband., V, 12.
[75] Lane, *Mod. Egypt.*, I, 242.

of service." One wealthy Chukchi gave his son-in-law "freedom of one day," which meant that the groom was free to catch as many reindeer as he could for himself on that day. "As a rule it is considered improper to pay for a bride 'as if she were a reindeer,' and the Chukchee always criticize the Tungus and Yakut on this point."[76] The Yakut groom has a heavy outlay for marriage, which is part of the bride-price; and it would be beyond his means (an ordinary marriage costing a hundred rubles—over thirty dollars) but that part comes back in the woman's dower.[77] Ostiak parents take a price but also give a dowry unless the bride is poor and the groom rich.[78] Among the Tungus, "several weeks after the marriage the newly wedded husband goes to his father-in-law and, as a rule, receives back from him as a gift a part of the reindeer paid for the bride—sometimes all of them, again none, their place being taken by other objects."[79] The Kirghiz give dower, which is always less than the purchase-price.[80] In Tibet, parents pleased with a marriage give the girl a dowry of cattle, sheep, a tent, or whatever they can afford.[81] In some cases, here and elsewhere, the dowry is composed of presents from many sources—as if the group endowered one of its members: "It is the custom for the men and women of a village to assemble when a bride enters the house of her husband, each of them presenting her with three rupees [about a dollar]. The Tibetan wife, far from spending these gifts on personal adornment, looks ahead, contemplating possible contingencies, and immediately hires a field, the produce of which is her own, and which accumulates year after year in a separate granary, so that she may not be portionless in case she leaves her husband."[82] The presence of this "portion" acts to stabilize the union. In Korea, where there is no purchase or dower, the bride receives a large trousseau.[83] In one district of India, "bone-money" (munda) can be demanded by the wife's father, if she or a child of hers dies, from her husband or his relatives. The munda is usually a buffalo. "The curious system of bone-money may be regarded as securing the protection of individuals under whatever circumstances they may be thrown, and the munda insures care for both wife and offspring."[84]

In southern Sumatra, when a girl is married with bride-price her father loses all right to concern himself with her condition; even if she is maltreated he may not interfere. There speedily develops an amelioration of this strictness, in the form of what is called the tali-kulo. This is an unpaid part of the bride-price. Twenty gulden (eight dollars) are given back to the groom as tali-kulo, symbolic of the fact that the girl's father has not yet wholly parted with her but may come to her assistance if she is maltreated by her husband.[85]

"It belongs to the peculiar customs of South Celebes that the bridegroom gets back a part of the marriage-gift as a small compensation for the expenses undergone by him, while another part is given to the blood-relations of the bride. The rest is pin-money for the prospective wife."[86] The bride-price be-

[76] Czaplicka, Aborig. Siberia, 72-73.
[77] Sieroshevski-Sumner, in JAI, XXXI, 84.
[78] Kondratowitsch, in Globus, LXXIV, 289.
[79] Hiekisch, Tungusen, 88-89.   [80] Russ. Ethnog. (Russ.), II, 188.
[81] Rockhill, Mongolia and Tibet, 156.
[82] Bishop, Tibetans, 95.   [83] Bishop, Korea, 115.
[84] Watt, in JAI, XVI, 355.   [85] Wilken, in VG, II, 236-237.
[86] Van Eck, in Ind. Gids, 1881, II, 843.

comes "a formality prescribed by religion" and tends to pass into the hands of the marrying pair; it "is not placed at the disposal of the father of the young woman but immediately after the wedding-celebration is turned over to her" and in addition "the father of the girl has to take care of the establishing of the young pair so that they can live according to their station." "The approach of the 'marriage season' in the Straits Settlements was responsible for the shipment of $125,000 of gold to that part of the world yesterday by the International Acceptance Bank. Further shipments are expected, and bankers said that an almost constant movement of gold to the Straits Settlements was likely for the next few months. The shipments have nothing to do with foreign exchange conditions and are not made in connection with ordinary commercial settlements, but are the result of wedding customs that prevail in parts of the Orient. In addition to a dowry, the father of the bride usually presents her with bracelets, necklaces, rings or other trinkets made of gold. Purchases are made of United States and other gold coins, which are melted and manufactured into ornaments."[87]

Among the Oregon Indians the suitor offers horses, blankets, or buffalo-robes for a girl; then her relatives "raise as many (or other property) for her dower, as the bridegroom has sent the parents, but scrupulously take care not to turn over the same horses or the same articles."[88] Similarly among the Tlinkit: "It is natural that this dower, which the man must return in case he casts off his wife without any fault of hers, assures the woman of a certain independence over against her husband."[89]

In Chaldæa, while marriage was really an act of purchase, the wife also brought a dower which is recorded in the marriage-contract.[90] There is no dower as such in Homer, nor more than the beginning of return-gifts to the bride; occasionally she gets a personal gift of a slave and sometimes richer presents, which were apparently her own and her children's property—they were not given to the groom.[91] The Hindu epic shows a contrasting picture where the daughter is given "with fitting bride-treasure";[92] the duty of making up a dowry rested on the brothers. Later on in Greek times, gifts became more common: Hermione says of the decorations she wears that they were given her by her father, together with a fine dower, "to insure me freedom of speech."[93] The giving of dowry came to be a religious duty among Hebrews and Mohammedans and in Greece its presence came to distinguish wife from concubine, as that of the bride-price has done elsewhere. This distinction existed in even higher degree in Rome, where a woman had legal claim on her father for dowry. The tradition persisted despite the repeated assertions of Justinian that the dower was a necessity only for persons of high class; long afterward the law "treated people who married without a dower as not being legitimately married and as necessarily being, they and their children, flecked with infamy. It is this tradition, it is thought, which is still active in France,

---

[87] Jacobs, *Groot-Atjeh*, I, 26; N. Y. *Times*, August 6, 1926.

[88] Schoolcraft, *Indian Tribes*, V, 654.

[89] Grosse, *Familie*, 76. [90] Maspero, *Hist. Anc.*, I, 734.

[91] Keller, *Hom. Soc.*, 213.

[92] Holtzmann, *Ind. Sagen*, I, 256; Bühler, *Manu*, IX, 118; Letourneau, *Prop.*, 335.

[93] Euripides, *Andromache*, 153.

though the *dot* is not a legal obligation.[94] The literature of the Romans, as well as of the French, plays about the dowry with insistence. In Plautus[95] the good young man sacrifices himself to get a dower for some dependent female, planning, after his labors, to sell himself to some richly endowered girl and settle down to well-deserved ease. French novels and plays carry this rather tiresome hero into a later stage.

The German wife "does not bring dower to the man but the man to the wife." The presents to the wife were substantial: oxen, a horse, arms; and the wife gave weapons to the husband. "This, they think, is the surest bond, these the mysterious holy objects, these the gods of marriage."[96] In the Law of the Saxons and among the Langobards, until the seventh century, the woman's guardian was paid; thereafter he got a small present and the rest went to the bride. Among the West Goths the gift is to the bride only. In Scandinavia, "the bride, in the most ancient times as still today, was fitted out for marriage by her parents or relations." The dower was specifically the woman's property, "over which the man had no right of disposition and which remained in persisting connection with the family of the woman." The man's creditors had not the slightest claim upon it. The man, according to East Gothic law, could use it only in case of famine, after he had used up all his own resources—and even so he must restore it—or as ransom for the wife if she had been captured in war.[97] Among the Irish, a girl's portion, consisting of cows, was made up by solicited contributions which people were afraid to refuse. These must be restored if the bride died childless within a certain time—a measure to prevent anyone from becoming rich by frequent marriages.[98] The evolution of the meaning of the Irish term is first purchase-money given for the bride and then dowry brought to a husband.[99] So-called "maidens' purses" are still made up by mining folk in the north of England, on Christmas Eve; they are stealthily thrown in at the girl's window to avoid any possibility of wounding her feelings.[100] In modern Greece "no young man ever thinks of marrying a girl who is not provided with a satisfactory dowry, and the marriage contract amounts practically to the purchase of the bridegroom. . . . It is quite an exceptional thing for a Greek to think of entering the wedded state himself until all his sisters are married." Immigrants send back money to endower the young women at home.[101]

The custom of planting trees at the birth of a daughter, which shall be her dower, is rather widespread.[102] In a number of instances the girl is encouraged to amass her own dowry by resort to a period of prostitution.[103] Finally, a curious case of undisguised husband-purchase is reported from India: the

[94] Westermarck, *Marriage*, II, 428 ff.; Schmidt, *Soc. Civ.*, 72; Maine, *Early Institutions*, 339.

[95] *Trinummus*, espec. II, 4; III, 2; V, 2, 3.

[96] Tacitus, *Germania*, 18; Von d. March, *Germanen*, I, 260-261.

[97] Weinhold, *Deut. Frauen*, etc., I, 325, 326, 331, 332; Westermarck, *Marriage*, II, 426.

[98] Gomme, *Village Life*, 204.   [99] Schrader, *Aryan*, 382.

[100] N. Y. *Times*, April 18, 1915.

[101] Fairchild, *Greek Immigration*, 39, 40, 93.

[102] Andree, *Eth. Parallelen*, 21.

[103] Codrington, *Melanesians*, 235; Bancroft, *Nat. Races*, I, 123; II, 676; Herodotus, *Hist.*, I, §93; Plautus, *Cistellaria*, II, 3, 20.

question of the groom-price is discussed and a certain part of it, usually half, is paid on the spot by the girl's family to clinch the bargain.[104]

Evidently it is the rich man who sets the pace in these dowry-developments. He thus keeps a hand upon the groom, for selfish purposes oftentimes, but again to ensure the stability of the daughter's or sister's marriage. The fact that the endowered wife is more independent, especially when the dowry remains wholly hers, is the burden of certain of the instances cited. The father may also set up an establishment for the two, at a time when the groom has spent his all in paying for his wife. Again the community may turn to and see that the new domestic economy has a fair start; this is still the sense of the "showers" and wedding-gifts. To be noted is the dowry which consists of a return of part of the purchase-price, thus constituting a transitional form or variation away from the bride-price. And finally it appears unmistakably that where the dowry-system prevails it is as humiliating not to be endowered as it is, under the bride-price, not to command a high figure. In a general way it can be said that the former is a later development in the series of property-adjustments now before us than the latter. It is correlative with increased wealth and a consequent opportunity to indulge in sentimental considerations that would not have occurred farther back in the course of evolution.

Purchase and dowry are the two ends of a series of correlations between marriage and property. We do not wish to dwell unduly upon this correlation or others in the same sense nor to leave out of all account the play of personal sentiment. The latter appears, nevertheless, in the guise of variation about a traditional procedure in the mores which is solidly based upon an enduring interest; and while it gradually softens rugged outlines, at least in some ages and cases, it is not that which blocked out the institution. As a preliminary to marriage, property-considerations had to be and still have to be attended to in some way; and the expediency of the way has determined, on a given stage, its survival as an adjustment. The ways which are now regarded as right, proper, and refined have been reached through variation and selec-

[104] Risley, *Ethnog. Ind.*, I, 82.

tion upon those which now strike us as crude, ridiculous, indecent, or despicable; yet the latter looked as desirable, in their setting, as ours do to us. Except by modifying and refining upon crudity, there was no way to attain to delicacy. If the rankly strong, coarse, and massive had not been there, as in the parallel cases of retaliation, enslavement, eidolism, or magic, there would have been nothing to refine.

CHAPTER XLVIII

FURTHER PRELIMINARIES TO MARRIAGE

§365*. Group-Consent and Test. Besides the property-arrangements there are other preliminaries to marriage which evince the interest of the society in the union of the sexes. The consent of the group must be forthcoming through the acquiescence of its representatives. One of the not uncommon preconditions to marriage, which shows the interdependence of the marital and the political, is the part played by the chief. As, in cases which have been reviewed,[1] he seems to be the owner of all the land, so does he sometimes appear to be the proprietor of all the women; then his consent may be needful to a marriage. He may even provide the wives himself or pay the bride-price for his retainers.

In West Victoria no marriage or exchange of wives can take place without the consent of the chief.[2] In the New Hebrides, marriage is arranged by the chiefs of tribes, the girl passing to her husband at puberty.[3] In 1815, when a prominent native made himself king of the Basuto, he gave his oxen for women whom he presented to his poorer subjects to win their adhesion; then the bride-price of all the daughters was eventually to be returned to him.[4] The king of Dahomi had a monopoly of all the women, whom he sold to his subjects.[5] The king of Uganda had seven thousand women, who were really a stock from which he provided his chiefs with wives, to win influence and popularity. His consent was a prerequisite to marriage.[6] In another region, when the prospective parties to a marriage are poor, the chief "oftentimes goes down into his own pocket, or rather into his own stalls."[7] Among the Niam-Niam a man does not pay for his wife but applies to a king or a magnate who gets him one; despite polygyny, marital obligations are strictly maintained.[8] In the absence of the sultan, five or six girls or women offered themselves to the German traveller Barth; for in the chief's absence "restraint was no longer necessary."[9] Among the Maori, the wife was chosen by the council of the place, the parties having nothing to do with it beyond giving their consent.[10]

A Wintun Indian usually has a maiden selected for him by the headman, who pays her parents money.[11] Powell[12] says that marriage by "legal appoint-

[1] §120, above. [2] Dawson, *Aust. Aborig.*, 35.
[3] Lawrie, in AAAS, 1892, 709. [4] Fritsch, *Eingeb. S.-Afr.*, I, 483.
[5] Waitz, *Anthrop.*, I, 147; Gomme, *Village Life*, 201, note.
[6] Johnston, *Uganda*, II, 632. [7] Volkens, *Kilimandscharo*, 251.
[8] Schweinfurth, *Heart of Afr.*, II, 27; Ratzel, *Vkde.*, I, 534.
[9] Goldstein, in *Globus*, XCII, 188. [10] Taylor, *Te Ika*, I, 43.
[11] Powers, in *Contrib. N. Amer. Ethnol.*, III, 238.
[12] In BAE, III, lix; Powell, in BAE, VII, 35.

ment" exists among all North American tribes; the young woman receives a husband from some other prescribed clan and the elders of the clan, with certain exceptions, control these marriages, so that personal choice has little to do with the affair. "The savage legislator sought to avoid controversy by regulating marital relations." When marriages are proposed, the virtues and industry of candidates and above all their ability to live properly as married couples and to supply the clan or tribe with a due amount of subsistence, are discussed long and earnestly; the young man or maiden who falls short in this respect may fail in securing an eligible and desirable match. These conditions are repeatedly rehearsed to the savage youth. Here is a real education for useful citizenship, an induction into the mores and the presentation of the standards which the youth should live up to. It illustrates the lodging of the regulative function in respect to marriage in the hands of the elders, who are the repositories of group-traditions and group-wisdom. It is a less crass case than where the chief assumes arbitrary control and is better illustrative of the inmixture of society in a proceeding between individuals which is at the same time of deep societal interest.

From time to time political regulation reappears in the more arbitrary form, as where one Roman Emperor decreed that no one should take a wife without his consent. This became the custom thereafter, in greater or lesser degree, among the barbarians; cities of the thirteenth century got exemptions from it in their charters.[13] The permission of lord or gild or community was long essential to marriage, as a guarantee of the interest of the group in the unions of its members.[14]

The acquiescence of the chief or the elders may be taken to represent that of the community. However, the group's consent rests ultimately in the mores, and in them are found numerous provisions for the test of virility, the passing of which alone enables a man to enter the marriage-relation. When one recollects that among many peoples the unmarried man is a nonentity or a perpetual minor, the importance of the test of marriageability is evident. The examples will show that it is imposed not infrequently at the hand of the girl sought in marriage and that she is often able to do her own choosing among suitors by making the test lighter for the man she likes—which is yet another piece of evidence against the current belief that woman has been hopelessly dominated throughout the ages. Further, it should be realized that tests are often coincident with puberty-ceremonies, so that the accompanying ordeals[15] are relevant to the present topic. Tests of eligibility to man's estate in general involve proofs of marriageability, for that is a salient feature of majority. There is

13 Grimm, *Rechtsalterthümer*, 437.
14 Schallmayer, *Vererbung*, 355-356; §§341, 365, above.
15 §163, above.

a kind of sexual selection in all these ordeals, whether of man or woman, that tends to eliminate the feeble or abnormal in body or mind from marriage, if not from procreation.

The qualities tested in man are those which go to make up virility according to current standards: chiefly prowess in war and the chase and ability to provide for a family.

The Bushman youth who wants a wife gives proof of skill and daring by bringing in game. There is often fighting and murder over the women.[16] Again, a youth may not marry until he has killed a rhinoceros.[17] In Madagascar the test is as follows. Placed at a certain distance from a clever spear-caster, the aspirant to marriage "is bidden to catch between his arm and side every spear thrown by the man opposite to him. If he displays fear or fails to catch the spear he is ignominiously rejected; but if there be no flinching and the spears are caught, he is at once proclaimed an 'accepted lover.' "[18] Again, when a girl has two suitors, they sit by her side while she presses a knife into the thigh of each. He who endures longest gets her.[19] It goes without saying that in this case the girl has some power of selection. A Galla girl will not marry a man who has not killed an enemy; he must present supporting trophies as a necessary preliminary to marriage.[20] In some cases the killing of a man allows the wearing of an ostrich-feather in the hair, which then means eligibility for marriage.[21] Said a chief of a tribe of Somals, voicing a literal conception about emplacement: "How can you desire that I shall marry a wife and bring a child into the world if I have not beforehand made a place for that child on this earth by removing another human being?"[22] Among the Arabs of Upper Egypt a man must undergo a flogging by the relations of the bride to test his courage; he must endure the ordeal, which is sometimes extraordinarily severe, with an expression of joy.[23]

Among the Chukchi of northeastern Siberia, the most usual method of getting a wife is by serving for her, the term used meaning "to be a herds-man for a wife"; the maritime tribes who have no herds use the same word. This service is a variety of test of the man; among the Koryak, no matter how wealthy he may be, he has to serve from three to five years, and is not treated as well as an ordinary servant would be. "The principal thought is not his usefulness, but the hard and humiliating trials to which he is subjected"; but if he gets through without quarreling with his prospective father-in-law, cattle are given him. The Chukchi have foot-races and contests of several kinds for the bride.[24]

In one caste in India, the maiden chooses the man who has loosed and brought to her a cloth tied to the horn of the fiercest bull. The animals are let loose and then terrified and bewildered by a great din. The suitor considers it a disgrace to be injured while getting the cloth. Again, a girl retires with her

[16] Hahn, in *Globus*, XVIII, 122; Ratzel, *Vkde.*, I, 71.
[17] Livingstone, *Mission. Travels*, 147.
[18] Sibree, *Great Afr. Isl.*, 251.
[19] Wilson and Felkin, *Uganda*, II, 310.
[20] Waitz, *Anthrop.*, II, 515.   [21] Peel, *Somaliland*, 219.
[22] Ernst, in *Umschau*, VIII, 110.   [23] Baker, *Nile Tributaries*, 120-121.
[24] Czaplicka, *Aborig. Siberia*, 72-74, 82-83.

suitor into the jungle and they light a fire. Then she takes a burning stick and applies it to his flesh. "If he cries out, Am! Am! Am! he is unworthy of her and she remains a maid. If he does not, the marriage is at once consummated. The application of the brand is probably light or severe according to the girl's feelings towards the young man." Much the same test occurs elsewhere, the youth being obliged, while being burned, to stand talking quietly with the girl and paying no attention to the torture.[25]

Among head-hunting peoples, like the Dyaks and Alfurs, the youth may not marry till he possesses one or more heads.[26] Qualification for admiration and marriage is supposed to be attained by getting the head of an enemy, but evasions occur. In one case a young man set out by himself to seek the necessary trophy and in a few days came back with it. "His relatives asked him how it was he was able to get to the enemy's country and back in such a short time. He replied gravely that the spirits of the woods had assisted him. About a month afterwards a headless trunk was discovered near one of their farms. It was found to be the body of his victim, an old woman of his own tribe, not very distantly related to himself!" It is especially necessary for a chief to have the orthodox trophy, though even here the requirement is conventionalized: the head of a woman or child, though a sort of debased currency, will serve the purpose.[27] Survivalistic practices connected with this requirement are found: "It was necessary in earlier times, before a man could take a wife, to steal a human head on one of the neighboring islands. Today this is not any longer demanded, but the bridegroom must, to give the appearance of going on a head-hunt, depart into the forest with several relatives and stay 180 days."[28]

Allied to the test of strength and courage is the so-called marriage by duel. Among the Australians, "a young chief who cannot get a wife, and falls in love with one belonging to a chief who has more than two, can, with her consent, challenge the husband to single combat, and, if he defeats him, he makes her his legal wife; but the defeated husband never afterwards speaks to her."[29] The right of the stronger once prevailed in the courting-festivals of the Malays and no one went without sword and shield.[30] In one Amazon tribe, "the women are for the most part the prizes of a fist-fight in which all the lovers of the marriageable girl participate under the condition that she shall go to the victor."[31] There was an Irish custom by which a girl was "horsed," that is, carried on men's backs. Then begins a hurling match, in which the person designated by her parents must beat all comers or she goes to the victor.[32] Tournaments where the victor wins the much-sought maiden have been exploited in poems and stories. Westermarck[33] has collected a number of instances of this test by duel; in some cases the women fight too, though their contest for a man naturally resolves itself into one of coquetry.

Cases of this sort could be multiplied. It is to be noted that such demonstrations prior to marriage are sometimes difficult to differentiate from details of the wedding-ceremony. For instance, to constitute a legal marriage, a Musk-

25 Thurston, *S. India,* 18, 22-23 (quoted); Gubernatis, *Usi Nuz.,* 79.
26 Wilken, in VG, I, 576; III, 150 n., 388; IV, 68 n., 85; Mucke, *Horde,* 78; §229, above.
27 Gomes, *Sea Dyaks,* 73, 74.   28 Pleyte, in *Globus,* LXXIX, 26.
29 Dawson, *Aust. Aborig.,* 36.   30 Ratzel, *Vkde.,* II, 433.
31 Spix u. Martius, *Brasilien,* 1074.
32 Gomme, *Village Life,* 215, 216.   33 *Marriage,* I, ch. XIII.

hogean Indian must, among other things, build a house, raise a crop and gather it in; then go hunting and bring home meat. When all this was done, and the product given over to the woman, the ceremony was ended, or, as the natives put it: "The woman was bound, and not till then."[34]

Test by riddle is a curious practice. Riddles occur in large number of folk-tales and are often their chief feature. The stories of Samson's riddle and that of the Sphinx show them as serious matters. "There is a class of stories in which the bride is won by the solution of a riddle. In another class the bride proposes the riddle, and the suitor who fails to answer it correctly is killed; or the suitor is obliged to propose one himself, and if the bride fails to answer it she must marry him; but if she succeeds, the suitor is killed. Evidently, where the penalty is death, riddles have a serious aspect and a significance which modern suitors do not fully appreciate or understand. And yet the use of riddles in courtship, described in European folklore, survives to this day in the plantation courtship among the negroes."[35]

The chief qualities that are tested in the primitive woman are industry and fecundity; she must be an effective partner in both maintaining and perpetuating the family. As one scans the cases where the bride-price is customary, the query rises: What is bought? It is not the privilege of sex-satisfaction, for that, though prostitution is rare, need not demand marriage; and even if chastity is imposed upon the woman, it is seldom required of the man. Yet along with this looseness of premarital relations goes often the strictest of regulation, at least for the wife, within the marriage-relation. What, then, is bought? It is sometimes stated that the bride-price is to cover the costs of the girl's rearing. This means that it is the price of something valuable possessed by the parents; and the construing of the bride-price as an indemnification for loss due to wife-capture amounts to the same thing.

The fact is that an investment in wives was as natural and obvious an expedient in living as one in cattle; what was bought was labor-force and reproductive capacity; and the investor felt that he had a just grievance if the woman purchased did not turn out to be a good worker and child-producer. If she did not, or if she exhibited a wrong attitude toward her purchaser, as in adultery, he could generally get his payment back, as for unsatisfactory goods, or at any rate require that she be replaced by a younger sister or other satisfactory substitute. Especially must a wife be able to bear children, in particular, sons. Conditions of success in self-maintenance, working out in the end to the need of

[34] Carr, in *Smithson. Rep.*, 1891, 528.
[35] Vance, in *Forum*, XXII, 256.

protection and support in old age, demanded the presence of children; and for the preservation of life beyond death they, especially sons, were regarded as quite indispensable. The possession of children came to minister powerfully to vanity as well; so that the desire for them, on economic, religious, dynastic, and other grounds, rooted in the very socializing forces themselves.[36]

Such views of the importance of children both account for the statement that the bride-price is paid for the sake of having offspring by a woman and counting them in the husband's tribe and also throw light upon the custom whereby the first-born child is surrendered to the wife's father as purchase-value for the wife;[37] herein is explained also the value often attached to the woman who has borne children prior to marriage. No doubt certain of the mutilations, tattooings, and other rites performed on and over women, for instance at puberty-ceremonies,[38] are intended in some way, magical or other, to ensure their fecundity; and the wedding-ceremonies do not fail to show preoccupation with this matter.

The test of woman as a worker has been brought out in preceding connections:[39] she must weed and plant a field within a reasonably short time or exhibit her skill in cookery or other specialties of her sex. Some of these tests get into the wedding-ceremony itself and some are involved, for man as well as woman, in the proposal of marriage.

The bride-show, elsewhere described,[40] amounts to a test of the woman, chiefly of her beauty, social accomplishments, and wealth rather than of her working-powers.

In Great Russia, after the proposal has been accepted, the go-between asked that the bride might be seen. This was sometimes refused, from pride or if the girl was not pretty, but generally consent was given and the man's mother or an old female relative was detailed as examiner. The girl was displayed in many ways. The "viewer" went into a decorated room where she stood in her best clothes and veiled or sat behind a drawn curtain and was allowed to walk and talk with her, to test her physical and mental qualities. If she were homely, her sister or another girl was shown in her stead. The groom could not see her till marriage and had to rely on his representative's account. If deceived, he could get divorce upon complaint, though this was rare. He had generally

36 §§11, above, and 409, below.
37 Smith, *Kinship*, 108; Starcke, *Prim. Fam.*, 146.
38 §163, above.
39 §§335, 361, above, 386, 387, below.   40 §361, above.

to put up with what he got and the only consolation given him was: if you
have not fully assured yourself, you should not marry.[41] Again the bride may
be tested for courage and self-control. She may be teased in rude fashion and
beaten but must not wail or repel any of her tormentors. The more blows she
gets without crying out, the more honorable it is for her and the more she
can boast.[42] At the door all the boys of the village push and pinch the bride,
who must not defend herself nor utter a sound.[43]

There is a special form of trial which is aimed chiefly at the
determination of the woman's fecundity and which has no parallel in the case of man, for the childlessness of a union is ascribed,
so far as our cases indicate, solely to the wife. The idea is that a
married couple simply must have issue. Primitive people are wont
to drive with relentless logic straight at some actual test, especially where issues seem to them of great significance; and marriage is perhaps the most significant issue of all.[44] So here; and
in this case it is the so-called marriage of trial or term which
determines beforehand the qualities of the wife and, to a much
less degree, of the husband. The parties live together as man and
wife until they are convinced that the union will be a success or a
failure, chiefly in the matter of fecundity but in other respects as
well; and then they act upon the evidence they get. The ceremony
comes after the trial or term.[45] If the woman bears a child or becomes pregnant, the marriage takes place. If a definite period of
trial is set, the relation is called a marriage of term. The contention that primitive marriage is made, not by romantic passion
but by concrete interest, is strengthened by evidence of this sort.
Perhaps trial-marriage really tests compatibility of temperament
also, though there is no evidence that it is intended to do that.
The mores call for a certain type of status known as marriage;
then are evolved tests that shall establish the probability of its
realization in the case of candidates who present themselves.[46]

In the Solomon Islands, the groom either takes the girl to his dwelling or
else he stays awhile with her parents, partly to show his ability to keep her,
and partly to see what kind of a house-wife she will make. If he is dissatisfied,
he is allowed to return her, the parents paying him for the time he has kept

[41] Kostomarov, *Gt. Russians* (Russ.), 228, 232; *Russ. Ethnog.* (Russ.), II,
123.
[42] Paulitschke, *Nordost-Afr.*, I, 200.
[43] Von Haxthausen, *Transkaukasia*, II, 22.
[44] §341, above.   [45] Smith, *Kinship*, 69, 141-143.
[46] Cases in Letourneau, *Marriage*, 67 ff.

her.[47] The marriage of a Bechuana is valid only after a child is born.[48] In West Africa, though ante-wedding sexual trials are not regarded as according to rule, they are very common. If not followed by the regular marriage-ceremony, they are adjudged to be adultery.[49] In one Uganda tribe, freedom of relations before marriage is common and if a young man likes a girl with whom he has so associated, he goes through the purchase-negotiations and marries her.[50] In Borku, "the young woman remains in her parents' dwelling, in whose neighborhood is set up a hut for the conjugal meetings of the young pair till the birth of the first child. If this event does not happen, the wife remains altogether in her parents' dwelling and her father must repay the purchase-price." In these regions, the wife is generally bought and in case of sterility returns home; then the payment is restored and the woman is turned over to another man for a determined price or she takes the position of a slave. "Among some tribes, however, it seems that the woman, if she has borne her husband five children, may at her volition return to her parents' dwelling."[51] The Berbers have a sort of annual marriage-market. "The ladies walk unveiled and the intending suitor goes with the one of his choice to seek her father or guardian to ask for her hand. The only engagement entered into is to bring her back to the same place on a market day if tired of her, so that she may better her lot. This is sworn to in a saint's shrine and a gift of a pair of slippers or some garment to her father seals the bargain."[52]

In Borneo, "when two young people take a fancy to each other, their intercourse is unrestrained. Should the girl prove with child, a marriage takes place; their great anxiety for children makes them take this precaution against sterility."[53] A young Kubu who wants to marry a girl lives with her for a time in secret union; if she appeals to him, he goes to her mother and the matter is arranged.[54] Among the Igorrotes, "after the betrothal, the parents of the bride permit the young man to live in concubinage with their daughter, for it is important above all to test her fecundity. If the bride becomes pregnant within a certain time, then only does the wedding take place; in the opposite case the bridegroom retires. Earlier, anyone who left his bride without reason was beheaded." This tribe lays great stress upon the chastity of its young women, who are always accompanied by older females of the family or by their fathers.[55] In view of this trial-custom, "in reality there appears to be little need for women in Bontoc to allure men through their curiosity."[56]

The importance of the child in a free union appears among the Tahitians. A man may, if he likes, make a second connection but if the woman becomes pregnant, he must put the child to death, afterwards either continuing his connection with its mother or deserting her. If he accepts the child and permits it to live, the pair are held to have entered into the marriage-state and usually continue to live together.[57]

Several Indian cases are cited by Starcke.[58] "The custom of trial-nights was

[47] Elton, in JAI, XVII, 94.
[48] Starcke, Prim. Fam., 239.
[49] Nassau, Fetichism, 6.
[50] Johnston, Uganda, II, 553.
[51] Nachtigal, Sahara, II, 177, 685.
[52] Meakin, in JAI, XXIV, 10.
[53] Roth, Sarawak, I, 116, 109; Gomes, Sea Dyaks, 127.
[54] Anon., "Kubus auf Sumatra," in Globus, XXVI, 45-46.
[55] Blumentritt, in Petermann's Mitth., Ergänzheft. LXVII, 27-28.
[56] Jenks, in AA, VI, 700-701.
[57] Cook, Voy. to Pacific, II, 157.
[58] Prim. Fam., 259-260, 282.

found in certain parts of the Inca empire, to the very great irritation of the missionaries, who set all their strength to combat this legal custom while they did nothing against the illegal conduct of the Spaniards with Indian girls and wives."[59] The Fuegian girl, before she is finally given away to her destined husband, is now and again sent to live with him for a time. This is before she is of marriageable age. If she feels insuperable aversion to him and persists in hating him, she is given to a man she likes.[60]

There is some evidence that the Greeks practised trial-marriage.[61] Experimental unions took place among the Irish pagans.[62] Amongst the Scottish Highlanders there was a custom called *hand-fasting;* that is, two chiefs agreed that the heir of the one should live with the daughter of the other as her husband for a year and a day; if at the end of that time, the woman had become a mother or at any rate if she was pregnant, the marriage was regarded as valid, even if unblest by a priest; if there was no sign of pregnancy the connection was dissolved and each party was at liberty to enter into another connection, either by marriage or hand-fasting.[63] Later there was a sharp conflict between law and the mores when southern enactments were enforced against the Highlanders.[64] In Scott's *Monastery*[65] the practice is attributed to lack of priests. "Mariachinage" is a term for premarital relations in a part of France. The practice is thought to favor marriage and not to reduce the birth-rate.[66]

To be clearly understood is the fact that when a system of trial is in the mores, it is attended by chastity and modesty quite as much as any other current arrangement. In the parts of Scandinavia where trial-marriage is in vogue, says a Norwegian of the very highest sensitiveness and refinement, there is no license or indecency of any kind connected with the system as such; if a young man is known to be visiting a young woman, all other suitors keep away, for he is known to have been accepted pending the test and she is meanwhile to be treated as a wife.[67]

There is a tendency to assimilate to trial-marriage a custom known as "bundling," which is really a phenomenon of courtship and will be treated under that topic.[68]

Premarital tests find their analogue in customs which appear

[59] Friederici, in *Globus*, XC, 305.

[60] Bridges, in *Voice f. S. Amer.*, XIII, 181.

[61] Becker-Hermann, *Charikles*, III, 328.

[62] Letourneau, *Marriage*, 246.

[63] Browne, *Hist. Highlands*, IV, 398; Skene, *Highlanders*, 166; Vinogradoff, *Hist. Jurispr.*, I, 244.

[64] Starcke, *Prim. Fam.*, 260; Westermarck, *Marriage*, I, 135; Stiles, *Bundling*, 17.

[65] Ch. XXV, note.

[66] Baudouin, in *Bull. Soc. d'Anthr. de Paris*, 1904, 80-87.

[67] Personal communication.   [68] §367, below.

after the marriage-relation has been formally established, or at least after formal betrothal. What is wanted in a wife or, indeed, in a husband, cannot be more clearly told than by a survey of the conditions resulting in the dissolution of marriage. The reasons for divorce show what marriage ought to be in the light of what it has not been; what is wanted in a wife or husband appears in the frustration of hopes and expectations. Divorce is a belated recognition of the fact that one or both of the parties, though it is generally the wife who is cast off, have failed to meet the test of actual experience in the relation. A marriage contracted with the possibility of divorce in view is really a trial-marriage; its kinship with the latter form will appear when we come to divorce.[69] Courtship, again, is a sort of experiment in determining the suitability of the parties to a proposed marriage, though the term covers tests less gross than those imposed by primitive peoples—among whom there is very little that we should call courtship, for they do not deal much in romance, compatibilities of temperament, "affinity," and the rest.

§366*. Chastity. Under the modern code, the greatest consequence is attached to the chastity and virginity of the bride who is to enter the state of wedlock for the first time. The assumption is that she is "pure," and an imbecile prudery has insisted even that she shall also be "innocent" in the sense of uninstructed, ignorant. No such stress is laid on the chastity of the man; the very fact that there is no word corresponding to virginity that can be used for man, so that a term like "virgin-man" or a circumlocution must be resorted to, is significant of the discrimination long current in the mores as respects the premarital life of the sexes. The "wild oats" of young men have been treated with tolerance or even with levity where sexual irregularities on the part of a young woman have been regarded with revulsion and horror. This discrimination goes back to the biological functions of sex, which involve inevitable consequences for woman without parallel for man.[70] Such an attitude toward female chastity and virginity, as the examples of premarital license[71] demonstrate, has not been of all places and times.

69 §§392, 393, below.   70 §§59-61, above.
71 §344, above.

"In the case of primitive man, chastity of a wife was not an indispensable condition of marriage."[72] With the Indian Archipelago chiefly in mind, "we can say that among the heathen peoples, with several exceptions, not the least value is set upon the chastity of young maidens, and that with some tribes abandon is even put at a premium—yes, is even regarded, in a certain sense, as a duty."[73]

The sentiment about virginity has become a highly idealized one. It is as if something mysterious that must remain untouched and at its climax until its moment of perfection and crisis has come. Nothing of this idealization is to be found in the primitive mind, any more than a belief about the purity of those who, in a negation of sex, avoid marriage altogether. There exists, in actuality, a common conviction that there is peril of a subtle sort connected with sex in woman; that she is "unclean" and dangerous to man—a notion traceable to a major source in religion.[74] Against such peril man seeks to protect himself, and particularly at the time of the first sexual relations sustained by a woman. Hence the performance of these first rites by some person such as a priest, whose position enables him to defy the mysterious danger. This is the defloration-custom, met with here and there around the world, and sometimes explained as a survival of communal rights in women. In the case of the *jus primæ noctis*, vested in some important personage, the latter—chief, lord, or priest—is thought to be the representative of a lapsing group-right.[75] This view seems to us highly speculative and as such was not included under the topic of survivals of group-marriage.

The case most often quoted is where the sisters of certain kings in India are deflowered by a man of the Nair caste. In such a case, the man is paid with rich presents and hangs a jewel about the girl's neck, "which she wears all the

---

[72] Starcke, *Prim. Fam.*, 171.   [73] Wilken, *Vkde.*, 294.

[74] §§374, 388, below; Sumner, *Coll. Ess.*, I, ch. III; Sumner, *Folkways*, §§559 ff.

[75] Lippert, *Kgchte.*, II, 11 ff.; Main, *Relig. Chastity*, Appendix, note XII; Letourneau, *Marriage*, ch. III; Letourneau, *Polit.*, 200. Other cases: Haddon, in JAI, L, 366; Miklucho-Maclay, in *Ztsft. f. Ethnol.*, XII, 89; Oliveira Martins, *Raças*, II, 26; Wilken, *Vkde.*, 294, 295; Wilken, in VG, I, 216, 217; Hrdlička, in BAE, Bull. XXXIV, 47; Herodotus, *Hist.*, IV, 68-70; Bruun, *Huleboerne*, 246; Saint-Martin, *Nord Afr.*, 43; Brunache, *Cent. Afr.*, 15; Reclus, *Prim. Folk*, 172-173; Wilken, *Vkde.*, 293 ff.; Stevens, in *Ztsft. f. Ethnol.*, XXVIII, 178; Nansen, *Esk. Life*, 168; Ratzel, *Vkde.*, II, 624; Bourke, in BAE, IX, 461; Von Martius, *Beiträge*, I, 113-114, 428, 485; Spix u. Martius, *Brasilien*, 1182; Cook, in AA, II, 479; Müller, *Sex. Leben*, 46, 47, 48.

rest of her life, as a token that she is now at liberty to dispose of herself to anyone she pleases as long as she lives.[76]

As for the specific *jus primæ noctis* (*droit du seigneur, droit de marquette*) of the mediæval lord, such an authority as Lea[77] says that it has been questioned without reasonable ground; and other specialists[78] agree with him as against those who variously explain it away.[79] Rudeck[80] states flatly that the *jus* existed *de jure* and *de facto*. Where serfs were at the mercy of their lords it is reasonable to suppose that any conceivable abuse may have existed; and in Russia and Poland, where all the abuses of the West were faithfully imitated, the "right" had wider extension than anywhere else. In many cases this practice as found in Europe does not go back to the notions that lay behind primitive defloration-customs and made the performance of the rites by the priest or other functionary a recompensed service rather than a "right."[81]

There is no "innate" feeling about chastity; the diverse convictions as to it are in the mores of the time and place as these have come into being with the evolution of the local societies. Alongside the laxity of some peoples is to be found in the code of others the most strenuous insistence upon chastity and virginity;[82] one of the most irrational and cruel tests of woman has been connected with the effort to establish her premarital virtue.

The chastity of a maiden and of a wife are two different things; also the conception of what is chaste varies widely in place and time. Proper sex-conduct for a woman does not always mean chastity of the unmarried as we understand it, while it generally does mean chastity of the wife as we conceive of that. It is not delicacy, it is sometimes even the brutal egoism of the man, that imposes restraint; the wife is "chastened for unauthorized unchastity but may be prostituted to the husband's profit."[83] Premarital license is generally followed by the requirement of strictest faithfulness in the wife. Starcke[84] believes that this requirement, coupled with very early marriage, is in part responsible for premarital chastity; the young girls must remain virgins because they are wives-to-be. This opinion is deserving of close attention, for it suggests the property-interest involved.

[76] Thurston, *S. India*, 127; Zimmer, *Altind. Leben*, 313.

[77] *Inquisition*, I, 269; Lea, *Sacerd. Celib.*, 354.

[78] Scherr, *Deut. Sittengchte.*, 237-238; Heusler, *Deut. Privatrecht*, I, 143; Schultz, *Deut. Leben*, 169; Wilutzky, *Mann u. Weib*, 41.

[79] Schmidt, *Jus Primæ Noctis;* Weinhold, *Deut. Frauen*, I, 300-301.

[80] *Oeffentl. Sittl.*, 144, 145.   [81] Starcke, *Prim. Fam.*, 125-127.

[82] Collection of cases in Westermarck, *Marriage*, II, 127 ff.

[83] Letourneau, *Morale*, 149-150; §383, below.

[84] *Prim. Fam.*, 212.

Ellis[85] holds that early betrothal led to chastity, for the betrothed girl is held virtually to wifely fidelity. "If, then, the great majority of girls were betrothed in childhood, it may readily be conceived that a notion might be formed that a bride ought to be a virgin, and be made of general application quite independent of betrothals. At present, the feeling of annoyance, which a Yoruba bridegroom experiences when he finds that his bride has been unchaste, is not due to jealousy or sentiment, but to a sense of injury, because his rights acquired by betrothal have been trespassed upon; but no doubt, in the course of time, the sentimental grievance would be produced. Whether this feeling ever extends to the lowest classes is uncertain, but at all events it has scarcely yet done so in Europe."

Finsch[86] says that wherever he went in New Guinea there "appeared the greatest morality and decency, in which respects Papuans could serve as shining examples to many civilized peoples"; conjugal morality is strict where the natives have not come into touch with civilization. "The Papuans regard the sexual relations as like other physical needs and make no artificial mystery of them; . . . as far as chastity goes, the Papuan girl can rival European maidens, educated as the latter are in artificial sham and prudery."[87] The Fijians and other islanders care much that a girl shall keep her virginity till marriage.[88] D'Entrecasteaux girls will not discard their grass-skirts, even in swimming.[89]

Bushwomen are superior in virtue to most of their less backward neighbors.[90] The Zulus are "mentally, morally, and physically, the superior native people of South Africa." They have an exceedingly high standard of morality, "the virtue of the women being a well known fact."[91] The Banziris of the Congo basin resist the strongest temptations; some cases of indecency in religious ceremonial are survivalistic.[92] "One at least of the Dwarf dances is grossly indecent in what it simulates, although it is danced reverently and as if the original *motif* had been forgotten and the gestures and writhings were merely traditional. Actually I never noticed any liking for deliberate indecency on the part of these Pygmies, who should certainly be described as strictly observing the ordinary decencies of life, perhaps rather punctiliously. Amongst themselves they are said to be very moral. Their women, however, soon degenerate into immorality when they come into contact with Sudanese or Swahilis. But even then they observe outward decorum and assume an affectation of prudishness."[93] In the "schools" where the African girls are taught to sing and dance, they learn that which "cannot be sung with honor, although they are chaste and modest in their daily conversations."[94] On meeting an African princess, Junker[95] was warned not to touch the bark fabric that enveloped her since this was "looked upon as a heavy insult." The Bahima

[85] *Yoruba*, 182.

[86] *Samoafahrten*, 81; Finsch, *Ethnol. Erfahr.*, II, 113.

[87] Miklucho-Maclay, in *Natuurkundig Tijdschrift voor Nederl.-Indië*, XXXVI, 298.

[88] Ratzel, *Vkde.*, II, 274.

[89] Jenness and Ballentyne, *D'Entrecasteaux*, 51.

[90] Fritsch, *Eingeb. S.-Afr.*, 444; Gentz, in *Globus*, LXXXIV, 158.

[91] Laidlaw, in *Amer. Antiquarian*, XXIV, 78 and ff.

[92] Clozel, in PSM, XLIX, 675.   [93] Johnston, *Uganda*, II, 543-544.

[94] Frobenius, *Masken*, 121, 122.   [95] *Reise*, III, 633.

are superior to their neighbors in morality "and there is generally chastity amongst the young women before marriage."[96]

In America, La Hontan[97] found that neither women nor men violated their marriage-duty. Indian girls were perfectly free and mistresses of themselves, but apparently without license. Mandan women were modest in deportment. "They were also noted for their virtue. This was regarded as an honorable and most valuable quality among the young women, and each year a ceremony was performed, in the presence of the whole village, at which time all the females who had preserved their virginity came forward, struck a post, and challenged the world to say aught derogatory to their character. . . . Mandan Indian women are beautiful and modest, and among the respectable families virtue is as highly cherished and as inapproachable as in any society whatever." The Omahas are even more careful. A young girl or even a married woman would incur suspicion by walking or riding alone. "No woman can ride or walk with any man but her husband or some immediate kinsman. She generally gets some other woman to accompany her, unless her husband goes. Young men are forbidden to speak to girls, if they should meet two or more on the road, unless they are kindred."[98] Likewise among the Cheyennes: "Under the most demoralizing and trying circumstances they have preserved in a remarkable degree that part of their moral code which relates to chastity, and public sentiment has been so strong in them in regard to this matter that they have been and still are noted among all the tribes which surround them for the virtue of their women."[99]

"Before the Pimas came into contact with 'civilization,' chastity was the rule among the young women, who were taught by compelling precept."[100] The sexual morality of the Seminoles "is a matter of common notoriety. The white half-breed does not exist among the Florida Seminole, and nowhere could I learn that the Seminole woman is other than virtuous and modest. The birth of a white half-breed would be followed by the death of the Indian mother at the hands of her own people. The only persons of mixed breed among them are children of Indian fathers by negresses who have been adopted into the tribe."[101] "There are no parents in all the world that guard their girls more carefully in order to preserve their chastity than the Thlingets of Alaska."[102] Though among most of the nations of Brazil virginity is not a matter of great moment, certain of them pay especial attention to it, exercising oversight "not over the maidens but over the young men."[103]

Among the aborigines of the Canary Islands, "one who lost her virtue was ostracized and for the rest of her life no one spoke to her."[104] In one district of the Balkans, "of a hundred swains among this simple people it would be hard to find ten who have had relations with a woman previous to their marriage; for, aside from the fact that it is held to be a sin, it is regarded among the people as the greatest shame for a young man."[105] In Albania the menace of the blood-feud stops all premarital looseness. The young man is not allowed

[96] Johnston, *Uganda*, II, 630.
[97] *Voy. dans l'Amér.*, II, 132.
[98] Dorsey, in BAE, III, 365.
[99] Mooney, in BAE, XIV, 1027.
[100] Russell, in BAE, XXVI, 182.
[101] MacCauley, in BAE, V, 479.
[102] Jones, *Thlingets*, 215.
[103] Von Martius, *Beiträge*, I, 112; Ehrenreich, in *Berl. Mus. Vkde.*, II, 28.
[104] Cook, in AA, II, 480.
[105] Rhamm, in *Globus*, LXXXII, 187.

to make love to the girls of his own tribe and if he approaches those of a neighboring tribe, the blood-feud ensues.[106] Our own mores of the present and recent past in regard to female and male chastity are well enough known.[107]

There is discoverable in our cases no exclusive or even regular correlation between insistence upon female chastity and anything else. Difference of code may appear where conditions of life seem to be practically uniform, as between two neighboring tribes; the presence of the father-family can offer no complete explanation of the custom, though it seems to be more generally and firmly enforced under that system, for chastity may be required under the mother-family and not under the other type; there is something in the correspondence of early betrothals, where there are such, and chastity, but not enough for very broad generalization. If the absence of definite, clean-cut correlations were decisive, we should be obliged to take the cases as facts, reference of which to a specific cause or set of causes is as yet impossible. Certainly the very variety of these cases reveals the difficulty and uncertainty of adjustments in matters related with sex and marriage. But there are certain wider aspects to the matter.

General evolutionary considerations readily explain the survival-value of chastity, as will presently be seen, once it is thrown into the arena as a variation; still it is always desirable, if possible, to indicate the provenance of such a variation. It seems reasonable to suspect that it came to be imposed along with the sharpening of the conception of property; one who has been impressed with the intimacy of the relationship between property and marriage naturally looks to that fact-derived and repeatedly fact-verified correlation when he faces a tangle like the one before us. Is not the chastity-taboo a parallel to the property-taboo? Let us first note the conditions attendant upon a strict application of the former. The common insistence upon fidelity in a wife, explicable as it is by reason of the fact that unfaithfulness results in property-complications incident to illegitimacy, is plainly a property-taboo.[108] That a man, especially where the *patria potestas* is marked, by owning his wife owns also her offspring, is sufficiently attested;[109] and, in such case, he is generally found to be highly resentful of any infringement upon his rights over his daughters

---

[106] Lane, *Shala,* 155.
[108] §384, below.

[107] Sumner, *Folkways,* ch. IX.
[109] §§381, 404, 409, 419, below.

or of any assumption by them of rights over themselves. He may allow what he wishes; he may assign them in hospitality to a guest; but he is very jealous of his authority. He sells them, with specifications explicit or understood as to their quality, and he is responsible in a definite, material way if they do not measure up to the specifications; he must replace a daughter who proves, on accepted tests, not to be satisfactory, or restore the price paid for her. Where daughters are property, even though they may resist by elopement, and where the conception of property has been sharpened into a pretty definite shape, the taboo against trespass reaches beyond a prohibition of mere abduction, which was early resented as an invasion of rights, to include sex-relations, unless these are expressly permitted by the father or other owner.

It cannot be demonstrated that the demand for chastity came from the suitor's side; it is more likely to have been prescribed from that of the father, as an extended safeguard to property. The inference is suggested, and writers have flown to embrace it, that chastity must have come in with the father-family.[110] The evidence available to us does not establish that position with any security, though cases of chastity under the patriarchate preponderate. As we see it, the daughter was tabooed by the authority over her, whether that was a man in possession of the *patria potestas* or somebody else. No corresponding prohibition was called for in the case of sons, for there was no sexual trespass that could be committed against them. Daughters were required to be chaste because of a developing sense of property-right in those who owned them. Those were the powerful who alone had a chance to make finer definitions of rights, thus satisfying their interests the better. Chastity, at first observed out of fear of punishment, came to be the mode and was then practised to win public approval.[111] Thus have many variations been set afloat; then they have been concurred in by lesser men, and if they have subserved the broad interests of society they have prevailed, carrying with them the conviction of their expediency and of the folly and sin of any other course of action.

The origin of the chastity-taboo must be inferential, but there

110 Lippert, *Kgchte.*, II, 87 ff.   111 Wilken, in VG, I, 194-195.

is nothing such about its expediency as revealed in the course of societal evolution. Here again it appears that a custom which is shocking to us has its share in the development of something else that we highly approve; bride-purchase is broadly correlative with premarital chastity.[112] Our approval or the reverse does not signify; it is the fact of the matter to which attention is called. Taking the long perspective of society's evolution into account, it may be said that insistence upon chastity goes with advancing civilization. While we may not know exactly how that policy was initiated, evidently it has been, in general, an expedient variation. As compared with unregulation, the restriction imposed has been, like others that have been and will be considered, superior in the interests of society; and it is not impossible to see why. For one thing, the imposition of premarital chastity militated against premature sex-relations and child-bearing, thus conserving vital forces for individual and society. And then, more broadly, it did for society something on the order of what marriage did:[113] it prevented irresponsibility and contributed to orderliness of social relations as respects property, inheritance, kinship-bonds, and legitimacy in general. In fact, the imposition of chastity is really one of the ways of safeguarding and defining the marriage-relation and the family; and if these latter are expedient, the imposition of chastity is called for as a supporting factor. It is a case of the maiden's status being set by that of the wife. Above all, perhaps, chastity was expedient as a discipline over sex-passion —as part, again, of the regulation exercised by the general institution of marriage of which, indeed, it is one manifestation. Discipline creates character, here as in other ranges. The requirement of chastity means that women and therefore men also, to some degree, must wait for marriage and may exercise their sex-functions only in the regular, authorized, and tested way. In that disciplinary respect alone it exhibits undoubted survival-value.

Some tribes, and they are of the lowest, restrict sex-relations but slightly, either in marriage or prior to it; others insist upon regulation in marriage but allow license beforehand (our cases showing no instances of the reverse of this); still others refuse license in any case. It follows that insistence upon premarital

112 Lippert, *Kgchte.*, II, 119.   113 Ch. XLI, above.

chastity is, as it were, an extension of marital regulation into the preparatory stage. All cases do not fall into this classification and into one based upon degree of civilization at the same time; in spite of that, however, and of the fact that there is always an oscillation between restriction and freedom, tightening and loosening, the evidence from racial evolution supports the policy of institution-building through restriction, in the premarital stage as well as in the status of matrimony.

Where people prize premarital chastity, they have been wont to adopt severe methods for securing and testing it. Girls are not merely secluded—a familiar process—but actually caged.

In New Britain, girls of the poorer classes wear a fringe across the shoulders until they are marriageable, while rich girls are veritably caged until that age in huts admitting no light and little air. There they stay for four or five years, in a cramped position, watched over by an old woman, and may be seen only by their own relations. They are taken out when fourteen or fifteen.[114] Similar cages are utilized in New Ireland, and the price of the girls is enhanced by the ordeal.[115] Seclusion is even more complete in some places in Borneo, amounting to solitary confinement. Physical development suffers by it; when freed, the girl appears bleached light yellow as though made of wax, and tottering on small, thin feet, which, according to native taste, is considered especially beautiful. This seclusion is not solely to secure chastity but also "to endow the daughter with the above-named pretty qualities, to make her name renowned, and at the same time through this to attract many rich suitors."[116] In Fiji, "when the time approached for young ladies of rank to be married, they were 'forbidden the sun' (tambu singa), that is to say, they were confined to the house for months so that they should not be exposed to the sun." The writer[117] thinks this was to preserve them from becoming prematurely the brides of the sun and cites the passage from Hamlet:[118] "Let her not walk i' the sun; conception is a blessing; but not as your daughter might conceive." In the Gilbert Islands there was a bleaching-process for the whitening of the girl's skin before she should become a bride. "After a few months of such treatment, in a seclusion which no sunray ever pierced, the rich and dusky olive tint left her skin, and she became pale with the dark paleness of some Spanish lady, who never leaves her house until sunset. . . . The whole idea underlying the bleaching process is closely connected with a race-memory of certain ancestral gods who, like the famous Tangaroa of Polynesia, were fair of skin and of a marvellous beauty."[119] As this illustration indicates, there were diverse or mixed motives for these seclusion-practices.

As for the preservation of virginity, there were devices even more drastic, involving operations on the body. The testing of the bride's virginity at marriage is often brutal in the extreme, besides being worth nothing as a proof;

[114] Danks, in JAI, XVIII, 284-286.   [115] Finsch, Ethnol. Erfahr., I, 145.
[116] Schwaner, Borneo, 77; Roth, Sarawak, II, cxcix.
[117] Hocart, in JAI, XLIX, 48.   [118] Act II, scene ii.
[119] Grimble, in JAI, LI, 42-43.

it is a striking case of the misery men have made for themselves by following in ignorance various notions that got into the folkways. In connection with this test at marriage there are precautions taken to avoid deception and other procedure is exhibited which savors more of a horse-trade than a marriage in our sense. The amount of suffering caused by the faithful accomplishment of these tests, which are no tests at all, followed by the dissolution of the union, persecution, and even execution, in case chance is against the girl, can be imagined.[120] Nevertheless it must not be lost sight of that the women themselves accept these tests and even confess misdemeanors that they never perpetrated when the evidence goes against them. They are in much the same state of mind as the mediæval persons who confessed that they had ridden through the air on broomsticks, had had intercourse with the devil, and other impossibilities, though they knew that a cruel death would follow upon their admissions.[121]

§367*. Courtship. Preceding betrothal comes, in modern mores, the period of courtship or wooing. This is a time of adjustment or even of test and trial, during which the parties can come, through greater intimacy, to some conclusion as to their mutual suitability and be the readier to face the inevitable further adjustments that attend upon the most intimate of all human relations. Courtship tests out the more delicate qualities, like good-breeding, which law and custom cannot handle but the presence or absence of which means everything to a marriage. This is, however, a modern development and is not represented to any considerable extent among primitives. Albeit special liking between the sexes has existed at all stages, it has had relatively little to do with marriage as an institution; indeed, it has often crossed and thwarted the latter. Considerations other than the concrete ones of working-power, property, and the like, which need no period of courtship to test, did not enter into the minds of those contemplating alliances, the less by reason of the fact that the contracting parties were often not the principals to the marriage at all. In child-marriages, not to mention those of the unborn or of the dead, the idea of courtship is incongruous. Hence the only regular antecedent to the betrothal is the proposal. Whatever relations

---

[120] Typical virginity-tests in Ellis, *Ewe*, 155-157; Ellis, *Yoruba*, 153-154; Nachtigal, *Sahara*, I, 738; Paulitschke, *Nordost-Afr.*, I, 201; Burckhardt, *Arabic Proverbs*, 114; Von Hahn, in *Globus*, LXXXVI, 32; Ratzel, *Vkde.*, II, 182; Gubernatis, *Usi Nuz.*, 235; Zimmer, *Altind. Leben*, 311; Kostomarov, *Gt. Russ.* (Russ.), 246; *Russian Ethnog.* (Russ.), II, 482; Letourneau, *Marr.*, 239.

[121] Sumner, *Coll. Ess.*, I, ch. IV.

of special intimacy may have existed between a young man and woman preceding an actual proposition are not to be distinguished in any special way. Only occasionally does anything like courtship appear. It will give a better picture of primitive courtship, such as it is, to set down the cases available along with those of proposal.

Before doing so, however, we wish to treat briefly of a custom which, because of some superficial similarities, has been aligned with trial-marriage, namely, *bundling,* or *tarrying.*[122] In its typical form it is really a species of courtship imposed by conditions of climate and housing; and it does hint at the kinship between courtship and trial-marriage. The only privacy available was at night or, in winter, in the unheated rooms of a cold house. In the latter case the lovers lay down together and covered themselves up.

Peters[123] says it was, in New England, a chaste Puritan habit and speaks strongly of the character of the Puritan girl, which resisted harmful consequences. Where lovers used the sofa in summer courtship, he says, they bundled in winter; and the latter was not so bad as the former. Old women were scandalized by preachers who inveighed against it. "The custom prevails amongst all classes to the great honor of the country, its religion, and ladies." Though the clergy thought bundling produced evil results, it was not until the end of the Revolution that the custom received its death-blow; and it died hard. Larger, better, and warmer houses were unfavorable to it. In 1788 a ballad in an almanac brought it under popular ridicule.[124]

Analogies, partial analogies, and alleged analogies to bundling are to be found in ethnography and history. In India there was a custom recalling "what is called bundling in Wales. The young man and girl, being together for the night, the girl is questioned next morning by her relatives whether she is pleased with her husband-elect. If she answers in the affirmative, it is a marriage; if not, the young man is immediately dismissed and the girl does not suffer in reputation if she thus discards half a dozen suitors."[125] The Afghans have a custom called the betrothal-game, like the custom known in Wales as bundling. The night is passed in "innocent endearments."[126] Among certain tribes of Farther India, courtship is carried on at night through holes cut in the floor or wall of the girls' sleeping-chambers. "Occasionally, if a horse or a buffalo is tethered under the house, a young man will mount on its back and have a comfortable seat while he does his courting. . . .The girls have distinctly the best of the game, as the young man is sometimes hanging in a precarious position outside in the cold night wind . . . while the girl, cosily wrapped in her blankets, squats in the house."[127]

122 Sumner, *Folkways,* §§576 ff.   123 *Hist. of Connecticut,* 325.
124 Stiles, *Bundling,* 75, 80; Burnaby, *Travels,* 144.
125 Thurston, *S. India,* 62.   126 Gomme, *Village Life,* 220.
127 Milne, *Eastern Clan,* 121-122, and ch. V, in general.

Among the Sea Dyaks, the girls receive their male visitors at night. "They sleep apart from their parents, sometimes in the same room, more often in the loft. The young men are not invited to sleep with them unless they are old friends, but they may sit with them and chat; if they get to be fond of each other after a short acquaintance and wish to make a match of it, they are united in marriage provided the parents on either side have no objections to offer. It is in fact the only way open to the man and woman to become acquainted with each other, as privacy during the daytime is out of the question in a Dyak village." If the parents do not like the man, "they use their influence with their daughter to ensure the utterance of the fatal, 'Please blow up the fire.'" It is said on good authority that these nocturnal visits but seldom result in immorality, for the Dyak girl is modest;[128] if the young man "dare to take a liberty with her person, she is sure to give an alarm and her relatives appear."[129] La Hontan[130] says of the Indians of Canada that if the lover is welcome when he pays a night visit, the woman blows out the light; if she covers her head, he withdraws. If she should have a child she would never be married. An analogy to bundling, which the author says arose from the lack of communications and winter storms that made it impossible to go home late, is reported from the Ukraine.[131] The custom of "Nachtschwärmen" or "nattloppen" (night-running) is charged with the fostering of immorality in Lappmark.[132]

Analogous practices occurred all over Europe under chivalry and the custom persisted among the peasantry, where it is often the betrothal, or leads to it.[133] "The German custom of spending continent nights before marriage in the arms of the intended is very old"; later the continence was in evidence only for a time.[134] In Holland of the seventeenth century there existed a similar practice called "queesten," which is aligned with Swiss, Tyrolese, German, Norwegian, and Swedish customs. But rarely did any harm result.[135] Night-wooing occurred in Scotland and is reported as having been universal amongst agricultural laborers. "Their daughters must have husbands and there is no other way of courting." "They have no other means of intercourse." It is against custom for a man to visit his sweetheart in the day-time.[136] In Wales in 1797 lovers practised bundling as they might take a walk, in the daytime, unblushingly and as a matter of course. Night-wooing by bundling was due to cold.[137]

Evidently there is here a case of adjustment of the mores, involving a practice that is approved and need not be attended with ill-results so long as it remains an inevitable or expedient adjust-

---

[128] Roth, *Sarawak*, I, 109; Gomes, *Sea Dyaks*, 120, 121.
[129] Roth, in JAI, XXI, 120.   [130] *Voy. dans Amér.*, II, 133.
[131] Krasinski, *Cossacks*, 281.
[132] Weis, in *Globus*, LXXVIII, 228.
[133] Weinhold, *Deut. Frauen*, I, 260, 261, 263, 264.
[134] Rudeck, *Oeffentl. Sittl.*, 146, 404, 405.
[135] Scheltema, *Vrijen*, 59-60; Schotel, *Huisgezin*, 228-229; Wilken, in VG, I, 513; Rhamm, in *Globus*, LXXXII, 324.
[136] *Royal Comm. on Marriage*, 1868, 172.
[137] Stiles, *Bundling*, 25 (where several primary sources are cited).

ment. Among Europeans, as among Dyaks, it disappeared as no longer needed when the conditions that summoned it into being had altered.

Courtship, as noted, is generally no more than a proposal; proposal is sometimes the single and sole act of courtship. When offered by parents or elders it contains nothing at all of courtship; nevertheless the immediate parties, including the woman, have more to say about a marriage, even among savages, than we are usually given to understand. Courtship is rather incidental, however, as the following cases will reveal. Illustrations of proposal show chiefly gifts of property and above all of food, the acceptance of which means consent. Such cases are so common that they are here reduced in favor of other types of proposal.

Though the Papuans do some "moonlight caressing," the official wooing takes place through the mother. The youth rolls a cigar which he smokes "solemnly half through and gives the stump to his mother with the request to deliver it to his heart's choice. Next morning the answer is obtained. If the girl has smoked up the stump, it means yes but if she gives it back intact, that means no. The latter, I think, occurs seldom, for before the youth sends the cigar-stump everything is usually arranged and smoothed out, both between the lovers and their parents." This proposal is a solemn act for which the lover prepares himself beforehand according to the rules for preparation for circumcision.[138] In the Solomon group, "a man wanting a wife cooks a dish full of yams and cocoa-nuts, and carries it to the house of the bride-elect, returning without having said a word. The next morning he goes after the dish. If the food has not been eaten, he is not accepted, and this he takes as an insult; if the bowl is empty and a couple of fathoms of money has been put in it, he is not accepted either, but is desired to be on friendly terms with the family. If the dish is entirely empty, he is accepted." Feasts by the groom and by the bride's parents make up most of the ceremony at marriage.[139]

The Chukchi display a sort of post-marriage courtship; they have "a custom of marrying young children, who then grow up together and are very much attached to one another later on, when they are actually married. This is the case in marriages between relatives or between members of two friendly families." They also marry a mere boy to an older woman. "The most curious side of this custom is that the age of the persons whose relatives marry them by exchange is of no account. . . . In some cases of this kind the wife may have a male 'marriage-companion,' and, having a child of her own, nurse it and her contracted husband together. This is done, as the Chukchee say, 'to ensure the love of the young husband in the future.' "[140]

The Algonquin, if his relatives and friends were willing, was permitted to offer his suit. Provided with a prepared pelt, he went to his prospective bride's dwelling and placed the skin at the back of it. If the girl's relatives had no

138 Hagen, *Papua's*, 241-242.   139 Elton, in JAI, XVII, 94.
140 Czaplicka, *Aborig. Siberia*, 72.

objection, her father ordered her to seat herself on the skin as a sign that the suit was acceptable.[141] Dakota courting "is always done in the evening and in the lodge. If the attentions of the young man are disagreeable to the young woman, she will get up and blow up the fire. The young man takes the hint and retires. If, on the contrary, she should be willing, she lets the fire alone."[142] Among certain coastal Indians of British Columbia, the wooing-customs include a four-days' fast of the lover.[143] In one Brazilian district, the man goes alone or with relatives, with presents for the girl's father. If the latter "takes several puffs from the cigar of the suitor's most eminent relative, or blows the smoke dignifiedly into the air, the suit has a favorable outcome." Elsewhere the wooing takes place through the suitor appearing, for several days, painted from head to foot and armed, before the hut of the chosen girl.[144]

In proposal there are a number of symbolic acts, which are echoed still, in expressions signifying rejection of a suit: to "get the mitten," "get the basket" (Korb bekommen), or "get the melon."[145]

By exception the proposal comes from the woman. Where the woman is higher in rank than the man, she must take the initiative; a queen may not be proposed to like an ordinary woman. Difference in rank does not, however, account for cases like the following. Among the Torres Straits tribes, "it is the usual, if not the invariable custom for the women to propose marriage to the men," but in the exchange of presents and food the groom's friends have to give the larger amount and he pays a bride-price. There may be some fighting, not very serious, between the girl's people and the man's. It was rather general that the husband should go to live with the bride's family.[146] A missionary-taught girl's proposal, written to one Peter and shown to an English scientist, reads: "Peta, what do you say? I try you. My heart he like very bad for you. You send me back a letter. Yes this talk belong me. Pita you Good-bye. Me Mageria." Peter replies: "Mageria I make you know. Me just the same, I want very bad for you. My talk there. If you true like me, all right just the same; good for you, good for me. Yes all right. Finish. You, Mageria. Good-bye. Me Pita."[147]

In the Ukraine, "when a young female has conceived an attachment for a youth, she goes to the house of his parents, where she tells the young man, in the presence of his parents, that 'the kindness she beholds depicted in his countenance, and the good qualities of his heart, inspire her with the hope that he will prove a good husband, and under this impression she has come to beg he will accept her as his wife.' If this initiatory announcement meets with hesitation or coldness on the part of the parents or their son, she sometimes renews her solicitation, either immediately or after the lapse of a few days; and then, if the young man assents to her proposal, the parents believe they would expose themselves to the wrath of heaven, should they withhold their compliance."[148] Cases occur in Bengal where the woman asks and the

[141] Leland and Prince, *Kulóskap*, 355.
[142] Beckwith, in *Smithson. Rep.*, 1886, pt. I, 256.
[143] Hill-Tout, *Brit. N. Amer.*, 183.
[144] Von Martius, *Beiträge*, I, 114, 217.
[145] Sienkiewicz, *Pan Michael*, 84.
[146] Haddon, in JAI, XIX, 356, 394.
[147] Hardy and Elkington, *S. Seas*, 43, 44.
[148] Krasinski, *Cossacks*, 250.

man cannot easily decline. On the wedding-morning he hides and is sought out by the bridesmen. "When found they wash him and lead him away, weeping as he goes, to his new home with his mother-in-law." The Zuñi girl also takes the initiative.[149] Among the Tarahumari of Mexico, "of marriage ceremonies there are few. The woman seeks the man."[150]

§368*. Betrothal. Many tribes have betrothal-customs which are in the nature of accessories to the making of a contract. "Where marriage is universally by purchase or exchange, there appears the betrothal, that is, the setting of the two individuals into relation with each other prior to the marriage."[151] This is the general sense of the custom in many cases also where marriage is otherwise than by purchase or exchange. Betrothal is often at so tender an age as to eliminate courtship altogether. The negotiations and ceremonies connected with it serve as a sort of rough synopsis of the marriage-preliminaries. As the parties are often strictly segregated from one another, the period of betrothal often bears no resemblance at all to our own form.

Among the Australians a young girl is betrothed in childhood to an old man; she is regarded as his property and violation of his rights in her, unless with his consent, is regarded as adultery.[152] Because of this peculiar custom of betrothing the young to the old, a young man has difficulty in getting a mature woman unless it is the widow of a dead elder brother. "A curious custom in regard to hair is associated with what may be described as a form of betrothal ceremony"; portions cut from the beard are exchanged as guarantees that the man whose beard is cut will give the man who receives the cutting, which he carries beneath his arm-band, his sister's daughter to wife. Sometimes the betrothal is effected through an intermediary, as there is a "strongly marked avoidance of son-in-law and father-in-law"; the father of the girl may place his child's arm in her future husband's hand, as an emblem of betrothal, and then receive presents from him; but "after this they do not look at one another." "At times, each woman has to present her hair to the man who is betrothed to her daughter, for the purpose of making him a waistbelt."[153]

In Melanesia it is the custom for girls to be betrothed at birth and grow up in the house of the betrothed;[154] a boy and girl are often betrothed by their parents at a very early age, and grow up recognizing each other as man and wife; and the boy's father works for the girl's father to cover the payment.[155] In the Loyalty Islands such a betrothal could be annulled by the man

149 Tylor, in *Nineteenth Cent.*, XL, 88.
150 Lumholtz, in *Inter. Cong. Anthrop.*, 1893, 107.
151 Hagen, *Papua's*, 224.   152 Ratzel, *Vkde.*, II, 68.
153 Spencer and Gillen, *North Tr. Cent. Aust.*, 504, 603, 77, note; Spencer and Gillen, *Nat. Tr. Cent. Aust.*, 40.
154 Ratzel, *Vkde.*, II, 274.
155 Guise, in JAI, XXVIII, 208; Codrington, *Melanesians*, 241, note.

through the payment of a fine.[156] In one place in New Guinea the following instance occurred: "The natives said that a man had refused to carry out a marriage which had been arranged by the parents. They said that by their custom the woman's friends had a right of damaging the man's gardens. They inquired if I, as resident magistrate, would sanction the custom. The unwilling bridegroom agreed that it was the custom, but that in this instance it should not be carried out because it was the woman who had refused to carry out the contract. A suggestion on my part that if they were both willing, they had better solve the difficulty by marrying, clearly pleased neither party. I then made it understood that if the garden was damaged I would accept a complaint from the man and treat it as a court case. On my next visit to the village I found that the garden had been damaged but the man declined to make any complaint."[157] This case illustrates both the binding nature of a betrothal and the tendency of the savage, even against his personal interest, to abide by the mores.

A curious variation of betrothal is shown in East Central Africa: "Two kinds of marriage are known: (a) Child marriage: a little boy, of his own free will, may declare that a certain little girl is his wife; by this simple act he acquires a prescriptive right to her. He visits his future parents-in-law and takes them insignificant presents. When he is of mature age, he gives a larger present, of the value of about 2,000 *djimbu* [shells], and then he is allowed to cohabit with her. Their children belong to the eldest maternal uncle. This form of marriage is attended by no special ceremony. If the girl, when of age, is unwilling, he cannot coerce her, but if she marries another man, the latter must make him a present of several thousand *djimbu*." Evidently this is a rude sort of betrothal and not a marriage, as the author denominates it. The other variety of union, adult marriage, is simply purchase of the usual order, where ten to fifteen thousand *djimbu* are paid to the owner, father or maternal uncle, of the girl.[158]

Among the Nagas, "the children of rich men are sometimes betrothed before they reach puberty, and though in such cases the actual marriage sometimes takes place before puberty, it is more common for a betrothal to take place and the marriage to follow when the parties are of a suitable age. . . . Such early marriages usually take place for more or less political reasons."[159] Wilken[160] treats of betrothal in the Indian Archipelago: he says that child-marriages are to be strictly distinguished from child-betrothals, that it is doubtful whether there was the same aim in both. In many places in the East Indies the girls are very loose of life before they are betrothed or married and the betrothal amounts to a taboo upon license. When they are betrothed, the parents watch them, and if there is any irregularity the girl's relatives have to pay damages to the groom's. Betrothal takes place not only before birth but before there is any prospect of a child at all.

Go-betweens, or marriage-brokers, are found in several lands. They are regularly employed among the Palaungs of Farther India.[161] In China betrothment is entirely in the parent's hands, and they use as a medium certain people "who are expected to be well acquainted with the character and circumstances of

[156] Creagh, in AAAS, 1892, 680; Ella, in AAAS, 1892, 627.
[157] Strong, in JAI, XLIX, 301.
[158] Torday and Joyce, in JAI, XXXV, 410.
[159] Hutton, *Sema Nagas*, 239.   [160] In VG, I, 473 ff.
[161] Milne, *Eastern Clan*, ch. VI and 400 ff.

the parties. Mothers sometimes contract their unborn progeny on the sole contingency of a difference of sex, but the usual age of forming these engagements is ten, twelve, or older, experience having shown that the casualties attending it render an earlier period undesirable."[162] Among the Armenians "the parents of the groom choose the bride and apply for her through a go-between, sometimes through the clergyman, who goes to the house of the bride with a lighted candle, which they take if they accept the proposal." Betrothal takes place without the presence of bride and groom, by the clergyman.[163] Other Armenians practise child-betrothal, babe-betrothal, and even antenatal betrothal.[164]

The betrothal-ring was used in ancient Rome; and the usage came thence to Germany. Siegfried is represented as exchanging rings with Brunhilde after sleeping with her three nights with a naked sword between them. In the Sagas, Olaf Trygvason sends one to Sigrid. The ring was used in the betrothal of Kaiser Otto, in 1209. The poems in general speak of the ring, with questions covering consent and will; the circle confirmed the arrangement. In Scandinavia the betrothed woman was taken on the knee—a common symbol of adoption—showing that she came into the power of the man as a child was in that of his father.[165] In Bulgarian custom, "the exchange of rings had binding force and it was regarded as a great disgrace to break a betrothal." Marriage followed speedily upon it, the wedding itself playing no especially essential rôle; the chief consideration was "that the parents or relatives give their consent or ultimately close up the business in accord with the prescription of custom."[166] In Albania there is a belief that Heaven protects betrothed persons more than others, and this leads to child-betrothal as a species of insurance; even antenatal betrothal occurs.[167]

The question whether betrothal confers the rights of marriage has been variously answered in different places and times. That women who have grown up in the belief that it does may be overreached and ruined by scoundrels has offered a theme for story-writers. In the old German law there was no distinction between betrothal and marriage: the distinction came in when the church was insisting strenuously upon its coöperation in marriage.[168] It is stated by others that the betrothed were throughout distinguished from the married and the betrothal from the marriage; that the infidelity of the bride was not regarded as adultery.[169] The Corsican youth seldom returns home the night of the betrothal. The subsequent civil and religious contract and ceremony merely ratify the betrothal-engagement. It is nothing unusual for the bride to have had a child or to be pregnant at marriage. "If the man dies before marriage, the children of the voluntary union are treated as fully legitimate, and are entitled to their due share of the inheritance, while the girl

[162] Williams, *Middle Kingdom*, I, 785.
[163] *Russian Ethnog.* (Russ.), II, 337.
[164] Seidlitz, in *Globus*, LXXVIII, 243, 244.
[165] Grimm, *Rechtsalt.*, 177, 178, 432, 433; Friedberg, *Eheschliess.*, 26-27, note; Weinhold, *Deut. Frauen*, I, 343; Gubernatis, *Usi Nuz.*, 102-103, 106, 165.
[166] Strauss, *Bulgaren*, 310.
[167] Peschel, *Vkde.*, 227; Lane, *Shala*, 41.
[168] Hagelstange, *Süddeut. Bauernleben*, 60, 61, 62; Schroeder, *Geschlechtl. Ordnung*, 53.
[169] Lehmann, *Verlobung*, 100, 102.

wears mourning and is regarded as a widow."[170] Modern conceptions of betrothal tend toward its entire differentiation from marriage.[171]

Several of the foregoing preliminaries to marriage have had their religious aspects, though the bulk of them are exhibitions of economic preoccupation. Food and property have been in evidence over and over again, indeed, and a perspective of the cases leaves one in the position of wondering whether, after all, marriage ought not to be classified as a form of societal self-maintenance. The religious idea will be seen to be present in greater intensity as we work on into the matrimonial status; it is not unrepresented, however, in specific preliminary ceremonials.

The period of betrothal is not seldom one of taboo on all relations between the betrothed. It is reasonable to interpret this inhibition as a precaution against premarital relations; yet the taboo as such always has a religious sanction[172] and definite religious scruple appears now and then. In New Guinea, "the time from the betrothal to the wedding is a really painful one for the pair, as they must have absolutely no relations with one another. So soon as they meet by chance they must turn their faces from each other; to smile or even speak with one another would be a misdeed."[173] Among very many East Indian tribes, the betrothed must not see one another at all during the betrothal-period, even though they have been previously free and intimate and though they both desire the marriage. As to the behavior during betrothal, the practice is one that does not allow, like ours, of the parties learning to know one another. Not only is there no courting, but the man and girl do not see or address each other; the parents attend to this. If the bride-to-be sees her affianced coming, she must get behind a tree or bush till he has gone by; if it is impossible to do this, as at sea, they must keep their heads averted. The girl must simulate repugnance to the young husband after marriage, and the author thinks that this custom has been carried back into the premarital period. In some cases there is more freedom; indeed, there may be a long engagement which may degenerate into concubinage; again, there is a sort of trial-marriage during the period after betrothal. Examples of all these forms are cited. The author[174] reporting this seems to think it a pretense of dislike and unwillingness on the part of the woman. Again, "the too familiar intercourse of betrothed persons is prohibited under the penalty of fine."[175] In Sumatra, even though the betrothal-period is a couple of years, the avoidance of meeting must be observed; if one sees the other approaching, he must take another way.[176] Among the Igorrotes, if a man should speak to his affianced before marriage it would be a gross violation of propriety and would cause the betrothal to be dissolved.[177] In Moslem Asia, among the half-civilized classes, "it sometimes occurs that the young man finds opportunity to cast a fleeting glance upon his future wife;

[170] Vuillier, Forgotten Isles, 240.
[171] Roguin, Mariage, 27, 28, 33.
[172] §268, above.
[173] Hagen, Papua's, 242.
[174] Wilken, in VG, I, 473-475, 523 ff.
[175] Roth, Sarawak, II, clxxxi.
[176] Jacobs, Groot-Atjeh, I, 40.
[177] Blumentritt, Igorroten, 95.

they arrange such meetings, though they are not allowed by the religion. I say a glance, for intercourse in words is unheard of." In view of this custom, the author[178] thinks, "the happy outcome of so many marriages must indeed seem a miracle." Among the Kazan Tatars separation of the betrothed is common.[179] Separation is unusual among the Slavs, but sometimes the betrothed bride remains two or three weeks under strict guard of the groom's sister, "who takes no step from her side."[180] The Ossetins of the Caucasus allow a man to see his betrothed only secretly, incidentally, or in the house of his relatives. It would be the grossest insult to ask him whether she is well or when the wedding will be.[181]

Premarital taboos are better understood when aligned with others that accompany the wedding and the early days of matrimony.[182] If the significance of marriage is such as to demand all the various preliminaries now before us, it is evident that people will not enter the state without an attempt to discover the will of the spirits. Here is a place where, even with the best calculation based upon the fullest data of a material order, the presence of the aleatory element is inevitable. It will have been noted that there is sometimes a marriage-broker[183] to refer to, who acquaints each party with the physical, mental, and moral qualities of the other and does all he can to effect a successful conclusion. He is sometimes the barber, as in British India, and again a special priest-like functionary, as among the Ghetto Jews.[184] But even his experience and shrewdness cannot be trusted to cope with the whole perilous situation. Besides all the religious and magical ceremonial which appears in connection with entrance upon wedlock, there is also some preliminary testing of the case by noting the omens, casting horoscopes, and the like, before the wedding. A few examples will serve to hold this aspect of the matter in mind until it can be taken up more thoroughly.[185]

A joint trading-journey is a novel and perhaps clever expedient for testing the luck of the proposed marriage. Among the Naga the couple go on such an expedition for twenty days. "If a fair profit is made, the omen is good and

[178] Vámbéry, *Sittenbilder*, 35-36.
[179] *Russian Ethnog.* (Russ.), II, 18.
[180] Rhamm, in *Globus*, LXXXII, 188.
[181] *Russian Ethnog.* (Russ.), II, 355.
[182] §§373, 374, 378, below.
[183] Saunderson, in JAI, XXIV, 305.
[184] Baden-Powell, *Land Syst.*, I, 151, note; Zangwill, *Ghetto*, 23, 80, 124; Antin, *Promised Land*, 34, 35.
[185] §§372 ff., below.

the marriage arrangements are proceeded with, but if the results are unfavorable the match is at once broken off."[186] This case might be classified,
perhaps, as a test of the man and woman and their ability to coöperate. If,
after a Hindu marriage is resolved upon, any relative of the bride or groom
dies, the omen is bad and the alliance not concluded. "It was thought that the
untoward occurrence foreboded either the death of the bridegroom or the barrenness of the bride."[187] A further set of omens was derived from the stock
source of the dream. "After the departure of the female go-between, the
parents of the bride begin to gather information about the groom, his property, his character, and so on, and they also pay the *mollah* [priest] a ruble
with the request that he record his next night's dream and interpret it. The
next morning they get from the *mollah* the explanation and interpretation of
his dream."[188] In Tibet, as in China, astrologers are consulted to see that the
horoscopes of the man and woman do not antagonize and "if the good and evil
of the life of the male harmonize in the calculation with those of the life of the
female, longevity is counted upon. If not, the happiness of the couple will be
short-lived." The formal proposal must be on an auspicious day during the
increasing lunation of the month. Domestic deities are propitiated before the
bride leaves for her husband's house and on her arrival there a ceremony is
performed to drive away all evil spirits that may have accompanied her from
her parents' house. She then gets a new name that is connected in some manner
with that of her mother-in-law.[189]

Out of the foregoing chapters on preliminaries to marriage
there is one general and covering consideration to be disengaged,
and that is the essential solidarity of the family. In a sense, it is
the family that marries, though in the person of the delegated individual. Regular marriage is a group-matter because the common
corporate maintenance-interests are so intimately involved; a
member does not live or marry unto himself alone. Relatives contribute not only assent and advice but also property; the group
shoulders a great deal of responsibility for the individual. It
might be said that that fact gives it the right to have its say in
the matter—only the truth is the other way around; for conditions of group-preservation involve responsibility and solidarity
and the forms of its expression are the results, not the cause or
justification, of the existing right and power of control. One who
is disposed always to center his interest upon the individual instead of the society is likely to remain blind to the real sense of
these matters.

[186] Godden, in JAI, XXVI, 175.   [187] Athalye, in JASB, I, 66.
[188] Von Stenin, in *Aus Allen Weltteilen*, XXIX, 62.
[189] Rockhill, in USNM, 1893, 725.

CHAPTER XLIX

THE WEDDING

§369*. Reason for the Ceremony. Ceremonial surrounds all the events of life which seem important to men. These occasions have to be dealt with in some manner; and after various stages of selection and concurrence, particular ways become established, for the most part unconsciously, in the mores of a group. These ways are not the product of reflection and rational selection any more than is the body of mores of which they form a part. However, there is expediency in them or they could not have persisted so universally over the earth; and it is the function of science, reviewing the cases, to reveal where this expediency lies. Though the ceremonies surrounding the entrance upon the status of matrimony are so multiform as to baffle description, they yield to classification. In general, they all converge upon a single final termination, consequence, or utility, namely, publicity. The expediency of publicity lies in the recognition and safeguarding of the group-interest as distinguished from the individual interest or even that of the family.

The interest of the group or society in the relations of the sexes has been seen to be a very vital one.[1] It will never cease to need emphasis. Even if the sex-relation had no consequences in the form of offspring, this interest would still be present. The quarrels between men which disrupt the societal organization and throw groups into conflict with one another are proverbially due to disputes over property and women. This has been recognized in the mores of property-tenure by the development of exhaustive rules about title.[2] It is a result of society's struggle for self-preservation that this was so; for otherwise society could not have concentrated its powers to maintain itself in the field of competition. The society that minimized these inevitable property-disputes by settling them speedily and without internal violence was the one to survive and to transmit its code. In the case of

[1] §§332, 340, above.　　　　[2] Ch. XIII, above.

property the societal interest thus made itself secure against the individual interest or that of component groups.

Marriage is not only indissolubly linked with property; it is itself a species of property-tenure. Whatever safeguards the group-interest enjoyed in the matter of property had to be paralleled in the case of marriage, even if marriage meant no more than an economic coöperation. But marriage is more than a form of industrial organization or of property; out of it comes, as a specific product, the adult society of a few years hence. Property-inheritance, with all the interests and conflicts involved, follows down the line of the family; so that it is incumbent upon the marriage-organization to provide adjustment, not only in the matter of property-relations but also in the case of such trouble-making factors as jealousy and other irritabilities directly connected with sex. The societal interest demands, even more urgently than in the case of property, that there shall be certain rules of the game. A set of limiting taboos develops and the institution takes on characteristic lines.

It is vital to society that the entrance of its members into the status of wedlock shall be generally known, so that they and their offspring can thereafter be "placed" in their setting as husbands, wives, children, families, with the result that their rights and duties toward each other within the relation and toward others outside it can fall under the local system of composition and regulation. Hence are required nowadays licenses, certificates, banns, and reports in the press as regards unions or proposed unions, as well as concerning births, testaments, divorces, and other details of "public interest"—all this in an age where publicity is harder to evade than to get. It is but rarely that a clandestine marriage is long kept secret. And when such records appear and it is known, for instance, that a certain man and woman have secured a marriage-license, the rest somewhat alter their attitude toward those persons, for they must now be shifted in the social classification. The engaged couple are "out of the market," as it is expressed, and are about to enter a new life-status with its own traditional code of conduct. It is also required that these public records shall be kept for future reference. No doubt there are good old couples who have lost their marriage-certificate, the witnesses to whose marriage are dead or scattered, and who could not possibly prove that they are not living together in sin were it not for the preservation of public records. The case of birth-certification is parallel.

Of such records the primitive people can possess none. All they can have is witnesses. Yet primitive marriage needs publicity quite as much as does civilized marriage. Hence the recourse to ceremonial. The more witnesses there are, and the more deeply the occasion has been impressed upon their minds, the more reliable the record and the more secure the rights that flow out of the new relation. An elaborate feast with plenty of strong liquor will raise up clouds of eagerly reminiscent witnesses to the fact that woman B is married to man A, for the ceremony, with its attendant bliss of carousing and brawling, will not soon be forgotten. The wedding was, then, a notification to all that such a woman belonged to such a man and was taboo to all others. It was of the utmost importance to societal peace and order that there should be a rite by which she should be known to have acquired this status. Further, the children born to her were his, in a number of cases irrespective of his actual paternity. He, she, and they were "placed" in society, and rights could be the more securely apportioned.

The wife of ceremony is the real or status-wife; the taking of a mere consort is unceremonious; authenticity and ceremonial go together. To wed, as etymology reveals, is to pledge; a wedded wife is a pledged, sworn, or guaranteed wife—pledged before all men. Such ceremonial was necessary in various other relations. It appears, according to the *Leges Barbarorum*, that no one could by a private act free a slave; there had to be a solemn ceremony, with the approval of king or church or in the presence of an assembly.[3] A third person was required to hear and witness mediæval sales and bargains and would be now, if people made such verbal contracts and broke or disputed their terms later on. This was so as to land; and in marriage only gradually did records supersede multiplied witnesses. Until they did, the public ceremony was indispensable.

In short, it is the ceremony that distinguishes marriage from non-marriage. By the ceremony the parties enter into a status

[3] Jenks, *Law and Pol.*, 251.

defined in the mores, carrying with it duties, rights, and guarantees of rights, for them and their legitimate offspring, at the hand of the society. Though it would be introducing a modern idea to call a concubine's children "illegitimate," yet they may not, in fact, inherit property or title at all or without special action. They have not the rights indissolubly inherent in the status proclaimed by the only recognized means of establishing publicity.

Ceremony is, then, a solemn determination explicitly expressed, less in words for the ear than in equally well or better understood action and symbolism for the eye. It makes sure of a deliberate and publicly avowed will. It will not do to say: "We have talked of it. We intend it. We have an understanding that we shall." The question is: Was there ever an explicit and complete act of will on both sides, resolved upon and publicly avowed? Consensus and fulfilment are all of marriage after the preliminaries to it have been settled. The essence of the matter is, of course, whether there has been fulfilment; and there have been attempts to secure publicity even of that.[4] These have occurred in very low savagery or where more developed peoples, having become obsessed by a certain "logical" mania, have wished to penetrate beyond the inferences from consensus and the obvious fact of joint life. Public examination of sexual intimacy always meets a bar. The most that can be insisted upon and certified to is the real consensus prior to fulfilment: it can and must be known that the parties involved have determined, not merely discussed, entrance upon matrimony, not something else. This is the point of the wedding-ceremony, whether primitive or not, and any ceremonial that will convey it so as to be understood by all is sufficient. The parties may join hands, tie their garments together, eat together, or perform mutual services that identify to any witness the status into which they plan to enter. In the church, questions are asked that evoke verbal expression, resulting in declarations such as "I take thee," with the formulas which reiterate the sense of marriage as understood; but in simpler times people acted out their consensus instead of talking about it. Hence the endless variety of ceremonial that has grown up around the entrance into wedlock. Much idealization has been superposed upon the public notification

4 Sumner, *Folkways*, §§417, 430.

which is the irreducible essence of the ceremony. Naturally the chance is seized upon to carouse and make merry; "marriage is the one great occasion in the native's life and he is therefore inclined to make the most of it."[5]

The fact is that people marry themselves by public declaration.[6] At most, "the benediction of the parents suffices without that of the priest; the domestic functions are enough without those of the church."[7] The current form of speech according to which some functionary "marries" a man and a woman to each other, although fixed in the language and apparently unavoidable, creates false notions about marriage. The whole question is as to the distinction in the mores between valid and invalid. The law of marriage is almost wholly judge-made and consists of dicta which owe their validity to the fact that the judge more or less correctly utters the views which are in the mores. The legislator is shut into a dilemma in his efforts to make those marriages valid which ought to be so at the same time that he pronounces other unions invalid; he necessarily fixes upon technical details which shall define validity. The finer and more specific or the more numerous those technical details, however, the greater the chance for error and fraud. Those details allow people of good faith to take measures for certainty, but if they are lacking while good faith is present on one or both sides, injustice may be done by letting the technicality determine validity.

§370*. Nature of the Ceremony. Instances of a total absence of ceremonial at entrance upon the status of wedlock—cases where the union of man and woman gets no publicity at all—are virtually non-existent. Absence of ceremony goes with feebleness of property-interests and weakness of societal organization, as might be inferred from what has just been set down in considering the reason for the wedding. In this connection it should be realized that puberty-ceremonies[8] provide a sort of substitute or, rather, prototype for the wedding; by them attention is sharply called to the identity of the youths who have reached marriage-

[5] Jenness and Ballentyne, *D'Entrecasteaux*, 108.

[6] The Quaker rite is an unadorned type of declaration. Case in N. Y. *Times*, April 27, 1924.

[7] Gubernatis, *Usi Nuz.*, 153.   [8] §163, above.

able age and who naturally pair off almost at once. The initiation-ceremony may be a marriage-ceremony,[9] as may those connected with childbirth.[10] In a small community where curiosity is rife and everybody's eye is upon everyone else this would be enough to secure complete publicity. In some of the cases where small attention seems to be paid to what might be called the actual wedding, the young man and woman have recently been specifically labelled as marriageable and so about to marry, so that the observed fact of their living together proclaims them man and wife. Even so, there is usually at least some little publication of the fact that a union has been contracted which is confirmatory of expectations. Furthermore, the marriage of ordinary people may be unceremonious where unions of those whose doings are more important to society are made much of.[11]

In southeastern Australia, "when a girl was old enough to be married, her father, accompanied by his brother, took her to her future husband's camp, and left her there with him."[12] There was here, at least, a procession of the girl and two recognized authorities and the inference as to what they were about was not a long one. No Tasmanian wedding-ceremony seems to have been described or witnessed by any European; "it was rarely the custom amongst them to select wives from their own tribes, but rather to take them furtively, or by open force, from neighboring clans."[13] The Siberian Soyots have no real marriage-ceremonies or, indeed, any ceremonies at all; they merely "drink themselves full."[14] "There are several peoples," says Wilken,[15] "who let the consummation of the marriage take place without any ceremony." He mentions one Papuan and two Malay tribes, but qualifies a little, reporting that in one case "the whole ceremony consists in this, that the young man receives from his father a blow-pipe and the girl from her mother an earthen pot." It is said of the Maori that they "seem to differ from almost every known tribe or nation in having no regular Marriage Ceremony."[16] Cowan[17] reports a reply of the headman of a small Maori village to the question: "What is your marriage ceremony here? Have you any *karakia?*" The answer was: *"Karakia!* This is my *karakia,"* said the old reprobate, grinning. He filled a tin pannikin with beer and held it up. "I say to Timi—that's the boy—'You drink this,' and then to Pare, the girl, 'You drink.' When they take a drink each, I say to them: 'Now, you are married.' . . . That's all my *karakia*—good enough, *ne!"*

"There is not always a feast and there is no regular marriage ceremony," when the Omaha groom has remained a bachelor until forty; but there are proceedings that are public enough to signalize the new status.[18] Among certain California Indians, "when a young man sees a maiden whom he admires, he

9 Haddon, in JAI, L, 243, 255, 275.   10 Rivers, *Todas,* 313.
11 Rivers, *Melan. Soc.,* I, 382.   12 Howitt, *S.E. Aust.,* 198.
13 Roth, *Tasmania,* 123-124.   14 Olsen, *Primitivt Folk,* 146.
15 *Vkde.,* 280.   16 Taylor, *Te Ika,* 335.
17 *Maoris,* 149.   18 Dorsey, in BAE, III, 260.

goes to her father's wigwam and lays down a quantity of shell-money. Both maintain profound silence, the old man feigning to take no notice whatever of the money, though he surreptitiously squints at it now and then. If he thinks there is not enough, or he does not like the youth, after a sufficient time has elapsed to suit the aboriginal ideas of dignity and red-tape, he reaches out his hands and returns it, and the suitor goes away without a word, or remains and adds another string. If accepted, the old Indian calls his daughter to him, joins her hand to her lover's makes them sit down together on the ground before his knees, and addresses to them a few words of advice. Thereupon they arise and go away husband and wife."[19] Apparently there are no witnesses.

Among the Arawaks there is really no specific marriage-ceremony, for proposal and wedding are one and the same. Doubtless there are many such cases reported as instances of no ceremony. The Arawak groom, first making sure that he will not be refused, goes to the house of the girl's parents, tells them how poor he is, and there is much ornate talk. If, at the end of these preliminaries, the girl sets food before the young man, consent is thereby given. When the lover has eaten the food, the marriage is concluded. Similarly if a father wants a certain man for his daughter, he sends him, by the hand of that daughter, something to eat; and if he eats of it, the marriage is made.[20] A list of Indian tribes which are alleged to have no marriage-ceremony is given by Westermarck.[21]

The part played by eating in even incipient ceremonial is to be noted. Primitive thought plays about food. Says a young Australian to a girl, "Djiitgun! What does the Djiitgun eat?" She replies: "She eats kangaroo, opossum," or some other game. This constitutes a formal offer and an acceptance.[22] In ceremonial of all sorts, food and eating play a prominent part. One has only to reflect upon modern examples to note that they still do: negotiations in business or politics take place over a table or are sealed by a dinner; there are still funeral baked meats and wedding-festivals; one of the mysteries of unification with deity takes the form of eating together.

The foregoing are cases of little or no ceremony or publicity; the immediate parties only are present and the society's interests are not represented by witnesses. If the society is very small, the fact that a man and woman live together is obvious and there is less need of advertising their status; then, as social relations within a society become more complex by reason of its growth or compounding, they must be regulated ever more exactly in the

[19] Powers, in *Contrib. N. Amer. Ethnol.,* III, 198-199.
[20] Schomburgk, *Brit. Guiana,* II, 459-460.
[21] *Marriage,* II, 593, and n. 1.   [22] Howitt, *S.E. Aust.,* 149.

mores. Other elements enter to create ceremony. Vanity is readily involved and as a consequence the ostentation of the wedding goes far beyond what is indispensable for the sake of the notification that woman B belongs to man A. Similarly in later times, ceremony takes on a religious character not present or not as marked in the primitive forms, so much so that it has come to be believed by not a few people that the essence of ceremony—in this case, the wedding—is the religious part of it. Here is one of the many instances where the essence of an institution, later so complicated as almost to defy analysis, comes out clearly in the simplicity of primitive cases.

Significant details of the wedding-ceremony will appear in sections immediately following, which deal with survivals and symbols in that ceremony; in this place are briefly illustrated several methods of securing publicity.

Westermarck's[23] assertion that secrecy of sex-connection is universal to mankind suffers a number of exceptions in cases where the crudest form of publicity occurs.[24] With such cases may be aligned the marriage, *teutonico more,* of the early Germans and the Middle Ages, whereby the jural consequences of marriage become completely valid in law from the moment when witnesses could assert that one coverlet had enveloped the pair. This usage was found in all ranks, enduring longest among princes, whose unions, involving more and greater interests, called for greater certainty.[25]

In the Solomon Islands marriage among the common people is attended by few ceremonies; but when the chief's daughter is married, certain dance-clubs are brought out and manipulated in various ways.[26] Among the Andamanese the marriage-ceremony requires that the bridegroom sit on the lap of the bride. Torches are brought that all present may bear witness that the ceremony has been duly performed.[27] In Korea there are ceremonial bowings by groom and bride; it is this reciprocal "salutation" which alone constitutes a valid marriage. After it, if the wife is repudiated, another cannot be taken. Though the husband has many concubines, he must treat the true wife, that

[23] *Marriage* (ed. 1891), 211; compare I, 568, of the three-volume edition. Many of the positive assertions of this author, made in the one-volume edition, appear in the three-volume revision either not at all or in a form much more vague and guarded.

[24] Von Pfeil, *Südsee,* 74; Fritsch, *Eingeb. S.-Afr.,* 365; Johnston, in JAI, XV, 11; Johnston, *Uganda,* II, 747; French-Sheldon, in JAI, XXI, 365; "Reise d. Prinz. Heinrich," in *Globus,* LXXII, 187; Von Bülow, in *Globus,* LXXII, 238; Ehrenreich, in *Ztsft. f. Ethnol.,* XIX, 30.

[25] Weinhold, *Deut. Frauen,* I, 399-401; Friedberg, *Eheschliess.,* 23; *Æneas Sylvius,* II, 95; Rudeck, *Oeffentl. Sittl.,* 141.

[26] Parkinson, in *Dresden K. Zoöl. u. Anth.-Ethnog. Mus.,* Abhandl., VII, pt. VI, 7.

[27] Man, in JAI, XII, 137.

is, the wife of ceremony, with respect.[28] In the Chin Hills region, the woman lives with her husband as a wife after entering the house with him in public.[29] In India the modern ceremonies are marked by "the following essential features: the night procession of the bridegroom to the house of the bride, tying the vestments of bride and groom together with a piece of consecrated cloth under which their hands are joined, winding a cord round their necks, marking their faces with paint, making them walk three times round the sacred fire, each time in seven steps, with repetition of prayers and Vedic texts. Noisy music during some part of the ceremony is held to be essential. In fact no one in India would believe in the validity of a marriage ceremony conducted without loud and often uproarious festivities." The high cost of weddings, according to a native, is a contributing factor to poverty in India.[30] These ceremonies can be followed back to a very primitive period.[31]

Among the Nairs, "the real marriage *de jure* and *de facto* is the *Sambandham*. 'Sambandham' is the Sanskrit word, meaning good and close union." The ceremony is most simple: a wise man is consulted who finds an auspicious date and informs the village elders. The Brahmin suitor brings some clothes which the wife wears, called *pudakas* and hands them over to the girl in the presence of her relations and neighbors, and it is announced that they are married. There is less ceremony if the suitor is a commoner man. When, however, "a stranger wants to marry in the family . . . all the formalities have to be gone through. Then all the village and all people in any way related are informed and, in the case of rich families, invited to a feast on the auspicious day."[32] Here is seen the necessity of wider publicity when one of the parties is not well known and also the tendency of wealthy people to mark the occasion in a way that will not be forgotten. Wilken[33] cites cases of weddings where the idea is to have ostentation as pronounced as possible; he says the original idea was publicity but that now there is nothing but display, in elaborate processions and showy feasts. Elsewhere this author gives some attention to the custom of offering the bride and groom something to eat; this is done by an old man or woman or, once only among the many cases cited, by a priest. No one gives any thought to the meaning of this usage, but the Letinese, having the idea that common drinking means blood-brotherhood, say: "You, man and woman, have become one in skin and in blood." Other tribes also see in the giving to the bride of something to eat her reception into the blood-bond: "Up to now you were an alien, now you belong to our blood" was said to the bride as food was thrust into her mouth. Similarly with the introduction of the man into the woman's family. "That the eating together, as a sacramental proceeding, must have a more or less religious character, is evident, though this comes into the foreground more with one people than with another." The Papuans of Geelvink Bay, like the old Romans, perform the ceremony before the images of the household gods, the ancestors; so too the Alfurs of Celebes, who make the meal eaten by the pair a sort of sacrificial one, as is

[28] Bishop, *Korea*, 117; Saunderson, in JAI, XXIV, 305.
[29] Carey and Tuck, *Chin Hills*, I, 189.
[30] N. Y. *Times*, Jan. 18, 1920.
[31] Monier-Williams, *Brāhmanism*, 380; Jolly, in *Grundr. d. Indo-Ar. Philol.*, II, 54.
[32] Panikkar, in JAI, XLVIII, 270-271.
[33] In VG, I, 572-573, 551, 552-553.

shown by the action of the priest who, before serving the pair, throws a little of the food to the four corners of the table and pours out a few drops of palm-wine there.[34]

The only Igorrot ceremony is the giving of certain counsels to the pair by an old man, in the presence of assembled friends, followed by a feast.[35] Among the Kubus, if the groom's gift is sufficient, "those who may be within reach are called. When they are seated under a tree, the father informs them that he has given his daughter So-and-so to So-and-so in marriage. One of the company then strikes the tree under which they are sitting, using his club for the purpose, and declares them man and wife. The ceremony is followed by such feast as can be provided, principally of the fruits with which the bride has been bought."[36] Among certain Malays, with whom dice-play and cock-fighting accompany all marriage-ceremonies, there is even a term which means to marry with a cock-fight.[37] In northern Sumatra, the groom is obliged to strip to the waist and sit on a mat; then, in the presence of four witnesses, he must make declaration in a loud voice. The witnesses are admonished to listen carefully.[38] A similar loud reiteration is required by the Arabs, the dialogue between the groom and the girl's father taking place within a circle of friends. Meanwhile the bride's procession has gone up and down the streets for six or eight hours.[39] The peace-chief of certain California Indians "causes the parties to enter into a simple covenant in the presence of their parents and friends, after which there is dancing and merrymaking for some time, together with eating and drinking."[40]

It has always been customary to carry away mementoes of a wedding. In Germany, up to the sixteenth century, the bride loosed the groom's garter and distributed pieces of it among the guests; and there was a similar French custom, called *don de la jarretière*. The French bride of the period gave under the table a ribbon of white or red silk instead of the garter, which was cut up and worn as a decoration at the wedding.[41] The bride's garter is a traditional talisman which is presented to some favored recipient. An informant[42] describes the case as follows:

"1. Its color should be yellow; this is almost invariable; but blue ones have been seen. 2. It must be worn by the bride on the left leg during the marriage ceremony; she may wear any number of them. 3. It must be worn by the recipient on the left leg constantly for one year (during the year it may never be removed, day or night, under any circumstances). During this period it must support the stocking without any assistance; but it is allowable to sew it around the edges, or lap it over on itself, in such a way as to prolong its usefulness. These conditions having been fulfilled, it is supposed (1) that, within one year after the year of constant wear, the wearer will be engaged to be married; and (2) that, within one year after said second year has elapsed, she will be married. This custom or superstition is probably practised throughout the United States; without special inquiry I have heard of it in

[34] §§150, 294, 295, above.   [35] Blumentritt, *Igorroten*, 95.
[36] Forbes, in *JAI*, XIV, 124.   [37] Wilken, *Vkde.*, 288.
[38] Jacobs, *Groot-Atjeh*, I, 42-43.
[39] Burckhardt, *Arabic Proverbs*, 114.
[40] Powers, in *Contrib. N. Amer. Ethnol.*, III, 157.
[41] Weinhold, *Deut. Frauen*, I, 400; Freisen, *Kanon. Eherechts*, 117.
[42] Letter of Dr. Samuel Peterson to W. G. Sumner, Jan. 18, 1899.

Connecticut, Ohio, and Tennessee." A remoter survival occurred in the case of the marriage of the former Crown Prince of Germany; strips of the same silk as the bride's garter, specially embroidered with the date of the wedding, were distributed among the guests as mementoes of the occasion.[43] Tylor[44] speaks of medals as wedding-souvenirs in France and thinks them derived from the old Frankish "marriage by the shilling and the penny (*per solidum et denarium*)." In Livland the bride gives her guests gloves or pieces of cloth, the latter being used as scarfs.[45]

Such instances bring us down to modern customs of gift-giving, where the gifts, as mere souvenirs, have no longer any significance as evidence of the publicity and so of the stability of the marriage.

§371*. Survivals and Symbols. Any ceremony of long standing is sure to contain survivals. Customs persist out of the past just because they furnish the solemn act, like "kissing the book," that can be proved and that constitute a juridical fact. If the only difference between illicit relations and marriage was permanency of intention, this *animus maritandi*, or intention of marrying, must needs be enunciated in solemn fashion. In fact, it had to be acted out in some way, not merely declared by word of mouth, in order to impress the fact through the eyes as well as through the ears of the witnesses. At first there was a pledge, oath, or vow, accompanied by or enacted in solemn ritual. The fuller ritual is of survivals the more solemn it is; nothing is so sacred as the old and time-hallowed practice, though it may not be understood at all by those who go through with it. Ritual loses nothing of solemnity or holiness through an incomprehensible, mystic character; it has been the practice of ancestors, now spirits or gods who like to see it preserved; a ceremony devoid of survivalistic elements loses in sanctity, impressiveness, and force. And so in the wedding-ceremony occur the semblances of capture, purchase, resistance, mourning by the bride—all in ritual form, constituting the only "right" things to do. To be knocked senseless and carried off bathed in blood is what saved the modesty of the Australian bride.

Survivals of capture, including mock-fights, have been listed above,[46] in direct connection with the actual abduction of which

[43] Assoc. Press despatch, in New Haven *Register,* Oct. 4, 1905.
[44] In *Nineteenth Cent.,* XL.
[45] *Russian Ethnog.* (Russ.), II, 194.   [46] §358, above.

they are the outcome and echo; in addition to these more obvious survivals of violence, there are other customs encountered in connection with the wedding-ceremony that should be aligned with them. The wedding is encased in conventionalities and make-believe and is nothing without them.

In one African tribe, when the bridegroom comes, the bride refuses several times; then he and his friends kill a goat or sheep and enter the house over its blood.[47] Resistance of the groom occurs among the Hill Tribes of India. Often the resisting parties have to be fed or the groom must drink with them before they yield. "It is not easy to correlate these customs under any one general principle. They partly suggest capture marriage, partly compensation to the relatives of the bride for the loss of her services, or they may be in part a survival of a stage of Beena marriage in which the groom became entitled to all the sisters." The mimic struggle between bride's and groom's relatives occurs, and the bride may run away and be recaptured by force.[48] "Among the Khonds the bride is carried off on her uncle's shoulders, while the young women of the village turn out and assault the uncle."[49] In one of the Hindu ceremonies, two unsheathed swords are crossed over the heads of the couple from behind,[50] this custom being paralleled in Italy where a knight held a drawn sword over the pair during the wedding.[51] "At a Kallan marriage the bride and bridegroom go to the house of the latter, where boomerangs are exchanged . . . there is a common saying still current: 'Send a boomerang . . . and bring the bride.' "[52] Among the Crimean Tatars, "it is the privilege of the old women to carry the bride into the house of her husband on a carpet, which is spread down for the purpose and on which she lies down when she gets out of the camel-wagon before the door. As the old women are weak and tottering, the bride often is hurt by striking against the wheel or the ground; nothing, however, can make the old women surrender their privilege."[53]

Among the Yakuts, "whether the stealing of women was the cause of the preceding hostilities, or the relatives gave the woman voluntarily in compensation for a man who had been killed, or for stolen cattle, is immaterial. In any case she was regarded as *booty*, and the wedding resembled a *peace negotiation and conclusion*. To this day, both the parties who come into relations with each other at a wedding behave to each other during the feast with respect, yet with a certain concealed distrust and jealousy. They are constantly on the look-out lest the others get the better of them in the gifts, or cheat them. The groom's party do not move at all; their horses are saddled, as are also those of the bride's relatives who have come to the wedding. A Yakut who was asked why he did not unsaddle his horse at a wedding answered, 'Differences are apt to arise at a wedding.' "[54] Wilken[55] holds that the giving and receiving of

[47] Stuhlmann, *Mit Emin,* 791.
[48] Crooke, in JAI, XXVIII, 239, 240; §363, above.
[49] Fawcett, in JASB, I, 235.   [50] Risley, *Ethnog. Ind.,* I, 89.
[51] Gregorovius, *Lucretia Borgia,* 112.
[52] Thurston, *S. India,* 559.
[53] *Russian Ethnog.* (Russ.), II, 94.
[54] Sieroshevski-Sumner, in JAI, XXXI, 86.
[55] In VG, I, 153, 175.

betel at a wedding is a symbol of conciliation—there is no longer any grudge because of abduction.

A Roman bride had her hair divided into six locks or *crines* with the point of a lance, called *hasta cœlibaris* or *doration*. The ancients had no idea of the reason for this; but "if, in a later time, the hair of the Roman bride was arranged with the *hasta cœlibaris*, it may be concluded that at an earlier time it was cut with this spear. . . . Into connection with capture is also to be brought the custom that the bride, arrived at the bridegroom's door, must be lifted by force over the threshold."[56] Of the symbolic barring of the way for the bridal pair by two threads, it is said: "Two things are mixed up in it. It is a bar, but not intended to be an effectual one, to the passage of the bridal pair. This may be a remnant of marriage by capture. It has analogies all over Europe. In France the procession is brought to a stand for a moment by a rope stretched across the streets. In Bohemia a chain is used in the same way, having in the middle a great loop of silk, or a rope adorned with flowers. In Texel a broom or a beam of wood is laid across the road; in the Rhineland a chain of flowers. In Aargau as soon as the bride, seated in the cart, has reached the end of her native village, the young men and maidens of the place bar her way with sticks, chains, and ropes. It is the business of the bridesman to cut a way through this barricade with the bridal sword."[57]

Gomme[58] rehearses a lengthy scene of the same sort connected with a village marriage in Lorraine. The bride's house is barricaded by her friends and the groom's party come, with music and gun-firing, as if to storm the house. Parleys and pretended assaults are in order. The whole thing degenerates into a singing contest, with much scuffling and scrambling and a final struggle over a goose roasting on a spit in the bride's house, which is secured by one of the groom's party who descends the chimney. Singing contests occur also in Russia.[59]

Ceremonial resistance and reluctance on the part of the bride, and sometimes, though much more rarely, of both bride and groom or of the groom alone, point back to a time when what is now counterfeit was actual. These cases link on to the preceding.

In the Andaman Islands, the bride sits apart, "attended by one or two matrons, and the bridegroom takes his place among the bachelors until the chief or elder approaches him, whereupon he at once assumes a modest demeanor and simulates reluctance to move; however, after a few encouraging and re-assuring remarks he allows himself to be led slowly, sometimes almost dragged, toward his *fiancée,* who, if she is young, generally indulges in a great display of modesty, weeping and hiding her face, while her female attendants prepare her by straightening her legs; the bridegroom is then made to sit on her thighs." When all present have seen and are ready to bear witness to the ceremony having been carried out in orthodox manner, the chief pronounces them duly married.[60] In New Guinea, the groom disappears on the

---

[56] Rossbach, *Röm. Ehe,* 286, 289, 291, 329-330.
[57] Peterson, "Pres. Address," in JASB, III, 330.
[58] *Village Life,* 222 ff.
[59] *Russian Ethnog.* (Russ.), II, 106.   [60] Man, in JAI, XII, 137.

wedding-day and having been sought out and seized by his friends along toward evening, is dragged to the bride's house.[61]

In one district of India, part of the ceremony is that the groom pretends to flee to Benares, there to lead an ascetic life. He is brought back by the father of the girl, who begs him to accept the hand of his daughter.[62] Among the Kirghiz the man is bound to act as if ashamed because he is a bridegroom.[63] Among the Dusun, it is etiquette for the bride, on the day following the wedding, "to run back to her father's house, and when a lot of women come from her husband's village to fetch her back, she would be considered bold and forward if she didn't pretend not to want to go, but she eventually lets herself be persuaded, and this little play has to be repeated several times before she is allowed to settle down as a married woman."[64]

Fries[65] has a rather extended description of Eskimo customs surrounding marriage which include a number of survivalistic features. "After having announced his choice before his parents and nearest relatives, the suitor sent to the bride's home a couple of old women who, without naming their errand, began to praise highly the bridegroom and his family. At this the young girl understood what hour had struck and, to all appearance much alarmed, ran away and tore her top-knot apart as a sign of her great anxiety. Her parents answered neither yes nor no to the suit but the envoys sought out the sweetheart and dragged her with violence, in which proceeding her top-knot came in to advantage as a handle, to the bridegroom's house. If she was over-stubborn and strong in her resistance, she was served with well-applied cuffs on the ears. Thus introduced into her new home, she sat on the bench with dishevelled hair and sorry mien, repeatedly utilizing every chance for flight, from which she was every time dragged back forcibly by the bridegroom, who sought with all sorts of knocks to inspire her with better ideas. All this belonged to the indispensable ceremonial, even if she was glad to join her destiny with that of her suitor. But if her dislike was real, she ran away so often that her lover at last got tired of seeking her or even, if his love was ardent enough, cut several slashes in the soles of her feet, in the happy hope that before the wounds should have time to heal her dislike might change into love. If in this her extremity in the strife with her persistent adorer, the woman cut off her top-knot, then it was clear to anyone that dissimulation had not taken place; but since, in and by that action, the woman renounced marriage for all the future, she very seldom seized upon this last recourse. . . . Even today a woman must show herself reluctant and indifferent to wooing; to a direct proposal of marriage there is very seldom any answer but no." At the wedding "the speaking of the yes, in the presence of others, is the hardest of all for the bride. Customarily, she answers the priest's question merely with her eyes, though that is regarded as equally conclusive. And after the act, which is carried out here with little celebration, the young pair are wont to hasten each to his place and seek to conceal his shame by feigning to be occupied with some everyday occupations." It is to be noted, in connection with this instance of rough handling, that the woman had, after all, the power of disposition over herself—at least to the extent of being able to avoid a detested match.

The classic case of reluctance-survivals is the Roman. "The *domum deductio*

[61] Krieger, *Neu-Guinea*, 173.   [62] Thurston, *S. India*, 1.
[63] *Russian Ethnog.* (Russ.), II, 188.
[64] Cator, *Head-Hunters*, 63.   [65] *Grönland*, 111-112, 113.

took place at the appearance of the evening star. The bride fled to the lap of her mother, clung closely to her, and had to be taken away by force." This custom is referred to "maiden modesty," and is alleged to be "only a symbol in the historic period."[66] In the Esth marriage, the bride selects four or six of her friends to go with her to sing invitations to the wedding. These songs of invitation which the companions render in the name of the bride, as well as all the songs of the bride during the wedding, are called "bride's complaints." The meter of them all is elegiac.[67] In White Russia, on the evening before the wedding, the relatives meet at the bride's house and sing, during which the bride is bound to cry.[68] The same custom obtained in Great Russia; the bride was bound to cry, expressing regret at leaving home and dread of the new life. The women sang sad songs.[69] In Connecticut weddings, at the end of the seventeenth century, "just before the pair joined hands, the bridegroom quitted his place, when the 'Bridesmen' would follow, seize him, and drag him back to his post of duty."[70]

There are several practices which hark back to primitive violence, generally with the bride as its object. It is difficult to say whether these acts are survivals of what was once done or merely indicative of future relations. It is likely that they are both at the same time. The survival passes easily into the so-called symbol when its original significance is forgotten and it is subject to interpretation and rationalization.[71]

Among the Berbers, the groom asked the bride to smell a stout stick, one end of which was perfumed with some sweet-smelling substance. "That meant that so long as she behaved well, her days would be happy and comfortable, . . . but if she should in the meantime try to go astray, she could be sure of being punished very severely."[72] Russian wedding-ceremonies have been marked by survivals of the use of the whip. The girl's father struck his daughter with a whip, saying: "By these blows, thou, O daughter, recognizest the authority of thy father. That authority now goes over into other hands. In my place thy husband will teach thee obedience with this whip." The whip is handed to the groom who says: "I do not expect to have need of it, but I take it and will keep it as a gift." He then sticks it in his girdle. Sometimes the woman fell at the feet of the man and put her forehead against his boots, and the man covered her head with the skirt of his coat as a sign of protection.[73] In a Russian folksong the husband gives the wife gifts which she ill-naturedly scorns; he then gets his whip and she succumbs and is sweet.[74] The Ruthenian groom gives his bride a light blow with the whip and after the party leaves the church he repeats the blow; he then drives the bride's brother

[66] Rossbach, *Röm. Ehe*, 329. [67] R.W., in *Globus*, LXXXIX, 257.
[68] *Russian Ethnog.* (Russ.), II, 106.
[69] Kostomarov, *Gt. Russians* (Russ.), 245-246.
[70] Weeden, *New Eng.*, I, 412. [71] §456, below.
[72] Bruun, *Huleboerne*, 78.
[73] Kostomarov, *Gt. Russians* (Russ.), 243, 244.
[74] Ralston, *Russ. People*, 11.

from her side with the whip and gives her a blow for the third time.[75] The same custom is reported from the Jewish ceremony.[76] In Croatia it has been the custom for the groom to give the bride a lusty box on the ear to signify his power over her.[77]

Other prefigurings of mastery are not merely symbolic but partake of the nature of imitative magic.[78] An ancient English custom provided that the groom's shoe was laid on the bride's head.[79] "The shoe, which in many mediæval marriage-customs appear as a gift of the groom to the bride, is to be interpreted as a symbol of mastery. The one who plies the slipper gives the orders"—*Wer den Pantoffel führt, gebietet*.[80] The groom may tread on the bride's foot to indicate mastery;[81] and there are several cases where the attempt is made by each of the pair to anticipate in this, thus qualifying for the dominant station in the new domestic economy. "At the wedding the bride can easily bring it about that she shall always be the ruling party in the marriage; to this end she must try, before the altar, to set her left foot on the right foot of the groom." Similarly in White Russia; but she must try to do it as if inadvertently.[82] In Great Russia a cup was thrown on the ground and bride and groom trod upon it, saying, "Thus be trodden under foot those who shall try to sow discord between us." It was the popular notion that the one who trod on the cup first would rule.[83]

Several instances may indicate the peculiar position occupied by the parents and close relatives in the wedding-ceremony, a position interpreted as recalling obsolete forms of family-organization, in particular, the mother-family.[84] An interminable amount of such interpretation, based upon more or less tenuous inference, could be constructed around the wedding.

The mother of the groom may take a prominent part in the ceremony;[85] in Cambodia, the bride-price is sometimes paid to the mother. This latter custom, with other facts, "attests to the existence in the past of the matriarchate."[86] In some cases the mother, in others the father, is excluded from the marriage-ceremony.[87] Prominence is given to the maternal uncle in the ceremony of several districts in India;[88] in Tibet he is consulted as the real arbiter of the girl's fate in marriage. Nothing can be settled without reference to him. When

75 Kaindl, in *Ztsft. d. Vereins f. Volkskunde*, XI, 284-285.
76 Klugmann, *Frau im Talmud*, 30, note.
77 Krauss, *Südslaven*, 385.   78 §302, above.
79 Gomme, *Village Life*, 221.
80 Weinhold, *Deut. Frauen*, I, 372-373.
81 Lippert, *Kgchte.*, II, 155.
82 Kaindl, in *Globus*, XCII, 286; *Russian Ethnog.* (Russ.), I, 106.
83 Kostomarov, *Gt. Russians* (Russ.), 244
84 §§415 ff., below.
85 Crooke, in JAI, XXVIII, 236-237.
86 Leclère, in PSM, XLIV, 777.
87 Anon., "Royal Marriage," in JASB, II, 311 ff.; *Russian Ethnog.* (Russ.), II, 188.
88 Thurston, *S. India*, 1-3, 81.

his leave is secured the marriage-proposal may be made formally to the parents. In one tribe, the maternal uncle of the bride makes her over to the maternal uncle of the groom.[89] Again, the father of the bride stands aloof from the marriage, saying that the daughter is the mother's property. Among the White Russians, it is the girl's mother who signifies consent; at one stage of the proceedings she must put on her jacket and cap wrong side out.[90] In some parts of Bavaria and Swabia the bride's mother may not take part in the wedding-festival but looks on in her work-day clothes. The bride is under the sponsorship of a brideswoman for the day.[91]

The details of ceremony hitherto cited are reminiscent in greater or less degree of capture, resistance, reluctance, harsh treatment of the bride, and so on. In general they represent ritual that no longer corresponds to the real feelings or relations of the parties concerned. It has not been arbitrarily invented and, since it goes back to antecedent actualities in the mores, it has been listed here as survivalistic. There is other ritual in the wedding-ceremony which, although it may present no evident reminiscence of earlier stages of the mores, likewise serves to fix attention in a solemn manner upon the character of the new relation in process of being formed. It may be called symbolic; but the symbolism in a time-honored ceremony is almost necessarily survivalistic.

There is, in particular, a set of observances employed in the wedding-ceremony which simply recalls graphically to principals and witnesses the set of mores surrounding wedlock. It might be termed educational. Owing to the desirability of having the location of rights in the new relation impressed on all parties concerned, the ceremony rehearses the salient aspects of their distribution and makes exposition of what is expected by society of those proposing to enter the traditional status. The wedding-ritual is symbolic of matrimony and intensifies the record. The mere rehearsal of an actual status is scarcely true symbolism; it is not, in any case, survivalistic.

The wedding-ritual is not seldom very complicated. From long and tiresome accounts[92] the reader derives little except a feeling of incredulity that such a meaningless mass of usages, songs, speeches, poses, and evolutions could be remembered. It is impos-

89 Rockhill, in USNM, 1893, 725.
90 Russian Ethnog. (Russ.), II, 123, 106.
91 Weinhold, Deut. Frauen, I, 397, note, 398.
92 As in Krauss, Bulgaren, 309 ff.

sible to catalogue these ceremonies and would be unprofitable if possible; we shall do no more than indicate their significance. Any one of the actions prescribed in the ritual may be the indispensable one. For the moment we are setting aside that in the ceremony which is specifically religious in character.

Symbolic of the union is the tying together of the bride and groom, the joining of hands, eating and drinking or smoking together, sitting on the same carpet or under the same canopy. Significant of sex-division of labor[93] and in particular of the place of the woman in the union are, besides the several symbolic acts of violence previously alluded to, ceremonies where she tends the fire, prepares and cooks food for her husband, washes his feet, and in general preserves a demeanor of humility, while he performs acts denoting authority and protection as toward one subject to him. In East Africa hoes are often given as presents, revealing the agricultural economy.[94] The Tibetan bride twists wool-fibers handed her by the groom into a thread, as "the ceremony of the first work of harmonious union."[95] The bride is seized by the groom, the *manus* of her passes over to him, through the clasping of her hand or the putting on of the ring. She is veiled or has her hair cut off or her ears bored or is even seriously disfigured as indicating that she is the property of one master.

Symbols of union and concord, of the "bitter-sweet" destiny of the married, of protection or adoption (as of a child), of fidelity, of the man's prospective generosity, and, above all, of hoped-for fecundity—these constitute the salient features of the ceremony which principals and witnesses are to remember. Blows are sometimes dealt to the former, as they are to youths at puberty ceremonies,[96] to stimulate their memories in the matter of the vows and engagements which they are taking. Dramatic performances sometimes serve to impress the situation more firmly; among the Indians these might include the acting out of the clan-legends,[97] while in Arabia[98] and in sixteenth- and seventeenth-century Germany[99] these representations were coarse and gross. Garlands and crowns are worn by bride and groom and there are well-wishes from the witnessing parties.

The endless variations of symbolism which play about the wedding-ceremony as celebrated throughout the world all center about publicity as the immediate interest of society in the occasion. While details of the ceremony may appeal to curious interest, some of them will be seen to be of a deeper scientific significance as their survivalistic character is better known.

[93] Ch. V, above.
[94] Dundas, K. R., in JAI, XLIII, 41, 42 ff.
[95] Rockhill, in USNM, 1893, 725.   [96] §163, above.
[97] Boas, in USNM, 1895, 360 ff.
[98] Burckhardt, *Arabic Proverbs*, 115.
[99] Weinhold, *Deut. Frauen*, I, 394, note.

§372*. Religious Aspects. That marriage is a crisis of life is clearly recognized by primitive peoples, though their point of view is not that of more developed societies and more analytical minds. They know that an inexpedient marriage can wreck at least two destinies. The tests of man and woman point to the significance attached to the marriage-relation. It is a rooted persuasion of nature-peoples that a marriage should be a "right" one according to their code. Yet there is always room for doubt; the outcome of any proposed alliance is problematical because it is impossible to foresee all the elements entering into it and to gauge their action. Even among less highly strung humanity, a union may seem perfectly expedient and yet turn out not to be so; results may not align themselves according to expectations legitimate in view of available knowledge. The luck-element enters largely and must be insured against. This involves the entrance of religion and the priest. The latter, however, does not make the marriage any more than he makes the property-relation; he safeguards as he can at the supreme crisis. Religion is invoked here just as in connection with any other important event of life, for at such a time the spirits are especially malevolent; they do not like to see men happy and prosperous. It is needful to evade or buy off their "envy,"[100] or, if that may not be, to refrain from entering a relation against whose happy consummation the daimons are implacably set. "It would be easy," says Frazer,[101] "to prove by a long array of facts that the sexual relation is associated in the primitive mind with many supernatural perils; but the exact nature of the danger apprehended is still obscure." Succeeding paragraphs will deal with the omens and auguries and the defensive and propitiatory methods employed to meet these perils.

The entrance of the aleatory element into marriage may be illustrated by partially anticipating a future topic.[102] One of the main objects of marriage is offspring. Beneath everything else is the urge of nature, and also that of society, by way of the mores, toward procreation. If the rest have children, the childless are set apart and feel it. In our day the disappointment connected

100 §§264, 265, 266, above.   101 *Golden Bough,* II, 359.
102 §§392, 409, below.

with a barren marriage is perhaps chiefly sentimental, including the frustration of domestic affections, the wounding of pride in the extinction of a family-name, and the like. The situation is sometimes expressed by saying that just as the bachelor is but half a man, so is a childless marriage no more than a half-marriage; that for the completeness of development and self-realization of man or woman not only marriage but a family is indispensable. We idealize upon the notion that happiness lies in the fulfilment of human destiny and harbor a variety of poetic sentiments that play about the whole subject.

Primitive people do not enter upon such ranges of sentiment; their reasons for desiring children are eminently definite and practical. They want from them support in the battle of life, especially in its last and losing phase; and they want such help in the life to come. The conviction that they must have children, somehow, is attested by the prevalence of adoption. Childlessness is a great curse, as fecundity is one of the highest of blessings. The tests of fecundity[103] witness to this set of the mores. If, however, a married couple have no children, they are not in the way of explaining the situation rationally, least of all of relieving it as a modern surgeon often can. To them childlessness is but one of the unreckonable and inexplicable ills of life. Hence it is referred at once to spiritual agency; in fact, it is often represented as being called down by a curse, that is, by invocation of the spirits who produce it;[104] to the least developed peoples even death, it will be remembered, is supposed not to be natural but induced by some supernatural agency.[105] The menace of a great calamity hangs over marriage and can be avoided only by daimonological measures; hence the entrance of religion into marriage, in the guise of some ritual or ceremony designed to ward off this misfortune.

Childlessness is not the only peril that menaces marriage; other impending ills call for the exercise of religious precautions. Most of the religious practices connected with marriage can be better treated under the general topics of religion, for they are no more than specific instances of general religious and magical procedure; in the present connection we shall merely set down a repre-

103 §365, above.
104 Kipling, *Courting of Dinah Shadd.*
105 §203, above.

sentative selection of cases in which religion enters into the beginnings of the marriage-relation.

§373*. Defensive and Propitiatory Measures. Foreknowledge
is a precondition to avoidance of ill. In addition to astrological research as to the expediency of a union, great care is expended upon the selection of a propitious day for the wedding.[106] To the present time and among people who publicly abjure "superstition," there is a prejudice against certain days, especially Friday or the thirteenth of the month.

In mediæval Germany, "marriages made under the waxing moon or at full moon had the guarantee of wholesome blessing. They still hold to this at the present day. . . . Marriages consummated on Thursday are . . . secure against all witch-work and magic."[107] Folklore contains many beliefs of this sort. Roman marriage-celebration began with the taking of the auspices; even one who thinks himself an arbiter of culture regards it as a disgrace to marry without them.[108] "Among the ancients nothing was done, publicly or even privately, without taking the auspices beforehand. From this custom, even now the auspices-takers are interposed in marriage."[109]

The Dyak divination takes the form of noting the will of the gods in the increase or decrease of pieces of betel-nut in a basket. If they should increase, the marriage will be happy; if they decrease, it must be postponed or relinquished altogether. "But as a matter of fact, they neither increase nor decrease, and this is interpreted to mean that the wedding is one upon which the spirits have pronounced neither a good nor a bad verdict." This instance is typical of many, the more so perhaps because of the degeneration into mere ritual of what was once taken more seriously. "I have been present at a Dyak wedding more than once, and what struck me most was the perfunctory manner in which everything was done. No one seemed to listen much to what the Master of Ceremonies had to say; all sat round talking and laughing as the mood suited them. The examining of the basket containing the pieces of split betel-nut was not awaited with any anxiety. Everything seemed to be done because it was the custom, and for no other reason."[110]

More specifically connected with marriage are certain omens supposed to be prophetic of the internal nature of the relation. The following cases are not so obvious as the survivals and symbols previously cited; they are more on the order of magic.

Among some of the Sahara peoples, "the first glance of the groom, after the wedding, should fall on the bride."[111] In Madras, "when the bride enters

---

[106] Many cases in Harvey, *Chinese Animism,* ch. VIII.
[107] Weinhold, *Deut. Frauen,* I, 374.
[108] Cicero, *Pro Cluentio,* V, 14; Cicero, *De Divinatione,* I, xvi, 28.
[109] *Valerius Max.,* II, i, 1.   [110] Gomes, *Sea Dyaks,* 124, 127.
[111] Pommerol, *Sahariennes,* 235.

the house she is directed to place the right foot first, as the placing of the left one is considered to be a bad omen."[112] Again, the pair play a game of odd and even. The party who wins will rule the other.[113] The Javanese bride and groom hurl a harmless missile at each other's heads and from the strength and dexterity shown in the throwing "they assert that the relation is revealed in which the married people shall stand to one another during their union."[114] Russian bride and groom try to step at the same time on the wedding-carpet, for the belief is that the one first to set foot on it will dominate.[115] Of the Czech couple the one who first sees the other has the mastery.[116] Again, "whichever one of the parties has his hand or thumb above at the wedding becomes the master. A bride treads upon the groom's foot to this end or sleeps on his trousers. . . . During the journey to the church the bride must not look about." The pair must keep close together so that nothing can come in to separate them; and the groom must carry the bride from the carriage to the middle of the floor so that she shall not touch the earth with her foot. "If the bride binds a little stick into the groom's neck-cloth, she hopes never to be beaten." They marry while the moon is waxing and most preferably on Friday. "The one whose wedding-ring falls to the ground at the marriage will die soon or will be unhappy; the one whose light burns longer will live longer."[117] "In general, through all Italy, it is held to be a good augury if something is broken on the day of the wedding."[118]

Omens often bear upon the question as to who is going to be married next. In North England the custom was for the bride to take off her stocking, which was thrown by a woman into the company. The person hit by it would be the next to marry. In another form the bridal pair sat in bed dressed except for shoes and stockings. The company entered and all the women stood in turn at the foot of the bed with back to it and tried to throw the groom's stocking with their left hands over their right shoulders so as to hit his face. The successful person would marry next. The men did the same thing with the bride's stocking.[119] The contemporary custom regarding the bride's bouquet is suggested. Of course what was originally ominous comes in time to be merely amusing and its persistence survivalistic. But it cannot be assumed that the amusement-motive was the original one where there is an invocation of chance or lot or any other appeal in the nature of divination or prophecy.

Exorcistic practices also attend the wedding; and fire and water play their usual rôle as banishers of evil influences. Baptism in some form is common. Defenses that may seem, on the face of them, obscure show significance in the light of cult-principles previously[120] developed.

[112] Naidoo, in JASB, II, 387.
[113] Nathubhai, in JASB, III, 389.
[114] Wilken, in VG, I, 497-498.
[115] Gubernatis, *Usi Nuz.*, 164.
[116] Tetzner, in *Globus,* LXXVIII, 341.
[117] Tetzner, in *Globus,* LXXVII, 221.
[118] Gubernatis, *Usi Nuz.*, 176.
[119] Clement, *Salischen Franken*, 238.
[120] Chs. XXV, XXVI, XXX, above.

In India and Ceylon water-sprinkling is common at a marriage,[121] and where, as among the Galla, the anointing of the bride with butter is practised, this "completely corresponds to the Oriental bath of the bride."[122] In Ponapé the future mother-in-law of the bride rubs coconut oil vigorously into her back and shoulders.[123] In India "the custom of the bridal couple bathing in water brought from seven different villages" is found among many castes. "The water is brought by married girls who have not reached puberty on the night preceding the wedding day, and the bride and bridegroom wash in it before dawn." This is called the "cuckoo water bath."[124] In the old Hindu wedding the groom led the bride toward the right three times round the fire and the water-jar.[125]

Peterson[126] gives full details of the Hindu marriage-ceremony which include a number of references to fire and water. The groom leads the bride by the right hand before the altar-fire and speaks certain formulas, "after which he must spread a mat west of the fire in such a way that the points of the blades of grass point to the north; on this they must sit, the bridegroom to the left and the bride to the right." Then comes the solemn joining together of hands, followed by the declaration, "I, M, take thee, N." "He must be looking west and she looking east. He must stand; she must sit." There is much in the formulas about the family-altar which she is to tend and the "purifying flame." "Now let him make her, standing to the north of the fire, take seven steps to the north or to the east. She must put her right foot foremost." The verse for the seventh step is, "With the seventh step, as is well-known, the marriage is irrevocable." Sacrifice and worship immediately sanction it. The taking of the fire to witness is one of the essentials to the marriage.

Wilkins[127] reports in even greater detail; we abstract certain significant points. An almanac is used to set a favorable day for a preliminary rite of anointing with turmeric. The groom bathes, puts on red-bordered cloth, and stands on a grindstone, while four women whose husbands are living, i.e., who are lucky, anoint him and touch his forehead with sacred water. Then he must carry about with him till marriage a pair of silver nutcrackers, and the girl a dye-case, to repel evil spirits. Abstemiousness on the wedding-day is required of all immediately concerned except the bridegroom's mother, who eats at least seven times. As the groom starts, a plate of rice and a pot of vermilion are thrown over his head by his father and caught by his mother. In the religious part of the ceremony, he wears a red silk robe and the closely-veiled bride is carried and seated on his left side. Ganges water is poured into his hand. Bride and groom place their hands in the water-vessel and are tied together with a garland. The girl's father then says: "I ———, give ——— to thee, ———," and the groom replies: "I have received her." Holy water is poured on the heads of the pair and they receive a blessing. Fire is called to witness when the vows are made. The groom then sprinkles a little water on the bride's

---

[121] Lewin, *S.E. India*, 176; Risley, *Ethnog. Ind.*, I, 82; Thurston, *S. India*, 4-5, 79-81, 101; Schmidt, *Ceylon*, 256.

[122] Paulitschke, *Nordost-Afr.*, 200-201.

[123] Christian, *Caroline Isl.*, 73; Pereiro, *Ponapé*, 118.

[124] Thurston, *S. India*, 79.

[125] Monier-Williams, *Brāhmanism*, 363; Gubernatis, *Usi Nuz.*, 156, note 1.

[126] "Pres. Address," in JASB, III, 323-328.

[127] *Hinduism*, 350-354.

head, and the two worship the sun. The groom puts a little vermilion on the parting of the bride's hair, puts his shoes on her feet, and then quickly removes them. Silk cloth is thrown over the heads of the pair and the groom draws aside the bridal veil, in many cases seeing his wife for the first time. Covering the pair with a cloth or canopy may, as in eating, be a measure to avoid the evil eye.[128]

In Rome the bride was received with fire and water (*aqua et igni accipi*) and her veil was called a *flammeum*.[129] Sprinkling was practised by the Moldavians also,[130] while among the ancient Germans the bride, arrived at the groom's house, was led or lifted over a vessel of water, then to the hearth, about which she walked thrice.[131] In Hungary the daughter kneels before her mother and receives the blessed water on her head; "it is a species of domestic sacrament." When the bride beats the groom with a sprig of blessed olive, the protective idea is doubtless present.[132] The Hottentot "priest" uses urine in purification where the more civilized people use water.[133]

The bridal veil is taken by some to be, like the mourning veil, a species of disguise from the spirits. It is hard to find another explanation that accounts for it better; under its protection the bride withdraws herself safely from the service and control of jealous family-spirits.[134] In the New Hebrides the bride's face is painted black or red.[135] The tearing off of the veil is often one of the last acts of the wedding-ceremony.[136] In the ceremony of the ancients a veil was held over the heads of bride and groom, and this custom persisted in France.[137] Among Russian Jews one of the presents of the bride to the groom was, along with a shroud, a veil to be worn at prayers.[138] In many cases the marrying parties are covered with a canopy, more or less rude, during part of the ceremony.[139]

Knots keep off the evil eye. In the girdle the Romans tied the "knot of Hercules." "The ancients most feared bewitchment through envy and the evil eye precisely when they were in luck. The wedding was reckoned as a happy event and therefore protection was here particularly necessary."[140] Again, all knots are loosened before the ceremony, in garters, shoestrings, strings of petticoats. "The precaution of loosening every knot about the new-joined pair is strictly observed" in Scotland. "It must be remarked that the custom is observed even in France."[141] In the reign of Queen Anne, there was "a curious superstition that every pin about the bride must be thrown away and lost.

128 §265, above.
129 Rossbach, *Röm. Ehe*, 361, 362, 364.
130 *Russian Ethnog.* (Russ.), II, 440.
131 Weinhold, *Deut. Frauen*, I, 407-408.
132 Gubernatis, *Usi Nuz.*, 155-156, 232.
133 Fritsch, *Eingeb. S.-Afr.*, 330, 331.
134 Lippert, *Kgchte.*, II, 145 ff.   135 Leggatt, in AAAS, 1892, 705.
136 Von Haxthausen, *Transkaukasia*, II, 22; Tetzner, in *Globus*, LXXVIII, 341.
137 Gubernatis, *Usi Nuz.*, 163.
138 *Russian Ethnog.* (Russ.), II, 413.
139 Weinhold, *Deut. Frauen*, I, 390.   140 Rossbach, *Röm. Ehe*, 278, 279.
141 Bourke, in BAE, IX, 569 (quoting Brand, *Popular Antiquities of Great Britain*, II, 143, and Pennant, "Tour in Scotland," in *Pinkerton's Voy.*, III, 382); Stoll, *Suggestion*, 421.

There would be no luck if one remained. Nor must the bridesmaid keep one, for should she do so she certainly would not be married before Whitsuntide."[142] Where it is in the mores that the younger brother or sister shall not be married before the elder, the most strenuous efforts are put forth to avoid such a calamity. The elder Hindu sister is wedded to a tree; then the younger can marry;[143] or the elder Jewess is hastily married beneath her, in one case to a boy "of whom little was known beyond the fact that he was inclined to consumption."[144] India is full of practices whereby an unlucky marriage is avoided by a prior marriage to some object.[145] With this may be compared the thrifty custom of avoiding the heavier expenses of a first wedding by marrying a Hindu girl to a bunch of flowers, which is then thrown into a well. Her next marriage will be a widow's second marriage and is much cheaper.[146]

The idea that the bride's foot must not touch the earth is worked out in the Hervey or Cook Islands as follows: "They are not content with mats wherewith to make a pathway for the bride to walk along. But should she be the eldest girl, the members of her husband's tribe lie down flat on the ground, while she walks lightly over their backs. This 'street of human bodies,' called in the native tongue *ara tangata,* extends from the bride's house to that of the bridegroom; and should the distance be so great that enough people cannot be found to make the pathway, then those on whom the bride has already stepped get up and quickly run on ahead, so as to lie down again and fill up the rest of the path.[147]

A stock method of averting daimonic attention is by appearing to be miserable or unlucky. The efficacy of vituperation and teasing in general has been mentioned elsewhere;[148] practices with the same end in view are to be found in the wedding-ceremonial.

The classic case is that of the coarse jokes and jibes employed by the Romans and called "fescennines."[149] The Chinese bride is asked embarrassing questions which she must answer.[150] In some districts of Russia the bride dances with the priest, the dance being accompanied by a song directed at the bride and containing indelicate jokes.[151] It would appear that some of the seemingly heartless treatment of the young wife may be accounted for along these lines. Chinese brides, for instance, "are often very young, always timid, and are terror-stricken at being thrust among strangers. There is a general indifference to the feelings of the poor child exhibited to the public gaze. In some places it is allowable for anyone to turn back the curtains of the chair and stare at her; in other regions, unmarried girls post themselves at a convenient spot and throw handfuls of chaff or hayseed at her, which will of course stick

[142] Ashton, *Queen Anne,* 33. [143] Jolly, *Recht u. Sitte,* 59.
[144] Antin, *Promised Land,* 35.
[145] Thurston, *S. India,* 34, 35, 36, 37, 41, 44, 47; Crooke, in JAI, XXVIII, 242; Risley, *Ethnog. Ind.,* I, 182; Hopkins, *Relig. Ind.,* 541; Jolly, in *Grundr. Indo-Ar. Philol.,* II, 61; Kohler, *Urgchte. d. Ehe,* 28.
[146] Hutchinson, *Marriage Customs,* 11.
[147] Hutchinson, *Marriage Customs,* 168-169.
[148] §266, above. [149] Lippert, *Kgchte.,* II, 20.
[150] Stevens, in *Ztsft. f. Ethnol.,* XXVIII, 176.
[151] Weinhold, *Deut. Frauen,* I, 390; Kaindl, in *Globus,* LXXXII, 356-357.

a long time to her oiled hair. When she reaches the house of her new parent, she is subjected to the same kind of criticism that would be given to a new horse."152 The fact that such rude treatment is ritualized, as it were, makes one hesitate to refer it merely to the love of bullying the helpless.

The custom of interposing resistance to the newly married is already familiar.153 It too is ritualized, which probably redeems it from being mere teasing. Those who plague the pair are the first to wish them happiness. "It is an old custom in Minorca to make the path of the newly married pair as difficult as possible. Young men stationed in the vicinity watch for their coming; when they appear, bushes will be set on fire, fresh walls will be built, and every sort of obstacle will be thrown in their way. Thus they learn that the path to happiness is difficult, while at the same time their home-coming will be celebrated by garlands of flowers. Fruit symbolizes the abundance wished to the married pair." Sometimes a wall is built against the door of the house occupied by the newly married on the wedding-night, and they are kept prisoners often till late the next day.154

The history of the wedding-ceremony shows that if a wedding is regarded as an occasion for some license of speech and action, if coarse jests are allowed and practical jokes are tolerated, the bride and groom can manage to pass it over as belonging to the occasion and therefore conventionalized; but it is also seen how these usages lower the dignity of the event and impair the conventionalization that confers solemnity. On the other hand, the abrogation of all such usages intensifies the latter form of conventionalization, and that heightens the decorum, protects the proprieties, sets aside all lewdness, and creates a sentiment of reverence for the marriage-relation.

The mediæval priest blessed the marriage-bed in order to exorcise demons from it, and the wedding-guests visited the spouses after they had retired because they thus witnessed the concubitus on which the law laid stress as making a marriage. The mores could carry even these usages and ward off annoyance and evil by conventionalization. It was a stricter conventionalization when such customs were abolished, after the religious and legal notions had suffered change. When people no longer believed that demons got an especial opportunity for working evil at weddings, the blessing of the bed was only a way of calling attention to what might better be ignored. Rationalization showed that the witnesses, despite their invasion of privacy, could not attest what the law referred to and that their presence was not necessary; then the visit to the spouses became a gratuitous annoyance. What brought such offensive usages to an end was the development of knowledge and enlightenment, not innate taste or an independent advance in refinement; the mores altered in adjustment to changed life-conditions.

152 Smith, *Chinese Char.*, 198.   153 §371, above.
154 Vuillier, *Forgotten Isles*, 103.

Several wedding-customs lie on the verge between the averting of evil influences and sacrificial propitiation. Fasting prior to the wedding is not uncommon.[155] Wilken[156] makes special mention of the practice of strewing grain at a wedding. It is an ancient Hebrew custom but is found commonly in the Indian Archipelago, except that here it is rice that is used. The interpretation has been along the line of symbolism, that the grain meant fecundity; it is accompanied often by invocation of the blessing of fruitfulness upon the bride. In the East Indies, however, the strewing of rice is not by any means confined to the wedding-ceremony; it takes place whenever it is desirable to evoke a spirit, for instance, when a person is unconscious and it is desirable to recall his soul. Such a soul often takes the form of a bird and, in particular, of a domestic fowl; and when the rice is strewn, the same call to the soul is made as is used to summon the chickens. The idea at the wedding, Wilken thinks, is to keep the souls of the parties within them, lest some evil spirit, prowling about intent upon working ill upon those who stand at a crisis of life and happiness, do them damage. In one case, a chicken is present to pick up the rice, the idea being that the soul-bird will thus be decoyed. It is a bad omen if the chicken refuses to peck at the rice. Rice-throwing is common in India,[157] and "the custom of throwing grain in the faces of the newly wed is as old as the Guanches."[158] The Bulgarians scatter grain and the Moldavians seeds and nuts.[159] Scattering of grain is, in general, one of the ways of diverting daimonic assault.[160]

Alongside ceremonial which is interpretable as exorcistic, at least in part, there is a profusion of usages which are wholly positive and propitiatory; these are sacrificial and are as numerous in variety as is sacrifice.[161]

"As a solemn joint sacrifice was the last part of the ceremonial in the father's house, another sacrifice is the first thing in the husband's house."[162]

[155] Wilkins, *Hinduism*, 350, 351; Hill-Tout, in *Amer. Antiquarian*, XXIV, 85-87.

[156] In VG, I, 563, 566, 567, 570-571.

[157] Thurston, *S. India*, 79-82, 100; Anon., "Royal Marriage," in JASB, II, 308, 309, 311 ff.; Collector of Sholapur, in JASB, V, 376-377; Modi, in JASB, III, 475, 480.

[158] Cook, in AA, II, 478.

[159] *Russian Ethnog.* (Russ.), II, 482, 440.

[160] Tylor, *Anth.*, 355.   [161] Ch. XXVI, above.

[162] Peterson, in JASB, III, 335.

A blood-offering in some form is common and the inference to antecedent human sacrifice is not a long one; in some parts of the world no marriage is valid, any more than other important relations, without the getting of a head.[163] In certain Hindu families, "it was customary for the bridegroom, at the marriage ceremony, to cut off the head of a human figure made of dough, with a knife supplied by the bride's family. That pointed to the fact that human sacrifice had at one time been performed at Hindu marriages."[164] Exuvial sacrifice is sometimes in evidence at a wedding: boys are circumcized as part of the ceremony in southern Tunis and the Indian girl's father cuts off a lock from the foreheads of the marrying parties, "a sign that marriage is completed."[165]

The ceremony of establishing "blood-brotherhood"[166] between bride and groom is found here and there. Among the Bechuana, the day after the pair goes to the groom's home, the shaman cuts their bodies in various places and rubs the blood of each into the wounds of the other.[167] The Papuans perform the same act after elopement and agreement[168] and it is found in Tibet.[169] Similarly each of the Rajput pair chews betel with which is mixed a tiny drop of blood drawn from the other's little finger; "this usage in which we may trace an interesting survival of primitive ideas is called . . . the joining of love."[170] Where bride and groom drink palm-wine out of a skull obtained on a head-hunting expedition[171] there is a combination of survivals.

The blood and flesh of animals then take the place of the human. After the Somal religious ceremony a sheep or goat is killed, and the woman dips the fingers of her right hand in the blood, streaks her forehead with it, and lays a piece of the animal's skin on her wrist. Then she may enter the blood-bespattered hut of the groom. This sprinkling of bride and house occurs also among the Galla; it and the anointing of the bride make the marriage irrevocable. Children born to the woman out of wedlock and even after the death of her husband—after which the wife cannot legitimately remarry—are regarded as his. This makes against divorce; even if, in case of a quarrel, the woman takes to prostitution and bears other children, these still inherit from the husband.[172] Among the Dyaks the bride and groom are touched with blood on the forehead and elsewhere, while the spirits are invoked to bless the pair with numerous offspring;[173] again the couple's hands are besmeared from a sword with the blood of a chicken and a pig, with invocations to the spirits.[174]

Blood, it will be recalled,[175] is one of the elements used, like water, as a protection from the spirits. In Rome the doorposts were smeared with the fat of a pig or wolf and thus made safe against hostile influences.[176] The South

[163] §§229, 365, above.   [164] Athalye, in JASB, I, 76.
[165] Bruun, *Huleboerne,* 145-147; Koch, in *Globus,* LXXXI, 105-106.
[166] §159, above.
[167] Ratzel, *Vkde.,* I, 188.   [168] Wilken, in VG, I, 489.
[169] Reid, "Farthest People," in *Cosmopolitan Mag.,* XXVIII, 451.
[170] Risley, *Ethnog. Ind.,* I, 83.   [171] Wilken, *Vkde.,* 394.
[172] Paulitschke, *Nordost-Afr.,* I, 200, 201, 204.
[173] Perelaer, *Dajaks,* 52.   [174] Bock, *Borneo,* 96.
[175] §227, above.
[176] Rossbach, *Röm. Ehe,* 351-352; Lippert, *Kgchte.,* II, 146; Sienkiewicz, *Quo Vadis,* 31, 99, 275.

Rumanian bride must, before she enters the groom's house, smear the threshold with butter that she may later in life have everything in superfluity.[177]

These cases are thus no more than special varieties of sacrifice. The stock forms, as connected with marriage, need no illustration here. It may be recalled that it is common for a bride to begin her married life with a sacrifice to the household-deities of the groom, an act which constitutes her introduction to the new set of ancestral gods which she is henceforth to serve.[178]

Not a little magic is performed in connection with the wedding, chiefly in order to secure, through an imitative representation, the salient objects of marriage.[179] Doubtless the symbols referred to above were often conceived of as exercising a magical effect in securing proper coöperation and harmony in the new relation and plenty of children to carry on the line and inherit the property.

One of the four ways for an Australian to get a wife is "charming by means of magic."[180] Magic is used also to protect the groom against the witchcraft that exists in woman:[181] "Let him take two threads, one blue and the other red, and lay them down across the track, so that the right wheel will go over the blue thread, and the left wheel over the red one. As he does this let him say, 'Blue and red are the two, and the witchcraft that is in her cannot pass them: her relations will now prosper, and her husband is in bonds.' . . . Let him now place in the lap of his wife the son of a woman who has borne sons only, all of whom are alive."[182] In Rome there was a marriage-god in whose lap the bride was set to ensure her fecundity.[183] In Great Russia there was a functionary at marriage whose duty it was to exorcise all evil spirits and sorcery, for marriage is a grand time for malevolent witchcraft. The bride solemnly walked about the bridal chamber, followed by fifteen or more persons, each carrying a part of the bed, and bearing in her hand a rod carved with magic marks.[184]

Though the shaman is at the wedding merely to attend to the luck-element,[185] he sometimes appears to be the center of ceremony, and the impression is somewhat as if religion made marriage.

The African shaman daily anoints and utters imprecations and formulas over a prospective bride for eight days.[186] "A Brahman performs the essential part

[177] Lazär, in *Globus*, XCIV, 318.   [178] Lippert, *Kgchte.*, II, 140 ff.
[179] §302, above.
[180] Spencer and Gillen, *Nat. Tr. Cent. Aust.*, 541.
[181] §388, below.
[182] Peterson, in JASB, III, 330, 335.   [183] Rossbach, *Röm. Ehe*, 302.
[184] Kostomarov, *Gt. Russians* (Russ.), 233.
[185] §341, above.
[186] Bastian, *Deut. Exped.*, I, 176, note.

of the marriage-ceremony by placing the bride's folded hands in those of the bridegroom";[187] and elsewhere the presence of a Brahman is needful at the essential and binding part of the ceremony.[188] In northern Sumatra the village priest discharges an important function in being present and blessing the union; the "whole long-drawn-out ceremony makes us think of . . . an amalgamation of religious prescriptions and antiquated custom."[189] Among the Yakuts the shaman formerly welcomed the groom when he entered and prayed the heavenly spirits to bless the newly married pair.[190] Again there is, at a marriage in the chief's family, a sort of religious ceremony where the priest prays over the pair.[191]

In the early Christian church, priestly benediction of marriage was not necessary and for widows sacerdotal nuptials were not allowed. The dogma that marriage is a sacrament developed from the phrase: "This is a great mystery."[192] Until 1563, marriage was valid without ecclesiastical benediction; the Council of Trent made it essentially a religious ceremony. One of the authors of this book has developed the relation of religion and marriage in the Christian church.[193]

Whether or not the shaman occupies the center of the stage, the religious element in the wedding is generally present and important. Certain Mohammedan Tatars had the custom that each guest smeared a piece of bread with butter and honey and ate it with dignity as in a religious ceremony; then came the real meal after the ritual one.[194] In Rome, "except for the wedding-day, the woman adhered to the old strict custom and wore the wreath only on the occasion of religious celebrations." The customs concerning the *lectus genialis* also witnessed to belief in the presence of the spirits, and were an added religious element in the Roman marriage-ceremony.[195] In Scandinavia the bride was consecrated with Thor's hammer.[196] In a Russian folksong, "a divine being is asked to come to the wedding, and to forge such a marriage as may be firm, strong, long-enduring, eternal—one on which the wind may blow without scattering it, and the rain may beat without washing it away, and which the sun may dry without turning it into dust."[197]

Priest and religion were, strictly speaking, incidental to the wedding rather than essential. The ceremony, as a sort of rehearsal of the status, was in the mores; the entrance of the priest and of religion took account of the aleatory element. It was very important that that should be done, but the doing of it was not at all the making of the marriage.

[187] Collector of Khandesh, in JASB, V, 59.

[188] Thurston, *S. India,* 60-61.

[189] Jacobs, *Groot-Atjeh,* I, 41-42, 67.

[190] Sieroshevski-Sumner, *Yakuts,* in JAI, XXXI, 83.

[191] Kubary, *Núkuóro,* 34.   [192] Ephesians, V, 32.

[193] Sumner, *Folkways,* 418 ff.; Sumner, "Mod. Marr.," in *Yale Rev.,* XIII, 249 ff.; Westermarck, *Marriage,* II, 576.

[194] Von Stenin, in *Aus Allen Weltteilen,* XXIX, 64; Pischon, *Islam,* 10, 11.

[195] Rossbach, *Röm. Ehe,* 292 (quoted), 367-370.

[196] Grimm, *Rechtsalt.,* 431.   [197] Ralston, *Russ. People,* 306-307.

§374*. **The Continuance of Precaution.** Succeeding the wedding itself is a varying period preceding the actual beginning of the status. People who are anywhere near the mating crisis are in special peril. Iphigenia calls to all men who want to marry and all women with child, as being particularly susceptible, to flee from the pollution that is abroad.[198] The climax of the crisis is the consummation of the union; all the interests surrounding fecundity and legitimacy center here. Hence the fasting of the Indian bride;[199] hence the blessing of the couch, with prayers for defense against phantasmal demonic illusions. Among other means of evading peril is the deferring of consummation, which amounts to misleading the lurking spirits that are ready to damage the health or fecundity of the parties and their prospective children. The custom is too widespread to be referred in reason to acculturation. We condense a long list of illustrations.

In West Victoria the newly married pair are attended by two companions for two moons. They are not allowed even to look at each other, the bride being called for the period a "not look around." She keeps head and face covered when her husband is present, and he turns away from her. The young people look in and laugh at them. If they need to speak to one another, they do it through their friends. After the termination of this period the bride is taken to see her own relatives for a week or two, the husband remaining behind, and when she returns the attendants are dismissed.[200] In other Australian tribes the period of deferred consummation is two months;[201] again, in a tribe very loose in sex-matters, two or three nights are demanded.[202] In Dutch New Guinea the pair are resolutely kept awake the night of the wedding, for those who do not sleep on the occasion will live long and happily, "and so every bridal pair gladly submit themselves to the torture."[203] In Africa the period may be four to eight weeks.[204] "Only upon the fourth day does the young husband succeed in gradually getting rid of the superfluous maidens" who guard the bride.[205] In the Sahara region, as in ancient Sparta, the husband must approach his bride clandestinely;[206] the Kabyles fine a man who does not defer his rights until he has conducted his wife solemnly to his home.[207] In modern Egypt the period of restraint is about a week.[208]

In India the waiting period may be a year, three months, seven days, or six

[198] Euripides, *Iph. Taur.*, 1226 ff.
[199] Hassler, in *Inter. Cong. Anthrop., Chicago*, 1893, 354.
[200] Dawson, *Aust. Aborig.*, 32.   [201] Smyth, *Vict.*, I, 84.
[202] Cunow, *Australneger*, 85, 98.   [203] Krieger, *Neu-Guinea*, 394.
[204] Volkens, *Kilimandscharo*, 251.   [205] Nachtigal, *Sahara*, I, 740.
[206] Pommerol, *Sahariennes*, 250-252.
[207] Hanoteau et Letourneux, *Kabylie*, II, 214.
[208] Lane, *Mod. Egypt.*, I, 241, 305.

days.[209] In ancient India it was never less than four days;[210] in the Brahmanic period, 1000-500 B.C., three to twelve days—some say one night and others that restraint occurred only if the husband was from another village.[211] During the period the pair must eat unsalted food, consisting of rice and milk.[212] Again, a string is placed about the bride's neck, to be removed by a special religious rite before consummation.[213] In one case, where the women shave the head until marriage and where it is considered a reproach to bear a child before the hair is long enough to be tied behind, the spouses are separated for a year after marriage.[214] Evidently, while this is a case of deferred consummation, the taboo is less directly explicable than in preceding instances. Surreptitious approach to the bride is found in India too.[215] Deferred consummation is, of course, rational where the bride is a mere child and there are beliefs concerning the sexual life of woman that lead to restraint over a period. The pair may begin to live together five or even seven years after the marriage, a period which "is fixed with reference to the physical development of the bride"; but there are cases where this rational procedure is not practised.[216]

Wilken[217] has made a collection of instances of deferment, running from one to one hundred and eighty days. He cites customs of keeping the newly married awake, noting that it is in part to avoid bad dreams, much as the Alfurs stop their ears before the marriage in order not to hear bad omens in the cries of birds. In general, the pair fear lest some evil spirit take advantage of the sleep to do them damage. The Sumatran husband is excluded by the old matrons for two or three days, "the bride holding it a point of honor to defend to extremity that jewel which she would yet be disappointed in preserving."[218] This interpretation links up with resistance-ritual. Restraint is common in northern Sumatra and nine days are passed by the bride under supervision of two duennas. "According to the Mohammedan rite they are really married, according to the Atjeh *adat*, not yet." Surveillance is not so protracted if the bride is older.[219]

American Indians practised the same deferment, sometimes for a year.[220] The Seri suitor must remain a "continent comrade" for that period as a pre-marital test.[221] Among the Cheyennes continence continues also after marriage; a "protective string" is respected for ten to fifteen days. They say it enables the pair to get used to each other. "Men tell me that they used to lie awake almost all night, talking to their newly married wives."[222] Abstention of one to four or more days occurs among certain Indians of Brazil.[223]

[209] Godden, in JAI, XXVI, 176; XXVII, 27, 28; Thurston, *S. India,* 51; Lewin, *S.E. India,* 127.

[210] Monier-Williams, *Brāhmanism,* 355.

[211] Hopkins, *Relig. Ind.,* 271; Zimmer, *Altind. Leben,* 313.

[212] Schmidt, *Jus Primœ Noctis,* 156 ff.

[213] Von Seidlitz, in *Globus,* LXXVIII, 244.

[214] Godden, in JAI, XXVII, 27-28.   [215] Lewin, *S.E. India,* 202.

[216] Risley, *Ethnog. Ind.,* I, 98, 82-83; Gubernatis, *Usi Nuz.,* 214.

[217] *Vkde.,* 288, 289; Wilken, in VG, I, 498-499, 501, 502, and note.

[218] Marsden, *Sumatra,* 269.

[219] Jacobs, *Groot-Atjeh,* I, 42 ff., 48, 60-61, 66.

[220] Wilutsky, *Mann u. Weib,* 202-204.

[221] McGee, in AA, IX, 375.

[222] Grinnell, in AA, IV, 14-15; Grinnell, *Cheyenne,* I, 145.

[223] Ehrenreich, in *Berl. Mus. Vkde.,* II, 29; Von Martius, *Beiträge,* 113.

The classic case of deferred consummation is that of Tobias,[224] and from it is derived the term "Tobias-nights." It was needful to exorcise a devil from the bridal chamber and so the pair prayed and were continent for three days. The Greeks, Romans, Germans, Scandinavians, Italians, and Turks also knew of the custom; perhaps the fact that the Argive bride dressed like a man was also an avoidance-measure.[225] In the eleventh and twelfth centuries the authorities recommended or enjoined a delay of one, two, or three days. In the canon law a marriage was clandestine unless there was abstinence for two or three days, such abstinence counting *pro reverentia benedictionis*.[226] "The demand of the Church, which at times appeared, that the young married pair, following the example of Tobias and his wife, . . . should refrain in the first or the first three nights . . . seems to have been little regarded in Germany. In France there was a dispensation from it in money." This was abrogated in 1409.[227] However, German tradition favored the practice; in the sagas, it is recalled, the groom and bride lay with a naked sword between them; and cases are cited from out-of-the-way places.[228]

Great anxiety was shown by the Russian bridal pair lest witchcraft intervene; they practised abstention for two days and all sorts of religious devices; and the prostitutes were not less sedulous in avoidance and exorcism.[229] Among the Slavs of former times, for three days the so-called *djevers*, generally brothers of the groom, lay ceremonially with the bride and the groom might not address her. Abstention lasted for two or three additional days. The groom feared to go near his wife during the first week.[230] This case links up with the preceding topic of expiation for marriage.[231]

One of the chief functions of religion among primitive people is the sanctioning of taboos. Of all the inhibitions surrounding the beginning of marriage, though perhaps the most striking is the one which has just been considered, there are yet others of a miscellaneous character that run over from the wedding into matrimony.

Among the Andaman Islanders, "it often happens that a young couple will pass several days of their honeymoon without exchanging a single word, and their bashfulness is so great that they sometimes do not even look at each other." They "do not leave the encampment in order to get food, or anything else that they may require, as the friends consider it a duty or privilege to supply all their needs until the shyness, consequent on the marriage, has worn off."[232] The words "bashfulness" and "shyness" are not used in our sense, as

[224] Tobit, VI, 2 ff.; Schmidt, *Jus Primæ Noctis*, 150.

[225] Gubernatis, *Usi Nuz.*, 214-215; Schmidt, *Jus Primæ Noctis*, 155; Plutarch, *Lycurgus*, §XV.

[226] Freisen, *Kanon. Eherechts*, 851, 129; Reichel, *Canon Law*, I, 351, note.

[227] Friedberg, *Eheschliess.*, 82, note.

[228] Pudor, "Geschlechtsleben," in *Pol.-Anth. Rev.*, V, 350; Weinhold, *Deut. Frauen*, I, 399; Schmidt, *Jus Primæ Noctis*, 155.

[229] Stern, *Russland*, 114-115.

[230] Rhamm, in *Globus*, LXXXII, 189.

[231] §343, above.   [232] Man, in JAI, XII, 138.

we shall see. In Africa the bride is sometimes shut up in a hut which her father has built for her; she may eat of the wedding-meal but may not be seen. This is reported of the negroes in general.[233] In South Africa, "at the marriage feast the bride is secluded, the groom not even being allowed to see her, but at the close of the preliminaries his friends are admitted to inspect her, and the veil is raised by one of her attendants."[234] On the Zanzibar coast the bride lives seven days in retirement; in Uganda the couple live in retirement for a month, during which time the bride wears a veil of bark and her husband must give a goat for leave to lift it. The wife and her girl friends eat the goat.[235] Elsewhere, "the bride keeps the house for two months without going to the field or taking any part in the household work, while the men do the sweeping and till the garden plot."[236] Among the Sahara women, the bride does not work for a year, sometimes two.[237]

At a Yakut wedding the bride and groom are hidden in corners and take no share in the festivities. He may not see her without great impropriety but she sees him through a crack when he goes to water his horses.[238] "In Rajput families of Tirhut it is considered contrary to etiquette for a young married couple to see each other by day so long as the husband's parents are alive, and in particular they must avoid being seen together by the husband's parents, and must not speak to one another in their presence."[239] In Madras it is customary that the bride and groom shall not look at each other, however much they may desire to do so; a sidelong glance is the most that custom and superstition permit.[240] Provision is sometimes made, by a screen, that the groom shall not see the bride at a certain stage of the wedding-ceremony.[241] Among the Kazan Tatars the newly married man avoids meeting his parents-in-law for several months.[242]

In Korea, "silence is regarded as the wife's first duty. During all the marriage day she must be speechless. If she says a word or makes a sign, she becomes an object of ridicule, and her silence must remain unbroken even in her own room, though her husband may try to break it by taunts, jeers, or coaxing, for the female servants are on the watch for such a breach of etiquette as speech, hanging about the doors and chinks to catch up and gossip even a single utterance, which would cause the bride to lose caste forever in her circle. This custom of silence is observed with greatest rigidity in higher classes. It may be a week or several months before the husband knows the sound of his wife's voice, and even after that for a long time she only speaks when necessary."[243] Among the Dyaks, during the first seven days "the young married people may not go out, and they are in duty bound to enjoy their honeymoon separate from the whole world. At real need they may go to the river to bathe . . . and then they must select such hours of the day that they stand the minimum chance of being seen by fieldworkers or passersby."[244] Staying at the house of the newly wedded wife is regarded by

[233] Ratzel, *Vkde.*, I, 154.
[234] Macdonald, in JAI, XIX, 272.
[235] Stuhlmann, *Mit Emin*, 37, 183.
[236] Clozel, in PSM, XLIX, 676.
[237] Pommerol, *Sahariennes*, 252.
[238] Sieroshevski-Sumner, in JAI, XXXI, 81, 83, 84, 86.
[239] Risley, *Ethnog. Ind.*, I, 82-83; §425, below.
[240] Naidoo, in JASB, II, 391.
[241] Thurston, *S. India*, 69-70.
[242] Von Stenin, in *Aus Allen Weltteilen*, XXIX, 65, 66.
[243] Bishop, *Korea*, 118.
[244] Perelaer, *Dajaks*, 54-55.

most people as a "brutal informality, likely to bring the good name of the young woman into danger."[245]

Among the Cherkes, a husband visits his wife only secretly; if he is seen he is treated with derision and so is she. This custom is especially strict in the first days of marriage. It is considered improper to see one's wife by day, to go into her house, or to talk with her in the presence of others. An Armenian bride, after marriage, covers her face all but the eyes and nose. She may speak to no one save her husband, sisters, and little children. She answers her parents-in-law by signs and her husband ought not to call her by name. Similarly among some Caucasus tribes.[246] After a Bulgar marriage, neither the groom nor bride goes from home; "the latter sits weeping at home and is comforted daily by her comrades, who cover her hands with a cloth so that they cannot be seen."[247]

All these ritual taboos cannot be referred to "shyness." If the parties have not been "bashful" before, why should they be after marriage? It seems to us, having in mind, among other things, the frequently easy-going relations of the sexes before marriage, that there is no great cause for shyness other than of the formal order, assumed as part of the traditional propriety of the occasion. There are writers who think that taboos like the above are rooted in some innate or instinctive sense of shame, or otherwise carry over into the explanation of them a set of considerations belonging to their own code. We believe that the retiring demeanor of the newly married, as illustrated by our cases, is a piece of ritual like the bride's resistance and despairing utterances. The thing to be shy about is the inviting of calamity by irritating the spirits that manage human destinies. If shyness means timidity, diffidence, or wariness in view of the definite or indefinite hazards surrounding a great life-crisis, then the term seems to us applicable, though not well chosen. All these taboos belong by their very nature to the religious aspects of marriage.

[245] Jacobs, *Groot-Atjeh*, I, 64.
[246] *Russian Ethnog.* (Russ.), II, 225, 340, 387.
[247] Strauss, *Bulgaren*, 315.

CHAPTER L

WEDLOCK: STATUS OF WOMAN

§375. Matrimony. Preceding chapters have dealt with usages connected with entrance into the life-status of matrimony. Regulations have determined who may marry whom, and they have prescribed the manner of marriage by fixing various norms of propriety that must be followed if the ensuing status is to be a "right" one. It is proper to elope or not to elope, to pay bride-price or to receive dowry, to practise antecedent chastity or license, to undergo test or to have no test at all. With entrance into matrimony comes a wedding-ceremony which gathers up and epitomizes these preconditions and also foreshadows the salient features of the status in which bride and groom are thereafter understood to be living. Inasmuch as all these preliminaries have that status in view, a survey of them must needs already have indicated what matrimony is to be. Evidently wedlock is the central feature of the organization for self-perpetuation. It is also a very complex life-status; one may bear in mind all the foreshadowings that he has encountered and still find enough other aspects of matrimony to engage his attention for an indefinite time.

Before we begin upon any of these, it is imperative to hook up into plain view the two main strands upon which the fabric of marriage is woven, lest they be lost to sight under the lesser threads that we have been tracing for some chapters back. These strands are the maintenance-factor and the sex-factor. Marriage is viewed in this book as primarily a form of coöperation in self-maintenance, as, indeed, the elemental type of coöperation between specializing unlikes. Because, however, the coöperators are of different sex, issues have risen in their association demanding specific adjustments not called for in uni-sexual organization. These adjustments, though they still go back to an ultimate root in self-maintenance, are immediately connected with conceptions about sex, offspring, and descent. It is the fact of bi-sexuality that lends a specific character to marital coöperation as compared with other forms of association in the struggle for existence. Marriage is a form of self-maintenance so shaped and colored by sexual considerations as to constitute an organization by itself, with marked characteristic features.

Thus the master-strand of marriage as of other societal organizations is still of the maintenance order, while the characteristic feature by which marriage is set off from other institutions is the sexual factor. The former strand has appeared and reappeared, for instance in the relations of marriage to property so much in evidence in the preliminaries to matrimony; the latter in the provisions about consanguine unions, pre-marital conduct, test of the woman, and others having to do with sex-relations and their sequels; while both have been represented in the summarizing ceremony of the wedding. It is to be expected that these two strands will remain determinative of the general pattern of matrimony.

A man and a woman, having been wedded, are now in a life-status. It is a social, not a natural one, and is, in so far, upon an artificial plane; what the processes of natural selection would by themselves have evolved as the biologically most expedient relation of the sexes cannot be known, for those processes have been superseded in the life of societies. The conjugal relation is conventional. In any society, at a time, there is a conviction as to what matrimony means, which could perhaps be formulated into a description of the status; but at the time nobody thinks of doing that. Marriage everywhere illustrates how mores, things everyone knows or does daily, do not get into formal record. They are always taken for granted. Only in a developed society does the fact come out more sharply that the marrying parties are really entering a life-status the nature of which is prescribed; for a man and woman who want to contract matrimony may not do so except as the law provides. This is on account of the state's guarantee of marriage and of property; what the status shall be, with the rights and duties of the parties, is set down in general lines by statute or common law. The man and woman may not marry otherwise nor can they alter at will the rights and duties that go with the status; if they try to do so the state will object or will not enforce. Law, however, is but the precipitate of the mores; behind it, and within and by the side of it, they prescribe all human relationships; rights and duties can be altered only in defiance of the force behind the mores, public conviction.

Though it is conditioned and determined by the mores, no such relationship of individuals in a status is thereby exempted from an internal antagonism of interests. The fact that the institution has to be built up by taboos which define the relation of the individuals as that of man and wife, witnesses to an original diversity of interests. Every prosperous institution must embrace antagonistic interests reduced to some degree of harmony. In the case of matrimony the interests are primarily those of the two contracting parties; then, right upon the heels of these, there are also and regularly to be considered the interests of the children presently to be born. Says Von Hartman:[1] "If we fix attention solely upon the felicity of the present generation, the value of marriage appears very doubtful. . . . And so we arrive at the conclusion that it is not at all the welfare of the marrying parties which should be advanced by the marriage but the weal of the future generation." Though this is an overstatement, it brings out a fact: that marriage cannot be a successful and permanent institution unless the interests of parents and offspring, inherently diverse as they are in important respects,[2] can be harmonized. Then come the interests of relatives and less closely connected parties. In the harmony of all these an extreme complexity of marital and family-relations has evolved which could never have been worked out rationally, which has grown up, rather, in the unconsidered, unconscious, automatic manner characteristic of the mores. When the human mind has managed to assume the control of these relations, and has applied its "logic" to them, then the race has been afflicted by whimsical and fantastic premises, contradictory to the sense of the institution as well as to nature, as, for example, the merit of celibacy and asceticism. Men have then experienced, in an atmosphere of fictions and incongruities and a murk of dogma, the curse of unhappiness that arises out of war with realities.

Lest one assume that what the mores dictate must be an expedient and adequate adjustment, exempt from the need of correction, he should recall, among other elements unfavorable to adaptation, an elusive variable that plays about the course of the mores, that sentiment which has been called

[1] *Phänom.*, 685.   [2] Spencer, *Prin. Soc.*, I, §§275 ff.

"pathos."[3] As here in evidence, it is a way of looking at marriage which is considered orthodox, proper, necessary, which every "respectable" person must profess in the phrases which have become current concerning marriage. Cant is almost inseparable from it. Pathos has hovered about tyrannicide in Greece, about revolution in the nineteenth century, about democracy in recent decades. It surrounds the system of monogamy and was much in evidence not so long ago in connection with the issue of seating Mormons in Congress. It sets itself against all variation, by a general taking of things for granted, and opposes free handling or discussion, thus checking criticism and slowing up selection. It is salutary in that it discourages reckless innovation; nevertheless, along with other forms of conservatism, it holds up the process of adaptation of the mores, which may then become inexpedient maladjustments.[4]

The antagonism of interests involved in the marriage-relation, as in any other, leads out into a definition of rights.[5] It was on account of the rights accruing in matrimony that society developed a ceremony or ritual by which the status out of which the prerogatives grew should be defined, impressed upon everybody, and its beginning be clearly signalized. The first set of rights distinguished come out of the clash and competition of interests between husband and wife. Since the race is divided into two sexes which associate perforce in antagonistic coöperation, the issue of adjustment is inevitable. No way has ever been found to settle it by formula, much less by some simple and "just" apportionment of rights. Inherent equality of the sexes is a dream and not of this earth.

§376*. Sex-Rights in Marriage. Almost insensibly, as one reviews the relation of the sexes in matrimony, does he find his attention centering upon the case of the woman. This is probably because he has been hearing all his life about woman's rights, about how she ought to have more of them, and about how she has been held down and oppressed by man, while man's rights have been taken to be a matter of course and nothing much has been said or written concerning them. There is no reason to resist this tendency to view the matter from the standpoint of woman's status. Indeed it is possible to contend that the evolution of wedlock can be followed best by taking the status of the wife as a gauge; that the position of man is readily inferred if hers is known; and that the

[3] §339, above.
[4] Another Bachelor, on "Courtship," in Atl. Mo., CXXVIII, 649 ff.
[5] Keller, Soc. Evol., 84 ff.; §§168 ff., above.

situation of the children is in many respects more closely assimilated to hers than to his. This is not to say, however, that the
stage of evolution reached by the status of the wife is an infallible
indicator as to the degree of progress and refinement attained by
the marriage-institution as a whole; nor does it mean that that
institution has developed solely out of restrictions laid upon the
man, he at first having had everything and later on less than all.
The element of truth in such correlations appears only when they
are subjected to a good deal of qualification; without it they are
likely to give a one-sided view of the facts. This being understood,
there is no reason why sex-rights in matrimony may not be envisaged by centering attention on the wife.

Furthermore, there is an economy of presentation attainable
by considering the status of woman outside of wedlock along with
that of the wife. The fact is that this topic of sex-rights speedily
eludes confinement within the range of matrimony and escapes
into the wider area of general societal organization. And, upon
reflection, it is clear that nothing is lost by treating the case in its
general aspects; for, since marriage has always remained the
center and focus of woman's destiny,[6] her life, whether she is married or unmarried, has been oriented from wedlock and has taken
its values from that status as from a sort of dominant chord.
Even the exceptional cases, such as enforced virginity, have recognized this orientation by the very quality of being in artificial con-
tradistinction to it. That orientation could not but exist with
biological conditions as they are and with the sex-mores forming
a girl's destiny toward marriage as they shape a boy's toward the
rougher and less circumscribed life of man. Since there rests upon
woman, in her special function as mother, a quite disproportionate share of the species-interest, which she can never evade as
long as she remains female, marriage determines her destiny,
whether she is in it or outside of it. Her rights outside of it are
gauged to those she is to have or has had within it. A study of the
general case inevitably includes all the essentials of the special.
Hence, in what is presently to come concerning the position of
woman, examples and conclusions will not relate to the wife alone.
The status of the prospective wife, the non-wife, or the widow

6 §§61, 62, above.

takes its tone from that of the wife, and the aspects of the code as it concerns them are, in turn, enlightening as to the status of the wife and the nature of wedlock in general. As soon as the girl emerges from childhood, and frequently long before that time, she enters the range of marriage-preliminaries, the nature of which is determined by what wedlock is conceived to be—which therefore prefigure that status; while at the other end of the scale is divorce or widowhood, both again envisaged from the standpoint of matrimony and revealing what it is by exhibiting, respectively, the conditions under which it ceases to be and the position of the woman who has fallen out of it. It is the status of the woman in wedlock which fixes her status outside it as well; and, conversely, the general status repeats the special.

There is no denying that in most recent times the enfranchisement of woman outside of marriage has begun to exert its influence upon the status of the wife; it is also true that if such an influence is now seen in operation, some prototype of it probably existed from time immemorial. But it has not been in evidence through the long earlier stages of evolution; if any such tendency existed, it was overgrown and repressed. The modern instance is as yet but a ripple on the surface, and may never become anything more, compared with the age-wide surges which we seek here to record.

This broad truth being understood, it follows that man has been freer and more independent in working out his destiny than has woman. Her fate centers more in self-perpetuation; man's in self-maintenance. Marriage was not to him the poet's "thing apart"; it was very important that he should be married;[7] but it was not his "whole existence" nor did it determine his destiny as it did that of woman. It might be said that woman surrenders more to the relation than does man and that she thus enters it at some comparative disadvantage. The truth of such a contention is demonstrable less by definite instances than by the consensus of all the evidence.

The broadest preliminary generalization is that when it was expedient for society that woman should get rights, she got them, and without agitation, just as children did. This generalization

---

[7] §341, above.

means something more than that woman got rights when she got them; it is an induction from many cases, the review of which should reveal why it has been expedient under certain circumstances and not under others for rights to be accorded to woman. The topic of sex-rights in marriage and out of it is an exceedingly intricate one, not to be dismissed, though it may be prefaced, by a sweeping generalization. Least of all may sex-rights be explained by a swelling deduction from some "self-evident" or "necessary" major premise. The question cannot even be discussed, much less settled, in any such manner, whereas it can be rationally examined, if not solved, by taking recourse to attested facts and allowing them to tell their story. We start, then, from the usual evolutionary position that, along with the rest of the mores, those which confer rights upon woman, or withhold them, represent an adjustment of society as a whole to its life-conditions. If usages in this respect are of long standing and wide of dispersal, the inference is that they are expedient under the life-conditions prevailing. There is here no question of progress or of moral judgment or of how individuals may rejoice, thrive, or suffer under any given system or of how we should feel under the circumstances; the only question regarding any system is: Was it expedient for the society at large, under prevailing life-conditions, and, if so, how?

§377. Status of Woman. No topic of the science of society is more difficult to treat with anything like conclusiveness than is the status of woman, for it has always been contradictory, as it is now. Woman's legal non-entity and her actual power or influence have always been in glaring contrast. Two ethnographers writing of the same tribe may draw two discordant but correct pictures. Isolated instances are even grotesque, as where wives held apparently in abject slavery are found to henpeck or even beat their husbands and to wield a considerable influence in the society. Woman's status appears to be a paradox.

One of the reasons why it seems so shifting, unidentifiable, and resistant of classification is because no specific content has been read into the term "status." When writers tell of the "high" or "low" status of woman in this society or in that, they are recording merely an impression. Evidently there are only two impressions possible about such a matter, namely, that of the outsider concerning a people and that of the people about themselves. The former is worthless for the securing of understanding because it simply assesses the usages of others according to the criteria of the observer; and the latter is of no utility because it does not discriminate. The outsider reports the status of women as high or low; the insider regards it as normal and right, if, indeed, he can be figured as thinking about it at all; neither says anything of scientific import, except that the insider's uncritical answer implies that the existing status is a satisfactory adjustment.

The term "status" when used in this impressionistic manner merely befogs the understanding. Suppose that we endeavor to put something definite into the term by agreeing that woman's status shall be considered to be the sum of her rights—her specific rights as objectively reported by either outsiders or insiders. There is a worldwide difference, for instance, so far as scientific utility is concerned, between the general statement that the women of tribe X are low of status, being badly treated and held in contempt, and the specific report that the women of tribe Y may be sold or killed at will by the males of their families. One is an opinion, subjective in an indeterminable degree, the other an objective fact. That woman has or has not the right to life is a real datum for the identification of her status, and a collection of such data affords a definite idea of her position in society. We arrive, then, at a method of determining the status of woman by listing a set of specific rights and observing whether she has them or not; and since the rights of the woman are set to the fore only as a device for more readily apprehending the broader issue of sex-rights, the status of man may be aligned in comparison.

From the evidence at disposal it is possible to construct a rough parallel-column exhibit of rights as possessed by the sexes that shall indicate contrasts in status. Perhaps the inductive quality of the generalizations represented in the following table would come out more convincingly if such summary were reserved until the discussion of its details had been completed; but for purposes of presentation it seems useful to insert at this point a sort of reconnaissance-chart of territory presently to be covered.

Prerogatives	Woman	Man
(1) Right to life	Yes*	Yes
(2) Freedom from seclusion.	Yes-No	Yes
(3) Freedom from public sex-control	Yes*	Yes
(4) Self-disposal (premarital)	No-Yes	Yes
(5) Self-disposal (consent to marriage)	Yes-No	Yes*
(6) Self-disposal (in wedlock)	No	Yes*
(7) Self-disposal (postmarital)	No-Yes	Yes
(8) Right to property in self	No-Yes	Yes
(9) Freedom from being owned by spouse	Yes-No	Yes
(10) Freedom from being given, lent, exchanged	Yes-No	Yes
(11) Freedom from being inherited	No-Yes	Yes
(12) Freedom from punishment for infidelity	No*	Yes*
(13) Right to own property	No-Yes	Yes
(14) Right to inherit property	No-Yes	Yes
(15) Right to hold public office	No*	Yes
(16) Right to hold religious office	No*	Yes
(17) Inviolability in war	Yes*	No
(18) Influence in family	Yes*	Yes
(19) Influence in kin-group	No-Yes	Yes
(20) Influence in territorial group	No*	Yes

"Yes" means "virtually always"; "No" means "virtually never"; "Yes-No" means "more often than not," i.e., a qualified positive; "No-Yes" means a qualified negative, i.e., more often no-right than right; "Yes*" or "No*" means just short of an unqualified positive or an unqualified negative, respectively.

Any such schematization must be rough, no more than typical, little qualified, and not self-explanatory. Item (1), for example, is clear enough; on the other hand, item (12) does not mean that man is never punished for adultery, but that he is not penalized merely for being unfaithful to his wife; if society chastises man A, it is for infringing upon B's rights over B's wife. Such explanations must be looked for in the discussions connected with the several items.

Whatever rights woman held, since they had to be conferred and guaranteed by society, were peace-group affairs.[8] The only exception in the list is item (17), which has an inter-group aspect and represents one of those variations away from unregulated warfare[9] indicative of the drift toward peace and of the development of an inter-group code. To all intents and purposes, however, what follows is concerned solely with in-group conditions. And it must not be lost to sight that there is no right unless support by the group, through public opinion, is present.

§378. Minimal Rights. The first right to be considered is that

---

[8] §170, above.　　　　　　[9] §§141, 142, above.

to mere existence.[10] It signifies, in effect, that the woman possessing it may not be killed by her husband. That the latter refrains from dispatching her simply because she is of value to him does not accord her a right any more than similar self-repression in the case of a slave; she has the right to life only when her death will be avenged or when society will punish her slayer.[11] If her fellow group-members will merely censure him, her right is slight; if, on the other hand, her kin will set out at once to exact blood-vengeance or if the tribal authorities will execute a wife-killer or even fine him heavily, her right is substantial. Naturally the captured woman, having no kinsmen at hand and not belonging to the group, possesses no right; by contrast, the regularly purchased wife has her father or uncle and brothers near at hand to supply the might that guarantees her right. The nearer they are, the better for her; still, even under exogamy, where her kinsmen are in another tribe, her murder would injure group-relations; and public opinion does not tolerate conduct provocative of war with a friendly tribe.

Only under conditions of low civilization is woman's right to life in abeyance, though it is often found to be less sturdily guarteed than that of man. To the few instances of no-right to life there are here attached several cases, likewise out of savagery, in which violence scarcely short of homicidal has been practised with impunity by the husband against the wife or by the father against a recalcitrant daughter.[12] There are in our collections no cases of the opposite tenor, where woman has the right to kill or mutilate man.

The Australian wife "is a slave, the beast of burden to the man; she is excluded from all rights, victim to the untamed brutality of her master."[13] This would seem to form a sort of base-line of rightlessness; but there is even here some qualification: "His wife he may treat or ill-treat pretty much as he chooses. . . . In the event of a man proceeding to kill his wife, however, the members of his tribe would interfere to prevent him, on the ground that her brothers would hold all the members of the tribe equally responsible with the husband for the act; and, in revenge, kill the first of his blood whom they might find in their power." The author[14] adds a detail of great significance to the picture: "In every way the female's looks to us a hard lot; and yet, not-

10 §172, above.
11 §§178, 182, above.
12 §419, below.
13 Semon, *Aust. Bush,* 231.
14 Curr, *Aust. Race,* I, 60, 61, 109, 110; Spencer and Gillen, *Nat. Tr. Cent. Aust.,* 195, 196, 426.

withstanding, I do not hesitate to say that they are, as a whole, fairly happy, merry, and contented." Of the Tasmanians it is recorded: "Like the majority of savages, they do not treat their women well"; the wives were "nearly all covered with scars" at the hands of their husbands, who would not, moreover, share in the labor.[15] The Papuan beats his wife, treats her with contempt, and kills her on slight provocation. In British New Guinea the woman, after marriage, is the property of her husband who "does with her according to his mood." A few years ago a missionary, endeavoring to rescue a woman who was going to be speared by her husband, was set right by an old female. "Why do you mix in this?" she said. "Don't you know that the Koiari men can kill their wives if they want to, and can then take another wife in place of the one killed?"[16] The New Hebrides woman may be killed by her husband "without fear of outside resentment. No brother or male relative would seek vengeance, as they would in a case of man murder."[17]

"The Fan woman is scarcely considered as belonging to the human species. Every Fan will tell you so plainly as it has been told me in apt terms. One day, tired of a dog that kept nipping at my heels and barking at my trousers, I let fly a kick at him: 'If you want to get mad, hit my wife, don't hit my dog!' To hit a woman involves no penalty; if it pleases a father or husband to beat his daughter or wife, to flog her, even without cause, no one sees anything amiss. Blood may run; it is no matter. She belongs so slightly to the tribe that law protects her in no way."[18] Among the Dinkas, "if a girl is killed by her father, brother, or any other whose property she is, there is no tribal authority to demand explanation or inflict punishment. . . . If a girl or woman is killed by her husband it is treated as an accident and misfortune to the husband, but he may have to pay a cow or more to propitiate the girl's family and stop talk. . . . The loss is his, and it is argued that it must have been an accident, as no Dinka would harm a cow, much less a woman, whose value may be many cows."[19] Here is a case where a woman gets at least the semblance of a right to life because she is a valuable possession.

When it comes to blood-money for murder the woman's life is valued at a third, a half, two-thirds that of the man's; in East Africa there was only one case where more was paid for a woman than for a man. In general the blood-money for a woman corresponds to the average bride-price, which witnesses again to the property-status of woman. But women are not killed casually and off-hand; "when a native speaks of killing a woman, he instinctively contemplates only death in childbirth resulting from illicit intercourse. He cannot conceive that a man should intentionally kill a woman, for this would not be done even in time of war, nor is it likely that a woman should be mixed up in brawls."[20]

There are few cases to be encountered among the Indians in which the woman might be said to lack the right to life; the only one at hand states that Brazilian women are sometimes feeble and sickly from the abuse they receive, and bear few children.[21]

15 Roth, *Tasmania*, 54–55.
16 Ratzel, *Vkde.*, II, 274; Krieger, *Neu-Guinea*, 297, 298, 299; Blum, *Neu-Guinea*, 27–28; Crawley, in JAI, XXIV, 219.
17 Somerville, in JAI, XXIII, 7; Lawrie, in AAAS, 1892, 709.
18 Trilles, *Fân*, 597–598.   19 O'Sullivan, in JAI, XL, 190.
20 Dundas, C., in JAI, LI, 241; and in JAI, XLV, 269.
21 Von Martius, *Beiträge*, I, 104; Rohde, in *Mitth. Berl. Mus.*, 1885, 15.

THE SCIENCE OF SOCIETY

In the foregoing instances the women are not to be conceived of as having done anything meriting punishment at the hand of society. In the ordinary course of life they have no right to life or to an uncrippled body. Punishment accorded to adultery, which often involves execution or maiming, is a different matter and is quite consonant with the guarantee of rights during proper behavior. It is also evident that a state of rightlessness as respects life and limb forms a sort of zero-line of rights in general, for human beings who are destitute of such minimal rights cannot well possess others.

§379*. **Liberty-Rights.** Under this heading are assembled a set of rights, conspicuous by their presence or absence, that have to do with personal freedom. Perhaps the most marked of these is denied to women when they are subjected to seclusion. It will be recalled that woman's sphere has been the home rather than the forum, and that there have been special occasions when, in preparation for marriage, girls have been actually caged for protracted periods.[22] Further than this, the married woman has not infrequently been expected to live in a seclusion varying from slight and periodic segregation immediately succeeding marriage or at sex-crises to the extreme of virtual post-marital imprisonment—a seclusion from which man is virtually immune. Though this is due in good part to the fact that woman is viewed as property, it falls into place as a non-right to liberty of movement. The practice of segregating the wife is usually, though incorrectly, ascribed to special peoples and localities, and is identified with the zenana of India or the Turkish harem; it is also supposed to attend solely upon polygyny. A few cases from widely separated parts of the world will recall the practice while dispelling the impression of its localization.

The seclusion of the wife may be quite as stringent as that of the girl upon whom premarital chastity is enforced, and even more so where jealousy is present. In the royal palaces in Dahomi more than five thousand women are immured; "it is unlawful for a man to look at the king's wives and women of the palace. The latter, when they leave the palace in the morning to fetch water, are preceded by one of their number wearing a bell around her neck, which she shakes vigorously at the sight of a man. At the sound of the bell every man must run off the road into the bush, and wait with averted face till

22 §§60, 61, 366, above.

the women have passed. If any accident happened, even a water-pot chanced
to be broken, the nearest male would be blamed and punished."[23] Again, the
woman's village is apart from the men's, the pathway to it being kept secret
from all outsiders; women are never to be seen in the main village, though they
are free to come and go and to do what they like except to visit the men's
settlement.[24] "An Egyptian wife who is attached to her husband is apt to
think, if he allow her unusual liberty, that he neglects her, and does not sufficiently love her; and to envy those wives who are kept and watched with
greater strictness. . . . They generally look upon this restraint with a degree
of pride, as evincing the husband's care for them; and value themselves upon
their being hidden as treasures."[25] This attitude, like pride in purchase-price,
has been regarded from the standpoint of another code as evidence of degradation, whereas it is quite normal and natural.

Among the Tungus and others, attacks on women may not be avenged by
blood unless made within the house, where the woman belongs. If she is anywhere else she is out of place and has forfeited protection.[26] A grown Tamil
girl may not leave the house without her mother's permission; even within it
she is secluded from the eyes of men as much as possible. If well brought up,
she may not look on a man at all. The place of seclusion is "no vulgar prison,
but a shrine." Bereft of its concealment, women would feel dishonored and
unprotected. They do not covet the public functions and "emancipation" for
which some Occidental women strive. "The very possibility of this blaze of
publicity shed on delicate high-bred womanhood is repugnant to the Oriental
mind."[27]

The "Hermit Kingdom" is the scene of strict seclusion of women. In Seoul
a bell tolls at eight o'clock in the evening, when the men retire to their houses
and the women come out, visit, and amuse themselves; at twelve the women
retire and the men can go abroad. "A lady of high position told the author that
she had never seen the streets of Seoul by daylight. . . . Absolutely secluded
in the inner court of her father's house from the age of seven, a girl at seventeen passes to the absolute seclusion of the inner rooms of her father-in-law's
house. . . . Absolute seclusion is the inflexible rule among the upper classes.
The ladies have their own court-yards and apartments, towards which no win-
dows from the men's apartments must look. No allusion must be made by a
visitor to the females of the household. Inquiries after their health would be a
gross breach of etiquette, and politeness requires that they should not be supposed to exist." Being touched by a strange man's hand has led to the putting
to death or suicide of daughters and wives; "and quite lately a serving-woman
gave as her reason for remissness in attempting to save her mistress, who
perished in a fire, that in the confusion a man had touched the lady, making
her not worth saving!" The author, in extensive journeying, "never saw one
girl who looked over six, except hanging listlessly about in the women's rooms."
One intelligent woman, referring to Western customs, said: "We think that
your husbands don't care for you very much!"[28]

In Borneo wives are sometimes hidden in a secret place in the forest. One of
the strictest rules of the head-hunters is that "no woman, young or old, shall
frequent the veranda after nightfall." Again, "if the women do not instantly

[23] Ellis, *Ewe*, 203.   [24] Burrows, in JAI, XXVIII, 41.
[25] Lane, *Mod. Egypt.*, I, 268, 466.   [26] Lubbock, *Origin of Civil.*, 77.
[27] Gehring, *Süd-Indien*, 73-74; Nivedita, *Indian Life*, 49.
[28] Bishop, *Korea*, 47, 114, 115, 119, 340.

run away and hide themselves as soon as a male stranger appears, they are struck by their husbands with a stick."[29] Markham gives a list of Amazon tribes that "are very jealous of their women and keep them apart." Among certain Indians, "should a travelling party arrive at a place where none but women are at home, they do not land, although they may chat with them from the canoe." Taboo against speaking to unrelated men is found among the Omahas.[30]

Seclusion was firmly established among the Greeks from Homer's time down and sentiments bearing upon it appear in the literature.[31] The *gynœcea*, or women's apartments, where the spinning and weaving went on, characterized Greek domestic arrangements and have their counterparts in ethnography and subsequent history. Veiling appears even in Homer. The aborigines of the Canary Islands forbade a man to speak to a woman whom he met in a solitary place. Sometimes there were separate roads for the sexes. Approach to the women's bathing-places was heavily penalized; to these spots a woman might go alone but nowhere else.[32] Mohammedan seclusion-customs are proverbial; Arab women in Algeria cling to the veil and claustration; this is their honor and dignity compared with nomad women. They object when their husbands, affected by French ideas, are willing to do away with the custom.[33] In Italy, and especially in Venice, seclusion long prevailed.[34] The Salic Law[35] notices the case of a girl abducted from the seclusion which is her proper place; and there was little freedom in Germany of the fifth and sixth centuries.[36] The tradition of seclusion lasts on even in modern Sicily.[37]

A minor form of seclusion imposed by the mores and rather widely known is veiling. Instances have already appeared incidentally, which have shown that the custom is not localized. In the Salic Law there is a fine for striking off a woman's outer cap so that it falls to the ground and that fine is doubled if her inner cap is loosened or her hair is caused to drop upon her shoulders.[38] Village-women wear veils where, probably owing to their inconvenience, nomad women do not; and women of the higher classes where those of the lower do not.[39] It is so much that women are protecting themselves by self-seclusion as that they are being protected by the men from general attention and covetousness. And it is understood that the habit of veiling goes back to other root-ideas besides.[40]

[29] Bock, *Borneo*, 21; Furness, *Head-Hunters*, 20; Stevens, in *Ztsft. f. Eth.*, XXVIII, 180.

[30] Markham, in JAI, XXIV, 260; Wickham, in JAI, XXIV, 205; Dorsey, in BAE, III, 270.

[31] Keller, *Hom. Soc.*, 221 ff.; Maspero, *Hist. Anc.*, III, 797; Euripides, *Electra*, 343-344; *Hecabe*, 974-975; *Phœnic. Maidens*, 1485 ff.; *Iph. Aul.*, 996, 1340 ff.

[32] Cook, in AA, II, 480.   [33] Pommerol, *Sahariennes*, 112.

[34] Burckhardt, *Renaissance*, 393; Molmenti, *Venezia*, I, 92; Yriarte, *Patricien*, 48-49, 52-53, 61.

[35] XIII, 5.

[36] Weinhold, *Deut. Frauen*, I, 251; Lichtenberger, *Nibelungen*, 380.

[37] Alec-Tweedie, *Sicily*, 97-98.

[38] Clement, *Salischen Franken*, 264.

[39] Huntington, *Pulse of Asia*, 129; Lane, *Mod. Egypt.*, I, 68; II, 349.

[40] §§224, 265, above.

Another limitation upon woman's freedom, in this case a public sex-control, is set in a number of places by the power of the men's secret societies. Women have undoubtedly been held in a subordinate position by that organization which men came to form as a consequence of their sex-specialization in hunting and war, namely, the regulative organization.[41] Under it the whole body of females are often treated as if they were nonentities under male control. They are alternately disciplined and protected as domestic animals might be. Though they may not be called chattels or slaves, they are treated as if, compared with men, they were upon a kind of sub-human plane. Under the protection accorded as well as under the discipline imposed they are denied liberty. One of the special agencies—in fact, the typical instrument—for public sex-control is the secret society.[42] Here may be cited several examples of its efficiency in suppressing any possible female assertiveness. It is noteworthy that there is no like agency which operates in the reverse direction, whereby organized females can control males; though they may have enjoyed a general ascendancy under matrilinear conditions, the women's secret societies are negligible relatively to those of men.

The men's secret societies have regularly imposed upon the weaker and unorganized women.[43] The newly initiated Australian youths take part in "frightening the women," by walking around the camp swinging their bull-roarers. The women and children suppose this to be an unearthly spirit returning to his abiding-place; they clamor and scream, to the immense delight of the novices. Bogies of various kinds have been invented to scare the women into continued submission.[44] The drum also is used to intimidate them: "there has been inspired in them so great a fear of it that every woman believes that the mere sight of a drum would be enough to kill her; even the sound frightens the women and drives them into the inmost parts of their huts. This fear has nothing to do with the idol-cult, religious observance, or the like but is merely a clever invention of the men, that they may carry on their festivals and hold their feasts undisturbed by the women and children."[45]

A significant group of African usages has to do with the control of women through the protection of husbands' rights. The best known is the *Mumbo-Jumbo;* it has a sort of specialized function, among the instruments for keeping public order, of disciplining the women. Mumbo-Jumbo is a mysterious deity represented as eight or nine feet tall, clothed in a long bark robe and topped with a bunch of straw. He is summoned when man and wife quarrel and commonly gives judgment in favor of the former.[46] Men also consulted

41 §§64, 65, 140, and ch. XVI, above.   42 §§161, 162, above.
43 Webster, *Secret Soc.*, 118-120.   44 Howitt, in JAI, XIV, 315.
45 Finsch, *Samoafahrten*, 106.   46 Frobenius, *Masken*, 145, 149.

an oracle from time to time, which advised the sacrifice of a couple of women; "for if this were not to happen off and on, the rest would become too high-spirited."[47]

The very protection accorded to women, for instance their seclusion, is a species of control of the inferior by the superior and witnesses by its exaggeration to their humility of status. Any such protection at least implies that they cannot take care of themselves. Thus the West Africans penalize what they call adultery, which "may be only brushing against a woman in a crowded market-place or bush path, or raising a hand in defense against a virago. It's the wrong word, but the customary one to use for touching women, and it is exceedingly expensive and a constant source of danger to the most respectable of men." Men whose means were not sufficient to pay the penalty exacted and who wished to save their family-property from liability for the balance, have given themselves up as pawn-slaves to their accusers. "There is undoubtedly great evil in this law, which presses harder on private and family property than anything else, harder even than accusations of witchcraft; but it safeguards the women, enabling them to go to and fro about the forest paths, and in the villages and market places at home, and far from home, without fear of molestation or insult, bar that which they get up amongst themselves."[48]

That the protection accorded to woman may be construed as a denial of rights is evidenced by the opposition of advocates of sex-equality to the various safeguards extended by modern laws over women in industry. They do not want the protection, regarding it as a concession to an inferior.[49] In connection with the privileges extended to a weaker sex there may be recalled the not infrequent inviolability of woman as a non-combatant in war, with the resultant phenomena of the female-intermediary between hostile forces and of the function of women in trade.[50]

Another set of rights and non-rights of woman is covered by her abilities and disabilities in the matter of sexual self-disposal. This topic too is closely connected with her status as property, as owned by others or by herself, but attention is centered for the moment upon her degree of freedom of action. The fact may first be recalled that usage varies considerably respecting her right of pre-marital self-disposal; in many cases she is free, while in others she is held with the utmost strictness to chastity.[51] The instances have exhibited man as under little or no control in this matter.

When it comes to self-disposal in marriage, that is, consent to union, woman is found to have had much more to say about the

47 Junker, *Afrika,* III, 118.
48 Kingsley, *W. Afr. Studies,* 434, 435.
49 N. Y. *Times,* Jan. 18, 1920; Feb. 29, 1920; May 16, 1922.
50 §§68, 76, 141, above.   51 §§344, 366, above.

matter than has sometimes been supposed. Her will is very often, if not predominantly, the determining factor. It is the savages and the most advanced races, says Westermarck,[52] who allow her the greatest freedom. The topic of elopement[53] furnishes a set of illustrations. If the woman takes the initiative and proposes,[54] she is evidently in control of her destiny to a considerable degree, though, of course, not more so than man. The following cases are chiefly instances of that prerogative, though they include others bearing upon her right of self-disposal.

Where what has been called marriage by charming, that is, where magical means are employed to attract love, is common, as in Australia, the woman as well as the man takes the initiative.[55] Proposal by the girl is common in parts of Melanesia; in Papua, "it is the hope of receiving a proposal that a man will go through endless adventures; it is to win the admiration of some good buxom girl that he risks his life head-hunting, and it is with pride and glory that he glances at his string of skulls which hangs from the poles of his hut, because he knows how brave the women will think him." This is in line with cases of test of the man. Girls are kept in retirement prior to the puberty-ceremonies and tattooed; then comes the day of exhibition, on which they have great freedom and choose their suitors by giving them betel. The girl may send to the man of her choice and ask him to visit her; and "very often then such a marriage leads to a second, in that the sister of the groom is given to the brother of the bride in exchange for the loss of her."[56] Elsewhere in New Guinea the girl invariably takes the initiative. The boy who admires her poses and leaps about before her to attract her attention; and if he succeeds she sends him an invitation. The joint consumption of betel is tantamount to betrothal, and eating together, later on, makes the parties man and wife.[57] A proposal by the man would make him a laughing-stock, and he would be called a woman.[58]

Among the Torres Straits Islanders, "as the women propose marriage to the men, girls hold a very independent position. . . . The missionaries discountenance the custom of marriage proposals by the women; there is not, however, the least objection to it from the moral or social side; it rather gives the woman standing."[59] Here again is a case of the inadvisability of correcting other peoples' mores on the basis of our own. The girl sends a string armlet by a confidential friend, who says to the happy man: "I've got something for you." "Show it to me," the man replies, if he is anxious; and "after learning the girl's name, and being satisfied that he is not throwing himself away, the youth will accept the armlet and in return make a present of two leglets to his fiancée." Again, the girl may send food, which the young man coyly refuses to

[52] *Marriage,* II, 310.
[53] §359, above; other examples in Westermarck, *Marriage,* II, ch. XXII.
[54] §367, above.
[55] Spencer and Gillen, *Nat. Tr. Cent. Aust.,* 556.
[56] §365, above; Hardy and Elkington, *S. Seas,* 37; Krieger, *Neu-Guinea,* 297.
[57] Guise, in JAI, XXVIII, 209.   [58] Müller, *Sex. Leben,* 38.
[59] Haddon, in JAI, XIX, 314, 315, 356, 396.

eat, pretending that he has no desire to be caught though he is really very proud to be noticed. The girl sends food day by day, "until her constancy makes the parents of the young man feel satisfied that he is not being led astray or fooled by a changeable woman." They then command him to eat. Thereafter the young couple meet face to face and the girl hands him fresh food which he eats, amidst signs of great joy on both sides at the act of condescension.[60] In the D'Entrecasteaux Islands, "a youth must never himself suggest marriage as an end to courtship. The girl would probably refuse him and tell her friends next day, when he would become the general laughing-stock. It is the girl who makes the suggestion. . . . Her young man visits her, and she places a cigarette in her bamboo pipe and lights it and inhales. Then she offers it to him, and after he has inhaled she says, 'Let us marry.' The youth is bound to consent, so they appoint a day and he sets about building his hut."[61]

Though a West African father can force his daughter to marry against her will, such marriages are troublesome and generally end in the man putting the woman away.[62] Here is a case of selection in the mores on the basis of expediency; women get rights because things work out better that way, not as the result of emotional or altruistic strains in the savage mind. If girls run off with their lovers, parents usually take no further trouble. But they must not be too finical, as is intimated by the moral of the folk-tale where, when girls refuse one young fellow after another, wild beasts turn themselves into men and carry them off.[63] No such admonitory story would be in point where women had little or no right of self-disposal. The Loango girl speaks the decisive Yes or No to the suitor;[64] no Dinka girl "is obliged to marry anyone unless she is herself willing."[65] African princesses have wide rights in choosing husbands; they may choose slaves and yet have children of princely rank or marry peasants who thereby become chiefs. They may dismiss their spouses at will and they have the control of their property.[66] Such cases show that the right to choose a husband goes along with the general enfranchisement of high social position.

In East Africa the women have large powers of self-disposal, despite certain superficial evidence to the contrary. "Often girls are bespoken while they are children, and in many cases dowry is then paid, without the girl having any voice in the matter. Hence it appears as if custom did not give them any liberty of choice as to husbands, and when it suits their purpose the elders will maintain that such is the case. But a little discussion will dispel any such idea, and I have repeatedly been assured by elders in all three tribes that this was not so formerly. . . . The native woman, however oppressed she may be, has certain rights, and the limitations of these have taught her to maintain them with a tenacity which is unexampled amongst the men. So soon as a man tampers with any of these rights he loses all control over his wife or daughter. The number of cases in which girls defy all authority, and the futile attempts of the elders to insist on forced marriages being maintained, are proof that the law never provided for such events; it was not so foolishly designed that

60 Hardy and Elkington, S. Seas, 41-43.
61 Jenness and Ballentyne, D'Entrecasteaux, 100.
62 Nassau, Fetichism, 8.
63 Ellis, Yoruba, 185; Ellis, in PSM, XLV, 775.
64 Pechuël-Lösche, Loango, 10.   65 O'Sullivan, in JAI, XL, 180.
66 Ratzel, Vkde., I, 598; Müller, Sex. Leben, 5.

it did not recognise that a permanent relationship between men and women must rest on mutual consent. . . . The proper method is undoubtedly for the suitor to approach the girl first, but after that he must agree with the father. It is distinctly recognised that mere inability to pay dowry should not be a reason to refuse a suitor chosen by the daughter, for there are many other ways of overcoming this difficulty. The father may, however, raise other objections, and then it becomes a conflict between paternal influence and filial independence. After careful observation, I have come to the conclusion that a girl has under native custom as much freedom of choice, and the father as much paternal influence, as is customary with us. An arbitrary decision and giving away of a girl is certainly contrary to good custom, but, on the other hand, submissive and often indifferent as the native female is, she is not likely to insist upon marrying one whom her father objects to. Nevertheless, this does happen."[67]

In the Indian Archipelago women have large freedom in self-disposal, even where there is a bride-price that is really a purchase-price. Girls are seldom coerced, for, they say, "if the girl is unwilling, what is to be done about it?" Abduction is carried out almost always with the girl's consent, that is, it becomes elopement; and if the parents are obstinate, she gets her will in that manner. Thus the East Indian union has a strong element of personal preference in it; money and politics enter chiefly in the alliances of the wealthy and the socially elect.[68]

Cheyenne courtship might last from one to five years; then they applied to the older people. If a girl refused that ended the matter. If pushed to wed a richer man, she could run off and marry her choice, though elopement was not in good form. However it was sometimes arranged with the girl's parents that she should elope. Girls were dutiful and sometimes evaded a distasteful union by suicide rather than offend by opposition.[69]

In Albania "a girl can escape the husband to whom she has been sold in one way only. Should she resolutely refuse to be married to him she may, by tribe law, swear perpetual virginity before twelve witnesses, and she is then free and has certain privileges."[70] In the Ukraine women have been, in recent times, the proposers. A woman attached to a youth goes to his parents' house and in their presence asks him to take her as his wife. If he consents, the parents think it a sin to oppose.[71]

If the woman exercises so notable a power of choice, she evidently is not utterly bereft of control over her own destiny. There is no point in extending illustration much beyond primitive life. In fact, the actual right of women to propose, in bald and direct form, has lapsed along with the development of civilization. The hardship they suffer in not being able to take the formal initiative has been much and romantically bewailed and we have been summoned to sympathize with her who "can only wait and hope." The

[67] Dundas, C., in JAI, XLV, 284-285.
[68] Wilken, in VG, I, 466-468.
[69] Grinnell, *Cheyenne*, I, 137, 139, 140, 141.
[70] Durham, in JAI, XL, 460.   [71] Krasinski, *Cossacks*, 250.

good old times of primitive innocence and naturalness have been yearningly recalled, along with the rest of the figments about the golden age and the noble savage. The fact remains that woman is emancipated now as never before; and though she may suffer a little through the loss of the actual proposing function, it is not so certain (we are told) that she does not virtually exercise, in an indirect fashion, most of the initiative ascribed to man and which he thinks he has.

Perhaps we can attach to this type of woman's self-disposal the fact that she may very seldom marry several men, while man has, through long stages of evolution, taken to himself a plurality of wives. Polyandry is rare, while plurality of female consorts is the typical system of many places and times. Further, a woman, having married a husband in regular form, is not permitted to have other informally taken consorts as man has done under the widespread custom of monogyny. To cover the whole case it might be said that woman has almost always been obliged to remain monogamous while man has been under almost no constraint in the mores to refrain from polygyny. Plural marriage is a topic to be encountered a little later on.[72] This situation anticipates to some degree what is immediately to follow.

Whatever may be the case with the unmarried, self-disposal while in wedlock is virtually interdicted to women, whereas men have been subject to little control. The fact is familiar enough that, however much freedom a woman has had before she became a wife, upon the attainment of that status the whole situation has been reversed and she has had no further rights of self-disposal. This is, again, largely because woman is property and man is not; and that property-status of hers is signalized by the not infrequent provision that she may or must have sex-relations with other men with her husband's permission or at his instance. So unmistakably, indeed, is adultery a matter of the infringement of man's property-right in the wife that it forms an excellent example of how his prerogative, established by the entrance of the pair into the prescribed status of matrimony, puts an end with virtual decisiveness to any rights of self-disposal the woman may have possessed while still outside the status. So far as the type of free-

[72] Ch. LIII, below.

dom under discussion is concerned, he loses virtually none while she sacrifices all. This illustrates the fact that matrimony is a status defined by a special distribution of rights. Because adultery is so distinctly an invasion of property-right in a wife, it is here merely recorded as a disallowed form of self-disposal and reserved for later treatment.

Post-marital self-disposal includes the case of the widow or divorced woman, which also is to be covered in a following chapter.[73] It will there be seen that she has few rights over herself as compared with man. When the husband dies, the widow falls temporarily or permanently into a condition of disability, provided, indeed, that she is not killed outright or driven by usage to mount, voluntarily, the funeral pyre of the deceased. She must "mourn" much longer than the widower, a duty which involves segregation and seclusion, together with much self-discipline. She may not re-marry at all, or only after a more protracted interval than in the case of man; and her re-marriage, when allowed, is frequently indistinguishable from a transfer of property to a brother or other heir. In regard to the divorced wife, it is typical that repudiation lies predominantly in the hand of the husband, being not seldom simply a return of an unsatisfactory purchase for which either a substitute or a refund is demanded. Under the mother-family and in other circumstances where, as in the *ambilanak* form,[74] the man enters wedlock in an inferior capacity, he may be dismissed by the parents of the woman; in general, however, he is the one who sends away, dismisses, or repudiates, while the wife has to run away. He stays where he is and acts in a positive manner to dissolve the status; she flees back to her erstwhile protectors who may have sold her in the first place. A repudiated wife is generally disgraced and branded as incapable or sterile; not so the repudiated or repudiating husband. There is nothing to prevent his re-marriage comparable to the suspicion under which she suffers. In short, the dissolution of wedlock by death or divorce is a much more serious matter for woman than for man.

§380*. Woman as Property. There is no question but that in history a woman has been the property of her father, brothers or

---

[73] Ch. LII.   [74] §363, above.

other male relatives, husband, or son; on the other hand, none of these males has ever been her property unless by some irregular extension of the term or by some rare exception. Females have had no property-right in males; the issue is as to how much of such right they have held over themselves. It may be said of the rights of woman hitherto considered that their number and degree form a rough measure of the intensity of her property-right in herself. Where she does not possess even the right to life, she evidently has no ownership in herself; where, on the other hand, she is exempt from seclusion and public control, may dispose of herself before marriage, and must be consulted as to her choice in marriage, she is much less of a chattel or slave.

If woman is spoken of as property, it is not always as property in the same degree. She is not always subject to destruction, rough handling, or sale at the caprice of a master, like the rightless slave, even though the fact of male ownership is unquestioned. The extreme of property in woman is the captive who has no more rights than any other piece of booty. If not valued as property, she is killed; for there is no power at hand to enforce even the right to life—that right which we have so often been adjured to believe a natural one. In something the same way, it makes considerable difference in woman's status if she marries outside her tribe and leaves her kin, for she thus loses such closeness of contact with the latter as would secure their constant scrutiny of her position. It will bear repetition that the farther a woman gets away, in marrying, from her kith and kin, the less guarantee has she for her rights as against her husband. And, again, the degree to which a woman is property and the number and degree of rights accorded her are inversely proportional. The obvious comparison is that between wife and slave. The captured wife is virtually in rightless servitude; when, however, a consort is acquired by the rendering of some equivalent in property, her status is more like that of a debt-slave.[75] That a man has given property for her raises her value in his eyes. Mores characterized by high intensity of property in women represent the crude, tough block of folk-ways[76] out of which have been shaped the later and more refined relations of the sexes. Here was, at any rate, something direct,

[75] §105, above.   [76] §177, above.

simple, and strong to start with, however repellent it may be to present-day taste.

The primitive way of arranging the relation of the sexes as regards rights sets the mode of evolution for that relation so decisively that all later-developed forms hark back to it. "In all primitive races woman has been the earliest domestic animal of man."[77] She is, among advanced mankind, so no longer; but the best she now is has evolved out of what she was then. Transitional forms exist to prove it. The cases now to come are selections, representative of many more, designed to exhibit property in women as it has come under observation. There exist in most of the evidence, where any context to bald statements or subjective opinions is available, such shadings from the extreme of man's property-right in woman as represent germs of rights. It is to be noted that the development of such embryo-rights is often incidental to the property-status. If a woman is spared as property of value, she advances a stage, slight and temporary though it may be, toward a right to life; that it is conferred indirectly and without specific intention does not affect its possibilities of ultimately insinuating itself into the code and attaining the guarantee of public approval. At any case the spared woman does not die but lives on, and the thin edge of the wedge has bitten in.

The Australian wife's value is reckoned according to her services as a slave: she is needed to carry water and wood and to prepare food. She can be kept, prostituted, exchanged, or given away.[78] Melanesian women have "the position of slaves who have some influence, either through personality or scarcity." They cook, cultivate, and carry burdens, and are sold for a trifle to strangers.[79] In the New Hebrides, "on marriage a woman's identity sinks *absolutely*, even as far as to cause her to lose the name by which she was called. She is then spoken of as 'the woman belonging to such a man.' She has no name."[80] Among the foregoing peoples, as we have learned, the wife is often killed at caprice and with impunity by the husband.

Bushwomen are servants and beasts of burden; if too weak to keep up with the march, they are abandoned.[81] "Throughout negro Africa women and slaves concurrently serve as domestic animals."[82] To the Kaffir, woman is, like any other property, a provision against the future. The man works in the diamond-

---

[77] Letourneau, *Prop.*, 65.

[78] Eyre, *Cent. Aust.*, II, 319, 321; Cunow, *Australneger*, 127; Ratzel, *Vkde.*, II, 66, 68, 70.

[79] Ratzel, *Vkde.*, II, 274.

[80] Somerville, in JAI, XXIII, 7; Lawrie, in AAAS, 1892, 709.

[81] Ratzel, *Vkde.*, I, 71.   [82] Letourneau, *Prop.*, 84.

mines until he gets enough money, when changed into cattle, to buy a European suit, a cooking-kettle, a rifle, and a wife. Later he returns, after setting up an establishment, and earns what more is needed to buy enough women to support him the rest of his life. He then retires from his labors and lives on his income. "To the Kaffir the woman he has acquired represents a stock of capital and he hopes to get his interest through her labor, as well as through the children she bears." The position of the Kaffir women is lower than that even of the Bushwoman. The youth sometimes wants a girl to whom he has taken a special liking; in that case he has to pay several oxen more than the usual price, "and since on the average, cattle lie nearer the heart than women, such a procedure is not common. . . . The only difference between women and cattle is that their lord and master may not kill them at pleasure or wound them severely on the body, for if he does the chief will demand of him an indemnity." Otherwise they belong to the husband's live stock. The Kaffir does not treat his women with cruelty any more than he does his beasts; "but affection, tenderness, conjugal love are unusual."[83] The women, while in an uncivilized state, do not object to polygamy: "The larger our number, the lighter our burdens" is a common expression. The husband may say to the wife who is ill and unable to work: "Did I not pay ten cows for you, and what are you doing to return them so that I may buy another wife? Go to work."[84]

Among the Dinka, "by marriage is meant the purchase of a girl by the payment of cattle to the father, guardian or owner of the girl. The payment gives to the buyer the possession of the girl and the right to all children borne by her." The women are proud of their price: "the desire to have a large 'marriage price' paid as their value, will influence them to accept marriage with men objectionable to them, and is the cause of a certain amount of unfaithfulness."[85]

Among the Siberian nomads a man can handle his wife as he likes, for she is his paid-for property. If he gets tired of her he beats her and returns her to her father, thus ending the union. But he has no right to kill her; if he does, he must send gifts to the lamas to get off. "Significant of woman's status is the fact that they have the same name for old reindeer and old women."[86]

Among the backward tribes of India, daughters are found reckoned into the heritage of their brothers just as if they were domestic animals. Women are so regarded that the use of a poisoned arrow, interdicted in general, is permissible if the mark is only a woman. The code of Manu represents woman as subject to father, husband, brother, or son all her life; the Mahabharata tells of a queen who was gambled away by her husband.[87] The Korean wife loses her name at marriage, is called "wife of so and so" or "mother of so and so," and is addressed as *yabu*, meaning "Look here" by her husband. She is a patient nonentity.[88] The Japanese woman was similarly reduced.[89] Sale of daughters and wives occurs in China. In one case, a man got into prison and deliverance

[83] Fritsch, *Eingeb. S.-Afr.,* III, 142, 112, 113.

[84] Tyler, "Kaffirs," in *Ill. Afr.* for Nov., 1895.

[85] O'Sullivan, in JAI, XL, 180.   [86] Olsen, *Primitivt Folk,* 146.

[87] Dalton, *Eth. Bengal,* 201; Woodthorpe, in JAI, XI, 199; Gehring, *Süd-Indien,* 79; Lewin, *S.E. India,* 176; 311; Naidoo, in JASB, II, 394; Risley, *Ethnog. Ind.,* I, 64; Monier-Williams, *Brāhmanism,* 387; Bühler, *Manu,* IX, 96; Wilutzky, *Mann u. Weib,* 50.

[88] Bishop, *Korea,* 118; Landor, *Corea,* 66.

[89] Hearn, *Japan,* 83-84; Tamura, *Warum Heiraten Wir?,* 84.

looked hopeless. "He accordingly sent word to his relatives to have his wife sold, which was done, and with the proceeds the man was able to buy his escape. The frequency of such sales may be said to bear a direct ratio to the price of grain." Trickery based upon the sale of a wife, represented as a sister, who later escapes to rejoin her "brother," is called ("with that keen instinct for analogy which characterizes the Chinese") "falconing with a woman." Regular deeds of sale are executed.[90]

Many Malay customs arise from the fact that the wife becomes a possession of the husband. But the desire for children is powerful and deep-seated in the mores and the woman gains by it in something the same way a female domestic animal of fine breeding qualities might profit by the high value set on her offspring. There is often less of direct oppression than of disesteem accorded her, and her destiny varies even within the same general locality. In one case, the man was seen to "take for himself all the fish and roots which his family had collected that day and silently eat the whole, leaving only the heads and the offal for his wife and children." Even when the woman was given food by a traveller, "she did not dare eat any of it if her husband was present; and even then, if her husband was not present, but another man was, she would withdraw from his neighborhood before she dared to eat and to give her children some of it." The women are sold but not into prostitution. If a man can get a very desirable object only in return for a daughter, she is given, "because the object he trades for is more valuable to him than the object sold and because he has the feeling that the girl . . . will be looked upon as in some sort a wife."[91] The Batak bride-price has wholly the character of a purchase-price, and the terms used for the wife support the implication. She is called "merchandise," "means to get food," "server of food," the last term witnessing to the custom whereby the man eats first while the wife serves him. Her position is quite inferior and wholly without rights. She possesses nothing and what she earns during the marriage belongs to the man. "The wife is . . . a piece of property, as well for the parents who sell her as for the husband who buys her, or for his brother or other relation to whom she passes, following the levirate-marriage, as a heritage." On Nias Island her position is a little better: "although her lot is hard work, she does it with zest for she is not treated as a slave but is, as a house-wife, if not reverenced at any rate recognized; and as to that her lot is not harder than that of most women of the lower classes in Europe."[92]

The women of Loyalty Island wait on their husbands and take the leavings, and on Yap Island the husband may sell his wife trickily, taking her under some plausible pretext to the place where the buyer lives, where she is held. The price is trifling if the buyer is a good friend of the husband. A New Zealand chief, "as token of his desire to make peace, sent to Sir J. Grey his two daughters as a present, and both he and they were greatly offended because they were not accepted."[93] The Maori "needed wives to till their sweet potato

[90] N. China Herald, "Nat. Hist. Chinese Girl"; résumé in JASB, II, 224; Doolittle, Soc. Life of Chinese, I, 107.

[91] Stevens, in Ztsft. f. Eth., XXVIII, 166, 167, 177, 178; Gomes, Sea Dyaks, 87.

[92] Wilken, in VG, I, 330, 331, 336.

[93] Ella, in AAAS, 1892, 628, 637; Waitz-Gerland, Anthrop., V, 106, 107; Senfft, in Globus, XCI, 143; Taylor, Te Ika, 194.

fields"; on being exhorted against polygamy, they said there would be less of it "when, like English gentlemen, they could replace them with cattle."[94]

The Eskimo woman is the property of her husband and at his disposition; her position is more stable if she has a child.[95] Grinnell[96] says that the Cheyenne woman "was in no sense the property of the man she married," but his cases seem not fully to support the statement. If a wife ran away, the husband had to be reimbursed, often the sum which he had paid for the wife, and the man could readily repudiate the woman. Tinneh women live on the refuse of the men's meals. In general, the Indian woman's lot is hard; in most respects the Aztec wife was the property of her husband.[97] Indians not seldom offered their women to travellers.[98] Schomburgk[99] tells a story of a pretty Carib wife, newly married, who had a severe toothache but went about doing her work, while her husband lolled, ate, slept, and played the flute all day in his hammock. She whimpered a little with pain from time to time at night and finally her husband leaped up and cut the cord of her hammock, spilling her on the ground and hurting her arm. She appeared in the morning with swollen and bandaged arm, yet with smiling face, and brought his breakfast to his hammock. He did not even glance at her. Schomburgk's anger at this performance elicited astonishment and wonder. In Brazil, "the woman is the subjected servant, the slave of man, a debasement which corresponds to the otherwise crude condition of the primitive Brazilians. Under compulsion the women have to attend to all the business of agriculture and domestic economy, and, surrendering all will, adjust themselves to every caprice and whim of the man."

In Sparta, "when a man has begotten enough children, it is quite proper and usual for him to sell his wife to one of his friends."[100] The idea that the children belong to the father as the calf to the owner of the cow is expressed in Shakespeare's *King John:*[101] the illegitimate son of a nobleman, the offspring of his wife by Richard Cœur de Lion, is declared legitimate. Says King John of his son: "In sooth, good friend, your father might have kept this calf, bred from his cow, from all the world."

§381. **The Marriage-Mark.** This is a sort of label indicative of the marriage-status. Part of the publicity desirable in the matter of marriage is secured by this means. In the case of the man, entrance into majority commonly carries marriage with it and the initiation-marks[102] are marriage-insignia. Married men are distinguished from unmarried also by the method of wearing the hair.[103] For women too there are general distinctions of this sort

94 Letourneau, *Prop.*, 65, 84.

95 Nansen, *Esk. Life*, 121, 170, 171; Holm, *Ethnol. Skizze*, 46; Turner, in BAE, XI, 178.

96 *Cheyenne*, I, 154.

97 Allen, in *Smithson. Rep.*, 1886, pt. I, 260; Hrdlička, in BAE, Bull. XXXIV, 51; Nadaillac, *Preh. Amer.*, 281, 311; Friederici, in *Globus*, XC, 305.

98 Lewis and Clark, *Travels*, I, 144; II, 164, 165, 416, 419.

99 *Brit.-Guiana*, II, 428-429.   100 Polybius, *Hist.*, bk. XII, §VI.

101 Act I, sc. 1.   102 §163, above.

103 Machon, in PSM, LII, 402; Geiseler, *Oster-Ins.*, 25, 29.

indicative of status in the community—conventional labels without special significance; but there are also special distinctions whose meaning is patent. They are like the brands set upon animal-property. Disfigurement of the wife, especially after adultery, is not uncommon,[104] as, for example, the shearing of her hair. Again, she must lay aside ornament, wear a veil, and otherwise render herself unattractive or withdraw into a sort of seclusion from men. There are many customs in different countries that set off the married woman in such manner as to discourage attention. She belongs to someone who will make trouble if she is appropriated.

Where this is done, she is evidently held in adverse possession by some man; she is the monopoly of an owner. Marks indicative of such a status are often true property-marks.[105] The infringement of such a relation of woman and man is adultery, which is assimilated to theft and is often punished by more serious disfigurement calculated to forestall further trespass.[106] No such disfigurement of the man, specifically with reference to his marriage-status, occurs either at marriage or in event of irregularities. The double standard is already in evidence. In many cases, then, the marriage-mark is for woman the badge of property-status. For her it denotes specific position and obligations. For this reason the topic of the marriage-mark is considered in connection with woman as property; but the following cases are not confined to the personal property-mark alone. They illustrate also and more broadly the advertisement of the marriage-status, enabling the married and the unmarried to be distinguished at sight and removing all excuse for inadvertent infringement of rights.

Shorn hair and a tattooed face mark the married woman in New Guinea. The hair is sometimes shaved with a piece of obsidian or glass bottle and kept shaved, though occasionally it remains long. Ornament is renounced and the small plain petticoat used by all women when at work becomes the characteristic dress. The wife becomes a mere onlooker at the dances. On the Murray Islands, "if a man and woman lived together without marriage, it would soon be known, and a friend seeing them constantly together would inform all the people. Having prepared a little paint he would then, in the presence of all the people, make a mark on each of their shoulders, after which they would be

104 §383, below; list of cases in Letourneau, *Marriage*, ch. XIII.
105 §§108, 121, above.   106 §184, above.

recognized as husband and wife."[107] In one district of central Africa married women are distinguished by a covering worn on the breast. Among the Zulus married women clothe themselves. In Kabylie the married woman might not go out bareheaded; "the headdress tells that she is subjected to the conjugal power." In parts of the Sahara the method of hair-dressing distinguishes maiden and wife.[108] Among the East Africans, "the 'mkia' is the special mark of the married woman; if, however, a young girl is going on a visit to another village, she can wear one on her journey, but must take it off directly she reaches destination, and not don it again till she leaves. This is done as a sort of artificial protective mimicry; by wearing the tail she is taken for a married woman, and is not likely to be molested by anyone she may meet on the way. . . . Among the Bantu tribes, married women generally wear a small black fringe of fibre in front, but the Ja-Luo married women very rarely wear anything in front, the requirements of decency are, in their opinion, quite fulfilled if they have the tail. Ja-Luo girls, in their villages, are quite nude, but when they go to market, or to a dance, they wear, for ornament, a small fringe of various coloured beads strung on fibre."[109]

In certain tribes of India, the married women have the bosom uncovered and wear long hair. Bracelets of solder or lead replace the brass ones worn by maidens. Distinctive bracelets of various styles are common. Again, married women mark the brow with vermilion and put on toe-rings, while widows shave the head and partially cover it. The one thing, in India, from which the wife will never part, "unless widowhood lays its icy hand upon her life, is that ring of iron covered with gold and worn on the left wrist, which is the sign of the indissoluble bond of her marriage—her wedding-ring in fact."[110] In Japan the eyebrows are shaved off and the teeth blackened. The style of hair-dressing indicates the status, and the custom is widespread of depriving a woman of ornaments when she is married. Among the Manchus, the front hair of the bride is pulled out with tweezers, a very painful operation, denominated "the opening of the face."[111]

In the Malay Archipelago the unmarried are distinguished from the married by the wearing of ornaments.[112] In Borneo, while tattooing is not permitted to unmarried girls, it is indispensable to the marrying woman. When a woman becomes a mother, here and elsewhere, she wears some mark indicative of it. In Sumatra, fillets and bracelets mark the virgin. The married woman must let her hair grow, as bangs are not proper for women who have two or more children. The sacrifice of ornamentation appears to be "the original object of the mutilation of the woman's hair. It takes place as soon as she comes to belong to a man, as soon as she need make no more conquests, in order to preserve the species, need not glitter any more and draw attention." If a

[107] Krieger, *Neu-Guinea,* 300; Waitz, *Anthrop.,* VI, 567; Chalmers, in JAI, XXVII, 331, 332; Guise, in JAI, XXVIII, 209; Hunt, in JAI, XXVIII, 11.

[108] Burrows, *Pigmies,* 15; Middlebrook, in *Globus,* LXXV, 270; Hanoteau et Letourneux, *Kabylie,* III, 218; Pommerol, *Sahariennes,* 173.

[109] Hobley, in JAI, XXXIII, 325 ff., 350-351.

[110] Nivedita, *Indian Life,* 39.

[111] Godden, in JAI, XXVII, 20; Carey and Tuck, *Chin Hills,* I, 170; Acworth, in JASB, II, 191; Waddell, *Himalayas,* 173; Tamura, *Warum Heiraten Wir?,* 39, 40, 43; Grube, in *Berl. Mus.,* VII, 24; Westermarck, *Marriage,* I, 311.

[112] Wilken, in VG, II, 269, note 119.

woman becomes a widow or separates from her husband, she may let her hair grow again. Polynesian married women wore a large piece of cloth about the hips but the unmarried only "the modest costume of Eve before the fall."[113] The aborigines of the island of Hainan tattoo a young wife with the mark of the family into which she is marrying. It is on her face and after death makes her recognizable to the ancestors as belonging to that family. With this Andree[114] aligns the slitting of the ear of a pig or a captive by Samoans and the tattooing of slaves by the Algerian Arabs, as indications of property in them. In America are found a difference in hair-dressing, painting, tattooing, or scarring and the use by maidens of a decorated girdle as compared with the mere string of the married women. Lip-stones are marks of the wedded state. "These stones must not be removed from the lips of a married woman, because they are a sign of wedlock, and their loss may be punished by death. They are not used for personal adornment, but serve as a kind of marriage certificate."[115]

The virgin daughters of David wore cloaks of many colors.[116] Jewish girls in Algeria were not allowed to wear footgear until married.[117] In Sparta and Athens women sacrificed the hair.[118] "The snatching away of the wreath or crown of the bride is founded upon the old German custom that the married woman may not any longer wear the hair loose but must put on the *Frauenbinde.*" Elsewhere a cap was placed on the head of the bride as a sign of marriage. She must wear it all her life, never taking it off except to comb her hair. Maidens wore no cap.[119] The White Russian bride's hair is to be cut off and redeemed by a payment. "The plait, or *kosa,* is a maiden's chief ornament, the cherished object of her care, the principal source of her girlish pride. Its unplaiting is a sign of the change which is coming upon her, for married women do not wear the *kosa.* Their back hair, if not cut short, is worn in two plaits, which are generally wound round the head, and concealed under a kerchief."[120] In Albania the marriage-mark is a belt.[121] A contemporary case is the sacrifice of the hair and the wearing of a wig by the Jewish woman—"the wig without which no virtuous wife is complete. For a married woman must sacrifice her tresses on the altar of home, lest she snare other men with such sensuous baits."[122] With this may be compared the traditional treatment of "woman's crowning glory" and of other personal attractions, and also of ornament, in the case of brides of the Church.

If one is inclined to question the bearing of such marriage-marks upon the issue of property in women, he might ask himself why the one sex bears them and the other not. Even now it is

[113] Roth, *Sarawak,* II, 94; Furness, *Head-Hunters,* 151, 153; Wilken, *Vkde.,* 36, 48; Marsden, *Sumatra,* 52; Jacobs, *Groot-Atjeh,* I, 43, 45, 46; Finsch, *Samoafahrten,* 355.

[114] *Eth. Parallelen,* 2d ser., 78.

[115] Fewkes, in *Smithson. Rep.,* 1895, 583; Speck, in HAI, II, 1006; Von Martius, *Beiträge,* I, 217, 289; Haseman, in AA, XIV, 341 (quoted).

[116] II Sam., XIII, 8.   [117] Casanowicz, in AA, VII, 357.

[118] Rossbach, *Röm. Ehe,* 290.

[119] Weinhold, *Deut. Frauen,* I, 400, 401; Clement, *Salischen Franken,* 201.

[120] *Russian Ethnog.* (Russ.), I, 106; Ralston, *Russ. People,* 272.

[121] Lane, *Shala,* 21.   [122] Zangwill, *Ghetto,* 15.

possible to judge of a woman's status, whether she is wife, fiancée, or unattached, by inspecting a certain one of her fingers; but there is no similar common criterion in the case of man. It is also in our mores, despite aberrations, that the married woman shall dress and act in a modest manner and shall not seek conquests as she might once have done. The modern woman does not sink supinely into the status of a possession, as women of other times and places have done; she does not renounce her youth and turn into the mere housewife, careless of herself and involved in an eternal round of "children, church, and kitchen." Except for the ring, her status as wife does not need to be indicated by any conventional mark.

§382*. Types of Disposition over Woman. It is evident that women were habitually stolen, as cattle or other property was, long before man-stealing became customary. Except under conditions of developed slavery,[123] there was little to evoke the latter. Wife-stealing, meaning the stealing of women to be wives, has been considered above;[124] but it is not precisely the same thing as the stealing of women who are already other men's wives, as a pair of citations will show. The distinction is of some little use to us here in helping to visualize the essential property-status of the wife.

If, on a Somal raid, a woman has been merely abducted, the abductor sends her relatives a sum in compensation; "but if a woman for whom her husband has paid a purchase-price is actually stolen with the purpose of using her as a worker, a conflict results."[125] In the Pelew Islands any woman met alone is subject to force and it does her reputation no harm; but murder is justified in the case of abduction of a wife, if the guilty party belongs to another community.[126]

If the wife is so special a piece of property that the stealing of her is particularly irritating, she is also, among some peoples, so distinctly the property of her husband that he may lend her at will. This power resides also in the father of the unmarried girl and extends to temporary sale into what we should call prostitution, though that term, like a number of others current today, does not cover the primitive relation[127] to which it is undiscrimi-

123 §§100-104, above.   124 §358, above.
125 Paulitschke, Nordost-Afr., II, 152.
126 Kubary, in Mitth. Berl. Mus., 1885, 77, 78.
127 §344, above.

natingly applied. Whether or not woman-lending is referable wholly to hospitality-customs, whether the women are or are not willing, whether it is or is not a mere case of ceremony on admission to the rights of the tribe,[128] it is a fact that normally the rôles of man and woman are never reversed so that she lends him. That would be, in very many instances, a case of property lending its owner.

Cases of wife-lending in view of prospective presents or out of sympathy are common in Australia. One Australian lent the least useful of his wives to a friend, saying, "Poor fellow, he is a widower, and has a long way to go, and will feel very lonely."[129] Often the lent woman must be one whom, according to their marriage-system, the visitor might marry. Again, a wife is given or lent to a poor man to win his adherence.[130] In Melanesia the feeling "that the intercourse of the sexes was natural where the man and woman belonged to different divisions, was shown by that feature of native hospitality which provided a guest with a temporary wife. . . . But the woman supplied to the guest was of necessity one who might have been his wife."[131] "The wife is fully the husband's property and may therefore be lent at will but her consent is necessary." If he kills or sells her, he must allay the feelings of her relatives by payment. Girls and wives are not infrequently forced to earn gifts and payments for relatives or husbands, especially amongst trading peoples.[132] The same connection with trade occurs in Africa, where the women are a sort of agency in bringing the parties together. In West Africa, "men can and do lend their wives, and the latter do not seem to have the right to refuse." Parents are often the more willing to lend a daughter if they are to retain the children whom she may have. Elsewhere it is a "habit of hospitality" to offer companions to strangers or to friendly chiefs who come on a visit. A rare case of "husband-borrowing exists among such mature Oromó girls as must remain single and yet want children."[133]

The Samoyeds used to lend wives, daughters, and sisters to guests.[134] In South India husbands traffic in their wives.[135] Borneo chiefs and their honored guests are provided with companions.[136] In the Pacific Islands chiefs and husbands can order women to go to strangers and there is not a little greed of

[128] Lippert, Kgchte., II, 17; Andree, in Globus, XLVI, 319.

[129] Howitt, S.E. Aust., 208, 217, 258, 266 (quoted).

[130] Fison, in AAAS, 1892, 694; Curr, Aust. Race, I, 109-110; Gason, in JAI, XXIV, 170; Spencer and Gillen, Nat. Tr. Cent. Aust., 267; Cunow, Australneger, 45; Ratzel, Vkde., II, 68.

[131] Codrington, Melanesians, 24.

[132] Von Pfeil, Südsee, 32; Krieger, Neu-Guinea, 297; Pöch, in Globus, XCII, 279.

[133] Frobenius, Masken, 223; Holub, Süd-Afr., II, 139; Ellis, Ewe, 202; Klose, Togo, 255; Conradt, in Globus, LXXXI, 337; Serpa Pinto, África, I, 284, 285; Stuhlmann, Mit Emin, 505; Sibree, Great Afr. Isl., 252-253; Paulitschke, Nordost-Afr., I, 209; II, 142 (quoted).

[134] Hiekisch, Tungusen, 90.   [135] Reclus, Prim. Folk, 283.

[136] Roth, Sarawak, I, 117; Veth, Borneo's Wester-Afdeeling, II, 251-252.

gain along with the extension of hospitality. The temporary making-over of wives constitutes "polygamy in another form."[137] Eskimo bond-brothers practise mutual hospitality and "neither family knows who is the father of the children." Lending for a season and exchange are found among the Central Eskimo.[138] Indians of the Five Nations provided companions for guests and on the northwest coast we see "the question of morality and immorality of the wife solely one of sanction by the husband."[139]

Among the ancient Hebrews, "as among other peoples, it was once the custom to turn over the women to the guest-friend. He is, as it were, the fellow-possessor."[140] Wife-lending was practised in Sparta and elsewhere in Greece.[141] Plutarch[142] goes into some length in describing Cato's opinions and acts in the matter of wife-lending. It was one of the first duties of hospitality in Canary and refusal was considered an insult.[143] Wilutzky[144] sees the custom world-wide, lasting in the Teuton nation down to the sixteenth century; this ancient German usage is represented by a survival, where sex-relations were tabooed, in the Netherlands.[145] In Russia, wives were held as security for loans, and if not redeemed within a specified time, were sold.[146] In England wives were once sold in the cattle-market and public house.[147] The modern press reports occasional reversions to such obsolete practices.[148]

The exchange of wives is sometimes, it will be recalled,[149] a survivalistic ceremonial.

In Australia, for example, "at times when there were great tribal gatherings wives were exchanged, but always within class limits. But they also resorted to this practice to avert some great trouble which they fancied was about to come upon them; for instance, they once heard that a great sickness was coming down the Murray, and the old men proposed exchanging wives to ensure safety from it. Yet at all other times men required wives to be faithful to their husbands, unless by their consent and command. In one case two men exchanged wives for a month."[150]

[137] Pereiro, *Ponapé*, 120; Finsch, *Ethnol. Erfahr.*, III, 239; Kubary, *Pelauer*, 51; Cook, in USNM, 1897, I, 717.

[138] Nelson, in BAE, XVIII, pt. I, 292; Boas, in BAE, VI, 579.

[139] Chalmers, *Polit. Annals of United Colonies*, I, 608; Niblack, in USNM, 1888, 240, 241.

[140] Maurer, *Vkde.*, I, 60.

[141] Xenophon, *Rep. Lac.*, I, 7, 8; Plutarch, *Lycurgus*, XV; Polybius, *Exc. Vat.*, XII, 6; Schoemann, *Griech. Alterth.*, I, 273.

[142] *Cato of Utica*, XXXVI, LXVIII; Letourneau, *Marriage*, 201-202, and ch. IV.

[143] Cook, in AA, II, 479-480.

[144] *Mann u. Weib*, 45 ff.; Schultz, *Deut. Leben*, 254.

[145] Weinhold, *Deut. Frauen*, II, 200.

[146] Kostomarov, *Gt. Russians* (Russ.), 153.

[147] Garnier, *Brit. Peasantry*, 380.

[148] N. Y. *Times*, Mar. 26, 1894, and Dec. 20, 1903.

[149] §§277, 343, above.

[150] Howitt, *S.E. Aust.*, 195; Smyth, *Vict.*, I, 77.

Perhaps such a reversion might with equal justice be called an exchange of husbands; the fact, however, that the initiative always proceeds from the man is significant of the lodgment of all control in his hands. Cases occur often enough where the exchange is no more than that of a piece of property, as the last part of the foregoing quotation indicates; and even where the operation has a religious significance, the wives are assimilated to other objects thus transferred.

Friends and relations exchange wives in Ponapé.[151] Exchange is a sort of hospitality-custom in East Greenland; but the limits of blood-relationship set for marriage apply to it also. Further, two men may arrange to trade wives and various other things for a shorter or longer period.[152] Of the Point Barrow Eskimo it is reported: "A curious custom, not peculiar to these people, is the habit of exchanging wives temporarily. For instance, one man of our acquaintance planned to go to the rivers deer hunting in the summer of 1882, and borrowed his cousin's wife for the expedition, as she was a good shot and a good hand at deer hunting, while his own wife went with his cousin on the trading expedition to the eastward. On their return the wives went back to their respective husbands."[153]

Where the wife is property, she is passed on, like other property, as a heritage. She must be the possession of some one, for she may not own herself any more than may a slave. The inheritance of women aligns them with property even more convincingly than do lending and exchange.

In the New Hebrides the widow[154] is the property of her husband's brother. He disposes of her; she is generally remarried; but he keeps the children, which are scarce and prized.[155] A Bechuana "became the owner of his father's wives, and took two of them for his own."[156] "A man inherits the wives of his dead brother and thenceforth regards them as his wives. . . . They hold, as inherited wives, a lower status and they rank only as a labor force." A grown son inherits his father's wives, generally with the exception of his own mother. If they have sons of their own the ownership is provisory and they are a labor-force; when their sons grow up, they may expel the step-father, saying, "Here is our father's place." The women submit by necessity and for protection, "for a man will treat his wives as his own only so long as they can work for him." If an inherited wife is old, she is turned over to her son for care, no matter how young he may be. Only the head-wife of a rich man and the one wife of a poor one are exempt from such unceremonious dismissal.[157]
The inheritance of a royal father's wives is a sign of the passage of his sta-

[151] Christian, *Caroline Isl*, 74.
[153] Murdoch, in BAE, IX, 413.
[155] Leggatt, in AAAS, 1892, 698.
[156] Livingstone, *Mission. Travels*, 203.
[157] Gutmann, in *Globus*, XCII, 32.

[152] Holm, *Ethnol. Skizze*, 56.
[154] §395, below.

tion. In Homer, the Suitors wanted Penelope, the characteristic possession of the absent king, as a step to the kingship.[158] Because Adonijah wanted Abishag, Solomon put him to death.[159]

If the wife is thus aligned with property, it follows that her issue are simply property derived from property. Where the father acknowledges or repudiates the child at birth he does so as the owner of the mother. In the Laws of Manu occurs an often quoted dictum that the possessor of the mother, even though he is not the begetter, is the owner of the son just as the proprietor of a cow is owner of her calf. This matter of the rights over children is to be reviewed in a later connection.[160]

§383*. Infidelity. This topic is an extension of a foregoing allusion to the power of self-disposal within wedlock. The wife's right in this respect has always been a vanishing or non-existent quantity in comparison with the husband's; she has been held to fidelity as he has not, and the double standard thus existing within matrimony has been reflected in life outside of it.

It is quite out of the ordinary that a husband, as in central Celebes, being surprised in adultery by his wife, commits suicide; much more commonly is it found that the wife is the only one from whom conjugal fidelity, a virtue solely feminine, is required.[161] "Adultery in our sense, on the part of the man, was unknown to the Peruvians."[162] Our standards are due very largely to the action of the Church which would not agree to any distinction between husband and wife as respects adultery and succeeded in enforcing its views upon Western mores.[163]

The salient consideration behind this contrast, going back as it does to biological fact, is that descent, inheritance, and succession are perturbed by the infidelity of a wife as they are not by that of a husband. The interest of society is always closely bound up with the definiteness and sureness of the parent-child relation. Hence society, through the mores, lays a heavier hand upon the sex through whose action its interest may more readily suffer a disservice. It does this without making any allowance for man-made sentiments regarding fairness and justice. In the light

[158] Keller, *Hom. Soc.*, 222-227.   [159] I Kings, II, 24-25.
[160] §§404, 405, 410, 419, below.
[161] Steinmetz, in AA (O.S.), VII, 58; Bishop, *Korea*, 116.
[162] Cunow, *Verf. Inkareichs*, 29, note.
[163] Freisen, *Kanon. Eherechts*, 617; Rudeck, *Oeffentl. Sittl.*, 166.

of the societal interest the mores securing adjustment to the condition of bi-sexuality evolved into the marriage-institution, with
matrimony as its central feature. Adultery and, later on, prostitution defeat that interest by striking at the institution; they are
therefore visited by penalties calculated to repress them. The code
that countenances wedlock as a harmonization of the interests in
the field cannot tolerate that which breaks it up in the matter of
important interest-relations—that which disharmonizes. Adultery
in particular, meaning illicit relations with a wife, becomes not
only a crime but a sin, for it strikes at genuineness of descent and
blood-kinship. The ancestral ghosts are keen to detect and punish
the sacrilege.

The nature of that which assails the marriage-institution in
such manner varies with the form of the institution. Where community of women within a group prevailed, the notion of adultery
was that someone not of the group associated with a woman of the
group;[164] for the monopoly over the women was scarcely more
than a group-monopoly and the group-right being about the only
one that could be infringed, must be protected. As the cases will
show, adultery was any action likely, or capable of being miscon-
strued as likely, to lead to an actual infringement of the conjugal
relation as existing in a given place and time. Hence there will
occur under this treatment of adultery cases of infringement upon
the rights of the father as well as of the husband. Naturally the
higher the social rank of woman, in the local society or generally,
the heavier have been the penalties for such infringement; for the
rights of the great are always more in evidence than those of the
small.

It must be understood that, although most races have set themselves against adultery, the driving motive has not been the one
that bulks largest in the mores of the present and which is played
up in literature, namely, a specific form of the sense of honor or,
to put it in its crudest form, jealousy. The modern ideal is that
the wife is sealed, sexually, to her husband and, though in a far
less degree, the husband to the wife. Fidelity to the relation demands not only that there shall be an exclusiveness in deed but
also even in intent and thought. The ideal marriage is an extreme

[164] Lippert, *Kgchte.*, II, 15; several cases in Letourneau, *Marriage,* 81, 209,
324.

of monopoly—a complete engrossment of the parties each in the other. If there is any vagrancy even in affection on the part of husband or wife, the relation is thereby marred and the existence of sex-relations outside of marriage is a personal disgrace and humiliation as well as a public scandal. This is not purely idealistic, at least in several modern countries, as witness the fate of a public man like Parnell, whose influence went when his private life was believed to be impure, or the exaltation of domestic virtue in the person of Victoria.

This insistence upon the mutual monopolization of husband and wife rests, not upon any instinct, but upon standards that are the product of a long course of societal evolution. Sexual jealousy is not innate any more than language or morals are. Some tribes show it and some do not; it is seldom reported by the ethnographers in a form comparable to that with which we are familiar in fiction if not in actuality. Sexual jealousy is not taken much account of in the primitive marriage-institution or in the sanctions with which it is surrounded. It is too individual and sporadic to call for institutional adjustment to its presence among society's life-conditions. The following cases include all the instances we have collected of such jealousy.

The Nagas of India are said to have each but one wife, "to whom they are strongly attached and of whose chastity they appear very jealous. The women . . . are said to be distinguished for the correctness of their behaviour."[165] The Veddahs show strong sexual jealousy; it appears that only the husband himself, "not even his brother, may ever go to his wife and child or give them any food."[166] The Botocudos contract brief unions, but "while they last they often give rise to outbreaks of jealousy and extreme passion on the part of the men. The women have not yet acquired the right to be jealous, a sentiment implying a certain degree of equality between the sexes. In case of real or suspected infidelity to their ephemeral masters, they are constantly subjected to most barbarous treatment, being beaten with clubs or hacked about with bamboo knives."[167] Another author[168] reports the same of the Botocudos and cites the secret tenderness of the Arawak for his wife; "if he is injured in this feeling he is capable of the most sweeping revenge." Of one Paraguay tribe we learn that "their feeling of jealousy goes to the extreme, and dominates all other feelings. It is the direct or indirect cause of all their crimes and all the personal and tribal quarrels. The stranger, whom they nevertheless fear, may

[165] Godden, in JAI, XXVI, 178.   [166] Sarasin, Weddas, 538, 462.
[167] Keane, in JAI, XIII, 206.
[168] Von Martius, Beiträge, I, 322, 693.

even sometimes run the danger of his life if he betrays too tender sentiments toward one of the damsels of the woods."[169]

It is by no means certain that the relatively few cases of reported jealousy are what we understand under that term. Of the Veddahs, just mentioned, and who have served as classic examples of primitive jealousy, it is stated on competent authority that they are jealous as a pure marital custom, just as the Singhalese are not jealous because it is not with them a marital custom.[170] Among the Pelew Islanders jealousy is less a sign of wounded feelings than of external propriety.[171] Among many of the Indians it is a sentiment unknown, with the result that sanctioned freedom of the wife is common.[172] The people who lend and exchange wives cannot be under the sway of jealousy as we know it; again and again customs will be encountered as the reader traverses this book which will contravene the significance of the sentiment as apprehended by certain writers.

Too much weight has been accorded to Darwin's argument about jealousy in animals, despite his honored name. If an animal or a man fights for fear that, if his female is taken away, he will have none—which often seems to be the motive—that is not "jealousy," as a husband feels it under monogamy. The resentment which civilized and uncivilized harbor at trespasses on property is far removed from "jealousy"; but this is the sentiment of the uncivilized about their wives. Genuine jealousy is a sentiment of dissatisfaction at having someone else draw away the personal devotion of a third person to one's self, when one has a right to such devotion. It is a modern and civilized sentiment, as is the exclusiveness of the sex-relation.

If it is conceded that the "instinct" of jealousy is not able to bear the weight of explanation, and if the materials dealing with the attitude toward and the treatment of adultery are surveyed without prepossession, it appears that, as an infringement of taboo, it has been generally resented and punished with a varying degree of severity.

Westermarck,[173] who is concerned to disprove primitive promiscuity, thinks that the punishments for adultery indicate jealousy and so make against the

[169] Machon, in PSM, LII, 405.   [170] Schmidt, *Ceylon,* 277.
[171] Kubary, *Pelauer,* 60.   [172] Niblack, in USNM, 1888, 347.
[173] *Marriage,* I, 300, 311.

looseness of relations which he dislikes. The word jealousy is sometimes employed in a sense not recognized by us and for which we should need some other expression such as "wounded vanity" or "resentment of encroachment upon property-right."[174] No issue can be joined if the counters in the game are to change their value at the will of one of the players.

There is no doubt about the general attitude of mankind toward adultery. It is hostile. Nevertheless we may as well face the exceptions and get them out of the way first of all; for while they are relatively few in number, they cannot be left out of the true picture.

In Australia, though sex-relations within the taboo—between parties forbidden to one another—are shameful and produce an uproar, adultery as we understand it is not much heeded. It is not dishonorable and concerns only the husband and the adulterer. The latter may be obliged to stand and let the former throw a spear at him.[175] In some parts of Melanesia the women have the right to do as they will, while in others they are only "fairly virtuous after marriage."[176] In the Uganda lake-region relations are loose and adultery frequent; in one of the tribes there is an utter license after marriage, the husbands are indifferent, and there is no restraint if the lover pays. Again, it is reported that the two sexes conduct themselves with excessive freedom and that in a single region may occur all grades of unrestraint.[177] Among the Galla the wife gives up all self-control and is faithless in return for small presents. A Somal man must give warning of his approach to his own house; one who, having given no sign of his presence, caught his wife in adultery was nonsuited before the judge when he sought divorce.[178] In Kuka the utmost looseness is regarded as quite natural and the Arab women in Algeria exhibited impulsive unrestraint overlaid by formal prudery.[179] Conjugal fidelity is not classed as the highest of virtues in later India.[180] Of the Todas, Rivers[181] writes: "I was assured by several Todas not only that adultery was no motive for divorce, but that it was in no way regarded as wrong. It seemed clear that there is no word for adultery in the Toda language. . . . Instead of adultery being regarded as immoral, I rather suspected, though I could not satisfy myself on the point, that, according to the Toda idea, immorality attaches rather to the man who grudges his wife to another. One group of those who experience difficulty in getting to the next world after death are the . . . grudging people, and I believe this term includes those who would in a more civilised community be plaintiffs in the divorce court." Neither sex in Timorlaut is strict about the marriage-relation.[182]

[174] Schroeder, *Geschlechtl. Ordnung,* 22, 23, 25.

[175] Cunow, *Australneger,* 43.

[176] Von Pfeil, *Südsee,* 74; Haddon, in JAI, XIX, 358.

[177] Stuhlmann, *Mit Emin,* 183; Johnston, in JAI, XV, 8; Burrows, *Pigmies,* 85; Schweinfurth, *Heart of Afr.,* II, 91.

[178] Paulitschke, *Nordost-Afr.,* I, 195, 249.

[179] Rohlfs, in *Mitth. J. Perthes' Geog. Anst.,* Ergänzband., V, 66; Pommerol, *Sahariennes, passim.*

[180] Bailey, in *Trans. Ethnog. Soc. London,* II, 291.

[181] *Todas,* 529-530.   [182] Forbes, in JAI, XIII, 20.

Homer,[183] unlike Vergil, has no sternness of censure for Helen; vengeance is
wreaked upon Paris and his family because he stole Menelaus's wife and property in contravention of the obligations of guest-friendship. In old Germany
the infidelity of a bride was not regarded as adultery, while in Transcaucasia
women who have borne children or those who have been married four or five
years may live unchastely, though previously their conduct has been irreproach-
able.[184] In the Elizabethan age it was as common for men of a certain class
"to debauch their neighbors' wives as for two yeomen to draw on each other at
a county fair, or for a craftsman to be butchered by his fellow in Smith-
field."[185]

These exceptional instances carry no great weight. Several of
them obviously reflect the moral judgment of the observers; others
are taken from societies where the institutions of property and
marriage are not well developed. The sharpness of the conception
of adultery varies with the definiteness and stability of both of
these institutions. Further, cases of this order form but a small
proportion when compared with instances of strict and stern
penalization of illicit freedom. This will come out when the penalties for adultery are reviewed. Many instances might be cited in
direct contrast with the preceding.

Looking at a New Caledonian chief's wife is punished as treason.[186] Among
certain African tribes, it is almost a crime for a married woman to give paint
to a man, for it implies undue familiarity and is sure to bring down the wrath
of the husband.[187] In the Congo region, "boys and girls from an early age
until puberty have free intercourse with each other, and I believe that later
there is no public condemnation if the girls are not betrothed. It is only when
money has been paid for the exclusive rights in her that adultery is condemned
—it is an infringement of another person's rights. It is rarely that one sees an
illegitimate child, either they have means of preventing pregnancy or of causing abortion. Then, again, likely young women marry at an early age, and
should a child be born soon after the marriage, the husband has no particular
objection."[188] Among the Dinka, "any man, who, *unknown to and without
consent* of the husband, has sexual intercourse with any of that man's wives
commits the offence of adultery." Again, though there are provisions that allow
of it, "a man who has sexual intercourse with a widow . . . commits adultery,
and her guardian demands the cattle fine from offender to be held 'in trust'
for his ward, the heir who is a minor, or may not yet be born. . . . All children, the result of adultery, become the property of the husband; or if borne
by a widow are held 'in trust' by the widow and the guardian for the heir,
whether a minor or not yet born."[189] The Niam-Niam women are modest and
retiring and many a man has been punished with the loss of fingers, or even

---

[183] Keller, *Hom. Soc.*, 228 (where full references to text are given).
[184] Lehmann, *Verlobung*, 102; Von Haxthausen, *Transkaukasia*, II, 24.
[185] Hall, *Eliz. Age*, 11.   [186] Letourneau, *Marr.*, 210.
[187] Burrows, *Pigmies*, 85; Schweinfurth, *Heart of Afr.*, II, 91.
[188] Weeks, in JAI, XL, 417.   [189] O'Sullivan, in JAI, XL, 187-188.

with death, for addressing a quite innocent word to the wife of a prince.[190] In Kabylie a kiss on the mouth "costs more than an assassination."[191]

The Laws of Manu[192] regard it as adulterous to address a wife from another outside village or to give her presents. The woman of high rank was to be devoured by dogs in a public place, the man burned on a red-hot bed. The Veddahs of Ceylon present a very remarkable trait in their constancy to their mates.[193] The Dyak women are generally faithful and adultery is especially uncommon when there are children; punishment falls in most cases and as a matter of course on the woman and consists in fines or a thrashing.[194] In one North Borneo tribe, "adultery is a crime unknown," and among others, astonishingly enough, it is punished by death to the man, who "is always considered the guilty and responsible party concerned." Among the Sea Dyaks adultery is uncommon, considering the density of the population.[195] A Balinese girl who had accepted a flower or some such trifle from a man, was executed despite all protests and offers to pay a fine on the part of the Englishman in whose family she lived.[196] On the Mentawei Islands a woman is free until marriage and is then under penalty of death for adultery.[197] In Rotuma, the natives could do what they liked till marriage. "After sixty years of missionary enterprise it is much the same. Indeed, the old men informed me that the stern laws and fines of the missionaries did no good, but really accentuated the evil. Then, they say, adultery was unknown, but now it is common with both sexes."[198]

Among the Omahas, in an extreme case, an adulterous woman was bound to a post and given up to twenty or thirty men and then abandoned by her husband.[199] Certain California Indians publicly disembowelled adulteresses and either destroyed one eye of the man or made him give his wife in exchange. In Yucatan both parties were stoned or shot with arrows; earlier the woman was impaled or disjointed.[200] Of the Indians of Mosquito Territory it is said that "they appear strict in observance of marriage state, and seem to be free from sexual disease consequent on adulterous intercourse."[201] In Peru capital punishment prevailed; in case of relations with a wife of the Inca, the man was burned, his relatives put to death, and his house destroyed.[202] The Ges tribes, though wild and low in culture, are remarkable for the purity of their family morals.[203]

Though Homer has no censure for Helen, the *Æneid,* representing the strong patriarchal mores of the Romans, pictures her as blameworthy.[204] In later Greece and in Rome the husband might kill with impunity both wife and paramour; but a husband's relation with a slave or a prostitute did not rank as a

190 Junker, *Afrika,* II, 461.
191 Hanoteau et Letourneux, *Kabylie,* III, 209.
192 Bühler, *Manu,* VIII, 356-357, 371-372.
193 Bailey, in *Trans. Ethnol. Soc. London,* II, 291.
194 Gomes, *Sea Dyaks,* 69, 70.
195 Roth, *Sarawak,* I, 130; Roth, in JAI, XXI, 131.
196 Wallace, *Malay Archip.,* 174.   197 Pleyte, in *Globus,* LXXIX, 26.
198 Gardiner, in JAI, XXVII, 409.   199 Dorsey, in BAE, III, 364-365.
200 Bancroft, *Nat. Races,* I, 350, 351, 412; II, 674.
201 Wickham, in JAI, XXIV, 207.
202 Prescott, *Peru,* I, 26; Letourneau, *Marriage,* 215.
203 Von Hellwald, in Reichenow, *Handwörterbuch, sub* "Gês."
204 Vergil, *Æneid,* II, 567 ff.

crime.[205] Aristotle and other writers, Greek and Roman, asserted the duty of husbands to observe the same fidelity they expected of their wives; they raised the question, at least, as to a single standard.[206] Adultery is very rare among the Bulgarians.[207]

With this conspectus of contrasting cases illustrative of mankind's attitude toward adultery before us, we may now inquire as to the nature of the crime as it appeared to the minds of that great majority of races who regarded it as such.

It is clear enough that some peoples inflicted upon those who infringed the taboos that made wedlock, a punishment so condign that adultery would seem to rank with the most dangerous and detestable of crimes. Most peoples punished it in some fashion; perhaps the commonest conception revealed in their attitude aligns adultery more closely with theft of property than with any other category of crime. It is for this reason that the topic of adultery is included in a section dealing chiefly with woman as property. The following instances, representative of the great majority of cases of adultery collected by us, show, in general, that woman's fault lies in the assumption of property-right in self-disposal, while the man is aligned with the trespasser upon land or other form of material possession. The feeling of the husband is not jealousy in the specific sense; Westermarck[208] juggles with the word, when he explains that since the jealousy of savages with respect to their wives is rather the feeling for the exclusiveness of a property-right than jealousy proper, the custom of lending wives does not prove that there is no jealousy. Nothing is gained by such confusion of terms. The savage husband cleaves to that adverse possession or monopoly which is the essence of property[209] either in things or in persons. He resents interference with his rights as accorded him in the mores; and because the invasion of the property-monopoly is dangerous to societal well-being, at any place or time, society backs him up. This view is strengthened by the fact that, as some of the cases will show, the father of the unmarried girl who is seduced, a man who can have no sexual jealousy as respects her, is compensated much as a husband would be.

[205] Schmidt, *Soc. Civ.*, 48.
[207] Strauss, *Bulgaren*, 302.
[209] §110, above.

[206] Lecky, *Europ. Morals,* II, 313.
[208] *Marriage,* I, 301.

"A wife is often regarded as not very different from other property and an adulterer is a thief. . . . In some parts of Africa he is punished as such, having his hands, or one of them, cut off."[210] "In all primitive societies adultery is assimilated to theft and becomes lawful when authorized by the proprietor or custom."[211] Woman is property; "to use her, therefore, without the authority of her owner, is a theft; and human societies have never been tender to thieves. . . . But adultery is not as ordinary theft. An object, an inert possession, are passive things; their owner may well punish the thief who has taken them, but him only. In adultery, the object of the larceny, the wife, is a sentient and thinking being—that is to say, an accomplice in the attempt on her husband's property in her own person; moreover, he generally has her in his keeping; he can chastise her freely, and glut his rage on her without any arm being raised for her defence. On the contrary, in letting loose his vengeance the husband will frequently have public opinion and law on his side, when the latter does not take on itself the punishment of the guilty one."[212]

Though it is impracticable to set up in parallel columns the punishments for adultery and for theft, still if one recalls the general attitude of evolving societies toward the latter and the common punishments for it,[213] and then realizes the specific features of property in human beings,[214] and the still more specific characteristics of property in wives as revealed in a survey of preliminaries to marriage, the wedding-ceremony, and the details of rights in marriage,[215] he should be able, despite their variation of detail, to grasp the sense of the following cases.

In Australia the injured husband may cast a spear at his injurer and cut his wife severely.[216] Tasmanian husbands severely punished wives' infidelities if unauthorized, on the ground of their right of ownership.[217] In Melanesia the stock penalty of death to the man was very generally mitigated by a fine. The woman was often made a harlot for the profit of the chief.[218] In New Guinea the injured party kills the adulterer, not because of wounded honor but because his property has been infringed; again, the coconut-trees belonging to the guilty party are cut down.[219] In New Britain, though there is a death-penalty, it is commonly commuted for shell-money; a husband may get his wife's money away from her by trumping up charges of adultery.[220] Again the aggrieved husband takes all the wives of his injurer, having first killed his own.[221] In the Solomon Islands, while no stain attaches to the man, the

210 Westermarck, *Marriage*, I, 300.
211 Letourneau, *Soc.*, 466; Lippert, *Kgchte.*, II, 121.
212 Letourneau, *Marriage*, 208-209.
213 §184, above.   214 Ch. X and §169, above.
215 Chs. XLVI-L, above, and the immediately foregoing paragraphs.
216 Spencer and Gillen, *Nat. Tr. Cent. Aust.*, 55.
217 Bonwick, *Daily Life*, 72.   218 Codrington, *Melanesians*, 243.
219 Krieger, *Neu-Guinea*, 300, 302; Blum, *Neu-Guinea*, 27.
220 Finsch, *Ethnol. Erfahr.*, I, 90; Danks, in JAI, XVII, 308.
221 Haddon, in JAI, XIX, 396.

woman's skull is cloven.[222] Again, the husband might kill both parties discovered *in flagrante delicto*, but under other circumstances he might simply divorce the woman and collect damages from the man. "This adultery price, like that paid for a widow, . . . must be paid; if the lover's own local group will not help him, he has to make the amount up as best he can. Only a portion of the adultery price . . . is kept by the aggrieved husband, the rest he shares among his clansmen."[223]

African punishments for adultery[224] include, beside disfigurement, execution and even dismemberment while alive, enslavement of the man, and marriage of the woman to a slave; and the punishment is the more severe in the case of the chief or status-wife. The Hottentots lent their wives readily but punished unauthorized freedom.[225] In South Africa the young wives of old men are apparently under no restraint.[226] In Ashanti a chief's wife is punished by death only in extreme cases; generally her family pays a sum for her redemption. If her family is powerful, her nose is usually cut off as a punishment.[227] Again, the husband may castigate her and recover damages from her paramour, the fine being large if the injured husband is of high rank. If the guilty man cannot pay, his creditor has the right to enslave him; or the adulterer may take the wife and her children, refunding her purchase-price and all expenses incurred in her behalf. Though in such case there is no fine, the woman becomes responsible to her new lord for the sum he has paid for her and may not leave him without payment in full.[228] Adultery can be committed only with a married woman; it is punishable by death or divorce but as a rule she is beaten and damages are recovered from her lover.[229] On the Ivory Coast, there is a sort of traffic in damages, the compensated party appearing to be quite content.[230] Where among the lower classes compensation is the rule, among the upper the two culprits are instantly put to death.[231] In the northern Cameroon region the woman is bound to a post and hacked to death by her husband's relatives, while the man, unless killed at once by the injured husband—which may be done with impunity—is fined.[232] In Angola, the wife who does not commit adultery, thus augmenting her husband's property by fines, is thought little of; and she may be ordered to do so.[233] The Mumbo-Jumbo society of West African regions has as one of its objects the prevention of unauthorized adultery.[234]

In Uganda adultery in the higher classes was once punished by being "chopped up alive together"; but it has come to be dealt with on the basis of fines. The wife is treated leniently in some districts, though the male offender is whipped. The husband is indifferent if the lover pays. This goes with affection and kindliness in family-relations.[235] Elsewhere the woman is killed if

[222] Somerville, in JAI, XXVI, 394.   [223] Seligmann, *Melanesians*, 80.
[224] List in Letourneau, *Marriage*, 211-214; Index to Pinkerton's *Voyages*, *sub* "adultery."
[225] Letourneau, *Marr.*, 210.   [226] Macdonald, in JAI, XIX, 272.
[227] Ellis, *Tshi*, 283.   [228] Ellis, *Ewe*, 202, 203.
[229] Ellis, *Yoruba*, 186.
[230] Anon., "Östl. Elfenbeinküste," in *Globus*, LXXXVII, 391-392.
[231] Kingsley, *W. Afr. Studies*, 454.
[232] Hutter, in *Globus*, LXXVI, 308.
[233] Serpa Pinto, *Africa*, I, 54, 144.   [234] Letourneau, *Marr.*, 128.
[235] Johnston, *Uganda*, II, 689; Johnston, in JAI, XV, 8.

the man is of another tribe; if he is not, she is enslaved or her father is fined.[236] Among the Akamba, the abduction of a wife is compensated for by handing over to the injured husband the amount of livestock he paid for the woman. "A case recently occurred . . . where the headman of a village had been carrying on a liaison with a young unmarried woman and she was taken ill and died while on a visit to his village. The matter of compensation was discussed at great length by a court of elders, and some held that the headman . . . should pay the father of the girl the damages due in case of murder, but eventually the majority decided that the father's claim should be assessed on the basis of the marriage value of the girl."[237] In northeast Africa, fines in goats are the rule, the woman being often left unpunished; if the husband kills the wife he must pay her parents. A man may reproach his wife for her fidelity, saying, "You are not even useful enough to bring a goat into my house."[238] Again, there is greater severity, as where the adulterer may be killed in the act or, if he escapes, lose his property by confiscation, two-thirds to the chief and one-third to the husband. The latter repudiates his wife, who is disgraced. The adulterer may return, though he is never sure of his life.[239] Again the man may pay a fine or take the poison-draught. The woman remains unpunished, unless she denies the charge, in which case she may undergo the same ordeal. If she lives, the man must pay her father and her; if she dies, her father must repay to her husband her purchase-price.[240] Elsewhere the male offender is not killed but the cause of the sin is burned; the adulterer excuses himself, placates the husband a little, and they remain friends.[241]

These African cases are representative of the treatment of adultery in ethnography. A few selected instances from other parts of the world may be added to enforce certain important aspects. In a number of cases "intercourse between both sexes is free and unrestrained until after marriage"; in India, however, "if a married woman goes astray, her seducer is not punished, but the woman is fined, and has her ears cut off."[242] In Sumatra, in the case of *flagrante delicto* adultery the husband is in duty bound to kill both culprits; if he kills the man only he is exposed to blood-vengeance from relatives of the slain, and the same is the case if he kills the woman only. If he kills neither, it is speedily known, for the people of the village constitute a coherent whole. If the man flees, it is enough if the injured husband presents a piece of his clothing in evidence, in which case the guilty party may not be killed but both culprits are brought to trial and condemned to death.[243] Among the Indians of the American northwest coast, the daughter constitutes property whose infringement is treated much as in the case of a wife. "If unmarried women prove frail, the partner of their guilt, if discovered, is bound to make reparation to the parents, soothing their wounded honor with handsome presents. A failure to do this would cause the friends of the offending fair one to use force to back up their demands and to revenge the insult. It must not, however, be supposed they would be induced to act this part, from any sense

236 Volkens, *Kilimandscharo*, 252; Abbott, in USNM, 1891, 389.
237 Hobley, *A-Kamba*, 80.
238 Paulitschke, *Nordost-Afr.*, I, 203; II, 11.
239 Stuhlmann, *Mit Emin*, 39, 93, 781.
240 "Kl. Nachrichten," in *Globus*, XCII, 147.
241 Vannutelli e Citerni, *L'Omo*, 195.
242 Lewin, *S.E. India*, 245.
243 Jacobs, *Groot-Atjeh*, II, 226.

of reflected shame, or from a desire of discouraging vice by making a severe example of the vicious, or that the girl herself has any visitings of remorse, or that the parents think her a bit the worse for the accident, or her character in any way blemished. Such are not their feelings, for the offender is simply regarded as a robber who has committed depredations on their merchandise, their only anxiety being to make the damages exacted as heavy as possible."[244] Among certain California Indians "no adultery is so flagrant but that the husband can be placated with money at about the rate that would be paid for murder."[245] The Pima husband sometimes shot the horse of the offending man and "then he felt all right."[246] "Suspicious jealousy, not of love but of their property-right, is an outstanding characteristic of the Arabs, on which they pride themselves. . . . Blood-relatives were just as jealous of their property-right in the maiden as the husband was of his in the wife."[247]

In Homer the adultery of Ares and Aphrodite was a matter for laughter, but Hephæstus demands the bride-price back from Zeus. "Adultery was a violation of contract with respect to the quality of the goods, plus encroachment from a third party upon the acquired property-rights; the first was atoned for by the mutual return of purchased article and price, and the latter by fines of considerable size. The fines due from Paris were collected in the ruin of his family and city and in direct reprisal; since he did not pay, his transgression descended in its consequences upon his community. Thus adultery-fines seem to have been a commutation of the talion-punishment or some other."[248]

Judging by these cases, it is wrong to assert that the woman was always, or nearly always, regarded as the sole culpable party and as the only one to be punished. When it was a matter of fining, she could not be so punished in the large number of cases where she owned no property at all or none sufficient to meet the charge. It may be said, however, that she is commonly visited by such punishments as are capable of being inflicted upon a possession that has no rights of its own: she is more commonly disfigured than is the man; she is severely thrashed,[249] exposed to torture,[250] her hair shorn or even her nose bitten off,[251] her ears split,[252] or some other deep humiliation is inflicted upon her.[253]

[244] Niblack, in USNM, 1888, 241.

[245] Powers, in *Contrib. N. Amer. Ethnol.*, III, 22.

[246] Russell, in BAE, XXVI, 198.

[247] Wellhausen, in *Gött. Gesell. d. Wissensft.*, 1893, 447-448.

[248] Keller, *Hom. Soc.*, 227-231 (where all references to text are given).

[249] Roth, *Sarawak*, I, 130.

[250] Stevens, in *Ztsft. f. Eth.*, XXVIII, 178-179.

[251] Starcke, *Prim. Fam.*, 122; Letourneau, *Morale*, 161; Westermarck, *Marriage*, I, 313; Rogers, *America*, 238; Schroeder, *Geschechtl. Ordnung*, 111, 114.

[252] Allison, in JAI, XXI, 315; Wilkins, *Laws of Canute*, I, 308.

[253] Schrader, *Aryan*, 388; Tacitus, *Germ.*, chs. XVIII, XIX.

Often the disfigurement for adultery is no more than a sort of exaggeration of the marriage-mark, which is a property-mark.[254]

In preceding connections[255] it has been emphasized that the consequences of sex bear more heavily upon woman than upon man. The degree to which these consequences are socially unfortunate for her depends entirely upon the local code. It is the interest of society, expressed in the form of public opinion, that is determinative. Because adultery or the bearing of an illegitimate child is disgraceful to a woman according to our code is no proof that it has been so in all ages and places. Out of all the variations in code, however, one incontrovertible fact stands forth:

"Marriage is the means to family-building. The man can transplant into his family by way of procreation no alien child as a part and a member; to a child whose natural father he may be he cannot give his wife as a mother. Only the wife is capable of incorporating into the family a child whose real father is not the *paterfamilias*. To this consideration, which rests the demonstration of its correctness on an unmistakable basis in nature, is to be ascribed the impunity found in many codes for so-called breach of the marriage-relation on the part of the man. What is called adultery in the man is a violation of marital duties, a neglect of the wife, but not a breach of marriage and is to be punished as the former, under certain circumstances, never as the latter." In marriage, on all stages of evolution, such a breach on the part of the woman was punished. The man's irregularity of sexual relations could never constitute such a breach; he is not guilty of it "but is merely an accomplice."[256]

In short, the conception of adultery and its punishments serves to emphasize the less privileged status of woman in most societies. The marriage-relation has been worked out in the mores as the expedient way of meeting the basic life-condition of bi-sexuality. Adultery is a breach of the code as thus formulated for a place and time. Punishment is accorded in proportion to the heinousness of the offense as that is conceived and to the powers and responsibilities of the offender. The treatment of adultery is therefore a gauge of woman's rights and duties, that is, of her status; and it supports in good measure the conception of the woman as property.

§384*. Other Rights and Disqualifications. The reckoning of woman as property, where man, except under enslavement, is not so regarded, is a central conception in a survey of her status

254 §382, above.   255 §§59 ff., 378, above.
256 Schroeder, *Geschlechtl. Ordnung*, 108, 109.

in wedlock and outside it, for it is a basic and primordial way of viewing her. Much that seems to us less crude and inhuman has resulted from alteration of this anterior code in adjustment to changed life-conditions. Even the primitive relation between woman and property presents aspects which exhibit her in possession of certain economic powers. Consider, for example, the fact that she may both own property and inherit it. Evidently the fact that a wife may hold independent possession of goods is one bearing upon her status. It is conceded that even a slave who may possess a peculium has rights beyond one who may not. Similarly the wife who, even though she is herself property, may own, is enjoying rights above one who may not.

It is not at all uncommon that a wife should have her own property; husband's and wife's possessions are not infrequently classified in the mores, the man generally owning the implements of war and the chase, the house and the land, while the woman disposes over the gear that goes with her special sex-occupations. Again, it is the usage in some parts of the world where the bride is endowered, that each spouse shall own what he or she brought into the marital union, while what they acquire by joint effort belongs equally to both. The former type of property tends to be inherited in the stock manner, whereas there may be in connection with the latter a freedom of disposal or bequest that represents a variation away from the system of inheritance typical of the society in question. The significance of cases of this sort will appear in connection with family-organization;[257] the facts are reviewed in good part in what immediately follows.

Says Von Pfeil[258] of certain Melanesians: "One might think that such an unconditioned property-right of the man in the wife should lead to a reduction of the latter to the plane of a superior domestic animal but that is not so. . . . The woman is sole owner of all the marriage-goods brought by her into the union and of all that she can earn during the union. . . . This prerogative of the wife to independent property has become so much of a customary right that a trespass on the part of the men is said to occur only in the rarest cases. . . . Through her material independence of her husband and the power of larger possession, that which is degrading in her position is wiped out, and so she stands over against the other sex in what is really a pretty independent status."[259] Sometimes the Papuan woman "exercises the right of veto with

257 Chs. LV, LVI, below.   258 *Südsee*, 33.
259 §§81, 121, 132, above.

regard to contracts that do not immediately concern herself."[260] In New Britain, husband and wife own shell-money quite independently of one another. The husband may despoil her of her stock, not directly by force, however, as that would be an invasion of her rights of property and an offense to public opinion. He trumps up a charge of adultery or of saying something derogatory, and threatens her unless she pays, which she does to avoid bodily harm.[261]

In East Africa, "judging from the position of women we might suppose them to be entirely debarred from inheritance. On the contrary, the widow appears to be always the nominal heir, and the actual heir cannot dispose of the property without her consent, which, though it may be nominal, is never disregarded. A woman by herself cannot, however, have the control of property. . . . In Ukamba and Theraka, if a man dies leaving no male relations, his property remains in the possession of his widow, but under the control of the clan. On the death of the widow the property cannot descend to a daughter of hers, and if she has no son it will be appropriated by a distant relative or by the whole clan. . . . In Kikuyu it appears that there is very little chance of property going out of the immediate family, for the widow will either be married to her brother-in-law, or she will be given a mate, . . . and any children she has by either of these become the lawful heirs. If a widow is too old to have a child, there is a curious means by which she can create an heir, namely, she may buy a girl out of her deceased husband's property, and this girl (who is called the 'wife' of the dead man) cohabits with any member of the clan. Her male children then become the direct heirs to the property, and this is justified by the argument that their mother was bought with the stock belonging to the deceased. . . . From the above we may conclude that a woman is in name always the heir to her husband's property, in which she has a certain right but no dominion. . . . A woman may be said to be regarded all her life as a minor. She has certain rights which extend even to possession of property, but she is never given the control of the same. Similarly a woman is held to all intents and purposes to be irresponsible, and her father or husband is, under all circumstances, liable for her actions, as he is for those of his children."[262] The case of the widow and her rights is given special place later on.[263]

In West Africa, "a wife's property is always separate from that of her husband, and at her death passes to her children"; in this region her position as regards rights of property is superior to that among the Bantu. Again, she inherits only clothes and cooking-utensils from her female relatives; there is no other heritage in question for her.[264] In the laws of Manu[265] the married woman had a sixfold property; namely, what was given before the nuptial fire, on the bridal procession, in token of love, by brother, by mother, by father. Property given to a woman at her marriage was inherited by her unmarried daughter and her children received, even during their father's lifetime, whatever was given her by her husband or his family. But the woman was enjoined

[260] Spencer, in *Cosmopolitan Mag.*, XVIII, 661.

[261] Danks, in JAI, XVII, 308.

[262] Dundas, C., in JAI, XLV, 295-296, 301.

[263] §395, below.

[264] Ellis, *Ewe*, 216; Kingsley, *Travels W. Afr.*, 484; Gutmann, in *Globus*, XCII, 32.

[265] Bühler, *Manu*, IX, 194, 131, 195, 199, 200.

not to hoard goods from her kindred or even from the property of her lord without his assent. For her were reserved also the ornaments worn during her lord's lifetime.

Among the Delaware Indians, the game brought into the house is property of the woman, while the man has a similar claim to the products of the garden.[266] "The Dakota woman owns the tipi. If a man has more wives than one, they have separate tipis, or they arrange to occupy different sides of one."[267] The Cheyenne woman had property of her own and it remained so; she could sell, give away, or devise by will. Some women were nearly as wealthy as the men.[268] Again, "husband and wife do not hold property in common, but each retains whatever they possessed before marriage, and also anything they may subsequently acquire." This may occur whether the woman lives with her husband or not.[269] Women have great authority in the interior of Oregon: "they have charge of the lodge and the stores, and their consent is necessary for the use of them; for after coming into their possession, these articles are considered the women's own."[270]

There are special sorts of gifts made in connection with the nuptials,[271] which remain the bride's property. Sometimes they are a sort of contribution to her expenses. The giving of a real "bride-treasure" is among Malayo-Polynesian practices; it is entirely different from parents' gifts.

In old Iceland the bride-gift was called *mundr,* and was her own property. The Lombards called this gift a *morgengap* (morning-gift, Morgengabe): it is "the post-nuptial gift made in the morning to a second wife in lieu of dower, when a woman of unequal rank is taken to wife without right of dower for herself and heirship for her children." A man must not give more than a quarter of his possessions in this manner. The original gift was clothing or household-gear; later it came to be money or land. It was given *in signum amoris* the morning after the wedding. Since it was given to widows it was no *pretium virginitatis.*[272] The giving to the bride of a little money figures, probably survivalistically, in the ceremonial of some peoples of India, and in England and France; "at a peasant wedding in Lorraine, at a certain point in the service, the groom places thirteen pieces of silver in the hand of the bride."[273]

Any list of representative cases taken from the life of primitive peoples shows that in a general way the man and wife have the personal property that goes with their respective functions in co-

[266] Loskiel, *Mission,* 77; Lippert, *Kgchte.,* II, 32, 33.

[267] Dorsey, in BAE, XV, 222.   [268] Grinnell, *Cheyenne,* I, 157.

[269] Allison, in JAI, XXI, 316; Harrison, in JAI, XXI, 473.

[270] Wilkes, *U.S. Exped.,* IV, 447, 457.

[271] §364, above.

[272] Lehmann, *Verlobung,* 61; Reichel, *Canon Law,* I, 346, note; Stammler, *Stellung d. Frauen,* 35-36; Weinhold, *Deut. Frauen,* I, 402; Weinhold, *Altnord. Leben,* 247.

[273] Gomme, *Village Life,* 220, 233.

operation.[274] But woman's property is not confined to clothing, ornament, and domestic paraphernalia; she may even hold land.

Certain Papuan tribes assigned the ownership of land to its women-cultivators; alienation was subject to approval by chiefs and heads of families. Elsewhere land was held by sons and daughters alike.[275] In Malabar the mothers, who always own the land, give it to their eldest daughters who let their oldest brothers manage it for all the brothers and sisters.[276] In Malacca, while woman could hold no office, she could own land. Though it went to her husband at marriage and she lost all right to it, she still owned exclusively all trees which she had planted or caused to be planted and could dispose of them to anyone during the life of her husband.[277]

At a council of the Six Nations, in 1788, Indian women appeared, the Indians declaring that it was the custom of their ancestors that women should be mistresses of the soil. Yet when the Delawares sold some land without consent of the Iroquois, an Onondaga chief reproved them harshly: "We conquered you. We made women of you. You know you are women and can no more sell land than women." Among the Iroquois, "the rights of property, of both husband and wife, were continued distinct during the existence of the marriage relation, the wife holding and controlling her own the same as her husband, and in case of separation taking it with her. . . . If the wife either before or after marriage inherited orchards, or planted lots, or reduced land to cultivation, she could dispose of them at her pleasure, and in case of her death, they were inherited, together with her other effects, by her children. . . . In this connection, and as showing the similarity of customs among the Indians, it is of interest to note that the Creeks claimed to have put petticoats upon the Cherokees, and at the treaty of Augusta, in reply to a statement of the Georgians 'that they had bought a certain piece of land from the Cherokees,' a Creek chief started to his feet, 'and, with an agitated and terrific countenance, frowning menaces and disdain, fixed his eyes on the Cherokee chiefs and asked them what right they had to give away their lands, calling them old women, and saying that they had long ago obliged them to wear the petticoat.'" Among the Wyandots the women-councillors apportioned the land among the householders. Women were the heads of the households and owned wigwam and lodge and all household-articles.[278] As is intimated in the foregoing paragraph, these Indians are involved in the peculiarities of relation that go with the mother-family.[279] It appears that while women owned the land, it was not in their power, in general, to give it away or to sell it.

In Scandinavia, "in the matter of woman's property-right, it is certain that she could not, in the oldest time, possess immovable property because upon it rested originally all the social obligations that . . . were not possible for woman wholly to meet. But in an early period these conditions were already altered. Even if allodial land was by inheritance passed over to the sons, the daughters received compensation . . . [sometimes] in other land, and in Ice-

[274] Lippert, *Kgchte.*, II, 69 ff.   [275] Chalmers, in JAI, XXVII, 334.
[276] Reclus, *Prim. Folk*, 175.
[277] Stevens, in *Ztsft. f. Eth.*, XXVIII, 167.
[278] Turner, *P. and G. Purchase*, 118; Morgan, *League of Iroq.*, 338; Carr, in *Smithson. Rep.*, 1891, 519, note, 522, note; Powell, in BAE, I, 65.
[279] §416, below.

land a daughter could now and then inherit a *god-ord,* that is, an estate with accompanying priestly and judicial dignity, although she could not personally exercise the latter" but must transfer it.[280]

As the instance just preceding indicates, one of woman's typical disabilities was that she was generally ineligible for any specified office in the regulative organization. This matter, though it has been touched upon already,[281] may be recalled and enforced by a few representative citations. Among them occur several which illustrate the one inter-group immunity listed among the rights tabulated above, namely, the inviolability of woman in war and her consequent ability to serve as intermediary in inter-tribal negotiations and trade. It will have been observed, further, that woman is prominent neither in the religious organization nor in those bodies which combine the religious and the regulative, the secret societies.[282] In short, her functions bear a distinctly non-public character.

There are some remarks by Henry Adams,[283] about the Virgin in the Middle Ages, which may serve to introduce the topic of woman's place in the community. He shows how the woman, especially the Virgin, is always the practical guide. When men were at their strongest, they yet bowed down before women. The Virgin was essentially "illogical, unreasonable and feminine," and had exclusive powers over poor and rich, sinners and saints. Protestant churches were "cold failures without her help." The Holy Ghost and the Son were powerless. The religion of the Virgin was, "in substance a separate religion." But why did the Virgin Mother, gentle and gracious, so exasperate the Pilgrim Father? "Why was the Woman struck out of the Church and ignored in the State? . . . These questions are not antiquarian or trifling in historical value; they tug at the very heart-strings of all that makes whatever order is in the cosmos. If a Unity exists, in which and toward which all energies centre, it must explain and include Duality, Diversity, Infinity—Sex!"

From this view of the matter, which rather transcendentally recalls certain contentions which we have made concerning the essential characteristics of the sexes, we may now descend, somewhat abruptly, to the bare facts that reveal woman's position in the political and religious organizations.

The use of women as spies or envoys in war and as factors in trade is not uncommon.[284] Australian women, especially wives of chiefs, are sent to recon-

---

[280] Wisen, *Qvinnan,* 14.   [281] §§152, 153, 157, above.
[282] §§377, 309, 320, 161, 162, above.
[283] *Mont-Saint-Michel,* 246, 261; §§58 ff., above.
[284] §§69, 76, 140, 141, 142, of the text and *Case-Book.*

cile tribal disputes.[285] Livingstone found many women present in an assembly summoned by the chief to receive him.[286] The Marutse showed a preference for female rulers, which led to a higher status of woman as compared with neighboring peoples among whom she was worker, beast of burden, and slave.[287] In one Sierra Leone tribe, woman has a "superior social rank," though no woman may occupy the throne.[288] In Ashanti the "queen-mother" may mix in state affairs and go out unveiled, though she is the only woman who may do so.[289] So-called "queens" are common in West Africa.[290] In equatorial Africa, women are the go-betweens in parleys and are sent to bring back the articles sent in declaration of war when they want peace.[291]

"Outside every village there is an open space called *Thomi*—the boys of the village are sent every morning to sweep it and light a fire there. The old men of the village sit there a great part of the day and eat and drink beer there. No woman is allowed to use the *Thomi* for her domestic pursuits or to sit there; if a woman broke this rule she would be beaten. It is said that this prohibition has existed for many generations and originated in the desire of the old men to have some place where they could talk over affairs without being overheard by the women of the village who could not keep counsel with regard to any business they overheard, but would generally tell their neighbours."[292] Again, "in matters concerning the tribe or community, women have little personal share, but where the family is so closely bound up with the State it is unavoidable that the influence of women within the family should be felt in all matters. Undoubtedly the actions and projects of the men are dependent to a great extent on the female element of the community, for the interests of the men are centered entirely in their families, and therewith principally in their wives. I would give no exaggerated impression of this point, but undoubtedly the unobtrusive and passive life of the native woman is still a remarkably telling factor, and one the extent of which we can never be sure of. . . . In matters of religion the tribe may appear to take little account of women. In Ukamba, however, there are certain *ithembo* to which only women are devoted, and it is remarkable that in all that is mysterious and awful the rites of the women seem to excel. Indeed in Ukamba the only mysteries that have led to disturbances have emanated from the women. They are superstitious and subject to the persecution of spirits to a far greater degree than are the men. The latter, however, in no way treat this fact lightly; it is not to them a matter of feminine weakness but of actual reality, possibly even female superiority. This side of the woman's life, therefore, vitally affects the men, and its practical consequences may, unfortunately, be the retarding of advance in the men as well. And it is well to bear in mind that we may enlighten the men and persuade them to much, but the real measure of actual advance for the tribe is that of the women, who will always abide as a drag on the men. I think I am justified in saying that this point is not always sufficiently reckoned with, but it will certainly be of greatest consequence in every endeavour to raise native society. Of this fact the following is a practical example: Some years ago a great attempt was made to introduce among the Akamba the use of iron hoes. The men were perfectly prepared to take up the new idea, but

285 Howitt, in JAI, XX, 72.   286 Ratzel, *Vkde.*, I, 368.
287 Holub, *Süd-Afrika*, II, 331.   288 Griffith, in JAI, XVI, 302.
289 Lippert, *Kgchte.*, II, 41.   290 Ratzel, *Vkde.*, I, 598.
291 Stuhlmann, *Mit Emin*, 391.   292 Hobley, *A-Kamba*, 32.

the women from superstitious motives declined to use the hoes, and the result was that the project completely failed. The use of iron in tilling the ground is believed to drive away the rains."[293]

Wilken[294] provides a good deal of information as to the political position of women in the East Indies. They have a very extensive influence upon the Bataks when it comes to questions of succession to office; they may even have occasionally a voice in the selection of chiefs and in councils stand beside the men and advise them. Schwaner[295] is quoted to the effect that women in Borneo often rule over the house and community with manlike strength, stir up war, and even lead in it; and though custom gives them no voice in council, they exercise great influence through their men. Further, Brooke is cited concerning conditions in Sarawak. "The women are in many cases, more adept politicians than their husbands, and their advice is often followed in serious business. . . . I gradually made many friends among the people, particularly the female part of the community. I soon learnt that great power and influence attached to their opinions on matters in general, and that to stand well with them was more than half any Dyak battle." Two old women had especial power; "in fact, they led one to suppose the whole country belonged to them, with every one in it. These old lasses, however, were not without some sterling qualities besides the tongue; for on more than one occasion . . . they were to be seen dressed in man's clothes, with swords and spears in hand, commanding the people, and working as hard as any of them."

In Borneo the women of certain tribes, having no right to interfere, yet participate in and have great influence over civil affairs and war; "some of the old hags carry great weight in the village discussions." Indeed the women may stir the men to war and even command forces. However, their power is exercised on account of the influence they have acquired over their husbands rather than directly.[296] In Polynesia, "just because of their lower status the women are kept, even in war, outside the party-lines, and thereby win a certain political importance." Thus the women attend undisturbed, for example, to the messenger-service in war and help to make peace. In New Zealand they were not excluded from the public councils.[297] In some places they might even inherit the chieftainship.[298]

The Iroquois "are the only tribes in America, north and south, so far as we have any accounts, who gave to woman a conservative power in their political deliberations. The Iroquois matrons had their representative in the public councils, and they exercised a negative, or what we call a veto power, in the important question of the declaration of war. They had the right also to interpose in bringing about a peace." It did not, however, compromise the general war-policy, if the body of the matrons expressed a decision in favor of peace. "This was an extraordinary feature in a government organized on the war principle, and among a race which, both in the domestic circle and in the corn-field, laid heavy burdens on their females."[299] Among the Wyandots the women-coun-

[293] Dundas, C., in JAI, XLV, 303.

[294] In VG, I, 258-259. He quotes Brooke, *Ten Years in Sarawak,* I, 70, 129-131.

[295] *Borneo,* I, 161.

[296] Schwaner, *Borneo,* I, 161; Roth, *Sarawak,* I, 92; II, clxii.

[297] Ratzel, *Vkde.,* II, 186.   [298] Kubary, *Núkuóro,* 34.

[299] Schoolcraft, *Indian Tribes,* III, 195-196.

cillors not only partitioned the gentile land, as has been seen, but settled many other matters.[300] The names of women appear among the signatures to treaties between some of the eastern tribes and the United States government.[301] "The Omaha woman worked hard. Upon her depended much of the livelihood of the people—the preparation of food, of shelter, of clothing, and the cultivation of the garden patches. In return she was regarded with esteem, her wishes were respected, and while she held no public office, many of the movements and ceremonies of the tribe depended on her timely assistance. In the family she was generally the center of much affection."[302] The Cheyenne women were the "rulers of the camp." They were far more conservative than the men but spurred them on to do their duty. There was real affection between man and wife. Women went to war as helpers and not seldom really fought; in general, however, it is as unusual for them to fight as to take part in councils. It is to be noted that they had quilling-societies, which fabricated quill-work of a sacred character; they look like gilds of skilled artisans.[303] On the northwest coast an old woman of rank usually steers the war-canoe.[304] "The old women are generally at the bottom of all rows, and also act afterwards as peace-makers, looking as innocent as lambs. The women are great diplomats and generally contrive to have their own way, and it is a great mistake to imagine that they are treated as slaves."[305] A remarkable feature of Nagualism was the exalted position assigned to women; they often held the highest posts in the organization.[306]

"In general, the position of the Persian women differs only very little from that of all Moslems, that is, they too do freely as they like, not only in the inner but also in the outer affairs, and often let their husbands feel their caprices in an acute manner. Examples are not lacking of their very active participation in the political and religious revolutions of the last decades, so that their inmixture has sometimes developed into intrigue dangerous to the state."[307]

Of these scattering cases the general implication seems to be that where women exercise a public function, it is either by exception or indirectly through their influence over their husbands or male kin rather than directly and as of acknowledged right. Instances which appear to run counter to this conclusion are often phenomena of the type of organization known as the mother-family or matriarchate, a system demanding separate treatment,[308] of which it need be said here only that there is "a difference which must not be overlooked between a respect for woman

---

[300] Powell, in BAE, I, 65.

[301] §157, above; Hewitt, "Women," in HAI, pt. II, 968 ff.; Farrand, *Basis*, 266-267.

[302] Fletcher and LaFlesche, in BAE, XXVII, 326.

[303] Grinnell, *Cheyenne,* I, 128, 157, 159 ff.

[304] Niblack, in USNM, 1888, 253.

[305] Harrison, in "Miscellanea," JAI, XXI, 472.

[306] Brinton, *Nagualism,* 32.   [307] Vámbéry, *Sittenbilder,* 23.

[308] §§416, 421, below.

and the observance of the female line of descent."[309] The fact is that women have never led much of a public life or occupied public office with any regularity and consistency, even under the so-called matriarchate. Their function has not been military, forensic, technically political, or external, for that destiny is negatived by the basic facts of sex and the sequels thereto. Particularly is this true within the range of the regulative organization as it approaches the territorial form or the state, correlative as that is with the patriarchate, conquest, slavery, developed agriculture, and the rest.[310] It might be said that woman's prominence varies with the degree of recognition accorded to kinship as a social bond.

This reflection suggests that her rights will be found most in evidence in the family and kin-group. Woman has been respected for what she could do; and her powers have always come out most strongly within the domestic range. Although weaker than man in obvious respects, she could, within that range, complement his activities in self-maintenance and hold up her end of the coöperative establishment. She has been traditionally the "priestess of the hearth."[311] Spencer[312] cites several instances to prove that the status of the sexes is equal where the work is equal, a plausible generalization were there any common measure to determine the equality. Perhaps it might be said that nowhere has woman proved herself more evidently man's equal than in the family, and that in no other rôle has she so regularly and consistently exhibited her indispensability as in that of wife and mother.

These powers within the domestic range, especially upon stages of culture where the family and kin-group were still the unit-clusters of society and the territorial régime yet afar off,[313] were sure to be projected, even though in an informal manner, into the wider societal life. The following cases are illustrative of the respect accorded woman within the family and its immediate environs, among the negroid races. By the inclusion of instances drawn from Asia, Malaysia, Oceania, and America, the picture would not be essentially modified.[314]

[309] Starcke, *Prim. Fam.*, 116.
[311] Clodd, *Magic*, 56.
[313] §§146-149, 185, 186, above.
[310] §186, above.
[312] *Prin. Soc.*, II, §455.
[314] Crawley, in JAI, XXIV, 119 ff.

It is unquestionable that where the man, in marrying, goes to dwell with the woman or her kin, the wife has a certain ascendancy.[315] This is found nowhere in Australia;[316] yet "the women are certainly not treated usually with anything that could be called excessive harshness." In the past woman was on a practical equality with man in the handling of sacred emblems and the performing of sacred ceremonies. "The great majority of the scars which mark the bodies of the women are self-inflicted, and, as a matter of fact, they are proud of them. . . . Taking everything into account, the life of one of these savage women, judged from the point of view of her requirements in order to make life more or less comfortable, is far from being the miserable one that it is so often pictured."[317] There is a central Australian story of a man who was cruel to his wife. She outwitted him, ran away home, and killed him when he followed her. The sentiment of the story is one of sympathy and admiration for her.[318]

In New Guinea there are tribes where woman upholds the respect she enjoys by power of speech and even of hand. Captives belong to the women: "should a woman throw her petticoat over a wounded man, he is safe from further molestation." Women are not handled like cattle; they have an existence fit for a human being and play a rôle, on their stage of culture, as important as that of our own women. They have a better lot than among the poorer classes among us. Some are even queens.[319] "The right of the husband is might, and that of the wife obedience!" but "the women appear to have had a good deal to say on most questions, and were by no means downtrodden or ill-used."[320] Women play a prominent part in the tribal life of the Mortlock Islanders: "the more women there are belonging to a tribe, the more numerous the marriages and offspring, the greater is the probability of its enduring safety. From this results the preferred status of the woman, which finds its expression in the fact that the oldest woman is regarded as the social head and is treated with peculiar respect. And so in the presence of a tribesman only good may be spoken of a woman of his tribe."[321]

The authority of the Andaman husband is more or less nominal and he is considerably at the beck and call of his wife.[322] "A Nicobarese wife is regarded by her husband in all respects as a helpmeet and equal, who, if she happens to possess any special merit or claim to superiority on account of her personal attractions, skill in household duties, or proficiency in other respects, is usually able to assert her authority without exciting any anger or opposition in her husband."[323]

"The Bushman's heart is not so full of his oxen as is the case with the landed Kaffirs and so there is still a place in it for wife and child."[324] The Hottentot women, according to the early Dutch travellers, were held in high esteem among all tribes, though they were obliged to do the hard work of the family. "An oath by a mother or sister was considered the most binding of any."[325]

315 §415, below.   316 Cunow, *Australneger*, 137.
317 Spencer and Gillen, *Nat. Tr. Cent. Aust.*, 50, 457; Spencer and Gillen, *North. Tr. Cent. Aust.*, 33.
318 Dunlop, in JAI, XXVIII, 28.
319 Hagen, *Papua's*, 226; Guise, in JAI, XXVIII, 213; Finsch, *Samoafahrten*, 257.
320 Haddon, in JAI, XIX, 357.   321 Finsch, *Ethnol. Erfahr.*, III, 306.
322 Man, in JAI, XII, 327.   323 Man, in JAI, XXII, 142.
324 Fritsch, *Eingeb. S.-Afr.*, 444.   325 Frere, in JAI, XI, 323.

Makololo wives are seldom required to labor "except in the way of beautify-ing their own huts and court-yards." A Banyai man, being requested to per-form a service, would reply, "Well, I shall go and ask my wife." "If she con-sented, he would go and perform his duty faithfully, but no amount of coaxing or bribery could induce him if she refused."[326] In Mashonaland, a good wife is valued according to her skill in beer-making.[327] Stuhlmann[328] notes that a Wahuma man kissed his wife on returning home—an unknown tenderness among negroes; elsewhere in the lake-region women do no work, but chat and smoke. Negro women, whether slave or free, do not work as hard as peasant and laboring women in Europe; they are sometimes consulted in important family-affairs and even interfere in their husbands' trading transactions.[329] In the rites of certain Africans connected with family life, at the puberty-cere-monies and mutilations of girls, or at births, men play a wholly passive rôle.[330] The Niam-Niam "display an affection for their wives which is unparalleled among natives of so low a grade"; a husband will spare no effort to redeem an imprisoned wife. Among other tribesmen, when asked to sell anything as a curiosity, the husband answers: "Oh, ask my wife: it is hers."[331] The women are fearless, can think and judge, converse, even wittily, and are far more cul-tivated than other negro women. "Among several of the mountain-tribes it is the wife who sways the domestic scepter in a manner hard to associate with the belligerent and proud character of these half-savage nomads."[332]

Sir Charles Dundas[333] sees the domestic position of the East African woman in a rather pleasant light; even as a female she has a certain prestige. "It may be well to point out here that in almost every ceremony, among the Akamba in particular, the act of cohabitation is introduced, and seems more or less to sanctify the ceremony. Sexual relationship thereby acquires a peculiar aspect of importance, and in a certain measure raises women above the position of mere drudges." Further, she knows how to cleave to her prerogatives. "In ministering to the wants of the family, the woman has reduced man to a state of considerable dependency on her in all domestic affairs, just as she is de-pendent upon him for bodily protection. In the course of ages this has gone so far as to foster a peculiar helplessness on the part of the men, which mani-fests itself in a somewhat childlike reliance of the husband in his wife. In fact, it may be said that the native is to all intents and purposes incapable of main-taining himself without the aid of a woman. But the material importance of the woman's sphere of labour is not without advantage to her, and she well knows how to use this. Hence in actual fact the husband is not in a position to enslave his wife, and down-trodden as she may appear, she holds her own so far as she considers right. The native woman certainly claims few rights, but their paucity has taught her to value them all the more. Hence it is, I think, that she has developed a tenacious character which resents with vigour any intrusion on her rights and sphere. Natives have often admitted to me, that there is no way of coercing a woman into what she has set her mind

[326] Livingstone, *Mission. Travels*, 204, 668.
[327] Bent, *Mashonaland*, 55.   [328] *Mit Emin*, 245, 619, 789.
[329] Brunache, *Cent. Afr.*, 56, 135.
[330] Gutmann, in *Globus*, XCII, 49-50.
[331] Schweinfurth, *Heart of Afr.*, I, 471-472; II, 41.
[332] Junker, *Afrika*, I, 146; II, 198, 296, 311.
[333] In JAI, XLV, 274, 302, 303, 304.

against. They warn against driving a woman to desperation, and I have in fact known of two cases in which women have resorted to suicide as a last resort."

Evidently the woman is not a mere passive drudge: "The most winning virtue that we discover in natives is the affection existing between parent and child. The tender treatment accorded to children is, if possible, carried to excess, for a native will ruin himself to indulge a prodigal son. It is in her children and in parental affection that the greatest stronghold of the woman lies. As wife and as mother she is treated with indulgence and consideration by all in the village; as provider of comforts she is looked to as the mainstay of the family. As such she takes her place, and it is probable that the last position she would assign to herself is that of a mere drudge. The situation was well put by an old woman who remarked to me, 'As long as there are women they will till their fields, for what would a woman be if she did not work?' " The fact is that "the native woman is neither drone nor drudge; she is an active partner. Between the two sexes there has been established a relation of mutual support, demanding reliance of the one upon the other. By courage and strength men supported and protected their homes, and by diligence and activity women created something worthy of protection. . . . I need scarcely say that among races with whom the State and the family cannot be distinguished the one from the other, the domestic influence of the woman reacts upon the State. None are better aware of this than the women themselves, and in view of this it may be surprising to us that they keep so strictly aloof from all public affairs. But if we reflect that it was by a division of labour that these women maintained their rights, we may not find it difficult to imagine that instinct enjoins upon them a respect for this partition of rights and duties. In so far as we are concerned the indirect influence of the women should be none the less carefully studied; in fact those who have to deal with native tribes can make no greater mistake than to regard the women as a negligible quantity in political or domestic matters. Indeed, because it is indirect, it is the more difficult to control, and therefore to us the more hazardous to overlook." Dundas always speaks from wide personal experience.

The west coast of Africa is the home of woman's rights.[334] The fierce warrior, we are told, is a passive figure in his own home; indeed, he may even be severely henpecked during the quieter periods between his heroic public performances. "The slipper-hero is as well known in Togo as among us, and must, also as with us, put up with both the (often palpable) corrections of his wife and the spicy jokes of his fellows and friends—who generally get on no better at home than does the victim of their jeers."[335] In Borku, tribesmen who have the reputation far and wide of robbers and cut-throats are powerless in their own houses.[336] Among the Teda, who have been taken as examples of primitive atomism,[337] women are highly respected.[338] Among the Tuareg they are the equals and in some respects the superiors of the men and sometimes hold most of the property.[339]

[334] Ratzel, *Vkde.*, I, 598.
[335] Pater, L., in *Globus*, LXXIX, 352. Other cases of the "Pantoffelheld" in Man, in JAI, XII, 327; Niblack, in USNM, 1888, 254; Von Haxthausen, *Transkaukasia*, II, 25.
[336] Nachtigal, *Sahara*, II, 93.   [337] §9, above.
[338] Mühlhofer, in *Globus*, XCII, 12.
[339] Duveyrier, *Touâreg*, 339-340, 429-430; Bruun, *Huleboerne*, 245-246.

What this evidence teaches is that there is a considerable degree of consideration and respect accorded to woman throughout the range of that section of the race which is generally regarded as the most backward in culture. It is clear enough that she has a number of miscellaneous rights in the family, and that they are not limited to the domestic range but extend outwards into the clan and tribe.

This subject should not be relinquished without some reference to the effect of the existence of the matrilineal system on the position of woman. The difficulty here is that that system is not yet before us.[340] Anticipating somewhat, we might say that when descent is reckoned exclusively in the female line, since both inheritance and succession follow that line, woman is undoubtedly thrown more into the foreground as respects property and social position. It seems that when the man went to live with the woman's kin he suffered in status and rights, as he did in the *ambil-anak* marriage and in cases where he was still serving out the bride-price.[341] As one author says,[342] "on *a priori* grounds we are inclined to assume that the position of woman in matrilineal communities is higher than in patrilineal societies of the same standard of culture. How strongly this opinion is held will be seen from the fact that even in other parts of South India, Malabar is spoken of as the 'Land where women rule.'" The writer, however, goes on to say that "it is impossible to make a general statement as to the relative status of women in matrilineal and patrilineal communities." The fact is that no mere system of reckoning relationship ever conferred rights; those were accorded, automatically, as a consequence of efficacy in the battle of life. The tracing of descent through the woman did not alter her biological qualities or make her a man. It may have offered her a greater opportunity by placing her in the foreground; but it did not enable her to seize and dominate societal situations with which she was by nature incapable of coping. The evidence available does not seem to warrant the correlation between the existence of the matrilineal system and of exceptional sets of rights for women. This is as far as we can go until the details of that system are reviewed.

[340] §§416, 417, below.
[341] §§361, 363, above, and 415, below.
[342] Panikkar, in JAI, XLVIII, 266-267.

The writer last quoted goes on to say that the Nair women of Malabar enjoy, under matrilineal conditions, "equality with men. They can hold property in their own right and enter the professions they choose. Traditions of scholarship and art are, perhaps, stronger among them than among men. Some of the best . . . poets and scholars have been . . . women, and at the present day the statistics of female education show a higher percentage of English-educated girls among them than among any other Indian community. . . . On the whole I am inclined to say that women in Malabar among the Nāyars at least enjoy, relatively to women elsewhere in India, greater liberty, with regard to individual conduct, family relationship and social life. This no doubt is due to the influence of matrilineal customs." Thus the writer is ready to accept the accountability of the matrilineal system in a special case while discreetly avoiding any broad generalizations. Presumably he knows both that his picture of the Nair women could be duplicated under the strictest patriarchal system and also that there are matrilineal communities which show a very low status for women. Wilken,[343] in discussing the Alfur bride-price, a patriarchal usage, notes that while it may look, from several angles, like a plain purchase-price, yet it is not so in its relations of rights. "Influence upon the relation of the wife to her husband, or upon the line of conduct of the latter in respect to the former, for myself, I have not been able to discover in the bride-price." The woman is far from being a slave or subject of her husband; she takes a certain rank in the kin-group and the spouses are on a footing of equality. They eat together, which is significant, and not alone in the kin-group but in the general community the woman does not lack great influence upon the course of affairs.

In the preceding paragraphs the rights and non-rights of women have been classified and described. The net impression, especially as fortified by reference to the tabular arrangement,[344] must be that she has had fewer prerogatives and less freedom than man. If status means condition as respects rights, her status has been regularly lower than his. From the standpoint of modern mores, her lot seems often to have been very sad and pitiable. Only exceptionally, however, has she felt it to be so, for she has lived along in the mores of her place and time and has known nothing different. Only the knowledge that others have what we have not can make us aware that we have not. Though it could not have been otherwise, it is nevertheless very striking to note with what content and even happiness and high spirits the savage women go forward over what seems to us a hard and painful life-journey. There is no lamentation over an unenviable lot; least of all is there resentment because tyrannical man has abstracted from tender woman her treasure of natural, god-given rights. He could not be

[343] In VG, I, 378-379.   [344] §377, above.

accused by her of taking away what she had never had. The main
reason why she saw none of these rights was because there never
had been any such thing; nor was she given to fashioning philosophical figments. There is no better example than her content
with her destiny to illustrate how the mores can make anything
right and prevent the condemnation of anything.[345]

To be sure, the bride kicked and struggled and howled when she
was brought to the threshold of matrimony. She protested vigorously and, indeed, too much. The whole performance was play-
acting and ritual, sound and fury, signifying nothing of her personal feeling. However delighted she might privately have been,
she had to make the normal concession to the code. There are, of
course, cases where the new wife was so badly treated that she
could not but resist, run away, or endure unhappily. That was
when she saw herself worse-treated than her fellows and had some
standard of comparison. Exceptional instances are bound to appear at all stages. In normal circumstances, it is only with the
coming of sophistication that woman begins to bemoan her hard
lot, that is, genuinely to bewail her entrance into marriage. A few
examples will indicate her reaction on a difficult destiny.

"To the outsider who has studied the life of the married women, marriage
would seem a grievous calamity to be avoided at all costs—at least a Papuan
one. The work of the married women is most arduous, and their whole existence seems to be taken up in waiting hand and foot on their loafing lords,
bearing children, and bringing them up. All the cares and worries of the
precarious lives of these natives seem to be thrown on to the shoulders of
wives, who bear it with a stolid philosophy that defies imitation."[346] Young
Yakut wives enter their husbands' families as subjects and have to endure the
traditional enmity of their sisters-in-law; they sometimes commit suicide on
account of their persecution at the hands of their husbands and his relatives.[347]
The Tamil mother-in-law is the terror of all young wives, for she is a cruel
tyrant, and is seconded by the husband's sisters. The young wife often runs
away.[348] The Greenland girl is forced by her father to marry; she always pretends to be forced, even if willing and glad.[349] Among the Knisteneaux Indians, the women's lot was one of drudgery, work, and pain. Therefore they
killed their infants and performed abortions to escape child-bearing.[350]

Cases as extreme as the last are rare, even among the rudest savages. European folk-songs frequently bewail the lot of the bride, and the lamentations

[345] Sumner, *Folkways,* ch. XV.
[346] Hardy and Elkington, *S. Seas,* 34-35.
[347] Sieroshevski-Sumner, in JAI, XXXI, 95.
[348] Gehring, *Süd-Indien,* 83.   [349] Holm, *Ethnol. Skizze,* 54.
[350] Mackenzie, *Voyages,* 87.

are not always mere ritual. The "gray of life" begins with marriage; the girl departs out of the *zadruga* of her father and enters that of the groom, whose sisters and mother commonly look upon the intruder with suspicious eyes."[351] Among the Slavs "the husband never helps out the wife, even when she is ill, for he holds woman's work to be demeaning." The beating of wives was common in one Russian district and was regarded as an injury even by its victims; yet in thirty-five years only two determined women found the courage to appeal to the law. Such facts make one doubtful whether he ought to classify certain parts of the Russian wedding-ceremony as survivalistic; perhaps they belong under the symbolic prefiguring of the status.[352] The relations with the parents-in-law forms one of the saddest phenomena of Russian peasant life. "Not seldom the home becomes a hell and the wife a true martyr." A parallel is found in Normandy: "Most of the dancing-songs, which portray the sufferings of wedlock, begin with the tear-deserving lot of wives. . . . In these songs there is no ray of happiness, no glimmer of content. The complaint is unbroken and echoes from all the provinces of France."[353] In Russia, again, the wailer is a person of much importance in the community; she it is who teaches the bride to mourn in becoming verse for her "maiden freedom."[354] It is not possible to tell just what part is played by pretense in these lamentations. Of Russian Karelia it is reported that "a bride radiant with happiness is an unknown sight here, for with the betrothal there begins for the bride the time of weeping, which lasts until the feast in the bridegroom's house. Even when she is quite content with her lot and looks to the future full of glad hope, she must yet, in order to satisfy custom, pour out copious tears, wherein her playmates afford faithful support. . . . Even at the present day in Livland, in the church play, Mary Magdalen, one often sees a bride in tears. Asked for the reason, she knows nothing to answer except, 'Why, I am betrothed.' "[355]

Evidently there is something more than mere ceremonial in all these expressions of apprehension in the prospect of marriage and the effusion of feminine tears at a wedding means more than the sentimental overflow often observed today. "The Russian woman, who exhibits, in comparison with man, a very small participation in crime, yet stands almost on a level with him in the matter of spouse-murder and that of relatives."[356]

It may be desirable to glance at the status of man before undertaking the difficult task of investigating into the reasons for woman's rights and disabilities. Reference to the rough tabulation of sex-rights reveals that he has practically every prerogative possessed by woman and in an enhanced degree. He enjoys a full right to life and a much greater share of liberty; his right to property in himself is, so far as marriage is concerned, complete; and so is his right to the ownership of all other kinds of property. His

[351] Tetzner, in *Globus,* LXXXVI, 91.
[352] §371, above.
[353] Rhamm, in *Globus,* LXXXII, 274-275.
[354] Ralston, *Russ. People,* 7, 65.
[355] Winter, in *Globus,* LXXVI, 316.
[356] Simkhovitch, *Russland,* 366.

prerogatives within the family and the kin-group are, in the aggregate, at least equal to woman's, while within the range of the regulative and religious systems they are far superior. He too takes his destiny as it comes to him, uncritically and contentedly. He doubtless harbors in his heart some complacency over the fact that he is a male; nevertheless he has grown up into the societal organization as unconsciously as has the woman. It is of vital import to any understanding of his status or hers to realize that no one, by the taking of thought, "created" it as it is, by conferring and withholding. Sex-status is a matter of adjustment, over ages of variation and selection in the mores, to the major life-conditions of maintenance-needs and bi-sexuality.

CHAPTER LI

STATUS OF WOMAN

§385. The Formation of Sex-Rights. There has been reviewed in the preceding chapter a set of facts relating to the status of woman; she has been found to have had, during the earlier stages of societal evolution, rights of several types in various degrees. The data presented now call for interpretation, for the *what* of the matter is of little more than curious interest unless something can be known about the *why* and the *how*. "Consider the *What*," says Goethe,[1] "consider more the *How*."

It has been asserted that the position of woman has varied in accordance with the services which she has rendered, in particular with the importance of her economic contribution to the domestic establishment.[2] Presumably this is a corollary of the more general proposition that rights and appreciation conceded to individuals and classes are a measure of services rendered to society. The proposition does not accord with experience except as it contemplates very long stretches of evolution. No one can seriously hold that rights are at any given time and place distributed on the criterion of utility to society. Since men began to reflect upon life, they have always been concerned over the non-correspondence of service and reward, of goodness and happiness. There has always been a host of forgotten men in the world; and "we must not overlook the fact that the Forgotten Man is not infrequently a woman."[3] If one recalls the facts about sex-specialization and co-operation,[4] he speedily arrives at the conviction that one of two complementary indispensables cannot well be more useful to society than the other. There is no way to measure the services of the sexes to society so as to support the conclusion that man has more rights than woman because his contribution to societal life is superior to hers. If, then, rights are distributed on the basis of utility to society there could not well be any discrimination between the sexes. There is not, in the mind of anyone who views

1 *Faust*, pt. II, act II, 427.
2 Sumner, *Coll. Ess.*, I, 65; Lippert, *Kgchte.*, II, 31 ff.
3 Sumner, *Coll. Ess.*, IV, 465 ff.; *Social Classes*, chs. IX, X, 145.
4 §§63, 69, above.

the long perspective; theoretically he would be disposed to accord
an equality at least in the algebraic sum of rights to man and
woman. But such a conclusion does not help in the explanation of
the distribution of rights as it has been and is. To account for
that it is necessary to renounce any single cause and try first to
identify the various factors that have actually been at work and
then to assess their effects. This is not an easy enterprise.

A beginning may be made by clearing away several misconceptions. One of the most persistent of these is that man originally
had all the rights and that woman got only what he was pleased
to donate to her. It is true that he had more prerogatives than
she, or than the child; it is also true that in modern times he has
voted this and that to her; but anyone who regards such facts as
proofs that he first deliberately and planfully seized everything
in sight and later, in remorse, "gave back" certain privileges
which she possessed in the good old times, has everything yet to
learn concerning the way human affairs are arranged.

For the sake of making graphic this contention about the rights-relation
within marriage, for it has an element of truth in it, let us assume an extreme,
perhaps never to be found in ethnography: that what woman and child get in
the matter of rights is disengaged, as it were, from a once-inclusive block of
man's prerogatives. Let the circle M indicate man's rights in marriage, and
assume them to be inclusive of woman's (circle A)—which would mean that
she has none except as he concedes
them. This extreme condition, though
never actually observed, for woman
has always been found to possess certain powers, has been approached, as
some of the cases cited have indicated. Among the husband's rights in
such a case would be found that of
life and death over the wife. Suppose
now that the taboo descends upon him
in this regard; then a portion of
woman's new circle (B) begins to
emerge outside of man's, the protruding part representing her right to life.
As she gets property of her own, as
the man loses more of his control over
her, the circle of her rights (C) comes
to stand more nearly clear of his. It
has never got completely clear, for
the husband has retained societal re-
sponsibilities or duties with respect to the wife which she has not needed to
reciprocate; and if society looks upon him as responsible for her—for her

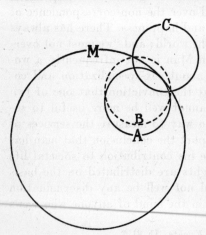

debts, let us say—it necessarily confers upon him certain rights of control or guardianship. In so far she remains, like an immature child, a minor. A similar case could be worked out for the child or the slave in the process of emancipation from the *patria potestas.* To make this figure correspond to actuality it would be necessary to begin with the circle of the inferior's rights already protruding somewhat beyond that of the superior's; for where there is any code at all, an in-group member must have some rights. In the case of the wife, circle A could refer only to a stolen woman; a good part of her attractiveness has been seen to inhere in the fact that the captor is under no limitation.

Lest this graphic device be taken to prove too much, it must be emphasized that such intimate relations as those within marriage and the family do not allow of clear-cut definition. Duties and responsibilities root somewhat in sentiment and cannot be dissected, classified, and coördinated with precision. They are not like relations outside of marriage and the family; when the effort is made to cause ordinary social relations to take on this familial character, it is significantly termed "paternalism"—a régime which is highly inadvisable in a state.[5]

Whatever the disparity of rights between the sexes, we can dispose at this point of the assertion that man was able to hold woman in whatever position he wished, that is, to grant or to withhold whatever rights he chose. If this were true, then what determined woman's rights was man's will or caprice. Under such circumstances, woman could never have attained the rights, often unquestionably superior to man's,[6] which she has come in the modern age to possess. No doubt, in primitive times of unchivalry, man could and did withhold; but he could do this only within limits. If he could have done capriciously what he willed, here or elsewhere, then there would be no basis for scientific treatment of these or other societal phenomena.[7] Beneath the action of men, and determining it, there have always existed laws of societal development evolved in the interest of society; and the moving factors in the evolution of the mores have not been the arbitrary choices of this or that individual, or sex, or constituent societal group, but the massive and impersonal forces of societal evolution. The phases of organization and institutions succeed each other under the unhurried, imperturbable impulsion characteristic of natural forces. They can be delayed somewhat, and at peril, by opposition, with the result, however, that they merely gather mo-

[5] Spencer, *Prin. Soc.,* I, §277.
[6] Saloman, "The Down-Trodden Sex," in N. Y. *Times,* Dec. 12, 1920.
[7] §460, below; Keller, *Soc. Evol.,* 24 ff.

mentum in the face of resistance and presently crush their way on. When, in the interest of society, the time was ripe for woman to get rights, always within the limits set her by nature, she got them despite the fact that man controlled the armies and, for the most part, made the laws. Provided such basic considerations are kept always to the front, woman's rights may perhaps be viewed to some advantage as being what accrued to her as the result of limitations imposed on man by the mores. He did not voluntarily submit to them. He was moved by no ideals of equity and fairness, for these grew up only in consequence of the development, through automatic selection, of usages representing adjustment by society to altered life-conditions—conditions residing fundamentally within the range of self-maintenance.

It gets us nowhere to proclaim that low valuation of woman was merely dominant man's lordly opinion of her, for his notions concerning her were also her convictions regarding herself. She acquiesced because she accepted the facts and the construction put upon them as undeniable. Woman is prone to be at least as critical of woman as man has been. The responsibility for the origination of these views can never be fixed; all that can be done is to take them as they stand and estimate their influence upon woman's rights and status. Man despised woman, and woman despised herself, for the lack of what he (and she) regarded, in him, as essential qualities: womanly weakness and timidity are the stock defects imputed by both sexes alike to men whom it is desirable to insult. Effeminacy has always been a standard reproach to a man and still is, although it has eventually come to be recognized that womanliness is as much a point of superiority in woman as virility in man. The savage could go into no such refinements; the struggle for existence loomed stark before him and demanded strength, quickness, courage, concentration of individual and collective power, and the rest of the positive, dramatic, virile virtues. Only as other qualities came to demonstrate their efficiency in that struggle did they enter consciously into account. On the earliest stages it was inevitable that the unspectacular activities of woman should be underestimated. Because in retrospect we see the essential value, even at the outset, of woman's coöperation, is no reason why the function of woman should have been promptly appreciated while it was in the process of development before unperceiving witnesses.

In this connection it is in point to remark that the conferring of a right is not invariably a service to the recipient. The right of citizenship carries with it an obligation to military service so offensive to some that they prefer to renounce the right. An immunity may be as great a blessing as a right; to give the latter when that involves the surrender of the former may even be an act of hostility. Further, there are rights of value that go with the absence of prerogatives in other directions so that by the acquisition of new rights older ones of much worth may be lost. If modern women are to compete on a par with men they cannot expect in the long run to enjoy the degree of chivalrous consideration, however slight that may seem to a radical soul, which has long been theirs. Such truths bear witness to the principle that, in the bewildering complexity of societal organization, much damage can be unwittingly done by incontinent actions upon the assumption that creditable intentions must always produce salutary consequences.[8]

A further misconception, allied to the foregoing, is revealed in some of our ethical theories and in the action based upon them. To judge by such standards, weakness and complaint are what win rights; it is the outcry about ideal justice, inherent rights, and pitiable oppression that summons us to do our "duty" by arranging life better for the feeble and unsuccessful. "In proportion as sympathy grows, the distinctions of strength disappear, and the woman, while perhaps not visibly happier, gathers around her an increasing dignity."[9] This sort of utterance gives us to understand that sympathy for weakness somehow develops out of latent instinct and sets all to rights. But nobody works upon that hypothesis when something tangible is at stake. Politicians do not try to awaken sympathy and pity for their candidate for office by asserting that he is a poor unfortunate who ought to be helped out. Sympathy and pity do not confer rights and elevate social status, even now; rather are strength and capacity of some sort the criteria of respect. It is necessary here again to get back to

[8] Sumner, *Coll. Ess.*, II, 67 ff.
[9] Sutherland, *Moral Instinct*, I, 236.

the actual, just as we have striven hitherto to rest our case upon realities of sex-differences in physique and code. When women have demonstrated strength they have won rights; otherwise, for all the elevating talk, they have not got them.

Pity and sympathy are a late development in the mores and are unstable even now. Sentimentalism is even more so. Respect for power and efficiency has been present from the outset and can always be counted upon. Sympathy and humanitarianism are luxuries going with a more secure societal organization and are represented but feebly among the stern necessities and the hazards of life nearer to nature.

In early Kentucky, "the female sex, though certainly an object of much more feeling and regard than among the Indians, was doomed to endure much hardship and to occupy an inferior rank in society to her male partner; in fine our frontier people were much allied to their contemporaries of the forest in many things more than in their complexion."[10] They were under compulsion to adjust to similar life-conditions.

To secure a right, woman had, then, to show power of some kind, for that was the only factor solid and impressive enough to enter with effect into the process by which her status was to be shaped.

§386. The Maintenance-Factor in Status. It goes almost without the saying that no society which systematically injures its women can survive in competition with those that do not. Female animals are not maltreated by the males. No evolutionist would expect any race to get ahead which kept its females in a state of strain, low vitality, and general misery and unhappiness. No expedient prosperity-policy ever included such items. The cases are very few where woman has not a right to life, and even where that right is in abeyance—where, that is, she has nobody to defend her by hand or voice—the instances of wife-murder are sporadic. If, again, a man has a right to cripple his women if he pleases, because no one will blame him, his own self-interest prevents him from injuring them; one should hark back to the savage who refrained from tapping his wife on the head with a club because that would mean an intermission of his meals.[11]

10 Butler, *Kentucky*, 135.   11 §67, above.

The conclusion of an eminent American naval officer[12] who, as a young man, studied the tribes of the American northwest coast is as follows: "In the approach to political and industrial equality of the sexes, and in the respect shown for the opinion of their females, these Indians furnish another refutation of the old misconception concerning the systematic mal-treatment of the women by savages. Such a thing is incompatible with the laws of nature. Good treatment of the female is essential to the preservation of the species, and it will be found that this ill-treatment is more apparent than real."

There may be some exaggeration of evident truth in such wide generalizations; nevertheless they indicate a sort of biological dead-line beyond which nature does not permit men to go.

The maintenance-factor and the sex-factor, both composite, enter to explain the distribution of sex-rights. The "maintenance-strand" runs back directly to sex-specialization in self-maintenance; if the reader will refresh his knowledge of that subject,[13] there will be small need of demonstration here. Perhaps we might center, in summary of results reached above, upon the fact that woman consistently occupied the background in societal life. She was indispensable to the economic well-being of the unit-cluster, the family; it is fair to say that though man is generally found delivering the initial assault upon nature which alone renders life possible and which woman could not accomplish, yet her coöperation in preserving and working up what he has won is nearly if not quite as indispensable for existence as his getting of it. There always fell to her a set of activities which were of a routine nature, unspectacular, domestic, unorganized. She did not get into the open. She did not hunt or fight and so did not attain to either weapons or discipline. Her stamp was industrial and domestic rather than militant and political. She could not rise to the occasion in time of peril as could man, and such crises were recurrent in savage life. Man has generally appreciated himself more and woman less in periods of violence, while woman has classified herself, so to speak, as the weaker and dependent sex by her incessant applause for masculine pugnacity and her adulation of a virile defender. Uniforms still speak to her of godlikeness. There is no question that Spencer[14] centered upon a very actual factor explanatory of the status of woman when he stated that her position

[12] Niblack, in USNM, 1888, 239.   [13] Ch. V, above.
[14] *Prin. Soc.*, I, pt. III, ch. X.

in a society varied inversely with the degree of militarism exhibited.

Woman, then, no less indispensable than man in sustaining society's everyday life, was not much in evidence at a pinch. It was the crisis-times, however, especially if they recurred at short intervals, that brought the heroic figure, warrior or hunter, to the front, while woman remained in the background. No one maliciously put her there, unless it may be charged upon Nature or God who made her a female. That was where she belonged, under the conditions; there was societal expediency in her undramatic occupancy of a humbler position. She was as well fitted to the domestic setting as she was incompetent to lead a public career. The destiny of the mother-family shows what happened to primitive society as a consequence of women getting more nearly into the center of the stage.[15] It would seem, then, that under the maintenance-conditions prevalent upon the lower stages of culture women did not and could not possess the visible and self-evident power shown by men; nor were their characteristic abilities staged in the focus of attention. They could not therefore attain the rights men had because they had not the powers men displayed.

§387. Woman and Tillage. This is what an examination of the maintenance-factor, as it operates in the distribution of sex-rights, reveals. It seems impracticable to carry analysis of that factor much farther. However, there is one asserted correlation between the status of woman and the stage of the extractive arts that calls for a little study. It has been suggested that her status is higher under an agricultural economy than among hunting or pastoral tribes; that tillage has always been her specialty and that her economic contribution to society and also her rights have been greater where she could pursue it relatively undisturbed by nomadic or militaristic tendencies on the part of the men.[16] Apparently that type of tillage is in mind which preceded man's encroachment, the application of the energies of animal and slave, and a superior organization.[17] It seems to us that there is here no very decisive correlation; for instance, the African cases cited in

15 §§421, 422, below.
16 Lippert, Kgchte., II, 73 ff.; §67, above.
17 §65, above.

STATUS OF WOMAN   1803

the last chapter, which include tribes of hunters, herders, and tillers, show that woman may attain about the same status under any
one of these forms of maintenance-organization. Perhaps an elaborate process of identification and checking up of small differences
might yield some confirmation of the asserted correlation; we shall
merely cite a selection of instances which may throw the issue into
relief within the general perspective.

The status of woman among the rudest hunting tribes is exemplified by the practice of the Australians and the African Bushmen. The natives of America, aside from certain more advanced
peoples like the Aztecs, the immediate subjects of the Incas, and
some tribes of eastern and western North America, were predominantly hunters. If agriculture, which can be developed only under
conditions of sedentary life, is woman's forte, it would appear that
the wandering life of hunters would afford her but few chances
to display her value as a coöperator in self-maintenance. It seems
fair to say that the prerogatives of the Indian woman were generally more extensive where tillage had been developed—higher,
at any rate, in the eastern parts of North America, where the
matrilinear system prevailed, than on the great plains where hunting was so productive.

"It is apparent," says Hewitt,[18] "that among the sedentary and agricultural
communities the woman enjoyed a large, if not a preponderating, measure of
independence and authority, greater or less in proportion to the extent of the
community's dependence for daily sustenance on the product of the woman's
activities." However, taking the Indian tribes north of Mexico together, hunters and all, this writer generalizes as follows: "One of the most erroneous
beliefs relating to the status and condition of the American Indian woman is
that she was, both before and after marriage, the abject slave and drudge of
the men of her tribe in general"; and he brings out strikingly the fact that
whatever arrangement was current represented an adjustment to tribal life-
conditions. "The essential principle governing this division of labor and responsibility between the sexes lies much deeper than apparently heartless tyranny
of the man. It is the best possible adjustment of the available means of the
family to secure the largest measure of welfare and to protect and perpetuate
the little community. No other division was so well adapted to the conditions
of life among the North American Indians."

This generalization is very significant, though it might be hard to
get every specific case under it. If woman discharged a function
so important to welfare, it is no wonder that she attained recogni-

18 *Sub* "Women," in HAI, II.

tion, even among the hunting tribes. To them her services in attending to the game and keeping the lodge were nearly if not quite indispensable, even though she did not provide a food-supply comparable to that raised by the women under tillage. Indispensability is a superlative, whatever the stage—a species of returns behind which it is impossible to go. Tillage and its conditions not being within the horizon—any more than skill in maintaining a salon in the interest of a husband's political ambitions—provided a wife did what fell to her with efficiency, her value was demonstrated. The same is true under the pastoral economy. The following instances exhibit the woman as a by no means negligible factor in the life of hunters and herders. There are numerous other contributions besides the product of tillage which women can make to joint welfare; consider only the labor and skill exhibited by the Indian squaw who takes over the deer's carcase brought in after strenuous exertions by the man and, while he recuperates for the next hunt, works it up into food and clothing.

Among the Eskimo of Point Barrow, who are typical hunters, and who exchange wives loosely with one another, "the women apparently stand on an equal footing with the men, both in the family and in the community. A man's wife is his constant and trusted companion in everything except the hunt, and he consults her on every important occasion."[19] Of certain Canadian tribes whose women are in an "abject state of slavery and submission," they yet "have considerable influence on the opinion of the men in everything except their own domestic situation."[20] The Iroquois woman is no drudge and at death her property in household-goods goes to her relatives.[21] Omaha men and women were equal in social standing. The woman had her work, and it was hard, but the men helped a good deal and even showed politeness and gallantry.[22] Tlinkit women take a full share in trade and are good at it. "They appeared in general to keep the men in awe and under their subjection."[23] "As between the sexes, the rights of the women are respected and the terms of equality on which the men and women live are very striking to most visitors of this region. . . . Women have usually as much to say as the men on other than ceremonial occasions, and their advice is frequently followed, particularly in affairs of trade."[24] In connection with these cases from the northwest coast it should in fairness be recalled that a greater degree of sedentariness attends upon a fishing as distinguished from a hunting economy; we have seen that fishing peoples may not be summarily classed with hunting tribes.[25]

"Because the California Indians were not a martial race . . . they did not

19 Murdoch, in BAE, IX, 413.
20 Mackenzie, *Voyages*, 147.
21 Hale, *Iroq. Rites*, 64.
22 Dorsey, in BAE, III, 266, 270.
23 Vancouver, *Voyage*, II, 409.
24 Niblack, in USNM, 1888, 240, 253.
25 §101, above.

make such abject slaves of their women."[26] Certain Nicaraguan tribes defer to the opinion and will of their wives. The writer attempted to settle a bill for damages sent in by an Indian but the latter refused to accept the money, "giving as a reason that his wife had forbidden him to do it. On being pressed to take it and told that she need not know it, he replied that 'the women knew everything,' and still refused."[27] Even among the Shingu Indians, the woman was in no unworthy position; the man was her lord and master but did what she wanted to have him do.[28] In the Amazon region female equality is to be found: "the women seem to be on a footing of perfect equality with the men, often scolding them and interfering in their trade."[29] Insight into the life of the Miranhas teaches "that the female sex, despite all slavish subjection, just because of its cheery diligence in caring for the domestic economy, possesses great power over the men."[30] Bororo men are apparently dominated by their women. Rohde[31] says that the Guatos men are "under the slipper" of their wives; he saw a drunken woman beating her husband and "he did not dare to lift his hand." In Argentina the husband treats his wife "extraordinarily well" and asks her counsel, despite the fact that women act with great levity as respects the marriage-bond.[32]

There may now be noted a few instances observed among tribes which are mainly pastoral. Huntington[33] emphasizes strongly the independence of the women of nomadic tribes. "The women of all races, so far as I know, both Mohammedan and non-Mohammedan, go about unveiled, and have a strong influence in the affairs of the community. Their relative strength of character is evident from the notable fact that when a Turkoman woman is married to a Persian, or a Kurdish woman to a Turk, the wife from the nomad stock, so it is said, usually rules the harem, and often rules the whole house. The universality of the contrast between the position of woman in nomadic and non-nomadic Mohammedan populations goes to show that the contrast is not the product of racial differences, but of nomadism." In Tibet, the position of woman is not injuriously affected by the fact that she does most of the work; the wife's opinion is always asked in household matters and those of trade. Her authority in the house is supreme and she joins freely in all discussions, being held in almost every walk of life the equal of man.[34] The most noted characteristic of the Mantzu is the position accorded to women, "who are as unfettered as in England and America, and on an absolute equality with men, possessing legal rights in respect of property, and sharing occupations and amusements with men."[35] Among the Soyots of Siberia, "aside from the usefulness which a woman shows in her work, marriage plays a slight rôle."[36]

[26] Powers, in *Contrib. N. Amer. Ethnol.*, III, 405, 406.
[27] Nutting, in *Smithson. Rep.*, 1883, 909, 910.
[28] Von den Steinen, *Zent. Bras.*, 332.
[29] Markham, in JAI, XXIV, 263.   [30] Von Martius, *Beiträge*, I, 544.
[31] In *Mitt. Berl. Mus.*, 1885, 15.
[32] Ambrosetti, in *Globus*, LXXIV, 245.
[33] *Pulse of Asia*, 128-129; the independence of the nomad woman is brought out in Kipling's story, *The Naulakha*, ch. XVII, and in *Kim*, ch. XIV.
[34] Rockhill, in USNM, 1893, 682.
[35] Bishop, in "Anth. Rev.," in JAI, XXVIII, 191.
[36] Olsen, *Primitivt Folk*, 147.

The Mongolian woman works while the man loafs; yet the women are to a great degree independent, are mistresses of the house and have equal rights with men.[37] The Mongols of Tsaidom are monogamists and their women enjoy an incomparably greater amount of freedom than the women do among the Mohammedan tribes of Central Asia.[38] Kirghiz and Kalmuk women are respected by the men for their share in the work and have influence as members of the society. They are not secluded and are treated with a certain chivalry.[39] "Among most Beduin tribes the women go unveiled"; Kurdish women "go about freely and mingle unabashed with the men."[40]

In the East Indies and the Pacific archipelagoes the typical form of self-maintenance is agriculture. It is impossible to say that greater respect and a higher social status for woman go with that form of the industrial organization, though its introduction seems to constitute a new point of departure in other important respects, inasmuch as it is accompanied by private property in land and by systematic slavery.[41] The presence of slavery, in fact, may reduce the actual importance of woman as an economic coadjutor, by relieving her of labors that are arduous and yet dignifying to her. Even if woman acquired merit by developing the beginnings of tillage, it does not follow that she will continue to hold her merit under an agricultural economy after men have taken it up themselves[42] or turned it over to slaves. A striking case is where the Bechuana woman was freed from field-labors by the introduction of the plow, the more so as the oxen that drew it were tabooed even to her touch;[43] perhaps, under such circumstances, she lost by her apparent gain from the advancement of the arts coupled with an enduring religious scruple. Perhaps woman's bane of hard labor was her blessing.

Sir Charles Dundas[44] draws a striking picture of the general usefulness of woman in East Africa: "Without doubt the most admirable figure in the village is the 'Kiveti,' the married woman. Stolid and apparently serenely indifferent to all that goes on around her she will always be found occupied one way or another. She milks the cows, tills the fields, threshes, pounds, and grinds the corn, fetches water, cuts and carries the firewood, besides many other duties which the men consider beneath their dignity to perform. Latterly when there has been no work in the fields the women have often been required to herd the cattle. . . . There seems to be no age at which the women are

37 Ivanovski, *Mongolei,* 12.   38 Hedin, *Through Asia,* II, 1082.
39 *Russian Ethnog.* (Russ.), II, 184, 445.
40 Hauri, *Islam,* 145.   41 §§103, 118, above.
42 §65, above.
43 Holub, *Sieben Jahre,* I, 422-423; Holub, *Capstadt,* II, 214.
44 In JAI, XLIII, 495-496.

excused from work. I have seen some who must have been well over seventy years of age working in the fields as untiringly as the youngest girls; often a woman lives alone with her son, a sturdy young loafer who is tired of his very indolence, but she is the one who keeps the wolf from the door. Yet the Kiveti never grumbles or seems to meditate upon the division of labour, so long as she has time for it all she is content to do it and although I have heard all sorts of complaints from women, I have never heard them object to their work. Apart from her labours, however, the woman has not much at which to grumble, indeed, it is often a question whether she is not the master in the long run. . . . The Kiveti is a strong-minded person, and will assert her rights with vigour. . . . It is beyond doubt, too, that the women have a strong influence in the village, as they could scarcely fail to have, being its main support. Latterly a great effort has been made to induce the Akamba to take iron hoes in place of the wooden Mue sticks, but they have obstinately refused to be induced to make such a change. The reason I think for this is that it is unlucky to use iron for tilling the soil and while it would not be difficult to persuade the men to abandon this belief, it is not they but the women who would have to use the hoes; the women, however, are most conservative, and if they decry the iron implements as harmful modern inventions the men will not, in fact cannot, oblige them to use these. On the whole one seems to notice that the excessive usefulness of the woman engenders in the man a regard for her which is rather pleasing, his attitude is one that implies great helplessness without her, and indeed the Mkamba without a woman to look after him is quite lost. He often talks of their sex as creatures of no account, but experience will tell you that if one wants anything it is always good to solicit the help of the Kiveti; even her lord's small store of cash is given into her keeping and she usually hides it away somewhere where he himself cannot get at it, consequently when the husband wants any money he frequently has to run to the field to get it from his wife." Among the Jibaro Indians the women have a special function of a religious order in raising manioc, which, like most other domesticated plants, has a woman's soul. "Like is best known by like."[45]

"The Javanese women are industrious and laborious beyond those of all the Archipelago, but their labor, instead of being a slavery imposed upon them by the men, becomes, through its utility to the latter, a source of distinction. Their faculties exercised in the various branches of domestic and agricultural economy, in which they are so often employed, places their understandings on many points above those of the men." They divorce husbands freely and the latter are infinitely more tame and servile than elsewhere in the Archipelago.[46]

Among the Dyaks the sexes "stand upon the footing of equality toward one another, not alone in the domain of private right but also of public. The accounts are of one voice concerning the high rank that woman occupies among this people."[47] "The gentler sex are even more important really than the men. They occupy positions, and are capable of exerting surprising influence. . . . I gradually made many friends among the people, particularly the female part of the community. I soon learnt that great power and influence attached to their opinions on matters in general, and that to stand well with them was more than half any Dyak battle. . . . The Sea Dyak women have no reason to murmur at their condition."[48] Among the rice-growing Sea Dyaks, the

[45] Karsten, "Jibaro," in BAE, Bull. LXXIX, 60; §214, above.
[46] Crawfurd, *Ind. Arch.,* 75, 79.   [47] Wilken, in VG, I, 381.
[48] Roth, *Sarawak,* I, 362-363; Roth, in JAI, XXI, 127; Bock, *Borneo,* 77.

women, who do nearly all the farm work, are more powerful and have a more exalted position in the tribe than women among the Kayans. Consequently, in Sea Dyak religion feminine ideals are far more conspicuous. What religious importance is given to women among the Kayans is centered about agriculture.[49] And her position allows her, together with other forms of independence, an important voice in matters of marriage.[50] The Macassars always inflict heavier fines for the murder of a woman than for that of a man of the same class.[51]

The women of the savage East Formosans, though kept in a subordinate position, contrive to have their full share of control and management of house and family.[52] In the Pelew Islands the taro-culture is the most important branch of agriculture and the most vital for the survival of the population; and it is wholly in the women's hands. "This may have contributed then, not insignificantly, to the preponderance of female influence in the social affairs of the people." For the women not only give the gift of life but also that which is most needful to support it, and so they are called the "mothers of the land" and are politically and socially superior to the men. The oldest women are treated as divinities while they still live and no chief would undertake to pass judgment without first taking counsel with the "mothers of the family." The richest women take great pride in their taro-patches and labor in them sturdily, not being demeaned at all by the uncommonly severe efforts put forth amidst dirt and sweat but with the utmost enthusiasm. As a matter of fact, these labors are such as to have a bad effect upon health and to render the hands unfit for finer labors such as weaving. The efficiency of a woman in producing taro "forms the most important factor in the contracting of a marriage." Conditions are not dissimilar in neighboring islands.[53] The women of the Gilbert Islands do not raise the taro, that and other heavy labors being the men's task, but they fish and not seldom accompany the men to war. They are independent, jealous, and generally faithful and the men who try to beat them must be prepared for a vigorous defense.[54] In the Ladrones and elsewhere in Micronesia women appear to hold a similarly high position, so much so that many men will not take a status-wife because custom favors the women too much.[55] The Samoan wife is treated with gallantry and respect.[56] On Easter Island, "as may be inferred from the preponderance of the male over the female portion of the community the latter are in great demand, and the supply not being equal to it, the women are a source of great solicitude; much consideration is shown them." "Family life itself is, in consequence of the good position of the wife, quiet, cheerful, and carefree."[57]

The foregoing cases show that woman attains rights and influence upon any stage of the extractive arts because there are always plenty of tasks besides tillage in which she can display

[49] Morris, in *Jr. Amer. Orient. Soc.*, XXV, 240 and ff.

[50] Nieuwenhuis, *Borneo*, I, 47, 77, 173; II, 276.

[51] Ratzel, *Vkde.*, II, 452.   [52] Pickering, *Formosa*, 72.

[53] Kubary, *Karolinen-arch.*, 159, 160; Kubary, *Núkuóro*, 35; Pereiro, *Ponapé*, 118.

[54] Finsch, *Ethnol. Erfahr.*, III, 30, 31.

[55] Waitz, *Anthrop.*, V, 107 ff.   [56] Ella, in AAAS, 1892, 628.

[57] Cook, in USNM, 1897, I, 716; Geiseler, *Oster-Ins.*, 41.

efficiency along lines adapted to her sex. It may be that she attains a somewhat higher position under the agricultural economy, but whether that is due solely to the fact that it is agricultural is doubtful. The case may stand as it is for a time, pending the consideration of the sex-factor as it operates to affect woman's destiny. Any general conclusions would be insufficiently based which did not take that second factor into full account.

§388*. The Sex-Factor in Status. If we hark back again toward our first account of sex-differentiation,[58] we shall recall a number of sex-characters in woman which have their immediate effects outside the basic range of maintenance, though they enter indirectly into that range. It might be said that woman, being as indispensable as man for the propagation of the race and the self-perpetuation of society, is as precious to nature as man can be, an obvious consideration that links up with Niblack's remark about ill-treatment of her being contrary to the laws of nature. Of course primitive men know nothing about the interests of nature and of society; what they feel is the necessity of having children, for both economic and religious reasons.[59] For the purpose of carrying on the family-line the only distinctions between women are, primarily, that between the barren and the fruitful, whereby the former fall utterly out of account, generally by repudiation, and that between bearers and non-bearers of sons, whereby in many cases the latter are visited with reproach and ignominy.[60] Such disabilities of women, however, as individual and not sex-phenomena, cannot enter into wide generalizations concerning status. The only inference permissible is that within the sphere indicated by nature as woman's normal field of activity she may attain recognition not only as a successful coöperator in self-maintenance but also as a mother of children. It is difficult to say just how far fecundity is effective in securing rights, though easy enough to conclude that barrenness results only in contempt and humiliating treatment.

In addition to her quality as child-bearer, woman has always exerted certain powers inherent in her sex. Despite all the attacks

[58] Ch. V, above.   [59] §§402, 406, 409, below.
[60] §§392, 409, below.

on sexual selection in the organic field,[61] there has always been accorded to the female animal some power of choice. How far this biological phenomenon may be characteristic of the human race in its earlier stages it is probably futile to ask; but there is no manner of doubt, as our cases have abundantly demonstrated, that human mating has been very largely at the will of the female. Consider the tests in courtship which the girl was entitled to apply and her power of self-disposal in marriage; also the prerogatives of the mother and daughters in the matrilineal family.[62] There is no doubt, despite much talk of "cave-man methods," that men have very generally had to take the attitude of the wooer rather than the dominator toward the weaker sex; and that led to female prerogative, however temporarily exercised.

Assertion of woman's choice and will in marriage occurs not only among peoples who are of a mild disposition toward their women but also among those whose females are ordinarily treated with roughness, entire lack of consideration, or even brutality.[63] It is doubtless to the interest of society that woman has a voice in her own disposition. In any case, woman as woman has always held a certain power over man; she has her methods, often by an indirection which he cannot readily follow, of getting her way with man; she has always held a power over him through the distribution of praise, blame, or ridicule. There is evidence enough that few men, young or old, are indifferent to their repute with the women of their group. Some of the tests of the man, preceding marriage,[64] are such that if he cannot withstand them no girl can be found who will marry him. Evidence is also forthcoming that the savage husband, even under the most strenuous patriarchal régime, is harassed, cajoled, controlled, ridiculed, even henpecked, by his wife or wives. How much of this power is original in sex-makeup, and so referable to the sex-factor rather than to adjustments in sex-conduct, probably cannot be known; yet it is perhaps under necessity of self-preservation that women have developed forms of attack that leave man bewildered—assaults that do not seem to call for or to admit of such resistance as would be meted out to another man. It is sometimes said that women take an unfair

61 Darwin, *Desc. Man,* section on "Selection in Relation to Sex."
62 §§359, 367, 379, above, and 416, 417, below.
63 §359, above.   64 §365, above.

advantage; that, their code being different from man's, the latter, supposing there is no code but his and not realizing the essential diversity of the sex-mores, feels himself unaccountably outgeneralled, aggrieved, and reduced. Whatever there is to this, and there is a good deal to it, occurs in its measure among primitive peoples, for man-nature and woman-nature are there from the outset.

In view of such considerations the presupposition is inadmissible that at first man had everything and woman nothing. She had her peculiar sort of power or might, as children did, and she got the rights corresponding to it. They were not extensive; in many cases they did not compare with man's; they were, under certain conditions, a vanishing quantity; but they were not non-existent. In considering female beauty, attractiveness, the capacity to flatter or to wound male vanity and reputation, one should not fail, however, to remind himself of their limitations in forming status. They do establish a certain ascendancy but, that once gained, there is nothing in them that tends to raise it much and to secure wider rights. It takes something more solid and durable to effect that consummation.

There is another characteristic factor entering into the status of woman which has been encountered only incidentally hitherto. It is wholly sexual in quality, resting squarely upon the view that there is something uncanny and wholly perilous in one sex which is unrepresented in the other. There results an appraisal of woman, in the mores, which through long ages has been largely decisive of her destiny. This is something quite different in quality from any contempt for woman because of her relative weakness or timidity. In addition, then, to the foregoing traditional grounds for the low appraisal of woman appears the fact that she is regarded as constituting, by reason of her special sex-functions, a menace to others and particularly to males. This has its relation to maintenance, as where the hunter or warrior must straitly refrain from any association or even conversation with a woman prior to activity in the field; but it is evident that the sex-element is feared as such, apart from any special influence which it may exert. Cases of notions and taboos connected with parturition will appear farther on;[65] for the moment the illustration of the

65 §§408 ff., below.

danger inherent in woman is to be found in the monthly courses. This phenomenon comes under the inexplicable and so belongs to the aleatory element and is referred to a spiritual source; and an avoidance-taboo is extended over the woman.[66] "For the time she is in exactly the same position as the mediæval leper."[67] Then this "uncleanness" (that term being used here in its ritual religious sense, meaning "possessed," "fraught with danger," "not to be touched," or even "holy")[68] that attaches recurrently to woman is ascribed to her as a constant characteristic; and it explains a good part of the fear, sense of mystery, disapproval, and even contempt, with which she is viewed. The sentiments harbored as to the intermittent function attach unremittingly to the sex that exhibits it. Into the experience of every growing girl this attitude enters as an element; and concealment and reticence come to characterize her behavior as it conforms to the existing sex-mores. She accepts the current belief about her sex, than which she can conceive of no other, and may even come to believe herself accursed because of her natural sex-function. Here is a strong factor making for the "instinctive" modesty of woman.[69]

This attitude toward woman is evidently of a primordial character, the result of an automatic, unconscious selection that must have been brought about by some ancient test of societal expediency. We cannot determine its origin with any precision and do not need to involve ourselves in speculation on that score. The factor is in the field where its working can be observed; and it is an important one for the topic of the status of woman.

The belief in the uncleanness of woman leads to the impact of various taboos upon her.[70] These, having largely to do with her seclusion during the most dangerous period, are extended to cover all forms of association with her; they may apply especially to priests.[71] In particular, she must have nothing to do with the food that other people are to eat. It is as if she were suffering from a contagious disease; there is the same sort of sentiment toward her that might be felt by the ignorant and superstitious at the present day toward a known typhoid-carrier or victim of smallpox—a

---

[66] §§208, 273, above.　　　　　[67] Ellis, *Man and Woman*, 14.
[68] §254, above.　　　　　　　　 [69] Ellis, in *Psychol. Rev.*, VI, 134.
[70] §§273, 317, above.
[71] Main, *Relig. Chastity*, Appendix, note XXIX.

compound of fear, loathing, resentment, and allied sensations, as
directed against one singled out for punishment at the hand of the
supernatural.

We do not feel it necessary to go into the fantastic and often unpleasant
details as portrayed in the numerous available cases. Crawley[72] has collected
much evidence and summarized it. But we wish to give some idea of the extension, geographical and through time, of the notion of female uncleanness. The
Australians are sedulous in isolating girls and women, and refer the phenomenon to a devil's curse for infidelity. "Boys are told, from their infancy, that
if they see the woman they will early become grey-headed, and their strength
will fail prematurely."[73] In New Guinea and Africa, as in Australia, the
women are marked to indicate their condition and in Togo there is a sort of
ritual baptism.[74] The prescriptions in India include penance and much ceremonial.[75] Among the Nagas, "it is strictly genna [tabu] for men to put on or
in any way use a woman's petticoat that has once been worn. To do so would
destroy all chance of success in war or hunting. It is equally genna to beat a
house with a petticoat, which has the same result on its inmates. One case the
writer knew of in which a chief had a somewhat serious family quarrel because his wife in a passion took her petticoat and beat his gun with it, and
exposed her nakedness to the gun. He has never been able to hit anything with
that gun since—a fact."[76] The Ostiaks use an identifying girdle and oblige
the mother to bear in a separate hut. A Soyot woman must not wade in water
above the knees lest she make it unclean; but there is no real modesty in our
sense.[77] In the East Indies the phenomenon is by some referred to the moon-
god; there are various taboos and a ritual bath.[78] In the Pacific Islands,
women and girls are confined in special houses, and there is the strictest taboo
on approach.[79] Eskimo and Indians are very strict in this matter; purification
is by smoke or bath. The notice taken of the beginning of the function is easily
confused with puberty-ceremonies in general. Fasting, averting of the face at

[72] In JAI, XXIV, 230 ff.

[73] Smyth, *Vict.*, I, 46; Spencer and Gillen, *Nat. Tr. Cent. Aust.*, 460-461;
Spencer and Gillen, *North. Tr. N. Cent. Aust.*, 601; Gason, in JAI, XVIII, 95;
Gason, in JAI, XXIV, 171; Eyre, *Cent. Aust.*, 295; Crauford, in JAI, XXIV,
181.

[74] Krieger, *Neu-Guinea*, 390; Hunt, in JAI, XXVIII, 11; Cator, *Head-
Hunters*, 194; Fritsch, *Eingeb. S.-Afr.*, 111; MacDonald, in JAI, XX, 138;
Ellis, *Ewe*, 153; Ellis, *Tshi*, 94-95; Bastian, *Deut. Exped.*, I, 168-169, 184-185;
Fies, in *Globus*, LXXX, 382; Conradt, in *Globus*, LXXXI, 337; Pommerol,
Sahariennes, 183; Hanoteau et Letourneux, *Kabylie*, II, 210.

[75] Thurston, *S. India*, 261-262; Risley, *Ethnog. Ind.*, I, 192; Godden, in JAI,
XXVII, 34; Haug, *Relig. of Parsis*, 242; Bühler, *Laws of Manu*, IV, 40, 46,
208; V, 108; Husain, in JASB, III, 140, 142.

[76] Hutton, *Sema Nagas*, 18.

[77] Kondratowitch, in *Globus*, LXXIV, 290; Olsen, *Primitivt Folk*, 146-147,
148, 149.

[78] Perelaer, *Dajaks*, 55, 227; Roth, *Sarawak*, I, 97, 98; Jacobs, *Groot-Atjeh*,
II, 84-85; Stevens, in *Ztsft. f. Eth.*, XXVIII, 170-172.

[79] Finsch, *Ethnol. Erfahr.*, III, 30, 130; Senfft, in *Globus*, XCI, 172; Kubary,
Núkuóro, 35.

meeting any one, and seclusion in a separate house are practised; and in South America the woman is beaten repeatedly.[80] Among the Guiana Indians, the women take a position in sitting that is the result of scrupulous concealment.[81] Antiquity held similar views and practised similar precautions. The Hebrews had an elaborate ritual that came down with the Old Testament; and the modern world has only gradually been emancipated from it.[82]

The fact that the calamities apprehended were not specific, but included the withering of plants, the sterilization of seeds, and other general ills, shows that the attitude here, as in the case of close in-breeding,[83] had little of the rational about it. The conviction that woman is periodically and mysteriously dangerous has been held with singular unanimity among many peoples. Very likely the actual effect of the resultant seclusion has been salutary, but even so that result was attained unaware. In any case the attitude exemplified was no less effective in determining the mores respecting woman's status because it was destitute of real reason, in so far, at least, as the considerations uppermost in the minds of those practising the various precautions were concerned. Into the estimate of woman there entered, then, fear and repulsion, in addition to considerable contempt. It doubtless might have been "fairer" otherwise; this is the way it was. Here were present a biological fact and function distinctive of sex which called for specific adjustments precisely as other sex-differences evoked other reactions and estimates mentioned in previous connections.[84]

§389*. Mistrust of Woman. Woman is an object of distrust-

[80] Holm, *Ethnol. Skizze*, 48; Boas, in BAE, VI, 596; Dorsey, in BAE, III, 267; Grinnell, in AA, IV, 13-14; Grinnell, *Cheyenne*, I, 130-131; Stevenson, in BAE, XI, 20; Kroeber, in AA, IV, 283; Russell, in BAE, XXVI, 183; Powers, in *Contrib. N. Amer. Ethnol.*, III, 31, 32; Niblack, in USNM, 1888, 370; Roger Williams, "Key," in *Mass. Hist. Soc.*, III (1794), 211; Sapper, in *Globus*, LXXVIII, 274; Von den Steinen, *Zent. Bras.*, 197; Von Martius, *Beiträge*, I, 645; Schomburgk, *Brit. Guiana*, II, 315-316; Hassler, in *Inter. Cong. Anthrop. Chicago*, 1893, 357.

[81] Roth, in BAE, XXXVIII, §935.

[82] Ellis, *Man and Woman*, 15, 262; Smith, *Relig. Sem.*, 133, 448; Müller, *Sacred Bks.*, IV, xcii; Geiger, *Ostiran. Kultur*, 236, 259-260; Gomme, *Folklore*, 63; Levit., XII, XXII, 4; Rohde, *Psyche*, II, 72; Ploss-Bartels, *Das Weib*, I, 263 ff.; Temesváry, *Geburtshilfe*, 3-4; Weissenberg, in *Globus*, LXXXIV, 143; Pliny, *Nat. Hist.*, VII, 13; Wuttke, *Deut. Volksaberglaube*, 368; Paturet, *Cond. Jurid.*, 12; Sumner, "Status of Woman," in *Coll. Ess.*, I, ch. III.

[83] §350, above.		[84] §69, above.

ful concern, not only at special periods of her sex-life but, under certain conditions, at any time. Not only that: men have never understood woman; she has seemed to them *varium et mutabile* and they have not known what to expect from her.[85] This uncertainty has bred mistrust, apart from fear, as of the uncalculable, and has led to a certain nervous fluctuation in attitude and action. Livingstone[86] remarks that by a selection of cases a people may be made to look kindly or heartless in disposition. Such is the case in respect to the treatment of women; it is possible to assemble instances that reveal her as hopelessly oppressed or as highly emancipated. We shall try to present the whole picture before we are done; but there is no doubt that she has suffered a handicap as compared to man from the fact that she has been so widely regarded with this strange mixture of contempt and fear. The element of fear in this combination has been of great significance, for women's mere physical inferiority cannot alone account for the attitude taken toward her. The folly of the notion that all women are bad and dangerous, so that one-half of the race is always pulling the other half down, needs no refutation to a reflective mind; that sort of a mind appears, however, only late in human evolution. If one wants to see things as they were, he will not project an evolved sophistication into the primitive period.

The following cases seem to us to be extensions of the mistrust of woman, as felt at certain periods of her sex-life, over all periods of her career as a sexual being. It is significant that "Zulu women observe the customs of *hlonipa*[87] in relation to the men, but when past the age of child-bearing they are called men and need do so no longer";[88] that is, the women stay under a sexual taboo as long as they are typically female in function,[89] while with the cessation of sex-life constraint relaxes.

In Australia, a man would not drink out of a place where a woman drank. "A woman must not on any account step over anything belonging to a man. For instance, if a man were making a fishing-line and left it on the ground,

85   Seid ihr nicht wie die Weiber, die beständig
            Zurück nur kommen auf ihr erstes Wort,
            Wenn man Vernunft gesprochen stundenlang!
                      Schiller, *Wallenstein's Tod*, Aufz. II, Auftr. 3.
86 *Mission. Travels*, 550.   87 §223, above.
88 Callaway, *Relig. Amazulu*, 441, 442, 443.
89 Crawley, in JAI, XXIV, 220.

and a woman stepped across it, he would throw it away." The shadow of a woman falling upon a novice at initiation would be evil magic.[90] A woman was thought not to have any spirit-part or to be reincarnated; she must not see the whirr-stick, a religious instrument of great potency.[91] Melanesian women may not cook food for a long time after confinement, must not see a boy who is undergoing the circumcision-rite, or look upon a man drinking *kava*.[92] It is degrading for a Melanesian chief to go where a woman may be above his head; hence the refusal to go below on board a vessel.[93]

In Africa and elsewhere, women have no names, just as they have no souls.[94] They may not make fire with the drill or be present during the forging process, lest the implements be spoiled. The king's cook must keep away from women; and celibate priests may not eat food prepared by a married woman. Women may not look on a dead member of the men's secret society and must withdraw from the village till after the funeral. Anyone struck with the cloth or skin that clothes a woman's body must die. "Therefore she protects her property from theft by touching each piece with her leather apron." Women must not set foot in the cattle-yard, much less tend the cattle or milk. In East Central Africa, "women kneel when addressing men, and go off the public path into the grass or bush when they meet any of the opposite sex as a sign of subordination and subjection." Among the Nile tribes, "after death women are seldom buried. Their corpses are generally thrown to the hyænas; men, on the other hand, are invariably buried, and generally in a trench dug outside the door of the house."[95] Where women are clothed and men are not, dress is unworthy of a man. Schweinfurth was known as the "Turkish Lady." In Madagascar there is a belief prevalent among the carriers of burdens that if a woman strides over their poles the skin of their shoulders will certainly peel off the next time they take up a load.[96]

In Siberia, a man might not warm bread with sticks which a woman had handled. The Yakuts have many contemptuous things to say about women. She spoils the guns of the huntsman and the tools of the craftsman. Women feel their own worthlessness and are submissive and patient under abuse, thinking all this to be in the order of things. The wife exalts her husband above herself even when she is superior and knows it. Samoyeds and Tungus disqualify woman in similar ways. Yukaghir girls must not cast a glance at the foot-prints of a man who is going off to hunt. Women must not pronounce the name of St. George, the men's saint; they use another term. Female infanticide is practised on the theory that if a girl is killed a boy will be born. Women defile a church; they themselves are convinced that the sacred images will not endure their presence.[97]

90 Howitt, *S.E. Aust.*, 402.

91 Spencer and Gillen, *North. Tr. Cent. Aust.*, 170; Eyre, *Cent. Aust.*, II, 320; Stuhlmann, *Mit Emin*, 378.

92 Chalmers, in JAI, XXVII, 328; Gray, "Tannese," in AAAS, 1892, 660, 661.

93 Codrington, *Melanesians*, 233, note.

94 §212, above; Crawley, in JAI, XXIV, 234.

95 MacDonald, in JAI, XXII, 118.

96 Johnston, in JAI, XV, 10; Serpa Pinto, *Africa*, I, 108, 109; Bastian, *Deut. Exped.*, I, 216; II, 212; Gutmann, in *Globus*, XCII, 49; Ratzel, *Vkde.*, I, 450; Schweinfurth, *Heart of Afr.*, I, 152; Sibree, *Great Afr. Isl.*, 288.

97 Patursson, *Sibirien*, 144; Sieroshevski-Sumner, in JAI, XXXI, 96; Hie-

The Lepchas believe that the troubles of the world have been caused by women. "The rainbow was made by our old first great-grandfather, our troubles were made by our old first great-grandmother !"[98] It may be noted here that the stories of Eve and of Pandora support this view and that in general it is the older female divinities, as in Homer, who are mischief-making and malevolent.[99]

Æschylus and, more frequently, Euripides, put into the mouths of their characters sentiments derogatory to woman. When all allowance has been made for dramatic circumstance, it yet remains significant that such utterances are critical of woman as such. No expressions of the sort are used as respects the male sex, however savagely certain male characters may be handled. Not only is "one man worth more than a myriad of women," in time of danger, but the general sex-characteristics of woman are reviewed with an appreciable degree of contempt. She is timorous, comfort-loving, vain, infirm of judgment, a creature of guile, prone to gossip and intrigue. "Oh, Zeus! In women what a race didst thou give!" The heroine—an Antigone, an Alcestis—stands forth in sharper definition by reason of the many critical comments upon female characters that are weak or wicked, or upon the sex in general. One of the most sustained characterizations is that by Eteocles in *The Seven against Thebes*:

> Neither in trouble nor in prosperous days
> Let me be housed with women! When they rule
> Their boldness is the bane of peaceful life,
> And once afraid, they bring worse misery
> To home and country. Even as you today,
> Coursing with senseless hurry to and fro,
> Set up a noise that genders heartless fear;
> Whereby the foreigners' advantage grows,
> And Thebes is ravaged inly by ourselves.
> So fares the man whom women dwell withal.[100]

In view of the rather full treatment, by one of the authors[101] of this book, of the status of woman in antiquity up to the time of Christ, it does not seem necessary to go into the detail of that period in the present connection. Under Islam, women were regarded as lower than men and as silly, superstitious, and frivolous; their status, even as wives of rich Turks and Persians, was not much different from that of the women of inner Asia. The curse of Islam is said to be that its view of women is so inextricably interwoven with its mores that no change to elevate woman within the societal system is possible. Theologues

kisch, *Tungusen*, 89; *Russian Ethnog.* (Russ.), II, 268, 353, 599; Von Stenin, in *Globus*, LXXVI, 167.

[98] Waddell, *Himalayas*, 295.

[99] Keller, *Hom. Soc.*, 202; Lippert, *Kgchte.*, II, 257 ff.

[100] Euripides, *Andromache*, 85, 272-273, 944-946; *Phœnissæ*, 198-201; *Hekabe*, 885; *Iphigenia among the Taurians*, 1005-1006, 1032; *Iphigenia in Aulis*, 1394; *Hippolytus*, 406-407; 616 ff., 664 ff.; Æschylus, *Suppliants*, 514, 749; *Agamemnon*, 483 ff., 1636; *Seven against Thebes*, 187 ff. (quoted from Campbell's rather free translation), 230 ff., 256.

[101] Sumner, in *Coll. Ess.*, I, ch. III.

turned an earlier respect for women the other way; the traditional view, ascribed to the Prophet, was that women generally go to hell.[102]

The Norse sagas exhibit women as witches and mischief-makers; they make swords unfit for battle. The *Roman de la Rose* and the old French comedy were full of disrespect. Upon such ideas the Church was enabled to fasten with power; the reason given for the decree of clerical celibacy of Gregory VII was the baseness of woman. Then, despised and feared as they were, women easily fell under the suspicion of the witch-persecutors. The *Malleus Maleficarum* calls woman a destroyer of friendship, an inescapable punishment, a necessary evil, a natural temptation, a desirable ill, a domestic danger, a delightful detriment, an evil of nature painted over with beautiful color. In the Middle Ages half the literature denounces woman as a suave, diabolical agency for man's ruin in this world and the next and the other half consists of the extravagances of chivalry in which she appears as the inspiration of all virtue. In Italy, "the most glorious thing that is said of the great Italian women of the time is that they had a man's spirit, a man's disposition. . . . The title 'virago,' which our century holds to be a very doubtful compliment, was at that time pure glory." Nature would continually bring forth men if she could; when a girl is born, it is an accident or defect of nature, as when one is born blind or halt.[103]

In Russia, woman was regarded as in some respects unclean; if she had to do with a food-animal, the meat would not taste good. "Death was usually represented by the Slavonians, unless under strong ecclesiastical influence, as a female being. "According to the Cossacks, the woman stands "immeasurably lower than the man in the whole spiritual endowment"; she is an "unclean vessel and container of every uncleanness"; the spirit of uncleanness gladly settles in her, whereas he fears the man. The South Slavs have the worst thinkable opinion of the female sex, revealed in numerous proverbs and figures of speech.[104]

Since a woman in her period will put a compass out of order or turn wine, suspicion fastens upon all strange women, who must keep out of places where they might do damage. Knox was the author of "The First Blast of the Trumpet against the Monstrous Regiment of Women," a most ungallant production. Upon the old woman in particular have the charges of witchcraft and the

[102] Ratzel, *Vkde.*, III, 153; Pischon, *Islam*, 30 ff.; Von Kremer, *Kgchte.*, II, 104.

[103] *Njala Saga* (Laing), 19, 59, 84, 138; Weinhold, *Deut. Frauen*, II, 200-201; Lichtenberger, *Nibelungen*, 368; *Roman de la Rose*, 18920, 19107; Lenient, *Satire*, 157; De Julleville, *Comédie*, 287, 300, 303; Scherr, *Deut. Frauenwelt*, I, 161; Sumner, in *Coll. Ess.*, I, ch. IV; Hoensbroech, *Papstthum*, I, 391; Hansen, *Zauberwahn*, 488-489; Burckhardt, *Renaissance*, 394; Castiglione, *Book of Courtier*, III, 11; Cook, *Fathers of Jesus*, II, 7-8, 159; McCabe, *St. Augustine*, 379; Lecky, *Europ. Morals*, II, 339; Legrand D'Aussy, *Fabliaux*, I, 251; Schultz, *Höf. Leben*, I, 459; Gide, *Condition de la Femme*, 209, 225, 229, 230, 242-243, 285; Stammler, *Stellung d. Frauen*, 10, 36, 38; Scherr, *Deut. Sittengchte.*, 113-114; Holt, in JAI, XXVIII, 162-163; Rudeck, *Oeffentl. Sittl.*, 34.

[104] Kostomarov, *Gt. Russians* (Russ.), 146; Ralston, *Russ. People*, 25 (quoted). Rhamm, in *Globus*, LXXXII, 274, 278-279, 323-324; Strauss, *Bulgaren*, 300.

miseries incident to taboos borne with cruel weight; she is of evil omen and helpless enough to be oppressed with impunity.[105]

The attitude toward women illustrated in the foregoing cases has no parallel for the other sex. It sets woman over against man as peculiar, abnormal, and inferior. Anything that may tend to identify him with her is to be avoided. Though he must associate with her in marriage, that must be done with as little risk as possible to himself. In so far as this attitude is taken, there is little inclination toward concern about her rights. It is next to impossible for a modern to realize the power of this sex-factor in the mores of primitive peoples, for it is almost wholly foreign to the thought of civilization. Yet no adequate appreciation of the position of woman in primitive society can be attained without a vivid comprehension of that factor.

§390. Adjustments in Woman's Status. It is as profitless to talk about progress in respect to woman's status as it is to bandy random words about the same subjective concept in any other field. There is nothing to gain by trying to estimate her status in terms of "high" and "low"; all that can be done is to count up the definite rights accorded to her under various circumstances and try to see how they constitute societal, not individual or sexwise adjustments to life-conditions as constituted by the triple environment of things, men, and spirits. When, however, her rights as conceded on the primitive stage are enumerated and compared with those of man, there is no question but that the case seems to make heavily against her. If, then, that list is scrutinized with the idea of comparing its items with those which must be set down in an alignment of sex-rights as accorded at the present time by a highly civilized society, it becomes evident that woman has acquired a number of rights during the course of societal evolution. Very likely some such contrast lies in the minds of those who assert that the position of woman is a gauge of the height of culture.

Entrance upon any attempted explanation of this contrast leads beyond the limits of primitive organization and so beyond the province of this book. We have never refrained, however, from

[105] Oliveira Martins, *Raças,* II, 27; Sharpe, *Witchcraft in Scotland,* 48; Klugmann, *Frau in Talmud,* 51.

suggesting the applicability to modern life of principles that have emerged from our studies; and in the present connection such suggestion seems in point. The principle to be applied is that of woman's status as an automatic adjustment to changing life-conditions. Let us begin by a comparison of primitive and modern conditions which will at the same time constitute a sort of summary of ground covered in preceding pages. In so doing, we shall work backwards through the table of sex-rights given above.[106]

In the religious organization woman has always been cast for a relatively insignificant part; and it would be difficult to show much prestige that she has won.

In the military organization, she has constituted the industrial arm, behind the lines, a function which the present generation has been taught by experience to appreciate; indeed it might almost be said that the women of 1914-1918 regained the importance in connection with war possessed by the savage women, even to the extent of battalions of Amazons. Woman, however, has almost never done direct fighting; her service has been relatively unspectacular, has been taken as a matter of course, and has not been much recognized. Womanish unwarlikeness and timidity, when ascribed to men, have conveyed deadly insult; when referred to as qualities of a woman, as of a deer, they have been descriptive merely, with some note of contempt. It is understandable that where militancy has prevailed strongly and unintermittently the sex without militant virtues has seemed of inferior serviceability and worth to society.

In government women have taken a comparatively small direct part, though it will be recalled that observers repeatedly remark upon the political influence wielded indirectly by them through their men; and the special powers of women under the mother-family system must be reckoned in. Here too, what women did is of the unspectacular order and much less regard has been registered for her than for man as a component of the regulative organization. It is undeniable that the attitude toward her has corresponded with rough fidelity to the facts. Nowadays, as is well known, woman in states of high culture is being accorded more political rights than she has had before. She is no longer

---

[106] §377, above.

confined to the kin-group but has prerogatives as a citizen of a
state.

The elemental service to society discharged by woman in connection with its self-perpetuation has generally been fully recognized, though in a matter-of-fact rather than in a sentimental
way. Poetic reflection upon primal facts is not the way of uncivilized or half-civilized man. Woman was not so much esteemed for
her motherhood as censured for sterility. There was no romancing
over this matter. Was a woman not a woman? And what did that
mean except that she would be a wife and bear children? That was
what women did, just as beavers built dams. The functions of wife
and mother were taken as a matter of course where nowadays a
couple that have a child seem to look upon it much as stout Cortez
is represented as gazing, of all men first, upon the Pacific, with a
"wild surmise." It would appear that such a momentous event had
never occurred before. Among savages, mothers were wanted and a
prolific wife was valued as a practical asset in life. Sophistication
has sometimes exaggerated the share of man and minimized that
of woman, as in Greece, where she was merely the "plowed field";
but primitive peoples, however slight their understanding of the
process of procreation, have judged by the obvious and have not
erred on the side of ascribing results solely, or even predominantly, to the male. It was rather the other way about.[107] Where
woman has enjoyed little or no recognition for anything else, she
has always had her dignity as an actual or potential mother just
as, conversely, no other defect has so lowered respect for her as
barrenness.

Of late, motherhood has been protected by industrial legislation of several
types. It is interesting to note a revolt against these once-lauded measures;
not long ago an adherent of woman's rights maintained that if the forty-eight
hour week was good for men it was equally good for women; and a subsequent
speaker stated that those who favored the forty-eight hour legislation were
trying to conceal its real purpose by waving the flag of maternity.[108] It sometimes seems from such utterances that there are women who do not contemplate service under that flag in the future.

Under modern culture the conception of woman as predestined
to wifehood and motherhood has changed. She is more of a per-

[107] §§334, above, and 411, 412, below; Lippert, *Kgchte.,* I, 81.
[108] N. Y. *Times,* Jan. 18 and Feb. 29, 1920; May 16, 1922.

sonality apart from her sex, and has a career-interest more like man's. This is a reflex of her economic situation. Changing maintenance-conditions have thrown the family as an industrial unit out of adjustment. We are told that the "companionate" is about to supplant the family and might believe, but for the ballast of the wholesome unemancipated, that society is swaying toward the impossible whim of depreciating motherhood.

"In one group of cases, we still have the initiation-ceremony [wedding] leading to the historic institution for reproduction and care of the young. In another, growing larger year by year, the same identical rites lead to a social unit which serves neither of these purposes—that is, the lengthy or permanent companionate." The author[109] says that the ablest strains tend to extinguish themselves, "if the family is to continue a handicap to an individual success which gets all the material rewards and social applause." The recognition of the companionate as a distinctive institution "has become fairly general only among the more radically minded," who tend to imitate the Russian experiment.

Perhaps even the "dual standard" of morality is disappearing, not, however, so much through tightening on the looser side as the reverse. Be that as it may, woman seems to have more rights in matrimony than she had in earlier times, though it would be hard to demonstrate that she is any more of a complementary help-mate than she has ever been.

Her rights to own and to inherit property are much more extensive now than formerly, and her property in herself is of about the same degree as man's. She is not owned by her husband, may not be given away, lent, exchanged, secluded, or inherited. There is no public agency for the control of women. Her consent is usually necessary to marriage and it is to her, in most civilized countries, that the initial proposal must be directed. She may not practise premarital license; on the other hand, she is not punished so severely for infidelity as when she was mere property. Divorce is not so fully in the hands of man. In short, woman has gained many rights to liberty and, of course, a right to life equal to man's—superior, in fact, where juries will not inflict capital punishment upon her.

Turning finally to the economic activities of woman, we find that they are passing beyond the domestic range. As regards that primordial maintenance-unit, the family, the attempt to say which

[109] Knight, "The Companionate and the Family," in *Jr. Soc. Hyg.*, X, 257 ff. See editorial on "The Familette," in N. Y. *Times*, Oct. 24, 1924.

of the pair of indispensable coöperators performed the superior service is like trying to settle the dispute between the belly and other bodily members, as propounded by the Roman conciliator. Woman has held her own in the family and has had little time for anything else; she has been accredited with so doing and, in a number of cases, has been exalted over man. That her "woman's work" has been thought degrading to man is irrelevant to the matter. There has been no scoffing at the utility of her camp-keeping or of her rudimentary tillage-activities among hunters or herders. That she has had to work hard has not meant that her status was degraded; that she has sometimes led a life of slothful ease in a harem does not prove that she enjoyed extensive rights or deference. Under the latter circumstances, all that has saved her from utter nonentity may have been the fact that she has borne sons.

It is the economic condition of modern woman that lies very plainly at the basis of her extra rights. Furthermore, that significant element in the sex-factor, fear and contempt with regard to certain of her sex-characteristics, has disappeared. Merely to mention this last relief accorded her is to explain much, provided that the reader has acquired any realizing sense of its weight upon her destiny. That the conviction of woman's uncleanness, held with an intensity of fear and detestation of which we can with difficulty form a conception, could ever have existed, a modern man, we say, finds it hard to believe. Though a medley of erratic notions derogatory to woman, and sufficient to counterbalance in part the correction of the uncleanness-fantasy, had been set afloat, yet it is reasonable to conclude that chances of all kinds were opened up to her when the suspicion of her on account of her sex-peculiarities had been dispelled by increase of knowledge. This represented to her a sort of negative gain; it meant that a hitherto well-nigh insuperable handicap was removed. That the sex-factor in woman's status, as represented by various erroneous notions about her, and taboos based upon them, has suffered significant alteration, needs scarcely more than mention. The significance of that change appears at sight. The maintenance-factor calls for more extended consideration; and it is really at the bottom of the changes in the sex-factor.

Reverting to woman's economic emancipation, we cannot but note that the passage of the industrial organization from its phase of domestic production to the factory system drew woman into the outside world, enabled her to supplant man, and gave her a chance to acquire legal rights. Women have come to see careers outside of marriage and the family; they can hope to support themselves. For this reason also they can face divorce with more assurance. The incursion of the discontented English women into the munition-factories resulted in a concession of rights for which they had long stormed in vain. In a very true sense, then, woman's increase in rights is due to mechanical inventions. More broadly, it is due to science, the master-agency of societal adjustment and only secondarily to the projection of science upon the world of things. It is a broad principle that the weaker always gain disproportionately by superior adjustments. To be able to make successively more rapid and expedient adaptations comes nearer deserving the name of progress than anything else; it is, then, the weaker who win by progress.[110]

Then the growth of wealth and luxury has made woman to be valued for her feminine grace and charm, which meant little to savages engrossed in the struggle for existence and prone to estimate all worth in terms of food-producing capacity, and has even emancipated her from the struggle for self-maintenance altogether. A man has come to be as proud of not having his wife labor as he once was complacent over her unremitting performances with a hoe. With the amelioration of the stress of maintenance and the development of luxury, taste changed, and woman profited by it. The element of chivalry, already alluded to, appeared in Western nations, constituting a very real and effective secondary factor in elevating ideas about women.

In the Middle Ages two opposite tendencies appear in the utmost exaggeration side by side: the denunciation and the idealization of woman. Both were largely religious in origin. Out of the latter, however, empty as it was of real conviction and content, out of the "spring-time poetry" and romance of writers in the north temperate regions of Europe and America, and probably also out of Virgin-worship, there has emerged an attitude toward women which has been carried far and wide over the earth. The emptiness and spuriousness of chivalry, as exposed by Cervantes, had no bearing upon the genuineness of the results reached under its influence, and did not prevent it from imposing upon

110 Sumner, "Who Win by Progress?" in *Coll. Ess.*, III, 167 ff.

later ages a very real conviction as to the consideration which ought to be accorded to woman. It is doubtless unnecessary to say that it is only a part of one race, even though that includes the dominant nations, which has arrived at any such general conviction.

The key to the whole situation as respects woman's evolving status lies, in the end, in maintenance-considerations. Mere availability in the struggle for self-maintenance can confer only the status of a tool or a domestic animal, that is, an unrelieved property-status; it can assure no rights to speak of. In such case there is nothing to lend value to women except scarcity of them. The demand for women as mere tools, or as work-animals, or as "plowed fields"[111] for propagation, never lent them a fulcrum by which to pry themselves up. To get ahead they must be more than inert implements; they must first play an active part in the industrial organization. Then as evolution went on, types of coöperation were called for and recognized which had no counterpart in the earlier stages; and in return for such finer types of usefulness, as for the former coarser ones, rights were forthcoming.

The development of the rights of woman has gone with the development of the maintenance-organization and constitutes a sort of function of that development, as is the case with other sets of what we have called secondary mores.[112] When maintenance was difficult and life one pressing and often violent exigency, certain virtues occupied the foreground. They were those of man. Those who did not possess them sought their shelter, much as the defenseless man commended himself to a powerful protector, and were assigned their places in the scheme of things, under the control of those who had the might and right. With the gradual strengthening of the maintenance-organization and the lengthening of intervals between life-and-death crises, society could be carried forward without so much regimentation of the weaker. More could be conceded to the latter, just as, at any time, people can afford to become "humanitarian" if they are better off.[113] This does not mean that men were looking for a chance to be humanitarian to their women; it simply signifies that with the relaxation of pressure the tautness of the regimentation slackened of itself, affording an opportunity for woman's self-assertion or

---

[111] Sophocles, Œd. Tyr., 1256.   [112] Keller, Soc. Evol., 62 ff.
[113] Sumner, Folkways, §§336, 337.

even for a careless good nature not seldom exhibited by savages not under stress. Easement in the stark struggle for existence allowed of selection in the mores upon a somewhat different basis. Society, in its own massive interests, shifted its basic adjustment. It became industrial instead of militant; and woman, carried along into the new phase, made a gain in status. Again, property-mores altered somewhat and marriage went over from purchase to dowry—another gain to woman. There came a change from polygyny to monogamy, likewise based largely upon property-considerations; and woman's position was improved. But all movement was not in a single direction: society abandoned the mother-family in favor of the patriarchate; it let the kin-group wane and adjusted through territoriality; and woman lost in both instances. The only covering generality is the one recently stated: that the mores about woman adjusted into consistency with the underlying maintenance-organization.

It was, in last analysis, the superior maintenance-adjustments which freed woman, at length, from the handicap of the sex-factor. Only with success in the struggle for existence and the winning of leisure does the opportunity come to mankind to correct in the light of understanding the errors and phantasms of the race's childhood. The hoary ideas about woman's uncleanness and the mistrust of the sex sedulously nursed up in religious speculation have died hard; but there never was any doubt about their demise as soon as science, another infant Hercules, could get out of its cradle.

Perhaps one might ask why a vagary like the notion of the uncleanness of woman could last so long. In putting that question it should not be lost to sight that, irrational in our sight as it seems—though not more irrational than the possession-theory of disease[114]—the notion had a certain practical value. It segregated woman and gave her time to recuperate when she needed it most, it taught restraint and subordination, it protected men from a weakening indulgence, it exercised a certain influence on population. Persisting vagaries, even though they seem at first sight to be nothing but folly, have been prevalent enough in the history of the race. Yet the very fact that society has endured is proof posi-

114 §315, above.

tive that human error has been held within some sort of limit and that the public opinion upon which men have acted has been kept in some sort of correspondence with reality.

A traditional attitude toward women, such as the one developed in connection with her sex-life, may last on for a long time, forming an obstacle of heavy inertia across the path of the elemental economic forces. Theoretical justification of that which has come to be a fact, in this case the misprision of woman, then stands in the way of further adjustment through rejection of the traditional attitude, now become a maladjustment. Thus the relative inferiority of woman was long supported by the legend that she was made from the rib of man, just as the enslavement of the negro was explained by the story that he rose from an ignoble descendant of Noah. Such traditions look like genealogical tricks and exhibitions of tendency in the chronicle;[115] they are in reality and in origin only the play of myth about actual conditions of life and of mores guaranteed by the societal system and in particular by religion. Later on recourse has been taken to the myths in order to shore up, under assault, the status to which they correspond. A handicap of this order can be overcome only by actual services to society, for they, even though they remain long unrecognized by men, are sure of eventual acknowledgment. They will be recognized in fact, in the mores, while they are still unconceded in principle and even though all theory makes against appreciation of them. This, we take it, is the explanation of the presence of female prerogatives in the face of theory and practice inconsistent with it. The theory, in the present case the daimonistic convictions about woman's sexual uncleanness, gives way at length by reason of the general undermining of daimonism, all along the line, at the hand of developing science; it lasts on for a time in a vague and attenuated form in a mistrust of women explicable only by myth and rationalization; but, as it loses power, the services of woman that have been submerged and lost to sight by reason of its presence, rise to the surface. Sometimes it almost looks as if sex-services were a sort of constant and their societal setting a variable whose play has lent now greater and now less import to the contributions of man or of woman. Perhaps Dundas

115 Gumplowicz, *Soc.*, 107.

and Weeks[116] have stated the general case when they tell how the African is hopeless and helpless without women, and can hardly imagine adult life as anything but a state of matrimony; that "a man cannot live without a woman."

It is not very risky to venture the contention that lack of correspondence between the way things are and the way men think they are is bound, in the long run, to be reconciled by a correction of public opinion. Usages and traditions that have clearly been maladjustments to actuality have been selected away, if need be by the extinction of the society exhibiting them.[117] The process takes time; but time seems to be the one thing of which there has always been plenty. In the long run the very existence of a society in competition with other societies depends upon a reasonably accurate adjustment, in the mores, to the perennial conditions of societal life. That such adjustments are made on a wrong theory is of no consequence whatever.

§391. Summary. First of all, whatever the disabilities or prerogatives of man or woman, neither sex was aware of anything morally reprehensible in existing conditions. There was turning and twisting when there was discomfort; sometimes the men organized to suppress the women and sometimes the latter revolted with enough energy and purpose to justify male concern;[118] but in general the sexes lived on together in uncomplaining acceptance of a code that had been worked out over long periods of automatic adjustment and was regarded as a traditional matter of course. Things were taken as they came because there was nothing different within ken with which to compare them and on the basis of which to criticize them. In particular, the primitive women did not pity themselves and seem to have been quite as content as those who have regarded themselves as emancipated and in a position to extend horrified sympathy. The view of women, their character and relation to men, and the mores as to their treatment, rights, and duties—and similar ideas as to children and the

116 Dundas, C., in JAI, LI, 249; Weeks, in JAI, XXXIX, 449; §342, above.
117 Keller, Soc. Evol., 62 ff.
118 Serpa Pinto, África, I, 24. Cases of such revolts are collected, with references, in Crawley, in JAI, XXIV, 119.

old—represent simply reaction on observation and experience in adjustment to what life seems to mean.

It is clear enough, next, that upon no stage of society's evolution have women, on whatever standards, been universally oppressed, any more than men have been, on any stage and on any standards, universally emancipated. It is inexpedient in the evolution of society that either sex shall be either wholly reduced or scot-free. The sexes are given by nature as a biological adaptation and not at random. Then they have to adjust to one another in such manner that society goes on. Adjustment must first be local; but even if a form could be perfect for a time and place it could not so remain for long. The details of adjustment must respond to the ever-shifting life-conditions amidst which, at a place and time, a society finds itself. Where different societies encounter similar life-conditions there appear of necessity, since there are not endlessly dissimilar ways of meeting similar situations, broad parallelisms and generalized types of adjustment. To recall an instance cited, if there are more women than men, the adjustment has regularly been polygyny. Then these types of adjustment, like organic types, may be set in evolutionary sequence, as we have been taking much pains to show. The question is never as to whether evolving usages seem to make progressively toward their acme in our own mores; the conception of progress should be set aside altogether; then the issue will be as to how the status of woman constitutes an adjustment or series of adjustments to the life-conditions of society prevailing at any given time and place. Amidst the complexities of this massive evolutionary process it is as futile to look for universals about sex-oppression and emancipation as it is irrelevant and impertinent to complain because the facts do not appeal to our taste.

The truth is that no universal is valid on the subject of the relation of the sexes except that those relations have evolved automatically as a phase of society's adjustment, through the mores, to its life-conditions. Society maintains and perpetuates itself, using its instruments according to their capacities—using them up, if that is more expedient. How have the sexes subserved these interests of society? Has one sex done it all, or almost all, and the other little or nothing—as adult age does what infancy and childhood cannot do? To ask such a question is to answer it. It is a mere rhetorical question. The sexes are upon a parity of indispensability to society's interest in both of its major forms: self-maintenance and self-perpetuation.

CHAPTER LII

DISSOLUTION OF WEDLOCK

§392*. **Divorce.** The dissolution of wedlock is to many high-minded people the putting asunder of that which has been joined together, if not by God, at any rate by the impersonal power behind the process of evolution. They see, at the culmination of a long course of development and as a triumph of advanced culture, the conception of marriage as a life-time relation of mutual devotion between one man and one woman. They observe this conception issuing in that of the monogamic family wherein children are procreated and nurtured under conditions making for steadfastness of affection, orderly upbringing, an atmosphere of happiness and virtue—in short, they see that incomparable achievement of humanity, the home. They believe all this to be good not alone for the individual but for society as well. Holding wedlock and the family in such esteem, divorce is to them an offensive reversion of the evolutionary process, destructive of the home, evil alike for parents, children, and society.

One can harbor an understanding sympathy with such an attitude and yet part company with those who hold it if they go on to censure the state or society for permitting feather-headed incompetents to mate under fleeting impulse, reproduce without responsibility, and separate light-mindedly. It is worth while to note, as was done in the case of marriage,[1] just how the state functions in this matter. Moral stress is laid upon being formally married because the relation is thus placed under the protection of society and is guaranteed as to its rights and perpetuity. Divorce is a dissolution of such protection and guarantees. The state, we have seen, does not marry people. It cannot enter into their reasons or lack of reasons for marrying. It defines the status of matrimony for those who may be interested and also the rights and duties of the contractants as to support, property, and legitimacy of offspring. Though it recognizes other rights and duties, and though courts adjudge them, no tribunal can enforce them; they are

---

[1] §341, above.

matters of conduct, private and conjugal, within the relation, and if either spouse is unwilling to perform the duties, coercion is impossible. Conjugal life goes on between two persons who are a world to themselves; neither the law nor even the mores can interfere. External authority cannot get hold of the inner relations; all it can do is to free the persons. In divorce the state can do no more than withdraw its power from the enforcement of rights and duties. It can decree alimony, that is, the support of the wife and the custody of children; it releases other rights, such as those of property and dower; it withdraws its hand from what it never could enforce, that is, the private and conjugal relations. In its own interest it must know what persons are entering the status of matrimony; it can let them out; but it cannot make them live as they have agreed to while they are in. It may also allow re-marriage under conditions, which means only that it will not put the parties in prison if they form new connections. The notion that the state divorces people is like the idea that the church marries them. They marry themselves when they consent together and begin conjugal life under the status of matrimony as defined. They divorce themselves when they withdraw from the relation. In the former case the church blesses; in the latter the state recognizes the disruption of the relation and readjusts rights and duties.

It is well to have such facts in mind, for they demonstrate that even in a highly organized society government and law can have but little to do with entrance into matrimony, existence within it, and exit from it. All these matters, in so far as control over them goes, are in the mores. It can occasion no surprise, then, to find primitive "divorce" highly casual and informal. In primitive marriage there is no contract or promise; that is very modern and does not exist even now where the ritual idea strongly prevails. It is the ritual that is gone through with that seems to make the relation. Primitive marriage, as a matter of the mores, is no more permanent than friendship, partnership, or other form of co-operation for a purpose. The causes for the dissolution of matrimony are, in general, those things which frustrate the main purposes of marriage; most broadly viewed, they include whatever thwarts self-maintenance or self-perpetuation. The woman is divorced because she is barren or is, by reason of weakness, sickness, laziness, or other defect, a poor worker; the man because he is a poor provider or is cruel or impotent. Where the coöperation of the parties to a marriage is not satisfactory, generally a new combination is readily formed. The woman is much more commonly blamed and divorced than the man, especially in case of an unfruitful union; it does not seem to occur to the savage, save under exceptional circumstances, that the man may be at fault. Divorce is also a modification toward polygyny; it breaks the "monotony of monogamy." It is quite incorrect to call a group monogamous where frequent divorces and re-marriages are possible. To be noted also is the fact that the passage of property, in the form of purchase-price or dowry, by acting as a bar to the dissolution of marriage, stabilizes the relation.[2] Where property passes, either for or with the wife, she is not cheap and is not so held. And while she is seldom dismissed if she is a child-bearer, adultery, as an act distinctly subversive of the marriage-relation, has very often constituted the decisive ground for repudiation.

In general, primitive people hold together in marriage while their interests are being served by it, and when they are not being served, they part without much difficulty. Divorce is either an unceremonious parting, a flight by the weaker party, or a dismissal by the stronger.[3] It may be posthumous.[4]

Among certain Australians, if a man sees that his wife likes another man better, he gives her up to him. There is no enmity between the two men, though the woman's relatives do not like it.[5] If a Papuan woman is a thief, she is cast off and the bride-price repaid; if the separation is for other cause, the husband gets nothing back.[6] If a woman has cause of grievance against her husband, she leaves him and returns to her mother's house. He has no further control over her and she has as much liberty as a single girl, only she may not rejoin her husband. A divorced woman invariably marries again in the course of a few months.[7] In New Britain the proceeding is similar, except that the husband may demand back what he has paid for the wife; and her friends may think enough of her to refund—which is rarely the case. The shell-money here used establishes the right of property, with power of alienation, even in women and children.[8] In the Murray Islands divorce was permissible for adultery on the part of the wife, but she could not divorce her husband.[9] In the Solomon

[2] §341, above.   [3] Starcke, *Prim. Fam.*, 258, 285.
[4] Cases in Crawley, *Mystic Rose*, 322.
[5] Cunow, *Australneger*, 101.   [6] Von Pfeil, *Südsee*, 30.
[7] Guise, in JAI, XXVIII, 209, 210.
[8] Danks, in JAI, XVIII, 293.   [9] Hunt, in JAI, XXVIII, 10.

Islands divorce, Somerville[10] thinks, cannot exist, since a wife is promptly tomahawked if she misbehaves herself and the husband may do as he pleases. The Andaman Islanders are exceptional in their ignorance of plural marriage or divorce; conjugal fidelity till death is the rule and matrimonial differences are settled with or without the intervention of friends.[11]

Divorce among negroes is said to be rare except where they have come into contact with Arabs or Europeans. Princesses can dismiss their husbands and the chief may grant a separation.[12] Yet we find that "a wife can, with her husband's consent, leave him at any time by refunding the head-money and the amount of all the expenditure he has ever incurred on her behalf"; if she has been ill-treated and can prove the facts before the headman, she need not refund. Children accompany the wife, who reimburses the father for their maintenance.[13] Again, after a wife flees with another man or refuses to live with her husband, he announces the fact to her family, stating that he has divorced her; then he has a right to receive back what he expended in getting her. The man has also the power to divorce without reason assigned but in that case is not reimbursed.[14] Elsewhere "the wife may be discarded if she neglects her hoeing or hacked to pieces if caught in an intrigue; the husband may be divorced if the wife can show a neglected rent in her petticoat or promptly executed if found making love to a wife whom his neighbor has determined to cast off because her children have died of the measles."[15] If a husband eats all the food, the wife may complain to her father, who gives her a bigger cooking-pot and urges her to cook more food so that there will be something left over for her. If the former situation then recurs, divorce ensues. On the other hand, since "love goes through the stomach," if the wife cooks poorly, love departs, and there is a sufficient reason for separation. Children remain to the man.[16] Again, it is the wife who dissolves the not very binding relation. The man to whom she goes must recompense the parents, the amount being lessened if the woman has had children. The women leave for the most trivial causes.[17]

In East Africa, "divorce and return of dowry [signifying bride-price, as used by this author[18]] may be taken as one and the same thing, for so long as a woman's father holds the dowry paid for her, the husband's claim cannot be challenged, and *vice versa*, the marriage is annulled so soon as the dowry is returned. There can be only two grounds for a divorce—either the wife runs away, or the husband voluntarily returns her. . . . The rules express clearly the fact that tribal custom discountenances divorce. It lies with the husband alone to grant this, and if he does so he invariably loses a part of what he paid. Altogether one must be impressed with the idea that marriage under native law is intended to be a very permanent union, particularly in respect to the first wife, who can never be the wife of more than one man. All this is especially in keeping with native society because of the importance of the family and clan, whose purity must be preserved. In addition to this we should consider many other customs which indicate that there is a religious relationship between man and wife which gives a very sacred meaning to marriage."

10 In JAI, XXVI, 407.

11 Man, in JAI, XII, 135.

12 Ratzel, *Vkde.,* I, 154.

13 Ellis, *Ewe,* 206.

14 Connolly, in JAI, XXVI, 145.

15 Macdonald, in JAI, XXII, 110.

16 Fabry, in *Globus,* XCI, 222.

17 Gutmann, in *Globus,* XCII, 31-32.

18 Dundas, C., in JAI, XLV, 288-290.

Among the Koryak of Siberia, "divorce was easily obtained, and it consisted in a simple separation. Remarriage is allowed, in the case of the woman, without the ceremony of capture and without the intercourse above mentioned"— the latter a sort of reversion that has been termed a purification-ceremony.[19] The Nairs of Malabar have a kind of marriage which, "though recognised as legal, has not the binding effect of a proper marriage. It is in theory dissoluble at will, and often it happens that, due either to misunderstanding or quarrel, either of the parties breaks off relations. In such a case, the marriage is deemed to have ended, and the aggrieved party can, without further formality, marry anybody else."[20]

Wilken[21] recurs repeatedly to the fact that, as in the Indian Archipelago, there can be no divorce where exogamy is practised under the father-family; the marriage under those circumstances is nothing but a purchase and cannot be undone, except only in case the wife is barren; then the parents must pay back the price or provide a substitute. "I recall that one man was condemned to several years of forced labor in chains and that, nevertheless, the attempt of his wife to get a divorce was rejected on the ground that he had bought her." The wife is so closely tied to the husband that a slave-family may not be separated in sale—not because of any right the slave has but merely by reason of the custom that binds spouses indissolubly. "I have," says one informant, "in my employ as a scribe a man who has seven wives one of whom he has not seen in four years, notwithstanding the fact that he has children by her and that she lives on one and the same river with him." Islam has changed this situation somewhat to the advantage of the man. Under exogamy and the father-family the woman leaves her kin-group for good and all and may not return; on the other hand, in cases of exogamy under the mother-family, and of endogamy, there is divorce on the slightest provocation or preference. The author quotes St. John[22] as follows: "Divorces are very common, one can scarcely meet with a middle-aged Dayak who has not had two, and often three or more wives. I have heard of a girl of seventeen or eighteen years who had already had three husbands. Repudiation, which is generally done by the man or woman running away to the house of a near relation, takes place for the slightest cause: personal dislike or disappointments, a sudden quarrel, bad dreams, discontent with their partners' powers of labour or their industry, or in fact, any excuse which will help to give force to the expression: I do not want to live with him or her any longer." Property follows, at divorce, much the same rules as at death. Childlessness is a common cause for separation and women who have no children are mocked and even punished; the East Indians prefer boys but say that "all girls bring money." If a wife does not bear children, her sister may be asked in her place; and if she dies before bearing, another girl may be demanded of the father-in-law in return for payment. Among certain Malays, who have the mother-family, "the first marriages, which are as a rule made by parents on both sides, without taking into consideration the leanings of the young people, are usually, after a few years, yes, even months, incontinently dissolved. The subsequent unions, in which the man can take a wife of his own choice, and likewise a woman a man, are more durable." Dyak divorces originate not seldom in the woman's initiative; "she

---

[19] Czaplicka, *Aborig. Siberia*, 89.   [20] Panikkar, in JAI, XLVIII, 271.
[21] In VG, II, 241-242; I, 388-390, 318, 319; Wilken, *Vkde.*, 201, 202, 291, 292.
[22] *Life in Forests of Far East*, 56-57, 165-166.

would run away to her parents and was not to be got back except through a large reconciliation-payment. Often this is a true speculation on the part of parents and daughters, in order to squeeze the man as much as possible."

"In all countries of the Archipelago, divorces may, by law or custom, be readily obtained. But, in all but Java, they are very seldom sued for; in Java there is a very wantonness on this point, which in some cases is hardly short of absolute prostitution." Java alone shows great laxity of morals as respects female virtue.[23] In Borneo, "many men and women have been married seven or eight times before they find the partner with whom they desire to spend the rest of their lives. These divorces take place at varied times, from a few days to one or two years after marriage. However, after the birth of a child, they seldom seek to separate, and if they do the husband is fined but not the wife." Thus the child acts as a bond between married parties, here as among more civilized peoples; in any case its presence proves the marriage to have been successful in one of its major aspects. Rather exceptionally, in some parts of Borneo, "by marrying both are united till death" and, in case of an infrequent divorce, those persons who were present at the wedding are summoned to declare the marriage dissolved.[24] A recent report concerning the divorcement and deposition of the Queen of Siam states that she was "unfitted for her royal duties." "Her failure to present the King with an heir was attributed . . . to her nightly conversations with 'invisible spirits from the ether.' The new Queen has been warned to have nothing to do with radio."[25]

In the Marshall Islands, divorce is frequent; if the wife does not please the husband, he simply sends her back to her relatives; but wives who have borne several children may not be sent away. They may even eat with their husbands.[26] On Ponapé, "in very many cases they do not need to go to that extreme [divorce], but frequently employ the custom they call *isipal,* which consists in exchanging wives among brothers and even among friends."[27] In the Pelew Islands, a maltreated wife may leave her husband for a time and seek the companionship of the free girls until the husband is sorry and buys her back. The women say: "The men are very bad to us; why should we not be just as free as they?"[28] Divorce for the Easter Islanders was very simple; "when the man said to his wife that he did not want her any more, the divorce was accomplished. The wife had quite the same right over against the husband."[29]

Eskimo divorce was simply at the will of the husband; if tired of his wife, he slept apart from her on the bench.[30] Elsewhere "the one who so desires leaves with little ceremony, but is sometimes sought for and compelled to return."[31] In general among the North American Indians, divorce, though discreditable, could easily be effected. "The marriage bond is loose, and may, with few exceptions, be dissolved by the wife as well as by the husband. The children generally stay with their mother, and always do in tribes having

23 Crawfurd, *Ind. Archip.,* 78.
24 Roth, *Sarawak,* I, 126, 128; II, clxxxi, clxxxii; Schwaner, *Borneo,* I, 199-200.
25 N. Y. *Times,* Dec. 27, 1925.
26 Finsch, *Ethnol. Erfahr.,* III, 130.   27 Pereiro, *Ponapé,* 119.
28 §344, above; Semper, *Palau-Ins.,* 319.
29 Geiseler, *Oster-Ins.,* 29-30.   30 Nansen, *Esk. Life,* 139.
31 Turner, in BAE, XI, 189.

maternal clans."[32] The Dakotas could divorce their wives during a certain dance; any one of the order practising the dance had only to rise and declare that his wife was divorced.[33] Of one tribe it is reported: "With great patience and submission the women are able so to adjust themselves to their husbands that separations seldom occur, and even when a man from time to time takes more wives they live in the most good-natured manner with one another and mutually support each other in the domestic labors."[34] Schomburgk[35] reports a dispute, leading to a separation, wherein the woman alleged that her husband gave her almost daily beatings and had sold all her property, while he accused her of laziness, for, at return from the hunt, he never found anything but empty pots—not even a drink of *paiwari*. Among the Bakairi divorce was very simple: the woman could go off, even against the man's will, but he might catch her again.[36] Some of the backward South American tribes show but few cases of separation or of repudiation of a wife; the bond is indissoluble and any attempt to break it is resisted by the whole community.[37]

In Chaldæa a man could at any time divorce his wife by a simple declaration, repaying her dower and sending her home; if, on the other hand, she renounced him formally she was drowned.[38] In the Laws of Hammurabi a woman who kills her husband—the only way she had of getting out of marriage, while he could divorce her—is to be hanged or impaled.[39] Among the ancient Hebrews, if a man finds in a wife something he does not like he shall send her away with a bill of divorcement and she may marry another.[40] In the New Testament, adultery is the only legitimate cause for parting.[41] Islam allowed wide latitude, though almost wholly from the side of the man. Later Moslems allowed separation and re-combination freely; some men of high rank had only one wife, while the common man, who also had one, changed often. The author quoted[42] knew of a man in Constantinople who had been married twenty-five times, and of a woman whose successive experiments had numbered seventeen. Considerable freedom in repudiating and changing wives was found in earlier Roman times;[43] and in ancient Germany divorce could be had with or without cause or by the will of either party, but especially of the man. The chief causes cited are bodily defects, crimes, impotency, and sterility.[44]

The general impression from the cases is that divorce has been rather readily attainable, especially by the man, this fact throwing considerable light upon the status of woman; that there is

---

[32] Lowie and Farrand, *sub* "Marriage," in HAI, I.

[33] Beckwith, in *Smithson. Rep.* for 1886, pt. I, 249.

[34] Von Koenigswald, in *Globus*, XCIII, 381.

[35] *Brit.-Guiana*, I, 228, 230-231.

[36] Von den Steinen, *Zent. Bras.*, 332.

[37] Von Martius, *Beiträge*, I, 233, 290.

[38] Maspero, *Hist. Anc.*, I, 736.   [39] Müller, *Hammurabi*, 128.

[40] Deut., XXIV, 1.

[41] Matt., V, 32; XIX, 9; Mark, X, 11; Luke, XVI, 18; I Cor., VII, 10-11.

[42] Pischon, *Islam*, 9, 10, 13.

[43] Dezobry, *Rome*, III, 17; Rossbach, *Röm. Ehe*, 134-136; Lecky, *Europ. Morals*, II, 306-307.

[44] Grimm, *Rechtsalterth.*, 454; Heusler, *Deut. Privatrecht*, II, 291.

nothing disgraceful about it, in the modern sense, and very little
evidence as to the presence of sexual jealousy; that what is now
known as "incompatibility" has been present from the outset,
although primitive people have used ruder terms for it; and that
the chief considerations deterrent of separation have been those
connected with property and children. When woman was property, of course she had no right to divorce any more than a slave
to manumission. In sum, it might be said that where, in a union,
the parties seem to be getting along satisfactorily as regards the
prime activities of self-maintenance and self-perpetuation, there
is little thought of divorce. Whether it will be permitted when
desired is a further question.

It appears, in a general way, that divorce decreases as societal
organization develops in firmness and integration. It has been seen
that the society at large has an abiding interest in all matrimonial
alliances between its members and that publicity of entrance into
the status of wedlock is secured by the wedding-ceremony.[45] The
more interests there are to be affected by the union of a man and
a woman, the more likely is the code to "place" them publicly in
their new status and, it may now be added, to hold them to it. The
society is not interested in their personal comfort in the relation;
it is deeply concerned, however, in the property-issues that inevitably attend the alliance, including especially that of inheritance.
Where such issues are in question, society cannot be indifferent to
casual termination of matrimonial relations any more than to
casual entrance upon the status. Much ceremonial at the entrance
to wedlock seems to make dissolution more difficult. It is significant that where informal consorts may be freely repudiated, the
wife of ceremony may not. Divorce does not demand the publicity
of the wedding; that is reserved for re-marriage. So far as the
termination of a union goes, it carries no such consequences as its
initiation. The children already born are "placed" in the matter
of their station and rights, and if the woman has further offspring
that is another affair. It is characteristic of any intensifying code
that it contemplates the settlement of issues once for all; the
presumption is that individuals will stay placed and not be rest-
lessly and irresponsibly moving about into new relationships, en-

45 §369, above.

tailing by such shiftings various dislocations in the societal order. And the more complicated and delicately adjusted that order becomes, as it develops to cover the progressively enlarged and increasingly interrelated network of individual and group-interests, the more must it subtract from personal freedom in the matter of deserting at will any specified station in life, to which formal assignment of the individual has been made. In general, then, the dissolution of wedlock through divorce appears to grow more difficult as the societal organization develops.

§393. Divorce as an Adjustment. Divorce can be viewed as an adjustment in the marriage-relation whereby the stringency of the latter is somewhat relieved. It has been pointed out that the human tendency in regulating anything has been first to tighten up and then to relax; to oscillate between a strictness that could not be borne and a laxness that has allowed the development of conditions that could not be tolerated.[46] There is plenty of truth in this estimate of human tendency and doubtless the history of divorce could be used to illustrate it. What interests us here is, first of all, that divorce is a relaxation of the restrictions surrounding the sex-relation. If carried to an extreme, it brings us back at once to something like monandry:[47] temporary and shifting relations between man and woman. It is nearly as capable, carried to the extreme, of neutralizing whatever has been built up in the course of society's evolution in the way of marriage and the family as is "free love" or the "socializing" of women. "Divorce," concludes one writer[48] who has collected voluminous modern instances of its terms and extension, "means the disintegration of the home and family. Upon these the State must rest, and without them it cannot flourish."

In general, when two persons wish to be divorced it means that they find the status into which they have entered not corresponding to their previous ideas or lack of ideas about it; or, perhaps more commonly, they do not find their mates in the relation what they had thought or imagined that they would be. All these things cannot be foreseen before marriage; there is always present a

[46] §340, above.   [47] §345, above.
[48] Snyder, *Geog. of Marriage,* 167.

considerable element of chance; but some of them can be. Certain of the qualities desirable in marriage have been objects of verification prior to marriage.[49] Others of them come to the test in courtship, though that period, where it exists, is too full of romance and imagination to allow of much sound judgment. Marriages seem to be about as satisfactory and stable, on the whole, where older and cooler heads make the arrangements; they take care that some, at least, of the material essentials are provided for.

Though it is impossible for the young, in any age, to know just what they are getting into when they enter matrimony, they can know one basic fact: that no human relation whatsoever is livable, not to say happy, unless those who share it are prepared to adjust themselves daily in ways that limit their personal freedom. If men are to fling out of an association in disgust the first time their interests are crossed, no human relations can be lasting or productive. The marriage-connection is simply the most intimate and delicate of all human relationships. There is in it more chance to wound as well as more chance to confer happiness; and the more sensitive and highstrung the mates in marriage the more those chances are multiplied. The best-disciplined spirits have seldom found the marriage-system of their time too stringent, so that they have demanded release by divorce.

Undisciplined characters, impatient of any restriction, are the ones who are always calling, by deed if not by word, for relaxation or "freedom." But it is by laying reins upon natural impulse that we have got ahead at all. Only by restriction has the institution of marriage, as well as other institutions, been formed and developed; only by adjustments of interests within the institution —by antagonistic coöperation, not by dissolving it—has success in living been attained.[50] There is no practicable liberty except liberty with responsibility and under law.[51] It is for this reason that divorce has always been a danger to the marriage-institution and also to the state. Its necessity varies inversely with the amount of knowledge available and utilized in contracting matrimony; thus it is a sort of reflection of the aleatory element.[52] Where people, like many of the savages, do the best they know how to avoid ill, divorce is an automatic allowance for a margin of

49 §365, above.   50 §340, above.
51 Sumner, Coll. Ess., II, 109 ff.   52 §195, above.

error that is inevitable. It is dangerous to mistake what is by its nature exceptional and corrective, for something positive and creative. The creative thing is knowledge of evolutionary processes, together with such adjustment to them through the deliberate curtailment of individual freedom that the making of allowances, like divorce, is reduced to the minimum. Dissolution of wedlock as an allowance for inevitable error is doubtless salutary in special cases; but divorce as a means of easily escaping the consequences of flightiness of mind, or of securing freedom from institutional restriction upon individual desire, leads back toward the crude stages from which, with pain and toil, we have emerged.

§394*. Widowhood. Marriage as an institution is, like property, the state, and other institutions, as long of life as is the race; but for the individual participants the inevitable dissolution of the marriage-relation, so far as human knowledge goes, comes with death. Marriages of the unborn and of the dead[53] are based upon notions which cannot be subjected to scientific test. Though in itself this form of dissolution is obviously no topic for discussion, the mores that have developed as to the status of the party surviving the disrupted relationship are significant of much. Perhaps the most telling aspect of the cases now to be cited is that they have to do almost exclusively with the widow. The death of the wife is an incidental matter, as it appears, compared to that of the husband; and the provisions as to the behavior and destiny of the survivor leave the man, for the most part, out of account. Almost never is he forced to accompany his wife to the spirit-world; he mourns but little; he is not much limited in the matter of a second marriage. His lot, in short, is not materially changed by the event; while the status of the widow is a sort of unique affair, needing definition of all sorts. Any such sharp distinction cannot but throw light upon the general status of woman. We shall first dispose of evidence as to the widower and then turn to the main case.

The Papuan widower must dye his hair black the rest of his life, and may not paint his face in bright colors, as hitherto. "But the worst thing for him is that henceforth he may no longer enjoy the best thing the Papuan table offers, namely, pork—not even after his re-marriage."[54] Again, he must cut off

[53] §342, above.   [54] Hagen, *Papua's*, 263.

his hair and blacken his whole skin, wear his dead wife's ornaments strung around his neck and her petticoat draped beneath his right arm.[55] His second marriage is, in New Britain, a very unpleasant affair for him. The female relatives of his wife fall upon his house, fences, plantations, and other property, and destroy them as far as possible, while he looks on helpless. The only attainable explanation is that "the women are angry on account of his first wife" and do not care to see her labor go to benefit the second.[56] In New Georgia a widower may marry again, provided that his late wife's mother is not alive; similarly with a widow, but not if the mother of her former husband is still living.[57]

On the Andaman Islands, "it is by no means unusual for a man, even though he be young at the time of his wife's death, to remain a widower for her sake for many years, or even till death. . . . It must, however, be admitted that as their customs allow of a widow or widower consorting with the unmarried of the opposite sex, a single life is not of necessity a virtuous one, or evidence of constancy and devotion to the memory of the dear departed."[58] In the Mentawei Islands "it is only allowed to widowers to marry again with widows, and vice versa."[59]

If an Eskimo wife dies, her husband must throw the skin, blubber, bones, and entrails of the first seal he catches into the sea; he may take the meat only.[60] Among the Natchez it was a law that every man who had married a girl of noble blood must be put to death as soon as she had expired.[61] This is a case, like many others cited or to be cited, where the deference paid is to the rank rather than to the sex. In the Homeric age, "re-marriage of men was rare, and only one step-mother is mentioned."[62] A more modern case of the widower's disability is where no "digamus" or husband of a second wife was admissible to holy orders; marriage after taking orders was strictly forbidden to the widower.[63]

When we come to the case of the widow, we encounter a series of prescriptions that clearly exhibit woman as an attachment of man rather than an independent person. If he is going to need her in the future life, it is frequently the practice to kill her or for her to commit suicide; if she survives, her mourning for him is protracted and painful. There is no reciprocal obligation worthy of mention. The woman is so plainly the man's property, his characteristic possession, that ghost-fear is to the fore and, until she is somehow detached from him, no one dares to have much to do with her. No such feeling is exhibited with respect to the widower, who, as a rule, mourns but briefly if at all and may re-marry at once or soon. The fear of a widow's influence for ill is not the fear of her

[55] Guise, in JAI, XXVIII, 211.   [56] Danks, in JAI, XVIII, 292.
[57] Somerville, in JAI, XXVI, 407.   [58] Man, in JAI, XII, 138.
[59] Pleyte, in Globus, LXXIX, 26.   [60] Boas, in BAE, VI, 615.
[61] Yarrow, in BAE, I, 187.
[62] Homer, Iliad, XXII, 477; V, 389; Keller, Hom. Soc., 227.
[63] Lea, Sacerd. Celib., 35, 36.

as a woman but as a dead man's relict, who may, as her husband's possession, allure him back to take vengeance upon his successor. The fear in question is therefore not of the living but of the dead. The widow is not only avoided and segregated but also maltreated. Her own choice of death, which she may gladly embrace, is often one between misery here or a continuance of her honorable wifely status by the side of her husband in the beyond.[64] Some cases of widow-sacrifice appear under the topic of the grave-escort.[65]

Main's *Religious Chastity* comes near to being a treatise on the widow. It cites many instances of widow's mourning and has an especially full chapter on "the haunted widow," showing how her deceased husband follows her up and does injury both to her and to his successor, if she marries. There is much on the immolation of widows and on their service in shrines as a substitute for such human sacrifice. The widow becomes a priestess. The argument moves from this point to the marriage of virgins with gods and to the wife-priestess or consort of the god, all of which is connected with religious prostitution and leads up to the idea of the sealing of women to the deity in chastity and virginity. An appendix contains numbers of cases in addition to those of the text.

In New Guinea, "if the husband dies, the widow usually goes back to her relations. Again, the widow, after the death of her husband and with her own consent, is strangled by her own relatives and buried with her departed."[66] In Fiji widows are strangled because a god lies in wait on the road to the spirit-world who is implacable to ghosts of the unmarried. Hence a male ghost must have a female ghost with him. The woman's brother strangles her with a cord that her husband's relatives leave on a piece of land, which thus becomes his. The dead wife is provided for by having her husband's beard, which he cuts off, put under her arm, as a proof that she is married.[67] The New Hebrides widows also were strangled, unless, as often, they committed suicide. They desired to die, for if they lived they would be despised; dying, they would, as they think, live on with their husbands. The son or other nearest relatives of the deceased perform the act.[68] In the Solomon Islands the strangling was done with a tissue of spider's web.[69] In West Africa, "formerly, in many tribes one or more of the widows were put to death, either that the dead might not be without companionship in the spirit world, or as a punishment for not having cared better for him in the preservation of his life."[70] Westermarck[71] cites many cases in Africa, America, and elsewhere; in one survivalistic instance the widow must lie on the funeral-pyre until the fire is lighted and the heat becomes unbearable.

The classic land for this type of human sacrifice is India, whence comes the term "suttee" or "good-wife." "The burning of widows begins rather late in India, and probably was confined at first to the pet wife of royal persons. It was then claimed as an honor by the first wife, and eventually without real

[64] Lippert, *Kgchte.*, II, 277.   [65] §229, above.
[66] Krieger, *Neu-Guinea*, 174.   [67] Fison, in JAI, X, 138.
[68] Ella, in AAAS, 1892, 628; Lawrie, in AAAS, 1892, 709.
[69] London *Morning Post*, Dec. 28, 1898, reproduced in JAI, XXVIII, 343.
[70] Nassau, *Fetichism*, 9.   [71] *Marriage*, I, ch. IX.

authority, and in fact against early law, became the rule and sign of a devoted wife. The practice was abolished by the English in 1829 [though it lasted on for some time thereafter]; but, considering the widow's present horrible existence, it is questionable whether it would not be a mercy to her and to her family to restore the right of dying and the hope of heaven, in the place of the living death and actual hell on earth in which she is entombed today."[72] If it did start with the noble families, it is a striking exhibition of fashion coming down from the initiation by the rich and powerful.[73]

In China, "since the beginning of our era, cases of widows destroying themselves in order to avoid being re-married, appear in the books in gradually increasing numbers. Evidently, from that time forth, the maxim, nowadays generally received as gospel, viz: 'As a faithful minister does not serve two lords, neither may a faithful woman marry a second husband,' has been a predominant principle of life. The astounding number of instances of such Sutteeism are regularly interspersed with others of betrothed girls, who took their lives to preserve their chastity on behalf of deceased future husbands with whom they had never enjoyed the pleasures of matrimonial life, nay, whose faces they had never yet beheld. . . . Sutteeism of widowed wives and brides has continued to flourish in China down to this day. Now as ever it meets with the same public applause; the aureola which covers the victim and her family is as eagerly coveted as it was in former ages. Hence, no doubt, many a woman is prevailed upon, nay compelled, by her own relations to become a suttee. There are but few Chinamen who cannot relate some case which has occurred of late years in their neighborhood."[74] Doubtless the Chinese cases have got a little away from the genuinely primitive motive but their connection with it is not to be mistaken.

Of a Maori widow it is said that "her proper course was to strangle herself."[75] Among the Natchez Indians and in Guatemala there was a practice of burning the widow on the pyre of the dead husband.[76] "Of the wives of the Caribs of the Antilles, the Darien and Peruvian savages, and of those of the Inca and the more eminent chiefs it is reported that, after the death of their husbands, they had to let themselves be buried alive with the corpses; but this is said to have happened only exceptionally and at their own choice."[77] In the Greek mythical period the wife often followed the husband to the grave, a custom shared by Thracians, Germans, Slavs, and others.[78]

Mourning in its ethnographical manifestations is, as we have seen,[79] formal and ritual, involving taboos of various description. It is protective for the survivors and especially for those closely connected with the dead. The intimacy of the relation of man and wife, and in particular the fact that the wife has often been the

---

[72] Hopkins, *Relig. Ind.*, 274.
[73] Jolly, in *Grundr. Indo-Ar. Philol.*, II, Heft 8, pp. 67-69.
[74] DeGroot, *Relig. Syst.*, II, 745, 747-748.
[75] Tregear, in JAI, XIX, 104.   [76] Brinton, *Myths*, 239-240.
[77] Von Martius, *Beiträge*, I, 124-125.
[78] Becker-Hermann, *Charikles*, III, 289; Weinhold, *Deut. Frauen*, II, 9.
[79] §§218, 221 ff., above.

characteristic and most intimate property of the husband, causes to devolve upon her an especial duty in this respect in event of the husband's death.[80] It will be noted also that she is thought to be rendered "unclean," that is, dangerous to others, by reason of her connection with the dead—a notion that works out into a roughness of treatment and a peculiar misery of life and status almost unparalleled except in the cases of lepers and other specifically "unclean" unfortunates.

In some parts of Australia widows are not allowed to speak for sometimes as long as a year; they communicate by gesture-signs.[81] Again, the widow smears herself with mud and sleeps beside a smoldering smoke. This is a form of exorcism, and a smoke must be made by her every time a stranger comes to camp. Should a woman be left a widow two or three times there rise sinister whisperings about her; she has a "white heart" and no one can expect to live long with such a woman.[82] In some tribes widows do not eat any female animals or only such animals as climb trees.[83] In New Guinea the widow wears mourning-garb all her life, whether she soon marries again or not; she must watch her husband's grave for a time, smear herself with a disfiguring substance, and otherwise indicate her condition.[84] She must stay with the corpse for a time, not leaving the house and having her wants attended to from without.[85] She must shave her head, blacken her body, and wear her husband's lower jaw-bone attached to her neck;[86] or she must carry his skull about with her during her widowhood.[87]

In Africa she does not leave the house during the time of mourning, paints herself red, shaves her head, and lays aside all clothing. Before being freed from these restrictions she is sprinkled with fetish-water. The period of mourning is, in one case, sixteen days.[88] Again, for six weeks, she may eat no beans, meat, or fish, and drink no palm-oil or rum. If she does, her husband will come and take her to the other world. She must be on guard against him for the whole period. "As a sign of mourning she goes about with head sunk and eyes cast down, and crosses her arms over her breast so that the left hand rests on the right shoulder, that 'no harm come to her through the dead.' Also she always carries with her a club to drive off the dead man in case he wants to approach her, for that would infallibly be her end. She even sleeps on the club, for otherwise the dead could take it away without her noticing it. When she 'eats and drinks, she first puts several coals upon the food and drink' to prevent her husband 'from eating and drinking with her, whereby she would die.'" She may answer no call but may smoke. She has at night a fire on which she stews something that makes an evil odor, to keep off the dead.[89]

[80] See Révéscz, in *Ztsft. Vergl. Rechtswiss.*, XV, 361, on the mourning-time for widows.

[81] Spencer and Gillen, *Nat. Tr. Cent. Aust.*, 500, 501.

[82] Parker, *Euahlayi*, 93-94.   [83] Palmer, in JAI, XIII, 298, 299.

[84] Hagen, *Papua's*, 262-263.   [85] Von Pfeil, *Südsee*, 79.

[86] Guise, in JAI, XXVIII, 211.   [87] Haddon, in JAI, XIX, 307.

[88] Klose, *Togo*, 301; Klose, in *Globus*, LXXXI, 190.

[89] Seidel, in *Globus*, LXXII, 22, and LXXIII, 357.

It is common, if not usual, in Tibet, for a widow to shave her head and become a nun. This custom obtains also among the Mongols.[90] A Korean widow wears mourning all her life. It has not been correct for a widow to re-marry, but the custom came to be tolerated and at length she got the right to re-marry.[91] "For a widow or a woman who has been divorced the bride-price is only half the standard amount, the idea being . . . that such women are only borrowed goods and must be given back to their first husbands in the next world."[92]

In Indonesia the widow must mourn in seclusion, without ornaments, and often disfigured.[93] If a widow re-marries before the last rites at the spirit-feast, "she is fined by the relatives of the deceased, for this is a slight upon his memory. The amount of the fine is just the same as if he were still alive and she had abandoned him for another; and her new husband is fined at the same time for seduction."[94] For months or even years, until the periodic festival of the dead, the Dyak widow must wear mourning-clothes, white first and then black, and cover the head.[95] Self-mutilation in mourning is found in Tahiti, and in the Gilbert Islands the widow stays close to the corpse for a considerable time, later carrying the skull about with her the rest of her life.[96]

Eskimo widows may not for six months taste of unboiled flesh, may wear no pigtails, and must cut off a portion of their hair; but they are not limited in their relations with the men.[97] In the Columbia River district, the widow carries the bones of her husband for some years. She is treated as a slave and all the laborious duties fall to her. She must obey the other women and even the children and the slightest mistake means heavy punishment. She must weed about her husband's grave with her fingers, while being cruelly beaten by her husband's relatives. To avoid this complicated cruelty she often commits suicide. If she endures three or four years, she is eulogized as a faithful widow and relieved of her miseries. Few women wish to risk a second widowhood. A reminder of the dead husband, made of rags or furs, is carried about by the widow in several Indian tribes.[98] Among the Sioux, "on the death of the husband the widow scarified herself, rubbed her person with clay, and became careless about her dress for a year. Then the eldest brother of the deceased married her without any ceremony, regarding her children as his own."[99] In California a devoted Indian widow never speaks, on any occasion or pretext, for several months, sometimes a year or more, or, in another district, she speaks in a whisper only. Sometimes the tarred head is the only sign of mourning. "It is only fair to say that the widow is generally more faithful to the memory of her husband than the widower to his wife's, and seldom disgraces human nature by remarrying in a week or two, as he not infrequently does."[100]

Among the Arawaks, at the death of a father of a family "the nearest relations of the dead appear and cut off the hair of his wives. These are also forced to lay aside their clothing during mourning." The hair must attain a

90 Rockhill, in USNM, 1893, 683.　　91 Bishop, *Korea*, 291.
92 Risley, *Ethnog. Ind.*, I, 145.　　93 Lippert, *Kgchte.*, II, 276.
94 Roth, *Sarawak*, I, 130; Roth, in JAI, XXI, 132.
95 Perelaer, *Dajaks*, 108.　　96 Ratzel, *Vkde.*, II, 337, 338.
97 Boas, in BAE, VI, 615.　　98 Yarrow, in BAE, I, 145, 185.
99 Dorsey, in BAE, XV, 232.
100 Powers, in *Contrib. N. Amer. Ethnol.*, III, 327.

certain length before the widows may put on the clothes and put off the widowhood.[101]

§395*. **The Lot of the Widow.** From the foregoing it appears that mourning bears much more heavily on the woman than on the man, and also that the former seems to be censured and held in contempt and fear by reason of the husband's death. For some time after that event she may be visited with neglect or cruelty; to encounter her is a bad omen;[102] and to her lot falls not infrequently a more protracted ill treatment, so that her destiny is one long-drawn-out misery. Not many examples are needed.

"The fate of a widow, on Duke of York at least, is a cruel one, for she becomes common property."[103] In Tibet, "widow" is a term of reproach and abuse; hence the women like polyandry.[104] In India there are twenty-three million widows, of whom two million became such in childhood and have to endure the destiny of widows.[105] The census of 1881 gave almost twenty-one million widows, of whom about six hundred and seventy thousand were under twenty years of age, over two hundred thousand under fourteen, and nearly eighty thousand under nine. The Tamil wife is blamed for the death of her husband, especially if it takes place soon after marriage, as due to a crime or sin committed by her in a former existence. She is pushed about, scorned, cursed, and objurgated, shut up in the inmost rooms, and condemned to sordid labors. "People avoid her glance, and merely to take the word widow in the mouth is regarded as a shame." She may not participate in festivals, least of all in a wedding. "If she is still a child, she must avoid also the games of her playmates. No bite of meat, fish, or candy, no drop of oil may pass her lips any more; two days in the month she must fast altogether and may not take so much as a swallow of water, even if she should lie in fever. And out of this fearful situation there is no escape except in death."[106] "The Indian word for widow is 'vidhva,' and to call a person by this name is considered a very gross abuse. This will show our treatment of widows and their wretched and despicable condition, and how the very word has come to be regarded as a term of reproach and abuse."[107] We have seen that the suttee may be preferable to widowhood. Even the grass-widow is subjected to renunciation of many things. Reforms have attained little success.[108] Among the Veddahs the widow is sexually free, yet is, among the more civilized tribes, the common property of the men.[109] In China, even "with the son of a widow, unless he be of acknowledged distinction, one should not associate himself as a friend."[110]

[101] Schomburgk, *Brit.-Guiana*, I, 227.
[102] §267, above.
[103] Danks, in JAI, XVIII, 292.
[104] Bishop, *Tibet*, 92.
[105] Niehus, in *Globus*, LXXXIX, 248.
[106] Gehring, *Süd-Ind.*, 84, 85, 86.
[107] Nathubhai, in JASB, V, 82; Kipling, *Naulahka*, chs. XIX, XX.
[108] Jolly, in *Grundr. d. Indo-Ar. Philol.*, II, Heft 8, p. 69.
[109] Sarasin, *Weddas*, 472.
[110] Legge, *Li Ki*, I, 78.

In Greenland they may rob a widow of all her husband's goods and cast her out to starve and freeze.[111] A Point Barrow widow who appeared to have no relatives was reduced almost to beggary, though her husband had been quite well-to-do; all his property and even his son were taken from her. But widows who have rich relatives, especially grown sons, are well cared for and often marry again.[112] Among the Indians the widow is likely to fall into misery, being shunned because her husband's ghost cleaves to her. His property is taken from her and no one will give her game because his weapons would not kill thereafter.[113] The Pima widow who has children is not wanted by another husband lest he burden himself with them. An Indian widow generally cultivates a small piece of ground which male friends and relatives plow for her.[114]

The Arabs think all who are connected with the marriage of a widow are ill-omened. For thirty days her new husband will not eat of her provisions or use her eating-vessels at meals.[115]

It is difficult indeed to find in savage life any custom to which there are no exceptions. Against the many cases where the widow's lot is sad and miserable may be set the few of the opposite tenor which have come to our notice.

In northeastern Africa, the widows live alone in their huts, are not recognizable by any mark, and are much freer than other women, especially in sex-relations. Their husbands' offspring remain with them and accompany them on a second marriage.[116] The Saharan Arab women of higher class lead a life devoid of interest or occupation unless they are widows with a minor son.[117] A Turkoman widow costs fifty or even a hundred camels where a girl costs five.[118] The Chinese widow, if she steadfastly refuses to marry again and lives a life of chastity and filial devotion to her parents-in-law, reflects great fame upon the house. "She is treated with much more affability than the other women in the house, and in this wise encouraged to persist in her purpose; indeed, the family know perfectly well that, should she change her mind and not live up to her original vow, they would be greatly dishonored and exposed to public ridicule."[119] In Samoa, widows and orphans are treated with compassion.[120]

In Greenland, where unmarried girls rarely become mothers, divorced and widowed women often do. The latter can sell their children to the childless or are taken in and even married for the children.[121] The widower's second wife must extol her predecessor and disparage herself.[122] In Carolina if an Indian widow has many children, the young men had to do all she could not do on her land.[123] Among the Karayá tribes, the unmarried and widowed of both sexes

[111] Cranz, *Grönland*, I, 232.
[112] Murdoch, in BAE, IX, 414.
[113] Loskiel, *Mission*, 83.
[114] Yarrow, in BAE, I, 99.
[115] Burckhardt, *Bedouins*, 152.
[116] Paulitschke, *Nordost-Afr.*, I, 205.
[117] Pommerol, *Sahariennes*, 396.
[118] Letourneau, *Marr.*, 116.
[119] DeGroot, *Relig. Syst.*, II, 757.
[120] Ella, in AAAS, 1892, 627.
[121] Cranz, *Grönland*, I, 191.
[122] Nansen, *Esk. Life*, 139.
[123] Carr, in *Smithson. Rep.*, 1891, 525.

were supported by the rest, the men in a special house, the women with relatives. The motive is stated to be the maintenance of family-purity.[124]
Among the Ossetes, the widow had the choice between several brothers who
wished to marry her, whereas the girl never had a choice but could avoid a
hated marriage only by suicide.[125] The Anglo-Saxon widow was protected by
legal penalties from any outrage or wrong.[126] In the old German law the
widow had greater independence of action than the unmarried woman.[127] In
Russia she was more independent and in a happier position than the wife; yet
she might be dispossessed by her sons and driven out to beg.[128]

The destiny of the widow offers a special case of property in
women and, in particular, a further extension of the topic of woman as a heritage.[129] When regarded as property and if not sacrificed at the funeral of her husband, the widow is passed over, along
with the rest of his possessions, to his heirs.[130] She naturally becomes the wife of her new owner; since, however, abhorrence of
incest prevents the marriage of mother and son, the widow is quite
commonly married to her deceased husband's brother. This is
known, in one of its forms, as a levirate marriage.[131] It seems to
us not to be a true type of the levirate but a simple case of inheritance. Something has to be done with the widow and she must
generally be under someone's guardianship; she is a species of
family-property and sometimes even of group-property. No such
arrangements are necessary in the case of the widower; it is the
woman's dependence that brings about her subjection and if she
comes under some man's protection or becomes his property, it is
primitive usage that she stands to him as a wife.

In Central Australia the "passing on of the widow to a younger, but never
to an elder, brother real or tribal is a very characteristic feature of these
tribes." If one such brother did not want her, she was simply passed on to
another, her acceptability depending largely on her age.[132] Elsewhere "a
widow is told by her late husband's brother or her mother when she may take
off her mourning, and the brother-in-law is sometimes allowed to marry her,
although he may already have one wife."[133] Among the Papuans of Geelvink

[124] Ehrenreich, in *Berl. Mus. Vkde.,* II, 28.
[125] Von Haxthausen, *Transkaukasia,* II, 53.
[126] Garnier, *Brit. Peasantry,* I, 99.
[127] Stammler, *Stellung d. Frau,* 37; Heusler, *Deut. Privatrecht,* I, 119.
[128] Kostomarov, *Gt. Russians* (Russ.), 154.
[129] §383, above.
[130] Letourneau, *Marr.,* ch. XV; Ratzel, *Vkde.,* II, 433.
[131] §§349, 383, above, and 406, below.
[132] Spencer and Gillen, *North. Tr. Cent. Aust.,* 510.
[133] Bonney, in JAI, XIII, 135.

Bay a brother must take his dead brother's wife; if he wants to marry her, he may; in any case, he must attend most carefully to her support. If the dead man left no brother, the widow goes over to the family of her husband, and they may, as they please, have her enter another marriage and get the bride-price attendant. It is clear that the woman in marriage leaves her tribe and goes over for good into that of her husband. Divorce is therefore impossible; separation occurs only at death.[134] In the Andaman Islands, widows generally marry again when the prescribed term is passed, this being due to a custom "which all but compels a bachelor or widower to propose to a childless widow of his elder brother or cousin . . . while she has no choice beyond remaining single or accepting him; should she have no younger brother-in-law (or cousin by marriage), however, she is free to wed whom she will."[135]

In Matabeleland, a man's widows "usually become his brother's wives, although it is not compulsory on the women; and if they choose they can marry again, but in that case the new husband must pay his father-in-law if a child is born."[136] "Only when a woman has become a widow does the Somal brother-in-law repudiate one of his legitimate wives in order to marry the widow." She may marry only one of her husband's brothers.[137] In West Africa, the deceased man's brothers are supposed to take his wives; if they object to this arrangement they may "leave the family." In Benin, a widow cannot marry without the permission of her son, if she have one; or if he is too young, the man she marries must furnish a female slave to wait on him instead of his mother. "When a man dies, his widows devolve upon his heir, whose wives they become, in name at all events, for it is not incumbent upon him to consummate the union. When a brother succeeds a brother it is more usual for the union to be consummated than when a nephew succeeds an uncle."[138] The curious African case should be recalled where a wife is found for an uneasy ghost but is married to the brother of the deceased.[139] In a great number of Kabyle tribes, the widow remains "hung" to her husband, and makes part of the inheritance; it is his heirs who dispose of her and provide for her needs.[140]

The Ostiak widow goes with her children to the parents of the dead man; "these may marry her off again as their own daughter. If the parents-in-law are dead, the widow goes to her own parents.[141] "At her husband's death the wife is taken over by his brother or nearest relative."[142] Among the Koryak "a widow marries a second husband without ceremony, but before any one takes her as a wife she must have intercourse with some one else, who is usually a stranger, as the fulfilment of the office is rather despised."[143] Thus any ill effects due to her uncleanness will be passed off upon the alien. In some tribes of India the custom prevailed of a widow marrying her deceased husband's brother;[144] among others "a widow can remarry any male member of

---

[134] Wilken, in VG, I, 359.　　　　[135] Man, in JAI, XII, 138.

[136] Decle, in JAI, XXIII, "Miscellanea," 84.

[137] Paulitschke, Nordost-Afr., I, 196, 205.

[138] Ellis, Ewe, 205; Letourneau, Marr., 313.

[139] §228, above; Hobley, in JAI, XLI, 422.

[140] Hanoteau et Letourneux, Kabylie, II, 156-157.

[141] Kondratowitsch, in Globus, LXXIV, 289.

[142] Prjevalski's Forskningsresor, 139.

[143] Czaplicka, Aborig. Siberia, 89.

[144] Godden, in JAI, XXVII, 28; Watt, in JAI, XVI, 355.

her husband's division except her husband's brother or his son. . . . A re-marriage must take place during a dark night."[145] Among the Saoras a widow is never turned out of her husband's family if she has a child and probably never if she has none. She is considered bound to marry her husband's brother or his brother's sons if he has no younger brothers.[146]

Among the Alfurs of Buru the widow falls to the husband's clan, any member of which has the right to marry her without bride-price; the preference is given to the nearest relative, who is generally the oldest brother of the deceased. If she should marry into another kin-group, her husband's kin would get a bride-price. In southern Sumatra, this marriage with a brother of the deceased is regular; the woman is a mere piece of property, to be passed on like any other. This is the theory; in the course of time it has been somewhat modified in practice. If the widow can repay the bride-price, she may go back to her parental kin-group, though she must leave her children behind. Again, she may sometimes marry again outside the husband's kin-group, on condition of repayment of her bride-price and relinquishment of any claim on the children. If they are too young to bear separation, they remain with her for the time being; when they are old enough to leave her, she is paid a sum for rearing them. The author quoted[147] reports that "among the peoples who have exogamy and the patriarchate we find it the rule that the wife, at the death of her husband rightfully and without any formality of marriage becomes the wife of one of his surviving brothers . . . but not seldom it is the son of another marriage who lays claim to the widow; that is, the step-son to his step-mother. As a heritage the woman falls therefore to the heirs of the husband, who naturally marry her without bride-price." "Among the Sumatrans, with or without children, the brother, or nearest male relation of the deceased, unmarried (the father excepted), takes the widow. This is practiced both by the Malays and country people. The brother, in taking the widow to himself, becomes answerable for what may remain due of her purchase money, and in every respect represents the deceased."[148] On the northwest American coast whoever inherits the property must marry the widow or, if married, pay indemnity to her relatives. If there is no male relative to marry her or if the indemnity is paid she may marry another.[149] In one Central American tribe, the widow belongs to the husband's relatives, and to marry again must pay them "widow-money." If she dies soon after marriage, her husband may reclaim the price he paid.[150] In the Inca empire, if a woman's husband died, "she became the wife of one of his brothers or she remained with that one of her sons who inherited the hacienda, assuming in respect to him a thoroughly subordinate position. The son was in every respect the master of his mother, "for she belonged, as a purchase, to her husband's estate."[151]

The case of Penelope, in the Odyssey, is a significant one, too complicated to be treated here in full.[152] But it may be noted that there were no husband's brothers in the family and that the supposed widow's son was master

[145] Scott, in JASB, IV, 363.   [146] Fawcett, in JASB, I, 231.
[147] Wilken, in VG, I, 46-47; II, 239-240; Wilken, *Vkde.*, 326, 327.
[148] Marsden, *Sumatra*, 260-261; 228-229.
[149] Niblack, in USNM, 1888, 254.
[150] Bancroft, *Nat. Races*, I, 731, 549, 277.
[151] Cunow, *Verf. Inkareichs*, 84, 85.
[152] Keller, *Hom. Soc.*, 222 ff., where full references are given.

of herself and the house; that he feared to send his mother away against her will, not only because the gods might be displeased but also because he would have to pay the fine due her father in such case. He had the power to give her in marriage and begged her to go, offering to give rich gifts with her. She put off her suitors by stratagem, striving to "do honor" to husband and son, and emerged a synonym for wifely faithfulness.

There is to be considered, finally, the re-marriage of the widow. The cases where that is not allowed at all, including of course all those of suttee or similar practice, are comparatively rare and not so primitive. In general, the re-marriage may come only after the completion of mourning, that is, after the ghost of the former husband has been laid; only then is union with the relict at all safe, and the ceremony is generally one with special features not present in the case of a girl.[153] If mourning is continued after the new marriage, it is doubtless, like some of the features of regular nuptials, in the nature of disguise or other precaution.[154] The following examples of re-marriage should enforce the evidence of preceding pages as to the widow's destiny.

In Victoria a widow with her children is supported till she can be exchanged for a young woman of another tribe. No sentiment is allowed to interfere; she is obliged to mate with the man chosen for her by her protector; "and though this mode of disposing of her may appear cruel and harsh, it is surely more humane than that neglect which a poor widow in a civilized country is sure to suffer." Again, after the mourning is over, childless widows are offered as wives, first to the husband's brothers, then to his first cousins; if, however, the widows have children, it is optional on their part whether they marry again.[155] Almost no widow-marriages take place among the Tamils of India; they are heavily penalized, the rationalized reason given being to hold open to all girls the chance of getting a husband.[156] It is stated that widow-marriage is at war with Hindu religion, not because the women married are widows but because the reformer-advocates of widow-marriage persist in trying to use a ceremony reasonable only for a first marriage; and details are cited.[157]

In Atjeh the widow may re-marry provided that, if pregnant, she shall wait till her confinement is past. The child belongs to her husband's family. Even if she is not pregnant, she must wait four months and ten days, though she may, during that time accept another man and go forward with arrangements. This period was prescribed by the Prophet,[158] in order to make sure, in case she might be pregnant, of the child's paternity. As a rule Atjeh women seldom re-marry so soon and are never forced. If a widow has a son of age, that is, fifteen or sixteen years old, he is his mother's guardian and she may not marry without his permission. Any man, married or unmarried, who is caught secretly

153 Main, *Relig. Chastity*, Appendix, note x.
154 §225, above.   155 Smyth, *Vict.*, I, 97.
156 Gehring, *Süd-Indien*, 78; Holtzmann, *Ind. Sagen*, II, 56-57.
157 Nathubhoy, in JASB, VI, 356.   158 Pischon, *Islam*, 10.

courting a widow or repudiated wife, is forced to marry her.[159] Re-marriages of widows, though not of widowers, have always been more or less stigmatized in China,[160] and various devices have been put into practice to restrain them and to reward continency.[161]

In British Columbia an Indian widow or widower "invariably takes another spouse within three months." The Tlinkits recognize a widow's right to support against the kin-group. Her husband's brother or his sister's son is bound to marry her; if neither is available, she may choose another man out of the kin-group of the deceased.[162] An Omaha widow must wait from four to seven years to re-marry, both out of respect to her husband's memory and also in order to wean her child if she has had one by him. Disregard of this restriction would lead to severe punishment at the hands of his relatives. Men used to wait the same time before re-marrying or else lose their ponies at the hands of the deceased's kindred; but now they do not wait over two years, and the women's period is shortened.[163] In one tribe of British Guiana the widow and children are the property of the brother or nearest relative; if the widow resists, after being thoroughly beaten she gets her freedom to choose whom she will. In a similar case the Arawak widow must buy herself off.[164]

A number of rules for widows entering wedlock, which set the case of the widow apart from that of the virgin, were in practice in Scandinavia.[165] The whole subject of second marriages has been covered, chiefly for other than primitive societies, by Jolly.[166] Westermarck[167] gives an important list of peoples who, together with practising only monogamy or but rarely polygyny, prohibit speedy re-marriage, not only of widows but also of widowers. Consideration of this correlation between two practices must be postponed until plural and single marriage have been reviewed, in the following chapter.

These cases of re-marriage of a widow serve to sharpen the impression, which has been taking form through this chapter, of the difference of treatment accorded to man and to woman in the event of the dissolution of wedlock. In general, it is the man who may repudiate the woman and who has to be restrained by property-considerations from so doing, whereas it is the woman who must bear the burdens incident to the dissolution of marriage by death. She must immolate herself or mourn miserably for a protracted time; as a widow she is regarded as disposable property or as a sort of culpable outcast. The death of a wife entails upon the man but a shadowy semblance of this destiny. Her re-marriage is hedged about with burdensome prescriptions and proscriptions

[159] Jacobs, *Groot-Atjeh*, I, 96-97, 225.
[160] Legge, *Li Ki*, I, 439, note.
[161] Medhurst, in *Trans. China Br., Roy. Asiat. Soc.*, IV, 18, 19.
[162] Grosse, *Familie*, 76. [163] Dorsey, in BAE, III, 267-268.
[164] Schomburgk, *Brit.-Guiana*, II, 447, 460.
[165] *Annaler f. Norsk Oldkyndighed*, 1849, 210-211.
[166] *Des Seconds Mariages*. [167] *Marriage*, I, ch. IX.

of various sorts, while he may contract another union with very little trouble. In order to fill out a true conception of woman's status and rights, it is necessary to annex the impression gained from this chapter to the conception of woman's status as summed up in the preceding ones.

CHAPTER LIII

PLURAL AND PAIR-MARRIAGE

§396. Numerical Limitation; the Status-Wife. The sense of the marriage-institution as an adjustment to conditions of life, and in particular to the condition of bi-sexuality, appears in all varieties of union; for in them all exists the coöperation of the sexes in self-maintenance and self-perpetuation. Preceding chapters have dealt with the questions as to who may marry, how marriage is accomplished, and in what manner rights are distributed in the relation. It has not been necessary to specify whether marriage is of this or that type as respects the number and sex-proportion of the spouses. Limitation set upon utter unregulation results primarily in monandry, whereby one man and one woman remain attached to each other for a brief season;[1] but the common limitation is one involving both numbers and time: polyandry, where one woman has several husbands, polygyny, where one man has several wives, and monogamy, where one husband has one wife —all of these forms differing from monandry in that they are institutional and at least relatively permanent. They involve ties that may not be lightly severed, for separation demands at least a minimal form of divorce or repudiation—some sort of reversal of the status publicly signalized by the wedding-ceremony, slight though the latter may have been.

Numerical limitation of spouses is analogous to the other types of limitation by which, as has been seen,[2] the institution of marriage has been formed. Restriction of the number of wives per man gives polyandry; that of the number of husbands per woman, polygyny; while restriction on both sides results in monogamy. It is now in place to review these three stock forms of mating in order to see in what respects they represent, within the general institution of marriage, adjustments to special life-conditions.

But before coming to that, it is advisable to get clearly in mind just what is meant by the term "wife." The fact that we do not need to trouble ourselves over the term "husband" is significant

[1] §345., above.   [2] §§347 ff., above.

of much respecting the status of woman. It is so seldom that a woman has more than one regular male consort that there is little object in seeking to distinguish between them. Under genuine monogamy the term "wife" is clearly understandable. Misconceptions rise chiefly where there is a multiplicity of "wives," that is, under polygyny; the ambiguity is general enough, however, to call for some clarification.

In brief, the "wife" is the consort of status; all the rest are mere consorts, relations with whom are incidental. The status-wife is the wife of ceremony and publicity; it is she who costs the bride-price or brings the dowry, that is, whose station is stabilized by the passage of property;[3] it is her children only who inherit, for she is the sole selected and publicly avowed agency for carrying on the family-line. In East Africa she is never the wife of more than one man, and through her the purity of the family and clan must be preserved.[4] She may or may not be the love-wife; for love is incidental to wedlock and is perhaps more likely to traverse the marriage-relation than otherwise. The love-wife, in any case, has none of the dignity that pertains to the status-wife, first wife, wife of ceremony, chief-wife, head-wife, or whatever else that consort may be called whose status is institutional.

One illustration may be cited here, by way of fixing this distinction for the time being and until, under the topic of monogyny,[5] it receives further definition. In Homer, "perhaps the clearest case of the distinction between head-wife and concubine lies in the Chryseis-Briseis episode. Agamemnon had a head-wife and Achilles expected one. Entirely apart from these conditions came the fondness for the captive of war, as if affection and marriage were quite distinct; the beloved captive was compared with the wife in a way which showed no real affection for the latter. Achilles's tenderness for Briseis has occasioned rhapsodies by those who forget that after all Briseis was no wife. It is clear, however, that in the home-land all the attributes of wife that would imply more than mutual tenderness would go to the ceremonially bought wives; they were recognized and sanctioned organs for the production of a line of descent and property-inheritance."[6]

This distinction, present in only a very small degree as between male consorts, should be borne in mind throughout the review of plural marriage.

3 §341, above.
4 Dundas, C., in JAI, XLV, 290.   5 §400, below.
6 Keller, *Hom. Soc.*, 218-219, where references to text are given.

§397*. Polyandry. As a form of plural marriage, polyandry is about as rare as the group-marriage with which it is connected by some writers.[7] It is not correct to speak of an occasional instance of ceremonial sex-relations between one woman and a number of men as polyandry,[8] though it may be a survival of that system. In reviewing the following cases it should be realized that nothing deserves the name of polyandry that is not at least a settled practice. It is also to be noted that when observers refer polyandry to a desire to keep down population, that does not mean that there exists a "population-policy."[9] Primitive people least of all think in terms of a society. In so far as polyandry is an expedient for checking population, it is numbers within a very local area that are the object of attention; even more likely is it that several men simply foresee that they cannot all have wives because they cannot afford them and so fall upon the expedient of sharing one wife. This adjustment to local and personal circumstances is far from being a population-policy.

There are a number of isolated instances where a woman has several mates, which could be added to somewhat by exhaustive search.[10] They amount to very little, in our judgment, and have been listed[11] chiefly to indicate just that. We cite but one instance.

"In Uganda polyandry is practised by two women only—the dowager queen . . . and the queen sister. These women had as many husbands as they chose, though they never went through any marriage ceremony, nor might they have children by them. Of these two women it is commonly said all Uganda is their husband; they appear to be fond of change, only living with a man for a few days and then inviting some one else to take his place."[12] Evidently this is no form of marriage.

Such instances would probably by themselves have led to no great amount of theorizing; the fact is that they have been assembled, by various theorists, for the most part because of their resemblance to conditions observed in Tibet, in parts of India, and in Arabia. These classic cases should be before us.[13]

[7] §346, above; Kohler, *Urgchte. d. Ehe*, 144; Zenker, *Gesellsft.*, I, 50; Starcke, *Prim. Fam.*, 138.

[8] Howitt, in JAI, XX, 62.   [9] §402, below.

[10] List in Zenker, *Gesellsft.*, I, 38, note; Achelis, *Entwickl. d. Ehe*, 28 ff.; Peschel, *Races*, 223; Mucke, *Horde*, 133, 134.

[11] *Case-Book*, §397.   [12] Roscoe, in JAI, XXXII, 36.

[13] Starcke, *Prim. Fam.*, ch. II; Westermarck, *Marriage*, III, chs. XXIX, XXX.

In Tibet junior brothers become inferior husbands to the wife of the elder, all the children belonging, however, to the head of the family. "The younger brothers have no authority, they wait upon the elder as his servants, and can be turned out of doors at his pleasure, without its being incumbent upon him to provide for them. On the death of the eldest brother his property, authority, and widow, devolve upon his next brother."[14] Where polyandry is not recognized, since only the eldest brother marries and the younger ones become monks, yet "there is not the least aversion to the idea of two brothers cohabiting with the same woman, and I believe it often happens in an unrecognized way, particularly among the landless classes, who send no sons into the monasteries." "Whatever the origin of polyandry, there is no doubt but that poverty, a desire to keep down population, and to keep property undivided in families, supply sufficient reason to justify its continuance. The same motives explain its existence among the lower castes of Malabar, among the Jats (Sikhs) of the Punjab, among the Todas, and probably in most other countries in which this custom prevails." Polyandry is said to account for the Tibetan's moderate, attentive demeanor toward women.[15] The women cling to polyandry: "they say, 'We have three or four men to help us instead of one' and sneer at the dulness and monotony of European monogamous life! A woman said to me, 'If I had only one husband and he died, I should be a widow.' The word 'widow' is with them a term of reproach and is applied abusively to animals and men."[16]

Cunningham[17] reports one wife for a family of brothers. The number of husbands, usually two, may be three or four. Only the poor practise polyandry; the rich often have two or three wives. But Kawaguchi[18] says that polyandry is prevalent among the higher classes in Lhasa, while free and unceremonious union is quite common among the lower. Prjevalski[19] finds that the rich have separate wives—one or two—and also concubines. There may be as many as seven husbands to one wife, who must, however, be kin, and properly brothers. Economic reasons are given: the Chinese tax each house in which there is a married woman, this making women the basis of taxation if married, while other women pay nothing. Hence the men club together with one wife. The behavior of the women is light; they are eager for money and husbands are often complaisant. Rubruck[20] says that if a woman's husband had no brothers she wore a head-dress with one horn; otherwise she added as many horns as he had brothers. In Tibet the unfruitful condition of the soil causes a dread of a rapid increase of population.[21]

Polyandry is "regarded in this pastoral country as an arrangement to protect the joint-family when its head is away for weeks, herding the cattle; and it is also viewed as a device to keep the common property within the family, in a country which cannot support a large population. Here, in Sikhim, it is usually a *fraternal* polyandry; that is, the conjoint husbands are usually brothers. And the practice is that if the eldest brother marries, his wife is the joint wife of all the brothers; while if the second brother marries, then his

[14] Starcke, *Prim. Fam.*, 134.
[15] Rockhill, in USNM, 1893, 727, 726, 677; Paske, in JAI, VIII, 195 ff.; Rockhill, *Land of the Lamas*, 212 ff.
[16] §395, above; Bishop, *Tibetans*, 92.
[17] *Ladak*, 306.   [18] In *Century Mag.*, XLV, 391.
[19] Zelenin, *Prjevalski* (Russ.), II, 430; Prjevalski's *Forskningsresor*, 217.
[20] *Eastern Parts*, 74.   [21] Starcke, *Prim. Fam.*, 136.

9

wife is common only to the second and younger brothers, and not to the elder.
. . . The children call the eldest of the conjoint brothers their 'father.' The
family relationships are therefore somewhat complicated, especially as it sometimes happens, when some of these ladies are the possessors of half a dozen
husbands."[22] Rivers[23] finds among the Todas great laxity in sexual matters
both before and after marriage. He thinks it may be the result of polyandry.
Sexual laxity tends toward sterility which is perhaps "a reason why polyandry
is so rare a form of marriage. The practice of polyandry must almost inevitably weaken the sentiment of possession on the part of the man which does so
much to maintain the more ordinary forms of marriage."

Among the stock cases of polyandry that of the Nairs is prominent.[24] They
are the ruling caste on the Malabar Coast and are militaristic. Their women
may not marry in a lower caste nor in the same household; "but within these
limits of the caste and the family the greatest liberty in sexual relations prevails." Marriage is for a day, and thereafter the bride "chooses two, four, even
as many a twelve husbands." Each lover remains at her command for twenty-
four hours. No Nair, it is said, knows his paternity. Starcke,[25] who summarizes
these customs, regards them as "final rather than primitive." Risley[26] admits
"that fraternal polyandry once prevailed in Malabar on a noticeable scale and
still prevails to a very small extent in certain parts of the country is not improbable." He protests, however, against tracing the custom to "primitive
bestiality" and launches out upon a general defense of the Nair, concluding
that the polyandry is "probably in most cases an expression of fraternal
benevolence on the part of the eldest brother" and due also to a militarism
that is favored by detachment from family-bonds and cares. In any case, their
peculiar usages are being given up in mortification over the ridicule heaped
upon them by other castes; and they want "a form of permanent marriage,
instead of the present trivial union and inheritance to children for those who
wish to avail themselves of such advantages."[27] "It is a point very keenly debated as to how far polyandry was prevalent among the Nāyars in olden days.
During the last fifty years no trace of such a system has been found. It is to a
certain extent true that there is extreme instability of marriage relationship
among the commoner folk even now. But for a woman to have more than one
husband at a time seems to have been against the moral ideas of the community even two hundred years ago. Nāyar ballads and poetry of that age
contain many passages where polyandry is spoken of as a barbarous and unknown custom. But though strict polyandry does not seem to have existed at
any time, traces of a system of supplementary spouses, very much like the
Pirauru custom among the Australians, exist even now. In the . . . allied
families . . . any woman of the same generation and in the same relationship
as cross-cousin is eligible for marriage, and even if she is married, the young
man whose spouse she might have been has certain rights—not distinctly conjugal, but still pertaining to it. He is the one who avenges her against insults.
Her children call him 'little father,' and he has the right of entering any part

Waddell, *Himalayas*, 197-198; Kipling, *Kim,* ch. XIV.

[23] *Todas,* 531-532.

[24] Starcke, *Prim. Fam.,* 83 ff.; Reclus, *Prim. Folk,* ch. IV; Letourneau,
Marr., 311-312.

[25] *Prim. Fam., * 83-84.   [26] *Ethnog. Ind.,* I, 137.

[27] Mateer, in JAI, XII, 290, 291, 293, 303; Mateer, in JASB, II, 318, 319.

of her apartments. Among the commoner folk a system of conjugal relationship may still exist."[28]

The contention that the Arabs practised fraternal polyandry takes its origin from a passage in Strabo:[29] "All the kindred have property in common, the eldest being lord; all have one wife." "This passage is strong testimony of the existence in Yemen of fraternal polyandry of the Thibetan type. It has recently been confirmed by the testimony of inscriptions brought from the same region. . . . The evidence of this type of marriage for Yemen is therefore indisputable." And the author[30] goes on to rehearse the arguments of Smith[31] for the existence of this type of polyandry in North Arabia. Smith lays much stress upon the levirate[32] as an outgrowth of fraternal polyandry.

Rivers[33] distinguishes the fraternal, or adelphic, polyandry of Tibet and the non-fraternal type of the Nairs, believing, however, that it is doubtful whether the latter should be called polyandry. "The Nayar practice was to a large extent the result of a custom of the Nambutiri Brahmins of the country, who only allow the eldest son of each family to marry, the other sons consorting with Nayar women; but as the children of these unions are Nayars, and stand in no definite social relations with their Nambutiri fathers, it is a question whether the practice should be regarded as marriage, at any rate if we regard marriage as, in its essence, an institution by means of which children are assigned the place which they are to occupy in the social community into which they are born." The fraternal form occurs also among the Todas and occasionally elsewhere in India, among the pastoral Bahima of Africa, and in the Marquesas Islands. It is reported of the ancient Arabs, Britons, and Canary Islanders, but may be only some form of sexual communism. Polyandry has been seen in the levirate-marriage, where a widow may be taken only by a younger brother of the deceased husband; but this levirate-system "is probably nothing more than a means of keeping the care of the children and any property belonging to the wife within the clan or family in one form or another. It is probably only very exceptionally that there is any relation between the levirate and polyandry."

In seeking to generalize upon the evidence presented, we are forced to conclude that it is composed largely of sporadic instances of sex-connection, mere tentatives thrown out as variations on a rather loose system. There are, indeed, no convincing instances of actual marriage between a woman and a second husband while the first is yet alive; all the ceremony there is goes with the original wedding. The additional so-called husbands are always secondary mates without much or any status; as they correspond to authorized concubines, the system seems to be a counterpart of monogyny.[34] However, since in several important cases

28 Panikkar, in JAI, XLVIII, 266.
29 Geog., XVI, ch. IV; Starcke, Prim. Fam., 127.
30 Barton, Semitic Origins, 64 ff.
31 Kinship, 135, 136, 138, 139, 86, 87.   32 §406, below.
33 Soc. Org., 43-44, 81-82.   34 §400, below.

such an arrangement seems to be supported in the mores, it is not reasonable to set polyandry aside forthwith as non-marriage. Particularly in view of the regularity of disposal of the children who are generally assigned according to some definite rule, is it impossible so to dismiss it; though, on that criterion, polyandry would seem to be a form of the family rather than of marriage.

If a number of theorists had not seen in polyandry some reflection, outgrowth, or survival of certain primordial mores, it would probably have been consigned to the category of odd and incidental variations. Thus McLennan[35] thought that in early times polyandry was the rule and monogamy and polygyny exceptions. Several writers regard it as a lineal descendent of group-marriage or even of promiscuity.[36] Smith,[37] like Rivers, distinguishes the two types of polyandry: where the wife receives lovers unrelated to one another and where she acts as consort to a set of brothers, the Nair and Tibetan types respectively. "The custom of the Nairs, which has been so confidently quoted as an undoubted instance of polyandry" is, according to Fison,[38] nothing but the Australian *pirauru*. If so, it is a somewhat limited form of group-marriage. It is as if a woman who had a wedding-ring might make marital arrangements at her own pleasure and bear children without question. Any man who is accepted must enter into an agreement and comply with conditions. No others are accepted. Both types represent, of course, a looser system of sex-relation than genuine monogamy or polygyny, though no looser than that of either of these forms when combined with concubinage—unless, indeed, a system is regarded as looser in that it does not restrain women more than men.

We are always less interested in inference as to origins of societal forms than in demonstration of their degree of expediency as adjustments. If polyandry be viewed in the large, it is readily seen to be unfavorable to the growth of population. To get numbers there must be many mothers. A relatively few males suffice for the production of numbers of infants. It is clear enough that the polyandrous community, unless protected by isolation of some sort, must fail in the competition with more fecund groups. In fact, a group may become polyandrous by reason of being weaker than its neighbors and consequently deficient in women by reason of their woman-stealing. It is obvious that where there is a sex-disproportion in favor of males and not enough women to go round the stress is in the direction of wife-sharing.

These two simple considerations seem to Huntington[39] largely to explain polyandry as it appears in Ladakh, a part of Tibet. It is an adjustment to a

[35] In *Fortnightly Rev.*, XXVII, 703.
[36] Kohler, *Urgchte d. Ehe*, 144; Zenker, *Gesellsft.*, I, 38, 50.
[37] *Kinship*, 122.
[38] In JAI, XXIV, 369; §346, above.   [39] *Pulse of Asia*, 63-64.

peculiar station. "This custom, like the prevalence of monasticism, as several writers have pointed out, is probably due chiefly to the limited amount of land available for cultivation, and to the consequent necessity for restricting population. If two brothers from a family of three have a single wife, and if the other becomes a lama, the entire family heritage of fields can be kept undivided, and a single house will serve for the whole family. But the question at once rises, what becomes of the daughters for whom there can be no husbands under such a system? There do not seem to be any. For some unexplained reason, girls appear to be less numerous than boys, as I was told by Dr. Shawe, an English physician, who has lived for years in Leh as a missionary. He knew of no cause, such as female infanticide, which could account for the anomaly." Strange cases of sex-disproportion occasionally occur. In the New Hebrides, according to a French settler of twelve years' standing, "a village near his place which he can once remember with fifty or sixty inhabitants now [1893] contains only nineteen of which but two are women."[40]

"Geographically," Huntington goes on, "the institution of polyandry is most interesting as a unique response to straitened physical conditions. In Ladakh the means of supporting life are scanty, and there is no opportunity to increase the amount of cultivated land, or the number of flocks. In most such lands the population increases until the pinch of want is felt, whereupon emigration ensues. In Ladakh the growth of population has been limited by the two peculiar institutions of polyandry and monasticism. Hence in a region where we should expect frequent movement of part of the inhabitants, there is the opposite condition of great fixity. Objectionable as both polyandry and monasticism are to modern western ideas, some method of limiting population seems to be a necessity in a land where opportunities are so restricted, and migration to unoccupied lands is so difficult. In Baltistan, just west of Ladakh, where physical conditions are similar, these institutions were overthrown some centuries ago by the introduction of Mohammedanism. Hence the people are constantly becoming too numerous, and the poorer ones are compelled to migrate to the most unproductive, and therefore heretofore unoccupied, corners of the regions round about them." And to the case of Tibet, as a region of destitution, might be added that of Arabia: "Down to the present time the nomads of Arabia suffer constantly from hunger during a great part of the year."[41]

Westermarck[42] generalizes to the effect that the chief polyandrous peoples live in sterile mountain regions, that is, in isolation.[43] "The dispersion or the aggregation of individuals and the proportion of the sexes in the species surely play the chief rôle in the production of promiscuity, monogamy, or polygamy. The conjugal form which has best assured the reproduction of the species, which is best adapted to circumstances of habitat, rivalries to be sustained, and other conditions—that useful form has necessarily become the object of selection, then a habitude and instinct."[44]

40 Somerville, in JAI, XXIII, 364.
41 Smith, Kinship, 283.   42 Marriage, III, 183.
43 §§352, 356, above.   44 Letourneau, Soc., 310.

Though polyandry is not specifically named in this generalization, it belongs there along with those that are. Westermarck[45] cites an authority who writes that any casual influx of wealth into Tibet breaks up the polyandrous family and causes separate households to be formed.

Another explanation, which is really based upon the preceding one, alleges economic considerations—the fear of dissipating the family-property;[46] again, the cause is said to be a peculiar theory of the family whereby "women are part of the household inventory and their position and treatment suffer correspondingly."[47] But this is no theory peculiar to polyandrous peoples. Nor can we lay great weight upon the "benevolence" of the eldest brother. As for the disproportion of the sexes, it may be true that when countries are settled it is usually by bodies of immigrants including more men than women; and perhaps that disproportion may have imposed polyandry for a time. However, even though "an indefinite portion of the race has suffered at different times from a serious inferiority in numbers of women to men,"[48] there is here nothing by which to explain Tibetan and other polyandrous systems.

It will appear in what follows that polygyny ordinarily goes with wealth where monogamy or even celibacy is the system of the poor, though it is true that there are exhibitions of polyandry among the noble and rich. We do not conceive of polyandry, even of the fraternal and more nearly institutional type, much less the mere taking of lovers, as always constituting an adjustment to the same conditions; it is very likely survivalistic in nature in a number of cases, as some writers insist. Nevertheless it seems to us to be in the main a response to straitened living conditions combined, in some significant cases at least, with so great a disproportion of the sexes as to have led investigators to look about for evidences of female infanticide, which are sometimes close at hand. Polyandry is, to our minds, somewhat off the main course of marriage-evolution. In fact, most alleged cases of it are not, strictly speaking, marriage at all. Only one husband has really any status that amounts to much. We do not regard polyandry as deserving much attention on its own account; still divagations of this sort have their bearing upon the definition of more salient and important matters, and the development of the latter cannot fail to lighten up the errant variations and forms in retrospect.

45 *Marriage*, III, 112, chs. XXIX, XXX.
46 Mateer, in JASB, II, 318.
47 Pitard, "Polyandrie," résumé in AA, III, 382.
48 Maine, *Early Law*, 212, 214.

§398*. **Polygyny.** If polyandry be set aside as a form of mating that is both rare and also obscure in its nature, the only form of plural mating which, strictly speaking, deserves the name of marriage, is where a man takes ceremonially two or more wives, who then enter approximately a parity of status. This occurs relatively rarely, though more frequently than where, in polyandry, the rôles of the sexes are reversed. In polyandry there is regularly one head-husband, in the person of the ruling eldest brother, for instance, while in polygyny there is almost always one chief wife to whom the rest of the consorts are subordinate. The general outline of the status of the chief wife, sketched above,[49] may have served to suggest also, as the cases of polyandry were reviewed, the status of the chief husband. The fact is that all cases of polygyny tend toward a form characterized by the dominance of one wife, and that pure polygyny, which would occur only under conditions of substantial equality in status of two or more wives, is much less common than has sometimes been supposed. Clarification upon this matter is urgent, for the terminology is so loose as to invite error. The fact, for instance, that there has regularly been one chief husband or wife—a single consort of status—has lent spurious color to the contention, which many people for sentimental reasons would like to believe, that the primitive form of marriage was monogamy. To accept that view is in so far to accredit the traditional dream of a golden age of innocence. Generalizations carrying any such implication should always be subjected to sharp scrutiny. Their prevalence forces us to pause for a moment over the question of terminology.

Suppose that two travellers visit the same tribe at different times. One, let us say, asks the chief how many wives he has and receives the answer, "One." The other inquires of the same potentate as to the number of his children and the reply is, "Fifty." The two make opposite reports as regards the tribe, the first asserting that it is monogamous, the second that it is polygamous. The difficulty is that the chief and the first inquirer understood different things by the term "wife"; the former was thinking of the status-wife, the latter of wife in the European sense. Nothing but confusion and darkening of counsel could result. It is therefore a wholly practical matter to be resolved as to the meaning of terms.

The word "polygamy" means simply "many marriages" and could as logically cover polyandry as polygyny; it is here discarded, except as it occurs in excerpts, in which it regularly means a plurality of female consorts, and gen-

[49] §396, above.

erally includes concubines. It covers both polygyny and monogyny as we understand those terms; and where there is no elucidating context it can only represent plurality of women, of varying status or none at all, attached sexually to one man. "Polygyny" involves the presence of two or more wives of status; the term means "many wives." "Monogyny," in our usage, is the same as "juridic monogamy";[50] it connotes a system which admits of only one wife of status, while allowing a number of consorts without status. The word means "one sole wife.' The jural relation of status belongs to one consort alone, while the subordinate consorts have few or no rights, and may be slaves. "Monogamy" is retained to mean about what it does nowadays, namely, a single marriage at a time; it does not exclude irregular sex-relations outside of the marriage-institution. It is quite misleading to employ the term, without qualification, to cover either monandry,[51] which is far more ephemeral and less institutional, or, as has so often been done, monogyny as just defined. For "pure monogamy," that is, an exclusive life-relation, we adopt the term "pair-marriage." Necessarily, in listing these terms, we have anticipated somewhat; but that has been inevitable.

An approach to the cases renders appropriate the warning that the sharp distinctions just indicated cannot be maintained intact; that is impossible, not alone by reason of the fact that they are not made by the authorities about to be quoted, but also because in treating of evolutionary forms as they pass, through zones of transition, from phase to phase of adjustment, man-made categories are distorted and split apart so that life escapes them. In particular we cannot hope to isolate very consistently the cases of genuine polygyny from those of monogyny, nor yet those of monogamy from those of pair-marriage. We can do no more than distinguish types; but the reader who has caught the above distinctions ought to experience no difficulty in detecting the types, while at the same time he can observe their interpenetration and their manner of merging into one another.

During any survey of the evidence as to polygyny, it should be borne in mind that this form of union is, in many important respects, the antithesis of polyandry, in that it tends to rise in adjustment to easy rather than to straitened circumstances of life and to a preponderance of females over males.

Rivers[52] surveys the spread of polygyny, remarking that it is the commonest form of marriage; "everywhere, so far as we know, it is not universal, but is the privilege of the powerful and rich." Evidently he includes under polygyny the form which we seek to distinguish as "monogyny." His survey is as follows: "The part of the world where the practice flourishes with the greatest luxuriance is Africa, where kings and chiefs may have even hundreds of wives, and it is here also that we find especially the feature that the wives have different establishments, and the children of different wives are distinguished by differences in the terms by which they address one another, own being distinguished from half-brothers. The practice occurs, or rather occurred, far less frequently in India, and is, of course, a widespread feature of Mohammedanism. It is frequent in Oceania, where, again, it is confined to the more impor-

[50] Durkheim, *Méth. Soc.*, 48.   [51] §345, above.
[52] *Soc. Org.*, 43.

tant members of the community. In some parts of Melanesia it is the privilege of the old" or is conceded to those who have taken ten heads in warfare.

In Australia, the possession by a man of "an extra wife has its advantages in the way of procuring food and saving him trouble, while if his other women object, the matter is one which does not hurt him, for it can easily be settled once and for all by a stand-up fight between the women and the rout of the loser."[53] The man, regarding his wives "more as slaves than in any other light, employs them in every possible way to his own advantage"; they seldom agree well with one another and each strives to be the favorite.[54] In another district, a man can have as many wives as he pleases: "I have heard of one with three; I have known some with two; but the generality of them seem content with one."[55] Again, each man may have two wives, one allotted him formally by the camp-council and the other a love-wife, each of due rank and from the proper group.[56] Ratzel[57] generalizes to the effect that polygyny is as common among the Australians as circumstances allow; in the fertile northwest a man may have as many as eleven wives, while in the poorer southeast he rarely has over two. The census of 1876 showed in South Australia 2203 men and 1750 women, so that polygyny left a good many men wifeless. While one authority calls the Tasmanians monogamous, a second asserts that "plurality of wives was the universal law among them," and cites one tribe in which "I scarcely ever knew an instance of a native having but one *gin*. On the contrary, two or three wives were the usual allowance."[58]

"The Papuan women are no friends of polygyny, and often they have influence and power enough to hinder the choice of a co-wife."[59] In what was German Melanesia, however, the boy who has reached maturity "may take as many wives as his money-bag allows him. . . . The women themselves are not at all against but very much in favor of polygyny and welcome very joyfully each new co-wife" as a participant in their labors. But polygyny is not so frequent as might be expected, for "the possession of *dewarra* [shell-money] is determinative."[60] In Melanesia, polygyny "is the rule, though a considerable number of wives is found only with rich and elder men. One wife is commonly enough for a Florida man, who says that he can neither manage nor afford more than one. . . . As a man advances in life and survives his maternal uncles, his brothers, and his cousins, the widows of these tend to accumulate around him; they are called his wives, live in houses round him and work for him, but he lives practically with two or three younger women whom he has taken for himself." On Leper's Island, "a man who has a young wife takes an elder woman, a widow, for a second, to look after the first."[61] In the New Hebrides, though polygyny prevails, only the rich can get several wives.[62] In the Murray Islands the first wife is regarded as the chief and superintends the work of the others.[63]

The African Bushman is poor enough to get on with one wife, though more are permissible;[64] more could profit him little if at all. The Hottentots

[53] Spencer and Gillen, *Nat. Tr. Cent. Aust.*, 556.
[54] Smyth, *Vict.*, I, 85.   [55] Parker, *Euahlayi*, 55.
[56] Roth, *N.W. Cent. Queensland*, 180.
[57] *Vkde.*, II, 68.   [58] Roth, *Tasmania*, 123-124.
[59] Krieger, *Neu-Guinea*, 173.   [60] Von Pfeil, *Südsee*, 26, 32-33.
[61] Codrington, *Melanesians*, 245. [62] Leggatt, in AAAS, 1892, 698.
[63] Hunt, in JAI, XXVIII, 10.   [64] Ratzel, *Vkde.*, I, 71.

used to have polygyny before their cattle died off; now "the Hottentot is happy if he can feed one wife."[65] One Herero wife is superior to the rest in rank and is called the "big" wife; but monogamy is common. Among the Zulu the sons of the chief wife are the heirs to property and in the case of a ruling family to the chieftainship. There follow two other wives, "who stand lower in rank, the wife of the right hand and of the left, whose houses likewise enjoy prerogatives and at the extinction of the house of the great wife succeed to its place."[66] A Bechuana chief who, turning Christian, repudiated all his wives but one, made enemies of all their relatives and destroyed his authority and the discipline of the tribe.[67] On the Zambesi, "the chief wife is *usually* the first wife, but not always, a man having the right to make any one of his wives his chief or head wife."[68] We are told that the high cost of wives has hit polygyny hard in South Africa. The Rhodesian government taxes all the wives after the first and the natives say that "it is not worth while to have more than one wife under such a system." Further, the cessation of intertribal wars which for centuries reduced the male population and put a premium on husbands has likewise contributed to the unpopularity of plural marriage. The Zulu word for buying wives or cattle is said to be waning in use.[69] The Salvation Army, which distinguished itself for common sense in the World War, has not insisted upon the repudiation by a converted Zulu of all his wives but one. "We knew as well as any one else that polygamy is not consistent with Christian principle; but neither could we see any Christianity in saving the soul of one man at the expense of ten or twenty women who had borne him children and who were absolutely dependent upon him for food and shelter."[70]

It is common in West Africa to invest wages or profits in wives, who thereafter support their owner.[71] Miss Kingsley,[72] supported by Bastian,[73] Ellis,[74] and Klose,[75] alleges that in West Africa polygyny "is an actual necessity, according to native custom; thus a wife after the birth of a child retires from her husband's companionship and devotes herself for the following two years to the cares of nursing." Sometimes this period is extended by religious scruples to four or five years. Again, at such a time, a woman may not prepare food except for herself. "This would place the man with only one wife in a peculiar position," as it is a general custom for all husbands, from the king downwards, to have their food cooked by one of their wives—a practice calculated to obviate the ever-present danger of dying by poison. One wife cannot, under their customs, do all that a husband has a recognized right to have done for him. Polygyny is "not an unmixed evil" and "at the present culture-level of the African it is not to be eradicated." Other authorities find the system an expedient adjustment to life-conditions. That polygyny "is injurious to domestic peace is also, I think, an error, as far as uncivilized peoples are concerned. It certainly has not that effect on the Gold Coast. No jealousy prevails amongst the women, because their affection, if they have any, for their lord and master, is quite passionless, and borders on indifference. . . . Wives con-

[65] Schmidt, *Deut. Kol.*, II, 229.
[66] Fritsch, *Eingeb. S.-Afr.*, 227, 92.   [67] Ratzel, *Vkde.*, I, 294.
[68] Decle, excerpt in JAI, XXIII, 421.
[69] N. Y. *Times*, Nov. 23, 1919.   [70] N. Y. *Times*, Aug. 31, 1924.
[71] Ratzel, *Vkde.*, I, 597.   [72] *W. Afr. Studies*, 559, 662.
[73] *Deut. Exped.*, I, 295.   [74] *Ewe*, 206.
[75] *Togo*, 254, 508; Klose, in *Globus*, LXXXIII, 312.

tinually urge their husbands to take other wives, or to purchase slave-girls as concubines; for in both cases the wife finds that her labour is lightened and her authority increased, while she does not suffer even a sentimental grievance." In fact, the women prefer polygyny to monogamy. The first wife is termed the "head-wife" (*muliere grande*),[76] the second, her assistant, is "mistress of the house," where the junior wives are called "trade-wives" or "wives of commerce," probably because they sell in the markets. It is unusual, except in the case of chiefs, for a man to have more than four or five wives; but in Dahomi the system is excessive, for a man's rank and position are gauged by the number of his wives.[77]

However, as polygyny is not an unmixed evil in West Africa, so is it also not a pure boon to the husband. Bastian[78] tells how his host led him "dejectedly through the tortuous and intersecting passages of his dwelling, in the innermost room of which he slept. He had reason to entrench himself with care, for twenty embittered female foes inhabited his court and rightly might he curse the hour on which his wealth had tempted him to surround himself with them."

In Uganda, "polygamy is universal, but it has not always been the custom to have an unlimited number of wives. In early years men were restricted to three wives, later on others were added because men began to regard them as property, and often bought women instead of keeping large herds of cattle, which only excited the envy and greed of those in high places. Women were much more easily concealed than cattle in the large enclosures or banana plantations, and there did not excite any feelings of envy in the owner's superiors."[79] Weeks[80] says that his "carefully considered opinion is that on the Upper Congo polygamy did not tend to large families, but the reverse. I have known a man with twenty-five wives have only one child really his own. Another man had eight wives and only five children, and they were all by one wife. Another had five wives, and he had four children by one wife and none by the others, but one had a child by another man, and he counted it as one of his own. I found the same state of things on the Lower Congo, viz., that polygamy meant small families, and the reason is not far to seek—a few old men owned most of the women and the strong young men were without wives, and this resulted in a great amount of adultery, and the women to screen their lovers prevented pregnancy or caused abortion." Naturally these observations do not refute the general expediency of polygyny as a producer of numbers. The author quoted goes on: "I have met many young men who were bachelors, and older men who had been widowers for years, but I do not for a moment think they practised celibacy. They were simply too poor to buy a wife, but probably not too poor to hire one for a time. Wherever I have lived I have noticed that polygamy has resulted in a few men having the women—and they the older men, while the virile young men have not been able to secure wives." This case should be carefully pondered, as it runs counter to conclusions long accepted. It is on good authority, but is unique in our collections.

---

[76] Bosman, *Guinea*, 169; Bastian, *Deut. Exped.*, I, 151; Conradt, in *Globus*, LXXXI, 336; Trilles, *Fân*, 137; Lippert, *Kgchte.*, II, 49.

[77] Ellis, *Tshi*, 288 (quoted); Ellis, *Ewe*, 204; Ellis, *Yoruba*, 182-183.

[78] *Afr. Reisen*, 182.   [79] Roscoe, in JAI, XXXII, 35.

[80] In JAI, XL, 418-419, and in JAI, XXXIX, 449.

The foregoing instances, assembled from ethnographic accounts of the eastern and western branches of the black race, are representative in all essentials of polygyny amongst the rest of the backward peoples. The following cases serve to complete the picture in some of its details.

The system is rare amongst the Hyperboreans of Asia, as women are scarce and food hard to get. Rich men have more wives, to take care of their cattle and other possessions, which are located in different places. Wives take more zealous care of property than indifferent hired persons. The Christianized Chukchi said that they could not get on without a plurality of wives because, for fear of contagious diseases, they were compelled to break up and scatter their herds of reindeer.[81] The Usbek who has several wives tries to keep them separated because if they live together they fight every day and scratch each other like cats. He is in the very worst position if they all have children, for these too quarrel and the result is hell and not family-life. This is not from jealousy, the Asiatic women having no notion of that as respects a husband; it comes from their desire for ease and influence over the household.[82] "The Reindeer Chukchee are mainly monogynists, but about one-third are polygynists. Many rich reindeer-breeders who have separate herds keep a wife with each herd, but frequently those who have only one herd have several wives. . . . The first wife is generally much older and controls the others, who are more like servants. If a wife has no children, she insists on her husband marrying another woman. . . . When the Cossacks first came among the Yakut, they found polygyny fully developed; but nowadays, as the Yakut have become poorer, and the *kalym* [bride-price] is somewhat large, it is not so much practised. Another reason for the decline of the custom is that girls die in infancy more frequently than boys, as they are not so carefully tended." The less civilized a community is the fewer women it contains.[83] "It is an indubitable fact that where polygamy exists it is the women who are its chief advocates"; the author[84] cites the case of the Mormons. "The men, on the other hand, consider it a great bother. I have heard many rich men to whom proposals were made for a third or fourth marriage say 'sufficient unto me are the evils of one wife.' "

Cases of polygyny among the Bataks are in good part a result of the levirate-union. Polygyny is limited by the high bride-price, and the Bataks dread the quarreling of the co-wives: "dissension between two lands has an end, but squabbling between the wives of one man is endless." A husband has to do what he can to prevent it by having separate quarters for each. The author[85] quotes Sibree on the meaning of the Madagascar term for polygyny: "So invariably has the taking of more wives than one shown itself to be a fruitful cause of enmity and strife in a household, that this word, which means 'the making an adversary' is the term always applied to it." In Sumatra a native

[81] Ratzel, *Vkde.*, II, 767; Hiekisch, *Tungusen,* 87; Sieroshevski-Sumner, in JAI, XXXI, 94.
[82] *Russ. Ethnog.* (Russ.), II, 640; 18.
[83] Czaplicka, *Aborig. Siberia,* 77, 112.
[84] Panikkar, in JAI, XLVIII, 266-267.
[85] Wilken, in VG, I, 329-330, 281-282; he quotes Sibree, *Madagascar,* 161.

may have several wives and a number of concubines. The third wife is subject to the first, the fourth to the second, while the concubines have to obey all four. The first has the most honorable position and lives in the best apartment, the rest occupying, in order of number, a graded series of progressively less desirable quarters.

In Greenland the hard life uses up the men before they are fifty, while the women live longer. It is estimated that eleven per cent of the deaths in Greenland are violent. Polygyny naturally results.[86] A woman who is tired of bearing children asks her husband to take a second wife. The missionaries demanded that a man should repudiate all his wives but one, which was a cruel hardship. In one case a baptized native divorced his younger wife but would not let her leave his dwelling, as her children would go with her.[87] Efficient hunters often have two wives when the first is unable to take care of all the skins or when two rowers are needed for his boat. There is no known case of more than two wives. "Although for every hundred men there are found a hundred and fourteen women, practically all the women are married. We know only one example of an older unmarried girl who, however, had a couple of children." They do not disapprove of an unmarried mother but of a childless wife.[88] Eskimo wives are not jealous; they smoke the same pipe, rub noses, and eat and sleep together; two are needed in order always to have one available as an indispensable coöperator.[89]

Morgan[90] says of the North American Indians: "The females are usually more numerous than the males from the destruction of the latter in war." The custom whereby a man marries along with an older sister all the younger ones is of common occurrence; and "polygamy is the natural result of the custom by which a sister's son or a brother falls heir to the relict of the uncle or brother, in addition to his own wife."[91] The practice, noted in Africa, of tabooing the pregnant wife leads here also to polygyny.[92] The question among the Indians seemed to be whether one wife could do all the work one man needed, particularly under an agricultural economy.[93] Omahas might have up to a maximum of three wives; the first wife, who was never deposed, must give consent.[94] A Sioux with one wife could not amass property, as she was constantly occupied in household-labors and had no time for preparing skins for trading.[95] The Pima maintained separate establishments for the several wives.[96] "There were in 1890 among about 600 married Apache men . . . 87 who had two and nine who had three wives each." Ten years later the efforts of the agents had considerably reduced these figures.[97] A law effective July 1,

[86] Cranz, *Grönland*, 201; Ratzel, *Hist. Mankind*, II, 101; Reclus, *Prim. Folk*, 31.

[87] Nansen, *Esk. Life*, 139, 170; Schell, in *Globus*, XCIV, 87.

[88] Holm, *Ethnol. Skizze*, 52-54.

[89] Hanbury, *Canada*, 69; Boas, in BAE, VI, 579.

[90] In *Smithson. Contrib.*, XVII, 238, 477-478; Mackenzie, *Voyages*, xcvii; Bancroft, *Nat. Races*, I, 197; Dorsey, in BAE, XV, 232, 242; McGee, in BAE, XV, 178.

[91] Kohler, *Urgchte. d. Ehe*, 134, note.

[92] Niblack, in USNM, 1888, 367, 368.

[93] Lippert, *Kgchte.*, II, 36.   [94] Dorsey, in BAE, III, 261.

[95] Dorsey, in BAE, XV, 225.   [96] Russell, in BAE, XXVI, 184.

[97] Hrdlička, in BAE, Bull. XXXIV, 49.

1897, by which certain Cheyenne and Arapahoe Indians must divest themselves
of from one to four extra wives, caused great excitement especially among the
squaws, each of whom strove by pleasing her husband to be the lucky wife.
Forty of these Indians had over a hundred squaws.[98] The Seri population,
being preponderantly feminine, polygyny naturally prevailed; there were always a number of unmarried widows but no bachelors of marriageable age.[99]

In British Guiana when the first wife becomes old, that is, attains twenty
years or so, the man seeks out a girl of seven or eight and puts her under the
tutelage of his older wife until she reaches maturity. All younger wives are
subjected to the first wife.[100] Only a part of the Bororo have permanent wives
and much woman-stealing goes on inside the tribe.[101] The old Peruvians had
only one consort possessing the dignity and rights of the true wife; their system was plainly monogyny. The head-wife was called "over-mother" or "settled wife." Here too occurred polygyny as the result of inheritance from a
brother.[102] In Tierra del Fuego, "owing to the almost general practice of
polygamy, many men are without wives, and live so all their days. And owing
to the general practice of giving young women to oldish men, the young men
frequently can get no wives but relicts."[103]

In the Old Testament the case where a man is to have two wives is discussed
as normal and regular.[104] Polygyny is presented without question or doubt.
Zoroaster had three wives who survived him.[105] That polygyny was common
in ancient Persia is well known; and it was an old Semitic tradition. Among
the Arabs, "in the midst of the wealth of the conquerors it became a worm
gnawing at the vitals of every nation which accepted Mohammedan doctrine."[106] Yet the conquerors needed numbers and polygyny is a numbers-
policy.[107] In Athens a native wife and foreign concubine were allowed.[108]
Ancient Scandinavians, Franks, Germans, Celts, Cymri, and others tolerated
concubinage.[109] It is stated that after the Peace of Westphalia bigamy was
tolerated in some German states on account of depopulation.[110] During the
late World War, in view of the losses of adult males, there was a revival of
discussion as to the merits of plural marriage.

§399. Some Features of Polygyny. Several of the salient as-
pects of polygyny, as they have appeared in the foregoing illus-

[98] Assoc. Press despatch, June 15, 1897.

[99] McGee, in BAE, XVII, pt. I, 279*.

[100] Schomburgk, Brit.-Guiana, I, 165; Spix u. Martius, Brasilien, 1339,
note.

[101] Von den Steinen, Zent. Bras., 500; Southey, Brazil, I, 128.

[102] Von Martius, Beiträge, I, 105, note; Cunow, Verf. Inkareichs, 83, 84,
notes.

[103] Bridges, in Voice f. S. Amer., XIII, 201; Ratzel, Vkde., II, 677.

[104] Deut., XXI, 15; Gen., XXXI.   [105] Jackson, Zoroaster, 20.

[106] Geiger, Ostiran. Kultur, 248, 249; Ratzel, Vkde., III, 152.

[107] Von Kremer, Kgchte. d. Orients, II, 114; Pischon, Islam, 9.

[108] Müller, Alt. Eherecht, 795.

[109] Grimm, Rechtsalt., 440; Müller, Sex. Leben, 37; Scherr, Deut. Sittengchte., 315-316; Rudeck, Oeffentl. Sittl., 176, 177; Jolly, Sec. Marriages, 173;
Holt, in JAI, XXVIII, 155; Gubernatis, Usi Nuz., 90.

[110] Westermarck, Marriage, III, 51.

trations, may be gathered up at this point. As sex-disproportion has been seen to promote polyandry, so does it, when existing in the opposite sense, favor polygyny. Wilken[111] remarks on a tendency among savages to a superfluity of women, citing examples, and concluding that female infanticide could do little more than equalize numbers. "Let us suppose a community in which for long periods together there is a large excess of females over males. There is no question that monogamy might be substantially maintained in such a community, by the precepts of some widely diffused religion, or by a morality derived from some former age or from some external source; but on the whole we should expect that such a community would, in some of its parts, be polygamous"— openly or secretly, lawfully or unlawfully so.[112] If, however, the sexes are numerically nearly equal, general polygyny is impossible; and the cases support this conclusion as they do the one just quoted. Particularly where the rich and powerful are polygynous, taking up the surplus of women where there is such and more than their share where there is not, must the ordinary run of men be content with one wife or even in some cases with none at all. Bigamy is probably the most common form of plurality of wives. It should be noted, however, that what is called monogamy is, where there is a rapid succession of divorces and changes of mate, no more than a "tandem" polygyny (or polyandry).

This monopolization of women by the noblest, richest, and bravest members of society is credited with a certain eugenic effect; "under the hypothesis that only the men with better heredity had more wives, polygyny might offer advantages over monogamy for generative evolution."[113] In any case, the women are often very unequally divided, "like money amongst us."[114] Perhaps wealth and social position were, in primitive societies, more nearly a gauge of individual quality. If so, it was expedient, as it always will be, that the superior strain should reproduce itself more rapidly than the inferior ones. This may constitute one of the survival-values of the system. It is doubtless obvious that polygyny is a numbers-policy and that one important way to secure rapid

[111] In VG, II, 43.   [112] Maine, *Early Law,* 210.
[113] Schallmayer, *Vererbung,* 341; Starcke, *Prim. Fam.,* 261; cases of "royal polygyny," in Main, *Relig. Chastity,* Appendix, note xi.
[114] Ratzel, *Vkde.,* I, 145.

increase of a society or a class is not to exclude a number of women from marriage but to have as many mothers as possible. Desire for children is one of the factors that makes for polygyny, causing even the ordinarily monogamous mores to be shaded toward tolerance of an extra wife. Further, if all the women could be regularly taken up into the institution there would be less likelihood of extra-institutional relations.

Westermarck[115] sums up the factors favoring polygyny as follows: danger to males; excess of female births; avoidance of periodic continence, due to taboos on the pregnant and nursing wife; attraction of youth and beauty, in the taking of a younger wife; taste for variety; the sterility of the wife, involving the dread of childlessness; the lowered fecundity of the long-nursing wife and the high infant mortality; the desire for women as laborers and as badges of distinction and as means of winning power. Inheritance-customs, whereby wives fall to brothers and sons, likewise produce polygyny; and Spencer[116] makes much of the fact that it habitually accompanies militancy. This matter of woman's labor deserves further elaboration. It is noteworthy that both sexes are found to favor polygyny on this score; the question as to whether one woman is sufficient as a complement to one man in self-maintenance has often been answered in the negative. It would appear from some cases that the more wives a man has the better off he is economically, for they support him in idleness; yet the unfortunate who can have only one wife because he cannot support more is a stock figure in ethnography.

The foregoing cases repeatedly emphasize the absence of sex-jealousy and the presence of friendliness between the co-wives; still there are instances of domestic discomfort and uproar that support the stock belief as to the home-life of polygynous peoples. The custom of separate establishments for the several wives is significant. Rivalry, jealousy, intrigue, and deception necessarily developed as the women were more valued for charm than for labor. To be noted is the fact that the quarreling is often stated to be over issues of ease of life and precedence rather than due to sex-jealousy. And out of the whole medley of relationships emerges clearly the status of the head-wife; to her other distinc-

115 *Marriage*, III, 64-84. 116 *Prin. Soc.*, I, §315.

tions as developed in our cases might be added the significant one that adultery with the chief wife is an offense all out of proportion with other such trespasses.[117]

Recalling the status of the chief wife brings us around again to the fact that most instances of polygyny are really cases of monogyny. Real polygyny exists only "where several women hold over against the one man a like jural position and where the children of all are regarded as begotten in perfectly valid matrimony."[118] Such cases have been found to be so rare that it has not seemed worth while to seek to set them apart. And though the marriage of ceremony and status is doubtless the "real" one, still the relation with women other than the chief wife comes well under our definition of marriage.[119]

§400*. Monogyny.[120] This form, doubtless the most common in the race's history, is characterized by the presence of one wife of status, or jural wife, together with an indefinite number of consorts who have no such status. Wife, concubine, and slave are the three ranks which ultimately, in higher civilization, become distinguished. The wife was superior or supreme long before she was sole. She is the wife properly speaking, taken by contract, with full customary ceremonies and under a status created by the mores, sanctioned by taboo, and enforced by the authority of the society. The concubine is a woman of inferior social status, taken in a relationship of an inferior grade, as defined and established by the mores. Taboo was generally lacking in this relationship and societal enforcement was weak. The slave-women were taken wholly by caprice. Concubinage has been said to "temper polygyny toward monogamy" and also to be one of the "polygamic palliatives" to monogamic marriage.[121] "The ideal transition from polygyny to monogamy is formed by the legal limitation of the wives and the preference accorded to a leading wife, the real mistress," whose marriage is hallowed by priestly benediction;[122] if present interest lay in evolution as progress from a "lower" to a

117 §§384, 385, above; Letourneau, *Marriage*, 211.
118 Geiger, *Ostiran. Kultur*, 247.   119 §338, above.
120 Sometimes called "juridic monogamy"; Durkheim, *Méth. Soc.*, 48.
121 Letourneau, *Marriage*, 154; Westermarck, *Marriage*, III, 155.
122 Müller, *Sex. Leben*, 37.

"higher" level, such a transitional form might seem to be a find. To call monogyny a transitional form means that one conceives of polygyny—where all the female consorts are equal, even if equal only to zero—as a prevalent and well-recognized type of marriage, existing prior to monogyny. The fact is worth reiteration that there is not nearly so much pure polygyny, on this understanding of the term, as has been supposed; most cases reported as polygyny are instances where attention is fixed upon mere plurality of female consorts, irrespective of whether they are upon a jural level—which they seldom are; whereas if interest is confined to the jural aspect of the relation, the very same cases may be reported as monogamy. Almost all forms reported as "polygamy," and a good share of those called "monogamy," are in reality monogyny. Some of the following instances will exhibit the tendency to look upon a combination of head-wife and subordinate wives as monogamy; but if mere plurality of consorts is considered, the cases are certainly not illustrative of monogamy, and if the jural relation is taken into account, they fall under monogyny. If marriage is to be viewed as an institution—not loosely as a term covering sex-relations, but with an eye to the status of the parties entering it—then monogyny stands out as its salient form.

The Bechuana are called polygynous; yet each has only one wife and her children have precedence.[123] In Guinea of the sixteenth century, "those who are rich have two wives perpetually exempted from labor, the first of which is the oldest and principal wife," head of the household. "The second is she who is consecrated to his god and thence called 'Bossum,' of whom he is very jealous. As for the remainder of his wives, he doth not watch them so narrowly, especially if he can get any money by them."[124] In Uganda if a deceased man is head of a family his body rests on a framework in the center of his hut; the head-wife also can claim such a framework; but the subsidiary wives, like the sons or daughters, are disposed along one of the side walls of the hut.[125] "Though the Mongol has only one lawful wife, he is allowed to take concubines who live with the wife in comradeship. There is no ceremony when they are taken. The real wife is regarded as the mistress and she rules the yurt [tent]. The children born to her have all the rights of the father. The children of the concubines are regarded as illegitimate and have no rights in the inheritance; yet such a child may be adopted with the consent of the authorities."[126]

[123] Ratzel, *Vkde.*, I, 294.   [124] Bosman, *Guinea*, 169.
[125] Johnston, *Uganda*, II, 693.
[126] Prschewalski (Prjevalski), *Reisen*, 58.

In Java and Madura there is an expedient by which the legal number of
four wives may be exceeded. "Since they have as a rule only one real wife,
there are three places over. They fill the three places by marriages with concubines; but when a man has, for instance, ten of these, he can be married to
three only of them at the same time. Therefore a man marries only those concubines whose society he chooses for the time being and as soon as he comes
to prefer that of another, he repudiates one or more of those to whom he is
married in order thereby to have one or more places vacant so that he can live
with a new one."[127] The concubine may never enter the house of the legal wife
or address her. The children of a slave or free concubine take the status of the
father. "They rank as consanguine brothers and sisters of the children of the
legal wives, inherit equally with these, and share in full in the same advantages; and when a concubine dies the father can even bring his children by her
into the house of his legal wife. They are then regarded as her children."[128]
The Sumatran *semando* or inferior marriage is accomplished by the payment
of a trifling ceremonial bride-price. A man cannot take a second wife since
he and the first wife own the property half and half.[129]

The Cambodian woman has many rights and must be treated by her husband
with consideration. "The woman can have but one husband, and he cannot take
a second wife or any additional one without the consent of his first wife. The
first wife is called the first wife, the second the middle wife, and the third the
end wife; those that follow are concubines. They are all hierarchically subordinated one to the other, but the great wife, the true wife, is mistress of the
house, and the others are only her followers and servants. If one of these encroaches upon her prerogatives, she can punish her; if she seeks to seduce the
husband and supplant the first wife in his heart, she can call her guilty rival
before the court and get judgment against her. The first wives sometimes
select the other wives for their husbands, often choosing such as will be agreeable companions to themselves; and women are numerous who have been able
to exert such influence over their husbands or exercise such power in the house
as to prevent the introduction of any other wives."[130]

Homeric marriage was distinctly of the monogynous type. "In the consideration of Homeric marriage, from the first advances on, a distinction must constantly and sharply be drawn between the feelings and customs connected with
the chief wife and those having to do with women whose personality did not
enter into economic and dynastic calculations. The importance of such calculations is paramount in Homer."[131] In the Scandinavian heroic age, marriage
was distinguished from irregular unions but did not exclude them. There was
generally only one house-wife (*adelkona*), though in several cases more than
one; but a man could have concubines without blame and the children of the
latter were not entirely excluded from inheritance. Marriage by purchase was
the legal marriage; hence the lawful wife, in distinction from one secretly
seduced or captured, was said to be won "by gift and payment" or "bought
with gifts," as in Homer. Thus did the gods get their wives.[132]

[127] Van den Berg, in *Bijd.*, XLI, 483-484.
[128] Jacobs, *Groot-Atjeh*, I, 78-79.   [129] Marsden, *Sumatra*, 270.
[130] Leclère, in PSM, XLIV, 779.
[131] Keller, *Hom. Soc.*, 218 ff., 211 (quoted), where full references are given.
[132] Geijer, *Svensk. Hist.*, I, 113.

"In general, the status of woman among all peoples who have attained a certain stage of civilization is the same where peculiar religious views like those of Islam or Christianity have not made it one-sided. As a rule only one wife ranks as the legitimate spouse and as the mistress of the house; but alongside her the man may have co-wives so far as his property allows and it is a matter of course that the female slaves of the house belong to him. The immorality that seems to lie in this relation, according to our way of looking at it, is not felt by a naïve folk; on the contrary, the slave-woman regards it as a disgrace if she does not 'find favor' with her master."[133] A few cases may be cited to bring out the position of the inferior consort or concubine.

In West Africa a slave girl may belong to a wife and, as her property "is always distinct from that of the husband, the latter cannot demand to use her as a concubine as a matter of right, but the wife ordinarily encourages him to take her," much as did Jacob's wives in the Bible story. Children born to her belong to the wife whose property she is.[134] Their status demands that "free born women must not smoke, eat or drink in the presence of their husbands; slave women can do so."[135] In India there is a regular agreement for concubinage, called "giving cloth." A valuable cloth being offered by the man, the girl asks her uncle, "Shall I receive it?" If he consents the same query is put to the mother. "A cheaper cloth is given to the woman's father, mother, brother, sister, and other new relatives."[136]

In Korea "concubinage is a recognized institution, but not a respected one. The wife or mother of a man not infrequently selects the concubine, who often is looked upon by the wife as a proper appendage of her husband's means or position, much as a carriage or butler might be with us. The offspring in these cases are under a serious social stigma, and until lately have been excluded from some desirable positions. Legally the Korean is a strict monogamist, even when a widower marries again, the children of the first wife retaining special rights."[137] "Among the Chinese concubines are bought for a small sum of money. They are treated like slaves, and are subject both to the man and to his lawful wife. Even their children regard the lawful wife as their mother, and treat the mother who bore them with contempt."[138] Among the Nahuas concubinage was legal. The Toltec chief could not have more than one wife; if she died before him, he could not re-marry or take a concubine.[139]

In ancient Chaldæa "the master had the right to take advantage of all his female slaves, and they seem to consider it the greatest misfortune for a slave not to have attracted the attention of her master, just as much so as for a free woman of rank to have found no husband." From a very ancient time a character in the popular poetry was the slave woman who had been disdained by her master. If he did not love her she became dangerous and magic was

133 Erman, *Aegypten,* I, 217. 134 Ellis, *Ewe,* 205.
135 Granville, in JAI, XXVIII, 107.
136 Mateer, in JAI, XII, 291, 294. 137 Bishop, *Korea,* 342.
138 Starcke, *Prim. Fam.,* 158. 139 Nadaillac, *Preh. Amer.,* 278.

necessary against her. The concubine had to wear a distinctive figure of stone or brick hung from her neck and bearing her name, that of her husband, and the date of the marriage.[140] Concubinage in Biblical, classical, and later times is familiar to readers of the records.

§401. Monogamy; Pair-Marriage. Monogamy, meaning strictly "one sole marriage," is the system where the wife of status, so long as she continues to be that, is the sole consort. The only way for a monogamous union to be terminated is by death or divorce. Law and public opinion, where monogamy is in the mores, will punish a second marriage which is not preceded by dissolution of the first in the recognized way; and while the law cannot penalize the contracting of a second alliance immediately following upon the attainment of freedom from its predecessor, public opinion is against such haste.

In the preceding connection it has been stated that conclusions concerning the existence of monogamy among tribes of low civilization should be viewed with a critical eye. When Westermarck draws such a conclusion as the one recently quoted, he is evidently thinking of what might be called monogamy under the constraint of circumstances rather than single union on the basis of conviction. It is a fact which will receive sufficient mention that in all ages and under all systems the poor have had to get along with one consort where the rich have had more or many. Such monogamy by force of circumstances turns immediately into monogyny or polygyny with a favorable shift of fortune. That is to say, monogamy is not in the mores and enforceable upon all. To call such a system monogamy is about like saying that abstemiousness characterizes a tribe most of whose members habitually lack a more than minimal supply of food. One must recall that no practice gets into the mores, much less into institutional form, concerning which there exists no conviction that it is expedient for societal welfare, so that all individuals are coerced to conform to it. Nor can it be said that monogamy under compulsion of circumstance tends to pass into monogamy by conviction; rather do the poor envy the rich and seek as opportunity offers to imitate them.

If these considerations are held in mind there is less harm in talking about the monogamy of primitive peoples; the difficulty always is that the reader who encounters the statement that monogamy has been the common practice of savages interprets the term in the sense in which he knows it and in so far seems to acquire evidence for a state of primitive innocence and rightness, to belief in which, very often, his prejudices incline him.

Monogamy makes for uniformity and for the closest sort of monopoly and restriction. It is cultural and artificial, being maintained as a system that is entirely "unnatural" by dogmas and institutions which, it cannot be denied, jeopardize the happiness

140 Lenormant, *Chaldean Magic*, 385; Maspero, *Hist. Anc.*, I, 735, 739.

of many. If monogamy is best for those who marry, it cannot be overlooked that it costs heavily to those who are ruled out. They pay for the extra happiness of the married by their own misfortune. Monogamy is monopoly, and wherever there is monopoly there are bound to be both "Ins" and "Outs."

Such monopoly becomes the more intense in the form of union which we call pair-marriage.[141] This is a term for the institutional form of wedlock in which the two parties are united upon an equal footing, the restrictions for the one being the same as for the other. In monogamy, men are supposed to be subject to the taboo equally with women, but they have never been so in practice. Pair-marriage even negatives sex-gratification outside of marriage. Further, the term cannot cover a series of unions with interpolated divorces, least of all for trifling causes; it includes, strictly speaking, only those whose contractants live up to the marriage-vow "until death." Such an absorbing sex-relation between two individuals has been observed among certain birds[142] and has been idealized upon in romance and poetry; it is a sort of selection by idealization out of monogyny, the chief wife becoming the unique consort. Pair-marriage has evidently existed but rarely at any period, even in the case of individual pairs, and has never formed a general system. What cases we possess of this form or of alleged approaches to it will be readily recognized among the following representative instances of monogamy.[143]

Most Australian tribes live in what is called monogamy "because the scantiness of the population and the complex character of the marriage laws render it difficult enough to find even one suitable wife. No rich man existing, there is no possibility for any one to procure himself a harem by purchase."[144] Some Papuans have only one wife; "the people therefore led a very moral life, a condition which I have found amongst all natives as yet untouched by civilization. Therewith reigned a decency which could serve as a model to many civilized men."[145] Their monogamy with no divorce, like that of the Land Dyaks, goes with an industrial type of society.[146] In Abyssinia there is a rare religious

[141] §§432, 433, below.
[142] Darwin, *Descent of Man,* II, 293; Letourneau, *Marriage,* 27; Lippert, *Kgchte.,* I, 72.
[143] List of uncivilized peoples amongst whom polygyny is alleged to be forbidden or unknown in Westermarck, *Marriage,* III, 5; see also Letourneau, *Marriage,* ch. XI.
[144] Semon, *Aust. Bush,* 231.　　　[145] Finsch, *Samoafahrten,* 107.
[146] Spencer, *Prin. Soc.,* I, §315.

form of marriage that binds the spouses, like the Roman patrician *confarreatio-*union, for the whole of life; but it is not popular.[147]

Among the Turkomans, "in consequence of the unequal division of the sexes the women stand much exalted in value; the Turkoman must pay a very high purchase-price for his wife and this circumstance leads to factual monogamy among the Turkomans; they may have several wives but actually have only one."[148] Among the lowest strata of population "there is little difference or none at all between the position of woman in Mohammedan Asia and that in Europe. . . . In the Mohammedan countries known to me—I do not shrink from the boldness of the assertion—among thousands of families is to be found at most one single one in which the legal permissibility of polygyny is taken advantage of. Among Turkish, Persian, Afghan, and Tartar peoples it is un-heard of—yes, unthinkable—since several wives involve also a greater domestic establishment, greater wealth and expense. Just as seldom and only quite sporadically, does it appear in the middle class. . . . In the high and highest circles, it is true, . . . this social evil luxuriates in a frightful manner; yet this is not so much a lawfully authorized polygyny as, rather, a consequence of the liberties which the master can take with the gang of female slaves neces-sary to luxury and prestige."[149]

The Lepchas of Hindustan usually have one wife each; this is a poor and outcast tribe.[150] In some cases in India there is a "sacramental monogamous marriage, by which a man is tied to one wife for ever," even beyond the grave.[151] A striking and seemingly incongruous case is that of the Veddahs, who have a "monogamy lasting to the death of one of the parties." Infidelity is rare and is punished severely. Polygamy and prostitution are absent. The explanation given is the small number of women and the very highly developed sexual jealousy. Such monogamy is assumed, on slight evidence, to represent the "primary form of sexualism."[152] In Japan, "with the progress of civiliza-tion, the general tendency was towards monogamy, although the ruling classes remained polygynous."[153]

Wilken[154] finds but one people in the Malay Archipelago who are clearly monogamous. "No Dyak can have more than one wife at a time." "Polygamy is considered very displeasing to the gods, and if a man does take to himself two wives, the other people of the village compel him to give one up, and sacri-fices are offered to the gods and spirits to avert any evil effects upon the com-munity for the crime."[155] Of a tribe in South Celebes it is reported that "they are low in intelligence, shy of strangers, truth-loving, do not know robbery and theft, live in monogamy, and have no religion, unless traces of tree-wor-ship be regarded as such." They are classified with the Veddahs as respects their monogamy.[156] The Philippine Negritos are reported to be monogamic and of good sex-morals.[157]

"That the Indians lean by preference to pair-marriage . . . is shown by the

[147] Müller, *Sex. Leben,* 38.   [148] Stieda, in *Globus,* LXXIV, 95.
[149] Vámbéry, *Sittenbilder,* 21 ff.   [150] Waddell, *Himalayas,* 99.
[151] Tylor (discussion), in JAI, XVIII, 271.
[152] Sarasin, *Wedda,* 458, 463, 473-474.
[153] Hearn, *Japan,* 78.   [154] *Vkde.,* 290.
[155] Roth, in JAI, XXI, 132; Gomes, *Sea Dyaks,* 127, 128.
[156] Sarasin, in *Globus,* LXXXIII, 280.
[157] Blumentritt, *Philippinen,* 10, 12.

words for 'spouse' in the languages of the Iroquois and Hurons. They use for husband and wife identical expressions, which Morgan translates by 'two-joined.'" Other Indians use terms meaning 'part of myself,' 'my cohabitant,' 'my aid through life.' Yet there are indications of a sort of group-marriage which has been yielding to the form of pair-union.[158] The Delawares questioned whether one woman could do all the work a man required; as they became agricultural they became monogamic.[159] Schoolcraft[160] finds the Iroquois purely monogamous and others almost purely so. This, he thinks, goes with parity of wealth and power and is correlative with the absence of slavery. It is reported that an Indian woman cast herself, with all her children, into the falls of the Mississippi because her husband took a second wife.[161] "Monogamy is the rule among the Pueblo Indians, and they do not obtain their wives through purchase. Indeed, in the household, the woman reigns supreme, and the man has but little to say."[162] "When a Miranha has brothers, he may take only one wife."[163] Certain Paraguay tribes are stated to be monogamous.[164]

To the writer of the first two chapters of Genesis monogamy seems to have been a fact in the mores. The early Mohammedan jurists "recognize expressly the right of the woman to impose the pre-marital condition that her husband shall marry no second wife and keep no concubine."[165] Aristotle[166] opposes all sex-relations outside of marriage. "Monogamy was, from the earliest times, strictly enjoined; and it was one of the great benefits that have resulted from the expansion of Roman power that it made this type dominant in Europe. . . . Partly by raising it into a sacrament, and partly by representing it as, in some mysterious and not very definable sense, an image of the union of Christ and His Church, a feeling was fostered that a lifelong union of one man and one woman is, under all circumstances, the single form of intercourse between the sexes which is not illegitimate."[167] An interesting modern case exhibits the reduction of the sex-proportion to a parity favorable to monogamy. "There is a dearth of women in High Albania. The people declare that it is because God knows that many men will be shot, and so provides an extra supply. I believe myself that one of the reasons is, that owing to the very young age at which girls are married, there is a cruelly high death-rate in child bearing. But in some of the tribes where church registers of baptisms and deaths have now been carefully kept for some years it really appears that a considerable excess of males is born and reaches maturity. Then the male death rate from gunshot wounds is high and thins them off a bit."[168]

[158] Bernhöft, *Verwdsftsnamen,* 19-20, 37, 54, 55.
[159] Loskiel, *Mission,* 101.
[160] *Indian Tribes,* III, 191; Westermarck, *Marriage,* III, 5, 82.
[161] Waitz, *Anthrop.,* III, 192. Other cases of resistance to polygyny are given. Müller, *Sex. Leben,* 37.
[162] Shufeldt, in USNM (Proceedings), 1892, 31.
[163] Von Martius, *Beiträge,* I, 427.
[164] Hassler, in *Inter. Cong. Anthrop. Chicago,* 1893, 366.
[165] Von Kremer, *Kgchte.,* II, 101.   [166] *Politics,* VII, 16.
[167] Lecky, *Europ. Morals,* II, 298, 347.
[168] Durham, in JAI, XL, 462.

The cases which have been reviewed make it clear that no one system of marriage would have been expedient for all places, times, and circumstances. It depends upon the swing of economic and some other conditions whether there will be polyandry, polygyny, or monogamy. And an obsolescent system may persist by tradition; the dicta of a "law-giver"—expressions of the expediency of one period—may win authority and be obeyed at a subsequent time when they are inexpedient. Polyandry is normal under peculiar conditions not often reproduced; it may spring up at any time and place under stress of poverty or a disproportion of the sexes. It cannot exist as an institution except where males greatly exceed females in number either through loss of women by raids, female infanticide, celibacy, or the special circumstances of emigrants or colonists. Polygyny is an adjustment resulting in numbers. The expediency of monogamy has been developed at some length by Spencer.[169] Where the sexes are nearly equal in number, it may even surpass polygyny in the production of offspring; marriage is more stable; the family bond is stronger and integrates the monogamic society; the development of ancestor-worship, once a strongly unifying bond, is promoted. There is a decreased mortality in offspring, once the barbaric stage is outgrown; children are better reared and quantity of reproduction is subordinated to quality; the position of both women and children is ameliorated; the passion of love is refined; the standard of living rises; those who have passed the reproductive period receive better care.

Whether or not these specific contentions of Spencer are accepted, it is clear that pair-marriage tends to become the ideal, if not the prevalent form in the mores, of somewhat advanced peoples. Lecky[170] thinks that "we have ample grounds for maintaining that the lifelong union of one man and one woman should be the normal or dominant type of intercourse between the sexes. We can prove that it is on the whole most conducive to the happiness, and also to the moral elevation, of all parties. But beyond this point it would, I conceive, be impossible to advance, except by the assistance of a special revelation. It by no means follows that because this should be the dominant type it should be the only one, or that

[169] *Prin. Soc.*, I, ch. VIII.   [170] *Europ. Morals*, II, 348-349.

the interests of society demand that all connections should be forced into the same die." Some of our cases have shown the ill results of insistence upon the immediate repudiation by polygynists of all wives save one. For civilized peoples, however, there exists no condition of life that calls for supersession of pair-marriage which is not overwhelmingly countered by the many conditions that demand its enforcement to a far more stringent degree than now obtains.

That it is probably impossible to decide what relation of the sexes is biologically most expedient, does not concern us here, for societal, not biological relations are the subject for study. Whatever the biological situation, relaxation toward any form of plural marriage is, in this age, as societally inexpedient as would be the abrogation of private property. Property-monopoly and sex-monopoly are kin expedients which have demonstrated their indispensability to society. It is instructive to notice that those who assault one of these forms of monopoly are presently led to attack the other. No better evidence as to the close connection of property and marriage could be found.[171]

Out of true pair-marriage there may develop also a certain fine flower of sex-coöperation that seldom takes root in any form of plural union, not even in monogyny or in a succession of monogamous pairings with divorces between. There is a privacy about pair-marriage which, though it allows of abuse and secret imposition and suffering, is yet conducive to refinement of feeling and of character. Polygyny "brings the privacies of conjugal life, which should remain secrets between husband and wife, before a larger circle and thus weakens feminine modesty and the delicacy of moral sentiment."[172] Men and women have gone on blunderingly seeking happiness in marriage for untold ages, and are still seeking it. Though fortunate pairs have sometimes found it in good measure at all ages and stages, a reliable set of precepts for its attainment has never been formulated. Happiness in marriage has been variously interpreted. Priam, for instance, was said to be fortunate in marriage because he had many children; only in the case of Hector and Andromache has the poet verged upon the

[171] Sumner, *Coll. Ess.*, II, 239 ff., especially 254-269.
[172] Von Kremer, *Kgchte.*, II, 112.

portrayal of that romantic love which was to be the product of many ages of evolution. Domestic comfort and fellowship are represented in the case of Odysseus and Penelope.[173] Says Odysseus to Nausikaa: "And may the gods give thee thy heart's desire, a husband and a home; and may they add concord, a noble thing. For nothing is better or finer than when two, man and wife, maintain a home in harmony of spirit"—"when wife stands not at variance with her lord."[174]

Such passages sound almost modern and rightly so but for their setting. The highest virtue of a woman in wedlock is devotion to her husband and children; that of a man is to cherish his wife and with her devote himself to their children. Pair-marriage calls for this and for that reason no other arrangement can compare with it for societal utility on advanced stages. Under it there is far less room for contention as to shares, spheres, or equality. In true pair-marriage the privacy alluded to above may work out into an understanding intimacy of one with the other, wherein a wedded pair supplement each other not alone in self-maintenance or in the rearing of children but in the life of sentiment and of the spirit. Inevitable differences in attitude and outlook due to sex may come, with indulgence and forbearance, to be matters of piquant interest and of mutual stimulation to the apprehension of less tangible values. This cannot well occur under other forms of mating. Thus may a relation that began its evolution in crudeness and coercion refine itself through the ages, and despite life's mischances, into the highest and most durable of earthly satisfactions.

173 Keller, *Hom. Soc.*, 219, 223-224, 233 (where all references to text are given).
174 Homer, *Odyssey*, VI, 180-184; Euripides, *Medea*, 15.

CHAPTER LIV

§402. "Population-Policy." The farther one penetrates into an involved subject like societal self-perpetuation, where all the strands endlessly interlace, the more frequently does he find that he has already trenched somewhat upon topics which are still to come. It is inevitable that foregoing chapters should have anticipated in part something of what is now to appear concerning children in their relation to marriage. The fact that it is generally her children only who inherit is, for example, one of the marks of identification of the chief wife. But these partial anticipations, seen aright, serve the important purpose of exhibiting the institution of marriage as an integral whole. Familiar strands should be noted even more carefully than others, for they are the master-filaments of the fabric.

Reproduction in nature is subject to neither limitation nor stimulation on the part of the reproducers. It takes place as nature dictates; and nature seems to be intent upon numbers. The limit of reproduction appears to be the generative capacity of the organisms. A powerful passion, engrossing to the neglect of other considerations, even that of self-preservation, urges bi-sexual beings to increase and multiply. If it is held in abeyance for certain periods, that is an expedient in the economy of nature which cannot be taken as a limitation on numbers. Death alone accomplishes diminution.

It is a necessary inference that earliest man was under the same natural compulsions and subject to the same sole and ultimate limitation as the rest of the animal-world. However, when mankind comes first within our range of vision, in the guise of the least developed tribes, they are thought by some to show a genuine "population-policy";[1] that is, to have developed expedients for increasing or for limiting numbers, as, for instance, magic and infanticide respectively. It seems to be assumed that this has been done deliberately, consciously, and as the result of reflection; the

[1] Sumner, *Folkways*, §§321 ff.

very term "policy" carries that implication. The truth of such a contention must be tested upon the cases presently to be cited; and in view of several broad considerations preliminarily to be noted.

Deduction from the conclusions reached as to the nature and origin of the mores,[2] as well as induction from a large body of facts, leads to the preliminary conviction that undeveloped societies can have no policies about numbers which are consciously held as the result of reflection. Whatever is done is by way of simple adjustment to life-conditions in response to easily visualized self-interest. The welfare of society is taken care of by the impersonal action of societal selection and adjustment, acting through or over the conglomerate of individual response. Some advanced groups attain to a sort of pooling of experience and action, say under some great stress, with a solidarity indicating that the status of all is consciously before the mind of many. Simple concurrence in the code, however, may lend a deceptive impression of rational agreement; one has to be on guard against such an impression, for common action may indicate common consciousness of conditions as little as does the habit of gulls when at rest all to face the same way. The sources of practices militating toward increase or diminution of population are—and not for primitive peoples alone—so various and often in motive so irrelevant to the result as respects numbers, that it seems very risky to align them in evidence for a deliberate population-policy, even when they have the superficial appearance of such.[3]

The nearest approach to a population-policy which we have encountered is a rite of the Lower Congo region. "When the elders of a village consider that the women are not bearing the usual proportion of children, they proclaim an 'N'Kimba.' The charm doctors, and other active agents of the rite, take up quarters in an isolated forest, where they are soon joined by numbers of voluntary initiates. . . . Full sexual license is permitted. . . . A complicated form of language is adopted. The initiate is supposed to die, and to be resurrected, and to have entered upon a new life. At the conclusion of the 'N'Kimba,' which usually lasts five or six years, the members of the craft take a new name, and do not recognize their parents and friends."[4]

An actual population-policy is represented by a bill introduced in the Angora Assembly whereby every Turk aged twenty-five must marry and each couple must have a child every three years. The deputy who introduced the

2 §§18, 19, 20, 21, above.   3 Keller, *Soc. Evol.*, 93 ff.
4 Ward, in JAI, XXIV, 288.

bill hoped the population of Asia Minor would be thus increased from eight to forty-eight millions. The bill was lost.[5]

The fact is that reproduction falls under restriction whenever it clashes seriously with self-maintenance; under that condition of maladjustment, so perilous to society's life, a consensus of many relevant and irrelevant motives leads to restriction. The simpler and more concrete cases of disharmony between self-perpetuation and self-maintenance can be visualized by men of simple understanding, whereas those involving the larger, less obvious interests of the whole society cannot. Because of misery, bitterly felt, conquered groups or slaves may dread and avoid reproduction; the ruling class may shrink from endangering their power or splitting up their property by increase; but even the best strains in a population, the least deficient in understanding, do not reproduce freely in the society's interest if so doing appears to endanger their own standards.[6]

Practices such as the various restrictions on mating, the prevention of conception, abortion, infanticide, cannibalism, the killing of the old, actually exist and their immediate effect is to keep down numbers; they, like the Malthusian checks, in their degree relieve the pressure of population on sustenance, that is, of self-perpetuation on self-maintenance. What is thus presented is, nevertheless, an immense, impersonal, unplanned societal process, deserving the name "policy" as little as does the procedure of nature as respects numbers in the world of plants and animals. Many of the limitations set on the sex-relation,[7] to take one set of cases, amount to restriction of births; this was their immediate effect, whether or not they operated, in the long run, to promote population. In any case, the issue as to population was incidental; how the sexes were to get along with one another was the dominant interest. Men could not take account of the incidental and remote consequences of their sex-arrangements, especially as these latter were themselves seldom if ever the product of conscious planning; but what men could not plan and foresee offered no difficulty in the working out of an impersonal process. In the societal range, as in the organic, selection may be figured, in Darwin's[8] words, as

---

[5] Assoc. Press despatch, April 23, 1923.
[6] Holmes, *Trend of Race*, 173 ff.
[7] §§347 ff., above.   [8] *Orig. of Species*, 77.

"daily and hourly scrutinizing, throughout the world, the slightest variations . . . silently and insensibly working, *whenever and wherever opportunity offers*," taking account of all those "slightest differences of structure or constitution" which, while they elude human apprehension, "may well turn the nicely balanced scale in the struggle for life, and so be preserved." What matter, then, if human intentions do not envisage the large results and if men contribute to them unintentionally and unwittingly? An agency transcending human wit is in the field and is competent to meet all demands upon it.

§403*. Restriction of Numbers. This survey of generalities may serve as a sort of outline-sketch within which the details may fall more obviously into place. First, then, come the cases of actual restriction; they are few, for limitation of numbers occurs as a comparative rarity among simple peoples. When the several forms of restriction have been covered, it will be possible to concentrate upon the prevailing belief as to offspring, namely, that they are a blessing of which no one can receive too much. We shall begin with representative cases of limitation.

Certain Australian tribes mutilate the breasts of women, "for the purpose of rendering their rearing children impossible."[9] Other natives perform operations on the male which result in diminished fertility, but it is not likely that, with the recourse of infanticide at hand, there is any idea of restricting population. The origin of the custom is referred by the natives to "some ancestor or other who first of all performed one or both of the operations, usually upon himself first and later upon other individuals. Since that time the natives have continued to follow his example, but why their ancestor first of all performed the ceremony they have not the vaguest idea."[10] Other writers have seen in such mutilations the purpose of restricting numbers to food-supply. "The stability of the Australian population is preserved by killing and exposing a certain proportion of infants, or by the castration or hypospadic mutilation of the boys before puberty. In some tribes every father of a family voluntarily submits to one of these radical operations after the birth of his second or third child. Personal sacrifice for public good could go no further."[11] But Roth[12] notes first that the marriage-taboos sufficiently retard the growth of numbers and also that the operations are not sure preventatives. He thinks

---

[9] Curr, *Aust. Race,* I, 76.
[10] Spencer and Gillen, *North. Tr. Cent. Aust.*, 329-330.
[11] Evans, in PSM, LII, 31; Cunow, *Australneger,* 31; Nadaillac, *Preh. Amer.*, 520.
[12] *N.W. Cent. Queensland,* 179.

them a rude preparation for marriage.[13] Again, the cannibalism in West Australia (where every tenth child born is eaten) is explained as "necessary to keep the tribe from increasing beyond the carrying capacity of the territory."[14] Sodomy through fear of overpopulation is reported from New Guinea.[15] It is clear enough that overpopulation comes speedily in the more sterile parts of Australia. It may be recalled that in 1899 the largest totemic group in the Alice Springs district consisted of forty souls on a hundred square miles; that a family of four needed a territory of ten square miles; and that this condition probably represented overpopulation.[16] Further adjustments to these difficult life-conditions will appear a little later, under infanticide.

Weeks[17] says that polygamists have few children in the Congo region because the old men monopolize all the women. In Bonny, West Africa, "a custom prevalent among these people, and common more or less to all other natives of the Delta, was the destroying of any woman if she became the mother of more than four children."[18] Among the Masai, "an increasing reluctance on the part of the men to settle down in the married state and beget children" has led to the drifting away of the women in increasing numbers to the trading-camps of foreigners.[19] Of course this is no more than love of ease on the part of the shirking men. In Tibet, "while the system of polyandry is keeping down population, the Tibetan government is worrying itself over its steady increase."[20] The people of the Antilles killed themselves by poison or the halter, and refused to have children to inherit their hard lot under Spanish domination.[21] The custom is widespread in South America for the old men to marry the young women and the young men the old women. The result is few children;[22] but this could hardly have been devised as a limitation on population. The Lenguas of Paraguay were dying out because each pair would have but a single child.[23] In Tierra del Fuego, "the struggle for mere existence is so bitter that unproductive members of the community are promptly swept away by cannibalism."[24] Reference to the review of this practice[25] will show that, however effective it may be in reducing numbers, it can scarcely be regarded as a population-policy.

More sophisticated peoples may adopt deliberate policies, as in the enforced migration of half a population, selected by lot, in the case of a famine, or in that of the *ver sacrum*.[26] In Corsica the Genoese were so detested that, in 1729, the girls of a city vowed never to marry as long as the enemy defiled the soil of the country. They said they did not wish to bear slave-children.[27] Once in Iceland, at a time of famine, it was decided to kill all the old and unproduc-

[13] Stuart, in *Jr. and Proc. Roy. Soc. N. S. Wales*, 115, 120.
[14] Whitmarsh, *World's Rough Hand*, 178.
[15] Beardmore, in JAI, XIX, 464.
[16] §29, above; Spencer and Gillen, *Nat. Tr. Cent. Aust.*, 9.
[17] Quoted in §398, above.
[18] Kingsley, *W. Afr. Studies*, 538.   [19] Johnston, *Uganda*, II, 829.
[20] Kawaguchi, in *Cent. Mag.*, XLV, 391.
[21] Peschel, *Races*, 151.
[22] Ehrenreich, in *Berl. Mus. Vkde.*, II, 27; Im Thurn, *Guiana*, 223.
[23] Hassler, in *Inter. Cong. Anthrop. Chicago*, 1893, 366.
[24] Nadaillac, *Preh. Amer.*, 520.   [25] §§290-292, above.
[26] §294, above; Herodotus, *Hist.*, I, §94.
[27] Vuillier, *Forgotten Isles*, 201.

tive and marriages of the poor were subjected to legal supervision. Exile was the punishment for marrying and having children without the lawful amount of means; the exiled might return when their means reached the required amount and when it was impossible for them to have more children.[28] In the seventeenth century cruel punishments were inflicted upon peasants who would not marry and beget children to inherit misery; in Holstein, in 1739, serfs were emancipated because they had lost courage to work or marry or, if married, had lost the natural desire for offspring—all through their experiences of wretchedness.[29] Modern cases occur where pregnancy is a sort of disgrace, so that women remain in seclusion during that period; or where to have children soon after marriage, or many children, is regarded as a mark of sensuality. Hence childbearing may be put off until several years have elapsed since marriage.[30]

What these miscellaneous cases reveal is scarcely more than the usual human twisting and turning in avoidance of discomfort, together with several practices which either do or may operate to limit numbers, though not so intended. There is a more positive, direct, and systematic method of limitation whereby children are put to death either before or after birth.[31]

§404*. Infanticide. Practices of abstention during the period of lactation have been noted in another connection;[32] religion has often imposed taboos which amount, in effect, to limitation on births.[33] Such usages may constitute indirect adjustment of numbers to life-conditions. Prevention of conception is to be found among primitive peoples, though it is rare. The commonest method of relieving the pressure of numbers, hailed by some as a true population-policy, is by killing the child either before or after birth. The cases of fœticide[34] and infanticide should be scanned with strict attention to the motives revealed; for only by so doing can one arrive at a tenable conclusion as to whether a "policy" as respects population and societal welfare is present or not.

Among the Papuans abortion is frequently and deliberately effected; there are very few half-breeds of European paternity.[35] "They love children but do not like to raise more than three," chiefly out of fear of shortage of food or

[28] Weinhold, *Deut. Frauen*, 92.
[29] Sugenheim, *Leibeigenschaft*, 511, 517, note.
[30] Temesváry, *Geburtshilfe*, 26; Von Fircks, *Bevölkrgslehre*, 313, note.
[31] Sumner, *Folkways*, ch. VII.   [32] §409, below.
[33] §§225, 277, 281, 374, 388, above.
[34] List of tribes using drugs to induce miscarriage in *Archiv. f. Anth.*, V, 451-455.
[35] Von Pfeil, *Südsee*, 31.

fondness for comfort.[36] "Children are burdensome. We are weary of them. We go dead."[37] "Abortion and infanticide were very common. If a woman did not want the trouble of bringing up a child, desired to appear young, was afraid her husband might think the birth before its time, or wished to spite her husband," she resorted to abortion.[38] It may be stated here, once for all, that the rude methods of primitive abortion often had as consequences death, invalidism, and permanent sterility. In the New Hebrides the women avoided the care of children; in New Britain children are not born for from two to four years after marriage, this being due to "a dislike among women to speedily becoming mothers."[39] Fœticide is common in the Solomon Island group and in the Torres Straits islands; a single woman will thus avoid shame and a wife the trouble of child-rearing.[40] Premature births are induced quite commonly in South Africa.[41] The absence of the practice in northeast Africa is commented upon as rather extraordinary.[42] Unmarried women of the Chin Hills procure abortion and it is common in northern India, though in later times it has been punished severely. In Malacca a husband might beat to death a wife who thus avoided the trouble of child-rearing. It was rarely done. An unmarried girl who strove thus to escape consequences was held in contempt by the other women and was not sought in marriage.[43]

In the Malay Archipelago the custom was common and had direful results in suffering, though "among the Dyaks wilful miscarriage is never resorted to under any circumstances."[44] In Atjeh, the natives themselves "assert that married pairs with many children are much in the minority; not alone outside of but also within marriage they make much use, according to their own admission, of means to avoid pregnancy or to secure abortion."[45] The women in central Celebes avoid lacerations sustained in parturition, regarding such as the greatest disgrace.[46] On the Gilbert Islands, though infanticide is not practised, abortion is, if there are already two children or if single women become pregnant.[47] Similar recourse for the unmarried occurs in the Nauru Islands.[48] The Yap women employ both abortion and contraceptives, lest they lose their comeliness; the former is regarded as shameful and a cause for divorce, though not legally punishable.[49]

Though desire for and love of children are universal among the Indians, yet "artificial abortion is practised among all the tribes visited, and is told of by the older men or women without much hesitation. The causes of the practice are shame or fear in the unmarried, and among married women inability through poverty to provide for the family, or a loss of many previous children,

---

[36] Krieger, *Neu-Guinea*, 165, 390.

[37] Von Rosenberg, *Geelvinkbaai*, 91.   [38] Codrington, *Melanesians*, 229.

[39] Leggatt, in AAAS, 1892, 704; Danks, in JAI, XVIII, 291.

[40] Elton, in JAI, XVII, 93; Haddon, in JAI, XIX, 359; Hunt, in JAI, XXVIII, 11, 12.

[41] Fritsch, *Eingeb. S.-Afr.*, 96; Büttner, in *Ausland*, 1882, 852.

[42] Paulitschke, *Nordost-Afr.*, I, 172.

[43] Stevens, in *Ztsft. f. Eth.*, XXVIII, 186, 187.

[44] Wilken, *Vkde.*, 209-211; Roth, *Sarawak*, I, 101; but see Perelaer, *Dajaks*, 37.

[45] Snouck-Hurgronje, *Atjèhers*, I, 73; Jacobs, *Groot-Atjeh*, I, 112-113.

[46] Riedel, in *Bijd.*, XXXV, 79.   [47] Finsch, *Ethnol. Erfahr.*, III, 31.

[48] Brandeis, in *Globus*, XCI, 77.   [49] Senfft, in *Globus*, XCI, 153.

or a desire to be rid of concomitant physical difficulties and necessary subsequent cares." It is commoner among the unmarried, despite the prevalence of premarital freedom and the fact that the unmarried woman is not particularly discredited by having a child. Attempts are made to induce artificial sterility. "One of the women applied to the writer for a 'medicine to make her have no more children.' When questioned as to the propriety of such a proceeding, the answer was that when one child after another is born and dies, or when a number of children, one after another, are born dead, something should be done to end this unfortunate state of affairs."[50] Among the Cheyennes, "it has long been the custom that a woman should not have a second child until her first is ten years old."[51] The Pima mother sometimes nursed a child till it was six or seven years old, during which time other children were sacrificed unborn to the nursing child, which the mother loved more "because she could see it."[52] Again, women forbore to go through child-birth in order not to spoil their bodies.[53] The Guacurus of Brazil were constantly diminishing because the women would bear no children till they were thirty, thus avoiding the privations of pregnancy and the trouble of child-rearing. Without children they could better bear the hardships of nomadic life and would not be abandoned by their husbands. One of the tribes allied to this people has nearly perished through this practice, there being now not over a hundred of them of pure blood.[54]

The usage was common in antiquity[55] and has not disappeared in more modern times. It is said to exist throughout Hungary, correlatively with a high birthrate, and to be carried on by all the nationalities to such an extent as to shock the observer. Women rejoice in sterility. The policy seems to be to have few children, in so far as they know of means to avoid offspring.[56]

It would appear that fœticide is carried on as a very obvious expedient for the easement of life, meaning generally the individual life of the woman, not the corporate existence. In by far the greater number of cases not the remotest concern for the society's welfare enters the mind of anybody. The practice is highly deleterious to health and, in general, is to be encountered mainly under conditions of isolation from societal competition. It is held to be directly accountable for certain cases of race-decline in numbers and strength, and appears as an expedient that is highly anti-social, a variation in the mores which, though it may have served as a sort of awkward adjustment under severe pressure of population on sustenance, was sure to be eliminated in competition with other variations, even with that of infanticide.

[50] Hrdlička, in BAE, Bull. XXXIV, 163.
[51] Grinnell, in AA, IV, 15.   [52] Russell, in BAE, XXVI, 186.
[53] Eden, First Three Books, 237.
[54] Spix and Martius, Brazil, II, 77; Von Martius, Beiträge, I, 231, 243; Koch, in Globus, LXXXI, 4.
[55] Lecky, Europ. Morals, II, 20-21.
[56] Temesváry, Geburtshilfe, 12, 13, 14.

Much more prevalent than the destruction of the embryo is that of the child after birth. Though it is not true that "all nations at a low degree of civilization follow the custom of exposing their daughters,"[57] the custom of infanticide has nevertheless been widespread both in space and time. It is obviously a check on numbers unless, indeed, the fact that some of the children are put to death means that the death-rate among the remainder is correspondingly lowered. The motives to infanticide are various and must be reviewed before the sense of the custom can be appraised.

Infanticide is very widespread among the Australians. An old woman of a South Australian tribe declared that if the Europeans had come a few years later they would have found Australia empty. Other natives asserted that half the children born were killed. Every child was killed which was born before his predecessor was able to run, as the mother could not carry two. Misshapen children were killed. At least half the children of white fathers thus perished. Mothers often killed children born of a marriage into which they had been forced. If, however, a child had been allowed to live, they were very affectionate toward it.[58] This summary of Ratzel's needs amplification. Says Curr:[59] "I am of the opinion that the Australian females bear on an average six children, or did before the advent of the whites, and whilst living in their natural state; and that they reared two boys and one girl, as a rule; the maximum being about ten. The rest were destroyed immediately after birth." Dawson[60] thinks that rarely more than four are allowed to grow up. Five is considered a large number to rear. "In all the tribes infanticide is practiced. There is no difference made in respect of either sex. The usual reason given for killing the child is that there is another one still being suckled by the mother. It is only on very rare occasions that any child, except a mere infant, is killed," though at times a healthy child may be put to death "for the purpose of feeding a weaker and elder one, under the idea that the strength of the former will pass into and benefit the latter." If once the mother has suckled the child, it is usually safe.[61] In Central Australia, "the number is kept down, not with any idea at all of regulating the food supply, so far as the adults are concerned, but simply from the point of view that, if the mother is suckling one child, she cannot provide food for another, quite apart from the question of the trouble of carrying two children about."[62] On the Murray River infanticide is practised "solely to get rid of the trouble of rearing children, and to enable the woman to follow her husband about in his wanderings, which she frequently could not do if encumbered with a child."[63] In Victoria the new-born that are slain are eaten; thus strength is supposed to be infused in the preceding child. Again the young of immature mothers are killed, as being weakly and not worth preserving; this amounts to a sort of survival of the fittest.[64] In the southeast, where infanticide is by starvation, "a mother would give all the

57 Ihering, *Evol. of Aryan*, 338.   58 Ratzel, *Vkde.*, II, 59, 61.
59 *Aust. Race*, I, 70.   60 *Aust. Aborig.*, 39.
61 Spencer and Gillen, *North. Tr. Cent. Aust.*, 608.
62 Spencer and Gillen, *Nat. Tr. Cent. Aust.*, 51, 264 (quoted).
63 Eyre, *Cent. Aust.*, II, 324.   64 Smyth, *Vict.*, I, 52.

food she had to her children, going hungry herself."[65] Again children were killed "to save trouble and privations in time of drought." The fate of the child "depended much upon the condition the country was in at the time, and the prospect of the mother's rearing it satisfactorily, no preference being shown for the male sex."[66]

The Australian cases are significant both in their number and because of the peculiarly difficult conditions of existence; nearly all the motives for infanticide co-exist in that region and most of them go back to considerations of self-maintenance.

Infanticide is widely practised among the Melanesians. The mother does it if she thinks herself insulted by her husband, and often also from vanity, to make herself appear young.[67] "No man likes a family of girls, and if a couple have no sons and three girls are born in succession, the last born might be killed."[68] In New Guinea, though the father is prone to evade the task of child-rearing, yet daughters are spared for the sake of their purchase-price in marriage. In general they do not like to raise over two children.[69] If a child is sickly and peevish its parents do not indefinitely tolerate the annoyance.[70] The beach-people of one of the Solomon Islands prefer to buy children of the bush-tribes; but infanticide is absent in these islands except in the case of illegitimate children.[71] In the New Hebrides abortion and infanticide are practised to escape trouble.[72] In the Torres Straits islands the custom was common: "Too hard work" was the reason for not rearing offspring.[73] In the Murray Islands, after the birth of a certain number of children the destruction-process commenced, lest the food-supply become insufficient. If children were all of one sex, some were killed from shame, it being held proper to have equal numbers of boys and girls.[74] In the Banks Islands female children were preserved over male, both "because of the family passing through the female side, as well as with the prospect of gain when the girl should be betrothed and married."[75]

As regards female infanticide, Wilken[76] (quoted elsewhere also, in a different connection) notes a tendency among savages to superfluity of females. He quotes Morgan[77] on the North American Indians to the effect that "the females are usually more numerous than the males from the destruction of the latter in war." The Blackfeet and Cheyennes are reported to have two females to one male; the Kubus of Sumatra have enough women so that each man can have two, three, or four of them. This seems hardly credible; in any case female infanticide, under such conditions, could do little more than equalize the numbers of the sexes.

In other parts of the world the inducements to infanticide are, in the main, the same as in the foregoing cases. It has been noted once or twice that children in any way abnormal were likely to

[65] Howitt, *S.E. Aust.*, 748.
[66] Bonney, in JAI, XIII, 125, 137, 225.
[67] Ratzel, *Vkde.*, II, 274.   [68] Seligmann, *Melanesians*, 704, 705.
[69] Krieger, *Neu-Guinea*, 292-293.   [70] Abel, *New Guinea*, 43.
[71] Elton, in JAI, XVII, 93; Ratzel, *Vkde.*, II, 274.
[72] Macdonald, in AAAS, 1892, 721.
[73] Haddon, in JAI, XIX, 314, 359.   [74] Hunt, in JAI, XXVIII, 11.
[75] Codrington, *Melanesians*, 229.   [76] In VG, III, 43, and note.
[77] "Syst. Consanguinity," in *Smithson. Contrib. Knowledge*, XVII, 477.

meet their fate immediately after birth. Considerations of a religious order thus led to the elimination of departures from the normal. The birth of two or more infants at the same time is distinctly exceptional; hence the case of twins offers a clear example of treatment of progeny which has nothing directly to do with economic considerations. Sometimes they are prized; the whole case is here illustrated.

Contrary to the assertion that in Australia twins are often born[78] is the statement that they are no less rare than amongst Europeans.[79] "Twins are usually destroyed at once as something uncanny, but apparently they are of very rare occurrence"; there is, however, "no ill-treatment of the mother, who is not thought any the less of."[80] Twins "are destroyed. To keep them would be a disgrace likening them unto dogs."[81] "Only one of the children was allowed to live, and even this one only in case the older children were able to follow the mother on her journeyings without help."[82] Hagen[83] mentions a single grown pair of twins that escaped death by chance. Again, if the twins are of one sex, they live; if of different sex, the girl, or sometimes the boy, is killed. "Every Papuan woman has a horror of the birth of twins, for in such case she will be jibed at by the other women of the village and compared with a bitch, which has a half dozen young at the same time; or they will hold her in suspicion of an immoral life, since, according to the local Papuan belief, twin-births are a consequence of adultery. Others blame the husband and say that he has broken a vow or taboo and therefore his wife is punished with twins."[84] In some places twins are acquisitions to be proud of; "the only sad thing about them is that they give much trouble"; again, "a woman who has twins or triplets is compared to a pig and is ridiculed."[85] In Florida Island "there seems to be something of a suspicion that two fathers may be concerned."[86] In New Britain, "if twins are born and they are boy and girl, they are put to death because of being of the same class and being of opposite sex, they were supposed to have had in the womb a closeness of connection which amounted to a violation of their marital class law."[87]

In East Africa, "the birth of twins is very unlucky, and in former times one was thrown into the bush; the natives, however, assure one that this practice ceased before the Government was established. When, however, a cow calves twins it is still more unlucky, and such a cow has to be slaughtered at once together with its calves otherwise nothing but sickness and death occurs in the village. The belief in this is still as strong as of old, and when a Mkamba kills his cow and its calves one can imagine how dire is the fate he is thereby warding off."[88]

[78] Jung, *Australien*, I, 98.   [79] Bonney, in JAI, XIII, 126.
[80] Spencer and Gillen, *North. Tr. Cent. Aust.*, 609; Spencer and Gillen, *Nat. Tr. Cent. Aust.*, 52.
[81] Gason, in JAI, XXIV, 176.   [82] Jung, *Australien*, 98.
[83] *Papua's*, 230, note.   [84] Krieger, *Neu-Guinea*, 293.
[85] Seligmann, *Melanesians*, 705.   [86] Codrington, *Melanesians*, 230.
[87] §353, above; Danks, in JAI, XVIII, 292.
[88] Dundas, C., in JAI, XLIII, 519.

The Nagas of India hold it advisable to destroy both twins.[89] Twins of different sex are sometimes regarded as born betrothed[90] but again they are regarded as an evil and killed, while their parents remain unclean for a year.[91] The Dyaks' beliefs cause them to be little pleased with twins, while in Atjeh it is the economic situation that makes them rather unwelcome.[92] In the Nauru Islands, where the mother-family prevails, if twins are of different sexes the boy is always killed.[93] On Duke of York Island if twins are of the same sex, they are allowed to live; if of different sex, both are killed.[94] The case is like a preceding one where intra-uterine proximity seems a violation of class-regulations in marriage.

In America, "twins are a mystery to the Teton, who think that they are of superhuman origin and must come from Twin-land. As they are not human beings they must be treated very politely and tenderly, lest they become offended and die in order to return to Twin-land."[95] The Pima receive twins with general rejoicing. "Every inhabitant of the village brings gifts and the mother feels assured that she will henceforth be a fortunate woman."[96] In British Guiana twin-births are extremely rare. Though Schomburgk[97] saw but two pairs of twins, their survival negatived the practice of killing one member of such pairs to avoid suspicion of infidelity or to evade ridicule. "In the birth of twins they saw something unnatural, unfortunate, and displeasing; ceremonies and sacrifices lasting several days were necessary after such an event."[98]

In one of the lays of Marie de France,[99] the notion is expressed that

> Woman never bore
> Two children at a birth, nor ever will,
> Except she serve two masters!

A jealous wife, of an "envenomed tongue," is figured as making use of the notion against another, and subsequently, by the irony of fate, herself bearing twins.

Misgiving at the advent of twins seems to have been confined chiefly to the more primitive tribes and peoples and not all of these show it. It is generally a matter of religion where it occurs.

§405. Causes of Infanticide. In view of the evidence it is impossible to share the view that infanticide has regularly been due to a fear of overpopulation and thus indicates an advance in social forethought.[100] No doubt impending overpopulation brought

89 Godden, in JAI, XXVI, 178.   90 §§348, 368, above.

91 Wilken, *Vkde.*, 208.

92 Grabowsky, in *Globus*, LXXII, 270; Jacobs, *Groot-Atjeh*, I, 105.

93 Brandeis, in *Globus*, XCI, 76.   94 Fison, in AAAS, 1892, 693.

95 Dorsey, in BAE, XI, 482.   96 Russell, in BAE, XXVI, 185.

97 *Brit.-Guiana*, II, 313.   98 Friederici, in *Globus*, XC, 305.

99 Luquiens, *Three Lays of Marie de France*, 26 ff.

100 Lippert, *Kgchte.*, I, 212-213; cases of infanticide varying inversely with the food-supply in Letourneau, *Soc.*, 134.

its load of misery, which was evaded, individually or family-wise, by the means available, including infanticide—a complex of local squirmings under pressure conveying a superficial impression of "policy." A number of our cases, however, reveal the custom in a setting of well-being. Often the standard of living plays the dominant rôle in the matter; it is too expensive or too much trouble to rear children, especially where the reasonably prosperous are lazy and pleasure-loving. In general, where the child is an asset rather than a liability, infanticide is likely to be restricted altogether or to be confined to one sex. The cases do not support in the latter event any selection of one sex over the other consistent enough to confirm hypotheses, for instance that of widespread polyandry as based upon general female infanticide.[101] Some of the evidence would support the contention that the prevalence of infanticide varies directly with the amount of illegitimacy;[102] this, however, is but one of many factors with which it is correlated.

Female vanity has much to do with the destruction of the child, born or unborn, as well as with the prevention of conception; and ethnocentrism is concerned to keep the blood pure. Where religious ideas lead to the destruction of freaks, twins, and the weak, there is doubtless a kind of selection in favor of the normal and strong.[103] Again, babes are buried with their dead mothers, not alone because in surviving they will constitute a burden on someone else but for fear of the especially malignant ghost of the woman who has died in child-bed.[104] Further, there is a belief that the strength lost by the immature mother can be restored to her by cannibalistic practice.[105] All these considerations, as well as those of self-maintenance, tend to weaken and to shorten the duration of the expression of mother-love.[106]

Before concluding the subject of limitation of numbers the Roman custom of the *ver sacrum*[107] should be recalled. This was a swarming off of bands of youths devoted as infants to the gods and to the luck which the gods might

[101] §397, above; Lippert, *Kgchte.*, I, 219; Westermarck, *Marriage*, II, 162-166; Starcke, *Prim. Fam.*, 131.

[102] Lippert, *Kgchte.*, I, 218.   [103] Lippert, *Kgchte.*, I, 206.

[104] §§219, above, and 408, below; Lippert, *Kgchte.*, I, 216; Letourneau, *Morale*, 119-125.

[105] §§291, 292, above.

[106] §336, above; Lippert, *Kgchte.*, I, 209, 211, 203.

[107] §§294, 295, above.

give, in a sort of mass-exposure. In the fifteenth century the same custom arose again, in an informal and unreligious phase, under similar conditions. It represents an easement of the population-land relation in a given region. In its origin this usage was a substitute for infanticide or exposure, by which these were transmuted into migration and colonization.

The representative cases here offered show at most—but they show that clearly—an unconscious adjustment to conditions of life as felt in the pursuit of what was conceived to be self-interest. This is no more a population-policy conceived in terms of society than is the tendency to refrain from buying at high prices an economic policy adopted with national interests in mind.

§406*. Sterility and Fecundity. Restriction of population is distinctly the exception among primitive peoples; few of them find it too much trouble to rear children. There is little or nothing corresponding to the conscious control over numbers which goes with a modern high standard of living.[108] In general, nothing is so important to simple peoples, next to bald self-maintenance, as the assurance of posterity. It is not that they want children for the sake of the society, any more than they renounce offspring in view of the society's interest; there is a multitude of varied considerations rooting in individual and family-interest which demands that there shall be children and which renders them an object of ardent desire. Someone has compared deliberate attempts to increase population to assisting a water-fall with an oar;[109] such an enterprise, whatever its degree of futility, is not in the minds of the simpler peoples. They are trying to meet the exigencies of life as presented and their only policy is to live up to the mores, which, over long periods and under the action of forces unperceived by the individual, are adjusting themselves to life-conditions encountered by society. Though conformity to code is action in society's interest, that action is quite unpremeditated.

Where the situation calls for numbers there is encountered the reverse of the sentiments and actions that result in limitation;[110] for then children become an asset instead of a liability. This situation, appearing regularly in the frontier-society of European

108 §§25, 38, above.
109 Bell, "Distilleries," *Overstone Tracts*, III, 515.
110 §402, above.

settlers and colonizers in the temperate zone,[111] occurs among savages also, provided conditions are favorable. In Togo, for instance, where there is much vacant land, many children are a blessing. Much labor is needed; there is a profusion of products that may be disposed of in trade; the children themselves can be sent to market.[112] Such cases go back to the fundamental relation of men to land.[113]

The incentives to increase in numbers are the same as those which promote socialization in general and more especially the accumulation of capital and property.[114] The savage looks upon children as an economic asset and as insurance against old age; he wants daughters to sell in marriage; his pride lies in the preservation of the family and line; and he needs children, especially sons, in view of convictions as to the spirit-world, which derive from ghost-fear. Illustrations of these incentives and of the detailed beliefs and motives connected with them appear in preceding connections as well as in the following pages.

Strongly indicative of the place offspring hold in the eyes of primitive people is the custom called "teknonymy," regular in Indonesia, of naming the father, and also the mother, from the child. The practice appears also in Africa and America. The Bechuana parents take the name of the child, and often address their children as Ma (mother), or Ra (father). Dr. Livingstone's eldest boy being named Robert, Mrs. Livingstone was, after his birth, always addressed as Ma-Robert, instead of Mary, her Christian name. When the father takes the child's name that means, according to Wilken, an emphasis on his paternity analogous to that of the couvade.[115]

Survivals and symbols in the wedding-ceremony bear witness to the fear of sterility and wedlock is frequently dissolved if that fear is justified in the event.[116] Magic is invoked, not only to ac-

[111] Keller, *Colon.*, 5 ff. [112] Klose, *Togo*, 256.
[113] §2, above. [114] §§11 ff., 81, 112, above.
[115] §212, of text and *Case-Book;* Wilken, *Vkde.*, 212 ff., where a number of examples are cited; Wilken, in VG, I, 106-107, 283; Furness, *Head-Hunters,* 42; Marsden, *Sumatra,* 286; Perelaer, *Dajaks,* 42; Hose, in JAI, XXIII, 170; Milne, *Eastern Clan,* 30; Creagh, in AAAS, 1892, 681; Livingstone, *Mission. Travels,* I, 140; Sibree, *Great Afr. Isl.,* 167.
[116] §§371-374, 392, above.

count for sterility but also to get rid of the curse.[117] For it is a veritable curse; some peoples in the Indian Archipelago believe that in the spirit-world the childless wife bears a snake in her bosom as a punishment.[118] It is perhaps unnecessary to stress this matter in view of the tenor of many cases gathered under various headings; we may re-illustrate, as peculiarly significant of the feeling that woman's function is the bearing of children, certain beliefs about the ghost of the woman who has died in child-bed.[119] These seem to reveal two conceptions of the matter: either that the woman is to blame because she has not fulfilled her natural function or that she has perished nobly, through no fault of her own, in the discharge of it. She is treated as sterile or not in accordance with the acceptation of the first or second of these views; in neither case, be it noted, does the importance of the child-bearing function fail of recognition.

In West Africa, women who die in child-birth are treated much as are those who bear twins. They are thought to have committed adultery with spirits and are not buried or thrown away; they are, as far as possible, destroyed.[120] Again, the child is buried with the mother in a case of child-bed death.[121] "The bodies of women dying in child-birth are taken out through the back of the house, and buried without any ceremony whatever."[122] "Spirits of men and women for whom no offerings have been made are said to wander about working mischief. If a man dies from accident, such as a fall from a tree, or is killed by man or wild beast, no ceremonies may be performed for him; nor in the event of a woman dying in child-birth; the spirit is supposed to wander about working mischief."[123] Such a spirit is "foredoomed, ye say, lest anguish lack, to haunt her home in death."[124] Among the Shans, "it is said that when a woman dies pregnant, her soul passes into torment, and her husband has to enter a monastery and become a priest for a certain time to secure her release."[125] The ghosts of such unfortunates cause all sorts of ills.[126]

In the East Indies this belief is rife; Wilken[127] explains that women dying without tasting the nearing joys of motherhood begrudge them to their fellows and are therefore most dangerous to pregnant wives. Among certain Dyaks the woman who dies in child-bed goes to the future abiding-place of the mur-

---

117 Spencer and Gillen, *Nat. Tr. Cent. Aust.,* 52, note; Basu, in JASB, III, 104; Von Scherzer, *Anfänge d. Industrie,* 29; Maspero, *Hist. Anc.,* I, 740; Weinhold, *Deut. Frauen,* II, 46-47; Roguin, *Mariage,* 46; Sébillot, in AA, IV, 91; Temesváry, *Geburtshilfe,* 9.

118 Wilken, *Vkde.,* 201.   119 §§219, 226, 227, above.

120 Kingsley, *W. Afr. Studies,* 148, 149; Seidel, in *Globus,* LXXII, 44.

121 Stuhlmann, *Mit Emin,* 539; Watt, in JAI, XVI, 355.

122 Godden, in JAI, XXVII, 36.   123 Painter, in JASB, II, 152.

124 Kipling, *Naulahka,* ch. X.

125 Woodthorpe, in JAI, XXVI, 23.   126 Niemann, in *Bijd.,* 1895, 343.

127 In VG, III, 319-320; Wilken, *Vkde.,* 202.

dered.[128] "The bodies of those Sea Dyaks who die from an outpour of blood and of women in child-birth, are not allowed to remain in the house, but are taken away at once and buried in the earth without ceremony and without a coffin. The bones of such are not collected."[129] Souls of women who have died in child-birth are especially intent upon hindering the birth or making it more difficult, and upon killing the child.[130] The case is about the same in Sumatra.[131] In Paraguay, "if a nursing mother dies, her corpse is buried in a squatting posture in the grave, and the child laid in her arms and buried with her. The ghost of the mother would otherwise appear every night, seek out the child, and disturb the living."[132]

Lasch,[133] who lists a number of peoples holding such beliefs, concludes that the primitive peoples generally regard the ghost of the dead woman as dangerous, restless, malevolent—an evil spirit, like that of the suicide; while among more advanced races, where the position of woman in the family and society is higher, her lot is a more honorable one. In Tyrol the belief is that the wife dying in child-bed goes immediately to heaven, or among the martyrs; she may for three days consort with the mother of God.

There is a custom called the "levirate," which is traditionally so closely associated with the Jews that the term has been derived from "Levi," though the proper etymology takes it back to the Latin "*levir*," meaning "husband's brother." In Deuteronomy[134] we read:

"If brethren dwell together, and one of them die, and have no son, the wife of the dead shall not marry without unto a stranger: her husband's brother shall go in unto her, and take her to him as wife, and perform the duty of an husband's brother unto her. And it shall be, that the firstborn which she beareth shall succeed in the name of his brother which is dead, that his name be not blotted out of Israel." There follow penalties to be exacted of the man who refuses this manifest duty.[135] This practice dates back to the most ancient time, and is thought by Maurer[136] to rest upon the ancestor-cult. Traces of it existed among the Arabs;[137] and instances, reproducing Deuteronomic injunctions, are to be found even in the modern press.[138]

Parallelisms appear in various parts of the world, though they may demand an interpretation differing from that given to the Hebrew case. "Spencer suggests that it is one of the results of inheriting women as one would inherit other property; to which Starcke justly replies that this view leaves unexplained the real

[128] Bock, *Borneo*, 103. [129] Roth, *Sarawak*, I, 140.
[130] Grabowsky, in *Globus*, LXXII, 269.
[131] Jacobs, *Groot-Atjeh*, I, 349-350.
[132] Koch, in *Globus*, LXXVIII, 220. [133] In *Globus*, LXXX, 108 ff.
[134] XXV, 5 ff.; Ruth, III, IV; Levit., XX, 21; XVIII, 16.
[135] Gen., XXXVIII, 8. [136] *Vkde.*, I, 150-151.
[137] Smith, *Kinship*, 87; Müller, *Sex. Leben*, 33.
[138] N. Y. *Times*, Aug. 1, 1901; Assoc. Press despatch, Feb. 8, 1897.

point of the custom, the counting of the children as the offspring of the dead brother."[139] When we come to see the importance assigned to children, and especially to sons,[140] we shall be ready to assign great weight to the latter contention. It is our hope in covering this topic not to sin as Barton correctly says sociologists are wont to do: "to heap instances together from every quarter of the globe, and assume that because their external character is similar one cause must have produced them all." Barton[141] himself, however, together with other experts in Semitic lines, thinks the levirate a sort of survival of polyandry[142]—a long inference at best. Ethnographical cases are gathered, it is true, from far and wide;[143] for the sake of learning what they teach, however, not of supporting a preconceived theory.

In West Victoria, when a married man dies, his brother is bound to marry the widow if she has a family, as it is his duty to protect her and rear his brother's children.[144] Among the Melanesians, "the Levirate obtains as a matter of course. The wife has been obtained for one member of a family by the contributions of the whole, and if that member fails by death, some other is ready to take his place, so that the property shall not be lost; it is a matter of arrangement for convenience and economy whether a brother, cousin or uncle of the deceased shall take his widow."[145] In this case the property-motive makes its appearance and the instance might be no more than the inheritance of the widow.[146] In the Torres Straits Islands, widows are free and may re-marry or not according to choice; "hence the Levirate is not in force."[147]

The "Greatest Ghost" of the Zulus ordained that "if anyone dies, his younger brother shall marry the wives of the deceased, that they may not be married by a man of another tribe."[148] "Among Zulus and Pondos, the brother or next of kin cohabits with the widow to rear children to the deceased; . . . the widow usually remains a member of her husband's family, and if she has children, enjoys their guardianship, and to a great extent the care of their property. She may return to her own people, but if she does, she has to leave the children behind and practically disinherit herself of her widow's rights. If there are no children, her late husband's relatives may lay claim to the cattle paid for her marriage, and in such case she retains no claim or interest in

---

139 Barton, *Sem. Orig.*, 66; Spencer, *Prin. Soc.*, I, §302; Starcke, *Prim. Fam.*, 152 ff.

140 §409, below.

141 *Sem. Orig.*, 66, 67, 68; Westermarck, *Marriage*, III, 207 ff.; Starcke, *Prim. Fam.*, 157, 158.

142 §397, above.   143 §§454, 455, below.

144 Dawson, *Aust. Aborig.*, 27.

145 Codrington, *Melanesians*, 244; Codrington, in JAI, XVIII, 308.

146 §§383, 395, above.

147 Haddon, in JAI, XIX, 358.   148 Fritsch, *Eingeb. S.-Afr.*, 139.

them."[149] The betrothed son and heir of a certain chief died at the age of eight, before his father. His brother married the girl. The son of this marriage turned out his own father, asserting that the latter had married his mother solely to produce an heir to the dead brother.[150] Starcke[151] sees in such a custom a parallel to the Hebrew practice: "among the Bechuanas, as among the Jews, when an elder brother dies, the brother next in age takes the wives," the children being regarded as children of the dead brother.

In West Africa, "formerly the Levirate was in force, and when an elder brother died the brother next in order of age married the . . . head wife, and so in succession from brother to brother. There was no obligation to marry the subordinate wives of a deceased elder brother, and they usually devolved upon the legal heirs. If the deceased were childless, the son first born of the new union of the younger brother with the widow was named after the deceased, and was considered to fill the place of a son; he did not, however, as among the Jews, succeed to the property to the exclusion of the Levir—his inheritance lay solely in the house of his actual father."[152] Among the Galla the levirate is practised.[153] In Abyssinia, if a man is emasculated in war, his brother at once takes his wife.[154] "The Malagasy have a practice similar to the Levitical law of the Jews; viz., that if the elder brother die childless, his next brother must marry the widow to keep his brother in remembrance."[155]

In Transcaucasia "the brother is in duty bound to marry his brother's widow, even when he is already married."[156] "The father or brother of the dead man may marry her, and this, indeed, is regarded as a duty and honour"; but if the dead man leaves no father or brother, the widow may live with other men, the children being "held to be just as legitimate as those born of the marriage which was dissolved by death." Among the Svanets if a man dies his wife goes to his next brother, if the latter is unmarried; if he is married, she goes to the next in age; if all are married, she is free to marry whom she will.[157] In Beluchistan, "the betrothal is held to be so holy that if the groom dies before marriage, his brother feels himself bound by the rules of honor and propriety to marry the bride. This is the noblest variety of the levirate, being on religious grounds. Still the same thing falls also under the category of inheritance."[158] "The Hindus combine the Levirate with the Ni-Yoga. According to this the childless wife may be espoused in her husband's lifetime."[159] Such espousal, where the sterility is attributed to the husband, is solemn and sacramental and all unnecessary contacts are avoided.[160]

Among the preceding cases occur instances that might well have gone simply under re-marriage of a widow;[161] and there are a number that similarly recall other aspects of marriage somewhat loosely related to the specific topic before us. They may assist the

[149] Macdonald, in JAI, XIX, 272.
[150] Bent, *Mashonaland,* 12.
[151] *Prim. Fam.,* 288, 154.
[152] Ellis, *Yoruba,* 185-186.
[153] Ratzel, *Vkde.,* I, 434.
[154] Letourneau, *Marr.,* 265.
[155] Sibree, *Great Afr. Isl.,* 246.
[156] Von Haxthausen, *Transkaukasia,* II, 53, 24; Starcke, *Prim. Fam.,* 155.
[157] *Russian Ethnog.* (Russ.), II, 267.
[158] Müller, *Sex. Leben,* 32-33.
[159] Starcke, *Prim. Fam.,* 142, 144.
[160] Oliveira Martins, *Quadro,* 26; Fawcett, in JASB, II, 336.
[161] §395, above.

reader in forming a conception of the difficulties of classification encountered by anyone who is dealing objectively with the products of societal evolution. It is not demonstrable that all the cases aligned by observers with the levirate are really akin to it; we have, at any rate, thrown together a set of instances upon the basis of which the nature of that custom can be examined.

The levirate, says Tylor,[162] appears in its various forms among a list of one hundred and twenty peoples, or about one in three of his collection. "On taking out its adhesions, it seems sufficiently accounted for as a custom of substitution, belonging to the period when marriage is a compact not so much between two individuals as between two families. . . . That the levirate forms part of this family transaction is consistent with other customs more or less associated with it; viz., that when a wife dies or turns out ill her family are bound to replace her by another, a rule which sometimes holds even for betrothal, and that the widow is not allowed to marry out of her husband's family unless by leave of his kinsmen, who have the choice of keeping her or parting with her, usually for a price."

It is evident enough from the tenor of cases previously cited[163] that the levirate-marriage may be "nothing else than the inheritance of the woman as of a thing by the brothers or other relatives of the deceased";[164] it may rest squarely upon property-considerations; but this explanation is not sufficient in all cases, least of all in those where the brother has a religious obligation to beget a son for the dead man. "The obligation was founded upon the ardent desire of having heirs to offer sacrifice, although, as Spencer suggests, the obligation sometimes arose from the inheritance of the property by the father's brother and the protection he afforded to it. In primitive times it was, undoubtedly, one and the same thing to inherit and to marry the widow, and the children afterwards born from the widow were . . . held to belong to the deceased." It is "probable that it was in this atmosphere that most of the Levir phenomena arose."[165]

Without doubt the levirate presents a special species of evidence as to the property-status of woman; it is cited here for its bearing upon the importance of offspring, which we conceive to be its typical feature. We do not see in it a survival of fraternal polyandry or of the primitive horde.[166]

§407*. Pregnancy and the Couvade. It would appear from the foregoing that augmentation of posterity is present in the

[162] In JAI, XVIII, 253. Lists of tribes practising the levirate, in Letourneau, *Marriage*, 328; Starcke, *Prim. Fam.*, 165.

[163] §353, above.   [164] Wilken, *Vkde.*, 331.

[165] Starcke, *Prim. Fam.*, 160, 152, 141; Schrader, *Aryan*, 388.

[166] Zenker, *Gesellsft.*, I, 50; Mucke, *Horde*, 235, 236. For a review of several theories of the levirate, see Starcke, *Prim. Fam.*, ch. III; Westermarck, *Marriage*, III, 207 ff.

minds of undeveloped peoples as a desirable, not to say indispensable objective. What they have at heart is only their own individual or familial interests; they want progeny for economic and religious reasons and to gratify personal pride and that of family. It is in the mores that they shall feel that want and they do not analyze or criticize the code under which they live. It is the code, not individuals thinking in terms of society, that takes care of the society's interests. Further details of all these matters will appear as there is passed in review a set of ideas and practices connected with the coming of offspring into the world. Despite the fact that this may appear as something of a digression, we see no way that is more direct of getting before us the primitive attitude toward reproduction.

The consideration of pregnancy and its treatment carries us at once into the range of the aleatory element, for here again emerges the need of explaining and dealing with the inexplicable.[167] It has been noted already that the pregnant woman is widely regarded as "unclean";[168] the taboo hangs over her and many limitations upon her conduct are enforced. These have in view, in part, her well-being during the crisis that is before her and are often insisted upon more strenuously in the case of a first pregnancy. Still it is the welfare of the child rather than of the mother that is the chief object of concern; this, which can be seen in the case of the taboos laid upon the woman, is even more evident from the fact that the husband is found to be subjected to all sorts of inhibitions during the period of his wife's pregnancy. Pregnancy-usages form an excellent hunting-ground for the collector of specimens of the *post-propter* fallacy and of imitative magic.[169] There appears also to be a certain vague credence in prenatal impressions. Practically all details of the regimen prescribed are of a religious order, although certain of them may appear in retrospect to have been of a rationally hygienic or prophylactic nature.

The prospective Australian mother is under certain taboos as to diet. If she eats meat, the unborn child is supposed to resent this by causing illness. During the first few months of pregnancy the husband does not kill large game; it

[167] §§194 ff., above.
[168] §378, above; cases in Crawley, in JAI, XXIV.
[169] §§199, 302, above.

is supposed that the spirit of the unborn child attends upon him and gives warning of his approach to large animals.[170] The Papuan mother eats or avoids certain foods that the child may be beautiful and strong, have thick hair and good teeth.[171] If she eats heavy or fat foods, the child will be a monstrosity, and dog's flesh must be avoided. Tobacco is forbidden; otherwise the child may be still-born.[172] Sex-intercourse must not take place until some time after the child's birth.[173]

In West Africa "everywhere are rules of pregnancy which bind both the woman and her husband." They must not eat the flesh of a pregnant animal, and must avoid the heart, liver, and entrails of all animals, lest trouble ensue for the unborn child.[174] Again, a pregnant woman must kill no animals, give the hand to no sick person, and must not see or eat the flesh of a big ape.[175] Amulets and talismans are used to secure the proper development of the embryo.[176] In East Africa, the pregnant woman wears over her eyes a deep fringe of tiny iron chains, "hiding her and preventing her from seeing clearly."[177] A special head-dress distinguishes the pregnant woman or she wears a noisy iron rattle upon the thigh.[178]

The Dyak woman must eat no fish or fruit during pregnancy, and both she and her husband must subject themselves to further taboos during the last month of it. They must not light or go near a fire, else the child will be spotted; they must eat no fruit, lest the child suffer abdominal sickness; they must make no holes in wood, lest the child be born blind; must not dive or hold things under water, lest the child be stifled in the mother's body and be born dead.[179] Restrictions upon both husband and wife come into force and have to be observed until the child has cut its first teeth. They must not cut creepers, lest the woman suffer hæmorrhage; nor cut cloth, handle a knife, bind up a parcel, dam a stream, tie up anything with string, drive a nail into a board, eat while walking, pass a hand through a window. The man may not nail up a wall or fasten together the planks of a boat; he must not plant a post or dig a trench. The woman must not plait or make mats. "It is unfortunate if the cord of the water-gourd used by the women, break when carrying water, but in case of such an accident, evil consequences may be averted if the woman step astride over the gourd or other vessel three times backwards and forwards. . . . To do any of these forbidden things would hinder the wife's parturition." The parents "must not pour out oil, lest the child should suffer from inflammation of the ears; or fix the sword (duku) in its hilt, lest the child be deaf; or break an egg, lest the head of the child should be abnormally large; or kill any animal, lest the child be deformed or its nose bleed; or scrape the shell of a cocoa nut, lest the child's hair should not grow. It is also forbidden to eat anything in a mosquito curtain, lest the child should be still-born; to carry stones, lest the child should be paralyzed; to bend into a circle any piece of wood, lest the child should not prosper. There are a great many other mat-

[170] Spencer and Gillen, Nat. Tr. Cent. Aust., 470, 471.

[171] Von Pfeil, Südsee, 17.   [172] Krieger, Neu-Guinea, 165, 293.

[173] Ella, in AAAS, 1892, 621; Fabry, in Globus, XCI, 223.

[174] Nassau, Fetichism, 192.

[175] Conradt, in Globus, LXXXI, 337.

[176] Bastian, Deut. Exped., I, 169.   [177] Johnston, in JAI, XV, 8.

[178] Von Götzen, Durch Afr., 191; Abbott, in USNM, 1891, 388.

[179] Perelaer, Dajaks, 38; Grabowsky, in Globus, LXXII, 270.

ters of a similar sort forbidden, but in the case of nearly all their restrictions, there are ways by which they can be circumvented, and no evil effects follow. For instance, the mother may do basket-work and make mats, provided some other woman begin the work for her, and the man may dig trenches or erect a hut provided the hands of others are first laid to it. A man may not kill an animal, yet, if he does kill anything, and runs away and then returns a few minutes afterwards, and makes some remark like this aloud, 'I wonder who killed this animal?' he has nothing to fear." This is the familiar case of cheating the spirits.[180] "The whole period of a woman's pregnancy is passed in fear lest the spirits (antu) should do harm to her or her unborn babe. If the mother has a bad dream or hears a bird of ill omen, at once a fowl is sacrificed to propitiate the spirits."[181]

The accounts exhibit the husband as occasionally subjected to taboos along with the wife; incidental mention has done but small justice to the restrictions laid especially upon him. We shall now review some of these, beginning with the custom of the "couvade."

"Couvade or male child-bed is the name given to a variable custom prevailing among many peoples, and which generally ordains that upon the birth of a child the father must go to bed and there behave as if he had endured the pangs of labor. Occasionally he is obliged to fast, almost always he is restricted in his diet, and generally he is not allowed to follow his usual vocations. In some cases his fast begins before his wife is confined, or even before marriage; in other cases the woman is also restricted to the use of certain foods. Simultaneously with the husband's lying-in, the wife gets up and resumes her domestic duties; but occasionally it happens that they lie-in together. The length of the state of couvade varies considerably, from a few days to several weeks, or up to the time that the navel string of the child falls off, or even up to the time at which the child can sit upright."[182]

It speedily appears that the term "couvade" has been used to cover a variety of customs centering about pregnancy and involving taboos upon both husband and wife. The indication is that the specific pseudo-confinement of the former is but one exhibition of a general tendency and practice. First comes a review of several cases of the specific couvade.

"In Cassange, at a birth, the husband goes to bed and has himself served by his wife, as is reported also of several Brazilian tribes and as was the case with the old Iberians."[183] In Togo, "as the mother must keep her confinement, so must the father too, by not leaving the hut, acknowledge his fatherhood."[184] In northeast Africa the father rests for several days subsequently to a birth,

180 §266, above.
181 Gomes, Sea Dyaks, 96, 97, 98; Pleyte, in Globus, LXXIX, 24; Ratzel, Vkde., II, 437.
182 Roth, "Couvade," in JAI, XXII, 204.
183 Bastian, Afr. Reisen, 194.   184 Klose, Togo, 251.

though the observer believes this to be only the reaction after days of joy, excitement, and dissipation.[185]

In India particular attention was sometimes shown to the man, not to the woman. The husband may take the prescribed stimulant. "Directly the woman feels the birth pains, she informs her husband, who immediately takes some of her clothes, puts them on, places on his forehead the mark which the women usually place on theirs, retires into a dark room where there is only a very dim lamp, and lies down on the bed, covering himself up with a long cloth. When the child is born, it is washed and placed on the cot beside the father. Assafœtida, jaggery [unrefined sugar], and other articles are then given, not to the mother, but to the father. He is not allowed to leave his bed, but has everything needful brought to him. . . . One of the men examined by me, who was more intelligent than the rest, explained that the man's life was more valuable than that of the woman, and that the husband, being a more important factor in the birth of the child than the wife, deserves to be better looked after."[186] Among the Alfurs in the East Indies, "after parturition the mother actually goes with the child to the river, both are cleansed and therewith the affair is at an end and the woman goes again about her business. The man, however, acts as ill as if he had just been delivered. He goes to bed and enjoys a number of delicacies prepared for him by his wife. . . . And so, in order to proclaim his fatherhood, the father counterfeits childbed and conducts himself like a lying-in woman."[187]

Tribes in southern California showed the specific type of couvade,[188] which appears commonly also in South America. "On the birth of a child, the ancient Indian etiquette requires the father to take to his hammock, where he remains some days as if he were sick, and receives the congratulations and condolences of his friends. An instance of this custom came under my own observation, where a man in robust health and excellent condition, without a single bodily ailment, was lying in his hammock in the most provoking manner, and carefully and respectfully attended by the women, while the mother of the new-born infant was cooking, none apparently regarding her."[189] "Like the old Tupis and the Caribs the men, at the birth of a child, lie several weeks long in the hammocks and receive the care of the woman who bore the child as well as the visits of the neighbors, for to the father only is the child ascribed, the function of the mother in the matter being compared to that of the soil that receives the seed."[190] Among the Abipones, when the mother is brought to bed, the father also takes to bed for some days.[191] Roth,[192] after sketching the geography of the couvade, cites a detailed description of the usage among the Surinam Caribs. "On the return of the mother and baby from the forest, where she has just been confined, back to the house to resume her household duties,

[185] Paulitschke, *Nordost-Afr.*, I, 193.

[186] Thurston, *S. India,* 547-548, 549.   [187] Wilken, *Vkde.,* 206, 207.

[188] Kohler, *Urgchte. d. Ehe,* 61, quoting a Spanish account of 1739; Sapper, in *Globus,* LXXVI, 351, 352.

[189] Thurston, *S. India,* 547 (quoting Brett, *Indian Tribes of Guiana*).

[190] Von Martius, *Beiträge,* I, 392, 588-589; Spix u. Martius, *Brasilien,* 1186, 1339, note.

[191] Markham, in JAI, XL, 81.

[192] In BAE, XXXVIII, 695-696. (He relies upon F. P. and A. P. Penard, *De Menschetende Aanbidders der Zonneslang,* I, 159, 160.)

the father takes to his hammock to be pampered. This takes place on the supposition that the infant's body proceeds from the mother, but the spirit, on the contrary, from the father, and that a mysterious connection binds the child's spirit to the father's for some weeks after birth. With newly born children the middle of the skull is very soft and pulsates with the respiration of the heart. In prematurely born children the attachments are even open, which perhaps has given cause for the supposition that the child before birth is nourished not through the navel-string but through the skull, and that its spirit penetrates through a little hole in the skull into its brains. As long as this spot is thus not hardened, it is believed that the little spirit is not yet entirely freed from that of the father. Thus it was supposed the life of the child depended entirely upon that of the father. He was also forbidden to undertake any heavy work or to hunt, because his arrow might strike the little infant. If he climbed over a tree trunk he always placed two little sticks as a sort of bridge for the child's little spirit that always followed him. If he crossed a river or creek, a calabash or fruit shell then served to facilitate the passage across of the child. He everywhere trod cautiously and carefully around, avoiding thorny places. And if he by chance met a jaguar he did not speed away, but courageously advanced on the beast. Verily his child's life depended on it. The little spirit nevertheless could get a fright and lose its way in the forest. Even at night the father had to take care to save his child pain. However badly something bit him, he must scratch very carefully, because his nails could harm the infant. And woe to him if he forgot himself and attempted, in too rough a fashion, to get rid of a louse that was worrying him, because the bare pate of his little darling suffered for it. There were likewise various foods that the father was forbidden to eat out of fear of hurting the child. Among other things, it was believed that water-haas meat caused spots. This abstention took place before as well as after the birth of the child. If the child, in spite of all the father's care, took sick, the latter then visited the piaiman [shaman] who, by calling upon the spirits in the usual fashion, speedily recognized the cause (generally a stranger) of the trouble. If the cause was not due to the snake spirit, the kanaima, the father was advised to make certain incisions on his breast and arms. Mixed with water, the infant was then given the blood to drink; or the evil spirit was, with the help of certain ants, bidden out of the child's body, or charmed away. . . . We believe that the custom of the couvade affords the proof or means whereby the man is placed in the position of determining whether it is his child or another's. For it is believed that if the father does not abide by the rules, the death of his infant results. If the infant lives, then everything is in order; if not, it must be an imputation that it is the offspring of its mother's prostitution. Verily, the guilty man will keep no couvade for fear of the righteous wrath of the deceived husband."

"The social manners of the Turanians are very astonishing in our eyes. The extraordinary custom of the Couvade appears to have originated among them. We hear nothing of it among Semitic people, but . . . Strabo mentions it among the Iberians; and Marco Polo found it in China."[193] "The custom of the couvade, in which the father took to his bed at the birth of a child and went through the pretense of being ill, was practiced, according to legend, in Ulster, Ireland; when an invasion of that province took place, the adult males of the region were laid up, and the conquest was easy."[194] Again, there was a

[193] Conder, in JAI, XVII, 147.
[194] Gomme, *Ethnol. in Folklore*, 133.

custom in Eastern Europe whereby the man lay in the wife's bed after the birth, thus "taking to himself the uncleanness of the child . . . whereby it became easier for the child."[195]

Among his collection of cases, Roth[196] has a number that are alignable with the foregoing; but most of them trail off into general taboos on the man which are not essentially different from those imposed upon the woman. A number are quoted from Wilken,[197] who treats the practice as it appears, with frequency, in the Indian Archipelago. Before citing any conclusions, we shall review representative cases that are associated with the couvade and sometimes classified under it.

In Melanesia perhaps only one case of "a proper Couvade" has been observed, "when the young father was found lying in after the birth of his child. . . . There is much however which approaches this." Both husband and wife abstain from some kinds of food that they think would hurt the child. The expectant father "will not eat pig's flesh, and he abstains from movements which are believed to do harm, upon the principle that the father's movements affect those of the child. A man will not do hard work, lift heavy weights, or go out to sea; he keeps quiet lest the child should start, should overstrain itself, or should throw itself about as he paddles." If he should eat shell-fish the infant would suffer from ulcers. "If during this time he goes to any distance, as to the beach, he brings back with him a little stone representing the infant's soul, which may have followed him; arrived home, he cries, 'Come hither,' and puts down the stone in the house; then he waits till the child sneezes, and he cries, 'Here it is,' knowing then that the soul has not been lost."[198]

It is reported that the couvade prevails among the Shingu Indians. This is substantiated by cases of male seclusion and food-renunciation. The custom keeps the man at home, in any case, to help take care of the child; he generally does this while the woman soon goes to work. The ground of it appears, however, to be not utilitarian but superstitious, and where it had fallen into decay the women complained, not because it hurt them but hurt the children. The father considers himself one with the new-born child; a Brazilian apothecary declared that if the child was sick the father took the medicine for it, in connection with which it must be remembered that they consider all illness of one person as the fault of some other.[199] Elsewhere, after a birth both the father and his father-in-law, if he dwells in the same house, abstain for a time from meat-food.[200] Fasting by the husband is a regular practice during the pregnancy and confinement of his wife and the week-old child is fumigated with cigar-smoke for a whole day by the shaman before being named.[201] They would

195 Temesváry, *Geburtshilfe*, 90.
196 "Couvade," in JAI, XXII; Letourneau, *Marr.*, 394; Man, in JAI, XVIII, 368.
197 "De Couvade," in VG, II, 141 ff.
198 Codrington, *Melanesians*, 228, 229.
199 Von den Steinen, *Zent. Bras.*, 334, 336.
200 Ehrenreich, in *Veröffentl. Königl. Mus. Vkde.*, 1891, II, 51.
201 Von Martius, *Beiträge*, I, 219, 428.

die of hunger before resolving to violate the mysteries of birth.[202] In Paraguay the father must eat only vegetables for eight days and must not wet his feet.[203]

These general taboos enforced by the mores on the husband are the genus, as it were, of which the specific couvade is a species. It belongs with them, and not apart, as is indicated by the grouping of it and them together in the minds of observers and systematists, and by the fact that all the varieties of conduct imposed upon the husband merge into one another by gradations not capable of sharp distinction. This is characteristic of all evolutionary products. We regard the "male child-bed" as a rather extreme variant of a general practice which is to be explained, along with the commoner cases, chiefly on the basis of the desire for healthy progeny.

Some writers have seen more than this in the couvade, thinking it to be a usage belonging to the transition between the mother-family and the father-family,[204] whereby the man asserts his parity of relationship with the child or even tries to appropriate the whole, assigning to the woman merely the function of the soil that receives the seed. There is no doubt at all that the relationship of father and child is stressed by all the customs which have been cited; that in itself, however, is no great evidence to prove the couvade a transitional form between mother-descent and father-descent. More significant is the correlation cited by Tylor,[205] who finds the great majority of his cases falling in the period of transition between the maternal and paternal stages and takes the couvade "to belong to the turning-point of society when the tie of parentage, till then recognized in maternity, was extended to take in paternity, this being done by the fiction of representing the father as a second mother." Wilken,[206] starting with the principle that the relation between mother and child is a physical fact while that between father and child is a juridic fiction, cites many examples of the custom, and concludes that it is due to the attempt to express the abstract conception of fatherhood under concrete form. If the mother has to renounce certain foods and acts, then the father does, and it comes to be thought that he must as a matter of course. The same notion is thought to be in play when the father takes his name from the child—as "father of So-and-So." Vinogradoff[207] concludes that "there is no evidence that the prevalence of the custom is the result of migration from one continent to another, and it must be regarded as a remarkable instance of the similarity of the situation and thought in different tribes."

However this may be—and we shall be better able to judge after looking into the organization of the family and descent[208]—

[202] Varnhagen, *Brazil*, I, 124.

[203] Hassler, in *Inter. Cong. Anthrop. Chicago*, 1893, 355.

[204] §418, below.

[205] In JAI, XVIII, 255; Frazer, *Totemism*, 78; Codrington, in JAI, XVIII, 311.

[206] In VG, I, 274 ff.   [207] *Hist. Jurispr.*, I, 198.

[208] Chs. LV, LVI, below.

there is certainly disclosed in all the cases of the couvade and those allied to it a conception of closeness of relationship between child and parents which is no longer represented. It is plausible enough to connect the couvade with ransom-sacrifices for the child.[209] It is still more evident, in our judgment, that we have here a consistent exhibition of imitative magic.[210] Imbued with the belief in his close connection with the child, "the father would naturally be very careful what he did, and what he ate, for fear the child should be injured."[211]

Whatever else of a more recondite nature the cases can be made to show,[212] the dominating reason for all the fasting and other self-abnegation is the desire for healthy and normal offspring. The accounts prove this, if they prove nothing else. It is for that reason that they are cited in this connection rather than another, though we have referred ahead and shall refer back to them as significant in other and lesser respects. As we go on to consider the primitive attitude toward offspring, the evidence will be found to accumulate that children are conceived to be not only a great blessing but an almost absolute necessity for the weal of individual and family. They are indispensable both during life on earth and after that life is over. They are worth whatever price in sacrifice and self-denial they may cost. All means, material and magical, must be called into requisition to secure and preserve them. Whatever else the practices connected with the couvade may be, they are expedients to secure this indispensable boon both in the earthly life and thereafter.

§408*. Child-Birth. The customs surrounding child-birth offer further evidence, both indirect and direct, as to the engrossing nature of the desire for normal and healthy children. Many of our topics might logically be classified under some other general heading; the usages connected with child-birth might be treated, for example, under religion or the family. But while the practices at-

209 §295, above; Lippert, *Kgchte.*, II, 313.
210 §302, above.
211 Starcke, *Prim. Fam.*, 52; Tylor, in JAI, XVIII, 256, note; Vierkandt, *Entstehungsgr.*, 150; Preuss, in *Globus*, LXXXVII, 399; Kaindl, in *Globus*, XCI, 62-63.
212 For a full treatment of the couvade, with citations of many cases, see Roth, "Signification of the Couvade," in JAI, XXII.

tending it witness to other preoccupations of life as well as to the attention accorded to progeny, they are cited in the present connection because it is here that the central reason for their being lies. Interest in the child underlies most of the usages which surround parturition.

Considering first the physical aspect of confinement and delivery among primitive peoples, we find a weight of evidence from many parts of the world to the effect that child-birth is easy and that the woman returns within a short time to her labors.[213]

Dr. Horley[214] compares the four to fourteen days needed for recovery by "an average healthy woman, not being a primapara, in the middle ranks of European life," with the half-hour or hour taken by the Kaffir or Indian woman for self-delivery. His examples may be extreme but they can be matched. The Australian women resume their usual avocations or continue the march in from two to twenty-four hours; they may sit up and ask for food an hour after confinement and walk two or three miles two days or even one day later.[215] The case is not very different with the Papuan and it is reported of the Andamanese women that no instances of difficult delivery are known.[216] Bantu women seem to bear with peculiar ease and the same is true of the Togo women and of other Africans.[217] The Tungus and Saoras[218] bear with the same ease; but it is stated that one of the reasons for the dying-out of the Veddahs is the death of women in parturition, which, by exception amongst savages, frequently occurs.[219]

"Parturition and childbearing among the Indian islanders is easy, expeditious, and safe, compared to what it is in Europe. A Javanese woman always expects to go abroad safely in five days after confinement." Few lives are lost in child-birth.[220] Other authors speak of the easy and quick confinement of the East Indians and Pacific islanders.[221] As a rule the Eskimo women suffer

[213] In Ploss-Bartels, *Das Weib* (10th ed., II, 58, 59), some doubt is expressed concerning the rapidity of parturition. The instances reported often have to do merely with the final period. But the conclusion favors the comparative ease and expeditiousness of the process.

[214] In JAI, XVII, 111.

[215] Curr, *Aust. Race*, I, 70-71; Eyre, *Cent. Aust.*, II, 323-324; Collins, *N. S. Wales*, 364; Matthews, reported in JAI, XXIV, 186.

[216] Hagen, *Papua's*, 229; Man, in JAI, XII, 87.

[217] Fritsch, *Eingeb. S.-Afr.*, 107, 204; Klose, *Togo*, 250, 509; Vortisch, in *Globus*, LXXXIX, 281; Lessner, in *Globus*, LXXXVI, 393; Stuhlmann, *Mit Emin*, 347; Paulitschke, *Nordost-Afr.*, I, 183, 192; Hanoteau et Letourneux, *Kabylie*, II, 210.

[218] Hiekisch, *Tungusen*, 91; Fawcett, in JASB, I, 223, 224.

[219] Stevens, in JASB, I, 135; Rütimeyer, in *Globus*, LXXXIII, 203.

[220] Crawfurd, *Ind. Archip.*, 36.

[221] Roth, *Sarawak*, I, 99; II, cxcvii; Schwaner, *Borneo*, I, 231; Roth, in JAI, XXI, 133; Veth, *Borneo's Wester-Afdeeling*, II, 225; Nieuwenhuis, *Borneo*, II, 88; Gomes, *Sea Dyaks*, 100; Marsden, *Sumatra*, 284; Blumentritt, *Igorroten*, 96; Ella, in AAAS, 1892, 621.

little; they "appear to be exempted from the curse of Eve, and deliver their children with as little concern as is exhibited among the brutes."[222] American Indian women make light of the pains of child-birth; labor is rapid and easy, though at times much pain is suffered and some die in labor.[223] Miller[224] tells of an Indian washer-woman who "had the washing well started on Monday morning when she said: 'Me feel heap bad, me go home; me think pappoose come.' Early the next morning she came back; the baby had been born and she was ready to finish the washing." The Shingu women dread child-birth and prevent it but return to work again very soon when they have borne a child.[225] Some South American Indians have killed mothers who have shrieked during labor, from the belief that the children would grow up to be cowards.[226] Recovery is very rapid.[227]

European peasant women often exhibit a recovery not much less rapid than that of savages; "as if nothing at all had happened."[228]

Obviously female animals in a state of nature must be able to bear easily or the mother or offspring or both must perish; and it is not so different with the primitive woman, who gets no great care or expert attention during parturition. If she cannot bear her children under the conditions she encounters, she leaves no hereditary tendencies toward difficult child-birth; only those who bear and recover easily leave offspring and so pass on their favorable tendencies. There is no counterselection here.[229] We have, however, the word of a noted specialist[230] to the effect that "a healthy Indian woman of normal physique, with a normal child, on the average suffers quite as much and as long as does the normal white woman under similar conditions." He thinks the Indian women are regularly well-built, healthy from outdoor life, strong, and very patient; and that, as compared with the whites, a larger proportion of the children are normal. This is an anthropological

[222] Nansen, *Esk. Life*, 151; Nelson, in BAE, XVIII, pt. I, 290; Turner, in BAE, XI, 271 (quoted).

[223] Mackenzie, *Voyages*, 141; MacCauley, in BAE, V, 497; Dr. Treon, in *Cincinnati Lancet Clinic*, Jan. 4, 1890; Donaldson, in *Smithson. Rep.*, 1885, pt. II, 531; Russell, in BAE, XXVI, 185-186; Stevenson, in BAE, XI, 143; Bancroft, *Nat. Races*, I, 111, 197, 242, 391, 412, 436, 513, 566, 703, 773; II, 267, 678; Miller, in *Globus*, LXII, 112.

[224] In PSM, L, 209, 210.

[225] Von den Steinen, *Zent. Bras.*, 334.

[226] Starcke, *Prim. Fam.*, 52 (quoting Lafitau, *Moeurs*, I, 592).

[227] Hassler, in *Inter. Cong. Anthrop. Chicago*, 1893, 355; Ambrosetti, in *Globus*, LXXIV, 245.

[228] Rhamm, in *Globus*, LXXXII, 275; Temesváry, *Geburtshilfe*, 97-98; Kohn, *Yakuts* (Russ.), 53.

[229] Schallmayer, *Vererbung*, 148 ff.; Keller, *Soc. Evol.*, 174-175.

[230] Hrdlička, in BAE, Bull. XXXIV, 55-56.

issue which we are not called upon to pursue farther, now that the general aspects of the physical process of child-birth are before us.

The consensus of evidence reveals no great concern, in the mind of either husband or wife, with regard to the latter's possible sufferings or death at confinement. They both expect her to suffer briefly and slightly, or at any rate endurably, and to survive. The chief concern is for the well-being of the child, and a good part of all the solicitude exhibited has to do with the aleatory interest involved. The element of the fortuitous permeates all the phenomena of parturition. The period is one of crisis when much happens that is inexplicable on the basis of any knowledge possessed by the savage; it is therefore a time for the imposition of taboos and the employment of other practices aimed at avoidance, exorcism, or propitiation of spirits.[331] Of the notion of the general uncleanness of women[232] we here encounter a specific case. Bearing in mind the ease with which savage women ordinarily bear their children, in the exceptional instance of difficulty one can readily infer an invasion by the supernatural element which tends to mark the woman in question as in some way abnormal or sinful and thus as an object of dread. Despite the truth of the contention that concern for offspring lies behind most child-birth practices, one of the salient aspects of the crisis is the reputed uncleanness of the woman at delivery; she is a danger to everyone and must be avoided both before and during her labor. If savage women were not wont to pass through the crisis safely and easily, it might be thought that they were sent off to bear their children alone lest they die in the house or within the community;[233] that they are avoided also for some time after as well as before and during child-birth, at a time when their health is fully restored, makes against that conclusion.

The Australian woman, though perfectly well, is considered unclean, and not allowed to touch anything belonging to any one. Her food is brought to her by some old woman. Her camp is only for her; and she is, as soon as her child is born, a thing unclean and apart.[234] In Australia, as in many other parts of the world, the birth must take place apart from the camp. One author[235] believes that "this is doubtless done to prevent a death in camp, which would

231 §§265, 341, and chs. XXV, XXVI, above.
232 §378, above.   233 §222, above.
234 Parker, *Euahlayi*, 39.   235 Bonney, in JAI, XIII, 125.

cause all to leave and seek another spot." That precaution may sometimes enter, though the tenor of the cases does not indicate its presence. The Papuan generally sees his wife and children only after some time subsequently to the birth. The less the wife comes into the house during her confinement-exclusion the better for all the inmates; in any case she must not use the customary steps, but climb up another log that has few and shallow notches. "They believe that the inmates would be visited by sickness if the woman entered the house by the customary way." One who meets the mother of an unweaned child, indoors or out, must avert his face from her lest he become sick. Such taboos are stricter and more prolonged in the case of a first birth.[236] Similar precautions, together with purification of mother and child in sea-water, are found elsewhere in Melanesia, except that in the Murray Islands, strangely enough, in view of the prevalent beliefs, "the woman was not considered unclean after child-birth, nor was any ceremony necessary for her readmission into society."[237] It is to be noted that if a Cameroons woman bears a dead child the uncleanness is double,[238] for it includes also that of the grave—the woman's body is that—and the corpse. In the Upper Yenesei region, while a bearing woman is not regarded by the Soyots as unclean, as she is among the Ostiaks, so that she must give birth in a separate yurt, still if several children have died in a yurt an expectant mother goes elsewhere to bear.[239]

The Greenland Eskimo is averse to having a birth take place in an igloo; in the case of one married pair, the husband had built several small snow-huts for his wife, on occasions when she mistakenly believed her confinement to be at hand. It appears that the taboo forbade the further use of a confinement-hut provided and tentatively occupied. The other Eskimo made merry over the discomfiture of the husband.[240] Central Eskimo taboos are observed more strictly and for a longer time if the child dies. In one locality the woman is permitted to re-enter her hut a few days after delivery but may not go through the regular entrance; an opening is cut for her in the snow wall. This custom recalls the "doors of the dead."[241] The Point Barrow and Bering Strait Eskimo carry their taboos into great and arduous detail, their custom of shutting up mother and child in a snow house in winter being perilous to the lives of both. In one case, in mid-winter, the woman "was put outside in a small brush hut covered with snow and her food handed her by her husband through a small opening. Despite the intensely cold weather, she was kept there for about two months."[242] The northern Indians regarded it as ill luck to have a child born in the house and turned the woman out as she approached confinement;[243] and

[236] Krieger, *Neu-Guinea,* 293-294; Von Rosenberg, *Geelvinkbaai,* 91; Parkinson, in *Inter. Archiv. f. Ethnog.,* XIII, 41.

[237] Somerville, in JAI, XXVI, 407; Leggatt, in AAAS, 1892, 597; Macdonald, in AAAS, 1892, 720; Hunt, in JAI, XXVIII, 11 (quoted).

[238] Conradt, in *Globus,* LXXXI, 337.

[239] Olsen, *Primitivt Folk,* 146-147.

[240] Personally communicated to one of the authors by the late George Borup.

[241] §223, above; Boas, in BAE, VI, 611.

[242] Murdoch, in BAE, IX, 415; Nelson, in BAE, XVIII, pt. I, 289; Hanbury, *Canada,* 68.

[243] Swanton, in BAE, XXVI, 429; Niblack, in USNM, 1888, 368.

the same avoidance of her presence is found in South America, together with the usual fastings and purifications.[244]

The Greeks and Hebrews regarded the bearing woman as unclean; and the idea persists among the Jews of southern Russia.[245] Elsewhere in eastern Europe the room in which a child was born was unclean for several days "in ancient times"; and the idea of woman's uncleanness at the time of parturition persists into recent days.[246]

As the foregoing instances have shown, the bearing woman is often left entirely to herself. Sometimes she is attended by an experienced old woman or friend; and there are a number of cases where aid, often rational, but generally very rough and ready, is afforded. We do not intend to go into these processes in the present connection, having alluded to them already in another place.[247] It seems clear, however, that in most cases the concern exhibited is rather for the well-being of the child than for the alleviation of the mother's condition; the idea of sparing the wife at the expense of the infant seems to be absent. It is true that among nature-peoples the wife appears to have less need of solicitude; in any case, there is an exceeding desire for children, and especially for sons, that scarcely brooks frustration at any cost.

In addition to the more rational processes that aim at easement of birth there is a mass of practices surrounding parturition, which may be called religious or magical; they link on to the usages connected with the perils supposed to be inherent in childbirth. A limited number of representative cases will serve to reveal this connection and will further illustrate the entrance of the religious element into self-perpetuation.

In case of difficulty in child-birth, the husband strips off all personal adornments and walks slowly up and down past the woman's camp, where his wife is, "with a view to inducing the unborn child to follow him, which, it is said, it rarely fails to do."[248] In many regions of New Guinea the wife is seated for hours before as hot a fire as she can stand; in New Britain charms are hung up to ease her labor, while in the Torres Straits Islands the sorcerer immerses some sacred object in the sea or the husband stands in the sea till his legs feel

[244] Schomburgk, *Brit.-Guiana*, I, 166; Von Martius, *Beiträge*, I, 427, 511, 537, 643.

[245] Euripides, *Electra*, 652 ff.; Maurer, *Vkde.*, I, 28; Weissenberg, in *Globus*, XCI, 361.

[246] Kostomarov, *Gt. Russians* (Russ.), 223; Temesváry, *Geburtshilfe*, 22.

[247] §§316, 317, above.

[248] Spencer and Gillen, *Nat. Tr. Cent. Aust.*, 466, 467.

cold, for the same purpose.[249] The Togo negroes, during a confinement, burn spices which cause coughing and sneezing; and women energetically wave horse and cow tails to ward off danger and illness.[250] Again, the fire is kept going for seven days and nights and, if it goes out, must be rekindled by the friction-method. When the newly-born is carried out for the first time by the mother, an old woman precedes her and dashes water from a basin against the ceiling of the house at the door so that mother and child are sprinkled. The village-women, standing outside, shout: "Quick! the child out of the rain!"[251]

The Ostyaks fumigate the successfully delivered woman with some powerfully smelling substance; devil-exorcisers attend the Bashkir mother.[252] The Naga mother "was wrapped in hot water blankets till faintness ensued" and the child immersed in almost boiling water.[253] Kipling[254] speaks of "the fourfold heated room, parched by the Birth-Fire's breath." The husband "goes on shampooing his own abdomen" to expedite his wife's delivery.[255] Again, a lamp with five wicks is waved about the wife's face; or, since the spirits avoid iron, a crowbar is laid across the threshold.[256] Similar means of exorcising evil spirits are employed in China.[257]

Wilken[258] refers to a large number of East Indian tribes who seek to drive off evil spirits by seating the woman and child with their backs to a blazing fire; the more roasting they can endure, the better. The process is repeated for a number of days. The spirits feared were the envious souls of women who had died in child-bed. Another means of warding them off was to cover the woman's body with fish-bones. All chests, doors, and holes in the house must be left open, as a closed object hinders delivery. This custom seems to partake of imitative magic and is very widely practised. "As soon as the child is born, a signal is given either by beating a bamboo with a stick or by striking a brass gong to announce the event. Then a fowl is waved over the heads of all present, including the infant and his mother. The fowl is then killed and the blood smeared on the foreheads of those present. It is afterwards cooked and eaten by the parents of the child and any friends that may be present." All sorts of practices having the general purpose of securing good luck and averting ill are found among the Sea Dyaks.[259] The dreams of the father during the period are ominous.[260] In Sumatra he may hinder the delivery by driving nails or wooden pegs; and the wife must confess all neglect of duties toward her husband if she wishes to have an easy time. He forgives by stepping over her body and blowing on her forehead. It is hard to see how the woman endures the hot and choking atmosphere of the birth-room.[261] In Malacca a great noise

[249] Krieger, *Neu-Guinea*, 390; Danks, in JAI, XVIII, 292; Hunt, in JAI, XXVIII, 11.

[250] Pater, L., in *Globus*, LXXIX, 352.

[251] Stuhlmann, *Mit Emin*, 37, 82, 184.

[252] Kondratowitsch, in *Globus*, LXXIV, 290; Von Stenin, in *Globus*, LXXX, 156.

[253] Godden, in JAI, XXVI, 178.   [254] *Naulahka*, ch. X.

[255] Thurston, *S. India*, 551.

[256] Kirtikar, in JASB, I, 397 ff., 403.

[257] "Kl. Nachr.," in *Globus*, LXXV, 199.

[258] *Vkde.*, 201-206.

[259] Gomes, *Sea Dyaks*, 100; Grabowsky, in *Globus*, LXXII, 272.

[260] Veth, *Borneo's Wester-Afdeeling*, II, 267-268.

[261] Jacobs, *Groot-Atjeh*, I, 118, 121, 142.

is made for ten minutes to a half hour after a birth in order to scare off evil spirits that may be trying to enter mother or child. The chance of these spirits is gone once the navel-strand is severed.[262] In Cochin-China likewise she is subjected to the heat which is regarded as so necessary through the Archipelago;[263] and Wake[264] finds the Siamese, Burmese, Maori, and even Malagasy exposing women to a burning heat which often causes death. The idea is to purify or to drive away a demon. The Maori call in a priest to repeat invocations if the delivery is difficult.[265]

The Eskimo never cut the navel-strand with iron or steel.[266] Cree women formerly drank water in which rattlesnake-poison had been boiled, to lessen the pains of parturition.[267] The Coroado shaman fumigates child and mother by blowing tobacco-smoke upon them.[268]

The Arabs protected child-birth from the evil eye and the spirits.[269] Ignorant moderns show the same fear of the evil spirits, witches, and the evil eye; births in Russia and elsewhere are kept secret because it is thought that delivery will thus be rendered easier, and various actions are prescribed to be performed by the man, whereby birth is hastened.[270] There is a notion in West Galway that no fire may be taken out of a house in which a child has been born until the mother is up and well.[271]

§409*. Solicitude for Posterity. Although the above cases have to do with the easement of the mother, they must not be interpreted, we repeat, as generally indicative of concern, least of all exclusive concern, for her. Whatever is dangerous for her is perilous also for the child; and it would appear that in most cases where relief is accorded to her it is the child that is the ultimate object of interest. There are few accounts explicitly indicative of sympathy with the woman in her suffering or of fear for her life, while there is a great deal of evidence, which is also quite explicit, to show that the fate of the child remains in the foreground as the dominating consideration, even when something is attempted by way of alleviating or hastening the parturition.

No doubt the treatment of the mother at child-birth is often harmful to the infant and some of the attempts to cause the child to conform to the local type of beauty, by head-flattening, nose-manipulation, and the like, may not conduce to its health and comfort;[272] but in general there is a positive purpose looking to its welfare in the most ill-judged procedure. In Melanesia, the

[262] Stevens, in *Ztsft. f. Eth.*, XXVIII, 192.
[263] Niemann, in *Bijd.*, 1895, 341.   [264] In JAI, XI, 24.
[265] Tregear, in JAI, XIX, 97.   [266] Reclus, *Prim. Folk*, 36.
[267] Hager, in AA, VIII, 37.
[268] Spix and Martius, *Brazil*, II, 247.
[269] Smith, *Relig. Sem.*, 428.
[270] Temesváry, *Geburtshilfe*, vii, 42-43, 54, 68.
[271] Gomme, *Village Life*, 112.
[272] Roth, *N.W. Cent. Queensland*, 183; Parker, *Euahlayi*, 52.

father scatters along the path little toy bows, to make a boy a strong bow-
man; "if it be a girl, he throws down bits of the pandanus fibre out of which
mats are made, for the mats which count as money are to be her work."[273]
The child is sedulously guarded against the spirit that steals infants and the
habit of giving it an insignificant or even indecent name is another measure
of protection.[274] A few hours after birth, the Andamanese baby has its head,
face, and body shaved and painted.[275]

Eskimo mothers lick their babies to wash them; and the Aleuts souse the
bawling child into water, even if the ice has to be broken to do so.[276] In northwest America, before it gets any food the child is caused, by squeezing its
stomach, to vomit.[277] The Sia mother and child go through a long and involved
ceremony, including purification by ashes, charcoal, and water, and the use of
the sacred corn meal and ears.[278] Here and farther south the child is exposed
to the sun and also "cured" by being held in the smoke of the mountain-cy-
press. With a fire-brand the medicine-man "makes three crosses on the forehead, if a boy, or four if a girl." The smoke of a corn-cob fire insures success
in agriculture.[279] The Fuegian child is bathed in cold water and the soft scrap-
ings of wood; only children with imperfections are killed, or those whose
mother has been deserted by her husband, or the youngest of a number of
daughters.[280]

The belief still exists in Europe that unbaptized children are particularly
exposed to the evil spirits. So the child is never left alone. In one locality the
three nights following birth are the most perilous; they are the period of
"child-guarding," are spent in entertainment and dancing, and obviously put
a strain upon the new mother.[281]

Partly out of concern for the child—though this is by no means
the only reason[282]—the period of suckling is prolonged among
many primitive peoples. It will be recalled that such protraction
of the nursing-period, being due very largely to the lack of a substitute food, is likely to be shortened when animal-milk is available.[283] But protraction of lactation is often purely religious in
nature. When it is put into effect because of solicitude for the
child, it amounts to limitation of numbers for the sake of quality.

Certain Australian mothers do not wean the children until they are over
three years old, and Papuan women nurse them till they can run about or
even up to the fourth year. Nursing is continued until a certain kind of fish
can be digested.[284] "A married man should not have intercourse with another

273 Codrington, *Melanesians*, 230.

274 §266, above; Krieger, *Neu-Guinea*, 294; Cayley-Webster, *New Guinea*, 59.

275 Man, in JAI, XII, 334.   276 Reclus, *Prim. Folk*, 38, 51.

277 Niblack, in USNM, 1888, 368.   278 Stevenson, in BAE, XI, 140 ff.

279 Lumholtz, in *Inter. Cong. Anthrop. Chicago*, 1893, 110; Lumholtz, "Tarahumari Life," in *Scribner's Mag.*, XVI, 298.

280 Bridges, *Voice for S. Amer.*, XIII, 181.

281 Temesváry, *Geburtshilfe*, 72-73.

282 Lippert, *Kgchte.*, I, 74.   283 §30, above.

284 Bonney, in JAI, XIII, 126; Von Pfeil, *Südsee*, 19; Guise, in JAI,

woman, be she single or married, during the time his own wife has a child at her breast, although lactation lasts for an average period of two years. The penalty for breaking this rule is the illness and perhaps death of the child."[285] In some of the islands children are suckled till three or over and often as long as they show an inclination for the breast.[286] In Fiji "after childbirth, husband and wife keep apart for three, even four years, so that no other baby may interfere with the time considered necessary for suckling children, in order to make them healthy and strong. . . . The relatives of the woman take it as a public insult if any child should be born before the customary three or four years have elapsed and they consider themselves in duty bound to avenge it in an equally public manner." This is also the case on the island of Sumba. The writer[287] relates a story of a white man, "who being asked how many brothers and sisters he had, frankly replied: 'Ten!' 'But that could not be,' was the rejoinder of the natives, 'one mother could scarcely have so many children.' When told that these children were born at annual intervals, and that such occurrences were common in Europe, they were very much shocked, and thought it explained sufficiently why so many white people were 'mere shrimps.' "

In East Africa there is an effective control of population due to wives living apart from their husbands while suckling, a period of two or three years.[288] If able to suckle them, the Andamanese women never wean their children and even nurse each other's infants.[289] The period is up to three years among the Yorubas, in Togo, and on the Gold Coast; and during that period the nursing wife is tabooed to the husband.[290] The Hyperboreans nurse for three years and there may therefore be two children nursing at the same time. A ten-year-old Tungus boy was observed in the act of nursing.[291] Similarly protracted suckling occurs among the Tibetans; Aino children are nursed four or five years; Toda children three or even six years; those of Sarawak three to five years; in Sumatra two years and a half; in Micronesia, into the third or fourth year; in Samoa two or three years. In the last case it is stated that the mothers suffer from the practice.[292] A foster-child in the Marquesas Islands has been known to remove a cigar from his mouth before beginning to nurse.[293]

Many are the practices adopted to secure the child's welfare; the following African case will recall a number of notions already reviewed. "When the cord drops off, it is handed, as a rule, to the father, who ties it to a kola or coconut tree; this tree is the property of the child when it grows up. . . . When the

XXVIII, 206; Somerville, in JAI, XXVI, 407; Leggatt, in AAAS, 1892, 697, 704.

[285] Seligmann, *Melanesians,* 704, 705.

[286] Jenness and Ballentyne, *D'Entrecasteaux,* 92.

[287] Wilken, in VG, III, 216.   [288] Lugard, *Brit. Cent. Afr.,* 66.

[289] Man, in JAI, XII, 81, 83.

[290] Ellis, *Yoruba,* 185; Klose, *Togo,* 251; Vortisch, in *Globus,* LXXXIX, 280-281; Bastian, *Deut. Exped.,* I, 169.

[291] Ratzel, *Vkde.,* II, 769; Prjevalski's *Forskningsresor,* 423; Hiekisch, *Tungusen,* 92.

[292] Rockhill, in USNM, 1893, 676; Hitchcock, in USNM, 1890, 465; Reclus, *Prim. Folk,* 202; Roth, *Sarawak,* I, 100; Jacobs, *Groot-Atjeh,* I, 165-166; Finsch, *Ethnol. Erfahr.,* III, 131; Ella, in AAAS, 1892, 621.

[293] Letourneau, *Soc.,* 139 (quoting Radiguet, *Derniers Sauvages*).

child's head is shaved, an elder takes some of the hair and adds it to the 'medicine' [used to rub the child]. . . . A child's milk-teeth are thrown on the roof; it is unlucky for children to be born with teeth; all spat when I mentioned the subject and denied that children born [in that region] . . . had teeth till some time after they had come into the world."294

Though we cannot regard the child as the factor that made marriage, there is no question about the importance of children in stabilizing wedlock. Preceding topics have contributed to the establishment of the fact: part of the test of the woman had to do with her fecundity; it was as a mother that she enjoyed respect and consideration; and her sterility was almost sure to lead to repudiation.295 There are enough good reasons why these things should be; and there is no uncertainty about the purport of examples of the feeling for children as it appears in ethnography.

Exceptional cases apart, mothers and fathers amongst the Australians show tenderness for children. The mothers often carry the corpses of dead children for ten or twelve months in the sack upon which they sleep.296 Whether this is a practice dictated by affection or by religious considerations, it is yet highly indicative of the consideration in which children are held. Between Andamanese spouses "complete confidence and genuine affection are never entirely established until they become parents, or at least until the wife is found to be *enceinte,* and even their relationship to each other is not regarded as being so close *prior* to the birth of a child as it is *after* that event."297 The Matabele husband pays for his wife only after she has borne a child; if he does not, the child belongs to the father-in-law.298 This shows what the husband is buying. Elsewhere in this region the girl at puberty receives a doll from her mother, which is evidently a sort of fecundity-fetish; she keeps it till she has a child and then is given another to keep till she bears a second.299 Again, great store is set upon children and the more valuable a woman has the more valuable she is.300 In Togo there is a superstitious fear of speaking of one's children, lest harm come to them.301 Among the Soyots of the Yenesei marriages are often unfruitful and children are so desirable that they are stolen. The race is on the decline and certain of the tribes, not many years hence, will be a "mere saga."302 In one of the backward tribes of Russia, a newly married woman is

---

294 Thomas, "Birth Customs of the Edo-speaking Peoples," in JAI, LII, 252, 253, 256, *et passim;* §§108, 254, 257, 276, 300, 404, above.

295 §§334, 335, 363, 365, 371, 374, 390, 392, above; Westermarck, *Marriage,* II, 31 ff.; III, 366 ff.; Lippert, *Kgchte.,* I, 70-71; Letourneau, *Marriage,* ch. IV.

296 Ratzel, *Vkde.,* II, 59; Palmer, in JAI, XIII, 298; Mathews, in AA, II, 500.

297 Man, in JAI, XII, 138.   298 Decle, in JAI, XXIII, 84.

299 Andree, *Eth. Parallelen,* 92.

300 Granville and Roth, in JAI, XXVIII, 106.

301 Klose, *Togo,* 509.   302 Olsen, *Primitivt Folk,* 151.

not allowed to speak to her husband's father, mother, or brothers till she bears a child. If the time is long, she is reproached by her father-in-law; and a childless woman is not treated with respect within her family or even by outsiders.[303] The Chinese bride is badly treated in many ways, "but all that changes at a stroke if she is of good hope." If she bears a son, all preceding troubles vanish.[304] A Cambodian woman "who has no children after several years of marriage is unhappy over the fact, and her fellow-women sympathize with her for it."[305] "A peculiarity, characteristic of all the Central Borneo tribes, that strikes the traveller, is the anxiety which they exhibit when a stranger happens to be in the neighborhood of small children; among the Punan, anyone who does not speak the language of the tribe may not touch a youngster, for otherwise it would become a numskull."[306] The Dyaks love children very much and the childless sacrifice to get fecundity.[307] Timorlaut fathers carry and fondle their children in the evenings, sniffing at them repeatedly.[308] The Greenlanders, as has been stated elsewhere, do not disapprove of an unmarried mother but of a childless wife.[309] A childless man considers the case so bad that he is glad if his wife bears a son of whom he is not the father. It is exceptional for women to practice abortion for the sake of remaining desirable to the men.[310]

In antiquity the motive of marriage was often offspring. The childless marriage has failed of its end. Childlessness is a curse for sin and offspring a reward of integrity and piety.[311] Woman as a mother, actual or prospective, was protected by special Hebrew laws.[312] The Homeric case is typified in Priam and Niobe, who were once fortunate in their many children and then miserable because of their loss. Having children, "thou hast not died, not even when dead, for children are to a man, though he is no more, a saving glory; and, like corks, they support the net, saving the spun thread from the depths."[313] The Salic Law recognized the rights and immunities of the bearing woman.[314] Even under the Directory in France it was the fashion for women to appear enceinte by wearing a *demi-terme*.[315]

These cases will serve to recall and enforce the views so widely held concerning the importance of children. The custom of adoption points in the same direction. The extent to which it is carried is rather astonishing to one who encounters the evidence for the first time.

[303] *Russian Ethnog.* (Russ.), II, 291.
[304] W.C.A., in *Globus*, LXXVIII, 263.
[305] Leclère, in PSM, XLIV, 779. [306] Nieuwenhuis, *Borneo*, I, 65.
[307] Grabowsky, in *Globus*, LXXII, 271.
[308] Forbes, in JAI, XIII, 20.
[309] Holm, *Ethnol. Skizze*, 54; Cranz, *Grönland*, I, 193, 201.
[310] Von Martius, *Beiträge*, I, 121. [311] Geiger, *Ostiran. Kultur*, 234.
[312] Exod., XXI, 22-25; Maurer, *Vkde.*, I, 51.
[313] Keller, *Hom. Soc.*, 233 ff. (where references are cited); Æschylus, *Choephori*, 504-508.
[314] Clement, *Salischen Franken*, 264. [315] Du Camp, *Paris*, VI, 388.

"If a man marries a girl who has had an 'illegitimate' child, he accepts and adopts the boy as his own."[316] As in the case of creating other artificial relationships, the adoption may be completed by the sucking of blood and other ceremonial.[317] An old man sometimes takes another wife, in case a son of his dies childless or unmarried, in the name of that son. The children she has are reckoned as the offspring of the dead son and as grandchildren of the real father. "This they do in order to assure the dead man a community in sacrifice with the living, which can be maintained only through sons."[318] There is here a generic likeness to the levirate. In Uganda "when the child is weaned it is sent away to some friend or relative who adopts it, and brings it up as his own child. . . . The child is taken away to the friend without any demonstration, in fact it is kept as secret as possible. The reason for adoption is to ensure the safety of the child. Should the father incur the displeasure of the King or his superior chiefs his goods and property might be confiscated, and his wives and children go into slavery, or if he incurred a debt his children were liable to be seized."[319] The adopted son may inherit only a fraction of his adopted father's property, as among the Kabyles, for the adoption does not render void all connections with the natural family.[320] The Ostyak adoption is very simple; it is done when the community is informed. The adopted son is treated just like a real one.[321] The case of the family where there are daughters but no sons, and where the daughter's husband takes the place her brother would have had, recalls the provisions of the *ambil anak*.[322]

The Alfurs and Dyaks practise adoption freely and the adopted child enters upon all the rights and duties of a real one, including the obligation of aid to parents and of helping defray the expenses at their death. Here too the symbol of blood-sharing occurs.[323] Adoption is highly developed among the Polynesians on account of the looseness of the family-bond; a man will adopt strange children, leaving his own to be adopted by someone else, and will accord to them the same care as if they were his own.[324] In Samoa, "the number of children seen in a family was small, occasioned, to a great extent, by the bad management and consequent mortality of children, and also a custom which prevailed of parting with their children to friends who wished to adopt them. The general rule was for the husband to give away his child to his sister. . . . The adopted child was viewed as 'tonga,' and was, to the family who adopted it, a channel through which native property (or 'tonga') continued to flow to that family from the parents of the child. . . . Hence the custom of adoption was not so much the want of natural affection as the sacrifice of it to this systematic facility of traffic in native and foreign property. Hence, also, parents may have had in their family adopted children, and their own real children elsewhere."[325]

"A pair of childless Eskimo frequently adopt a child, either a girl or a boy,

[316] Somerville, in JAI, XXVI, 407.
[317] Paulitschke, *Nordost-Afr.*, I, 193-194; Letourneau, *Soc.*, 366.
[318] Gutmann, in *Globus*, XCII, 3.   [319] Roscoe, in JAI, XXXII, 32.
[320] Hanoteau et Letourneux, *Kabylie*, II, 190.
[321] Kondratowitsch, in *Globus*, LXXIV, 289.
[322] §363, above; Tamura, *Warum Heiraten Wir?*, 7.
[323] Wilken, *Vkde.*, 330; Wilken, in VG, I, 386 ff.; Schwaner, *Borneo*, I, 215.
[324] Ratzel, *Vkde.*, II, 182; Pereiro, *Ponapé*, 119.
[325] Turner, *Samoa*, 83.

preferably the latter. This is done so that when they die there will be some one left whose duty it will be to make the customary feast and offerings to their shades at the festival of the dead. All of the Eskimo appear to have great dread of dying without being assured that their shades will be remembered during the festivals, fearing if neglected that they would thereby suffer destitution in the future life."[326] The Hidatsa Indian, like many another man on his stage of culture, "usually marries his brother's widow unless she object, and he may adopt the orphans as his own children."[327] An adopted child is treated in all respects like a real one.[328]

In Chaldæa foundlings or other children were adopted by the childless.[329] In Homer[330] the predicament of the childless old man is strikingly brought out in several connections; and a defender in old age was sometimes adopted, even if he were some other man's son. Rohde[331] states flatly that "to dedicate to the adoptive father and his ancestors a lasting and regular cult, and then to care for their souls—this is the true and original sense of all adoption"—an overstatement, of course, by one who is impressed by the undoubted strength of the religious element entering into adoption.

The religious importance of children comes out much more clearly in the case of sons, as generally they alone are able to carry on the ancestor-cult. It is utterly impossible for us to comprehend to the full the concern with which a man without sons, among ancestor-worshippers, views his hapless state. In brief, his whole future existence in this world and, above all, in the next, is in a state of more than jeopardy; it is hopeless.

The interest of the Eskimo in these post-mortem ceremonies has appeared above. In one African district it is believed that "whoever has to descend into the world of the dead without having begotten a son, is dissipated like smoke in the morning wind." He gets no sacrifice and his name is uttered in no prayer. To avoid this a man takes a second or third wife. These people "tell of a man who always begot only girls. He announced at last that his latest born was a boy, and had her dressed and reared as such. This girl-boy became a brave warrior and acceptable above all to the chief until they found out her sex. Summoned before the chief for examination, the father went first to God and asked for aid. And God comforted him and changed the sex of the girl, so that he overcame his accusers in the trial."[332] In India there are twelve varieties of sonship, representing a very high valuation placed upon male issue; the explanation is that sons are workers for the father and that they perform the ghost-cult.[333] The ancestors of any man who has not a son to perform in their honor the sacrifices to the manes are excluded from the celestial abode. It is necessary to have a son to "pay the debt of the ancestors." "By a son, a man gains heaven; by the son of a son, he obtains immortality;

[326] Nelson, in BAE, XVIII, pt. I, 290.
[327] §§395, 406, above; Dorsey, in BAE, XV, 242.
[328] Dorsey, in BAE, III, 265, 281.   [329] Maspero, *Hist. Anc.*, I, 740.
[330] *Iliad*, IX, 435 ff., 492 ff.; XXIV, 485 ff.; Keller, *Hom. Soc.*, 236.
[331] *Psyche*, I, 251.   [332] Gutmann, in *Globus*, XCII, 1.
[333] Jolly, in *Grundr. d. Indo-Ar. Philol.*, II, Heft 8, pp. 71, 73, 74.

by the son of this grandson, he rises to dwell in the sun." "If, on the contrary, a member of the family dies without a male child, the celestial dwellings are closed to him, and his parents and grandparents, for whom they had already been opened, are expelled forever." A son may pray for his dead father, while a daughter is of no account. If a man had only daughters, he could charge one of them to bear him a son and could make such a son his own by a mental formula: "Let her son become mine and accomplish the funeral ceremony in my honor."[334] Zangwill,[335] weaves this religious motive into a story of the modern Jew, who married because he wanted an heir. "Not to inherit anything, but to say *Kaddish* for him. *Kaddish* is the most beautiful and wonderful mourning prayer ever written. Rigidly excluding all references to death and grief it exhausts itself in supreme glorification of the Eternal and in supplication for peace upon the House of Israel. But its significance has been gradually transformed; human nature, driven away with a pitchfork, has avenged itself by regarding the prayer as a mass, not without purgatorial efficacy, and so the Jew is reluctant to die without leaving some one qualified to say *Kaddish* after him every day for a year, and then one day a year."

The religious incentive to procreation is thus exceedingly strong; in addition there is a general desire for children that is not at all religious in nature. It is highly materialistic. Perhaps this may come out best in preliminary by a comparison of cases where boys or girls respectively are preferred. Apart from the religious considerations the question as to which sex is preferable is largely a matter of the economic utility involved.

In parts of Melanesia it is regarded as most unfortunate not to have girls growing up to take over the care of the household and to bring in the bride-price. Parents would let boys go to school, "but it touched the prospective food supply when it came to giving us the little girls." The women were turned over to those recruiting a labor-force for Queensland, for a consideration. Yet the Torres Straits Islanders object to having girls because they ultimately marry and work for other men.[336] The Andaman Islanders do not like to let their boys set up a separate establishment because they are so useful in many ways; they do not raise any objection in the case of the girls who represent but a small material loss. "One sees how strongly the economic interest works upon the relation of parents and children."[337]

For the Basuto wife to bear all boys is a financial calamity: girls are salable and are capital. On the Gold Coast daughters are wanted for service and bride-price.[338] In Uganda, where the wives bear few children, the advent of a second son is an occasion of great rejoicing. In Central Africa girls are wel-

[334] Bühler, *Manu,* IX, 137, 127; Letourneau, *Marr.,* 333, 415; Jolly, *Seconds Mariages,* 11.

[335] *Ghetto,* 64.

[336] Von Pfeil, *Südsee,* 30; Krieger, *Neu-Guinea,* 292; Abel, *New Guinea,* 53; Somerville, in JAI, XXIII, 7; Haddon, in JAI, XIX, 390.

[337] Grosse, *Familie,* 52.

[338] *Archiv. Antrop.,* XXXI, 459; Vortisch, in *Globus,* LXXXIX, 280; Lessner, in *Globus,* LXXXVI, 393.

come and tenderly treated. Boys may be preferred, especially by a widow, as protectors but the girls are more useful in work and as salable brides.[339] Again, "the sons are a much desired labor-force; the daughters bring in marriage-goods."[340] The Hovas take great pride in male children.[341] In Darfur, girls are preferred as salable; among the Kabyles, on the other hand, there is no such celebration at the birth of a daughter as at that of a son.[342]

In Korea a very cheap wedding costs about seventy-five dollars, so that several daughters are a misfortune; and in China a girl is likely to be unwelcome. The fortunate ratio is five sons to two daughters. The latter are not available for the performance of ancestral rites.[343] In India, because of the cost of a wedding, "even to the well-to-do, to have many daughters is a curse. In proportion to the position of the family, the father has to spend on his daughter's marriage, running into debt from which he seldom frees himself." The conch blown when a son is born is silent at the birth of a daughter and the parents receive condolences instead of congratulations. "It is believed by an average Hindu that a male child is the fruit of the propitiation of ancestors." Where girls are sold, two men have been known "to quarrel desperately over the ownership of a female orphan child of ten or eleven years, to whom both were related and to whose guardianship both laid claim."[344]

In the Malay Archipelago, in general, a son is wanted more than a daughter as a first-born; yet with the girls there is the bride-price to be considered. Says the Alfur of Celebes: "Only girls bring money." In Central Borneo girls are preferred: "they help in the work all their lives and later bring a son-in-law into the kin-group." "Sons are a curse and daughters a blessing to their parents . . . for this curious reason: that when the sons grow up they look to the parents to help them with the . . . wedding portion, and when married they leave their home to live in the house of their father-in-law." In Atjeh sons are preferred, chiefly from an economic view-point; among the Mohammedan tribes the woman is regarded rather as a thing than as a person.[345] In Formosa a man wants daughters who will bring him sons to support his old age.[346] Polynesians kill girl babies as useless for war; they worship fishing and navigation. In the Loyalty Islands boys are preferred, though girls are a source of profit, not only in the shape of the bride-price but also in that of the husband's continued gifts to his wife's relatives.[347]

An Eskimo must have sons for his old age; he may even ask the shaman or a European to beget a son for him.[348] Indian wives sometimes prefer boys to

[339] Johnston, *Uganda,* II, 690; Brunache, *Cent. Afr.,* 66; Gutmann, in *Globus,* XCII, 1; Paulitschke, *Nordost-Afr.,* I, 172; Vannutelli e Citerni, *L'Omo,* 195; Stuhlmann, *Mit Emin,* 797.

[340] Fabry, in *Globus,* XCI, 222.   [341] Ratzel, *Vkde.,* III, 511.

[342] Ridgeway, *Standards,* 44 (quoting an Arabic traveller); Hanoteau et Letourneux, *Kabylie,* II, 211.

[343] Bishop, *Korea,* 117; "N. Chinese Herald," in JASB, II, 220; Reid, in *Cosmopolitan Mag.,* XXVIII, 443.

[344] Risley, *Ethnog. Ind.,* I, 95; Wilkins, *Hinduism,* 10, 339; Chaube, in JASB, V, 72; Meade, in JASB, I, 283.

[345] Wilken, *Vkde.,* 201, 202; Nieuwenhuis, *Borneo,* I, 63, 82; Roth, *Sarawak,* I, 125; Jacobs, *Groot-Atjeh,* I, 165.

[346] Tylor, in *Nineteenth Cent. Mag.,* XL, 87.

[347] Ratzel, *Vkde.,* II, 126; Creagh, in AAAS, 1892, 681.

[348] Cranz, *Grönland,* I, 193.

girls and sometimes girls to boys for the sake of help in the household-duties. Boys were wanted more consistently when there was fighting in prospect or that they might become great foot-racers or governors. The question always is as to which are likely to be more useful. The Fuegians prefer boys since they are a source of strength and protection when they grow up.[349]

The ancient Aryan received the son with joy, the daughter with repugnance.[350] The professional dancing girls of Egypt considered a son as a calamity; he could not enter the profession.[351] In Poland of the tenth century the price of woman was high and that of food low; hence a man with daughters was rich and one with sons poor.[352] The Ossetes celebrate the birth of a boy only; and "the Albanians believe that an owl sitting on a house means that a death is about to take place there, or that one of the inmates is about to be delivered of a daughter!"[353]

There are some cases to be found of the sale of children; they are relatively few and the tribes who practise the custom do so under rather special circumstances. The bearing of the sale of children upon a preceding topic dealing with the making of marriage,[354] lies less in the absolute than in the relative. It is not so much that the parent does not love the child at all as that he loves his own life and ease more, or lusts irresistibly for luxuries or novelties or for the thrills of gambling.

In Togo there is said to be a great superfluity of people in proportion to the food-supply. Therefore the tribesmen "are said frequently to have brought their own children to market or to have caught and sold strange children, in order to feed their own." Letourneau reports other cases from West Africa, notably one where the grown children "avoid the author of their being as far as possible; sometimes they even lay snares for him and, if they can, retaliate by selling him instead." This is probably an effect of the slave-trade. Botocudo fathers, before the abolition of slavery in Brazil, kidnapped their own children and sold them for rum and tobacco. "The sale of wives and of children in China is a practice not confined to years of peculiar distress, but during those years it is carried on to an extent which throws all ordinary transactions . . . [of the sort] into insignificance." In February, 1922, "General Booth announced at a meeting in London that the Salvation Army in China, by his instruction, had bought a hundred girls from their parents at thirty shillings each in order to save them from a life of shame." In antiquity and among the ancient Teutons, the sale of children was often practised.[355]

349 Hrdlička, in BAE, Bull. XXXIV, 52, 53; Oliveira Martins, Raças, II, 46; Bridges, in Voice f. S. Amer., XIII, 201.

350 Ihering, Evol. of Aryan, 35.

351 Burckhardt, Arabic Proverbs, 145.

352 Lippert, Kgchte., II, 114 (quoting Ibrahim ben Jakub).

353 Von Haxthausen, Transkaukasia, II, 54; Peterson, in JASB, III, 336.

354 §334, above.

355 Klose, in Globus, LXXXIII, 314; Letourneau, Property, 83; Smith, Chinese Char., 204; "N. Chinese Herald," in JASB., II, 220; N. Y. Times, Feb.

The conception of the child as of property that may be disposed of at will is exceptional; in general people want their own children for themselves for the very good reasons indicated in preceding and following paragraphs. Even in the case of the daughter who brings in a bride-price, evidence enough has been cited to show that she has something to say about her own destiny. However, this issue is not fully before us until the nature of the father's special position and power in the family, under the system of *patria potestas*, has been examined.[356]

§410*. Treatment of Children.[357] Lippert[358] remarks very justly that it is not easy to train our children because the motives of our precepts are, for the most part, beyond their perception; yet a boy will obey the lightest order of a skilful game-keeper or fisherman because he sees it justified by immediate and visible success or failure. Among the uncivilized, he finds, though children are generally treated with the greatest consideration and allowed the fullest liberty, and though the notion of authority and discipline is not yet developed, they obey willingly or, rather, follow the example of the parent, whose actions are mostly directed toward immediate and concrete ends. In a word, the requisite discipline, for people living so near to nature, is afforded by the immediate experiences of life. Where one of our boys cannot understand why he should study grammar, for example, the savage child knows by personal, immediate, and hard experience that disobedience to the suggestions of an older hunter results in loss of life or injury, or, at any rate, the escape of the game upon which he has hoped to feed. This explains the apparent paradox presented by ethnographers: that the primitive children are not disciplined much or at all by their elders and yet are generally obedient and unspoiled. It is the protection from the consequences of inexpedient conduct that ruins a child's behavior; and in primitive life such protection cannot be extended very far.

I, 1922; Keane, in *JAI*, XIII, 206; Marx, in *Beitr. z. Assyr.*, IV, 40; Exod., XXI, 7; Grimm, *Deut. Alterth.*, 461, 487; Biot, *Esclavage*, 107, 264; Stammler, *Stellung d. Frauen*, 14.

[356] §§359, 360, 386, above, and 419, below.

[357] Todd, *The Primitive Family as an Educational Agency*, and Miller, *The Position of the Child in a Simple Society*, are thorough studies.

[358] *Kgchte.*, I, 226, 227.

Lippert[359] thinks also that there is a correlation between the treatment of children and of the aged. Perhaps, upon comparison, our two sets of instances[360] may throw light upon this contention.

The Australian child, as a rule, "has his own way from morning till night, and becomes the most self-willed little imp under the sun. Correction is rarely thought of; but should the parental temper on any occasion be ruffled, it generally results in a severe blow with the back of the tomahawk on the head of the child." "That the Aborigines are affectionate is well known; but it is not well known that they are generally very judicious in the treatment of infants and young children." Children "are not spoilt by this kind treatment, a word from a parent being generally sufficient to check any wrong-doing, and the greatest respect is shown by the children to their parents."[361] The same kindliness to children, and even to women, is reported of the Tasmanians.[362] Young Papuan children are much pampered; but they acquire a self-control that puts white children to shame. The mother may not punish a male being and the father is passive. There is no education except through imitation. This forms a great contrast with the strict military education of South Africa and the Central African habit of constantly inculcating by precept. "If the child strikes its mother, the Papuan father often rejoices over his brave son." A Solomon Island native "never strikes his own child, and concedes to all its wishes." "Andamanese children are reproved for being impudent and forward, but discipline is not enforced by corporal punishment."[363]

The Bushmen leave their children to themselves and they begin early to depend upon themselves. The Hottentots treat their offspring well.[364] In the Niger region, children practically do as they like and generally the natives of western and central Africa treat them well. In Uganda they receive some little discipline and in East Africa they begin to make themselves useful at an early age. Among the Arab Sahara tribes they are treated with tenderness.[365]

Hyperborean children are very quiet, good-natured, and resigned; their mortality is great because of ignorance and neglect of the laws of health but the parents seem to love them. Parental affection is strong in Tibet. Though "Chinese children have no proper discipline," they fall in with the custom of filial piety, which is the virtue basic to most others. Unconditional obedience is

359 *Kgchte.*, I, 242 ff. (*passim*).

360 §428, below; for copious instances of the treatment of children, see Pinkerton's *Voyages*, XVIII, Index, 87.

361 Curr, *Aust. Race*, I, 71; Smyth, *Vict.*, I, 51, 129; Bonney, in JAI, XIII, 125; Spencer and Gillen, *Nat. Tr. Cent. Aust.*, 51.

362 Roth, *Tasmania*, 46.

363 Von Pfeil, *Südsee*, 19, 21, 24, 25; Hagen, *Papua's*, 230, 232; Semon, *Aust. Bush*, 332; Krieger, *Neu-Guinea*, 295, 296, 390; Parkinson, in *Intern. Archiv. Ethnog.*, XIII, 41; Finsch, *Samoafahrten*, 321; Elton, in JAI, XVII, 94; Leggatt, in AAAS, 1892, 697; Haddon, in JAI, XIX, 316; Man, in JAI, XII, 93.

364 Ratzel, *Vkde.*, I, 72, 105; Lichtenstein, *S. Afr.*, II, 230.

365 Granville and Roth, in JAI, XXVIII, 107; Hutter, in *Globus*, LXXVI, 307; Phillips, in JAI, XVII, 219; Brunache, *Cent. Afr.*, 135; Junker, *Afrika*, II, 297; Johnston, *Uganda*, II, 879; French-Sheldon, in JAI, XXI, 371; Pommerol, *Sahariennes*, 222, 223, 224.

demanded of the Japanese child and honor and love for parents, brothers, and sisters. Lapp children are generally treated with indulgence and do about what they like.[366]

The Dyaks spoil their children: "the more mischievous a boy is the prouder they are of him, and prognosticate great things for him when he gets older." Children are rarely if ever punished. Only when ill is a child heard to cry. Occasionally tyranny breaks up the good relations of parents and children. If a child has been punished it must be smeared with blood that its soul may not become sad and throw itself away, causing death. Throughout the Archipelago the civilized islanders show the best relations between parents and children. In the Philippines children are never beaten, yet are taught respect for their elders.[367] The case is similar among the Pacific Islanders: the children in the Marshall Islands "have their free will, but behave very well." In Rotuma the "sole method of correction is by laughing and making fun of them." In New Zealand children sit in all the councils and are seldom checked. Once and once only, Taylor saw a man whose child was very troublesome in church take him up and run out with him to a river close by, in which he kept ducking him until he ceased crying.[368]

Eskimo children are not disciplined by words or blows; they are treated with the greatest indulgence; but they are still and quiet. Nansen is forced to conclude that the absence in them of naughtiness, quarreling, and fighting is due to the peaceableness and good humor of their race, which is not nervous or irritable. It is remarkable to note the unanimity of opinion expressed concerning these children. Even among the youngsters at play there is the greatest harmony; they are not petulant or fretful and seldom deserve punishment.[369] The Onondaga Indians, though more indifferent to children, do not strike them "lest the evil spirit carry away the soul of the child." The Seminoles are entirely devoted to their offspring, as are the Indians of the northwest coast of the continent.[370] Indian children in the schools are seldom guilty of more than minor transgressions. In play they both laugh and cry less, though by no means stolid or voiceless. Severe chastisement, even of step-children, is unknown unless the parent or guardian is intoxicated.[371] California Indians sometimes berate children in passion but do not chastise; the same is reported from Mexico.[372] Much the same situation is recorded of a number of South American

[366] Ratzel, *Vkdc.*, II, 769; Bishop, *Tibetans*, 95; Smith, *Chinese Char.*, 173; Crasselt, in *Globus*, XCII, 57; Wiklund, *Lapparna*, 35.

[367] Roth, *Sarawak*, I, 102, 103; Roth, in JAI, XXI, 120; Gomes, *Sea Dyaks*, 103; Nieuwenhuis, *Borneo*, I, 81-82, 83; Grabowsky, in *Globus*, LXXII, 271; Forbes, in JAI, XIII, 20; Crawfurd, *Indian Arch.*, 82; Blumentritt, *Igorroten*, 96.

[368] Finsch, *Ethnol. Erfahr.*, III, 31, 131, 242, 307; Gardiner, in JAI, XXVII, 408; Kubary, *Núkuóro*, 33; Ella, "Samoa," in AAAS, 1892, 622; Taylor, *Te Ika*, 338.

[369] Cranz, *Grönland*, 196; Nansen, *Esk. Life*, 103, 154; Holm, *Ethnol. Skizze*, 50; Fries, *Grönland*, 118; Boas, in BAE, VI, 566; Turner, in BAE, XI, 191; Murdoch, in BAE, IX, 417.

[370] Henning, in *Globus*, LXXVI, 198; MacCauley, in BAE, V, 491; Niblack, in USNM, 1888, 240; Allison, in JAI, XXI, 316.

[371] Hrdlička, in BAE, Bull. XXXIV, 85, 87.

[372] Powers, in *Contrib. N. Amer. Ethnol.*, III, 153; Lumholtz, "Tarahumari Life," in *Scribner's Mag.*, XVI, 298.

tribes,[373] though among certain others children are treated with neglect and indifference.[374] A modern case is the severe treatment accorded to Russian children after the prescriptions of the Greek orthodox church.[375]

The benevolent attitude toward children born to wedded parents, as brought out in this chapter, is not always maintained in such degree toward those whose origin is outside of whatever the local form of wedlock may be. Despite any natural tendency to love children as children, and despite the numerous cases where illegitimacy injures neither mother nor child,[376] the mores that guarantee marriage are now and again strong enough to suppress its expression in the case of the offspring of a tabooed relation. It is true that tribes which care little about pre-marital chastity do not consistently discriminate very strictly against the offspring of license;[377] yet some of them do, for consistency is not a primitive virtue. Though "Bastaard" is a title rather of dignity than of shame in the case of some half-breeds,[378] birth outside of marriage, even among very backward peoples, is sometimes the reverse. It must be kept in mind that illegitimacy is, strictly speaking, definable only with relation to the ceremonial marriage and wife. The following cases, representing the extent of our collections, may serve as a sort of qualification upon the general indiscriminatingly high value set on children.

In New Georgia, the prospective unmarried mother hides in the bush to bear her child. Occasionally such children are kept alive; "I know," writes the author,[379] "of one grown-up bastard, whom no one looked after, and who lived as a sort of slave." Such a child is called a child of the thicket and is said to be born without belongings.[380] In Kabylie the mother may sometimes be spared but not the child.[381] In Borneo "the illegitimate children are hated and despised and can later on enter matrimony only with great difficulty." In Sumatra such a child has no right to existence and is killed immediately after birth, if

[373] Ehrenreich, in *Berl. Mus. Vkde.*, 1891, II, 28; Schomburgk, *Brit.-Guiana*, I, 167; Von den Steinen, *Zent. Bras.*, 178, 503; Von Martius, *Beiträge*, I, 644; Von Wied, *Bras.*, II, 39; Koch, in *Globus*, LXXXI, 106; Ambrosetti, in *Globus*, LXXIV, 245.

[374] Von Martius, *Beiträge*, I, 122, 124, 125; Spix u. Martius, *Brasilien*, 1226; Von Wied, *Bras.*, I, 144; Bridges, in *Voice f. S. Amer.*, XII, 181.

[375] Simkhovitsch, *Russland*, 362; Kostomarov, *Gt. Russians* (Russ.), 155.

[376] Sieroshevski-Sumner, in JAI, XXXI, 97; Finsch, *Ethnol. Erfahr.*, III, 31, 131; Nansen, *Esk. Life*, 164; Keller, *Hom. Soc.*, 234.

[377] §§344, 366, above.   [378] Ratzel, *Vkde.*, II, 114.

[379] Somerville, in JAI, XXVI, 394.

[380] Codrington, *Melanesians*, 236, note.

[381] Hanoteau et Letourneux, *Kabylie*, II, 56.

not before. Among the Karoks of California, "notwithstanding their vicious system of intercourse between young people, bastards are universally shunned and despised. They and the children for whose mothers no money was paid—illegitimate, according to the Karok idea—constitute a class of social outcasts, Indian Pariahs, who can intermarry only among themselves." A similar situation exists among the Hupa, another grossly immoral tribe.[382] In Colombia the illegitimate child "is reputed a bad animal and is so called, and the mother is so disgraced that no Indian will marry her."[383] The Hebrew law provided that a bastard to the tenth generation should not enter into the congregation of the Lord.[384]

It is evident that both nature and society have provided, through instincts and mores respectively, for the presence and preservation of posterity. In the evolution of society there have been tried out unconsciously not only various relations between the sexes but also between procreators and procreated. The whole case of adjustment should presently be before us when the several forms of family-organization have been surveyed.

There are some general aspects of the relation of parents and children that may be gathered up at this point. Numbers and quality are evidently antagonistic to each other at any stage. If there is just so much power at disposal, a quantum of it can be used on each of a hundred persons or twice as much on each of fifty. Under existing methods there is an immense waste in all these adjustments and probably must always be under any devisable application of rational procedure. The loss from mortality at all ages of preparation before any return is obtained is one of the dead weights against which the human race has to strive. Then there is the antagonism between the interests of parents and offspring. The parents give; the children receive. The higher the civilization and the standard of living, the surer it is that the children will never repay anything of a material order to the parents. There is no call for them to repay. All capital spent on human beings is sunk. If the young should repay their parents by services or capital the parents would soon die and the capital would be lost. One generation pays for the next; it does not pay back to the last. In this way the society keeps up an advancing fight, as a corporate body, against the limitations of its existence. One great reason why the tribes of low civilization gain little in

[382] Powers, in *Contrib. N. Amer. Ethnol.*, III, 23, 75, 76.
[383] Nicholas, in AA, III, 613.   [384] Deut., XXIII, 2.

the course of centuries is that there is no continuity in their effort; whatever they gain they lose again. Even the most advanced societies have no adequate process for securing what they win, and so incur great losses, chiefly through political folly. The effort of parents to give their children better chances than they themselves had, in thousands of cases fail to bear fruit; nevertheless it tends to continuity of societal struggle for fuller control of the conditions of existence.

The fact that capital spent on men is sunk is the great reason why slavery was an economic anomaly in a capitalistic state. The abolition of slavery was no loss in man-power to the Southern States as a society. The next day all the laborers, capital, and land were there just as much as before. Some relations between men had been cancelled and the beneficiaries of those relations had lost the benefits. The case had no resemblance to that of a fire or inundation which annihilates work done. It was not like the abolition of contracts of rent or debt, for there never were any contracts. Slave-breeders expected to get back from the adult laborer the capital spent in bringing him up, including risk-rate and profits. Fathers in Connecticut might just as well keep accounts of expense against their children and carry the sum on their books as an asset. If at one time such debts were collectible, assignable, realizable, they would be thought of as part of the wealth of the population; if some day they were made incollectible, it would be just like the abolition of slavery; but it would be in reality only a recognition of the fact that adults must sink part of their earnings in rearing children in any capitalistic community. A man might as well carry on his books an account of the capital consumed by himself as a credit and asset to himself. Since abolition the negro father has acquired, along with the other prerogatives of freedom, the right to pay for rearing his own children. Many of them, as the vital statistics of southern cities show, have thought it more trouble than it was worth. White masters, in slavery times, would not have given food to negro children if they had not expected to sell them and get back their outlay; they would not have cared whether the negro babies lived or not. This was the only semblance of consideration which the slave-owner had given to the slave, legally speaking: he insured his existence. He undoubtedly had an equitable claim, arising from the existence of the institution, to get his expenditure back again. This he lost by abrupt change during a political convulsion.

The antagonism between the interests of parents and children appears most distinctly when the care of the children and work for them has put an end to any attempts of the parents to win further culture for themselves. This antagonism is not absolute, for there is a margin in favor of the parent unless the features of the case are exceptionally unfortunate. The antagonism between numbers and quality and that between parents and children offset one another; the latter is least when the number of children is least, this coinciding with the conditions of high quality for the offspring. Therefore, in high civilization, what perfects the man coincides with what perfects his children and the interest of the individual coincides with that of society; to have few and superior children brings societal duty and individual self-realization and evolution all into harmony. In this case, moreover, the joy in children is the greatest, for their strength and success are of a kind which gives the deepest satisfaction to parents who are themselves persons of high standards.

The modern view of the relation of parents and children has done much to raise the standard of living. Formerly the notion was that children owed obedience and all possible service to their parents because the latter were the "authors of their being." The relationship of parent and child was supposed to be entirely explained by this phrase and the rights and duties arising out of it were construed accordingly. Thus were all the rights accorded to the parent and all the duties to the child. In the modern and certainly more correct view, an adult who brings a new person into the world does not win any rights over him by so doing; on the contrary, he or she contracts the heaviest responsibilities that mortals can ever incur. The parent takes on the duties; all the rights are with the child. Obedience and respect of child to parent are not due as a return for procreation but for care, discipline, affection, and devotion spent in assisting the child to win in the living of his life. The parent owes all this and there is no return in kind. The relation is always one of sacrifice on the part of the parent, and filial affection and piety are due as a recognition of the fidelity with which the sacrifice is performed. Any attempt to shift parental duty to the shoulders of the "State" upsets and nullifies some of the highest of the human and social virtues.

CHAPTER LV

FAMILY-ORGANIZATION

§411. **The Blood-Bond.** People who habitually associate with each other are held together by various bonds; they have various ways of belonging to one another. The typical bond that has united human beings throughout the evolution of the race has been the tie of common blood, or consanguinity. On the early unregulated stages where group-isolation prevailed, the blood-bond is virtually equivalent to that of propinquity, for those who lived in proximity in isolated communities mated together. It is scarcely possible that any other bond is so ancient and it is certain that no other has been so durable and tenacious.

For the origin of the blood-tie it is possible and necessary to go back to the mother and child[1]—indeed, it may almost be said, to the doe and her fawn or to the she-wolf and her cub. There is no object, however, in invading the animal-kingdom except by way of noting the essentially animal-like nature of the mother-child relation. Helplessness and need on the one side; instinctive protectiveness and support yielded under a dominating stress of feeling on the other—this is what nature has arranged, whereby the higher types of animal shall be perpetuated. One who starts with a tie so self-evident can reasonably hope not to be charged with building upon unwarranted assumptions. The mother-child bond is a fact of observation, as is also the mother-love that lends to that bond the strength which it possesses.

The unborn child belongs with and to the mother just as any other part of her body belongs to her. At birth there is removed from her something that has been part of her and which still remains connected with her until artificially separated. Thereafter she and her child must be together periodically or the child will die; it is true that some other agent may take the mother's place in nursing the child but that seldom happens among savages. No two other human beings are so associated by nature as are the mother and child; theirs is a primordial and an unique form of

---

[1] Lippert, *Kgchte.*, I, 76 ff.

relationship. As regards duration and closeness of relation to the children, no matter what the notions about the share of the parents in procreation might have been, man's connection was far less intimate and realistic than that of the mother who bore the infant, cared for it, and nursed it for several years. The phenomena connected with this relationship which captured the attention of primitive men is the presence of blood. It would seem, as many passages in this book have indicated, as if primitive men were veritably obsessed by blood; consider the rôle played by it in magic and religion. The origin of this obsession can be inferred with some degree of safety: in religion it probably goes back to the location of the soul in the vital fluid;[2] and in the matter of kinship as based upon common blood there is no other source so nearly primordial as the mother-child relationship. It is perhaps profitless to speculate about the relative antiquity of origins; in the present case, however, since the mother-child association is in nature, it is quite likely that in our consideration of it we are at the main source of the stream of ideas and usages about blood.

However that may be, it seems that the stoppage of a periodic flow of blood by impregnation and a degree of effusion at birth suggested to childlike intelligences, unversed in physiological matters, the idea that offspring must be formed out of the maternal blood or, at any rate, must have that blood in its veins. The fact that the embryo has a heart and circulation of its own, even if that fact had been known, would not have injured the common-blood theory. In fact, nothing has ever shaken it seriously prior to the modern discoveries concerning the function of the placenta; doubtless most people still believe that the mother's blood flows through the embryo. It was all but inevitable that the relation of belonging to one another, existing between mother and child, came to be identified with community of blood. There was no such enforced association between father and child and if there had been there was no obvious physical process or element to typify or symbolize the bond. "A rooster," say the Sumatrans, in explanation of their matrilineal arrangements, "lays no eggs."[3] Insistence upon the father's relation to the child and the relegation of the

---

[2] §213, above.   [3] Wilken, in VG, II, 119.

maternal function to the reception of the seed were no more than a fiction developed for a purpose.

If consanguinity existed between mother and child, then, as a sort of corollary, it must exist between child and child. Brothers and sisters were of the "same blood," provided they had the same mother. Hence the mother and her brothers and sisters were consanguine; and so a woman's children were related by blood, not only to her and to each other but to her brothers and sisters. All were descended from some mother of a preceding generation and therefore had the same blood in their veins. The husbands who came in, up and down this line, all had their own relationship to their several mothers, brothers and sisters, maternal uncles and aunts, and maternal ancestors.

"Relationship by maternal descent is closest of all, and thus it is that a man is more closely related to the illegitimate son of his mother than to a half-brother. In matters of blood money, for instance, all sons of the deceased's mother have an equal share, but half-brothers can only receive a part by gift."[4]

"The fact that descent is reckoned exclusively in the female line may appear strange to a superficial view but is in nowise so if one keeps his eye on the fact that the relation between mother and child is more natural than that between father and child—that the former is a physical fact about which there can exist no doubt, while the latter, on the contrary, is more in the order of the mores and sets in the foreground, as a necessary precondition, an established marriage-union." The author[5] quotes the Roman pronouncement: "The mother is always sure, even if she conceives in prostitution, but the father is merely the person whom the wedding designates," and concludes: "If one keeps this in mind, it is without doubt no over-venturesome statement to assert that female descent was earlier known than male."

§412. Descent. It seems strange, at first sight, to find relationship reckoned exclusively in the female line; but reflection upon the facts reveals such a set of the mores to be, under the circumstances, natural and indeed inevitable. It might be added that under a régime of unregulation of unions and of ignorance or error concerning the source of children[6] there could be no such precision of conception in the case of fatherhood as there could not but be in the case of motherhood. The exclusion of the male line of descent, attested over and over in ethnography and represented by many survivals upon the later stages of evolution, is

4 Dundas, C., in JAI, XLV, 301.   5 Wilken, in VG, I, 307.
6 §§334, 343, 347, above.

one of those unexpected discoveries that reward candid explorers after the truth with new and significant clues.

When people live in association it is of great importance that they shall be able to recognize and designate their degrees of relationship to one another. No one thought this out. The exigencies of life as it had to be lived stressed in that direction; then the automatic process of societal evolution, being called into action, worked out the expedient adjustment. The need of tracing descent roots largely in the institution of property, which is seen, here again, to be intimately related with marriage and the family;[7] and it originates also in the regulative system. The members of society have to be "placed" so as to be identified and found at need. The question as to who shall inherit property and political and social position is one that cannot be evaded by any society, for upon its orderly settlement depend internal peace and cohesion. Since men are ready to quarrel over masterless possessions or for unappropriated prestige, the only safe policy, in the earlier stages of evolution at least, was to have them assigned. No society does well to remove stimuli to activity and competition; yet there must be some stability or all is chaos. There are plenty of opportunities for the enterprising without staging a general scramble for every deceased person's property and position.

Especially in the case of property is it disastrous to permit unregulation. It is the confidence that he can leave his property to certain persons that has provided many a man with a strong motive for accumulation. Until he could be assured of a private and transmissible title to property, no one cared to concentrate energy upon the building of permanent structures, upon land-improvement, or upon the planting of long-lived vines and trees.[8] It was only by the possibility of inheritance that greater accumulations of capital were attainable; and whatever may be said of inherited fortunes in a later day, their prototypes of an earlier time were certainly highly expedient for the development of civilization. Pride has been immensely stimulated by the prospect of founding and passing on family-wealth and social position; the prospect of achievement along those lines has been one of the durable and productive impulses of self-gratification.[9]

7 §341, above.   8 §§122-124, above.
9 §§449, 450, below.

There is therefore good reason for the development of a system of relationship as a basis upon which inheritance may securely rest. Even if the whole kinship-group once inherited in a communal way, that was preferable to uncertainty; but in the actual ethnographical cases it is to persons standing within a much more limited circle of kinship that heritages fall. Since the bond of blood is the kinship-bond, inheritance could not but follow, in cases where consanguinity was recognized solely through the mother, the female line; and so a man's heirs would naturally be, not his own children but his brothers and sisters and, in the younger generation, his sisters' children.

Descent was also the basis, along with age, upon which marriage was permitted or disallowed. When unions have come to be tabooed within certain degrees of kinship, the usage of exogamy is present. If, again, kinship is recognized solely through the mother, then a number of combinations, which upon somewhat later stages would be regarded as incestuous and also upon modern criteria are cases of close in-breeding, are freely conceded. This is one of the reasons, alluded to above,[10] why it is foolish to refer the primitive taboo upon certain cases of consanguine union, where savage ideas happen to coincide with our own, to an appreciation of the asserted ills of close in-breeding—overlooking in the meantime the obtuseness of the nature-man in not noting any ill effects in other alliances which, on his theory, he permits but which we know to involve exactly the same degree of in-breeding as those which he abhors.

Rivers[11] finds that most of the misunderstanding surrounding the issue of father-right and mother-right is due to the confusion of the three terms descent, inheritance, and succession. The first should be taken to apply to membership in a group, and that alone; the second has to do with transmission of property; the third with transmission of office. The three do not always go together; a man, for instance, may belong to the social group of his mother, and yet receive the property or office of his father.

§413. The Family. In addition to its significance as the basis upon which marriage-unions and inheritance-customs were formed, the blood-bond has had a function which may be regarded as inclusive of all minor and accessory ones: it has exercised a deter-

[10] §§348, 349, 351, above.   [11] *Soc. Org.*, 85.

minative influence upon family-organization. Where descent has
been reckoned solely in the female line, a type of family is encountered which differs markedly from that existing where descent
solely through males is recognized as well as from that in which
relationship is reckoned in both lines. Where descent is through
the female line we have the so-called "mother-family"; where it is
by way of the male line, the "father-family." With considerable
exaggeration the former has been called the "matriarchate" and
with very little over-statement the latter is termed the "patriarchate." The patriarchate, or at least the conception it conveys, is no
new thing; "patriarch" is a current term; but matriarchate and
"matriarch" are rare, relatively modern expressions and are de-
viously misleading. "Mother-family" and "father-family" are both
plainly descriptive of sets of observed and verified facts; they
mean types of family occurring in conjunction with and largely
resultant from the reckoning of relationship respectively through
the female and the male line. They are "matrilineal" and "patrilineal," involving "mother-right" and "father-right."

It is an error, however, to conceive of the family as made by
lines of descent; it was only formed upon them. As a type of association it was made as others were.[12] The effect of ideas about
descent in molding the form of the family will come out as we go
on and it will appear, in particular, that the recognition of the
male line was correlative with a profound alteration of family-
organization. Descent-ideas are interwoven all through the evolution of the family and some such generalities concerning them as
have just been given should be carried into the study of the topic
now under consideration. The same is true of certain other matters treated at greater length in the preceding chapters; it has
been impossible in reviewing the status of women and of children
not to anticipate something of family-organization. The reader
has been allowed, perforce—for all things cannot be treated at
once—to infer what he would from the cases cited and the conclusions drawn from them; some such body of facts and inferences
must be present as a background for the understanding of that
combination of sexes and ages which constitutes the unit-cluster
of society. For the family is that unit. In its very lowest terms a

12 §§6, 10, above.

human society must consist of a man, a wife, and enough children to replace the parents; less than this would not meet the definition of a society.[13]

Everyone knows what the word "family" means in current usage. If, however, the term is to cover the various evolutionary forms out of which our own has developed, as well as contemporary forms existing alongside our own, the current conception is not general enough.

To illustrate: marriage is not the family-bond in East Greenland; the natives hold that all blood-kin must help each other in all cases.[14] In West Africa the family is not based upon relationship but upon power; a man's family consists of those whom he controls and so includes junior members of all descriptions and also, like the Roman *familia* with its *famuli,* a number of slaves.[15] Among the Somals daughters are often not reckoned as members of the family because they are to be sold and so alienated. "Under family in the narrower sense the Somal understands, rather, all the hands that earn for him. Under this conception of things it happens very often that old men marry quite young wives, in order always to be getting fresh forces for the increase of material wealth."[16] The function of the family as a peace-bond is illustrated in the case of the Fuegians: "family influence is the one great tie which binds these natives together, and the one great preventive of violence."[17]

The family is characterized by joint work, dwelling, eating, owning, subjection. It is a mass-phenomenon automatically evolved in the face of the problem of living. "The wide range and contradictoriness of the folkways in regard to family life show how helpless and instinctive the struggle to solve the problem has been."[18] There can be, in fact, no inclusive definition of the family that is not a definition of a miniature society. It too is a group of human beings living in a coöperative effort to win subsistence and to perpetuate the species. It exhibits, on a reduced scale or in embryo, the phenomena of the larger society of which it is a constituent unit. If a start is made with this inclusive conception of the family, we shall cover all cases and may then go on to sharpen the definition, or at least to distinguish more definite types of family-organization, as the cases are spread before us.

[13] §3, above.   [14] Holm, *Ethnol. Skizze,* 45-46.
[15] Ellis, *Tshi,* 88, note.
[16] Paulitschke, *Nordost-Afr.,* II, 143.
[17] Bridges, in *Voice for S. Amer.,* XIII, 201.
[18] Sumner, *Folkways,* §362.

"In ordinary language, and largely also in works supposed to be of a scientific kind, the term 'family' is used to denote four different kinds of group: (i) the small group of parents and children; (ii) the bilateral group, consisting of persons related through both father and mother; (iii) the unilateral group of persons related through the father only; and (iv) a fourth group, of a unilateral kind, consisting of persons related through the mother only." The author[19] proposes to use the term "kindred" for the bi-lateral group: "When I speak of a kindred, I shall mean a group consisting of persons related to one another, other than by marriage, through both father and mother." He calls the third and fourth types "joint family," distinguishing them as patrilineal and matrilineal respectively. Trilles[20] repeatedly insists upon the fact that all social forms rest in the end upon the family as an unique basis; it constitutes the node or primordial cell, or the pivot on which the whole organization revolves. In the constitution of the Fan society, "the man is nothing and counts for nothing, except as he forms part of the family, the first social cell." The family, says Wilken,[21] "was originally based upon force rather than on descent; of descent man had primordially no conception. Besides, through adoption and other arrangements, even through inclusion of whole groups, . . . strange elements were sometimes brought into the tribe."

A single example may clarify conceptions at this point. Among certain tribes of Melanesia, which have clans, called *pangua,* "within the *pangua* the unit is the *ikupu* which represents a family group, though often this term must be understood in the broadest possible sense. Thus while small weak *ikupu* may be composed of only a few householders, strong *ikupu* commonly consist of from thirty to fifty households. But, however large an *ikupu* may become, its members, other than those introduced by marriage or adoption, are always able to trace their origin to a common ancestor who may, however, be so remote that his name may have been forgotten by all except a few old men." Copious illustration is given. "The actual birth of an *ikupu* seems to take place somewhat as follows: As the parent *ikupu* becomes larger and stronger, parties are naturally formed in it, and groups consisting of families closely united by blood and marriage begin to cling together more and more, and to hold somewhat apart from the general life of the community. This goes on, and probably nothing is said until one day an individual with somewhat more force of character and perhaps ambition than his neighbours, suggests building a *ngove.* In this he naturally seeks only the assistance of his relatives and friends. If the rest of the *ikupu* offers no strong objection, and if above all they can be assured that a feast will be given and that the thing will be managed decently according to Papuasian standards, the split takes place."[22]

When an author proposes such detailed studies as those of Rivers, it is natural enough that he should wish to draw finer distinctions not strictly necessary in a more general study. Those distinctions should be noted and kept in mind; nevertheless, as the last quotation shows, it is common enough to speak of a family-group when a kin-group is meant, and the term "family" is often extended to cover such a family-group. If we were to try to adhere to strict categories we should have to fill our citations with brackets explanatory of the terms used by authorities quoted. While calling attention, therefore, to stricter

19 Rivers, *Soc. Org.,* 15, 16.　　　　20 *Fân,* 14, 15, 137, 138, 139.
21 In VG, I, 293, note.
22 Seligmann, *Melanesians,* 336, 337, 340-341.

usage, we cannot be held to it ourselves; it is probable that the meaning of the terms used will appear clearly enough for present purposes.

The family is an organization of force and authority, with inequalities, combinations of powers, and discipline. It is a domain of restriction, not of freedom, and from the point where its beginnings come into the ken of science, it reveals the exploitation of some human beings by others.[23] It has been an industrial and regulative organization and has often constituted also a cult-association. It was once not narrowed down to the marriage-tie, though it was formed upon the blood-bond. Inequalities of age and sex could not, at the beginning or at any later time, be eliminated from any societal group; and upon inequalities rested predominance and authority. Women might control if by virtue of circumstances they possessed superiority; then, again, adults always governed the young and the old generally exercised over the younger an influence based upon experience and tradition. In the family this matter of inequality and of dominance generally worked out in such manner that the organization of diverse and unequal powers came under the headship of the man. Despite the so-called "matriarchate" or "gynæcocracy," this has been the type of the family. There was no perception of the late-appearing values of pair-marriage. If there were more wives than one and they were differentiated into the trio of status-wife, love-wife or concubine, and labor-wife or slave, the organization became, under primitive conditions, more complex and efficient. As for the last type of consort, it is to be noted that whatever may be reported about the rules of marriage at any time and place, a man might have a woman captive from outside the group and its rules. If there were other slaves also, the family was still further heightened in structure and intensified in action. Experience led to the realization, by those in control, of the advantages of power and to the adoption of ways by which power could be developed and used.

It is evident that the family-institution and the marriage-relation, though they are most closely allied and blended, are not identical. Marriage is a sex-combination in self-maintenance, with a characteristic, distinguishing, and vital element of self-perpetuation. The family is a miniature societal organization, in-

[23] Ratzenhofer, *Soc. Erkennt.*, 143.

cluding at least two generations, and is characteristically formed upon the blood-bond. Marriage and the family have always reacted determinatively upon one another; in general it has been the latter which, in its changes, has forced alterations upon the former. In a sense, the family may even be said to have preceded marriage; for an endogamous group living in an extreme of unregulation as regards sex-unions might still be called a family. Whenever the family as an organization had to respond to the life-conditions presented and to the type of the struggle for existence, in every case the notion of what was wanted in a wife and of her relations to her husband changed. If he was an inveterate warrior, she must be a specialized producer. Other relations within the family suffered parallel modification. Organization of the family on the basis of mother-rule or father-rule involved characteristic views of the marriage-relation together with all preconditions and sequels connected with it.

The family was also the domain of personal rights, for these were a definition of limits imposed by the mores upon power. Such rights are the stages in the reduction to harmony of the individual and group-interests in the family. Society has been very slow to interfere with the control of a man over his wife, child, or slave, for the anterior code which accorded him power, sometimes nearly absolute in degree, was stubborn against alteration. It has always been the case, as it is now, that though the mores and laws concede rights to wives, yet they cannot get them if husbands do not grant them; for the process of remedy is slow, costly, and difficult and is attended with publicity and even public scandal. This is well recognized and also resented by agitators for woman's rights.

These considerations lead to the general conclusion that the family is the inclusive institution and that the matrimonial relations of man and woman lie within it. That is to say, the family is the societal unit within whose boundaries fall all the mutual relations of the individuals composing it; and when the individuals are of different sex and mate together in some form regulated by the group-code, their relations are those of matrimony.

§414*. Primitive Family-Organization.[24] For all practical

[24] A classic sketch of the varieties and history of family-organization is

purposes mankind may be thought of as characterized by family-organization formed on the blood-tie. Still it is instructive to follow up what clues there are as to the earliest and loosest forms of that association. In trying to reconstruct the formative period of relative unregulation, one finds himself facing "temporary monandrous groups in local contact with each other, the whole forming . . . a type of the primitive horde."[25] Highly speculative writing has been done in the attempt to visualize that type of society and much tenuous theorizing has been born of the constructions thus imagined. Whatever the primal, loosely-knit group may be called, it was organized less upon the basis of the blood-bond than upon age-differences. This is the system of the so-called "generation-grades," alluded to in a former connection,[26] whereby all who were of approximately equal age were brothers and sisters, the older generation being fathers and mothers, the younger, sons and daughters. These grades formed a basis for the taboo of sex-unions outside of the age-stratum, that is, marriage must be with those of one's own grade. Though of curious interest, the system is not of much significance except in so far as echoes of it persist into later stages. Its existence at one time should at least dispose of the assertion that the family as based upon the blood-tie alone is primordial.

A striking feature in the early evolution of family-organization is the subordination of the individual to the group; he is lost in his family or, rather, he has never emerged from it. In the matter of property, the system of sharing or holding in common by the family is widespread; there are even cases that reveal virtual family-property in women.[27] Family-solidarity is evidenced also in the joint responsibility of the group for the misdemeanors, secular or religious, of its members.[28] Furthermore, in a number of cases, it is to all appearance not the individual but the family that does the marrying.[29] "We usually consider family ties and family property from the point of view of successive generations and of

given by Morgan, *Anc. Soc.*, pt. III. Criticisms in Lippert, *Kgchte.*, I, 85 ff.; Gomme, "Prim. Horde," in JAI, XVII, 118-133. See also Post, *Familienrecht.*

[25] Gomme, in JAI, XVII, 128; ch. XLIII, above.

[26] §353, above; Lippert, *Kgchte.*, I, 82 ff.

[27] §§114, 119, 120, 127, 128, 129, above.

[28] §§176, 178, 182, 274, above.   [29] §§163, 361, 364, 365, above.

inheritance. This is, however, by no means a necessary or even a natural mode of approaching the subject. In ancient life the principal fact governing these relations was the continuity of a family organization, and there was no compelling reason for dissolving it in connection with the death of a particular member, even if the member in question happened to be the ruler or manager of the concern. . . . In connection with this prevailing idea, we find among all the branches of the Aryan race manifestations of the so-called united family or *joint family* arrangement. The most extensive and best described practices of this kind are to be found in India and among the Southern Slavs, but there are many traces of similar institutions in the history of the Germans, of the Eastern Slavs and of Romance nations."[30]

"In most tribes of the Bantu the unit in the constitution of the community is the family, not the individual. However successful a man may be in trade, hunting, or any other means of gaining wealth, he cannot, even if he would, keep it all to himself. He must share with the family, whose indolent members thus are supported by the more energetic and industrious. . . . If an individual committed theft, murder, or any other crime, the offended party would, if convenient, lay hold of him for punishment. But only if it was convenient; to this plaintiff justice in the case was fully satisfied if any member of the offender's family could be caught or killed, or, if the offence was great, even any member of the offender's tribe." The dismissal of extra wives, in West Africa, imposes on them no special shame or hardship but it is difficult for a man to get rid of them. "The real trouble is that they are not his to dismiss without family consent. The family had a pecuniary claim on them, and the heathen members thereof are not willing to let them go free back to their people."[31] "In Ceylon . . . it was the family and not the individual that was supposed to marry; it was this collective unit that had children; and they belonged vaguely to the whole family by the same right as the domain, which was never divided." Again, in Java and, to a certain extent, in China, expulsion from the family is a grievous penalty, a sort of excommunication.[32] "After the death of Patroclus, Achilles took no more prisoners, and the blood-vengeance descended upon all the offender's blood-kin and community, upon women and innocent children." And the Greeks in the story play especial and enthusiastic havoc with the brothers and other kinsmen of Paris, the original offender.[33]

It appears from much evidence scattered through this book, as well as from cases like those just cited, that the family-organiza-

30 Vinogradoff, *Hist. Jurispr.*, I, ch. VI, 261 (quoted).
31 Nassau, *Fetichism*, 156, 157.   32 Letourneau, *Prop.*, 103, 173.
33 Keller, *Hom. Soc.*, 283, 308, where references are given; Homer, *Iliad*, XXIV, 493-498.

tion was once a larger as well as a looser structure than it later became. The primitive type is frequently one which, as previously stated, has been called the joint-family. Nothing can bring this primitive type home to the modern mind more forcefully than a reference to the existence and wide extension of the joint-house, or long-house, a structure large enough to hold many families or even a small tribe, with relatively small compartments for married pairs, their children, and their property.

In Sarawak a community of not less than four hundred souls lived in a building a little short of six hundred feet long. The longest Sea-Dyak house on record was seven hundred and seventy-one feet long.[34] Joint-houses have been found in Melanesia, among Ostiaks and Cossacks, in parts of India and Farther India, in Japan, in Borneo and elsewhere in the Malay Archipelago, in Micronesia and Polynesia, in North America (among the Eskimo, Aleuts, Haidahs, Iroquois, Pueblos, Guatusos, and others), in South America (especially in Brazil and Argentina), and among the aborigines of the Canary Islands. The names "pueblos" or "casas grandes" witness to the joint-house type, and the lake-dwellings or pile-dwellings are related forms.

Whether people were led to herd together in such joint establishments for the sake of safety,[35] or for other reasons, their life could not but be vitally influenced by the propinquity. They belonged together and there was less divergence of interests than would otherwise have existed. It is said that the arrangement declined among the Sengirese with the increase of wealth.[36] There seems to be no doubt that such communalism is economically and politically a poor adjustment sure to disappear except in isolation.[37]

In New Guinea, a house is never occupied solely by a man, with wife and children; "aunts, uncles, and cousins of many removes are included in the family circle."[38] The Yakuts have no word for a family consisting of man, wife, and children. Their term means house-mates or *familia*.[39] In India "the family in early as well as modern times has rarely been a divided one." The son hands over all his separate earnings to his father to be amalgamated with the general stock of family-property. The property is thus a joint arrangement, whose whole status is somewhat shaken by the introduction of will-making.[40] In the Nicobar Islands, as the family grows, and sons-in-law move

[34] Roth, *Sarawak,* II, 16, 17.
[35] Roth, *Sarawak,* II, ch. XXXIX, 17.
[36] Hickson, in JAI, XVI, 140.   [37] §129, above.
[38] Abel, *New Guinea,* 28.
[39] Sieroshevski-Sumner, in JAI, XXXI, 75.
[40] Nathubhai, in JASB, III, 410.

into the house, quarters become too narrow and a neighboring dwelling is erected; each hut is a small community.[41]

Among the Dyaks a whole blood-related group stays together, and the marriages of the males result in constant increase. "It is incredible how many fathers, mothers, children, grandchildren, uncles, aunts, brothers, sisters, nephews and nieces . . . swarm about in such a Dyak house-hold; and that all live and move in one dwelling, under one roof." Counting in the servants and pawns there may be up to three hundred souls.[42] "The custom of living in such a way, close together in a confined space, in which a great many disadvantages as regards personal freedom, ease, cleanliness, morality, etc., must inevitably be inherent, has something unnatural about it, not on a par with the inborn inclination of the natives for liberty and freedom from restraint, and is contradictory to the normal manner of life of their ancestors. . . . The practice of herding together in long houses prevents mental and moral improvement and hinders advance in gardening and planting and agricultural development generally."[43] The system of joint-houses in Polynesia and neighboring islands is unfavorable to the family; the more it is developed the weaker the family-bond. The legitimate wives and the unmarried women quarrel all the time about the attention of the men.[44] On Easter Island, "several families occupy the same dwelling; men, women and children lie down together like dogs in a kennel, and with about the same ideas of what constitutes the comforts of life."[45] "The Araucanians inhabit large family dwellings, which is also often the case with other tribes, and as long as they all dwell together, there is great cohesive power in the family group; but as soon as the local bond is dissolved, the kinship is no longer recognized."[46]

"The family group, or joint undivided family, constitutes the typical feature of the Aryan community."[47] The Ossetes of the Caucasus have clan-houses; all the members of the clan are consanguine and regard themselves as descended from a common ancestor, whose name they bear. At first everything was common but the system was undermined by individualism.[48] The East Finns and various tribes under Russian control show the joint-family; the single family is rare and is the result of Russian influence.[49]

There is much to be said for Morgan's[50] view that the individual family was too weak an organization to face the struggle for life until the economic and regulative system had been further developed. This conclusion falls in with the contention brought out while considering the system of communal property,[51] that only with the development of organization and civilization can the

[41] Svoboda, in *Intern. Arch. Ethnog.*, V, 185, 192.

[42] Perelaer, *Dajaks,* 122-123.

[43] Roth, *Sarawak*, II, ch. XXXIX, 25.

[44] Ratzel, *Vkde.*, II, 189.   [45] Thomson, in USNM, 1889, 454.

[46] Starcke, *Prim. Fam.*, 47.

[47] Starcke, *Prim. Fam.*, 95 and ff.; Schrader, *Aryan,* 393, 394; Jolly, in *Grundr. d. Indo-Ar. Philol.*, II, Heft 8, pp. 76, 77, 78.

[48] Letourneau, *Polit.*, 389-390.   [49] Abercromby, *Finns,* I, 179 ff.

[50] In *Contrib. N. Amer. Ethnol.*, IV, 63, 112.

[51] §128, above.

smaller group or the individual take his own insurance into his own hands. It should be clear enough that the family gets its joint form largely along with property and for the same underlying reasons; in fact, the joint-family has been of necessity, and more than partially, portrayed in the section on common property.[52] It is significant to find the joint-family in extreme form where self-defense is a matter of concern and where wealth is small, that is, where there is less power and confidence in the struggle for self-maintenance. It is the expedient adjustment under the circumstances. Such considerations present the joint-family as an organization based upon the blood-tie but resisting reduction to its constituent elements, namely, single families.

§415*. Sex-Ascendancy. Whether the family-group is larger or smaller, degrees of relationship by blood must be determined within it and, as is readily understandable, there is a considerable difference in the family-organization according as descent is reckoned in the female or in the male line. To the sex which carries descent and what goes with it a distinct importance is accorded. But before we are quite ready to enter upon the comparison of the relative status of carriers and non-carriers of descent and the results of such discrimination between the sexes, it is necessary to recognize and set aside one disturbing factor the presence of which often confuses the issue in particular cases.

The presence of economic or social inequality as between the parties contracting matrimony is always capable, irrespective of descent, of determining their relative status in the union. Witness the case of the *ambil-anak* marriage,[53] where a rich man with daughters only can ignore the non-payment of the regular *jujur*, or bride-price, and receive a son-in-law into his own house on terms of relative inferiority. Some of the following examples will recall this type very distinctly. In general in human relations it is the inferior who goes to the superior; one might even say that attending upon another instead of having him come is a recognition of his position or power. The king summons; he does not go. In any case, though there are a few illustrations to the contrary, where a man went to live with a woman and her kin he accepted a

---

[52] Ch. XII, above.   [53] §363, above.

status of less liberty and fewer privileges than where he brought the woman into his own family. For that sacrifice there were compensations or he would not make it. Sometimes he stayed with the wife's family only temporarily until he could serve out the brideprice; but while he remained on the servant's or debtor's plane he was an inferior and was treated as such. The fact that the woman usually goes to the man, after the payment by him of the brideprice, and then remains his inferior if not his property, is a further, less striking illustration of the same general principle. The tracing of descent through one line or the other affects this class of cases only indirectly if at all; but they can muddle the discussion of matrilinear and patrilinear family-organization by introducing the "matrilocal" and "patrilocal" conceptions, unless they are allowed for and excluded. Even Vinogradoff[54] can write, concerning the question of the paternal and maternal systems, that "the main fact is residence."

"If we scan carefully the accounts according to which 'a man marries into the family of a woman,' we find that his status here resembles that of a serving slave more than that of a spouse."[55] This is a good generalization, though there are exceptions. "Two kinds of marriage have been distinguished, according as the wife goes to live with her husband, or the husband goes to live with his wife. These two kinds are known as *patrilocal* and *matrilocal* respectively. As a general rule patrilocal marriage is associated with father-right and matrilocal marriage with mother-right, but the association is far from invariable. Even when marriage is patrilocal, the married couple often reside with the wife's people for a time, or the wife may return to her parents' home for the birth of her first child, this and other similar customs suggesting the influence of ideas derived from mother-right."[56]

"It is usual throughout Melanesia for a married couple to live with the husband's people. . . . A bride is taken to her husband's village, sometimes even while she is still a child." Yet Melanesia is regarded as a "characteristic area of communities with mother-right." There is evidence "that even in the part of Melanesia which has social institutions of the most archaic kind, there is no association of matrilocal marriage with matrilineal descent."[57] The Bushman, though he joins his wife's family for a considerable time and brings in food to it, yet is by no means a slave to his parents-in-law.[58] Most cases, however, go the other way. In South Africa the husband who removes to his wife's village is obliged, when in his mother-in-law's presence always to sit with his knees in a bent position. "If he becomes tired of living in this state of vassalage, and wishes to return to his own family, he is obliged to leave all his children behind—they belong to the wife." He gives nothing for his wife and has

54 *Hist. Jurispr.*, I, 195.　　　55 Mucke, *Horde*, 126.
56 Rivers, *Soc. Org.*, 90.
57 Rivers, *Melan. Soc.*, II, 126; I, 207.
58 Fritsch, *Eingeb. S.-Afr.*, I, 445.

no status. "From the temptations placed here before my men, I have no doubt that some prefer to have their daughters married in that way, as it leads to the increase of their own village."[59]

Among the Yakuts of ancient times, the first child ought to be born in the house of the woman's parents; the husband would then take wife and child home at the same time. This was considered a condition of good fortune.[60] In Ceylon the woman may go to the man or the man to the woman; in the latter case he has no more rights than a stranger and may be dismissed by the woman's father for no cause and without consulting the wife.[61] In Cochin China "at a marriage the pair generally lives several years with the parents of the wife, a very common usage among all Indo-Chinese peoples except the Annamites."[62]

"It needs no demonstration that under endogamy it must be a matter of complete indifference whether in marriage the man goes to live with the woman or the woman with the man." They are in the same community. Under exogamy, however, where the wife is from another group, she is parted from her relatives. In such a case the children must belong to the man and the family be patrilineal. On the other hand, if the man abides, or, in any case, associates at intervals with the woman, in her own group, the children follow her and the system is matrilineal.[63] "In Rotuma the husband very generally, though by no means universally, came to live with his wife, the children belonging to her." This, like adoption, was a method of recruiting the *hoang*, the social group of the woman. "It was the duty of a girl to attract a man who would enter her *hoang*; but in cases of great chiefs, or owners of family names, or when men belonged to a rich *hoang*, the girl would enter his *hoang*. When a wife dies in the *hoang*, if the husband did not belong to it, as the corpse was carried out through one door of the house, he was pushed out of another, signifying that he had no right to it. This seems to point to a system of matrilocal marriage, such as is commonly associated with matrilineal descent."[64]

From such cases it can be seen that the fact of the man going to the woman or the woman to the man had some effect in determining descent along one line or the other; nevertheless, to refer the existence of the matrilineal or patrilineal system solely to the localization-situation is to exaggerate a single factor and one which is, as ensuing evidence will show, a relatively minor one.

On Timor Island, "the men of Saluki can marry with the women of Bidauk, and take them back with them to Saluki, but they must purchase them, and it is not in their option to remain in Bidauk with their wives' relatives instead of paying. On the other hand, the men of Bidauk can marry with the women of Saluki, but the man must go to Saluki and live in the house of the woman, and he has not the option of paying for her at all."[65] By this arrangement, evidently, Bidauk gets the property and Saluki the population.

[59] Livingstone, *Mission. Travels*, 667-668.
[60] Sieroshevski, *Yakuts* (Russ.), I, 567, note 2.
[61] Schmidt, *Ceylon*, 254, 255.
[62] Niemann, in *Bijd.*, XLV, 340.   [63] Wilken, in VG, I, 372.
[64] Williamson, *Cent. Polyn.*, II, 122.   [65] Forbes, in JAI, XIII, 416.

Where the Samoan man goes to live with his wife's family, he becomes a serf and an underling; this happens sometimes when ordinary arrangements for a match fall through.[66] In New Zealand a man often went to live with his father-in-law and became one of the tribe to which his wife belonged. In case of war he might have to fight his own relatives. The usage is so common that a wife will go back to her relatives without her husband if he refuses to go with her; young men who have tried to break through the custom have lost their wives.[67] Among certain California tribes, though a man goes to live at his wife's or father-in-law's house, he retains power of life or death over the woman. Then there is a "half-marriage," where the suitor does not wait until he has accumulated all the shell-money which the girl's father demands: "instead of taking the woman as a slave into his house, he must live in her house as her slave."[68] The Lapps, even in the eighteenth century, retained a custom whereby a man went to the house of his wife's parents for a year.[69]

Though some of the above cases might plausibly be explained as survivals of descent in the female line, the economic motive is evidently dominant. In the agricultural community, Starcke[70] thinks, the father opposes the departure of his daughter "and seeks to induce her wooer to become one of his household." Daughters are valuable workers and the father must in any case be paid for loss of their services; if the man cannot do this the father may be quite reconciled to renunciation of the bride-price if he can retain the daughter and acquire her husband and children. Such motives could evidently exist upon any theory of descent; and explanation on such a basis is more obvious and direct than on that of the female or male line. In the presence of much insubstantial theorizing it is well, however, to recognize the fact that sex-ascendancy in the family is not a matter solely of the line upon which descent is reckoned. The economic and social factors must be kept constantly in mind in reviewing family-organization by descent.

§416*. The Mother-Family. The reason for beginning with the mother-family, as the prior number in the series of evolutionary forms of family-organization, is that relationship through the mother is definite and obvious; further, we accept Tylor's[71] contention that that type of family must be antecedent inasmuch as

[66] Ella, in AAAS, 1892, 625.
[67] Taylor, Te Ika, 337; Starcke, Prim. Fam., 90.
[68] Powers, in Contrib. N. Am. Ethnol., III, 382, 56.
[69] Lippert, Kgchte., II, 38.   [70] Prim. Fam., 100.
[71] In JAI, XVIII, 250 ff.

it reveals no survivals of the father-family, while the latter shows not a few reminiscences of the matrilinear system. At the same time we cannot share his opinion that it was the simple fact of the dwelling of the man in the wife's home, or the reverse, that determined the various usages which, taken together, form the father-family and the mother-family; nor yet do we agree that the blood-kinship idea called for an amount of observation and inference of which very primitive people were incapable. All such contentions are perhaps better left until an accumulation of information along several lines has had time to create a series of impressions on the mind.

In reviewing evidence for the existence of the mother-family, one must not expect to find a type cleanly defined in all of its details. Tylor[72] puts at twenty the number of genuinely matriarchal peoples in existence. In most cases the maternal family is in the process of transformation toward the paternal form and often there is nothing left of it except certain usages inconsonant with the latter system and inexplicable except as survivals of an older type. In our cases we begin with those which are most characteristic and follow them up with others of a more transitional order.

Again, it is necessary to retain in mind the distinction between descent, inheritance, and succession, the latter two having to do with transmission of property and of office respectively. It will not do to conclude from either as to the existence of descent in one line or the other, though it is entirely unlikely that property or position will be found to descend in the female line while descent is patrilineal. This is one of the reasons for assigning priority to the mother-family. Where descent, inheritance, and succession do not accord, it is likely that the latter two are becoming patrilineal under a weakening mother-family. Hence the purest types of the mother-family are those in which inheritance and succession, as well as descent, are matrilineal.

Connected particularly with descent is the question of authority. Whatever social or political ascendancy may accrue to wo-

---

[72] For the distribution of the mother-family, see Tylor, in *Nineteenth Century Mag.*, XL; Rivers, in *Hastings's Encyclop. Relig. and Ethics*, VIII, 851 ff.; Lubbock, *Orig. of Civ.*, 104 ff.; Kohler, *Urgchte. der Ehe*, 55 ff.; Grosse, *Familie*, 161 ff.; Cunow, *Australneger*, 139 ff. Tylor lists what he regards as the best typical cases.

man because she holds the key-position in the matter of descent
or even inheritance, it is not to be thought that she actually rules.
What we have in the mother-family is an oldest living ancestress
and her female descendants forming a group in which the ancestress is only roughly parallel to the patriarch in the father-family. Anyone who has come to appreciate the essential sex-differences and their sequels will be slow to believe that there ever was
a "metrocracy" or "gynæcocracy" except under extraordinary
conditions and for limited periods. He will note that woman sometimes obtains a position of dignity and even of some power that
is well attested and he will observe that there is a certain degree
of correlation between the presence of the maternal family and
that status;[73] but he will not be ready to refer the latter solely to
the former without due allowance for contributing causes. The
preceding account of the status of woman has shown that the
topic is a complicated and difficult one and has recalled the danger
of assigning societal results to single causes.

With these preliminary suggestions we shall go to the cases.
It is particularly necessary to apprehend the numerous shadings
which they show before trying to sum up the various aspects of
the mother-family. Though matters of inheritance and succession
cannot be suppressed, even were that desirable, without mangling
citations beyond measure, what should be gathered chiefly from
the following instances are, first, the evidence for the reckoning of
descent in the female line to the exclusion of the male, and, second,
the effect of so doing upon the identity of those composing the
family-group and, as such, exerting the ultimate influence upon
family-organization.

"A good example of complete mother-right is that of the Khasi of Assam.
Here descent in the clan is matrilineal; the house and other property belong
to the woman, and are inherited by daughters; and the chief is succeeded by
his brother, or by the son of his eldest sister. The husband and father only has
authority in those special cases in which, some time after his marriage, he
removes his wife with her children from her house, and takes them to another
house." It will be noted that when Rivers[74] thus singles out a case of complete
mother-right, he fastens attention upon the fact that inheritance and succession harmonize with descent. "Other complete examples of mother-right occur
in Sumatra, where we find the extreme case in which the husband does not live
with his wife: she dwells with her brothers, and is only occasionally visited

---

[73] §384, above.　　　　　[74] Soc. Org., 92.

by her husband. Descent, inheritance and succession are all matrilineal; property and rank, however, are enjoyed by the brothers before they pass to the sisters' children." The one genuine matriarchal people in the Archipelago, the Menangkabau Malays of central Sumatra, form a group composed of mothers and their children, uncles, aunts, grandmothers and great-aunts, that is, all "who are derived from the same womb," or, as the Alfurs put it, "those who have sucked the same milk." The clan, they think, is derived from a common mother. Says Wilken[75] of this system, after remarking that man and wife do not live together at all, much less form a kin-group: "Each remains in his family, in his kin-group, with his brothers and sisters, and with them forms a kin-group. This group does not comprise, therefore, man, wife, and children, but brothers, sisters, and sisters' children. At the head of the group stands the eldest brother who exercises control also over his sisters' children, as belonging to his kin-group. The uncle on the mother's side, the *mamak,* is, in his rights and duties, the real father of his sisters' children. . . . The father, as not belonging to the kin-group, has nothing to say about his children. In his turn, however, he stands, at least if he is an elder brother, at the head of the kin-group of his brothers and sisters and the latters' children. At the death of the eldest brother the next oldest becomes head . . . until all the brothers are dead. Then comes dissolution: each sister with her children forms a new kin-group and if she too dies, then the children again form a group with the eldest son at the head. Thus the group is not always composed of brothers, sisters, and sisters' children but sometimes of the mother with her children. The former is the normal form, however, and the latter the transitional. Really the woman always belongs, at any rate if she is married and has children, to two kin-groups, namely to that of her brothers and sisters and to that of her children, which is coming into being. But the latter group remains dependent so long as the former still remains and becomes independent only when the other has ceased to exist by reason of the death of all the brothers. With this arrangement the right of inheritance is consistent." A man's property goes to his brothers, sisters, and sisters' children, in which case boys and girls share alike. The father leaves nothing to his children; when a man dies, his kinsmen go to his wife's house to get all he may have left. The father can give things to his children, but it must be done before his brothers and sisters as witnesses or the last bit will be demanded and taken back. When a man, under the prevailing exogamic system, has several wives in different localities, whom he visits periodically, his headquarters are always with his own blood-kin. He is always an alien to the groups of his wives. What work he does in the house or field during his sojourn accrues to the wife's advantage, his own property being all under the surveillance of his mother and sisters and inheritable by his sisters' children.

A final illustration of the mother-family in its purest form is offered by the American Indian; this system, together with its political and social sequels, occurs in North America in a high degree of perfection. The more advanced tribes that had agriculture and totem-groups had the mother-family: the Iroquois, Hurons, Mohegans, Cherokees, Creeks, Choctaws, Mandans, Minitarees.

[75] In VG, I, 313-319; *Vkde.,* 323-325. This author deals with the mother-family in the Archipelago in several monographs collected in VG, I, 121 ff.; II, 161-308; and especially I, 287-406. The titles of these appear in the Bibliography of this book, under Wilken's name.

"The Hurons and the Iroquois had a perfect matriarchate";[76] descent among the latter was female as to tribe, clan, and nationality. We may review but briefly the now familiar facts concerning descent and inheritance typical of any mother-family and enlarge a little upon the extraordinary power of the women in the family and community, for inside the house they had rule; outside it they had influence; and in regard to the land they tilled they had power and authority. The classic on the Iroquois system is that of Morgan,[77] but we shall use chiefly the condensed summaries of the *Handbook of American Indians*. It is to be noted preliminarily that "all the Iroquoian tribes were sedentary and agricultural, depending on the chase for only a small part of their subsistence"[78]—a condition favorable to the economic activities of women.[79]

Starting with what Hewitt[80] calls the "brood-family," we find it to have been "composed of the progeny of a woman and her female descendants, counting through the female line only; hence the clan [a development of this family-germ] may be described as a permanent body of kindred, socially and politically organized, who trace actual and theoretical descent through the female only. . . . Custom, tradition, and the common law do not regard the wife or wives of the household as belonging to the clan of the husband. By marriage the wife acquires no right of membership in her husband's clan, but remains a member of her own clan, and, equally important, she transmits to her children the right of membership in her clan; and she acquires no rights of inheritance of property either from her husband or from his clan. On the other hand, the husband acquires no rights from his wife or from her clan, and he, likewise, does not become a member of his wife's clan."[81] In all cases, the woman confers her tribe and nationality upon her children. If a Cayuga marries a Delaware woman, his children, unless formally naturalized with the forms of adoption, are Delawares and aliens; if a Delaware marries a Cayuga woman, her children are Cayugas and of her tribe of the Cayugas.[82]

The "long-house" system of the Iroquois is pretty well known. The dwelling itself was usually forty to sixty feet long and fifteen to eighteen broad, with a common hall through the center, from door to door. The rest of the house was divided into equal compartments opening on the hall, and in the center of the latter were six to ten fire-pots, each of which was used by the two families occupying opposite compartments. The size of a village was estimated by the number of these houses, the largest settlements numbering one-hundred-and-fifty and also by the number of fires. The idea revealed in this Iroquois communal house runs through the architecture of the Indian family.[83] The head of each house was a woman; she owned all the household goods and children, and in case of separation retained the latter.[84] Husbands were admitted by

---

[76] Hewitt and Swanton, "Kinship," in HAI, I, 649; Lowie and Farrand, in HAI, I, 809; Morgan, in *Smithson. Contrib. Knowledge*, XVII, 139, 165.

[77] "Systems of Consanguinity," in *Smithson. Contrib. Knowledge*, XVII; Morgan, *League of Iroq.*; Morgan, *Anc. Soc.*; Hale, *Iroq. Rites*.

[78] Hewitt, "Iroquoian Family," in HAI, I, 617.

[79] §§67, 387, above.

[80] Articles on "Iroquois" and on "Family," in HAI, I, 618, 451.

[81] §149, above.

[82] Morgan, in *Smithson. Contrib. to Knowledge*, XVII, 165, note, 139.

[83] Morgan, in *Smithson. Contrib. to Knowledge*, XVII, 153, note.

[84] Hale, *Iroq. Rites*, 64, 65.

the senior matron on sufferance, as it were, and could be dismissed by her forthwith if she were dissatisfied. "The stores were in common, but woe to the luckless husband or lover who was too shiftless to do his share of the providing. No matter how many children, or whatever goods he might have in the house, he might at any time be ordered to pick up his blanket and budge; and after such orders it would not be healthful for him to attempt to disobey. The house would be too hot for him; and, unless saved by the intercession of some aunt or grandmother, he must retreat to his own clan; or, as was often done, go and start a new matrimonial alliance in some other. The women were the great power among the clans, as everywhere else. They did not hesitate, when occasion required, 'to knock off the horns,' as it was technically called, from the head of a chief, and send him back to the ranks of the warriors."[85] The wife "was really the head of the household; and in this capacity her right, when she chanced to be the oldest matron of a noble family, to select the successor of a deceased chief of that family, was recognized by the highest law of the confederacy."[86] It is worth noting that "female descent did not prevent the subjection of women" among the Iroquoian Creeks; but as a rule their rights were clearly defined.[87]

Hewitt[88] has summed up the evidence for the high position of woman among the Iroquois and tribes similarly organized. She "controlled many of the fundamental institutions of society; (a) descent of blood or citizenship in the clan, and hence in the tribe, was traced through her; (b) the titles, distinguished by unchanging specific names, of the various chieftainships of the tribe belonged exclusively to her; (c) the lodge and all its furnishings and equipment belonged to her; (d) her offspring, if she possessed any, belonged to her; (e) the lands of the clan (including the burial grounds in which her sons and brothers were interred) and so of the tribe, as the source of food, life, and shelter, belonged to her. As a consequence of the possession of these vested rights, the woman exercised the sovereign right to select from her sons the candidates for the chieftainships of her clan, and so of the tribe, and she likewise exercised the concurrent right to initiate the procedure for their deposition for sufficient cause. Being the source of the life of the clan, the woman possessed the sole right to adopt aliens into it, and a man could adopt an alien as a kinsman only with the tacit or expressed consent of the matron of his clan. A mother possessed the important authority to forbid her sons going on the warpath, and frequently the chiefs took advantage of this power of the woman to avoid a rupture with another tribe. The woman had the power of life or death over such alien prisoners as might become her share of the spoils of war to replace some of her kindred who may have been killed; she might demand of the clansmen of her husband or from those of her daughters a captive or a scalp to replace a loss in her family. Thus it is evident that not only the clan and the tribal councils, but also the League council were composed of her representatives, not those of the men. There were chieftainesses who were the executive officers of the women they represented. . . . Part of their duty was to keep close watch on the policies and the course of affairs affecting the welfare of the tribe, to guard scrupulously the interests of the

[85] Morgan, *Anc. Soc.*, 455, note.   [86] Hale, *Iroq. Rites*, 64.
[87] Lowie and Farrand, "Marriage," in HAI, I, 809.
[88] "Women," in HAI, II, 971; Hewitt, "Iroquoian Family," in HAI, I, 617; Hewitt, "Family," in HAI, I, 452.

public treasury, with power to maintain its resources . . . and they had a voice in the disposal of the contents of the treasury. Every distinct and primordial family . . . had at least one of the female chiefs, who together constituted the clan council; and sometimes one of them, by reason of extraordinary merit and wisdom, was made regent in the event of a vacancy in the office of the regular male chief. Hence, in various accounts mention is made of 'queens' who ruled their tribes. In view of the foregoing facts it is not surprising to find that among the Iroquoian tribes,—the Susquehanna, the Hurons, and the Iroquois—the penalties for killing a woman of the tribe were double those exacted for the killing of a man, because in the death of a woman the Iroquoian lawgivers recognized the probable loss of a long line of prospective offspring." This provision may be compared with that prevailing on the northwest coast, which exacted for a woman's death only half the penalty imposed for killing a man.

Tylor[89] connects with the maternal system the custom (teknonymy) of naming a father after his child; and he cites the practice of the Crees. "Among these people the young husband coming to live with his wife's parents, must turn his back on them and does not speak to them (especially ignoring his mother-in-law) until his first child is born, whereupon he takes its name and is called 'father of So-and-so,' and henceforth he attaches himself more to his parents-in-law than to his own parents. That is, he is ignored until his child, being born a member of the family, gives him a status as the father of a member of the family."

The foregoing citations indicate the main outlines of the mother-family and fill in some of the details. In various parts of the world the latter differ considerably but without affecting the broad type; there follow several illustrations of minor variations.

"If you were a New Guinea boy, or girl, your mother's brother would rank as your father, and her sister as your mother; your first cousins on your mother's side would actually be your brothers and sisters."[90] Again, in Melanesia, "at the same time all the father's brothers are called fathers, and the father's sisters mothers; in fact, all on both sides who are near the father's and mother's generation are called fathers and mothers, except the maternal uncles, who alone have a distinctive name."[91] Such a situation reveals the emergence of the idea of blood-kinship through the mother from out the older system of age-grades.[92]

Melanesia has been "regarded as a characteristic area of communities with mother-right." The author[93] quoted uses the region, however, to illustrate the complexity of the subject, and will be cited later on by way of illustration of transitional forms reaching out toward the father-right. He connects the mother-line with exogamy and the dual organization: "In the area of Melanesia included in my survey, matrilineal descent is almost universal wherever definite exogamy is practised by means of a social mechanism of clans or moieties. The dual organisation is invariably matrilineal. . . . So far as structural form is concerned, it is clear that in the region of Melanesia with

89 In JAI, XVIII, 248.   90 Abel, *New Guinea,* 28-29.
91 Codrington, in JAI, XVIII, 309.   92 §353, above.
93 Rivers, *Soc. Org.,* 91 ff.; and *Melan. Soc.,* II, 91.

which I deal, descent is almost universally matrilineal wherever it is proper to speak of descent at all." Codrington,[94] a standard authority, who seems always reliable when he is recording actual observations, states that "a man's sons are not of his own kin, though he acts a father's part to them; but the tie between his sisters' children and himself has the strength of the traditional bond of all native society, that of kinship, through the mother. The youth, as he begins to feel social wants, over and above the food and shelter that his father gives him, looks to his mother's brother as the male representative of his kin." Certain head-hunters are devoted to their mothers; "their father they may like, or they may not; they recognize no duty toward him; but their mother is something holy to them, whatever she is like, and no one is ever allowed to breathe a word against her."[95]

In East Africa, "a man is said to belong to his mother's clan and, consistent with this principle, inheritance goes in the female line. The main object is to conserve the property of the clan. A strict rule on the subject does not exist, but the normal course is for a man to select as his heir the most capable son of a full sister who was born next before or after himself. In default of such an heir the next entitled is sister's daughter's son, and last of all a brother. In absence of any such heirs some other male descended from a sister is selected."[96] Seligmann[97] cites the Beja of the Sudan as nomads who count genealogy in the female line. "Property passes to the sons of sister and daughter to the prejudice of the son of the deceased. To justify this custom they say that there can be no doubt as to the parentage of the son or daughter of a sister and that these must belong to the family, whether their mother had gotten them by her husband or by another man." Thus far the account is from a traveller of about 1500 A.D. "Here is a perfectly definite account of a pagan, nomad, pastoral people with matrilineal descent." They have dropped that form but without much change in the other mores as recorded four hundred years ago. "Moreover, even a slight acquaintance with the people is enough to show that they retain indisputable traces of a former matriarchy." These appear in their marriage-customs, as the author goes on to show.

A striking case of the maintenance of matrilineal mores for economic reasons is found in Malabar. "The alliance between the Malabar Brahmins and the Nāyars is a social fact of very great interest. In no other part of India is a Brahmin allowed to marry out of his own caste. In Malabar, on the other hand, among the Nampudiris or the Aryan immigrants, only the eldest member of the family can marry among the Brahmins, the others being forced to marry among the Nāyars. The permanence through ages of matrilineal descent among the Nāyars is due to this fact. The Brahmins, being of a superior caste, and the Nāyar wife of a Brahmin being unable to live in her husband's family, the system tended to be matrilineal as well as matrilocal. Also, since the children of such a marriage are Nāyars and not Brahmins, though the father is a Brahmin, the system remained wholly unilateral without any definite bilateral development. . . . The peculiar custom of the Malabar Brahmins of not allowing their junior members to marry among their own caste introduces a complication into the Nāyar system. The idea underlying such a prohibition is evidently the preservation of the big estates which the Nampudiris own. Since the Nāyar sons of the Malabar Brahmins do not inherit anything from

[94] *Melanesians,* 34; and in JAI, XVIII, 308, 309.
[95] Cator, *Head-Hunters,* 184.   [96] Dundas, C., in JAI, LI, 270.
[97] In JAI, XLIII, 649-650.

their fathers, their estates remain undivided and descend only to the eldest son. Primogeniture has been the custom in every country where the preservation of big landed property in the hands of a few was aimed at. The undivided family among the Nāyars is also meant to conserve their possession of the land and maintain the political influence resulting from it. A point of utmost importance which should always be kept in mind in this connection is the interaction of economic and social forces. The interest of the Nampudiris to keep their property undivided led to their custom of primogeniture, and this again induced them to use their temporal power and sacerdotal influence to perpetuate the matrilineal system among the Nāyars. Also, the desire to preserve the family estates as a whole, kept the Nāyar families from being divided, making thereby a change to patrilineal system altogether impossible."98

An astonishing case is that of the Todas, who hold to female descent among their buffaloes. "The Todas regard their buffaloes so much as fellow creatures that any of their ideas concerning the relations of their buffaloes to one another should not be without interest to the student of social regulations. . . . We have various groups of buffaloes, and each buffalo—certainly each female buffalo—belongs to the same group as its mother. There is complete promiscuity, and the buffalo belongs to its mother's group because paternity is unknown or disregarded. . . . If they had attached importance to paternity nothing would have been easier than to regulate breeding, to record paternity, and even to have developed a system of male descent among their buffaloes such as exists among themselves." They have no names for male animals. "The nature of what may be called the social regulations of the buffaloes shows that the Todas take little interest in the part played by the male in the process of mating, and . . . this lack of interest is almost as great among themselves. Side by side with the strictest regulation of marriage as a social institution, such great laxity prevails in regard to sexual relations that the Todas may almost be said to live in a condition of promiscuity."99 It is inferred that they have continued to follow, in the case of their animals, a theory and system which they themselves have had to modify.

In a number of places in his collected works, Wilken100 cites features of the mother-family, but chiefly, perhaps, in his treatment of the Sumatran system. He lists the East Indian districts where the mother-family or traces of it occur and finds that such survivals fall in more or less with linguistic divisions. The name of the blood-kin group, signifying "from one belly," "from one mother," sometimes betrays a former reckoning of kinship; and so does the distribution of the *heerendiensten,* or services to the chief. "The outstanding rule about it is that only those who have wives are held to the discharge of *heerendiensten,* and that those are exempted from it who are not yet married, whatever their age. If the wife dies, then the husband is free of all possible obligations; if, on the other hand, the husband dies, then the wife remains involved in the obligation of service in the sense that one of the sons replaces the father. Only in case there are no children or that these are not yet old enough, is the woman, evidently only as a concession to her weakness, exempted. . . . Of itself this rule leads us back to the times of the matriarchate, when the woman was head of the clan, and the man, an alien in the house of his wife, belonged to the clan of his mother and sisters, in which, too, he held

98 Panikkar, in JAI, XLVIII, 265.
99 Rivers, *Todas,* 548-549.   100 In VG, II, 163 ff.

a subordinate position. If the man died, yet the clan remained in being and the existing obligations must be met; if, on the other hand, the woman died, then the clan was dissolved and so the obligations came of themselves to nothing."

When an East Indian matrilineal group becomes too large it divides into two dwellings, which then form a *kampong*. Each group is under the direction of the oldest male among the blood-kin; its members, say the Malays, "are family-comrades, they have a single crown and single root, they have debts and claims in common, they share shame and honor." Property goes over undivided from generation to generation; community of blood is the basis for complete community of life. But no two members may marry, and this taboo leads to exogamic relations between the kin-groups of the kampong. The mother raises or lowers the child to her social status, which the father cannot do. In one locality the groom is purchased as is the bride under the patriarchal system, and the same term is used for the matriarchal as for the patriarchal marriage, namely, "to sell someone something," the "something" being generally the wife but in this extreme case the husband. The author is inclined to believe that where a woman chooses her husband there is a reminiscence of this situation. Finally, there is a Batak case where a sister's son may marry a brother's daughter, but not a brother's son a sister's daughter—a curious variation of the cross-cousin union. This is explained as follows. Under the mother-family the brother regards his sister's children as his own, but not the sister the brother's as her own. Sisters' sons would not therefore avoid marriage with brothers' daughters, while brothers' sons would not marry girls who stood as children to their father. Gradually the idea would gain strength that one union was allowable, the other not. This illustrates the possible extensions of the matrilineal idea and system.

Grinnell[101] says that under the Cheyenne matrilineal system a man went to live with his wife's clan and could become a chief in it. "A man might live in several groups during his life, a woman in but one." Says Jones[102] of the Tlinkit: "The children belong to the totem of the mother, and, of course, receive their caste from her. The father has no authority over his own children. The maternal uncle of the children has far more to say about them than the father. The aunts on the maternal side have, also, all authority over their nephews and nieces. They are regarded as mothers and are so called by their nephews and nieces. When the mother dies the father must relinquish his children to their maternal uncles and aunts. If the father were to inflict any injury on his child, his tribe would have to pay damages to his wife's tribe. . . . Uncles are especially indulgent toward their nephews. In fact the more liberties they take the better the uncles like it. No uncle would think of imposing restrictions on his nephew in his own home, and the nephews walk in and out of the homes of their uncles as if they were real sons."

There has been some little dispute concerning the priority of matrilineal institutions to paternal in North America. It does not seem to us to shake the general proposition that normally the former are antecedent.[103]

[101] *Cheyenne*, I, 91.   [102] *Thlingets*, 44-45.
[103] Boas, in USNM, 1895, 333-335; Boas, in JAI, XL, 535-536; Discussion,

A great deal of material was presented by the earlier writers on the "matri-archate"—who, indeed, knew but little ethnography—from ancient history, legend, and mythology. It is of widely varying value, and is illustrated in the *Case-Book*. Perhaps it is the Orestes case that is most typical of such evidence. "The stories of Orestes and Clytæmnestra, of Alcmæon and Eriphyle, are deep-rooted in matriarchy—both look back to the days when the only relationship that could be proved, and that therefore was worth troubling about, was that through the mother; and hence special vengeance attends the slayer of the mother."[104]

One more aspect of the matrilineal system needs illustration, namely, the location of authority. Wherever it is, it is in the hands of men. This disposes of the idea of "woman-rule" or "matriar-chate" in the strict sense. There is really no *matria potestas*.

"In many communities with matrilineal descent the father or father's father is definitely, so far as the clan is concerned, the head of the household, but in other cases the head of the household is the mother's brother. The household in these cases consists of the man and his brothers, his sisters and their children, but not the children of the man himself or of his brothers, who will belong to the households of their wives. In this case authority in the household is exerted by the brothers, or, looked at from the point of view of the children, by the mother's brothers. The husbands of the sisters will not form part of the household, or, if members of the household group, permanently or temporarily, are without authority, and rank in this respect behind the brothers of their wives. Similarly, the brothers or mother's brothers, who are the dispensers of authority in their own houses, will be without authority, or occupy only a subordinate position, in the households of their wives and children. This kind of organization has been termed the *Avunculate*, in order to indicate the important position occupied by the maternal uncle."[105]

The close relationship between children and their mother's brother has been brought out incidentally in several of the foregoing cases; it is clear that he is the male adult most closely related to the child and he has been seen to have been, in several parts of the world, the mother's strongest support and partisan. Both property and social position have frequently passed from maternal uncle to nephew. There is no explanation for such customs unless we may believe that kinship is or has been reckoned in the female line. Even where a strong patriarchate is in evidence, the maternal uncle may still figure in certain junctures as a prominent person.[106] The uncle-nephew relation deserves special illustra-

sub Hartland, in AA, XX, 224-226; see also the views of Spencer and Gillen, *Nat. Tr. Cent. Aust.*, 36, note; Wilken, in VG, I, 228, note (by Wilken's editor); Rivers, *Soc. Org.*, 96.
104 Harrison, *Greek Relig.*, 246-247.
105 Rivers, *Soc. Org.*, 88-89.   106 Ratzel, *Vkde.*, I, 294.

tion in addition to the incidental notice it has received by reason of its significance in connection with the mother-family.[107]

In a small number of Australian tribes the control over the daughter's hand falls, not to the father but to the mother and her brother.[108] Again the mother's brother decides whether her infant shall be killed or not.[109] In Melanesia, while descent follows the mother, "it must be understood that the mother is in no way the head of the family. The house of the family is the father's, the garden is his, the rule and government are his; it is into the father's house that the young bridegroom takes his wife, if he has not one ready of his own. The closest relationship, however, according to native notions, is that which exists between the sister's son and the mother's brother, because the mother who transmits the kinship is not able to render the service which a man can give."[110] This last phrase contains the whole case as respects authority and power; the female is not the equal of the male and no system can make her so, when it comes to the capacity to discharge such functions. In northeastern Melanesia the purchase-price for a child that is sold goes to the mother's brother. A young man's bride is selected, never by his father but by his maternal uncle, elder brother, or the chief. In practice the youth confides his wishes to the proper intermediary. The bride-price is received by the bride's mother's brother, the mother getting only a share. If there is no uncle, the girl's brother or nearest male relation takes his place.[111] In the New Hebrides, a boy belongs to his mother's tribe and her full brother instructs him; if he goes with his father he is scolded and sent to his uncle. If a man is in danger or is ill he invokes the ghost of his father or maternal uncle.[112] In the Torres Straits Islands the nephew may despoil his maternal uncle of anything he wishes. Such customs, found in a tribe with paternal descent, are probably "vestiges of a previous condition in which descent was maternal, and the brothers of the mother were regarded as nearer kin than the father."[113]

This last case merges into the Fijian *vasu*, whereby a nephew is granted the most extraordinary rights as against his mother's brother. "The vasu has certain privileges with regard to his uncle, and can make free with his property to an extent which would be surprising if we did not know the vasu-right to be a survival of inheritance through the mother under which the sister's son becomes the heir, to the exclusion of the son."[114] Starcke[115] makes considerable point of the custom: "However high a chief may rank, however powerful a king may be; if he has a nephew he has a master, one who will not be content with the name, but who will exercise his prerogative to the full, seizing whatever may take his fancy, regardless of its value or the owner's inconvenience in its loss. Resistance is not thought of, and objection only offered in extreme cases. Thokonanto, a Rewa chief, during a quarrel with an

[107] Rivers, *Soc. Org.*, 93-96.   [108] Cameron, in JAI, XIV, 352.
[109] Bonney, in JAI, XIII, 225.
[110] Codrington, *Melanesians*, 34; and in JAI, XVIII, 308, 309.
[111] Von Pfeil, *Südsee*, 21, 28, 29.
[112] Macdonald, in AAAS, 1892, 722, 729.
[113] Rivers, *Soc. Org.*, 93; and in *Man*, I, 171-172.
[114] Fison, in JAI, X, 339; Thomson, in JAI, XXIV, 380.
[115] *Prim. Fam.*, 91-93; Mucke, *Horde*, 229; Grosse, *Familie*, 185.

uncle, used the rights of Vasu, and actually supplied himself with ammunition from his enemy's stores." No son would venture to put forth such claims. "In the Banks' Islands the sister's son . . . has certain rights with his maternal uncle . . . corresponding to those of the Fijian *vasu*, but by no means conspicuous or important."[116]

The African chieftainship may be hereditary in the direct line, but in case of doubt the descendant of the chief's sister is preferred.[117] In southern Africa, "the general tendency towards the female line of descent makes it easy for the sister's son to inherit the kingly power."[118] Said a chief of the Gold Coast, explaining the nephew-inheritance: "My sister and children are my blood relatives, but whether the children my wives bear are so or not, I cannot tell."[119] In the Lake regions the maternal uncle owns his nephews and can sell them if he likes. "This avuncular right cannot be gainsaid, and may be exercised despite the protests of father and mother thus set aside."[120] The maternal uncle is very influential in giving the names to a newly born nephew.[121] In the fourteenth century, Sudanese names were derived from maternal uncles and nephews inherited, "a custom I witnessed nowhere else except among the infidel Hindoos of Malabar."[122]

A story is told of a Samoan chief "who, in visiting his uncle in effect asked the latter to give him a bread-fruit storage house which the uncle had recently constructed at ruinous expense. The uncle did not consent; so the chief kidnapped his wife 'as is the custom in these cases.' The uncle, longing to have his wife back, eventually decided to give up the house; but, as this was not, after what had occurred, enough, he went to the nephew chief with a present of pigs, and ultimately the wife was restored, and the bread-fruit house was handed to the chief; but the uncle was ruined." In connection with this tale it was stated "that if a nephew took a fancy to his uncle's gun, he would go and take it, and in case of difficulty, would report the matter to his mother, who would enforce compliance by her brother (the uncle) by pronouncing a curse upon his family." A consul reported that, during fighting, "men used often to bring guns to his house to save them from their nephews, and sometimes slept with guns lashed to their legs; but the nephews had come and taken them away even then. This right of a nephew was said to be connected with 'a custom called *vasu*, which prevailed in the islands, as regarded the rights of a nephew to his uncle's property,' these rights being confined, however, to the children of the eldest sister."[123]

Morgan[124] writes of the uncle as follows: "The relationship of uncle in Indian society is, in several particulars, more important than any other from the authority with which he is invested over his nephews and nieces. He is, practically, rather more the head of his sister's family than his sister's husband. It may be illustrated in several ways from present usages. Amongst the Choctas, for example, if a boy is to be placed at school his uncle, instead of his father, takes him to the mission and makes the arrangement. An uncle, among the Winnebagoes, may require services of a nephew, or administer correction,

116 Codrington, in JAI, XVIII, 309.   117 Ratzel, *Vkde.*, I, 404.
118 Starcke, *Prim. Fam.*, 74.   119 MacLeod, in JAI, XXI, 75.
120 Letourneau, *Prop.*, 93 (quoting Barton, *Lake Regions, Cent. Afr.*, I, 37).
121 Stuhlmann, *Mit Emin*, 82.   122 Ibn Batuta, *Travels*, 234.
123 Williamson, *Cent. Polyn.*, II, 153-154.
124 "Syst. Consang.," in *Smithson. Contrib. Knowledge*, XVII, 158.

which his own father would neither ask nor attempt." The Tsimshian system shows nephew-inheritance: "Property—embracing a man's hunting-ground, fishing-ground, his house, canoes, slaves, etc., as well as his name, the dancing-privileges, traditions, songs that belong to the same—is inherited first by the nephews; if there are none, then by the deceased's mother or aunt. A woman's property is inherited by her children. When a man dies, his widow keeps her children and her own personal property; while the personal property, as well as the family property of the deceased, goes to his own family."[125]

The Arabian idea that character is transmitted from the maternal uncle (chal) to the nephew is very pronounced. Formulas of appreciation and of imprecation are: "God repay his chal!" or "God damn his chal!" The uncle is blamed for his nephew's misdeeds or at any rate for two-thirds of them; the younger man is responsible for only one-third.[126] Tacitus[127] speaks of the honor enjoyed by the maternal uncle as compared with the father; relationship by blood to the former is closer and holier. Nephews are preferred as hostages, as inspiring a stronger attachment and interesting the family on more sides. In the North, sons were gladly intrusted to the mother's brother.[128]

§417. Some Features of the Mother-Family.

Although the statements about the mother-family are individually correct, the sum of them, to modern understanding, may be misleading. Where ethnographical descriptions emphasize one aspect of it at a time there is an element of distortion. A large part of the controversy waged over the subject is due to the fact that, although all might agree in accepting the sequence: father-family (meaning really monandry)—mother-family—father-family, yet some are talking of the first two members of the series and others of the last two when they dispute as to the priority of mother-family or father-family.[129] If, now, monandry be distinguished from the father-family, it seems clear enough that mother-descent and the mother-family arose out of primitive monandry by direct evolution. The woman at the fireside, with the children issued from her body, was the settled part of society and the institutional growth began to form about her and her children—not about the man, who was wandering, unstable, unregulated. Institutional development tended to integration and closer adjustment on the lines set for it by the facts of the case and the forces operating in it.

Beliefs about the share of the parents in procreation are thought to have had significance in the formation of the mother-family. Uncivilized peoples have obvious reasons for thinking the

---

[125] Boas, in BAE, XXXI, 499.
[126] Wilken, in VG, II, 33-36.
[127] Germ., XX.
[128] Weinhold, Altn. Leben, 285.
[129] Hildebrand, Recht, 22.

share of the mother far greater than that of the father. If we locate ourselves at their standpoint, the logic of the mother-family is unmistakable; mother and child, brother and sister, are united by a physical and historical fact. Then child and maternal uncle are united almost as directly and clearly, although by two links instead of one. The father is in a position at one side, inferior and incidental, perhaps uncertain. There is abundant evidence that such is the view of his position.

Nevertheless it is necessary to guard unceasingly against the "category-fallacy"[130]—against assuming that all the facts of societal life will fall unerringly into the categories into which some have been tentatively cast in order to get them somehow classified and relieved of original confusion. In one case it may be reported that children know only their mothers and them only up to a certain age, after which they forget the relationship and it is replaced by a sense of belonging to the group;[131] and yet one happens immediately upon an instance such as the following, reported by Howitt[132] of the Australians: "These aborigines, even while counting 'descent'—that is, counting the class names—through the mother, never for a moment feel any doubt, according to my experience, that the children originate solely from the male parent, and only owe their infantine nurture to their mother. . . . The daughter emanates from her father solely, being only nurtured by her mother." This is the view of the highest tribes in this continent. There are very few statements on the specific point as to which of the parents is thought to have the greater share in procreation; evidently it was open to endless and incontrovertible argument on any theory of parenthood. It is not the theory, then, which is determinative; people who are not trained to analysis might well feel that the share of the mother was greater and longer at the same time that they conceived that of the father to be more creative and essential. Then, too, there is often that doubt as to the identity of the father.

Another point upon which it is not possible to insist dogmatically is as to where authority is lodged. "The subject of authority

130 §456, below.
131 Sieroshevski, *Yakuts* (Russ.), 568.
132 In JAI, XII, 502; Cameron, in JAI, XIV, 352.

is by no means simple. Authority may be divided between the father and the mother's brother, that of the latter being often the greater; or it may be divided between the mother and her brothers; or, in exceptional cases, it may rest with the mother."[133] What emerges with distinctness is the infrequency with which women are found clothed with it.

What is found is that female descent controls all genealogical relations and all institutions which depend upon genealogy, while male descent appears in connection with civil and military institutions. A boy is born into his mother's clan; at puberty he is introduced, by initiation, into his father's tribe.[134] Peace-rulers come from clans by birth; war-chiefs from tribes by election. The Galla represent the most noteworthy case of a modern people with the mother-family, which is also warlike. Property-inheritance is likely to be a genealogical matter, whereas succession to political position tends to break away from the blood-tie.[135] So intimately is the former connected with the family-bond that the whole subject of property-inheritance could be treated under the section of family-organization. Furthermore, the presence of the mother-line of descent is no guarantee of a high status for women: the Fijian may kill and eat his wife, and other matrilinear peoples hold woman in profound contempt.[136]

Thus the presence of the mother-family is not competent to explain all attendant societal phenomena with precision and without reservation; the reckoning of descent in the female line is but one of the factors that enter to determine the type of a society. Our understanding of societal evolution is much clarified by the knowledge of the existence and characteristics of this form of adjustment, which is so strange to us when we first encounter it; the tendency of those who first discovered it to strain and exaggerate its influence upon society is easily understandable. There is the more occasion for discretion and scientific reserve in estimating its place in the evolutionary series of societal forms. Its main features are before the reader; it is now in order to examine the transitional forms that lead over to the father-family. These

[133] Rivers, *Soc. Org.*, 159.   [134] Howitt, in JAI, XIV, 144.
[135] Paulitschke, *Nordost-Afr.*, I, 257.
[136] Waitz, *Anthr.*, VI, 627; Stevens, in *Ztsft. f. Ethnol.*, XXVIII, 175.

will be found, as is generally the case with such bridging types, to throw as much or perhaps more light upon the forms which they connect than is to be gained by separate study of those forms themselves.

CHAPTER LVI

THE TRANSITION TO THE PATRIARCHATE

§418*. **Transitional Forms.** Before any attempt to generalize further concerning the aspects of family-organization presented in the foregoing chapter, there should be presented a set of cases which look to be transitional between the mother-family and the father-family. Some of these will bear little better evidence of transition than a number which have been cited above, for it is impossible to construct exclusive categories here or elsewhere in the study of mores and institutions; but in this connection the eye will be fixed upon modifications of the matrilinear system rather than upon the distinguishing characteristics of that system. There are enough cases to allow of utilizing a fresh set to cover the transitional features.

The general type of the Australian family is the maternal. An Australian tribesman, "in speaking to me of the practice of betrothal, said that a father could do what he liked with his daughter, because the child is his, and 'he only gives it to his wife to take care of for him.' This, which is at variance with the Dieri custom, where the mother has full disposal of her infant daughter, is an indication of an advance toward paternal descent."[1] Among the Dieri the sons take the father's class and name and the daughters the mother's. The father is the family-head but does not eat of his offspring as the females must.[2] Tylor[3] speaks of the Kurnai as departing from the "ordinary Australian matriarchal rule of female descent" through the practice of elopement, their "only mode of marriage." Their departure from the normal Australian type means that "they have made some part of the transition from the matriarchal to the patriarchal system." A curious case is where, "if the infant is a boy, the nearest relative is the father; if it is a girl the nearest relative is the mother."[4]

"It is . . . clear that it is only correct to speak of the greater part of Melanesia as matrilineal if the application of that term be limited to descent. In the matter of succession, the part of Melanesia with which I deal is patrilineal throughout. Inheritance occupies an intermediate position, and here the evidence is clear that, in that part of Melanesia which the general argument of this book has shown to possess the most archaic institutions, inheritance is, or was till quite lately, altogether matrilineal. In the most advanced communities, on the other hand, it is mainly patrilineal, while various islands which occupy intermediate positions in order of development also occupy intermediate positions in the matter of inheritance, showing various stages of progres-

---

[1] Howitt, *S.E. Aust.*, 198.   [2] Gason, in JAI, XVII, 186.

[3] In discussion of Howitt, in JAI, XV, 421.

[4] Dawson, *Aust. Aborig.*, 38.

sion from the maternal to the paternal line. It is beyond all doubt that the direction of change in Melanesia has been from the matrilineal to the patrilineal mode. . . . If, as seems to be the case, the social groupings in clans and moieties has the regulation of marriage as its chief social function and has little or no influence in the determination of rank or wealth, it is perfectly natural that men should be moved to bring about the transmission of their property or honours to their children, while they still allow them to belong to the social group of the mother. There would not have been the motives for changing the mode of descent which seem to have had so great an influence on inheritance and succession. If increasing recognition of fatherhood has thus been the essential factor in determining the change towards patrilineal institutions, it also becomes natural that succession should have advanced farther in this direction than inheritance. Those who are especially interested in succession are men of influence in the community who might be expected to have more power to change the nature of a social institution than would be possible in such a matter as the transmission of property which intimately affects other persons. Further, the vested interests interfered with by a change in the mode of inheritance would probably affect a wider circle of persons than would be involved in the transmission of rank. . . . The conclusion . . . is that there has been a progressive change from an early condition of society organised on the dual basis with matrilineal descent towards one in which the clan organisation has disappeared and marriage is regulated solely by relationships which can be traced genealogically."[5]

In the New Hebrides, a sign of transition from the older to the newer system is seen in the fact that in the spirit-world a man's ghost is said to be treated by that of his mother with contempt and hatred but by that of his paternal aunt with kindness.[6] One of the Torres Straits tribes "is in the intermediate condition between a matriarchal and a patriarchal system. The proposal of marriage by the girls, the tendency for the man to live mainly with his wife's people, and possibly the fair condition of the women may be regarded as matriarchal conditions—on the other hand, relationship is from the father, and the life of the wife is at her husband's disposal."[7]

Among African tribes, children often belong to the tribe of the mother, though among the herders the patriarchal rule prevails.[8] The only branch of the Bantu race among whom "no certain traces of totemism and but a few of mother-right are found" are the Amazulu and certain allied tribes, the most advanced of all the Bantu stock.[9] "All the Makalaka children cleave to the mother in cases of separation, or removal from one part of the country to another. . . . The Bechuanas, on the contrary, care nothing for their mothers, but cleave to their fathers, especially if they have any expectation of becoming heirs to their cattle."[10] It is worth while to note all cases where father-right appears to be correlative with a pastoral life.

In Dahomi the common people reckon relationship and inherit property through the mother, while the higher classes have father-right. "This, which

[5] Rivers, *Melan. Soc.*, II, 87-88, 101, 102.

[6] Leggatt, in AAAS, 1892, 698; Macdonald, in AAAS, 1892, 723, 729.

[7] Haddon, in JAI, XIX, 355; Thilenius, in *Globus*, LXXXI, 331; Hunt, in JAI, XXVIII, 6.

[8] Ratzel, *Vkde.*, I, 156.

[9] Hartland, in *Folk-Lore*, XII, 15 ff.

[10] Livingstone, *Mission. Travels*, 333.

carries with it a proprietorship of a father in his children not recognized else-where, has very probably been brought about by the exercise of arbitrary power." There is no doubt that descent was formerly reckoned universally in the female line. "Among the Yoruba tribes descent is through both parents with succession in the male line, and marriage is forbidden both in the father's and mother's family so long as relationship can be traced. A man's heirs are his sons, among whom the property is equally divided. If a man have no sons, his brothers inherit. The old ideas concerning blood-descent still, however, exercise some influence, and children by the same father, but different mothers, are not generally considered proper blood relations. Thus, going from the Tshi tribes to the Yoruba, from the least cultured to the most cultured we find a gradual but regular change from kinship and descent through mothers only, to kinship and descent through both parents."[11] In West Africa sometimes the initiation-ceremony consists partly in the symbolic killing and burial of the youth who has been torn away from his mother; then he is resurrected as a man, into the male organization, and becomes related to his father's god.[12]

Among the Yakuts there are many sibs which trace their descent by tradi-tion from women, although kinship is now through males.[13] In one tribe in India the boys become the property of the father on his paying the mother a small sum of money when the child is named and enters his father's tribe; girls remain with the mother and belong to her tribe.[14]

Wilken[15] sees in abduction and elopement a factor working steadily to un-dermine the maternal system. In the South-West Islands the man regularly follows the wife, and the children are hers; but if he abducts her, the children are his. It is really elopement, for the young pair hide in the bush and the blood-kin of the woman, arming themselves, hunt them. When they are found the parents of the groom are visited and restitution demanded. The parents deny that they have encouraged the son in his enterprise, beg forgiveness for him, and promise property-compensation. The maternal system, though the recognized rule, is always liable to pass into the paternal system by capture, which brings wife and children into the husband's hands.[16] Wilken[17] thinks the custom of female proposal, especially by the peculiar method of asking the man into the house and making him pay for its internal decorations if he refuses,[18] is a relic of the matriarchal régime. This author rather specializes in transi-tional forms between the two systems; several other of his illustrations may be cited. In connection with the naming of children, chiefly among the Alfurs of Celebes, he notes first that the name would follow the conception of rela-tionship and that that must be closer in the case of the mother, especially if she nursed the child into the third or fourth year, as is common among sav-ages. When the change was approaching the father was anxious to assure what he should leave to his own children; therefore he wanted to mark the child as his at its birth. What could secure this end more readily than to name himself after the child, as "father of So-and-so"? This custom, therefore, arises out of

[11] Ellis, *Yoruba*, 188, 298-299 (quoted).
[12] §163, above; Lippert, *Kgchte.*, II, 342.
[13] Sieroshevski-Sumner, in JAI, XXXI, 75.
[14] Lubbock, *Origin of Civil.*, 106.   [15] In VG, I, 479.
[16] Tylor, in JAI, XVIII, 260.
[17] In VG, I, 516-518, 108, 109-111, 120; II, 173 (quoting Tylor, in *Academy*, XXVIII, 67).
[18] §368, above.

an original uncertainty about fatherhood. Later, he thinks, the mother adopted the same sort of designation. Also, in respect to the father, there was less need of establishing blood-kinship to the child than of demonstrating ownership over the mother, for this conferred a right to the child. Even the Manangkabau Malays, among whom the mother-family is as pure as anywhere in the Archipelago, when they moved out of their original home began to take on the patriarchal character; and even when they have not migrated, some adjustment in that direction has come to pass. "Gradually in a number of regions the rule has evolved that at least half of what the man has himself earned can accrue by gift . . . to the benefit of his own children." Among the Sumatrans of several centuries ago, "in marrying, the husband goes to the house of the wife and afterwards belongs to her family, therefore they prefer getting girls to boys"; but here, too, there has been some adjustment. While "the titles and dignities of the man go over to the brothers, then to the sisters, and not seldom directly to the latter; and while in governmental positions it is the eldest son of the eldest sister who is the regular successor; yet it is a notable exception to the original right of inheritance that what a man earns for himself is inherited by his own children," or, more generally, that "not only his sister's children but also his own have rights to his possessions."

Wilken quotes as follows: "The Hon. J. W. Powell mentioned from his own observations of American tribes a visible cause of the change from female to male kinship—the necessity of tribes spreading over the country for hunting. The husband thus removing his wife from the neighbourhood of her uncles and brothers in the matriarchal settlement, naturally gets her and their children into his power, and a kind of patriarchalism with male kinship sets in." This sounds a little like the pronouncement of Kohler:[19] "The first man who brought his wife into servile dependence and therewith inaugurated the period of husband-control, the first who, thousands of years ago, stole the first wife, was unwittingly a benefactor of mankind, for he leaped the chasm that separates mother-right from father-right." This is, again, a reference to the connection between the local and linear systems.[20]

"A Chocta once expressed . . . a wish that he might be made a citizen of the United States, for the reason that his children would then inherit his property instead of his gentile kindred under the old law of the gens [clan]. . . . Usages would distribute his property after his death among his brothers and sisters and the children of his sisters. He could, however, give his property to his children in his life-time, in which case they could hold it against the members of his gens. Many Indian tribes now have considerable property in domestic animals and in houses and lands owned by individuals, among whom the practice of giving it to their children in their life-time has become common to avoid gentile inheritance. As property increased in quantity the disinheritance of children began to arouse opposition to gentile inheritance, and in some of the tribes, that of the Choctas among the number, the old usage was abolished . . . and the right to inherit was vested exclusively in the children of the deceased owner."[21]

In the Greek, Roman, Celtic, and German legends the ordered patriarchate of later times does not appear. In one myth Hercules is the woman-hater who undertakes to relieve men of the last relics of woman-rule. Much has been

---

[19] In *Ztsft. f. vergl. Rechtswiss.*, VI, 321 (quoted by Wilken, in VG, II, 343-344).

[20] §415, above.

[21] Morgan, *Anc. Soc.*, 162-163.

made, as was intimated above, of the Klytemnæstra-Orestes story, since Bachofen first turned his attention to it.[22]

"Among the Basque people today there is prevalent the idea that motherhood, and not father-hood, is the initial point of birth-right." The oldest daughter has in recent times had precedence over all sons in inheritance. In general the eldest born, male or female, has inherited. "If it was a daughter, then she was, in the capacity of exclusive heiress, head of the house and of the possessions of the family. Even after her marriage she remained under the roof where she first saw the light of life, her husband came to live with her, lost his name to take that of his wife, while the children too were named after the mother. Only in case the first-born was a son did the family progress in the male line and did the children get the name of the father and stand under his control."[23]

Markedly exceptional instances are always worth noting. There is one in which a writer[24] thinks he sees an adjustment tending away from the paternal system and toward the maternal. The case is very intricate, and acculturation from matrilinear systems to the north is not improbable. The original organization has suffered disturbances of several kinds. "It seems to my mind that this exceedingly intricate law . . . can not be explained in any other way than as an adaptation of maternal laws by a tribe which was on a paternal stage." The exceptionality of this case sets in relief the normality of the transition in the opposite direction.

§419*. The Father-Family. If the father-family were not so well known—known to the exclusion of any other form—it might have been well to describe it before reviewing types of family-organization transitional to it. To speak of foremothers instead of forefathers would seem to us odd and outlandish. The fact is that the father-family needs little description except to exhibit certain of its extreme manifestations. Relationship is reckoned in the paternal line—not often, however, to the utter exclusion of the maternal, for the mother's relation to the child was always too obvious to be ignored unless arbitrarily and deliberately. The chief characteristic of the father-family is the rule of man; if the mother-family never really becomes a matriarchate or metrocracy or gynæcocracy, the father-family well deserves the title of patriarchate or androcracy; and within it are securely nourished the germs of the regulative system.[25] We turn to a limited number of representative cases.

[22] Wilutzky, *Mann u. Weib*, 86-87; *Diodorus Sic.*, III, 54; Lippert, *Kgchte.*, II, 75; Starcke, *Prim. Fam.*, 117; §416 of the *Case-Book*.

[23] Gomme, *Ethnol. in Folklore*, 135; Buschan, in *Globus*, LXXIX, 118; Wilken, in VG, I, 245-246; §416 of the *Case-Book*.

[24] Boas, in USNM, 1895, 333-335; Boas, in *Science*, XII, 195.

[25] §§152-154, above.

In Australia "we find side by side with tribes who retain uterine succession, other tribes who are still nomad hunters, ignorant of agriculture, but.who reckon descent through males."[26] To Starcke[27] such cases mean that the lowest tribes have male descent and hence disprove the priority of the maternal line to the paternal; but such examples exhibit monandry[28] rather than any settled and regulated form of organization and should not be confused with the father-family. In parts of Melanesia the wife is generally bought, is identified with her husband's family, and at his death goes to the brother or some other kinsman of her husband.[29] The Papuan girl may go to her future parents-in-law immediately after attaining to puberty, to be married several years later on.[30] The cattle-raising peoples of South Africa have a strong patriarchate; the wives are rated as children of the men.[31] "The father rules supreme in all things, and the children are surnamed after him and belong to his tribe. . . . At marriage a woman becomes a member of her husband's tribe."[32] In East Africa, "a full claim to children is established only by payment of dowry [meaning bride-price] in full. Excepting for this, the father has undisputed claim to his children, and this rule applies to legitimate children as well as to those born by his wife of adulterous unions; he may reject illegitimate children, but if he retains them they have all the rights of his own offspring. As a rule the husband is also entitled to illegitimate children born of his wife prior to her marriage."[33] In Uganda, they are so sure of derivation from the father that "a person speaking of himself prior to birth says, 'Whilst I was still in the calves of my father's legs.' A man's seed is always said to be in the calves of his legs, and a man with large calves is admired and spoken of as being able to beget children."[34] In West Africa family-headship "descends to a son; if there be none, to a brother; or, if he be dead, to that brother's son; in default of these, to a sister's son. This headship carries with it, for a man, such authority that, should he kill his wife, he may not be killed; though her relatives, if they be influential, may demand some restitution."[35] In some tribes of Central Africa, a woman, after she has borne three or five children, can be ransomed out of marriage and go back to her father.[36] Among the Somals and some allied pastoral tribes of East Africa there are no traces at all of the mother-family.[37]

The patriarchal régime is strong among the peoples of the Eurasian steppes.[38] The Ossetes have the strictest father-family: a man may marry his mother's sister but not the remotest cousin who has the same name. Blood-revenge for a father's relatives extends to the remotest cousinship.[39] The firmly established family, in ancient India, formed "the secure foundation of the state, and the community. At its head stands the home-father as house-master." "The Indo-European family most resembles the Roman *familia*, i.e., it

[26] Howitt and Fison, "Mother-right to Father-right," in JAI, XII, 33.
[27] *Prim. Fam.*, 27.   [28] §345, above.
[29] Wilken, in VG, I, 400.   [30] Pöch, in *Globus*, XCIII, 141.
[31] Ratzel, *Vkde.*, I, 294; Lippert, *Kgchte.*, II, 29.
[32] Macdonald, in JAI, XIX, 267.
[33] Dundas, C., in JAI, LI, 260.   [34] Roscoe, in JAI, XXXII, 40.
[35] Nassau, *Fetichism*, 5.   [36] Nachtigal, *Sahara*, II, 685.
[37] Paulitschke, *Nordost-Afr.*, II, 142.
[38] *Russ. Ethnog.* (Russ.), I, 251, 287, 327; Lippert, *Kgchte.*, I, 180.
[39] Von Haxthausen, *Transkaukasia*, II, 27.

consists of women, children, and slaves, under the *potestas* of a single house-master." The wife came to him by capture or purchase.[40]

The patriarchate in the East Indies is quite fully treated by Wilken.[41] All the exogamous tribes are of the patriarchal type, however common the survivals of the mother-family, except certain Sumatran Malays. The Batak joint-house is occupied by those related in the male line. Since the Batak daughter leaves her tribe for good when marrying, her father, anticipating this, addresses her in the distant form (like the French second person plural) which is used regularly with non-tribesmen. Here the woman goes over to the man's tribe so fully that at his death she falls to his brother. She is merely a thing, a piece of property, less than a slave. Her marriage is dissoluble only by death. Children inherit only from the father; the mother's possessions go to her brothers and sisters and after them to her brother's children. Yet among these Bataks there are women, especially elderly ones, who exercise a great influence in their families. These people practice the "matriarchal marriage" as a sort of pledge due to the non-payment of the bride-price. This is evident from the name *mandingding* which signifies to live with a creditor, in the same place and with the obligation of supporting him in pressing business. In fact, even in the matriarchal marriage-form this is the position of the man over against the family of his wife. The Batak form is typical of the strong patriarchate. A variant appears in the Nias Islands, where the woman is not excluded from inheritance and where the children inherit from father and mother alike. Among the Alfurs it is the tribe that pays the bride-price and receives it. The bride goes to her husband's tribe; then, if he dies, any member of his tribe has the right to marry her without bride-price. In one district of Borneo, "when the wife dies the man has not a single duty more towards her family to fulfill. But this is not the case with the wife under the same circumstances, especially if her husband was rich. Then the wife is under obligation to marry the brother of her deceased husband, or, if he is failing, one of the nearest blood-kin, so that the former property of the husband shall remain undivided in the family. If however she feels no desire either to enter matrimony again or to accept the proper person as husband, she can satisfy by giving back all her husband's property to his blood-kin." The *ambil-anak* marriage[42] is a sort of desperate effort to keep up the patriarchate. In southern Sumatra the duty of keeping up the stock, in the absence of male issue, is imposed upon the daughter, "who is put on a par with a son and thus also has all the rights of a son." Her marriage is *sine manu;* no bride-price is demanded and none would be accepted, even if offered. The children, in another part of the island, belong to the man just as the offspring of an animal while it is owned. They reckon, not from the time of conception but that of birth, in deciding to whom the child belongs. As among the Hindus and ancient Arabs, the child of which a woman is pregnant at the time of marriage belongs to the husband; that it should be of his begetting is not essential. Conversely, the husband can lay no claim to a child of whom his wife is pregnant at the time of divorce.[43]

The father-family was strongly intrenched in the ancient empires. "The wife vanished, so to speak, into the house of her husband." Without a father's con-

---

[40] Zimmer, *Altind. Leben*, 305; Schrader, *Aryan*, 393.

[41] *Vkde.*, 325 ff.; "Verwantschap," in VG, I, 431, 463; "Erfrecht op Nias," in VG, I, 407-410; "Prim. Vormen," in VG, I; "Zuid-Sumatra," in VG, II.

[42] §363, above.   [43] Wilken, in VG, II, 245-246.

sent, the union contracted by a Babylonian son was concubinage. Long genealogies in the male line were kept.[44] The Hebrew and Arabic languages unite the conception "people" and "kin on the father's side" in one word, which seems to indicate the widening of the patriarchal family into a political body. In the Book of Leviticus[45] occurs a list of near relatives for whom one may mourn. The wife is not mentioned. "There prevailed then a well-marked system of father-right, based on the old conception of stocks, which, again, stands in the closest relation with ancestor-worship."[46] Baal-marriage (master-marriage) is where a man takes his wife to his home and becomes her master, by capture or purchase. The laws are in his hands, descent is in the male line, and he may divorce at will.[47] Everyone is familiar with the Biblical "patriarchs" and their powers; and the Aryan patriarchate is traditional.[48] The Homeric patriarchate is clearly marked and its father-rulers are of the type of the Old Testament.[49] The very phrase "patria potestas" is indicative of the Roman system.

"Among the Germans we find the legal arrangement that the man stood at the head of the family only so long as he was sturdy and able to protect it against every evil, in particular as long as he was able to use weapons; then he must retire, the oldest son living in the house took his place, and father and mother came under his mund [guardianship] like his own children and younger brothers and sisters. A similar situation seems to have developed also with the Vedic people."[50] "The German could make over his wife by will, give her away, or sell her as an item of inventory together with house and estate. . . . He could severely chastise his wife if she deserved it, and even kill her."[51] The male line among the Germans is shown by the fact that father and husband, "the former and present owners" of the woman, struggle for the possession of the child.[52]

Among the Slavs the lord and ruler is the paterfamilias; "but a tradition sanctified through centuries, the right of the kin-group, does not permit the rule of the house-father to degenerate into caprice. And in this kin-group right we see the distinction of the zadruga [of the South Slavs] from the purely patriarchal despotism of the head of the Russian joint-family."[53] Again, the young wife, not being allowed, "out of shame," to call house-mates by their right names, gives them special ones that have effect only in her relation with them. According to a fiction, developed logically in all directions, she must act as if she were in a strange land among unknown people. Her situation recalls to the author[54] an anecdote from a Dutch province. "The housewife is dead and buried. At evening the peasant is sitting with his children about the hearth. For a while all remain in silent reflection, but finally the father breaks

[44] Schrader, Aryan, 377; Maspero, Hist. Anc., I, 733; Kohler and Peiser, Bab. Rechtsleben, II, 7; Herodotus, Hist., II, 142; Meyer, Aegypten, II, 160, note, 169.

[45] XXI, 1 ff.   [46] Maurer, Vkde., I, 148, 153.

[47] Smith, Kinship, 75; Wellhausen, in Gött. Gesellschaft d. Wissenschaft, 1893, 446; Buhl, Israeliten, 29; Klugmann, Frau im Talmud, 60, 61.

[48] Starcke, Prim. Fam., 96, 97.

[49] Keller, Hom. Soc., 207 ff.; Euripides, Electra, 945 ff.

[50] Zimmer, Altind. Leben, 326-327.   [51] Weinhold, Altnord. Leben, 240.

[52] Starcke, Prim. Fam., 106; Wilutsky, Mann u. Weib, 93-94.

[53] Simkhowitsch, Russland, 361, 362, 363.

[54] Rhamm, in Globus, LXXXII, 192, 271, 279.

the silence with the words: 'Children, now we are once again quite by ourselves, for mother was, after all, only a relation by marriage.' "

Among the Celts two powerful factors make for male ascendancy: "the natural preponderance of strength accruing to the armed sex in primitive communities, and the settlement in separate households which led to permanent marriages and to the establishment of patriarchal administration within the limits of the household, and on the basis of the land assigned to it."[55]

"The principle of association in the father-family," says Lippert,[56] "is rule, not kinship." Marriage develops an exclusion and monopoly unheard of before. Even in the Iroquois long-house each pair had its room or stall and all "the vice of monopoly" as to property and wife developed in it as vigorously as in a New York street today. This situation did not alter with the change in family-organization. Wife and children are the man's property and upon his wife and daughters fidelity and chastity come to be imposed. Marriage is some form of grant by the father or some breach of his authority. Though the blood-tie through the mother may last for some time, there is no doubt where the power is. One need not go so far as to say that "paternal right calls up terrible ambitions, creates inequalities, extreme disparities betwixt those who are nearest," while "the matriarchate is a law of equality, incites to neither hatred nor jealousy, tends to tranquillity and peace, apportions equally."[57] This quotation is highly impressionistic in tone. It is fair to assert, though, that the father-family, just because it did evoke ambitions and disparities, had capabilities looking toward organization, control, war, conquest, and enslavement, not possessed by the maternal form.

In the present connection there is no need to expatiate upon the wider bearings of the patriarchate; we turn, therefore, to a few examples of the father's power in the family. If woman attained to some social importance because she was the recognized channel of blood-kinship, there is no reason why man's position of undoubted social power should not, along with advance in knowledge of biological processes and in exclusiveness of sex-relation, have won for him at length a parity of parenthood. Some writers see in the couvade[58] an effort by man to insist upon and demonstrate his relation to the child. Perhaps there was some such at-

[55] Vinogradoff, *Growth of Manor*, 12.
[56] *Kgchte.*, II, 78, 87, 339, 529; Wilutzky, *Mann u. Weib*, 123.
[57] Reclus, *Prim. Folk*, 176.   [58] §407, above.

tempt to reconcile his real title, which was power, with traditional notions about blood-relationship; the essential fact is, however, that he gets control and presently, under the strong patriarchate, the theory itself is wrenched about, so that the man is the real progenitor and the woman no more than the "plowed field" that receives the seed, the temporary receptacle and nurse of the man's child and heir.

"It is necessary," says Wilken,[59] "to form a just idea of the *patria potestas* among nature-peoples. It would be wrong to regard it as unlimited. However strange it may sound, the despotism of the father in the kin-group, far from being peculiar to the lowest evolutionary forms of society, is precisely a characteristic of a higher civilization." In view of the preceding cases and discussion we should not be unprepared for this statement. Despite the fact that woman is often man's property and is treated with great cruelty, a grown son and not infrequently a grown daughter have a liberty in savage societies and in high civilization which is not accorded on the intermediate stages.[60]

Take first an exceptional case of the extreme application of paternal power. The Australian father makes a demonstration of his control when he gives his daughter in marriage. He picks out an elderly husband for her; "if she resists the mandates of her father, he strikes her with his spear; if she rebels and screams, the blows are repeated, and if she attempts to run away, a stroke on the head from the waddy or tomahawk quiets her. The mother screams and scolds and beats the ground with her kan-kan [fighting stick]; the men, women, and children in the neighbouring huts come forth to see the sight; the dogs bark and whine; but nothing interrupts the father, who in the performance of his duty is strict and mindful of the necessity of not only enforcing his authority but of showing to all that he means to enforce it. Seizing the bride by her long hair, the stern father drags her to the house prepared for her by her new owner. . . . If she attempts to abscond, the bridegroom does not hesitate to strike her savagely on the head with his waddy; and the bridal screams and yells make the night hideous. If the girl is energetic, and absolutely refuses the man to whom she is assigned, she causes a disturbance that can be quelled only by the authority of the old men. The young fellows seize their weapons, and one or two who may have had friendly feelings towards the bride begin to throw their wonguims [boomerangs]. These striking his frail dwelling, rouse the husband, and he rushes forth, fully armed, to do battle with his rivals. A general fight follows, and the old husband often is wounded, and so deeply marked as to be able, after the lapse of many years, to number his wives, living and dead, by his blemishes. During the fight, and when the husband is fully occupied, the bride rushes to her mother, and with streaming

59 In VG, I, 463; Westermarck, *Marriage*, II, 278 ff., 326 ff.
60 Ch. LII, above.

eyes and heaving breast begs vainly for protection and help, which her mother dare not give her. As soon as the old men have quelled the disturbance, the father again seizes her hair and drags her to the wiam of her husband, gives her a few blows with his waddy, and there leaves her. If she is still determined to escape, and makes the attempt, the father will at last spear her in the leg or foot, to prevent her from running. Beaten, frightened, and at last completely conquered, she resigns herself to her hard fate, thinks no more of the young men who have in past times shown her kindness, and becomes a willing and obedient drudge to her new master."[61]

This case is the more significant by reason of the picture it gives of incipient or sporadic resistance to a code which assigned the young women to the old men—a custom which would seem to belong to the category of harmful mores[62] and is found very infrequently.

The filial piety doctrine of the Chinese is well known, though it is extended to cover both parents. "If for three years he does not alter from the way of his father," says Confucius of the son, "he may be called filial."[63] "Originally the Japanese *pater-familias* was at once ruler, priest, and magistrate within the family. He could compel his children to marry or forbid them to marry; he could disinherit or repudiate them; he could ordain the profession or calling which they were to follow; and his power extended to all members of the family, and to the household dependents. . . . Any affection powerful enough to endanger the cohesion of the family would be condemned. A wife might therefore be divorced because her husband had become too much attached to her. . . . Again, the sale of a daughter, in time of extreme need, might save a house from ruin; and filial piety exacted submission to such sacrifice for the sake of the cult. . . . It must be remembered that the individual was not legally considered in former times: the family only was recognized; and the head of it legally existed only as representative." The young man was not permitted to choose a wife. "The community would not tolerate insubordination in such matters: one example of filial revolt would constitute too dangerous a precedent."[64]

Among certain California Indians the power of the man approached that of the Australian.[65] "Among the ancient Peruvians the paternal power lasted into the twenty-fifth year; it was limited by the Incas."[66]

Patria potestas was existent in Chaldæa[67] and in other ancient states.[68] The Roman system has given us the term, and under the spell of that system the patriarchate has been projected by writers ignorant of ethnography far back into the primitive times.[69] The Roman father "was owner of all that belonged to the family, priest of the domestic cult, and avenger of blood." It is enough to say that his power was as nearly absolute in the family as can well be imagined, even covering the issues of life and death. He had all the rights and

[61] Smyth, *Vict.*, I, 76-77.
[62] Sumner, *Folkways*, §29; §428, below.
[63] Smith, *Chinese Char.*, 173.
[64] Hearn, *Japan*, 81, 79, 82, 84, 85, 102; Westermarck, *Marriage*, II, 328.
[65] Powers, in *Contrib. N. Amer. Ethnol.*, III, 270.
[66] Von Martius, *Beiträge*, I, 123, note.
[67] Maspero, *Hist. Anc.*, I, 732.
[68] Jolly, in *Grundr. d. Indo-Ar. Philol.*, II, Heft 8, pp. 76, 77, 78.
[69] For example, by H. S. Maine; McLennan, *The Patriarchal Theory*, for a statement and refutation of Maine's views.

no one else had any.[70] Lecky[71] sums up as follows: "The child was indeed the absolute slave of his father, who had a right at any time to take away his life and dispose of his entire property. He could look to no time during the life of his father in which he would be freed from the thraldom. The man of fifty, the consul, the general, or the tribune, was in this respect in the same position as the infant, and might at any moment be deprived of all the earnings of his labour, driven to the most menial employments, or even put to death, by the paternal command."

Elsewhere in Europe the power of the father has appeared in strength, though not in so extreme a form. In heroic Sweden a father could take up and recognize his child, or he could condemn it to exposure; if he took it up, he caused it to be baptized and named in the presence of his kinsmen. He had similar power in Iceland and among the Norsemen.[72] The ancient German father also had the right to take up his children or not; the child lay on the ground before him until he had declared his will.[73] The Russian father was sovereign and judge; he married off his son without reference to his wishes. The South Slav daughters and mothers had one duty: "to be silent and to obey."[74] The French and Belgian fathers possess a trace of the old *potestas;* and in the fifteenth century, in England, "every poor man that hath brought up children to the age of twelve year waiteth then to be holp and profited by his children."[75]

Upon such historic cases of the paternal power, especially upon those preserved in the Scriptures and in the records of classical antiquity, have been formed prevalent ideas of what the earliest forms of family-organization must have been. Until relatively recently the immense stretches of prehistoric evolution, long ante-dating the stages familiar to us, have remained unknown; and even now, when we are aware of the once unheard-of facts about the matrilineal system, it is possible to be misled and to conceive of the father-family as, after all, primordial.[76] Such error rests upon a failure to distinguish between two different things: monandry and the father-family. Monandry[77] is no system of family-organization but rather the rude beginning of sex-association; there is more excuse for confusing it with promiscuity than with the father-

[70] Rossbach, *Röm. Ehe*, 12 ff.; Grupp, *Kgchte.*, I, 107-108; Schmidt, *Soc. Civ.*, 55, 56, 58, 59, 60, 63, 222, 223, 224, 418, 419, 422; Ihering, *Evol. of Aryan*, 44; Westermarck, *Marriage*, II, 332; Gubernatis, *Usi Nuz.*, 81, note 2.

[71] *Hist. Europ. Morals*, I, 298.

[72] Geijer, *Svensk. Hist.*, I, 113; Dasent, *Burnt Njal*, XXII.

[73] Heusler, *Deut. Privatrecht*, I, 120-121; Stammler, *Stellung d. Frauen*, 13; Lippert, *Kgchte.*, I, 224.

[74] Oliveira Martins, *Quadro*, 46; Simkhowitsch, *Russland*, 359; Starcke, *Prim. Fam.*, 157.

[75] Roguin, *Mariage*, 57; Green, *Town Life*, I, 194.

[76] Keane, *Ethnol.*, 9, note 4.   [77] §345, above.

family. The latter is the system that was able to survive selection and to reach down into modern times; it has done so because it represented, as we shall try to show, a closer adjustment to the facts of life: to conditions surrounding self-maintenance and self-perpetuation.

§420. **Comparisons and Contrasts.** Now that the characteristics of the two systems of family-organization have been set before us in the cases, it is possible to gather together certain comparisons and generalizations which reveal, among other things, the revolutionary nature of the change from mother-family to father-family. There are those who regard it as the most profound revolution in the history of human society. This change did not take place all at once, be it remembered, but over incalculable stretches of time. During this secular period, as was inevitable, there were parallelisms and repetitions, at different stages, of similar phenomena referable to similar causes and including traditional features carried over from one stage to another. It is clear that the confusion and controversy that have reigned concerning the whole subject of family-organization are due less to the undoubted presence of true parallelisms that represent adjustment to similar circumstances than to the sketchy identification of partial similarities as complete ones. A striking instance of this procedure is the alignment just alluded to of monandry and the father-family; another is the assumption that the mother-family is always a complete system.

"When men have taken up such a notion as that of blood-relationship through the mother, they have built upon it the strictest logical inferences, maxims, customs, doctrines of right. When they change the fundamental notion they do not at once alter all these deductions, for the latter have won the force of traditions. In spite of contradictions, a later system grows up alongside the older one and the two are reconciled to each other by the method of accommodation or compatibility. Sometimes one doctrine is taken as the basis for one set of actions and another for another set. The result is inconsistency and irrationality."[78] The history of institutions is full of facts from which this observation is derived; that is the reason why the phenomena are so misleading and difficult to interpret. The history of the transition from the mother-family to the father-family is perhaps the ranking illustrative instance. Transitional stages are numerous and different groups stopped at various points for long periods; features of one system are found mingled with those of the

[78] Lippert, *Kgchte.*, I, 80.

other in incongruous combination or contorted into mutual adjustment by
accommodation.

The mother-family came naturally to be, by spontaneous
growth out of antecedent conditions. The mother-clan persists
indefinitely without any interruption, unless it dies out entirely.
A father-family, on the other hand, necessarily breaks up every
three or four generations at longest. The former is stable and
enduring, like the sex upon which it is based;[79] the latter is active
and variable, prone to movement, raiding, and eventually to conquest. In its broadest features the mother-family is conservative,
traditional, and tends to equality in many respects, whereas the
father-family is enterprising, progressive, sets free individual
energy, and therefore promotes inequality.

The limited communalism of the mother-family, chiefly as respects food,
wastes capital where it does not prevent its accumulation; the energy of men
is not stimulated. Its garden-culture by women is only a premonition of agriculture; tillage proper does not begin until men take it in hand. The mother-
family has little history because its character is a perpetuity of sameness.
There is slight division of labor in it and therefore little societal organization.
It is exogamy and the father-family which begin competition, combination,
coöperation, and organization.[80] The evolutional movement which we call progress gains momentum with the father-family. War under the mother-family is
caused by bickerings over emplacement and blood-revenge; captives are killed
or tortured and only exceptionally adopted or enslaved. War has the character
of raiding merely. In the father-family, war is less impulsive and is more
organized and planned for a purpose by the authority on the ground, and is
prosecuted more perseveringly. Its purpose is plunder and, at length, conquest,
and its results subjugation, domination, enslavement, and eventually the construction of territorial states. Slavery is the connecting link between the economic and militant forces in the evolution of society. Since family-organization moves at the same time through the change which we are now viewing,
the total organization of society undergoes a transformation which is difficult
to embrace and understand with due allowance for all the elements in it.
    It is instructive to follow some one specific usage through the various types
of organization. Consider the matter of wife-getting.[81] In monandry gifts or
services rendered by the groom to the bride's father had the character of
means to conciliate or win favor. In the mother-family they were gifts to win
the woman and her female elders or were stipulated contributions by the man
to the common welfare. When the man took his wife out of her home, he paid
to her uncle, brother, or clansmen a fee, which looks like purchase, as expiation
or atonement. Capture might occur on any stage and might lead to *connubium*.
Closely allied to capture is abduction or elopement, the proper sphere of this
form being within the range of permitted marriage; it does not include cases
of real violence or of violation of the woman's will or that of her guardians,

79 §§58 ff., above.   80 Lippert, *Kgchte.*, II, 163.
81 Ch. XLVI, above.

and it is a crime when it involves transgression of any taboo. The woman is not foreign; she is in the same peace-group as the man. Here are manifest differences from capture; the whole matter takes on an institutional character when the girl's guardian is aware of what is happening and when a comedy is played which is satisfactory to all because it saves trouble, breaks the trammels of vexatious usage, saves expense, or is otherwise expedient. Abduction is like capture in that in its institutional form it requires expiation, that is, leads up to purchase.

If a man and woman merely agree to become man and wife and do so, there is no formality as of an institution; it is when the woman's father, in whose control she is found, must be asked to consent that institutional construction really begins. The demand for the woman and the reply of the father are necessarily somewhat formal; and so are the delivery of the bride in public by her father and the leading home of the wife by her husband. They constitute a wedding. Marriage in the mother-family never could be in any high degree institutional because these formal steps had no parallel in it. In the true mother-family there is no real wedding. Abduction and elopement belong to the transition from the mother-family to the father-family. The situation of the man in the mother-family was accepted by the man as a fact of the traditional order rather than as a satisfactory arrangement. There was one type of variation, however, which could excite comparison with the result of making him discontented with his lot, namely, the possibility of obtaining a slave-consort by capture alongside the wife of status. This possibility stimulated the idealization which operates to dissolve the old and bring in the new. The mother-family in its developed form amounted to a considerable restriction on man's liberty. When capture with tribal exogamy was a growing custom which the men liked and the old traditions inside the group had been weakened though not overthrown, there was a stage at which all parties had a deep interest in abduction or elopement inside the nation. In real capture there was no bride-price. In peace-capture, even from a foreign group, there was only a piece of rough play; a composition was paid in order that it might not be a breach of intertribal peace. In abduction and elopement a bride-price became the essential thing, the rest being a comedy. The fees for taking home a tribal wife or for elopement and abduction or for capture of an extra-tribal wife were the origin of purchase.

If we follow out the consequences of these changes in the method of wife-getting we shall see typical differences between the mother-family and the father-family and shall collect tests which will contribute to the analysis and understanding of transitional phenomena.

(1) The status of woman in the mother-family was such that she was mistress of the situation so far as wife-getting was concerned. The man came as a suitor and his status among her relatives depended upon their good will, they being on her side. In the father-family the man was master and was free to use his physical and other superiorities, the woman being a stranger who must win friends and favor.

(2) In the mother-family the women could dismiss the man or determine the duration and conditions of the union. In the father-family the man could

divorce the woman at pleasure; he dismissed her and sent her back home if he was dissatisfied with her. If she was a real captive she had no status or rights. If she had been purchased the man would lose what he paid for her, unless he could, by showing that she was defective, require a substitute or reimbursement. He was, however, in any case only dealing with his property; hence he could lend, sell, or give away his wife and his male relatives inherited her.

(3) There was no adultery in the mother-family unless the stipulations between the woman and her husband bound her to some exclusive relation to him. No such obligation was in the institution. The agreement of the two determined in each case the nature of the union. In the father-family a woman who had been captured or bought belonged to her husband indefinitely, that is, as long as he pleased. Fidelity, chastity, and allied qualities came into being as definite moral ideas and duties of a woman. Her honor came to inhere in fidelity. The numerous cases in which women were under no restrictions at all until marriage but were thereafter held strictly to marital fidelity belong to transitional stages. There never was any notion of adultery for men until pair-marriage was established by law of church or state, because pair-marriage rests upon a voluntary mutual covenant to maintain exclusive sex-relations with each other and rests upon that promise, not on any authority outside of themselves. The state does not enforce the covenant when it is broken; it merely dissolves the union. Adultery has never yet, in the mores of any people, meant the same for men and women.

(4) If the mother gets the children in case of dissolution of the union we recognize a feature of the mother-family; if the father, of the father-family.

(5) If a man who proposes marriage, or his representative, deals with the woman or her mother, maternal uncle, brother, or clan, it is a feature of the mother-family; if he deals with her father or grandfather, of the father-family.

(6) The usages that a man must serve in the family of the woman for a time before marriage or must undergo tests of his worth are ambiguous. Sometimes servitude is a form of purchase. If the husband remains in the house of his father-in-law after marriage it is a reversion to or modification of the mother-family. In the mother-family a woman may of her own right put her suitor to the test; in the father-family the father may do that.

(7) In monandry, polyandry, and the mother-family the relation of husband and wife is one of covenant between the two. In the father-family there is no such covenant; the man has dominion over the woman by force and right under law and custom. The bridegroom and the bride's father might make a covenant and confirm it by property-pledge. The bride could generally assent or refuse.

(8) Not every gift is a bride-price, for gifts run through all manner of variation. In the mother-family the husband makes gifts or payments to the wife or her representatives. In the father-family he gives them to her father. If there is an outfit or dower the father provides it.

(9) In the mother-family the woman accepts a husband; but she may also invite one. When the woman asks the man it is a feature of the mother-family.

(10) It would seem that the determination of which relatives-in-law are to be ignored or avoided[82] should follow different lines in the two forms of the family but the means to specify the difference are not available.

82 §425, below.

(11) The couvade belongs to the father-family or to transitions thereto; where it exists the tie between the child and its father are supposed to be close, real, and intimate.

(12) The levirate belongs to the father-family; in that usage the woman is and remains, even after his death, in her husband's family, like his property.

(13) In the mother-family rank and status must be derived from the mother, so that if a free man marries a slave-woman the children are slaves; if, on the other hand, a princess marries a slave-husband the offspring are royal. In the father-family the wife takes the rank of the husband and the children derive their status from him, though there are inconsistent variations.

(14) The joint-family or joint-household appears in both family-forms. In the father-family it is, however, far less stable and of a very different character, for it is held together by joint property-interests, both in possession and use. It is always precarious. In the mother-family the joint-household is a form of society, a natural fact, and it has notable consistency.

(15) In the mother-family the woman has the property and her children inherit from her, not from their father. His property goes to his brothers and sisters and to his sisters' children. When a man's children inherit his property it is a feature of the father-family. In that form the woman leaves her property at her home; in fact, she has none except her outfit or dower and her children cannot inherit more than that, at least, from her. Hence we find that heiresses take husbands in a manner resembling that of the mother-family, lest the property pass out of their group. In transition from one form of the family to the other, husband and wife join their property or hold it severally and their children inherit from both.

Too much caution cannot be observed in the use as criteria of the features of the two forms here given. Innumerable inconsistencies in cases which are fully open to study warn us that inferences may not be drawn too confidently. Nevertheless there emerge from such comparisons and contrasts broad outlines of a trustworthy order. The fact stands out with the utmost prominence that the institution of marriage was created by force. Monandry and the mother-family were loose and voluntary. It was in subjection that the institution took form, as one of inequality and dominion; it has been softened through the ages without, however, being relaxed into a relation of equality.

It is evident that innumerable varieties are to be found in the transitional forms between mother-family and father-family; survivals of the older system and early stages of the new produce anomalies and inconsistencies. Before the new is realized there are bound to be series of compromises. It is clear also that all institutions of property and all jural customs must come into consistency with the developing father-family; blood-revenge could not apply at the same time to the kin in the father-line and those in the other line, unless the group were endogamous.[83] It was the friction of this complicated change which made the process long and slow and the phenomena inconsistent; the motives of interest

[83] Pollock and Maitland, *Eng. Law*, 238.

for the men were contradictory and there was no guiding mind to reconcile them in principle. The results worked out automatically under the play of interest as it was felt by men and checked up by the imperturbable forces of societal evolution.

§421*. The Mother-Family as an Adjustment. Generalization upon the facts now before us reveals the mother-family, not as an ethnographical curiosity but as a practical arrangement into which a good many peoples have gravitated and by which they have lived. Any evolutionarily-minded person would conclude at once that the system had sense and expediency in it and that it constituted, in its day, an adjustment of no mean consequence. It is also evident that this adjustment did not meet the exigencies of life as well as the father-family; for it is nowhere found to be as persistent as the latter; it seldom or never supersedes the latter, though it has itself been almost universally replaced by the father-family; and it nowhere exhibits itself as a unit comparable in concreteness, consistency, and independence with the patriarchal organization. It occurs, indeed, fragmentarily and in survivals rather than as a rounded whole, instinct with vitality. It is met with chiefly in comparative isolation. It seems, further, to have no destiny in the sense of higher organization along its own lines; it does not pass into the state-form, as does the patriarchate. Apparently civilization and higher organization cannot proceed until it has been transformed in its essentials—transformed, that is, into the father-family. Consequently, whatever may be thought as to its relation in time with the patriarchate, there is no question that it is antecedent to the latter in the evolutionary sequence. It is more primitive, cruder, less stable and durable, less powerful, less adjustable. It has the appearance of an adaptation to a passing phase of life-conditions rather than to circumstances of an enduring or perennial character; yet that passing phase must have been of wide prevalence or the mother-line would not have appeared so generally over the world.

It is our business to identify the conditions, whatever their span of persistence, in response to which the mother-family evolved. This is, however, a difficult and uncertain matter, for we do not find a well-knit system operating amidst the conditions to which it is an adjustment but rather a set of survivals existing amidst circumstances that have called forth the father-family. The life-conditions to which the mother family constituted an adjustment are largely a matter of inference and we do not go in very much for inferential reconstructions; but there are certain broad considerations concerning the mother-family which seem to us to admit of little question and at the same time to contribute significantly to an understanding of family-organization in particular and of institutional organization in general.

The outstanding condition to which the mother-family formed an adjustment was the conception of blood-relationship as reckoned solely through the mother. Most of the evidence for the mother-family is, strictly speaking, no more than evidence for the female line of descent. The mother-family was an organization expressive of blood-kinship rather than one primarily economic or regulative. People who were born together were classified according to the amount of common blood which they were believed to retain by reason of their descent from a common ancestress. All this goes back to obvious physical phenomena and to simple and natural interpretations;[84] yet the latter proved later to be quite mistaken. However long the conception of relationship solely through the female may have lasted, in point of time, it proved itself, at length, to be merely a passing condition.

While it lasted, nevertheless, the custom had established itself of transmitting property and position down the female line, and this led to a characteristic type of economic and political organization, as the foregoing paragraphs should have indicated. In short, the forms of self-maintenance were colored, so to speak, by considerations rooting in ideas concerning self-perpetuation and projecting themselves into family-organization. The maintenance-forms thus molded revealed themselves eventually as maladjustments. Then the theory of descent upon which the family-organization rested was altered to fit the actualities of existence and whatever remained of the superseded theory or practice became survivalistic.

§422. Readjustments in Family-Organization. The mother-family was not a winning organization because it could not sur-

84 §§411, 412, above.

vive the process of selection and could persist only where it was isolated from competition with an intenser, more closely-knit régime. Let us look into the defects of the mother-family system as compared with the form that succeeded it.

First, as to the relative powers of the sexes under the system: the woman was at least the transmitter of power, and it has been assumed that she occupied, as such, a strategic position from which to win status and influence for herself. We have not been able to see, however, that woman's status, meaning her sum of rights as compared with man's, has been vitally affected by the system of family-organization.[85] The power of woman under the mother-family has been much exaggerated. The notion of mother-right, having been wholly lost to history and tradition, seemed exceedingly strange when it was re-discovered, for there was no such thing in the Bible, which afforded what was once our only knowledge of the most ancient times. Bachofen and others, in the ardor of discovery, saw in the matrilineal phenomena much that was not there except to an overheated fancy. That there ever was a time, among savage peoples, when women exerted a real mastery is quite untrue. The fact that, under the mother-family, woman was the acknowledged channel of descent, and so of inheritance and even succession, seems to have won for her no exceptional rights and powers. It is probable that the case of the Iroquois has figured too prominently in the envisagement of the system; it undoubtedly represents an extreme. Yet, with that case in mind, the following passage can be written by an author[86] who credits the matrilineal organization with having secured an exceptional status for woman:

"In so far as the man appears only as a guest in the house, and, by reason of his functions there resembles a serving member of the household, while the permanence of the establishment is represented by the woman—only thus far may we properly speak of a dominance by the woman in the house and in the group or horde that grows out of it."

Those who fix the eye upon the somewhat precarious and even servile status of the husband in the Long-House and upon the dignities of the matron who heads it, are prone to ignore the presence of the brothers and other males whose interests are centered

---

[85] Chs. L, LI, above.   [86] Lippert, *Kgchte.*, II, 23, 29.

in it. They will return from wherever they may be to fight for it, even against their own sons.

The difficulty with the matrilineal system is not so much in the distribution of powers between the sexes, although in so far as the women held them they were in less efficient hands owing to the fact that discipline and practice in organization were taught by hunting and war;[87] the inadequacy of the system lay in the defect that, although the powers were generally lodged in the brothers and other males of the kin-group, they lacked concentration, for these males had to go abroad for their own matings and were not definitively settled upon the terrain on which the powers were to be displayed. Neither economic direction nor regulative policy could be integrated by controllers who were intermittently absent. Both economic and political organization were sure to be stunted under such circumstances. There was lack of continuity and gathered momentum. This was strikingly revealed when it came to armed conflict, for war is a crucial test of any system; but even in the peaceful course of economic life there arose for advancing peoples a set of conditions as respects industry and property, adjustment to which was beyond the capacity of the mother-family system.

We are assured on the best of authority that the mother-right is out of place, when a tribe gets much beyond the hunting-stage. If "a hunting tribe settles down to agriculture, uterine succession soon becomes extremely inconvenient. Property does not now consist in game which roams over the whole territory. It consists chiefly in agricultural produce grown in particular localities. Residence becomes fixed, and the tribe which formerly migrated, either as a whole, or in parts, from one place to another of the common hunting grounds, dwelling in mere temporary huts, now takes to living in villages which have to be fortified against invaders; and since invasion has to be continually guarded against, the lands in the neighborhood of the stronghold are the most highly valued. . . . Under these circumstances we find a growing disinclination on the part of the heirs of a man's body, to surrender the inheritance to his sister's children, . . . the necessary arrangement under uterine succession. Thus in some agricultural tribes who still retain that line of descent, the agnates redeem the inheritance by payment to the sister's children; other tribes meet the difficulty in other ways, so as to enable the son to take the father's land, and it may be laid down as a general rule that when property becomes fixed and localized, the tendency is to inheritance from father to son, or at least to inheritance by a group of agnates, and ultimately to the abandonment of uterine succession. . . . Even among hunting tribes we find this tendency with regard to property which is localized." Thus swans' eggs, in well-known Aus-

[87] Ch. V, above.

tralian breeding-places, "are claimed by certain families . . . and even by a few individuals, to the exclusion of the rest of the community."[88]

Further, there seems to exist a sort of incompatibility between a pastoral civilization and the mother-family. The Biblical tradition presents the Patriarchs as owners of flocks and herds and the Ten Commandments reveal the depth of the Israelites' dominant interest in domestic animals. The correlation between cattle-raising and the patriarchate is noted by Spencer[89] and Lippert;[90] the latter, whom we follow to a considerable distance throughout this and other sections of this book, striving to profit by his keenness and suggestiveness without ascending with him in his occasional flights of conjecture, holds that the rule of woman, in so far as it ever existed, was finally undermined when the men got control of a food-supply that was both of high quality and steady, this forcing woman into a protected position. It might be added that the wandering life of the pastoral nomad militated against her pursuit of rudimentary tillage.

In short, when the economic situation became more complicated and intense, it called for man's direction because it demanded intenser organization; and that control could not be extended so expediently under the mother-family as when man was uninterruptedly present, with all his interests centered upon the scene of his economic activity.

As has been intimated, it was not primarily the economic organization of which he was capable that man was called upon to summon into being. In consequence of the possession of qualities rooting ultimately in inevitable physical, mental, and social sex-difference, he was the warrior as well as the hunter; and out of the activities of the chase and of war he derived, as has been repeatedly remarked, not only weapons but also discipline and power of organization.[91] Even where the mother-family was of a pronounced type, the fighters were males and the leaders only exceptionally females—so exceptionally that overmuch has been made of each case encountered. The leader was the brother or son of an influential matron, not her sister or daughter. In short, the maternal organization was obliged to recede in time of war, even where the women, as among the Iroquois, once more, could and did depose war-chiefs.

This war-situation is decisive by itself, and we shall recur to it; but before so doing there are to be introduced a few scattering

88 Howitt and Fison, "Mother-right to Father-right," in JAI, XII, 32.
89 Prin. Soc., I, §319.
90 Kgchte., II, 73 ff.; 1-140, passim; 505 ff.; I, 77 ff.
91 §§64, 65, 66, 143, 145, 153, 155, 157, above.

indications illustrative of the tendency to move away from the mother-right.

"The maternal husband," says Tylor,[92] "emancipates himself from his inferior position whenever the social pressure is removed, and he can become a paternal husband"; and he illustrates from the life of the matriarchal Pueblo Indians, parties of whom "leave the villages and go forth to camp on distant spots where some small stream makes the arid alkaline soil cultivable. The consequence is that the wives and children fall under the control of the husbands and fathers, and the first step is taken in the transformation from mother-right to father-right."

It would seem that whatever ruffled the placid course of events under the maternal system might relieve the "social pressure" of tradition and allow of disintegration.

Self-assertion, rooting largely in vanity, always led the strongest to set the fashion. The break-up of the old system, as we now know, was heralded by the infringement upon it represented by wife-capture. The captive wife was a trophy, had no rights because she had no power or defenders, and was at her captor's will. She was not of the maternal family but outside it and her owner was subject to no part of the code which weighed upon him. He was enviable and imitable. He had started a variation that appealed to the men. If he had also invited an expedition of revenge by the woman's kin-group, that could be composed into a *connubium*. Marriage by capture, exchange, or purchase are terms descriptive of the relation of tribes to one another in the matter of their women.[93] The appearance of woman as property by capture or purchase changes her status from what it had been; indeed, the term "woman-rule" is clear only by contrast with her status of subordination which is more familiar to us.

"It is evident that anything which disturbs the social organization tends to radical change, and there can be no complete showing of the probable causes of the change in the line of descent without a consideration of these disturbing causes. Prominent among them," the authors[94] quoted go on to say, "is the custom of elopement, which has become so frequent as to have grown up into a custom of widespread prevalence; among the Gippsland Kurnai it is even the recognized form of marriage."

"Far more effective than violence in converting family rule to the father's side was the introduction of friendly and equitable means of compensation . . . for as soon as the rule is admitted that resistance is to be merely formal, the weaker gains the power of equitable retaliation. Next comes acquisition

[92] In *Nineteenth Century,* XL., 94.   [93] Lippert, *Kgchte.,* II, 35, 39, 86.
[94] Howitt and Fison, in JAI, XII, 39.

of the wife by service in her family. . . . If the service comes before the marriage, as is common, for instance, in the Malay Islands, and familiar to us in the story of the patriarch Jacob, the transaction becomes simply one of payment in labour. If evidence is needed to show that we are here on the track of change from maternal to paternal, and not the contrary, it will be found in the fact that the man's residence in the woman's family may be for the rest of his life, or for any shorter period, down to the morrow of the wedding. But he habitually begins in his wife's house and ends in his own, whereas for the couple to set up in the husband's house and remove to the wife's is almost unknown. Last comes actual purchase for goods and money—a custom as much above low savagery as below high civilisation, which improves on rougher methods by estimating the current value of personal attractions, and the pretensions of a rich and powerful family, for their daughter's hand."[95]

Wilken[96] makes a good deal of the bride-price as a gift in reconciliation and therefore survivalistic of ruder methods of wife-getting. "Where the patriarchate has just evolved out of the matriarchate, it is not based upon the conception of blood-relationship between father and child. It is simply the control over the wife that forms its foundation. The marriage is then really a purchase. To the man now belongs the child not because he has begotten it but because he is the master or owner of the wife, because he has the woman in his power through having paid the so-called bride-treasure, in other words, through purchase."

In other ways too does the man strive to squirm out from under an oppressive system. For example, "the father feels the awkwardness of a social system which reckons his children as members of mother clan and forces him to bequeath his rank and possessions to his sisters' children, or other members of his own group, rather than to his children. The Navajoes and Nairs, and ancient Egyptians avoided this unpleasant condition by giving their property to their children during their own lifetime, and the Shawnees, Miamis, Saks, and Foxes avoided it by naming the children into the clan of the father, giving a child a tribal name being equivalent to adoption."[97] Morgan[98] cites a number of Indian tribes that have attempted to shift inheritance so that a man's own children might have his property.

The war-weakness of the matrilineal society, to which we now recur, is correlative with a relatively feeble and incoherent regulative organization. The latter comes to its test in armed strife. No regulative system is viable which cannot withstand the shock of war; and war is bound to come and to effect its characteristic function of selection among the mores,[99] including those of regulation. Though if human groups are widely scattered, with few

[95] Tylor, in *Nineteenth Cent.*, XL, 95.

[96] In VG, I, 191, II, 223-224 (quoted); Schroeder, *Geschlechtl. Ordnung,* 33, 34; Grosse, *Familie,* 168-169; 171-172.

[97] Thomas, in *Am. Jr. Soc.*, III, 773.

[98] *Anc. Soc.*, 531-532, 162, 163, 169, 170, 171.

[99] Keller, *Soc. Evol.*, 62 ff.; Keller, *War to Peace,* ch. XIV.

contacts, endogamy is inevitable,[100] on the other hand, the very existence of exogamy witnesses to a growing density of population, with consequent attrition provocative of strife. The matrilineal régime may have been well enough in isolation, but it was not an organization capable of securing adjustments when numbers were coming into that contact which means the development of civilization.

It is a commonplace that a situation marked by recurring warfare tends to concentrate and consolidate government, that is, in the primitive instance, the power of the war-leader; to assure him of permanent tenure, the privilege of selecting his assistants and training them, and, at length, of designating his successor. Even under the maternal system, the war-power residing primarily in brothers and sons, uncles selected nephews, not nieces, to assist them; then, when the defects of that system had weakened it until a man had some chance to have his children by him, both inheritance and succession went to sons and organization became the more coherent and strong.

If one desires to see the two systems of father-right and mother-right in confrontation, let him turn back to the paragraph in which are assembled the preconditions of state-formation incident to and correlative with the existence of one and the other organization.[101]

In view of the inadequacies of the matrilineal system that have been presented—and they could readily be resolved into a number of minor constituent details—that once-expedient societal adjustment was doomed to decline as having become a maladjustment to inevitably changing conditions. The theory of descent through the mother could not stand up against the facts of life. If it could not, then it was so much the worse for the theory, however much resistance there might be or however long it might last on in survivalistic form. Plainly the matriarchate could not make and consolidate conquests or support slavery,[102] for its regulative power was insufficiently strong, durable, and consolidated. Under the strict mother-family there is no real organization. Its presence was one of the correlated factors which prevented the Iroquois Confederacy from becoming a real state. Division of

[100] §§347, 355, 356, above.   [101] §189, above.
[102] Lippert, *Kgchte.*, II, 275.

function is present, but it is imperfect and there is no sufficient
coöperation on the large scale; rather is it family-wise. Exogamy
began the movement of competition and higher adjustment which
worked out, under the father-family, into the germs of the state.[103]

Vinogradoff[104] sums up the results of his studies of the matrilineal and
patrilineal families as follows. "The position of the mother in the family is
based on the patent fact of generation, and the elemental affection between
mother and children. . . . Matrilineal institutions develop under the influence
of a sharply marked division of labour between males and females. . . . In
matrilineal arrangements the mother of the family leans on the support of her
brother, instead of leaning on the support of her husband. . . . The father's
position in the family is primarily connected with appropriation and lordship.
. . . The transitions from matrilineal to patrilineal institutions are gradual
and depend to a great extent on the condition of settlement. . . . The patriarchal order has advantages in competition with the matriarchal, on account of
its greater solidity and discipline." The author goes on to say that "the institution of the family centre determines the formation of systems of relationship
on the lines of affinity by blood (cognation), affinity through household ties
(agnation) and affinity by consciousness of reincarnation (totemism)." This
statement is anticipatory of our following chapter. Such a "formation of
groups of kinsmen reacts powerfully on the evolution of matrimonial unions by
producing . . . safeguards for contractual marriage."

What has been said concerning the inadequacy of the mother-
family system to support the strains incident to intenser competition between societies really throws into relief the winning qualities of the patriarchal régime. The latter was, briefly speaking,
what the former was not, in the matter of adjustment to rising
life-conditions of society. At this point it is useful to recall the
comparisons and contrasts between the two systems which have
been recently presented,[105] for all of them are in point and might
be cited over again. In general, the drift was away from all the
features of the mother-family as maladjustments and toward the
contrasted ones of the father-family; for all the features of each
system could not but cleave together.

The mother-family is so far back on the line of evolutionary
development that the prospect of deriving from the study of it
any suggestions as to modern conditions must be slight. It cannot
be shown to be one of those felicitous systems of the noble savage
and the good old times; the theory at the basis of it has collapsed
under the light of knowledge. In a sense it is nothing but a curios-

103 Lippert, *Kgchte.*, II, 163; Oliveira Martins, *Quadro,* 61.
104 *Hist. Jurispr.*, I, 212.		105 §420, above.

ity the details of which interest only the specialist. If, however, anyone wants to understand the process of societal evolution in its long perspective, he should ponder upon the reversal in adjustment represented by the transition from mother-right to father-right in family-organization, for it is undoubtedly one of the most striking cases of the right-about-face ever executed by mankind. We have entered into detail respecting family-organization only so far as to exhibit this aspect of the matter; we have noted that the father-family must have had a superior survival value to society over the mother-family, as shown by its wide prevalence in succession to the latter; and we have reviewed the very good reasons for its superiority. It is to be noted, finally, that in any period of transition, the forms of the family, of property, and of political organization all march together for the sake of expediency and under the strain of consistency in the mores;[106] exceptions have the form of incomplete transitions or survivals[107] which are mischievous when maintained, by religion or the influence of class or rank, in the face of altered life-conditions.

[106] Sumner, *Folkways*, §5.

[107] Tylor, in JAI, XVIII, 258, makes an attempt to depict graphically the persistence of features of the mother-family.

CHAPTER LVII

RELATIONSHIPS AND FAMILY-LIFE

§423*. Terms of Address. People who associate together and are obliged to address each other have to have names and designations; it is necessary that everyone shall be identified and "placed" in society, so that it is known who he is and where he belongs. Throughout the world men have labelled each other with personal names which have become part and parcel of personality;[1] and they have also placed themselves, by classification of some sort based upon their relations to one another as apprehended. They have used terms indicative of the degree of mutual belonging recognized by them. Such terms have signified proximity in space, equality or difference in age, contrast in sex, connection resulting from marriage; they have above all registered degrees of the blood-tie.[2] That they are not merely forms of address is proved by the fact that without them there are no terms of relationship; that the bond of relationship conveyed by them is verified by the passage of property and other heritage, that is, by inheritance and succession; and that they define ranges of rights, revenge, share in booty, marriageability, and of various taboos.[3] Notions of duty and allegiance attach to the relationship defined by such terms, although the kin-group may, in some instances, be neither a peace-group nor a friendship-group, and despite the fact that the blood-tie may be no more than a vague tradition of common descent.[4]

These designations have been evolved in the face of need for them under local circumstances; it is therefore to be expected that they shall not be identical for all peoples. Much confusion over a subject tortuous enough without it has been introduced by failure to realize the simple fact that differing circumstances and ways of

[1] §212, above.

[2] Lippert, *Kgchte.*, I, 6, 82; Wellhausen, *Skizzen*, III, 182, 194, 196.

[3] Westermarck, *Marr.*, I, 242 ff.; Fison, in JAI, XXIV, 369; Cunow, *Australneger*, 176; Peschel, *Races*, 232; Lippert, *Kgchte.*, II, 9; Mucke, *Horde*, 21-25; Kohler, *Urgchte. d. Ehe*, 14, 15, 66, 80; Starcke, *Prim. Fam.*, ch. V; Letourneau, *Marr.*, ch. XVII, sec. V; Von Martius, *Beiträge*, I, 93; Rivers, *Soc. Org.*, 52 ff.; Kroeber, in JAI, XXXIX, 77 ff.

[4] Curr, *Aust. Race*, I, 69; Sieroshevski, *Yakuts* (Pol.), 248, 434.

looking at things must evoke divergent needs for designations and therefore terms of different signification. Under a system of age-grades,[5] for example, where fatherhood is not well understood, men of a preceding grade are all called by a certain term which has been rendered as "father." There is no harm in this if the situation is understood; the terms that savages use must be translated into their nearest understandable equivalent. Sometimes, of course, there is no equivalent; thus the English term "maternal uncle" could not possibly convey to a person living under an inveterate patriarchal régime what it means to a member of a matrilineal society. Again, our term "aunt" may be covered by the primitive designation "mother," and "cousin" by "brother" or "sister." It is plain, upon examination of terms of address that savages are at the same time both less and more definite than we are; they have felt no need of differentiating where our forebears have, and they have adjusted by a special term to some call for identification and placement that those who made the English language did not hear. The savages cover with one term several relationships as understood by us; and again they discriminate degrees which we do not distinguish: one Hawaiian term, for example, covers son, sister's son, brother's son, brother's son's son, brother's daughter's son, sister's son's son, sister's daughter's son, mother's sister's son's son, mother's brother's son's son; yet, despite this apparent parsimony of terminology, there are separate terms for husband's brother's wife and husband's sister, where we have the one appellation, sister-in-law.[6] This being the case, the study of terms of address is exceedingly beset by danger of misunderstanding and error. We do not intend to pursue it into any detail but only to bring out its broad significance; and first there must be spread before the reader a number of concrete instances.

Spencer and Gillen[7] issue the following warning concerning the interpretation of their Australian cases: "It will at once be seen that the one striking feature, common to the whole series, is that the terms used by the natives apply not to the individual but to the group of which the individual is a member. Whilst we are of course obliged to use our ordinary terms of relationship, such as father, mother, brother, wife, etc., it must always be remembered that this is merely a matter of convenience, and that, for example, the words *oknia*,

5 §353, above.   6 Lubbock, *Orig. Civ.*, 60-64.
7 *North. Tr. Cent. Aust.*, 95.

which we translate by father, or *mia* by mother, *okilia* by brother, and *unawa* by wife, by no means whatever connote the meaning of our English terms. . . . Strictly speaking, in our sense of the word they have no individual terms of relationship, but every person has certain groups of men and women who stand in a definite relationship to him and he to them. If he should pass out of his own tribe into another, the very fact that he is a member of a particular subclass causes him to stand in a definite relationship to the various groups of individuals in that tribe. . . . The savage Australian, it may indeed be said with truth, has no idea of relationships as we understand them. He does not, for example, discriminate between his actual father and mother and the men and women who belong to the group, each member of which might have lawfully been either his father or his mother, as the case may be. Any wrong done to his actual father or mother, or to his actual father-in-law or mother-in-law, counts for nothing whatever more than any wrong which he may have done to any man or woman who is a member of a group of individuals, any one of whom might have been his father or mother, his father-in-law or mother-in-law."

In Australia, all the "fathers" are men belonging to the particular group to which one's actual father belongs; all the "mothers" belong to the same group as that to which one's real mother belongs; and all the "brothers" belong to one's own group. "That is, it is the age-strata that are laid off, for the sake, it is believed, of preventing marriage between them. A Kurnai will call 'wife' not only his own consort but his brother's."[8] "Although a given person applies the name *mama* to a large number of individuals, if he is asked 'Who is your *mama?*' he immediately replies by giving the name of his actual father, unless his own father dies during his infancy, in which case he gives the name of his foster father. In the same way, if asked for his *maeli* he gives the name of his father's father, although there are a number of other men to whom he applies the same term. Each term, therefore, has, what we may call, a primary and specific meaning. The primary meaning of *mama* is 'father,' and that of *maeli* 'father's father.' The primary meaning of the native term corresponds very closely to our own use of relationship terms in English. . . . Just as we use the word 'cousin' so the . . . native uses his word *mama*, . . . speaking of a large number of different related persons by the one name, but distinguishing in thought, though not in words, those of his 'fathers' who are more nearly related to him from those who are more distantly related. In the modern blackfellow English he speaks of his 'close-up' and his 'far-away' 'fathers.' The same is the case with every other term of relationship. . . . Although the use of the terms of relationship is based on actual relations of consanguinity and affinity, it is so extended as to embrace all persons who come into social contact with one another. If we take any single member of the tribe, then every person with whom he has any social dealings whatever stands to him in one or other of the relations denoted by the terms in use and may be addressed by that term. In this way the whole society forms a body of relatives. In the Kariera tribe, a man or woman never addresses anyone, except young children, by a personal name, but uses the appropriate relationship term. . . . Yet in all this system of widely extended relationships the real relations of consanguinity are never lost sight of. The natives preserve their genealogies carefully in their memories. . . . When a stranger comes to a camp that he

[8] Spencer and Gillen, *Nat. Tr. Cent. Aust.*, 56; Cunow, *Australneger*, 25, 52; Mathews, in AA, IX; Ratzel, *Vkde.*, II, 65.

has never visited before, he does not enter the camp, but remains at some distance. A few of the older men, after a while, approach him, and the first thing they proceed to do is to find out who the stranger is. The commonest question that is put to him is 'Who is your *maeli?*' . . . The discussion proceeds on genealogical lines until all parties are satisfied of the exact relation of the stranger to each of the natives present in the camp. When this point is reached, the stranger can be admitted to the camp, and the different men and women are pointed out to him and their relation to him defined. . . . If I am a blackfellow and meet another blackfellow that other must be either my relative or my enemy. If he is my enemy I shall take the first opportunity of killing him, for fear he will kill me. This, before the white man came, was the aboriginal view of one's duty towards one's neighbour." Again, "two persons are brothers or sisters or brother and sister if, during the whole or a part of their infancy they have belonged to the same family group—i.e., if they have been fed and cared for by the same parents. It may sometimes be convenient to use the term 'blood-brothers' to denote two children born of the same mother while she was the spouse of one and the same husband."[9]

The Papuan child calls several women, among them his mother's sisters, "mother," though there is a term for the actual mother.[10] "To the Melanesian man it may be almost said that all women, of his own generation at least, are either sisters or wives—to the Melanesian woman that all men are brothers or husbands." In a story a man discovers two children of his dead sister and brings them to his wife. "Are these," she asks, "my children or my husband's?" and the answer is: "Your husband's, to be sure; they are my sister's children."[11] In New Britain the children belong to the mother's class and often call the maternal uncle "father" and the maternal aunt "mother."[12] In the New Hebrides there is no word for aunt; one's mother, mother's sisters, and the wives of his father's brothers are one's mothers. The sister of a man's father or the wife of his maternal uncle are his mothers-in-law. All male cousins through a paternal uncle or maternal aunt are brothers, though there are separate words for such brothers as are younger or older than one's self. A woman can have no brother-in-law; her eligible husbands are her cousins, the sons of her father's sister or her mother's brother. The name which a woman gives her husband applies also to all his brothers. A husband and wife have to be especially modest and decent in the presence of her brother or his sister. A man calls all his own and his brother's girls his daughters and a woman her own and her sister's girls her daughters.[13]

"Kinsfolk are grouped according to generations. Take an individual man as a starting-point and work outwards from him. His parents include his real parents together with all their brothers and sisters; every man amongst them he will call *kamaku* (my father) and every woman *inaku* (my mother). Their 'parents' again are his 'grandparents,' and he will name each one *kubuku* (my grandparent) without distinction of sex. . . . Retracing your footsteps you find the same system ruling the converse relationships. My children (*natuku-weavo*) include the children of all my brothers and sisters; my grandchildren (*kubukuweavo*) include their grandchildren, the same word, let it be noted,

9 Brown, in JAI, XLIII, 150, 151; in JAI, XLVIII, 223; and in JAI, LIII, 425 ff.

10 Von Pfeil, *Südsee*, 25.   11 Codrington, in JAI, XVIII, 306.
12 Danks, in JAI, XVIII, 294.   13 Gray, in AAAS, 1892, 672.

signifying both grandparent and grandchild. . . . There is more variety in the terms applied to the kinsfolk of one's own generation, for two distinct systems of classification are in vogue, one based on sex, the other on age. . . . Upon this system of consanguinity depend the marriage regulations. Within the kin marriage is strictly forbidden, and the prohibition extends to our '-in-law' relations. Outside these limits there are no restrictions whatever, and a man may take his bride from anywhere."[14] " 'Tis but my sister Nehi, my father's brother's child," says one of the characters in a Strong's Island story.[15]

In India, "if a matrilineal community is divided into two exogamous sections, as children belong to their mother's section, they look upon their mother's sisters, who also belong there, as their own mothers; while the males of their mother's generation, but belonging to the opposite section, being the potential husbands of their mothers, are naturally looked upon as fathers. In a typically patrilineal society the mother, the mother's married sisters, the father, father's brothers and the children all belong, or come to belong, to the same section; hence the classification under consideration follows more easily. Therefore, the grouping together of the mother and sisters on the one hand and of the father and his brothers on the other in kinship-terminology may be taken as an indication of the former existence of dual organization."[16]

It is not possible, if it were advisable, to rehearse the copious detail of American Indian relationship collected by Morgan,[17] but a few cases may be added to his. Among the Dakotas "the grandparents as a rule take care of the children and are called father and mother. Uncles and aunts are always addressed as father and mother."[18] Among the patrilineal Omahas, "it is plain that kinship terms are used with considerable latitude, and not as we employ them. Whether Ego be a male or female, I call all men my fathers whom my father calls his brothers or whom my mother calls her potential husbands. I call all women my mothers whom my mother calls her sisters, aunts, or nieces, or whom my father calls his potential wives. I call all men my brothers who are the sons of such fathers or mothers, and their sisters are my sisters. I call all men my grandfathers who are the fathers or grandfathers of my fathers or mothers, or whom my fathers or mothers call their mother's brothers. I call all women my grandmothers who are the real or potential wives of my grandfathers, or who are the mothers or grandmothers of my fathers or mothers, or whom my fathers or mothers call their father's sisters. I, a male, call all males my sons who are the sons of my brothers or of my potential wives, and the sisters of these sons are my daughters. I, a female, call those males my nephews who are the sons of my brothers, and the daughters of my brothers are my nieces; but my sister's children are my children as their father is my potential or actual husband. I, a male, call my sister's son my nephew, and her daughter is my niece. I, a male or female, call all males and females my grandchildren who are the children of my sons, daughters, nephews, or nieces. I, a male or female, call all men my uncles whom my mothers call their brothers. And my aunts are all females who are my fathers' sisters as well as those who are the wives of my uncles. But my father's sisters' husbands, I being a

[14] Jenness and Ballentyne, *D'Entrecasteaux*, 64, 66.
[15] Becke, *Pacif. Tales*, 221.   [16] Ghurye, in JAI, LIII, 81.
[17] In *Smithson. Contrib. to Knowledge*, XVII.
[18] Beckwith, in *Smithson. Rep.*, 1886, pt. I, 257.

male, are my brothers-in-law, being the potential or real husbands of my sisters; and they are my potential husbands when Ego is a female."[19]

Among the Omaha, "kinship terms played an important part in all social intercourse. They not only designated the actual relationship between persons but the custom of never addressing anyone—man, woman, or child—by his personal name or of using a person's name when speaking of him, if he chanced to be present, made the use of kinship terms a practical necessity. These terms were also applied to what may be called potential relationships, that is, relationships that would be established through marriage made in accordance with tribal custom. If the wife had sisters, these women held a potential relationship to her husband, as they might become his wives either during his wife's lifetime or at her death. According to tribal usage a man had the potential right to marry his wife's sisters and also her nieces and her aunts. On the other hand, a man was under obligation to marry his brother's widow. Should he fail in this respect, he was liable to suffer in person or property, either by the act of the woman herself or by that of her near of kin, in order to force him to recognize or make good her rights. Because of these potential relationships the children of the wife called all those whom their father might marry 'mother' and all their father's brothers 'father.' Moreover, all the children of such relationships called one another 'brother' and 'sister.' There was no cousinship. All the brothers of the mother were called 'uncle' by her children, and the father's sisters were called 'aunt.' The regulation of marriage implied in these potential relationships was explained to be for the purpose of 'holding the family intact, for should the children be bereft of their own mother they would come under the care of her close kindred and not fall into the hands of a stranger.' This interpretation seems borne out by the approval still expressed when a woman weds the brother of her late husband or a man marries the sister of his dead wife or the widow of his brother; even when there is a marked disparity in the ages of the parties, it is said, 'The marriage does not make a break in the family and it shows respect for the dead.' The interweaving of actual and potential relationships greatly extended the family connection and supplied the proper terms for familiar and ceremonial address. . . . In the Omaha language the term for relationship, or the accent on the word, was varied according to the sex of the speaker and according to his or her relation to the person spoken of, as (1) when a father or mother was spoken of by a son, (2) when addressed by a daughter, (3) when spoken of by a male relative, (4) when spoken of by a female relative, and (5) when spoken of by a person not a relative."[20]

It is noteworthy that the old terms become survivalistic, appearing in ceremonial, for instance, in smoking, where the pipe is passed in a prescribed way. "The terms 'father,' 'grandfather,' 'son,' 'brother,' 'elder brother,' 'younger brother,' which are exchanged at that time do not now indicate clan relationship . . . but are survivals of a time when they did. A youth of 18 may be called 'grandfather' by a man of 60, and when Hahawe passes the pipe to Wiki and calls him 'my elder brother,' and Wiki responds 'my younger brother,' neither of these priests means that the other is his clan relative—it is the relationship of the sacerdotal standing of one to the other that is indicated. The

[19] Dorsey, in BAE, III, 254. The author presents these relations in chartform.

[20] Fletcher and LaFlesche, in BAE, XXVII, 313, 314.

terms are survivals of a time when they meant blood kinship, for when the ceremony was limited to the clan, Wiki, the chief, was 'elder brother,' or 'father,' or 'grandfather,' to the man who thus addressed him. The formal address survives, although the man using it may now belong to a different clan from that of the chief."[21]

One may reasonably doubt after much study whether he has mastered one of these systems, much more whether he understands the underlying factors which brought them into being; yet they were evolved by savage and barbarous men and appear to be readily and accurately usable by them. Inasmuch as they never could have planned or devised the system complete, it must have been worked out, with all its consistency and "logic," by experience over unreckonable time. Why should men elaborate such terms of address and develop them into such a system? Why should peoples all over the world have done the same thing, with inconsiderable variations? That question may be answered with another: Why should men have elaborated language into a structure so coherent and consistent that study of it reveals regularity and orderliness comparable to those found in nature? The answer to the one question is the answer to the other; all such queries amount to interrogation as to the evolution of the mores. Terms were evolved where there was a felt need of them; when there was no such evocation there were no terms evolved. Differences in terminology correspond therefore to differences in life-conditions, including among these such forms of organization as are already in the field; for example, Rivers[22] finds the essential distinction between the system used by many primitive peoples—of throwing together in one category a number of relations whom we distinguish—and ours to be "that the former is founded on the clan or other similar social group while our own is founded on the family." Older men were flung together into the category "father" because it did not matter, even granted that it was known, who was one's real father; then, as it came to matter, the "close-up" father was distinguished from the "far-away" one. This is the broadest generalization from the cases and is in no way invalidated because it is impossible, and may always be impossible, to specify in any given instance the precise reason for a looser or tighter classification.

21 Fewkes, in BAE, XIX, pt. II, 1007.
22 *Melan. Soc.*, 6.

Somewhat more specifically, all systems provide for distinctions of sex and of age. Here an obvious but none the less important fact comes into account, namely, that sex-division is an ultimate and inalterable one while age-division is relative. As one goes through life he traverses the age-grades. At a time, the persons on these stages might be called sons, fathers, and grandfathers, but the personnel of the grades alters, and there is little sense in the terms unless interest had previously been centered on kinship. Every time one turns his back on kinship and tries to account for these usages by age, and especially by terms of address derived from age, he is forced back upon kinship to explain the usages as to age. Plainly the age-distinction is no creative fact unless connected with sex-distinction, marriage, and kinship. If a man divides his fellow-tribesmen into older and younger when he addresses them, that is no division of the tribe into objective or real groups; all depends on who is the speaker. Sex, however, is objective and changeless; the identity of the speaker is irrelevant. It appears that the terms of kinship and address were indispensable to educate children from the earliest years in the intricacies of the marriage-rules; that is a practical reason for the evolution of the terms.

It is evident that economic and political circumstances modified the kin-tie and that propinquity or dispersion respectively intensified or weakened it. Terms of relationship, used by us to describe nearness or remoteness of blood-tie, connote error if employed in relation to these primitive systems, for these do not contemplate grade of blood-kinship but only marriageableness. Our system is individual; theirs are group-systems.

By a simple transition kinship-terms furnish terms of address, especially for the expression of affection, intimacy, and respect. The terms "uncle" and "aunt" are so used among ourselves, and royalties address each other as "cousin." A large number of cases occur in which terms of relationship are used to express the relation of friendship, intimacy, or alliance between tribes. The members of the Six Nations described each other as father, son, brother, to indicate seniority and precedence in the confederation.[23] On account of the general taboo against the current use of

23 Morgan, in *Smithson. Contrib. Knowledge*, XVII, 203.

names, terms of relationship are the usual forms of address among savages.[24] This leads to an extension of relationship-designations to cover remote kindred. The constant use of them is an education in the local kin-system which helps to account for an ability to wield it in spite of its complications. For the student it is better to forget his own relationship-terms, such as cousin, and try to watch the primitive connotations.

§424. Significance of Nomenclature. A distinction has been drawn between the primitive system illustrated in the preceding topic and that to which we are used. Relationship-systems, according to Morgan,[25] the classic author on systems of consanguinity and affinity, "resolve themselves into two ultimate forms, fundamentally distinct. One of these is *classificatory*, and the other *descriptive*. Under the first, consanguinei are never described, but are classified into categories, irrespective of their nearness or remoteness in degree to *Ego;* and the same term of relationship is applied to all the persons in the same category. Thus my brothers, and the sons of my father's brothers are all alike my brothers. . . . In the second case consanguinei are described either by the primary terms of relationship or a combination of these terms, thus making the relationship of each person specific. Thus we say brother's son, father's brother, and father's brother's son." The system is curious enough to modern eyes, but it has been supposed to have a deeper significance than appears upon its rather grotesque surface; "terms of relationship have usually been regarded principally as material from which conclusions as to the organization of society and conditions of marriage could be inferred."[26] Its lack of precision in distinction has been thought to afford evidence as to primitive uncertainty about descent and unregulation of sex-relations.[27] Perhaps the recent survey by Rivers[28] offers the most dispassionate view of the mat-

[24] Eyre, *Cent. Aust.*, II, 214.

[25] *Anc. Soc.*, 394; details in Morgan, in *Smithson. Contrib. Knowledge*, XVII.

[26] Kroeber, in JAI, XXXIX, 82.   [27] §§343, 344, 346, above.

[28] *Soc. Org.*, 192 (quoted), 52 ff.; *Melan. Soc.*, I, 6-11, 38-40, 43-45. For a denial of the existence of a real classificatory system, see Kroeber, in JAI, XXXIX, 77 ff.

ter; his conclusion may be stated in advance of a short synopsis of his work.

"My object . . . has been to support the view that the features of the classificatory system of relationship, as we find them at the present time, have arisen out of a state of group-marriage, while pointing out that this system lends no support to the view that the state of group-marriage was preceded by one of wholly unregulated promiscuity. . . . The classificatory system, in one form or another, is spread so widely over the world as to make it probable that it has had its origin in some universal, or almost universal, stage of social development, and I have attempted to indicate that the kind of society which most readily accounts for its chief features is one characterized by a form of marriage in which definite groups of men are the husbands of definite groups of women."

"The really characteristic feature of the European system is that the terms referring to the family are used exactly and with definite meanings, while all others are loose and inexact, and this is definitely connected with the preponderant importance of this family in our society. Our system is clearly dependent on the family in the strict sense." The primitive system called classificatory, on the other hand, belongs with the moiety and clan. "A child born into a community with moieties or clans becomes a member of a domestic group other than the family in the strict sense; and this is reflected in the terms of kinship that he addresses to those around him. The system of relationship found in these circumstances is called classificatory because whole groups of relatives are classed with the father, mother, brother, sister, and so forth, and receive the same terms of address. That is to say, relatives are grouped in classes. Thus, a person will give to a large number of men the term which he applies to his own father; to a large class of women he gives the same name as that he uses for his mother; and this applies even to the relationship of husband and wife. Thus, the distinctions of uncle, aunt, and cousin that play so fundamental a part in our system of relationship are largely obliterated in communities with moieties and clans." A savage "will denote as father a group consisting of the first, second (and third) cousins of his father in the male line. It is also an almost universal feature of the system that he will class with his father the husbands of his mother's sisters, and of all those whom the mother would call sister." Nevertheless, "it must be realized that, so far as we know, every people who use the classificatory system of relationship distinguish the actual father, i.e. the social father, not necessarily the physiological father, from the other persons with whom he is classed; but the persons grouped together as father may, on the other hand, be just as important as the real father in so far as social duties and privileges are concerned. Similar groupings occur in the case of the mother." Every son of one called father or mother will be classed with the brothers, and every daughter of these persons with the sisters.

Wherever there are exogamous groups practising this system, the term "father" is extended to all the men of one's father's clan of the same generation as the father and to all the husbands of the women of the mother's clan of the same generation as the mother, even when it is impossible to show any genealogical relationship with them. "The grouping together of relatives and members of clans and moieties is one of the chief characteristics of the classificatory system." There is also a distinction by age, as between, for example, brothers and sisters, own and classificatory.

The system is not merely one of nomenclature, a collection of terms of address pure and simple; "it is now thoroughly established . . . that these terms connote definite social functions, specific duties, privileges, and restrictions on conduct, and that these social functions apply to relatives in the classificatory sense, as well as to relatives in the much narrower sense which the terms would bear among ourselves." The special relation between a man and his mother's brother is instanced.[29] Taboos exist which lead to customs of avoidance, especially between a man and his wife's mother, and the provisions about cross-cousin marriage are also in evidence.[30] Certain of the features of the system "are only to be explained as the outcome of the dual organization of society in which it was obligatory for certain relatives to marry. It is quite certain that, in Australia for instance, certain marriages between relatives, principally the cross-cousin marriage, were the only forms of marriage that could be constructed, that, speaking generally, other forms of marriage simply did not exist."

With particular respect to Melanesia, the author remarks that he accepts the fundamental similarity of classificatory systems throughout the world and has concentrated upon the differences within that area. "On attending to these differences, one fact becomes at once apparent. In Oceania, contiguous peoples often differ more widely from one another in their method of denoting relationship than others who live far apart, and some of the closest resemblances occur among widely separated peoples." A number of examples are cited. "People who seem alien to one another in race show a greater resemblance in this respect than people who differ little from one another in physical appearance or in general culture. This at once suggests that the nature of systems of relationship depends on forms of social structure rather than on differences of race. . . . My aim . . . will be to show that all the diverse features of Oceanic systems of relationship are due to social causes and depend on differences in the social conditions out of which they have sprung." Again, "just as I have supposed that the father's sister and the wife of the mother's brother have been classed with the mother to make their non-marriageable status clear and unambiguous, so do I suppose that this has been the essential motive producing the classification of the brothers and sisters of the consort with brothers and sisters, and of fathers and mothers of the consort with fathers and mothers. The fact that men and women address one another as brothers and sisters, or as parents and children, provides, according to Melanesian ideas, the clearest of all possible indications that they are ineligible as consorts in marriage or as partners in extra-marital sexual relations. . . . The chief general conclusion to be drawn from the survey . . . is that the forms of Oceanic systems of relationship are directly dependent upon features of social organisation, and especially upon forms of marriage." Further it is concluded "that distinctions in nomenclature are definitely associated with distinctions in conduct."

Fison[31] protests against the assertion that the classificatory system is a mere "system of addresses." There are many tribes who never employ the terms; again, if they are not terms of relationship, the millions of people who use

29 §416, above.   30 §425, below.
31 "Classificatory System of Relationship," in JAI, XXIV, 369.

them have no such terms at all, for these are the only ones they possess; further, it is impossible to suppose that the obligations and prohibitions conveyed by the terms could be conveyed by a mere system of addresses. Take, for instance, the taboo between the Fijian *veinganeni* (brother's or sister's children of different sex). Any woman whom a Fijian calls *ngane* is strictly forbidden to him; her touch would bring pollution to him and marriage with her would be regarded with horror by all the tribe. The author thinks no mere terms of address could involve such prohibition; these classificatory terms "are the necessary outcome of the exogamous intermarrying divisions found in Australia and elsewhere; and the fair inference is that, wherever we find the terms, these divisions are, or have been, in the past."

It is evident enough that the tangled terminology—tangled as it appears to one viewing it without the clarifying suggestions of such careful students as Rivers—is not an exhibition of whim, caprice, or accident but has been evoked in response to societal needs under the existing life-conditions. And whether or not the classificatory system will bear the weight of sponsor for an antecedent little-regulated sex-life, it unquestionably casts much light upon earlier stages of societal organization. We repeat that the presence or absence of terms of relationship means the presence or absence of that for which the terms stand; where a relationship is recognized, there the appropriate term will not fail to disclose itself. Further, there is no disposition shown to ignore the basic human differentiation of sex; it was always taken into account in terms of address. There are few or no terms, like "Geschwister," to include adults of both sexes as the word "child" covers the sexually immature. Age, too, is a criterion of distinction that was enforced upon even the least reflective mind; it also lay in nature and was to be found in all places and times. The next principle of relationship was the blood-tie, which, though it too is in nature, was susceptible of more than a single interpretation. If it is conceived to pass through the female line alone, as is most natural among the most ignorant peoples, then the system of nomenclature is found to emphasize the closeness of relationship upon the mother's side and to set off the father and his kin—to indicate the consanguinity of those taken to be related by blood as compared with the affinity[32] of those brought into relations by marriage. Under the father-family the conditions are reversed;[33] and when

[32] Morgan, *Anc. Soc.*, 394.
[33] Cunow, *Australneger*, 154, 156; Tylor, in JAI, XVIII, 263.

it is conceived that the tie of blood proceeds through both father and mother, they are combined.

Again, the small endogamous group could have but a simple nomenclature as compared with the exogamous, for in the former consanguinity is all that need be taken account of, whereas with exogamy comes the need of new terms for the affinities created.[34] "By the lively intercourse which is always kept up between the settlements, it cannot fail that marriages between members of different tribes should be of frequent occurrence and that many ties of affinity and consanguinity should thus be created. These relations, however, as distances increase, quickly become less common."[35] The reflection of the rise of exogamy found in terms of address is but another indication of the profundity and significance of the change from endogamy to out-marriage.[36]

Morgan[37] generalizes shrewdly upon the systems of consanguinity and affinity which he has investigated in such detail. Without following him in his arduous research, we may still apprehend the truth of his general results. Of three systems which he distinguishes he writes:

"Since we have the right to suppose that each one expresses the actual relationships which existed in the family at the time of its establishment, it reveals, in turn, the form of marriage and of the family which then prevailed, although both may have advanced into a higher stage while the system of consanguinity remained unchanged.

"It will be noticed, further, that these systems are natural growths with the progress of society from a lower into a higher condition, the change in each case being marked by the appearance of some institution affecting deeply the constitution of society. The relationship of mother and child, of brother and sister, and of grandmother and grandchild have been ascertainable in all ages with entire certainty; but those of father and child, and of grandfather and grandchild were not ascertainable with certainty until monogamy contributed the highest assurance attainable. A number of persons would stand in each of these relations at the same time as equally probable when marriage was in the group. In the rudest conditions of ancient society these relationships would be perceived, both the actual and the probable, and terms would be invented to express them. A system of consanguinity would result in time from the continued application of these terms to persons thus formed into a group of kindred." The systems of consanguinity "do not rest upon nature, but upon marriage; not upon fictitious considerations, but upon fact; and . . . each in its turn is a logical as well as truthful system. The evidence they contain is of

[34] Cunow, *Australneger,* 50, 154.   [35] Boas, in BAE, VI, 462.
[36] §§355, 356, above.
[37] *Anc. Soc.,* 392, 393, 394, 396, 397, 398.

the highest value, as well as of the most suggestive character. It reveals the condition of ancient society in the plainest manner with unerring directness."

The divisions and branches of any such system are complex to the last degree. "With such a mass of divisions and branches, embracing such a multitude of consanguinei, it will be seen at once that a method of arrangement and of description which maintained each distinct and rendered the whole intelligible would be no ordinary achievement. This task was perfectly accomplished by the Roman civilians, whose method has been adopted by the principal European nations, and is so entirely simple as to elicit admiration. The development of the nomenclature to the requisite extent must have been so extremely difficult that it would probably never have occurred except under the stimulus of an urgent necessity, namely, the need of a code of descents to regulate the inheritance of property." Here again we discover the powerful property-interest at the bottom of institutional development;[38] with such a vital interest involved even primitive arrangements are likely automatically to develop a perfection that astonishes the investigator.

"Systems of consanguinity are neither adopted, modified, nor laid aside at pleasure. They are identified in their origin with organic movements of society which produced a great change of condition. When a particular form had come into general use, with its nomenclature invented and its methods settled, it would, from the nature of the case, be very slow to change. Every human being is the centre of a group of kindred, and therefore, every person is compelled to use and to understand the prevailing system. A change in any one of these relationships would be extremely difficult. This tendency to permanence is increased by the fact that these systems exist by custom rather than legal enactment, as growths rather than artificial creations, and therefore a motive to change must be as universal as the usage. While every person is a party to the system, the channel of its transmission is the blood. Powerful influences thus existed to perpetuate the system long after the conditions under which each originated had been modified or had altogether disappeared. This element of permanence gives certainty to conclusions drawn from the facts, and has preserved and brought forward a record of ancient society which otherwise would have been entirely lost to human knowledge."

This last passage, written by Morgan almost fifty years ago, might well have been composed in the light of the most modern ideas about the evolution of society and its institutions. It gives what is needed in order to set the systems of relationship in their proper position. In general they are a set of labels for various degrees of mutual belonging as between individuals. They are not primary at all but have followed upon basic adjustments of family and society to life-conditions as presented. They sharpen considerably the outlines of those forms of adjustment.

§425*. Relationship-Mores. In the general considerations now before us lies the sense of a number of miscellaneous notions and

[38] §§131-135, above.

customs having to do with the behavior of relations to one another. These may be reviewed by sample and with brevity.

A feature which has always stimulated curiosity is the peculiar arrangement as respects cousin-marriage whereby certain persons in this relationship to one another may marry and others may not. Children of two brothers or of two sisters are generally sternly tabooed to one another, while those of a brother may marry those of his sister. Since they are all biologically equally related, this case is very significant of the absence, in provisions about exogamy, of any biological considerations.[39] The cousins who are the offspring of a brother and of a sister have been called "cross-cousins,"[40] and the question puts itself in this form: Why may cross-cousins regularly marry where other types of cousin may not? This query has been answered by reference to the dual division and to the provisions characteristic of mother-family, father-family, and transition from the former to the latter.

Let us first hear Wilken[41] on this subject. Under the mother-family system, the children of two sisters are regarded as closely related; they may call each other brother and sister; and their union is incestuous. Similarly, under the father-family, the children of two brothers would be closely consanguine and so tabooed. As for the marriage of brother's children under the mother-family, it may take place provided the brothers have married into different groups so that the children, following the mother, are not group-comrades; and the same is true of children of sisters under the father-family, under the same conditions. Where this is the case, the cross-cousins are under no disabilities; in fact, the cross-cousin union is often the preferred one. Among the Bataks, who are exogamous, a man normally marries the daughter of his mother's brother, and the wife or betrothed may be called by that title, even when she does not stand in that relation; so a woman calls her lover "son of father's sister." It is a transgression of the mores (adat) to marry a father's sister's daughter, however; that is, in this case, while a union between a brother's son and a sister's daughter is tabooed, that between a sister's son and a brother's daughter is allowed. This is explained by the lasting-over of mother-family taboos into the patrilineal system; then, as under the mother-family, a brother would look on his sister's children as his own; but the sister could not have arrived at the same attitude toward those of her brother; they, having been alien to her under the former family-system, remain so. It is clear, in any case, that the transition from one form of family to another made certain allowed unions incestuous and vice versa, while the cross-cousin union remained allowable, for in it, barring few exceptions, the "totem" was always "crossed." The author quoted cites many cases from the East Indies in illustration.

Rivers[42] adds the feature of the effect of dual organization. "It is an almost

[39] §§273, 348, above.   [40] Tylor, in JAI, XVIII, 263.
[41] In VG, I, 452, 455, 456, 457; II, 227-228, 342-343, 348, 349-351.
[42] Soc. Org., 67-68; and Melan. Soc., I, 13.

universal feature of the classificatory system that the children of brothers are classed with the children of sisters. A man applies the same terms to his mother's sister's children which he uses for his father's brother's children, and the use of this term, being the same as that used for a brother or sister, carries with it the most rigorous prohibition of marriage. Such a condition would not follow necessarily from a social state in which there were more than two social groups. If the society were patrilineal, the children of two brothers would necessarily belong to the same social group, so that the principle of exogamy would prevent marriage between them, but if the women of the group had married into different clans, there is no reason arising out of the principle of exogamy which should prevent marriage between their children, or lead to the use of a term common to them and the children of brothers. Similarly, if the society were matrilineal, the children of two sisters would necessarily belong to the same social group, but this would not be the case with the children of brothers, who might marry into different social groups. If, however, there be only two social groups, the case is very different. It would make no difference whether descent were patrilineal or matrilineal. In each case the children of two brothers or of two sisters must belong to the same moiety, while the children of brother and sister must belong to different moieties. The children of two brothers would be just as ineligible as consorts as the children of two sisters."

"All the nations which have advanced to a knowledge of the relationship of cousin have restricted it in every instance to the children of a brother and sister"; they thus show "that if it was developed at all, the direction of the advance was predetermined by the elements of the system."[43]

Cases in point occur in a previous connection;[44] a few may be cited here. In the New Hebrides a man may marry his father's sister's daughter but not his father's brother's daughter, who is his sister; he may take his mother's brother's daughter but not his mother's sister's daughter, who is his sister. If they are related to each other through parents of the same sex, a pair may not marry.[45] Among the Hovas, "marriages regularly take place between brothers' children and between brothers' and sisters' children; but it is forbidden that children of sisters who have the same mother shall marry, and the prohibition extends to the fifth generation, that is, to the great-great-great-grandchildren of the sisters. Undoubtedly this is to be regarded as a survival, a limitation of a former exogamy with descent in the female line."[46] In Sumatra, "of two brothers the children may not intermarry. A sister's son may marry a brother's daughter; but a brother's son may not marry a sister's daughter."[47] Among the Caribs, "the father's brothers are called fathers; the children of brothers, of sisters, and of brothers and sisters are called brothers. Children of brothers do not marry, while those of sisters do."[48]

Whether such marriages are forbidden or allowed depends, then,

[43] Morgan, in *Smithson. Contrib. to Knowledge*, XVII, 179, 180.
[44] §§348, 349, above.   [45] Gray, in AAAS, 1892, 672.
[46] Wilken, in VG, I, 397.   [47] Marsden, *Sumatra*, 228.
[48] Von Martius, *Beiträge*, I, 354, note.

upon consanguinity as apprehended; and apparent contradictions are due to diverse ideas as to the line of descent and relationship.

In circumstances arising under conditions such as foregoing paragraphs have portrayed, there may be a peculiarly close relation developed between brothers or brothers and sisters.

For instance, among the Dieri, "if there is some trouble in the 'fighting place' with a man, his elder brother hastens to it, and calls on the adversary to deal with him." Similarly when some native has been judicially condemned to death, "the penalty of death does not fall upon the offender, but on his eldest brother at that place."[49] "It is the custom of the Mangbattu rulers to keep a sister with them. She remains single, remains always in the neighborhood of her brother, and upholds his interests." Only the sister remained seated in the king's presence, asserting that her brother had no control over her.[50] In the Yakut legends and folk-tales, "we see that in ancient times the feeling of attachment in the brother and sister tie was far more strongly developed than in the marriage tie, or even in the parent and child tie. The first of these prevailed over all others. They often called the wives of the legendary heroes 'sisters,' using a distinct name for older sister, and another for younger sister. Almost every hero, whether good or bad, has by his side sisters, who act as his protectors and comrades. The folk tales contain many cases of the devoted service of sisters to brothers."[51] In the Kiowa marriage, "the brother of a girl has as much to do with the decision of the case as her parents, and continues to claim a sort of guardianship over her even after her marriage."[52] "The relation of the sister to the brother among the South Slav tribes is peculiar. . . . It is of a special tenderness and intimacy and is regarded as much more pure and noble than that of a wife to a husband. The brother is the natural protector of the sister, and her pride."[53] Several similar European cases are cited by Wilutzky.[54]

Williamson[55] considers this brother-sister relation as it appears in Polynesia: "writers refer to the very great deference and respect which a man had to show to his sister. In some cases it is obvious that this only refers to sexual avoidance, and in others there is nothing to indicate that more than this is involved; a few of the statements, however, seem to carry the matter further. . . . Kindness, respect and protection . . . are one matter; and manifestations of respect, suggesting an idea that she was a superior being, might be merely a matter of avoidance. But a right on her part to require him to treat her with submission and to follow her counsel in family matters, and a right to dominate the decisions of his family council, is a very different matter." The author thinks the explanation must be sought in "a lingering partial continuance of matrilineal descent."

This citation brings us to the subject of avoidance between relatives. Particularly in the case of relatives-in-law does one

[49] Howitt, *S.E. Aust.*, 327.   [50] Junker, *Afrika*, II, 505.
[51] Sieroshevski-Sumner, in JAI, XXXI, 89.
[52] Mooney, in BAE, XVII, pt. I, 232-233.
[53] Rhamm, in *Globus*, LXXXII, 279.
[54] *Mann u. Weib*, 91, 95.   [55] *Cent. Polyn.*, II, 102, 105, 172.

encounter a set of customs some of which are quite strange to him. However, before coming to these, it is in point to note that, along with the above relations of mutual helpfulness and affection between persons so close as brother and sister, there appear also phenomena of strict avoidance, where the parties mutually shun contact with one another.

"In Lepers' Island a brother and sister never see one another after the girl is tattooed about the time of puberty. It is the girl who leaves the house of her parents and goes to live with her mother's brother. She will only do so, however, if she has a brother, and if there are only girls in the family they continue to live with their parents. If after the separation brother and sister meet on a path the girl will get out of the way and both will look down so as to avoid seeing one another. They will never say each other's names nor will they speak of one another. When a woman has married and had children it may happen that her brother will want to go to her house to see his nephew and in such a case the boy's mother will leave the house before her brother enters it. The avoidance even continues after death, for if one dies the other will not enter the house where the corpse is lying but will mourn outside." A native of another island "said that he had asked the people why brother and sister avoided one another but without result. He was inclined himself to think that its object was to avoid the possibility of sexual relations, being no doubt influenced by the undoubted relation between avoidance and sexual relations in other parts of Melanesia including his own island."[56] In San Cristoval, one of the Solomon Islands, in the Arosi district, restrictions are common upon the intercourse between actual brothers and sisters. "This is natural as they cannot marry, and free intercourse means possibility of marriage. . . . These restrictions are extended to cross-cousins. . . . At any rate in Arosi a boy must never speak to his cross-cousin: if he wants something from her he must get a friend to go and ask for it; he must never play with her; if they meet by chance on a path she will step aside into the bush and let him go by and they must not look at one another; he must never take food from her even if he is hungry, nor must he eat food she has cooked; if she is in a house he does not go in, but stands near the house, and when she observes him she goes out and then he can enter; he must not go on a voyage with her in a canoe or boat, and he must be very careful never to touch anything of hers—her bag, her lime-box, her sleeping mat, or to tread upon the last. The meaning of these restrictions is quite plainly seen when it is remembered what the mark of betrothal is in Arosi. If a boy feeds a girl and she eats the food this is consent to marry."[57]

"There is little doubt that these customs of avoidance are connected in many cases with the potentiality of sexual relations; two relatives to whom sexual relations are forbidden have to avoid one another altogether. Moreover, there is little doubt that, where relatives now avoid one another, sexual relations were formerly

[56] Rivers, *Melan. Soc.*, I, 213.   [57] Fox, in JAI, XLIX, 117.

allowed, if they are not habitual, and the theoretical interest of these customs arises out of this possibility. Much of the evidence for the former prevalence of group-marriage or organized sexual communism is derived from customs of this kind. It is clear, however, that sexual relations do not furnish a complete explanation of these customs, for they frequently occur between members of the same sex."[58]

The general case of avoidance may be said to be that between relatives by marriage, and most general among these, perhaps, is the usage of avoidance between a man and his wife's mother.[59]

The Australians have a term "mura" meaning a woman whom the man in question may not marry. "These women were . . . those who are strictly prohibited from speaking to or having any intercourse with the man in question, to whom they were tribally mothers-in-law," that is, mothers of girls whom a man might marry.[60] A man might not look at his mother-in-law, nor even in her direction. "If his shadow happened to fall on her, he would have to leave his wife, who would return to her parents. A case happened in Jervis Bay which I heard of, where a man in a drunken state accidentally ran up against his mother-in-law, and the *Gommera* made him leave his wife. The law is one of those told to the novices at the initiation ceremonies, and strongly impressed on them. . . . A woman from the time her daughter was married must not see her son-in-law, or even hear his name spoken. If she heard anyone mention his name, she would put her fingers in her ears and say, '*Gungowa*,' that is, 'Be quiet.' " If a woman should look at or speak to her daughter's husband, or his brother, "it was thought that her hair would turn white. In order to prevent such consequences, a woman would, when the son-in-law sent game by his wife to her husband, rub charcoal over her face, especially over her mouth, and she could then safely eat of the game without suffering any harm."[61] The Australians say: "A man cannot even look at his wife's mother."[62] "The mother-in-law can never speak to her daughter's husband, or enter his wuurn. If she meets him, she must cover up her head with her rug, walk in a stooping position, and speak in whispers while he is near. To such a length is this remarkable law carried, that it is not departed from even while one of them is dying. After death, however, the living looks upon the dead. The aborigines, who show great willingness to give explanations of their laws and habits to those persons they respect, cannot give any reasons for this very extraordinary custom, which is said to be observed all over Australia, and in several island groups in the Pacific Ocean."[63]

"In the Bank's Islands the rules of avoidance and reserve are very strict and minute. As regards the avoidance of a person, a man will not come near his wife's mother; the avoidance is mutual; if the two chance to meet in a path, the woman will step out of it and stand with her back turned till he

[58] Rivers, *Soc. Org.*, 66.
[59] A number of cases in Clodd, *Magic*, 53-55, 63; §273, above.
[60] Spencer and Gillen, *Nat. Tr. Cent. Aust.*, 57, 504, 558, 559.
[61] Howitt, *S.E. Aust.*, 199, 257, 266.   [62] Howitt, in JAI, XII, 503.
[63] Dawson, *Aust. Aborig.*, 32-33; Ratzel, *Vkde.*, II, 65.

has gone by, or perhaps if it be more convenient he will move out of the way." Again, "a man would not follow his mother-in-law along the beach, nor she him, until the tide had washed out the footsteps of the first traveller from the sand. At the same time a man and his mother-in-law will talk at a distance." Other cases of avoidance are few in this latter region.[64] In the New Hebrides the mother-in-law, in avoidance, covers her face and hides.[65]

Among the Bushmen the man avoids his wife's mother and the wife her husband's father. Similarly among the Kaffirs, where even the names of the avoided persons are suppressed in favor of new words, constituting an example of the *hlonipa*-custom.[66] Fritsch[67] thinks this usage is due to fear of improper relations, for it precludes any temptation to such. "When a man marries he must be very reserved in the presence of his mother-in-law, whom he may address, but only on necessary subjects. A newly married woman may not see her father-in-law unless she is veiled, and cannot speak to him under any pretext. The time during which these various restraints must continue varies with the rank of those interested, from a few weeks to many months, or until there are children, after which normal conditions follow."[68] "A man can never look at his mother-in-law or at his wife's aunt; neither can a woman look at her father-in-law."[69]

In Uganda the wife's mother is under a serious ban. "She must not enter her daughter's house, and she must not speak to her son-in-law. Should they meet accidentally on the path, she must turn aside and cover her head with her clothes. If her wearing apparel is not sufficient to cover her head, the exactions of etiquette may be met by sitting on the haunches and covering the eyes and part of the face with the open hands. When the son-in-law has passed, she may go on her way. She may pay a visit to her daughter, but she cannot enter the house. She remains twenty yards off; the daughter goes to her and they sit and talk. If the son-in-law is indoors, and not in view from outside, the mother-in-law may shout 'Ofya' (that is, 'How dost thou?') and the son-in-law may answer her from inside the hut; but it would be a *gross* breach of etiquette either to carry the conversation further, or for the mother-in-law to look in at the door, or her son-in-law to glance at her from within the hut." Again, "a married man with a child must on no account call on his mother-in-law without wearing a piece of goat skin, which, though quite inadequate for purposes of decency, is nevertheless, a very important thing in etiquette." To call on the lady in question "in a state of absolute nudity would be regarded as a serious insult, only to be atoned for by the payment of goats. Even if under the new dispensation a man wears European trousers, he must have a piece of goat skin underneath."[70] This is a striking instance of survival.

In the Congo region, "*Bokilo* means . . . any relation-in-law. *Bokilo* is a noun derived from *kila* . . . to prohibit, tabu, . . . and indicates that all bearing the relationship of *Bokilo* can have no intimate relationship with one another. It is highly probable that at one time they were not allowed to speak to each other. It is certainly regarded now as incest for any persons bearing the relationship of *Bokilo* to cohabit with one another. A son-in-law may not look at a mother-in-law, and a daughter-in-law must not look at a father-in-law. When absolutely necessary they may sit a little apart with their backs

[64] Codrington, *Melanesians*, 43.
[65] Macdonald, in AAAS, 1892, 723.
[66] §223, above.
[67] *Eingeb. S.-Afr.*, 445, 114.
[68] Macdonald, in JAI, XIX, 273.
[69] Decle, quoted in JAI, XXIII, 84.
[70] Johnston, *Uganda*, II, 688, 781.

to each other and talk. Some have told me that this is to guard against all possibility of them coming together, 'For a person you never look at you never desire.' Others have said: 'Well, don't you see, my wife came from her womb.' I am strongly inclined to think that the former is the real reason."[71]

Among the Votyaks "a bride must hide from her father-in-law and in his presence must conceal her face with a kerchief. For a whole year she must not say a word to him or even mention his name. In his presence, or in that of her elder brother-in-law and the oldest sister-in-law, she may not appear bare-headed or bare-footed. The same takes place in the behavior of the son-in-law towards his wife's father and mother."[72] Again, a married woman may never be seen by her father-in-law, nor a married man by his mother-in-law until he has a child.[73]

Tylor,[74] Andree,[75] and Wilken[76] cite many examples of the avoidance of the mother-in-law, together with sayings about her which bring us up to the modern jibes connected with her. "Mother-in-law and daughter-in-law are a tempest and a hailstorm." There is no other case of avoidance of which we know which is at once so widespread over space and also through all stages of civilization. Before, however, attempting to draw any conclusions from this widespread example of avoidance-customs, we should have before us the other and less common types.[77]

Kaffirs exclude women from their feasts in the kraal out of respect for their deceased fathers-in-law.[78] "The custom of covering the face and head with a cloth in the presence of men, particularly in that of the father-in-law, has, according to Ostiak information, the object of preventing seduction."[79] In Korea, "with the father-in-law the law of silence is extremely rigid. The daughter-in-law often passes years without raising her eyes to his, or addressing a word to him."[80] In ancient India a woman owed great respect to her father-in-law.[81] In connection with such cases it should be stated that a father sometimes married his son of tender years to a mature woman and then himself had children by her.[82]

In one Australian case whereas a man may speak to his tribal elder sister at a distance of forty yards, with a younger sister he must be at least a hundred dred yards away. Elder or younger sister may go to their brother's camp and if he is present, they, sitting in the darkness where their faces are not discernible, may converse with his wife. "We cannot discover any explanation of

[71] Weeks, in JAI, XL, 367-368. [72] Abercromby, *Finns*, I, 194, 195.
[73] Müller, *Ugrische Volksstämme*, I, 308.
[74] *Early Hist.*, 290-292. [75] *Eth. Parallelen*, 159 ff.
[76] In VG, I, 170 ff.
[77] Post, in *Globus*, LXVII, 174 ff.; Starcke, *Prim. Fam.*, 237.
[78] Kropf, *Kaffir-Engl. Dict.*, 148.
[79] Kondratowitsch, in *Globus*, LXXIV, 290.
[80] Bishop, *Korea*, 118. [81] Zimmer, *Altind. Leben*, 327.
[82] Letourneau, *Soc.*, 335; Sumner, *Folkways*, §378; Kaindl, in *Globus*, LXXIX, 155.

the restriction in regard to the younger sister; it can hardly be supposed that it has anything to do with the dread of incest, else why is there not as strong a restriction in the case of the elder sisters?"[83]

The Yukaghir of Siberia call this usage *nexiyini,* which means "they are bashful (in the presence) of each other." "Among relatives by affinity the following persons must avoid each other: (a) The father and his son's wife. (b) The elder brother or elder male cousin, and the wife of the younger brother or male cousin. (c) The elder brother or the elder male cousin, and the wife of the younger brother's or younger male cousin's son. (d) The elder brother or the elder male cousin, and the wife of the son of his younger sister or of his younger female cousin. (e) The mother and her son-in-law. Besides this, the father does not speak to his daughter's husband nor the elder brother to his younger sister's husband. Persons who are *nexiyini* should not address each other directly, should not look into each other's faces, and should not uncover their bodies in the presence of each other, nor even bare the legs above the knees. . . . On inquiring as to the origin of this custom, Jochelson was told 'Our fathers did so,' or 'Wise men know that it ought to be so.' One may suppose that these restrictions consciously aimed at exogamy. . . . The Yukaghir say that in former times marriage was forbidden only between first cousins, and that they do not consider second cousins as consanguineous relatives. The myths often refer to consanguineous marriages, especially between brother and sister." One traveller knew, of his own experience, of a union between brother and sister.[84]

In Hindustan and the Deccan the terms "brother-in-law," "father-in-law," together with "sister-seducer" and "daughter-seducer" were terms of abuse; "the pith of the taunt lay in the imputation of cowardice, the most despicable of vices."[85] A married Hindu woman must not look at or address her husband's elder brother.[86] In China there is no relationship between the husband's relatives and those of the wife.[87] Among the Sea Dyaks the newly made bride may not enter her mother-in-law's room until "she has first been led over the threshold by that austere relative herself, or by some female relative deputed by her to perform the office." Again, "the respect paid by a son-in-law to the father of his wife is greater than that paid to his own father. He treats him with much ceremony, must never pronounce his name, nor must he take the liberty of eating off the same plate, or drinking out of the same cup, or even of lying down on the same mat."[88] In Sumatra, the son-in-law must avoid his parents-in-law, and not enter their part of the house or speak to them except under direst necessity.[89] Among the Alfurs of Celebes it is forbidden that a man shall name his parents-in-law. In referring to persons with the same name as these, he says "just like my father-in-law or mother-in-law" or "I may not name that name." Sometimes he uses a circumlocution; and this goes so far that he avoids names of objects which sound like those of his parents-in-law; if his father-in-law "is called Kalalo, then he must never use *kawalo* (horse) but *sasakejan.*" This custom is quite well represented in the Indian Archipelago.[90]

[83] Spencer and Gillen, *Nat. Tr. Cent. Aust.,* 88, 89.
[84] Czaplicka, *Aborig. Siberia,* 91-92.
[85] Kitts, "Abuse," in JASB, II, 73; Spencer, *Study of Soc.,* 160.
[86] Wilkins, *Mod. Hinduism,* 18.
[87] Von Mollendorff, *Chinese,* 15.   [88] Roth, *Sarawak,* I, 112, 125.
[89] Jacobs, *Groot-Atjeh,* I, 69.   [90] Wilken, in VG, I, 172, 173.

Among the Omahas, "in former days it was always the rule for a man not to speak to his wife's parents or grandparents. He was obliged to converse with them through his wife or child, by addressing the latter and requesting him or her to ask the grandparent for the desired information. Then the grand-parent used to tell the man's wife or child to say so and so to the man. In like manner a woman cannot speak directly to her husband's father under ordinary circumstances. They must resort to the medium of a third party, the woman's husband or child. But if the husband and child be absent, the woman or her father-in-law is obliged to make the necessary inquiry."[91] "If an Omaha enters a tent in which the husband of his daughter is seated, the latter conceals his head with his robe, and takes the earliest opportunity to withdraw, while the ordinary offices of kindness and hospitality are performed through the female, who passes the pipe or the message between her father and husband."[92] Among the Assiniboin, "the names of the wife's parents are never pronounced by the husband; to do so would excite the ridicule of the whole camp. The husband and father-in-law never look on each other if they can avoid it, nor do they enter the same lodge. In like manner the wife never addresses her father-in-law."[93] Even among the Fuegians "sons-in-law and daughters-in-law treat with considerable deference their fathers and mothers-in-law."[94]

Hocart[95] has a strange sort of custom to report from Fiji which he aligns with certain relations between kin. "*Tauvu* is a relationship between two groups, whether tribes or sub-divisions of a tribe," characterized by privileges of appropriation and ill-manners. It is somewhat like the *vasu*-relationship between nephew and maternal uncle. It allows appropriation of property with-out leave and the use of abusive language without resentment being roused. He cites examples. There is a parallel in kinship-relations between cross-cousins. Improper jests and general impudence are permitted. He thinks that two tribes that are *tauvu* used to intermarry; "the same rules govern the behaviour of *tauvu* and cross-cousins because both are cognate relationships," that is, relationships through descent from a single ancestor or ancestress.

Though it is evidently impossible to get at the significance of all the avoidance-customs of which the above are fair representa-tives, there is no doubt that the taboo on sexual relations ex-plains some of them, as it does in the case of brother-sister avoid-ance; but then there are a number where the avoiding parties are of the same sex. Probably there is at bottom of many of these a collision of interests or a reminiscence of such. What was once a real adjustment, though its reason for existence may be obscure, might later have become a ceremonial, as is common enough throughout societal evolution. Rivers[96] thinks he finds a key in the existence or previous prevalence of the dual organization.

[91] Dorsey, in BAE, III, 262.
[92] Donaldson, in *Smithson. Rep.*, 1885, pt. II, 72.
[93] Dorsey, in BAE, XV, 225.
[94] Bridges, "Firelanders," in *Voice for S. Amer.*, XIII, 201.
[95] In JAI, XLIII, 101-108.   [96] *Melan. Soc.*, II, 169-171.

"All these regulations seem to have underlying them a common principle; they all seem to indicate that relatives by marriage must not approach or touch one another when at a disadvantage, as when sitting down or carrying a load. There seems to be implied in these rules the idea of hostility and the possibility that one relative may injure the other, and this appears to be especially strong in the attitude of a man towards his wife's father. This implied hostility is evidently to be connected with the condition of hostility between the two moieties of the community. . . . The head occupies a very peculiar position in these customs of avoidance. . . . The conclusion so far reached is that rules of avoidance between relatives by marriage are connected with two ancient social conditions: sexual communism and a condition of hostility between the members of the two moieties of the community."

Tylor[97] is not very clear in his conclusions as to this mutual avoidance. "There is a well marked preponderance indicating that ceremonial avoidance by the husband of the wife's family is in some way connected with his living with them; and *vice versa* as to the wife and the husband's family." The barbaric custom differs from the most primitive. "Here the husband is none the less on friendly terms with his wife's people because they may not take any notice of one another. In fact, the explanation of this ceremonial cutting may be simpler and more direct than in civilized Europe. As the husband has intruded himself among a family which is not his own, and into a house where he has no right, it seems not difficult to understand their marking the difference between him and themselves by treating him formally as a stranger."

A survey of the cases as a whole reveals that avoidance is very largely sex-wise. In so far as this is the case, we have before us a sex-taboo. In general, if the persons of different sex who avoid one another were to mate, they would transgress that taboo; and we know of no instances of avoidance between parties who are free to mate together. Avoidance looks like a sort of supplementary sex-taboo laid upon persons who are not related by consanguinity but by affinity. Growing up in a kin-group, the individual picks up of himself or has inculcated in him the taboo in so far as it affects his relations with his group's membership; but perhaps restriction, as it covers the new propinquities into which marriage throws him, needs to be extended and emphasized somewhat. In point of fact the avoidance-usages appear to be, and in some cases are stated to be, precautionary and prophylactic. We do not pretend that they are all thus explicable but we call attention to the correlation between them and the regular sex-taboos;[98] and we see no other correlation with economic, religious, or other mores which is, in cases where the sexes avoid one another, as marked.

Where the avoidance-customs interpose between persons of the

[97] In JAI, XVIII, 247.   [98] §§348, 349, above.

same sex, it is pretty clearly an issue of authority and prestige. When the father-in-law ignores or humiliates the son-in-law, he is in so far manifesting his own superiority of position. Such cases shade off into actual tyranny over an alien who is working out the bride-price instead of paying it and removing his wife to his own people. He is an inferior and is so treated. And the exactions of the mother-in-law over her son's wife bear the same stamp. It is characteristic of this type of avoidance that it is not so necessarily reciprocal; it is for the inferior to stand aside, while the superior goes his way undisturbed.

The salient case of the mother-in-law and son-in-law seems to combine the two types that have been distinguished. It has been interpreted as a survival of the mother-right, wherein the mother manifests ceremonial resentment, originally real, at the loss of her powers of disposal over her daughters and of control over the men who enter her group to marry them.[99] Such an explanation is highly inferential and even fanciful; it seems to us that one might as well believe that the same factors which are said, both in jest and in earnest, to produce the traditional antipathies between a woman's husband and her mother were present from the beginning. There is doubtless something of truth in either contention but not much chance for verification. However, the two avoiding individuals are of different sex and, though it is of less consequence among savages than among us, may easily be of about the same age; and their mutual avoidance is not far from being a sex-taboo.

Doubtless it would be possible to explain certain special cases by showing their expediency under local conditions, if it were not generally impossible to observe those conditions and hazardous to attempt to reconstruct them. We do not see how we can go farther in the explanation of these to us strange folkways than to regard them as adjustments for the safeguarding of sex-taboos or for the assertion of authority. In the former case the issue is thus shifted, as from corollary to proposition, to the explanation of the taboo.[100]

§426*. Artificial Relationship.

The adoption of children has been alluded to in a former connection,[101] and it has been noted

---

[99] Lippert, *Kgchte.*, II, 94, 97, 157 ff.

[100] Ch. XXXI and §§349, 350, above.   [101] §409, above.

that the *ambil-anak* marriage is a species of adoption.[102] The practice of concluding artificial relationship extends much farther than the construction of a parent-child tie; witness the blood-brotherhood.[103] It is significant that the idea of kinship through the blood is so ingrained that those who adopt each other try to make themselves, by interchange of blood, actually consanguine.[104]

In New Guinea the wedding of a pair, who have first eloped, consists in the cutting of the forehead by all participants until the blood flows. It is a sign that they all belong to one another.[105] "The midwives enter into a peculiar relation with the newly-born; they are addressed as 'mother' by the child until the child, if a girl, is itself married or, if a boy, leaves the mother's house to live with the men." If two chiefs like one another, they decide to become relations. Then marriage may not take place between their people because relationship is too close.[106] In the Andaman Islands, "it is said to be of rare occurrence to find any child above six or seven years of age residing with its parents, and this because it is considered a compliment and also a mark of friendship for a married man, after paying a visit, to ask his hosts to allow him to adopt one of their children. The request is usually complied with, and thenceforth the child's home is with his (or her) foster-father: though the parents in their turn adopt the children of other friends, they nevertheless pay continual visits to their own child, and occasionally ask permission to take him (or her) away with them for a few days." This custom of adoption results in the taboo of marriage between those who become related through it; and it assists also in so confusing relationships that they are not recognized beyond the third generation.[107]

On one occasion Livingstone[108] became a blood relation to a young woman by accident. He was removing a large cartilaginous tumor from her arm, when some blood spurted up into the doctor's eye. She said: "You were a friend before; now you are a blood-relation; and when you pass this way, always send me word, that I may cook food for you."

In India relationship exists between those who are joined together by the cake of sacrifice or by the same libation of water.[109] Here is a religious relationship.[110] A Brahman may not adopt any child whose mother he might not have married.[111] In the Pelew Islands, "since it is only the woman who founds a family, only she may adopt or accept children." Trading of children is found here also.[112] There is, in general, no distinction between the real and the adoptive parent.[113]

The Central Eskimo reckon into the family adopted children, widows, and old people. "If for any reason a man is unable to provide for his family, or if a woman cannot do her household work, the children are adopted by a relative

102 §363, above. 103 §150, above.
104 Starcke, *Prim. Fam.*, 143. 105 Krieger, *Neu-Guinea*, 392.
106 Von Pfeil, *Südsee*, 18, 26.
107 Man, in JAI, XII, 125 (quoted), 126, 141.
108 *Mission. Travels*, II, 526. 109 Starcke, *Prim. Fam.*, 96, 102 ff.
110 §349, above. 111 Mateer, in JAI, XII, 295.
112 Kubary, *Pelauer*, 59; Semper, *Palau-Ins.*, 117.
113 Letourneau, *Marriage*, 296.

or a friend, who considers them as his own children. In the same way widows with their children are adopted by their nearest relative or by a friend and belong to the family, though the woman retains her own fireplace."[114] It is well known that the Iroquois and others adopted captured enemies; the relatives of those slain in battle might sacrifice by torture, enslave, or adopt prisoners.[115] Among the Omahas, an uncle by adoption had all the rights of a real uncle. "For example, when Mr. La Fleche's daughter Lusette wished to go to the Indian Territory to accept a situation as a teacher, and had gained the consent of her parents, [the Indian chief] Two Crows interposed, being her uncle by adoption, and forbade her departure."[116]

The Kwakiutl go to great lengths in forming an artificial relationship when inheritance of a name is in question. "The law of descent through marriage is so rigid that methods have developed to prevent the extinction of a name when its bearer has no daughter. In such a case a man who desires to acquire the use of the crest and the other privileges connected with the name performs a sham marriage with the son of the bearer of the name. . . . The ceremony is performed in the same manner as a real marriage. In case the bearer of the name has no children at all, a sham marriage with a part of his body is performed, with his right or left side, a leg or an arm, and the privileges are conveyed in the same manner as in the case of a real marriage."[117] Among the Shingu Indians the man who puts on a boy's symbol of manhood for him the first time becomes related to him by marriage, and marries either the boy's sister or aunt.[118]

An Egyptian picture represents a goddess as giving the breast to a king, thus adopting him into the divine family according to the ceremony of adoption.[119] In Egypt adoption was a mode of making a will in favor of an outsider.[120] In the Roman family relationship by rites existed; a client was a sort of artificial kinsman.[121]

Among the southern Slavs "artificial kinship stands so high as a bar to any union that even spouses, with a view to amicable separation, take recourse to the establishment of brotherhood to secure immediate annulment." Artificial relationship, "apart from being formally concluded by food or cup, by interchange of blood, weapons, or amulets, arises also *ipso jure* through the nursing relation, common pilgrimage, Jordan-bath, or the best-man relation." In one case, "in a Montenegrin frontier-village, a priest consecrated six neighbors of a murdered girl to be her blood-brothers, for the purpose of stern blood-vengeance on the guilty Dalmatians."[122] Among other Slavs, a man may ask a woman whom he specially respects to adopt him as a son. He and she fast for several days, and then in the presence of witnesses she gives him the breast. They esteem this relationship very highly and consider it closer than any blood-tie, so that marriage between the persons or their children is tabooed.[123]

[114] Boas, in BAE, VI, 580.
[115] §§140, 141, 188, above; Letourneau, *Marriage*, 292.
[116] Dorsey, in BAE, III, 265.   [117] Boas, in USNM, 1895, 359.
[118] Von den Steinen, *Zent. Bras.*, 501.   [119] Maspero, *Hist. Anc.*, I, 263.
[120] Paturet, *Cond. Jurid.*, 27.   [121] De Coulanges, *Cité Ant.*, 59.
[122] Ciszewski, rev. in *Globus*, LXXII, 163.
[123] *Russ. Ethnog.* (Russ.), II, 316; Hahn, "Milchverwandtschaft," in *Globus*, LXXII, 116.

Foster-relationship, as may have been gathered from foregoing cases, likewise plays a considerable rôle in undeveloped societies.

In South Africa, where adoption is not practised, the foster-relation is common. A rich man often maintains a number of children of poor parents, "to drink milk." These foster-children get as much care and affection from their foster-parents "as is represented to have existed among the Highlanders of Scotland."[124] The practice virtually represents the native system of poor-law, for the rich are bound to help the poor; yet there is a real relationship formed. Of the Nair child we read: "No kind of food except the mother's milk is given to it, and, if the mother died at the birth of the child, it is generally given the milk of some relations or even of outsiders who have children of almost the same age. The person whose milk the child thus drinks, though she be an outsider, is considered equal to its own mother, and her children are considered the same as own brothers. There is a story of a . . . king who as a child lost his mother and was therefore fed on the milk of an attendant woman, refusing to punish her son after repeated acts of treason on the ground that an ocean of milk flowed between them which a drop of blood would pollute for ever."[125] In Sumatra, "foster-relationship is conceived to exist when a child has been suckled three times by the nurse." This relationship and that of blood are so closely associated in the local Mohammedan law that a non-member of the family is but seldom allowed to nurse a child of the family. If the mother cannot nurse her child, her mother undertakes to do it.[126]

"If kinship means participation in a common mass of flesh, blood and bones, it is natural that it should be regarded as dependent, not merely on the fact that a man was born of his mother's body, and so was from his birth a part of her flesh, but also on the not less significant fact that he was nourished by her milk. And so we find that among the Arabs there is a tie of milk, as well as of blood, which unites the foster-child to his foster-mother and her kin. Again, after the child is weaned, his flesh and blood continue to be nourished and renewed by the food which he shares with his commensals, so that commensality can be thought of (1) as confirming or even (2) as constituting kinship in a very real sense."[127] In the Moslem law there is no marriage between foster-relations.[128]

In ancient Scandinavia he who fostered another's child was his inferior. Harald Harfagar sent his son to the King of England; the boy was put in the king's lap and left, which forced the king to foster him. Harald was greatly pleased at this, "for it is a common observation of all people that the man who fosters another's children is of less consideration than the other."[129] In Ireland teachers and pupils were regarded as in a sacred relation. The teacher was the foster-father and is expressly declared to have had the same *patria potestas* as a real father, and to have been entitled to support through life.[130]

124 Macdonald, in JAI, XIX, 268.
125 Panikkar, in JAI, XLVIII, 273-274.
126 Jacobs, *Groot-Atjeh*, I, 22, 159, 166.
127 Smith, *Relig. Sem.*, 274; Winckler, *Hammurabi*, 31, 32; Von Kremer, *Kgchte.*, II, 113.
128 Tornauw, *Moslem. Recht.*, 64.
129 Laing, *Heimskringla Saga*, I, 393; *Laxdaela Saga*, 84; Leo, *Island*, 480.
130 Maine, *Early Law*, 10.

"This custom of fosterage was another pleasing feature of patriarchal sway."[131]

Cases of artificial relationship are significant chiefly of the strength of the blood-tie; for in the joining of such bonds there is regularly an attempt to reproduce, at least symbolically, the conditions characteristic of the bond of consanguinity.

§427*. Family-Life. It remains to present in this chapter, which gathers up several aspects of the general section not readily classifiable elsewhere, some idea of family-life as it is lived by undeveloped peoples. There is a strong tendency to assume that their domestic relations are analogous to our own, a tendency strengthened by the sentiment that has been read into those Biblical tales, like that of Ruth, which have represented to many the only glimpse accorded into the earlier life of the race. Romantic writers have introduced false ideas about the way savage life is led. Anyone who has read this far in our book needs no injunction about being critical of such imaginative reconstructions. We turn to a set of representative instances from which the true picture of family-life in uncivilization may emerge.

There are some cases of domestic affection—relatively few, so far as our collections reveal—in addition to those alluded to under the status of women and of children.[132]

In Central Australia, "almost everything that is said is prefaced by the appellation of father, son, brother, mother, sister, or some similar term, corresponding to that degree of relationship which would have been most in accordance with their relative ages and circumstances. Often, besides, they add 'dear,' to say nothing of the hugs and embraces given and received. . . . The natives are very fond of the children they rear, and often play with them and fondle them."[133] "Though young women are often compelled to marry men of whom they know nothing their marriages are usually happy ones. Quarrels between husbands and wives are rare, and they show much affection for each other in their own way."[134] Parents-in-law are accorded much consideration.[135]

In New Guinea, conjugal love is often very noticeable. There was one case where a young couple used to go to meet each other as the woman returned from the field or the man from fishing; and there was an old couple who were as affectionate as in youth. Others fought and threw pottery all the time.[136] As for the relation to children, "without being very demonstrative, the parents

131 Garnier, *Brit. Peasantry*, 166.
132 Ch. LII and §410, above.
133 Eyre, *Cent. Aust.*, II, 214.
134 Bonney, in JAI, XIII, 129.
135 Gason, quoted in JAI, XXIV, 170.
136 Hagen, *Papua's*, 243.

like them well enough, and the child is not at all hardly used—although, be it remembered, the family pig has a deeper place in the adults' affections. In times of stress it is to be feared it is the pig that is first considered, probably because it is so important an article of diet. The devotion to this animal goes far further than that of Pat, for it is not unusual to see a Papuan woman acting as foster-mother to a young pig."[137] "It may be said that generally man and wife get on well together, and are united by their great fondness for their children." It might be added that the Melanesians have a special term for parents whose children have intermarried, for which no equivalent exists in English, but which may be translated "fellow-wayfarers." The existence of the term connotes a recognized fellowship hitherto non-existent.[138]

Among the Herero, woman's position is higher than among other South African negroes, "conjugal love does not belong among the uncommon occurrences and the wife is not reduced wholly to the position of beast-of-burden."[139] Miss Kingsley[140] finds sex-affection weak where other associative ties and affections are strong. Among the tribes near the mouth of the Congo, "a man never maltreats his wife and the children are tenderly loved by their mothers."[141] Affection for parents and children is developed among the Dyur much more decidedly than in any other Central African tribe known to Schweinfurth.[142]

In domestic life the Lepchas are gentle and especially kind to their children and elders.[143] Among the Khonds of Bengal any accusation or insult on the part of the husband against his wife would be more than sufficient reason for her to take her own life.[144] "Among the traits by which the Veddahs distinguish themselves from the Cingalese are the praiseworthy strictness and cleanness of their conjugal life and the friendliness with which the women are treated; they live only in monogamy and hold true till death separates them. Characteristic also is it that while the Cingalese is not jealous, the Veddah, on the contrary, is so in a high degree: strangers do not easily get to see Veddah women."[145] Cambodian children respect their parents but are more familiar with their mothers. This continues through life; the king salutes his mother on his knees, as his mandarins salute him.[146]

In Borneo, "I particularly noticed the younger married men standing behind their nice little wives at night when we were at dinner. They folded their brown arms around their necks, and whispered loving gossip into their ears, evidently well contented with themselves and with each other; and, perhaps, their love is as real and as ardent and as true here as it is in high places where dress clothes are worn."[147] In Celebes "the husbands and wives are much attached to one another and eat, when alone, together."[148] In Micronesia it was a violation of accepted morals for a husband to strike his wife or to insult her in public. If an insulted woman is noble the punishment is the same as for

[137] Pratt, *New Guinea*, 330.
[138] Codrington, *Melanesians*, 244, 37.
[139] Fritsch, *Eingeb. S.-Afr.*, 228.   [140] *W. Afr. Studies*, 168.
[141] Henning, in *Globus*, LXXII, 102.
[142] *Heart of Afr.*, I, 212.   [143] Waddell, *Himalayas*, 100.
[144] Reclus, *Prim. Folk*, 260.   [145] Schmidt, *Ceylon*, 277.
[146] Leclère, in PSM, XLIV, 777.   [147] Roth, *Sarawak*, I, 129.
[148] Riedel, in *Bijd.*, XXXV, 79.

murder. It is the greatest insult to a husband to speak ill of his wife; indeed it is not permitted even to name her.[149]

As the Greenland husband and wife grow older they learn to like one another; divorce rarely occurs if there are sons.[150] Concerning the Indians of the northwest coast "it is the universal testimony . . . that 'they treat their wives and children with much affection and tenderness.' "[151]

It might be noted that forms of expressing affection are a matter of the mores. The kiss, for example, is regarded by most primitive peoples as foolish or disgusting. "To blacks, kissing is a 'white-foolishness,' also handshaking: in olden times even to smell a stranger was considered a risk." In the D'Entrecasteaux Islands, "kissing is quite unknown. The natives were horrified one day when they saw a missionary kiss his wife. They thought he was trying to bite her." It is reported that to the Japanese kissing is so repugnant that they erected a huge bamboo screen around Rodin's "The Kiss," when on exhibition in Japan, in order that "the sensibilities of the public may not be shocked."[152] Snuffing with the nose or rubbing noses is much commoner; in India, "instead of pressing lip to lip, they apply the mouth and nose to the cheek and give a strong inhalation. In their language they say 'Smell me,' instead of 'Give me a kiss.' " Of certain Borneans we learn that "in their language the verbs *to smell* and *to kiss* are the same."[153]

The aspect of family-life which seems strangest to us is the element of separation in it; in fact, it does not look to one like family-life at all, any more than does the joint-family previously described.[154] It is a fact that almost deserves the name of a principle that kindly feeling thrives on proximity. That absence makes the heart grow fonder is a sentimental and doubtful saying that certainly does not apply to savage men of short memory. It took absentee-ownership to bring about the worst exhibitions of the slave-system.[155] In any case, it is a fact that family-life among a number of primitive peoples precludes much intimacy between husband and wife and is not characterized by the kindly feeling or

[149] Ratzel, *Vkde.*, II, 186.   [150] Cranz, *Grönland*, I, 194.
[151] Niblack, in USNM, 1888, 238.
[152] Parker, *Euahlayi*, 126; Jenness and Ballentyne, *D'Entrecasteaux*, 96-97; §367 of *Case-Book;* N. Y. *Herald Tribune*, May 18, 1926.
[153] Lewin, *S.E. India*, 118; Furness, *Head-Hunters*, 13; Hopkins, "Sniff-Kiss," in *Jr. Am. Orient. Soc.*, XXVIII, 20 ff.; Peschel, *Races*, 22, 237; Codrington, *Melanesians*, 354; Gentz, in *Globus*, LXXXV, 80; Ellis, *Ewe*, 207; Ellis, *Tshi*, 288; Granville and Roth, in JAI, XXVIII, 107; Brunache, *Cent. Afr.*, 78; French-Sheldon, in JAI, XXI, 383; Sibree, *Great Afr. Isl.*, 209; D'Enjoy, in *Bull. Soc. d'Anth. Paris*, ser. IV, tome 8, fasc., 2; Tamura, *Warum Heiraten Wir?*, 52; Ratzel, *Vkde.*, I, 592; Man, in JAI, XVIII, 368; Finsch, *Ethnol. Erfahr.*, III, 29; Becke, *Pacific Tales*, 179; Holm, *Ethnol. Skizze*, 55; Lumholtz, in *Scribner's Mag.*, XVI, 299; Von Martius, *Beiträge*, I, 96; Spix u. Martius, *Brasilien*, 1216.
[154] §414, above.   [155] §104, above.

real affection seen in several of the rather exceptional cases cited above. Husband and wife might speak different languages and have different mores. They had different work and food and they ate apart. They might have diverse totems and gods. They might not even be friends. One must recall the instances illustrative of the position of woman[156] in order to attain to a fuller understanding of the nature of family-life.

The husband and wife use their own tribal languages in West Victoria; so that all conversation is carried on between them "in the same way as between an Englishman and a French woman, each speaking his or her own language."[157] Men and their wives in Melanesia and Polynesia are generally strangers to each other, occupying separate houses.[158] The man "goes about in the forest and on the shore and sees as little as possible of the wife; but the counterpart to the lacking tenderness is at least a quiet peacefulness and noisy, scolding marriages are a great exception."[159] After the first night the husband usually sleeps in the assembly-house and where there are barracks for both men and women the pairs meet in the forest at trysting-places.[160] It is to be noted how generally over the world the men live virtually by themselves in the so-called men's houses.[161]

"The woes of daughters-in-law in China should form the subject rather for a chapter than for a brief paragraph. . . . Parents can do absolutely nothing to protect their married daughters, other than remonstrating with the families into which they have married, and exacting an expensive funeral if the daughters should be actually driven to suicide." Suicides of young wives are excessively frequent, and in some regions scarcely a group of villages can be found where they have not recently occurred. "What can be more pitiful than a mother's reproaches to a married daughter who has attempted suicide and been rescued: 'Why didn't you die when you had a chance?'" The demands of propriety keep family-members apart in an arbitrary way. The beating of the wife belongs to good form.[162] The Manchu bride "stands in absolute dependence upon her mother-in-law to whom she owes unconditional obedience." When a Chinese girl marries she is no longer the daughter in her own family but some one else's daughter-in-law. When she goes home, it is on a business basis. She takes sewing which her own family must help her do; or she takes children who are thus kept out of the way of her husband's family and must be supported by the maternal grandmother. Where daughters and their children are numerous these visits are a constant source of terror and tax. Hence fathers and brothers discourage them, though the mothers may secretly invite them.[163]

In Borneo, "during the time that a child is still nursing at the mother's breast, there is that instinctive, protective parental affection observable in all mating animals; but after the child is weaned and is able to toddle, it is al-

156 Chs. L, LI, above.   157 Dawson, *Aust. Aborig.*, 40.
158 Crawley, in JAI, XXIV, 231.   159 Von Pfeil, *Südsee*, 30.
160 Krieger, *Neu-Guinea*, 301, 392.   161 §162, above.
162 Smith, *Chinese Char.*, 201; De Groot, *Relig. Syst.*, I, 3; Legge, *Li Ki*, I, 77, 470 ff.; Williams, *Middle Kingdom*, I, 795; Klugmann, *Frau im Talmud*, 55.
163 Grube, in *Veröffentl. K. Museum f. Völkerkunde*, VII, 27; Smith, *Chinese Char.*, 199.

lowed to ramble pretty much where it will, and to take its educational bumps and tumbles without parental worry. Mother Nature provides the only clothes it wears, and, after her own healing, scarifying fashion, darns the rents and tears that they may receive. Among the young boys and girls there is a sort of playmate affection, whenever self-sacrifice is not necessary, and where the one who plans the game or sport always expects to be and is the principal player. Between adults, be they the nearest of kin or be they even lovers, I think I am safe in saying that there is no such thing as unselfish love; a youth would never think of resigning a comfortable place in a boat to his father, or to his mother, or to his sister, or even to his sweetheart. When a man comes back from a long, and perhaps dangerous, expedition, he does not fall into the arms of his family amid tears of joy and welcome; but he walks up the notched log and stalks along the public veranda, looking neither to the right nor to the left until he deposits his burden opposite his own door, and there he sits down, lights a cigarette, and tries to act and look as if he had just come in from the rice-field after a day's work. There is not a greeting of any kind whatsoever exchanged on either side: but after a while, and little by little, an admiring group of men and boys gather round and slowly he unbends, telling scraps of news about friends or foes in the country whence he is come, until at last he is haranguing the people and acting 'Sir Oracle' in the centre of a circle of gaping mouths and unwinking eyes. It is the same were he about to start off on an expedition; no kerchiefs are waved to him nor do eyes stream with tears as his canoe pushes off from the shore; he goes down to the boat with his parcels in just the same matter-of-fact manner as if he were only going to cross the river for fire-wood."[164] "The husband appears seldom or not at all in public with his wife alone; he may not walk with her unless there are more persons along. A transgression in this respect would be looked upon as a defect in form, as uncultivated."[165] Young wives are always being ordered about and scolded by their husbands' mothers: "I have known cases where husband and wife have separated simply because the mother-in-law has made the life of the wife unbearable."[166]

Among the Mohammedan Arabs "that which we call 'family life' seldom or never exists"; servile deference of wife, children, and slaves is in the order of events. The husband does not eat with his wife but is served by her; and he never goes about with her. In more barbaric times he was the guardian of her honor; "she sees in the degree of his jealousy the measure of her worth to him and from this point of view learns to value even his blows."[167]

Slavic life reveals little harmony in families; all members of a joint-family often live in strife. Folk-songs play about the poisoning of wives by husbands. The bride becomes the slave of her parents-in-law; she seldom sees her husband alone, by reason of the taboos, and finds her friends in his brothers, especially the elder ones. "Often it might inspire pity in a stone, how sadly the mother mourns her son, or the sister her brother. But it would be a shame for the wife if she wanted to mourn her husband, and still more for a bride to mourn her groom."[168]

[164] Furness, *Head-Hunters*, 141-142.
[165] Jacobs, *Groot-Atjeh*, I, 71. [166] Gomes, *Sea Dyaks*, 125.
[167] Pischon, *Islam*, 15, 32, 33; Wellhausen, *Ehe*, 451-452.
[168] Kostomarov, *Gt. Russians* (Russ.), 158; Ralston, *Russ. People*, 21; Krauss, *Südslaven*, 8; Rhamm, in *Globus*, LXXXII, 191, 192, 193.

Family-life, as we know it, has evidently evolved out of a domestic existence highly repellent to our mores, being in this respect not so different from the rest of the societal forms which have been reviewed. Attachments ran along other lines than the ones which we are accustomed to regard as primordial and inevitable. This could scarcely be otherwise in the light of the undeveloped family-organization, the status of women and children, the ideas of descent, and the other underlying and conditioning factors which we have come to know. In particular is to be noted the custom whereby boys and men lived together in the club-house, an institution of a religious and political character which has been noticed elsewhere.[169] So long as the substructure of the family and its organization remained what they were in adjustment to life-conditions under uncivilization, the domestic relations were bound to show what seems to us an astonishing oddity. As one reflects, however, upon the life-conditions encountered by struggling mankind and the notions that filled the minds of unenlightened men, the wonder is rather that the family-relations of undeveloped peoples show as much kindliness as they do; and then he notes that there was, after all, a high survival-value in intra-group peace and good feeling and in a stress toward cheerful coöperation that was bound, in time, to wear away the roughnesses and reduce the friction. With the alleviation of the struggle comes the opportunity for the development of the higher forms of emotional life.

§428*. Treatment of the Old. This last consideration is illustrated in the treatment accorded to the aged. The old and weak are a severe burden upon people who are struggling for existence and they have come to lack just that quality of strength which savages understand and respect. It is no wonder, therefore, that they are often put to death or abandoned, especially when their people must keep on the move in order to sustain themselves. On the other hand, age is surrounded by a certain menace, to us wholly superstitious; for the old are presently to die and become ghosts capable of taking vengeance. Also the old are the repositories of tradition and wisdom and the conservators of the mores, which lends to them a prestige that is seldom ignored. Further, it must

169 §162, above.

not be imagined that even the killing of the old is regarded by the victims as an unfriendly act; for the religious views of savage peoples are often such as to lead to a desire for death. If the deceased is to enter the future life as he left this one, he does not always wish to postpone departure so as to be decrepit in the next world. The killing of the old is in many cases an act based upon direct and logical inferences from eidolism; they are sent to rejoin their ancestors and they wish to go. The entrance of the religious factor, where the aged are expedited, not because they are burdensome but by reason of some belief that it is for their benefit, makes their execution an extreme and ultimate service of respect and honor. There are no ideas about the sanctity of human life or that no one but God has a right to terminate existence to stand in the way of merciless logic in the face of sharply sensed conditions and unshakenly accredited beliefs.[170]

Strange to record, the treatment of old women seems to be kindlier, according to our standards, than that of old men; it is possible that the closer relationship to the mother, which has appeared under several of the foregoing topics, is responsible for this.[171] On the other hand, where the old are killed from duty or as a favor, with the safeguarding of their future status in mind, woman is of so much less account than man that her exemption is an evidence of indifference rather than of preferment.

With these preliminary considerations in mind we turn to the cases, and first to a set illustrative of the honor accorded to the old. Along with these should be aligned the evidence for the political importance of the elders as developed elsewhere.[172]

In parts of Australia, the aged are well treated, and certain superior foods are reserved for them. It has been noted that the old men often have the rights to the young women. Disrespect to the old is considered a great fault.[173] In the D'Entrecasteaux Islands, along with the tender treatment of children goes respect for age. "Children are invariably well treated; no man would dream of beating his own child, while to lay a hand on another's would inevitably lead to a brawl. The old are reverenced and cared for with a tenderness that would shame many a more civilized people. It is touching to mark the respect

[170] Sumner, *Folkways*, ch. VII; Lippert, *Kgchte.*, I, 229 ff.
[171] Lippert, *Kgchte.*, I, 325.   [172] §§153, 159, above.
[173] Spencer and Gillen, *Nat. Tr. Cent. Aust.*, 51; Parker, *Euahlayi*, 79; Smyth, *Vict.*, I, 137; Ratzel, *Vkde.*, II, 22.

which even the children feel towards them, and the promptness with which they obey their wishes."[174]

Rivers[175] has a chapter on Melanesian "Gerontocracy"; he makes a good deal of this topic, seeming to regard the lodgment of power in the hands of the old men as a regular stage in the development of Melanesian society. There are many anomalous cases of relationship, such as where a woman's children are considered as younger brothers and sisters of her father, or where "it was a normal occurrence for a man to marry the granddaughter of his brother, using the term brother either in the English or the classificatory sense," which, the author thinks, are inexplicable except under what he calls a gerontocracy. He goes on to show how a man might marry a woman two generations older than himself, explaining all these curious cases as due to the dominance of the old men. He thinks it was once possible for them to monopolize all the young women of the community, "the young women of each moiety becoming as a matter of course the wives of the elders of the other moiety." Whatever may be thought of his theory, certainly he assembles much evidence for the dominance of age throughout Melanesia, as well as in Australia.

In the Andaman and Nicobar Islands the old are treated kindly and allowed to live as long as they can.[176] The Herero father is much respected, keeping his title to his property even when his son has taken over the care of it. The milk-pails and joints of meat are brought to him to bless. There is great reverence for a father's grave.[177] The Gold Coast negroes and their neighbors have great respect for old age; public opinion is very strong on this point.[178] In the Sudan "respect of the young for the old has become a compelling social law," and the same is true among the tribes toward the east.[179] The Hovas of Madagascar have an exaggerated respect for age; if two slaves have a load to carry, the younger tries to carry the whole.[180]

A Kalmuk youth does not sit down before old people or show himself before them without a girdle. The old may not be contradicted.[181] Old age is honored among the wild tribes of India and in Borneo the young men restrict themselves in the assemblies to saying "Amen" to all that the elders wish.[182] Cranz[183] found the Greenlanders taking good care of their aged parents. The Omahas and Ponkas "never leave aged and infirm people in the prairie. They were left at home until the return of the hunting party." They addressed the thunder-god as grandfather, "the term of highest respect in the language."[184] On the northwest coast, "they have great respect for the aged, whose advice in most matters has great weight. Some of the older women, even bond women in former times, attain great influence in the tribe as soothsayers, due as much to

[174] Jenness and Ballentyne, *D'Entrecasteaux*, 202-203.
[175] *Melan. Soc.*, II, ch. XVII, and index, *sub* "gerontocracy."
[176] Man, in JAI, XII, 93; Man, in JAI, XVIII, 384.
[177] Ratzel, *Hist. of Mankind*, II, 468.
[178] Vortisch, in *Globus*, LXXXIX, 281; Granville and Roth, in JAI, XXVIII, 109.
[179] Nachtigal, *Sahara*, II, 176; Vannutelli e Citerni, *L'Omo*, 448.
[180] Ratzel, *Vkde.*, II, 511.
[181] *Russ. Ethnog.* (Russ.), II, 445; Von Haxthausen, *Transkaukasia*, II, 35.
[182] Lewin, *S.E. India*, 256; Nieuwenhuis, *Borneo*, I, 102.
[183] *Grönland*, I, 197.
[184] Dorsey, in BAE, III, 274; Fletcher, in JAI, XXVII, 441.

their venerable appearance as to any pretense they may make of working medicine charms."[185] The Mayas of Yucatan revered parents and respected elders and so did the Ges of South America. "According to the laws of the Incas, the old who were not capable of other employment had to scare off the birds from the fields and in return were, together with the blind, dumb, and lame, maintained at public cost."[186]

It is naturally the cases of a tenor opposite to this of deference and honor which require fuller illustration, for it is fair to say that, whether good treatment of the old was motived in affection, in ghost-fear, or in other less understandable notions, yet it is really characteristic of mankind. The exceptional cases, while not great rarities,[187] serve to illustrate adjustments under rather special conditions. It is particularly to be borne in mind in scanning them and in reflecting over their meaning, that respect for age and killing of the aged are by no means incompatible. We have not sought to separate the instances where the death of the aged is due to contempt for age and irritation at its burdensomeness from those where death is conferred as a sort of boon, and at their own request, upon those who are held in honor. It is not necessary to do so if the compatibility of an attitude and an action, to us utterly irreconcilable, be kept steadily in mind.

Among the Murray River people an old woman who broke her thigh was left to die as the tribe did not want to be bothered with her. People were treated in the same way when helpless and infirm. "When old people become infirm, and unable to accompany the tribe in its wanderings, it is lawful and customary to kill them. The reasons for this are—that they are a burden to the tribe, and, should any attack be made by an enemy, they are the most liable to be captured, when they would probably be tortured and put to a lingering death. . . . Very often the poor creatures intended to be strangled cry and beg for delay . . . but all in vain. The resolution is always carried out," and at the hand of a relative deputed for the purpose.[188] In New Guinea the old are buried alive. "Nothing seems more inhuman than the practice of burying sick and aged people alive, yet it is certain that when this was done there was generally a kindness intended. It is true that sometimes the relatives of the sick became tired of waiting upon them, and buried them when they thought they ought to be ready for it; but even in such cases the sick and aged acquiesced. It was common for them to beg their friends to put them out of their

[185] Niblack, in USNM, 1888, 240.

[186] Le Plongeon, in PSM, XLIV, 662; Von Martius, *Beiträge*, I, 126, note, 274.

[187] Examples in Sumner, *Folkways*, §§330 ff.; Letourneau, *Morale*, 113 ff.; Tylor, *Anth.*, 409-411.

[188] Eyre, *Cent. Aust.*, II, 321; Dawson, *Aust. Aborig.*, 62.

misery."[189] The Solomon Islands represent "a community where no respect whatever is shown by youth to age."[190]

In the New Hebrides, the custom of burying old men alive, "which has prevailed evidently since the beginning of the race, is only kept alive by the old men; the younger ones show an absolute distaste for it. Directly a man or woman shows signs of decrepitude or helplessness, those who are nearest to that stage themselves tell him that his time has come, and that his burial will take place on such and such a date. On the arrival of the day, the grave for the intended victim is dug, and, in front of a large crowd, the old man is led or carried to it—if he be too weak to get into it himself. He is then stretched out at full length, and, whilst incantations are sung, the earth is thrown over him, and willing hands soon have the ground level and solid above him, and the old man is left there to die. The spectators of this ghastly scene then adjourn to a feast, which is to many of them the most important part of the ceremony. In some cases the buried man has had sufficient strength left in him to upheave the earth and rise out of his grave, and has even attempted to join the feast, but he has been still considered dead, and no one has given him food. If he be strong enough and can obtain food for himself, he is buried again and again, until at last he has to die from pure exhaustion, if nothing else. Should, however, a very tough customer be met with, and it is found that he refuses to die, and each time gets out of his grave, he is strangled before being buried again; for once his death sentence has been passed it must be carried out—he is a dead man from that hour and nothing can save him. I may add that directly the man is buried his property is divided amongst the villagers, so that if he were allowed to come back he would be a homeless wanderer, and no one would have anything to do with him."[191]

A Greenland man "upbraided his mother-in-law because she was so old that she was good for nothing, and said that he could not understand why she did not die. Thereupon she went down to the shore and drowned herself."[192]

A classic case is the one related by Catlin:[193] "The tribe were going where hunger and dire necessity compelled them to go, and this pitiable object, who had once been a chief, and a man of distinction in his tribe, who was now too old to travel, being reduced to mere skin and bones, was to be left to starve, or meet with such death as might fall to his lot, and his bones to be picked by the wolves! I lingered around this poor old forsaken patriarch for hours before we started, to indulge the tears of sympathy which were flowing for the sake of this poor benighted and decrepit old man, whose worn-out limbs were no longer able to support him, their kind and faithful offices having long since been performed, and his body and his mind doomed to linger into the withering agony of decay and gradual solitary death. I wept, and it was a pleasure to weep, for the painful looks and the dreary prospects of this old veteran, whose eyes were dimmed, whose venerable locks were whitened by an hundred years, whose limbs were almost naked and trembling as he sat by a small fire which his friends had left him, with a few sticks of wood within his reach and a buffalo's skin stretched upon some crotches over his head. Such was to be his only dwelling, and such the chances for his life, with only a few half-picked

[189] Codrington, *Melanesians*, 347.   [190] Woodford, *Head-Hunters*, 25.
[191] Hardy and Elkington, *S. Seas*, 145-147.
[192] Holm, *Ethnol. Skizze*, 139.
[193] Donaldson, in *Smithson. Rep.*, 1885, pt. II, 429, 430.

bones that were laid within his reach, and a dish of water, without weapon or means of any kind to replenish them, or strength to move his body from its fatal locality. In this sad plight I mournfully contemplated this miserable remnant of existence, who had unluckily outlived the fates and accidents of wars to die alone, at death's leisure. His friends and his children had all left him, and were preparing in a little time to be on the march. He had told them to leave him; 'he was old,' he said, 'and too feeble to march.' 'My children,' said he, 'our nation is poor, and it is necessary that you should all go to the country where you can get meat; my eyes are dimmed and my strength is no more; my days are nearly all numbered, and I am a burden to my children; I cannot go, and I wish to die. Keep your hearts stout, and think not of me; I am no longer good for anything.' In this way they had finished the ceremony of exposing him, and taken their final leave of him. I advanced to the old man and was undoubtedly the last human being who held converse with him. I sat by the side of him, and though he could not distinctly see me, he shook me heartily by the hand and smiled, evidently aware that I was a white man, and that I sympathized with his inevitable misfortune. . . . This cruel custom of exposing their aged people belongs, I think, to all the tribes who roam about the prairies, making severe marches, when such decrepit persons are totally unable to go, unable to ride or to walk, when they have no means of carrying them. It often becomes absolutely necessary in such cases that they should be left; and they uniformly insist upon it, saying, as this old man did, that they are old and of no further use, that they left their fathers in the same manner, that they wish to die, and their children must not mourn for them."

"The old German right allowed the son to expose his parents, when feeble with age, and give them over to starvation." It often came to pass. At a time of famine in Iceland it was decided to kill all the old and unproductive. The old Swedish "family-clubs," which used to be kept in the churches, were used in ancient times solemnly to put to death the aged and hopelessly sick and the same sort of sacrosanct instrument was kept in temples elsewhere in Europe. "Aubrey has preserved an old English 'countrie story' of 'the holy mawle which (they fancy) hung behind the church dore, which, when the father was seaventie, the sonne might fetch to knock his father on the head as effete and of no more use. . . . Sir Percival, in his adventures in quest of the Holy Grail, being at one time ill at ease, congratulates himself that he is not like those men of Wales, where sons pull their fathers out of bed and kill them to save the disgrace of their dying in bed."[194]

Though many centenarians are to be encountered in Russia, "the old are looked upon rather with fear than with respect." People over a hundred years old are called by a term that means "beings who practise evil magic-arts"; they are believed to be able to kill men with the breath; "in times of epidemics they were held responsible for the calamity and were condemned to death by fire."[195]

Some cases of killing the king or the priest doubtless go back to the execution of the father. Frazer's *Golden Bough* was written with the idea of explaining the slaughter of the priest of Nemi and his unrivalled set of instances include many which might enforce the ones here presented. He carries the custom off into religious and political developments and sequels which do not belong to primitive life.

[194] Gomme, *Ethnol. in Folklore*, 136.   [195] Stern, *Russland*, 476.

Any discussion of the treatment of the aged should be aligned with the facts about the treatment of children and of women, for the covering question is as to how the physically weak are to be handled amidst the exigencies of life. Killing the old is parallel in several respects with infanticide[196] and there is an element of human sacrifice in both. The former, however, is distinctly more of a population-policy, or maintenance-measure, than is infanticide, for the old are more of a burden and there is little or nothing to hope from their preservation. Though they have experience, which the child has not, they are often in a condition where they are unable to profit anyone by it. They often see this themselves, as did the old Indian chief. They are virtually worthless and no practical considerations could speak for their preservation.

Mere sentiment is not highly developed among primitive peoples; for its expression it needs considerable ease of mind as respects the struggle for existence. It is unable to withstand the pressure of menacing circumstance, even among civilized men; Fremont and his party left their weak and dying members, one by one, after lighting a fire for them, to perish in the snow[197] much as the savages have done under like pressing circumstances. The difference is that the civilized man feels the pinch only occasionally, while the savage senses it, near or afar, almost all the time. It is noticeable that the arctic peoples and those whose livelihood demands constant movement are represented largely among the killers of the old and infirm. It seems entirely probable that the effort to disburden themselves was the prime cause for the killing of the old among the most backward peoples, and so among mankind.

The services which age can render to the kin-group are clearly not so obvious where the struggle for existence is intense. There is nothing more highly prized later on in the evolutionary stages than the seasoned wisdom and knowledge of tradition and precedent of which the old are repositories. It is evident that the treatment of the aged corresponds broadly to the services which they are thought to render. Their status is dependent upon the recognition of their value that accompanies basic changes in the socie-

196 §404, above.
197 Thayer, *New West*, 231 (quoting Fremont's letter to his wife).

tal organization. Among people not so primitive the mores come to enjoin quite generally the care of the old, and that cannot but mean the care of even the useless aged. Nevertheless, there is no opportunity for the development of this humanitarian aspect of the issue until men have freed themselves from the constant menace of failure in the struggle for existence by accumulating capital and otherwise erecting barriers against nature and the aleatory element. Then after a time the ancient customs, which are generally the only adjustments expedient under their conditions, dwindle away, persisting only in the form of unrecognizable and rationalized survivals and at length the evolved code confronts the primordial one in direct antithesis. It follows that those who practise the former must look upon the latter with horror and upon those isolated groups who still practise it as inhuman or perversely rebellious against "the moral sense" or some other fictitious substruction.

CHAPTER LVIII

RETROSPECTIVE

§429. The Maintenance-Substructure. The societal forms considered in the last seventeen chapters, while they all have their roots in the industrial organization and their intimate connections with property, the regulative system, and religion, would not have been evolved except for the presence of human bi-sexuality. In a true sense marriage is the form taken by societal self-maintenance when the element of sex is injected into it, just as religion is the form displayed on the entrance of the aleatory element and of the conception of the spirit-environment. Maintenance is the generic activity of society, of which the industrial, regulative, religious, and marital organizations are specific manifestations. The presence of the element of sex means that the race is split into halves which, wholly dissimilar, must coöperate if society is to exist and reproduce itself; and that is something that society insists upon doing. While it is true that the sexes, in their thoroughgoing differentiation, have never comprehended each other, still their qualities are readily seen upon analysis to be complementary and to have constituted the basis for effective, albeit antagonistic, coöperation, when once the necessities of living have forced man and woman into unplanned association. The basic fact is that the sexes, different though they are, must associate and somehow get along together. The several forms of marriage are the ways evolved for accomplishing that manifest destiny.

These institutional forms have developed in the usual way out of blocks of mores representing accretions about cores of interest. Out of a mass of scrambling and groping tentatives have been carved, by the cutting blade of societal selection, sets of regular and traditional procedure. Out of unregulation has sprung regulation. The sexes must coöperate along lines demonstrated ultimately by survival, though proximately by public opinion, to be expedient ones. Interests of spouses, children, parents, kindred, and group-members in general must be and are, in effect, somehow harmonized. When the groups are small and loosely organized, there are fewer of these interests in the field and the regulation is not so intense; as societies enlarge and evolve a wider, more complex, and closer organization, the regulation of marriage takes on a more comprehensive and at the same time more intense form and the characteristic institution develops sharper and harder outlines. The successive adjustments to a progressively more complicated set of societal life-conditions fall into an evolutionary series the study of which reveals the essential nature of the marriage-institution.

Regulation is exercised over the personnel and the manner of marriage—what we have called the who, the how, and the how many—and over the status of the parties brought into the relations of wedlock. It prescribes the way of entering, of occupying, and of terminating that relationship. In so doing it cannot reach, however, beyond the relatively superficial, visible, public aspects of the case; it is incapable of penetrating into the subtle privacies, for they are too multiform, insubstantial, and intangible to submit to the necessarily rough classifications upon which law and even the mores must perforce rest. Regulation can lay off circles within or outside of which marriage may not take place; it can prescribe a variety of ceremonial and ritual in the absence of which union is not valid; it can enumerate the number of pairings into which male or female may enter; it can fix spheres of rights and duties within the status of matrimony and set up criteria for its assessment. In doing all this it must needs, however, deal with ages, classes, numbers, material possessions and considerations, and ritual acts rather than with individual differences, motives, moods, and other imponderables. Nevertheless the roughness of its rubrics and its inevitable undiscriminating indifference to the finer shadings of individual relationships have by no means nullified its efficiency in securing society-wise adjustment to the permanent life-condition of sex. This can be readily perceived and appreciated by anyone whose mind is not obsessed by the all-importance of the individual and his "psychology" and "choices," that is, by anyone who is able to distinguish a science of society that deals with aggregates from an amorphous composite of random observations with no distinctiveness or excuse for existence.

From one very revealing point of view the various relationships established by marriage may be regarded as no more than a special framework convenient to the pursuit of group-maintenance. Kinship-designations are names for the several stations occupied by individuals in the joint organization; they fix the relations of its members as respects the distribution of property and other forms of power; they are somewhat like the military terms which place the individual components of an army as corporals, sergeants, and the rest. If it were not for this very material and practical service in locating the individual within the field of coöperation in living which is discharged by terms of relationship, of what use would they be? The savage has no interest in labelling persons for the mere pleasure of attaining orderliness. The conception of blood-kinship affords a set of designations that are convenient counters in the real game of society's self-maintenance. The condition of bi-sexuality imposes sex-wise coöperation plus cohabitation; the coming of children means the development of the family as a characteristic maintenance-unit; the passage of time brings with it inter-family relations and larger kindred aggregates, which are still maintenance-combinations, as indicated by their corporate responsibility and solidarity. Thus both the smaller and the more extensive kin-groups may reasonably be regarded as maintenance-organizations formed upon and making use of the framework of real or fictitious relationship. It is because these coöperative bodies, from the smallest family up, have as one of their chief functions, though it is by no means their only one, the rearing of the next generation that they do not belong strictly under societal self-maintenance. If, however, they are distinguished and set apart from other types of maintenance-combinations on the basis of this particular feature of self-perpetuation, it is the more necessary to keep in mind their essential function as maintenance-expedients. It is the variations in life-conditions, chiefly economic, which make and slowly modify the marriage-institution, producing the innumerable minor variations which are encountered along the course of its evolution.

§430*. The Function of Idealization. There can be no object in rehearsing by way of formal summary the argument of the foregoing chapters on societal self-perpetuation; unless certain large aspects of the subject can be disengaged and reinforced, as in the preceding paragraphs, there seems to be no call for a retrospect. There are, however, several aspects of modern marriage the consideration of which amounts to recalling certain important factors and lines of development touched upon hitherto but not pursued into their later phases as far as, not without profit, they might be.

It must be understood that the outward forms of modern Occidental marriage are largely a heritage from the Old and New Testaments as interpreted by ecclesiastical authorities. Just because the fundamentals of the marriage-institution in any age are a function of the mores of that age, moderns have taken from the Scriptures only what has seemed appropriate and have rejected, ignored, or interpreted what has been felt to be inconsonant with contemporary mores. They have also read into the Bible, if some sanction has seemed to be required for the modern code, what is not there at all. Nevertheless the outer forms of modern marriage among Christian nations have been largely molded, as we have said, by ideas derived from what is now known as the Near-East. Perhaps the most high-minded conception of matrimony according to modern standards is the fusion of life and interest of a man and woman, with special reference to the procreation and rearing of offspring, although the enhancement of their own happiness in life enters as a real and legitimate part into the constitution of matrimony and into their purposes in entering it.

The marriage-institution is a legitimate field of idealization.[1] If idealization means something of what Tyndall[2] called the scientific use of the imagination it can have no evil effects at all. Idealization in the form of a straining after better satisfaction has had and has so much to do with the evolution of marriage that its scientific importance on this domain must be recognized. It is not, therefore, a flat condemnation of youthful enthusiasm to point out that, when matrimony is contemplated, young people are almost always under the dominion of unrealities and unrealizable ideals; it belongs to youth and to the situation that they should be so. The sage who should warn them that they are likely to find their golden dreams all delusions would show no wisdom and perform

1 §462, below.   2 In Fragments of Sci., ch. XXX.

no service to them or to society. Their ideals have often been false, having been adopted in ignorance, especially by women. They may be formed from novels which are written from all sorts of motives but rarely from a desire to present true ideals of wedlock. According to many popular tales every boy and girl ought to expect some grand convulsive experience of love, which comes of itself, cannot be reasoned with, and must be obeyed. That divorces are more frequent on this system than they were when parents chose the spouses of their children is not strange, for it is as fantastic as the frank extravagance of the old romances and far more delusive. Fortunately foolish notions are quickly corrected and become the subject of ridicule before they do any harm. If the ideal is dissipated after marriage the case is more serious.

Indeed, novels have been wont to deal either with the entrance into wedlock—wooing, betrothal, and wedding—or with the dissolution of wedlock—adultery and divorce. Wedlock is represented in them only through the parents and other relatives who fill subordinate rôles in relation to the parties who are, generally more or less spasmodically, "in love." If the representations which are given of these people who have been in wedlock for a number of years, and of their relations to each other, were grouped together and studied, in contrast with the accounts of the lovers, their relations to each other, and their purposes and promises up to the wedding on the last page, the deductions which would offer themselves would be of the gloomiest. The lovely sweetheart and winsome bride of one novel is the mother-in-law of the next.

Though ideals in matrimony produce effort and experiment out of which something better may come, they suffer the fate of all ideals when brought to the touch of experience. They wither away. Generally those who have cherished them are the first to laugh at them; but it by no means follows that the ideals do not give way to something far more genuinely satisfactory and contributory in a higher degree to happiness. This is what happens to most people in matrimony. They reduce their expectations here as they do elsewhere in life; they learn renunciation and contentment here as they do there; they find out how to get what satisfaction they can from what is real, being taught by experience that in this life they can get no other. Parenthood brings with it a new set of ideals which largely supersede those of an earlier period. It is true that care for children draws parents together; nevertheless their interests, after they have children, very often center more in the offspring than in each other. The vicissitudes of life also change ideals, for they change character. A man and woman who have undertaken to go through life together will find that the elements in their problem of individual happiness cannot remain the same over twenty or thirty years. Their happiness will depend on how they meet the new requirements, often painful, which these changes will present to them. Some fortunate life-partners there are, however, who, after stripping from their ideals that which is childish and silly, do find the rest realized; and others there are, who, if they lose some ideals, realize others beyond anything they had hoped for. Some favored pairs have attained happiness to an extent which few mortals know.

The modern family—father, mother, and children—also involves an ideal which is rarely realized. It is conceived of as a group quite independent and separate from others, its privacy being a special feature of its character. It is assumed in the ideal that all the interests in it are reduced to harmony and that it is a domain of peace, concord, and affection. In it the members are supposed to coöperate in mutual services and favors, winning subsistence, accumulating capital, educating the younger, producing joy in life, and creating an arena of domestic felicity which is a retreat from strife, labor, and care and a seat of sentiments and codes entirely different from those which rule the shop and the market. Misfortune, poverty, and illness damage this ideal. Divorce ruins it. The domestic group is only temporary, for the grown-up children scatter and new families are formed.

Now, however, comes another aspect of the entire subject. Our age has become saturated with optimism. For more than a century the world-beatifiers have been filling our heads with the notion that each one of us ought to be "happy" here, and that if we are not, somebody else is to blame for it; also, so much being established, that society is proved to be at fault and ought to rescue us from our troubles and make us happy. All the people who are pursuing popularity and living by it take up the chorus to this lament and demand. When, therefore, these prophets have gone far enough with the subject of matrimony to show its glorious beauty provided you succeed in it, they drop the subject as exhausted. On the contrary, it is hardly begun. If we respect the youthful enthusiasm of lovers and, recoiling from the charge of killing joy, say nothing to discourage it, the result is that in many cases we have in fact laid a trap for those whose disillusionment is bitter. The domain of ideals is necessarily also the domain of disillusionment and disappointment.

§431. **Unrealities.** Though all our civilization is crusted over with conventions, falsehoods, deceitful pretenses, and inveterate errors, this is true of marriage more than of anything else, especially since the topic has so long been tabooed by reason of notions of propriety that it is impossible to discuss it publicly in the manner which is necessary to correct error and reform abuse. It is not to be regarded as an imputation on our civilization to say that it is veneered with conventionalities and the rest. Those who hold the opposite opinion on this point embrace the dogma that nothing is wrong which is natural and then inveigh against the artificiality of civilization. Many of them go on from this dogma until, without being led to perceive their own error, they find themselves advocating unregulated bestiality. Of course the test of the dogma is in the application of it to modesty, decency, propriety, chastity, and other desirables. Whenever art modifies nature it always introduces an element of artificiality, so that when the product is compared with unmodified nature the difference appears as falsehood of one degree or another.

It is necessary to note here in passing the immense range of variety which is presented by the mores at different ages and in different societies. The most astounding contrasts are furnished by the notions and customs concerning modesty, propriety, and chastity at different times and places. Hence these notions and customs all present themselves to us as conventions. Unreal or destitute of rationality though they may be, they stand because the members of the society accept them, bend to them, pass them on to their children. Later on there develops a revolt against them, like the contemporary reaction against loose divorce, which modifies them, at first among the classes which cultivate the higher standards and later amongst all classes. Religious and philosophical dogmas, with ecclesiastical sanction, frequently have the same effect; often too they introduce arbitrary and pharisaical constraints which produce new mischief. Anybody, however, who attempts to go back up the stream of tradition and to strip off all which is conventional and false, will arrive at the point from which the stream started, that is, crude unregulation. The denunciations of conventionality and falsehood are quite wasted.

The divorce court is warning us every day that thousands of people who try matrimony fail to make a satisfactory experience out of it; and there are plenty of other instances around us where people are too high-bred to publish their misery to the world. The feeling of the optimists toward these cases seems to be that the unfortunates had their liberty and must bear their own consequences. In a large degree this view is justified; where it breaks down is in the fact that there is no due knowledge to check the liberty and to furnish a true moral ground for the responsibility. The trouble arises, not so much from the conventionalities, accepted fictions, and tolerated falsehoods as from ignorance and error. The amount of this ignorance and error about a matter of the first societal importance is amazing, even when due account is taken of the conventional mystery with which the matter is surrounded.

The function of educating people in notions of love, courtship, and the ideal of matrimony has been left mainly to stories and dramas; and these are, aside of their tendency to idealize, of all grades, approaching the subject from all sides and seeking to find in it those aspects which are interesting. Hence they are often sensational and appeal to vicious propensities. With the democratization of modern society and the abolition of the older arbitrary restraints on marriage, the way of true love runs smoother and furnishes therefore less material for those romantic and dramatic episodes which used to give the romancer or playwright his opportunity. In the newspapers sympathy is generally given to young people who make a runaway match or otherwise defy parental authority.

Out of this literature there results an education on all these topics which is full of error; there is also a vacuum of ignorance because no correct knowledge is imparted. The most immoral books we have ever read have been some inferior American novels sold on railroad trains and questioned by nobody. They have contained no vulgar incidents and no characters of the recognized immoral types, yet may be called immoral in the strictest sense of the word because the views of life presented are totally false and impossible, the sentiments suggested by them are extravagant, overstrained and irrational (like those, for instance, in *Camille*), and the ethics about love are at least dubious. It is these influences which bring men and women up to matrimony with false and impossible notions and prepare them for speedy disillusionment, misery, divorce, a new attempt to reach the impossible, and so on.

The difficulty of saying things and at the same time not saying them is one which it is impossible to overcome. Certainly the welfare of society now depends to an important degree on raising the taboo on these subjects to such an extent that more correct ideas in regard to them can be inculcated; but if anyone tries it, some yellow journalist who regularly corrupts public morals by sensational publications will suddenly think that he sees a chance to go over to the high moral line, for a change, and will denounce a prudent and careful attempt to do something useful of this kind as a violation of public ethics.

§432. **Modern Pair-Marriage.** Loose divorce undoes monogamy as completely as a return to polygyny; monogamy tainted by adultery and easy divorce is worse than plain plurality. Of course it is not monogamy at all, but a falsehood of a far different order from those conventions which were mentioned above. It is a network of deceit totally different from the conventional deceit involved in modesty and decency. It exposes children to homelessness and to evil communications; the offspring of divorced persons are a large component amongst the inmates of reform and industrial schools. A polygynist at his worst is bound by his system to support all his wives so long as they live and to give his children all the care and education he can, according to his means and social station.

In our society polygyny is regarded simply as an abomination. This is an expression of the mores and is not a rational opinion.

Here is one of the most important of the cases in which the mores serve as a fortification of healthful societal observances on grounds of authority, dogma, tradition, or prejudice, and without rational reflection and conviction. There are rational grounds in favor of pair-marriage and they are very strong although they are not yet clearly understood. The phrase "purity of the home" does not go very far toward explaining them, useful as it is to a legislator eager for glory as the champion of a great "moral" and popular movement, where also he will have no antagonists to meet. In all matters concerning the sex-relation the race is enclosed between two limitations. On the one side is the idealization to which there is no limit of satiety whatever, every attainment only opening the way to new desire; on the other are the renunciation and self-denial, in short the temperance, which is the condition of health and peace, of long life and vigor, of robust and healthful offspring, and of a vigorous and enduring society.

Temperance favors vigorous offspring. Therefore pair-marriage favors it. Temperance in eating and drinking, regarded societally, are trivial compared with temperance in matrimony. The intoxication of passion and the whirl of emotion which are excited by some products of literature and art react on physical vigor with exhaustion and disgust, while thrift and temperance in the mild satisfactions of home conserve and strengthen. The stimulus of variety encourages expenditure; the indifference of familiarity conduces to moderation. These are reasons why pair-marriage is socially expedient—if it is real; every one of them is vitiated if a pretended pair-marriage is corrupted by illicit relations or broken by easy divorce. If we sing pæans to our glorious system of the "purity of the home" under pair-marriage and if, in horrified contempt, we inflict punishment upon polygynists while we know that illicit relations amongst ourselves are constant and widespread facts, then we have presented to us a social hypocrisy for which there is no apology. It is no defense of plural marriage to hold that the "purity of the home" is infinitely more in peril from this hypocrisy in monogamic societies than it is from polygyny in certain restricted localities.

All this criticism is far nearer the truth in connection with another and perhaps the greatest advantage of pair-marriage, its

effect upon the status of women. In polygyny wives are set in
rivalry with each other for the favor of the husband, a rivalry
which, if they have attained to sensitiveness, they can prosecute
only at the expense of dignity and individuality. It is under pair-
marriage alone that a woman can take her place by the side of her
husband as an equal and help-meet; here it is that she wins a
sphere of her own in which she may develop to the utmost her skill
and talents as woman and reach a dignified position of work and
achievement. She can then command the respect of her husband by
what she contributes to the joint interest and can defend her opinions and wishes as to wise conduct in conjugal life, upon a plane
of equality. Feminine cunning then becomes nothing worse than
coquetry and tact. All this, however, is a high and beautiful literary ideal, the realization of which is hindered by an infinite variety
of facts: weaknesses of human nature, faults of character, illness,
poverty, interferences of other interests, and so on. All falls to
the ground if the pair-marriage is not real. The ideal, again,
might be far more nearly attained under polygyny than under
pretended but false monogamy.

We have come in our time to expect that all sorts of social benefits should accrue to us without cost and stay by us without care.
It is so with liberty and religion and also with pair-marriage and
the family. The trouble is not that we must all the time fight
somebody who is trying to rob us of them; it is that we must use
them aright ourselves if we want to keep them. Pair-marriage
costs self-denial if it is desired that it shall be maintained in its
purity; that appears to be the reason why it is so imperfectly
realized anywhere. It is also a system of restraint upon self-will.
In the past, dogmas and ecclesiastical regulations have multiplied
restraints and have caused great misery to many mortals during
their short span on earth; yet even when all these arbitrary features are done away with, the monogamic marriage-institution is
a system of stringent limitations. If some are so contented inside
these limitations that they do not feel them and are not aware of
their existence, to others they become intolerable. Here in America, where marriages are contracted by the young people themselves with scarcely any interference from parents, the divorce
courts furnish ample proof that pair-marriage is no solution of

the old difficulties. Why not? It is because pair-marriage turns out to be a yoke which the pairs have not the discipline of character to bear.

Woman gains more specifically than man by the change to pair-marriage; he loses on the side of selfish indulgence and wins only the higher moral goods which are less obvious and less welcome. Man's share in debasing the system is pretty well recognized; it is not always realized that woman too has her part in its degradation. For woman, though with more to lose, is often at fault for the failure of pair-marriage. She gains, as we have said, in dignity, independence, range of education, power, and worth. The question arises concerning her, however, as it arises for all mortals when they gain anything: Is she worthy of it? What will she do with it? Anyone who wins a higher position, with power and security, may lapse into idleness, indifference, neglect of duty, defiance of remonstrances, and may set up exacting and arbitrary claims of right up to the full theory of the situation, without yielding to its duties. When women so use the prerogatives which they win in pair-marriage, the result may be divorce, that is, revolt against the institution, or the man may fall back into monogyny.

§433. The Pair-Marriage Monopoly. It should also be noticed, in connection with the exactions of a highly evolved type of wedlock, that marriage is still a monopoly. Very little attention has ever been paid to this fact except by some social sects which have revolted against the institution. These and their antagonists fight their battles over property and rarely see that every issue which is raised about property has its parallel in respect to marriage; that every victory which radicals may win about property will turn at once to defeat because it will react on marriage. Property is said to be due to force. This is not true without due limitation and explanation, but marriage is as completely and unquestionably a product of force as property ever was. Property is monopoly; so is marriage. If this fact condemns property, it also condemns marriage. One monopoly has various grades; so has the other. One has been historically evolved; so has the other. The motive of one has been to enable men to pass their existence on earth with the greatest possible measure of satisfaction; this also has been the motive of the other. The two are intertwined and their modifications have been such as to adapt them to each other at all stages of civilization.

The monopoly in marriage does not consist simply in the fact that a woman who becomes a man's wife is, under the father-family, forbidden to all others. If there were just as many men as women in a society and each man and woman could be paired off with the one best suited to him or her, the ideal of a purely mono-gamic society might be reached. The very statement of the conditions shows why this ideal never can be attained. Moreover, even if we imagine it won, it would be unstable; the lapse of a short time would overthrow its ideal perfection. In fact, excluding new countries with their predominating male immigration, there are more adult women than adult men in settled society. Also when we consider the lofty ideal of a monogamic society which we have formed, the faith which we place in it, the interests which hang upon it, our methods of securing a satisfactory pairing-off which will give stability to the institution are both ridiculously and tragically inadequate. The consequence is that the institution of pair-marriage is one into which only a part of the society ever can enter. The rules by which it is constituted and by which its integrity is maintained, form a complete barrier of exclusion from all its benefits against those who have not entered it and at the same time impose upon them heavy obligations of self-denial and sacrifice for which there is no compensation whatever.

Since a wife and family cost far more under real monogamy than under polygyny, the expense involved under the former system is another restriction upon the numbers who can enter it. In the older countries, with denser population, a large fraction of the population is condemned to celibacy; even in America a tendency in the same direction, as the standard of living rises and the competition of life becomes more intense, is distinctly to be noted. In short, the monogamic marriage-institution in its purity, however high and refined a societal organization, is not possible for all. It is im-practicable and unthinkable except for a limited number who, favored by circumstances, can get into it. Thousands force their way in without knowing or heeding the conditions of entrance;

then they and their children suffer for it and phenomena are presented—abandoned wives, foundlings, vagrancy, prostitution, pauperism—which, under lower organizations of marriage and the family, were unknown. These phenomena often arrest the attention of social philosophers and reformers who attribute them to anything but the true cause and attack them by any but the appropriate remedies. They are the attendant evils inseparable from a step in advance in the societal organization.

Any monopoly is an advantage to those who are inside it; its victims are those who cannot get in. As was said above, the monopoly of pair-marriage, regarded as a societal institution, is maintained by laws and mores which are a life-constraint on the adult unmarried and for which there is for them no compensation whatever. It is astonishing that in such discussion of marriage as takes place little heed is ever paid to this aspect of the matter. The dogmas of chastity and sex-morality are universal through the community and the unmarried are expected to conform to them; nevertheless the dogmas are all made with a view to the welfare of society through married people and children. The unmarried not only have missed all that phase of life which comes under marriage but they are expected to take all the burden and fulfil all the sacrifice which falls upon them in order that the walls and buttresses of pair-marriage may remain intact, to the benefit of those who are inside and who are enjoying the benefit. Men, with the exception of a small minority, do not submit as do women to such a demand.

It follows that the victims of pair-marriage are women who do not marry. This is the one commanding reason why no arbitrary limitations should be put upon them in the pursuit of happiness in any other ways that they may choose. A woman of fifty whose friends in the older generation who loved her are all dead and in her own generation are all married and indifferent, if she is poor and trying to fight the battle of life alone, is one of the saddest spectacles our civilization affords; yet the social reformers have all been at work to rescue the able-bodied laboring man who has wages, a family, a trade, and a vote. Thousands of unmarried women care nothing for marriage or for a husband; what they yearn for is children. The mores of monogamic society forbid them ever to have any. That such a prohibition is plainly called for in the interest of society does not remove the disharmony between that interest and the one felt by the individual.

Probably unmarried women do not often feel wronged. They are too well drilled and disciplined; they are trained to inhibitions from the earliest childhood and such restraints are strengthened by imitation and affection. Boys are so trained also, but girls have been subjected to a greater number of limitations and the habit of conforming conduct to approved standards has become the norm of life. All this applies especially to their own status, to their relations to men in or out of marriage, and to all which concerns the sex-relation. They have acquiesced and submitted without reflection or struggle in whatever loss or sacrifice the existing societal system has brought to them individually, and they have done it so instinctively that they have not been conscious of the source of their pain and disappointment and resentful of its tyranny. There are at present some signs of change in respect to these matters, but it will take a long time to alter the mores in their stronghold among the masses.

In summary, then, we find that pair-marriage is a type of the sex-relation which stands at the end of an evolution as long as human existence. Survivals of all earlier forms are mixed up in it. It is by far the most complicated of them all, by virtue of the variety of combinations which it makes with other facts and circumstances of life and especially because it belongs to a highly developed and complicated civilization. On one side it is favorable to health, because it imposes temperance; on another, it may be unfavorable to society because of the practice of preventing procreation in view of the expense entailed. It brings to all who enter it intelligently and wisely, if they have well-disciplined characters, a great number and variety of chances of happiness. To those who enter it ignorantly or carelessly and with ill-disciplined characters, it is sure to cause misery far beyond what they would suffer in any lower form of the sex-relation.

We are all living within a mental horizon which is created for us by the traditions, customs, institutions, ideas, and doctrines of the society in which we were born. These furnish us with our notions and standards of what is right; and they have clustered

around the sex-relation probably in greater number and with
greater imperativeness than around any other interest of men.
They have often been arbitrary and sometimes irrational; yet
they have been tabooed from discussion. These facts are irritating
and tend to provoke revolt. Formerly men and women grew into
them as into the order of nature; there was nothing else with
which to compare them and it was rare for anyone to revolt
against them or even to criticize them. Modern people, however,
educated as they are to demand the earth, find fault with everything which does not minister to their luxury and vanity. When
two persons of this habit of mind try to live together in wedlock
in this world of ours, they do not succeed, for the relation demands concession and self-effacement from both parties. Here
then we have a series of observations which afford ample reason
for the high valuation of pair-marriage and also reveal that system as at best but imperfectly realized in society.

PART VI

SELF-GRATIFICATION

PART VI

SELF-GRATIFICATION

CHAPTER LIX

PLEASURE

§434. **The Element of Pleasure.** Behind the evolution of the institutions previously considered in this book has lain the impulse of iron necessity. About the primordial interests that impel to societal self-maintenance and self-perpetuation there have gathered blocks of mores out of which the taboo has wrought the institutions of industry, war, property, government, and marriage; and fear of the supernatural has impelled to the development of religion. These are the fundamental institutions of society which men have been coerced to form. They are all expedients for insuring life against starvation, violence, and other menacing and destructive elements. It is through them that society continues its existence. They are adjustments to the inevitable conditions of life.

They do not, however, include the whole of human activity. There is yet another and more positive interest which has appeared over and over, though incidentally, in preceding chapters. The race has not been engrossed in the evasion of ill to the exclusion of positive outreachings after self-gratification. It has not been always at a tension in the struggle for existence; the spur of necessity has not always been dug deep into its flanks; there has nearly always been some leisure that could be spent in doing what men wanted to do instead of only what they must do. Every society, no matter how backward its development, shows some folkways that serve neither self-maintenance nor self-perpetuation, either exclusively or in the main, but merely self-gratification.

It is a safe generalization that the primordial needs must be met at least to a minimal degree before there is any chance for developing the arts of pleasure. In extreme cases of destitution, where a population is starving and in terror of its life, there is no pleasure for anybody and the animal-needs stand out stark and sole. If a wretched people drugs itself to offset its misery, that is hardly self-gratification. On the other hand, where there is plenty of food and no care for the future, mankind normally turns to pastimes and follies or to more refined diversions. There occur all grades of correlation between the degree of success in satisfying primordial needs and the degree of development of pleasure-getting activities. The gratification-element is often no more than an accompaniment to success, real or fancied, in economic, religious, or other adjustment. When such adjustment is more than passably secured, it passes into self-gratification. It is pleasant to have a superfluity of food, extensive property, many wives and children, much merit accumulated with the gods. It not only relieves care and promotes ease and confidence but it tickles vanity to have a superiority in such respects over one's fellows—to display a standard of living that is distinctive and confers prestige. The pleasure-getting element thus enters largely into strainings after material possessions, wife and family, civil and religious security.

It is a fact that men strive no less to get pleasure than to attain the more fundamental things; they will even put forth effort to attain the luxury where they will go without the obviously useful. "How humiliating it is," exclaims one writer,[1] "that so much more is accomplished in the domestication of pigeons and fowls for sporting purposes than in that of the creatures most important in economic life." Nevertheless there is a wide and general truth in the contention that the struggle for pleasure and luxury may begin only where the effort in mere self-maintenance leaves off, granted that it is often impossible to say just where the one passes into the other. All human institutions are shot through with the workings of the pleasure-interest.[2]

Certain Australians are so involved in the struggle for existence that their amusements "have always consisted in practising those arts which were necessary to get a living."[3] The Papuans, who are somewhat better off, are fond of play and playthings, like the rest of the blacks; they make toy boats and houses as soon as they are a little more prosperous.[4] Conversely, art sinks with the decline of prosperity; Junker[5] expects native art to go under, judging from what he has observed, in the struggle for the preservation of mere existence, and artistic products to be succeeded by those which meet an extremity of need.

[1] Vierkandt, *Natur- u. Kultur-völker*, 134.
[2] Powell, in BAE, XIX, lv ff.; Welling, in AA, 1-40.
[3] Smyth, *Vict.*, I, 180.   [4] Schmidt, *Deut. Kol.*, II, 382.
[5] *Afr.*, II, 514; Vierkandt, *Natur- u. Kultur-völker*, 138-140.

Although there is no question but that self-gratification attaches to or grows out of adjustment in self-maintenance and
self-perpetuation, being attained oftentimes by no more than a
quantitative increase in the satisfaction of basic needs and so
appearing to be an incidental or even accidental sequel to economic, political, domestic, or religious organization, nevertheless
the pleasure-element is of such significance that it must be distinguished if one wishes to acquire a true perspective of societal
evolution. It is worth while to rob property or religion of one of
the topics that logically belong to it for the sake of displaying to
advantage the drive of the pleasure-impulse. To begin with, however, we shall concentrate upon certain matters which evidently
do not belong primarily to any of the sections which have hitherto
been covered: upon the so-called "play-instinct"; the sense of
form, color, sound, and rhythm; the special tastes, both physical
and mental; and upon vanity in both its cruder and more refined
forms.[6]

There is one other consideration of major importance that
needs preliminary mention. In surveying the field of self-gratification the salient fact that enforces attention is that there have
here been developed no real institutions.[7] There is no structure
for the realization of self-gratification corresponding to property in self-maintenance or marriage in self-perpetuation; no
accretion of mores about a core upon which the taboo has been
formatively at work. The taboos connected with self-gratification
are time-taboos[8] rather than prohibitions laid upon the practice
itself, that is to say, such and such a form of self-gratification is
seldom interdicted altogether, but only for a period. There is
nothing here comparable to the abolition of incestuous unions or
of cannibalism. Nothing is lopped off for good and all from the
accretion of mores. This fact doubtless explains why the taboo
has not operated, in this range, in its regular function as the
institution-builder. There are scattered forms of self-gratification,
each with its own relatively petty history, but they form no consistent evolving whole. There is no relationship between betel-
chewing, the game of chance, the victor's trophy, and the min-
strel's song except that they all serve, in their several ways, the

6 Tylor, *Anth.,* ch. XII; Sumner, *Folkways,* ch. XVII.
7 §47, above.   8 §273, above.

pleasure of man as distinguished from his fundamental and vital needs. This fact that the various types of self-gratification are not genetically connected and do not arrive at institutional form obliges us to make of this section of our book a series of relatively disconnected episodes in societal evolution, whereas in former sections there has always been a master-factor to which all side-developments could be related somewhat as the corollary to the proposition. Forms of self-gratification are by no means absolutely isolated and sporadic societal phenomena; there are none such; but there is no major strand upon which they can be strung that is comparable with the aleatory element in religion or the condition of bi-sexuality in self-perpetuation. The best we can do is to distinguish, in these two chapters, the type of pleasure-getting that responds to an appeal of the senses and that which caters to vanity. These two will be found to overlap; as types, however, they stand apart from one another sufficiently to be thrown into contrast.

§435. Pastime and Play. There are characteristic gratificacations of the special senses of taste, sight, hearing, touch, and smell. To these we shall presently come. About pastime and play there is a sort of general appeal to the senses which we have no interest in trying to analyze. Doubtless there is in mere idling, in stretching the muscles, in diverting the mind, and so on a goodly element of plain utility as well as of positive pleasure. We seek no distinctions here, for the fact is one of common knowledge and, wherever the line may be drawn, the presence of the pleasure-element is assured.

To judge from the accounts of very backward peoples, one of the simplest forms of self-gratification, one of the chief ways of employing leisure won by getting somewhat ahead in the struggle for maintenance, is sleep. It must be understood that what looks like slothfulness is not always pure inertia; and that much of the sleep and loafing observed by travellers is relaxation called for by previous strenuous exertion.[9] However, savages do show "periods of blank unreceptiveness, when the mind is not working, and the individual is in a kind of state of coma. This state is induced

9 §§52-54, above.

by rest and having nothing to do. . . . A very noticeable thing
with most Bantus is that work induces work, and leisure induces
laziness of both mind and body." It is the call for new adjustment
that stirs to activity: "there is nothing that upsets a native so
much as new conditions."

The author quoted[10] goes on to say: "I believe that the native is capable of
assuming a state in which the mind is absolutely detached and not working,
and when in such a state, he is only recalled by a start to his present surroundings. . . . The life of the head man of a village in Nyasaland, when not engaged in the strenuous pursuit of his official duties, is something like this. At
sunrise he crawls out of his hut and sits outside. After a short time his wife
crawls out and offers him some food. He eats this and then makes his way to
a tree, perhaps a hundred yards from the village. Under this he sits in deep
abstraction, till about noon a child brings him some food and water. After
partaking of this he moves a little so as to get the afternoon shade. He then
sits in deep meditation till sunset, when he crawls into his hut and goes to
sleep. "Sometimes he is joined by a few other old men under his tree. They
hardly ever speak to each other, and if they say anything, it is to make some
obvious remark as, 'There is a dog,' 'Yes, it is a dog,' 'Oh,' 'Ah,' and a further
period of silence."

Sleep is perhaps the simplest expedient for passing time, for
evading boredom or forgetting care; the race has developed many
others also, of a more positive order. The very term "pastime,"
or the expression "to kill time," is significant; indeed, it sometimes
appears that men are bent upon hurrying through life to the
grave, so eager do they seem to have time pass quickly. It is characteristic of life, as Shakespeare[11] long ago noted, that time
passes rapidly when men would prefer to prolong it and with
incredible slowness when they would like to have it over with and
gone. In any case pleasure and the swift passing of time are associated in human experience to the extent of being represented in
English, at any rate, by the same term; whereas boredom, in the
German language at least, is signified by *Langeweile*. There is
no doubt that pure ennui, on higher stages of civilization, has led
to inventions for passing time. Even the bath was a diversion; and
hunting, fighting, crusading, gambling, and general adventure-
seeking were the much-sought spice of life.

We are not interested in such torpid joys as sleep or mere
vacancy of mind. Most human beings, given leisure, will seek for
some positive gratification. The leisure of maturity as well as of

[10] Stigand, *Elephant*, 155, 156, 157.   [11] *As You Like It*, Act III, sc. ii.

childhood turns instinctively to play.[12] Play may be said to call upon energy which might be lost in vacuous idleness, to train it somewhat, and to store it up for later use. It is, in fact, a phenomenon of that surplus, over and above mere living, out of which gains in culture are made. And play is not so strictly restrained by tradition and ancestral usage as is the serious and regular work of life; there is more chance for variation and experiment and also for idealization. Part of children's play is in nature, releasing energy and promoting physical growth and adjustment; much of it, however, is social, for it is highly imitative and results in transmission of the mores. The pleasure is largely in the imitation; boys rehearse the activities of men and girls prefigure their inevitable destiny. Sport keeps up the virtues of war and supports the taste for adventure and romance; it is debatable whether a serious proportion of the energy spent on it is subtracted from better purposes.

Effort is put forth spontaneously under the play-interest that must be painfully evoked in the case of work; indeed, if work can be disguised as play, it is performed with vigor, enthusiasm, and ease. It is evident that in play is involved an attitude of mind, an interest that goes typically with youth. Whether any given activity is work or play is a question of the absence or presence of the gratification-interest. It follows that if this interest changes, the character of the activity is altered; every serious man comes to see in work, in difficult, tiring labor, one of the durable satisfactions of life. This is quite different from the gratification attained in the pursuit of pet avocations or hobbies. Savages undertake useful enterprises under compulsion rather than voluntarily, while highly cultured men, unless they are triflers, spend their lives in such undertakings as their chief pleasure and do what merely distracts them only on special occasions when they can win some leisure.

That play has an important bearing upon societal life, that it confers survival-value upon a society, has been intimated in what precedes. It is interesting to note that in the play of children there have been preserved, in survivalistic form, a number of the serious usages of the past. Shooting with the bow and arrow,

[12] Tylor, "Games," in JAI, IX; Groos, *Play of Animals;* Groos, *Play of Man;* Culin, in BAE, XXIV; Powell, in BAE, XVII, pt. I, xxix.

after it has been discarded by adults, is preserved in children's play; even in the dances of adults discarded weapons may appear;[13] and games and formulas used in "counting out" and otherwise are reminiscent of a time when neither the game nor the formula was child's play.[14] The play of children reflects the fact that they begin, like the savage, without mores or morals, and execute, as they move toward adult age, a sort of recapitulation of the race's history.[15] Reflection over the phenomena of even juvenile play and make-believe has in it the possibilities of arrival at truth now seen to inhere in the once lightly-esteemed study of legend and folklore.

If the playfulness of young animals "is based upon the fact that certain very important instincts appear at a time when the animal does not yet need them"; if play "is at least an expression of definite instincts leading to the better adaptation of animals to the surrounding conditions of life";[16] then there is no reason for looking upon children's play as any the less an evolutionary adjustment. In particular do juvenile sports, though they are pursued for no such purpose but only for pleasure, teach the indispensable lesson of discipline and regard for the rights of others which primitive people, even in extreme youth, learned straight from life and which modern children are kept from acquiring where the home is run on the principle of a hot-house. The fact is that there is no game without rules; it is the rules that make the game, or the difference between games. Rules automatically appear when children are at desultory play, being invented to suit occasion. All pastimes have risen to the character of recognized games by the general concurrence in certain regulations. These rules mean discipline; participation in games—"playing the game"—is conditional upon their good-natured acceptance. No one is a "good sport" who will not cheerfully acquiesce in them; when they cost him something he must be a "good loser." Because children—and grown-ups as well—want so much to participate, they submit willingly to discipline that they would resist were not their interests so deeply involved in the self-gratification in prospect. It is a curious fact, too, and one that bears emphatically

13 Tylor, *Anth.*, 244, 306; Von den Steinen, *Zent. Bras.*, 231, 234.
14 Bolton, *Counting-Out Rhymes*, 26, 41.
15 Keller, *Soc. Evol.*, 220-222.　　16 Groos, *Play of Animals*, 75, 76.

upon the nature of play, that the man who has not learned to be a "good sport" in his games is likely not to be such elsewhere; incredibly enough, many a vital defect of character is betrayed first in sport, later to be confirmed in ranges where self-revelation is under stricter suppression. The play of human beings is worth attention as an expedient in molding societal life; it can be and has been organized into a powerful educational device. Yet it has, we repeat, no original basis or motive in any one of these things but only in self-gratification.

To catalogue the games and pastimes, even of savages, would be a difficult undertaking and, for our purpose, a profitless one. Pleasure in the release of physical energy has lasted, in some races, well on through life. Athletic sports are practised by many primitive peoples, some of their games, like lacrosse, being strenuous to a high degree. Where physical play is less a matter of animal-spirits and more one of exercise, diversion, relaxation, or the preservation of physical and mental fitness, the social relations involved continue to minister to self-gratification. The great bulk of human pastimes are not, however, play of the athletic order; they occupy and minister to the mind, or at least to the nervous system, rather than to the body.[17] There is an element of emotional pleasure, especially in team-play, over and above any sense-gratification. Pastimes come thus to relieve the monotony of life and the emptiness of mind that are such factors of discomfort when men have emerged from mental torpor into a degree of alertness. To primitives, mere talk or "palaver" is entertaining, and oratory, especially where the words flow thick and fast, is a great diversion.[18] Then, too, there is a sense of humor in many savage peoples which finds its gratification in jests running all the way from the broad to the subtle. This element appears all through the practices of self-gratification.

Some Papuans, we are told, are wholly discontented to be positively idle. "*The time of the people seems to be fully occupied.* They had great harvest festivals; they kept their gardens of yam, bananas, sugar-cane, and taro, in good order; trade expeditions were frequent; they made their own fishing-nets and kites; built houses and cut out canoes; taught their children legends, songs,

17 Dellenbaugh, *N. Amer.*, ch. XI.
18 Elliott, cited in JAI, XXIII, 81; Vierkandt, *Natur- u. Kultur-völker*, 129; Keller, *Hom. Soc.*, 264.

and games; they scorned a Tolelewa—lazy man (according to their ideas of laziness); despised the Abisida—beggar-woman."[19]

It is especially to be noted that many games have a religious tinge. "Back of each game is found a ceremony in which the game was a significant part. The ceremony has commonly disappeared; the game survives as an amusement, but often with traditions and observances which serve to connect it with its original purpose. The ceremonies appear to have been to cure sickness, to cause fertilization and reproduction of plants and animals, and, in the arid region, to produce rain. Gaming implements are among the most significant objects that are placed upon many Hopi altars, and constantly reappear as parts of the masks, headdresses, and other ceremonial adornments of the Indians generally. These observations hold true . . . of the athletic games as well as of the game of chance. The ball was a sacred object not to be touched with the hand, and has been identified as symbolizing the earth, the sun, or the moon. In the ring-and-pole game, the original form of the ring was a netted hoop derived from the spider web, the emblem of the Earth mother. The performance of the game was bound up with ceremonies of reproduction and fertility. In the kicked-stick and ball-race games of the S.W., the primary object seems to have been to protect the crops against sand storms within the circuit traversed."[20] "Preceding and accompanying the game there was much ceremonial of dancing, fasting, bleeding, anointing, and prayer under the direction of the medicine-men."[21] Grinnell[22] has a chapter on the games and amusements of the Cheyenne, showing how, in many cases, they were directly or indirectly connected with religion.

It must not be thought that even so insignificant a game as cat's-cradle is without its serious aspect. In New Guinea it is more than mere amusement; it is ritualistic, in connection with the construction of a food-house and also magical in the discovery of theft.[23] "Cat's-cradles, which they also teach them, were formerly played only in the season when the yams were growing, for they were thought to assist their growth. Now, for no apparent reason, the belief has changed, and they are thought to injure them, so no one is allowed to play the game till after harvest. It is a favourite amusement with the children. and the number of figures they can make is perfectly amazing."[24] This pastime is equally well known to natives of Central Africa, North America, and Torres Straits.[25]

It goes almost without the saying that pastimes existed which were merely such. "Dearly as the Delaware loved the glory and excitement of war, the milder diversions of sports and games found a warm place in his affections. A form of lacrosse; the game of 'snow-snake,' in which polished wooden wands were thrown for great distances across the snow; an amusing football game,

[19] Bromilow, in AAAS, 1909, 483.   [20] Culin, "Games," in HAI, I, 484.
[21] Mooney, in HAI, I, 127.   [22] *Cheyenne*, I, 312 ff.
[23] Jenness, "Papuan Cat's Cradles," in JAI, L, 301.
[24] Jenness and Ballentyne, *D'Entrecasteaux*, 168.
[25] Cunnington, "String Figures and Tricks from Central Africa," in JAI, XXXVI, 123; Parkinson and Haddon contribute articles to the same number of the JAI, 132 ff. and 142 ff. Compton, in JAI, XLIX, 236, furnishes a bibliography. An inclusive treatment is Haddon, K. (Mrs. Rishbeth), *Cats' Cradles from Many Lands.* Barton, Holmes, and Haddon give accounts of native children's games, in JAI, XXXVIII, 259 ff., 280 ff., 289 ff.

in which women contended with men, the men kicking and the women throwing the ball; the mocassin game, in which a bullet was hidden under one of a row of mocassins and the opponent required to guess which—all were popular, whole communities attending and betting against one another. Besides these there was the game of bowl and dice; the 'scatter game,' resembling jackstraws; a game played with a hoop and javelins, and another with bows and arrows."[26]

Bathing is one of the commonest forms of self-gratification in certain parts of the world. "The personal cleanliness of the Indian is proverbial. Thus, in Demerara, . . . a part of their idle hours they pass in bathing and swimming in the rivers, which they do in companies, without distinction of sex, several times a day. . . . The Surinam Indians are a very cleanly people. They greatly delight in bathing, which they do twice at least every day, men, women, boys, and girls, promiscuously together. They are all excellent swimmers without exception. Among these parties not the smallest indecency is committed, in either words or actions."[27]

One of the stock pastimes of savages is tale-telling, the repetition of stories about men and gods out of which develop myth, legend, and folklore. Here is a powerful agency for the transmission of the code, by which the mores are inculcated in the young and perennially recalled to the adults.[28] Proverbs or even riddles, containing folk-wisdom in condensed form, are circulated among delighted hearers. It goes almost without the saying that in such records lies the germ of history; in them there is to be found much that is of value to the scientist for the reconstruction of the prehistoric past.[29] It is not to be denied that primitive tales frequently display a strongly imaginative element and almost always witness to keen powers of observation.

Of the East Africans it is reported that "their love of animal folklore is a well-known characteristic of the Bantu race throughout Africa from Zululand to Uganda. . . . The general type of story is usually the meeting of a savage animal with a harmless one, and the eventual triumph of the harmless animal by some simple trick. These stories are told in the evening, when the members of the village congregate and gossip after their meal is finished; one will start and tell a story, and then another will tell one, and so on; they try to outvie one another by striving to see who can recount the greatest number; the children sit round, and, as the same stories are heard over and over again on different occasions, they become firmly imprinted on their memories, and are thus perpetuated from generation to generation."[30] Similarly on the Upper Congo, "the greedy man, the coward, the thief, the scamp who disregards the feelings of others, and rides rough-shod over all the social and communal institutions, the man who is impotent—not able to beget children, the man who is accused

26 Harrington, in AA, XV, 216.   27 Roth in BAE, XXXVIII, §932.
28 Keller, *Soc. Evol.*, ch. VII.   29 Tylor, *Anth.*, ch. XV.
30 Hobley, in JAI, XXXIII, 337.

of witchcraft and will not take the ordeal, and the incestuous are all put into the songs which are sung at the village dances, and there is no more powerful factor in influencing the native to good or evil than the mention of his name in an impromptu song at the village dance. The paragraph in our newspaper is read by comparatively few people, and only a small percentage of those who read it know the person mentioned, but the song is sung, night after night, by all the village—the very neighbours of the one thus held up to ridicule, or honour. The village song incites to deeds of reckless daring in times of war, it brands and shames the cowards, and it restrains considerably the rascals, while it maddens to the verge of suicide the impotent."[31]

Tale-telling easily runs out into romance and pure imagination. The whole domain is one of self-cajolery. Romances and poets have always created worlds in which earthly limitations were set aside; in which fortunes came by luck, obstacles vanished at the waving of a fairy wand, people who were not princes proved to be such, and in which the story ended with the assurance that its characters were happy ever afterward and lived long in health and prosperity. Although the taste as to details has changed, the love of romance and illusion is as great as ever. The Golden Age, the Millennium, Utopia, are all efforts to paint this world in all its glory as it would be if all limiting conditions were set aside, all ills and hardships abolished, and, as a consequence, prosperity made constant and uniform.

Much of the pleasure attained through games and pastimes, as well as through a number of forms of self-gratification yet to be noticed, lies in the gratification of what some writers call the "social instinct." We see no instinct here[32] but regard sociability as a developed product of use and wont, in the mores. There is no doubt that the propinquity of their fellows and the consequent privilege of being off guard, appealed strongly to early men, when once they had been forced into association; and it is a commonplace that many human joys come only in the proximity of others —only, it may be, among crowds of others. Vanity itself, in its myriad forms, cannot be satisfied in isolation.

§436. Gaming. Men have always taken joy in competition, not alone as competitors but also as observers. The matching of bodily and mental powers, especially between superior performers, has always awakened and enthralled interest. Contests be-

[31] Weeks, in JAI, XXXIX, 447. [32] §§4 ff., above.

tween animals, human athletic rivalry, the display of mental agility in verbal battles—all these have been important sources of self-gratification. They have been strongly tinctured with an educational element, for the essence of the game is, as we have noted, its rules, code, and discipline; even the non-participant learns something of sportsmanship from looking on. In any case the bystander, even more than the principal, has an outlet for his excitement in wagering upon results. This is the specific form of gaming which we have in mind—betting upon the outcome of a competition, first, and then upon the element of chance itself.

Theoretically these two types of wager are distinguishable, though they run together in practice. One may study the bodies of two horses and compare their records and then be ready to wager upon the correctness of his judgment. If he is a specialist on race-horses, where his opponent is not, or if he has access to information not open to the other man, he is betting on a sure thing, in so far as the entrance of chance can be excluded. This is a different matter from wagering upon the fall of uncogged dice, where no one can well have information not possessed by another and where the presence of the luck-element is precisely the sense of the game. In one case there is a matching of knowledge and judgment; in the other a mere luck-wager. Where knowledge ends, luck begins; and an engrossing passion of men has been the love of playing with the unreckonable and unpredictable that lies beyond the range of knowledge, that is, with the aleatory element.[33]

This tendency is deep-seated in basic conditions of living. Men have always dreamed of getting something for nothing instead of something for something, that is, an equivalent of product for effort put forth. One of the chief joys of the child, and of the grown-up too, for that matter, is to "find something"; to chance upon some article and possess it without paying for it. In the savage this tendency is particularly marked and unrestrainedly followed. To him a game like chess could give no pleasure, not only because it is too hard for him but also because there is little luck in it and no wager involved; on the other hand, he will squat all day over the engrossing fall of the bones or nuts that are his dice, provided there is a chance to win property. He is not looking for

[33] §195, above; Spencer, *Stud. Soc.*, 306.

intellectual pleasure or the satisfaction of intellectual curiosity. To him no game is a real game that is not a gamble—that does not touch upon self-maintenance in some intimate way.[34]

Hence most savage games are those of chance; though the wager on judgment is present to some degree, it is submerged by the flood of luck-wagering. The following examples will reveal the current mode.

Seligmann[35] cites what seems to be a remarkable exception. "The result of the most careful inquiries showed that formerly the Koita knew nothing of any game in which a gambling element occurred, nor did anything in the nature of betting exist. Yet at the present day all the young, and some of the middle-aged men of all the sections of the tribe with which I am acquainted, are inveterate gamblers, willing to stake not only the whole of their wages but their personal property as well. As far as I know, they have adopted but one method of gambling. One of their number holds a pack of cards from which he takes a card, and bets are made on the colour or suit of the card turned up." It would appear here that gambling was introduced from without to a people in a state of primæval innocence. More commonly by far, the natives have their own indigenous gambling games, and are devoted to them. Of the Tsimshians it is reported: "Many men pass their time gambling. They paint their faces to secure good luck. Some men play until they have lost all their property. They will gamble away even their wives and parents, although it is not clear what this means, since the relatives certainly retain their liberty."[36]

Gambling, says Junker,[37] is something to which the African "is so given over that with him, as with civilized man, it degenerates into an untamable passion." "The Ba-Yaka appear to be particularly addicted to this form of pastime. . . . They are the worst gamblers I ever met."[38] Malays are great gamblers and so are the Polynesians, who will risk everything, including their arm and leg bones after death, and even themselves, on a cast.[39] In parts of the Malay Archipelago and the Philippines every man of any consequence has his fighting-cock and is all ready to put up a wager on him at any time. If his house catches fire, the cock is the first treasure to be rescued.[40] Small boys carry beetles around in grass cages and match them with one another for some childish stake.

Among the Hudson Bay Eskimo "gambling is carried on to such a degree among both sexes that even their own lives are staked upon the issue of a game. The winner often obtains the wife of his opponent, and holds her until some tempting offer is made for her return. The only article they possess is frequently wagered, and when they lose they are greeted with derision. The

[34] "Betless horse-racing" has been twice tried and has twice failed in one of the western states. N. Y. *Times,* Feb. 6, 1924.

[35] *Melanesians,* 135.

[36] Boas, in BAE, XXXI, 409-410.				[37] *Afr.,* III, 129.

[38] Torday and Joyce, in JAI, XXXVI, 47.

[39] Ratzel, *Vkde.,* II, 134.

[40] Furness, *Head-Hunters,* index; Worcester, *Philippine Isl.,* 284-286; Scheltema, in *Jr. Amer. Folklore,* XXXII.

women, especially, stake their only garment rather than be without opportunity to play."[41] The Indians of North America are great gamblers.[42] Horse-racing, with wagers inevitably accompanying it, was a favorite Indian pastime. The following excerpt not only illustrates the trait before us but also supports the assertion made by experts on the American Indian that he is not always the grim figure of tradition. Dellenbaugh[43] quotes Col. Richard Dodge,[44] who "describes an amusing race that took place near Fort Chadbourne, Texas, between a horse of a Comanche chief and three horses of the officers of the garrison, which illustrates the Amerind cleverness in the jockeying line. It took several days of manœuvering to bring the chief to the point, and then a race was arranged with the third best horse of the white men. The distance was four hundred yards, and property to the amount of sixty dollars a side was wagered on the result." "At the appointed time," writes Dodge, "all the Indians and most of the garrison were assembled at the track. The Indians 'showed' a miserable sheep of a pony with legs like churns; a three-inch coat of rough hair stuck out all over the body, and a general expression of neglect, helplessness, and patient suffering struck pity into the hearts of all beholders. The rider was a stalwart buck of one hundred and seventy pounds, looking big and strong enough to carry the poor beast on his shoulders. He was armed with a huge club, with which, after the word was given, he belabored the miserable animal from start to finish. To the astonishment of all the whites, the Indian won by a neck. Another race was proposed by the officers and, after much 'dickering,' accepted by the Indians, against the next best horse of the garrison. The bets were doubled, and in less than an hour the second race was won by the same pony, with the same apparent exertion and with exactly the same result. The officers, thoroughly disgusted, proposed a third race, and brought to the ground a magnificent Kentucky mare, of the true Lexington blood, and known to beat the best of the others at least forty yards in four hundred. The Indians accepted the race, and not only doubled the bets as before, but piled up everything they could raise, seemingly almost crazed with the excitement of their previous success. The riders mounted; the word was given. Throwing away his club, the Indian rider gave a whoop, at which the sheep-like pony pricked up his ears and went away like the wind, almost two feet to the mare's one. The last fifty yards of the course were run by the pony with the rider sitting face to his tail, making hideous grimaces, and beckoning to the rider of the mare to come on. It afterwards transpired that the old sheep was a trick and straight pony, celebrated among all the tribes of the South." "Yet," comments Dellenbaugh,[45] "some people think the Amerind has no sense of humour." The humorous element, though it too has its bearing upon self-gratification, should not be allowed to obscure the fact that this case is one of gambling in an incidental setting of the amusing.

"Every one is familiar with Tacitus's[46] description of the ancient Germans who, when they had lost everything else, staked their freedom and their life on the last throw. H. M. Schuster[47] gives a long list of examples of Germans

---

[41] Turner, in BAE, XI, 178.

[42] Andree, *Eth. Parallelen*, 2d ser., 105; Niblack, in USNM, 1888, 344.

[43] *North. Amer.*, 329, 330.   [44] *Plains of Great West*, 329, 330.

[45] *N. Amer.*, 330.   [46] *Germania*, ch. XXIV.

[47] *Das Spiel, seine Entwicklung und Bedeutung im deutschen Recht* (Wien, 1878).

staking freedom, wife, and children, the clothes on their backs, life itself, yes, even their souls' salvation when their passion for play was at its height. That this is a universal Aryan trait is shown by the Indian poem of Nala and Damayanti. . . . Konrad von Haslau, says Schuster, testifies to having seen and heard 'how on the one hand dice are honoured, greeted, and kissed, and have offerings made to them, while on the other they were beaten and abused as if they possessed life. Often the player who has lost by them takes revenge by picking out the spots or smashing the dice with a stone or biting them in two to make them suffer.' "[48] This is a performance of the same order as the punishing of the fetish when things go wrong.[49]

One should bear in mind the evidence cited while considering the debt-relation and debt-slavery,[50] as indicating the savage's interest in playing with the aleatory element. Likewise in our special treatment of that element we have sought to indicate the place of the gambling interest.[51] In later times, while gambling has persisted in its cruder and more obvious forms, it has developed in addition certain new aspects, as in financial speculation. Man has never ceased and never will cease, unless his nature is completely altered, to take pleasure in playing with the chance of getting something for nothing or more for less, without the exertion of acquiring it in the ordinary, humdrum way.

It is evident that one of the attractive elements in gambling is the passage of property; nevertheless one would miss a most significant impulse in human nature if he failed to realize the fascination in merely playing with chance, where there are no stakes at all. It may amount to a veritable appetite and intoxication. It would sometimes appear as if a habit-forming drug were somehow latent in the situation. Anyone who has reflected upon the matter realizes that a prosperous gambling business must rest upon some sort of solid basis of calculation according to which a system has been devised which cannot lose; there is always, nevertheless, a feeling that the bank can be broken and the system beaten—a sentiment which is periodically galvanized by some freak of chance against which no system, however prudently devised, can provide. There are always those who, though they realize the truth of the matter, take keen pleasure in trying to win, even in the privacy of their own homes over the evening solitaire-table. To the addict there is an interest in experiencing the mild excitement both of

[48] Groos, *Play of Man,* 211, 216.   [49] §§244, 276, 277, above.
[50] §§83, 105, above.   [51] §194, above.

getting ahead and of falling back in the game, and even in facing the inevitability of eventual failure. It is somewhat more than a pastime merely to toy a little, and not at all seriously, with chance.

This gambling impulse is catered to and kept vigorous by the very nature of human life. Men have to meet the unpredictable at every turn; every road of experience and thought leads to the unknown. From the stock-dealer to the laboratory scientist, men are always hoping for the happy chance that means material success or illuminating discovery. A whole section of human institutional development,[52] as we now know, centers about the aleatory element. It is so menacing and terrible in many of its manifestations that there is no self-gratification to be had out of it; but the picture is not complete until it is seen that there inheres in it likewise much that has afforded mankind both innocent and noxious self-gratification.

§437*. Sense-Gratification: Taste. Gratification of the senses, over and above the satisfaction resulting from adequate bodily maintenance, might be taken to represent the first approach to luxury. Bodily comfort is secured by bathing where there is no question primarily of cleanliness but of the exhilaration attendant upon, say, the sweat-bath.[53] Oiling and even painting the body are often less for show than for creature comfort, for example as defense against insects. There are many scattering forms of self-gratification which we shall not attempt to catalogue. Perhaps we should begin here with gluttony, which is merely an extreme of the satisfaction of hunger. In it is exhibited the passage of self-maintenance into self-gratification and at length into the dissatisfaction attendant upon satiety. To be noted is that what appears to be mere gluttony is not always such. Backward peoples often oscillate between starvation and repletion; in the absence of security in the preservation of supplies, the only safe thing to do is to eat as much as possible. Such cases of primitive improvidence are illustrated above.[54] Though it is not so easy to determine in a given case whether a prodigious performance in eating deserves

52 Part IV of this book.   53 Lippert, Kgchte., I, 355-356.
54 §80, above.

the name of gluttony or not, yet, despite this qualification, there is much over-eating for pleasure.

The Bushmen eat enormously when they can get food and then sleep it off. They are lazy and hard to move, preferring, up to a certain point, starvation to effort.[55] Three Africans eat easily, in a single night, a fat ram; five men eat a young calf in a day and a half. Women and children are not behind in such feats. They roll about on the ground to aid digestion.[56] The Green Corn Dance of certain Indian tribes is a tremendous gorge. During the week or ten days while the corn is soft and pulpy, all hunting and war are dispensed with; "and all join in the most excessive indulgence of gluttony and conviviality that can possibly be conceived. The fields of corn are generally pretty well stripped during this excess, and the poor improvident Indian thanks the Great Spirit for the indulgence he has had, and is satisfied to ripen merely the few ears that are necessary for his next year's planting." After certain ceremonial, "an unlimited license is given to the whole tribe, who surfeit upon it and indulge in all their favorite amusements and excesses until the fields of corn are exhausted, or its ears have become too hard for their comfortable mastication."[57] The orgies of the Australians over a stranded whale—"gorged to repletion with putrid meat—out of temper from indigestion, and therefore engaged in constant frays—suffering from a cutaneous disorder by high feeding"—are the extreme of beastly gluttony.[58]

Most social functions are, even yet, accompanied by eating, drinking, or other gratification of appetite. They are convivial. Feasts and festivals have in them always the element of self-gratification, even though their immediate object is religious or political. Festivals at harvest and vintage are occasions of gluttony and drunkenness, though they always or regularly bear a religious character. Feasts at weddings and funerals are often ruinous to the parties giving them; puberty-ceremonies and others of a public order represent a menace to economic well-being.

"Still more pernicious to the natives and still more ruinous to their welfare are the feasts they are obliged to celebrate, in consequence of their superstition not unfrequently causing misfortune of their whole family." These feasts are very numerous and the expense attendant is considerable. "The frequent repetition of such meetings and the extravagance with which their attractions are enjoyed, contribute much to the moral corruption of the natives. There drunkards and libertines receive their education, and idlers and gamesters are made. Business suffers considerably by them, the household concerns are neglected; women and girls are misled into a dissolute life, cause is given for quarrels and law-suits, and the transgression of the laws often originates from them."[59]

[55] Lichtenstein, S. Afr., II, 46, 195.   [56] Schmidt, Deut. Kol., II, 228.
[57] Donaldson, in Smithson. Rep., 1885, pt. II, 314, 315, 316.
[58] Grey, Journals, II, 278.   [59] Roth, Sarawak, II, clxxiii.

This case will stand for many and will recall other examples of festivals and celebrations cited in other connections elsewhere in this book.

Ordinary food makes no such appeal to the senses as do certain condiments, narcotics, and stimulants which may or may not conduce to bodily welfare. Typical of the condiments are salt, honey, spice, and, much later, sugar; while coffee, tea, tobacco, alcoholic preparations, opium, and hashish represent the toxic elements which possess little or no food-value. The popularity of the condiments is due to the savor which they lend to food. In the earliest days there must have been a sameness and lack of variety in diet of which one can now have little conception; of a consequence anything which served to lend piquancy to its taste was highly valued; onions, garlic, and pungent "bitter herbs" are found discharging this function.[60] Of all the early condiments, salt is the most popular and widespread; the word "sauce" is derived from it.[61]

Salts, indeed, as constituents of the body, must be acquired in some way. A supply of salt, says Möller,[62] is indispensable for mammals; but the author cannot refer exclusively to common salt, for there are certainly animals and human beings who do not have it.

The cows of the negroes give little milk; only by feeding them salt could more be obtained.[63] Dr. Livingstone[64] speaks of being "drawn on by a keen craving for animal food, as we had been entirely without salt for upward of two months." Elsewhere he speaks of the need of salt or, in default of it, of milk or meat, to counteract "the bad effects of a purely vegetable diet." Later, being deprived of salt for four months, at two distinct periods, Livingstone "felt no desire for it, but was plagued by very great longing for the above articles of food." The Sarasin brothers[65] cite authority to the effect that people who eat purely animal-food are ignorant of or indifferent to salt, while the vegetarians show an irrepressible longing for it as an indispensable article.

There are a good many peoples who do not have common salt. The salts they get come generally from ashes. Thus the Tasmanians dipped meat in the ashes before carrying it to the mouth;[66] and many other tribes have leached their salt out of wood-ashes.

[60] Lippert, *Kgchte.*, I, 619.
[61] Möller, *Salz*, 27.
[62] *Salz,* 9; Hehn, *Salz.*
[63] Stuhlmann, *Mit Emin,* 499.
[64] *Mission. Travels,* II, 524; I, 28 ff.
[65] *Weddas,* 448.
[66] Roth, *Tasmania,* 103.

This condiment, such as it is, is "the greatest delicacy of Central Africa."[67]

"Lye enters into almost all the food preparations of the Cherokees, the alkaline potash taking the place of salt, which is seldom used among them, having been introduced by the whites."[68] "The only salt in use among the Indians of Virginia was the ash of stick weed and hickory."[69] The natives of the Shingu region get salt by burning plants with large leaves that grow in stagnant water and leaching the ashes.[70] On the west coast of Jutland it was got, by a great expenditure of wood, from peat.[71] Such cases could be multiplied. Those at our disposal refer to districts of Melanesia, central and southern Africa, northeast Asia, the Malay Archipelago, Micronesia, Polynesia, North and South America, and the Canary Islands (aborigines). Homer[72] refers to people who do not know salt, which he calls "divine"; they are inlanders who would mistake an oar for a winnowing-shovel; and the writers of antiquity occasionally refer to such peoples.

Even though natives have inferior salts of their own, it does not take them long to appreciate the qualities of the salt of commerce. It comes to them as a notable luxury. When they have encountered it, especially where it has been rare, the enthusiasm for it is very great.

The Abongo had little interest in Lenz's[73] trinkets and wares; only when they saw salt "did they become more alert and begged hard for a little gift." "The negroes living between the Gambia and the Niger suck pieces of salt as eagerly as our children suck sugar-plums. It is there said of rich people that they eat salt at their meals." It is the symbol of goodness; "they even say: 'sweet, like salt.'"[74] In East Central Africa, salt "is particularly prized, and is also used as currency; it is made from the ashes of water-plants, but imported salt, especially that in crystalline form, is greatly preferred. . . . The natives believe that imported salt falls from heaven in Europe. Salt is eaten as a stimulant on a journey, and salt water is also drunk on these occasions. Geophagy is common, as is the case among the neighbouring Ba-Yanzi." The place of salt in the currency is exhibited in the following table:

"10 *djimbu* [small shell] = 1 *mitako* (brass rod, length 16.5 cm., diam. 3 mm.).
20 *mitako* = 1 fowl.
100 *mitako* = 1 'salt' (from 1 to 1½ kg.).
2 'salts' = 1 he-goat.
4 'salts' = 1 big she-goat.
10-20 'salts' = 1 female slave.
20 'salts' = 1 male slave."[75]

[67] Stuhlmann, *Mit Emin,* 477; Schweinfurth, *Heart of Afr.,* I, 269.
[68] Mooney, in BAE, VII, 330.   [69] Bruce, *Va.,* I, 167.
[70] Von den Steinen, *Zent. Bras.,* 106.   [71] Lund, *Norg. Hist.,* I, 19.
[72] *Odyssey,* XI, 122-125; XVII, 455-457.
[73] *Westafr.,* 108.
[74] Peschel, *Races,* 170; Paulitschke, *Nordost-Afr.,* I, 160; II, 190, note.
[75] Torday and Joyce, in JAI, XXXV, 403; and in JAI, XXXVI, 283.

"A Dyak once having eaten salt can *never* do without it; this article tames a savage more than aught else, human or divine." This is the opinion of Sir Charles Brooke. Of the interior Borneo tribes it is said: "Their incessant necessity to procure salt forces them to submit to the wishes and demands of their oppressors."[76] The civilized Veddahs quickly accustom themselves to salt and "it becomes for them a new need."[77] By exception, though salt is rare among them, the taste of Guiana Indians for it is far from general; they think it damages health.[78]

Salt, as an important article, becomes emblematic of hospitality and blood-friendship was strengthened by eating it together. The covenant of salt appears in the Bible.[79] The Roman salt-cellar was a symbol of family-life. Sprinkling with salt was a form of purification; it was also medicinal, as in the Old Testament, and holy from its use in embalming. It appears with some frequency in connection with witchcraft.[80] It became money, was monopolized by rulers, and was paid to Roman proconsuls and proprætors in set quantities, as *salarium*, that is, *salary*. That salt comes chiefly from the sea is evident from its etymology; there are only two European languages in which the name for salt does not go back to the Greek term for "sea" (*hals;* Latin *sal*).[81]

Honey, as the only concentrated natural sweet, has been to primitive peoples the object of much attention; it was a symbol of desirability to the ancient Hebrews, who longed for the "land of milk and honey." Its comparative scarcity impelled men to an adjustment with regard to its ownership; the bees' nest or the branch supporting it or even the tree in which it hung became one of the earliest pieces of immovable private property. It was used as a preservative of meat and an intoxicant, mead, was made from it. It became an article of sacrifice to the dead and the household-gods were anointed with it. It was thought to have power over spirits and to be therapeutic. Mediæval taxes were payable in honey and princes had their bee-agents. The commonest thing except corn to be given by manorial tenants in tribute was honey; and pious people donated their honey to a monastery.[82]

[76] Roth, *Sarawak*, I, 387.   [77] Sarasin, *Weddas,* 448.
[78] Roth, in BAE, XXXVIII, §§250-252.
[79] Levit., II, 13; Num., XVIII, 19; II Chron., XIII, 5.
[80] §308, above.
[81] Stuhlmann, *Mit Emin,* 421, 426; Möller, *Salz,* 5, 7, 8, 27, *et passim;* Zangwill, *Ghetto,* 225; Koshimoto, in PSM, XLVI, 213; West, "Symbolism of Salt," in PSM, LII, 244; Mason, *Woman's Share,* 146; Tylor, *Anth.,* 282; Peschel, *Races,* 170; Andriessen, "Münzen," in *Ausland,* LXV, 43.
[82] Lippert, *Kgchte.,* I, 63, 621, 627-628; Johnston, *Uganda,* II, 872; Sarasin, *Weddas,* 417, 446; Seymour, *Hom. Age,* 389; Keller, *Hom. Soc.,* 46, 131-132; Zangwill, *Ghetto,* 144; Campbell, quoted in AA, IX, 13; Staehr, *Artels,* II, 52; Vinogradoff, *Villainage,* 289; Garnier, *Brit. Peasantry,* I, 99.

Other sweets were less widespread and less concentrated. Sugar scarcely comes within our range of treatment. An eccentric case of procuring sweets is reported from Australia. "Another sweet liquid is obtained by mischievous boys from young parrakeets after they are fed by the old birds with honey dew, gathered from the blossoms of the trees. When a nest is discovered in the hole of a gum tree, it is constantly visited, and the young birds pulled out, and held by their feet till they disgorge their food into the mouth of their unwelcome visitant."[83]

There is no object in cataloguing the other condiments that played their part in rendering the monotonous diet of savage life more palatable.[84] It may be recorded, by way of curious interest, that earth is sometimes eaten for its piquant taste. On the Upper Congo, "the people ate a black, nice smelling mud called *nguna*. It was prepared by the Libinza people in thoroughly dried balls and sold to the Boloki folk at Monsembe, who, if they ran short of it, would break a Libinza made saucepan and nibble off pieces of it until they were able to renew their supply of mud balls. The only reason given was that it was nice to eat. Pregnant women ate a light clay."[85]

A word needs to be said, in preliminary, regarding the spices as a whole. Generally they were locally held, as in the case of turmeric,[86] to be medicinal; and a number of them have turned out to be not mere luxuries alone but wholesome stimulants to digestion.[87] However, to realize the importance assigned to the spices in human history one must consider the estimation in which pepper and the rest of the East Indian condiments were held prior to the Discoveries. Alaric's ransom of Rome was said to have been three thousand pounds of pepper.[88] The demand for the spices is reflected in the keenness of the mediæval Italian merchants in opening and utilizing the trade-routes to the East and in the efforts of Portuguese, Spanish, Dutch, and British to penetrate to the East by sea. Europe wanted spices and the demand was a large factor in the Discoveries; the manipulation of the trade in spices, tea, coffee, sugar, and other Eastern luxuries has been an

[83] Dawson, *Aust. Aborig.*, 21.   [84] Lippert, *Kgchte.*, I, 619.
[85] Weeks, in JAI, XXXIX, 457.
[86] Dymock, "Narcotics," in JASB, II, 44, 47; Dymock, "Turmeric," in JASB, II, 447.
[87] Bordier, *Géog. Méd.*, 14–15; Ratzel, *Vkde.*, I, 333.
[88] Gregorovius, *Rome*, I, 127.

important factor in the making of post-Discovery history.[89] Colonial policy was directed toward the acquisition and control over luxuries, not necessities; and the lands that promised little along those lines, such as temperate North America, were esteemed as not worth the effort of occupation. The story of the Discoveries and of subsequent conquest and so-called colonization is a grand commentary on the tendency of men to put forth effort and endure hardship for the sake of what they have not had, do not need, but insatiably want. It is a sort of epic of self-gratification.

§438*. Intoxicants and Narcotics. Of all the luxuries that men have ardently striven for, under the impulsion of physical appetite, the leading class is that of the poisons—the intoxicants. The substances that contain toxic elements are myriad: there are some, such as coffee, tea, maté, and tobacco, that are only mildly stimulant or narcotic; then there are others, on the order of opium or hemp (hashish, from which comes the word "assassin") that have powerful effects upon the nervous system. A large number of the intoxicants are such by reason of the fermentation of sugar or starch, resulting in the production of alcohol; according to the percentage of this product the corresponding stimulant may range from ardent spirits ("burning daimons," "fire-water") to light wines with very little power of inebriation.[90] The effect of these drugs and milder poisons upon the taker runs all the way from a mild nerve-quieting to the opium-dream and the frenzy that leads to running amuck; in them all, however, there is a certain relief from the ills of life and a gratifying effect upon the nervous system. It is no wonder that they were worshipped as fetishes[91] or even gods, for there was but little comprehension of the price at which the relief or the transport of pleasure was bought.

It is probably not going too far to say that almost any substance that can readily be used as an intoxicant has been so employed. Native stimulants and narcotics have generally been mild, because the methods of distillation or other preparation have been

89 Keller, *Colon.*, chs. II, III, X, XI, XII, *passim.*
90 Ranke, *Mensch*, I, 332-337, has a discussion of the various types of intoxicant.
91 §254, above.

defective; the white man has not so much introduced the native to alcoholic stimulants as provided him with compounds in which the content of alcohol is high and its quality low. Still even this is not always true. "Philanthropists in England," says Sir Harry Johnston,[92] "who have never visited Africa seem to imagine that the negro of the far interior who is carefully shielded from contact with European forms of alcohol is a total abstainer. On the contrary, he is far more frequently drunk on his own fermented liquors than is the case with the negro of the west coast, who may have easy access to European gin, rum, whiskey, or wine."

Addiction to the worst of these poisons has constituted a quality of unfitness of which societal selection has not been slow to take advantage; the disappearance of the savage in contact with civilization has been much hastened in several regions of the earth by self-poisoning through alcohol and other toxics, the pursuit of self-gratification having been at the expense of both societal and organic well-being. This is an extreme case; milder counterparts of it appear in connection with almost all forms of pleasure-seeking. There is no question about the immense enthusiasm of men in the pursuit of this form of self-gratification; no science of society could give a correct representation of society's evolution and life if it took no account of this element. Statistics of domestic and foreign trade reveal the enduring importance of the demand for intoxicants, both mild and strong.

It is somewhat inexact to refer to the use of intoxicants as a gratification of taste. As a matter of fact, it is rather the rule that they are not relished on first acquaintance;[93] and it is not the sensation of the palate that is sought by addicts to stimulants but the exhilaration and intoxication itself. This might be called an acquired taste or appetite, however; and there is no harm in classifying the stimulants and narcotics under taste-gratification if the facts of the case are appreciated.

Figures have been assembled to indicate roughly the popularity of these instruments of self-gratification. Coffee leaves are used as the basis of a decoction drunk by two million people, while the drinkers of the common coffee number many millions more. Paraguay tea (*maté*) is drunk by ten million and as many more consume coca. Millions use chicory, pure or with coffee and cocoa

92 *Uganda*, II, 591.
93 London, *John Barleycorn*, 37, 60, 98, 112, 340.

either as chocolate or in some other form. One hundred million chew betel or some of its substitutes; three hundred million eat and smoke hashish; millions use opium. Hundreds of millions drink tea. All the known people of the earth are devoted to the use of tobacco.[94] In short, not a people is found which does not use some means of narcotic enjoyment. Drug-addicts might be included in this list. Though such statistics cannot aim at exactitude, they certainly witness to the importance of the element of taste-gratification.

It is possible to cite many narcotics and stimulants whose names are not known except to the specialist, in support of the foregoing statement about the virtual universality of the use of such articles. Lippert[95] lists a number. The Australian used twigs of a bush called *pitcheri;*[96] Africans employed several plants of unfamiliar name;[97] Americans make powders of certain weeds, leaves, and tree-bark which they snuff,[98] and the coca and *kola* are very popular in South America.[99] Hemp is used in the East, Near East, and Africa,[100] and in the East Indies. There are also other narcotics derived from vegetable forms whose names mean nothing to the layman.[101] The ravages of opium in China and the East need not be illustrated.[102] Most of the stimulants are habit-forming, some being deleterious to the digestive and nervous systems and others apparently harmless. Nachtigal[103] says he came to miss the guro-nut preparation more than tea, coffee, or tobacco but never noticed any ill effects whatsoever. Generally, as has been noted in its place,[104] such drugs are regarded widely as fetishes with which magic can be accomplished. "We learn the great importance which men attach to the use of narcotic stuffs in conjuring. . . . They regard an ecstatic condition as necessary and know the means of inducing it."[105] The Indian *peyote* is one of the less well-known stimulants.[106]

Typical of the milder stimulants are the betel-nut and tobacco. The former is chewed throughout the East Indies, Australasia, and part of southern Asia —in general, throughout the Malay race. It was used very commonly in southern China in bygone centuries but has been supplanted by tobacco and

[94] Ratzel, *Vkde.,* I, 337.　　　　[95] *Kgchte.,* I, 625.

[96] Howitt, in JAI, XX, 76.

[97] Ratzel, *Vkde.,* I, 101; Livingstone, *Mission. Travels,* 597-580; Kingsley, *Travels West Afr.,* 667; Paulitschke, *Nordost-Afr.,* I, 166; Nachtigal, *Sahara,* I, 667, 669.

[98] Donaldson, in *Smithson. Rep.,* 1885, pt. II, 410; Von Martius, *Beiträge,* I, 389-390, 410-411.

[99] Bordier, *Géog. Méd.,* 71, 162 ff., 170; in AA, III, 613-614; Andriessen, in *Ausland,* LXV, 43.

[100] Ratzel, *Vkde.,* I, 335; Dymock, "Narcotics," in JASB, II, 40, 41; Dymock, "Use of Bhang," in JASB, II, 469, 481; Johnston, *Uganda,* II, 674; Stuhlmann, *Mit Emin,* 751.

[101] Moszkowski, in *Globus,* XCIV, 315; Wereschagin, in *Globus,* XXIV, 2, 23, 34.

[102] Scheltema, in *Am. Jr. Soc.,* XIII, 79 ff., 224 ff.; Scheltema, "Opium en Nog Wat," in *Ind.-Gids,* January, 1914.

[103] *Sahara,* I, 667, 669.　　　　[104] §§299, 301, above.

[105] Lehmann, *Overtro,* III, 7.

[106] Mooney, "Peyote," in HAI, II, 237; Hrdlička, in BAE, Bull. XXXIV, index *sub* "peyote."

opium.[107] It contains alkaloids of whose action the organism becomes tolerant, it is supposed by Samoans to be a cure for fever, and is known by Europeans to be therapeutic in other connections.[108] In Farther India, "the constant chewing of betel-nut with lime discolours the teeth of nearly all the girls and women, sometimes completely spoiling their appearance when they open their mouths, as the teeth are chocolate in colour. They have a certain amount of excuse for the custom, as they often suffer from toothache, and they believe that betel-chewing helps to destroy the 'worm' that they think makes holes in the teeth."[109] The betel plays the same part in ceremonies of peace-making as the pipe and rum-glass do elsewhere and is presented in token of civility or affection. "It is likewise given in confirmation of a pledge, promise, or betrothal," as a challenge or an invitation to undertake some difficult affair. A man proposes by asking a girl for a chew and bride and groom chew in common. Betel is the head of the adat (mores), of the customary law, and of counsel.[110]

Even if tobacco was known prior to the discovery of America,[111] it amounted to little until introduced from the New World; it has since shown, in a comparatively short time, the most amazing spread. Of the Melanesian it is said: "There is only one thing the loss of which would draw a tear from the shallow well of his eyes—American tobacco. Alcohol and sugar have no allurements for him; only the narcotic weed seems to possess the charm to soothe the savage Kanaka's breast."[112] "They are all smokers and 'from the beginning' tobacco has been grown and smoked."[113] "Two things appear to the native almost as necessary as his food—betel-nut and tobacco. Abundance of both makes life rosy, their absence robs it of all pleasure. Sometimes the natives assert that they could not live if they were deprived of tobacco. . . . Betel-nut is quite indispensable, even more so perhaps. Many a native would rather lack food all day than betel-nut. . . . Two things constitute perfect friendship —the eating of food together and the sharing of betel-nut and tobacco. . . . A whale-boat crew with a stick of tobacco will row twice as far in the same time as a crew with none. The tobacco appears to renew their strength, while the betel-nut takes away hunger and thirst. . . . On the average about three-fourths of their wages goes in tobacco."[114] "Previously to their communication with Europeans the Andamanese had no knowledge of smoking, but so rapidly have both men and women acquired the habit that when away from home and unable to obtain tobacco, they fill their pipes with *pan* leaves rather than endure the privation. So confirmed and excessive has the tobacco habit become that it is almost impossible to get them to do any work without its use."[115]

Of the West Africans it is reported: "There is not a single thing Europe

107 Wilken, *Vkde.*, 11-13; Ratzel, *Vkde.*, I, 336; DeGroot, *Relig. Syst.*, I, 153.
108 Dymock, "Narcotics," in JASB, II, 39; Wilken, *Vkde.*, 12.
109 Milne, *Eastern Clan*, 108.
110 Ratzel, *Vkde.*, II, 448; Wilken, *Vkde.*, 13; Dymock, "Narcotics," in JASB, II, 37; Finsch, *Ethnol. Erfahr.*, II, 326.
111 Wiener, *Africa and the Disc. of Amer.*, II.
112 Von Pfeil, "Duk Duk," in JAI, XXVII, 182; Von Pfeil, *Südsee*, 157; Pratt, *New Guinea Cannibals*, 192, 195.
113 Chalmers, in JAI, XXXIII, 120.
114 Jenness and Ballentyne, *D'Entrecasteaux*, 163-164.
115 Man, in JAI, XII, 112; Man, in JAI, XXIII, 232 ff.

can sell to the natives that is of the nature of a true necessity, a thing the natives must have or starve. There is but one thing that even approaches in the West African markets to what wheat is in our own—that thing is to-bacco."[116] In Uganda both sexes and all ages use tobacco. "The fighting men take snuff, the old married men chew tobacco, and the old women smoke it. The Lumbwa people make tobacco juice by keeping macerated tobacco leaves soaked in water in a goat horn slung round the neck. Closing one nostril with a finger, they tilt the head on one side, and then pour the liquid tobacco juice out of the horn into the other nostril. Both nostrils are then pinched for a few minutes, after which the liquid is allowed to trickle out."[117] In India the bowls of pipes have "a small bamboo receptacle beneath for the tobacco juice, which is collected, mixed with a little water, and carried about in a small tube from which sips are taken." The women are sometimes compelled to supply, from their incessant smoking, nicotine water for the men.[118] In Borneo, tobacco is the next important item after food and is received in trade even when salt is refused. "Children begin its use long before they shed their milk-teeth."[119]

"Although tea and tobacco do not, like alcoholic spirits, produce any evil physical consequences, yet they exert very disadvantageous economic effects; for the sensual, light-minded Tungus with incredible extravagance squanders his most valuable article of exchange, sable (out of which he has still his tax to pay), for these objects and for other articles of luxury, thus falling into debt and becoming quite impoverished as time goes on. It is chiefly the sly Yakuts who furnish him with all the luxuries and in so doing live like true parasites at the cost of their consumers," taking an exorbitant payment in sable-skins.[120]

The use of tobacco by the native American is familiar to most people; a wooden Indian used to grace the front of most tobacco-stores. "On the arrival of the first Europeans in North America the natives were observed to make offerings of the smoke of some plant, generally believed to be tobacco, to their many deities and spirits; by it disease was treated, and the smoke ascending from the pipe was regarded as an evidence of such an act as the sealing of an agreement or the binding of a treaty. Tobacco was likewise offered in propi-tiation of angry waters, to allay destructive winds, and to protect the traveler." The plant was credited by European writers of the Discoveries period with wonderful properties; it was supposed to cure not diseases alone, but wounds. It came to be called "herbe sainte," "yerba sancta," and "erba santa croce" by French, Spanish, and Portuguese respectively. "Tobacco was cultivated in most tribes by the men alone, and was usually smoked by them only; among the Iroquois and some of the Pueblos trade tobacco was not smoked in solemn ceremonies." "The plant was commonly used throughout Europe as an antidote against the plague and other diseases. Its cultivation, to the exclusion of other vegetal products, brought the colonies of Virginia and Maryland on more than one occasion to the verge of starvation." Among the Indians, "no important undertaking was entered upon without deliberation and discussion in a solemn council at which the pipe was smoked by all present. The remarkable similarity in smoking customs throughout the continent proves the great antiquity of the

[116] Kingsley, *W. Afr. Studies,* 339.   [117] Johnston, *Uganda,* II, 872.
[118] Woodthorpe, in JAI, XI, 197; Carey and Tuck, *Chin Hills,* I, 183.
[119] Hiller, in *Bull. Geog. Soc. Phila.,* III, 59.
[120] Hiekisch, *Tungusen,* 86.

practice." There was no higher courtesy than to offer to light one's tobacco for him.[121] "The Indians . . . believed that it had the power to increase virility: the warriors who had several wives used it freely, while unmarried ones either partook of it sparingly or not at all."[122] The Guiana Indians made much of tobacco.[123]

Two billions of dollars a year are spent on tobacco in the United States— about twice the amount accorded to education. It is evident that an interesting and significant history of tobacco could be written; here, however, we content ourselves with the above facts and those already cited which stamp this narcotic as a fetish-plant.[124]

The toxic power of most of the substances heretofore noted, excepting hemp or opium, are relatively slight and harmless. No race has perished from the use of these milder narcotics or stimulants; all peoples have used them and mankind still exists. Some of them have conferred benefits upon their users, either as prophylactics, medicines, or otherwise. This cannot be said of the Siberian narcotic drink that is made out of bilberry juice and that of the deadly *amanita muscaria* mushroom, a fungus with which the shamans intoxicate themselves in their professional activities.[125] Of all powerful intoxicants the most widespread are the alcoholic drinks. To list them in their great variety or to recount the peoples that use them is impracticable. It is more enlightening, perhaps, to review the few instances which we have encountered of peoples who are said to have had no intoxicants prior to contact with civilization.

According to Tylor,[126] the Australians, North Americans, and Hottentots knew no fermented drinks. This statement is not precise as respects the Indians,[127] and does not mean that the Australians had no form of intoxicant at all. It is stated that honey-wine was known in New South Wales.[128] The Tasmanians, we are told, drank water only; yet they collected a saccharine liquor from a tree which, if allowed to stand for some time, "ferments and settles into a coarse kind of wine or cider, rather intoxicating if drunk to excess."[129] In some regions of Melanesia the natives had not learned to make intoxicating drinks, though the juice of the wild sugar-cane, palm-sap, and other possibili-

[121] McGuire, "Tobacco and Pipes," in HAI, II, 257-260, 603-604, 767-769; McGuire, "Smoking Customs," in USNM, 1897, 361 ff.
[122] Bruce, *Va.*, I, 161 ff.
[123] Roth, in BAE, XXXVIII, §§282 ff.
[124] §§248, 254, above.
[125] §311, above; Ratzel, *Vkde.*, I, 335; Bourke, *Skatalog. Rites,* ch. XI.
[126] *Anth.*, 268; Lippert, *Kgchte.*, I, 630-631.
[127] Hough, "Fermentation," "Foods," in HAI, I, 456, 468.
[128] Ratzel, *Vkde.*, II, 54.   [129] Roth, *Tasmania,* 98, 108.

ties were at hand. Alcoholic drinks are repugnant to some of the natives.[130] The D'Entrecasteaux Islanders made no intoxicating beverage and did not gamble.[131] "Until the time of their first communication with Europeans, the Andamanese had no conception of liquor and its effects. They coined a word for a drunken person—'staggerer.' "[132] The South African Maschukulumbe were indifferent to intoxicating drinks, and certain negroes of West Africa "have no intoxicating drinks"—they know how to make one but scarcely ever use it. The Monbuttoo have plantains, but fermented drink made from them is almost unknown. The Somals have a sort of beer but do not know spirits.[133] The Hyberboreans in general have no strong drink of their own; like the Eskimo, they have nothing to make it with.[134] The wild Veddahs do not know alcohol and the more civilized do not like it.[135] China long ago forbade alcoholic drinks[136] and they are unknown to a number of Malay peoples. The well-known taboo of spirits to Mohammedans affects the Archipelago; then the impulse to self-gratification leads to the use of hemp and opium.[137]

So far as known, the New Zealanders had no intoxicating drink; they have taken up tobacco-smoking with passion. Certain of the Caroline and Gilbert Islanders knew no intoxicants and there were none on Easter Island.[138] The Indians of the northwest coast of North America formerly had no spirits and refused the brandy offered by Russians as a "scandalous" liquor which would take away their senses. The Virginia Indians had no knowledge of spirits, except the juice of the crushed maize-stalk, "unless the infusion of hickory nuts with water can be so regarded. The liquid they seemed most to enjoy was the water that had been standing long in ponds exposed to the sun." "So far as known mescal was not fermented by the Indians to produce an intoxicating drink before the coming of the Spaniards." Intoxicants were unknown among the Shingu Indians of South America.[139] Again, singing was wholly prohibited by certain Indians by whom it was regarded as a sign of drunkenness,[140] which they seem to have abominated; but "the Guiana Indians are well versed in the manufacture of fermented liquors" of all sorts.[141] Of an Arabian district it is reported that "no drink but water is known hereabouts, though date-tree wine might easily be manufactured, and the old poets and writers of Northern Arabia often mention it; but it has now gone out of fashion, and even remembrance."[142]

[130] Finsch, Samoafahrten, 261; Von Pfeil, Südsee, 41-42; Somerville, in JAI, XXVI, 381; Somerville, in JAI, XXIII, 382.

[131] Jenness and Ballentyne, D'Entrecasteaux, 209.

[132] Man, in JAI, XII, 112.

[133] Holub, Capstadt, II, 212; Lenz, Westafr., 200; Schweinfurth, Heart of Afr., II, 88; Paulitschke, Nordost-Afr., I, 163.

[134] Ratzel, Vkde., II, 728.   [135] Sarasin, Weddas, 411.

[136] Schallmayer, Vererbung, 206.

[137] Wilken, Vkde., 10, 11, 17; Jacobs, Groot-Atjeh, I, 254-255; Nieuwenhuis, Borneo, I, 104.

[138] Ratzel, Vkde., II, 167; Finsch, Ethnol. Erfahr., III, 26, 204; Cook, in USNM, 1897, I, 716; Hough, "Mescal," in HAI, I, 845.

[139] Niblack, in USNM, 1888, 344; Bruce, Va., I, 167; Von den Steinen, in Mitth. Berl. Mus., 1885, 187.

[140] Sapper, in Globus, LXXXVII, 130.

[141] Roth, in BAE, XXXVIII, §§256 ff., 282 ff.

[142] Palgrave, Cent. and E. Arabia, 49.

In contrast with these few and not always clear cases of the absence of fermented drinks, the instances where natives know how to make them and use them enthusiastically are legion. *Yangona* is prepared with much formality by the Fijians,[143] and *kava* and palm-wine are widely in use in Melanesia and the Pacific Islands.[144] In Africa intoxicating drinks are made from millet, maize, bananas, and sugar-cane; and wherever the palm grows they top it for palm-wine. Honey is fermented into a sort of mead and from less familiar vegetal sources other decoctions are derived which turn their users "into devils." Banana-wine is typical of Uganda. Spirits are less in use in East Equatorial Africa than in the west, this being referred to the presence of Arabs.[145] "Nearly all [East African] natives, including most of the Mohammedan tribes, are, with the exception of the Somali and the warrior castes of the Nilotic tribes, passionately addicted to drink. There is much truth in what has been written: that the whole population of Tropical and Subtropical Africa is drunk after sunset. Many kinds of fermented liquor exist. . . . *Pombe*—beer made either from bananas or from maize and millet—is the curse of the African native. Entirely unable as he is by constitution to resist temptation, he drinks as long as the state of his finances and the existing provisions permit. It has always seemed to me as if the effects of intoxication on a native were different from what they are on a European. They may be similar when he gets hold of whiskey; but they undoubtedly differ in cases of drunkenness produced by pombe. In a native who has got drunk on pombe, the effect is none the less violent because it is less apparent in the beginning. Its climax is reached some twenty-four to thirty-six hours after the libation has ceased, and manifests itself in a nervous irritability which often leads to disastrous consequences. Some individuals in this state, although sober to all appearances, become a grave danger to their neighbors. . . . It is probable that the shortness of memory, with which most natives are afflicted to quite a remarkable degree as regards things which do not touch them directly, is due in part to this racial vice and in part to the abuse of the elixirs mentioned above."[146] In East Africa, "the honey barrels are always marked with the mark of the clan (not of the family), and their possession is most sacred. Often they are further protected by a spell laid at the tree, which causes a thief to be bitten by snakes on descending from the tree. Formerly, if a man was caught three times stealing hives he was killed: to be found in the tree was regarded as equivalent to having committed the theft. . . . The honey is not used much for eating, but

[143] Weld, in PSM, XLVIII, 232.

[144] Gray, in AAAS, 1892, 648, 661; Ratzel, *Vkde.*, II, 166, 167; Finsch, *Ethnol. Erfahr.*, II, 66; III, 250; Christian, *Caroline Isl.*, 188-191; Semper, *Palau-Ins.*, 49; Pereiro, *Ponapé*, 112 ff.; Becke, *Pacific Tales*, 67, 227.

[145] Ratzel, *Vkde.*, I, 213; Fritsch, *Eingeb. S.-Afr.*, 90, 189, 332, 352; Holub, *Capstadt*, II, 123-124; Holub, *S.-Afr.*, II, 343; Bent, *Mashonaland*, 55; Serpa Pinto, *Africa*, I, 146, 147, 245; Klose, *Togo*, 473; Ratzel, *Vkde.*, II, 540; Rohlfs, in *Mitth. J. Perthes' Geog. Anstalt*, Ergänzband. V, Ergänzheft. 25, p. 10, note; Junker, *Afr.*, I, 198 note, 262, 309, 367, 448 note, 481 note; II, 137, 330, 355-356; III, 49, 399; Johnston, *Uganda*, II, 673; Stuhlmann, *Mit Emin*, 177; Ratzel, *Vkde.*, I, 201, 460; Abbott, in USNM, 1891, 394; Vannutelli e Citerni, *L'Omo*, 195, 440, 441; Schweinfurth, *Heart of Afr.*, II, 68; Paulitschke, *Nordost-Afr.*, I, 164, 165; Ratzel, *Vkde.*, III, 141; *Russian Ethnog.* (Russ.), II, 179.

[146] Coudenhove, in *Atl. Mo.*, CXXVIII, 167-168.

is destined almost entirely to be made into the much loved honey beer, 'Njoki.' But for this I am afraid that the Akamba would not bother much about the honey collecting. . . . Mostly the beer-drinks end in everybody being wildly intoxicated, and then as often as not a fierce fight ensues, and it is on such occasions that perhaps 90 per cent of the murders committed occur."[147] Of course the natives very speedily learned to use strong intoxicants, whether or not they had them before the Europeans came. "For a dram the Hottentot is at any time ready to serve, while for a bottle of raw spirits he will ride as a messenger all night, will sell his wife, or commit a murder." They liked tobacco so well that they cultivated it without incitement from the missionaries.[148]

The Soyots of the Yenesei make kumyss from mare's milk, less often from that of the reindeer. They get the condensed steam from out of the spout of a vessel of boiling fluid by chilling. "We were treated, and judged that the kumyss contained twenty-five to thirty per cent of alcohol." The Soyots drink themselves full of the warmish product just out of the still. They have fearful tobacco, which they snuff, especially at greeting. It is hard on a European if there are many hosts. They pass the pipe about like the Indians, and infectious diseases are thus spread. The Kirghiz too make kumyss.[149]

The Tibetans drink barley-wine or *chang*, and various forms of beer are common in India.[150] *Saki, arrack,* and other names of liquors distilled from rice, date-juice, and other grains and fruits are more or less familiar.[151] Even the Ainos have their fermented drink from rice and millet.[152] Palm-wine is common in the Malay Archipelago, and also a combination of arrack and honey which is very intoxicating.[153] Perelaer[154] mentions a Dyak drink called by him *toewak,* made out of rice, sugar, and betel-nut and always in evidence on festal occasions. He says it has a peculiar effect upon a European; "it does not make him drunk but *stopelgek,*" which is to say, crazy enough for a strait-jacket.

When we come to North America, we find a pretty general absence of fermented liquors. The Greenlanders have taken to coffee with the enthusiasm of novices. Indulgence in it has become a vice.[155] What liquors the Indians had were generally drunk unfermented or reduced, like the sap of the maple, to sugar.[156] Yet there were some distilled beverages, usually ardent and strongly alcoholic—*tesvin, mescal, pulque,* and *maguey*—prepared from various plants and fruits.[157] The Tarahumari of Mexico say that the agave, from which they make an intoxicating drink, was the first plant created by their god.[158] "I saw

---

[147] Dundas, C., in JAI, XLIII, 502-503.

[148] Schmidt, *Deut. Kolonien,* II, 228.

[149] Olsen, *Primitivt Folk,* 84, 85, 91; *Russian Ethnog.* (Russ.), II, 179.

[150] Rockhill, in USNM, 1893, 706; Cunningham, *Ladak,* 306; Waddell, *Himalayas,* 74, 75, 76; Waddell, *Buddhism,* 265; Carey and Tuck, *Chin Hills,* I, 183, 184; Woodthorpe, in JAI, XI, 64.

[151] Williams, *Middle Kingdom,* I, 808; Bourke, *Skatalogic Rites,* 75.

[152] Hitchcock, in USNM, 1890, 458.

[153] Wallace, *Malay Arch.,* 216, 368; Veth, *Borneo's Wester-Afdeeling,* II, 294; Bock, *Borneo,* 85; Semon, *Aust. Bush.,* 494, 495; Wirth, in AA, X, 363; Brandeis, in *Globus,* XCI, 62.

[154] *Dajaks,* 22.   [155] Nansen, *Esk. Life,* 95.

[156] Ratzel, *Vkde.,* II, 609.

[157] Hrdlička, in BAE, Bull. XXXIV, 26-27; Bruce, *Va.,* I, 167, note.

[158] Lumholtz, in *Scribner's Mag.,* XVI, 35.

men empty at one draught calabashes that certainly contain from two to three quarts, then hurry off to a tree, squeeze in their stomachs, relieve themselves of what they had drunk, and directly afterwards accept from the hand of the woman waiting for them the newly filled calabash, again to guzzle its contents at one pull. In the drinking of paiwarri, the Indian is never satisfied, and here also the dance and song, if one can apply that name to a villainous bawling, continue until the intoxicating liquor is drained to the last drop."[159] The so-called "manzanita cider" is all consumed before it has time to ferment, so that they do not get intoxicated, but other compounds are carefully fermented.[160] Farther south the toxic element seems to have been more appreciated: *pulque, peyote,* and other intoxicants flourished; "but the worst of all is that made of the alder tree."[161] The South Americans seem to have been more enterprising than the northern tribes in producing intoxicants. In British Guiana there was a drink prepared from maize, sweet potatoes, and the juice of the sugar-cane; and mandioca entered largely into the making of intoxicants.[162]

Dr. Mayo[163] suggests that a pure water-supply promotes temperance and that much of the drinking of intoxicants has been due to the need of a sterile beverage. "The drink habit is one of the many forms of individual protection resorted to by nature to save man from filthy diseases which cause death, or that which is worse than death, intellectual deterioration." This is an interesting observation by a wise man upon modern conditions but it does not cover the ethnographical facts.

In connection with the great majority of these intoxicants there is found the same sort of ceremonial, often highly religious, that has been encountered in the case of tobacco and other similar articles. They are all of a fetishistic quality by reason of the ecstasy or inspiration which they induce.[164] Drunkenness is what is wanted by the celebrants; in some cases all must by custom

[159] Schomburgk, *Brit. Guiana,* I, 207; Roth, in BAE, XXXVIII, 470.

[160] Powers, in *Contrib. N. A. Ethnol.,* III, 376; Dellenbaugh, *North Amer.,* 360.

[161] Bourke, "Distillation," in AA, VII (o.s.), 297; Lumholtz, in *Scribner's Mag.,* XVI, 438; Hough, "Pulque," in *Proceedings of USNM,* XXXIII, 577-592; Brinton, *Races,* 259; Brinton, *Nagualism,* 7, 9, 10; Hrdlička, in AA, VI, 73, 74; Nadaillac, *Preh. Amer.,* 268, note; Sapper, in *Globus,* LXXVI, 349; Sapper, in *Globus,* LXXVII, 5; Wickham, rev. in JAI, XXIV, 203.

[162] Ratzel, *Vkde.,* I, 335; II, 608 ff.; Schomburgk, *Brit.-Guiana,* I, 201-202; Appun, "Getränke," in *Globus,* XVIII, 268; Brown, *First Republic,* 409; Von den Steinen, *Zent. Bras.,* 212, 433; Koch-Grünberg, in *Globus,* XC, 117-118; Spix u. Martius, *Brasilien,* 1220, 1221; Von Koenigswald, in *Globus,* XCIII, 379, and in *Globus,* XCIV, 45; Schmidt, in *Globus,* LXXXII, 97-98; Frič, in *Globus,* LXXXIX, 233; Koch, in *Globus,* LXXVIII, 219; Koch, in *Globus,* LXXXI, 6, 45, 71-73.

[163] In N. Y. *Times,* Feb. 15, 1924.   [164] §§254, 311, above.

become drunk or at least feign drunkenness. That "only three instances of drunkenness occur in the action of the Homeric story, and a heavy punishment follows each,"[165] is a highly exceptional piece of evidence. The element of self-gratification is always present and strong in the use of intoxicants; they are employed to get rid of care by the only animal that feels care.[166] Any additional burden of living which is not yet familiar in the mores becomes, when imposed, a personal load of care and anxiety for the individual. There are penalties of progress, especially for the less adjustible. It is reported that the savage becomes less carefree—often, indeed, sullen and morose—when contact with white men has thrown him out of adjustment. Though such increases of care, absolutely considered, are not great in the case of the uncivilized, still the sense of oppression produced by any slight increment of worriment is very considerable upon minds less disciplined to the bearing of such loads. The savage is at least as eager to banish his seemingly slight cares as the civilized man is to get rid of his heavier ones.

The deleterious effects of intoxicants upon native peoples are obvious enough; that there is some little compensation here is not always realized. In Portuguese Benguela "brandy discharges for men the same function that in Europe oil discharges for machines. Without it nothing moves."[167] In dealing with South African natives it is said that beer "clears the moral atmosphere and is a useful valve."[168] It is only by the enlistment of an ardent interest that results can be attained. That the interest is in the large an inexpedient one does not affect this fact.

§439. The Strain after Luxury. Now that the more material forms of self-gratification have been outlined and before going on to the æsthetic arts, it is in place to gather up a few generalities which look both backward and forward. The most important of these is that the advance of civilization allows an increasing amount of energy to be expended in self-gratification; in fact, a considerable portion of the race, having been emancipated by on-sweeping culture from the mere struggle for existence and being

---

165 Preuss, in *Arch. f. Anth.*, XXIX, 169; Seymour, *Hom. Age*, 227.
166 Lippert, *Kgchte.*, I, 622, 624-625.   167 Serpa Pinto, *Africa*, I, 67.
168 Guyot, in *Bull. and Mem. Soc. d'Anthrop. de Paris*, Ser. V, t. 2, p. 367.

safe enough as regards the vital and primordial needs, has its eye fixed upon self-gratification almost alone. It is after more and better and is not content with what it regards as a bare sufficiency. It is seeking a higher standard of living, not mere existence and self-perpetuation. Even among uncivilized peoples there are classes that are thus emancipated and assured of leisure which can be used to plan for more leisure and for new forms of self-realization.

Viewed from this angle, self-gratification looks like a sort of sublimated self-maintenance—like something that supervenes upon success in providing for regular and routine wants. The possibility of competing for it is, from one aspect, a sort of prize for success in self-maintenance, though it is not to be denied that enfranchisement may so run out into license that privilege may destroy the strength that won it. From another point of view, again, self-gratification becomes the forerunner of self-maintenance. For after it has been enabled to reach forth beyond maintenance, the latter moves out into the area opened up by the former; what has been novel and exciting becomes regular and routine; what have been luxuries become necessities; the element of gratification fades out of them along with their novelty and they are taken as a matter of course. Consider the case of sugar, once a rare luxury, now so much of a necessity that one nation may be rationed in behalf of another. Take the telephone or the automobile. Says a French official: "The Eiffel Tower is a necessity. If there were no Eiffel Tower, it would be necessary to construct one."[169] Of the original satisfaction in the attainment of a luxury all that is left is discomfort in its absence; joy in the getting is replaced by grumbling at deprivation.

The human race, with what looks like strange perversity, has over and over again spent its greatest enthusiasm upon that which is not bread; nevertheless the arts which have been developed in the service and under the special stimulus of pleasure-seeking or vanity have been turned in the next stage to the service of self-maintenance. Uncivilized peoples who grasp at beads and other trifles, when merchants first come among them, learn later to appreciate tools, weapons, and fabrics and even arrive at length at

[169] N. Y. *Times*, May 6, 1923.

a knowledge of the processes by which such products are made.[170] The desire for luxurious foods is a spur to effort and trade; it brings about contact with other races and consequent acculturation. The taste for luxuries leads nomads over to civilization.[171] Luxuries break the way for utilities.

"It is everywhere the way of uncivilized men to strive more energetically for that which the more experienced civilized man has learned to regard as a superfluity, ranking it after the necessary and useful and even regarding it as a hindrance and obstacle to the necessary and useful." Barbarians have usually imitated the luxuries in dress of the civilized before they have assimilated more important things. Men have cared more for, and worked harder to get, the seasonings of food than the food itself.[172] "Nothing is more significant for the frivolity, improvidence, and hand-to-mouth life of the uncivilized man than the misproportion between ornament and clothing, luxury and necessity."[173] Such observations would seem to fasten upon the uncivilized man a weakness peculiar to his stage of culture and enlightenment; but the observing reader will note, upon a moment's reflection, that we are here dealing with a permanent trait of humanity. It is the uncommon and luxurious thing that stimulates mankind to the effort or self-denial necessary to attainment.

The following examples simply illustrate the tendency as it appears among primitive people whose sets of values differ from our own. In New Guinea, "the most cherished ornament . . . is the necklace of dog's teeth, which is prized by the Papuans beyond any article of 'trade' that the traveller can give them. Not even a knife or an axe is so welcome, nor can the traveller get so much work out of the Papuan for any steel implement as he can for one or two teeth." There is, again, the desirable nose-ornament. "Very few young blades can afford to possess one, and accordingly it may be lent, either for a consideration or as a very special favor. The possessor of one of these ornaments could easily buy a wife for it, and sometimes it is paid as a tribal tribute by one who may have to pay blood-money, or is unable to give the statutory pig as atonement for a murder."[174] The Papuan feather headdress, sixteen feet high and used in the tribal dance, taking a generation to make, is an heirloom and rare.[175] Again, "the Papuan of New Guinea is very fond of

170 Finsch, *Samoafahrten*, 62; Keller, *Colon.*, 29.
171 Lippert, *Kgchte.*, I, 620; Ratzel, *Vkde.*, III, 47, 57.
172 Lippert, *Kgchte.*, I, 364, 422, 620 ff.
173 Ratzel, *Vkde.*, II, 38.
174 Pratt, *New Guinea Cannibals*, 295, 297-298.
175 Pratt, in *Nat. Geog. Mag.*, XVIII, 569.

red paint, it is more to him than rouge to the actress or wool to our British ancestors when Cæsar first came to Britain. For a handful of red paint one may obtain sufficient bread stuff and vegetables of the country to stock a Covent Garden market."[176]

Bent's[177] negroes saved and carried along his empty tin cans to make ornaments; when given an old pair of boots the recipient took out the brass hooks and eyes to fasten as ornaments on his loin cloth and threw the rest away.

Clay-eating is performed by ladies in India because they fancy it improves the complexion.[178] With a Saora, "ornament precedes use." A head-man in a village will appear, in cold weather, with a mere scrap of thin cloth upon him, whereas he will present himself before the Governor's agent, in blazing hot weather, wearing a thick scarlet blanket with signs of great satisfaction.[179] Certain Assamese are beyond measure lazy and negligent in agriculture; at the end of the summer they are at the point of starvation; yet they cultivate opium and tobacco with great zeal, being extravagantly fond of them.[180] Aleutians and Fuegians, cold and miserable, lusted first of all for ornament.[181] Of the poorest villagers he met with on the Shingu River, Von den Steinen[182] says that "in spite of their poverty, they cared more for pearls than they did for knives."

Nansen[183] thinks it harmful for the East Greenlanders to touch the rim of civilization. They make a four years' journey to Cape Farewell for the sake of a half-hour in the depot of purchase—to buy tobacco or tea or to give good furs which they could use for their native dress in exchange for the cheap and shoddy European costume which they all prefer. They would not make this journey to get useful things.

The attainment of a higher standard of living opens perspectives of new wants to be satisfied; for few people rest and gloat upon what they have. The perfect adjustment, moreover, is never secured, since that which must be adjusted to—the body of life-conditions—is always changing. The very rise in the standard of living is bound to bring those who have secured it into new life-conditions; then they begin to feel new symptoms of maladjustment and the struggle begins all over again. It is no more than a stagnating society that is not intent on raising its standard of living. This "divine discontent" is a wide-reaching principle. The struggle for self-gratification, in this sense of an inveterate reaching-out for what is just beyond, is a thing too general to be confined under any special category; it is a covering condition of all life and evolution. Goethe[184] portrays the human spirit that can-

[176] Cayley-Webster, *New Guinea*, 50, 53.
[177] *Mashonaland*, 214, 215.
[178] Thurston, *S. India*, 552.
[179] Fawcett, in JASB, I, 218.
[180] Cooper, in *Globus*, XXVI, 60.
[181] Lippert, *Kgchte.*, I, 378, 374.
[182] *Zent. Bras.*, 113.
[183] *Esk. Life*, 186.
[184] *Faust*, pt. II, act V, 375-394, 481-531, 876 ff.

not be brought to say to the present moment: "Stay! Thou art so fair." Faust has always the presentiment, which saves him in the end, of a fairer moment just beyond; the episode of his death and the rescue of his immortal part is the last and profoundest word from one of the few who have possessed supreme insight into human life. And Faust does not stand for the individual alone; the people too that "exerts itself in continual striving" is the one that will be saved in the struggle.

Self-gratification is the domain on which idealization is born and nursed to great strength. Men are reaching out for a fuller realization of some satisfaction which has been experienced in some degree already.[185] "All idealism consists in this, that people want to spring over the immediate, attainable steps of evolution in order forthwith to arrive at a distant future which cannot at once be reached."[186] The eternal delusion lies in the fact that we think we decide the shape things are to take, whereas it is the things that shape us. "We are all so educated to the need of illusion that life without it seems flat, just as unseasoned food seems uneatable to one who is used to seasoning. . . . Most men love error more than the consciousness of ignorance or doubt, especially where it is a question of the ultimate 'purpose' of life as a whole. . . . As for the influence of illusion upon human happiness, it is like the effect of certain narcotics: one who has accustomed himself to them, needs them; one who has not, is no less happy without them."[187] The fascination of the drama, as of poetry and fiction, when literature has been developed, is in idealization. The loftiest drama and its literary allies may dwell on the fate of mortals caught in the vast machinery of earthly existence so that their wills and notions serve only to give zest to the cruelty of the tragedy in which they perish; but for the drama and its allies to be popular, they must portray and prophesy smooth eventualities. They remain on the plane of romance where it is possible for men to get rich without labor and for princes to marry beggar maids without unpleasant consequences. The ordinary man does not like tragic or otherwise unpleasant endings. This is the extreme of

185 §§339, 430, above.   186 Gumplowicz, Soc. u. Pol., 110.
187 Schallmayer, Vererbung, 232, 311; London, John Barleycorn, 12, 223, 305 ff., 315 ff.

idealization and we like it while we laugh at it and know it is false.

Though never primary, the imaginative element, when it is once brought into play by anterior causes, in itself becomes a new cause. It wins great power when it acts in the same way on a number of persons or a whole group, as in a crusade, in war for glory, in exploration, in *Minnedienst* or chivalry, and so on. It lends zest and stimulates interest to otherwise commonplace things. It throws a glamor over life. For its freest activity prosperity is needed, with leisure, freedom, ease, and a sense of power to do great things. Though the fundamental cause is the favorable conditions, yet the group's success is regularly attributed to its heroes, to current religions and philosophies, or to political institutions and dogmas. Then glory, national vanity, and a sense of achievement stimulate the imaginative element to new and higher flights. The horizon of thought is a mirage of golden illusions by which the vanity of men and nations is served.

There is no doubt that civilization develops a fringe of emancipation from primordial needs, especially from the hunger which sanctions self-maintenance; it is a zone of high possibilities for society's advancement and refinement. Finer powers are liberated and produce characteristic results. It seems a pity not to leave the case at that and to refrain from recalling the tough truth that, despite all acclaimed conquests over nature and lordship over their own destiny, most human beings spend the bulk of their lives doing what they do not choose to do or refraining from what they would like to do.

§440. **Line and Color.** It is said of the Chinese that they used to pass around delicate fabrics, when entertaining guests, for them to feel of, thus catering directly to the sense of touch; and there are many perfumes which have been compounded by peoples of some cultural development for the gratification of the nostrils. The lower stages of civilization show little appeal of this sort to the senses involved; but primitive peoples have with considerable unanimity taken pains to please the eye and ear. They have experimented with line, color, sound, and rhythm. Interested as we are in the societal rather than the technological aspects of human activities, in the satisfaction of the primordial and vital needs that suffered no denial and about which the imperative mores gathered rather than in habitudes that worked out into no massive societal structures, we shall pass over the fine arts rather summarily. Of these drawing, painting, and music have had rather less in the way of broad societal consequences than have dancing and acting; and this despite the fact that from the age of the cave-dwellers and from the lowest stages of civilization men have practised a delineation and coloring which is not by any means without its artistic appeal. Says Wallace[188] of the Papuans: "If these people are not savages, where shall we find any? Yet they have all a decided love for the fine arts, and spend their leisure time in executing works whose good taste and elegance would often be admired in our schools of design!"

Satisfaction in line, form, color, sound, and rhythm and in the imitation of things seen and heard is an original factor in the field with which the student of the science of society has to reckon but which he is not called upon to account for any more than for the play-tendency of children. There seem to be basic performances in art that please all, probably because all eyes and ears are essentially alike. Be this as it may, it is the societal results of the presence of the pleasure-factor rather than the nature or origin of that factor which enlist our present attention; for its consequences, by no means confined to the range of self-gratification, appear throughout the societal system and especially in the cult.

In the opinion of one writer,[189] the love of ornament is an older motive than worship; the latter set new tasks and higher aims for the art. Again, it is held that æsthetic ideas are derived and secondary; that nothing is done primarily to make an object beautiful. Finsch[190] says of the artistic products of the Papuans that they are accidents of whim or fantasy to which no deeper significance can be ascribed. "The negro knows nothing of the beauties of nature. Where it is warm and he has plenty to eat, he is well content."[191] There is in West Africa "the usual want of definiteness in expressing colours. . . . Colours are . . . grouped into three classes, light, dark, and reddish. To express different shades of colours with exactness recourse is had to natural objects." Illustrations are cited which are not unlike parallels to be found in Homer.[192] Totemistic notions caused animal carvings and then these became decorative. Symbols also led in the same direction: the seal is the symbol of plenty, not a totem; then the seal-figure becomes a decoration.[193] The Núkuóro

[188] Malay Archip., 510.   [189] Lippert, Kgchte., I, 34.
[190] Samoafahrten, 102.   [191] Stuhlmann, Mit Emin, 408.
[192] Ellis, Yoruba, 216-217; Keller, Hom. Soc., 76.
[193] Boas, in USNM, 1895, 392; McGee, in BAE, XVII, pt. I, 176*.

Islanders ordinarily use no ornament; "only at the religious festivals and the dances connected with them do they rub themselves with turmeric, put an ornament in the ear, and employ a special coiffure."[194] Drawing and coloring, and especially sculpture and architecture, being largely at the service of religion, became stereotyped by that association. It was undoubtedly priestly leisure that allowed of systematic progress in them.[195]

Brief illustration of artistic ornamentation may be taken from accounts of American Indian practice. "In painting, as in engraving, symbolic designs seem to originate largely with the men and the nonsymbolic with the women, although the distinctions between the work of the sexes probably vary with the social organization and state of culture." The origin of the designs seems to reflect something of the original sex-division of labor, or to denote the function of the individual somewhat as does the marriage-mark. "Considerable diversity in the ideas associated with decoration arises from differences in the spheres of activity of the men and the women. Delineative elements having their origin in myth and ceremony, in military occupations and the chase, and in pictography generally, are largely the creations of the men; the activities of the women are connected in a great measure with the domestic establishment, and embellishments employed in the strictly domestic arts consist in large part of designs derived from nonsymbolic sources or those which have associated meanings obtained traditionally, or from dreams, or such as are invented to please the fancy. However, articles made by the women for the men, as clothing and certain ceremonial objects, may be embellished with subjects pertaining to masculine activities. So different is the point of view of the two sexes that designs identical in origin and appearance, used by the men and the women respectively, have wholly distinct interpretations. It would seem that where a marked difference exists between the decorative work of the men and the women, especially among the more primitive tribes, that of the women is less distinctly symbolic than that of the men, less graphic in character, and more fully dominated by simple esthetic requirements."[196] Again, the designs reflected the experiences of life, and even the dreams or prayers of the decorator. "The horses of warriors were often painted to indicate the dreams or the war experiences of their riders. . . . Sometimes a man painted his robe in accordance with a dream, or pictured upon it a yearly record of his own deeds or of the prominent events of the tribe."[197]

It is never easy to say whether certain colors are employed for æsthetic reasons or because they are lucky or otherwise connected with religious ideas. Take the case of red, which to many tribes is virtually a fetish. Since to the Papuan red is lucky, red bushes are planted amongst the taro, to get good harvests. Red is only exceptionally the war-color. It is also the favorite color in the New Hebrides.[198] In China, too, it is lucky, drives away evil spirits, and dispels all inauspicious influences resulting from contact with death; in India, on the other hand, it is the death-color.[199] The Maori used it as the taboo-tint;

[194] Kubary, Núkuóro, 11.

[195] Spencer, Prin. Soc., III, chs. IX-XI.

[196] Holmes, "Ornament," in HAI, II, 152, 154; ch. V and §381, above.

[197] Fletcher, "Adornment," in HAI, I, 18, 19.

[198] Krieger, Neu-Guinea, 186; Finsch, Samoafahrten, 89; Turner, Samoa, 308.

[199] Grube, in Veröffentl. aus d. Königl. Museum f. Vkde., VII, 13; DeGroot, Relig. Syst. China, I, 6; Holtzmann, Ind. Sagen, II, 304.

their idols, sacred stages for the dead, offerings and sacrifices, graves, chiefs' houses, and war-canoes were thus painted. "In former times the chief anointed his entire person with red ochre; when fully dressed on state occasions, both he and his wives had red paint and oil poured upon the crown of the head and forehead, which gave them a gory appearance, as though their skulls had been cleft asunder."[200]

Among the American Indians, "the predilection for red, already remarked in connection with feathers and cloth, finds expression also in a very wide use of red paint for sacrificial purposes. Paint, like any other article, might be offered loose to a supernatural being, but usually it was daubed upon the stone, tree, or other object to which it was desired to show respect. . . . Red paint was usually smeared upon objects considered sacred, and Ntlakyapamuk women always painted their faces red when they went to gather berries or to dig roots on certain mountains, or just before they came in sight of certain lakes."[201] "This sacred red paint is a bright red ocher, about the color of brick-dust, which the Paiute procure from the neighborhood of their sacred eminence, Mount Grant. This is ground, and by the help of water, made into elliptical cakes about 6 inches long. It is the principal paint used by the Paiute in the Ghost Dance, and small portions of it are given by the messiah to all the delegates and are carried back by them to their respective tribes, where it is mixed with larger quantities of their own red paint and used in decorating the faces of the participants in the dance, the painting being solemnly performed for each dancer by the medicine-man himself. It is thought to ward off sickness, to contribute to long life, and assist the mental vision in the trance."[202] Among the Hopi, red was the war-color and sacred to the sun; black was the mourning-color and white that of peace.[203] Red had a ceremonial character in certain Brazilian tribes and was worn by an expectant mother.[204] Under the title of "The Psychology of Red," Ellis[205] notes that "everywhere, even in the folklore of modern Europe, we find that blood is a medicine, as it is also among the primitive aborigines of Australia."

One can hardly fail to suspect that the sacred character of red is somewhat connected with blood, especially as a red tint has been seen, here and there throughout our cases, to be a sort of substitute for blood.

The same color may have two opposite significations, as, for instance, white. "To the Iroquois and to many other Indians white as a color was auspicious, and its use in ritual and ceremony therefore indicated peace, health, welfare, and prosperity—ideas expressed by white wampum when ceremonially employed; on the contrary, black as a color was inauspicious, and its use therefore indicated hostility, sorrow, death, condolence, and mourning—ideas expressed by dark or purple wampum when ceremonially employed; nevertheless the dark or purple variety of wampum was commercially much more valuable than the white kind, and the darker its shade the more valuable it was. Commonly the ratio was as one to two."[206] Yellow is an auspicious color in India and among the Arabs.[207]

[200] Taylor, *Te Ika*, 209, 210.
[202] Mooney, in BAE, XIV, 778.
[204] Von Martius, *Beiträge*, I, 638.
[206] Hewitt, in HAI, II, 907.
[207] Dymock, in JASB, II, 443, 444; Von Kremer, *Kgchte.*, I, 152, note.
[201] Swanton, in HAI, II, 404-405.
[203] Matthews, in HAI, I, 325, 326.
[205] In PSM, LVII, 523.

One has only to recall the facts about the amulet-ornament[208] to apprehend the close connection between decoration and religion. It is profitless to discuss which of the two motives, vanity or ghost-fear, comes first. The interest involved lies in the interpenetration of self-gratification with religion, marriage, and other institutional forms rather than with any question of priority. It is dangerous to assume that any case is one of pure self-gratification. Men's motives seem sometimes to be solely æsthetic, as when the potter draws on his clay or the weaver works into his basketry lines and patterns that have no utility at all, either real or fancied; again and again, however, those additions are found to be significant beyond their superficial appearance, constituting, it may be, a protection against the evil eye or a fetishistic design.[209] Many cases have taught us that what we are likely to interpret as ornamentation by rhythmical repetition of lines and dots is really a series of pictures of objects or of personal marks of the makers, conventionalized through long usage; and that these marks were very often originally selected for an entirely unæsthetic reason—in order, for instance, to keep a vessel from breaking. The ornamentation is not an original attempt to satisfy any æsthetic "instinct." The same is true of tattooed lines and designs. It is asserted that the patterns on Oriental rugs are really conventionalized representations of things and ideas which have come down from great antiquity and that they often have cabalistic significance.[210]

A single example may indicate the pursuit of art for art's sake among a primitive people. "Throughout Melanesian New Guinea the artistic tendency attains its highest expression in wood carving and in each community there is at least one expert in this art. These experts are hereditary craftsmen, having been taught their trade by their fathers or maternal uncles, and in turn take as pupils their own or their sister's sons. They are shown special consideration, and are fed by the men by whom they are employed, and there is no doubt that their work is appreciated by their fellows, many of whom also carve, though their work is generally inferior to that of the experts. Apart from their appreciation of decoration the Papuo-Melanesians undoubtedly delight in the effort involved in its production and a man with nothing particular to do will take up some half-made or partially ornamented utensil and work leisurely at it in a way that certainly betokens pleasure. . . . Although art,

208 §§248, 254, 265, 301, above.
209 §265, above; Westermarck, in JAI, XXXIV.
210 Pommerol, *Sahariennes*, 355.

and especially decorative art, plays a much larger part in the life of the majority of Papuo-Melanesians than it does among ourselves, certain motifs are unaccountably absent. In the first place the sexual element is scarcely to be found, not only is there an absence of pornographic detail in art, but even the female genitalia themselves are seldom represented. This reticence is the more surprising since Papuasians betray no such reserve in their speech, while the utmost freedom in sexual affairs is allowed to the unmarried. Again, landscape is never represented and plants only rarely, in spite of the fact that among the Massim many clans have totem plants as well as totem animals."[211]

The American artist, Cox,[212] suggests that the prehistoric paintings may have had "a magic purpose, and have been intended to give the delineator power over the thing delineated." He holds, however, that "man must have learned to make an image of things before he can have thought of that image as giving him power over the things themselves. He must have made the first images in obedience to some deeply implanted instinct, and that instinct one must believe to have been another form of the instinct of imitation which controls the play of children and which originated the art of acting." It is risky to assert that one thing "must have" preceded another; but the natural connection between playing, acting, and delineation is unmistakable. Cox goes on to define painting as "the selective representation on a plane surface of objects or actions, real or imagined, by means of spaces, lines, colors, and variations of light and dark, all of which elements, as well as the materials employed, have been subjected to some principle of order for the attainment of unity."

The decorative motive played about the more massive institutional forms as the attainment of security in the satisfaction of more vital needs gave it liberty. It is broadly true that men pleased themselves by adding touches, useless even to their own credulous minds, to the useful and practical, but that they were unable, until a considerable degree of security in self-maintenance had been attained, to command the leisure and freedom from care necessary to the giving of consistent attention to the development of art as art. The primitive prototypes of the fine arts entered into the general life of society as distinctly subordinate factors; nevertheless the impulse was there and awaited fuller expression when conditions became favorable. The history of primitive art or architecture, like that of industrial processes, belongs to historical anthropology.[213] Some light will be thrown upon primitive decoration and taste when the topic of ornamentation and clothing is reviewed.[214]

[211] Seligmann, *Melanesians,* 36, 38.   [212] *Concerning Painting,* 6, 7, 62.

[213] General treatment in Grosse, *Beginnings of Art;* Haddon, *Evolution in Art;* Holmes, various works on American art; "Art," in HAI, I; Wilson, *Prehistoric American Art,* in USNM, 1896; Thomas, *Source-Book,* with references.

[214] §§447, 459, below.

§441. **Rhythm.** The allied arts of poetry, music, and dancing have exercised considerable influence upon societal development. Mere language, by gesture or the spoken word, is a practical instrument belonging in the first instance to self-maintenance; and mere sound by itself signifies little; what transforms both of them into gratification-elements is really rhythm, whether it be perceived through the ear or through the eye. The nervous structure of man is such that rhythm exercises a powerful influence upon him. Rhythmical sound pleases and even evokes or stimulates rhythmical motion; of the Saoras it is reported that "music has great effect on them, and seems to compel them to give vent to the emotional excitement it creates in rhythmic motion."[215] Effort is rendered less arduous if it is put forth in a tempo set by sound. The big racing canoes of Borneo are paddled in rhythm with the beating of an experienced director.[216] African carriers always get along better if they are allowed to accompany and assist their marching by chants and songs. The function of rhythm in military evolutions is better known than is its connection with various forms of labor.[217] Rhythmic sound or motion can even induce hypnosis. To sentiments expressed in meter are added an elevation, impressiveness, lightness, abandon, tenderness, or ferocity which common means of expression do not convey. Rhythm and tone can create states of mind, as instrumental music, unaccompanied by words, has often demonstrated. These are strange and unaccountable phenomena but that they occur is a commonplace. People like to feel them; and much of the race's time has been devoted to producing rhythm and experiencing its interesting effects. Men like to play with it.

It is not alone for the æsthetic pleasure derived from music that it is so consistently practised. Take the case of the drum and of singing. The former has been met with as a sacred instrument, the designating mark of the shaman; but it is far more than that. Each East African clan has its special drum beat. "In Uganda the drum is an indispensable instrument, it is a musical instrument, it peals forth the news of death, of birth, of joy, of war; to its sound the feet of the pedestrian are kept going, burdened porters are encouraged to press forward by it, and chiefs are known in the distance by the beat of

215 Fawcett, in JASB, I, 236.
216 Furness, *Head-Hunters*, cut opp. 76; Gomes, *Sea Dyaks*, 81, 225, 226; Roth, *Sarawak*, II, chs. XXV, XXVI; Haddon, *Head-Hunters*, ch. XXV.
217 Bücher, *Arbeit u. Rhythmus*, ch. II.

their drums. In short, it is to Uganda what the telegraph is to England."[218]
In the Congo region the drum is used for communication over considerable
distance. "One drum, the *lokole*, was used for 'talking.' By it they could signal
messages, they could abuse their enemies, and warn their friends. When I asked
some lads how it was done, they took their sticks and imitated the syllables of
some words and so went through a sentence. . . . Warnings, threats, and
abuse each had their own sets of sounds or notes, that were struck in various
order. Urgency in warning, vehemence in threats, and fierceness in abuse were
shown by the rapidity and strength of the beats. . . . Their mourning was said
to be musical, for while they admired one whose *crying* was in tune, they
jeered at another who had no rhythm about her wailing, and imitated her
unmusical weeping to the amusement of all present." Singing is combined with
drumming and has sometimes the same function. "Their songs are generally
topical, and as they paddle up or down river they give all the latest information of interest to the villages they pass. I have often been amazed at the
rapidity and accuracy with which news was spread in this way. . . . This
singing answered another purpose. It gave warning to the village that a canoe
was approaching and that the folk in it were friendly. A canoe of any size that
approached a town without singing and drumming was regarded as an enemy's
canoe and was treated as such, i.e., spears and stones, etc., would be thrown at
the occupants of it."[219] Thus there appears always to be a possible utility to
primitive art which attaches to it, to whatever æsthetic end it may be applied.

Not much of our space needs to be devoted to primitive poetry
and music;[220] there is little in them but the germ of later developments—monotonous repetitions of a few vocal or instrumental
sounds or endless reiteration of set phrases of a more or less
rhythmical character. They are often strikingly like the verses
and chantings that modern children affect; they are upon the
child-level and juvenile taste sees nothing amiss in them. The singing of the Hyperboreans is said to sound just like white men's
sobbing—so do the emotional efforts of certain operatic stars,
for that matter. There is no doubt about the taste of many very
backward tribes for singing, however, and some of the songs are
old enough to contain references to "articles which those of this
generation do not possess and would not understand the use of."[221]
Singing is often linked with rhythmic motions of the body and
passes into the dance. Although many songs are of a highly magical or religious character, even the Fuegians have those which are
sung by the people for amusement.

Professional singers have been in evidence for many ages. They

[218] Roscoe, in JAI, XXXIII, 29.
[219] Weeks, in JAI, XL, 404, 402-403.
[220] Wallaschek, *Prim. Music;* Myers, "Music," in *Anth. Ess.*, 235 ff.
[221] Patursson, *Sibirien,* 146; Worcester, *Philippine Isl.*, 496.

have been nomads or even vagabonds in their manner of life, or
have attached themselves to the rich and powerful whom they
have entertained or flattered. There was in this vocation even less
of specialization than in others. The mediæval jongleur is typical
of the itinerant entertainer: he was also a sort of animated news-
sheet, covering everything from foreign relations to agony-
columns.

"Poet, mountebank, musician, physician, beast-showman, and to some extent
diviner and sorcerer, the jongleur is also the orator of the public square, the
man adored by the crowd to whom he offers his drugs and his couplets. Questions of morals and politics, tooth-ache, pious legends, scandalous tales of
abbés, noble ladies and cavaliers, gossip of grog-shops and news from the Holy
Land were all in his domain."[222]

§442*. Dancing and Acting. The matter of rhythm can be
presented for our purposes by focussing attention upon the dance
and its derivatives, for it is in connection with rhythmical motion
that rhythmical sounds are commonly produced. First of all, respecting the dance, it is not at all certain that it belongs under
self-gratification rather than under religion; it will be recalled
that the buffalo-dance, the war-dance, the snake-dance, and other
well-known primitive types are part of the cult or of magic.[223]
Folk-dances were organized in the Middle Ages at times of deep
depression, as during visitations of the plague, to keep up the
spirits of the people.[224] To many the dance, as they understand it,
is a method of sexual provocation, a view portrayed in Lord
Byron's poem on the waltz. If this be so, the sex-element has been
imported, here as elsewhere, since primitive times, for among backward peoples and in ancient times the dance is reverential, even
when it is described as bacchanalian or obscene, and it is generally
performed by one sex alone or by both sexes apart from one another. There are no embracings and whatever sexual elements are
present belong generally to the religious festivity of which the
dance is likely to be the part most innocent of license. Sex among
primitive peoples is, as has been stated elsewhere,[225] something
about which there is little suggestion; it is a matter of course
somewhat as among animals. If some of their dances have an

222 Lenient, *Satire*, 23; Lichtenberger, *Nibelungen*, 400.
223 §§278, 302, 314, above.   224 Angerstein, *Volkstänze*, 7, 8.
225 §334, above.

erotic tinge, that aspect is more than likely to be ceremonial and ritual merely. If we carry back into these facts, for purposes of criticism, our own taboo on the sex-relation and all which pertains to it, we simply destroy the evidence as to early mores and ideas.

Of late there has been a movement to stop the Pueblo Indian dances on the ground that they are demoralizing and "are as indecent as it is possible for dances to be." This accusation is repelled by a noted authority[226] as "based on the grossest misinformation." The indecency of most primitive performances is in the eye of the observer.

It can hardly be thought that dancing was original in religion, however closely it seems to cling to the cult; it seems to have been, in origin, a pleasurable set of movements catering to the sense of rhythm. If the men liked it when alive, their ghosts did not cease to get pleasure from it; they liked to see it as they enjoyed viewing funeral-games. It is but a step to the notion that the daimons could be propitiated by the spectacle. The frequency of the dance in religion signifies merely that it was a prime pleasure of men and therefore a superior means of propitiation of the spirits. Then it could not but be connected with magic, rain-making, puberty-ceremonies, fortitude-tests, initiations into secret societies, ritual of such organizations, and all similar ceremonial.

One must not think of the savages as æsthetically appreciative of mere grace of movement any more than of mere palate-sensations in the case of an intoxicant. The fact is that the dance can defensibly be classified as an intoxicant;[227] what was wanted in many of the dances was elevation of spirit or even frenzy rather than a satisfaction of æsthetic yearnings. The primitive dance is often in the highest degree violent and exhausting. "If only the negro would show the lasting quality in work that he develops in the dance!"[228] One leader after another is dragged off in a state of collapse from his exertions. Gyrations induce vertigo and the minds of both performers and audience appear to be unhinged. The fetish-element is in evidence, for the dancers exhibit many of the marks of possession.[229] Still the fact that the dance is pleas-

226 Hodge, in N. Y. *Times,* Dec. 20, 1923; Oct. 26, 1924.
227 Lippert, *Kgchte.,* I, 632.
228 Conrau, in *Globus,* LXXV, 250.   229 §§246, 311, above.

urable and diverting, as well as edifying and religious, must not be lost sight of.

The following cases are selected from a considerable number as presenting significant features of the dance. "The leading amusement of the Australian aborigines is the . . . corroborree, which somewhat resembles pantomime, and consists of music, dancing, and acting." It is both a spectacle and a dance. In Australia the women have their own dances, "which they practice for their own pleasure when no men are present."[230]

To make rain, a number of finely ground emu-bones are placed in water, "the bones being about eleven inches long, pointed at both ends, and about a quarter of an inch in diameter. The whole circle then starts to chant, and the man on the inside ring picks one of the bones out of the water and thrusts it through a fold of skin over the muscle of the upper arm of the man opposite, then the one who has been pierced puts a bone through the arm of the man in the inner ring. When they have put the bones through the skin of the arm, they push some through loose flaps of the thigh" and through the skin of other bodily parts. "This is kept up until all the bones are used. The resulting blood is caught in the *pirrha* and the performers drink it after the ceremony. . . . These ceremonies read impressively, but to one watching them they seem futile. There is so much time taken up in preparation and so little in performance that one wonders at them ever starting. I think that the innate love of display and dressing-up that is so large a part of the aborigines' pleasure is responsible for much."[231] "In these performances all the animals represented are totems of the tribe, and the performers themselves, whenever possible, belong to the particular groups whose totem animals they represent. . . . Proceedings which outwardly appear to be merely imitations of the actions of different animals are really part of the instruction of the novices in the sacred lore connected with the totems and the ancestors of the various clans."[232] Mimetic dances are numerous in the D'Entrecasteaux Islands; the hunt is portrayed and also the ways of the animals.[233]

Malinowski[234] cites the curious case of the purchase of a dance; for even such a ceremony may constitute property, as was indicated earlier in this book. In the Trobriand Islands "important ceremonial visits are paid, in which a whole village calls on another officially, under the leadership of the chief. Such visits are sometimes connected with momentous transactions, such as the buying of dances, for these are always monopolies, and have to be bought at a considerable price. Such a transaction is a bit of native history, and will be spoken of for years and generations. I was fortunate enough to assist at one visit connected with such a transaction, which always consists of several visits, on each of which the visiting party (who are always the sellers) perform the dance officially, the onlookers learning the dance in this way, and some of them joining in the performance. All big official visits are celebrated with considerable presents, which are always given to the guests by the hosts. The latter,

---

[230] Dawson, *Aust. Aborig.*, 80; Curr, *Aust. Race*, I, 90; Smyth, *Vict.*, I, 166 ff.
[231] Horne and Aiston, *Cent. Aust.*, 115-116.
[232] Webster, in JAI, XLI, 484, 485.
[233] Jenness and Ballentyne, *D'Entrecasteaux*, 169 ff.
[234] In JAI, XLVI, 374.

in their turn, will visit their former guests and receive the return gifts." The last lines of this quotation exhibit a special form of entertainment characteristic of many primitive peoples.

Melanesian dances are like Polynesian and have lost their religious character; it is even asserted that these peoples have no religious dances. One Papuan dance showed how a flock of aquatic birds settles upon a piece of drift-wood floating on the sea and is at length driven off by bigger birds. One of the dances strenuously objected to by the missionaries is of little interest to the natives; "they call it 'the dance belong women'; and were it such an immoral proceeding, surely the men would crowd to see it."[235] The so-called Duk-Duk dance of the Melanesians is largely a means of curing the sick.[236]

The Herero show some sex-license in their dances but in general "they are of a mimetic nature, though war and the hunt play no such important rôle as among the Zulus and Xosa. Rather, therefore, do they exalt their precious cattle, whose behavior and movements they seek to imitate in their dances."[237] Again, in South Africa, there is a dance whose object is sex-excitement and which may be performed only at behest of the king. It is danced by two or four men, one of each pair appearing as a woman. "The costumes are royal property, so that it was impossible to get them." Other South Africans have a puberty-dance by the girls who have arrived at that stage. It is kept up for weeks, lasting always till toward midnight, and serves "to bind more intimately the bonds of friendship among the girls born in a locality who are of about the same age." They have also elephant, lion, and leopard dances after a successful hunt and dances at weddings, in connection with which they injure themselves with too much corn-beer.[238] Although the dance in Southwest Africa "has often a religious, or what is of about the same significance, a medicinal aim—the healing of the sick, the exorcism of evil spirits, the rousing of the dead—the dances often have also the character of pure enjoyment. At the bottom of every particular dance lies a definite idea. Chiefly it is a matter of representation from the life of animals or of hunting-scenes or even, as with the songs of the Herero, of an imitation of peculiarities of Europeans—for instance, how these wage war, make brick, or build houses. . . . In another dance the basic idea is the discovery and removal of a wild bees' hive. During the dancing about in a circle they indicate with arms, hands, and gestures the removal and conveying to the mouth of the precious luxury. From time to time several persons strike wildly about them with their arms to represent the beating off of the bees that surround them or indicate by a loud 'Ow, ow' sound that they are stung."[239]

The West African war-dance is a tumultuous affair, including a sham battle and much pantomime. Such a dance or one connected with fishing, which may seem to unite the men in a purely pleasurable way, may well have originated in exorcistic or propitiatory rites.[240] Johnston[241] speaks of a dance that "is said to be of an obscene nature, though, as I have said before, the obscenity

[235] Ratzel, *Vkde.*, II, 228; Hagen, *Papua's*, 273; Hardy and Elkington, *S. Seas*, 54.
[236] §§316, 317, above; Dall, in BAE, III, 100.
[237] Fritsch, *Eingeb. S.-Afr.*, 235.   [238] Holub, *Süd-Afr.*, II, 200, 258.
[239] Gentz, in *Globus*, LXXXIV, 156-157.
[240] Lenz, *Westafr.*, 196; Karutz, in *Globus*, LXXIX, 361, 362.
[241] *Uganda*, II, 753-754.

appears to lie in the stereotyped gestures, and not in the thoughts or intentions of the people at the time of dancing." Other dances occur on the occasion of a death, at an initiation-ceremony, after a wedding, and to bring rain. In India, actors are dressed and painted in imitation of the deities they represent. "The worst dances that I have ever seen have been in front of an image and as part of the rejoicings of a religious festival. Crowds of men, women, and children sit to watch them the whole night through."[242] In a Mortlock Islands dance, which is plainly indecent to European eyes, "no immoral outbreaks take place"; but dances of passion are common throughout Polynesia.[243] Japanese dancing, says Hearn,[244] "is something utterly different from what usually goes by the name,—something indescribably archaic, weird, and nevertheless fascinating. . . . Japanese dancing girls, be it observed, do not dance: they pose. The peasants dance."

The Eskimo drum-dance is really a combat in vituperative songs. But they regard it also as an entertainment and dance it for pastime, with singing and bodily contortions. "The most important festivals are apparently semi-religious in character, and partake strongly of the nature of dramatic representations." Masks of undoubted age are used in these dances.[245] American Indian dances are numerous and various.[246] They are largely pantomimic, sometimes include jests and horse-play, and involve a large element of fortitude-testing. The Indian war-dance, where "each warrior in turn jumps through the fire, and then advances shouting and boasting, and taking his oath, as he 'strikes the reddened post'" is familiar in American history and literature. Dances that involve self-torture, such as the sun-dance of the Sioux, which was forbidden by the Government after 1883,[247] have a distinct religious significance; they have been alluded to above.[248] The so-called "crazy dance" of the Arapahos went with the Ghost-dance religion, and "was performed only in obedience to a vow made by some person for the recovery of a sick child, for a successful war expedition, or some other Indian blessing."[249] The Snake-Dance of the Mokis and at Walpi is a rain-inducing ceremony.[250] A dance may even become a piece of property; a man may acquire it through marriage from his father-in-law; he then controls it and only with his consent may it be shown. A dance may be acquired also by killing its owner.[251] Of the Omaha it is said that "there was no ceremony in the tribe that corresponded to the drama, the acting out of a myth, a legend, or a story. There were dances and movements which were dramatic in character as when . . . a man acted out his warlike experience." Some examples of what might be called approaches to the dramatic are given.[252] The Salish had "dream-dances"—"we say 'dancing,' but

[242] Wilkins, *Mod. Hinduism*, 225.

[243] Finsch, *Ethnol. Erfahr.*, III, 309; Thomson, in USNM, 1889, 469.

[244] *Japan*, 222, note.

[245] Nansen, *Esk. Life*, 189; Murdoch, in BAE, IX, 365.

[246] Hewitt, "Dance," in HAI, I, 381-382; Donaldson, in *Smithson. Rep.*, 1885, pt. II, 314 ff.; Malkus, "Ind. Dances," in N. Y. *Times*, April 8, 1923.

[247] Dorsey, in BAE, XI; Schwatka, in *Century Mag.*, XVII; Beckwith, in *Smithson. Rep.*, 1886, pt. I, 250.

[248] §282, above.   [249] Mooney, in BAE, XIV, 1033.

[250] Bourke, *Snake Dance;* Fewkes, in *Smithson. Rep.*, 1895, 693; Fewkes, in BAE, XV; Crane, in *Atl. Mo.*, CXXXVI, 188 ff.

[251] Boas, in USNM, 1895, 421, 424.

[252] Fletcher and LaFlesche, in BAE, XXVII, 369 ff., 466.

these so-called 'dances' were rather dramatisations of their dreams, than dancing in our sense of the word."[253] The difference between the white man's drama
and the red man's is analyzed in a somewhat self-consciously literary and
oracular manner by D. H. Lawrence.[254]

Lumholtz[255] describes very fully a funeral-dance of the Tarahumari of
Mexico. "Dancing is an essential part of the Tarahumari's worship; it is not
for his pleasure; it is in order to secure rain and good crops and to ward off
evil that he dances." The Tarahumari words for dancing mean, literally, "they
are going to work." Among the Bororo of Brazil there are dances in imitation
of animals, with all their noises and movements. Both men and women take
part in the dance of the jaguar-skin. Women are not to see the skin which one
of the men, carrying it on his back, makes every exertion to show them. The
anxiety of the women is the point of the dance.[256]

Though not all primitive dances are violent, the effect of the
rhythm is very likely of itself to produce excitement, even if the
participators are in other respects sober; and it is the excitement
that affords most of the pleasure. The rhythmical movements are
almost always accompanied and guided by singing, slapping,
pounding, or drum-beating; indeed primitive music gets much of
its reason for being from its association with the dance. The tom-
tom of the medicine-man is, as an auxiliary to his gyrations,
almost the badge of his profession. The effect of music accompanying pantomime to heighten the effect is well recognized by the
producers of motion-pictures.

The drama seems at first sight to have sprung directly from the
cult; there was, however, an intermediate stage and that was the
dance.[257] It has been seen how closely the dance is related to religion; and dancing and play-acting have been almost indistinguishable in uncivilization. That the primitive dance is mimetic
is at once apparent to anyone who has looked into the subject
even superficially; imitation of the ways of animals and rehearsal
of their life-cycles form a favorite theme. Several types of dance
are nothing but imitative magic,[258] for example, the buffalo-
dance[259] and the war-dance, in which hoped-for successes are rehearsed. Such cases, as we think, may be merely acted prayers,

253 Hill-Tout, in JAI, XXXIV, 328.   254 N. Y. Times, Oct. 26, 1924.
255 Tarahumari, "Dances," in Scribner's Mag., XVI, 440.
256 Von den Steinen, Zent. Bras., 494.
257 Tylor, Anth., 298 ff.; Havemeyer, Drama of Savage Peoples (where
many cases are given at some length).
258 §302, above.
259 Description and plate in Donaldson, in Smithson. Rep., 1885, pt. II,
358 ff.

wherein the daimons are shown, beyond peradventure of misunderstanding, just what is wanted. Again, there may be a portrayal of episodes in the life of the gods, a performance staged at some place or time peculiarly associated with the activity of some special spirit.

Ridgeway[260] thinks that anthropology can render service to the classical scholar by relieving him of some of his longstanding errors, such as the traditionally close connection of the drama with Dionysus and the vintage. "Down to recent years it has been universally held that Greek tragedy arose in the worship of Dionysus, the Thracian god of wine, and that it was at the vintage festivals that tragedies were always performed. But now we know better. The festivals of Dionysus all fall in winter and spring, not in the vintage season. Some four years ago I pointed out that tragedy originated in Greece long before the Thracian god Dionysus ever was worshipped there, and that in Greece, in India, in Thibet, in China, in the Malay peninsula, and wherever there is a native tragedy, it has originated in the worship and propitiation of the dead. Such too is the origin of the early mediæval Christian drama, as for instance the passion plays still represented by that periodically performed at Ober Ammergau." Miss Harrison[261] believes that the "tragedy," the "mustsong," was derived really from the "bean-fest-song."

It is clear that religion, dramatic dances, music, songs, emotional suggestion and excitement, and sex-stimuli are intertwined in even low barbarism or savagery. In festivals and in the dramatic representations accompanying them there is frequently a certain relaxation or reversion from the moral status created by the mores to the ancient, "natural" ways, especially because the new manners are a reflection on the ancestral code and as such will displease the ghosts. Civilized people too relax, for a holiday, the discipline of ordinary life and make allowances in the theater for what would not be tolerated on the street or in the home; that an expression or action is in jest or is not real is an excuse for what is a little beyond the limit otherwise observed. If the reversion by Australian natives to primitive sex-mores with the purpose of satisfying notions of duty to religion and to ancestors[262] comes to us as an incomprehensible violation of what we regard as primary instincts, evidently the only way to understand it is to take the standpoint of the mores of the place and time. Many dramatized myths have presented acts such as later mores could not tolerate; they are put under conventional standards for the pur-

260 In JAI, XXXIX, 18.   261 *Greek Religion*, 421.
262 §344, above.

pose of representation, as we put the Bible stories and Shake-speare under conventional rules by themselves.

This conventionalization[263] can explain much, and it can be carried far enough to effect harm. A usage of self-gratification which is consonant with the mores, religious views, and world-philosophy of a people need work no corruption on them, for it is under taboos and conventions; whereas if all restraints are re-moved, it enters into their life for just what it is in its character: sensual, cruel, bloody, obscene. What had been, for instance, merely savage and bloodthirsty when the Romans were warriors became base and cowardly when they never incurred risks of any sort. Condemned criminals were compelled to enact rôles (Prome-theus, Dædalus, Orpheus, Hercules, Attis), in which the character represented suffered torture and a frightful death, and to be exe-cuted in that way incidentally in order to entertain the crowd.

Returning to the actual passage of the dance into the drama, we find that to pantomimic acting is added a vocal feature in the form of words chanted in accord with the tempo of the dance. A protagonist recites certain sentiments to which the rest respond in chorus; or two leaders chant antiphonally to each other and to the chorus. Then the part of the chorus has but to dwindle as the share of the protagonists increases in order to have the genuine play emerge. Paraphernalia such as masks and stature-increasing foot-gear develop to accentuate the presentation. It is instructive to notice that the words "chorus" and "orchestra" have to do, in their Greek forms, with dancing and that other theatrical terms are similarly revealing as to origins; that the meters of the Greek plays correspond to the walking, running, or swaying motions of the actors or chorus. The very terms for the stressed and un-stressed parts of the metric "foot" are, respectively, "thesis" and "arsis," meaning a "setting-down" and a "lifting." Further, the Greek plays, which were certainly the beginnings and models of occidental drama, reveal their source in the festival and dance, even if they were originally the worship and propitiation of the dead, as is likely, by their connection with Dionysus, who becomes the deity of the theater.

Several centuries ago, Europeans were highly diverted by pup-

263 §§324, 326, above.

pet-plays and the populace has hung about the Punch and Judy booth at fairs with untiring pertinacity; now such entertainment, except for occasional whims and conscious posturings of enthusiasts, has been relegated to the juvenile sphere. There has been a continuous refinement of dramatic representation, with periodic relapses and reversions. When the highest types of poetry, music, and acting have come to be associated with the drama and the opera, self-gratification in sound and rhythm has been lifted far above its humble beginnings. The professions of poet, musician, dancer, and playwright have disengaged themselves and a certain institutional character has been diffused somewhat vaguely over the theater and its connections.

When one looks in perspective at the proverbs, tale-telling, and other means of self-gratification, realizing that the proverbs and maxims in action, when set in a dramatic story, sink into the memory and win a zest that no philosophy can give; that the taboo is doubly effective when impressed by weighty authority and enforced by a tale of calamity; that the myths may be actually, in a sense, creative, and truer than history by virtue of the fact that they are experience generalized—he observes that the usages of self-gratification discharge a function over and above mere entertainment. They shape, formulate, and crystallize the folkways, delineate the code, give definite statement to standards, specify what is right and proper, differentiating so that it can be remembered between what should be done under certain circumstances and what should not. Ceremonial in general discharges a function covering these desirables. Much of ceremonial is, in part at least, entertainment; but that type which is, to appearance, much more frivolous than the religious variety—than such a serious rite as that of initiation, for example—yet attains the same results from a slightly or totally different angle. It renders standards tangible, understandable, unforgettable.

CHAPTER LX

OSTENTATION AND PRESTIGE

§443. Vanity. In our original canvass of the forces lying behind institutional development,[1] hunger, love, and ghost-fear have been distinguished as the impulses to self-maintenance and self-perpetuation; and vanity has been named as the typical force underlying activities in self-gratification—with the proviso, however, that it is only the most prominent of several allied impulses. These latter, together with the results of their influence, have now been reviewed: the senses or appetites or instincts leading to play, pastime, and gaming, to the struggle for luxuries catering to the palate, the eye, and the ear, to satisfaction of the sense of rhythm, and to the diversions of the theater. The way is now cleared for the consideration of vanity by itself.

Vanity is a sentiment which, like hunger, love, and ghost-fear, is capable of indefinite refinement—a process which, in the present instance, has been so long and so effectively in operation that certain evolved forms of vanity resemble the original sentiment about as distantly as a refined product of plant-breeding resembles the wild parent-form. Self-respect and a delicate sense of honor are very far from vain show and crass boasting. On the other hand, just as crude religious sentiment has persisted along with highly generalized and even etherealized forms, so have the primitive exhibitions of vanity lasted on alongside the evolved types.

In its essence, vanity seeks self-distinction, exaltation of personality, recognized superiority of various sorts, admiration, and applause, and out of attainment of these at the hand of fellow-men it derives a deep and enduring satisfaction. In no other range of societal phenomena is the subtle reaction of the societal and the individual element so evasive as here. There could be no play of vanity except in a society, yet vanity is above all other sentiments that one which begins and ends in self. The individual desires distinction; yet vanity makes him wish not to be distin-

[1] §§11-14, above.

guished by anything which will bring upon him contempt or social disapproval—unless, indeed, he can be so bad as to transcend the lower grades of disapproval and gain an evil eminence that the foolish will acknowledge. The criminal can generally reckon on a distinction and notoriety and even an ill-judged admiration that offset censure. Aside from such pathological cases, the boldest individual departs only a little from the societally regulated uniformity. Ambition for recognition leads to the most strenuous and unremitting effort and makes nothing of labor or pain endured in self-assertion; it is one of the most powerful of driving forces and is capable of overcoming even the inertia of the most primitive savage. The possibility of distinction and applause can be visualized by many men whose foresight is in other respects rudimentary and to whom the prospective satisfaction of other wants, both the primordial ones and the more refined and spiritual, makes unavailing appeal.

It is obvious that the development of vanity, in that it promotes ambition, has high selective value both for the individual who has it and for the class or society characterized by it. If it is present, it is sure to result in the elevation of the standard of living. "Every constraint which man puts upon himself out of vanity exerts a taming and subduing influence which has no parallel among animals. Such a moral subjugation of the still wholly naked savage begins with the high valuation he sets upon his individuality . . . and in this range vanity performs actual miracles of a moral kind."[2] Though vanity may be regarded as a vice and a weakness, yet the surest sign of decline in an individual, especially in a woman, is to cease to care how she looks; it is even said that when the women become indifferent in this matter it is a sign of tribal decline.[3] Of a certain people in Brazil it is reported that they wear no tribal designation and are in that respect like a number of hordes "that can no longer maintain their nationality in war."[4] Pride is gone. There is no doubt, either, that vanity leads to foresight and saving in order to attain the means of its satisfaction. Other services of vanity and pride will appear in the examples.

Vanity stimulates the individual to produce variations for selec-

[2] Lippert, *Kgchte.*, I, 343.   [3] Ploss, *Weib*, I, 39 (1885 ed.).
[4] Von Martius, *Beiträge*, I, 351.

tion to work upon; and group-vanity in the form of ethnocentrism is one of the main factors promoting that conflict and competition without which there can be no selection resulting in the survival of the fitter.[5] The Latin race, asserts the Spaniard, in rather belligerent italics, "is no less necessary than the Anglo-Saxon, that humanity may attain its further destiny"; and the Portuguese speaks of his nation as "a people, the freest in the world, that extends its liberty even to Africa."[6] It will be recalled that the institution of property has certain of its deepest roots in vanity.[7] To the eye of the evolutionist there is here a factor of the highest societal import, which has contributed powerfully to shape the course of society's evolution. Its activity has been so general that its effects are to be found scattered broadcast over society's life rather than assembled about the nucleus of any single interest to form a classifiable body of mores capable of being shaped into a specific institution. It will appear, as we go on through this chapter, that the vanity-element is intertwined very intimately with the other socializing forces,[8] with ghost-fear, for instance, and its expressions and derivatives. Some of the practices of self-gratification, tattooing for example, when all the motives for them are passed in review, may seem to belong elsewhere than under the chapter-topic of ostentation. If this is so, it is no matter; for the gratification-element should be seen in its full setting; and if it has evolved out of other and more serious interests, which still color its manifestations, that too is part of the picture. When we come, presently, to the permeation of the vanity-element throughout the societal structure,[9] we shall be able to indicate one last set of those cross-strands that bind together horizontally, as it were, the several institutional series which have had to be treated one at a time and, so to speak, longitudinally.[10]

§444. Fashion and Ostentation. The topic of fashion has been treated with some elaboration by one of the authors of this book.[11]

5 Keller, *Soc. Evol.*, 51-52, 58 ff.; Spencer, *Study of Soc.*, ch. IX, espec. 205, 213 ff.
6 Fabié, *Legisl. Españ.*, 50; Serpa Pinto, *África*, II, 58.
7 §113, above.   8 §§11 ff., above.
9 §450, below.
10 Chs. VIII, IX, X, XXXI, §§260, 261, above.
11 Sumner, *Folkways*, §§185 ff. and index, *sub* "fashion."

It belongs really in a survey of the mores and not peculiarly to self-gratification; it is a department of the mores, a set in the social mode of activity along defined lines, and it may affect any form of human activity. It extends all the way from dress and ornament to ideals of character and favorite objects of enthusiasm and devotion. In large part its manifestations and successive phases seem to be only the rolling over and over of cloud-shapes in which all change is merely relative readjustment of the constituent elements one to another, with no reference to guiding lines drawn from point to point in any all-encompassing horizon.[12] Though a tendency to concurrent preference or adherence, with consequent concurrent action, is often capricious and fantastic, yet it generally has a cause in the attempt to realize interests. Then come social contagion and imitation; the crowd falls into line and follows the path which has been lightly worn by a sparse vanguard. Thus fashion varies from the concurrence of many in a whim to the sanction by the multitude of a great faith or action which has been started by the few. If in the one view fashion seems contemptible, in the other it is highly important and expedient.

Fashion is readily seen to be a mode of transmission of rising variations in the mores. Those who follow it are practising a sort of imitation, sometimes enthusiastic but oftener simply enforced by fear of the penalties of non-conformity. Fashion pure and simple, therefore, does not belong especially to self-gratification any more than solely to clothing and ornament.

Nor is it confined to any stage of development. "The savage," says Schweinfurth,[13] "is voluntarily even more of a slave to fashion than any of the most refined children of civilization." This, to our way of thinking, would read better if it ran: "The savage people suffer pain to gratify vanity just as civilized people do."[14] The uncivilized are veritable slaves of fashion. We civilized people keep up that servitude, only we view most of our fashions with seriousness and gravity, whereas we find primitive modes laughable because they are not ours and seem obvious and childish or perverted and repellent. The nose-ring is ridiculous and even disgusting; the ear-ring is charming and dainty. Deforming the foot

[12] Keller, *Soc. Evol.*, 247-248.   [13] *Heart of Afr.*, I, 293.
[14] Von den Steinen, *Zent. Bras.*, 179.

is regarded as repulsive, though it does not directly threaten health, whereas waist-deformation has been thought proper, and doubtless will be again, even though it interferes directly with bodily welfare. The Chinaman, being patronizingly set aright in the matter of putting food on the graves of the dead on the ground that the dead cannot eat it, is entitled to his retort: "Why does the Christian put flowers on the graves of the dead? They cannot smell them." If the retort of the Oriental is regarded as irrelevant, inasmuch as our practice is now rationalized, yet much of the attention shown to the dead is due to the desire that others shall see and approve the sentiments we harbor and the correctness of our expression of them in memorials of various types. Mankind is prone to pose before fellow-men, and almost any occasion will do.

"*Bijang abwi*—great style! But style of what sort? Because bijang covers the things of ornament—a necklace is bijang; and the things of manner—a studied gesture is bijang. A mannered person is bijang, and a man on a bicycle is bijang. And while a man on a wheel is undoubtedly consumed with pride, there is another word for this flaming emotion. The pride, I suppose, is the inner exaltation, and the bijang is the air of distinction which is the fruit of that spirit. I know bijang when I see it. It is a conscious emphasis in ornament, or carriage, or deportment." These West Africans said, when this missionary stood and told them of the word of God, that the performance was "Bijang abwi!"[15]

There is no place where distance and detachment from our own ways are more needed, in order to see the truth, than in the consideration of fashion and modes of ostentation. The reflective person will view modern instances with a more seeing eye when he has pondered somewhat over the naïve vanity of savages or children. He will then no longer confuse a change in mode with a difference of essence. A few representative instances of primitive fashion and vanity will do to begin with.[16]

In Melanesia, "the fashion in pipes, and all other kinds of trade, changes at different times and varies in different localities. Sometimes nothing but perfectly plain pipes are demanded; at other times they must have the representation of a ship in full sail or an anchor impressed upon them. At one time they must have a knob, at another, knobs are out of fashion; now white pipes are in fashion, and again nothing will suit but red ones. . . . Today everyone smokes white clay pipes and the dealer is stormed with demands for white

[15] Mackenzie, in *Atl. Mo.*, CXXXI, 488.
[16] Sumner, *Folkways*, §§187, 188.

ones. Four weeks later no one wants any more of them; now all must have them brown; not one more white one does the dealer sell; if he has no brown ones, so much the worse for him. Four weeks later, again, no one wants any pipes at all; now they all run around with red umbrellas."[17]

Savages are capable of enduring great discomfort in order to be in fashion; there is the "African belle whose great copper rings on her limbs get so hot in the sun that an attendant carries a water-pot to sluice them down now and then."[18] Sometimes leg-rings "are so heavy that the ankles are often blistered by the weight pressing down; but it is the fashion, and is borne magnanimously." And "the gentlemen who wish to imitate their betters do so in their walk; you see men with only a few ounces of ornament on their legs strutting along as if they had double the number of pounds. When the writer smiled at the sight of one of these men, the people remarked, 'That is the way in which they show off their lordship in these parts.' "[19] Rich Herero women load themselves with iron ornaments up to a weight of thirty-five pounds. The slow, slouchy gait enforced by the carrying of this weight "is looked upon in Damaraland as peculiarly aristocratic."[20]

In the Congo a queen was observed who wore "a brass collar round her neck weighing from sixteen to twenty pounds, and compelling her every now and then to lie down and rest, these ornaments being permanently fixed on."[21] Scarcely less cumbrous were certain hats of gigantic size and fantastic shape that were worn in Uganda. They were as much as three feet high, consisting of a basket-work foundation plastered on the exterior with white kaolin, sometimes with stripes or patterns of black mud.[22] The wealthy wives in another tribe are often laden with iron to such a degree that without exaggeration, the writer[23] asserts, they carry close upon fifty pounds of metal. Elsewhere women wear around the hips strings of pearls bound in a bundle the weight of which makes them wabble as they walk.[24] Galla women carry about two or three kilograms of ornament.[25]

Some lower class women in India wear on the leg a brass, collar-like ornament which is fitted on with a hammer while they writhe upon the ground in pain. "These women would rather undergo the torture of putting the ornaments on than be without them. The heavier the ornament, the more beautiful the wearer is considered." Similarly with bangles reaching sometimes from wrist to elbow.[26] Fashion in a region of southern India called for the baring of the left thigh, both in front and behind, and also for the shaving of the head; "any relaxation of either custom would lead, it is believed, to the destruction of the tribe by tigers."[27] Thus does religious belief support custom.

A short, tight sarong or skirt, worn by Bornean women, enforces a mincing gait regarded as very graceful. Dyak dandies spend much time and great pains

[17] Woodford, *Head-hunters*, 178; Hagen, *Papua's*, 213-214.
[18] Tylor, *Anth.*, 243.
[19] Livingstone, *Mission. Travels*, 205, 298-299.
[20] Büttner, *Walfischbai*, 29 (235 of vol. entitled "Kamerun"); Tate, in JAI, XXXIV, 139.
[21] Phillips (discussion), in JAI, XVII, 235.
[22] Johnston, *Uganda*, II, 729-730.
[23] Schweinfurth, *Heart of Afr.*, 153; Johnston, *Uganda*, II, 808.
[24] Stuhlmann, *Mit Emin*, 23.　　[25] Paulitschke, *Nordost-Afr.*, I, 93.
[26] Mitra, in JASB, III, 370.　　[27] Thurston, *S. India*, 528.

in twisting about the loins a strip of cloth a yard wide and, in the case of exquisites, up to twelve or fourteen yards long. "It requires considerable practice to dispose gracefully of so much cloth about the person but more time is spent by these young dandies of the forest than one might imagine, in order that they may appear to the best advantage."[28]

Fashion, almost a synonym for whim or caprice, may yet show a stubborn persistence in survivalistic form, provided some religious idea such as the placation of ancestors enters into it as a sort of preservative. Consider the following examples of retention of the old.

Though the Africans of the west coast ordinarily dress in imported cloths, on all solemn occasions, such as a palaver, they costume themselves in leaves. Under his clothing the African sometimes wears the loin-string or even the apron. "Both skins and bark-cloth . . . are rapidly being replaced by the calico of India and America. It is, however, still the custom in Unyoro that a man and woman of whatever rank must, for at least four days after the marriage ceremony, wear native-made bark-cloths. . . . Until the trade with Arabs became an established thing in the country about forty years ago, the upper classes wore nothing but bark-cloth, and even at the present day the use of this cloth is *de rigueur* for certain purposes and certain occasions. I believe it is considered a matter of etiquette that all princesses and women about the king's court should wear nothing but bark-cloth. A Muganda man begins his clothing by winding a strip of bark-cloth round the hips and passing it between the legs, even though he may wear garments or a pair of trousers over this." It is said of a tribe of India that they were once allowed only an apron of twigs and leaves over the buttocks; it was a mark of their deep degradation. "But now, when no longer compulsory, and of no use, as it is worn over the clothes, the women still retain it, believing its disuse would be unlucky." Malay women, when they have adopted the Chinese costume, often wear a survival of the old fashion, for example, a string, now entirely useless but representing the ancient girdle. In like manner Andaman women wear the ancient bunch of leaves under the dress.[29] Other examples have appeared in the discussion of the old as the holy, under the topic of religion.[30]

It must be realized that fashion in dress is but one rather crass exhibition of the general phenomenon. The literature of any period runs on a fashion; the heroes and heroines of novels conform through a period to accepted types. Fashion dictates the virtues which shall be esteemed and the vices which shall be tolerated from one generation to another; also the doctrines, political and other,

[28] Schwaner, *Borneo,* I, 221; Roth, *Sarawak,* II, 54.

[29] Ratzel, *Vkde.,* I, 591; Stuhlmann, *Mit Emin,* 515, 652; Junker, *Afr.,* I, 149-150; Johnston, *Uganda,* II, 581-582, 648; Thurston, *S. India,* 524-525; Ratzel, *Vkde.,* II, 391.

[30] §324, above.

THE SCIENCE OF SOCIETY

that shall be accepted or condemned. Gestures, attitudes, usages like kissing, shaking hands, bowing, smiling in conversation, are arbitrary and conventional, controlled primarily by fashion, ultimately by taste. Like ornament and decoration, they add an element of grace and pleasure to the intercourse of men and make it easier. They therefore contribute to its utility.

Individuals and classes are always outbidding ordinary fashion in order to secure special distinction. Although fashions of primitive peoples partake of the stereotyped character of all their usages, nevertheless the mode is a domain in which the play of caprice and variation ranges as on native soil. There is less of the stereotyped here than in the more settled, institutional field. It is a matter of great importance that among the conservative tribesmen something should be variable and elastic, thus giving a chance for adjustment.

It is the unusual and non-customary that attract attention. When none are beautified, decoration is a distinction; when all become decorated, non-decoration may confer prestige. Napoleon, after he had surrounded himself with a band of marshals in most gorgeous uniforms, himself dressed with great simplicity; he had conferred the ornament, was too great to need it himself, yet remained the most conspicuous of all. "Nobody wears it," is at one time a reason why nobody will; "Everybody wears it," at another time, is a reason why all with one consent reject the article in question as common. The reason is the same in both cases. In the former, except for leaders, and perhaps even for them, it would be a cause of unfavorable preëminence; in the latter, it confers no distinction and that prize must be won by a change. At other times, "Nobody wears it" is a reason for wearing it—to win distinction. Again, "Everybody wears it" is a reason for wearing it —so as not to be odd.

It is evident that there is here an advance and then a retreat, an action and then a reaction, as so often in the evolution of the mores. For our purposes we may confine ourselves to the positive effort to outbid and outdo the rest in some selected and popular direction. Cases already before us have foreshadowed such rivalry, as where, when iron ornament is the fashion, the heaviest-laden is the most distinguished. The applause that attends victory in such a contest of ostentation is doubtless to most human beings one of the sweetest of earthly satisfactions.

The truth is that it is difficult to isolate cases of ostentation from their connection with religion, marriage and the family, and the other institutional developments. Yet there are some exhibitions of it that are more purely for vanity's sake than others; bodily ornament and deformations, badges and gauds, forms of address, and memorials of honor are examples of such. War for glory as distinguished from war for plunder belongs to self-gratification and vanity. Some of these items have been abundantly illustrated by Spencer[31] under the topic of ceremonial. Our instances will be confined chiefly to one or two types of ostentation, preceded by a few miscellaneous cases indicative of the boundless scope of the topic.

At feasts in the Fiji Islands the chiefs wear as much tapa or bark-cloth as possible. The ends are allowed to fall as a train behind. A case is mentioned where one chief wore two hundred meters of it.[32] Again, "a native wearing a calico loin-cloth and a top-hat poised on his woolly head and kept in position by a string round his chin is not an uncommon sight. Another may be seen wearing a pair of knee-breeches, a tennis shirt, with the collar turned up, and a trader's hat. Another, perhaps dispensing with the breeches, will wear only the hat and shirt. To meet a burly native with elaborate ear-rings, an ivory spike through his nose, and his face well marked, with a collar and dickey hanging round his neck, seems absolutely ridiculous, but the proud possessor of such a costume will strut about as if he were the best-dressed man in the islands. The humour of their costumes, needless to say, does not strike them, and their less-clothed neighbours look on them with envy, whilst the girls bill and coo at the sight of them—such is fashion."[33]

Rivers[34] finds much ostentation in the *kolekole* connected with the Melanesian secret societies. He cites a number of instances. "The chief features of a *kolekole* are the dance, the killing of pigs and the payments to those who participate, and every one will try to excel his neighbour in the splendour of the dance, the number of the slaughtered pigs and the liberality of payment. The whole behaviour of the people seems to be exactly of the same kind as when among ourselves people endeavour to gain social kudos by the splendour of weddings or funerals which may occur in their families. . . . It is probable, however, that the association with the *Sukwe* and *Tamate* societies is very close and deeply seated, and that the *kolekole* performances are means whereby the general population is allowed to participate to some extent in the ceremonial of these bodies." On the island of Pentecost, this author says, a rich man, after drinking kava, "will take sugar-cane in his mouth and after spitting

[31] *Prin. Soc.*, pt. IV, vol. II, §§343 ff.
[32] Ratzel, *Vkde.*, II, 232.
[33] Hardy and Elkington, *S. Seas*, 173-174.
[34] Rivers, *Melan. Soc.*, I, 130, 132, 138, 212.

this out, will take a second piece, shoot it out of his mouth and utter a long drawn out cry which is a sign to everyone that he is a rich man." In the Trobriand Islands, "vanity, display of wealth, of valuable, finely ornamented objects, is one of the ruling passions of the Kiriwinian. To 'swagger' with a large wooden sword, murderous looking, yet nicely carved and painted white and red, is an essential element of the fun to a Kiriwinian youth in festive paint, with a white nose sticking out of a completely blackened face, or one 'black eye,' or some rather complex curves running all across his face."[35]

Among the African Bahima "there is a difference between the women and the men; the former have a slight bend or stoop from the hips, this is artificial and is affected from an idea of its gracefulness—their back and shoulders are perfectly straight: the reason for walking with the bend may be accounted for by their extreme stoutness, and the lack of exercise. A Muhima beauty must be like a prize ox; too fat to walk, the women struggle along a few yards, and then stop to rest; the method of resting is to place a hand on either knee in a stooping posture for a few moments."[36] In Madagascar, as has been noted in another connection,[37] long strings of soot hanging from the inside of a house's roof are never brushed down. They prove antiquity and respectability, and the word for "soot" means "venerable from age."[38] In the Sahara women ride on camels in a big tent-like structure, in which they are shaken about in discomfort. They cling to it from vanity. It is for the young and attractive. Old women walk.[39] The Soyots of the Yenesei saw nothing in coin money except a novel sort of ornament. They always reckon values in squirrel-skins. Olsen[40] once paid a shaman in Russian silver coins. He wanted to know how many squirrel-skins they were worth, and gave them to his wife to hang on her ears. A social whim is manifested in Borneo by the passion for the possession of ancient jars, imported long ago and now objects of affection and superstition. The secret seems to lie in the fact that these jars are means of ostentation and social prestige, for they are not used and are set out only on state occasions. The sentiment in regard to them enters into the mores and even affects political power.[41] A Polynesian had his wife cooked over a fire which he had made her prepare and light herself; then he carved and ate her—all this without rancor or wrath, merely to acquire notoriety, to advance beyond the commonplace.[42]

Ostentation as connected with the potlatch has been cited in another connection. Of course the possession of wealth and property has always afforded the chance of display.[43] Cases not so extreme as those of self-destitution are common. "In 1883 the writer was invited to attend a feast of furs to be given by one of the most energetic of the . . . Indians of northeast Labrador. This man had been unusually successful in the capture of fur-bearing animals, and, to prove his wealth, displayed it before the assemblage and gave a feast in consideration of his ability."[44] The widows and children of the richest deceased Tinneh Indians are left in poverty because all the property is distributed at death for ostentation and glory.[45]

[35] Malinowski, in JAI, XLVI, 375.   [36] Roscoe, in JAI, XXXVII, 94.
[37] §324, above.   [38] Sibree, Great Afr. Isl., 159.
[39] Pommerol, Sahariennes, 382.   [40] Primitivt Folk, 94.
[41] Veth, Borneo's Wester-Afdeeling, 263.
[42] Pritchard, Polyn. Reminiscences, 371.
[43] §§81, 83, 113, above.   [44] Turner, in BAE, XI, 322, 323.
[45] Allen, in Smithson. Rep., 1886, pt. I, 265.

"Palaung girls are either dressed entirely in new clothes or entirely in shabby ones. . . . A girl once said to me, 'If I wear a new hood and a dirty old dress . . . people would think that I possessed no new clothes except the hood.' "[46] Among certain native tribes in Russia, the women, before putting on a new garment, dip it into a mixture of ashes and grease and thus turn it into a filthy, greasy rag. The reason for this is that if a woman puts on a clean garment evil tongues will say that it is clean because its mistress never sees either meat or sheep's fat; so the richer a woman is, the filthier and greasier is her dress.[47] For about a century after the settlement of Connecticut, "it was discreditable for those who had a competency to eat shad. It was disreputable to be destitute of salt pork, and the eating of shad implied a deficiency of pork."[48]

Any form of ostentation will do which distinguishes the individual or class practising it from the common herd. Evidently the forms are as numerous as there are opportunities for variation from the general code. The cases cited are representative of such departures in various directions. Being strange, they seem grotesque and ridiculous; but reflection reveals that the type they belong to has by no means passed away. A dispassionate observer from another planet would find them no more and no less ridiculous than the display of a higher civilization.

§445. Alterations of the Body. Among the multitudinous forms of ostentation, there has been selected for fuller illustration the habit of improving upon the body in various ways in order to lend it a beauty which it could not otherwise possess. The notion of beauty is not primary and cannot be defined in any way which will make it so without ignoring or doing violence to facts. That is beautiful which pleases taste. Taste, however, is not settled by dispute or debate; it is in the mores and is transmissible as they are, through imitation and education. Taste is not an independent reality but is relative and personal or local. Standards of beauty differ widely and may have little in common; they may be opposite and contradictory. The facts show that the notion of what is beautiful follows fashion and does not lead or create it any more than does the knowledge of what is healthful or useful or convenient. Ethnography, as preceding and following cases indicate, furnishes no evidence that human beings possess an innate æsthetic sense or instinct or that the idea of the beautiful is objective and

[46] Milne, *Eastern Clan,* 109.
[47] *Russian Ethnog.* (Russ.), II, 406.   [48] Judd, *Hist. Hadley,* 313.

real. That idea is a product of the notion of what is right and correct according to the standards set by the fashions. There are in these fields no ultimate tests of truth.

Types and standards of beauty as well as of propriety, distinction, and style have a wide societal influence. Those who conform to the types are selected for honor and win position and power, while others are despised, neglected, excluded, and more or less completely eliminated. Warriors, athletes, millionaires, military men, ecclesiastics, and other types may be the ones which at a time and in a particular society are public favorites. Others will ape the external forms, at least, and the manners of the favorite type and young people will be trained by their parents or will be driven by their own enthusiasm to model themselves upon that which is most esteemed. If in a modern state militarism is in fashion, fathers show greater pride in those sons who develop military tastes.

It is fortunate that fashion as to all these social matters is, in civilized societies, so mutable, for this brings it about that if one thing is favored for one time, another is favored for another. If the mode should run long on a certain type, the result would be societal distortion; for the process of selection would intensify, with time, in the favored direction; the more militarism prevailed, the more would men take to the military career and the stronger, from generation to generation, would societal selection in favor of militarism become. China has been cited as a case of distortion by selection in favor of industrialism.

It is important to notice that many of the bodily mutilations have, like circumcision, a religious origin; they represent exuvial sacrifice and are often the visible sign of proper relations with the spirits. Mutilations leave scars which fall into ceremonial uniformity, presently becoming the marks of a justified and chosen people, of a cult-bond uniting a set of worshippers. Thus they come to be tribal marks indicative of membership.[49] It is readily seen that they are sure to be the objects of eager striving and their attainment certain to confer gratification along with distinction. It is a rare case where, as among the Baganda, all mutilations are absent and the threatened imposition of a rite like cir-

[49] §§229, 298, above; Spencer, *Prin. Soc.*, II, ch. III; Lippert, *Kgchte.*, II, 339.

cumcision has halted the advance of a religion.[50] There is little or nothing of the hygienic about the imposition of any of them, though they may work out that way; in fact, a number of the bodily alterations are attended by harmful results.[51] Yet the mores can make such alterations the object of envy and admiration.

When primitive people have got into their heads an idea of the desirable and admirable and distinctive, they do not delay or hesitate in trying to realize it. To preserve the tribal type they are quite ready to cut off all variations from it. Selection is practised on children through infanticide.[52] The idea is to realize the perfection of the accepted local type or even to intensify it, as later examples will show, by deformations.[53] It is part of the general attitude of ethnocentrism[54] to esteem that type above all others.

"The negroes give the preference to the thickest and most prominent lips; the Kalmucks to turned-up noses; and the Greeks, in the statues of heroes, raised the facial line from eighty-five to one hundred degrees, beyond nature."[55] "Australian mothers flatten their children's noses by pressing with the hand on the point, or laying it flat on the face. The natives laugh at the sharp noses of Europeans, and call them 'tomahawk noses,' preferring their own style."[56] To a Papuan, female beauty calls for a big nose and a dark-brown, smooth skin.[57] Kaffirs, when they flatter their chiefs by calling them "black" are perhaps "thinking more of the conception of the imposing, the terrible, than of the beautiful" but to be thus black is evidently desirable. The Kirghiz think that their race, the Mongolian, "offers the most finished type of human beauty, because the bony structure of their face resembles that of a horse—the greatest masterpiece in all creation."[58]

So pronounced is the taste for the local physical characteristics that Darwin[59] was led to conceive of race-types as due to different standards of beauty. It is probable, rather, that the race-types were responsible for the standards. Darwin cites a number of instances illustrative of the difference in the notion of beauty among different races.

A list of ethnic mutilations and deformations—for to civilized

[50] Johnston, *Uganda*, II, 640.
[51] Bordier, *Géog. Méd.*, 411 ff.; Puccioni, "Deformazioni," in *Arch. p. Anthro.*, XXXIV, 355 ff.
[52] Lippert, *Kgchte.*, I, 206 ff., 400-404.
[53] Tylor, *Anth.*, 240.   [54] Keller, *Soc. Evol.*, 58 ff.
[55] Humboldt, *Nouvelle Espagne*, I, 90, note (from Cuvier).
[56] Palmer, in JAI, XIII, 280, note.   [57] Hagen, *Papua's*, 241.
[58] Letourneau, *Soc.*, 80.   [59] *Descent of Man*, end ch. XX.

taste they are describable by those terms—would be a long one. Our cases aim only at sufficient illustration and are designed also to enforce previous statements about the pain and trouble which people are willing to undergo for the sake of the vanity and ostentation involved. It is proverbial that human beings will suffer for the sake of pride what they will not endure for any other interest. Contemporary examples rush to the mind and perhaps they are as good as any from savage life. But there is a directness, naïveté, and ruthlessness about what savages do that is peculiarly impressive; indeed, as one scans the evidence it is borne in upon him that the nervous system of the backward peoples must be considerably less sensitive than our own or they could not endure so cheerfully the tortures to which they subject themselves. However, it must be realized that pride is doubly efficacious in such cases; not only are the mutilations desirable but there is also the chance to win special distinction by showing contempt for suffering as well as to lose all standing by cringing and crying out. And it must be admitted that they do not have to encounter the non-physical but no less poignant agonies that attend the more sophisticated person's struggle to realize ambition. They bore their teeth through the nerve-cavity, with a dull instrument, and that is excruciating enough; but they are not called upon to work through the mental and spiritual Golgothas that are traversed by the more sensitive and intense human souls.

Not all bodily alterations are painful. The re-shaping of parts is often a matter of time and patience rather than of suffering. There is one element common to all these practices: they impose upon the untamed savage the necessity of discipline; he must at least hold still while he is being beautified; and discipline is certainly one of the basic requirements for life in society.[60]

The various types of cranial deformation have been exhaustively catalogued and classified by Topinard.[61] Pressure is applied to the soft skulls of infants during the first weeks of their lives and the head is rounded or flattened according to local taste. "The child was laid on its back, and the head surrounded with three flat stones. One was placed close to the crown of the head, and one on either side. The forehead was then pressed with the hand, that it might be

[60] §§143, 330, above.
[61] *Anthrop.*, 744 ff.; Wilken, "Het Afplatten van het Voorhoofd bij de Al-foeren van de Minahasa," in VG, IV, 199 ff. (many cases and methods are cited).

flattened. The nose, too, was carefully flattened. Our 'canoe noses,' as they call them, are blemishes in their estimation."[62] The piercing of nose, ears, lips, and sometimes cheeks is very widespread. Into the perforations of the ears, feathers, knives, rings of great weight, and even casual articles, such as half-smoked cigars, are inserted. A Melanesian woman was seen with a little dog hung to her ear, one of his feet being attached to the lobe. Ear-lobes are so distended, sometimes by springs, as to rest on the shoulders and great care has to be taken in running races and other activities lest they get caught and rent asunder; for even if the torn lobe grows together, the two ears are no longer symmetrical as to length, which destroys their beauty. In Sumatra a girl's teeth must be filed and her ears bored before she may marry; and in Brazil the future husband does the ear-boring. It is thought by some that the ear was bored first in blood-sacrifice or the establishment of blood-brotherhood and then something put in to keep the hole open and visible, as a sign of the covenant.[63] Slitting the lips for the insertion of a plug or labret creates a deformity in very truth. One of Livingstone's native friends said of some women whose lips were bored: "These women want to make their mouths look like those of ducks." The circumference of the distorted lip reaches seventy-five cm. (over twenty-nine inches) according to actual measurement and "the woman seen at a distance and in profile, seems to be holding two saucers between her teeth." Eating is very difficult "and the woman is, to all practical intents, dumb." The labret is uncomfortable; yet it is a mark of honor and people who so regard it hesitate at nothing to get it and to celebrate its attainment lavishly. Among the Thlinkits, the labret "is a piece of bone or silver varying in size according to the rank of the person wearing it, that is inserted into the lower lip just below the mouth. It is worn as a sign of womanhood. . . . Only women of high caste are allowed to wear it. Slaves were strictly forbidden its use. As the woman who wears the labret grows older, its size is increased, so that a woman's age may be known from the size and kind of labret she wears." The Portuguese word "Botocudo" means one who is plugged or bunged.[64] Among a number of Central African tribes the left nostril is pierced and a ring worn in it; "a woman piercing the right ala nasi would be laughed at and called a fool."[65]

Mutilations of the teeth[66] are extraordinarily cold-blooded. The drawing or knocking out of certain of the teeth, chiefly incisors, is widely practised. False teeth are sometimes inserted. In South Africa, "the custom is so universal that a person who has his teeth is considered ugly, and occasionally when the Batoka borrowed a looking-glass, the disparaging remark would be made of boys or girls still retaining their teeth, 'Look at the great teeth.'" Again, they

[62] Turner, *Samoa*, 80.

[63] Wilken, *Vkde.*, 31; Ratzel, *Vkde.*, II, 237; Thurston, *S. India*, 374; Pratt, in *Geog. Mag.*, XVIII, 560; Furness, *Head-hunters*, 154 ff. (cuts); Marsden, *Sumatra*, 53; Von den Steinen, *Zent. Bras.*, 501, 180; Roth, "Guiana Indians," in BAE, XXXVIII, §§503-506; Lippert, *Kgchte.*, I, 394; II, 330.

[64] Cuts in *Nat. Geog. Mag.*, XIX, 723, 724, and in Grandidier, abstracted in *Literary Digest*, June 16, 1923; Livingstone, *Mission. Travels*, 618; Dorsey, in PSM, LIII, 173; Jones, *Thlingets*, 68; Von Martius, *Beiträge*, I, 267; Von Koenigswald, in *Globus*, XCIII, 37; Tylor, *Anth.*, 242.

[65] Stannus, in JAI, XL, 316.

[66] Ihering, in *Ztsft. f. Ethnol.*, XIV, 213 ff.

are filed to a point or according to some other pattern. Though such practices go with other mutilations in which blood is let as an offering to spirits, yet the increase of beauty is perhaps the main motive. In one case the idea is to grip more effectually the arm of an adversary. Teeth filed to a point, a phenomenon common to the whole of central Africa, are thought by some to be an evidence of cannibalism. The idea of being like, or unlike, certain admired and despised animals also appears; one tribe wanted to be like oxen and not like zebras.[67] Trilles[68] asked certain elders about the connection between pointed teeth and cannibalism. They always laughed "à gorge déployée." One old chief replied: "True, we point our teeth in order to tear better; you, however, keep them large in order to cut better!" The Africans of the Cameroons region could identify the skulls of murdered fellow-tribesmen "by means of the condition and deformation of the teeth."[69]

Wilken[70] devotes one of his enlightening monographs to the mutilation of the teeth, chiefly in the East Indies. They may be filed off clear to the gum, as part of the ceremonial of wedding, puberty, or mourning. He thinks filing is an ameliorated form of breaking, and exuvial sacrifice of a *pars pro toto,* like the hair-offering. A tooth may be demanded as a sign of subjection. Most East Indians, however, file their teeth for beautification, just as they blacken them or ornament them with gold. Blackening is now very widespread in the Archipelago, though in the old literature of Java white teeth are admired. He cites numerous examples.

Great pains are taken with the decoration of the teeth. Some tribes spend much time cleaning and polishing them with bits of wood the ends of which have been crushed to separate the fibers into a sort of brush. Malays blacken the teeth by chewing betel. "No mouth is thought handsome that is not engaged in chewing the betel"; hence blackened teeth are common and admired. It is probable that the custom is preservative. "White teeth are universally considered disfigurements, and he or she, who for a few days neglects to renew the stain, is sure to be jeered at by all companions with the scoffing remark that white teeth are no better than a dog's. I have had that reproach cast at me many a time by little children." Kazan Tatar women, along with painting their nails and blackening their eyebrows and lids, color their beautiful teeth red.[71]

Furness[72] mentions an "ineffably excruciating" mandate of fashion observed in Borneo. "The Ibans, not content with blackening the teeth, actually drill holes through and through the faces of the six front teeth, and therein insert plugs of brass, whereof the outer end is elaborated into stars and crescents. Then they finish up by filing the teeth to sharp points! No dentist's chair can

---

[67] Wilken, *Vkde.,* 233 ff.; Schweinfurth, *Heart of Afr.,* II, 6; Livingstone, *Mission. Travels,* 571 (quoted); Torday, in JAI, LI, 379; Hobley, *A-Kamba,* 18; Ratzel, *Vkde.,* I, 178, 328, 387, 389, 399, 454, 495, 527, 559; II, 395; Roth, in BAE, XXXVIII, §502; Lippert, *Kgchte.,* I, 400.

[68] *Fân,* 244.   [69] Malcolm, in JAI, LIII, 399.

[70] "Mutilatie der Tanden," in VG, IV, 4 ff.

[71] Ratzel, *Vkde.,* I, 72; II, 396; Crawfurd, *Ind. Archip.,* 103 (quoted); Peal, in JAI, XXII, 245; Furness, *Head-Hunters,* 157 (quoted); *Russ. Ethnog.* (Russ.), II, 5.

[72] *Head-Hunters,* 157-158, 156; Gomes, *Sea Dyaks,* 38, 39; Hose, in JAI, XXIII, 167.

hold a more hideous torture than this. The drill—usually no more delicate an instrument than the rounded end of a file—bores directly through the sensitive pulp of the tooth, tearing and twisting a nerve so exquisitely sensitive that but to touch it starts the perspiration and seems the limit of human endurance: yet an Iban will lie serene and unquivering on the floor while his beauty is thus enhanced by some kind and tender-hearted friend. Of course, the tooth dies and becomes a mere shell, tanned inside and out by repeated applications of the astringent blackening; the gums recede, exposing the fangs of the teeth and sometimes portions of the alveolar process—I need not add that the mouth of a middle-aged Iban is anything but attractive." A small hammer is used to fix the plugs in tight. "I am told that it is not often a man can bear to have more than one or two teeth operated on at a time."

Binding of parts of the body is quite common. "A more ridiculous sight could not be seen than a young native with his waist so strapped in as to form an enormous, ugly bulge above and below his belt, but it is greatly admired by the girls." Armlets and other bindings are put on early in life and with the growth of the wearer cut deeply into the body. From the waist of a strong young man of about twenty-seven a girdle was removed which showed a length of only sixty-five centimeters, or a little over twenty-five inches. Women of some tribes wear corsets and compress the breasts from early years. Certain Indian tribes in northern Canada practised compression of the feet of boys, though not to the extent of interfering with walking. The Chinese foot is well known. Constriction of the leg, especially of the calf, was common in parts of South America; the pipe-stem leg was regarded as beautiful. The ideal of a certain tribe of Guiana is a prominent abdomen.[73] An extraordinarily large number of interferences with the sex-organs appears in ethnography; and, as in Australia, those who have been operated upon take precedence of all others, hold the most important positions, and influence the government of the tribe.[74] Circumcision[75] is typical of this class of operations.

Skin and hair are the objects of much attention. Numerous examples attest the fact that the oiling and painting of the skin is largely for the sake of protection from cold, heat, wind, and insect-bites. Ashes and dirt are often plastered upon the body with no thought of ornamentation. Butter was used by certain negroes and the ancient Aryans purely for anointing the skin.[76] Such a coating amounts to clothing and the decorative element may or may not be added. Then there is, of course, the actual decorative motive, with its attempt to please, impress, or terrify. Here too there is a mixture of factors, for the religious element enters into the designs and colors assumed in prospect of war, festivals, and ceremonial; and so does the political, when it is the tribal symbol or totem that is represented.[77]

[73] Hardy and Elkington, *S. Seas,* 41, 105; Finsch, *Samoafahrten,* 90; *Russ. Ethnog.* (Russ.), II, 215, 235; Rae, in JAI, XVI, 200; Mason, *Woman's Share,* 184; Schomburgk, *Brit.-Guiana,* I, 260; Martin, in *Bijd.,* XXXV, 67; Koenigswald, in *Globus,* XCIV, 29-30; Ratzel, *Vkde.,* II, 569.
[74] Howitt, in JAI, XX, 85.
[75] §§163, 229, 298, above; Roth, "Guiana Indians," in BAE, XXXVIII, §507.
[76] Stuhlmann, *Mit Emin,* 54; Schrader, *Aryan,* 319.
[77] Boas, in *Globus,* LXXIV, 194; Koch, in *Globus,* LXXXI, 40; Lippert, *Kgchte.,* I, 375 ff.

It is chiefly to the scarring and tattooing of the skin that interest here attaches. It seems clear enough that the latter of these
processes is a refined development of the former; and, further,
that while scarring is relatively infrequently referable to self-
gratification, its sequel seems to have lost much of its connection
with religion and other more serious interests and to be associated, to a considerable extent, with art for art's sake. There is
no doubt that, whatever the origin of these skin-markings, they
are admired and confer distinction.

Scarring is a rude and coarse method of marking and is not generally, if
ever, accompanied by the use of color. One of its root-motives may be the imitation of honorable scars attained in battle by some hero. Cuts are kept open
for months by irritating substances, so as to leave finally an elevated scar a
quarter of an inch or more high.[78] "Cutting for the dead," as it is called in
the Bible, and other more developed forms of exuvial sacrifice or self-torture[79]
are practices of religious origin and character. The scars resulting from cutting or burning, located on some particular bodily area and conventionalized,
become tribal marks, identifying cult-comrades. In addition, men are proud
of them and it is certainly partly in view of the adornment that the great pain
involved is gladly endured. We are told that, when borne by men, they exert an
attraction on the women and that a correctly scarified woman is the first to
be wanted and brings the largest price. Since the scars denote the woman's
position, "there is no danger of a . . . girl losing her 'marriage-lines.' "[80]
Naturally scarring is to be found chiefly among backward peoples, for as soon
as a tribe gets ahead somewhat, its scarring is covered by clothing and gradually disappears or develops so as to deserve the name of tattooing.[81]

§446*. Treatment of the Skin and Hair. What has been said
about the causes for scarification applies directly or indirectly to
tattooing,[82] for there seems but little doubt that the latter originated in the former. The suggestion is strong "that in their ultimate origin the *stigmata* are nothing more than the permanent

[78] Sinclair, in AA, X, 375; Basedow, in JAI, XLIII, 294.

[79] Levit., XIX, 28, XXI, 5; Deut., XIV, 1; I Kings, XVIII, 28; Jer., XVI,
6; XLI, 5; XLVII, 5; XLVIII, 37; §§229, 282, 297, 298, above.

[80] Tremearne, "Nigerian Head-Hunters," in JAI, XLII, 149-150.

[81] Tylor, *Anth.*, 238; Ratzel, II, 41; Smyth, *Vict.*, I, 295; Wilken, *Vkde.*,
252; Somerville, in JAI, XXVI, 365; Parkinson, in *Dresden K. Zoöl. u. Anth.-
Ethnog. Mus., Abhandl. VII*, pt. VI, 14-15; Pratt, *New Guinea Cannibals*, 50;
Finsch, *Ethnol. Erfahr.*, I, 96, 128, III, 76; Ward, in JAI, XXIV, 294; Pater
L., in *Globus*, LXXIX, 351; Fabry, in *Globus*, XCI, 199; Burrows, *Pigmies*,
125, 126; Johnston, *Uganda*, II, 728; Ratzel, *Vkde.*, II, 567; Von den Steinen,
Zent. Bras., 179.

[82] Joest, *Tätowiren;* Sinclair, in AA, X.

scars of punctures made to draw blood for a ceremony of self-dedication to a deity,"[83] though one must expect to find the evidence of a religious significance less direct in the evolved tattoo than in the parent-form, scarification. There is no doubt that the tattoo-design retains all the force of a tribal mark; we have seen elsewhere[84] that the ghost fares ill who cannot show his identifying tattoo on his way to the spirit-world. There is no denying, however, that tattooing has struck many travellers as highly ornamental; it is reported, in particular, that a body which is elaborately tattooed does not appear naked.[85] Colors are employed in such manner as to indicate engrossment with æsthetic considerations; designs that may once have meant something definite have been conventionalized and their meaning lost. Whatever the original motive for tattooing, it has worked out into self-gratification.

It is worth while to reproduce a list of what investigators have thought to be the motives originally and later involved in the practice, though we believe that the basic religious interest will show through most of them. It is significant that the same devices represented in tattoo-patterns are often seen on posts, canoes, weapons, utensils, and other forms of property. The tattoo-marks are said to distinguish between free and slave rank and between high and low social status in general; to certify to bravery exhibited under the ordeal of getting them; to indicate personal prowess, especially in war. They are religious symbols, therapeutic and prophylactic against disease. They are tokens of disgrace, of wifehood, of marriageability. They identify the individual, charm the opposite sex by magic, inspire fear in the enemy, render a person invulnerable, and bring good fortune. They are, finally, devices of secret societies.[86] Another list, fuller but not classified very well, mentions patterns that indicate rank, title, position, slaves, subjects, tribe, societies, clubs, name, signature, warlike deeds, number of enemies or whales killed, maturity, occupation, adoption, brotherhood, wifehood, a social feast, husband's achievements, children, mourning, and disgrace or crime. They are charms against all manner of evil influences and also sex-charms.

[83] Smith, *Relig. Sem.*, 334, note.   [84] §§163, 295, 298, 365, above.
[85] Lippert, *Kgchte.*, I, 399; Fraser, *Stevenson's Samoa*, 132-133.
[86] Mallery, in BAE, X, 418.

They mark a person as not subject to taboo but as having magical or supernatural power.[87] All these lists end with "etc."; it is evidently no mere poetic exaggeration when Oliveira Martins[88] writes about the skin being a civil register, an autobiography, a ledger, and even a gospel; on it "religion is written by the side of the chronicle and the code." The case of the tattoo is a fine example of the folly of trying to account for a complicated societal phenomenon by a single cause,[89] for it exhibits the play of many factors in producing a single result.

Darwin[90] was well within the truth when he wrote: "Not one great country can be named, from the Polar regions in the north to New Zealand in the south, in which the aborigines do not tattoo themselves." Our interest centers less in the extension of customs than in the ideas connected with them. The following cases of tattooing are a few out of many which may help to set the usage before us as one probably rooting in religious ideas, working out into almost pure self-gratification, and yet maintaining connections always with the economic, political, and family-organizations.

Tattooing of a rude order is undergone by Australian women who have lost a child. In New Guinea it dedicates to the spirits the part of the body that is decorated and protects it from profane glances; it is also done purely for beautification and to identify the famous warrior. Some of the designs are heritable from father to son. A woman not tattooed as marriageable "has no attraction whatever in the eyes of the young men." The operation is painful; girls are overpowered by female relations and forced to submit; the fevered face is dipped frequently into the sea-water. In some locations it is the image of the totem that is tattooed upon the leg of man or the small of the back of the woman. In the Andamans, "they say that the skin becomes more sensitive after tattooing, which is considered ornamental and also as proving courage and power of bearing pain."[91]

In the Congo region, "the tattooing was begun in earliest childhood by the parents, but not more than sufficient to show that the boy or girl belonged to the tribe. Later on in life the boys and girls would have the cicatrices enlarged, and at the age of eighteen or twenty and onwards the person who wished to be thought fashionable would work away at his tattoo every week or so, cutting

87 Sinclair, in AA, X, 382-383.   88 Raças, II, 94.
89 Lippert, Kgchte., I, 397-399; Wilken, Vkde., 251; Sinclair, in AA, X, 384.
90 Descent of Man, 655.
91 Eyre, Cent. Aust., II, 343; Krieger, Neu-Guinea, 377; Finsch, Ethnol. Erfahr., II, 303, 305; Guise, in JAI, XXVII, 207; Woodford, Head-hunters, 31; Abel, New Guinea, 35; Hardy and Elkington, S. Seas, 31; Haddon, in JAI, XIX, 392; Man, in JAI, XII, 331.

it deeper and putting wads in the cuts to cause the flesh to stand up."[92] In Central Africa cicatrization formerly had significance as indicating tribal affiliation or initiation, or as commemorating events; now it is mostly decorative.[93] Among the Malays, "if we differentiate as we ought the practice of tattooing (*i.e.*, of decorating the person with punctured designs filled with pigment) from the various forms of scarification and raised cicatrices or keloids, we shall feel a considerable measure of doubt as to the extent to which any form of tattooing, properly so called, exists among the tribes of the Malay Peninsula. . . . Of the practice of skin-scarification, on the other hand, as well as of face-painting, there is abundant evidence."[94] In Farther India, "the tattooing of the outside of the leg does not hurt the boy much, but the doing of the inside is very painful. Leaves are heated and applied to the freshly tattooed surfaces to allay the irritation. Occasionally a man may be seen with only one leg tattooed, because his courage has failed; in such a case he probably says that he learned in a dream that it would be unlucky to have the other leg tattooed. . . . It is a proud day for a boy when he can sing to a girl, 'Dost thou love me, the tattooed one?' "[95]

Of the moon-figure upon the Borneo woman's hands it is said that, as she passes to the next life, "her tattooing becomes luminous like a fire-fly's light, and that without it she would wander in total darkness. . . . Believe one who has tried it," Furness[96] goes on, "when I say that the pain of the Kayan operation, even for small designs, is very considerable; when endured for more than an hour, it becomes torture." This author goes into graphic detail in describing the operation in which, when it is a question of finishing quickly, the needles are repeatedly driven into the sore and swollen flesh of tender parts of the body. In the case of a girl who has had an unexpected and desirable offer of marriage and cannot take her time in acquiring the extensive and elaborate decoration, the operation is driven through with extra torture. "The instant that the poor wretch of a girl is released from the hands, and toes, of her tormentor, she runs with the swiftness of agony to the river, there to soothe with the cool flowing water the frightful, burning ache. The absorption of so much foreign matter by the lymphatics often induces high fever; suppuration also not infrequently results from the septic manner in which the operation is performed; this naturally injures the sharpness of the lines. After one session, the tattooing is not resumed until the skin is entirely healed, unless an approaching marriage necessitates the utmost speed; should a woman have a child before her tattooing is completed, she is lastingly disgraced." This author reproduces and explains a number of patterns.

Tattooing in Borneo has much to do with the recording of feats, chiefly military. One chief who ran away in a fight, showing his back to the enemy, had two square marks tattooed on his back and was deposed. This engraving of records on the skin causes Roth to make the remark that "we may justly conclude that tatuing among the natives of Borneo is one method of writing." The Dyaks explained their marks as having connection with religion and as sometimes indicative of family and clan; while the Kayans' tattooing has "wholly the character of ornament to the body." Formosans grant colored lines

---

[92] Weeks, in JAI, XXXIX, 101.   [93] Stannus, in JAI, XL, 317.
[94] Skeat and Blagden, *Malay Penin.*, II, 28.
[95] Milne, *Eastern Clan*, 96, 97.   [96] *Head-Hunters*, 149, 152, 153.

on chest or forehead for the taking of a head. Some authorities record twenty-nine lines and one old chief boasted of ninety-five.[97]

Polynesia and Micronesia are classic regions of the tattoo; in fact, the word "tattoo," like "taboo" is derived from this part of the world. In Samoa a young man was in his minority until he was tattooed; he could not think of marriage and was constantly exposed to taunt and ridicule, as being poor and low-born and as having no rights to speak in the society of men. When a youth reached the age of sixteen, he and his friends were all anxiety that he should be tattooed. The Maori specialize on face-tattooing, in order to look fierce to the enemy and also to conceal age—for tattooing makes the old look young and the young old. The motive of decoration was also present. Poor man's tattooing showed few, straight, and coarse marks, while the rich man could display his opulence on his face. The ultimate reason for the custom was religious and the performance was often connected with religious rites. "A funnel is used to feed a Maori chief when his face is being tattooed, for, owing to the inflammation caused by the operation, he then has to be fed on liquid food, being unable to move his jaws." To tattoo a person fully was a work of time; to do too much at once would endanger his life. A taboo extended over the operation, lest evil befall. And "to have fine tattooed faces was the great ambition of young men, both to render themselves attractive to the ladies, and conspicuous in war: for even if killed by the enemy, whilst the heads of the untattooed were treated with indignity and kicked on one side, those which were conspicuous by their beautiful *moko* were carefully cut off, stuck on the *turuturu,* a pole with a cross on it, and then preserved; all of which was highly gratifying to the survivors, and the spirits of their late possessors." Here is a case of gratification-seeking that extends beyond death. That the tattoo-mark may be highly individualized is shown by the following: "Some missionaries once bought a certain piece of land from a chief, and the tattoo marks upon the face of the seller of the land were copied on to the deed of sale, serving thereby as his signature to the contract."[98]

"The ancient practice of tattooing the skin is gradually declining among the Society Islanders generally. The missionaries have been much opposed to the custom, and among the laws framed for these islands was one which made tattooing criminal. . . . We felt much regret, not unmingled with indignation, when we beheld, in the house of the royal chief of Raiatea, a native woman, of naturally agreeable features, disfigured by an extensive patch of charcoal embedded in her cheek—a punishment inflicted upon her by the judges for having slightly tattooed herself. While we were regarding this spectacle, a second female showed us her hand, which afforded a similar instance of judicial severity; we could only cling to the hope that British missionaries had not given sanction to such barbarities."[99]

The marks of the North Americans were, we are told, little more than a tribal fashion. Figures of birds and beasts were delineated on their faces.

[97] Roth, *Sarawak,* II, 83, 87, 92, 291; Schwaner, *Borneo,* I, 220, 223-224; Bock, *Borneo,* 76; Nieuwenhuis, *Borneo,* I, 234; Gomes, *Sea Dyaks,* 37; Ratzel, *Vkde.,* II, 393; Wirth, in AA, X, 361.

[98] Sinclair, in AA, X, 374, 385; Turner, *Samoa,* 88; Ella, in AAAS, 1892, 624; Ratzel, *Vkde.,* II, 135, 136; Taylor, *Te Ika,* 320, 321; Roth (transl. of Crozet), in JAI, XXI, 206; Letourneau, *Soc.,* 72.

[99] Roth, in JAI, XXXV, 293.

With the Haidas tattooing was a fine art and their figures "serve to identify the individual with his or her totem." Rank and family-connections are known by the variety of designs. Thus the patterns are, as it were, heraldic. "Tattooing appears to have been practised among nearly all the Indian tribes, though chiefly in connection with mystic rites, and for the exorcism of demons believed to cause disease." In one tribe "women had tattooed upon the forehead a small round spot, by which, in case of war, they could be identified by their friends, and ransomed." Again, there were "short transverse marks tattooed along the inner side of the forearm, by which the value of strings of shell money was estimated"—a sort of scale of linear measure. In Nicaragua, slaves were tattooed on the face. Numerous marks in the form of a cross had, we are told, "nothing whatever to do with Christianity." Because the missionaries set their faces against body-markings, it was generally possible to distinguish the heathen Indian at sight. Tattooing, at first distinguishing men and women of high family, was extended later to mark the whole tribe. One tribe of Brazil tattoos the inner arm in the belief "that a slight loss of blood from this part makes them sure bowmen." Women are tattooed where men are not, as is the case in several other parts of the world.[100]

Among the alterations of the body practised by mankind the treatment of the hair deserves a prominent place. Men have taken an enormous amount of time and pains both to get rid of it by depilation and shaving and to preserve and enrich its luxuriance. Depilation, except for certain mourning-ceremonies, is almost never practised upon the hair of the scalp. Hair on the face— beard, eye-brows, eye-lashes—is plucked out by a number of peoples but otherwise it is only the hair of the trunk and limbs that receives this discouragement. A hint as to the reasons for the usage is afforded by the fact that peoples with light body-hair regard hirsuteness as a monstrosity evoked by evil spirits;[101] it departs from the tribal type and is therefore ugly and abnormal. Emphasis upon the familiar norm leads to the eradication of even the little facial and bodily hair that appears. This does not apply to the eye-lashes, of course, for all tribes have them; here is found the notion that some benefit to sight or some other advantage is secured by their removal. In general, however, depilation is for self-gratification.

[100] Mallery, in BAE, X, 419; Wood, *New Eng. Prospect,* 74; Niblack, in USNM, 1888, 257, 258; Dellenbaugh, *N. Amer.,* 58; Hoffman, *Begin. of Writing,* 36, 37; Mallery, in BAE, IV, 67; Sapper, in *Globus,* LXXVIII, 271; Martin, in *Bijd.,* XXXV, 25; Von den Steinen, *Zent. Bras.,* 188; Von Martius, *Beiträge,* I, 333, 387, note; Koch, in *Globus,* LXXXI, 75; Roth, in BAE, XXXVIII, §§509, 510.

[101] Hiekisch, *Tungusen,* 63; Nieuwenhuis, *Borneo,* I, 128.

The Melanesians exterminate the hair from the body. Some East and West Africans pluck out all the hair on the body, "so that it is difficult to say what character it assumes." One of the tribes near Lake Albert removes both eyebrows and eyelashes and the Pygmies, though they have little vanity and love of ornament, the latter. Again the hair of the arm-pits is pulled out. The Sahara Arab women despise the French women because they do not practise depilation and refer the sterility of marriages to its omission. In East Africa all the hairs on the face, including eyelashes and eyebrows, are pulled out, it being "considered ridiculous to leave these. . . . The practice of pulling out the eyelashes accounts, I think, for so much eyesickness which one notices among the Akamba; according to them, however, it has the opposite effect."[102]

Tibetan men pluck out their beards with tweezers; the lamas sometimes have full beards. In the Chin Hills "The women object to hair on the face and the slender growth is consequently plucked out with nippers by all young men." "The prejudice in favor of a smooth face is so strong that in the whole course of my experience I have never met with a single bearded or moustached Sea-Dyak, although it cannot but be manifest to a close observer that were they only so disposed, they could produce a thicker crop than the Malay." Aged and infirm men who do not care much about their personal appearance show bristly chins. "The universal absence of hair upon the face, on the chest, and under the armpits would lead the superficial observer to infer that this is owing entirely to a natural deficiency, whereas it is due in great measure to systematic depilation." Eyelashes also are plucked out by both sexes, which, according to Sir Charles Brooke, "often brings ophthalmia and weakness of eyes." Elsewhere in Borneo the women remove all bodily hair and the men eyebrows and eyelashes. To some natives one writer "pointed out that both eyebrows and eyelashes are a protection to the eyes from dust and glare. But my remarks made little impression on them. Among the Dyaks, as elsewhere, fashions die hard."[103]

Most of the head-shaving, apart from mourning-customs, is only partial and is intended to throw into relief the pattern of the hair that is left. Many peoples attach great importance to coiffure, spending much time, energy, and patience and enduring considerable discomfort in working the hair into a selected shape. It is oiled to brilliancy or even stiffened by gums and other foreign substances into a condition where it can be molded or carved into odd, desirable, and conspicuous forms. Manifestly such a product of diligence and art must not be disarranged or disfigured by resting it upon anything hard or in rubbish that might adhere to it. Hence the anxious possessors of a superb coiffure, when sleeping, really suspend it in the air; that is, they repose with the neck propped up on a crutch-shaped support and with the head hanging.[104] It is the only way to preserve a crowning glory. It is evident enough that the hair is manipulated chiefly for the sake of self-gratification.

[102] Ratzel, *Vkde.*, II, 234; Johnston, *Uganda*, II, 617-618; Brunache, *Cent. Afr.*, 59; Stannus, in JAI, XL, 319; Tate, in JAI, XXXIV, 134, 139; Stuhlmann, *Mit Emin*, 315, 321, 471, 621; Volkens, *Kilimandscharo*, 218; Pommerol, *Sahariennes*, 400; Dundas, C., in JAI, XLIII, 498 (quoted).

[103] Rockhill, *Mongolia and Tibet*, 125, note; Rockhill, in USNM, 1893, 696, 697; Carey and Tuck, *Chin Hills*, I, 166; Roth, *Sarawak*, II, 81; Nieuwenhuis, *Borneo*, I, 69; Gomes, *Sea Dyaks*, 39-40; Furness, *Head-Hunters*, 158.

[104] Lippert, *Kgchte.*, I, 343-344; Wilken, in VG, IV, 116 ff.; Bacon, *Japanese Girls*, 77, note.

The variety of patterns of hair-arrangement is beyond description. Various areas of the scalp are shaved or left unshaved; the hair is clipped or left long; twisted into knots and spirals or combed straight; colored or merely oiled. All through East Africa there are notable coiffures, each tribe having its peculiar one, and on the west coast only the Bushmen and Hottentots seem to pay no attention to their hair. To build up some of their constructions takes eight to ten years. Clay and varnish are worked into the hair to give it body and stiffness so that it can be molded or carved.[105] The Hudson's Bay Company is gradually getting certain Indians to give up their immense pigtails which, by a great addition of fat, feathers, and other extraneous matter, become very heavy and offensive. Pictures only can give an idea of the limits of grotesqueness to which the treatment of the hair has gone.[106] The Spanish governor, General Arolas, managed to discipline certain refractory Moros by having their heads shaved in fantastic and demeaning patterns as a penalty for misdeeds. This assault on their vanity was far more effective than savage punishment.[107]

There are comparatively few cases where the whole head is shaved regularly, not for a time only or an occasion. In New Britain it is done to get rid of parasites. The instrument is sometimes a bit of glass. The Andaman Islanders used to shave the head almost entirely; now fanciful patterns have come to be adopted.[108] Maspero[109] knew a native Copt, over eighty years old, who shaved his head with a stone razor, although all his neighbors used razors of metal. After the operation his skull was scraped almost raw and he covered it with leaves to reduce the inflammation. The hair is reddened by several African peoples, in many parts of Polynesia, and by several Brazilian tribes.[110] The tonsure, found in many parts of the earth, was very widespread amongst the South American aborigines before the Discovery. From "coroa," meaning "crown" or "tonsure," the Portuguese called many heterogeneous tribes "Coroados" or "crowned."[111]

The American negro has ceased to take pride in woolly hair; the columns of newspapers read by the colored population, from Massachusetts to Texas, are full of advertisements of "anti-kink" nostrums, with illustrations of long, flowing hair.

The pride which men of the white race have taken in the beard is a familiar fact of history and of contemporary observation.[112] Some representatives of other races also cherish this ornament. In West Africa, where the beard is rare, a man who has one is called a "big daddy" and enjoys much consideration.

[105] Lippert, *Kgchte.*, I, 381.

[106] Many illustrations occur in Ratzel, *Vkde.*; Holub, *Capstadt*, II, 207 ff.; Holub, *Süd-Afrika*, II, 294 ff.; Stuhlmann, *Mit Emin*, 240 ff.; Junker, *Afr.*, I, 253, 297, 376, 406, *et passim*; Schweinfurth, *Heart of Afr.*, II, 6; Johnston, *Uganda*, II, 804, 843; Dundas, C., in JAI, XLIII, 498.

[107] Worcester, *Philippine Isl.*, 191.

[108] Finsch, *Ethnol. Erfahr.*, I, 97; Fison, in JAI, XIV, 20, note; Man, in JAI, XII, 77, 78; Tylor, *Anth.*, 88.

[109] *Hist. Anc.*, I, 50.

[110] Junker, *Afr.*, I, 261; Paulitschke, *Nordost-Afr.*, I, 107; Ratzel, *Vkde.*, II, 140; Von Martius, *Beiträge*, I, 250.

[111] Von den Steinen, *Zent. Bras.*, 174; Von Koenigswald, in *Globus*, XCIV, 29.

[112] Lippert, *Kgchte.*, I, 383 ff.

The longest beard Stannus saw was about fourteen inches from chin to tip and was kept rolled up. The heavily bearded Australians are solicitous about the hair of the face and in New Guinea, among people scarcely before met by the whites, were found even false whiskers. The Seminole Indians commonly wore a moustache, "and a few have a bold looking combination of moustache and imperial."[113] The consternation produced by Peter the Great's decrees concerning shaving, although some opposition to the beard had been registered before his time, can well be imagined.[114]

It is perhaps worth while to recall that long and carefully kept finger-nails are an obvious sign of leisure and superiority. Nails several inches long mark the primitive aristocracy in some regions; and people of distinction and old men sometimes tint the beard and nails saffron color.[115]

§447*. Ornament and Clothing.

By ornament is here meant beautifying attachments to the body or those which hide or neutralize defects, not the remodelling of bodily parts. It is reasonable, doubtless, to regard paint as such an attachment. The earliest ornamental attachment is likely to have been also an amulet with religious signification, and even the weapon was an ornament;[116] but much of adornment is for vanity's sake alone or even to inspire fear[117] and any other meaning is generally lost in the course of time. To rehearse the endless varieties of bodily ornamentation, from wooden tails[118] to coronets, attained by attachments to the skin, ears, fingers, neck, waist, and limbs would be impossible and also pointless. Further, quantity as well as uniqueness of attachments constitutes ornament.[119]

There are very few peoples who are reported as indifferent to ornament and it is almost unparalleled to find it stated flatly that such and such a people wears none.[120] The people of one African tribe who asserted that they had no ornament, were probably concealing the little they had.[121] "There is no doubt about the dwarf-peoples, that the lower they are and the more un-

---

[113] Finsch, *Ethnol. Erfahr.*, I, 96, 97; Thomson, in AAAS, 1892, 424; Stannus, in JAI, XL, 319; MacCauley, in BAE, V, 486.

[114] Stern, *Russland*, 21 ff.

[115] Tylor, *Anth.*, 240, 241; Junker, *Afr.*, II, 312; Friederici, in *Globus*, XC, 304; *Russ. Ethnog.* (Russ.), II, 396.

[116] §§112, 265, above; Lippert, *Kgchte.*, I, 297-298; Schultz, *Höf. Leben*, II, 6.

[117] Lippert, *Kgchte.*, I, 366.

[118] Godden, in JAI, XXVII, 20; Lippert, *Kgchte.*, I, 409.

[119] Lippert, *Kgchte.*, I, 410 ff.

[120] Rütimeyer, in *Globus*, LXXXIII, 204; Sarasin, in *Globus*, LXXXIII, 279.

[121] Lessner, in *Globus*, LXXXVI, 337.

touched, the less ornament, decoration, and disfigurement do they employ. The lowest and completely wild Wambutti . . . wore no ornament at all."[122]

It is to be noted, as a broad generality, that "among the most uncivilized peoples it is the men who are more decorated than the women; . . . on the other hand we see how among more highly developed peoples the women have retained ornaments that have fallen into disuse among the men."[123]

Everyone who knows the ardor with which ornament as a form of luxury is sought, often in preference to articles of necessity, can easily realize the disciplinary value of that seeking and of the pains and trouble cheerfully taken by otherwise rather inert savages in the pursuit of adornment. We do not conceive that this point needs further elaboration and shall consider ornament chiefly in its connection with the development of clothing. The former seems clearly to precede the latter; very commonly ornament is found where clothing deserving of the name is not, whereas there are few or no clothed people to be heard of who do not wear ornament. It is obvious that clothing serves a practical purpose in the cooler lands and sometimes in the warmer ones; in general, however, the costume of the warmer countries is much less useful than ornamental. Clothes in the latter regions are cloths rather than specialized garments and are worn for display rather than for utility; the desire for ostentation often leads to the envelopment of the body in yards of heavy material, to the intense physical discomfort of the spiritually exalted wearer.[124]

Whatever is attached to the body, barring actual mutilation to secure such attachment, since it demands natural support against slipping off, will obviously tend to appear at or below such incurvings as the neck, waist, wrists, and ankles. The cord or girdle about the waist seems to be the most common nucleus of bodily covering. Originally a mere cord and of no thinkable value as clothing, it forms a support upon which ornament of various description can be hung and still be seen by the wearer. To a lesser degree the neck-cord performs the same service. Gradually the consequent but unpremeditated covering of the pelvic regions and, to a lesser degree, of the chest becomes the mode. It is a deroga-

[122] Davids, in *Globus*, LXXXV, 118.
[123] Wilken, *Vkde.*, 36.   [124] Lippert, *Kgchte.*, I, 411 ff.

tion to vanity and self-respect not to have what the rest have and not to be similarly covered, just as it is an enviable distinction to have more. Poverty is humiliating, a state to be ashamed of, and to be uncovered is an evidence of it or, at least, of lack of manners. No one is ashamed of his naked hands as such; if, however, all the rest are white-gloved, those hands look large, exposed, red, and ugly. Nudity of the parts of the body not usually uncovered is demeaning and disgraceful and readily becomes indecent;[125] then the body must be covered for reasons which, at first sight, seem quite removed from the securing of its protection or the satisfaction of vanity.

It seems clear enough, then, that clothing has taken its origin largely in ornament and so goes back to the motive of ostentation. The original practical value of clothing, in the warmer regions where mankind is most reasonably conceived to have taken origin, is very slight. Of course when men have at length migrated into cooler lands, there is a practical reason for clothing and the northern type of "clothes" as distinguished from "cloths"[126] is developed; further, it is not to be denied that the primitive breech-clout had its practical reason for being.

A sort of suspensory is very common among savages. Its utility is religious as well as practical, for the slight concealment it affords is widely designed as protection against the evil eye.[127] There is a good deal, too, in the suggestion that the Dyaks wear the loin-cloth, in a number of folds, to keep the abdomen warm—a precaution which all travellers in the tropics must imitate with flannel, day and night, for fear of dysentery.[128] There is no doubt that the girdle is a practical convenience for the carrying of weapons and other paraphernalia. Girded loins are believed by many peoples to confer strength: "the Igorot says he wears a girdle because it makes him stronger, and with it he can travel faster and farther"; women too have their need of a loin-covering.[129] Even rain-coats are to be found discharging their practical function.[130]

Clothing of this protective type belongs under self-maintenance; here interest rests solely in its ornamental character. It almost always reveals that quality, whether or not it is indispensable for

[125] Lippert, *Kgchte.*, 17 ff., 66, 408 ff. [126] Lippert, *Kgchte.*, I, 413, 424.

[127] Ratzel, *Vkde.*, II, 231; Fritsch, *Eingeb. S.-Afr.*, 58, 168-169; Wilken, *Vkde.*, 37, 51; Von den Steinen, *Zent. Bras.*, 191, 192, 194, 195, 431, 432, 504.

[128] Bock, *Borneo*, 78.

[129] Jenks, in AA, VI, 701, 703, 704; VII, 173.

[130] Von Pfeil, *Südsee*, 48; Niblack, in USNM, 1888, 267, 268; Boas, in USNM, 1895, 319.

protection, as even a superficial observer of fashion and costume realizes.

It likewise appears that the so-called sense of shame is nothing innate or inherent, a truth abundantly attested by the unabashed nudity of many native peoples. There are a number of tribes who wear little or no clothing and who seem quite destitute of the "sense of shame" as it is commonly understood;[131] and some who do wear clothing for protection lay it aside when indoors. However, scarcely any of these peoples renounce ornamentation.

Cook found the Tasmanians quite naked; the early explorers could not understand how they could live in such a climate without clothing. Yet both sexes decorated themselves with feathers and flowers.[132] Papuan decorations afforded little concealment and several Melanesian groups went about, both sexes, "clad only in their virtue." Of another group of islanders, it is said: "They wear no clothing, not even the T bandage customary in the Solomon Islands." In New Britain the women are "no more covered than Eve in Paradise." Occasionally bunches of fresh leaves are bound on in front and rear. Some of these naked tribes know how to make very handsome costumes.[133] Complete nakedness is reported in South Africa, while in the equatorial regions men will be naked and women clothed and *vice versa.* In Togo nakedness is encountered. In the Congo Basin, "girls continue totally naked until they are married; three cowries, a few pearls, or a little bell hanging in front of their bodies and held by a belt of pearls or a leather strap, emphasize their nudity." Women thus decorated were chaste and repelled any advances of Europeans, whom they regarded as slaves. Indifference to the waist-cloth on the part of Sudanese women and children is common. Elsewhere women of low degree go without clothing. In Uganda, nakedness is often met with, though waist-belts and necklaces may be worn.[134]

"Among the Eastern Nagas in several tribes the women used no clothing, in others the men." The summer dress in Formosa is *nil* and on the sea-coast one tribe "sported as the only apology for dress a trinket in the hair and an earring." Except for chiefs, male Pelew Islanders used to go "without exception stark naked.[135]

131 Cases in Westermarck, *Marriage,* I, 548 ff.

132 Roth, *Tasmania,* 21, 141, 144.

133 Wilken, *Vkde.,* 45; Von Pfeil, *Südsee,* 48; Finsch, *Ethnol. Erfahr.,* I, 91, 126, III, 386; Finsch, in *Mitth. Berl. Mus.,* 1885-86, 60; Cayley-Webster, *New Guinea,* 345, 399; Woodford, *Head-hunters,* 31; Codrington, *Melanesians,* 108; Ella, in AAAS, 1892, 637.

134 Holub, *Capstadt,* II, 253; Junker, *Afr.,* I, 286, 297-298; Schweinfurth, *Heart of Afr.,* II, 104; Ratzel, *Vkde.,* I, 492, 640; Serpa Pinto, *Africa,* I, 196, 197; Smend, in *Globus,* XCII, 247; Clozel, in PSM, XLIX, 675; Henning, in *Globus,* LXXII, 103; Brunache, *Cent. Afr.,* 264; Stuhlmann, *Mit Emin,* 515, 765; Johnston, *Uganda,* II, 43, 840, 852-853.

135 Godden, in JAI, XXVII, 21; Wirth, in AA, X, 361; Kubary, *Pelauer,* 209, note; Kubary, *Núkuóro,* 10.

The Eskimo of East Greenland were naked or nearly so in their dwellings.[136] Most North American Indians were pretty fully clothed except upon occasion; yet the men sometimes "wore nothing whatever in mild weather, and even in winter the dress of some, especially in the more southerly regions, was far from elaborate. . . . In war the body was generally naked in many tribes." In Markham's list of South American tribes, men are found wearing a girdle of woollen thread or a loin-cloth and the women nothing at all. A small gourd and belt are all that is worn in one Colombian tribe. Again, men go for religious reasons quite naked and women wear a slight apron, or *vice versa;* or there is no dress at all except paint. It is difficult to get the naked women to put on an apron to go to church. In general it is the men only who are clothed and that very scantily. "In the intimacy of their villages, far from all civilization, the Toba go for the most part stark naked."[137] Letourneau[138] collects a number of cases proving that not the slightest feeling of shame existed in various tribes. It might be added that clothing is put on, rather than left off, to excite passion.[139]

Recurring now to the idea of clothing as adornment, that motive is found prominent in even the minimal coverings of the most backward peoples. These are assumed when the individual has passed childhood, not because he or she then arrives at sex-maturity and must give up normal child-nudity but because at that time individuality is first attained and must be proclaimed.[140] It is to be noted how consistently the slight coverings are ornamental and how readily they are laid aside when the time for display is past.

Australian women wear small aprons formed of strands of string suspended from a waist-string; and the man is little better clothed in his "waist belt made of human hair—usually provided by his mother-in-law" and carrying some religious significance. Women, elsewhere in Australia, cast aside their one garment, an apron of feathers, after the birth of a child. In New Guinea, "the neck is decked with ornament, and very richly too, in the form of all kinds of trinkets made of teeth and shells, as well as little bags and chains. These are hung about it in such manner that they all bunch up together on the breast, which for that reason is often completely covered and does not any longer look naked at all. I have here learned to appreciate that in reality ornament can become a piece of clothing and that the latter can come out of the former." A boy's assumption of dress is an occasion of feasting and depends upon his friends' willingness to provide the same; therefore some friendless big boys have to go naked. Elsewhere young women wear only "flimsy grass mats made

[136] Nansen, *Esk. Life,* 165; Holm, *Ethnol. Skizze,* 46.

[137] Hough, "Clothing," in HAI, I, 310; Dellenbaugh, *N. Amer.,* 155, 156; Markham, in JAI, XXIV, 255, 281; De la Rosa, trans. in AA, III, 617; Von Martius, *Beiträge,* I, 217, 271-272, 388, 427, 504; Spix u. Martius, *Bras.,* 1196, 1224, 1312, note; Koch, in *Globus,* LXXXI, 77.

[138] *Morale,* 143 ff.

[139] Westermarck, *Marriage,* I, 553 ff.   [140] Lippert, *Kgchte.,* I, 443-444.

of streamers, and tied round their waists—which from a point of decency would be equal to a piece of mosquito netting." When the missionaries insisted upon the women wearing calico gowns it was an amusing sight "to see the girls and women arriving at the church, for—on entering the courtyard—they pulled these European costumes over their half-nude bodies; but it was still more comic to see the way they pulled themselves out of them directly the service was over." Yet these women were extremely modest. "Madame de Stael speaks of certain children being *vétu du climat'*: the same expression may be applied to the Andamanese, for neither sex wears what we would understand as clothing. They wear ornamental circlets, garters, etc., of bone, wood, or shell." "Despite full nudity the natives are extremely decent and modest people whose morality may serve as an illustration to show that nakedness and modesty may very well exist side by side. . . . It is certain that nakedness rather dulls than excites sensuality, which therefore stirs much less often among these people than is commonly assumed."[141]

In general, negroes wear as much clothing as the means at hand will allow; in spite of the temperature they put on all they can to be imposing. "Pleasure in viewing himself over and over again in the mirror belongs to the negro like his dark skin-color!" Lippert makes a good deal of this quantity-ostentation in dress. The Xosa's leather girdle is essentially for ornament and is as a rule not used for the suspension of any apron; it is richly adorned, though solely with beads, buttons, and other trinkets, while the Zulu suspends tails of wild cats from his belt so that he has, front and rear, a thick bundle of such ornaments. Again, in South Africa, "they go completely naked, only the women are accustomed to hang little iron bells on a strap about the waist." "In explanation of the women's nudity . . . a chief once informed me that 'concealment is food for the inquisitive.' " On the Congo the women string pearls upon a thin cord about the hips, which is their only clothing. The natives of the eastern horn of Africa revel in foreign cotton goods, wearing great quantities purely for vanity's sake. The women cover about eighty per cent of the body, the men only sixty. In the Uganda region the people are quite indifferent to nudity; "clothing is only worn for warmth or for ornament, and not for purposes of decency." One of the naked tribes is "the most moral people in Uganda." Much of the clothing is like the veil which often causes the stranger "to imagine a defective face perfectly charming." Such ornamental deception is not uncommon: we read of a young buck as

> one of those
> Who slyly put soft clay
> Into their moccasins
> That they may be admired
> By folk of lesser size,
> And win the love of squaws.[142]

[141] Spencer and Gillen, *Nat. Tr. Cent. Aust.*, 27, 30; Smyth, *Vict.*, I, 275; Hagen, *Papua's*, 169; Codrington, *Melanesians*, 232; Hardy and Elkington, *S. Seas*, 174, 55, 56; Man, in JAI, XII, 329; Finsch, *Ethnol. Erfahr.*, I, 92.

[142] Ratzel, *Vkde.*, I, 225; Vortisch, in *Globus*, LXXXIX, 279; Lippert, *Kgchte.*, I, 410; Fritsch, *Eingeb. S.-Afr.*, 59, 128; Holub, *S.-Afrika*, II, 293; Ward, in JAI, XXIV, 293; Thonner, *Afr. Urwald*, 21; Paulitschke, *Nordost-Afr.*, I, 80, 81, 84; Johnston, *Uganda*, II, 862-864; Lane, *Egyptians*, I, 63; Leland and Prince, *Kulóskap*, 94.

"A friend, bartering for two bead necklets, which constituted the full-dress of a jungle girl, had no difficulty in securing one, but no bribe would tempt her to part with the second, as, in its absence, she would be naked." The Tamils say of a maiden who wears no jewels to attract beaux that she is "not dressed."[143] A Kayan chief has to wear a head-cloth where a common man does not, to preserve his dignity. "Even to-day the Bontoc men and women exhibit no shame before their fellow Igorot when, while at work . . . they remove their clothing to keep it clean and dry." It is for show, not for use or for the covering of the body. "At no time does the woman manifest shame regarding her always naked breast. As a psychological phenomenon," the author goes on, "shame induced by nakedness is impossible and shame alone never caused a primitive people to adopt its first form of covering for the person." Letourneau cites the report from the South Seas of how the native women swam out naked to the ships and then put on their finery and opened their parasols.[144] It is as embarrassing to an Indian woman to be seen without her labret as for a European to be seen with bare bosom. Slaves were forbidden to wear this ornament.[145]

One modern case may be added; it has to do with shoes. "When a Scotchman rises from the lowest to the middling classes of society, they become to him necessaries. He wears them to preserve, not his feet; but his station in life."[146] We are ashamed to go barefoot. Sometime some philosopher will probably enunciate the proposition that shoes were invented on account of "innate shame" at exposing the feet,[147] and we shall have another "instinct."

To enforce the evidence for the origin of clothing in self-gratification, it is possible to cite representative instances of its use in ceremonial, that is, on public occasions when it will be seen. Whether or not ceremonial clothing has religious significance, there is much ostentation and self-gratification involved in the wearing of it upon public occasions.

In New Britain, clothing is worn at the dance, though not at other times. "One bunch of leaves is bound about the waist in front and another in the rear, with a string. This . . . very primitive covering of the privates amounts, therefore, only to ornament." In one part of Africa, "however little ornament the people commonly wear on the body, various and manifold are the appurtenances which they use at the dance and the objects with which they bedeck themselves at their festivals. Hats and caps of the most heterogeneous description are in use for that." In Borneo, "people burden themselves at home with as little covering as possible, while on festal occasions adornment through the extension of clothing is the important thing."[148] "The Hyperborean man and woman go almost as naked in their hut or underground house as their con-

[143] Thurston, *S. India,* 531; Gehring, *Süd-Indien,* 72.

[144] Nieuwenhuis, *Borneo,* I, 121; Jenks, in AA, VI, 700; Letourneau, *Morale,* 146, 147 (quoting Beechey).

[145] Niblack, in USNM, 1888, 257.   [146] Senior, *Pol. Econ.,* 36, 37.

[147] Von den Steinen, *Zent. Bras.,* 199.

[148] Finsch, *Ethnol. Erfahr.,* I, 112, 113; Lessner, in *Globus,* LXXXVI, 337; Nieuwenhuis, *Borneo,* I, 119.

geners farther south. It is when they venture forth that they exhibit the highest invention in dress." Certain Canadian Indians "usually carry a *dress suit* to put on in the evening, or on arrival at a trading station." The dancing-dress of the Bakairi is like a bathing-garment in one piece, though these people wear no clothing on ordinary occasions.[149]

It is, of course, no revelation that human beings dress up for ceremonial public functions, for it is only in the presence of their fellows that men can satisfy vanity and reach out toward prestige. The fact needs to be pointed out rather than illustrated; it is often the primitive phase of a common custom that sets it off in perspective and shows the whole world kin.

§448*. Clothing as Adjustment. It is impossible to dismiss the subject of clothing without referring to its evolutionary aspects. That the amount and character of the clothing worn by a people represents an adjustment to life-conditions is a proposition that would be accepted, perhaps, out of hand. Nevertheless, such adjustment has often in particular cases been interfered with by vanity of one type or another. That contemporary fashions often oppose obvious and salutary adjustments in the matter of dress is enforced upon us by both reformers and satirists. Rational selection appears to have no force in this range of the mores; it is the pinch of necessity only that can make people adjust to something more elemental than the mode: such sad experience as made the Portuguese mothers in Brazil cease to lap their sickly infants in fine clothes, concede to them rather the virtual nudity of the Indian babies or, more broadly, such stress of circumstances as led to the general adoption by European settlers of the mores as respects not only clothing but many other matters practised by the natives round about them.[150] The colonists prospered when, in facing new life-conditions, they adopted methods that had been tested out on the spot by long selection.

The reverse was often true; Europeans have suffered because, for a time at least, they refused to adjust in the matter of clothing and otherwise to new environments. A notable case is that of the Germans at the outset of their colonial career.[151] Nor was it

[149] Mason, in USNM, 1894, 264; Rae, in JAI, XVI, 200; Von den Steinen, *Zent. Bras.,* 302.
[150] Southey, *Brazil,* I, 345; Keller, *Soc. Evol.,* ch. IX.
[151] Keller, *Colon.,* 577.

always the Europeans alone who suffered by reason of such malad-justments; it was not seldom the native, who had a misfit forced upon him either because automatically the environment he was used to was considerably altered by the presence and activities of the Europeans or because the latter forced or persuaded him to give up tried and settled folkways in favor of others to which the white men were predisposed. It would seem sometimes as if the civilized men have hated to see the native enjoying himself in his own way and have assumed a paternal and self-righteous attitude of correction toward him, as illustrated in the Spanish sovereigns' admonition to the Indians "that they should not bathe as often as they were accustomed, because the Royalties were informed that it did them a great deal of harm."[152]

The civilized have usually been keen, among other things, to have the native clothe himself in accordance with their ideas of propriety rather than his own; and his vanity has generally co-operated with them. His unclothed condition has been regarded as "immoral," especially by the missionaries. This change in the matter of dress has not seldom been extremely damaging to him; for it has involved a maladjustment that cost him dear. "No one of the false notions which we have to attack has been more disas-trous to the healthful development of man than the alleged close and intimate connection between clothing and morality. It hangs like a leaden weight on all efforts to advance to better adjust-ments, and nevertheless it is seen upon closer examination to be utterly false."[153]

Whatever may be said of the white man's motives, they rested ultimately, where the result was not merely an inevitable outcome of race-contact, upon a solid basis of vanity or ethnocentrism, the reflex of which was contempt for the mores of others and particu-larly of a "lower" race. Thus vanity came to interfere with long-tried adjustments in customs of covering the body or of leaving it uncovered. It should be particularly noted in the examples that it was the partial rather than the wholesale adoption of the Euro-pean code which wrought much of the harm—the adoption of the clothing without the hygienic customs, for example. The fatal re-sult presents a fine illustration of how all the mores go on together,

152 Fabié, *Legisl. Españ.*, 52.
153 Fritsch, in *Pol.-Anth. Rev.*, II, 873.

representing in their ensemble, not in their detached detail, the society's adjustment to life-conditions. This is the fact of the "strain toward consistency" in the mores.[154]

The assumption of clothing by the Tasmanians "occasioned many deaths; they were sometimes drenched with rain—perspiration was repressed, and inflammatory diseases followed." Among the Australians, "the idea of making any kind of clothing as a protection against cold does not appear to have entered the native mind, though he is keen enough about securing the Government blanket when he can get one, or indeed any cast-off clothing of the white man. The latter is worn as much from motives of vanity as from a desire for warmth; a lubra [woman] with nothing on but a straw hat and an old pair of boots is perfectly happy. The kindness of the white man who supplies him, in outlying parts, with stray bits of clothing is by no means conducive to the longevity of the native." The clothing he gets is passed around from one to another. "The natural result is that no sooner do natives come into contact with white men, than phthisis and other diseases soon make their appearance, and in a little time all that can be done is to gather the few remnants of the tribe into some mission station where the path to final extinction may be made as pleasant as possible." "A departure from this primitive mode of covering, and the adoption of the white man's costume, have weakened the constitution of the aborigines, and rendered them very liable to colds and pulmonary diseases." "The acceptance of European dress, or rather European rags, which their imitative spirit induces them to wear, proves injurious to this race, as to all other nations living in a state of nature and on such inferior cultural level. The use of clothes has to be learned and for savages who hardly ever change them and wear the same things in heat and cold, letting them dry on the body when wet through, clothes prove a very questionable gift of civilization. . . . It has been universally proved, and is admitted by every person of colonial experience, that the careless introduction of European dress among primitive nations and people of low culture is a most dangerous experiment. The native will at once become vain of the one costume he has been able to purchase, and anxious not to be seen in anything but the 'latest fashion.' Proud of his new raiment, he keeps it on his body by night and by day, sleeps in it when he is drenched by rain, runs with it in and out of the sea at random, remaining at the same time ignorant of the beneficent qualities of soap and water. The missionaries of the London Missionary Society therefore limit their dress reforms to a piece of cloth, which they make the lads who work for the mission wear around the loins. The women . . . wear grass-frocks, thus making further interference unnecessary."[155] These missionaries were exceptional in their understanding of the situation.

Says Miss Kingsley:[156] "If the question of the abstract morality of introducing clothes, or introducing liquor, to native races, were fairly gone into, the results would be interesting—for clothing native races in European clothes works badly for them and kills them off." Nansen[157] presents a melancholy picture of the results of missionary meddling in the case of the Eskimo: they

[154] Sumner, *Folkways*, §5.
[155] Roth, *Tasmania*, 173; Spencer and Gillen, *Nat. Tr. Cent. Aust.*, 17, 18; Dawson, *Aust. Aborig.*, 9, 60; Semon, *Aust. Bush*, 222, 353.
[156] *Travels W. Afr.*, 675. [157] *Esk. Life.*, 83, 87.

were persuaded to live in separate houses, to wear heavy clothing indoors, and to refrain from changing from the winter-dwelling to the summer-tent—all with disastrous consequences.

Under whatever motive man adopted clothing—and the evidence all points to self-gratification as the predominant consideration—the expediency of his mores was always being tested up by automatic forces of which he had little or no comprehension. Clothing is a good case to illustrate the operation of that automatic selection which ceaselessly passes upon the survival-value of mores and institutions.

§449*. Prestige. Satisfaction in recognized superiority is one of the keenest pleasures of the individual; and class-pride and national self-esteem must be counted in.[158] There is even a sort of species-pride, which is wounded by the truth that mankind is related to and descended from the animals and which lashes out in rage at science and the scientists who have established the fact. From the savage on up the ambitious have sought to exalt themselves, by some form of exclusiveness, from the common herd. It has been pleasant to be feared or held in awe by others. The chief knows that; it is hardly necessary to mention the regulative organization, with its offices, gauds, and ceremonial as a favorite range of the hunter after prestige. Children who converse in jargon, in order to impress their fellows with the secrecy and exclusiveness of some fleeting organization which they have formed, are striving for prestige along lines pursued not much less naïvely by secret societies of adults. In all ages secrecy and mystery have been favorite, successful, and also cheap devices for securing prestige. The man who can look portentous and say nothing stands a good chance of getting recognition; if he can occasionally utter some platitude in a resonant and impressive voice, his prestige is assured. People are readily impressed by what they do not understand, provided that it is set forth with sufficient unction, ostentation, sound, and fury. Such methods of prestige-getting were well known on the primitive stage, especially to the sacerdotal class.[159]

Otherwise prestige is attained by establishing connections with

[158] §§163-166, above.   [159] §320, above.

those who have exhibited superiorities or are thought to have done so. To be related to greatness is to be great one's self. To be called by his patronymic was a glory to the Homeric Greek; the leader names each man "from his paternal race, glorifying all."[160] Genealogical researchers with imagination are still in demand. Societies of the descendants of this and that are so much in evidence that one caustic critic proposed an association of "The Mothers-in-Law of the Stamp Act." It would appear that prestige is viewed as a sort of contagion which one may take if he exposes himself sedulously enough. During the French Revolution, when a law was passed requiring the withdrawal of all nobles not imprisoned to a distance of several leagues from Paris, many who were not noble but wanted to be thought so retired also.[161] From primitive times it has been possible to observe a type of human group assembled about some great man who is basking in the not disinterested adulation of a host of seekers after fame or after a combination of fame and food.

Of course the sweets of prestige lie in the sense of power and importance. Few human beings are immune to flattery; self-assessment is difficult and one is glad to accept at its face-value the favorable estimate of others. It is not at all infrequent to find a man prouder of what he can do only passably well than of what he performs surpassingly; thus Goethe thought his scientific performances were his best title to fame.[162] In any case prestige is a danger to the living man, for it verges upon the character of an intoxicant or a habit-forming drug. The accomplishments recorded by ancient rulers upon the monuments are preposterous and not a few kings have proclaimed themselves gods. The constant lift of flattery gets the feet of all but the elect off the ground. All pride may be renounced; but then it slips in under the guise of self-satisfaction in demonstrated humility. In view of the seduction of common sense which the thirst for prestige effects in nations as well as individuals, it is no wonder that the hard-headed Franklin broke out about "the pest of glory."[163]

That which most impresses the savage is power; he has no sympathy with what he considers weakness and privately and openly

[160] Homer, *Iliad*, X, 68-69.   [161] Duras, *Prison Jr.*, 101.
[162] Eckermann, *Gespräche*, III, 59 (Feb. 19, 1829).
[163] Cited in Sumner, *Coll. Ess.*, I, 292, 313, II, 56.

despises and ridicules much of what we call altruism or humanitarianism. Fearfulness is the greatest dignity he knows. Colonial administrators have learned this.[164] Great native conquerors have practised it and have been deified because of their ferocity. Kipling's[165] figure of the Norse leader, "red as a red bear," who was looked upon by his men as a god, and "who cheered them and slew them impartially as he thought best for their needs," is a true type. The exaltation of war and the military hero has directed the ambition of young men through the ages. Trophies, such as heads, scalps, or eagle-feathers standing for "coups," as among the American Indians, have rewarded effort and established prestige. Such considerations are developed by Spencer,[166] and have appeared here and there through our treatment of war and government. It is to be noted that there exists, along with the religious motive for a practice like head-hunting, the intense desire for a trophy which will elevate its taker into manhood.[167]

A pair of cases will enforce the savage viewpoint. Among the Asabs of the Niger, "an *Obu,* which literally means a Killer, is a man who has done some deed considered brave by his fellows. The deed accounted highest is the slaying of another man; but a person may become an *Obu* in three other ways, (i) by buying a man and killing him, (ii) by killing a man when he is sick, (iii) by killing a tiger (*aworo*) or a leopard (*ubido*). . . . In connection with the *Obu* the following peculiar custom is worthy of note. A man who slays another publicly, the deed being publicly confessed, plants a cotton tree in the public street. In this tree the spirit of the slain resides, and forms a witness to confront any slanderer who dares impugn the bravery of the planter. These cotton trees may not be cut down, but are not sacred in the ordinary sense of the word, *e.g.,* no sacrifices are made to them."[168] Among the Omaha Indians "sometimes after an attack on the camp, an arm, leg, or head was brought from the neighboring battlefield and boys were made to strike or to step on the mutilated portion of the dead enemy, as though they were taking honors. This discipline was thought to stimulate a desire to perform valorous acts by familiarizing the youths with scenes of war." This tribe recognized six grades of honors which "could be taken on the body of an enemy: (1) The highest honor was to strike an unwounded enemy with the hand or bow. This feat required bravery and skill to escape unharmed. Only two warriors could take this honor from the same person! (2) This honor required the warrior to strike a wounded enemy. Only two could take this honor from the same man. (3) To strike with the hand or bow the body of a dead enemy. Only two could take

164 Lippert, *Kgchte.*, I, 51; Keller, *Colon.*, 578 ff.
165 "The Finest Story in the World," in *Many Inventions*, 143, 147.
166 *Prin. Soc.*, II, chs. II, VIII, IX.
167 §§163, 229, 365, above.
168 Parkinson, in JAI, XXXVI, 319.

this honor from the corpse. (4) To kill an enemy. (5) To take the scalp. This honor ranked with no. 3, since the dead man could not resist, although the friends of the slain might rally around the body and strive to prevent the act by carrying the man off. Two could scalp the same enemy. (6) To sever the head from the body of an enemy. . . . For the first grade the warrior was entitled to wear in his scalp lock, so arranged as to stand erect on the head, the white-tipped feather from the tail of the golden eagle. As the sign of having won the second grade, the warrior could wear the white-tipped feather from the tail of the golden eagle fastened to his scalp lock so as to project horizontally at the side of the head. The third-grade honor entitled the man to wear the eagle feather so as to hang from the scalp lock." The other three grades form a descending series of honors.[169]

§450. Scope of Self-Gratification.

As has been intimated, the gratification-element forms a sort of fringe about or growth upon all societal institutions. Though the primordial appetites of hunger and love drive to satisfaction by the discomfort that attends them, their satisfaction yields pleasure. The pleasure is the counterpart of the pain. For long ages of evolution the race seems to have had an eye almost single to the avoidance of pain; then, with the development of capital and superfluity it was able to turn more and more from what might be called negative strivings to the positive pursuit of the more and better. Where it could attain demonstrable security, as in industrial self-maintenance, its efforts turned more confidently to self-gratification; where it could never be definitively reassured, as in its relations to the aleatory element as embodied in the spirits, negative methods of avoidance have continued to be characteristic. In all cases, however, men reach out for self-gratification where they may, as will be seen in the following outline of the entrance of the gratification-element into the evolution of the industrial and regulative organizations, war and property, marriage and the family, and religion. This outline will amount mainly to an assembling of aspects of these topics that have appeared incidentally throughout foregoing sections and will constitute the last of our cross-sectional surveys. As it is intended to be a contribution to perspective, it does not aim at exhaustiveness of detail; and it will ignore such physical sensations as come from the mere satisfaction of hunger and love, as well as the routine comfort that arises from a sense of security for the immediate future, not only from hunger, exposure, and

[169] Fletcher and LaFlesche, in BAE, XXVII, 434, 437, 438.

various specific dangers but from the menace of the spirit-world as well.

Superiority can be demonstrated wherever there is a competition with unequal distribution of reward; and vanity may be tickled by any form of ascendancy. There is, moreover, no place in the societal structure where competition is not going on, revealing superiorities or inferiorities as it goes and thus preparing the conditions under which pleasure-seeking and vanity thrive. There are few or no human necessities that do not afford a basis for the development of luxuries and few forms of effort that cannot be transformed into play, pastime, or art. The gaming-element affords at least a veneer of pleasure to many activities otherwise uninteresting. In general, therefore, one might expect to find the self-gratification element highly pervasive of all societal phenomena—indeed, to put the matter in lowest terms, to find it highly pervasive of the mores.

Among the incentives to the prime activity of labor[170] is the desire for luxuries, including finer food and clothing, ornament, and intoxicants. There is also the possibility of demonstrating superiority that will gain reputation. Some writers have spoken of an "instinct of workmanship," meaning pride in product. It is a mere fantasy to imagine that there is an instinct here; the driving force is the hope of applause, and that from an audience not composed of one's self alone. Again, the element of self-gratification enters into sex-division of labor, if the men do what interests them at the expense of the women[171] or if the masters accord to themselves the light and noble labors, leaving the undesirable tasks to slaves. In inter-group exchange, it is the luxury rather than the necessity that is in demand, this being particularly marked in frontier-trade.

It is not hunger alone that leads to the accumulation of capital; desire for luxury and distinction plays an important part. The potlatch should be recalled. The debt-relation is oftener created by the desire for social distinction or as the result of gambling than otherwise.[172] Many domesticated animals are useless except for sports or other pleasure or for purposes of osten-

170 §54, above.   171 §65, above.
172 §§81, 83, above.

tation. Slavery is largely a matter of the standard of living and to have reduced a powerful rival to servility is one of the keenest satisfactions to vanity.[173] It is not going too far to say that one of the deepest roots of property lies in vanity; certainly the amulet-ornament was one of the very earliest articles of private possession; and it was upon some criterion of desirability that the unique and pleasing thing was selected from the common, to become a private possession rather than part of the communal holding.[174]

The entrance of the gratification-element into the military and regulative organizations is highly characteristic. First there is war for glory as distinguished from war for booty or territory. It is possible to contrast these two types, even though they never occur pure any more than do economic and political earth-hunger.[175] There is always glory, meretricious or genuine, in a fight, for it is a competition out of which men emerge with unequal degrees of renown. No one needs to be told about the glory-element in war, for literature, sacred as well as profane, is full of evidence and is itself, in good part, a glorification of warriors, from Achilles and Joshua to Napoleon and the latest national military hero. War is godlike, and even the Christian deity is acclaimed in hymns as a god of battles. "The Lord is a man of war."[176] What need to say that war is the field *par excellence* for the culling of prestige among one's fellows? War is also a great game, with supreme stakes, full of chances to develop art and to gamble with chance. It has adventure in it and novelty; it offers relief from monotonous labors—and also engenders a distaste for them that interferes with a return to industry. It is as full of romance as it is of suffering. Perhaps the supremely imbecilic exhibition of fighting as glory-hunting lies in the records of mediæval chivalry —a set of mores portrayed in romances by Scott and many others and ridiculed in Don Quixote and lesser works.[177] The impression made by a uniform upon civilians and especially upon women, is still sufficiently strong; the play of boyhood is full of the military element. If all the detail of evidence as to the hold which war main-

[173] §§100, 105, above.   [174] §§110, 112, 113, 129, above.
[175] Sumner, "Earth-Hunger," in *Coll. Ess.*, II, 46, 51 ff.
[176] Exod., XV, 3.
[177] Clemens, *Connecticut Yankee;* Doyle, *White Company.*

tains over the race were assembled, it would make an astonishing exhibit.[178]

The regulative organization being in good part the offspring of the military, the incitement to activity within it is largely the desire for prestige. The young man attains dignity and privilege by the very fact of entrance upon his majority, succeeding the puberty-ceremonies; and his initiation into the secret society is a goal to be reached by the most rigorous and unremitting of effort. Every office up to the chieftainship is a tribute dear to vanity, for one thus becomes a regulator instead of an undistinguished unit among the regulated. In fact, every man who has emerged from childhood into majority becomes thereby a master as compared with the minors, the women and the children, as well as with such men as cannot meet the tests of manhood. There is satisfaction of pride in belonging to the ruling class; poetry and literature have made much of the "blood of kings." To be part of the aristocracy and thus able to look down upon one's fellows has always been attended with an expansive and intense gratification. The prestige of class has a story of its own and there is no end to the degrees of appeal to vanity involved.

All these coarser joys are susceptible of refinement into gratifications of a nobler stamp. It is somewhat the fashion, especially in the present age, to strive for the refined satisfactions of public service. Not a few of those who stand forth as public servants are impelled, though they may dissemble it, by the ancient motive of vanity and there are a goodly number of public men who will not serve society at the price of their own unpopularity. Despite all this, however, there is always a body of the high-minded who take as their motto the famous saying that "public office is a public trust" and who will live up to that trust despite personal consequences. It is true that most men who are big enough to do that are wise enough to realize that they will be justified by the verdict of history; but when men have reached the stature where they can forego popularity, the gratification they have in mind is the approval of their own sense of honor and right, which is the loftiest and most durable gratification of all. The run of those who give sums to charity or to the support of culture or ideals are not

178 Davie, *Evol. of War*, ch. XI.

attracted by anonymity; but there are always those who seek to avoid rather than to court applause.

Between the undisguised joy of the savage in popularity and power and the delicate satisfaction derivable from the use of influence to conserve the interests of society lies a long evolution whose details would demand much space to review. Our only object here is to note the opportunity for the gratification of vanity and pride offered by the regulative organization. From chiefs, judges, councillors, and other leaders all the way down to petty bosses and officers, all are more or less in the public eye. Some wear badges and uniforms to keep them conspicuous and are addressed by titles which distinguish them. Such titles, purely honorary as they are, may be borrowed from the military organization and the costumes worn, like the wigs and robes of judges, generally carry the impressiveness of antiquity. They all render the "public man" conspicuous. That means that they single him out from among his fellows; and it is indeed a stoic and a Roman soul that gets no satisfaction from such a position. The regulative organization has offered chances for the gratification of vanity, legitimate and other, hardly second to any others in the societal system.

The same might be said of ecclesiastical preferment and office; from prophet, patriarch, or pope to village priest the religious office confers distinction. The highest glory and power accorded to living man have undoubtedly attended religious headship. To rehearse the titles and other distinctions and the honors that have fallen to the mediators between gods and men, from the shaman on through to the sacerdotal functionaries of a high civilization, is sufficient proof of the fact. Religious leaders have been sainted and deified much more frequently than have secular rulers, just as the religious life has been the object of more concern and anxiety than any other. Where the man who could win battles and rule strongly has received his reward in fame, the one who could save souls and secure for them an eternity of felicity has seemed a very god. Interest has always centered strongly on the life to come; and so, although the man who could make earthly existence more endurable or happier was like a god, still he could not vie with the one who could assure endless life beyond the grave.

It should be recalled that the arts of pleasure have had a dis-

tinctly religious aspect;[179] perhaps it would be correct to say that
it was mainly religious performances that worked out into those
arts. Painting, sculpture, music, dancing, and the drama, if they
did not originate among the priesthood, yet found in it the leisure
class that had time and inclination to develop them. People who
are not pious are not infrequently highly religious because of the
æsthetic elements that belong to church ritual and ceremonial.
The poets have emphasized the appeal of the holy dusk, the
stained glass, the incense, the organ, the solemnity inhering in
survivalistic dress, language, and manners.

Peace of mind is one of the highest of satisfactions; and it is
religion, again, that has secured a good measure of security,
where there was no other means of attaining it, from the concern
with which men have always faced the aleatory element. One of
the high survival-values of religion lies in this service. The preceding section on religious evolution[180] details a number of the processes by which men have insured themselves against mischance.
The act of insuring might well have been painful and renuncia-
tory but the result was at least relative immunity and happiness.

Again, the ceremonies themselves, together with the cessation
of labor involved in connection with festivals and other observances, formed a set of diversions that were eagerly anticipated
and entered upon or viewed with zest. In his degree the veriest
savage attained to something of the pleasure in religious ceremonial that the most highly cultured now derive from the more
evolved and artistic product. By magic as well as by propitiation
gratifying results could be attained; and when the whole plane
of religion had been so raised through the evolution of belief that
the divinity came to be thought of as good and benevolent, then
believers were set in a relation with the universe that theoretically
freed them from sin, death, and calamity. They were redeemed
souls to whom the vicissitudes of earthly life were as nothing in
the certitude of endless bliss. Many men have undoubtedly attained to this supreme satisfaction.

The element of self-gratification connected with marriage and
the family is bound up, first of all, with sex. Reference is not to
the mere gratification of sex-passion, for that is a physical mat-

[179] Lippert, *Kgchte.*, I, 34.   [180] Part IV.

ter, nor to the child-parent relation in so far as it is a sequel to the organic process. Rather is the memory directed to what has already been written about the enthusiasm, romance, and idealization surrounding marriage and to the relation between marriage and vanity.[181] Perhaps it is worth while to insist yet again upon the universality of the love-interest, as indicated by the insatiable appetite of the modern reader for love-episodes. Weddings are traditional occasions of joy and also of ostentation. The test of the man and of the woman reveals vanity-satisfying superiorities. Pride and ostentation appear in connection with the bride-show, bride-price, dowry, family-alliances, and many other of the preliminaries to the status of matrimony. The woman can please herself to a large degree in the choice of a husband.

A happy marriage is the source of what are perhaps the deepest of earthly satisfactions; and when to a well-assorted union children are born, the satisfaction to love and to vanity is enhanced many fold. Prayers of men and women have regularly petitioned for children. By their arrival, and especially by the birth of sons, the wife's status has been elevated and her happiness and prestige assured; and wife, husband, and all the ancestors have been rendered secure as to the life to come. The importance of children for happiness is beyond calculation and the satisfaction in their presence is indicated by the tender treatment so regularly accorded them, even by the rudest savages. Something of the pleasure derived from offspring can be inferred from the miseries resulting from childlessness and the concern over its possibility. "Mother" and "father" are terms of honor, and when the head of a big family becomes a "patriarch," his prestige is approaching that of the chief and priest. The *patres conscripti* were the old men—the *senatores* or *gerontes*—in whom resided the dignity of the state.

§451. Retrospect of Self-Gratification. Looking back over the last two chapters, we recall that the positive element of self-gratification is grafted upon the institutional stocks that have developed under the primordial impulsions of painful coercion. Perhaps the figure would be better if self-gratification, an element present

181 §§339, 341, 430, above.

in some degree from the outset, is figured as a slighter growth which, twining about the heavier trunks, flowers among their highest branches. Yet the figure is inadequate. While a certain amount of a given good may constitute self-maintenance, added increments of the same confer self-gratification. Then additional quantities may, as amounting to too much of a good thing, cause satiety and pain. Of some things, for instance music, it may be said that they are not at all indispensable to self-maintenance but are, even in minimal amount, purely pleasure-giving. Still, as has been seen, there are few indeed of the activities listed under self-gratification that are not at least regarded as being of prime utility in living in the triple environment of things, men, and spirits. The gratification-element somehow enters into the very structure of all the heavier institutional stocks. It is really neither a parasitic growth nor a graft.

Whatever it is, to conceive of it as the prime impulse in societal evolution and to think of human beings as beckoned forward by pleasure rather than impelled by pain or the prospect of it, is nevertheless an error. Grim necessity demanded that hunger should be stilled; cold, violence, and other damaging influences be warded off; the next generation be begotten and reared; the spiritual beings that dispensed ill fortune be evaded, exorcised, or bribed. All this was serious business. The reward for performing these activities was relief of discomfort through adjustment; the penalty for not performing them was that which hangs over maladjustment in the rigorous competition of societies. The guerdon is existence; the retribution is death.

But the effort that men put forth under stress and fear is capable, except in the most inhospitable environments, of securing something more than satisfaction of the primal instinct of self-preservation alone. Men succeed in unequal degrees and are correspondingly applauded. Surpluses appear and the beneficence of their presence is felt. Capital removes living from the neighborhood of the dead-line and endows it with a measure of freedom and leisure. Until the essentials of livelihood are pretty well assured, the gratification-element has small encouragement; when they are once taken care of, it expands to become one of the most powerful factors in further development. It has immense possibilities for societal life, for, according to the turn it takes, it may plunge a society into degeneration, causing it to lose what it has gained in solid achievement and be selected away; or it may refine the society's life and react, largely through idealization, upon its economic, political, domestic, and religious institutions as a stimulus to variation and so to better adjustment. The gratification-element seems to be one whose powers and possibilities are released progressively along the course of evolution.

The struggle for self-gratification, motived in vanity, ambition, and other forces, along with their more refined derivatives, is one of the major forms of competition out of which comes selection. Inventiveness stimulated by the effort to attain eminence in some selected line is fecund of those variations without which selection would have nothing to work upon. Pride in the ancestral or national code strengthens the agencies that secure its further transmission. Thus the struggle for prestige enters inevitably and powerfully into the process of societal evolution. Since, however, the ambitions of men do not lead them to strive unerringly for that which will promote society's welfare, definitive selection has to be worked out by the automatic and impersonal forces that ultimately settle societal destiny. It is enlightening, sobering, and also reassuring to realize that there exists beneath all the vanity, ambition, fashion, and crazes of men and societies an elemental current which these surface-flurries never reach or agitate and which flows on serene, irresistible, and powerful to support its freightage of human life.

PART VII

GENERALITIES

CHAPTER LXI

CONDITIONS BEARING UPON THE STUDY OF SOCIETAL EVOLUTION

§452. The Way of Science. The way of science is the path of "trained and organized common sense." There is no other course by which to arrive at a genuine science of society, or of anything else, than to gather a mass of facts and then strive to learn what they have to teach. It is stated by a competent scientist[1] that if a set of facts has been lucidly classified and their sequence and relative significance recognized, the function of science has been discharged. This book contains a diligently assembled body of facts which have been classified, thrown into sequence, and their significance considered and re-considered over a number of years, with the hope of contributing toward a real science of society. Here is the sum and substance of our method.

The science of society, like other sciences, aims to learn what is and how it has become. Entirely foreign to it is the formulation of imaginative constructions, or the weighing and comparison of such, as set forth in literature, legislation, or popular discussion. Many edifying suggestions about the way to live in society have been made by poets and philosophers long before any conception of a science of society existed. Such suggestions can never be more than views which turn out to be more or less wise and useful. The science of society confirms some of them in part and proves others to be worthless; its own results are of a wholly different order and have a very different warrant. The history of intuitions and guesses about societal matters affords ample proof of one thing only: from the fact that, to men's minds, it seems easy and natural, and even "stands to reason," that things must follow a certain course, there arises no guarantee whatsoever of their having done so. The aim of science can never be the proposal of *a priori* views or even the verification of them; it is the presentation of ascertained facts in such coördination that they can become, through induction, matters of knowledge.

[1] Pearson, *Gram. Sci.*, 6.

Since it is in the natural sciences that the way of science has been most undeniably justified of its results, it is toward these disciplines that one who is intent upon arriving at similarly verifiable attainments in the study of society naturally turns for suggestion and instruction. Everyone who has come to sense the need of accuracy, objectivity, and reiterated test in the investigation of societal phenomena looks with envy upon the methods of natural science and wishes to emulate them so far as possible.[2] If a student of the social sciences no more than acquaints himself with the life and work of some outstanding natural scientist, like Darwin or Pasteur, he is better equipped, by reason of the leading he gets as to attitude toward materials and ways of handling them, than he could otherwise be. The unproductiveness of the study of society when approached from the direction of philosophy has been repeatedly and dismally demonstrated. In the order of the evolution of science, the social sciences rest squarely upon the development of the natural sciences, as societal evolution follows upon organic.

There is no intention of launching here upon a description of scientific method; but the sense and limits within which "science" is legitimately used in the present range of study need to be stated with discrimination, especially since "social science" is to be judged so immediately, peremptorily, and inconsiderately by its practical applications. Any practical activity of man must be exercised subject to the laws of mechanics, physics, or chemistry, as these reign in the natural world; its success depends upon the intelligent adjustment of any enterprise to the conditions set for it in the physical laws to which it is subject. All activities in the world are capable of intelligent adjustment to life-conditions in the same way, granted a knowledge of facts, a recognition of their relation to one another, and a comprehension of the significance of such facts and relations when construed with respect to the matter in hand. This is the sense of "science" when applied to the phenomena of human society.

Though the ways of science are everywhere essentially the same, yet there are differences of application according to the range of phenomena in which science is employed. Phenomena being set

2 Keller, *Soc. Evol.,* 1 ff.; Keller, "Sociol. and Sci.," in N. Y. *Nation,* CII, 475-478.

apart in groupings for convenience of examination, scientific procedure must be somewhat modified in adjustment to materials and so must yield results of different quality according to the range in which it is exercised. The phenomena dealt with by a science of society are less concrete and positive than those of the physical world and their relations are more complex, shifting, and elusive. Such relations can seldom or never be expressed mathematically except as an academic exercise; they are highly contingent and are qualitative rather than quantitative. The best that can be hoped in forecasting is a high degree of probability as contrasted with the certainties of the laboratory sciences. In the domain of the social sciences, "science" must always be understood as no more stringent than the class of phenomena permits; nevertheless, it can be insisted upon, such as it is, in wholesome contrast to the sentiment, myth-making, speculation, conventional agreement, or personal views from the standpoint of some selected world-philosophy, which have largely controlled in this domain.

It is quite idle to pretend to treat societal phenomena strictly by the methods of natural science; such pretense issues in mere affectation. In society, controlling force is ever exerted by fashion, custom, mores, and institutions. Societal expediency under existing circumstances of environment, as well as the constraint imposed by what has been passed down by tradition, even when it is no longer expedient, are among the decisive factors in societal evolution. It is not that mere "accident" occurs. Every societal effect is due to an adequate cause. But no investigation can establish the exact causal relation in all cases, or even in many. Presumably it can never be known, for example, why certain peoples have no pottery. Hence there is in the mores an appearance of caprice. The notion of the evil eye makes mores; it may be irrational, but they are real and positive. Historical causes, such as the vanity of kings, the ambition of prelates, the whims of democracies, the rivalries of statesmen, the love of women, are "accidental," inasmuch as they are not consecutive or predictable; they belong to the aleatory element, like the blunder of a general in battle. Though the prime impelling necessities of hunger, love, vanity, and ghost-fear must be conceived of as in their nature positive and definite, and perhaps even mathematical to some degree, their complexity defies analysis if that is attempted by quantitative methods. In history, though men always seem to be trying to live so as to win satisfaction of their needs and to avoid pain and harm, yet in different places and times they have not had the same notions as to what they needed or as to what pain and harm were; much less have they harbored the same conception as to the comparative desirability of things. The most primitive is by no means the nearest correct; in general, it is the contrary that is true; it is through long effort, change, variety, experiment, error, relapse, readjustment, that men have forged along the road of culture—so that culture means the accumulated product of efforts to solve the problem of the art of living and to win a stock of knowledge about the meaning of things in the world which can be handed down from generation to generation. The student of the social sciences has to follow all the operations of this imposing evolutionary process; to train his mind to recognize their sense, manner, and consequences; to apprehend their success or failure as affecting the welfare of mankind.

In point of time the art regularly precedes the science. The practice of the art produces habitual methods which are in the nature of general inferences from experience about the best way or the right way to perform the acts. There is here some insight into the natural conditions, under the law of economy; the underlying aim, whether visualized or not, is to get a desired result with the least expenditure of energy and capital—to work along lines of least resistance. This insight and judgment are expressed in empirical rules which are the germ of the science. The art itself is controlled by maxims, for it is an affair not of truth but of wisdom, and maxims are rules of practical wisdom or expediency. They are always relative. The science is unintermittently criticizing and correcting the empirical rules by bringing greater intellectual power and a better method to discern the truth of the natural conditions. Extended knowledge when applied to the art brings new experience, in verification or refutation, upon which the science begins its operations anew.

Men lived in society for ages before there was any approach to a science of society, when medicine-men, poets, law-givers, sages, and philosophers set forth rules of right living for group-prosperity. Their injunctions proceeded from various motives and were especially shaped by powerful convictions which they had adopted, generally in view of some distress experienced by the society in a crisis of the societal movement, also in the selfish interest of the expounders and their friends. The injunctions had no root in knowledge. This did not prevent them from alleviating the pressing distress; for many a happy adjustment was stumbled upon. Yet if they did attain such success it was not because they were intelligently in control of the case. Even an equivocal outcome, however, if plausibly exhibited as a success, might lead to the adoption of a long-standing policy. The prestige of the lawgiver's name gave authority to his dicta long after the case had entirely changed; it suffices to name Confucius, Zoroaster, Moses, Manu, Sakyamuni, Solon, Lycurgus, Mohammed, to recall the fact that great numbers of men have been and still are directed in their thinking and acting by the views and ordinances of law-givers and culture-heroes who spoke with only very limited knowledge of the society of their own times and localities and no knowledge at all of others. Millions of men in different societies still think themselves bound by loyalty to accept and act upon the prescriptions of great law-givers, believing it wicked to question or test the said pronouncements; and adherents of various ancient systems are still thrown into bitter antagonism to one another.

This is not to say that the work of the law-givers has been an unrelieved curse to mankind. Before science was, something had to fill the place reserved for it in the fulness of time. All societies in all ages have had common elements on which ordinances might act beneficially. Not seldom, what men have needed was a decision of some sort and it might almost be said that an erratic injunction, so long as it dissolved a state of uncertainty, was better than none at all. Nor were all the pronouncements beside the mark when it came to practical utility; ritual religious observances which were in origin irrelevant have had useful hygienic and sanitary effects. The stiffest dogmatic rules have undergone inevitable relaxation by interpretation and others have become obsolete. Reforms have marked the history of all law-codes, philosophies, and religions—re-shapings in which all that was necessary to win a modification in fact was to treat the letter of the dogma with respect. Nevertheless, the benefits of authoritative systems have been accidental, incidental, partial, irrational, mixed with restriction and other harm, especially after a lapse of time allowing of change in life-conditions. Hence the history of science as applied to society, like that of other sciences, has shown a constant negation of and war against what has come down in tradition. The progress of the science has been backwards, as it were; that is, with face to the past and back toward the direction of advance. It has been like that of an army always fighting rear-guard actions against a defeated but tenacious foe. A science has to go through this stage before it can emancipate itself from aimless groping and tradition and face forward toward free and original examination of facts, with the resulting possibility of constructive activity in the formulation of principles and laws.

All fruitful investigation proceeds by alternate steps of experience or observation and of generalization. Analysis and comparison, however rudely made, of a set of facts, even though these be unsystematically observed, suggest a bond of connection which, if true, would set them in an intelligible relation to one another. Having won this much, men may turn back to the facts again and test the inference upon them. It never verifies exactly but always needs modification to make it fit at all closely. It may then be re-applied to a wider range of experience or observation and the process repeated indefinitely. The many-sidedness of societal phenomena brings it to pass that different generalizations may seem to be suggested at different times or to different persons. The mental picture and the expression in language seem to need endless correction as advance is made to wider and deeper knowledge. It follows that it is illusory to pile up facts of history and statistics in the hope that "laws" will issue out of them by some sort of immanent necessity or spontaneous formation. Such store of brute facts crushes the student. It is only by constantly reverting to the process of generalization that men know what facts they want, and in what sequence and order it is most expedient to get them— what facts will be most significant and what ones may be discarded. That a thing is trite or a truism is often asserted as a mode of setting it aside with contempt; on the contrary, such are deserving of faithful attention. The most successful investigations have been those in which this process has been conducted with the greatest sagacity and the judgment best trained as to where to look. Undoubtedly it is at this point that imagination serves science.[3]

The process of investigation just sketched is also the way to put to productive use the results won by science, that is, by repeated alternation between the employment and verification of generalizations which have been reached, on the one side, and, on the other, the construction of new generalizations from patient study of the facts. The notion of eternal verities which have been formulated so that they never need be touched again is wholly antithetic to science. It is true that principles are reached at length which have been so often and variously tested and corrected that they are trustworthy for a period, or within a certain society; but beyond such limits the proof of the vitality and utility of a conclusion is that it is constantly undergoing correction, re-definition, and development. We are familiar with this truth in regard to legal doctrines and the principles of natural science; it is equally true as to political dogmas, ethical rules, and societal generalizations. What has happened in actuality, however, is this: the conclusion from experience, instead of being carried back at once as an engine for the new ordering of facts, has been made the starting-point for philosophical deduction, so that systems have been constructed on a small and shifting basis of fact, the remoter inferences from which have been endowed with authority because they are parts of a revered system, and have been imposed as arbitrary rules for action upon men who felt that they must obey. This process is one which has wrought untold mischief in human society. Men have been forbidden to think and know and have been held in separation and antagonism for which there was no reason at all. It is only by virtue of emancipation from such traditions, with freedom to approach things as they are, that a few sons of men may be properly described as enlightened; it is not by reason of the contents of any rival systems which they profess. It follows that no speculative system is to be viewed otherwise than with deep suspicion.

The science of society does not often have the chance, which is

[3] Tyndall, "Scientific Use of the Imagination," in *Fragments of Science*.

a commonplace with the natural sciences, of studying simple and
direct cases of cause and effect, nor can it simplify complexities
by experimental isolation. What it studies above all is group-
reaction in adjustment. Nor can it deal wholly impersonally with
its materials, though the object of the student should be to occupy
unwaveringly as impersonal an attitude as he can. This is one of
the main reasons why he should approach the study of the society
in which he lives and of which he cannot but be a sentient part,
through the examination of primitive and other more remote societal phenomena toward which he can with less difficulty maintain the scientific attitude.[4]

There is no doubt that the most satisfactory method of verification is by
experiment in a laboratory where conditions can be controlled. In the social
sciences experimentation is notably out of the question. To make an experiment it would be necessary to dispose of the time and perhaps the happiness
of a number of persons. Furthermore, because the forces which come into play
are numerous and very complicated in their action, and the conditions complex
and composed of elements which are delicate to the verge of imponderability,
it would not be possible, even with a group of human beings under control,
to set up an experiment in which natural conditions would be successfully
reproduced. It would also be out of the question to exclude or render constant
other elements than the one to be tested, because all the elements are inseparable. Communistic sects which have isolated themselves in order to try out
their tenets in isolation afford proof of these impossibilities; not one of them
has had the character of a true experiment or has proved anything except the
impracticability of isolation for experiment. Sometimes a case occurs independently which has something the character of an experiment, like that of
the Pitcairn Islanders[5] who tested the law of population and the effects of in-
breeding to some extent. Such examples would be important objects to study
had they occurred under such circumstances that competent investigators could
have got at them. The great difficulty is that if nature performs such an
"experiment," she does not announce that she is going to do so, and it is
generally over before men become aware of what she is about. Colonies in a
new country show a sort of societal experiment. The earliest history of the
Anglo-American settlements tested the notion that land is a boon of nature,
also the squatter theory of government, fiat money, and a variety of other
theories and projects. In a few cases experiments can be made with children in
school, which may have some value. The "typical instance" is another resource
that social scientists may lay some weight upon, though in its nature it is an
exaggeration and is therefore, like analogy, much misused in controversy because it is striking.

A further difficulty in the study of society is that a societal

4 §§454, 455, below; Keller, "Soc. and Sci.," in N. Y. *Nation*, CII, 475-478.
5 Hermann, "Pitcairn," in Petermann's *Mitth.*, XLVII, 225 ff. A full bibliography is given.

force so often shows opposite effects. This occurs in nature too, but is there less vividly sensed because the fallacy that consequences must follow purposes is checked up more sharply. In a society a new or disturbing force produces effects on lines radiating from the center of disturbance, and to degrees which depend upon the nature of the societal medium at the time and place of action. Hence it is no conclusive refutation of an explanation to show that, while in one case the cause effective in another case was at work, it produced no similar effect. Conversely, "the extremes of opposite operations often in civilized society produce the same or similar results."[6] Societal causes penetrate into a web of relations and the parts of the web differ in strength and adjustment. The consequences are therefore various and contradictory. The causes are also complicated; no societal force ever acts alone or "other things equal," although we are obliged to try to conceive of them as so acting. Everything displaces something else; "other things being equal" is merely an academical expression. There are also differences in circumstances which cannot all be included in a record of a case; yet a very minute variation in these may determine on which line the force is to work out.

In nature, a nerve-stimulus may produce a reaction or lame the nerve; exposure to the weather may harden or kill; it is said that deep-sea fish either lose their eyes or develop them abnormally and that species of plants spreading into a desert either become dwarfed and shrunken or humid and pulpy. There are various lines of adjustment. It would be incorrect to speak of the case of a society as analogous, for there is here a true parallelism. Social pressure makes the rich richer and the poor poorer; oppression may either reduce people to despair or incite them to revolt. The presence of wild animals big enough to be dangerous may train and educate the men who are their rivals or it may make the territory uninhabitable; the absence of such competitors may leave men undisciplined or it may give them a chance.[7] Abundance in nature assures men the leisure necessary for advance in the arts, or it may make them lazy so that they do not advance at all. Dire distress crushes or steels. Says Sir James Brooke:[8] "I may mention, too, that the effect on the Dyaks of a freedom from oppression has been just the reverse of what I expected. The freedom from oppression, the reduction of taxation, the security for life and property, has made them lazy. I always thought that it would have made them industrious, and eager to improve their condition."

Hence we cannot say whether idleness is the sister of luxury or of want, nor whether money (capital, wealth) is the root of all evil or of all good. Competi-

6 Von Pfeil, *Südsee*, 113.
7 Muñiz and McGee, in BAE, XVI, 21; Peschel, *Races*, 328.
8 Quoted in Roth, *Sarawak*, 70.

tion works either downwards toward nonentity or upwards toward excellence. What men have done they like to do, or they are sick of doing. A man wishes to be distinguished; he dislikes to be singular. He wants a fashion early, although it draws notice because it is striking and may be ridiculous; he rejects an oddity of fashion because it would attract notice. One wants what everyone has when not to have it is a sign of not knowing what is the right thing; he wants not to have what everyone has, when it is common. One wants what no one has when it is a distinction; he does not want it when it is a stigma. The constant force in all these cases is vanity. Again, appeals to public opinion at one time fall dead; at another time the same appeal seems to enthuse the whole society. What we, on our criteria, call good and bad are mixed in all the impulses which are infused into society. There is nothing good which has not its attendant ill; consider bigotry and fanaticism in religion. Nor is there anything bad which has not its attending good; consider war, slavery, despotism, polygamy. The critical question at any time is whether the good or the bad elements in the societal tendencies of a period will propagate more rapidly.

It is clear from the above that the best that the social sciences can hope for in the way of procedure is about the worst the natural sciences have to put up with. In a general way we do not care to deal with what has been called "methodology." Anyone who tries to learn what scientific method is can readily do so. If science is "trained and organized common sense," then the method of science is to train and organize that incomparable quality; it is not necessary to develop a pomp and foppery of method to clothe the process withal. The learned world has heard a good deal within the last generations about "method," "historical method," "statistical method," "laboratory method," "seminar method." Every one of these has some basis of wisdom and utility. Each has been heralded as the sole correct and admissible mode, that is, has been made into a fetish and a fad. Such fads distract science, encourage busybodies, and educate in affectation and empty form. When a scientist begins to talk a good deal about method instead of demonstrating it in practice without saying much about it, legitimate inference leads to the conclusion that he has not been working much of late or has mined out his vein. Advice as to the way to employ the tools of the expert is often suggestive to the beginner; but demonstration of what they will do is what really counts. The danger is that when a student focusses his attention upon "methodology" he is getting perilously near to playing with subjective concepts and dismally away from dealing with objective fact. He falls easily into the terminology and mood of logic and philosophy and acquires a taste for reasoning about results reached by workers rather than for laborious personal investigation. He is then likely to clothe his ineffectuality in arrogance or condescension toward those who are enduring the burden and heat of the day. He is liable to become an illustration of the famous maxims;[9] "These wisdoms are for the luring of youth towards high moral altitudes. The author did not gather them from practice, but from observation. To be good is noble; but to show others how to be good is nobler—and no trouble."

§453. **Pitfalls.** In attempting to use the approved methods of science in the study of society there are several false paths into which the present authors erstwhile strayed. We have since been sedulous to avoid them. One of the ways to find out where a thing is, is first to discover where it is not. The sincere student has to spend a deal of energy and incur considerable soreness of heart, first and last, in acquiring a scent for vacuity.

Many students of society have felt that, before they could go ahead, they must settle for themselves questions such as that of free-will *versus* determinism; some have even thought that they must come to some conclusion as to the relation of God to the Universe; not a few have anxiously sought an unearthly precision of terminology. In this book not the least concern has been felt whereby we should try to define what we mean by "facts," "reality," "self," or "ideas." The aim has been to use current terms with current connotations, except where the science calls for its own terminology; what is meant by such terms is what they signify to such as have not lost their bearings in the actual world through much contemplation of "ultimates" and "absolutes," or immersion in "free meditation." If the senses report that an object is hard, the possibility is not here contemplated that it is really soft or merely a cerebral disturbance. We are warned of the unreliability of the eye and other sense-organs; nevertheless we— and also those who warn us—go on relying upon them in practice. Faulty as they are, they are the best we have. The race has got where it is by depending upon them and not by floating about in a state of solemn or tearful depression because they are not perfect; experience shows that we somehow pull through by relying upon

---

[9] Clemens, *Pudd'nhead Maxims*.

them and never get anywhere by ignoring them. It is an inveterate habit of the race to put confidence in that which it lives by.

No seer need rise to make proclamation that the pursuit of any human conception comes to a halt in the grim void of mystery that surrounds existence. Here we are, sentient beings, paying daily in pain for being such, cleaving to a flying ball of matter which is but part of a hurtling system of spherical clods hung, we know not how, in endless space. The unknown and the unknowable bring up the background of every vista. Mystery pervades all things. This is a fact and cannot be ignored by any intelligent being; it is well to have caught a glimpse of it. Most scientists have done so, not soulfully, but in the course of their regular business, and stand aside in awe. As a fact entering into the making of institutions it must be taken into account, and we have done that.[10] There is no profit, however, in perennially contemplating, with lack-luster eye, the circumscribing mystery itself. To do that is like peering endlessly into a chasm; it is likely to result in vertigo or even autohypnosis. Over the unplumbed depths of the unknowable there may be figured a surface, thin if you like, of what we call reality. On this film men have lived and moved, pursued their interests, succeeded or failed, for the most part serenely unconscious of the grisly depths beneath. Upon it they have developed society and its institutions. Experiences have been accumulated and selection has passed upon variations in life-policy. Men know what they mean by "fact," "man," "woman," "birth," "death." If it is superficial to insist upon remaining upon this superficies, dealing with things objectively, and taking current terms at their face-value, then our method is deliberately superficial. It aims to deal with things as they are, in the race's ordinary experience and practice. Even if the equipment of the senses common to all men is inadequate to apprehend the transcendental, mystical, and super-sensual, it can yet respond to common sense.[11]

Myth-making and metaphysics flourish in the discussion of questions such as that of "manifest destiny," where verification is impossible, and they form a concretion of doctrine about many an objective core that is completely concealed thereby; but they cannot withstand the dissolving test upon the crude but palpable actualities of life. Much ranting is done against "commercialism" and "materialism"; no person of discernment takes it seriously, for all know

[10] Ch. XX, above.   [11] Goethe, *Faust*, I, 1830-1833.

it is but the howling of the "Outs" at the "Ins," and that if the former get in they will act exactly as the present insiders do. Especially when monetary interests become involved does there come into play a factor before which the myth-making and philosophizing wither.

Much muddlement is due to metaphysical blurring of terms. It is contended that there is no "law" or "natural law" in society. This is because of the old metaphysical conception of law as an independent power in nature, whereas it is only a formula in human words to state and hold fast observed sequences and relations. Everyone knows what "I see a man" means, unless he has been led to fuddle his mind by asking himself: "What do you mean by 'I'? What do you mean by 'see,' and 'man,' and 'a'?" From the standpoint of science such queries are chatter, and the bedevilled worker, plagued by the buzzing of it, might be excused for lashing out with the savage: "This makes our heads swim! Better to think of nothing and be at peace. Enough of this!"[12]

It is fatal to the genuine study of society, further, to become absorbed in the motives of individuals. Any real science of society will obviously study what it professes to study, namely, a society. In so doing it must watch what really happens, that is, consequences as distinguished from purposes or motives.[13] The consequences of human action have no necessary relation with the motives, purposes, and intentions of the man or men who bring about the action. The purposes of the agents arise in their own inner selves and are a product of all the complex components of human nature. The consequences, on the other hand, are a product of natural forces which may be set at work by human agency but which, once started, produce their own results according to their own laws. A science of society studies the nature, laws, and consequences of the natural forces in its field, not the inferred motives of men; it studies what men actually have done, not what they may be imagined to have thought; hence it is a fallacy to believe that it is psychological as regards the character of the phenomena which it studies. The psychological element, which is usually interpreted as including the ethical, dogmatic, philosophical, speculative, sentimental, or "logical" elements, demands stringent criticism wherever it shows itself in societal affairs; on account of the irresponsible ease with which it can be handled, societal questions

---

[12] §209, above.   [13] Sumner, *Coll. Ess.*, II, 67 ff.

are now a field for caprice and arbitrary or precipitate opinion not infrequently clothed in accomplished rhetoric or apparent erudition. One of the chief functions of a science of society is to rescue this branch of human interest and put it under the guarantees of science which have won so much for mankind in other domains.

"Indeed," writes Vinogradoff,[14] "no analysis of social life based on the consciousness of isolated individuals can be found productive of positive results. . . . This appropriation by the psychologists of a special set of questions on the borderland of both studies is after all only a matter of convenience and should certainly not lead to the absorption of sociology by psychology. And yet it is at such a rectification of frontiers that the more ambitious among the psychologists are aiming: they claim the right to subject social phenomena and relations to their own results and standards, and, for the purpose of such an annexation, they are ready to discard the most conspicuous features of psychological observation—introspection, and to extend the definition of psychology to the study of human behaviour in all its aspects. The consequences of such a shifting of ground cannot be said to justify the claims of the initiators of social psychology in this wide sense. Social creations, like language or religion, are approached with more valour than discretion, and instead of a critical examination of data and of careful inferences, we are treated either to sweeping assertions about instincts or to a restatement of facts gleaned from occasional linguistic, mythological or folklore studies. . . . Social intercourse, though arising between individuals, develops on lines of its own and does not simply follow the promptings of individual psychology."

Rivers,[15] himself a psychologist and one who looks forward, though with a sort of chastened hope, toward a future science of social psychology, has realized, as a consequence of his anthropological studies, that the identification of motives is still a long way off. "It is only when our knowledge is far more extensive and exact than at present that we can hope to disentangle the exact part which motives of different kinds have taken in the genesis of social customs, but one of the most important means by which we can hope to gain this increased knowledge is the study of the ways in which the contact of peoples has contributed to form the varieties of human culture. . . . Indeed, . . . it is because we can only hope to understand the present of any society through a knowledge of its past that such historical studies as those of which this book is an example are necessary steps towards the construction of a science of social psychology."

Another pitfall into which the unwary are likely to slip, to their grief, is the attitude of defense of a thesis. Before there was much scientific knowledge people exercised their minds and played with intellectual processes by guessing at truth and then defending their surmises by isolated cases selected out of experience for the purpose, and set forth with rhetoric, logic, dialectic, and elo-

[14] *Hist. Jurispr.*, I, 62, 64, 66.   [15] *Melan. Soc.*, II, 595-596.

quence, with frequent use of analogies and parables. Poets still
do this and so do philosophers. Debaters whose object is not the
truth but a plausible forensic display, employ the same practice.
The race is far from having outgrown it and the method comes
easily and naturally to anyone. It is all survivalistic since the rise
of science. A scientifically-minded man is always suspecting some
fallacy lurking in the major premise upon which the thesis rests,
especially if the latter is adopted emotionally, to be "defended"
against criticism. "I must begin," writes Darwin,[16] "with a good
body of facts and not from a principle (in which I always suspect
some fallacy)." To proceed with deductions from a major premise
once accepted, without incessantly carrying that premise back to
facts for test, is to create a dogma.

This may be illustrated by a diagram. Let the line AB represent objective
facts and the line CD conclusions from the study of facts. Then the course
of scientific procedure is from AB to CD, along the line EF, forming the conclusion F, then back to fact for verification (FG), then up to a further conclusion H, and so on. Perhaps the line CD should rise somewhat to represent

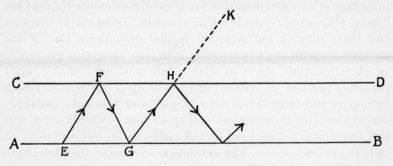

the advancing scope of the conclusions. In the formation of a dogma, however,
presently no further return is made to AB but the course of deduction leads
on to K, far away from fact, and into the realm of the metaphysical and intui-
tional. This is a representation of what scientific method is and is not.

The persistence of scholasticism in the mores, that is, of a
tendency to "reason" about things instead of investigating them,
is patent to any observing teacher who is not himself a "reasoner."
Students are always inquiring as to the "argument" for or
against this or that position, and if they are given a smart logical
quibble they are often quite satisfied. The answer that there is no

16 *Life and Letters,* ed. by F. Darwin, II, 371.

"argument" in the case but only supporting or controverting facts seems to evoke a certain incredulous depression. They do not want to buckle down to laborious study; they seem to put confidence in a creative "logical" process. This is like depending upon a coffee-mill to provide a breakfast beverage. It is a survival out of the dominance of the school-men. Many people seem to accredit the logical process with the power to discover new truth; that you can put a few facts in at one end, grind them over into equations or syllogisms, and extract at the farther end more than you put in. It is so very much easier to "reason" than to dig; the human mind seems to fly to the former and to drag itself with distaste and reluctance toward the latter.

This tendency encounters halcyon days in the societal range, for it cannot there be checked up sharply as in the physical domain. The assertion that everyone has a right to an opinion, supposing the case to be one arising in a chemical laboratory, is manifestly absurd, while in matters social and political even the prize-fighter's pronouncements are quoted, much more those of the "social philosopher" who is adept at camouflaging major premises and then spinning out a set of logical deductions. One of the cleverest ways to beg any question is to stow the major premise in an adjective: thus, the "Christian" state must fight, that is, must persecute heretics. So natural and so strong is this tendency both to employ and to be taken in by "logic" and "reason" that every one who aspires to an understanding of society should set a special guard over his soul lest he fall victim to his own verbosity or to that of someone else. The antidote is to demand the facts, both of one's self and of others, and to learn to identify the empty juggling of words that has so long bedazzled men's minds and led their judgment astray. Logic is nothing but an arrangement of things, easily degenerating into a sort of game with words as counters, with high-sounding categories and pretentious meticulosities. It is a thing of manner, not of matter, of posturing rather than of action, and one who gets involved in it is like a self-conscious æsthete who thinks only of how he says a thing, regardless of the content of his utterances.

At its best, logic is an art of exposition. Men's minds have been observed to respond to certain presentations better than to others, so much so that a clever exposition of nonsense, if dressed with a show of logic, will be accepted for a time as against an awkward setting forth of truth. Especially is logic evoked to justify a view or course of action which men wish to take; its subtleties are so manifold that it can readily be made to support anything; men can even fool themselves with it when they know better. Further, flaws can be picked in any argument that leads to a distasteful conclusion. It is evident that we are in the presence of a highly treacherous instrument, a good servant but a bad master. There is every reason why a scientist should know how to present his case in a skilful manner; he will do so if he has it clearly in mind and is not an illiterate, without any schooling in *non-sequiturs* and *elenchs*. He is after the truth, not dallying with words or trying merely to discomfit, ingenuously or not, some adversary. Above all, when faced by "logical" opposition, he should recall the sterling advice: "Always dig out the major premise"; and should not allow himself to forget that, in the end, the race has never been persuaded by logic but by "shovelfuls of facts."

Yet another danger-signal should be set up to warn the student of society to beware of "reasoning from analogy" himself or allowing anyone else to beguile him by such method. This case is not unlike the preceding one. Parable and analogy are devices of presentation common in undeveloped civilization and always well-suited to convey meaning to childlike minds, whether the latter are housed in an infant's body or in that of an adult, as among peoples of backward culture; and since they convey ideas easily to the simple they cannot fail to transmit them to those who are not simple. They will always remain indispensable instrumentalities in exposition; in fact, that is their characteristic function; they are an expedient for transmission of truth and have nothing directly to do with its discovery. Let anyone note the tendency of preachers to use analogy, if he wishes to observe its typical utility. Even as a device in exposition, however, analogy has its dangers. It is very easy to assail anything more pretentious than an illustration; all one has to do is to find an inconsistency. Flaws can therefore always be picked in an analogy, for no two things ever exactly superpose. This is why philosophical and pulpit "argumentation," when it leans heavily upon analogizing, as it so often does, invites attack and readily succumbs to it, even though its positions may be well taken. Henry Adams[17] speaks of analogies, "which are figures intended to serve as fatal weapons if they succeed, and as innocent toys if they fail."

The main contention here is that the use of analogy is directly contrary to approved scientific procedure. The object of science is to collect all the facts and relations possible and then to derive an induction which shall ignore or distort the meaning of not even the least of them; the analogy, on the contrary, if it is to be effective, must be confined to one selected fact or relation. The more clever the selection, the closer the similarity, the more effective is the analogy. There can be no real reasoning from analogy; it is a misnomer. The analogy is often, indeed, factitious, being no more than a figure of rhetoric; accidental or entirely external resemblances are taken as indices of a "causative communalty of properties"; and these resemblances, "which have at most a didactic value," have been regarded as possessing a "heuristic value."[18] In short, the use of analogy by a scientist is risky; it is full of suggestion and is insidious. Even a Spencer falls in love with his biologic analogy; granted that he held himself clear of reasoning from it, he certainly conveyed to many of his followers who had less acumen a profound faith in the use of it as a means of attaining truth.

We put the case against analogy without qualification thus far, because we believe it to be so disastrous to the social scientist—especially in his first years, when he is tempted to eke out scanty materials with showy but insubstantial matter and manner—to fall under its seductive spell. Nevertheless it would be a one-sided presentation to pass over the legitimate scientific use of analogy, in which it is employed under recognition of its lethal qualities and always with critical control. The truth of this matter is something as follows. Here is the limitless field of phenomena—the macrocosm and the microcosm—all manifestations of some great energy such as that of the Earth-Spirit at the loom of Time. Men arbitrarily divide up the phenomena into various ranges, for purposes of study. Science enters and exploits some of these ranges before it can do so in the case of others. Consequently laws are

[17] *Mont-Saint-Michel*, 294.   [18] Majewski, *Sci. de la Civ.*, 30.

discovered in some ranges while others are yet in the inchoate stage of exploitation and still others scarcely explored at all. Now, while working in one of the newer ranges or in one that has been exploited unscientifically, an investigator observes the analogy between the relations of the phenomena under his eye and those of the phenomena, better reduced to order and shown to be subject to law, of a neighboring range. It suggests itself to him that there may be identical laws in his own range. Perhaps a synthesis arrived at in an allied field impresses him as being so wide-reaching that it is likely to apply in his own area of observation. There is certainly a growing feeling among scientists that a kind of oneness exists in natural processes; no doubt the evolutionary theory has been as much responsible for this conviction as has any other factor.

There is no reason why the scientist should not take suggestion due to obvious analogies, where of other guidance or hint there seems to be none, and employ it for what it is worth, that is, with full consciousness of the deceptiveness of what may be merely superficial likeness and always under the unremitting scrutiny of the critical faculty. It should ever be realized that, even if the same principle obtains in different ranges, it will probably appear in the new range in a mode and on a plane that differentiate it almost specifically, perhaps, from its other manifestations. The proper corrections and qualifications are to be made with clear eye and cool intelligence before it is accepted or heralded. To get across the boundary into the new range, such a principle has to be generalized and then re-applied under adaptation to the diverse conditions encountered. This cannot be done by "reasoning from analogy," for the analogy is sure to break down sooner or later under conditions of the earthly diversity of all things. What has to be done is to try out the essence of the process discovered in the better-worked field upon the phenomena of the newer or virgin range.

We hasten to illustrate. The Darwinian theory of evolution amounted to a great synthesis in the field of natural history. Obvious analogies existed between that range and the domain of societal phenomena. A number of writers, Lilienfeld and Schäffle prominent among them, hastened to denominate society an "organism" and to try to apply biological terminology to societal phenomena. This was attempting to work the analogy direct. Spencer, as has been intimated, was the source of much of this sort of thing, in that his development of the biological analogy was so suggestive to the minds of a number of his contemporaries and adherents who did not possess the corrective in range of knowledge and sensitiveness of critical faculty which kept Spencer from being wholly carried away. Counters were borrowed from biology; a term like "counterselection" was invented to cover cases where societal selection merely diverged in mode, in the field of societal phenomena, from the mode of selection under nature;[19] there has been much mention of "social heredity."

The use of a term like "social heredity" is a mere analogical word-play. Heredity has to do with the germ-plasm, which never carries mores or institutions. There is no object, in science, in playing that words are tokens upon which whimsical values can be stamped over the accepted ones. A new conception calls for a new word; otherwise the old image and superscription will always be showing through. It is current usage that determines the circulating value of a word. Take the case of society as a "mechanism"[20] or an "organism." Let it be required of a thousand persons selected by chance to say whether society is either one of these, and the answer will be: No. Many of these persons could be muddled by a clever "logician" or word-juggler into believing that they were mistaken; but their native hue of common sense would have to be sicklied o'er before that came about.

The upshot of these reflections on analogy is, then, that there can be no direct scientific utility in it; that it is a device for exposition of positions taken, not for the discovery of new truth; that it is useful as offering suggestion from one range to another; but that it must always be employed with critical circumspection.

What the evolution theory, rightly used, has afforded in the way of suggestion and guidance outside the range within which it was first demonstrated has constituted the subject-matter of a Darwin anniversary volume;[21] and its services in particular to the social sciences are related by Vinogradoff.[22] "No event in the history of scientific thought has had a greater influence in shaping the habits of mind of researchers and philosophers than the rise of Darwinism. The biological view of evolution focussed in that expression has come to dominate not only natural science, but also the study of man and of society. . . . Three ideas emerge as especially powerful in this respect: the idea of gradual adaptation to circumstances, the idea of a continuous connection between the lowest and the highest forms of animal and human life, and the idea of a transformation of individual faculties through the life of social groups. In their combined effect these three leading ideas constitute the mainstay of the

19 Spencer, *Prin. Soc.*, I, §269, end; Keller, *Soc. Evol.*, ch. VI.
20 Majewski, *Sci. de la Civ.*, ch. XXXI.
21 Seward (ed.), *Darwin and Modern Science.*
22 *Hist. Jurispr.*, I, 136, 137, 138.

doctrine of evolution which has set its stamp on the scientific thought of the last seventy years. . . . Yet, though even the most rudimentary forms of culture known to us are very complex and replete with various accomplishments, we are justified in considering them at early stages and in tracing the incipient forms of social organization and law in their arrangements. These cultural origins supply us not only with simpler combinations and more clearly defined natural conditions, but they possess the inestimable advantage of presenting themselves in a very great number of instances and varieties which shade off one into the other and offer welcome opportunities for comparative investigation. This is so much the case, that comparative jurisprudence has almost become synonymous with a study of primitive societies, although, of course, such a connotation is by no means rendered necessary by the aim of the study."

The science of society, like other sciences, is after nothing else than the truth; and any method of attaining to the truth which experience has shown, by verification, to be effective, provided such a method is applicable to societal phenomena, is to be drawn upon freely. In general, we say, the student of society, especially in his years of apprenticeship, runs least danger by adhering as closely as possible to the positive methods exemplified in the natural sciences. Above all and at every stage it should be kept before the mind that true science always looks forward to and provides for its own correction, and that one of the surest signs of a spurious process is the absence of any such provision.

§454. Evidence. It will have been noticed that this book draws the bulk of its evidence from the life of prehistoric societies, including under that term the contemporary societies of primitive men who have no history in the strict sense. Our evidence is largely ethnographical; few instances are cited from the life of modern cultured peoples. Further, we do not attempt to construct by inference a remote past for which there is no direct evidence. The section of societal evolution here drawn upon begins where the first direct evidence begins—first, that is, as respects series and not at all necessarily in time—and seldom extends far into the strictly historical range. This restriction at both ends of the line is partly deliberate and partly inevitable; the explanation to be offered for it is, however, in no sense apologetic.

The fact is not so obvious as not to need pointing out that the range covered by the evidence here used is by far the longest stretch of societal evolution. History is short, even though it be dated from the first written or ideograph records; if man has been on earth only two hundred thousand years, it covers not over some five per cent of that period. Doubtless it would be better to make requisition upon the whole stretch of society's evolution if that were possible. We think it is not—at least not yet. We are content, in plotting the curve of that course, to utilize only so much of a segment as appears to us most trustworthy, and we are here noting, preliminarily, that this segment is not much short of the whole. It might be considerably shorter without irreparable loss; in undertaking to determine the nature and line of development of an evolutionary product it is not indispensable to know the whole course of its career, from the beginning up to and including the present, any more than it is requisite to know the whole course of a projectile in order to plot its flight. A section considerably short of the whole is enough to judge by, when it is a question of perspective rather than of an exhaustive catalogue of detail.

Conviction as to that matter has led us to some degree of indifference as to societal origins; and we are the readier to adopt this point of view because of the practical impossibility of securing precise and verifiable evidence as to these origins. The origin of primitive customs, and so of societal institutions, "is always lost in mystery, because when the action begins the men are never conscious of historical action, or of the historical importance of what they are doing. When they become conscious of the historical importance of their acts, the origin is already far behind."[23] All that one needs to do in order to appreciate the virtual impossibility of a science of society that must rest upon clarity as to social origins, is to read the literature concerned with some such topic as the origin of exogamy or of totemism.[24] What we have done is to begin with facts of observation, together with such simple and self-evident inferences as we think these facts easily support. Since the origins are lost in mystery, especial significance attaches to the earliest state of human society of which positive knowledge can be obtained, for that becomes our starting-point. In taking strict account of the most simple and primitive conditions much weight is laid upon ethnography and historical anthropology.[25]

23 Sumner, *Folkways*, §§7, 8.
24 For example, Lang, *Social Origins; The Secret of the Totem.*
25 §459, below.

In the endeavor to realize the conditions with which, so far as concrete evidence goes, the race started, we are bound to begin with the most primitive cases known to us in ethnography. It is not at all necessary, we contend, to determine the very origins of society, even if we could do so, any more than it is needful in organic evolution to be resolved as to the origin of life. We simply wish to get back as far along the line of the evolution-series as the facts and modest inferences from them will warrant, in order to have as extended a perspective as possible at the present stage of knowledge. Once, when the knowledge of all really primitive societies was very slight, it was the custom to construct *a priori* theories as to how it must have been at the beginning. Most peoples have legends about the creation and the early conditions of the race, which are mostly guess-work, with a plentiful sprinkling of constructions carried back from the conditions and mores of the constructors. Later philosophers attempted to disclose the "noble savage" by stripping from civilized man what they conceived to be the trappings of civilization. Since such a social philosopher was often a combination of a romancer and a critic of contemporary society, the primitive condition of the race, as he imagined it, was a laughable travesty upon the unwitting savages and the life which, as we have since learned, they really lead.

But with the opening up of the world since the Discoveries Period, there have come into being the sciences of prehistoric anthropology and especially of ethnography, which have revealed the actual facts about the life of peoples upon an undeveloped stage of socialization and civilization. Hence it is no longer necessary to cudgel the imagination or to venture upon *a priori* guesses in order to have a conception of savage life. Use of the comparative method has also enabled us to interpret scientifically, in the light of ethnography, much of the evidence that once lay almost useless in legend, tradition, and ancient literature. The field of the imaginary reconstructor has now been shifted much farther back, into the dim region of inference concerning the origins of the societal forms which appear full-fledged in the simplest societies of which we know. We do not mean to follow these attempts at reconstruction very far, for we are always seeking for sequences rather than for origins, and the sequences can be made out within the range of facts actually known to us.

On the hither end of the series, further, we do not feel under obligation to bring lines of development up to include contemporary forms. Practical considerations appear here, as in the case of the origins. Here, as there, the evidence needed for verification is absent and the views of specialists conflict. Let the student of society depend upon whatever historian he will, he is still sure to be charged with knowing no history. Yet he must have recourse to treatises; life is not long enough for him to be able to verify his own historical data. Though historical materials contain copious evidence for a science of society, the student of that science can scarcely gather it for himself; the life of a developed society, with a history, is so complex that no man can live long enough to allow him to rise from a critical study of actual historical materials and sources to generalizations upon the evolution and life of society. The historians, besides having small interest in several kinds of evidence for which the social scientist is eager, are by no means in agreement as to facts and the simplest relations of facts, even those exhibited on the relatively restricted stage of a single nation's history. Hence it is the part of caution to await some consensus among specialists before venturing much into the field of history, especially modern history. Though in time this range of knowledge is bound to furnish abundant evidence for a science of society, we do not trust ourselves to it very confidently at present, while theoretically we do not need it any more than we require precision as to societal origins.

Still less do we care to have recourse to the "commanding evidence" of contemporary life. By a study of contemporary society there may be attained a cross-section of societal life, but not a "longitudinal" or evolutionary view. It is the latter in which we are interested; the other is set aside under the separate category of demography.[26] In so doing we run counter to the common understanding as to the nature of social science, or "sociology," and to the current "sociological" practice of generalizing from a set of contemporary conditions to which it is designed at once to apply such generalization with the purpose of securing "progress" or some other desirable consummation. Practically, as any intelligent observer knows, there prevails the greatest diversity of interpretation, and even of description, of present-day social conditions; the specialists, both real and self-styled, give us no consensus to depend upon. Even statistics,[27] the employment of which lends such an appearance of mathematical exactitude, are not utterly reliable, much less susceptible of a single or generally accepted interpretation.

Theoretically, the science of society is as indifferent to contemporary conditions, looked upon as evidence, as it is to inferences as to societal origins. These latter are untrustworthy because they are largely speculative, and, like all speculation, not verifiable; the former are unreliable because of the inevitable and ineradicable bias with which we all view that which, since we live in the midst of it, touches us immediately. We constantly admit

26 §459, below.   27 §458, below.

the superior exactitude of "the verdict of history"; yet those who propose to make a business of depending upon that verdict should fortify themselves against the fate of being scouted as unpractical, or academic, or backward-looking, or worse. From this attitude respecting the contemporary it follows that the science of society is also indifferent to social programs. As the societal origins are lost in mystery, so the societal destinies are no more than an object of fruitless speculation. If the business of the "sociologist" is to construct utopias, as the somewhat unlearned, but confident H. G. Wells[28] tells us, then we enter an extra disclaimer to the title.

The essential fact of the matter, especially as respects contemporary evidence, is that what is most needed in any scientific study of society is the austerity of distance and detachment; for no man of us is capable of so insulating himself from the social currents that flow about him as not to have his immediate judgment concerning contemporary things deflected this way and that. We are all creatures of circumstance; the displays made by those who lay claim to the power of self-detachment from environment form an edifying commentary upon that truth. But judgment clears rapidly as we pass into spheres of observation which the subjective element can less readily enter. One of these spheres is the study of peoples remote in place, time, or culture. This means the study of the earlier historical and the primitive or non-historical peoples.

In dealing with evidence from such sources we are much less likely to pass a "moral judgment," that is, to measure things and men by our own code—a procedure that vitiates all our results. To pass a moral judgment in chemistry—to say that a mixture of saltpeter, sulphur, and charcoal "ought" not to explode if fire is applied—would be laughable; to be depressed because a fly has six legs instead of a dozen would argue an unsettled mind. Similarly in a theoretic science that has to do with the evolution and life of society, it is impertinent to be a pessimist or an optimist, and entirely out of order to pass the moral judgment—constantly to use "ought" and "must" about society's nature and doings, instead of "is" and "can." By confining the study of human society

[28] In *Sociological Papers*, III, 367.

chiefly to those examples of it which can be viewed and appraised dispassionately, this tendency is reduced.[29]

It is probably unnecessary to contend that every science works out into an applied or practical phase, which is really an art. If the test of science is prediction, it must ultimately measure itself against conditions and institutions of the present, with a view to their better adjustment in time to come. But there is no gain to be won by confusing the theoretic and applied in the physical sciences, or the investigative and the therapeutic in the social sciences. The physicist whose mind is always intent upon the felicity to be won for the race by somehow securing the abolition of friction is not likely to have a place among the world's benefactors; nor is the social scientist who has an eye ever upon present-day problems of social betterment likely to contribute much to a science of society except whimsical imaginings. Inventors of efficient mechanical devices are an asset to a nation, and originators of efficient societal agencies would be no less; but there are very few or no persons in the complex life of these days who can originate anything practical without a solid background of preparatory study of fundamental principles and theory.

A large part of the effort consciously and conscientiously expended to uplift society has failed—and in failing has involved disillusion and disappointment to worthy intention—because of lack of background on the part of the uplifters. One who is convinced of this is the more ready to emphasize the importance of securing distance and detachment, as a condition favoring coolness of judgment, through the study of materials that can be approached in the scientific spirit. The study of society cannot go far without showing more accomplishment in the line of pure science; and, to attain that, investigation must set out with a renunciation of any final program or purpose of societal betterment, except as the course of quiet, unhurried, unexcited study shall reveal the one great formula for societal adjustment on rational lines, namely, to know what a society is, and is not, and what can and cannot be done with it. In any case, our aim is to investigate the nature and recorded evolution of society rather than to advise forthwith as to its manipulation.

[29] See quotation from Vinogradoff under the preceding section.

§455. Quality of Evidence. In resting great weight upon the evidence from ethnography a writer encounters criticisms of a various order. We do not intend, as a rule, to engage in any controversies over legitimacy of procedure, but to let our results witness to the degrees of validity of our methods—believing that to be the only conclusive demonstration. However, concerning ethnographic evidence, as well as much testimony from the range of historical anthropology, we may briefly record, in positive form, the reasons for our faith in it.

Let it be recalled that, in studying primitive phases of societal evolution, one is dealing, not with a small section of that evolution but with by far the longer stretch of it. Granted that a section may be significant of the whole, this section is quantitatively the most promising. The quality also of the evidence derivable from the life of primitive societies is regarded by us as of the highest. The adjustments of society which we call civilization form a much more complex aggregation than does the culture that went before; but the difference is in degree, not in kind, and the essential nature of the several institutions produced by adjustment in the mores does not change. The essence of property is now what it was in the beginning. As in geology, the same forces remain always at work, without catastrophic intervention to alter the course of orderly and continuous development. In geology it is possible to work back from what is to an explanation of what was; the past can be explained by the present; so too might it be in the study of societal evolution, if results were as convincingly verifiable. In view of the human tendency to carry back our own ideas and mores into stages where they could not possibly have existed, it is safer to undertake to explain the societally complex by working up from the simple than the reverse. We are all biassed in the matter of our contemporary mores where we can be judicial in dealing with contemporary rocks.

Preoccupation with historic method causes some to doubt the validity of evidence not capable, for the most part, of chronological arrangement, and not to be accurately dated. But here we have to do with a science,[30] which is interested in genetic series rather than in sequence in time or proximity in space. It is an

---

[30] §457, below.

approved method in science—approved because it verifies—to arrange its materials irrespective of place and time. Few dates occur in science, though history, true to its origin in chronicle, has always made much of them. The interest for the science of society lies in the adjustment of mores and institutions to life-conditions of society; it is largely a matter of indifference as to when and where such adjustments took place. Non-acquiescence in such a contention is a rejection of the comparative method that has proved valid and useful throughout science.

All research must pick its facts in the sense of choosing what sort of evidence it shall seek and of looking for it where it is likely to be found. There is no point in prowling vaguely through the whole field of phenomena. The mineralogist does not spend time in digging on coral islands if he is after metals and facts about them. Looking for the sort of materials you need is a quite different matter from selecting some facts and rejecting others in defense of a thesis[31]—which is not a part of science, because the essence of science is search for truth, not self-justification in the matter of some "intuition." The science of society, in making use of ethnography and historical anthropology, is intent upon finding out how society adapts itself through its mores and institutions, in their several phases, to life-conditions. If it encounters cases of such adjustment in different places and times, these are highly instructive parallelisms, to be promptly seized, appropriated, and set in their proper places in an evolutionary series.

Further, it is a matter of indifference to the science that primitive institutions may represent cases of degeneration. Evolution, though popularly confused with progress, includes what may be, from a selected point of view, retrogression.[32] Evolution means only adaptation. If life-conditions alter in one sense, the resulting societal adjustments approach our own and are taken to be progressive; if in the other sense, they depart from ours and are called retrogressive. It is all a question of the point of view whether institutions seem to be one or the other. The point of view, however, is a shifting and unreliable thing. If, on the other hand, evolution is regarded as adaptation to life-conditions, the

31 §453, above.
32 Keller, "Soc. Evol.," in Lull and others, *Evol. of Man*, ch. V.

point of view is dispensed with, and along with it go any and all of those subjective or moral judgments which are, by their nature, unscientific. Adjustments come into effect by the action of inevitable evolutionary factors; they could not be otherwise. Whether they represent to our eyes progress or degeneration is a matter of no scientific significance.

The so-called cases of degeneration fall, at all events, into a stock position in the same evolutionary series up through which they are supposed to have come. The African hunting-tribe gets cattle and "rises" to the pastoral stage; it loses the cattle in some manner—by rinderpest, perhaps—and "reverts" to the hunting-stage. But its adjustments to the hunting-conditions, now resumed, though doubtless somewhat modified by brief elevation to something "higher," are as valid cases of response to life-conditions as if the tribe had never seen cattle. The case of the frontier-society is instructive along the same lines.

The whole matter is one of adjustment. The savages of nowadays are under pressure to adjust to conditions not dissimilar to those of our remote ancestors and with the same lack of accumulated knowledge of facts and forces. "We should get a correct idea, in the main, of life in Sweden one or two thousand years B.C. if we should go into the house of a Greenlander or a Lapp of the present day." All savages on the same grade of life show resemblances in their adjustments, from tools up to societal institutions.[33] "The effect of the present evidence may be stated as confirming and extending the argument, familiar on neolithic ground, that the condition of modern savages illustrates the condition of ancient stone age peoples, representatives of a stage of culture at once early in date and low in degree."[34]

The simpler structure is taken to be the more primitive, just as the use of copper is inferred to have preceded that of bronze; it is of little moment whether it was once reached in the course of evolution, and then preserved under isolation, or whether it represents a reversion from a once more developed form. The sequence of types is what science is after, whether the types are those of organic or of societal structure. If a group of Europeans go to

[33] Montelius, *Sver. Hist.*, I, 18, 19; Nilsson, *Scand.*, 152.
[34] Tylor, in JAI, XXIII, 152.

Alaska and are there forced, under the prevailing life-conditions, to live as the Indians or Eskimo do, then the type of society and of societal institutions which they show is in so far classifiable with those of the Indians or Eskimo, and is scientifically significant in just the same way. Suppose that the Bushmen of Africa were once less primitive than they are now, but, upon being driven into the desert, adapted themselves to the new set of life-conditions, losing something of what they had before—what of it? They are primitive in a high degree now, and illustrate how man had to live under unfavorable life-conditions; their type is of much significance as showing just that, for the simpler members of the sequence of societal forms are precisely what we want to know about, to start with.

Thus we do not regard the general objections to reconstruction of primitive stages out of types of retrograde societies as of any importance. Granted common sense in the reconstructor, this simply becomes a part of the comparative method and verifies freely in the new truth which it reveals. In any case there has been an unwarranted outcry in this matter; a great many of the examples of primitive society show no evidence at all of retrogression. They have developed in isolation and have never been forced to adapt themselves in an increasingly complex manner. For all we know they may have been where they are for millennia, living all that time after a manner not much dissimilar to the one presented by them at their discovery. The reasons of the objectors to ethnographic evidence are often just what they are in the case of dissenters from the evolutionary theory; they do not like the results and want to explain them away somehow; they have in the back of their minds a feeling that nothing can be true that is distasteful, together with an idea about "progress" that evolution does not confirm; they begin with the ethics and the ideals and hate to believe anything that seems to corrode them. It has been easy enough to proclaim that this or that migration of peoples "must have" taken place, so as to explain with less rearrangement of accepted ideas the unwelcome phenomena which they exhibit; in such manner geologists before Darwin's time used to lift up lost land-bridges and let them sink because not to have done so would have entailed at least a painful search for less obvious causes of geographical distribution. It has been easier to say that this or that item in societal life "must have" been the result of acculturation or of preservation out of a higher culture once possessed (presumably before the "fall of man"); but nothing is harder than to prove the truth of any one of these agreeable impressions. And what gives added confidence to one who ignores the objectors is to find the cases of parallelism existing between primitive societies that no one seems to have the hardihood to call retrograde and those over which, when they are introduced into a sequence, certain wiseacres wag the head most mournfully.

Further, there seems to be present in the objections raised against the evolutionary method of series-making another form of deep-seated sentimental bias, again somewhat like that harbored against series in organic evolution which reveal the ancestry of man. The process is disliked when it arrives at a certain type of result; otherwise it is not regarded as accursed. Few object to a series covering the successive adjustments in the arts of life; they do not see anything repulsive in the evolutionary chain of forms of money or of medicine; it is when the family-tree of the state, or of marriage, or of religion comes into account that certain sages begin to look dismal and to question the validity of evidence—particularly the significance of the earlier members of the series. There abides in many minds, we repeat, an ineradicable vestigial belief in the descent of man from some better estate, whereas all that science has to tell supports the contention that he began in the utmost destitution and savagery, and that human societies have either risen by virtue of the forces in them, or have stayed pretty much as they were because of the lack of forces in them, or have been reduced by reason of the play of superior forces outside of them, in the environment of things and men. In all these cases we have differing degrees of adaptation and differing societal forms as evidence thereof—forms which we may arrange without further scruple in an evolutionary series.

Confidence in the use of ethnographic and other primitive evidence is heightened by the reflection that it produces results which have withstood the tests of reality as these have been developed in experience. These results are at the same time a justification of the science of society. The credit of this demonstration of results

THE SCIENCE OF SOCIETY

belongs, above all, to Herbert Spencer, and can never be taken from him. It has worked out, in brief, to a conception of society as a unified whole—as a great entity, self-maintaining and self-perpetuating, something more and greater than the sum of its parts, whose evolution and life are susceptible of investigation, whose forms pass from phase to phase, from the most primitive up to the most sophisticated, remaining yet constantly interdependent in the most intimate and intricate of relations. The local form of society is seen to be an adaptation to environment, and the phases of institutions are found to be due to mutual adjustments between them. Democracy did not simply happen, nor was it revealed; it is a characteristic form under certain conditions—and so were and are communalism, polygyny, fetishism. Property and marriage are seen to be closely interlocked; likewise property and religion, religion and government, government and economic organization, economic organization and property. Fossil forms of institutions—survivals—exist, as in organic evolution, and afford links with phases of the evolutionary far past. In short, the conception of the nature of society and of the rise and decline of societal institutions has come to be a broader one, and it has entered into and vitally affected all subsequent study and thought along social lines.

In reaching such results Spencer made systematic use of materials from primitive life; and discriminating readers will readily discern that he would have attained to those results with great difficulty, if at all, and with much less surety, had he, after the order of his predecessors, rejected primitive materials or known nothing about them. He was not alone, moreover, in getting effects by thus availing himself of an unexploited series of data; by their researches into primitive institutions, Tylor, Frazer, and many others have served the interest of men in knowing the nature of human society.

There is an excellent general reason for the various successes gained by using ethnography and historical anthropology. Fractions, we know, are most readily handled when in their simplest, lowest terms. You can do next to nothing with the highly complex fraction as it stands; you reduce it and see it in its lowest terms; if then it turns out to equal zero, or one, or one-third, you can readily deal with it. The case is not so different with the institutions of society. Try to dig out the nature of money from the complexities surrounding an assault upon the gold standard, and you are foiled; study the primitive mechanism of exchange for a time, and the essential services of that adjustment in the mores, which we call money, become clear. Then follow up along the line of its evolution and note its growing complexities, correlative to the demands put upon it by life-conditions that are steadily becoming more involved and exacting, and you have gained an insight, otherwise denied, into the nature of an important societal agency. The governmental or regulative system of a modern state is most complex; that of an African tribe is very simple; nevertheless the former is in the same series as the latter and is descended from it through an unbroken line of gradual evolutionary transitions.

This analogy and these illustrations may serve to carry the point, at any rate with those whose minds are attuned to the conception of evolution, that evidence as to the earlier and simpler phases of the institutions of society is highly useful, if not indispensable, to the understanding of them. It is becoming every year increasingly evident that the best, and perhaps the only, way to know the nature of anything is by finding out how it came to be— its development or evolution. In any case, the conclusive demonstration of our position does not reside in logical or dialectical exercises; it is a matter of results actually attained by recourse to assembled evidence.

As regards ethnographic evidence, in addition to the fact that the use of it makes for distance and detachment, we venture to assert that it possesses a degree of contemporaneity, or of applicability to contemporary conditions, that is not recognizable at first sight. To be specific, there is little doubt in our minds that the topics of "Folkways" can sometime be almost completely illustrated out of the case-records of scientific observation of contemporary social conditions in this country. Among our negroes and immigrants are to be observed many survivals of primitive usages, or even the usages themselves. Such phenomena, however, have been recorded hitherto, for the most part, more or less as curios, or in a mood of contemptuous or horrified reprobation,

THE SCIENCE OF SOCIETY

just as the mores of primitive peoples were reported aforetime. They have been unintelligible, or have been misinterpreted, because the observers have had no evolutionary background before which to set them. The practical result has been failure in the attainment of social adjustment, no matter how excellent the intentions displayed; for it is solely by knowledge that unexceptionable purposes are transmutable into expedient consequences. Primitive notions and points of view underlie and even permeate much of what we call culture; they lurk in the minds of many whom we are wont to consider most cultured. Much more commandingly do they govern the lives and ways of the masses who constitute the real body of a nation and generate its characteristic mores. This is particularly true of a country like the United States, with its admixture of races and codes. As a matter of plain common sense, programs of assimilation or "Americanization" of alien racial elements should begin, not with perfervid ethnocentrism but with objective study of that which is to be assimilated. If contemporary mores are ever scrupulously recorded and thereafter objectively analyzed in the light of societal evolution, an inexhaustible mass of the most significant evidence for the science of society will be disclosed. But there is not much to be gained by surveys of such contemporary ethnography before the key to its interpretation has been provided by the study of the long course of evolution traversed by the mores prior to the beginning of this last brief period of civilization.

There is another variety of prehistoric evidence of which we have been able to make less use than we could have wished; this is the testimony of legend and folklore. Tylor[35] has set forth in a suggestive chapter the historical value of tradition and Frazer has recently dealt with the folk-lore of the ancient Hebrews. The value of such evidence lies chiefly in the fact that it is given unconsciously. If one is able to realize that while the thought of such a poet as Homer is entirely devoted to his theme, which may be as fanciful as you will, he yet must of necessity provide for it a setting taken from the ordinary facts of life as he sees them, it becomes clear at once that this setting is constructed without deliberation and is likely to be quite veracious. In such records there

[35] *Anth.,* ch. XV.

is often a military, aristocratic, or priestly bias, inherent in the circumstances of the chronicler, which leads to a certain selection of incidents and characters; the life of the common people may be suppressed somewhat or wholly; nevertheless, especially in the case of the longer legends, and above all in Homer,[36] there is afforded a quantity and quality of evidence about periods concerning which we should otherwise be but meanly informed, that the student of society's evolution cannot afford to pass over. Concerning the theme of the legendary material one may, as a scientist, be almost wholly indifferent; but he can have no such attitude toward the setting. He need not believe that gods came down on the battlefield; but he must see that the story of the plague in the Greek camp reveals the Homeric theory of disease and cure. The handling of such materials demands caution and common sense; given these, the results to be expected are second to none others.

The following quotations are assembled by way of enforcing several of the foregoing contentions about evidence and also of suggesting corollaries to them. Veth[37] says that "the increasing acquaintance with the interior of Borneo teaches us more and more to recognize in that island a world in the small," in which there is not lacking any single form of culture, half-culture, or barbarism. And Wilken,[38] referring to the same Malay region, contends "that there are many phenomena in our modern civilization which can be explained only as survivals of older situations, and that we have to go to school to the nature-peoples in order to comprehend these phenomena in their true significance, that is to say, in their living state." The comparative method alone can reveal verities here, and it allows also of the relegation of the recounter's personality to the background; for it affords a footing upon which to stand in judgment over him, so that the issue becomes: "non quis sed quid"—not so much who is speaking as what he says.

Rivers,[39] as usual, is worth hearing on issues of evidence. "The unity which is so apparent to one who studies simple cultures in the field is a necessary feature of any society. It is only the more obvious to the ethnographer who works in Oceania or Africa than to the student of civilized institutions, because the simpler character of Oceanic or African society makes the interdependence more obvious. . . . Anthropology, in fact, stands midway between the sciences that study Nature on the one hand, and history and other humanistic studies on the other. Its methods are, or should be, those which it shares with the

---

[36] Keller, "Sociology and the Epic," in *Am. Jr. Soc.*, IX, 37 ff. Henry James speaks of "the detached impersonality of legend." Beer, *Mauve Decade*, 229.

[37] *Borneo's Wester-Afdeeling*, II, 293.

[38] In VG, II, 329, 333.

[39] "Unity of Anthropology," in JAI, LII, 13, 14; and *Melan. Soc.*, II, 440-441. Rivers is a judicious acculturationist. See his *Medicine, Magic, and Religion*.

students of Nature, while its subject-matter covers largely the same ground as history, literature, art, and religion."

Of survivals this author notes the following. "One of the most striking features of social and religious institutions is their tendency to persist, but in altered form. A leading characteristic of the aspects of human culture which form the special subject of this book is their extraordinary plasticity. Indigenous elements of culture and practices introduced by immigrant peoples have persisted in a remarkable way, though often with modifications which would make their recognition almost impossible if it were not for the intermediate links which have been preserved in the wonderful variety of Oceanic culture. Occasionally, as in the case of circumcision, a rite once practised seems to have wholly disappeared, but as a rule it is persistence rather than loss which is characteristic of the social and religious aspects of human culture. Material culture is far less plastic. An indigenous weapon or utensil found to be less formidable or less useful than one introduced by an immigrant people will not as a rule be greatly modified, but will be displaced entirely by the superior object. Similarly, an introduced object unsuited to a new environment will as a rule be found incapable of much modification and will disappear. Such an object, whether indigenous or introduced, may continue to be used in sport or may become an object of religious rites, and by such survival in sport or ceremony material objects may be of the utmost value in the analysis of culture; but with this exception a material object tends either to persist with little change from its original form or to disappear; it does not undergo the exceedingly various modifications to which the less material elements of human culture are subject. One kind of persistence is, however, frequent in material objects. A special feature of a material object will often persist in a form which shows that it once had a definite meaning and purpose. A canoe may have protuberances and angles which can be shown by intermediate links to be the survivals of structures which once served to protect the canoe from injury by shallow reefs or provide a means for pulling it from the water. Such survivals may be of the greatest use as indications of past history and of cultural influences; they do not depend, however, on any active process of the interaction of peoples, but are only the results of modification or even of degeneration in a new physical environment. The survival of features of a material object in degenerate form are often only the precursors of the degeneration or even disappearance of the object itself, and there is reason to believe that this disappearance of material objects is far more frequent and complete than in the case of elements of social and religious culture."

Fox and Drew[40] have something to say concerning the evidence derivable from the mere tales of the natives. "We venture to think that there is no better method for getting true information about natives than that of listening to their stories. Every native has a story to tell. Boys are as good as old men in this respect, or even better in many cases, as they have freshly heard the stories from their mothers. Some boys know quite a number of tales. In this way many things are mentioned, about which the natives might otherwise be reticent; and if the story-teller is not interrupted he may be questioned afterwards about certain customs he has mentioned in the course of his story, which he will willingly try to explain to make the story clear. For example, in these . . . stories, we learnt of a sacrifice quite new to us, that of a coconut on land-

[40] "Beliefs, San Cristoval, Solomon Islands," in JAI, XLV, 209.

ing from a voyage. When the canoe touches the shore, the first duty is to climb a coconut tree. Only one nut is taken, each of the voyagers touches it, and it is put in the bow of the canoe and left there, after which the travellers may eat food. In the stories many customs that have died out are referred to, customs which one would not be likely to hear of in any other way."

That there are innumerable survivals in the mores and in institutions no one who has read this book will be disposed to deny. Societal phenomena are shot through with persisting items which had their expediency once, have it no longer, but still remain. The vast significance of such reminiscences of the evolutionary past has become familiar to any student of natural history, and we believe unshakenly in their significance in the range of the science of society. The reader will have been able to gain his own impressions as to this matter from the text of this book. We shall recur briefly to survivals in connection with symbolism, in the following section. In this place we need only to say that we subscribe without reservation to the following quotation from the *Origin of Species*,[41] holding that societal survivals, within their range, are equally significant with the rudimentary and aborted organs of which Darwin speaks.

"Rudimentary organs may be compared with the letters in a word, still retained in the spelling, but become useless in the pronunciation, but which serve as a clue for its derivation. On the view of descent with modification, we may conclude that the existence of organs in a rudimentary, imperfect, and useless condition, or quite aborted, far from presenting a strange difficulty, as they assuredly do on the old doctrine of creation, might even have been anticipated in accordance with the views here explained."

It is the evolutionary point of view that leads us also to a high estimate of evidence from the life of the frontier-society.[42] Frontier-conditions call for adjustments of a peculiar order, which represent a return, in some measure, to the primitive. Then there ensues, under favoring circumstances, a rapid rehearsal or recapitulation of stages of societal evolution culminating in the attainment, by the former frontier, of a status on a parity with that of the older and parent societies. When the evolution of frontier society has once been worked out systematically from the evolutionary point of view, it will provide evidence of a peculiar value for the science of society. Many preliminary collections of data, and

[41] 474 (of the one-volume edition).
[42] Keller, *Soc. Evol.*, ch. IX; *Colonization*.

much analysis and comparison of the same, will have to be made before this source of evidence lies accessible.

§456. Animal-Series, Category-Fallacy, Symbols. Though we lay great weight upon evolutionary series, we have yet a strong objection to the construction of series that begin in the animal-kingdom and run on to include human societal phenomena. It is a source of much error, we believe, to confuse the two modes of evolution, the organic and the societal. We accept unreservedly the derivation of physical and mental man from an animal-ancestry, and there is in our minds no doubt that the germs of our mores and institutions lie obscurely, occasionally even plainly, in animal-ways. But we regard societal evolution as upon so developed a plane that, in order to secure a series including both animals and man sufficiently continuous to mean very much, we should have need of transitional forms of which we possess no actual knowledge. For example, we see no accomplishment, except of the most vague description, in the stock method of Letourneau, followed in his many books on the evolution of marriage, property, and other institutions, wherein he makes a practice of starting out with chapters on "Property among the Animals" or "Commerce among the Animals." We see no force in the argument that the primordial form of marriage must have been monogamy because, as asserted, the series of animal-forms of sex-mating runs up to culminate in anthropoid "monogamy," thence to pass directly over to man. There is much use of analogy in such statements.

If such a series were continuous and unbroken in direction, it would carry more weight. As a matter of fact, the purest pair-mating in the animal-range occurs among certain birds, and thus far down the evolutionary scale, while the mammals are largely indiscriminate. Ravens may accumulate odds and ends that might whimsically be called property, but horses and cows do not make such collections. And it must not be forgotten that there is yet a considerable break in the biological series of transitional forms between anthropoid and man. It is clear enough that they are related, and physical forms of transition are found. But no one has any idea about the social relations of *pithecanthropus*, and it is next to certain that such knowledge will remain always sealed to us. Derivation of body and mind may be accepted and a series completed, some time, between animal and man; in a general way it is acceptable that human behavior is a developed form of animal-behavior; but when it comes to the connection of particular human institutions with their animal-prototypes, we have crossed from one plane of evolution into another, and it is risky and also useless to try to make direct and simple connection. Animals, whether human or not, mate; it is a biological necessity. But other animals than man do not marry. Marriage is mating under the mores; and animals do not show mores. Mating belongs to organic evolution, marriage to societal; and while the one phase of the general evolutionary process leads broadly into the subsequent one, they are specifically distinct when it comes to their precise processes and results. Though breadth of perspective is to be gained by realizing the broad correspondence, nothing of a scientific order is to be expected from the attempt to prove that relationship closer than it is. Series constructed within the organic field have led us to much enlightenment; we believe that series constructed within the societal range will continue to issue in a notable increase of insight into the nature of society; but when it comes to confusing the two sets, the result is a sphinx-like creation that may put embarrassing riddles to the passer-by.

Another error into which students have been prone to fall is the so-called "category-fallacy." One matter at least about which the evolutionist should be immune from illusion is that of classification of forms. It is the essence of evolution that there shall always be blurred outlines and zones of transition. Form passes into derived or related form by gradations that are almost imperceptible. No evolutionist could have been led to accept, for example, the contention that the stone and bronze "ages" were successive, sharply defined epochs. Nor ought anyone who has appropriated the evolutionary viewpoint to be disturbed by the use of the term "stage," as in hunting stage or pastoral stage. These ages and stages are simply categories of a classification which is useful for purposes of analysis and exposition; they refer to types of societal life, and to types only. You have to classify institutions by types just as you classify plants or human races by types. Very likely no purely pastoral people was ever observed; but there is a distinctly pastoral type and it is typical not only in its form of self-maintenance, but in its more derived mores, such as the domestic or religious, as well.

Nevertheless, one of the most constant and mischievous causes of error in the present range of study is the tendency to create and then fall down and worship the category. Endogamy and exogamy, when they first became known, seemed to be strange and unique arrangements. The conception of them being once attained, the tendency arose at once to round it off in each case into a distinct form with a sharp definition, thus making it a category. Fuller acquaintance with the phenomena dispels the strangeness and the antithesis between such notions and our own. Group-marriage and classificatory relationship, mother-family and father-family, and various forms of property in land are other examples. The mischief of this fallacy is that arguments are confidently deduced from the definition of the category and also that controversies are roused which, after raging hotly for a time, turn out to have had no point or issue. What seem to be clear and specific differences when we have few facts lose their distinct separateness when we get many. Then categories which seem almost to have become permanent landmarks, such as the "stone age," or "hoe-culture," collapse like the flimsy artificial structures which they are.

Classification by types is wholly necessary in this field; the science of society cannot but be schematic. Much time and effort is wasted in futile controversy through a neglect of this fact. Institutions are flexible; mores vary constantly. While there are striking uniformities, sequences, persistences, in societal matters, there is also wide variation. The phenomena often present themselves in masses; then again they are interlaced and delicate; and inasmuch as the forces at work cannot always be discerned and the relative component value of some can be no more than roughly conjectured, there is an element of our own ignorance which appears in the form of chance or even caprice. Hence, whenever we try to present the case, we are between two difficulties: if we try to do justice to the variations and "exceptions" we are lost in an infinity of detail and can win no definite conceptions; if we present only the commanding features, the uniformities and sequences, and generalize these, the presentation can be no more than schematic, formal and academical, unfaithful to reality. The student needs concepts with firm outlines; he cannot get on without them; he has to have a sketch-map of the territory that does not show every petty hill and depression; he must see the woods and not always the individual trees. Yet he must be aware that in contact with stark realities he may never meet with specimens of topography or of institutions to correspond. There will be encountered only variety, individuality. Just as in anatomy the "man" who is presented is a schematic representation of the species, to whom no real person may correspond, so here: human societies will be found not to fit exactly into the categories which have to be formed in order to gain any understanding at all, but to group themselves about generalized central types. If students can resolutely keep in mind that such types are artificial devices and not revealed verities, such as species were formerly thought to be, there is no harm. The defects of schematic representation, which is an indispensable device in science, are not inherent in it but in the unintelligent use of it.

It is useful to construct a series of stages of culture. No people ever went exactly through it. It is made up of phenomena presented in many societies, set in order and sequence of development. This order contains an element of arrangement contributed from the mind of the series-maker, not from fact. It is schematic. It would be quite wrong, having constructed such a series, to argue from it that the history of a society could never present gaps, or inversions, or transfers in the order set down. It is equally foolish to assert that the schematic representation is deceptive or useless because the history of every group shows departures from it. The concept of civilization as a whole, with typical relations of parts, growth, aberrations, revivals, and survivals, is a result worth reaching; and its value rests in the fact that the best command of the whole is won by ranging under this concept as wide and full knowledge of detail as can be won. It is only by falling in love with some classification and assuming its categories to be clean-cut, inclusive, and durable, to be natural instead of highly artificial, that one slips into this "category-fallacy."

There is a class of so-called explanations of societal phenomena which have not been systematically brought under the evolutionary interpretation, but which we think belong there. It is the current explanation of a number of social practices to say that they are "symbols." This is no explanation at all. It merely sets the inquiry back one degree; for the next question that is directly challenged is: Why this symbol rather than some other? The Russian peasant touches his bride with a whip. Symbolical? Evidently; but why this particular symbol? Because a real practice of the more or less remote past lies behind it. The wedding-ceremony is saturated with such usages indicative of the status that is being initiated.

That plain symbolism exists even in low savagery is not to be denied. What it is and how much it is worth is not always possible to discover. Sometimes it seems as arbitrary as the language of flowers; again, it is as rational as cries of joy or terror. Upon closer examination of symbols it becomes clear, nevertheless, that many of them are simply survivals, that is, practices once in active use and which persist in a more or less shadowy manner, though their utility and even their sense have been lost. They are as much survivals as are certain rudimentary organs in the body, or as is the cut of an evening coat.[43] There is a strong presumption that most if not all symbols, as they occur among primitive peoples, at least, are survivals. That is the answer to the question as to why certain symbols rather than others are encountered. The language of every people is shot through with unrecognized survivals, some of which can be identified as such upon investigation, just as the surface of the earth is full of fossil forms whose significance lay unrecognized previous to systematic study. And when the significance of the societal fossils is at length disclosed and made available to science, it is likely that there will ensue an enlightenment parallel to that attained in the physical world from the serious study of fossil forms.

By way of brief illustration: in Homer,[44] the soul of a man is represented as gladdened because an enemy has been killed to serve as his escort to the spirit-world. Seymour[45] comments as follows: "This need not be interpreted literally any more than Romeo's words to Tybalt, 'Mercutio's soul | Is but a little way

43 Tylor, Anth., 15; see §455, just preceding.
44 Iliad, XIII, 416.   45 Homeric Age, 480.

above our heads; | Either thou or I or both must go with him' (*Romeo and Juliet*, iii, 1, 131)." Now, with all respect, both personal and professional, to an eminent colleague, we contend that there is here nothing but darkening of counsel. The allusion to Shakespeare confutes nothing; the fact that this idea of a grave-escort[46] is employed in connection with Mercutio's soul does not destroy the inference as to the Homeric belief but confirms it rather. It is certainly no refutation to cite other cases from other ages.

Some day, when a treatise shall have been written by a student of the science of society who is also philologically trained, upon the survivals of the past that are embedded in everyday language, we shall become aware of the number and significance of these fossil indications and cease to dismiss them as "mere symbols." At present, in the youth of the social sciences, there is much reasonable criticism of the unsystematic and almost promiscuous employment of survivals as evidence.[47] As yet the chartings in this range of inquiry and the appraisal of its quality of data have not been worked out. But in many instances the significance of survivals is self-evident; and it has been our purpose to utilize them in what we believe to be such cases.

§457. **Relation with History.** The introduction of this topic is not for the sake of controversy or of justifying the existence of a science of society; it is for the purpose of illustrating once more the attitude here taken toward the study of society. Least of all do we wish to put up fences and trespass-warnings or to repel charges of encroachment or thieving made by sensitive neighbors. Let the truth come out, whoever quarries it, and wherever.

"A teacher," wrote Henry Adams,[48] "must either treat history as a catalogue, a record, a romance, or as an evolution." He was groping toward the last of these alternatives, without, however, having a very clear idea of what it meant. Darwinism seems to have passed over his classical, even though wistful soul, without making any productive impression. History is the name for the flow and sequence of events in time. Any connection of antecedent and consequent, cause and effect, between the occurrences is due to forces behind the history, in the societal organization, and it is there they must be sought. This is what but few historians have

---

46 §229, above.   47 Rivers, *Soc. Org.*, 96.
48 *Education*, 300.

done. The contention here is that the science of society contrasts with history much as a science with an art.[49] It is characteristic of a science that it is general in both place and time. Upon geology or physics there rests no limitation in these respects. The area of scientific observation may be circumscribed, as when one speaks of the geology of Connecticut; and in the history of science there may be distinguished, say, the geology of the nineteenth century; but to subtract from the generality of geology as a discipline would be to deny it the typical and identifying features of science. It will be noted in the last sentence that when time-limitation is set on a science, the result is a history of that science. The covering truth is that history deals with localities and definitely marked times: the history of France; the history of the reign of Louis XIV. It is a picture of what happened at a time and place. It has but one course and does not admit of comparison; yet what is oftenest required for the interpretation of an historical event is a comparison of it with the same situation changed in the respect of a single act. The composition of such a picture is an art rather than a science; it is perhaps a descriptive science; but it does not belong to the same species as the recognized analytical and synthetic sciences.

True to its origin in chronicle, history is written about chronology and makes much of dates. The science of society, in common with other like disciplines, is largely indifferent to temporal sequences and their mile-stones; it seeks only to establish genetic derivations and sequences; where history is descriptive and chronological, the science of society is analytical and evolutionary. Not only does it not limit itself as to place and time; it does not concede even that all the occurrences in the same society at the same time belong together, for some may be earlier in the evolutionary series than others. The forces at work, moreover, and their mode of operation are often more clearly perceived in the whole race than in the smaller parallel cases of detail in the organization of a single group.

It is in adherence to this typically scientific procedure that the science of society has experienced some of its bitterest assaults from historians, to whom scientific method has meant little more

[49] Gumplowicz, *Soc. u. Pol.*, §10.

than an orderly handling of material, and who have thought history a science because at length it came happily to employ, in dealing with its materials, processes that are objective and not productive of distortion due to bias. It is evident enough that an evolutionary discipline which seeks for sequences and laws in the life of human society is sharply enough contrasted with the story of a given society at a given time, no matter how great the fidelity shown by the recounters of the latter in imitating routine scientific procedure.

Again, the science of society, in its evolutionary sweep, has explored the life of peoples who have no history in any technical sense. Historians have never given more than passing notice to ethnography or the evidence from legend and folklore. This was natural enough, for they did not possess the methods of science that are alone capable of developing that range of evidence. Historical observations, so far as made at all within that range, have been unproductive because their scientific value had not been realized. Curiosity led otiose amateurs to win a certain desultory and casual knowledge of prehistorics, ethnography, and historical anthropology, but nobody thought of writing a scientific book, say on the evolution of marriage and the family, of any one of the arts, or of religion, or of analyzing legend and folklore to find out something about the evolution of societal forms and institutions. Science does not stop with the "what," but always strains toward the "how."

A science wishes to investigate not solely "just how it has been," but, further and most important, "just how it has come to be." Because of its scientific and evolutionary character the science of society has been able to make use of the comparative method as no antecedent disciplines dealing with societal life have done. This method has been established as a normal and successful way of handling the facts of that life; its range has been extended clear beyond the comparatively few and feeble attempts to employ it that preceding centuries and older disciplines had, almost unconsciously, made. Aristotle compared the few political forms known to him and doubtless saw no reason for much inquiry into those of the barbarians; but the science of society makes requisition upon Kaffir *induna* and Iroquois *sachem* alike—upon Malay *adat*,

Homeric *themis*, Roman *mos.* In biology the human vertebrate is not studied to the exclusion of the rest, as grander and nobler and alone worth attention; the elephant and the mouse, the lion and the lamb—all are equally objects of study, with the understanding of the evolution and life of the vertebrate group in view. So in the science before us: the Christian religion is not studied by itself as alone worthy of attention; Buddhism and Voodooism, Mohammedanism and Fetishism—all are equally objects of concern with the understanding of the evolution and life of a particular societal institution in view.

There is one supreme service which the science of society, because of its characteristic approach and methods, has been competent to perform in bringing men to a realization of essential truth. We have alluded to it before; we do not hesitate to advert to it again. It is something that history, for all its seniority, never did or could do. Through the science of society the race got its first view of human society as a whole. It is this startling vision, probably, which accounts somewhat for the pæans and rhapsodies sung by shining-orbed prophets of the new revelation—seers who emotionally staked out preposterous claims for the science of society as the master-science—to the utter detriment of the science and to the ruin of "sociology." Inasmuch as the science of society, in its character of science, is general in place and time, and as the comparative method is one distinguishing trait going with that character, it follows from the use of that method that the science of society is bound to see human society as a whole and, so seeing it, is sure to catch a better view of the articulation of its parts than could otherwise be attained. This is a view that is thoroughly worth while. It cannot be denied that the scientific conception of society as a unified whole, whether it be regarded as mechanism, organism, superorganism, or organization, has profoundly affected the thought of the race. Certainly there was something here to study that was unique in the world of observed phenomena. In short, chiefly by reason of the work of Spencer, the conception of the nature of society and of the rise and decline of societal institutions came to be a broader one that has entered into and vitally affected all subsequent study along societal lines. This could not have happened had the newer of the social sciences perished from the earth in the chrysalis stage. Naturally enough, much of the more general and vital suggestion that came out of this conception of society and societal evolution is not recognized as of any particular time or source. It has passed into current thought as a mode of it, and many people know of and use it naturally who perhaps have never heard of Spencer or any other of the thinkers who have coöperated in working out the conception.

§458. **Relation with Statistics.** For reasons briefly assigned, earlier in this chapter, we have employed virtually no contemporary statistics; these reasons need a little more development. As statistics are to some a sort of fetish, their real nature and serviceability should be firmly apprehended.[50] Biologically speaking, though human life consists of a set of processes which can be enumerated and described, yet the diversity in the life-experiences of these processes by different persons is very wide indeed; in a large population no two might be found whose experiences of physiological and pathological contingencies would be the same. Still more, if we turn to biography, it is evident that the life-story of individuals varies so much that we are safe in saying that it could never have been the same for any two. Nevertheless resemblances in the lives of persons of the same class, occupation, or other classification are such that they can be grouped together and their similar reactions upon similar conditions taken as mass-phenomena. All are born and die; not all marry; not all the married have children. These are broad and general likenesses that say little; and from this point on, the groups whose life-facts are the same are smaller and overlap each other. Similarly within the range of social life; here the individuals, acting under career-interest, avail themselves of their opportunities and put forth their energy to win the environmental reaction which they desire. The variety of act, though enormously wide, is restrained within limits set by the facts of the environment and by human nature. The phenomena are multifarious but they run into currents of consentaneous action in which there is no convention or contract.

Among one hundred thousand persons born at the same time in a given society there will be a certain proportion of males to females. They will die off in a certain series and the rate will not be the same for the males as for the females. A certain proportion of them will marry and will show a certain birth-rate. These are facts of observation, not laws; they are ascertained subsequently to their occurrence and are found to repeat themselves so that their recurrence is anticipated. Reasons for them, we do not know; we can perceive only how general tendencies are favored by one influence and prevented by another.

Far more important are the fluctuations to which these phenomena are subject under the influence of societal changes where a causal connection is within the range of our observation; *e.g.*, the decrease of the marriage-rate and the birth-rate as a consequence of war, or their increase with a rise in wages or a fall in the price of food. In the case of the supposed hundred thousand born at the same time, consentaneous actions will be efforts for education, for a place in the industrial organization, for property, for amusement, for friendships and affection, for distinction, for power, for security as to the other world. Results in attainment are reached which are ascertainable in figures. Statistics can be obtained for illiteracy and for grades of school-training, for the number who fail and become paupers or criminals, or who are disabled by accident, or who choose this or that occupation, or who give up and commit suicide or become tramps, hermits, or cranks. In a given state of the society these figures will exhibit constancy, but once more the instruction for us is in their fluctuations as these correspond to changes in the state of the society. It is in these changes that we may discern causal relations, become familiar with societal forces, and ascertain laws. Evidently it is in the nature of the case that these phenomena should show conformity to a law of probability; that is the only sort of law which can be formulated in this domain.

The way to get from the statistical data to the theoretical law in each case is the great difficulty, especially as there is no routine process by which it can be arrived at. Statistics belong to description and present the case which it is desired to analyze in terms of the most positive detail. As this is the first essential to correct analysis, statistics should stand in the front rank of interest and importance. They should hold the facts for us in the firmest grasp and in a form suitable for analysis, and the analysis should lead us into the relations of parts, the proportion of components, and the play of forces. The material is there; it is a question of handling. It always requires insight, sagacity, and independent grasp of the case to identify the controlling forces and estimate their magnitude and their relation to each other. Though all the elements of the problem are present, its solution calls for a large personal element. It would seem that societal problems could scarcely be made more simple or more universally every-man's-affair than by the utilization of statistics.

Inasmuch, however, as statistics belong to description and observation, they present a status at a moment of time. Although at any given juncture the status is conceived of as an equilibrium, in practice it is only on the way toward an equilibrium of the forces in action at the time, which equilibrium never is reached because the action of new forces intervenes. Statistics in themselves never have a background or perspective. They do not say anything about development. Zero is zero, but it is often very important, even in mathematics, to know what a certain zero came from, that is, what was there before, now disappeared. The exaggerated view of statistics which is very commonly held is like asserting that a photograph or a geometrical diagram is the only true picture. Statistics are static only, and the dynamics are in the changes. The key to the interpretation of statistics is generally to be found in those attendant circumstances which cannot be measured arithmetically. Evolution is like a stream in time; statistics are like a cross-section at a moment. It has been suggested that statistics need something in the nature of a parliamentary inquiry to give them a background against which they can be interpreted.

This is only another form of the great difficulty already experienced with statistics, namely, their bulk, which makes it impossible to grasp them. If one begins with a few, generalizations seem easy and firm. Questions of detail arise, and more figures are sought. They open new doubts and incidental questions; then comes a call for still more statistics or a re-classification of the old ones. Instead of striding toward stricter and more positive conclusions one is marching into obscurity and doubt. Skull-measurements are a good illustration; at the end of them we are told that there is still an unmeasurable, indefinable impression made by a skull upon an experienced observer which must be taken into account. But the measurements were invented and have been made precisely in order to get away from the indefinable, unverifiable impression which the observer obtained from looking at the skull. All statistics of societal experience run into the same dilemma: in the pursuit of the sense of the figures we must either multiply them until we are buried under them or discard them all. With a few selected statistics one can prove anything; with an exhaustive array of them it would take a life-time to reach a petty result—often a triviality or a truism. Statistics contain no secrets, in the way of laws, which can be extorted from them; much less do they reveal anything by their own voice. They only describe what is, either as data or as tests to be used in verification. That in civilized countries about 105 males are born alive for every 100 females is a fact; it is not a law. We know of no cause for it. That life uses up men faster than women through the prime of life is, if true, not a cause or reason. Under other societal conditions it may not be true; but what connection can we see between those conditions and that fact? Analysis, comparison, generalization and deduction are operations of scientific method for which there are appropriate canons. These operations have their own warrant. They must be employed upon the data with due skill. Without them nothing will issue from the statistics. Gathering figures and measurements is no royal road to the understanding of society's life; they are only the paving-stones. When obtained, they are of small use because men have not yet learned how to handle and place them. The only way to do that is to start with a background not to be acquired in the accumulation or scrutiny of lists of figures.

§459. Classification of the Social Sciences. It remains, in dealing with the scientific character of the discipline which we are studying, to outline its relations with the rest of the social sciences. There is no accepted classification; and so it is indispensable to know in what sense the terms are used by any speaker or writer. Nor is there any technical designation for the whole group of the social sciences, though "sociology," "anthropology," and "ethnology" are sometimes so used. A classification in chart form is here proposed.[51]

PROPOSED CLASSIFICATION OF THE SOCIAL SCIENCES

HISTORICAL AND DESCRIPTIVE   ANALYTICAL AND DYNAMICAL

Anthropology treats of the Human Group, of its relations to its habitat, and of membership in it.

It includes numbers 1, 2, 3, 4, and 5, below.

NATURAL SCIENCE BRANCH

1. SOMATIC ANTHROPOLOGY (DESCRIPTIVE) OR ANTHROPOGRAPHY. The Natural History of Man. *Craniometry. Anthropometry.* Description or race features by anatomy and physiology. Monstrosities and aberrations. *Human Palæontology.*

2. SOMATIC ANTHROPOLOGY (DYNAMICAL) OR SOMATOLOGY. *Anthropogeny. Craniology.* Classification of races by anatomical and physiological features. The human race as a total and its relations to other animal forms. Laws of descent, variation, and development. Influence of diet, flora, fauna, climate, and territorial features on the physical development of man. Migrations. Acclimatization.

HISTORICAL SCIENCE BRANCH

3. ETHNOGRAPHY. Description of existing nations (not races) and tribes, with manners, customs, etc., by which they are characterized.

4. ETHNOLOGY. Analysis and comparison of national traits; discrimination of races; generalization of traits of human nature. (It contributes material to sociology.) *Palæoethnology.*

5. HISTORICAL ANTHROPOLOGY. *Prehistorics.* Domestication of plants and animals. History of the utilization of natural materials and forces. *Archæology.* Description and history of forms of society. History of institutions, arts, sciences, manners, customs, rites, ceremonies, and language; of religion; of property; of ideas; of marriage and family-organization; of the societal

6. SCIENCE OF SOCIETY (SOCIOLOGY). The Science of Society, a science of generalization, using the results of Anthropology. It treats of the evolution and life of society under the heads: Organization; I. Self-maintenance (Industrial Organization, Property, Regulative Organization, Religion); II. Self-perpetuation (Marriage and the Family);

---

[51] The accompanying classification is one which was printed and issued, with corrections and amplifications, year by year, to the classes in the science of society in Yale College. It was always labelled "Not Published," as its originator, the senior author of this book, wished to have it remain tentative. With some changes, especially in the arrangement of No. 6, it is as he left it.

organization and of classes or groups in it. *Folklore.* Contributions of superstition, vanity, and the arts of war to industry and the arts of peace.

7. DEMOGRAPHY. Description of the actual status of a society, at a point of time, in respect to the chief elements of its structure and functions and the phenomena of its life. Vital statistics and facts. Institutions of religion, charity, correction, recuperation, education, and culture, police, courts of justice, army and navy. Statistics and facts of crime and vice; also of social entertainment, recuperation, and cultivation. Status of groups employed in modern forms of industry. Census.

9. ECONOMIC HISTORY. History of the industrial organization and its evolution. History of agriculture, commerce, finance, transportation, and insurance, and of modes of traveling and transmitting intelligence as aids to the supply of material needs.

11. COMPARATIVE POLITICS. Description and comparison of the institutions and organs of the civil organizations in different States.

III. Self-gratification (Vanity, Amusement, Æsthetics).

8. DEMOLOGY. Generalizations as to the maintenance and cultivation of a society. Causes and nature of crime, vice, and social disease. *Criminology.* Tests of restorative, amendatory, prophylactic, educational, and creative agencies. *Penology.* Effects of Military service, taxation, and social burdens. Generalization of the phenomena of population in particular groups. Generalizations as to a census—what is wanted and how to get it. The inductions of a census.

Maxims and principles of social amelioration. *Societal Policy.*

10. POLITICAL ECONOMY. Investigation of the conditions of providing in the greatest possible measure for the physical needs of man by societal organization.

Systematized maxims and principles of finance and taxation, and of the art of political economy.

12. POLITICAL SCIENCE. Generalizations as to the State and rights. Analysis of political institutions. Generalizations as to constitutions, legislation, and administration. Systematized maxims of civil welfare. *Statecraft. International Law. Jurisprudence.*

Numbers 9 and 11 are branches of 5 which have become independent; 10 and 12, similar branches of 6.

CHAPTER LXII

CONCLUSIONS AND APPLICATIONS

§460. Some Conclusions out of the Experience of the Race.
Out of studies covering a considerable stretch of society's evolution there is derivable a sort of residue or precipitate in the form
of general impressions, which represent the effect of the impact of
thousands of facts. Many of these turn out to be simple and
homely truths or even truisms, so that, in the end, one may have
the feeling that he has done no more than demonstrate the obvious.
He may comfort himself, perhaps, by the reflection that it is often
precisely the obvious that most needs demonstration, so that there
may be some rational grounds for accepting it. There is also the
category of the spuriously obvious, the emptiness of which requires showing-up. In any case, here, toward the end of our treatment, and before considering interferences with and corrections of
the natural order, we are setting down some of the general impressions or conclusions derivable from long association with such
facts as this book contains. They will be recorded without much
comment, since the grounds for holding them have been spread
over many preceding chapters.

The existence of the human race on earth, and of human society, is conditioned by forces in nature and in society. It is subject to law. If men could do what they chose to do, there could be
no laws and so no chance for the development of science. The
power of man to control the forces that play about his little life
is extremely limited and consists in the skill which he develops in
adjustment. He can act on few of the forces and then only under
conditions: either before they come into operation, or by choosing
which of them shall be set in motion, or, very near their inception,
by modifying them slightly in form or direction. By such slight
interferences, however, ultimate results may be greatly changed.
These results cannot be altered at all after the forces have acted,
any more than a field of potatoes can be changed into a field of
wheat because its owner regrets that he did not plant the latter
instead of the former.

Even the slight modifications of the conditions of life which are in the power of man to make are won only when a number of men, by consenting, will bend their energies in a common direction. This consensus has been brought about only after the discipline of repeated bitter experience. Even under high civilization, the most that can be accomplished, by argument and discussion, for the purpose of bringing about an intelligent convention, is to hasten to some slight degree the taking to heart of the lesson of experience. The progress of the race means nothing more than an attempt to make the best of things which by no means suit mankind with means which are, at best, inadequate to secure satisfaction; and such advance as has been made has been won by infinitesimal degrees, under the handicap of repeated and long-continued retrogressions.

Mankind has never advanced at all save by patient, steady exertion against those obstacles which have been nearest and open to attack only in their minutest details; there have been no sweeping revolutions. The grand moral elements in this process, which fill the eye and swell the heart of the historian or humanitarian when he embraces centuries in a glance, have been secondary products which followed upon the detail adjustment; they never have been, and never can be, the object of direct human effort and all attempts to reach them in that way have resulted not alone in missing them altogether but also in neglecting and losing the humble, inglorious, commonplace, but only real progress. A most important service of a science of society is to make it possible for re-formers to understand the methods by which and the limits within which human efforts can realize human hopes.

Here are some of the general conclusions derivable from a dispassionate study of society's evolution. They forbid us to engage in grandiose schemes for recasting society and point us to small, immediate, and arduous efforts to adapt the means we control to the problems nearest before us, as the only sound method of readjustment, while they limit the scope of science to the investigation of what is and has been, and the reason why it is and has been thus and not otherwise.

A scientific study of the race's history shows men struggling for self-preservation against difficulties, restraints, and obstacles, which finally conquer the individual, though not the society, in death. All advances in adjustment have to be won by a more than lavish expenditure of effort. The race has not been tempted forward by delights held out in advance; it has been forced onward in its adjustments, like animals, by necessity. When man came into existence here, he found himself such and such a being and his earthly home such and such a place. He might use anything he could find, appropriate, and control, in or on the earth, to sustain his life. The effort to use the stores of nature, however, for resisting and making headway against the obstacles of life, could not be carried on by individuals, each for himself, with no bearing or relation between his efforts and those of the rest. Success in living demands an aggregation of force which can be attained only by higher development of the individual, by an accumulation of the supplies which sustain human energy, and by progressively intensified organization. These conditions all imply limitation of freedom and the acceptation of care and anxiety concerning the future; but they allow of a new variety of liberty, namely, self-determination under the modes and limits imposed by the organization of existing society, or liberty under law. This organization is not that of an army, in which order and liberty exclude one another, but that of industry, in which the tasks are minutely divided and their relation to one another is close; there is a wide choice among them, as there is not in an army, and some liberty in the method of performing the one chosen. Nevertheless, further advance always costs more of the same kind of restraint while it confers a higher degree of the same sort of liberty.

With the passing of strict group-responsibility for the individual, a distinct increment was added to the latter's liberty. As civilization advanced, with its new adjustments as respects individual freedom, customs and institutions rose which emancipated the individual from that close responsibility for and with his fellow-men under which he lives on lower stages of culture. Greater scope was accorded him, especially in the struggle for self-maintenance and the competition with his fellows; he came under a new set of conditions covering the whole range of industrial effort, competition, and reward. He was allowed to get what he could and keep it; in theory, at least, he was no longer forced to share it with the rest. Society came to employ its power to guarantee him that reward, and that is all society was or is supposed to do. That guarantee enabled him to choose the course which he judged best for his own success, whatever others might do, and insured him the advantage, or the penalty of miscalculation, for himself, whatever might be the fate of others. Those who denounce "individualism" and want to persuade the individual to enter into some convention by which he shall surrender this privilege and these guarantees and try to attain some other vague standard of justice, established *a priori*, are running counter to the course of society's evolution.

Despite the evolution of liberty described, the fact that the individual is a human being like the rest locks him into the movement of the race, so that he must share the issues of their wisdom and their folly, their knowledge and their ignorance, their prudence and their thriftlessness.

The competitive struggle and the need of the race as a whole to sustain itself against the obstacles of life, has forced all the adjustments which combine to form civilization. Only at an advanced and high point in this course does the stimulus of want and necessity give way, as a spur to effort, to the attraction of a possible greater good, conceived of as realizable, by exertion, in the future. Then the higher demand of the human being on life raises the minimum or zero-line of existence, so that the pressure of competition from increasing numbers is felt at a higher level, while there is yet a good margin above pure and genuine distress; and the two together—the ambition for further development and the apprehension of want while it is still remote—advance the arts and restrain population, giving the former a chance to precede, and securing greater comfort for all.

The history of the race is one long reiteration of the lesson that the welfare of man rests on industry and prudence. If there were on this earth a fountain of youth, or a plant which would distil the elixir of life, or a drug which would heal all diseases, the science of life and the art of living would be very different from what they are. If we could invent perpetual motion we could abolish labor. If the law of the diminishing return were not true, we might all be still in the original home of the race, and there might have been no migration, transportation, or commerce. If two and two could make five we could feed five men with two plus two loaves of bread or keep five laborers at work with two spades and two pickaxes—that is, capital would not limit industry. If a demand for commodities were a demand for labor, we should be getting rich by consuming and not by saving and there would be an end of economy. If action and reaction were not equal, we could increase prosperity by tariff taxes. As it is, when we have defined the negative barriers which limit our powers, we are wise not to dash against them, but to turn back to what we can do. Nature offers us materials by means of which we may satisfy more or less of our needs and may satisfy each of them more or less well; but the condition of this satisfaction is labor. She puts in play around us forces which may help us or may destroy us, and she never explains herself. The condition of welfare is to observe, to reflect, to foresee; the penalties of the neglect of labor and prudence are hunger, cold, disease, and death. These are inflicted without explanation or remorse. Those at fault suffer and perish; and the race may take warning and go on more wisely. From the lowest stage of civilization to the highest, industry and prudence, though varying in their application, remain the essential conditions of success in the struggle for existence, while idleness and improvidence always carry the same penalties. No effort can avert the penalties, though it may divert them from the guilty to the innocent.

Whenever population increases so as to press upon the means of subsistence offered by the land at disposal on the existing stage of the arts, there ensues in the community a crisis involving the chances of an advance or a retrogression. It is true throughout the societal order that every new opportunity of advance brings with it a chance of retrogression, and every new power acquired involves as much harm from abuse as profit from use. When the population reaches the limit, the first escape is offered by migration. This, however, costs pain and loss, dissolves sentimental ties, breaks up habits and customs, renders acquired experience less valuable, and makes it necessary to undergo risks and dangers until new experience is won. Old ills with which men have learned to cope are left behind and new ones have to be encountered. An alternative escape is by an advance in the arts; and it involves the same disagreeable consequences, only in different application. The penalty of failure to advance by one or the other of these paths is that the community loses physical vigor, becomes inferior to its neighbors, has to yield its lands to them, is pushed into a corner, and perishes.

The race thus advances by those who have vigor, energy, and intelligence enough to take the courses which are open, and the rest are left behind. The fittest to survive are they who appreciate

the new order of things and adapt themselves to it, and they do
survive. We perceive the same law among the lowest savage tribe
migrating from an old home, or passing from hunting to herding,
and among a highly civilized people at the introduction of new
machinery. Any interference to prevent the survival of the fittest
tends only to promote the survival of the unfittest.

In the unit-cluster of the family and in its extensions into larger
associations, there is always some division of labor, if only between
the sexes, and some coöperation, that is, an industrial organization. The members of the community show differences of structure,
capacity, taste, and desire, out of which arise differences of function in the work of the community. Hence appear mutual services,
rights, and obligations. The functions are interwoven in their
activity, supporting and supplementing one another, so that the
community as a whole, by carrying on a combined assault upon
nature, wins more than its constituent number of isolated individuals could. If the numbers are not too great for an economical
division of function on the existing grade of organization, the
product of the society's organized labor will enhance its development and its power. If it has outgrown its organization, it must
divide into two or organize more highly.

Human society then, by the diversity of its parts, their specialization, the distribution of functions, the mutual service and support of the parts, and their solidarity, is a true system or organization. It has a life different from that of the individual and not
simply aggregated or multiplied from the life of individuals. The
quality of a combination is not the sum of the qualities of its components; no one could predict the characteristics of gunpowder
from those of sulphur, charcoal, and saltpeter. One cannot juxta-
pose cells and judge what they will make. Similarly the juxtaposi-
tion of human qualities does not guarantee the quality of a society.
The development of histology does not render physiology less indispensable. There is a body to study as well as a cell, a society as
well as an individual; and the body and the society are things with
lives and laws of their own.

Hence forces arise in the societal organization which are characteristically societal forces. They come into being because a
society of humans of different sexes and ages, of various attain-

ments, divergent tastes and desires, yet with certain broad and fundamental similarities, has grown up. These forces operate in accordance with law, as all things do; and they produce phenomena which follow certain sequences. The forces combine, or cross, or counteract each other, in all possible ways and degrees, and the phenomena vary with the circumstances of the physical world or with the material on which the forces act.

It is these societal forces, the conditions under which they come into action, the laws under which they operate, the effect of modifying circumstances, the resistances they encounter, their combinations with one another, and the limit of man's control over them, that call for investigation. We cannot be satisfied with the position of science while it leaves any of these elements the subject of loose conjecture, or pretends to do them justice by giving them careless recognition in passing. We may call the laws in question natural laws because they come into action whenever conditions are fulfilled which are established in the nature of things, and because they follow an unchangeable sequence in all times and places and for all men. Arbitrary interferences never destroy the force or alter its laws; they only divert its course and alter its incidence.

The existing societal system in the most highly civilized countries is the product of a long development. It is, and it is what it is, by virtue of the forces which have been at work in history. It is disputed whether the natural laws of human society would suffice to produce a better state of things if all interferences were withdrawn. A "better" state of things can have no other meaning, as the term is used, than one in which there would be less discontent amongst men with their lot on earth. We find that, along with greater possibilities than ever before for the satisfaction of human needs there is as much or more discontent now than ever before. Such a result is a natural and necessary concomitant of the fact already observed, that civilized man, living behind the barriers of culture, is in a position to be moved more by desire for an ideal and possible future good than by present and pressing distress. If wants are expressed by the numerator of a fraction and satisfactions by the denominator, what is found is that both have greatly increased; that, however, the value of the fraction may have changed only slightly, if at all. Discontent is the spring of effort. It will not be quenched unless men become satiated with all the goods they can conceive of, which is impossible. It will exert its due effect in advancing civilization if each individual who is discontented is allowed to exert himself to the best of his ability to overcome what is unsatisfactory in his position or to attain to the good he desires. The notion of quenching discontent and individual initiative by passing resolutions and laws may be dismissed as a mischievous delusion.

The foregoing considerations have been reviewed with the idea of presenting the setting within which men can, with any hope, undertake the manipulation of societal destiny—can, in a word, interfere with the natural course of things in societal evolution. It may not be disputed that the advances in civilization of the last three centuries have been marked by a progressive lessening of arbitrary administrative, legislative, and police interferences with societal laws; nor can it be denied that a fair prejudice against all such interferences has been aroused; nor can it be refuted that any interferences, to be wise and beneficial, must be controlled all the time, in form, method, and degree, by a scientific knowledge of societal laws. There is no need or desire, therefore, for any dogmatic assertion that interferences are not and never can be wise and beneficial. It is enough to say that the grand desideratum for mankind is to see the natural laws in full operation in order to study them. It will then be possible to find out by experience of them what our interferences may accomplish and what they must avoid, just as we have learned how to act, for our own good, in the presence of the laws in the physical world. We can then, under the same conditions which we seek in determining similar questions in other fields, consider what interferences to attempt. In the meantime we are driven to separate the effects of the natural laws from those of the interferences, in history, as best we can.

§461. **Interferences.** Since the matter of interferences with the natural course of things has arisen, we may as well go forward to meet it at once. There are here three possible policies: to let things take their course as they will; to meddle indiscriminately; to interfere discerningly. The first of these has never been put into practice by anyone; the second is the common mode; the third is the only hope men have. The first is the extreme of revolt, in theory, against the second, and has been the way-breaker for the third. It has been called *laissez-faire* or *laissez-aller*. In the course of frenzied opposition to it, it has become an epithet; as "atheist" covers "agnostic" and other possible terms descriptive of the critical mind in religion, so *laissez-faire* covers any position critical of any pet uplift-program formulated by ignorance and sentimentality. All that *laissez-faire* ever meant in practice is what the sign, "Hands Off" upon swiftly running and delicate machinery means. Such a warning does not refer to the engineer, who knows what he is about, but to the cane-poking crowd and even to the occasional rambling fool or victim of locomotor ataxia who is likely to lose his balance and fall in. In their natural irritation with meddlers, men like Spencer may have called for an exaggeration of the let-alone policy; it is not to be wondered at; but anyone who can read has only to scan the lives of such men to find models of genuine labor and self-sacrifice in the interest of social expediency. The difference between them and their impassioned critics lies not in motives but in that link between purposes and consequences which alone can make the latter correspond to the former, namely, knowledge.

Laissez-faire should be set aside as representing nothing but a figure of straw that has been much and ferociously knocked about. Between the other two contrasting policies of indiscriminate meddling and discerning interference no one would disclaim lip-loyalty to the latter. Many of the most officious and offensive meddlers have the loftiest motives and are the nuisance and peril which they are through pure ignorance backed by indefatigable zeal; and even their benightedness is not wholly their fault, for their hearts tell them that something must be done and their minds are both undisciplined and understocked with expedients. There is no body of principles to refer to, because the self-proclaimed students of society have never got down to the dog-labor necessary to collect and classify the facts; much less have they been able, in the absence of scientific materials, to rise to guiding generalizations. Pareto,[1] commenting upon the popular uplift-type of sociology,

[1] Communicated by Professor J. H. Rogers.

said that it ought to be given in a temple, "avec un peu de musique de temps en temps." For practice there is little background in theory. Hence a pathetic dependence upon intuition, "standing to reason," and, at best, rule of thumb.

It will be a long time before the science of society arrives at any possibility of application remotely comparable with that of the laboratory sciences. Nevertheless there are certain broad conclusions which can be drawn as to the possibilities of application within this range of science. Here again is the basic issue as to what can and what cannot be done with a society.

The question as to the practical value of a science of society opens up the general case of the relation between science and the mores. Since the mores reside in the masses, or the "crowd," the issue is as to how far the masses are influenced by science. The answer is: very little, directly. Indirectly, however, that influence is inevitable, irresistible, and transformative. That it acts with a deliberation exasperating and, indeed, intolerable to those impatient to see results, is irrelevant. The scientist who deals with society needs, together with the telescopic eye, always patience, and then more patience. If there is to be a bridge here he must not expect to see its span rise out of thin thought to be dotted presently with appreciative beneficiaries; for a long time all the work that counts will be done on the caissons and piers, which will be largely out of sight, perhaps beneath the surface altogether. Together with patience, the real contributor of labor and thought must practice self-abnegation and renunciation. He will not see the promised land, if there is one; but he may throw his small strength into the only sort of a drive that will ever realize Canaan for the generations to come. He can rest assured, not as the result of a vision but of cold calculation, that if there is any hope at all it lies in the conscientious accumulation of scientific knowledge.

The masses are hard to influence. Thrills of emotion run through them and gather force as they go. The masses can be stampeded by adroit suggestion and may commit infamous acts of cruelty and folly; again, they may show magnanimity. In any case, they are freakish. No one has learned their ways so as to predict them. All that one can be sure of is that their action will be spontaneous and unreflective. The same view of a man or a situation is tossed from one to another until the nickname or epithet is found which expresses the idea. Inventions are arrived at in this same manner. The crowd wants the concrete, dramatic, graphic, as children do; personal and anecdotic features, as well as gossip, command its attention. Hence popular literature selects those features for presentation. It is the art of the journalist to give the people what they want; by reading their favorite newspapers one can see what they like. Among their wants is that of some hero, but they also crave scapegoats and butts.

Here is no favorable environment for the acceptation of science. Calculus has never directly influenced the ways, ideas, faiths, and practices of any group, nor has the law of the conservation of energy. The same is true of the discoveries in electricity and magnetism; not until an art, in the form of the telegraph, was invented were mores affected. The Röntgen rays are a case of a discovery which was immediately applicable in surgery—against disease, one of the most universal interests of mankind—but they were at the end of a long series of laboratory-finds of which the crowd knows nothing. Discoveries must become arts and be included in the routine of life before they affect mores. Pure science must always go through the stage of application before it can make general appeal. Here is opened a chasm between men of scientific education and the crowd, for the minds of the former have been trained to work on scientific processes and to value scientific truth entirely aside from its applications. Here is the real gulf between the practical man and the theorist. It is a profound fault of modern society to underrate theory and exalt the practical man; the latter often boasts that he is up with the times whereas the most salient fact about him is that he is not up with the times.

Evolution, in good part, on account of its supposed bearing on religion, has interested the crowd. The terminology of it has got into literature and has affected the thinking even of those who reject it with horror. To realize this one should note that the ecclesiastics at the Council of Trent were not able to conceive that what they had received from the last preceding generation had not all been given just so by Jesus Christ himself. They had no historical sense of perspective. They were men whose minds had not been trained to think of sequences and lines of development. In the mental operations of many of the untrained of today the same attitude is discernible; they have remained unaffected by one of the greatest feats of science; their beliefs take no account of it even when they profess to have accepted what they take to be evolution. Nevertheless, the thought of the world has become permanently tinged with the concept of adjustment to life-conditions, which is the broad sense of evolution.

What has science to do, then, with the mores? The first impression produced on the mind by phenomena is very often erroneous. It is necessary to train the intellect to resist first impressions and to look deeper. There is need of investigation and verification, in order to form judgments and thus to accumulate knowledge and develop mental power. That the sun moves from east to west is an obvious commonplace open to everybody's perception; yet the true relation of the sun and earth can be understood only by mental effort. The leading minds of centuries were under tension to find out the truth of this matter; the concepts connected with it were beyond the grasp of untrained intellects. It would seem that, to begin with, phenomena enveloped man in delusion and his own mind betrayed him. He started off, for instance, with the grand phantasm of the ghost-theory as his world-philosophy, and may be said to have found his way out of it by advancing backwards; he has modified and corrected the notions which came down to him by tradition; he has never until recently faced forwards to find out the truth by free investigation of problems posed independently of tradition. These processes of criticism and systematic search constitute science. No man can investigate more than a minute part of the field of knowledge for himself; for the rest he must accept the authority of his colleagues when once they have shown themselves worthy of trust.[2] There are vested interests of church and state the guardians of which are sure to meet him with all possible opposition. And then too the masses hold, in the mores, all the traditional errors and they dislike to be forced to change their notions. Knowledge can be used and enjoyed by those who have it, and it gives them power and superiority; this goes far to explain the "inequalities" in modern society. It is when discoveries affect life-philosophy that they necessarily pervade the society. Then the fact becomes important that only very slowly, and from

[2] "You fulminate," writes Darwin (letter of April 30, 1861, in *More Letters,* II, 443), "against the skepticism of scientific men. You would not fulminate quite so much if you had had so many wild-goose chases after facts stated by men not trained to scientific accuracy. I often vow to myself that I will utterly disregard every statement made by any one who has not shown the world he can observe accurately."

the top downwards, can the masses be imbued with a new life-philosophy.

It should be realized, further, that men have always practised artificial delusion upon one another, both innocently and intentionally; enthusiasts, dreamers, men of craft, politicians, demagogues, have moved the masses by suggesting to them utopias and other visions of bliss or by exciting their vague fears of unknown ills. They have always played upon the imaginative element, and can regularly affect the masses far more than the master of science with his demonstrations. Defense against fraud requires the same arms and armor as defense against delusion.

But if scientific discoveries do not get into the mores, scientific methods do. In the course of time the upper sections of the masses have become so habituated to seeing these processes verified in experience that they are not altogether frightened by new truths or the necessity of readjustment of old concepts. They trust and use the methods in respect to all interests of life; they live by them and know it. Such habits of mind slowly but steadily invade the lower strata. So far as this takes place the mores are influenced and science has then effected its most important results. The masses get a popular and approximate notion of the difference between reality and unreality; unconsciously they acquire habits of rudimentary criticism and investigation. The old world-philosophies, with their fantastic conceptions, are displaced from their ascendancy in control over the mores; the outlook upon the world is altered; the notion of what are real "interests" is metamorphosed. Therefore the motives which will move men and to which appeal may be made with a certainty of response are of a different complexion. It is a fact of the mores, we have seen, that the evolution theory has largely entered into the current language and has affected the popular thinking of our day, although the notions of evolution which are current are crass and sketchy, if not erroneous, and the current phrases are imperfectly understood. However inadequately evolution may be apprehended, it controls, so far as it goes, the conception of interests and therefore the whole attitude of men toward life, its activities, and its problems.

In the Middle Ages, daimonism and projectivism controlled the notion of interest, or at least traversed the primary notion of interest which each should struggle to realize for himself, during his earthly career, so far as he could. Under the evolution-theory there are no transcendental interests. These must be defined in terms of utility in the struggle for maintenance. In the second step of the series: "act–thought–act," science is supplanting all transcendental philosophy. Science, as it becomes a more universal possession or habit of mind of group-members, tends always to raise the mores to a more rational and purified character.

It follows from the above that for any science the first practical measure is to develop its principles as far and as accurately as possible. To do that it is necessary that there shall be a number of hard-working students in whose horizon practical results do not figure, who shall be devoted to "pure science." There is at present much impatience among social experts with any who wish to belong to this class. The pure science has no more to do with the solution of the "social problem" than meteorology with the bringing about of uniform mild weather or the abolition of storms. Nevertheless, the science of society, like meteorology, if it teaches what the forces in the situation are, and how they act, allows of avoidances and adjustments that make for insurance against calamities. People are not societally-minded; they do not think in terms of society. It is no wonder, for the accepted social philosophers who have thought in that manner are very few, and no such point of view has been passed down, as it were from above.

Popular sentiment is focussed on rights and not on duties; it sees only half of the situation as respects organization. A man will keep a yelping dog in a crowded neighborhood and will remain oblivious to the discomfort of others unless forced, reluctantly and resentfully, to abate the nuisance. The human race is still far from knowing how to live in society. If knowledge of what a society is and what it is not, and, as a result, apprehension of what can and cannot be done with it, ever becomes popular, the millennium will be at hand. As it is, people are saturated with the same hoary, vain hopes and ambiguous fears that Spencer[3] catalogued more than fifty years ago. The happy throng which was just now singing pæans to progress cries out that progress is poverty.

[3] *Study of Soc.,* ch. I.

They thought that it was universal wealth, happiness, peace, and love; they find that it is only a change of name for toil, care, pain, loss, and the perishing of the unfit. Current literature seems to prove the existence of the notion that you can talk down, or ignore, societal forces, or that if you can show them up by revealing how unpleasant they are, they will withdraw in confusion. It is common for the discontented to demonstrate how immensely strong capital is in order to justify the measures they propose to restrain it. If it is as strong as they say, their measures are like efforts to dam ocean-currents with reeds.

§462. **Correctives to Thought.** Current thought upon societal subjects evidently is in need of correctives. The only efficacious antidote to irresponsible thinking and grotesque enterprise is a thorough inoculation with scientific spirit, and the chief item to be inculcated out of scientific procedure is to go to the facts. Comparatively slight study of ethnographical or historical evidence should render anyone immune to mere plausibility by evoking in him a critical attitude. Acquaintance with the facts is the only real corrective to muddled thinking, provided, of course, that the facts are seen in some perspective and are not merely contemporary statistics. Nevertheless it is worth while to list some miscellaneous misapprehensions which should be cleared up by the actual study of society's evolution.

Among the correctives which must be furnished by pure science, if at all, is the accurate placing of ideals. This it can do by providing criteria upon which their realizability can be forecast. In the present instance, a distinction is to be drawn between two types of the exercise of the imagination, to be designated by the terms "idealism" and "idealization." Idealism is here taken to be the mere play of the imagination, yielding phantasms that have no connection with fact; it is therefore an abomination in science. The real question about this process is whether man can create something in thought, and then, having made such addition to his mental possessions, can, as a matter of course, realize it in fact, although there is no process for bringing about a connection between the mental creation and actuality. The method of creating ideals and trying to work up to them in societal affairs is very popular. It is a form of utopia-making. When an undisciplined and unseasoned mind has labored for awhile over a societal problem only to find that its elements are both stubborn and elusive, he throws it aside impatiently and lets his imagination run to the construction of another state of things in which the recalcitrant elements would be so changed that they would admit (as he thinks) of an easy adjustment to produce what he regards as desirable societal arrangements. This is in the manner of an ethical philosopher who should dwell upon the blessings to mankind if gravitation, instead of acting inversely as the square of distance, should act inversely as the cube of it. The farther he goes with this speculative process, the farther he has to go, because the whole societal system hangs together. He ends, therefore, with a scheme for the reorganization of society. It is evident that he has shirked the real and difficult task and has indulged himself in a proceeding which is easy and futile. The process ranks with day-dreaming in the individual case and has like day-dreaming no product except demoralization and enervation of character. Oft-repeated experience goes to prove that any attempt to realize an ideal which has been deduced from a philosophical theorem will not only fail of the end contemplated but will produce unexpected results with the net consequence of confusion and disturbance in the normal process of societal growth.

Idealism is a sort of doctrine. Idealization is different; it is an actual and useful process—the link which connects needs with desires. The former are objective and real; the latter are the needs enlarged and refined by an imaginative element which is capable of expansion to infinity. Idealization plays a part in all the departments of societal interest. Hunger is need of food; idealization carries it up to desire for condiments, intoxicants, narcotics, and for abundance, luxury, and excess. Love is a need for the other sex; marriage and the family constitute the richest of all fields for idealization.[4] In every stage of civilization there has always been a floating vision of these things, cherished by all though experienced by few, which has steadily elevated the institution from epoch to epoch. Vanity is a need for distinction, admiration, self-aggrandizement, power; every step of it is a stimu-

4 §§338, 430, above.

lus to the next, which presents itself to the imagination, upon the basis of what is being enjoyed, as a chance of still higher felicity. The aleatory element in life lies half in the struggle for existence, half in ghost-fear; the immense fascination of this element to man has always been its appeal to the imagination, the idealization of material welfare through luck, that is, gratuitously. To a higher civilization the notion of the other world has taken the form of an idealization of this world. Idealization has kept human powers strained in effort. The words sacred, holy, purified, refined, elegant, testify to idealization.

A further suggestion which a pure science of society can afford as to the art of living comes out of a clarification of the relation between the individual and the societal interest. Inasmuch as all the ends of the individual are attained in and through the societal organization, it would seem that individual and society must have harmonious interests; yet their interplay involves contradictions and inversions. As previously intimated, men are jealous of the former interest and unappreciative of the latter. There is no doubt that the individual wins more as a member in a peace-group, sharing in all its advantages, than he would by relying upon his own powers in a system of general hostility. His own interest is, in the long run, that of society; nevertheless he is called upon to limit his freedom, obey the mores, yield to authority, and otherwise permit the societal to prevail over the individual by living within the code of his society; and in the short run, which is the only stretch ever visible to the unreflective, this is often felt to be a hardship. In many and recurring cases, besides, he strongly suspects that by living in the manner prescribed he is not serving the interests of society at all but only those of some group in power. He may believe theoretically that the individual must be sacrificed to the species, but may suspect that those who can get the power constitute themselves the species. The antagonism of petty combinations of men in pursuit of special interests to both individual and group-interests is one of the elements productive of disharmony between the two.

Consider the relations of the individual and the group-interest when the latter demands war, that is, when it appears to require hostile relations with other groups. Here the individual drops pretty much out of account. On low civilization, power in war goes with numbers; the multiplication of numbers is the prime societal interest, and the rules of "right" action—for instance, rapid propagation or even plural mating—which the group imposes upon its members by authority, tradition, custom, and taboo, are such as, according to the prevailing theory, will maintain its numbers. Hence violence is forbidden and the guardians of order, law, and authority become highly arbitrary and even domineering. Under the highest civilization, on the other hand, brute numbers are relatively less determinative of power in war. The comparisons which are often made of the population, or the rate of increase of population, in order to prognosticate success in war, are less conclusive. Capital is now a component in war-power, perhaps more important than numbers. If one state has more numerous armies and another more or better capital in armaments and in power to command with speed the latest and best equipment, the victory of the former is not so sure. Also the higher the civilization the more the quality of the men counts, this component referring not only to the officers and their training and talent, but to the type of the "man behind the gun." The shift in emphasis, however, does not relieve the individual of arbitrary infringement upon his peace-time rights.

Numbers and quality of men being always in antagonism, so must the individual and the societal interest be, so long as the latter demands only numbers. Given a certain power in the struggle for existence, it can be spent in a small amount on each of a great number or in a large amount on each of a small number. Further, the strain of rearing many children limits the individual development of the parents by subtracting from the time and capital which they can spend upon themselves. In all stages of civilization, individual aggrandizement is in such antagonism to group-aggrandizement until the latter is sought in quality and not in numbers. And yet alarm is periodically raised over the possible effects of the limitation of numbers which is an essential condition of the attainment of societal quality.

The basic fact here is that we are in the presence of a sliding adjustment between the two types of interest. The omnipotence of the group and the anarchistic liberty of the individual are the two poles between which the societal constitution has varied since there was any sort of association at all, entrance into which meant sacrifice of personal liberty. The healthful adjustment of the two elements is set at any time by the life-conditions of the group; it is not a matter of dogmatic philosophy. Because these life-conditions change, the adjustment is always unstable and readjustment is perennially called for by the voice of discontent. The expedient policy is clear enough along general lines, however difficult in its specific applications; its guiding principles are two: to grant freedom of activity in the pursuit of self-selected ends; and to secure discipline to regulate the relations of these efforts, on the part of different individuals, to one another in the interest of peace and harmony. When the societal element predominates over the individual, there is a negation of freedom and a struggle for equality in spite of individual differences of achievement. This verges toward socialism. When the individual element preponderates over the social, there is lack of discipline; societal organization dissolves; the individual of talent loses societal security and disappears in an atomistic horde once more, as in the ages after the destruction of the Roman Empire of the west. Here is a swing toward anarchism. Socialism and anarchism are thus diametrically opposed one to the other; they seem destined to divide civilized men for a long time to come.

An analogous sliding adjustment is to be seen in the swing between competition and monopoly. Every societal cluster is a monopoly, for its benefits are for its members only. It is also in competition with other clusters having similar purposes. Combination into a higher unit eliminates competition and widens and secures monopoly. This process is natural and goes on as far as the development of the arts at the time allows. If two individuals carry on the struggle for existence side by side against nature, they are in the competition of life with one another. Each may get a poor return and be in misery. If they combine and organize their effort against nature, they win more. They share in peace inside their group, but are in competition with similar groups. Higher combination repeats the process. Monopoly and competition, therefore, instead of being two hostile and opposite methods, mutually exclusive, are only two phases of the societal process, as it is repeated over and over again from the combination of a man and a woman in savagery up to a railroad pool or a trust at the top of civilization.

A fact that is not well understood by those who wish to interfere with the operation of societal forces is that societal institu-

THE SCIENCE OF SOCIETY

tions are largely instrumentalities for reducing antagonisms to harmony. Perhaps the root of this difficulty lies in the non-realization of the fact that coöperation is antagonistic in nature. It is true that similarity of interests socializes. But a far wider and stronger case is that in which socialization arises from interests which are primarily antagonistic. This has been called antagonistic coöperation.[5] It is out of antagonistic coöperation that societal harmonies arise. Two parties which are competitors, with primarily diverse and antagonistic interests, and consequently with mental or emotional hostility one to the other in their hearts, set aside their differences and unite for the sake of satisfying, by joint effort, some preponderating interest which they have in common. This is the strongest form of organization. It is illustrated from the bottom to the top of civilization. In fact, the two attitudes of each member of society, the individual and the societal, are antagonistic one to the other, while, as we have seen, they complement one another and are indispensable one to the other. Antagonistic coöperation is founded in the most elemental relations. Infanticide has appeared at times as a phenomenon of the antagonism between the individuality of the parents and the perpetuation of the society, where the latter has been denied recruits because the former evaded care. The combination of laborers and capitalists at the top of the capitalistic civilization is another case of antagonistic coöperation. "Politics makes strange bedfellows" is a proverbial saying that reveals an apprehension of such a relation. The history of civilization furnishes innumerable cases between any pair of extremes.

The combination of man and woman had utility and sense because the two together could win more in the struggle for existence than the sum of what they could win separately. The picture here presented of dissimilar and unequal efforts combined against a primary disinclination, for the sake of a higher gain, is fundamental to organization. It is repeated over and over again in every man's everyday experience.

McGee[6] shows how, in the desert, plants and animals are forced into coöperation with each other to keep up the struggle for existence against the environment, with the result that they form complex communities of creatures helping

5 §16, above.   6 In AA, VIII, 350.

and depending upon one another. The case shows with what persistency all things endowed with life cling to it and manifest what seems like high intelligence and ingenuity. The man-animal too exhibits an automatic and instinctive struggle for existence which looks like a rational determination not to die if it can be avoided, just as much as any other animal. Such action is as if guided by intelligence, but what evokes it is a power less wavering than intelligence. It is especially astonishing to see the emergence of coöperative effort between organisms which, though strange and even hostile, sink their differences for joint advantage. Such organization is, of course, unplanned and automatic. It is "in the nature of things." It is as spontaneous and inevitable, once given a society of men, as is the formation of the crystal or the breathing of the new-born child. It belongs among the first mass-phenomena, the first products of evolution in its societal mode.

In a sense all coöperation is antagonistic, for none is possible without the sinking of individual differences in interest. But it is desired here to emphasize that important set of cases where nothing short of a predominant and vital common interest could secure the socialization of otherwise discordant elements. For, coöperation once secured by such a *force majeure*, the composition of minor differences—further socialization—is likely to proceed apace.

It is to be noticed that individuals are unequally dependent on society, and can never contribute equally to its success. The law of distribution of social reward may be by equality or by some rule of proportion to contribution. The abler members may therefore find themselves working inside of it only in order to give something to the less able. They speedily sense the antagonism of interests involved; then they will try to break out of it in order to win individual independence again and profit by their own ability and individuality. "The strong man is most powerful alone." For this reason the law "from each according to his ability, to each according to his wants" is a law of dissolution for any organization of men, whatever its size or purpose, and whether natural or artificial.

If antagonisms are to be composed in a society, that does not by any means signify that the strong individual should not be permitted to defend his interests but must always yield to the persistent whinings of the weak and flabby. At the present time the highest requirement of the individual is moral courage to resist and strength of character to abide by his own judgment, when that has been arrived at by the acquisition of enough knowledge to confer the right to an opinion. There is no proper composition of interest-collisions unless both sides are afforded the chance, and take it, to present their claims in the most emphatic manner. And it must not be lost sight of that variation lies in the enterprising individual, who is likely to break away from the crowd, and that variation is the leader-off in any process of evolutionary adjustment. The individual may not be suppressed with safety. As it is, the press pretends to speak for the people, but it adds all its own defects and vices to those of the crowd. Democracy is a system in which the voice of the multitude is endowed with fetishistic authority. Popularity is made the test of truth and wisdom. The gulf between policy and conviction is widening and the individual is forced to choose between truckling to the crowd for ease, smoothness, and prosperity, and standing for what he thinks right in spite of abuse and unpopularity. The tyranny of the crowd always favors half-culture—neither ignorance nor thorough knowledge— and it cultivates mediocrity. The most available man is the one who is most colorless and characterless, especially if he can talk on a plane of elevated truism. The prophets of the present are those, we are told, to whom God reveals himself in platitudes. The net result is that society has greater and greater need for men of individual power and character, and that it is at the same time driving them away and scolding them because they do not come.

It is quite as possible that the collective element may become excessive and produce evil as that the individual element may do so. The fashion of the day runs, in increasing degree, to undue exaltation of the former, and inasmuch as that element acts through morals or ethics, this abuse wins a presumption of right by calling itself ethical. In fact, civilization might be more properly connected with that civil security under which men dare to stand independently and act with individual self-determination, escaping from all the minor combinations in which liberty and independence are sacrificed for security. When the individual dares to stand alone he gives exercise to all his idiosyncrasies. We must regard civilization as an outcome of all human action in which antagonisms have been reduced to resultants, contrasts have been softened in wider combinations, and concurrent elements have come together, so that the product may be conceived of as if it were a product of natural forces. We can never get a standpoint outside

welfare, lies in the failure of most reformers to identify the point at which to begin operations. They have not known where to take hold and have not had the patience or the will to find out. They have built, as it were, a roof before there was any foundation or substructure; they have then elevated it upon tall but shaky supports (consisting of assumptions and prophecies) incapable of withstanding even the stirring of dialectical breezes set in motion by other visionaries, much less the piping gales that sweep the world of realities. They have regularly confined their efforts to the remodeling of superstructures, seeking to re-shape and beautify, in accordance with their taste, religions, property-systems, marriage-practices, forms of government. Missionaries have been prominent in such enterprises.

The basic object to which any existing form of life does and must consecrate its energies is to the continuance of its existence. "The first task of life is to live."[7] That is naturally its first interest. A society presents the collective pursuit of self-maintenance as its enthralling interest and activity. To operate upon the terms of self-maintenance is to go to the root of the matter.[8] Anybody who is eager to improve the socital system, as a whole or in any of its details, is on safe ground only as he follows the roots of any practice or institution which he designs to modify down into their branchings in the soil of the maintenance-substratum. If a science of society arrives at any degree of confidence in its conclusions, it is here.

This statement, positive as it is, does not imply the absence of any reverse influence, from religion and the other secondary institutions upon the maintenance-organization. It has been repeatedly noted in foregoing pages that love, vanity, and ghost-fear often traverse that organization, exercising what is at times a dominant influence upon forms taken by the very struggle for existence itself. Asceticism, altruism, and sacrifice are policies which are hostile to individual self-maintenance. Such practices sometimes appear as collective phenomena. Ghost-fear has led to acts such as destruction of capital, which were directly disastrous to self-maintenance, and religious precepts have been obeyed which were against prosperity in the struggle for existence. Hindus and Chi-

[7] Sumner, *Folkways*, §1.   [8] Keller, *Soc. Evol.*, 140 ff., 240 ff.

of this civilization from which to criticize it. It comes to us with the same authority as the flora and fauna which we find sharing the world with us as products of biological evolution.

There is a complicated network of bonds in which everyone is held in a highly civilized society. He makes the alliances which he must make, classifying his interests and serving the most important while he sacrifices others, and especially sacrificing his preferences and sentiments, his "liberty," at every turn. In politics the parties are denounced for immoral conduct because those which are farthest apart in "principle" unite for victory over a common enemy, although they hate each other still. The party-leaders exhort their followers to sink their differences and seek harmony and the politician's art consists largely in conciliating and compromising differences which arise. To him organization is life and he is seeking to develop those more comprehensive interests which are strong enough to embrace and resist the disrupting force of minor ones. The current relations between employers and employees form, we have said, a case of antagonistic coöperation: some tell us that their interests are antagonistic, others that their interests are harmonious, and both point to phenomena in proof. The interests in question are primarily antagonistic and the mutual sentiments are not affectionate. But the two parties have a common interest, to earn a living, which they cannot satisfy separately. They come together and compromise their antagonisms in coöperation.

Antagonistic coöperation is the strongest and most pervasive form of organization throughout the whole societal structure; no combination of sentiment and affection can compare with it. When the terms of the adjustment have been carried to the point where the parties think that neither could do better; when habit and custom have made the bearings familiar so that they appear "right"; and when institutions have grown up to serve the functions at proper junctures; then the antagonistic coöperation works smoothly and without question and the original antagonism is lost to sight. What is seen is a harmony which seems to be a part of the order of the universe. The life of a highly civilized society is still, as regards all its broadest and most fundamental operations, a vast set of such harmonies, the product of centuries of struggle and adjustment; and the great problems of society today involve new struggles, working on to new adjustments which are to issue at last in new harmonies embracing interests as yet unprovided for by adequate societal usages and institutions, and therefore subject to vicissitudes entailing waste and loss.

A prime difficulty in the way of discerning interference with the "natural course of things," in the effort to promote societal

nese defeat themselves in that struggle by universal and early marriages and consequent overpopulation—mores referable chiefly to ghost-fear, since the motive is to provide for the sustenance of one's soul after death. Spain is a case of a state that ruined its prosperity in good part by loyal adherence to political and religious ideals, which, accepted on authority, were destructive errors.[9] Nations have often sacrificed real material welfare for national vanity.

It is not, therefore, true that self-maintenance always overrides every other motive or interest of the group; nevertheless it is the prime motive and interest which prevails normally and in all but the exceptional cases and it gives shape to everything else. The intellectual interests conform to the economic necessities; the political institutions shape themselves to the economic powers and to the requirements of economic operations; notions of right and wrong and conceptions of rights are a product of economic relations which have been adopted because expedient and successful; philosophical and religious dogmas are a result of reflection on experiences furnished by the operation of existing systems of societal economy. It is in the next following stage that the secondary elements, intellectual, political, ethical, philosophical, and religious, come back into the economic system with authority and may override economic interests.[10] "If we wish to test the truth of the proposition that it is the economic motives which always and everywhere occasion social movement, as well as advance all civil and social development, we may take the first historical event we choose, or we may study any civil commotion we wish and inquire as to its causes. We always find the economic impulses and motives at the bottom of these events. It cannot be otherwise, since everywhere and always material necessities stand in the first line of causes of all human doing or refusing to do."[11]

An interesting piece of direct testimony is given in the case of the Yakuts. Their old kin-groups are breaking up. The disintegrating forces are economic, and against them the old kin-tie avails only to maintain for a time a few arbitrary regulations to prevent the separation of the men of the same family into different groups.[12]

"The whole history of the past offers us the spectacle of economic forces

[9] Keller, *Colon.*, 168 ff.   [10] Lippert, *Kgchte.*, I, 21.
[11] Gumplowicz, *Soc.*, 122.
[12] Sieroshevski, *Yakuts* (Russ.), 436.

making sport of legislative devices, whether the devices were invented by aristocrats or democrats, and whether they had the purpose of maintaining or preventing certain inequalities of condition." The author[13] quoted has shown that the French Revolution was due to the fact of a great increase in the population, and consequently in the price of food, from the middle of the eighteenth century. This produced bread-riots in the mob of Paris and at the same time enriched the peasants, especially if they were copyholders, and the nobles if they were landlords; for there ensued a rise in the rent of land. The copyholders, being strengthened, wanted to throw off the feudal burdens which remained and the tenant farmers resented the increase in rent. Thus the distress of the consumers and the prosperity of the producers concurred.

Another generality, of a corrective order, derivable from the study of societal evolution—one useful for the discerning interferer to cherish—is that every form of society which comes into existence and lasts on is expedient relatively to its time. It is evidently idle to sit in judgment on phases of societal evolution. The proceeding has no sense. Often the phenomena are like storms or epidemic diseases. The Crusades were an undertaking which absorbed the interest and wasted the energy of Europe for centuries. The religious faith of the age was entirely out of adjustment to its knowledge and its other interests. Projectivism[14] pushed men on to secure a guarantee against the terrors of endless punishment for sin. The result was a societal storm. Nevertheless, given the facts in the notions of the time, the Crusades were a perfectly legitimate product of them and no man or doctrine could have intervened to prevent the error. Moral judgments, therefore, are idle. There are epidemics of folly and cruelty, such as witchcraft, sorcery, or anti-semitism, which take possession of a society and have to spend themselves before they can be brought to an end.

The taste of the same society changes from period to period. What interests one age revolts another. The coarseness, cruelty, and pruriency of the Middle Ages offends us because the set of our time is toward humanitarianism. The mores in regard to what is decent, proper, and modest never stand still, but from time to time undergo changes for which no rational ground can be assigned. Artists, poets, novelists, essayists, often give a trend to the sentiment of a society if they are not widely at discord with its pet notions and current traditions, and want to influence it

[13] D'Avenel, *Hist. Écon.*, I, 209; Maine, *Early Law*, 321.
[14] §206, above.

only to a slight extent in a certain direction. All these phenomena of society evidently deserve study and discussion but they by no means invalidate the proposition that the phases of evolution of a society are necessary, like the stages of growth of a man. The follies and phantasies of society, like those of a man, are a part of itself and are products of its character and of its contact with the world; they are evidently elements in the societal evolution itself. We now abhor slavery, polygamy, feudalism, witchcraft, and trial by torture, but they were all stages in the way to what is. Their historical expediency is quite independent of our present estimate of them.

We speak of classical, mediæval, or modern civilization. We do so because there is an essential consistency in the faiths and institutions of a period, and this tendency toward consistency appears as a force which modifies the details of the societal system. Charlemagne, Barbarossa, and others tried to force mediæval cities to be what Roman cities had been, but a mediæval city conformed to feudalism. Democratic elements in the cities struggled vaguely to formulate modern ideas of republican independence, but the age could not think out a system that did not include a lord. At the beginning of the period there was a great variety of status in which men stood in the society—grades of freedom, as we should now construe them. They were all swallowed up and systematized into the typical classes of the thirteenth century, because by that time nobody could understand what a man was unless he was in one of the typical classes of fully developed feudalism. All notions of what was "right" or what "ought to be" conformed to these fundamental institutions. All new questions were decided accordingly; that is to say, all new developments were constrained to take a form consistent with the prevailing societal theories and the existing societal system. The introduction of the Roman law amounted to a forced interjection of foreign elements which, we are told,[15] was a "national misfortune."

Here, however, we easily fall into another fallacy. We may be sure that what we ourselves have and do is also only a stage on the way to something else. We are wrong in our tendency to think that what we have attained is the crown of things, or that, because we can see and are astounded at the errors (as we esteem them) of the past, therefore we are making none such now. The very opposite is the correct conclusion. If we see errors in the past, posterity will see them in our acts. It cannot be otherwise than that institutions and usages of today will be maladjustments with respect to some future time just as certainly as feudalism and coarse public exhibitions are errors to us.

[15] Maurer, *Frohnhöfe,* IV, 484; Michael, *Gchte. d. Deut. Volkes,* I, 324.

If the contention that all phases and stages of societal evolution are expedient relatively to their time is not true, then it is in vain for us to discuss societal topics at all, for history would be no better than heraldry—a mass of uncoördinated and arbitrary relations; on the other hand, if the proposition is true, then our own settled societal institutions and organization are as fully justified as any others, past or future, and the attempt to pass wholesale judgment upon them, abolish them, and invent others, is vain.

It is a corollary from this proposition that no subsequent generation can ever be held bound to make good to any of its contemporaries any wrong (as the subsequent generation construes it) which the ancestors of the former once did to the ancestors of the latter. The now living generation of whites are not bound to make good to now living blacks any wrong done by former whites to former blacks through enslavement. The same may be said of present Englishmen and present Irishmen. The former men did good and ill as they judged best, and are dead. We inherit the fruits of their wisdom and folly and go on, making the best of it and in our turn acting well and ill. A reversal of judgment and penalty would turn time and effort all backwards. It is another corollary that it is no proof how things ought to be now to show how they were once or "originally." To show that property in land or other property was once or originally communal is no proof that it ought to be so now. Neither is it any proof that a usage or institution—property, for instance, or marriage—ought to be abolished if one can show that it arose in violence.

It is impossible that we should ever formulate any sharp definition of the limit of arbitrary intervention by man in the course of societal evolution. This, however, is very different from asserting that men can mold societal affairs as they see fit, and it is far from announcing that in any given case the only task before them is to make up their minds forthwith as to what they think best to do about it. The stronger the science the narrower its dictum as to what is the "right" thing to do in a given case. The element of chance or accident is due to our ignorance. As our knowledge extends this irrational element is reduced to rationality. If we knew all the components of every case, with their magnitude and relation to each other, we should see the one right and only thing to be done in each instance. We should be set free from doubt, fear, hesitation, and anxiety. Then we should have lost all "free will."

The saying is attributed to Laplace that an intellect which knew all the forces existing, at a given moment in nature, and could grasp them in mathematical formulæ, could reckon out all the events of the future.[16] This suggestion gives us the correct standpoint for understanding our apparent power to interpose arbitrarily in the course of things. We are all ignorant and in our consequent hesitation and doubt there is opportunity for acting upon each other. We are, as it were, moving about in the dark. Since no one knows where he ought to go, anyone who adopts a decision may collide with others and push them out of their courses. If we were all in the light we should move simply and directly to our purposes, without collision and friction. The range of choice or determination open to us is in any case quite narrow and in very many eventualities we have no choice at all. While a societal movement is in its earliest stages and the forces have not acquired momentum and have not worn channels for themselves (for we must use figures drawn from other fields of observation) it is possible for men who are well trained and well informed to influence consequences greatly by scattering, combining, or deflecting forces.

The traditional duties to act in a given direction which are obeyed by masses of men who inherit the same religion or philosophy enter as component forces into the subsequent evolution of the society. They are difficult to overcome—in fact, it is well-nigh impossible even to join issue with them. They have to be accepted as virtual constants and reckoned with as such. The refusal of men to do what is considered women's work or the taboo against eating prohibited foods, which has become senseless, may in an appropriate crisis be decisive for the welfare or fate of the group, despite the most fervid and frantic protests and the most cogent arguments. The reflex action of all philosophies, codes, maxims, and doctrines drawn from previous experience is a component in subsequent action. The great mass of any society live an unreflective life within the traditions which have been inherited by their generation, which create for them a mental and moral horizon out of which they never can project themselves in order to form independent judgments of what it is right or wise to do. Their consentaneous action is a mighty and steady current against which reformers, philosophers, and others find it very hard to exert an influence.

16 Gumplowicz, *Soc. and Pol.,* 107.

§463. Pure Science. Mankind is set down in the midst of a world of matter and force, forming a part of it and obliged, as a condition of self-preservation and self-realization, to take account of his surroundings. He cannot create or destroy matter, nor can he cause forces to act otherwise than as prescribed by the laws of their being. He cannot will that stone shall float or that water shall run up hill. As the condition of successful dealing with the forces in the field, he must first learn what they will inevitably and inexorably do under the circumstances, and then adjust his behavior accordingly. From the outset the race has been obliged to pursue, as it best could, an inquiry into the nature and action of forces in the inorganic and organic world; and its findings have been preserved in the form of an ever increasing fund of knowledge, in the light of which succeeding generations have been able to order their living in progressively more apt adjustment to more and more complicated life-conditions. Naïve conclusions have been corrected and, in their corrected form, verified and re-verified until they have been proved fit to live by. Experiences have been collected and compared, in the course of the practical business of living, and conclusions of wider scope have been drawn. The results of experience and experiment have been periodically brought into alignment by superior minds and out of the process has been shaped the form of comprehensive law.

The earlier acquisitions of knowledge were turned to instant use; they were wrought out for the sake of immediate application to imminent life-necessity. There was no chasm between the theoretic and the practical, for the former was not recognized as existent; all was empirical and there was no possibility of rising to perspectives and syntheses. This immediate application of isolated conclusions of limited scope has in it an element of error and uncertainty; it is shortsighted; and the race, although unconscious of this fact, unwittingly moved away from the specific toward the general. Students of the nature of things got farther away from the domination of the immediate and practical, and began, at length, to investigate at the instance of intellectual curiosity rather than of material interest.

In so doing they stumbled upon the major instrument of all adjustment as performed by men, namely, pure science; for pure science confers an insight into the nature of things which nothing else can give, and men had to be aware of the nature of things before they could perform adequate adjustment to them. It is not to be denied that the results attained by pure science, or what is so called, have often been and still are so remote from the practical as to seem to have no bearing at all upon actual living. It is true, too, that men, starting with science, have become absorbed in speculation and vagary, have got their feet off the ground and have floated away into regions of metaphysical spindrift. But this is not science at all, and if from such forays there have been brought back only illusions and delusions, to plague the race and to set it upon false and ambiguous paths, the fault is not that of science, but of the desertion of science. For pure science is the most practical thing, the agency most gravid of actual benefits, in the world. Let one consider the homely blessings to humanity that issued out of Pasteur's absorption with the highly theoretic and academic question of spontaneous generation. In its true form, pure science has always revealed the very strongest of survival-values in the struggle that the race has always had to wage amid the conditions of earthly existence. As army-organization has perforce and automatically developed out of the fighting chiefs a general staff that seldom or never comes to personal grips with the enemy, so has society, perforce and automatically, developed a body of investigators into the deeper and more comprehensive aspects of the battle of life; and, in the one case as in the other, that conflict cannot be prosecuted, except as a series of disconnected raids and skirmishes, without the central and perspective-taking agency.

All men seek, in this world of chance and change, after steadying-points, immutabilities, absolutes. Most of the alleged absolutes upon which the race has tried to rest, have proved to be illusory, for they have been arrived at by metaphysical or myth-making processes, that is, by some form of unverifiable guess-work. But the laws of nature and society, though less satisfying than the self-persuasions of transcendental yearning, verify over and over again. In fact, modest as they are, they are yet what the race has actually existed by. Whatever the devotional relations to a Final Cause, it is through a progressively clearer understanding of secondary causes and their effects that men have lived on into what they have become; and there never has been a time when they have not eventually, if not promptly, seized upon and appropriated what scientists, dealing wholly with secondary causes, have been able to demonstrate. Furthermore, the understanding of the verifiable has resulted in enlargement of spirit as well as in contributions to practical well-being. There is a temper and a "bite" to this apparently delicate and even tenuous-seeming instrumentality of pure science which enable it to cut through knotty impediments that turn the edge of grosser tools. The most expeditious way to get practical results in science is to see that it is cultivated in its purest and most highly theoretical form.

When mankind developed pure science, however, there was opened up to human minds the hardest labor they would ever be called upon to perform. The comprehensive view does not come cheap; it is no revelation; nor can it be conveyed, by the laying on of hands or the baptism of words, upon a passive subject. It is not a mere tale to be told. The unifying element to be apprehended is the universal reign, within the field of observation, of order and law; and this apprehension rests upon the acquisition and genuine appropriation of masses of hard-won facts. There is then something capable of being set in order, again by the exercise of limitless labor and patience. The race has revolted at the toil and strain involved. It is easier and pays better to have visions and exhort on the strength of them than to study unostentatiously, disinterestedly, and doggedly. It is more popular to mouth offhand about what society "ought" to do than to strive, through long vigils, to find out what society can do, or what can be done with society. It is more interesting to buzz about, catching half-glimpses at contemporary things and then talking learnedly, with splashes of local color, to uplift-organizations, than to wrestle with tough masses of evidence.

It has been so much easier to guess and talk, and then to do, or to adjure someone else to do, something definite and "practical." Hit-or-miss therapeutics long preceded treatment in conformity with the facts and laws discovered by the anatomist and physiologist. The chief trouble with "sociology" is that it is not qualifying as a science by subordinating its types of therapeutics to that which corresponds, within its range, to anatomy and physiology. There are not enough patient devotees of the pure science in proportion to the number of expositors, exhorters, and prophets. What the study of society needs, to entitle it to the respect, consideration, and deference for which so many "sociologists" clamor in vain, is to be anchored deep and secure in principle. It needs the orientation that can be derived only from evolutionary perspective. It needs more work and less talk. The art of living reacts upon the apprehension of and the adjustment to immutable conditions; and a knowledge of the conditions is always a prior necessity. There is every justification and call for studies of society which shall be purely scientific; coldly scientific; so austerely unmindful of contemporary "problems" as deliberately to seek distance and detachment from them. Under some Darwin of the future, such studies can result in the apprehension of societal laws; then the race can make a farsighted and accurately planned campaign against its problems instead of a series of desultory and disconnected engagements. What is now needed is some such collection of scientific materials as Darwin found at hand, a collection assembled by many patient and obscure workers intent, not upon self-glorification, but the discovery of truth.

The following incident deserves reflection. The coal-operators refused to have a labor man on the Anthracite Coal Commission of 1902. Roosevelt[17] relates: "After hours of patient negotiation I finally found that the operators really objected to the labor man being appointed *as such;* and as they wished some one of the commission to be what they called a 'sociologist,' I finally appointed a labor man and called him a sociologist, which, rather to my amusement, and greatly to my relief, gave entire satisfaction to both sides." Could a labor man have been called a chemist, to the satisfaction of both parties? How is it that anybody, no matter who, can be jocosely labelled a "sociologist"?

§464. Insight. The value of any science will always be measured, in last analysis, by its utility for living; there is, however, another less tangible product of faithful scientific study which should not be passed over because it is immaterial. This is insight. The astronomer of parts stares through his telescope at the farthest visible star. Once it was not to be seen. It is thousands of light-years away. Beyond it there are doubtless unopened vistas

[17] "Grover Cleveland and the Coal Strike," in *Outlook,* LXXXIX, 883.

of space, and the mind recoils with a certain terror before the thought. It feels that tingling shudder or thrill which the incomparable seer[18] calls "mankind's best portion." But the astronomer knows about the universe that which is still more impressive, namely, that throughout its extent all is law and orderliness. Laymen cannot fully appreciate this mighty disclosure because it comes to them merely second-hand; but an outsider who has firsthand knowledge in some other range of science can attain a not inconsiderable degree of insight even when compared with that of the specialist who has been laboriously self-enlightened.

The microscopist as well as the macroscopist penetrates into the region of awe and thrill. He sees now what was not visible before; he notes the concentrated possibilities of the chromosomes; he peers some distance into life-processes. He knows that there is an infinity of the unknown beyond his vision. It is a staggering thought. Like the astronomer, again, he finds that within the microcosm is law and orderliness. He knows why the astronomer is overborne by a sense of awe and mystery, for that is his own condition, reached by another road. It is no trouble for him to conceive that at the end of every serious study lies the same experience, and that the identity of the experiences reveals the universe as a range of order and law.

Anyone can mouth these words, "law" and "order." Many do. But unless one has qualified, by self-discipline, much as the ascetic equipped himself, for the real vision, the terms are mere vocables, signifying nothing. All such may be dismissed with the injunction to go forth in their glory, for genuine insight could only distress them.[19]

This matter of insight, or overwhelming perspective, might be illustrated from chemistry, physics, geology—in fact, from any one of the natural sciences. The contention is that it is one of the givings of the science of society as well, to the toilsome student who is also possessed of some measure of intellectual or spiritual scope. Aware of the intricate complexity of human society and also of the stages of its evolution, he can no more uncover its mainsprings than can a biologist disclose the essence of life itself. His vista too ends in the inexplicable and the awe-inspiring. He

[18] Goethe, *Faust,* II, 1660.　　　[19] Goethe, *Faust,* II, 2195-2196.

also detects throughout the range of his science the presence of law and regularity, in exhibitions no less impressive than the precession of the equinoxes or the process of fertilization and cell-division. He attains the same species of satisfaction to an inquiring mind, and if he is possessed of the requisite sensitiveness to larger matters, he gets the same sort of glimpse into the ordering of the universe that is vouchsafed his fellows in the natural sciences.

He is under some disadvantage, however, as compared with them, when it comes to conferring even a pale reflection of his vision upon his fellow-men. Almost anyone can be fleetingly impressed by the astronomer or the biologist; but it would not be so if men had telescopic or microscopic vision, for then they would take the circling of the planets or the movement of the polar bodies as casually as they now take the rise and fall of exchange. To understand commonplaces is not felt to be necessary. The marvels of societal organization are regarded as matters of course, not calling for examination, in order that they may be understood, but merely for manipulation in accordance with their apparent suitability or the reverse for the realization of human desires.

Real wonder comes only after study has revealed the inexplicability of the obvious and commonplace. Take the case of language. Men use it continually with as little appreciation of its nature as the pauper in the tale had for the Great Seal of England when he used it to crack nuts with. Consider, however, the fact that language has grown, like the rest of the mores, by casual accretion and alteration, wholly automatically; and then note that any tongue is an incomprehensible exhibition of the reign of law and order in the universe. The grammatical rules are all made after the act and are merely expressive of the regularity of the automatic process. They are the formulations we make of the way things go; and then we grandly turn about and triumphantly show that things have gone as they have gone. There is profit in that, except for the attendant paranoiac mood of grandeur and triumph; the opposite frame of mind would better befit us.

Through the device of a small disc of stamped metal a man can command the services of many of his fellow-men in different parts of the earth, without any one of the human beings thus brought into a coöperative relation being remotely conscious of the far-reaching and societal bearings of the action by which he becomes party to such relation. All over the world men are raising products, not for the race but for immediate profit; otherwise they would not exert themselves; and yet they are providing for distant strangers. They are busy transporting things, yet with no idea of serving others. The presence of pepper on a New England table unites its user in the coöperative relation with some Malay whom he will never see, as well as with the long chain of men who handle the product from the time it leaves the East until it arrives in the West. This concept of the solidarity of mankind is part of the insight derivable from even a slight knowledge of the facts.

The covering marvel is the reign of law and order in the general institutional structure, life, and evolution of human society. Organisms—plant, animal, and human—are marvellous enough in their delicate and complicated structure. Then, in human society, one can observe a set of the most complex of these brought together in association, all striving to satisfy individual needs, and yet existing together, under the most diverse and entangled conditions, in relations of extraordinary peace and harmony over relatively extended areas and periods. How is this marvel brought about and maintained? Certainly if it is by forces less than supernatural, then there is no longer any need of assuming miracles in the world; for this eventuality is more wonderful than any stock miracle that could be cited. Some inkling of the automatic process by which such results are brought to pass should have been gained from preceding parts of this book. Without attempting any poetic flights, we should wish simply to recall the long series of automatic adjustments in the mores which constitute the industrial organization, property, the regulative organization, religion, and marriage. No one planned them out. Men were simply trying their best to live at all, or with less discomfort, in the face of the physical, social, and supernatural environments, in the presence of the element of chance, and of the condition of human bi-sexuality. Then what they have worked out, in the form of institutions, is seen, upon faithful examination, to have the rationality and the "logic" of the results of natural processes. All this, genuinely apprehended at the end of a long and arduous engrossment with bodies of facts, represents what might be called the immaterial reward of the study of society.

Insight, it seems, is rare, visiting only those who have painfully learned enough to stand intelligently aghast before the limitless vista of the unknown. If so, it consorts with a sense of frustration and with humility rather than with satisfied vanity and self-assurance. It engenders a mood of awe and of reverence in the face of incomprehensible power. There is more here than the mere satisfaction of intellectual curiosity; there is a quiet disclosure, not sudden and catastrophic but cumulative day by day, of the order of the universe. Though this is a revelation that evokes no faith, in the technical sense, it yet makes for strength of heart and reassured steadfastness of spirit.

END OF VOL. III.